LOUISIANA CIVIL CODE

WITH OFFICIAL LEGISLATIVE COMMENTARY

2016 Student Edition

LOUISIANA CIVIL CODE

WITH OFFICIAL LEGISLATIVE COMMENTARY

2016 Student Edition

MELISSA T. LONEGRASS

Harriet S. Daggett-Frances Leggio Landry Professor of Law
Bernard Keith Vetter Professor of Civil Law Studies
LSU Paul M. Hebert Law Center

WEST
ACADEMIC
PUBLISHING

© 2016 LEG, Inc. d/b/a West Academic
    444 Cedar Street, Suite 700
    St. Paul, MN 55101
    1-877-888-1330

Printed in the United States of America

ISBN: 978-1-62810-349-6

PREFACE

This volume contains the official text of the Louisiana Civil Code of 1870, complete with revisions and amendments through the 2015 Regular Session of the Louisiana Legislature. References to the enacting and amending legislation are provided alongside the text of the law. To maintain the simplicity of this text, code provisions that either are vacated or have been repealed are listed simply as "blank."

In this Louisiana Civil Code: Student Edition, readers will find the official legislative commentary accompanying the articles. Although these comments do not have the force of law, they provide historical background, explanations, and references to jurisprudence, all of which may be useful to the understanding and interpretation of the Code. Insofar as the official commentary places the law in its historical and legal context, it can be immensely helpful to novice readers of the Civil Code, and in particular, to law students.

Law students will also benefit from the provision of electronic updates to the Civil Code for the two legislative sessions following the date of this edition. These electronic updates ensure law students access to all legislative revisions made during the usual three years of legal education without the need to purchase a revised print edition of the Civil Code. Thus, each edition of the Louisiana Civil Code: Student Edition is designed to shepherd law students through their studies, from the first semester to the completion of the state bar examination.

It is my sincere hope that this volume will serve students of Louisiana law, not only as a useful pedagogical tool, but also as a first introduction to the most significant compilation of Louisiana's private law: the Civil Code.

MELISSA T. LONEGRASS

October 2015

TABLE OF CONTENTS

PRELIMINARY TITLE

CHAPTER 1—GENERAL PRINCIPLES

Art. 1. Sources of law

The sources of law are legislation and custom.

Acts 1987, No. 124, § 1, eff. Jan. 1, 1988.

REVISION COMMENTS—1987

(a) This provision is new. It does not change the law. Articles 1 and 3 of the Louisiana Civil Code of 1870 make it clear that the sources of law in Louisiana are legislation and custom. However, as in all codified systems, legislation is the superior source of law in Louisiana.

(b) Article 1 declares that the sources of Louisiana law are legislation and custom. Legislation is defined in Article 2 and custom is defined in Article 3, infra. According to civilian doctrine, legislation and custom are authoritative or primary sources of law. They are contrasted with persuasive or secondary sources of law, such as jurisprudence, doctrine, conventional usages, and equity, that may guide the court in reaching a decision in the absence of legislation and custom. See Yiannopoulos, Louisiana Civil Law System Sections 31, 32 (1977). The distinction of sources of law into primary and secondary sources is a matter of theory of law; for this reason, this distinction is not mentioned in text.

(c) In Louisiana, as in other civil law jurisdictions, legislation is superior to any other source of law. Article 1 of the Louisiana Civil Code of 1870 (Article 2 of this projet), declaring that legislation is a formal expression of legislative will, has been interpreted to establish the supremacy of legislation and to exclude judicial legislation. It is only in cases not covered by legislation that a lawyer or judge may look for solutions elsewhere. See Yiannopoulos, Louisiana Civil Law System Section 32 (1977). Article 1 does not derogate from the principle of the supremacy of legislation. This provision serves as an introduction to Articles 2 and 3. Article 2 continues to have the meaning that it had in the 1870 Code.

(d) Article 1 makes no reference to sources of law such as the Constitution of the United States, federal legislation and executive orders, international treaties, and the Louisiana Constitution. These sources of law are the prius of all Louisiana legislation and need not be mentioned in Article 1 of the Civil Code.

Art. 2. Legislation

Legislation is a solemn expression of legislative will.

Acts 1987, No. 124, § 1, eff. Jan. 1, 1988.

REVISION COMMENTS—1987

(a) Article 2 reproduces the substance of Article 1 of the Louisiana Civil Code of 1870. It does not change the law.

(b) Article 1 of the Louisiana Civil Code of 1870 declares: "Law is a solemn expression of legislative will." This does not mean that legislation is the only source of law in Louisiana, that is, that all rules of law are to be found in enactments of the Legislature. In the French text of the Louisiana Civil Code, Article 1 reads: "La loi est une declaration solemnelle de la volonté legislative," which ought to be translated: "Legislation is a formal expression of legislative will." The new provision defines legislation rather than law, and leaves room for sources other than legislation.

Art. 3. Custom

Custom results from practice repeated for a long time and generally accepted as having acquired the force of law. Custom may not abrogate legislation.

Acts 1987, No. 124, § 1, eff. Jan. 1, 1988.

REVISION COMMENTS—1987

(a) The first sentence of Article 3 reproduces the substance of Article 3 of the Louisiana Civil Code of 1870. It does not change the law.

(b) According to civilian theory, the two elements of custom are a long practice (longa consuetudo) and the conviction that the practice has the force of law (opinio necessitatis or opinio juris). The definition of custom in Article 3 reflects these two elements.

(c) The second sentence of Article 3 is new.

(d) Legislation and custom are primary sources of law. Article 1 supra. However, as in all codified systems, legislation is the superior source of law in Louisiana.

Art. 4. Absence of legislation or custom

When no rule for a particular situation can be derived from legislation or custom, the court is bound to proceed according to equity. To decide equitably, resort is made to justice, reason, and prevailing usages.

Acts 1987, No. 124, § 1, eff. Jan. 1, 1988.

REVISION COMMENTS—1987

(a) This provision reproduces the substance of Article 21 of the Louisiana Civil Code of 1870. It does not change the law.

(b) The term "natural law" in Article 21 of the 1870 Code has no defined meaning in Louisiana jurisprudence and is not reproduced in this revision.

Art. 5. Ignorance of law

No one may avail himself of ignorance of the law.

Acts 1987, No. 124, § 1, eff. Jan. 1, 1988.

REVISION COMMENTS—1987

(a) This provision is based on Article 7 of the Louisiana Civil Code of 1870. It does not change the law.

(b) Ignorance is inexcusable for laws that are in force. It may be excusable as to laws that have been properly enacted by the legislature but are not yet in force. For example, the legislature may enact a new title of the Civil Code in the summer with an effective date of January 1 of the next year. Reichenphader v. Allstate Insurance Co., 418 So.2d 648 (La.1982), is legislatively overruled to the extent that it suggests that ignorance of law is inexcusable even as to laws that have not yet been in force.

(c) Ignorance of law is distinguished from error or mistake of law. Cf. C.C. Art. 3078 (1870); C.C. Art. 1950 (Rev.1984); La.R.S. 14:17; Spanish Civil Code Art. 6. Error of law may be a ground for relief when the law so provides. Ignorance of law does not exclude good faith in matters of prescription. Cf. C.C. Arts. 3480, 3481 (Rev.1982).

Art. 6. Retroactivity of laws

In the absence of contrary legislative expression, substantive laws apply prospectively only. Procedural and interpretative laws apply both prospectively and retroactively, unless there is a legislative expression to the contrary.

Acts 1987, No. 124, § 1, eff. Jan. 1, 1988.

REVISION COMMENTS—1987

(a) This provision is new; it reproduces the substance of Article 8 of the Louisiana Civil Code of 1870 and accords with Louisiana jurisprudence interpreting the source provision. It does not change the law.

(b) According to a well-settled rule of statutory interpretation, a substantive law applies prospectively only, unless it expressly or impliedly provides that it be applied both prospectively and retroactively. Of course, retroactive application of substantive laws is possible only to the extent that it is constitutionally permissible.

(c) According to a well-settled rule of statutory interpretation, procedural and interpretative laws apply both prospectively and retroactively unless they violate vested rights or obligations of contracts. See Ardoin v. Hartford Acc. & Indemn. Co., 360 So.2d 1331 (La.1978); Barron v. State Dept. of Public Safety, 397 So.2d 29 (La.App.2d Cir.1981, writ denied 401 So.2d 1188).

(d) Article 6 makes no reference to so-called remedial legislation because of the multiplicity of meanings assigned to it. A remedial law may be procedural, interpretative, or substantive. A procedural law is remedial in the sense of dealing with the remedy rather than with the right itself. An interpretative law is remedial in the sense of remedying an error or ambiguity in the prior law. In both situations the new law may, in principle, apply retroactively even in the absence of express language to that effect. However, a substantive law may also be, and often is, called remedial when it remedies an existing social problem resulting from a gap, silence, or deficiency of the prior law. In such a situation, the new law should not be applied retroactively, absent a contrary and constitutionally permissible legislative directive. See Rodriguez v. Brown & Root, Inc., 410 So.2d 325 (La.App. 4th Cir.1982); Manuel v. Carolina Casualty Ins. Co., 136 So.2d 275 (La.App.3d Cir.1961); Tessier v. H.S. Anderson Trucking Co., 713 F.2d 135 (U.S.App. 5th Cir.1983).

Art. 7. Laws for the preservation of the public interest

Persons may not by their juridical acts derogate from laws enacted for the protection of the public interest. Any act in derogation of such laws is an absolute nullity.

Acts 1987, No. 124, § 1, eff. Jan. 1, 1988.

REVISION COMMENTS—1987

(a) This provision is based on Articles 11 and 12 of the Louisiana Civil Code of 1870. It does not change the law.

(b) The word "individuals" in Article 11 of the 1870 Code meant "private persons," that is, individuals as well as entities possessing juridical personality under the Civil Code, such as partnerships and corporations. "Laws enacted for the protection of the public interest" is sufficiently broad to include laws made for the preservation of good morals. For this reason, Article 7 does not specifically mention good morals.

(c) The second paragraph of Article 11 of the Louisiana Civil Code of 1870 contains a self-evident proposition, that a private person may renounce a right or privilege unless renunciation is expressly or impliedly forbidden, affects the rights of others, or is contrary to public good. For this reason, that paragraph has not been reproduced in this revision.

(d) The term "prohibitory law" in Article 12 of the Louisiana Civil Code of 1870 meant rules of public order. Whatever is done in contravention of a rule of public order is an absolute nullity. The words "laws enacted for the protection of the public interest" have the same meaning as "laws for the preservation of public order."

Art. 8. Repeal of laws

Laws are repealed, either entirely or partially, by other laws.

A repeal may be express or implied. It is express when it is literally declared by a subsequent law. It is implied when the new law contains provisions that are contrary to, or irreconcilable with, those of the former law.

The repeal of a repealing law does not revive the first law.

Acts 1987, No. 124, § 1, eff. Jan. 1, 1988.

REVISION COMMENT—1987

This provision reproduces the substance of Articles 22 and 23 of the Louisiana Civil Code of 1870. It does not change the law.

CHAPTER 2—INTERPRETATION OF LAWS

Art. 9. Clear and unambiguous law

When a law is clear and unambiguous and its application does not lead to absurd consequences, the law shall be applied as written and no further interpretation may be made in search of the intent of the legislature.

Acts 1987, No. 124, § 1, eff. Jan. 1, 1988.

REVISION COMMENT—1987

This provision reproduces the substance of Article 13 of the Louisiana Civil Code of 1870. Changes in phraseology and terminology, made in the light of Article 2046 of the Civil Code as revised in 1984, do not change the law.

Art. 10. Language susceptible of different meanings

When the language of the law is susceptible of different meanings, it must be interpreted as having the meaning that best conforms to the purpose of the law.

Acts 1987, No. 124, § 1, eff. Jan. 1, 1988.

REVISION COMMENTS—1987

(a) This provision is new. It is based on Article 18 of the Louisiana Civil Code of 1870 and Article 2048 of the Louisiana Civil Code as revised in 1984. It does not change the law.

(b) This provision expresses the principle of teleological interpretation.

Art. 11. Meaning of words

The words of a law must be given their generally prevailing meaning.

Words of art and technical terms must be given their technical meaning when the law involves a technical matter.

Acts 1987, No. 124, § 1, eff. Jan. 1, 1988.

REVISION COMMENT—1987

This provision reproduces the substance of Articles 14 and 15 of the Louisiana Civil Code of 1870. Changes in phraseology and terminology, made in the light of Article 2047 of the Civil Code as revised in 1984, do not change the law.

Art. 12. Ambiguous words

When the words of a law are ambiguous, their meaning must be sought by examining the context in which they occur and the text of the law as a whole.

Acts 1987, No. 124, § 1, eff. Jan. 1, 1988.

REVISION COMMENT—1987

This provision reproduces the substance of Article 16 of the Louisiana Civil Code of 1870. It does not change the law.

Art. 13. Laws on the same subject matter

Laws on the same subject matter must be interpreted in reference to each other.

Acts 1987, No. 124, § 1, eff. Jan. 1, 1988.

REVISION COMMENT—1987

This provision reproduces the substance of Article 17 of the Louisiana Civil Code of 1870. It does not change the law.

CHAPTER 3—CONFLICT OF LAWS

Art. 14. Multistate cases

Unless otherwise expressly provided by the law of this state, cases having contacts with other states are governed by the law selected in accordance with the provisions of Book IV of this Code.

Acts 1991, No. 923, § 1, eff. Jan. 1, 1992.

REVISION COMMENTS—1991

(a) Role and function of this Article. This Article replaces Civil Code Articles 14 and 15 (Redesignated 1987) which contained virtually all the choice-of-law rules of the Code. The new choice-of-law rules are now placed in a newly-created Book IV of this Code, Arts. 3515 et seq., infra. In addition to serving as a cross-reference to these new rules, this Article delineates the scope of Book IV and establishes its residual nature vis-a-vis other more specific provisions of Louisiana legislation.

(b) Role and function of Book IV. The scope of Book IV encompasses all multistate cases or "cases having contacts with other states", whether these contacts pertain to the domicile of the parties, the transaction or the occurrence giving rise to the dispute, or the location of its object or subject matter. These contacts may implicate the laws of the involved foreign states in a way that raises the potential of a conflict between their laws and the law of this state. Book IV establishes the principles for determining whether such a conflict actually exists in a given case, and, if so, how it should be resolved. Through these principles, a court will determine whether the provisions of the first three books of the Civil Code as well as other Louisiana laws should apply to a particular case "having contacts with other states", and if so to what extent.

The residual nature of the provisions of Book IV is established by the introduction phrase of this Article "[u]nless otherwise expressly provided by the law of this state". This phrase means that the provisions of Book IV are not intended to supersede more specific choice-of-law rules contained in other Louisiana statutes, such as the Insurance Code (see La.R.S. 22:611 et seq.), the Commercial Code (see, e.g., La.R.S. 10:1–105, 10:9–103), the Consumer Credit and Consumer Protection statutes (see e.g., La.R.S. 9:3511, 51:1418), and the Lease of Movables Act (La.R.S. 9:3302 et seq.). When applicable those rules, being more specific, should prevail over the provisions of Book IV.

Arts. 15 to 23.   [Blank]

BOOK I—OF PERSONS

TITLE I—NATURAL AND JURIDICAL PERSONS

Art. 24. Kinds of persons

There are two kinds of persons: natural persons and juridical persons.

A natural person is a human being. A juridical person is an entity to which the law attributes personality, such as a corporation or a partnership. The personality of a juridical person is distinct from that of its members.

Acts 1987, No. 125, § 1, eff. Jan. 1, 1988.

REVISION COMMENTS—1987

(a) This provision is new; it expresses ideas that are inherent in the Louisiana Civil Code of 1870. It does not change the law.

(b) According to the Romanist tradition, persons are divided into natural persons and juridical persons. A natural person is a human being. Only human beings may be natural persons. A juridical person is an entity to which the law attributes personality, such as a corporation or a partnership. See La.C.C. Art. 427 (1870) and La.C.C. Art. 2801 (Rev. 1980). An unincorporated association may possess legal personality for certain purposes. See La.C.C. Art. 446 (1870); Lord v. The District VIII Baptist Convention, 391 So.2d 942 (La.App.2d Cir.1980).

(c) According to civilian doctrine, juridical persons are classified either as private persons or public persons. A public person is governed by rules of public law; a private person is governed by rules of private law. The state and its political subdivisions have dual personality. At times they act as public persons in a sovereign capacity and at times as private persons in the capacity of a citizen or a private corporation. The property that the state and its political subdivisions own is known as "public property." This property consists of two categories of things: public things, namely, things that the state and its political subdivisions own in their capacity as public persons; and private things, namely, things that the state and its political subdivisions own in their capacity as private persons. See C.C. Art. 450 (Rev.1978).

(d) The personality of a juridical person is distinct and distinguishable from that of its members. La.C.C.Art. 435 (1870). Hence, the patrimony of a juridical person is distinct and distinguishable from the patrimony of its members. La.C.C. Art. 436 (1870). The capacity of a juridical person is governed by provisions in its charter, governing legislation, and customs.

Art. 25. Commencement and end of natural personality

Natural personality commences from the moment of live birth and terminates at death.

Acts 1987, No. 125, § 1, eff. Jan. 1, 1988.

REVISION COMMENTS—1987

(a) This provision is new. It is based in part on Article 28 of the Louisiana Civil Code of 1870. It does not change the law.

(b) A natural person exists from the moment that he or she is born alive, subject to the exception established in Article 26, infra. Cf. La.Civ.Code Arts. 28, 955, 956, 963 (1870). A human being that is born dead is considered never to have existed. Live birth suffices. There is no requirement that the child be born capable of living. See La.Civil Code Art. 956 (1870). Articles 960 and 961 of the Louisiana Civil Code of 1870 seem to establish a requirement of viability. However, these articles ought to be interpreted in accordance with Article 956 (1870). See Yiannopoulos, Louisiana Civil Law System Section 50 (1977).

(c) Death marks the end of human personality. For the definition of death, see R.S. 9:111.

(d) For the personality of a human embryo in vitro, see R.S. 9:121 to 133.

Art. 26. Unborn child

An unborn child shall be considered as a natural person for whatever relates to its interests from the moment of conception. If the child is born dead, it shall be considered never to have existed as a person, except for purposes of actions resulting from its wrongful death.

Acts 1987, No. 125, § 1, eff. Jan. 1, 1988.

REVISION COMMENTS—1987

(a) This provision is new. It is based on Articles 28, 29, and 956 of the Louisiana Civil Code of 1870. It does not change the law.

(b) The term "Children in the mother's womb" in Article 29 of the Louisiana Civil Code of 1870 has advisedly been changed to "An unborn child." An "unborn child" may be a person even if it is in a test tube (rather than its mother's womb). Question may arise as to the time of birth of a "test tube" baby.

(c) An unborn child may be plaintiff in an action for the protection of its property rights. Malek v. Yekani-Fard, 422 So.2d 1151 (La.1982). If the child is born alive, it may be plaintiff in an action seeking recovery for prenatal injuries. See Vicknair v. Hibernia Building Corporation, 468 So.2d 695 (La.App. 4th Cir.1985); Bunch v. Mercy Hosp. of New Orleans, 404 So.2d 520 (La.App. 4th Cir.1981); P.J. Pace, "Civil Liability for Pre-Natal Injuries," 40 Modern L.Rev. 141 (1977); Johnson, "Tort Liability for Prenatal Injury," 24 Tul.L.Rev. 435 (1950); Note, 52 Tul.L.Rev. 893 (1978).

(d) The parents of a still-born child may maintain an action for its wrongful death under Article 2315 of the Civil Code of 1870 despite the language of Article 28 of the same Code. Danos v. St. Pierre, 402 So.2d 633 (La.1981). When a child is born dead, the fiction of its personality from the moment of conception is wiped out; however, this does not condone the fault of a person who caused the loss of the foetus. In effect, the still-born child is considered as a person for the purposes of a wrongful death action. Under Article 26, the death of an unborn child on account of the fault of a person gives rise to an action for wrongful death under Article 2315 of the Civil Code.

There is no wrongful death action "for the loss of a foetus not conceived at the time of the mother's traumatic injury." Jilek v. Colonial Penn Ins. Co., 468 So.2d 671 (La.App. 4th Cir.1985).

(e) A newborn infant whose brain was severely and irreversibly damaged at birth and who was in a comatose state was recognized as a person in In re P.V.W., 424 So.2d 1015 (La.1982). That infant had the "right to discontinuance of artificially sustained life through the mechanical invasion of the child's body" (id. at 1020). It is implicit in the court's decision that the child was born alive.

(f) For actions for wrongful life, see Foutz, "Wrongful Life: The Right Not to Be Born," 54 Tul.L.Rev. 480 (1980).

(g) For the personality of human embryos in vitro, see R.S. 9:121–133.

Art. 27. General legal capacity

All natural persons enjoy general legal capacity to have rights and duties.

Acts 1987, No. 125, § 1, eff. Jan. 1, 1988.

REVISION COMMENTS—1987

(a) This provision is new. It is based on Article 33 of the Louisiana Civil Code of 1870. It does not change the law.

(b) Every natural person is the subject of rights and duties. This incident of natural personality is known in civilian literature as "general legal capacity." The general legal capacity of a natural person is contrasted with his capacity to acquire rights and assume obligations by virtue of juridical acts. For contractual capacity, see La.Civil Code Arts. 1918–1926, as revised in 1984. For testamentary capacity, see La. Civil Code Arts. 1470–1492 (1870).

Art. 28. Capacity to make juridical acts

A natural person who has reached majority has capacity to make all sorts of juridical acts, unless otherwise provided by legislation.

Acts 1987, No. 125, § 1, eff. Jan. 1, 1988.

REVISION COMMENTS—1987

(a) This provision is new. It is based on Article 1782 of the Louisiana Civil Code of 1870 and on Articles 1918 and 1922 of the same Code, as revised in 1984. It does not change the law.

(b) Articles 1918 and 1922 of the Louisiana Civil Code, as revised in 1984, deal with contractual capacity only. Article 28 has a much broader scope. It establishes the general principle that a person who has reached majority has capacity to make all sorts of juridical acts, unilateral or bilateral, unless, of course, he labors under some special incapacity (e.g. interdiction, deprivation of reason) or unless a special capacity is required by legislation for the making of a juridical act. Article 28 thus deals generally with the capacity that majority alone confers on a person; the Article does not confer capacity on interdicts or other incompetents.

(c) The capacity to enter marriage is governed by Title IV of Book I of the Civil Code. Impediments to marriage are not matters of capacity to make juridical acts.

(d) For the capacity of minors to make juridical acts, see C.C. Arts. 370–376, 381–385 (1870) and C.C. Art. 1923, as revised in 1984.

Art. 29. Age of majority

Majority is attained upon reaching the age of eighteen years.

Acts 1987, No. 125, § 1, eff. Jan. 1, 1988.

REVISION COMMENTS—1987

(a) This provision is new. It is based on Article 37 of the Louisiana Civil Code of 1870. It does not change the law.

(b) Persons who have reached the age of majority enjoy contractual capacity unless they are interdicted or deprived of reason at the time of contracting. See C.C. Art. 1918, as revised in 1984.

Art. 30. Presumption of death

When a person has disappeared under circumstances such that his death seems certain, his death is considered to have been established even though his body has not been found.

Added by Acts 1990, No. 989, § 3, eff. Jan. 1, 1991.

REVISION COMMENTS—1990

(a) This provision is new. It reproduces Article 34 of the Swiss Civil Code. See also Article 39 of the Greek Civil Code.

(b) This provision determines the standard of proof in cases in which a person disappeared under circumstances that make his death a certainty, yet his body has not been found. Under this provision, the death of a person is proved by a preponderance of the evidence.

(c) R.S. 9:1441 establishes a legal presumption of death that is applicable to persons missing while on active duty in one of the armed services of the United States. The statute provides: "A person on active duty in one of the armed services of the United States, who has been reported missing under circumstances which have induced the armed services to which he was attached to accept the presumption of his death, shall likewise be presumed dead under the law of this state." On the basis of this presumption, a Louisiana court may render a judgment of declaration of death.

Art. 31. Existence of a person at time of accrual of a right

One claiming a right that has accrued to another person is bound to prove that such person existed at the time when the right accrued.

Added by Acts 1990, No. 989, § 3, eff. Jan. 1, 1991.

REVISION COMMENTS—1990

(a) This provision is the same as Article 76 of the Louisiana Civil Code of 1870. Cf. Article 37 of the Greek Civil Code. It does not change the law.

(b) This provision expresses the fundamental principal of civil law that rights may be acquired only by the living. Thus, a person who claims that another person acquired a right must prove that the acquirer of the right lived at the moment of the accrual of the right. Of course, this burden of proof must be carried only as to persons "whose existence is not known".

Arts. 32 to 37.   [Blank]

TITLE II—DOMICILE

Art. 38. Domicile

The domicile of a natural person is the place of his habitual residence. The domicile of a juridical person may be either the state of its formation or the state of its principal place of business, whichever is most pertinent to the particular issue, unless otherwise specifically provided by law.

Acts 2008, No. 801, § 1, eff. Jan. 1, 2009. Amended by Acts 2012, No. 713, § 2.

REVISION COMMENT—2008

This Article is new. It is based on Civil Code Article 38 (1870). The word "parish" is no longer used in the definition of "domicile." The suppression of "parish" will make the definition of domicile relevant for both in-state and out-of-state applications.

Art. 39. Domicile and residence

A natural person may reside in several places but may not have more than one domicile. In the absence of habitual residence, any place of residence may be considered one's domicile at the option of persons whose interests are affected.

Acts 2008, No. 801, § 1, eff. Jan. 1, 2009.

REVISION COMMENTS—2008

(a) This Article is new. It is based on Article 38, second paragraph, of the Louisiana Civil Code of 1870 and provisions of modern civil codes. Cf. Quebec Civil Code Art. 77 and 78; Greek Civil Code Art. 51; cf. Italian Civil Code Art. 44.

(b) For Louisiana jurisprudence illustrating the difference between domicile and residence, see McClendon v. Bel, 797 So.2d 700 (La.App. 1 Cir. 2000).

Art. 40. Domicile of spouses

Spouses may have either a common domicile or separate domiciles.

Acts 2008, No. 801, § 1, eff. Jan. 1, 2009.

REVISION COMMENTS—2008

(a) This Article is new; it is based on Article 82 of the Quebec Civil Code and Article 108.1 of the French Civil Code.

(b) Civil Code Article 98 declares: "Married persons owe each other fidelity, support, and assistance." Unlike the Quebec Civil Code, the Louisiana Civil Code does not impose on spouses the obligation to reside together.

Art. 40.1.   [Blank]

Art. 41. Domicile of unemancipated minor

The domicile of an unemancipated minor is that of the parent or parents with whom the minor usually resides. If the minor has been placed by court order under the legal authority of a parent or other person, the domicile of that person is the domicile of the minor, unless the court directs otherwise.

The domicile of an unemancipated minor under tutorship is that of his tutor. In case of joint tutorship, the domicile of the minor is that of the tutor with whom the minor usually resides, unless the court directs otherwise.

Acts 2008, No. 801, § 1, eff. Jan. 1, 2009.

REVISION COMMENT—2008

This Article is new. It is based on Civil Code Article 39 (1870), first clause, and Article 80 of the Quebec Civil Code. The first paragraph of this Article is applicable when the parents of the minor are married to each other and the minor is under parental authority. The second paragraph of this Article is applicable when the parents of the minor are divorced or widowed. That paragraph is also applicable when parents exercising parental authority have placed the minor under tutorship.

Art. 42. Domicile of interdict

The domicile of a full interdict is that of the curator. A limited interdict retains his domicile, unless otherwise provided in the judgment of interdiction.

Acts 2008, No. 801, § 1, eff. Jan. 1, 2009.

REVISION COMMENT—2008

This Article is new. It is based on Civil Code Article 39 (1870), second clause and Article 81, second clause of the Quebec Civil Code.

Art. 43. Domicile of person under continued or permanent tutorship

The domicile of a person under continued or permanent tutorship is that of his tutor.

Acts 2008, No. 801, § 1, eff. Jan. 1, 2009.

REVISION COMMENT—2008

This Article is new. It is intended to apply when a developmentally disabled person is under continued or permanent tutorship. See C.C. Arts. 354–362.

Art. 44. Change of domicile

Domicile is maintained until acquisition of a new domicile. A natural person changes domicile when he moves his residence to another location with the intent to make that location his habitual residence.

Acts 2008, No. 801, § 1, eff. Jan. 1, 2009.

REVISION COMMENTS—2008

(a) This Article is new. It is based on Civil Code Article 41 (1870).

(b) For the deletion of the word "parish," found in Civil Code Article 41 (1870), see comments under Article 38 (Rev. 2008). For the domicile of persons displaced from their place of residence by a gubernatorially declared state of emergency, see R.S. 18:101(F) and 451.3.

Art. 45. Proof of intent to change domicile

Proof of one's intent to establish or change domicile depends on the circumstances. A sworn declaration of intent recorded in the parishes from which and to which he intends to move may be considered as evidence of intent.

Acts 2008, No. 801, § 1, eff. Jan. 1, 2009.

REVISION COMMENT—2008

This Article is new. It is based on Civil Code Articles 42 and 43 (1870).

Art. 46. Person holding temporary position

A person holding a temporary position away from his domicile retains his domicile unless he demonstrates a contrary intent.

Acts 2008, No. 801, § 1, eff. Jan. 1, 2009.

REVISION COMMENT—2008

This Article is new. It is based on Civil Code Article 44 (1870) and broadens its principles to include positions other than public offices.

TITLE III—ABSENT PERSONS

CHAPTER 1—CURATORSHIP OF THE PROPERTY OF ABSENT PERSONS

Art. 47. Curator of an absent person's property

An absent person is one who has no representative in this state and whose whereabouts are not known and cannot be ascertained by diligent effort.

When an absent person owns property in this state, the court may, upon petition of any interested party and a showing of necessity, appoint a curator to manage the property of the absent person.

Acts 1990, No. 989, § 1, eff. Jan. 1, 1991.

REVISION COMMENTS—1990

(a) This provision is new. It changes the law in several respects. According to Article 47 of the Louisiana Civil Code of 1870, the appointment of a curator is mandatory if the terms of the article are satisfied. Under this Article, a curator may be appointed at the discretion of the court upon a showing of necessity. The court may act only upon petition by a person having a legitimate interest. See R.S. 13:3421 et seq.

(b) A curator may only be appointed if the absent person owns property in this state. The word "property" includes movables and immovables, corporeals and incorporeals. See Yiannopoulos, Civil Law Property § 1 (2d ed. 1980).

(c) In the light of contemporary needs, however, the curator should have both power of administration and power of disposition. The curator should exercise his power of disposition with the permission of the proper court in accordance with the provisions of the governing legislation. See R.S. 13:3437 through 3440. The words "to manage" are used in this Article to indicate that the curator has powers of administration and disposition over the property of the absent person.

(d) The appointment of a curator is predicated on "necessity". The petitioner must show that the appointment of a curator to manage the property of the absent person is necessary for the protection of the interests of the absent person, of the interest of the petitioner, or of the interests of third parties.

(e) This Article defines the term "absent person." For the definition of "absentee" as used in the Code of Civil Procedure, see C.C.P. Art. 5251(1). Civil Code Article 3556(3) is repealed.

(f) A person, whether dead or alive, is an absent person if his whereabouts are not known and cannot be ascertained by diligent effort. To prove that the whereabouts of a person cannot be ascertained by diligent effort, it must be shown that such an effort has in fact been made or that it would be futile to do so. When there is a strong probability that the absent person is dead, a proceeding for the declaration of death may be instituted. See Article 54, infra.

Art. 48. Powers, rights, and duties of curator

The curator has power of administration and disposition over the property of the absent person as provided by legislation.

When the absent person is a spouse in community, the curatorship is limited to his separate property.

Acts 1990, No. 989, § 1, eff. Jan. 1, 1991.

REVISION COMMENTS—1990

(a) This provision is new. It changes the law as it provides that the curator has power of disposition over the property of the absent person. This power exists and may be exercised as provided by legislation. See R.S. 13:3437 through 3440.

(b) For letters of curatorship, see R.S. 13:3435. For management of the community property, see Articles 2355, 2355.1, 2356, and 2374, infra.

Art. 49. Legal capacity of absent person

The establishment of the curatorship does not deprive the absent person of his capacity to make juridical acts. Nevertheless, his acts of disposition of immovable property are not effective towards third persons and the curator unless filed for registry in the public records of the parish in which the immovable property is located.

Acts 1990, No. 989, § 1, eff. Jan. 1, 1991.

REVISION COMMENTS—1990

(a) This provision is new. It expresses the principle of Louisiana law that an absent person continues to enjoy full legal capacity to make juridical acts. Indeed, the establishment of the curatorship is not like an interdiction.

(b) Although an absent person has full legal capacity to make juridical acts, third persons acquiring rights in immovables from the curator of the absent person's property ought to be protected in the absence of information in the public records that the immovable property has been disposed of by the purportedly absent person. Accordingly, this Article provides that acts of disposition made by a purportedly absent person after the establishment of the curatorship of his property are not effective towards third persons unless filed for registry in the public records of the parish in which the immovable property is located. With respect to movables, delivery takes the place of registration.

Art. 50. Termination of curatorship of right

The curatorship of the property of the absent person terminates of right when he appoints a person to represent him in this state, when his whereabouts become known, or when he dies.

Acts 1990, No. 989, § 1, eff. Jan. 1, 1991.

REVISION COMMENTS—1990

(a) This provision is new. The curatorship of the absent person's property terminates of right, that is, without the necessity of a judgment, when he appoints a person to represent him in this state, when his whereabouts become known, or when he dies.

(b) The curatorship terminates of right when the absent person reappears anywhere in the world. It is the same when the absent person appoints a representative in any part of the world to represent his interests in Louisiana. For the protection of the interests of third persons who are ignorant of the termination of curatorship, see Article 53, infra.

Art. 51. Termination by judgment of declaration of death

The curatorship of the property of the absent person also terminates when a judgment of declaration of death is rendered.

When an absent person has no known heirs and is presumed dead, it shall be the duty of the curator to initiate proceedings for a declaration of death.

Acts 1990, No. 989, § 1, eff. Jan. 1, 1991.

REVISION COMMENTS—1990

(a) This provision is new. It is based in part on Article 53 of the Louisiana Civil Code of 1870.

(b) When an absent person has no known heirs and is presumed dead, it shall be the duty of the curator to initiate proceedings for the declaration of death. In such a case, the curatorship shall terminate when a judgment of declaration of death is rendered.

Art. 52. Effects of termination of curatorship

Upon termination of the curatorship, the curator is bound to account for his management and to restore the property to the formerly absent person or to his successors.

Acts 1990, No. 989, § 1, eff. Jan. 1, 1991.

REVISION COMMENT—1990

This provision is new. When the curatorship terminates, either of right or by judgment, the curator is bound to account for his management upon the demand of the formerly absent person or his successors. The curator is also bound to restore the property to the formerly absent person, if he has reappeared, or to his successors if the absent person has been declared to be dead. In the last case, the property of the absent person will devolve under the laws of succession.

Art. 53. Validity of acts of curator after termination of the curatorship

When the curator acquires knowledge of the termination of his curatorship, he is bound to file a notice in the curatorship proceeding that his authority to manage the property of the formerly absent person has ceased.

Acts of administration or disposition made by the curator after the curatorship has terminated are valid toward third persons unless notice of the termination of the curatorship has been filed in the curatorship proceeding.

Acts 1990, No. 989, § 1, eff. Jan. 1, 1991.

REVISION COMMENTS—1990

(a) This provision is new.

(b) After termination of the curatorship, whether of right or by judgment, the authority of the curator to manage, dispose, or encumber the property of the former absent person terminates. Nevertheless, acts of administration or disposition made by the curator after the curatorship has terminated are valid toward third persons unless notice of the termination of the curatorship has been filed in the curatorship proceeding. This accords with the public records doctrine. Third persons are entitled to rely on the absence in the curatorship proceeding of a notice that the curatorship has terminated.

(c) When the curatorship terminates by judgment, the recordation of the judgment in the curatorship proceeding constitutes notice of the termination of the authority of the curator to manage, dispose, or encumber the property of the absent person. Thus, the nullity of the acts of the curator may be asserted against third persons.

CHAPTER 2—DECLARATION OF DEATH

Art. 54. Absent person; declaration of death

One who has been an absent person for five years is presumed to be dead. If the absence commenced between August 26, 2005, and September 30, 2005, and was related to or caused by Hurricane Katrina or Rita, the absent person who is not currently charged with an offense that is defined as a felony under the laws of the state of Louisiana or the United States of America shall be presumed dead after the passage of two years. Upon petition by an interested party, the court shall render judgment declaring the death of the absent person and shall determine the date on which the absence commenced and the date of death.

Acts 1990, No. 989, § 1, eff. Jan. 1, 1991. Amended by Acts 2006, No. 258, § 1.

REVISION COMMENTS—1990

(a) This provision is new. It is based in part on Articles 57, 60, and 70 of the Louisiana Civil Code of 1870, Articles 39 and 40 of the Greek Civil Code, and corresponding provisions of other modern civil codes.

17

(b) The presumption of death that Article 54 establishes is applicable to all matters, including the opening of the succession of the absent person and the recovery of the proceeds of his life insurance. See Ledet v. State Department of Health and Human Resources, 465 So.2d 98 (La.App. 4th Cir.1985).

Art. 55. Declaration of death; effect

The succession of the person declared dead shall be opened as of the date of death fixed in the judgment, and his estate shall devolve in accordance with the law of successions.

Acts 1990, No. 989, § 1, eff. Jan. 1, 1991.

REVISION COMMENTS—1990

(a) This provision is new. It is based on Article 70 of the Louisiana Civil Code of 1870 and on provisions in modern civil codes.

(b) The judgment of declaration of death determines the date of death. The succession of the person who is declared dead is opened as of that date and devolves on the persons qualifying as his successors on the date of death.

Art. 56. New evidence as to time of death

If there is clear and convincing new evidence establishing a date of death other than that determined in the judgment of declaration of death, the judgment shall be amended accordingly.

Persons previously recognized as successors are bound to restore the estate to the new successors but may keep the fruits they have gathered.

Acts 1990, No. 989, § 1, eff. Jan. 1, 1991.

REVISION COMMENTS—1990

(a) This provision is new. It is based in part on Article 71 of the Louisiana Civil Code of 1870.

(b) If, after the judgment of declaration of death is rendered, new and convincing evidence is gathered which establishes a date of death other than that determined in the judgment of declaration of death, the judgment shall be amended to show a new date of death. In such a case, the succession of the deceased will be re-opened and shall devolve on persons who were capable of receiving at the time of the newly determined date of death.

(c) If the re-opening of the succession results in the institution of new successors, the new successors will have the right to recover the estate from those who possessed it as successors under the previous date of death. The obligation of the former successors is to restore the property that they received as successors with the exception of gathered fruits. If they are unable to restore the property in kind, they will be bound to return its value at the time of restoration. There is no recourse against third persons.

Art. 57. Reappearance of absent person; recovery of his property

If a person who has been declared dead reappears, he shall be entitled to recover his property that still exists in the condition in which it is found from those who took it as his successors or from their transferees by gratuitous title. He may also recover the net proceeds of things alienated and for the diminution of the value of things that has resulted from their encumbrance.

Acts 1990, No. 989, § 1, eff. Jan. 1, 1991.

REVISION COMMENTS—1990

(a) This provision is new. It is based in part on Article 73 of the Louisiana Civil Code of 1870.

(b) If a person who has been declared dead reappears, he shall be entitled to recover his property only from those who took it as his successors or from their transferees by gratuitous title. The property must be restored in the condition in which it exists, as it may be burdened with real rights in favor of third persons. If property has been alienated, the claimant will be entitled to recover the net proceeds. If the property has been encumbered, the claimant will be entitled to recover for the diminution of the value of things that has resulted from the encumbrance.

(c) With respect to fruits, the persons who were placed in possession of the claimant's property as his successors are considered to be possessors under Civil Code Article 486 (Rev.1979). If in good faith, they shall be entitled to keep the fruits they have gathered. Likewise, with respect to improvements made on immovables, the persons who were placed in possession of the claimant's property shall have the rights of possessors under Civil Code Articles 496 and 497 (Rev.1979).

(d) When property has been alienated or encumbered by the persons who were placed in possession of the property of a person declared dead, there is no recourse against third persons.

(e) This provision contemplates recovery of the property of a person who has been declared dead upon his reappearance. For the recovery of a succession opened in favor of such a person, see Article 58, infra.

Art. 58. Succession rights of person presumed dead or declared dead

A person who is presumed to be dead or who has been declared dead at a time a succession would have been opened in his favor cannot be a successor. The estate of the deceased devolves as if that person were dead at the time of the opening of the succession.

Acts 1990, No. 989, § 1, eff. Jan. 1, 1991.

REVISION COMMENTS—1990

(a) This provision is new. It is based in part on Article 77 of the Louisiana Civil Code of 1870.

(b) A person who is presumed to be dead or who has been declared dead at the time a succession is opened in his favor may not be an heir or legatee. A declaration of death is not required for application of this Article.

(c) If a person presumed to be dead or who has been declared dead is called to a succession as the only heir or as the universal legatee, the succession passes to persons who succeed in his default. If the person who is presumed to be dead or who has been declared dead concurs with other heirs, he is represented by his descendants.

Art. 59. Reappearance of absent person; recovery of his inheritance

If the person who is presumed to be dead or who has been declared dead reappears, he shall be entitled to recover his inheritance in the condition in which it is found from those who succeeded in his default and from their transferees by gratuitous title. He may also recover the net proceeds of things alienated and for the diminution of the value of things that has resulted from their encumbrance.

Acts 1990, No. 989, § 1, eff. Jan. 1, 1991.

REVISION COMMENTS—1990

(a) This provision is new. It is based in part on Article 79 of the Louisiana Civil Code of 1870.

(b) This provision contemplates an action by a person who was presumed to be dead or who had been declared dead at the time of the opening of a succession in his favor. Since he could not be a successor, other persons succeeded in his default. Article 58 supra. If the person who is presumed to be dead or who has been declared dead reappears, he shall be entitled to recover his inheritance from those who succeeded in his default. This may be an action for the recovery of an entire estate or a share in an estate ("petition d'heredite"). The rights of a formerly absent person will be determined as of the time of the opening of the succession in his favor. This may result in the displacement of a person as heir or in the diminution of an heir's share in the succession.

(c) The claimant is entitled to recover his inheritance in the condition in which it exists, as it may have been encumbered with real rights in favor of third persons. The claimant may also recover the net proceeds of things alienated and for the diminution of the value of things that result from their encumbrance. Cf. Article 57, supra. Rights to fruits and improvements are determined by application of Civil Code Articles 486, 496, and 497 (Rev.1979).

(d) If the absent person reappears within two years from the date of the finality of a judgment of possession, he should have the same rights that omitted heirs have under R.S. 9:5630.

Arts. 60 to 85.   [Blank]

TITLE IV—HUSBAND AND WIFE

CHAPTER 1—MARRIAGE: GENERAL PRINCIPLES

Art. 86. Marriage; definition

Marriage is a legal relationship between a man and a woman that is created by civil contract. The relationship and the contract are subject to special rules prescribed by law.

Acts 1987, No. 886, § 1, eff. Jan. 1, 1988.

REVISION COMMENTS—1987

(a) This provision effects no change in the substance of the source provisions, Articles 86 through 89 of the Civil Code of 1870. In particular, the import of Article 86 of the Civil Code of 1870 remains unchanged: the law views marriage as purely a civil matter, and not as one subject to the operation of religious or ecclesiastical law. The term "civil" in former Article 86 has been retained in order to emphasize that continuity of policy.

(b) The provisions of this revision, as a general rule, are not intended to overrule the established jurisprudence holding that certain laws regulating marriage and the relationship of husband and wife are matters of public order from which the parties may not derogate by contract. See, e.g. Holliday v. Holliday, 358 So.2d 618 (La.1978) (obligation of support); Favrot v. Barnes, 332 So.2d 873 (La.App. 4th Cir.1976), reversed on other grounds 339 So.2d 843 (La.1976) (sexual obligation). See also C.C. Art. 11 (1870).

(c) The marriage contract differs from other contracts in that it creates a social status that affects not only the contracting parties, but also their posterity and the good order of society. It is thus subject to legislative control, independent of the will of the parties. Rhodes v. Miller, 189 La. 288, 179 So. 430 (1938). Accordingly, it has been held that constitutional strictures against the impairment of contractual obligations do not apply to incidents of the marriage contract. Hurry v. Hurry, 144 La. 877, 81 So. 378 (1919); Maynard v. Hill, 125 U.S. 190, 8 S.Ct. 723 (1888). Laws governing marriage and divorce may thus be given retroactive effect without constitutional impediment. Stallings v. Stallings, 177 La. 488, 148 So. 687 (1933).

(d) The relationship of marriage is not a legal entity, separate and distinct from husband and wife.

Art. 87. Contract of marriage; requirements

The requirements for the contract of marriage are:

The absence of legal impediment.

A marriage ceremony.

The free consent of the parties to take each other as husband and wife, expressed at the ceremony.

Acts 1987, No. 886, § 1, eff. Jan. 1, 1988.

REVISION COMMENTS—1987

(a) This Article reproduces the substance of Article 90 of the Civil Code of 1870. A valid marriage is created if the requirements of this article and Article 91, infra, are satisfied. Physical consummation is not necessary.

(b) A person may contract marriage if he is not prohibited from doing so by Articles 88, 89, or 90, infra. This rule applies to minors as well as majors, in the sense that once a minor has contracted marriage that marriage is valid. This revision does not change the prior jurisprudential rule that the Louisiana statutory provisions imposing an age requirement for marriage in general and special third-party consent requirements for marriages of minors are only directory to officiants. State v. Golden, 210 La. 347, 26 So. 837 (1946). Under R.S. 9:211 [repealed; see, now, Ch.C. art. 1545], certain officiants are enjoined, on pain of withdrawal of their privilege to perform marriages, from performing marriages in which one or both of the parties is a minor.

(c) Instead of referring to "the forms and solemnities prescribed by law," as did Article 90 of the Civil Code of 1870, this Article uses the more specific term "ceremony". This change is intended to emphasize that the only essential "formal" prerequisite to a valid marriage is a ceremony conducted in accordance with Article 91, infra. Thus the parties' failure to procure a marriage license will not prevent the creation of a valid marriage. See Succession of Jene, 173 So.2d 857 (La.App. 4th Cir.1965); Holmes v. Holmes, 6 La. 463 (1834); Art. 91, comment (a), infra.

(d) The requirement that the parties express their consent to be married at a ceremony precludes the confection of common-law marriages in Louisiana. See Liberty Mutual Insurance Company v. Caesar, 345 So.2d 64 (La.App. 3d Cir.1977), cert. denied 347 So.2d 1118 (La.1977); Succession of Marinoni, 177 La. 592, 148 So. 888 (1933). Louisiana courts, however, have traditionally recognized the validity of common-law marriages contracted in other states whose laws sanction such unions. E.g., Brinson v. Brinson, 233 La. 417, 96 So.2d 653 (1957).

Art. 88. Impediment of existing marriage

A married person may not contract another marriage.

Acts 1987, No. 886, § 1, eff. Jan. 1, 1988.

REVISION COMMENTS—1987

(a) This provision does not change the law.

(b) A bigamous marriage is an absolute nullity. It is void from its inception, cannot be ratified, and can be challenged by anyone with an interest, collaterally or directly. See Article 94, infra; Prieto v. Succession of Prieto, 165 La. 710, 115 So. 911 (1928); Summerlin v. Livingston, 15 La.Ann. 519 (1860).

(c) An undissolved marriage is an impediment to either spouse's subsequent marriage. A bigamous, incestuous, or otherwise absolutely null union is not. A party to such a union may lawfully marry even though the nullity of his prior union has never been judicially pronounced. Coon v. Monroe Scrap Material Co., 191 So. 607 (La.App. 2d Cir.1939).

(d) A bigamous union may produce civil effects if either or both of the parties contracted it in good faith. See Article 96, infra.

Art. 89. Impediment of same sex

Persons of the same sex may not contract marriage with each other. A purported marriage between persons of the same sex contracted in another state shall be governed by the provisions of Title II of Book IV of the Civil Code.

Acts 1987, No. 886, § 1, eff. Jan. 1, 1988. Amended by Acts 1999, No. 890, § 1.

REVISION COMMENTS—1987

(a) This Article reproduces the provision of Article 88 of the Civil Code of 1870, as amended by Acts 1975, No. 361, Sec. 1, which provided that only marriages contracted between a man and a woman would be recognized by law.

(b) Under Article 94, infra, a purported marriage contracted in contravention of this article is an absolute nullity.

(c) A purported marriage between persons of the same sex is not an impediment to either party's subsequent marriage to another person.

(d) A purported marriage between persons of the same sex cannot give rise to a putative marriage. See Article 96, infra.

Art. 90. Impediments of relationship

A.   The following persons may not contract marriage with each other:

(1) Ascendants and descendants.

(2) Collaterals within the fourth degree, whether of the whole or of the half blood.

B.   The impediment exists whether the persons are related by consanguinity or by adoption. Nevertheless, persons related by adoption, though not by blood, in the collateral line within the fourth degree may marry each other if they obtain judicial authorization in writing to do so.

Acts 1987, No. 886, § 1, eff. Jan. 1, 1988. Amended by Acts 2004, No. 26, § 1.

REVISION COMMENTS—1987

(a) This Article changes the law in only one respect. See comment (e), infra.

(b) The phrase "collaterals within the fourth degree" includes aunt and nephew, uncle and niece, siblings, and first cousins. See C.C. Art. 901 (rev.1981). Marriages contracted by these collaterals before September 11, 1981, were legal under former Civil Code Article 95 as retroactively amended by Acts 1981, No. 647. Though not continued as part of the Civil Code, that validating provision has been carried forward in Section 5 of the act embodying this revision (Acts 1987, No. 886).

(c) The prohibition of marriage between close relatives appears to spring from an ancient taboo found in most societies. It is difficult to determine with certainty whether this prohibition is ultimately based on empirical observation of the harmful genetic effects of such marriages, or on moral considerations growing out of the need to preserve peace within the family and to expand family fortune and influence through intermarriage with other family or tribal groups, or on a combination of these two factors.

(d) Under Article 94, infra, a marriage that violates any of the prohibitions of this article is absolutely null. Such a marriage may nevertheless produce civil effects in favor of a party who has contracted it in good faith. See Article 96, infra.

(e) The third sentence of this Article is new. It resolves a question that the law previously left unanswered. See C.C. Art. 214 (Rev.1978). A judge of a court of competent jurisdiction may authorize a marriage between collaterals unrelated by blood but legally related by adoption. In deciding whether to do so, the judge should consider whether the policy of preserving family harmony will be advanced or impeded by the proposed union. No other exception to the prohibitions listed in this article may be made on account of adoption. If collaterals within the fourth degree marry without the authorization required by this article, their marriage is absolutely null under Article 94, infra. Such a union may nevertheless produce civil effects in favor of a party who contracted it in good faith. See Article 96, infra.

Art. 91. Marriage ceremony required

The parties must participate in a marriage ceremony performed by a third person who is qualified, or reasonably believed by the parties to be qualified, to perform the ceremony. The parties must be physically present at the ceremony when it is performed.

Acts 1987, No. 886, § 1, eff. Jan. 1, 1988.

REVISION COMMENTS—1987

(a) This Article clarifies but does not change the law. It reflects the prior jurisprudential rule that the articles of the Civil Code of 1870 that set forth the formalities of marriage were only directory to officiants. An officiant's failure to comply with any other ceremonial provision than is imposed by Article 87 and this Article may subject him to civil sanction (see R.S. 9:201 et seq.), but it will not invalidate the resulting marriage. Succession of Jene, 173 So.2d 857 (La.App. 4th Cir.1965); Landry v. Bellanger, 120 La. 962, 45 So. 956 (1908); Sabalot v. Populus, 31 La.Ann. 854 (1879).

(b) Other ceremonial provisions, including those relating to the issuance and presentation of marriage licenses, the registration of officiants, the requisite number of witnesses to the ceremony and their qualifications, and the written act of celebration of the marriage, appear in the Revised Statutes. See R.S. 9:201 et seq.

(c) A "person . . . reasonably believed by the spouses to be qualified" to perform a marriage ceremony may include any member of the class of persons generally recognized as empowered to perform such ceremonies, whether or not properly registered to do so. The expression may be broadly construed to prevent the annulment of marriages for technical reasons reasonably beyond the control of the intended spouses.

Art. 92. Marriage by procuration prohibited

A marriage may not be contracted by procuration.

Acts 1987, No. 886, § 1, eff. Jan. 1, 1988.

REVISION COMMENTS—1987

(a) This Article does not change the law.

(b) A marriage contracted by procuration, that is, with a party absent and represented by another person, is absolutely null. See Article 94, infra. The parties must personally express their consent to take each other as husband and wife at a ceremony, and the officiant must be able to examine them to satisfy himself that their consent is freely given.

Art. 93. Vices of consent

Consent is not free when given under duress or when given by a person incapable of discernment.

Acts 1987, No. 886, § 1, eff. Jan. 1, 1988.

REVISION COMMENTS—1987

(a) This Article carries forward the most important provisions of its sources, Articles 90 and 91 of the Civil Code of 1870 and the associated jurisprudence.

(b) As used in this Article, "duress" includes not only executed violence, but also threatened violence, if the threat is pending at the time consent is given. This usage is in keeping with the jurisprudence decided under the source provisions, Articles 90 and 91 of the Civil Code of 1870. See Fowler v. Fowler, 131 La. 1088, 60 So. 694 (1913); Quealy v. Waldron, 126 La. 258, 52 So. 479 (1910). Threats of criminal prosecution, as well as of violence, may render the consent procured thereby ineffective. Grundmeyer v. Sander, 175 La. 189, 143 So. 45 (1932). Applying by analogy Articles 1856 and 1857 of the Civil Code of 1870, the courts have traditionally drawn a distinction between charges warranted by the facts and those not: only marriages contracted under threat of the latter have been invalidated. Lacoste v. Guidroz, 47 La.Ann. 295, 16 So. 836 (1895). See C.C.Art. 1962 (Rev. 1984). Threats to reputation or fortune may be sufficient to invalidate a marriage under this Article. See C.C.Art. 1959 (Rev. 1984).

(c) This Article adds a new instance in which the Civil Code views a party's consent to marriage as not freely given: when the spouse is "incapable of discernment" at the time the marriage is contracted. Mere ignorance of the law is not sufficient to render a party's consent unfree. Insanity may do so. As under prior jurisprudence, under this Article insanity is viewed as creating a lack of free consent, rather than a lack of capacity to contract marriage; so only the insane spouse may seek annulment of such a marriage. Stier v. Price, 214 La. 394, 37 So.2d 547 (1899); Sabalot v. Populus, 31 La.Ann. 854 (1879). Under Article 95, infra, the spouse of a person of unsound mind has no standing to bring an action to have the marriage annulled.

(d) A "person incapable of discernment" may include, but is not limited to, a person under the influence of alcohol or drugs, a mentally retarded person, or a person who is too young to understand the consequences of the marriage celebration.

CHAPTER 2—NULLITY OF MARRIAGE

Art. 94. Absolutely null marriage

A marriage is absolutely null when contracted without a marriage ceremony, by procuration, or in violation of an impediment. A judicial declaration of nullity is not required, but an action to recognize the nullity may be brought by any interested person.

Acts 1987, No. 886, § 1, eff. Jan. 1, 1988.

REVISION COMMENTS—1987

(a) This Article continues the prior rule that bigamous and incestuous marriages are absolutely null. It clarifies the law governing nullity of marriages between persons of the same sex and marriages contracted by procuration or without a ceremony.

(b) This Article and Article 95, infra, codify the prior jurisprudential rules regarding the differing effects of absolutely and relatively null marriages. While a relatively null marriage ceases to have legal effect only from the time that its nullity is judicially declared, an absolutely null union is devoid of legal effect from the moment of its inception. Burrell v. Burrell, 154 So.2d 103 (1st Cir.1963); Succession of Minvielle, 15 La.Ann. 342 (1860). Thus, a party to an absolutely null union may lawfully contract a second marriage without having the first judicially annulled. Coon v. Monroe Scrap Material Co., 191 So. 607 (2d Cir.1939); Patterson v. Gaines, 47 U.S. (6 How.) 551, 12 L.Ed. 543 (1848); 1 M. Planiol, Traité élémentaire de droit civil, no. 1046 (La.State Law Ins. transl. 1959). The parties to an absolutely null union may be accorded the civil effects of marriage, however, if a court declares one or both of them putative spouses. See Article 96, infra.

(c) The absolute nullity of a marriage may be raised in a direct action or collaterally, either as the basis of a claim, or as a defense to a claim of another. McCaffrey v. Benson, 38 La.Ann. 198 (1886); Summerlin v. Livingston, 15 La.Ann. 519 (La.1860); Succession of Minvielle, 15 La.Ann. 342 (1860). See also Farrell v. Farrell, 275 So.2d 489 (1st Cir.1973). Because the prohibitions giving rise to absolute nullity are matters of public order, the class of persons who may raise the issue is broadly defined. A bigamist may assert the nullity of his bigamous union. Clark v. Clark, 192 So.2d 594 (3d Cir.1966); Burrell v. Burrell, 154 So.2d 103 (1st Cir.1963). The same right is extended to either party to a marriage that is invalid by reason of the existence of any of the other listed impediments. See Rhodes v. Miller, 189 La. 288, 179 So. 430 (1938); 1 M. Planiol, supra, no. 1035.

(d) The retrospective provision of Article 113 of the Civil Code of 1870 concerning "fugitive marriages" has been suppressed in this revision. However, in order to protect the interests of persons who have relied on the most recent such exception, a section of the act embodying this revision (Acts 1987, No. 886, § 5) retroactively validates all marriages between collateral relations contracted prior to September 11, 1981, the effective date of Acts 1981, No. 647 (which similarly amended Article 95 of the Civil Code of 1870).

The prospective fugitive marriage provision of Civil Code Article 113 (1870) has also been suppressed because it is unnecessary. The only situation it addressed is that in which Louisiana domiciliaries who lack capacity to marry in this state contract marriage in another state or country and then return here to live, intending to remain here. In that case the second paragraph of Civil Code Article 10 (1870) (redesignated as Art. 15 in 1987 [subsequently revised; see, now, C.C. art. 3520]) applies, and is dispositive.

There is no reason to apply a different rule to a fugitive marriage performed in another state, rather than a foreign country.

Art. 95. Relatively null marriage; confirmation

A marriage is relatively null when the consent of one of the parties to marry is not freely given. Such a marriage may be declared null upon application of the party whose consent was not free. The marriage may not be declared null if that party confirmed the marriage after recovering his liberty or regaining his discernment.

Acts 1987, No. 886, § 1, eff. Jan. 1, 1988.

(a) Limiting the right to challenge a relatively null marriage to the party whose consent was not freely given is consistent with former Civil Code Article 110 (1870) and with general obligations law. See C.C.Art. 2031 (rev. 1984). Stier v. Price, 214 La. 394, 37 So.2d 847 (1948); Succession of Barth, 178 La. 847, 152 So. 543 (1934).

(b) A spouse may confirm a marriage to which he did not freely consent because such a marriage is only relatively null.

(c) This Article changes prior law by substituting the broader term "confirm" for the phrase "cohabit together" used by Article 111 of the Civil Code of 1870 in specifying the means of validating a relatively null marriage. Louisiana jurisprudence has generally defined the term "cohabitation" as necessarily including sexual intercourse. Ford v. Ford, 292 So.2d 275 (2d Cir.1974); State v. Brown, 236 La. 562, 108 So.2d 233 (1959); State v. Freddy, 117 La. 121, 41 So. 436 (1906). Proof that the parties have lived together as man and wife will continue to be persuasive evidence that the one whose consent was initially defective subsequently intended that a valid marriage should subsist, but the use of the broader term in this Article also permits the application of certain general obligations principles regarding confirmation of contracts. For instance, under Civil Code Article 1842 (rev. 1984) a party who had married under duress could confirm the marriage by express declaration.

(d) Under the language of this Article a spouse's legal representative may not confirm the spouse's marriage. The right to do so is limited to the spouse himself, once he has recovered his liberty or regained his discernment.

Art. 96. Civil effects of absolutely null marriage; putative marriage

An absolutely null marriage nevertheless produces civil effects in favor of a party who contracted it in good faith for as long as that party remains in good faith.

When the cause of the nullity is one party's prior undissolved marriage, the civil effects continue in favor of the other party, regardless of whether the latter remains in good faith, until the marriage is pronounced null or the latter party contracts a valid marriage.

A marriage contracted by a party in good faith produces civil effects in favor of a child of the parties.

A purported marriage between parties of the same sex does not produce any civil effects.

Acts 1987, No. 886, § 1, eff. Jan. 1, 1988.

(a) This Article reproduces the substance of the source provisions, Articles 117 and 118 of the Civil Code of 1870, and the associated jurisprudence, but changes the law in one respect: It provides that under certain circumstances a person who has contracted a bigamous marriage in good faith will be deemed a putative spouse even after he ceases to be in good faith.

(b) The jurisprudence decided under Articles 117 and 118 of the Civil Code of 1870 held that, where only one of the two parties to a null marriage had contracted it in good faith, the civil effects of the putative marriage terminated as of the moment at which the good faith spouse learned or should have learned of the existence of the impediment. Howard v. Ingle, 180 So. 248 (2d Cir.1938) (dicta); Evans v. Eureka Grand Lodge, 149 So. 305 (2d Cir.1933); Patton v. Cities of Philadelphia and New Orleans, 1 La.Ann. 98 (1846); Clendenning v. Clendenning, 3 Mart. (N.S.) 438 (La.1825). That rule had its source in Spanish law. See Projet of the Civil Code of 1825, 1 La.Legal Archives 10 (La.State Law Ins.1937); Patton v. Cities of Philadelphia and New Orleans, supra. This Article abrogates the traditional Louisiana rule in one very specific situation: where a party has acted in good faith in contracting a marriage that is absolutely null because the other party was already married at the time of contracting. In that situation the party whose prior undissolved marriage is the cause of nullity is the one who has the dispositive power to rectify the nullity (by divorcing his former spouse and remarrying his present one). The other party cannot do so. Accordingly, the second sentence of this Article permits the spouse who has acted in good faith and whose prior marriage was not the cause of the nullity to enjoy the civil effects of marriage even after he ceases to be in good faith. This additional period ends when the party benefitted by it contracts a valid marriage (whether with the other party to the null union or with a third party), or when the nullity of the bigamous marriage is judicially recognized, whichever occurs first.

(c) The special extension of time granted by the second sentence of this Article does not benefit a good faith party who has contracted an absolutely null marriage in ignorance of the continued existence of a prior marriage of his own. The equitable considerations that justify the extension do not apply in such a case.

(d) This Article is not intended to disturb the prior jurisprudence construing the term "good faith" in this context. The "good faith" contemplated by this Article is an honest and reasonable belief that there exists no legal impediment to a marriage. Jones v. Squire, 137 La. 883, 69 So. 733 (1915); Smith v. Smith, 43 La.Ann. 1140, 10 So. 248 (1891). Such a good faith belief may arise from an error of law, as well as of fact. Succession of Pigg, 228 La. 799, 84 So.2d 196 (1955) (putative wife relied upon husband's fraudulent divorce from first wife); Funderburk v. Funderburk, 214 La. 717, 38 So.2d 502 (1949) (putative wife relied upon null divorce obtained in a court of improper venue). Whether good faith exists is a question of fact dependent upon the circumstances of each case. Succession of Chavis, 211 La. 313, 29 So.2d 860 (1947). The jurisprudence has also held that good faith is presumed; that the burden of proof rests on the party who challenges its existence; and that any doubt as to the good faith of the parties to a marriage must be resolved in favor of the one who claims good faith. Succession of Pigg, supra; Funderburk v. Funderburk, supra; Jones v. Squire, supra. The spouse who is shown to have been a party to a previous undissolved marriage, however, bears the burden of proving that he contracted his second marriage in good faith. Gathright v. Smith, 368 So.2d 679 (La.1978).

(e) This Article is not intended to affect the jurisprudence governing the question whether the parties to an absolutely null union need have gone through a marriage ceremony in order to be deemed putative spouses. See, Succession of Rossi, 214 So.2d 223 (4th Cir.1968), cert. denied 253 La. 66, 216 So.2d 309 (La.1968); Succession of Cusimano, 173 La. 539, 138 So. 95 (La.1931); Succession of Marinoni, 164 So. 797 (La.1936). The holding of Succession of Marinoni, supra, could, in a proper case, form the basis for the application of the putative marriage doctrine to a marriage that was absolutely null under Article 94, supra, because contracted without a ceremony. The ultimate decision whether to follow Succession of Marinoni in preference to the two contrary cases previously cited, however, is left to the discretion of the court under this revision.

Art. 97. Civil effects of relatively null marriage

A relatively null marriage produces civil effects until it is declared null.

Acts 1987, No. 886, § 1, eff. Jan. 1, 1988.

REVISION COMMENT—1987

This Article is new, but it does not change the law. In Louisiana the relatively null marriage has long been regarded as valid until annulled by a judicial decree rendered in a direct action of nullity brought by a proper party, as defined in Article 110 of the Civil Code of 1870 (see Article 95, supra). Succession of Barth, 178 La. 847, 152 So. 543 (1934); State v. Loyacano, 135 La. 945, 66 So. 307 (1914); see also Delpit v. Young, 51 La.Ann. 923, 25 So. 547 (1899).

CHAPTER 3—INCIDENTS AND EFFECTS OF MARRIAGE

Art. 98. Mutual duties of married persons

Married persons owe each other fidelity, support, and assistance.

Acts 1987, No. 886, § 1, eff. Jan. 1, 1988.

REVISION COMMENTS—1987

(a) This Article reproduces the source provision, Civil Code Article 119 (1870), almost verbatim. It does not change the law.

(b) As used in this Article, the term "fidelity" refers not only to the spouses' duty to refrain from adultery, but also to their mutual obligation to submit to each other's reasonable and normal sexual desires. The jurisprudence has held that the latter obligation is a necessary concomitant of marriage. Favrot v. Barnes, 332 So.2d 873 (La.App. 4th Cir.1976), writ denied 334 So.2d 436 (La.1976), reversed in part on other grounds, 339 So.2d 843 (La.1976), cert. denied, 429 U.S. 961, 97 S.Ct. 387 (1976); Phillpott v. Phillpott, 285 So.2d 570 (La.App. 4th Cir.1973), writ refused 288 So.2d 643 (La.1974); Mudd v. Mudd, 206 La. 1055, 20 So.2d 311 (1944).

(c) The jurisprudence decided under the source provision has held that the spouses' duty to support each other is limited to furnishing the necessities of life. Smith v. Smith, 382 So.2d 972 (La.App. 1st Cir.1980); Hingle v. Hingle, 369 So.2d 271 (La.App. 4th Cir.1979); see 1 M. Planiol, Traité élémentaire de droit civil, nos. 904–905 (La.State Law Ins. transl. 1959). Nevertheless, the term "support" has been construed to include the cost not only of food, clothing, and shelter, but also of operating such conveniences as telephones, home appliances, and an automobile. Bernhardt v. Bernhardt, 283 So.2d 226 (La.1973) (construing C.C.Art. 160 (1870)). The duty to render assistance, insofar as it is separate from that of support, includes the personal care to be given an ill or infirm spouse. 1 M. Planiol, supra, no. 917; James v. State Through Board of Administrators of Charity Hospital, 154 So.2d 497 (La.App. 4th Cir.1963).

(d) Under R.S. 9:291 spouses may not sue each other during the existence of their marriage to enforce the obligations imposed by this Article. However, either party to a divorce suit has the right to seek enforcement of the other party's support obligation by petitioning the court for an interim support award.

(e) The spouses' duties under this Article, as a general rule, are matters of public order from which they may not derogate by contract. E.g., Favrot v. Barnes, 332 So.2d 873 (La.App. 4th Cir.1976), writ denied 334 So.2d 436 (La.1976), reversed in part on other grounds, 339 So.2d 843 (La.1976), cert. denied, 429 U.S. 961, 97 S.Ct. 387 (1976).

(f) Under this revision the spouses are free to live together as necessary to fulfill their obligation mutually to support, assist, and be faithful to each other. Cf. C.C. Art. 120 (1870), repealed by Acts 1985, No. 271.

(g) The property rights of married persons are regulated by their matrimonial regime, either a regime adopted by matrimonial agreement or the regime imposed by law under Book III, Title VI of this Code [C.C. art. 2325 et seq.].

Art. 99.   Family authority

Spouses mutually assume the moral and material direction of the family, exercise parental authority, and assume the moral and material obligations resulting therefrom.

Acts 1987, No. 886, § 1, eff. Jan. 1, 1988.

REVISION COMMENT—1987

This Article is new. It states a general principle of equality between the spouses in the moral and material direction of the family. See C.C.Art. 227 (1870) (spouses' mutual obligation to support children of their marriage).

Art. 100.   Surname of married persons

Marriage does not change the name of either spouse. However, a married person may use the surname of either or both spouses as a surname.

Acts 1987, No. 886, § 1, eff. Jan. 1, 1988.

REVISION COMMENTS—1987

(a) This Article is new. It resolves a conflict in Louisiana jurisprudence. Compare Succession of Kneipp, 172 La. 411, 134 So. 376 (1931) (legal surname of a married woman is her maiden name) with Wilty v. Jefferson Parish Democratic Executive Committee, 157 So.2d 718 (La.1963) (legal surname of a married woman is her husband's surname).

(b) Under this Article the legal name of each spouse remains unchanged by marriage, although the spouses are entitled to use each other's names as a matter of custom. Thus, the legal name of a spouse cannot be changed on his birth certificate, as maintained by the state registrar of vital statistics, simply as a result of the marriage. See R.S. 40:34. Only a name change effected by an action under R.S. 13:4751–4755, or by an adoption pursuant to R.S. 9:421–462 [repealed in part; see, now, also, Ch.C. art. 1167 et seq.], or by virtue of a legitimation under R.S. 40:46(A), can be given this ultimate legal effect. R.S. 40:34(A)(1)(a)(v) (rev. 1979); See also R.S. 40:75. However, either spouse may validly sign documents either with his spouse's surname or with a combination of his and his spouse's surname.

(c) As regards the wife's name, the rules adopted by this Article are those followed in French law (1 M. Planiol, Traité élémentaire de droit civil, no.'s 390–392 (La. State Law Ins. transl. 1959)); and the same rules are applied to the husband under this revision. It has been held that these rights continue after the marriage has ended. Welcker v. Welcker, 342 So.2d 251 (La.App. 4th Cir.1977), writ denied 343 So.2d 1077 (La.1977). Contra, 1 M. Planiol, supra, No. 395.

CHAPTER 4—TERMINATION OF MARRIAGE

Art. 101. Termination of marriage

Marriage terminates upon:

The death of either spouse.

Divorce.

A judicial declaration of its nullity, when the marriage is relatively null.

The issuance of a court order authorizing the spouse of a person presumed dead to remarry, as provided by law.

Acts 1990, No. 1009, § 1, eff. Jan. 1, 1991.

REVISION COMMENTS—1990

(a) This Article reproduces the substance of the source provision, Article 136 of the Civil Code of 1870, omitting unnecessary material. It does not change the law, except as provided in comment (d), infra.

(b) The omission of the redundant phrase "legally obtained" that followed "divorce" in the source Article is not intended to change the law.

(c) The source Article's reference to the effect of separation from bed and board has been omitted because this revision does not provide for legal separation.

(d) This Article specifies a judicial declaration of nullity as a means of terminating only relatively null marriages because such a marriage is valid until its nullity is judicially declared. An absolutely null marriage, on the other hand, is null from its inception; so as a general rule no action, judicial or otherwise, is necessary to terminate it. See C.C. Art. 94 (1987).

(e) The last clause of this Article refers to R.S. 9:301 (1990).

TITLE V—DIVORCE

CHAPTER 1—THE DIVORCE ACTION

Art. 102.   Judgment of divorce; living separate and apart prior to rule

Except in the case of a covenant marriage, a divorce shall be granted upon motion of a spouse when either spouse has filed a petition for divorce and upon proof that the requisite period of time, in accordance with Article 103.1, has elapsed from the service of the petition, or from the execution of written waiver of the service, and that the spouses have lived separate and apart continuously for at least the requisite period of time, in accordance with Article 103.1, prior to the filing of the rule to show cause.

The motion shall be a rule to show cause filed after all such delays have elapsed.

Acts 1990, No. 1009, § 2, eff. Jan. 1, 1991. Amended by Acts 1991, No. 367, § 1; Acts 1993, No. 107, § 1; Acts 1995, No. 386, § 1; Acts 1997, No. 1380, § 1; Acts 2006, No. 743, § 1, eff. Jan. 1, 2007.

REVISION COMMENTS—1990

(a) This Article changes the law. A petition filed under this Article precedes the spouses' living separate and apart.

(b) A petition filed under this Article sufficiently states a cause of action for dissolution of marriage if it declares that the plaintiff desires to be divorced from the defendant, and alleges the jurisdictional facts called for by Article 10(A)(7) of the Code of Civil Procedure, and one or more of the bases for divorce venue specified in Article 3941 of the Code of Civil Procedure. See also C.C.P. Art. 3951 (added 1990). The petition need not allege marital breakdown, fault on the part of the other spouse, living separate and apart for a period of time, or any other basis for the plaintiff's demand.

(c) No answer need be made to a petition filed under this Article. The defense of reconciliation and the various procedural defenses implicit in this Article and Article 3952 et seq. of the Code of Civil Procedure (added 1990) should be raised at the hearing on the rule to show cause provided for in Code of Civil Procedure Article 3952 (added 1990).

(d) The one hundred eighty day waiting period required by this Article is not waivable.

(e) An action under this Article may be defeated by proof that the parties have reconciled during the one hundred eighty day period. See C.C. Art. 104, infra (rev.1990). What constitutes reconciliation under this Article and Article 103 is a question of fact to be decided in accordance with jurisprudential guidelines. See Millon v. Millon, 352 So.2d 325 (La.App. 4th Cir.1977); Jordan v. Jordan, 394 So.2d 1291 (La.App. 1st Cir.1981).

(f) Code of Civil Procedure Articles 3941 et seq. govern the procedures for obtaining a divorce under this Chapter.

(g) The rule to show cause required by this Article is the sole means whereby a final judgment of divorce may be obtained under this Article. In particular, a motion for summary judgment or judgment on the pleadings may not be employed for this purpose. C.C.P. Art. 969 (rev.1990).

(h) Under new Article 3954 of the Code of Civil Procedure (added 1990) an action under this Article is deemed abandoned if the motion for entry of judgment called for by this Article is not filed within one year of the service, or execution of a valid written waiver of service, of the original petition. [The time period was changed to two years in 1991.]

REVISION COMMENT—1991

The reference to "execution of written waiver of the service" is added in order to coordinate this provision with new Article 3957 of the Code of Civil Procedure, added in 1991.

Art. 103.   Judgment of divorce; other grounds

Except in the case of a covenant marriage, a divorce shall be granted on the petition of a spouse upon proof that:

(1) The spouses have been living separate and apart continuously for the requisite period of time, in accordance with Article 103.1, or more on the date the petition is filed.

(2) The other spouse has committed adultery.

(3) The other spouse has committed a felony and has been sentenced to death or imprisonment at hard labor.

(4) During the marriage, the other spouse physically or sexually abused the spouse seeking divorce or a child of one of the spouses, regardless of whether the other spouse was prosecuted for the act of abuse.

(5) After a contradictory hearing or consent decree, a protective order or an injunction was issued during the marriage, in accordance with law, against the other spouse to protect the spouse seeking the divorce or a child of one of the spouses from abuse.

Acts 1990, No. 1009, § 2, eff. Jan. 1, 1991. Amended by Acts 1991, No. 918, § 1; Acts 1997, No. 1380, § 1; Acts 2006, No. 743, § 1, eff. Jan. 1, 2007; Acts 2014, No. 316, § 1; Acts 2015, No. 221 § 1.

REVISION COMMENTS—1990

(a) Subparagraph (1) of this Article reproduces the substance of former R.S. 9:301 (1989) without change. It is intended to provide an alternative to an action under Article 102, supra, for spouses who have lived separate and apart for the requisite period of time and who do not wish to wait an additional six months to be divorced (as would be necessary if they instituted proceedings under Article 102 at the end of their period of living separate and apart).

(b) Subparagraphs (2) and (3) of this Article reproduce the first two grounds for immediate divorce contained in former Civil Code Article 139 (1870) without substantive change.

(c) Subparagraph (1) of this Article is not intended to change the prior jurisprudential rule that the one year living separate and apart required by former R.S. 9:301 (now this Article) must have been voluntary on the part of at least one of the parties. Adams v. Adams, 408 So.2d 1322 (La.1982).

Art. 103.1.   Judgment of divorce; time periods

The requisite periods of time, in accordance with Articles 102 and 103 shall be as follows:

(1) One hundred eighty days where there are no minor children of the marriage.

(2) Three hundred sixty-five days when there are minor children of the marriage at the time the rule to show cause is filed in accordance with Article 102 or a petition is filed in accordance with Article 103.

Added by Acts 2006, No. 743, § 1, eff. Jan. 1, 2007. Amended by Acts 2010, No. 604, § 1, eff. June 25, 2010; Acts 2014, No. 316, § 1.

Art. 104.   Reconciliation

The cause of action for divorce is extinguished by the reconciliation of the parties.

Acts 1990, No. 1009, § 2, eff. Jan. 1, 1991.

REVISION COMMENT—1990

This Article codifies the prior jurisprudence holding that an action for divorce under former Civil Code Article 139 or R.S. 9:301 (now Article 103, supra) could be defeated by proof that the parties had reconciled. E.g., Whipple v. Smith, 428 So.2d 1114 (La.App. 1st Cir.1983), writ denied 433 So.2d 154 (La.1983); Humes v. McIntosh, 225 La. 390, 74 So.2d 167 (1954). What constitutes reconciliation is a question of fact to be decided in accordance with established jurisprudential guidelines. E.g., Millon v. Millon, 352 So.2d 325 (La.App. 4th Cir.1977). Under this revision reconciliation may also defeat a divorce action under new Civil Code Article 102, supra.

Art. 105.   Determination of incidental matters

In a proceeding for divorce or thereafter, either spouse may request a determination of custody, visitation, or support of a minor child; support for a spouse; injunctive relief; use and occupancy of the family home or use of community movables or immovables; or use of personal property.

Acts 1990, No. 1009, § 2, eff. Jan. 1, 1991.

REVISION COMMENTS—1990

(a) This Article is new, but it does not change the law. It states in a single Article the general rule that either party to a divorce action may move the court to determine the incidental issues raised by the divorce.

(b) Under this Article a party may move the court to determine the relevant incidental issues either while the divorce action is pending, or for the post-divorce period, or both. This revision does not provide for an interlocutory judgment of separation (compare former C.C. Arts. 138, 139 (1870), R.S. 9:302 (repealed by this revision)); so it is not necessary to pretermit consideration of post-divorce dispositions until the final hearing on the divorce issue itself. The court may do so, however, in its discretion in order to afford the parties time to develop necessary evidence.

(c) In making a determination under this Article the court should consider the factors listed in the relevant provisions of Chapter 2 of this Title or of Title 9 of the Revised Statutes.

Arts. 106 to 110.   [Blank]

CHAPTER 2—PROVISIONAL AND INCIDENTAL PROCEEDINGS

SECTION 1—SPOUSAL SUPPORT

Art. 111.   Spousal support; authority of court

In a proceeding for divorce or thereafter, the court may award interim periodic support to a party or may award final periodic support to a party who is in need of support and who is free from fault prior to the filing of a proceeding to terminate the marriage in accordance with the following Articles.

Acts 1997, No. 1078, § 1, eff. Jan. 1, 1998. Amended by Acts 2006, No. 749, § 1, eff. June 30, 2006.

REVISION COMMENTS—1997

(a) This Article is new. The term "spousal support" is used in this and the remaining articles of this Section instead of "alimony" in order to emphasize the changes effected by this Section. One of the principal changes in prior law made by this Article is the separation of the termination of an interim allowance and the entitlement to a final award from the divorce judgment. An interim allowance may extend (or be awarded) after the divorce judgment, and final periodic support may be awarded before the divorce judgment. See C.C. Art. 113, Comment(d), infra. Under prior law, alimony pendente lite terminated at the time the divorce judgment became definitive. See Wascom v. Wascom, 691 So.2d 678(La. 1997).

(b) This Article states the basic principle that a court may award support to a party to an action for divorce out of either the assets or earnings, or both, of the other spouse in accordance with the needs of the claimant and the ability of the other party to pay. See C.C. Art. 231 (1870). Article 112, infra, provides the standards to be followed in making final awards. In addition to the two fundamental criteria stated here, the court must consider all relevant factors, which may include any of the nine factors listed in that Article. Article 113, infra, authorizes interim awards after the court considers the needs of the claimant and the ability to pay of the other party in light of the standard of living enjoyed by the parties during the marriage.

(c) A condition for the award of final periodic support is the claimant's freedom from fault prior to the filing of a proceeding to terminate the marriage. Fault continues to mean misconduct the rises to the level of one of the previously existing fault grounds for legal separation or divorce. See C.C. Art. 160 (Rev. 1982 and 1986); Adams v. Adams, 389 So.2d 381(La. 1980). See also Allen v. Allen, 648 So.2d 359 (La. 1994). However, unlike prior law this Article is explicit that the fault of the claimant that precludes an award of spousal support must have occurred prior to the filing of the "proceeding to terminate the marriage"—for example, prior to the institution of an action for divorce.

(d) The use of the term "periodic" in this Article reflects a change effected by this Section as a whole. The authorization given the court in former Civil Code Article 112(B) (Civil Code Article 160 prior to its redesignation in 1991) to award alimony in a "lump sum" when the parties consented thereto has been suppressed as inappropriate in this Article. The awarding of rehabilitative support, with or without the parties' consent, is permitted under the terms of Article 112, infra. See comment (d) thereto.

(e) Nothing in Section 1 of this Chapter is intended to overrule the jurisprudence that permits a good faith party to an absolutely null marriage to claim support upon the declaration of its nullity under the same conditions as a divorced spouse. Galbraith v. Galbraith, 396 So.2d 1364 (La.App. 2d Cir. 1981); Cortes v. Fleming, 307 So.2d 611 (La. 1973). See C.C. Art. 152 which explicitly authorizes such an award.

(f) This Article does not carry forward the second sentence of former Civil Code Article 112(A) (rev. 1982 & 1986), but that omission does not change the law. The omitted sentence was introduced into the text of that Article in 1964 (in somewhat different form) in an attempt to clarify the rights of our courts in relation to spousal support provisions of divorce decrees rendered by courts of other states. See Acts 1964, No. 48, Sec. 1; prior C.C. Art. 160, comment (b) (West Supp. 1984); Acts 1979, No. 72. When a spouse who has established a valid domicile in any state obtains a divorce there, the full faith and credit clause of the United States Constitution requires that the courts of every other state recognize the validity of that judgment, even if it was rendered by a court that did not have personal jurisdiction over the defendant spouse. Williams v. North Carolina, 325 U.S. 226, 65 S. Ct. 1092 (1945); Williams v. North Carolina, 317 U.S. 287, 63 S. Ct. 207 (1942). Under the Supreme Court's later holding in the case of Vanderbilt v. Vanderbilt, 354 U.S. 416 (1957), however, such a judgment is void to the extent that it purports to affect the right to support of the spouse who was not subject to the rendering court's jurisdiction; and therefore to that extent it is not entitled to full faith and credit in other states. 354 U.S. at 419; see also Lewis v. Lewis, 404 So.2d 1230 (La. 1981). Accordingly, a court of another state that obtains personal jurisdiction over both spouses may award support to either of them in contravention of the foreign decree. Our courts may exercise this latter right on the authority of the Vanderbilt decision itself. There is no need for the Civil Code to contain a provision paraphrasing the holding of that decision.

Art. 112.   Determination of final periodic support

A.   When a spouse has not been at fault prior to the filing of a petition for divorce and is in need of support, based on the needs of that party and the ability of the other party to pay, that spouse may be awarded final periodic support in accordance with Paragraph C of this Article.

B.   When a spouse has not been at fault prior to the filing of a petition for divorce and the court determines that party was the victim of domestic abuse committed during the marriage by the other party, that spouse shall be awarded final periodic support or a lump sum award, at the discretion of the court, in accordance with Paragraph C of this Article.

C.   The court shall consider all relevant factors in determining the amount and duration of final support, including:

(1) The income and means of the parties, including the liquidity of such means.

(2) The financial obligations of the parties, including any interim allowance or final child support obligation.

(3) The earning capacity of the parties.

(4) The effect of custody of children upon a party's earning capacity.

(5) The time necessary for the claimant to acquire appropriate education, training, or employment.

(6) The health and age of the parties.

(7) The duration of the marriage.

(8) The tax consequences to either or both parties.

(9) The existence, effect, and duration of any act of domestic abuse committed by the other spouse upon the claimant, regardless of whether the other spouse was prosecuted for the act of domestic violence.

D.   The sum awarded under this Article shall not exceed one-third of the obligor's net income; however, where support is awarded pursuant to Paragraph B of this Article, the sum awarded may exceed one-third of the obligor's net income.

Acts 1997, No. 1078, § 1, eff. Jan. 1, 1998. Amended by Acts 2006, No. 749, § 1, eff. June 30, 2006; Acts 2014, No. 316, § 1; Acts 2014, No. 616, § 1.

REVISION COMMENTS—1997

(a) This Article retains much of the substance of its source, former Civil Code Article 112 (Civil Code Article 160 prior to its redesignation in 1991), but changes the law in a few respects.

(b) The first seven factors listed in this Article are essentially the same as those listed in former Civil Code Article 112 (rev. 1982 & 1986). They were first introduced into that Article by Act 72 of 1979 and, except for factors (4) and (6), seem to have originated in the 1978 decision of the Louisiana Supreme Court in the case of Loyacano v. Loyacano, 358 So.2d 304, 310–311 (La. 1978) (holding that trial court had not abused its discretion in reducing wife's previous alimony award, in light of the relevant factors), vacated on other grounds sub. nom. Loyacano v. LeBlanc, 440 U.S. 952 (1979), reinstated 375 So.2d 1314 (La. 1979). See also Sonfield v. Deluca, 385 So.2d 232 (La. 1980). Factor (3) is intended to be broad enough to permit the court to consider the attorney's fees obligations of either or both parties in making a spousal support award, and the child support obligations of, or child support payments received by, either party as well.

(c) The sixth factor listed in this Article, coupled with the word "duration" in the first sentence of the Article, permits the court to award rehabilitative support and other forms of support that terminate after a set period of time. The absence from Article 111, supra, of the word "permanent," which was formerly found in the source provision before "periodic alimony" (see former C.C. Art. 112, as amended 1982 & 1986), emphasizes the authority of the court in this regard, thus legislatively overruling Teasdel v. Teasdel, 493 So.2d 1165 (La. 1986), and Hegre v. Hegre, 483 So.2d 920 (La. 1986). The appropriateness of a rehabilitative award depends upon the capacity of the recipient spouse to become self-supporting, in light of the relevant factors listed in this Article. See Rovira v. Rovira, 550 So.2d 1237, 1239 (La.App. 4th Cir. 1989), writs denied 552 So.2d 398 (La. 1989). The duration of such an award should be determined primarily by the amount of training or other preparation that the recipient requires in order to secure employment that will meet his needs, as similarly defined. See K. Spaht, "Developments in the Law, 1979–1980, Persons," 41 La. L. Rev. 372 (1981); Geter v. Geter, 404 So.2d 1283 (La.App. 2d Cir. 1981). Cf. Ducote v. Ducote, 573 So.2d 560, 562 (La.App. 5th Cir. 1991) (assessing time needed for recipient to become self-supporting in payor's action to terminate permanent alimony). Other factors may also form the basis of a fixed-duration award, but it is contemplated that such awards will ordinarily be based upon the assumption that certain facts (such as employment of the recipient) will occur within the term fixed in the judgment awarding support. If those facts have not occurred at or after the expiration of the specified term, the recipient may seek modification of the judgment upon proof that circumstances have changed since the awards were made; i.e., that the facts that the court assumed would occur did not. But see comment (g), infra.

(d) The eighth factor listed in this Article is new. Inter alia, it affords the court a means of assessing the degree to which a spouse's habituation to dependency during the marriage has impaired his earning capacity.

(e) The ninth factor listed in this Article codifies prior jurisprudence. Hamiter v. Hamiter, 419 So.2d 517 (La.App. 2d Cir. 1982), writ denied 423 So.2d 1140 (La. 1982) (tax consequences to wife);

Meyer v. Meyer, 371 So.2d 1304 (La.App. 4th Cir. 1979) (tax consequences to both parties); Bernhardt v. Bernhardt, 283 So.2d 226 (La. 1973) (tax consequences to wife). See, e.g., 26 U.S.C.A. Secs. 71, 215, 1041.

(f) The one-third limitation on final spousal support contained in former Civil Code Article 112 has been carried forward in this revision but with the qualification that the limitation is to be calculated on the net income of the payor. The court may not therefore award final spousal support in excess of one third of the payor spouse's income. See Slayter v. Slayter, 576 So.2d 1121 (La.App. 3rd Cir. 1991) and Robinson v. Robinson, 412 So.2d 633 (La.App. 2d Cir. 1982).

(g) The factors listed in this Article should be considered whenever the court makes or modifies a final spousal support award. Except as provided in Civil Code Article 117, infra, the court may make such an award at any time either during the process or after the rendition of the final judgment of divorce.

(h) When a former spouse seeks an initial award of spousal support after the entry of the associated divorce judgment, the court may consider the period of time that has elapsed since the entry of that judgment in deciding whether to make the award, or in setting its amount or duration. That period is not explicitly included in the list of factors given in this Article, but it is implicitly included by virtue of the presence of factors (4) and (6). These factors together imply that a former spouse with significant potential or actual earning capacity should not be able to claim spousal support indefinitely absent countervailing incapacitating factors. See Johnson v. Johnson, 442 So.2d 901 (La.App. 3d Cir. 1983), writs denied 445 So.2d 451 (La. 1984) (former wife's alimony claim instituted three years after divorce rejected where the cause of her increased need was her decision to stop working and go to nursing school). The same reasoning can be applied in actions to change spousal support awards previously made. See, e.g., Ware v. Ware, 461 So.2d 467 (La.App. 5th Cir. 1984) (termination of alimony upheld where former wife who had earning capacity and work experience had not made serious attempt to secure employment for eight years); Teasdel v. Teasdel, 454 So.2d 886 (La.App. 4th Cir. 1984) (termination upheld where former wife who had never worked had been receiving "generous" alimony and other payments for fifteen years without seeking employment). Actions to change previous spousal support awards differ from initial claims for spousal support, however, in that initial actions are also governed by the peremptive periods of Article 117 of the Civil Code, while actions for modification are not.

Art. 113.   Interim spousal support allowance pending final spousal support award

A.   Upon motion of a party or when a demand for final spousal support is pending, the court may award a party an interim spousal support allowance based on the needs of that party, the ability of the other party to pay, any interim allowance or final child support obligation, and the standard of living of the parties during the marriage, which award of interim spousal support allowance shall terminate upon the rendition of a judgment of divorce.

B.   If a claim for final spousal support is pending at the time of the rendition of the judgment of divorce, the interim spousal support award shall thereafter terminate upon rendition of a judgment awarding or denying final spousal support or one hundred eighty days from the rendition of judgment of divorce, whichever occurs first. The obligation to pay interim spousal support may extend beyond one hundred eighty days from the rendition of judgment of divorce, but only for good cause shown.

C.   Notwithstanding Paragraph B of this Article, if a claim for final spousal support is pending at the time of the rendition of a judgment of divorce pursuant to Article 103(4) or (5) and the final spousal support award does not exceed the interim spousal support award, the interim spousal support award shall thereafter terminate no less than one hundred eighty days from the rendition of judgment of divorce. The obligation to pay final spousal support shall not begin until after an interim spousal support award has terminated.

Acts 1997, No. 1078, § 1, eff. Jan. 1, 1998. Amended by Acts 2001, No. 738, § 1; Acts 2003, No. 1092, § 1; Acts 2014, No. 316, § 1; Acts 2014, No. 616, § 1.

REVISION COMMENTS—1997

(a) This Article is new and changes the law in part. See Comment (e), infra. It has a purpose equivalent to that of former Civil Code Article 111 (Civil Code Article 148 prior to its redesignation in 1991). Under this Article, the court may award an interim support allowance based on the needs of the party claiming it and the ability to pay of the other party, considered in light of the standard of living enjoyed by the parties during the marriage.

(b) The purpose of an interim allowance is to maintain the status quo without unnecessary economic dislocation until a determination of the amount of final support can be made and until a period of time for adjustment elapses that does not exceed, as a general rule, one hundred eighty days after the judgment of divorce. Generally, the same purpose was attributed to alimony pendente lite under former Civil Code Article 111 by the court in Arrendell v. Arrendell, 390 So.2d 927, 930 (La. App. 2d Cir. 1980): "(I)t is designed to preserve and continue the status quo insofar as maintenance and support are concerned. It relates to facts as they have existed during the time the parties were living together and as they actually exist at the time the litigation commences, not to future possibilities and capabilities." Accord: Ridings v. Ridings, 595 So.2d 343, 345 (La.App. 2d Cir. 1992).

(c) The phrase "[u]pon motion of a party" permits a party to seek an interim allowance without first demanding final spousal support. The reason for permitting an award of interim allowance without a pending claim for final spousal support is that a spouse may not be entitled to final support under Articles 111–112, but nonetheless may be entitled to an interim allowance under this Article.

(d) The phrase "when a demand for final support is pending" permits a party to seek and be awarded an interim allowance when that party has filed a demand for final support. Under Article 111, a party may seek and be awarded final spousal support before or after the divorce judgement is rendered. See C.C. art. 111, Comment.

(e) An award of interim allowance, whether or not there is a pending claim for final spousal support, may not extend beyond one hundred eighty days from the rendition of the judgment of divorce, unless the obligee shows good cause for an extension. Unlike alimony pendente lite, which was terminated by a judgment of divorce (see Wascom v. Wascom, 691 So.2d 678 (La. 1997)), the claim for and termination of an interim allowance is independent of the divorce judgment.

(f) Under Code of Civil Procedure Article 2592 (rev. 1990), a demand for the relief authorized by this Article may be maintained by summary process. A rule to show cause is the usual vehicle.

Art. 114.   Modification or termination of award of periodic support

An award of periodic support may be modified if the circumstances of either party materially change and shall be terminated if it has become unnecessary. The subsequent remarriage of the obligor spouse shall not constitute a change of circumstance.

Acts 1997, No. 1078, § 1, eff. Jan. 1, 1998. Amended by Acts 2001, No. 1049, § 1.

REVISION COMMENTS—1997

(a) This Article supplements and clarifies the similar provisions of former Civil Code Article 112 (rev. 1982 & 1986).

(b) An award of periodic support is subject to modification or termination if either party applies to the court and proves a substantial change of circumstances. R.S. 9:311 (1992). However, the subsequent remarriage of the obligor shall not constitute a change in circumstances. The recipient of a rehabilitative or other fixed-duration periodic award may also seek to have it modified or extended under this Article. See comment (c) to Article 112, supra. The court should make the determination whether periodic support will be modified or terminated based on the changed circumstances of either party. The court should consider the relevant factors listed in Article 112 or 113, supra, depending upon whether the award to be modified or terminated is an interim or final award.

Art. 115.   Extinguishment of spousal support obligation

The obligation of spousal support is extinguished upon the remarriage of the obligee, the death of either party, or a judicial determination that the obligee has cohabited with another person of either sex in the manner of married persons.

Acts 1997, No. 1078, § 1, eff. Jan. 1, 1998.

REVISION COMMENTS—1997

(a) This Article supplements and clarifies the relevant provisions of former Civil Code Article 112 (rev. 1982 & 1986). It does not change the law.

(b) Under this Article, the obligation to pay periodic spousal support, whether or not it has been reduced to judgment, is automatically extinguished without need of judicial intervention, by the death of either party or the remarriage of the obligee. Similarly, the obligation of support is extinguished when it is judicially determined that the recipient has cohabited with another person in the manner specified in this Article. See comment (e) to this Article, infra. These rules represent extensions of prior jurisprudential and statutory holdings relative to alimony awards. E.g., McConnell v. Theriot, 295 So.2d 60 (La.App. 4th Cir. 1974), writ denied 296 So.2d 834 (La. 1974) (remarriage of obligee); Cortes v. Fleming, 307 So.2d 611 (La. 1974) (death of payor); Succession of Carter, 32 So.2d 44 (La.App. 1st Cir. 1947) (same).

(c) This Article does not affect the holding of Keeney v. Keeney, 30 So.2d 549, 211 La. 585 (1947), to the effect that periodic spousal support terminates when the recipient contracts another marriage even when that marriage is absolutely null. That holding is, if anything, more appropriate now than when it was rendered. The supreme court based its decision in the Keeney case on the absurdity of the results of the opposite holding—including the possibility that a party to a null marriage might continue to receive alimony from his former spouse even while enjoying the de facto economic benefits of the subsequent null union. After the date of that decision, however, the law created a stronger basis for it; namely the legal right of a putative spouse to receive permanent alimony from the person with whom he contracted the null marriage. See C.C. Art. 152 (rev. 1993); Galbraith v. Galbraith, 396 So.2d 1364 (La.App. 2d Cir. 1981), writ denied 401 So.2d 974 (La. 1981); Cortes v. Fleming, 307 So.2d 611 (La. 1974). That jurisprudential rule has not been disturbed by this revision; so the vast majority of divorced spouses who have contracted invalid second marriages (i.e., those who have done so in good faith) will continue to be protected without the necessity of their former legal spouses being kept perpetually subject to contingent support liability.

(d) A relatively null subsequent marriage terminates the obligation of support under this Article because such a union produces all of the civil effects of marriage until it is declared null. See C.C. Art. 97 (rev. 1987).

(e) As used in this Article, the phrase "cohabited . . . in the manner of married persons" means to live together in a sexual relationship of some permanence regardless of whether the cohabitants are prohibited from marrying. See Article 89. It does not mean just acts of sexual intercourse. The use of this quoted phrase obviates the difficulties of proving absence of concealment that were inherent in the term "open concubinage" used in former Civil Code Article 112 (as amended by 1982 La. Acts, No. 580). See, e.g., Petty v. Petty, 560 So.2d 629 (La.App. 4th Cir. 1990); Gray v. Gray, 451 So.2d 579 (La.App. 2d Cir. 1984), writ denied 457 So.2d 13 (La. 1984). The phrase "in the manner of married persons" does not require that the cohabitants be capable of contracting marriage under Chapter 1 of Title IV of this Code.

Art. 116.   Modification of spousal support obligation

The obligation of final spousal support may be modified, waived, or extinguished by judgment of a court of competent jurisdiction or by authentic act or act under private signature duly acknowledged by the obligee.

Acts 1997, No. 1078, § 1, eff. Jan. 1, 1998.

REVISION COMMENT—1997

This Article recognizes that final spousal support is not a matter of public order about which couples are forbidden to contract under Civil Code Article 7. Instead, spouses are permitted to contract concerning final spousal support at any time before or during marriage, or after divorce. See McAlpine v. McAlpine, 679 So.2d 85 (La. 1996). However, this Article does impose a requirement of form that may be satisfied by authentic act or act under private signature duly acknowledged by the obligee. This Article applies to the modification or extinguishment of final spousal support. It does not apply to an interim allowance.

Art. 117. Peremptive period for obligation

The right to claim after divorce the obligation of spousal support is subject to a peremption of three years. Peremption begins to run from the latest of the following events:

(1) The day the judgment of divorce is signed.

(2) The day a judgment terminating a previous judgment of spousal support is signed, if the previous judgment was signed in an action commenced either before the signing of the judgment of divorce or within three years thereafter.

(3) The day of the last payment made, when the spousal support obligation is initially performed by voluntary payment within the periods described in Paragraph (1) or (2) and no more than three years has elapsed between payments.

Acts 1997, No. 1078, § 1, eff. Jan. 1, 1998.

REVISION COMMENTS—1997

(a) This Article establishes that the obligation to support a former spouse under the provisions of this Chapter is subject to a peremptive period of three years to date generally from the signing of the judgment of divorce. If there has been an award of spousal support made either before the judgment of divorce or during the peremptive period, the period begins to run anew from the day a judgment terminating the prior judgment of support is signed. The same rule applies if, instead of a prior judgment awarding support, the obligor has recognized the obligation by voluntary payments to the other spouse: the period begins to run from the date of the last payment.

Prior to the effective date of this revision, the obligation to support a former spouse not reduced to judgment was not subject to either a prescriptive or peremptive period. On the other hand, the right to obtain a judgment for arrearages of support has been, and continues to be, subject to a five year prescriptive period. C.C. Art. 3497.1 (added by Acts 1984, No. 147).

(b) A peremptive period, unlike a prescriptive period, is not subject to interruption or suspension, nor may it be renounced. C.C. Art. 3461 (rev. 1982).

The right to enforce the obligation provided in this Chapter is timely exercised when an action asserting the right is filed before the expiration of the peremptive period. See Comment (c) to C.C. Art. 3461 (rev. 1982). For other effects of a peremptive period, see C.C. Arts. 3458–3460 (rev. 1982).

(c) Under this Article, if voluntary payments are made by an obligor, the peremptive period begins to run from the date of the last payment. The payment to which this Article refers is one that constitutes a recognition of the obligation of spousal support, not merely a gift from the obligor proceeding from a spirit of liberality.

The voluntary payment contemplated by this Article is likewise not one made pursuant to a contract between the parties, but instead is made by unilateral action of the obligor. If there is a contract between the obligor and the obligee as to payments to be made in satisfaction of the obligation of support, the right to enforce the conventional obligation is subject to the general prescriptive period of ten years. See C.C. Art. 3499 (rev. 1983). The contract between the obligor and the obligee may result from consent explicitly or tacitly given by the parties. See C.C. Art. 1927 (rev. 1984).

Art. 118. Other remedies affected

Failure to bring an action for divorce pursuant to Article 103(4) or (5) or final spousal support pursuant to Article 112(B) shall in no way affect the rights of the party to seek other remedies provided by law.

Added by Acts 2014, No. 316, § 1.

Arts. 119 to 120.   [Blank]

SECTION 2—CLAIM FOR CONTRIBUTIONS
TO EDUCATION OR TRAINING

Art. 121.   Claim for contributions to education or training; authority of court

In a proceeding for divorce or thereafter, the court may award a party a sum for his financial contributions made during the marriage to education or training of his spouse that increased the spouse's earning power, to the extent that the claimant did not benefit during the marriage from the increased earning power.

The sum awarded may be in addition to a sum for support and to property received in the partition of community property.

Added by Acts 1990, No. 1008, § 2, eff. Jan. 1, 1991. Amended by Acts 1991, No. 367, § 1.

REVISION COMMENTS—1990

(a) The articles of this Section are based on Civil Code Article 161 as enacted by Act 780 of 1986.

(b) This Article restates the basic elements of the cause of action created by the 1986 act, including the discretionary character of the remedy. This cause of action is not based upon classification of an education or training as community property, nor is the claim subject to the same factors as spousal support.

(c) Under this Article the court is empowered to compensate a divorcing or former spouse for financial contributions made during the marriage to the education, training, or increased earning power of the other spouse. The court may do so by making a special monetary award, over and above those authorized by the preceding section of this Chapter, to the spouse who made the contributions. In making such an award the court should keep in mind that the relevant equitable considerations weigh most heavily in favor of the contributing spouse in cases where the timing of the divorce prevents him from realizing benefits from the contributions during the marriage. The usual situation that has prompted the making of awards of this kind in other states has involved a wife who supported her husband through professional school, only to be divorced by him shortly after his graduation. E.g., In re Marriage of Washburn, 677 P.2d 152 (Wash.1984); Lundberg v. Lundberg, 318 N.W.2d 918 (Wisc.1982). Usually the wife has had little opportunity to share in the husband's enhanced income, and ordinarily little or no community property has accumulated to be divided between them. Thus, the only way to compensate her is by means of a monetary award akin to support, but different from support in that it is not affected by the various factors that govern such an award. See Haugan v. Haugan, 343 N.W.2d 796 (Wisc.1984) (holding that trial court should have awarded wife compensation for her contributions to support of husband while he was in medical school). In particular, fault on the part of either spouse that contributed to the breakdown of the marriage is not relevant to a claim under this Article.

(d) "Financial contributions" include direct educational or training expenses paid by the claimant for the other spouse—such as tuition, books, and school fees. The term also includes financial contributions made to satisfy the living expenses of the supported spouse. For examples of how the figure that represents the supporting spouse's financial contributions can be calculated, see DeLaRosa v. DeLaRosa, 309 N.W.2d 755 (Minn.1981), and Reiss v. Reiss, 195 N.J.Super. 150, 478 A.2d 441 (Ch.Ct.1984).

(e) The limitation on awards under this Article expressed in the phrase "to the extent that the claimant did not benefit during the marriage ..." reflects the basic equitable consideration underlying this section. See comment (c) above. A spouse who contributed financially to the education or training of the other spouse in a marriage of significant duration may have already benefitted during the existence of the marriage by an improved standard of living or an accumulation of community property.

(f) This Article rejects the approach of treating the degree, trade, or license acquired by the supported spouse as marital property subject to distribution. The only Louisiana appellate court that has been presented with this issue has avoided it. Harmon v. Harmon, 486 So.2d 277 (La.App. 3d Cir.1986), writ denied, 489 So.2d 916 (La.1986) (holding that the question whether a wife had "a cause of action to partition a professional medical education" was moot because previously settled, indirectly, by agreement of the parties). Such claims have also not received widespread approval in other states. See Mahoney v. Mahoney, 182 N.J.Super. 598, 442 A.2d 1062 (N.J.Super.App.Div.1982). The second paragraph of this Article is intended to make clear that the contemplated award is not spousal support or a disposition of community property.

(g) Under the terms of this Article a spouse may assert a claim under this Section only after an action to dissolve his marriage has been filed. He may do so for three years after the resulting divorce judgment is signed. See Article 124, infra.

COMMENT—1991

This Article is amended to remove a reference to actions for separation from bed and board, which are no longer available in this state under the law as amended by Acts 1990, No. 1009. See C.C. Arts. 101–105 (1990).

Art. 122.   Nature of action

The claim for contributions made to the education or training of a spouse is strictly personal to each party.

Added by Acts 1990, No. 1008, § 2, eff. Jan. 1, 1991.

REVISION COMMENTS—1990

(a) This Article is new. It was not included in former Civil Code Article 161, enacted by Act 780 of 1986. It clarifies the law.

(b) Under this Article and Civil Code Articles 1765 and 1766, the obligation recognized by this Section is neither transferable nor heritable prior to being reduced to judgment. Under this Article and Code of Civil Procedure Article 428, a pending action under this Section abates when either spouse dies.

Art. 123.   Form of award; effect of remarriage or death

The sum awarded for contributions made to the education or training of a spouse may be a sum certain payable in installments.

The award shall not terminate upon the remarriage or death of either party.

Added by Acts 1990, No. 1008, § 2, eff. Jan. 1, 1991.

REVISION COMMENTS—1990

(a) This Article is new. It was not included in former Civil Code Article 161 as enacted by Act 780 of 1986. It clarifies the law.

(b) This Article, drawing upon the spousal support example, makes available a special kind of money judgment that is likely to be used often in this context. This Section contemplates an award that will tend to be greater the earlier it is made in the defendant's career, because of the importance of the "realized benefit" factor discussed in comments (c) and (e) to Article 121, supra. Thus, a mechanism is needed whereby the award can be structured so as to shift some of its cost from the judgment debtor's early working years to his later, more productive ones. This Article provides that mechanism. Cf. R.S. 9:2801(3)(c).

(c) The periodic award made available by this Article is intended to be merely an alternative to the type of lump-sum money judgment normally awarded in other kinds of cases. A judgment under this Article is still a money judgment for a specified sum, not an open-ended award. Thus a judgment under this Article is similar to a spousal support award in only two ways: (1) It is payable periodically; and (2) it may be enforced by an action to make past-due installments executory under Code of Civil Procedure Article 3945 (rev. 1990). It is not, like a spousal support award, modifiable in light of changed circumstances, and under the second sentence of this Article it is not terminated by the death or remarriage of either party.

Art. 124.   Prescription of spousal claim for contributions

The action for contributions made to the education or training of a spouse prescribes in three years from the date of the signing of the judgment of divorce or declaration of nullity of the marriage.

Added by Acts 1990, No. 1008, § 2, eff. Jan. 1, 1991.

REVISION COMMENT—1990

This Article reproduces the substance of Paragraph B of former Civil Code Article 161 as enacted by Act 780 of 1986. It does not change the law.

Arts. 125 to 130.   [Blank]

SECTION 3—CHILD CUSTODY

Art. 131.   Court to determine custody

In a proceeding for divorce or thereafter, the court shall award custody of a child in accordance with the best interest of the child.

Acts 1993, No. 261, § 1, eff. Jan. 1, 1994.

REVISION COMMENTS—1993

(a) This Article simplifies the relevant language of the source article, former Civil Code Article 131 (1992), but does not change the law. It retains the best interest of the child as the overriding test to be applied in all child custody determinations. The primacy of that test has been statutorily mandated in Louisiana since 1979 (C.C.Arts. 134, 131(A) (1992); Acts 1979, No. 718), and the best interest principle itself has been jurisprudentially and legislatively recognized at least since 1921. See Kieffer v. Heriard, 221 La. 151, 58 So.2d 836 (1952); Brewton v. Brewton, 105 So. 307 (La.1925); prior C.C. Art. 157, as amended by Acts 1921, First Ex.Sess., No. 38. The best interest standard is the fundamental principle governing all the articles of this Section.

(b) Under this Article an action to determine custody may be instituted either in conjunction with or after the associated divorce action. An action may be brought in one of the venues provided by Code of Civil Procedure Article 74.2. See also Code of Civil Procedure Article 3822, providing for venue in habeas corpus actions. A custody action does not have to be brought in the same venue as the associated divorce action. See C.C.P. Art. 74.2(A). See also Howard v. Howard, 409 So.2d 279 (La.App. 4th Cir.1981) (Custody action has basis independent of divorce for venue purposes.).

(c) Under Article 2592 of the Code of Civil Procedure (rev. 1990), an action to determine child custody is triable by summary process, whether instituted in conjunction with or after the associated divorce suit.

(d) This Article should be followed in actions to change custody as well as in those to initially set it. An additional, jurisprudential requirement is imposed in actions to change custody decisions rendered in considered decrees, however. In such actions the proponent of change must show that a change of circumstances has occurred such that "the continuation of the present custody is so deleterious to the child as to justify a modification of the custody decree, or . . . that the harm likely to be caused by a change of environment is substantially outweighed by its advantages to the child." Bergeron v. Bergeron, 492 So.2d 1193, 1200 (La.1986). Accord: Smith v. Smith, 559 So.2d 48 (La.App. 4th Cir.1990). This burden of proof is imposed by the jurisprudence as a means of implementing the best interest standard in light of the special considerations present in change of custody cases.

(e) An action to fix custody brought in a court of this state may form the basis for a plea of lis pendens in relation to another such action instituted in the same or a different court between the same parties for custody of the same child. The fact that one of the claims is associated with a divorce action does not change this result (Compare State v. Aucoin, 174 La. 7, 139 So. 645 (La.1932).), because custody actions are now treated as independent causes of action, and not merely as matters ancillary to divorce actions. See C.C.P. Art. 74.2; Fournier v. Fournier, 475 So.2d 400 (La.App. 1st Cir.1985) (custody action not "incidental" to separation suit for venue purposes); Howard v. Howard, 409 So.2d 279 (La.App. 4th Cir.1981) (same). See Lewis v. Lewis, 404 So.2d 1230 (La.1981) (Child support order rendered in Louisiana separation suit had independent basis and so would be given effect over later foreign divorce judgment.).

Art. 132.   Award of custody to parents

If the parents agree who is to have custody, the court shall award custody in accordance with their agreement unless the best interest of the child requires a different award.

In the absence of agreement, or if the agreement is not in the best interest of the child, the court shall award custody to the parents jointly; however, if custody in one parent is shown by clear and convincing evidence to serve the best interest of the child, the court shall award custody to that parent.

Acts 1993, No. 261, § 1, eff. Jan. 1, 1994.

REVISION COMMENTS—1993

(a) This Article changes and supplements the relevant portions of the source provision, former Civil Code Article 131(A) (1992).

(b) Under this Article the agreement of the parents, if any, regarding the allocation of custody is controlling when it is consistent with the child's best interest. The agreement may include an agreement for sole custody in one parent, joint parental custody, or even an award of custody to a third person. If there is no agreement, or if the agreement is not in the best interest of the child, the court must award joint custody, unless custody in one parent is shown by clear and convincing evidence to be in the child's best interest. This latter provision is intended to strengthen the preference for joint custody provided for in former Civil Code Article 131(A).

(c) The second sentence of this Article governs the decision whether to award joint custody. The legal effects of joint custody, once it is awarded, are addressed in R.S. 9:335 (1993).

(d) As of 1989, 36 states had statutes that explicitly authorized joint custody. Of those 36 states, 12 states declared a general presumption in favor of joint custody, 5 states declared a presumption in favor of joint custody where both parents agreed to it, and the remainder made joint custody an explicit option without any presumption for or against it. 10 "Fairshare" No. 3, at 6 (March 1990).

Art. 133.   Award of custody to person other than a parent; order of preference

If an award of joint custody or of sole custody to either parent would result in substantial harm to the child, the court shall award custody to another person with whom the child has been living in a wholesome and stable environment, or otherwise to any other person able to provide an adequate and stable environment.

Acts 1993, No. 261, § 1, eff. Jan. 1, 1994.

REVISION COMMENTS—1993

(a) This Article reproduces the relevant portions of the source provisions, former Civil Code Article 131(A) & (B) (1992), without substantial change. The redundant dual test for divestiture of parental custody found in the source article has been replaced with a similar, but briefer, provision.

(b) The requirement of proof that parental custody would result in "substantial harm" to the child that is stated in this Article represents a change in the terminology of the test for divestiture of parental custody. The new language, which is not entirely new to Louisiana law (Pittman v. Jones, 559 So.2d 990, 993 (La.App. 4th Cir.1990); In the Matter of Stewart, 602 So.2d 212, 214 (La.App. 3d Cir.1992)), has been adopted because it represents an efficient means of giving effect to a parent's paramount right to custody of his child as against any nonparent. The primacy of that parental right was recognized by the Louisiana jurisprudence long before it was given effect by the legislature in 1982. See prior C.C. Art. 146 as amended by 1982 La.Acts, No. 307; Wood v. Beard, 290 So.2d 675 (La.1974). Prior to the 1982 introduction of the two-part statutory test that parental custody be shown to be "detrimental" to the child and that divestiture be "required to serve the best interest of

43

the child," the courts had followed the jurisprudential formula: "the parent . . . may be deprived of . . . custody only when (he) has forfeited his or her right to parenthood, . . . is unfit, or . . . is unable to provide a home for the child." Deville v. LaGrange, 388 So.2d 696, 697–98 (La.1980). See also Jones v. Jones, 415 So.2d 300 (La.App. 2d Cir.1982) (Use of best interest standard was improper in custody contest between parent and nonparent.). That jurisprudential language was of course substantially different from the statutory language adopted in 1982, and at least one court accordingly held that the 1982 enactment had changed the law, giving the courts "more freedom or latitude to pursue the goal of insuring that the best interest of the child is served in resolving custody disputes between parent and nonparent litigants." Boyett v. Boyett, 448 So.2d 819, 822 (La.App. 2d Cir.1984). A similar argument (although most likely to the opposite effect) could be made again under this revision, which does indeed change the terms of the relevant test significantly. However, it is clear that the heart of the parental primacy concept, the rule that a nonparent always bears the burden of proof in a custody contest with a parent, was not disturbed by the prior statutory enactment, and likewise has not been affected by this revision. See Love v. Love, 536 So.2d 1278 (La.App. 3d Cir.1988); Boyett v. Boyett, supra; Deville v. LaGrange, supra.

(c) The use of the singular "person" in this Article (Cf. items (3) and (4) of former Civil Code Article 131(A)) is in accordance with standard drafting practice (C.C. Art. 3506(2) (1870)), and is intended to rule out any inference that this Article might require the awarding of joint custody between nonparents under the specified circumstances. An award of joint custody to nonparents is not precluded, however. Cf. Schloegel v. Schloegel, 584 So.2d 344 (La.App. 4th Cir.1991) (award of joint custody between child's father and maternal grandmother upheld as within trial court's discretion).

Art. 134.   Factors in determining child's best interest

The court shall consider all relevant factors in determining the best interest of the child. Such factors may include:

(1) The love, affection, and other emotional ties between each party and the child.

(2) The capacity and disposition of each party to give the child love, affection, and spiritual guidance and to continue the education and rearing of the child.

(3) The capacity and disposition of each party to provide the child with food, clothing, medical care, and other material needs.

(4) The length of time the child has lived in a stable, adequate environment, and the desirability of maintaining continuity of that environment.

(5) The permanence, as a family unit, of the existing or proposed custodial home or homes.

(6) The moral fitness of each party, insofar as it affects the welfare of the child.

(7) The mental and physical health of each party.

(8) The home, school, and community history of the child.

(9) The reasonable preference of the child, if the court deems the child to be of sufficient age to express a preference.

(10) The willingness and ability of each party to facilitate and encourage a close and continuing relationship between the child and the other party.

(11) The distance between the respective residences of the parties.

(12) The responsibility for the care and rearing of the child previously exercised by each party.

Acts 1993, No. 261, § 1, eff. Jan. 1, 1994.

REVISION COMMENTS—1993

(a) This Article preserves the list of factors formerly found in Civil Code Article 131(C)(2) (1992) but changes their import. Under the former provision the listed factors were to be considered by the court in determining whether the evidentiary presumption in favor of joint custody imposed by that article was rebutted. Under this revision the factors are simply provided as a guide to the court in making the fundamental finding as to what disposition is in the best interest of the child.

(b) The list of factors provided in this Article is nonexclusive, and the determination as to the weight to be given each factor is left to the discretion of the trial court. This would seem to represent a change from the source provision, which required the court to reach its decision only "after consideration of evidence introduced with respect to all" the factors listed in the article. C.C. Art. 131(C)(2) (1992). That unequivocal language was added to the text of that article in 1983 (by Acts 1983, No. 695, eff. Aug. 30, 1983), and there does not appear to have been any decision thus far reversing a trial court's decision for failure to consider all of the listed factors. See also Turner v. Turner, 455 So.2d 1374, at 1377 n. 2 (La.1984) (checklist only intended "to provide guidance for the courts"). The appellate courts have reiterated the traditional rule that a trial court's custody award will not be disturbed absent a manifest abuse of discretion. Goldman v. Logue, 461 So.2d 469 (La.App. 5th Cir.1984); Stewart v. Stewart, 460 So.2d 59 (La.App. 1st Cir.1984); see also Fulco v. Fulco, 259 La. 1122, 254 So.2d 603 (La.1971) (traditional discretion rule). This revision does not change that rule.

(c) The illustrative nature of the listing of factors contained in this Article gives the court freedom to consider additional factors. See Turner v. Turner, 455 So.2d 1374 (La.1984) (court allowed, even obligated, to consider additional factor of inability of parents to get along); Goldman v. Logue, 461 So.2d 469 (La.App. 5th Cir.1984) (same); Krotoski v. Krotoski, 454 So.2d 374 (La.App. 4th Cir.1984) (Trial court properly considered fact that if primary physical custody was granted to mother in California, grandparents would be available to assist in caring for child, whereas the father in Baton Rouge could only provide a stranger to the child to assist him.). In general, the court should consider the totality of the facts and circumstances of the individual case. Theriot v. Huval, 413 So.2d 337 (La.App. 3d Cir.1982).

(d) This Article should be followed in actions to change custody, as well as in those to fix it initially. But see comment (d) to Article 131, supra.

(e) The language used in factor (2) of this Article is intended to reproduce the substance of former Civil Code Article 131(C)(2)(b).

(f) Factor (6) of this Article has been amended in order to state what is believed to be the better rule on the much-litigated issue addressed by it. Its predecessor, factor (f) of Civil Code Article 131(C)(2) (1992), read simply "(t)he moral fitness of the parties involved." The language added here brings the statutory provision into line with the fundamental principle that the purpose of every custody award is to secure the best interest of the child, not to regulate the behavior of his parents. Stephenson v. Stephenson, 404 So.2d 963 (La.1981) (upholding award of custody to wife whose past adulterous behavior was not shown to have had any detrimental effect on the children); Cleeton v. Cleeton, 383 So.2d 1231 (La.1980) (same). See also Monsour v. Monsour, 347 So.2d 203 (La.1977) (same: primary consideration was welfare of child, not past misconduct of custodian). But see Bagents v. Bagents, 419 So.2d 460 (La.1982) (upholding change of custody from mother who had lived in open concubinage in the custodial home). The rule embodied in this Article should apply not only to past misconduct, as in the cases just cited, but also to continuing immorality that does not harm the child. See Rollins v. Rollins, 521 So.2d 647 (La.App. 1st Cir.1988), writ denied 522 So.2d 573 (La.1988) (joint custody not modified where there was no showing that mother's discrete illicit relationship had detrimental effect on child); Montgomery v. Marcantel, 591 So.2d 1272 (La.App. 3d Cir.1991) (change of custody to sole custody in wife due to father's living in concubinage reversed in absence of evidence of detrimental effect on child); Peters v. Peters, 449 So.2d 1372 (La.App. 2d Cir.1984) (upholding judgment refusing to take child from custody of mother who was living in concubinage with man she planned to marry); Peyton v. Peyton, 457 So.2d 321 (La.App. 2d Cir.1984) (upholding equal joint custody award where both parents were engaged in discrete sexual relationships that had no adverse effect upon the child).

(g) Factor (9) of this Article permits the court to consider the preference of the child as to custody "if the court deems the child to be of sufficient age to express a preference." This formula has been preserved unchanged from the predecessor provision, former Civil Code Article 131(C)(2)(i). Under Article 601 of the Louisiana Code of Evidence (West 1992) and R.S. 13:3665 (1968 and Supp.1992), on the other hand, the general test for testimonial competency of a child is not his age, but whether the court finds him to be "of proper understanding." Because of the kinds of conclusions that these provisions require from the trial judge, these two tests overlap to a considerable extent, but they are not identical. In Watermeier v. Watermeier, 462 So.2d 1272 (La.App. 5th Cir.1985), writ denied 464 So.2d 301 (La.1985), the court applied the general competency provisions in holding that a child of five years and seven months could testify in a custody hearing. The decision in that case, however, did not state whether the child had testified about factual issues or about his preference as to custody. Arguably, a very young child's statement of preference might reasonably be deemed admissible even though his testimony as to matters of fact would not. This revision leaves that question to be answered by the courts. See, e.g., Matter of Fox, 504 So.2d 101 (La.App. 2d Cir.1987), writ denied 504 So.2d 556 (La.1987) (six-year old is too young to express reasonable preference). The procedural rulings of the Watermeier decision (permitting the court to question the child in chambers with the parties' attorneys present solely as observers) are unexceptionable.

(h) Factor (11) of this Article permits the court to take into account the distance between the residences of the parties, a consideration that is often important both as it affects the welfare of the child and as it affects the practicalities of the post-divorce relationship of the parents with the child. See, e.g., Doyle v. Doyle, 465 So.2d 167 (La.App. 3d Cir.1985), writ denied 467 So.2d 1136 (La.1985); Lachney v. Lachney, 446 So.2d 923 (La.App. 3d Cir.1983), writ denied 450 So.2d 964 (La.1984). The Louisiana Legislature elaborated upon this factor, which was also in former Civil Code Article 131, in 1986 when it enacted a special provision to the effect that the presumption in favor of joint custody would cease to exist if a parent moved out of state. That provision has not been retained in this revision because the presumption has not, and because the matter is sufficiently provided for by the inclusion of factor (11) in this Article. See former C.C. Art. 131(K) (1992). See also Meyers v. Meyers, 561 So.2d 875, 878 (La.App. 2d Cir.1990); Edwards v. Edwards, 556 So.2d 207, 209 (La.App. 2d Cir.1990) (mother's remarriage and impending removal from state constituted change of circumstances sufficient to justify termination of joint custody award).

(i) Factor (12) of this Article is new. It is a significant factor that was not included in former Civil Code Article 131 but which has sometimes been considered by Louisiana courts. See Edwards v. Edwards, 556 So.2d 207, 209 (La.App. 2d Cir.1990); Quinn v. Quinn, 412 So.2d 649 (La.App. 2d Cir.1982), writs denied 415 So.2d 941, 945 (La.1982); Nale v. Nale, 409 So.2d 1299 (La.App. 2d Cir.1982). See also Garska v. McCoy, 278 S.E.2d 357 (W.Va.1981); Neely, "The Primary Caretaker Parent Rule: Child Custody and The Dynamics of Greed," 3 Yale Law & Policy Review 168 (1984). The responsibility for child rearing previously exercised by the parties may be evaluated by identifying which of them had primary responsibility during the marriage for the following duties concerning the child: (1) preparing and planning meals for the child; (2) bathing, grooming, and dressing him; (3) purchasing, cleaning, and caring for his clothes; (4) obtaining and providing medical care, including nursing and trips to physicians; (5) arranging for social interaction among the child's peers after school, e.g. transporting the child to friends' houses or to girl or boy scout meetings; (6) arranging alternative care, e.g. baby-sitting, day-care, etc.; (7) putting the child to bed at night, attending to the child in the middle of the night, waking the child in the morning; (8) disciplining him, including teaching him general manners and toilet training; (9) obtaining and providing education (religious, cultural, or social) for the child; and (10) teaching him elementary skills, e.g. reading, writing and arithmetic. Garska v. McCoy, 278 S.E.2d at 363.

COMMENT—2012 REVISION

The facilitation of the relationship between the child and the other party described in factor (10) may include a party's willingness to make travel arrangements and facilitate electronic communications that allow the child meaningful time with both parties and that minimize the negative impact of long-distance parenting on the child.

Art. 135.   Closed custody hearing

A custody hearing may be closed to the public.

Acts 1993, No. 261, § 1, eff. Jan. 1, 1994.

REVISION COMMENTS—1993

This Article is based on former Civil Code Article 131(G) (1992). It changes the law, affording the court greater flexibility in choosing the setting for a closed custody hearing.

Art. 136.   Award of visitation rights

A.   A parent not granted custody or joint custody of a child is entitled to reasonable visitation rights unless the court finds, after a hearing, that visitation would not be in the best interest of the child.

B.   A grandparent may be granted reasonable visitation rights if the court finds that it is in the best interest of the child. Before making this determination, the court shall hold a contradictory hearing as provided for in R.S. 9:345 in order to determine whether the court should appoint an attorney to represent the child.

C.   Under extraordinary circumstances, any other relative, by blood or affinity, or a former stepparent or stepgrandparent may be granted reasonable visitation rights if the court finds that it is in the best interest of the child. Extraordinary circumstances shall include a determination by a court that a parent is abusing a controlled dangerous substance.

D.   In determining the best interest of the child under Paragraphs B and C of this Article, the court shall consider:

(1) The length and quality of the prior relationship between the child and the relative.

(2) Whether the child is in need of guidance, enlightenment, or tutelage which can best be provided by the relative.

(3) The preference of the child if he is determined to be of sufficient maturity to express a preference.

(4) The willingness of the relative to encourage a close relationship between the child and his parent or parents.

(5) The mental and physical health of the child and the relative.

E.   In the event of a conflict between this Article and R.S. 9:344, the provisions of the statute shall supersede those of this Article.

Acts 1993, No. 261, § 1, eff. Jan. 1, 1994. Amended by Acts 1995, No. 57, § 1; Acts 2009, No. 379, § 2; Acts 2012, No. 763, § 1, eff. June 12, 2012; Acts 2014, No. 586, § 1.

REVISION COMMENTS—1993

(a) This Article reproduces former Civil Code Article 132 as amended by Acts 1992, No. 782. The third paragraph of the source Article has been amended to reflect the designation scheme followed in this revision, without changing the law.

(b) The first paragraph of this Article restates the test for parental visitation established in the leading case of Maxwell v. LeBlanc, 434 So.2d 375 (La.1983). That case set forth a comprehensive body of rules governing visitation, all of which were jurisprudential in nature, because Louisiana did not have statutory provisions concerning child visitation prior to 1988. (Acts 1988, No. 817 enacted prior C.C. Art. 146.1, later redesignated as C.C. Art. 132.) Nevertheless, this Article is not intended to affect the Maxwell case, except for the court's declaration that visitation is a "species of custody," which is no longer strictly true, since visitation has an independent basis under this Article.

(c) The first paragraph of this Article applies to parents of illegitimate, as well as legitimate, children. Maxwell v. LeBlanc, supra, at 377. There may be special facts militating against visitation in such cases that are not present in most cases involving legitimate children, however. See id. at 379–380.

(d) The second paragraph of this Article provides a general rule regarding visitation of nonparents, of which the provisions of R.S. 9:344 and 9:345 (rev. 1993) may be seen as more specific applications. Accordingly, this Article defers to those statutes in the areas that they address.

(e) Relatives by affinity—i.e., by marriage—may be given visitation rights under the second paragraph of this Article under extraordinary circumstances when the court finds it to be in the best interest of the child to do so.

Art. 136.1. Award of visitation rights

A child has a right to time with both parents. Accordingly, when a court-ordered schedule of visitation, custody, or time to be spent with a child has been entered, a parent shall exercise his rights to the child in accordance with the schedule unless good cause is shown. Neither parent shall interfere with the visitation, custody or time rights of the other unless good cause is shown.

Added by Acts 2008, No. 671, § 1.

Art. 137.   Denial of visitation; felony rape; death of a parent

A.   In a proceeding in which visitation of a child is being sought by a parent, if the child was conceived through the commission of a felony rape, the parent who committed the felony rape shall be denied visitation rights and contact with the child.

B.   In a proceeding in which visitation of a child is being sought by a relative by blood or affinity, if the court determines, by a preponderance of the evidence, that the intentional criminal conduct of the relative resulted in the death of the parent of the child, the relative shall be denied visitation rights and contact with the child.

Added by Acts 2001, No. 499, § 1. Amended by Acts 2010, No. 873, § 1, eff. July 2, 2010; Acts 2012, No. 763, § 1, eff. June 12, 2012.

Arts. 138 to 140.   [Blank]

SECTION 4—CHILD SUPPORT

Art. 141.   Child support; authority of court

In a proceeding for divorce or thereafter, the court may order either or both of the parents to provide an interim allowance or final support for a child based on the needs of the child and the ability of the parents to provide support.

The court may award an interim allowance only when a demand for final support is pending.

Acts 1993, No. 261, § 6, eff. Jan. 1, 1994.

REVISION COMMENTS—1993

(a) This Article clarifies the law by providing explicit Civil Code authorization for courts to make child support awards in connection with divorce actions. Prior to this revision that authority was not expressly conferred upon Louisiana courts by any legislation, although the underlying substantive obligation of support was provided for in the Civil Code (See C.C. Arts. 227, 240 (1870)), and the guidelines for determination of child support amounts enacted in 1989 of course assumed that courts had that power. (See R.S. 9:315–315.15 (1992).)

(b) This Article and the other Articles in this Section of the revision are essentially codifications of the fundamental principles governing child support that have been followed in prior jurisprudence, and so these Articles do not change the law in any substantial way. (But see comment (d) to Article 142, infra.) For the same reason, this and the succeeding Articles of this Section also function as general statements of the principles of law that are given particularized expression in R.S. 9:315–315.15, which were prepared and drafted separately from this revision by the Louisiana Legislature in 1988–89, and adopted by it as Act No. 9 of the Second Extraordinary Legislative Session of 1989. Those statutory Sections provide a detailed set of guidelines for courts to follow in arriving at decisions as to the amount of child support to award in "any proceeding to establish or modify child support filed on or after October 1, 1989" (R.S. 9:315.1), which necessarily includes, of course, all proceedings addressed by the Articles of this revision. Those statutory guidelines should therefore be followed in all such cases as an initial matter, with resort being had to these Articles when necessary for the sake of clarity, or when a party seeks to overcome the rebuttable presumption in favor of results achieved under the statutory guidelines that is provided by R.S. 9:315.1(A), or when the court deviates from those guidelines under R.S. 9:315.1(B) and (C), or when the guidelines are inapplicable, or in any other situation where resort to first principles is necessary.

(c) In principle the parents' duties to support their children are equal, as reflected in this Article by the use of the plural term "parents." See also C.C. Art. 227 (1870); Castille v. Buck, 411 So.2d 1156 (La.App. 1st Cir.1982). Thus an order of approximately equal physical custody to each parent might seem to obviate any monetary child support judgment against either. In reality this will seldom be the case, however, because of differences in the incomes and situations of the former spouses. Under R.S. 9:315.8(C), the share of the total cost of child support for which each parent is responsible is proportional to his percentage share of the total income of both parents. Thus, one parent can be ordered to pay substantially more than the other when he can afford to do so, and such an order is necessary to afford the child the requisite standard of living. Such an order is particularly appropriate when sole, rather than joint, custody is ordered. See comment (e), infra; Cox v. Cox, 447 So.2d 578 (La.App. 1st Cir.1984). Similarly, under R.S. 9:315.8(E), a court may adjust a child support award downward to reflect time spent by the child living in the home of the payor. Accord: Flournoy v. Flournoy, 546 So.2d 617, 621 (La.App. 3d Cir.1989) (under prior, jurisprudential, law). And under R.S. 9:337 (this revision), a court may, in or in conjunction with a joint custody implementation order, make a special monetary award to one spouse in order to enable that spouse to maintain adequate housing for a child.

(d) In determining the amount of child support to be awarded, the court must consider the needs of the child and the ability to pay of the parents. See R.S. 9:315.2(D) and 315.8 (parties' incomes are starting point in computing total child support obligation), and R.S. 9:315.3 through 315.6 and 315.8(A) (child care costs and extraordinary expenses associated with child also considered). See also Dickinson v. Dickinson, 461 So.2d 1184 (La.App. 3d Cir.1984); Byrd v. Guilbeau, 442 So.2d 887 (La.App. 3d Cir.1983); Ducote v. Ducote, 339 So.2d 835 (La.1976). These standards are fundamental and must be applied, but the court may also consider other circumstances in those cases where it must decide whether to deviate from the statutory child support guidelines. See R.S. 9:315.1(B) and (C). In the past, the trial court was free to consider the totality of the circumstances presented in every case (Marcus v. Burnett, 282 So.2d 122 (La.1973)), and its decision would not be disturbed on appeal unless the court was found to have clearly abused its discretion (E.g., Foquet v. Foquet, 442 So.2d 787 (La.App. 5th Cir.1983); Bettencourtt v. Bettencourtt, 407 So.2d 804 (La.App. 4th Cir.1981).), but that may no longer be true given the presumption in favor of the results mandated by the new child support guidelines that is imposed by R.S. 9:315.1(A). Under R.S. 9:315.1(B), as amended in 1992, moreover, the court must reach certain findings and give specific oral or written reasons, on the record, whenever it decides to deviate from the statutory guidelines. Accord: Montgomery v. Waller, 571 So.2d 765 (La.App. 2d Cir.1990). See also R.S. 9:315.10(B) (Court may use its discretion in setting amount of basic child support obligation of persons with combined monthly adjusted gross income greater than highest level shown in schedule given in R.S. 9:315.14, but support amount in such a case cannot be less than maximum shown in schedule.).

(e) Under R.S. 9:315.2, 315.8, and 315.3, the factor of the parents' ability to provide support, that is, their "combined adjusted gross income," is the primary factor and the starting point in determining the "total child support obligation" and hence the amount of child support to be awarded. That approach is consistent with this Article and the prior jurisprudence, even though the prior jurisprudence usually claimed to give primacy to the factor of the child's need. The measure of that need, however, was usually stated as the sum necessary to afford the child the same standard of living as he had enjoyed prior to the divorce (E.g., Garcia v. Garcia, 438 So.2d 256 (La.App. 4th Cir.1983).), or as he would enjoy if he were living with the non-custodial parent (E.g., Ducote v. Ducote, 339 So.2d 835 (La.1976).), and the courts did not hesitate to apply that test when the means of the non-custodial parent permitted, even where doing so would result in an award clearly in excess of the child's otherwise reasonable needs. Garcia v. Garcia, id.; Fellows v. Fellows, 267 So.2d 572 (La.App. 3d Cir.1972). Assessing a child's "need" on the basis of his parents' standard of living was of course tantamount to basing the child support decision primarily on the parents' income, as is now done expressly in the statutory child support guidelines (modified to a degree by the consideration, built into the tables in R.S. 9:315.14, that the percentage of income spent on a child decreases as income increases).

(f) Under R.S. 9:315(6)(b) and 315.9, unemployment or underemployment of a parent will not diminish his portion of the parents' total child support obligation below that which would be dictated by his "potential income", except in specified circumstances. That is consistent with this Article and prior jurisprudence. The courts have usually held, for example, that unemployment is not a ground for excusing a parent from paying child support unless the parent is shown also to be unemployable. E.g., Lopez v. Breau, 462 So.2d 1333 (La.App. 3d Cir.1985); Sykes v. Sykes, 308 So.2d 816 (La.App. 4th Cir.1975). See also Siciliani v. Siciliani, 552 So.2d 560, 562 (La.App. 2d Cir.1989) (not error for trial court to look to father's past income where his current and future income was uncertain and appeared much less than his established earning capacity).

(g) A parent's obligation of support is owed to his child, but the child is usually an unemancipated minor in divorce actions and therefore does not have the procedural capacity to sue. C.C.P. Art. 683 (1992). Thus the usual practice has been for the parent who expects to be the child's custodian or domiciliary parent to raise the child support issue in the divorce proceedings. Under Civil Code Article 105 (rev. 1990), either party may take this step without being appointed tutor of the child, and under Code of Civil Procedure Article 2592(8) either party may do so by summary process. See also former R.S. 9:309(C) (rev. 1992) (R.S. 9:315.22 in this revision). The usual procedural vehicle is a rule to show cause. This accords with prior jurisprudence. (See Dubroc v. Dubroc, 388 So.2d 377 (La.1980).), and with R.S. 9:315.8(D), under which the child support award is to be made payable directly to the appropriate parent. When that is done, the payor of support may discharge his obligation only by making the required payments to that parent, absent an agreement on the part of the latter to permit payment to a third party on the parent's behalf. E.g., Feazell v. Feazell, 445 So.2d 143 (La.App. 3d Cir.1984). To be enforceable, such an agreement must be in the best interest of the child, or at least not work to his detriment. See, e.g., Feazell v. Feazell, id.; Dubroc v. Dubroc, 388 So.2d 377 (La.1980).

(h) R.S. 9:337 (this revision) governs allocation of the income tax dependency exemption between joint custodians of a child. It changes the law by allowing, rather than requiring, the court that awards custody to make that allocation. Cf. former C.C. Art. 131(A)(1)(c)(ii) (1992).

(i) This Article is not intended to restrict the availability of child support orders to divorce actions. See C.C. Art. 227 (1870); R.S. 9:291 (1992).

Art. 142.   Modification or termination of child support award

An award of child support may be modified if the circumstances of the child or of either parent materially change and shall be terminated upon proof that it has become unnecessary.

Acts 1993, No. 261, § 6, eff. Jan. 1, 1994. Amended by Acts 2001, No. 1082, § 2.

REVISION COMMENTS—1993

(a) This Article recodifies the prior jurisprudential test applicable to actions to change child support, which was first codified as former R.S. 9:311(A) by Acts 1985, No. 41. It does not change the law. See, e.g., Bernhardt v. Bernhardt, 283 So.2d 226 (La.1973); Custard v. Custard, 424 So.2d 474 (La.App. 5th Cir.1982). The change in circumstances referred to in this Article is a change that occurs after the initial award is made. See Bernhardt v. Bernhardt, 283 So.2d 226 (La.1973); Kuhn v. Kuhn, 420 So.2d 1026 (La.App. 5th Cir.1982); Howell v. Howell, 391 So.2d 1304 (La.App. 4th Cir.1981).

(b) As under the source statute, under this Article the stated criteria for changing child support are the same as those for changing spousal support. See Civil Code Article 114 (rev. 1993). However, a special substantive rule that is often applied in situations where a party seeks a modification or termination of a child support award has been that any "voluntary act by a parent that renders it difficult or impossible to perform the primary obligation of support and maintenance of his children" cannot be countenanced as a ground for release of the parent, in whole or in part, from that obligation. Laiche v. Laiche, 237 La. 298, 111 So.2d 120, 122 (1959). Accord: Lustig v. Lustig, 552 So.2d 516, 517 (La.App. 2d Cir.1989); Toups v. Toups, 573 So.2d 1164 (La.App. 5th Cir.1991). See also R.S. 9:315(6)(b) and 315.9 (effects of voluntary unemployment). For examples of the types of voluntary acts that do not constitute a change of circumstances, see Boudreaux v. Boudreaux, 460 So.2d 703 (La.App. 3d Cir.1984) (incurring business debts); Dugas v. Dugas, 374 So.2d 1278 (La.App. 3d Cir.1979) (buying house). But see Daigle v. Daigle, 448 So.2d 207 (La.App. 1st Cir.1984) (holding that general rule did not apply where father had contracted increased debts in question in a good faith effort to keep his business operating; Romagosa v. Romagosa, 464 So.2d 1129 (La.App. 5th Cir.1985) (payments suspended temporarily under supervision of court). This Article is not intended to change the prior jurisprudential approach.

(c) This Article contemplates that judicial action will be necessary to modify or terminate child support awards in most cases. However, a payor of child support may lawfully cease making payments in a situation where R.S. 9:315.22(A) or (B) (this revision) applies. This Article, moreover, is not intended to change the prior jurisprudence recognizing another basis for extrajudicial modification of child support awards. That basis is the agreement of a custodial or domiciliary spouse "to suspend his right to compel the other party without custody to turn over to him in advance money necessary for the child's maintenance" in a manner that "meets the requisites for a conventional obligation" and "fosters the continued support and upbringing of the child." Dubroc v. Dubroc, 388 So.2d 377, 380 (La.1980). Accord: Lavergne v. Lavergne, 556 So.2d 918, 921 (La.App. 3d Cir.1990) (Evidence did not establish that parties had "clearly agreed" to modification).

(d) Under this Article, whenever a sole custody arrangement is changed to joint custody, the court may consider reducing the child support entitlement of the former sole custodian, provided that the change in the legal situation gives rise to an actual change of circumstances sufficient to justify doing so. See, R.S. 9:315.8(E); Chaudoir v. Chaudoir, 454 So.2d 895 (La.App. 3d Cir.1984); Plemer v. Plemer, 436 So.2d 1348 (La.App. 4th Cir.1983). Compare former C.C. Art. 131(A)(1)(c)(i): "An award of joint custody shall not eliminate the responsibility for child support." Under R.S. 9:315.11 the enactment in 1989 of statutory child support guidelines did not constitute a change of circumstances for the purposes of changing child support.

(e) The Louisiana Supreme Court has held that the change of circumstances test may be abrogated by agreement of a child's parents, that is, the parents may by agreement empower the court to change the support award in the future without requiring the usual showing. Aldredge v. Aldredge, 477 So.2d 73 (La.1985). This Article is not intended to change that holding.

COMMENT—2001

The amendment adds materially to describe the change in circumstances necessary to obtain a modification or termination of child support. The language overrules Stogner v. Stogner, 739 So.2d 762 (La. 1999). See also R.S. 9:311.

Arts. 143 to 150.   [Blank]

SECTION 5—PROVISIONAL AND INCIDENTAL PROCEEDINGS IN ACTIONS OF NULLITY

Art. 151.   Proceeding for declaration of nullity of a marriage; interim incidental relief

In a proceeding for declaration of nullity of a marriage, a court may award a party the incidental relief afforded in a proceeding for divorce.

Acts 1993, No. 108, § 1, eff. Jan. 1, 1994.

REVISION COMMENTS—1993

(a) This Article is new. It fills a gap in the former Civil Code and statutory law.

(b) This Article affords the parties to a nullity action the same right to claim interim incidental relief as the parties to a divorce action. In the case of a marriage that is relatively null, that right is ultimately based on the existence of the marriage. See C.C. Art. 97 (Rev. 1987). In the case of an absolutely null marriage, on the other hand, the right to claim incidental relief is based exclusively on this Article, unless a party is deemed entitled to the civil effects of marriage as a putative spouse under Civil Code Article 96. (But see Art. 151, comment (d), infra.).

(c) This Article is intended to govern only claims for relief pending the nullity action. Relief that is intended to continue in effect past the effective date of the judgment of nullity is governed by Article 152.

Art. 152. Proceeding for declaration of nullity of a marriage; final incidental relief

After the declaration of nullity of a marriage, a party entitled to the civil effects of marriage may seek the same relief as may a divorced spouse.

Incidental relief granted pending declaration of nullity to a party not entitled to the civil effects of marriage shall terminate upon the declaration of nullity.

Nevertheless, a party not entitled to the civil effects of marriage may be awarded custody, child support, or visitation. The award shall not terminate as a result of the declaration of nullity.

Acts 1993, No. 108, § 1, eff. Jan. 1, 1994.

REVISION COMMENTS—1993

(a) This Article is new. It fills a gap in the prior statutory law.

(b) This and Article 151 govern claims for incidental relief in nullity actions. Article 151 governs claims for incidental relief pendente lite, which a party may be granted irrespective of the nature of the alleged nullity, and of whether he was in good or bad faith in contracting the marriage. This Article governs claims for post-judgment relief, which is available only to parties to relatively null marriages and to parties to absolutely null marriages who are deemed entitled to civil effects as putative spouses under Civil Code Article 96 (Rev. 1987).

(c) The first sentence of this Article affords parties to relatively null marriages and putative spouses the same rights to claim incidental relief as are enjoyed by a lawful spouse in a divorce action. In the case of the putative spouse, this disposition reflects the established principle that "(t)he words 'civil effects' (in Civil Code Article 96) are used without restriction, and necessarily embrace all civil effects given to marriage by the law." Smith v. Smith, 43 La.Ann. 1140, 1149, 10 So. 248, 250 (1891). See generally Blakesley, "The Putative Marriage Doctrine," 60 Tul.L.Rev. 1 (1985). These civil effects include spousal support, and a putative spouse may receive such support whether the other party was in good or bad faith in contracting the null marriage. Galbraith v. Galbraith, 396 So.2d 1364 (La.App. 2d Cir.1981), writ denied 401 So.2d 974 (La.1981); Cortes v. Fleming, 307 So.2d 611, 613 (La.1973).

(d) The second sentence of this Article reflects the temporary nature of the rights granted by Article 151 as to certain classes of persons.

(e) The last sentence of this Article reflects the view that the rights and obligations of parents toward their children arise from the fact of parenthood, and not from the marriage of their parents. See Civil Code Articles 240, 245; R.S. 9:399.

Arts. 153 to 158.   [Blank]

CHAPTER 3—EFFECTS OF DIVORCE

Art. 159.   Effect of divorce on community property regime

A judgment of divorce terminates a community property regime retroactively to the date of filing of the petition in the action in which the judgment of divorce is rendered. The retroactive termination of the community shall be without prejudice to rights of third parties validly acquired in the interim between the filing of the petition and recordation of the judgment.

Acts 1990, No. 1009, § 2, eff. Jan. 1, 1991.

REVISION COMMENTS—1990

This revision reproduces two of the three significant rules formerly stated in Civil Code Article 159, omitting unnecessary language. The substance of the former provision of Article 159 concerning attorney's fees and costs incurred in a divorce action is now to be found in amended Civil Code Article 2357 and in new Article 2362.1. These provisions do not change the law.

Arts. 160 to 161.   [Blank]

TITLE VI—OF MASTER AND SERVANT [REPEALED]

Arts. 162 to 177.   [Blank]

TITLE VII—PARENT AND CHILD

CHAPTER 1—FILIATION

Art. 178.   Definition

Filiation is the legal relationship between a child and his parent.

Acts 2009, No. 3, § 1, eff. June 9, 2009.

REVISION COMMENT—2009

This Article is new but the definition of filiation is consistent with doctrine. See J.R. Trahan, Glossae on the New Law of Filiation, 67 La. L. Rev. 387, 388 n. 1 (2007); and Katherine Shaw Spaht and William Marshall Shaw, Jr., The Strongest Presumption Challenged: Speculations on Warren v. Richard and Succession of Mitchell, 37 La. L. Rev. 59 (1976). See also Gérard Cornu, Droit Civil: La Famille No. 195, at 313 (7th ed. 2001); Francesco Messineo, 2 Manuale di Diritto Civilee Commerciale: Diritti Della Personalità, Diritti Della Famiglia, Diritti Reali § 62, No. 1, at 145 (9th ed., Milano, 1965); Eduardo A. Zannoni, 2 Derecho Civil: Derecho de Familia § 793, at 283 (2d ed., Buenos Aires, 1989); Caio Mário da Silva Pereira, 5 Instituições de Direito Civil: Direito de Família No. 410, at 173–74 (7th ed., Rio de Janeiro, 1991); and Jean Carbonnier, Droit Civil: La Famille: L'Enfant, Le Couple 181–82 (20th ed. 1999). This Article introduces the subject matter that follows in Title VII, including how the legal relationship of parent and child is established, see Civil Code Article 179 (Rev. 2009), infra, and the legal consequences thereof.

Art. 179.   Establishment of filiation

Filiation is established by proof of maternity or paternity or by adoption.

Acts 2009, No. 3, § 1, eff. June 9, 2009.

REVISION COMMENT—2009

There are two methods for establishing the filiation of a child to his mother and father: by proof that a particular person is his father and a particular person is his mother under the provisions of Chapter 2 or by adoption under Chapter 3. Proof of maternity or paternity may consist of evidence including factual circumstances that create presumptions of paternity, testimony, documents, or the results of scientific tests.

Arts. 180 to 183.   [Blank]

CHAPTER 2—FILIATION BY PROOF OF MATERNITY OR PATERNITY

SECTION 1—PROOF OF MATERNITY

Art. 184.   Maternity

Maternity may be established by a preponderance of the evidence that the child was born of a particular woman, except as otherwise provided by law.

Acts 2005, No. 192, § 1, eff. June 29, 2005.

REVISION COMMENTS—2005

(a) This Article clarifies present law by explicitly establishing that the mother of a child is the woman who gives birth to the child, and that maternity may be proved by any evidence at any time. Civil Code Article 196 (1870); Civil Code Articles 193–197, which concerned proof of legitimate filiation.

(b) Evidence of maternity includes all facts and circumstances establishing that a child was born of a particular woman, including testimony of witnesses to the fact of birth, documentary evidence (including formal or certain informal acknowledgment), and scientific evidence.

(c) For exceptions provided by other laws, see R.S. 9:121–133; R.S. 40:32 (definition of "biological parents" to include husband and wife providing sperm and egg for in vitro fertilization by physician and fetus is carried by surrogate birth parent who is blood relative of either the husband or wife); R.S. 40:34(B)(1)(h)(v) and (B)(1)(j) (birth certificate reflect mother and father as married couple who donate gametes when child born to a gestational surrogate by in vitro fertilization who is a relative of the husband or wife).

SECTION 2—PROOF OF PATERNITY

SUBSECTION A. THE PRESUMPTION OF PATERNITY OF HUSBAND; DISAVOWAL OF PATERNITY; CONTESTATION; ESTABLISHMENT OF PATERNITY

Art. 185. Presumption of paternity of husband

The husband of the mother is presumed to be the father of a child born during the marriage or within three hundred days from the date of the termination of the marriage.

Acts 2005, No. 192, § 1, eff. June 29, 2005.

REVISION COMMENTS—2005

(a) This Article does not change the law. Under this Article the presumption of the husband's paternity applies to a child born during the marriage of his mother or within three hundred days of its termination.

(b) The presumption that the husband of the mother is the father of the child has been referred to as the strongest presumption in the law. See, e.g., Tannehill v. Tannehill, 261 So.2d 619 (La. 1972); Williams v. Williams, 87 So.2d 707 (La. 1956); Katherine Shaw Spaht and William Marshall Shaw, Jr., The Strongest Presumption Challenged: Speculations on Warren v. Richard and Succession of Mitchell, 37 La.L.Rev. 59 (1976). Under Article 187 (rev. 2005), the husband can disavow paternity of the child, but he may do so only by clear and convincing evidence, and his testimony requires corroboration. See also former C.C. Art. 187 (rev. 1976). The mother, under limited circumstances, is also permitted to contest the presumption under this revision. See Civil Code Articles 191–194 (rev. 2005). Under this Article the presumption that the husband of the mother is the father of the child continues to be among the strongest in the law.

(c) Four other presumptions of paternity exist under this revision. The first is that a man who marries the mother and with her concurrence, acknowledges the child as his is presumed to be the father under Civil Code Article 195 (rev. 2005). This presumption is as strong as that of the paternity of the husband of the mother who conceives or bears a child during marriage; it can only be rebutted in a disavowal action by the same evidence required under Civil Code Article 187 (rev. 2005), and the action must be brought within a relatively short period of time. The other three presumptions of paternity are either qualified or narrowly focused: (1) the presumption of paternity of a man who executes an acknowledgment can only be invoked by the child, which constitutes a change in the law for an acknowledgment by signing the birth certificate (see C.C. Art. 196 (rev. 2005) and former C.C. Art. 203(B)); (2) the presumption of paternity arising under R.S. 9:397.3(B)(2)(b) when tissue or blood tests results establish a 99.9% probability of paternity requires the institution of an action and a high probability of paternity (see R.S. 9:396; 398.2); (3) the presumption of paternity created for child support purposes only arises when the mother of a child identifies the father. See R.S. 40:34(E); C.C. Art. 196, Revision Comment (g).

Art. 186.   Presumption if child is born after divorce or after death of husband; effect of disavowal

If a child is born within three hundred days from the day of the termination of a marriage and his mother has married again before his birth, the first husband is presumed to be the father.

If the first husband, or his successor, obtains a judgment of disavowal of paternity of the child, the second husband is presumed to be the father. The second husband, or his successor, may disavow paternity if he institutes a disavowal action within a peremptive period of one year from the day that the judgment of disavowal obtained by the first husband is final and definitive.

Acts 2005, No. 192, § 1, eff. June 29, 2005.

REVISION COMMENTS—2009

(a) This Article clarifies the law. This Article contemplates that a child may be born within three hundred days of termination of a marriage, and the date of his birth may occur after his mother has remarried. See former Civil Code Article 186 (1870). It, just as prior law did, resolves the dilemma of overlapping presumptions that can arise under Civil Code Article 185 (Rev. 2005).

(b) When "dual paternity" is created by the effect of overlapping presumptions, this Article provides that if the first marriage terminates and a second is contracted before the birth of the child, the first husband is presumed to be the father of the child. To do otherwise would be for the law to presume in effect that the mother committed adultery during the first marriage.

(c) The last paragraph of this Article is new. The source is German Civil Code § 1600 and, to a lesser extent, Swiss Civil Code Article 257. This provision assures that when the husband to whom the presumption of paternity ultimately applies, or his successor under Civil Code Article 190 (Rev. 2005), has successfully disavowed the paternity of the child, the other husband will be presumed to be the father of the child. Such a result does not necessarily follow without explicit statutory language. Protection of the child from the social stigma of illegitimacy and the necessity of proving paternity justifies the result.

(d) Under the last paragraph of this Article, if the presumption that applied to the first husband is rebutted in a disavowal action, then the presumption that had applied to the second husband and been displaced will be resurrected. In fairness to the second husband, however, this provision permits him to disavow the paternity of the child within one year from the day that the judgment of disavowal became "final and definitive," which means final and no longer subject to appeal. Louisiana Code of Civil Procedure Articles 2166 and 2167 describe the effect of these terms.

(e) The period of time for instituting the second disavowal action is explicitly peremptive, rather than prescriptive as in Civil Code Article 189 (Rev. 2005). The reason the period is peremptive is that the first husband to whom the prescriptive period applied has a year to institute the action with potential suspensions and interruptions and the other husband was notified and made a party to the disavowal action. See R.S. 9:401 (2006). The desirability of a relatively short period of time for resolving paternity, and thus the status of the child, justifies the peremptive nature of the time period afforded to the second husband to institute a disavowal action.

(f) Indispensable parties to this action include the person presumed to be the father of the child and the person who will be presumed to be the father if the action is successful. See R.S. 9:401 (2006). See, generally, Ebey v. Harvill, 647 So.2d 461 (La.App. 2 Cir. 1994), where the first husband of the mother, who was the presumed father of the child, was held to be an indispensable party to a paternity action by the mother against the second husband.

(g) This Article does not apply to "dual paternity" created by the existence of a presumed father and a biological father to whom the presumption of Civil Code Article 185 (Rev. 2005) does not apply. Such cases are governed by the provisions of Civil Code Articles 197 and 198 (Rev. 2005).

Art. 187.   Disavowal action; proof

The husband may disavow paternity of the child by clear and convincing evidence that he is not the father. The testimony of the husband shall be corroborated by other evidence.

Acts 2005, No. 192, § 1, eff. June 29, 2005.

REVISION COMMENTS—2005

(a) This Article only changes the law by changing the explicit standard of persuasion that must be satisfied by a husband in order to disavow the paternity of a child born to his wife or former wife. Under former Civil Code Article 187 (rev. 1976) the husband could disavow paternity if he proved by a preponderance of the evidence facts that reasonably indicated that he was not the father. For a representative example of the jurisprudence interpreting that language, see Mock v. Mock, 411 So.2d 1063 (La. 1982). Former Civil Code Article 187 also required proof of facts susceptible of independent verification by physical evidence. This Article omits that requirement, but imposes the higher burden of persuasion, clear and convincing evidence, upon the husband who seeks to disavow. The continuing strong policy of favoring the legitimacy of children supports imposition of the higher burden. See Succession of Lyons, 452 So.2d 1161 (La. 1984).

(b) This Article makes it clear that corroboration by other evidence is required when the testimony of the husband is offered to rebut the presumption of paternity. The husband need not testify, of course; but if he does, his testimony must be supported by other evidence. Other evidence includes: scientific or medical evidence, including the results of blood tests or DNA prints, or medical evidence of sterility; evidence of physical impossibility due to location at the probable time of conception; or tangible evidence and testimony of lay witnesses. For a jurisprudential example, see the Mock case, supra. See also R.S. 9:396 et seq. (blood and tissue-type test results) and C. Blakesley, Louisiana Family Law, Chapter 6 (Butterworth 1993).

Art. 188. Disavowal precluded in case of assisted conception

The husband of the mother may not disavow a child born to his wife as a result of an assisted conception to which he consented.

Acts 2005, No. 192, § 1, eff. June 29, 2005.

REVISION COMMENTS—2005

(a) This Article only changes the law governing disavowal actions by extending its application to all forms of assisted conception to which the husband consented, not just artificial insemination. Assisted conception includes in vitro fertilization and embryo transfer.

(b) The provision of former Civil Code Article 188 that denied the husband's right to disavow if he married a pregnant woman knowing that she was pregnant has been suppressed in this revision. The suppression of this provision eliminates the need for an exception to it where the husband was deceived into marrying a pregnant woman believing the child was his.

Art. 189. Time limit for disavowal by the husband

The action for disavowal of paternity is subject to a liberative prescription of one year. This prescription commences to run from the day the husband learns or should have learned of the birth of the child.

Nevertheless, if the husband lived separate and apart from the mother continuously during the three hundred days immediately preceding the birth of the child, this prescription does not commence to run until the husband is notified in writing that a party in interest has asserted that the husband is the father of the child.

Acts 2005, No. 192, § 1, eff. June 29, 2005.

REVISION COMMENTS—2005

(a) The only change in law made by this Article is that the period of time for instituting a disavowal action under this Article is explicitly prescriptive, overruling Pounds v. Schori, 377 So.2d 1195 (La. 1979) (former Civil Code Article 189, the predecessor to this Article, contained a peremptive period for the disavowal action). The husband may file the disavowal action at any time within one year after he learned or should have learned of the birth of the child, with one exception contained in the second paragraph of this Article. The special "suspension" of the time period that appeared in former Article 189 if the husband "for reasons beyond his control is not able to file suit timely" is no

60

longer necessary because the time period is prescriptive subject as a general rule to both suspension and interruption. See C.C. Arts. 3462–3472.

(b) The second paragraph of this Article provides an exception to the general rule that the husband must file his disavowal action within one year of actual or constructive knowledge of the birth of the child. If the husband lived separate and apart from the mother continuously during the three hundred days immediately preceding the birth of the child, the prescriptive period within which the husband must institute his action only begins to run when the husband is notified in writing that a party in interest has asserted that he is the father of the child. The fact that the prescriptive period only begins to run from this notification does not preclude the husband from instituting an action in disavowal before the period begins.

Art. 190.   Time limit for disavowal by heir or legatee

If the prescription has commenced to run and the husband dies before the prescription has accrued, his successor whose interest is adversely affected may institute an action for disavowal of paternity. The action of the successor is subject to a liberative prescription of one year. This prescription commences to run from the day of the death of the husband.

If the prescription has not yet commenced to run, the action of the successor is subject to a liberative prescription of one year. This prescription commences to run from the day the successor is notified in writing that a party in interest has asserted that the husband is the father of the child.

Acts 2005, No. 192, § 1, eff. June 29, 2005.

REVISION COMMENTS—2005

(a) This Article clarifies the law. Similarly to its predecessor, former Civil Code Article 190 (1999), this Article permits a successor whose interest is adversely affected by the failure of the husband to institute an action to disavow the child to do so within a prescriptive period of one year. The commencement of prescription pursuant to this Article begins to run at different times depending upon whether or not the prescription of Article 189 (rev. 2005) commenced to run against the husband before his death. For the definition of "successor," see Civil Code Article 3506.

(b) If prescription has commenced to run against the husband but not yet accrued before his death, the prescriptive period of this Article commences with the death of the husband. By contrast, if at the time of the husband's death prescription has not yet commenced to run either because he did not actually or constructively learn of the birth of the child or because he had not yet been notified in writing that his paternity was being asserted, the prescription of this Article commences to run when the successor is notified in writing that a party in interest has asserted that the husband is the child's father.

Art. 191.   Contestation and establishment of paternity by mother

The mother of a child may institute an action to establish both that her former husband is not the father of the child and that her present husband is the father. This action may be instituted only if the present husband has acknowledged the child by authentic act or by signing the birth certificate.

Acts 2005, No. 192, § 1, eff. June 29, 2005.

REVISION COMMENTS—2005

(a) This Article is new. Under many statutory schemes regulating disavowal of paternity the mother of a child is permitted to disprove her husband's paternity. See, e.g., French Civil Code Articles 318, 318.1; Uniform Parentage Act § 6(a); Quebec Civil Code Article 275; Cal. Civil Code § 7006.

(b) The provisions of this Article permit the mother of a child to contest her former husband's paternity, and thus rebut the presumption of Civil Code Article 185, under certain limited circumstances. The mother is permitted to file the contestation action only if she seeks to establish the child's paternity to her present husband. The restricted right of the mother to file an action to contest her former husband's paternity serves to align more closely biological and legal paternity in instances when the child's status will not be adversely affected by the social stigma of birth outside of marriage if the action is successful. In the situation contemplated by this Article, the mother's action serves to establish legally the child as a member of an intact family, whose stability is marked by the marriage of the mother and alleged father.

(c) This Article accomplishes a compulsory joinder or cumulation of two different actions that can be instituted by the mother of a child—one to disprove the paternity of her former husband, and the other to establish the paternity of her present husband. See C.C.P. arts. 641 et seq.

(d) Civil Code Article 195 (rev. 2005) creates a presumption of paternity when a man marries the mother of a child and formally acknowledges the child, but only if the child is not filiated to another man.

(e) Under this Article, the judgment in the action of contestation and establishment rebuts the presumption of Article 185 (rev. 2005) and Article 186 (rev. 2005) and establishes the paternity of the present husband.

Art. 192.   Contestation action; proof

The mother shall prove by clear and convincing evidence both that her former husband is not the father and that her present husband is the father. The testimony of the mother shall be corroborated by other evidence.

Acts 2005, No. 192, § 1, eff. June 29, 2005.

REVISION COMMENT—2005

Under this Article the mother must prove by clear and convincing evidence that her present husband is the father of the child and that her former husband is not. The reason for requiring clear and convincing proof that her present husband is the father (compare Civil Code Article 195) is that there is a legal presumption that the mother's former husband is the father, which the mother is also seeking to rebut. The consequences of the contestation action differ significantly from the actions permitted the child or the biological father under Civil Code Articles 197 and 198 (rev. 2005): in a contestation action, the former husband will no longer be considered by law as the child's father; instead, only the mother's present husband will be considered the legal father. Under Civil Code Articles 197 and 198, the child or the father is seeking to establish paternity without affecting in any way the child's established filiation to another man.

Art. 193.   Contestation and establishment of paternity; time period

The action by the mother shall be instituted within a peremptive period of one hundred eighty days from the marriage to her present husband and also within two years from the day of the birth of the child, except as may otherwise be provided by law.

Acts 2005, No. 192, § 1, eff. June 29, 2005.

REVISION COMMENT—2005

The contestation action must be instituted within one hundred eighty days of the marriage of the mother to her present husband and before the child has attained the age of two years. This short time period encourages the mother to act expeditiously in the interest of all of the affected parties, in particular the child. The time period for instituting this action is similar to that of French Civil Code Article 318.1 in that both actions must be brought within six months of the inception of the marriage. This Article departs from the French article, however, in requiring that the action be instituted before the child has attained the age of two years. Under French Civil Code Article 318.1 the action must be instituted before the child has reached the age of seven years.

Art. 194.   Judgment in contestation action

A judgment shall not be rendered decreeing that the former husband is not the father of the child unless the judgment also decrees that the present husband is the father of the child.

Acts 2005, No. 192, § 1, eff. June 29, 2005.

REVISION COMMENT—2005

This Article assures that there will be a successful contestation action only if the mother is also successful in establishing by clear and convincing evidence that her present husband is the father. The compulsory cumulation of the two actions is reflected in the interdependence of the resulting judgments. A judgment recognizing that the former husband of the mother is not the father can be rendered only if at the same time a judgment is rendered recognizing that the present husband of the mother is the father. There are two purposes served by permitting contestation by the mother of her husband's paternity: to align biological and legal paternity more closely and to establish the child as a member of an intact family resulting from the marriage of the mother and alleged father. This Article insures that both purposes will be fulfilled in any successful action under this Subsection.

SUBSECTION B. PRESUMPTION OF PATERNITY BY SUBSEQUENT MARRIAGE AND ACKNOWLEDGMENT

Art. 195. Presumption by marriage and acknowledgment; child not filiated to another man; proof; time period

A man who marries the mother of a child not filiated to another man and who, with the concurrence of the mother, acknowledges the child by authentic act or by signing the birth certificate is presumed to be the father of that child.

The husband may disavow paternity of the child as provided in Article 187.

The action for disavowal is subject to a peremptive period of one hundred eighty days. This peremptive period commences to run from the day of the marriage or the acknowledgment, whichever occurs later.

Acts 2005, No. 192, § 1, eff. June 29, 2005.

REVISION COMMENTS—2005

(a) This Article establishes a new presumption of paternity that corresponds to the circumstances of former Civil Code Article 198 (rev. 1979). Former Article 198 recognized legitimation by subsequent marriage as a method of establishing paternity. By creating a presumption of paternity under circumstances that previously constituted legitimation by subsequent marriage, this Article overrules such cases as Chatelain v. State, DOTD, 586 So.2d 1373 (La. 1991), and O'Brien v. O'Brien, 653 So.2d 1364 (La.App. 4 Cir. 1995) (father who signed birth certificate and married the mother was not presumed to be father of child born before marriage).

(b) This Article creating a presumption does not apply if the child born prior to the marriage is filiated to another man. Civil Code Article 197 (rev. 2005) permits the child whose filiation is already established to prove his filiation to another man by an action instituted during the other man's lifetime or within one year of his death. By contrast, under Civil Code Article 198 (rev. 2005), the father of such a child can establish his paternity only if he institutes the action within one year of the child's birth with one narrow exception. Compare Succession of Mitchell, 323 So.2d 451 (La. 1975). Furthermore, in a contestation action brought by the mother under Articles 191–194 (rev. 2005), the presumption does not apply and the mother must prove the paternity of her present husband by clear and convincing evidence.

(c) The presumption created by this Article, like that of Articles 185 and 186 (rev. 2005), may be rebutted only by an action instituted within the short time period specified by this Article, and only by clear and convincing evidence that the man who married the mother after the birth of the child and acknowledged the child as his is not in fact the child's father. The time period within which the husband must institute an action to disavow under this Article is six months rather than one year, as provided in Article 189 (rev. 2005). It is also peremptive rather than prescriptive. See Articles 2458, 3447, 3449, and 3462–72.

(d) The presumption created by this Article arises when, subsequent to the birth of a child, the mother marries a man who formally acknowledges, or has acknowledged, the child as his with the mother's concurrence. Prior law provided that a child was legitimated by the subsequent marriage of his parents if the child was formally or informally acknowledged before or after the marriage. This Article requires a formal acknowledgment, which may be made at any time. An informal acknowledgment consisted of a writing not the equivalent of an authentic act in which the father referred to the child as his, or conversations and other similar conduct to the same effect. See IMC Exploration Co. v. Henderson, 419 So.2d 490 (La.App. 2 Cir. 1982).

(e) The concurrence of the mother required by this Article is a juridical act. See C.C. Art. 2347, Revision Comment (c).

SUBSECTION C. OTHER METHODS OF ESTABLISHING PATERNITY

Art. 196.   Formal acknowledgment; presumption

A man may, by authentic act or by signing the birth certificate, acknowledge a child not filiated to another man. The acknowledgment creates a presumption that the man who acknowledges the child is the father. The presumption can be invoked only on behalf of the child. Except as otherwise provided in custody, visitation, and child support cases, the acknowledgment does not create a presumption in favor of the man who acknowledges the child.

Acts 2005, No. 192, § 1, eff. June 29, 2005. Amended by Acts 2006, No. 344, § 1, eff. June 29, 2005.

REVISION COMMENTS—2005

(a) This Article is new, although it resembles former Civil Code Article 203(B)(2) (rev. 1997). Under this Article a man who acknowledges a child creates a presumption that he is the father which operates in favor of the child only. Such an acknowledgment is created by an authentic act in which the father acknowledges his paternity, or by his signing the child's birth certificate as father. The man who executes the acknowledgment or signs the birth certificate will not create a presumption in his own favor that he is the father of the child.

(b) Under former Civil Code Article 203(B)(2) (rev. 1997), a presumption of paternity was created only when there was an acknowledgment made by signing of the registry of birth or baptism, and that presumption was explicitly declared rebuttable by a mere preponderance of the evidence. To be sufficient to rebut the presumption, however, evidence of certain facts "susceptible of independent verification or of corroboration by physical data or evidence," had to be provided. That language was identical to the description found in former Civil Code Article 187 (rev. 1989) of the proof required for a husband to disavow a child of his wife born or conceived during the marriage. This Article changes the law in that, under this revision, no presumption is created by signing the baptismal registry.

(c) This Article changes the law as to a child acknowledged by authentic act: it creates a rebuttable presumption of paternity in favor of the child only, whereas former Civil Code Article 203(B)(1) (rev. 1997) created "a legal finding of paternity" but for limited purposes. Under former Civil Code Article 203(B)(1), formal acknowledgment by authentic act was "deemed to be a legal finding of paternity" that was "sufficient to establish an obligation to support . . . without the necessity of obtaining a judgment of paternity." The presumption created by this Article applies generally and is not restricted to issues of child support. Prior to the 1997 revision of former Article 203 declaring an acknowledgment a legal finding of paternity, the jurisprudence recognized the relevance of blood tests to establish the biological link between the child and the father who had acknowledged him. See Succession of Robinson, 654 So.2d 682 (La. 1995) (administrator's motion to compel blood tests of illegitimate children acknowledged in statutory will upheld); O'Brien v. O'Brien, 653 So.2d 1364 (La.App. 4 Cir. 1995) (man who had acknowledged child by placing his name on birth certificate permitted to seek declaratory relief that he was not the biological father); McKinley v. McKinley, 631 So.2d 45 (La.App. 2 Cir. 1994). See also Comment (e), infra.

(d) The presumption created by this Article must be distinguished from the presumptions under Sections 1 and 2 of this Chapter. There is no similar limitation in this Section as to who may bring the action to rebut the presumption created by this Article. See Civil Code Articles 189 and 195 (rev. 2005). Likewise, there is no time period during which an action to challenge the presumption of this Article must be instituted.

(e) Under former Civil Code Article 206 (1997) an acknowledgment could be revoked without cause within sixty days (or less) of its execution in a judicial hearing; thereafter, the acknowledgment could only be revoked upon clear and convincing evidence of fraud (C.C. Arts. 1953–1958), duress (C.C. Arts. 1959–1964), material mistake of fact (C.C. Arts. 1949–1952), or "that the person is not the biological parent of the child." This revision repeals Civil Code Article 206. See R.S. 9:392(A) (before execution of acknowledgment notary required to provide in writing explanation of the consequences of a failure to acknowledge and the legal consequences of an acknowledgment, including the right to revoke). See also Faucheux v. Faucheux, 772 So.2d 237 (La.App. 5 Cir. 2000); Jones v. Rodrigue, 771 So.2d 275 (La.App. 1 Cir. 2000).

(f) R.S. 40:46.1 establishes a hospital-based voluntary acknowledgment program, but the statute only requires the signatures of the two parents and the signature of a notary who authenticates their signatures. If the form for such an acknowledgment does not provide for the signatures of two witnesses, it does not constitute an acknowledgment by authentic act, and thus does not have the effect accorded to such an acknowledgment under this Article.

(g) R.S. 40:34(E) adopts a procedure for the identification of the father of a child born outside of marriage, notice to the alleged father, the creation of a presumption of fatherhood for support purposes only if he fails to contest the identification, and the effect of blood tests results at a contested hearing. That statute creates a limited exception to the provisions of this Chapter and is unaffected by this revision. See Comment (c) to Article 185 (rev. 2005).

(h) Under prior law, an acknowledgment of fatherhood by an authentic act or by signing the child's birth or baptismal certificate was referred to as a formal acknowledgment. Prior law distinguished the effects of such formal acknowledgments from those of informal acknowledgments. The formal acknowledgment of a child by his father relieved the child of the necessity of establishing paternity by an action timely instituted under former Civil Code Article 209 (rev. 1984). An informal acknowledgment, which consisted of writings by the father and his conversations referring to the child as his, did not relieve the child of the necessity of instituting a paternity action. The same result obtains under this revision.

REVISION COMMENT—2006

"Except as otherwise provided" in this Article refers to other related statutes that give an authentic act of acknowledgment, such as that contemplated in R.S. 9:392, the effect of a legal finding of paternity in compliance with 42 U.S.C. 666. For example, see the provisions of R.S. 9:392, 392.1, 393, 400, 405, 406, R.S. 40:34(B)(1)(a)(iv) and (h)(iv).

Art. 197.   Child's action to establish paternity; proof; time period

A child may institute an action to prove paternity even though he is presumed to be the child of another man. If the action is instituted after the death of the alleged father, a child shall prove paternity by clear and convincing evidence.

For purposes of succession only, this action is subject to a peremptive period of one year. This peremptive period commences to run from the day of the death of the alleged father.

Acts 2005, No. 192, § 1, eff. June 29, 2005.

REVISION COMMENTS—2005

(a) This Article, for the most part, codifies prior jurisprudence interpreting former Civil Code Article 209 (rev. 1981), which recognized that a child may institute an action to establish his paternity even though the child's filiation to a man other than the subject of the action has been established. For example, even though the child is presumed to be the child of his mother's husband who has not disavowed the child under Civil Code Article 189, the child may prove in an action that another man is his father. See, e.g., Succession of Mitchell, 232 So.2d 451 (La. 1975) (children presumed to be children of mother's first husband but legitimated by subsequent marriage as to her second husband); Griffin v. Succession of Branch, 479 So.2d 324 (La. 1985) (children presumed to be children of mother's husband permitted to institute a paternity action to establish filiation as to the decedent); Smith v. Cole, 553 So.2d 847 (La. 1989) (child presumed to be child of mother's husband permitted to institute paternity action against another man for support). If the child establishes paternity under this Article, all of the civil effects of filiation apply to both the child and the father.

Civil effects of filiation include the right to support, to inherit intestate, and to sue for wrongful death.

(b) Louisiana currently is the only state which recognizes that a child may establish his filiation to more than one father. The United States Supreme Court concluded that the United States Constitution did not prohibit a California statute from denying the biological father such a right. See Michael H. v. Gerald D., 109 S.Ct. 322 (1989). But see Lawrence v. Texas, 123 S.Ct. 2472 (2003), which does not directly concern the biological father's right to establish his paternity but rejects part of the rationale of the decision in the Michael H. case.

(c) Under this Article, all relevant evidence is admissible to prove paternity. Examples of such relevant evidence include blood tests, an informal acknowledgment, and cohabitation of the mother and father at the time of conception. See former Civil Code Article 209, Comment (b) (rev. 1981). Compare Jenkins v. Mangano Corp., 774 So.2d 101 (La. 2000) and State, Dept. Soc. Serv. v. Bradley, 779 So.2d 786 (La.App. 2 Cir. 2000). Furthermore, if the results of the blood or tissue sampling indicate "by a ninety-nine and nine-tenths percentage point threshold probability that the alleged father is the father of the child," the alleged father is presumed to be the father. R.S. 9:397.3(B)(2)(b).

(d) The burden of persuasion applicable to paternity actions under this Article remains, as under prior law, by "clear and convincing evidence" if the alleged father is dead and by a preponderance of evidence if the alleged father is alive. The latter burden is not explicitly stated here because it is the general burden of persuasion in civil matters. The distinction in the burden of persuasion based upon whether the alleged father is dead or alive is best explained by the fact that "[a]fter the death of the alleged parent, whose knowledge concerning the fact or probability of his filiation to the child is superior, the [estate's] vulnerability to fraudulent claims is significantly increased." Katherine Shaw Spaht, Developments in the Law, 1981–1982—Persons, 43 La.L.Rev. 535, 537 (1982).

(e) The time period for bringing the paternity action under this Article is limited to succession matters only. This is a change in the law. The time for instituting a paternity action for the purpose of exercising the right to support, to sue for wrongful death, or to claim Social Security benefits or the like, is not limited by this Article. Prior law required that a paternity action under former Civil Code Article 209 (rev. 1984) be instituted within nineteen years of the child's birth or within one year from the alleged parent's death, whichever first occurred. If the action was not timely instituted, the child could not thereafter establish his filiation for any purpose, except to recover damages under Civil Code Article 2315. That was a harsh result not justified by any policy consideration. For the particular purpose of succession, on the other hand, there is a time limit on instituting the action—to facilitate the orderly disposition of estates and the stability of land titles.

(f) The time period during which the paternity action must be instituted for succession purposes is longer than that of prior law. Under former Civil Code Article 209 (C) (rev. 1984), the action also had to be instituted within nineteen years of the child's birth. Under this Article the child, regardless of his age, has one year from his father's death to institute the action.

Art. 198.   Father's action to establish paternity; time period

A man may institute an action to establish his paternity of a child at any time except as provided in this Article. The action is strictly personal.

If the child is presumed to be the child of another man, the action shall be instituted within one year from the day of the birth of the child. Nevertheless, if the mother in bad faith deceived the father of the child regarding his paternity, the action shall be instituted within one year from the day the father knew or should have known of his paternity, or within ten years from the day of the birth of the child, whichever first occurs.

In all cases, the action shall be instituted no later than one year from the day of the death of the child.

The time periods in this Article are peremptive.

Acts 2005, No. 192, § 1, eff. June 29, 2005.

REVISION COMMENTS—2005

(a) This Article replaces C.C. Art. 191 (2004) and clarifies that the avowal action is strictly personal to the alleged father. See C.C. Arts. 1765–66. See also Mouret v. Godeaux, 886 So.2d 1217 (La.App. 3 Cir. 2004), which applied C.C. former Article 191. Even before the enactment of Article 191, the jurisprudence recognized the right of the father to institute an avowal action as a predicate to, or simultaneous with, the exercising of parental rights. See, e.g., State ex rel. Williams v. Howard, 898 So.2d 443 (La.App. 1 Cir. 2004); Putnam v. Mayeaux, 645 So.2d 1223 (La.App. 1 Cir. 1994).

(b) Proof of paternity under this Article may be made at any time, as a general rule, by any relevant evidence, the same type of evidence used in an action by or on behalf of a child to prove his paternity under Article 197 (rev. 2005). See Comment (b) to that Article. The standard of persuasion is a preponderance of the evidence.

(c) The alleged biological father may obtain a court order for blood tests without first instituting the paternity action permitted by this Article. R.S. 9:398.2 (1995). Even though the statute authorizing the court order provides that in such action the court shall not make a determination of paternity, the test results are admissible in any subsequent action filed by the parties relating to the filiation of the child. R.S. 9:398.2(E).

(d) Although the general rule is that the avowal action may be brought by the alleged father at any time, this Article does establish time periods during which this action must be instituted in two instances: (1) if the child is presumed to be the child of another man or (2) if the child dies. All of the time periods established by this Article are peremptive, rather than prescriptive and thus are not subject to interruption or suspension. Contrast Putnam v. Mayeaux, 645 So.2d 1223 (La.App. 1 Cir. 1994) (no applicable prescriptive period for avowal action; one year and three days was a reasonable time); Geen v. Geen, 666 So.2d 1192 (La.App. 3 Cir. 1995) (fifteen to nineteen months not an unreasonable time); Demery v. Housing Auth. of New Orleans, 689 So.2d 659 (La.App. 4 Cir. 1997); T.D. v. M.M.M., 730 So.2d 873 (La. 1999) (six years was not too long to wait to bring avowal action).

If the child is presumed to be the child of another man, the alleged father must institute his action within one year of the child's birth, to which there is one exception. See comment (e), infra. If the child dies, the action must be instituted no later than one year from the death of the child. These restrictions imposed upon the alleged father's rights to institute the avowal action recognize first, that state attempts to require parents to conform to societal norms should be directed at the parents, not the innocent child of the union (see Trimble v. Gordon, 430 U.S. 762, 97 S.Ct. 1459 (1977)), and second, that a father who failed during a child's life to assume his parental responsibilities should not be permitted unlimited time to institute an action to benefit from the child's death.

(e) The time period of one year from the child's birth imposed upon the alleged father if the child is presumed to be the child of another man requires that the alleged father act quickly to avow his biological paternity. Requiring that the biological father institute the avowal action quickly is intended to protect the child from the upheaval of such litigation and its consequences in circumstances where the child may actually live in an existing intact family with his mother and presumed father or may have become attached over many years to the man presumed to be his father.

(f) The only exception to the time period of one year for the institution of an avowal action by the biological father is if the mother in bad faith deceives the father concerning his paternity. In such case the father may institute the action within one year from the day he knew or should have known of the birth of the child or within ten years of the child's birth, whichever first occurs. See former C.C. Art. 191 (2004) and R.S. 9:305.

(g) The Department of Social Services, which is providing services in accordance with 42 U.S.C. 666, is not bound by the time periods in this Article. See R.S. 9:395.1.

CHAPTER 3—FILIATION BY ADOPTION

SECTION 1—EFFECT OF ADOPTION

Art. 199.   Effect of adoption

Upon adoption, the adopting parent becomes the parent of the child for all purposes and the filiation between the child and his legal parent is terminated, except as otherwise provided by law. The adopted child and his descendants retain the right to inherit from his former legal parent and the relatives of that parent.

Acts 2009, No. 3, § 1, eff. June 9, 2009.

REVISION COMMENTS—2009

(a) This Article does not change the law as to the effect of an adoption. It severs the legal relationship between the person who is adopted and his legal parents and relatives with a few exceptions and establishes the legal relationship of child and parent between the person who is adopted and the adoptive parent.

(b) Among the exceptions to the severance of the legal relationship between the person adopted and his legal parents and relatives are: (1) the retention of the right to inherit by the adopted child from his former legal parent and other relatives of that parent (this Article, second sentence), (2) the retention of the legal relationship between a child who has been adopted and a legal parent if the legal parent is married to the adoptive parent (Children's Code Article 1256 and La. R.S. 9:461), and (3) the right of the parents of a legal parent at the time of the adoption to seek visitation with the child (Children's Code Article 1264).

SECTION 2—ADOPTION OF MINORS

Art. 200.   Adoption of minors

The adoption of minors is also governed by the provisions of the Children's Code.

Acts 2009, No. 3, § 1, eff. June 9, 2009.

REVISION COMMENT—2009

Even though the Children's Code regulates extensively the process of the adoption of minors and contains provisions as to the effect of the adoption once a judgment is rendered, the Civil Code also provides for the effect of an adoption. See Civil Code Articles 199, supra, and 3506(8) (defining children to include those who have been adopted).

Arts. 201 to 211.   [Blank]

SECTION 3—ADOPTOIN OF ADULTS

Art. 212.   Adult adoption requirements

A person who has attained the age of majority may be adopted without judicial authorization only when the adoptive parent is the spouse or the surviving spouse of a parent of the person to be adopted.

In other proposed adult adoptions, the court, upon the joint petition of the adoptive parent and the person to be adopted, may authorize the adoption of a person who has attained the age of majority if the court finds after a hearing that the adoption is in the best interest of both parties.

Acts 2008, No. 351, § 1, eff. Jan. 1, 2009.

REVISION COMMENTS—2008

(a) This Article changes the law. The former provision, R.S. 9:461, (as amended 1988), permitted any adult to adopt another person age seventeen or older by simply executing an authentic act of adoption. This Article permits only a stepparent, during the lifetime or after the death of his spouse, to adopt a major child of his spouse simply by executing an authentic act with spouses' concurrences, if applicable. See Article 213. Such an adoption has no effect upon the spouse who is or was the legal parent and that parent's relatives, who retain their legal relationship to the child. See R.S. 9:461.

(b) All other proposed adoptions of an adult "child" by another adult require judicial authorization of the adoption; that judicial authorization, obtained during a hearing initiated by a joint petition (see the second Paragraph of this Article) of the person to be adopted and the adoptive parent, requires proof that "the adoption is in the best interest of both parties." Under the former provision, R.S. 9:461, the only time a court hearing was required for the authorization of an adult adoption was if the person to be adopted was older than the adoptive parent. In such a case, the standard to be applied by the court at the hearing was the same as the standard articulated in this Article.

(c) The requirement of judicial authorization for an adult adoption is intended to assure that the adult adoption does not involve either circumstances that suggest undue influence has been exercised over either party or a situation where one party took advantage of the other party whose mental or physical circumstances increase his vulnerability to the slightest imposition. Compare this policy with the purpose of the requirement of judicial supervision of a matrimonial agreement during the marriage of the spouses as imposed by Civil Code Article 2329. Katherine S. Spaht and Cynthia Ann Samuel, Equal Management Revisited: 1979 Legislative Modifications of the 1978 Matrimonial Regimes Law, 40 La. L. Rev. 83–145 (1979).

Art. 213. Adult adoption; form

The adoptive parent and the person to be adopted shall consent to the adoption in an authentic act of adoption.

The spouse of the adoptive parent and the spouse of the person to be adopted shall sign the act of adoption for the purpose of concurrence in the adoption only. The act of adoption without this concurrence is absolutely null. The concurrence does not establish the legal relationship of parent and child.

Neither a party to an adult adoption nor a concurring spouse may consent by procuration or mandate.

Acts 2008, No. 351, § 1, eff. Jan. 1, 2009.

REVISION COMMENTS—2008

(a) The consent of the parties to the adult adoption must be expressed in an authentic act designated in this Article as an authentic act of adoption.

(b) This Article imposes a new requirement for adult adoptions: the consent of the spouses of both the adoptive parent and the person to be adopted. This consent is described more accurately as "concurrence," which is a juridical act (see Civil Code Article 2347, Comment (c)), because the concurrence, unlike the two parties' consent, "does not establish the legal relationship of parent and child."

(c) An adult adoption without the concurrence of a spouse is an absolute nullity. See Civil Code Article 2030. The requirement of the concurrence of the spouse of the adoptive parent and the spouse of the person to be adopted is a rule of public order, the violation of which results in the absolute nullity of the act of adoption. The public order involved in a spouse's concurrence is not simply the protection afforded the spouse who must concur, but also the protection of the broader family, i.e. other children, other ascendants, and other collaterals. An adoption creates for all purposes the relationship of parent/child between two persons not so related, i.e., for the purposes of reciprocal intestate succession, forced heirship, wrongful death and survival actions, as well as the life-time obligation of support owed by and to needy descendants and ascendants. Civil Code Article 229 (1870). Thus, the consequences of an adoption for the spouse of either party, but especially the spouse of the adoptive parent, are significant and serious.

(d) Consistent with the seriousness of an act of adult adoption, neither the parties nor a concurring spouse may consent by procuration or mandate. See Civil Code Articles 2987 and 2989. See also Civil Code Article 92, which also prohibits a party from consenting to marriage by procuration.

Art. 214.   Adult adoption; recordation requirement

The adoption is effective when the act of adult adoption and any judgment required to authorize the adoption are filed for registry, except as otherwise provided by law.

Acts 2008, No. 351, § 1, eff. Jan. 1, 2009.

CHAPTER 4—FILIATION OF CHILDREN BY ASSISTED REPRODUCTIVE TECHNOLOGY [RESERVED]

CHAPTER 5—PARENTAL AUTHORITY OF MARRIED PERSONS

SECTION 1—GENERAL PRINCIPLES OF PARENTAL AUTHORITY

Arts. 215 to 220.   [Blank]

Art. 221.   Authority of married parents

The father and mother who are married to each other have parental authority over their minor child during the marriage.

Acts 2015, No. 260, § 1, eff. Jan. 1, 2016.

REVISION COMMENTS—2015

(a) This Article introduces the subject of parental authority, which exists during the marriage of the parents. The Articles in this Chapter establish a regime, or system of rules, governing the relationship of parent and child. The Articles that follow not only prescribe rights and responsibilities of parents to their children and children to their parents but also provide instruction concerning the proper conduct of good children and good parents.

(b) Parental authority as used in this Article does not refer to the authority of a parent in its broad sense, that is the authority that lasts throughout the lives of both parent and child (see C.C. Art. 236 (Rev. 2015)), but instead refers to such authority in its limited sense that lasts until the majority or emancipation of the child, or the termination of the marriage of the child's parents. See C.C. Art. 235 (Rev. 2015).

(c) Fathers and mothers enjoy parental authority over their child during their marriage, with a few exceptions. See C.C. Arts. 232 and 234 (Rev. 2015). Compare C.C. Art. 216 (1870). By contrast, if the father and mother of the minor child never married or if they divorced, the regime of tutorship exists rather than the regime of parental authority. C.C. Arts. 256 and 246 (1870).

Art. 222.   Representation of minor

Parental authority includes representation of the child and the right to designate a tutor for the child.

Acts 2015, No. 260, § 1, eff. Jan. 1, 2016.

(a) This Article makes explicit that parental authority includes representation of the child. Despite the reference in the title to representation, C.C. Art. 235 (1870) provided simply that fathers and mothers may "appear for [their minor children] in court in every kind of civil suit. . . ." The Code of Civil Procedure recognizes the father and the mother as the proper parties plaintiff and defendant for their minor child. C.C.P. Arts. 683, 732, and 4501. However, C.C. Art. 235 (1870) did not contain a general rule of parental representation of the minor in juridical acts but instead referred only to the parents' acceptance of any donation made to their child. C.C. Art. 1472 (Rev. 1991).

(b) Representation means that the parent may represent the minor child in "legal relations." C.C. Art. 2985 (Rev. 1997). See W. Holmes and S. Symeonides, "Representation, Mandate, and Agency: A Kommentar on Louisiana's New Law," 73 Tul. L. Rev. 1087 (1999). Of course, only the child may enter into some legal relations, such as marriage (C.C. Art. 92 (Rev. 1987) and Ch.C. Arts. 1543 et seq.), making a will (C.C. Art. 1476 (Rev. 1991)), and other legal relations subject to exceptions made by law (see e.g., R.S. 40:1299.35.5). See also Carey v. Population Services, International, 41 U.S. 678, 97 S.Ct. 2010, 52 L.Ed.2d 675 (1977).

(c) Parental authority includes the right of a parent to designate a testamentary tutor as permitted by C.C. Art. 257 (1870). The designation can be made by authentic act as well as by testament. See C.C. Art. 219 (1870).

Art. 223.   Rights and obligations of parental authority

Parental authority includes rights and obligations of physical care, supervision, protection, discipline, and instruction of the child.

Acts 2015, No. 260, § 1, eff. Jan. 1, 2016.

(a) This Article introduces the rights and obligations of parents over the person of their child. Principal among these rights and obligations is the physical care of the minor, this right and obligation that was implicit under C.C. Art. 218 (1870). The right to physical care of the child reflects the parents' paramount right to custody of their child, recognized in the jurisprudence. See Reinhardt v. Reinhardt, 720 So.2d 78, 79 (La.App. 1 Cir. 1998), writs denied 745 So.2d 22 (1999); Troxel v. Granville, 530 U.S. 57, 120 S.Ct. 2054, 147 L.Ed.2d 49 (2000). Furthermore, this right makes possible in a practical way the rights and obligations of supervision, protection, and instruction.

(b) The parental rights and obligations of supervision and instruction provide the means of performing the parents' obligation of moral and material direction of the child. See C.C. Art. 99 (Rev. 1987). The right to physical care of the child assures parents the opportunity to supervise and instruct their child and to provide for their child's health and safety.

(c) C.C. Art. 235 (1870) imposed an obligation upon the parents to protect their child but contained no language explicitly creating a right of protection. This revision incorporates both a parental right and obligation to protect the child.

SECTION 2—OBLIGATIONS OF PARENTS

Art. 224.   Parental obligation of support and education

Parents are obligated to support, maintain, and educate their child. The obligation to educate a child continues after minority as provided by law.

Acts 2015, No. 260, § 1, eff. Jan. 1, 2016.

(a) This Article is the first of three Articles imposing obligations upon the parents toward their child and third persons. The obligation of parents to support and maintain their minor child under this Article is identical to its predecessor, C.C. Art. 227 (1870), but distinguishable from the obligation of parents who enjoyed a usufruct over their child's property under C.C. Art. 224 (1870). Parents with a usufruct over their minor child's property were obligated to support and maintain their child "according to their situation in life." C.C. Art. 224 (1870). Nevertheless, C.C. Art. 227 (1870) was interpreted as imposing a responsibility upon parents to support their child in accordance with their standard of living during their marriage. See Comment (c) to C.C. Art. 141 (Rev. 1993).

(b) The parents' obligation to educate their minor child continues after minority for a child who "is a full-time student in good standing in a secondary school or its equivalent, has not attained the age of nineteen, and is dependent upon either parent" and when the child "has a developmental disability, as defined in R.S. 28:451.2, until he attains the age of twenty-two, as long as the child is a full-time student in a secondary school." This does not change prior law. See C.C. Art. 230 (1870); R.S. 9:315.22(C) and (D).

(c) Although a parent is obligated to support, maintain, and educate his minor child, the unemancipated child may not enforce the obligation against any person who has parental authority. R.S. 9:571 (Rev. 2015). Nevertheless, in a proceeding for divorce, or while the spouses are living separate and apart, a spouse who seeks custody of a child may also assert a claim for child support. C.C. Art. 105 (Rev. 1990), Arts. 141–142 (Rev. 1993); R.S. 9:315–315.26. See also R.S. 9:291 (claim for child support if living separate and apart).

Art. 225.   Parental liability for child's offenses and quasi-offenses

Parents are responsible for damage occasioned by their child as provided by law.

Acts 2015, No. 260, § 1, eff. Jan. 1, 2016.

REVISION COMMENT—2015

This Article does not change the law; it merely replaces C.C. Art. 237 (1870) and recognizes the liability of parents for damage "occasioned by their minor child" as provided in C.C. Art. 2318. This liability rests upon the authority of the parents over the person of their child—the rights to and obligations of the physical care, supervision, protection, discipline, and instruction of the child. See C.C. Art. 223 (Rev. 2015) and Turner v. Bucher, 308 So.2d 270 (La. 1975).

Art. 226.   Parental obligation of direction

Parents have a moral obligation to provide moral, social, and material direction for their child.

Acts 2015, No. 260, § 1, eff. Jan. 1, 2016.

REVISION COMMENTS—2015

(a) Parents assume the moral obligation of providing moral, social, and material direction to their child. C.C. Art. 99 (Rev. 1987) explains that, by marrying, spouses mutually assume the moral and material direction of their children.

(b) Moral direction includes instruction and exhortation concerning moral obligations and common moral principles. Social direction is more expansive and contemplates, for example, instruction concerning acceptable conduct within the broader community and the necessity of considering and balancing the needs of others and the community against the individual's desires. Instruction concerning basic economic matters, such as living within one's means, falls within the purview of material direction.

(c) C.C. Art. 223 implicitly and Art. 228 (Rev. 2015) explicitly impose obligations upon the child to obey his parents and upon the parent to instruct his child, with the concomitant right to correct the child in a reasonable manner, all for the purpose of assuring a legally practical means of accomplishing the parents' obligation to provide direction for their child.

SECTION 3—OBLIGATIONS OF CHILDREN

Art. 227.   Parental control

A child owes assistance to his parents and may not quit a family residence without the consent of both parents, except as otherwise provided by law.

Acts 2015, No. 260, § 1, eff. Jan. 1, 2016.

(a) The explicit obligation a child owes to assist his father and mother is new. Assistance includes, at the least, the personal care of an ill or infirm parent, just as the obligation of assistance reciprocally assumed by spouses includes such responsibility. C.C. Art. 98 (Rev. 1987), Revision Comment (c). In addition, assistance more broadly defined includes cooperating and participating in the daily tasks required for the efficient functioning of the family and other responsibilities that are consistent with the purposes and goals of family life. This obligation of assistance, however, does not include monetary support.

(b) As long as the minor is unemancipated, he may not leave the family home without the consent of both parents for the purpose of establishing a residence separate from his parents. "Quit" does not refer to a temporary absence. On this point, this Article makes no change in the law. C.C. Art. 218 (1870).

Art. 228.   Child's obligation of obedience; parental correction

A child shall obey his parents in all matters not contrary to law or good morals. Parents have the right and obligation to correct and discipline the child in a reasonable manner.

Acts 2015, No. 260, § 1, eff. Jan. 1, 2016.

(a) This Article restates the substance of C.C. Art. 217 (1870). The child's obligation of obedience serves as the foundation for the parental right of correction. See C.C. Art. 223 (Rev. 2015).

(b) Consistently with its predecessor, C.C. Art. 218 (1870), the second sentence of this Article bestows upon parents the right to correct their child in a reasonable manner. This right to correct is essential to compliance with the parental obligations with physical care, supervision, protection, and instruction. Since acculturation of children occurs principally within the family, the law recognizes the necessity of reasonable discipline by those who love the child to instill character, self-discipline, and virtue.

SECTION 4—AUTHORITY OVER THE PROPERTY OF THE CHILD

Art. 229.   Administration of the property of the child

Each parent has the right and the obligation to administer the property of the child. The parent must do so as a prudent administrator and is answerable for any damage caused by his fraud, fault, default, or neglect. An action for failure to perform this obligation is subject to a liberative prescription of five years that commences to run from the day the child attains the age of majority.

Acts 2015, No. 260, § 1, eff. Jan. 1, 2016.

(a) This Article departs from its predecessor by granting the right to administer the minor child's property to either parent. Under C.C. Art. 221 (1870), the father was the administrator of the minor's estate unless he was interdicted or absent (an absent person under C.C. Art. 47 (Rev. 1990)). See also C.C.P. Art. 683 (as amended 2012) and Art. 732 (as amended 2004), which as a general rule made the father the proper party plaintiff and defendant for the minor child during the existence of parental authority. Upon enactment in 1987, however, C.C. Art. 99 recognized that parental authority was to be exercised equally. See 1987 Revision Comment to C.C. Art. 99 (Rev. 1987).

(b) The standard of care imposed upon the parent who administers the minor child's property is that of a prudent administrator, and the administration must be for the benefit of the minor child. Usufructuaries (C.C. Art. 576), spouses who are co-owners of former community property (C.C. Art. 2369.3), managers under a negotiorum gestio (C.C. Art. 2295), and tutors (C.C.P. Art. 4262) are subject to the same standard. Furthermore, this Article imposes the standard of care in the context of the principle that the property be administered for the benefit of the child. In this respect, the responsibility of the parents resembles the responsibility of those who administer the property of another, such as the trustee who has a duty to administer the trust solely in the interest of the beneficiary; R.S. 9:2082.

Consistent with the standard of care imposed upon the parent who administers the minor's property, this Article imposes liability upon the administering parent "for any damage caused by his fraud, fault, default, or neglect." Similar language appears in C.C. Art. 576 (liability of usufructuary to the naked owner) and Art. 2369.3 (liability of a spouse to the other spouse for failure to manage former community property prudently).

(c) Acts of administration differ from acts of alienation, encumbrance, or lease. The ability of the parents to act alone without court approval in matters affecting the minor child's property depends upon the nature of the act: either parent may administer the child's property without court supervision; a parent may dispose of the child's property only with prior court approval (See C.C. Art. 230 [Rev. 2015]), except as otherwise provided by law (see R.S. 9:572 (Rev. 2015)). Administration contemplates preservation or protection of acquired rights or the exploitation of them without changing the substantial character of the minor's patrimony as a whole. Disposition is any other act that is not administration.

In the different, yet analogous, regime of tutorship, the Code of Civil Procedure contains detailed articles governing when the tutor needs court approval. Nevertheless, those articles do not provide a complete solution to the problem of distinguishing between the two types of acts: some acts that require court approval are purely administrative. Other acts are of such gravity that a requirement of court approval might be expected; yet there is no legislation specifically requiring it. This Article clearly contemplates a difference between administration and disposition that more nearly reflects the classic distinction. See Katherine Shaw Spaht, Family Law in Louisiana, 714–715 (2000).

Art. 230. Alienation, encumbrance, or lease of the property of the child; expenditure of fruits

Either parent may alienate, encumber, or lease the property of the child, compromise a claim of the child, or incur an obligation of the child for his education, support, and maintenance only with prior court approval, except as otherwise provided by law.

Nevertheless, a parent may expend, without court approval, the fruits of the child's property for the shared benefit of the family, excluding major children not living in the household, or for the expenses of the child's household or property.

Acts 2015, No. 260, § 1, eff. Jan. 1, 2016.

REVISION COMMENTS—2015

(a) In contrast to Article 229 referring to acts of administration, this Article, as a general proposition, requires the parent to obtain court approval in the manner provided by C.C.P. Art. 4501 (Rev. 2015), if the act contemplated by the parent is an alienation, encumbrance, or lease of the minor child's property, including the compromise of a claim of the child, or if the act includes incurring an obligation of the child. All such acts must be for the purpose of education, support, or maintenance of the child. See C.C. Art. 224 (Rev. 2015).

The procedure for obtaining court approval is intended to provide protection to the minor child. See C.C.P. Arts. 4271 and 4501 (Rev. 2015). If a parent does not obtain court approval of a transaction when approval is required, the transaction is relatively null. See C.C. Arts. 2031 and 2033 (Rev. 1984); Snowden v. Huey P. Long Memorial Hospital, 581 So.2d 287 (La.App. 3 Cir. 1991). See also Succession of Hellmers, 637 So.2d 1302 (La.App. 4 Cir. 1994); and Carter v. Fenner, 136 F.3d 1000 (5 Cir. 1998).

(b) R.S. 9:572 (Rev. 2015) permits a parent to take certain actions without prior court approval, such as alienation of the minor's movable property if the sum received does not exceed $15,000.

(c) A major exception to the requirement of court approval for alienation of the minor's property is the expenditure of fruits of the minor's property for two purposes—expenses of the child's household, such as electricity, water, rent, or for the shared benefit of the family. "Family" as used in this Article is family in its limited sense under C.C. Art. 3506(12), which consists of "father, mother, and children." Nonetheless, this Article further restricts the meaning of family to exclude major children not living in the household, even though they are included within the broad definition of "children" in Article 3506(8).

(d) The second paragraph of this Article is intended as a substitute for the former parental right of enjoyment, which was a form of usufruct enjoyed by parents during the existence of parental authority. See C.C. Arts. 223–226 (1870). Prior law restricted the type of property of the minor child subject to the right of enjoyment, by excluding, for example, property earned by the minor's own labor and industry or donated to the minor (C.C. Art. 226 (1870)). But property subject to the parents' enjoyment made them the owners of the fruits of the property. As a consequence of being owner of the fruits produced from such property of the minor child, the parents could expend those fruits as they saw fit, for any purpose. This Article changes the law: although it does not create a parental right of enjoyment subject to the rules of the law of usufruct, it does permit the parents to use the fruits from all of the minor's property but only for limited purposes which are described in the Article.

(e) Code of Civil Procedure Article 4521 (Rev. 2015) contains further protection, in the interest of the minor, when his property consists of a judgment or settlement, as in the case of the minor child's personal injury recovery. The court has authority to order the funds from a minor's personal injury recovery to be deposited in the registry of the court, to be expended only for certain authorized purposes, or to be placed in trust. In addition the court has authority to impose other restrictions upon the use and withdrawal of such funds as it deems necessary to protect the interest of the minor in accordance with the provisions of C.C.P. Article 4521 (Rev. 2015).

(f) The right of parents to expend the fruits of the child's property for authorized purposes without court approval under this Article is forfeited if one of the parents is declared unworthy to succeed and his child inherits under the provisions of C.C. Art. 946(B).

Art. 231.   Parents' obligation to deliver and account

Parents are bound to deliver the child his property at termination of parental authority.

Parents shall also give an account of their administration when ordered by the court. The action to compel an accounting is subject to a liberative prescription of five years that commences to run from the day the child attains the age of majority.

Acts 2015, No. 260, § 1, eff. Jan. 1, 2016.

REVISION COMMENTS—2015

(a) At termination of parental authority for a cause provided in C.C. Art. 235 (Rev. 2015), the parents are obligated to deliver to the child his property in their possession and/or under their control. In addition they are bound to "give an account of their administration. . . ." just as a tutor must. See C.C.P. Art. 4392. For example, they must explain what happened to the child's property that is no longer in their possession or under their control and for what purpose any proceeds were expended.

(b) The action instituted by the child to obtain an accounting from the parents at termination of parental authority is a summary proceeding. See C.C.P. 2592(9) (Rev. 2015).

(c) The action to enforce the obligation to deliver the child's property is not subject to liberative prescription. See Yiannopoulos, Property (Civ.L.Treat., vol. 2), Section 279, at 557–558 (4th ed. 2001). In contrast, the action by the child to compel an accounting is a personal action that prescribes in five years from the day the child attains the age of majority.

(d) The obligations of the parents contained in this Article are governed by general principles of the law of obligations in determining if the obligation of the parents is joint or solidary (C.C. Arts. 1786–1788, 1794–1806 (Rev. 1984)), and if joint, whether divisible or indivisible (C.C. Art. 1789 (Rev. 1984)).

SECTION 5—PERSON HAVING PARENTAL AUTHORITY AND OF ITS DELEGATION AND SUSPENSION

Art. 232.   Parental authority

Either parent during the marriage has parental authority over his child unless otherwise provided by law.

Under extraordinary circumstances, such as if one parent is mentally incompetent, interdicted, or imprisoned, or is an absent person, the other parent has exclusive authority.

Acts 2015, No. 260, § 1, eff. Jan. 1, 2016.

REVISION COMMENTS—2015

(a) Under this Article, which changes the law in part, parental authority may be exercised by either parent. The predecessor of this Article, Civil Code Article 216 (1870), acknowledged that parents shared this authority, but "[i]n the case of difference between the parents, the authority of the father prevails." Nevertheless, the jurisprudence never applied the Article strictly. See Wood v. Beard, 290 S.2d 675 (La. 1974). Article 99 of the Civil Code, which was later legislation enacted in 1987, provides that spouses by the act of marrying "mutually assume the moral and material direction of the family, exercise parental authority, and assume the moral and material obligations resulting therefrom." The Revision Comment to C.C. Art. 99 (Rev. 1987) explains that that Article "states a general principle of equality between the spouses in the moral and material direction of the family." This Article explicitly recognizes the general principle of equality of the parents in the exercise of parental authority by permitting either parent acting alone to exercise any facet of this authority, with certain specified exceptions. See the second paragraph of this Article and C.C. Art. 234 (Rev. 2015).

(b) An instance under this Article for the exercise of one parent's exclusive authority occurs when there are extraordinary circumstances, such as the mental incompetence, commitment, or imprisonment of the other parent or the other parent is an absent person under C.C. Art. 47 (Rev. 1990). The illustrative list of extraordinary circumstances is similar to that contained in C.C. Art. 2355 (Rev. 1979).

The list of extraordinary circumstances in this Article differs from that contained in C.C. Art. 2355 (Rev. 1979) in the following respect: this Article includes interdiction of a parent. Interdiction may be full or limited. If a parent has been fully interdicted (See C.C. Art. 389 [Rev. 2000]), the second paragraph of this Article applies. If the interdiction of a parent is limited (see C.C. Art. 390 [Rev. 2000]), the second paragraph applies only if the judgment of limited interdiction places parental authority in his curator. See C.C. Art. 395 (Rev. 2000), which distinguishes the effect of a full and a limited interdiction.

Art. 233.   Delegation of parental authority

Parents may delegate all or a part of their parental authority to others as provided by law.

Parents delegate a part of their parental authority to teachers and others to whom they entrust their child for his education, insofar as may be necessary.

Acts 2015, No. 260, § 1, eff. Jan. 1, 2016.

REVISION COMMENTS—2015

(a) As under prior law, parents may delegate all or a part of their parental authority. This revision recognizes the right of parents to delegate their authority under the following circumstances: (1) upon execution of a mandate granting provisional custody under the provisions of and for the purposes contained in R.S. 9:951–954; (2) upon a voluntary transfer of custody to other responsible adults under the provisions of Children's Code Articles 1510 et seq.; (3) upon an express grant of authority to a person with whom the parent places the child, for example, a babysitter, neighbor, or grandparent; or (4) when the circumstances are such that it is customary for parents to delegate a part of their authority, for example, the child's overnight visits in the homes of friends.

(b) C.C. Art. 220 (1870) permitted parents to delegate a part of their authority to teachers and others to whom they entrusted their children for education. This revision recognizes that by virtue of the provisions of R.S. 17:223 (discipline of pupils; suspension from school; corporeal punishment), parents by the very act of enrolling their children in school in effect do delegate a part of their authority to teachers and others for the purpose of educating their child. The Article thus accomplishes a legal delegation of parental authority implicit in the provisions of Title 17 of the Revised Statutes.

(c) A delegation of parental authority does not relieve a parent of liability for a child's offenses or quasi-offenses under C.C. Art. 225 (Rev. 2015) and Art. 2318 (Rev. 2008). See C.C. Art. 2318 (Rev. 2008).

Art. 234.   Parental authority; custody award

Parental authority continues during marriage, unless modified by a judgment awarding custody to one parent, by a joint custody implementation order, or by a judgment awarding custody to a third person.

An ascendant, other than a parent, who is awarded custody has parental authority. The authority of a third person who is awarded custody, other than an ascendant, is governed by the rules of tutorship, unless modified by court order.

Acts 2015, No. 260, § 1, eff. Jan. 1, 2016.

REVISION COMMENTS—2015

(a) This Article is new. It provides that the general rule [is] that parental authority continues until the parents' marriage terminates unless modified by a court order. A court order of custody modifying parental authority may be rendered during the marriage pursuant to a rule to show cause while the parents are living separate and apart (R.S. 9:291) or after a petition for divorce has been filed (C.C. Arts. 105, 131, and 136). A custody award may also be made in a proceeding for a judicial separation in a covenant marriage. See R.S. 9:308(D).

(b) The reference to a modification by a joint custody implementation order includes the possibility of the designation under R.S. 9:335(B) of a domiciliary parent, a term that is defined as the parent with whom the child primarily resides. This designation necessarily modifies parental authority because the "domiciliary parent" has sole authority to make all decisions affecting the child unless the implementation order specifically modifies this authority. If no domiciliary parent is named but the implementation order is detailed and provides for decision-making by one or both parents as contemplated by R.S. 9:335(A), the order modifies parental authority. If no domiciliary parent is designated and no specific allocation of decision-making authority is contained in a joint custody implementation order, parental authority is unmodified according to R.S. 9:335(C).

(c) The reference to a modification by a judgment awarding custody to one parent contemplates the possibility that a custody award to one parent conveying authority over the child can modify parental authority. A sole custody award to one parent may be modified by the provisions of a court order and affect the authority of the custodial parent. The terms of the judgment determine the extent to which parental authority is modified.

(d) For a parent without parental authority because of a sole custody award to the other parent or the provisions of a joint custody implementation order, certain rights and obligations nonetheless continue. For example, a parent awarded visitation under the provisions of C.C. Art. 136(A) may discipline and correct the child absent a contradictory provision in the court order of visitation. Likewise, the noncustodial parent remains obligated to support, maintain and educate the child, an obligation that is often enforced by a child support award under C.C. Art. 141 and R.S. 9:315 et seq. These rights and obligations attach to parenthood, more generally, and are not limited to a narrower concept of parental authority.

(e) If the court awards custody of the child to a third person during the existence of parental authority, as it may under C.C. Art. 133, the general principle adopted by this Article is that, with one narrow exception, the third person has the authority of a tutor under C.C. Arts. 246 et seq. The only exception to this general principle is for ascendants, other than a parent, awarded custody of the child. An ascendant awarded custody of a minor child during the existence of parental authority exercises such authority. Although the ascendant with custody has the authority of a parent, the custody award to the ascendant does not displace the obligation owed by a parent to the child to support, maintain, and educate the child, C.C. Art. 224 (Rev. 2015) nor does the ascendant assume a more onerous obligation of support than the reciprocal obligation imposed by C.C. Art. 237 (Rev. 2015) owed by all ascendants and descendants to each other.

SECTION 6—TERMINATION OF PARENTAL AUTHORITY

Art. 235.   Termination of parental authority

Parental authority terminates upon the child's attaining the age of majority, upon the child's emancipation, or upon termination of the marriage of the parents of the child.

Acts 2015, No. 260, § 1, eff. Jan. 1, 2016.

REVISION COMMENTS—2015

(a) This Article does not change the law: parental authority terminates when the child reaches majority or is emancipated, or when the marriage of the parents terminates. See C.C. Arts. 221 and 246 (1870) and C.C. Art. 101 (Rev. 1990).

(b) Parental authority also terminates upon a judgment of separation from bed and board in a covenant marriage (R.S. 9:309). Parental authority is suspended upon the appointment of a guardian under the Children's Code (Ch.C. Art. 682) or upon the rendition of some other judgment by public law which removes the child from the care and custody of his parents or interferes with either or both parents' authority over their child. See, e.g., C.C. Art. 234 (Rev. 2015); Williams v. City of Baton Rouge, 252 La. 770, 214 So.2d 138 (La. 1968); Redd v. Bohannon, 166 So.2d 362 (La.App. 3 Cir. 1964).

(c) Parental authority lasts until the child reaches majority at eighteen years or is emancipated. A child may be emancipated by judicial emancipation, marriage, or authentic act. See C.C. Arts. 365–369 (Rev. 2008).

CHAPTER 6—OBLIGATIONS OF CHILDREN AND PARENTS AND OTHER ASCENDANTS

Art. 236.   Filial honor and respect

A child regardless of age owes honor and respect to his father and mother.

Acts 2015, No. 260, § 1, eff. Jan. 1, 2016.

REVISION COMMENT—2015

The duty of a child to honor and respect his parents is not limited to the minority of a child. See C.C. Art. 215 (1870). Although no direct sanction for the breach of this obligation exists, the purpose of this Article is both hortatory and instructive as to the conduct of a good child at any age. Of course, if the child is a forced heir and the disrespectful act is sufficiently extreme, the parent is permitted to disinherit the child. See C.C. Arts. 1617 and 1621 (Rev. 2001).

Art. 237.   Obligation of providing the basic necessities of life; ascendants and descendants; exceptions

Descendants are bound to provide the basic necessities of life to their ascendants who are in need, upon proof of inability to obtain these necessities by other means or from other sources, and ascendants are likewise bound to provide for their needy descendants, this obligation being reciprocal.

This obligation is strictly personal and is limited to the basic necessities of food, clothing, shelter, and health care.

This obligation is owed by descendants and ascendants in the order of their degree of relationship to the obligee and is joint and divisible among obligors. Nevertheless, if the obligee is married, the obligation of support owed by his descendants and ascendants is secondary to the obligation owed by his spouse.

Acts 2015, No. 260, § 1, eff. Jan. 1, 2016.

REVISION COMMENTS—2015

(a) This Article contains the provisions of former C.C. Art. 229 (Rev. 1979). It imposes a reciprocal lifetime obligation upon ascendants and descendants, relationships determined in accordance with C.C. Arts. 899–901, to provide the basic necessities of life, which explicitly are limited to food, clothing, shelter and health care. This obligation exists only when the obligee proves that he is unable to obtain these necessities "by other means" or "from other sources."

(b) The needs of the obligee, referred to in C.C. Art. 238 (Rev. 2015), are to be measured by the basic necessities of life explicitly delineated in this Article as food, clothing, shelter, and basic or essential health care.

(c) The phrase "by other means" includes the capital resources and the earning capacity of the obligee. See Levy v. Levy, 536 So.2d 742 (La.App. 3 Cir. 1988); Landeche v. Airhart, 372 So.2d 598 (La.App. 4 Cir. 1979).

(d) The phrase "from other sources" includes public assistance.

(e) For the first time this Article provides a ranking of those descendants and ascendants who owe this reciprocal, lifetime obligation. Furthermore, this Article also directs that, if the obligee is married, the obligation of support owed by one spouse to the other (see C.C. Art. 98 (Rev. 1987)) primes the limited obligation owed by ascendants and descendants. See Matheny v. Matheny, 205 La. 869, 18 So.2d 324 (La. 1944); Lyons v. Landry, 293 So.2d 674 (La.App. 1 Cir. 1974); McCole v. McCole, 383 So.2d 55 (La.App. 2 Cir. 1980); and Simon v. Simon, 127 So.2d 769 (La.App. 3 Cir. 1961). The ranking of obligors imposes the obligation first upon the spouse, then upon the descendants and ascendants closest in degree of relationship to the obligee. To determine the closest in degree of relationship to the obligee, see C.C. Arts. 900 and 901 (Rev. 1981).

(f) This Article specifically provides that this obligation is strictly personal, not heritable (see C.C. Arts. 1766 and 1765 (Rev. 1984)) and as a consequence may not be enforced by a third person. This Article is explicit that the obligation is joint and divisible among obligors, not solidary. See C.C. Arts. 1786, 1788, 1789, and 1790 (Rev. 1984).

Art. 238.   Amount of support

The amount of support shall be determined in accordance with the needs of the obligee, as limited under the preceding Article, and the means of the obligor.

Acts 2015, No. 260, § 1, eff. Jan. 1, 2016.

REVISION COMMENTS—2015

(a) This Article incorporates the content of former C.C. Art. 231 (1870), which contained the general rules for the award of alimony.

(b) C.C. Arts. 233 and 234 (1870) have been suppressed.

Art. 239.   Modification or termination of support

The amount of support may be modified if the circumstances of the obligor or the obligee materially change and shall be terminated if it has become unnecessary.

Acts 2015, No. 260, § 1, eff. Jan. 1, 2016.

REVISION COMMENT—2015

This Article incorporates the provisions of C.C. Arts. 232 (1870), which provided for the change or termination of an alimony award if the need of the obligee or the ability of the obligor to pay changed or the award became unnecessary. See Comment (a) to C.C. Art. 238 (Rev. 2015) and C.C. Art. 142 (Rev. 2001), Art. 114 (Rev. 2001), and Art. 115 (Rev. 1997).

Arts. 240 to 245.   [Blank]

TITLE VIII—OF MINORS, OF THEIR TUTORSHIP AND EMANCIPATION

CHAPTER 1—OF TUTORSHIP

SECTION 1—GENERAL DISPOSITIONS

Art. 246.   Occasion for tutorship

The minor not emancipated is placed under the authority of a tutor after the dissolution of the marriage of his father and mother or the separation from bed and board of either one of them from the other.

Amended by Acts 1924, No. 72.

Art. 247.   Kinds of tutorships

There are four sorts of tutorships:

Tutorship by nature;

Tutorship by will;

Tutorship by the effect of the law;

Tutorship by the appointment of the judge.

Art. 248.   Modes of establishment of tutorships

Tutorship by nature takes place of right, but the natural tutor must qualify for the office as provided by law. In every other kind of tutorship the tutor must be confirmed or appointed by the court, and must qualify for the office as provided by law.

Amended by Acts 1960, No. 30, § 1, eff. Jan. 1, 1961.

Art. 249.   Accountability of tutor

For every sort of tutorship, the tutor is accountable.

SECTION 2—OF TUTORSHIP BY NATURE

Art. 250.   Persons entitled to tutorship

Upon the death of either parent, the tutorship of minor children belongs of right to the other. Upon divorce or judicial separation from bed and board of parents, the tutorship of each minor child belongs of right to the parent under whose care he or she has been placed or to whose care he or she has been entrusted; however, if the parents are awarded joint custody of a minor child, then the cotutorship of the minor child shall belong to both parents, with equal authority, privileges, and responsibilities, unless modified by order of the court or by an agreement of the parents, approved by the court awarding joint custody. In the event of the death of a parent to whom joint custody had been awarded, the tutorship of the minor children of the deceased belongs of right to the surviving parent.

All those cases are called tutorship by nature.

Amended by Acts 1924, No. 196; Acts 1981, No. 283, § 1; Acts 1982, No. 307, § 1, eff. Jan. 1, 1983; Acts 1983, No. 695, § 1.

Art. 251.   [Blank]

Art. 252.   Unborn and posthumous children

If a wife happens to be pregnant at the time of the death of her husband, no tutor shall be appointed to the child till after his birth; but, if it should be necessary, the judge may appoint a curator for the preservation of the rights of the unborn child, and for the administration of the estate which may belong to such child. At the birth of the posthumous child, such curator shall be of right the undertutor.

Arts. 253 to 255.   [Blank]

Art. 256.   Illegitimate children

A.   The mother is of right the tutrix of her illegitimate child not acknowledged by the father, or acknowledged by him alone without her concurrence.

B.   After the death of the mother, if the father had not acknowledged the child prior to the mother's death, the court shall give first consideration to appointment as tutor either of her parents or siblings who survive her and accept the appointment, and secondly, the father, always taking into consideration the best interests of the child.

C.   If both parents have acknowledged their illegitimate child, the judge shall appoint as tutor the one by whose care the best interests of the child will be served. However, if the parents are awarded joint custody of such acknowledged illegitimate child, then the cotutorship of such child shall belong of right to both parents, with equal authority, privileges, and responsibilities, unless modified by order of the court or by an agreement of the parents, approved by the court awarding joint custody.

Amended by Acts 1974, No. 90, § 1; Acts 1979, No. 536, § 1; Acts 1983, No. 215, § 1, eff. Sept. 1, 1983.

SECTION 3—OF THE TUTORSHIP BY WILL

Art. 257.   Surviving parent's right of appointment

The right of appointing a tutor, whether a relation or a stranger, belongs exclusively to the father or mother dying last.

The right of appointing a tutor, whether a relation or a stranger, also belongs to a parent who has been named the curator for the other living spouse, when that other living spouse has been interdicted, subject only to the right of the interdicted parent to claim the tutorship should his incapacity be removed by a judgment of a court of competent jurisdiction.

This is called tutorship by will, because generally it is given by testament; but it may likewise be given by any declaration of the surviving father or mother, or the parent who is the curator of the other spouse, executed before a notary and two witnesses.

Amended by Acts 1974, No. 142, § 1.

Art. 258.   Right of appointment where parents are divorced or separated

If the parents are divorced or judicially separated, only the one to whom the court has entrusted the care and custody of the children has a right to appoint a tutor for them as provided in Article 257. However, if the parents have been awarded joint custody of the children, then the right to appoint a tutor for them belongs to the parent dying last, but either parent may appoint a tutor of the property of the children as provided in Article 257. In the event that both parents appoint a tutor of the property of the children, the tutors shall separately administer that portion of the children's property which is attributable to the respective parent's estate. The court shall decide which tutor shall administer that portion of the children's property which is not attributable to either parent's estate.

Amended by Acts 1960, No. 30, § 1, eff. Jan. 1, 1961; Acts 1983, No. 695, § 1; Acts 1992, No. 680, § 1.

Art. 259.   Option of acceptance of tutorship

The tutor by will is not compelled to accept the tutorship to which he is appointed by the father or mother.

But if he refuses the tutorship, he loses in that case all the legacies and other advantages, which the person who appointed him may have made in his favor under a persuasion that he would accept this trust.

Art. 260.   [Blank]

Art. 261.   Illegitimate child

The father or mother who is entitled to the tutorship of the illegitimate child, according to the provisions of Article 256, can choose a tutor for him, whose appointment, to be valid, must be approved by the judge.

Amended by Acts 1979, No. 607, § 1.

Art. 262.   Appointment of several tutors; order of priority

If the parent who died last has appointed several tutors to the children, the person first mentioned shall be alone charged with the tutorship, and the second shall not be called to it, except in case of the death, absence, refusal, incapacity or displacing of the first, and in like manner as to the others in succession.

SECTION 4—OF THE TUTORSHIP BY THE EFFECT OF LAW

Art. 263.   Qualified ascendants; collaterals by blood; surviving spouse

When a tutor has not been appointed to the minor by father or mother dying last, or if the tutor thus appointed has not been confirmed or has been excused, then the judge shall appoint to the tutorship, from among the qualified ascendants in the direct line, collaterals by blood within the third degree and the surviving spouse of the minor's mother or father dying last, the person whose appointment is in the best interests of the minor.

Amended by Acts 1976, No. 429, § 1.

Arts. 264 to 269.   [Blank]

SECTION 5—OF DATIVE TUTORSHIP

Art. 270.   Occasion for tutorship

When a minor is an orphan, and has no tutor appointed by his father or mother, nor any relations who may claim the tutorship by effect of law, or when the tutor appointed in some of the modes above expressed is liable to be excluded or disqualified, or is excused legally, the judge shall appoint a tutor to the minor.

Amended by Acts 1960, No. 30, § 1, eff. Jan. 1, 1961.

Arts. 271 to 272.   [Blank]

SECTION 6—OF THE UNDERTUTOR

Art. 273.   Necessity for appointment

In every tutorship there shall be an undertutor.

Amended by Acts 1960, No. 30, § 1, eff. Jan. 1, 1961.

Arts. 274 to 277.   [Blank]

Art. 278.   Liability concerning minor's legal mortgage

The undertutor who fails or neglects to cause to be inscribed in the manner required by law, the evidence of the minor's legal mortgage against his tutor, shall be liable for all the damages which the minor may sustain in consequence of such failure or neglect; and this claim for damages shall not be prescribed so long as the minor's right of action exists against his tutor.

Art. 279.   [Blank]

Art. 280.   Termination of undertutorship

The duties of the undertutor are at an end at the same time with the tutorship.

SECTION 7—OF FAMILY MEETINGS [REPEALED]

Arts. 281 to 291.   [Blank]

SECTION 8—OF THE CAUSES WHICH DISPENSE OR EXCUSE FROM THE TUTORSHIP

Art. 292.   Excuse by reason of office or function

The following persons are dispensed or excused from the tutorship by the privilege of their offices or functions:

    1.   The Governor and the Secretary of State;

    2.   The judges of the different courts of this State and the officers of the same;

    3.   The Mayor of the city of New Orleans;

    4.   The Collector of the Customs;

    5.   The officers and soldiers attached to the regular troops, whether on land or sea service, employed and in actual service in this State, and all the officers who are intrusted in this State with any mission from the Government, as long as they are employed;

    6.   Preceptors and other persons keeping public schools, as long as they remain in the useful and actual exercise of their profession;

    7.   Ministers of the gospel.

Art. 293.   Waiver of excuse by subsequent acceptance of tutorship

The persons mentioned in the preceding article, who have accepted a tutorship posterior to their being invested with the offices, engaged in the service, or intrusted with the mission which dispenses from it, shall not be admitted to be excused on that account.

Art. 294.   Subsequently acquired excuse

Those, on the contrary, who shall have been invested with offices, who shall have engaged in the service, or shall have been intrusted with commissions, posterior to their acceptation and administration of a tutorship, may, if they do not choose to continue to act as tutor, be excused from the tutorship, and apply for the appointment of another tutor to supply their place.

Art. 295. Excuse for remote relationship

No person, who is not a relation of the minor by consanguinity, or who is only related to him beyond the fourth degree, can be compelled to accept the tutorship.

Art. 296. Excuse for age

Every person who has attained the age of sixty-five years, may refuse to be a tutor.

The person who shall have been appointed prior to that age, may be excused from the tutorship at the age of seventy years.

Art. 297. Excuse for infirmity

Every person affected with a serious infirmity, may be excused from the tutorship, if this infirmity be of such nature as to render him incapable of transacting his own business.

He may even be discharged from the tutorship, if such infirmity has befallen him after his appointment.

Art. 298. Excuse for prior tutorships

The person who is appointed to two tutorships has a legal excuse for not accepting a third.

A parent who has been appointed to one tutorship shall not be compelled to accept a second tutorship, except it be that of his own children.

Amended by Acts 1974, No. 163, § 3.

Art. 299. Time to present excuse

The tutor, who has excuses to offer against his appointment, must propose them to the judge who has appointed him, within ten days after he has been acquainted with his appointment, or after the same shall have been notified to him, which period shall be increased one day for every ten miles distance from his residence to the place where his appointment was made, and after this delay he shall no longer be admitted to offer any excuse, unless he has sufficient reason to account for such delay.

Art. 300. Provisional administration pending consideration of excuse

During the time of the pendency of the litigation relative to the validity of his excuses, the tutor who is appointed shall be bound provisionally to administer as such, until he shall have been regularly discharged.

Art. 301. Parent's unconditional obligation of tutorship

The causes herein expressed, or any other, cannot excuse a parent from the obligation of accepting the tutorship of his children.

Amended by Acts 1974, No. 163, § 3.

SECTION 9—OF THE INCAPACITY FOR, THE EXCLUSION FROM, AND DEPRIVATION OF THE TUTORSHIP [REPEALED]

Arts. 302 to 306.   [Blank]

SECTION 10—OF THE APPOINTMENT, RECOGNITION, OR CONFIRMATION OF TUTORS, OF THE PERSONS WHOSE DUTY IT IS TO CAUSE TUTORS TO BE APPOINTED AND OF THE LIABILITY OF SUCH PERSONS

Art. 307. [Blank]

Art. 308. Duty to apply for appointment

In every case where it is necessary to appoint a tutor to a minor, all those of his relations who reside within the parish of the judge, who is to appoint him, are bound to apply to such judge, in order that a tutor be appointed to the minor at farthest within ten days after the event which make[s] such appointment necessary.

Art. 309. Minors exempt from taking application

Minor relations are not included in the provisions contained in the preceding article.

Amended by Acts 1974, No. 163, § 3.

Art. 310. Liability for failure to make application

Relations who have neglected to cause a tutor to be appointed, are responsible for the damages which the minor may have suffered.

This responsibility is enforced against relations in the order according to which they are called to the inheritance of the minor, so that they are responsible only in case of the insolvency of him or them who precede them in that order, and this responsibility is not *in solidum* between relations who have a right to the inheritance in the same degree.

Art. 311. Action for damages; prescription

The action which results from this responsibility can not be maintained by the tutor but within the year of his appointment.

If the tutor neglects to bring his action within that time, he is answerable for such neglect to the minor.

Arts. 312 to 321. [Blank]

Art. 322. Minor's legal mortgage on tutor's property

The recording of the certificate of the clerk operates as a legal mortgage in favor of the minor for the amount therein stated, on all the immovable property of the natural tutor in the parish.

Amended by Acts 1960, No. 30, § 1, eff. Jan. 1, 1961.

Arts. 323 to 332. [Blank]

Art. 333. Sale of mortgaged property by one claimant; inscription of legal mortgage of remaining minors

Whenever a special mortgage is given by a tutor to secure the rights of two or more minors, any of the minors, on attaining the age of majority or being emancipated, may cause the sale of the mortgaged property to satisfy the indebtedness of the tutor to him, after having discussed the other property of the debtor, in the following manner:

If the judge is of the opinion that the mortgaged property is sufficient to satisfy all of the demands of the major and minors, he shall order the sale of so much of the property as will satisfy the demand of the major, if susceptible of division, and the property so sold shall be free of the mortgage in favor of the remaining minors.

If the judge is of the opinion that the mortgaged property is not sufficient to meet the demands of the major and minors, or that it is not susceptible of division, he shall order the sale of the whole of the mortgaged property, and the release of the mortgage of the major and minors. The proceeds of the sale, after defraying the expenses thereof, shall be divided equally among the major and minors, giving each his virile share. The portion to be paid the minors shall be paid to their tutor.

When the judge orders the sale of the property, he shall order the inscription of the minor's legal mortgage in the manner heretofore provided. This inscription shall be made in the parish where the tutor resides within three days of the order, and in all other parishes where the tutor has immovable property within thirty days of the order.

Amended by Acts 1960, No. 30, § 1, eff. Jan. 1, 1961.

Arts. 334 to 335.   [Blank]

SECTION 11—OF THE ADMINISTRATION OF THE TUTOR

Art. 336.   Alienation of minor's immovables

The prohibition of alienating the immovables of a minor, does not extend to the case in which a judgment is to be executed against him, or of a licitation made at the instance of the coheir, or other coproprietor.

Acts 1966, No. 496, § 1.

Art. 337.   [Blank]

Art. 338.   Interest

The sum which appears to be due by the tutor as the balance of his accounts, bears interest, without a judicial demand, from the day on which the accounts were closed.

The same rule applies to the balance due to the tutor.

Acts 1966, No. 496, § 1.

Art. 339.   Agreements between tutor and minor

Every agreement which may take place between the tutor and the minor arrived at the age of majority, shall be null and void, unless the same was entered into after the rendering of a full account and delivery of the vouchers, the whole being made to appear by the receipt of the person to whom the account was rendered, ten days previous to the agreement.

Acts 1966, No. 496, § 1.

Art. 340.   Prescription of minor's action against tutor

The action of the minor against his tutor, respecting the acts of the tutorship, is prescribed by four years, to begin from the day of his majority.

Acts 1966, No. 496, § 1.

Arts. 341 to 353.   [Blank]

SECTION 12—OF CONTINUING OR PERMANENT TUTORSHIP OF PERSONS WITH INTELLECTUAL DISABILITIES

Art. 354. Procedure for placing under tutorship

Persons, including certain children, with intellectual disabilities or mental deficiencies may be placed under continuing or permanent tutorship without formal or complete interdiction in accordance with the following rules and the procedures stated in the Louisiana Code of Civil Procedure.

Acts 1966, No. 496, § 2. Amended by Acts 2014, No. 811, § 30, eff. June 23, 2014.

Art. 355. Petition for continuing or permanent tutorship

When a person above the age of fifteen possesses less than two-thirds of the average mental ability of a normal person of the same age, evidenced by standard testing procedures administered by competent persons, the parents of such person, or the person entitled to custody or tutorship if one or both parents be dead, incapacitated, or an absent person, or if the parents be judicially separated or divorced, may, with the concurrence of the coroner of the parish of the mentally deficient person's domicile, petition the court of that district to place such person under a continuing tutorship which shall not automatically end at any age but shall continue until revoked by the court of domicile.

Acts 1966, No. 496, § 2. Amended by Acts 1974, No. 714, § 1; Acts 1991, No. 107, § 1.

Art. 356. Title of proceedings; procedural rules; parents as tutor and undertutor

The title of the proceedings shall be Continuing Tutorship of (Name of Person), A Person with an Intellectual Disability.

(1) When the person to be placed under the continuing tutorship is above the age of fifteen, and under the age of majority, the proceeding shall be conducted according to the procedural rules established for ordinary tutorships.

(2) When the person to be placed under the continuing tutorship is above the age of majority, the proceeding shall be conducted according to the procedural rules established for interdictions.

(3) Upon the petition of both parents of the mentally deficient person during their marriage one parent shall be named as tutor and the other as undertutor, unless for good reasons the judge decrees otherwise.

Acts 1966, No. 496, § 2. Amended by Acts 1974, No. 714, § 1; Acts 2014, No. 26, § 1; Acts 2014, No. 811, § 30, eff. June 23, 2014.

Art. 357. Decree, place of recording, notice

If the prayer for continuing or permanent tutorship be granted, the decree shall be recorded in the conveyance and mortgage records of the parish of the minor's domicile, and of any future domicile, and in such other parishes as may be deemed expedient. The decree shall not be effective as to persons without notice thereof outside of the parishes in which it is recorded.

Acts 1966, No. 496, § 2.

Art. 358. Authority, privileges, and duties of tutor and undertutor; termination of tutorship

The granting of the decree shall confer upon the tutor and undertutor the same authority, privileges, and responsibilities as in other tutorships, including the same authority to give consent for any medical treatment or procedure, to give consent for any educational plan or procedure, and to obtain medical, educational, or other records, but the responsibility of the tutor for the offenses or quasi-offenses of the person with an intellectual disability shall be the same as that of a curator for those of the interdicted person and the tutorship shall not terminate until the decree is set aside by the court of the domicile, or the court of last domicile if the domicile of the person with an intellectual disability is removed from the State of Louisiana.

Acts 1966, No. 496, § 2. Amended by Acts 1979, No. 216, § 1; Acts 2014, No. 811, § 30, eff. June 23, 2014.

Art. 359.   Restriction on legal capacity

The decree if granted shall restrict the legal capacity of the person with an intellectual disability to that of a permanent minor, except that after the age of eighteen the person, unless formally interdicted, shall have the legal capacity of a minor who has been granted the emancipation conferring the power of administration as set forth in Chapter 2, Section 2 of this Book and Title.

Acts 1966, No. 496, § 2. Amended by Acts 1974, No. 714, § 1; Acts 2014, No. 811, § 30, eff. June 23, 2014.

Art. 360.   Parents' rights of administration

In addition to the rights of tutorship, the parents shall retain, during the marriage and for the minority of the child with an intellectual disability, all rights of administration granted to parents of children without an intellectual disability during their minority.

Acts 1966, No. 496, § 2. Amended by Acts 2014, No. 811, § 30, eff. June 23, 2014.

Art. 361.   Contest of decree restricting legal capacity

The decree restricting his legal capacity may be contested in the court of domicile by the person himself or by anyone adversely affected by the decree, and upon evidence which would justify the full emancipation of a minor above the age of eighteen the decree shall be rescinded and set aside.

Acts 1966, No. 496, § 2.

Art. 362.   Persons subject to interdiction

Persons subject to mental or physical illness or disability, whether of a temporary or permanent nature, of such a degree as to render them subject to interdiction, under the provisions of Title IX hereof, remain subject to interdiction as provided in Articles 389 to 399, inclusive, and such other laws as may relate thereto.

Acts 1966, No. 496, § 2.

Arts. 363 to 364.   [Blank]

CHAPTER 2—EMANCIPATION

Art. 365.   Emancipation

There are three kinds of emancipation: judicial emancipation, emancipation by marriage, and limited emancipation by authentic act.

Acts 2008, No. 786, § 1, eff. Jan. 1, 2009.

REVISION COMMENT—2008

This revision establishes an emancipation regime under which a minor can be emancipated by a judgment of a court, by marriage, and by an authentic act. Emancipation by authentic act, however, may be limited.

Art. 366.   Judicial emancipation

A court may order for good cause the full or limited emancipation of a minor sixteen years of age or older. Full judicial emancipation confers all effects of majority on the person emancipated, unless otherwise provided by law. Limited judicial emancipation confers the effects of majority specified in the judgment of limited emancipation, unless otherwise provided by law.

Acts 2008, No. 786, § 1, eff. Jan. 1, 2009.

REVISION COMMENTS—2008

(a) This Article is analogous to the provisions in former Civil Code Article 385 (enacted by Acts 1976, No. 155) that provided for emancipation that relieved the minor from the time prescribed by law for attaining the age of majority. See C.C. Art. 385 (enacted by Acts 1976, No. 155).

(b) Among other effects, full judicial emancipation empowers the minor with capacity to incur conventional obligations and to make donations. Unemancipated minors lack capacity to make many donations, see C.C. Art. 1476 (Rev. 1991), and to contract, see id. C.C. Art. 1918 (Rev. 1984).

(c) By providing that a fully emancipated minor is treated as a major "unless otherwise provided by law," this Article clarifies that laws regulating the conduct of those "under age eighteen," are not affected by emancipation.

(d) This Article is new in that it provides for limited judicial emancipation. This provision gives a court in an emancipation matter discretion to tailor a judgment of limited emancipation to the needs of the minor and his parents or tutor. For example, if a minor needs capacity to contract in order to further the needs of his business, a judgment of limited emancipation could confer upon him only that capacity. He would be treated as a minor in all other respects.

(e) Although a court has much discretion to tailor a judgment of limited emancipation to suit the needs of the minor and his parents or tutor, a judgment of limited emancipation might include restrictions on capacity similar to those contained in the 1870 Civil Code, such as (1) limitations on the minor's capacity to alienate immovable property, C.C. Art. 373 (1870); (2) limitations on the amount of the minor's conventional obligations, see C.C. Arts. 371–372 (1870); and, (3) limitations on the minor's capacity to make donations, see C.C. Art. 374 (1870).

(f) This Article permits a court to emancipate a minor "for good cause."

(g) "Good cause" warranting emancipation may exist when the minor's parents need to be protected. For example, emancipation might be appropriate if a minor has run away from home and cannot be found. Emancipation would protect the minor's parents from liability for the acts of an absent child over whom they have no control.

(h) "Good cause" warranting emancipation may exist when the minor needs the capacity to enter into juridical acts. For example, emancipation might be appropriate if a minor is operating a business and needs to contract with vendors or suppliers without parental assistance.

(i) "Good cause" warranting emancipation may exist if the parents of a mature and responsible minor give the minor "corrupt examples," "ill treat him excessively," or "refuse him support." See C.C. Art. 368 (1870).

Art. 367.   Emancipation by marriage

A minor is fully emancipated by marriage. Termination of the marriage does not affect emancipation by marriage. Emancipation by marriage may not be modified or terminated.

Acts 2008, No. 786, § 1, eff. Jan. 1, 2009.

REVISION COMMENTS—2008

(a) This Article retains the concept of emancipation by marriage. See C.C. Art. 379 (1870). However, it effects a significant change in the law by rendering the minor "fully emancipated" by marriage. Under the former law, a married minor below the age of sixteen obtained only the power of administration through marriage. See id. C.C. Art. 382 (1870).

(b) As used in this Article, the term "marriage" includes both lawful marriages and putative marriages.

(c) This Article reproduces the substance of C.C. Art. 383 (1870). Therefore, termination of marriage by divorce or by the death of the emancipated minor's spouse (or otherwise) will not affect his emancipation.

90

Art. 368.   Limited emancipation by authentic act

An authentic act of limited emancipation confers upon a minor age sixteen or older the capacity to make the kinds of juridical acts specified therein, unless otherwise provided by law. The act shall be executed by the minor, and by the parents of the minor, if parental authority exists, or by the tutor of the minor, if parental authority does not exist. All other effects of minority shall continue.

Acts 2008, No. 786, § 1, eff. Jan. 1, 2009.

REVISION COMMENTS—2008

(a) This Article retains the concept of limited emancipation by authentic act. It increases the age of eligibility for emancipation from fifteen to sixteen. The limited emancipation by authentic act does not relieve the parents from liability for the damages occasioned by their minor child. See Civil Code Article 2318 and the Comments thereto.

(b) Within the authentic act of limited emancipation, the parties may provide that the emancipated minor has the capacity to execute all juridical acts, or certain kinds of juridical acts, or only specific juridical acts.

(c) The requirements for an "authentic act" are set forth in Civil Code Article 1833.

Art. 369.   Emancipation; when effective

Judicial emancipation is effective when the judgment is signed. Emancipation by marriage is effective upon marriage. Limited emancipation by authentic act is effective when the act is executed.

Acts 2008, No. 786, § 1, eff. Jan. 1, 2009.

REVISION COMMENT—2008

Emancipation is wholly prospective, has no retroactive effects, and does not affect the validity or invalidity of an act made by the emancipated person prior to the emancipation.

Art. 370.   Modification and termination of judicial emancipation

The court may modify or terminate its judgment of emancipation for good cause.

A judgment modifying or terminating a judgment of emancipation is effective toward third persons as to immovable property when the judgment is filed for registry in the conveyance records of the parish in which the property is situated, and as to movables when the judgment is filed for registry in the conveyance records of the parish or parishes in which the minor was domiciled at the time of the judgment.

A judgment modifying or terminating a judgment of emancipation does not affect the validity of an act made by the emancipated minor prior to the effective date of modification or termination.

The termination of judicial emancipation places the minor under the same authority to which he was subject prior to emancipation, unless otherwise ordered by the court for good cause shown.

Acts 2008, No. 786, § 1, eff. Jan. 1, 2009.

REVISION COMMENTS—2008

(a) "Good cause" exists whenever the reason justifying emancipation—or any other meritorious reason-exists for termination or modification.

(b) Through the use of the term "may," this Article leaves termination or modification of judicial emancipation to the sound discretion of the court. For example, a court could exercise its discretion to convert a full emancipation into a limited emancipation.

(c) This Article clarifies that the termination or modification of emancipation is wholly prospective and has no retroactive effects.

(d) This Article does not change the law regarding the supervisory regime to which the minor will be subject following a termination of emancipation. Under the 1870 Code, "revocation of emancipation places the minor under the same authority to which he was subject previous to his being emancipated." See C.C. Art. 378 (1870). However, this Article clarifies that a court has discretion to place the minor under different authority.

Art. 371. Modification or termination of limited emancipation by authentic act

The parties to an authentic act of limited emancipation may modify or terminate the limited emancipation by making a subsequent authentic act. In addition, a court, for good cause, may modify or terminate limited emancipation by authentic act.

An authentic act or judgment modifying or terminating limited emancipation by authentic act is effective toward third persons as to immovable property when the act or judgment is filed for registry in the conveyance records of the parish in which the property is situated and as to movables when the act or judgment is filed for registry in the conveyance records in the parish or parishes in which the minor was domiciled at the time of the act modifying or terminating limited emancipation by authentic act.

An authentic act or judgment modifying or terminating a prior act of limited emancipation does not affect the validity of a juridical act made by the minor prior to the effective date of modification or termination.

Acts 2008, No. 786, § 1, eff. Jan. 1, 2009.

Arts. 372 to 388. [Blank]

TITLE IX—PERSONS UNABLE TO CARE FOR THEIR PERSONS OR PROPERTY

CHAPTER 1—GROUNDS FOR INTERDICTION

Art. 389.   Full interdiction

A court may order the full interdiction of a natural person of the age of majority, or an emancipated minor, who due to an infirmity, is unable consistently to make reasoned decisions regarding the care of his person and property, or to communicate those decisions, and whose interests cannot be protected by less restrictive means.

Acts 2000, 1st Ex.Sess., No. 25, § 1, eff. July 1, 2001.

REVISION COMMENTS—2000

(a) This Article changes the law. Under prior law, full interdiction was appropriate when the defendant was "subject to an habitual state of imbecility, insanity or madness," or when the defendant "owing to any infirmity", was incapable of taking care of his person and administering his estate. See Civil Code Articles 389 and 422 (1870). This Article changes the law by making eligibility for interdiction dependent upon functional inability and is uncomplicated by considerations of "insanity", "madness", and the like.

(b) For a person to be interdicted under this Article, the inability to make reasoned decisions regarding the care of his person and his property must result from an infirmity, including among others, chronic substance abuse. Advanced age alone is not an infirmity. Consequently, a person who is merely caring for his person and property in an imprudent manner, but who does not suffer from an infirmity affecting his ability to make reasoned decisions, is not a candidate for full interdiction. However, categorizing the infirmity from which a person suffers is significantly less important than evaluating his functional ability to make reasoned decisions and to communicate those decisions. A decision is not unreasoned merely because it appears risky, unwise, or imprudent.

(c) A person lacks the ability to communicate reasoned decisions only when he cannot convey his thoughts in an understandable manner to other persons. Thus, a person who can consistently communicate his reasoned decisions through any form of verbal or nonverbal communication is not a candidate for full interdiction.

(d) A person is unable consistently to make reasoned decisions if, for example, he suffers from an infirmity which intermittently deprives him of reason. A person who experiences periodic deprivations of reason can inflict substantial harm to himself or his property during such bouts and is a candidate for full interdiction. In short, that a person suffering from an infirmity may experience lucid intervals does not render him ineligible for full interdiction.

(e) Full interdiction is a last resort and, as a result, is warranted only when a person's interests cannot be protected by less restrictive means. A person's interests can be protected by less restrictive means if, for example, his interests (1) are currently being protected by other legal arrangements, including a procuration, mandate, or trust, or (2) could be protected by other legal arrangements, including limited interdiction, see Civil Code Article 390 (Rev. 2000). If the court determines that less restrictive means can protect the defendant's interests, the court should deny full interdiction.

(f) Full interdiction is distinct from civil commitment. See Vance v. Ellerbe, 150 La. 388, 90 So. 735, 740 (1922). Civil commitment requires compliance with the standards and procedures set forth in the mental health law. See R.S. 28:1 through 28:173.

(g) The petitioner in a full interdiction proceeding shall prove by clear and convincing evidence all facts justifying interdiction. See Code of Civil Procedure Article 4548 (Rev. 2000).

Art. 389.1.   [Blank]

Art. 390.   Limited interdiction

A court may order the limited interdiction of a natural person of the age of majority, or an emancipated minor, who due to an infirmity is unable consistently to make reasoned decisions regarding the care of his person or property, or any aspect of either, or to communicate those decisions, and whose interests cannot be protected by less restrictive means.

Acts 2000, 1st Ex.Sess., No. 25, § 1, eff. July 1, 2001.

REVISION COMMENTS—2000

(a) This Article reproduces the principle that a right not specifically restricted in the judgment of limited interdiction is retained by the limited interdict. See Civil Code Article 389.1 as enacted by Acts 1981, No. 167.

(b) A person is a candidate for limited interdiction if he is consistently unable to make reasoned decisions regarding the care of his person or property, or any aspect of either, or to communicate those decisions. If he is consistently unable to make reasoned decisions regarding the care of both his person and his property, or to communicate those decisions, he is a candidate for full interdiction.

(c) Various Louisiana laws, including Civil Code articles within this Title, refer to "interdicts" and "curators of interdicts." To the extent that doing so is consistent with the terms and purposes of the judgment of limited interdiction, such legislation should be applied to "limited interdicts" and to "curators of limited interdicts."

(d) A judgment of limited interdiction does not deprive a limited interdict of the capacity to make a disposition mortis causa. See Civil Code Articles 395 and 1482 (Rev. 2000).

Art. 391.   Temporary and preliminary interdiction

When a petition for interdiction is pending, a court may order a temporary or preliminary interdiction when there is a substantial likelihood that grounds for interdiction exist and substantial harm to the health, safety, or property of the person sought to be interdicted is imminent.

Acts 2000, 1st Ex.Sess., No. 25, § 1, eff. July 1, 2001.

REVISION COMMENTS—2000

(a) This Article is based upon Civil Code Article 394 and Code of Civil Procedure Article 4549 as amended by Acts 1997, No. 1117. It does not change the law.

(b) A court can order either full interdiction or limited interdiction on a temporary or preliminary basis.

(c) For purposes of this Title and other Louisiana legislation, a temporary or preliminary interdict is an interdict, a temporary or preliminary curator is a curator, a temporary or preliminary limited interdict is a limited interdict, and a temporary or preliminary limited curator is a limited curator.

(d) The terms temporary interdiction and preliminary interdiction parallel similar terms used in the context of injunctive relief. See Code of Civil Procedure Articles 3601–3613.

CHAPTER 2—GENERAL DUTIES OF CURATORS
AND UNDERCURATORS

Art. 392.   Curators

The court shall appoint a curator to represent the interdict in juridical acts and to care for the person or affairs of the interdict, or any aspect of either. The duties and powers of a curator commence upon his qualification. In discharging his duties, a curator shall exercise reasonable care, diligence, and prudence and shall act in the best interest of the interdict.

The court shall confer upon a curator of a limited interdict only those powers required to protect the interests of the interdict.

Acts 2000, 1st Ex.Sess., No. 25, § 1, eff. July 1, 2001.

REVISION COMMENTS—2000

(a) This Article is new. It sets forth in general terms the duties of care and loyalty that the curator owes to the interdict.

(b) Code of Civil Procedure Articles 4566, 4567, and 4569 (Rev. 2000), contain provisions setting forth more particular duties of curators.

(c) In making decisions regarding the interdict, the curator should consider the interdict's preinterdiction expressions of will set forth in any preplanning documents, wills, or other directives. Moreover, the curator should consider the interdict's preferences, religious beliefs, and values to the extent known to the curator.

(d) To the extent reasonably possible, a curator should encourage the interdict to participate in decisions and to develop or to regain the ability to care for his person, to manage his affairs, or both.

(e) The term "affairs" is used throughout this title to refer to interests of the interdict that are distinct from his person. This term includes the interdict's estate, property, and business, but may include other interests as well. The use of this term is consistent with the terminology used in the mandate Articles, see Civil Code Article 2989 (Rev. 1997), Comment (d), and confirms that interdiction serves to empower the curator to protect the interdict from harm to all his interests.

(f) A curator's duties and powers commence upon his taking an oath and furnishing security, irrespective of when letters of curatorship evidencing such qualification are issued.

Art. 393. Undercurators

The court shall appoint an undercurator to discharge the duties prescribed for him by law. The duties and powers of an undercurator shall commence upon qualification. In discharging his duties, an undercurator shall exercise reasonable care, diligence, and prudence and shall act in the best interest of the interdict.

Acts 2000, 1st Ex.Sess., No. 25, § 1, eff. July 1, 2001.

REVISION COMMENTS—2000

This Article changes the law. It sets forth generally the undercurator's duties of care and loyalty. Code of Civil Procedure Article 4565 (Rev. 2000), contains provisions setting forth the particular duties of undercurators. The undercurator has no particular duties, either expressed or implied, other than those specifically set forth in that Article.

CHAPTER 3—EFFECTS OF INTERDICTION

Art. 394. Pre-interdiction juridical acts

Interdiction does not affect the validity of a juridical act made by the interdict prior to the effective date of interdiction.

Acts 2000, 1st Ex.Sess., No. 25, § 1, eff. July 1, 2001.

REVISION COMMENTS—2000

(a) This Article is new.

(b) This Article relates only to juridical acts predating interdiction. Whether a pre-interdiction juridical act creates, modifies, transfers, or terminates a personal or real right turns on the substantive law potentially giving effect to the act.

Art. 395. Capacity to make juridical acts

A full interdict lacks capacity to make a juridical act. A limited interdict lacks capacity to make a juridical act pertaining to the property or aspects of personal care that the judgment of limited interdiction places under the authority of his curator, except as provided in Article 1482 or in the judgment of limited interdiction.

Acts 2000, 1st Ex.Sess., No. 25, § 1, eff. July 1, 2001. Amended by Acts 2001, No. 509, § 1, eff. June 1, 2001; Acts 2003, No. 1008, § 1.

REVISION COMMENTS—2000

(a) This Article is new. This Article provides an exception to the general rule that natural persons have the capacity to make juridical acts, see Civil Code Article 28 (Rev. 1987). In addition, it explicitly acknowledges that specific legislation may override this general lack of legal capacity of an interdict.

(b) A juridical act is a lawful volitional act intended to have legal consequences. It may be a unilateral act, such as an affidavit, or a bilateral act, such as a contract. It may be onerous or gratuitous. See Civil Code Article 3471 (Rev. 1982), Comment (c) (citing 1 A.N. Yiannopoulos, Louisiana Civil Law System Coursebook Section 77 (1977)); 1 Planiol & Ripert, Treatise on the Civil Law, pt. 1, no. 265, at 187 (La. St. L. Inst. trans., 12th ed. 1939).

(c) The interdict lacks capacity to make a juridical act including an act purporting to create, modify, transfer, or extinguish rights and obligations, whether personal or real.

(d) A juridical act by an interdict is a relative nullity. See Civil Code Articles 1919 and 2031 (Rev 1984). Likewise, a marriage contracted by an interdict would lack consent and, thus, would be a relative nullity. See Civil Code Article 93 (Rev. 1987).

(e) This Article qualifies the general rule that an interdict lacks capacity to make juridical acts with the proviso "except as otherwise provided by law". Other statutes expressly reserve to interdicts the limited capacity to make specified juridical acts. See Code of Civil Procedure Article 4554 (Rev. 2000), (reserving capacity of an interdict to seek termination of interdiction). Moreover, this Article specifically reserves for an interdict the capacity to make and to revoke a disposition mortis causa. Nevertheless, the proponent of a testament executed by an interdict shall prove the testator's capacity by clear and convincing evidence. See Civil Code Article 1482 (Rev. 2000).

(f) Because interdiction affects only the interdict's capacity to make juridical acts, it has no effect on obligations that do not arise through an exercise of will. For example, an interdict remains responsible for obligations arising under tort law or family law.

Art. 396. Effective date of judgment of interdiction

A judgment of interdiction has effect retroactive to the date of the filing of the petition for interdiction.

Acts 2000, 1st Ex.Sess., No. 25, § 1, eff. July 1, 2001.

REVISION COMMENTS—2000

This Article reproduces the substance of Civil Code Articles 400 and 401 (1870).

CHAPTER 4—MODIFICATION AND TERMINATION OF INTERDICTION

Art. 397. Modification and termination of interdiction

The court may modify or terminate a judgment of interdiction for good cause. Interdiction terminates upon death of the interdict or by judgment of the court.

A judgment of preliminary interdiction granted after an adversarial hearing terminates thirty days after being signed, unless extended by the court for good cause for a period not exceeding thirty days. A judgment of temporary interdiction granted ex parte terminates ten days after being signed. On motion of the defendant or for extraordinary reasons shown at a contradictory hearing, the court may extend the judgment of temporary interdiction for one additional period not to exceed ten days.

Acts 2000, 1st Ex.Sess., No. 25, § 1, eff. July 1, 2001.

REVISION COMMENTS—2000

(a) This Article is new. This Article does not change the law with regard to the termination date of a final judgment of interdiction. This Article, however, does change the law with regard to the termination date of a judgment of temporary interdiction by permitting a court to extend the life of an ex parte judgment of temporary interdiction for an additional ten day period. A separate hearing must be held prior to the granting of such an extension.

(b) For the procedures associated with modification or termination of a judgment of interdiction, see Code of Civil Procedure Article 4554 (Rev. 2000).

Art. 398. Effective date of modification or termination of a judgment of interdiction

An order modifying or terminating a judgment of interdiction is effective on the date signed by the court.

Acts 2000, 1st Ex.Sess., No. 25, § 1, eff. July 1, 2001.

REVISION COMMENTS—2000

This Article reproduces the substance of Civil Code Article 420 (1870).

CHAPTER 5—RESPONSIBILITY FOR WRONGFUL FILING OF INTERDICTION PETITIONS

Art. 399. Responsibility for wrongful filing of interdiction petition

A petitioner whose petition for interdiction is denied is liable for resulting damages caused to the defendant if the petitioner knew or should have known at the time of filing that any material factual allegation regarding the ability of the defendant consistently to make reasoned decisions or to communicate those decisions was false.

Acts 2000, 1st Ex.Sess., No. 25, § 1, eff. July 1, 2001.

REVISION COMMENTS—2000

(a) This Article is based upon Civil Code Article 419 (1870). This Article retains a cause of action against those who file unwarranted petitions for interdiction. However, this Article changes the law. It requires that the petitioner knew or should have known that a material factual allegation was false. In contrast, Civil Code Article 419 (1870) premised liability on proof that the petitioner acted from motives of interest or passion.

(b) This Article does not limit or restrict other remedies that may be available to the defendant, including court-imposed sanctions or delictual damages.

Arts. 400 to 426. [Blank]

TITLE X—OF CORPORATIONS
[REPEALED]

Arts. 427 to 447.   [Blank]

BOOK II—THINGS AND THE DIFFERENT MODIFICATIONS OF OWNERSHIP

TITLE I—THINGS

CHAPTER 1—DIVISION OF THINGS

SECTION 1—GENERAL PRINCIPLES

Art. 448. Division of things

Things are divided into common, public, and private; corporeals and incorporeals; and movables and immovables.

Acts 1978, No. 728, § 1, eff. Jan. 1, 1979.

REVISION COMMENT—1978

This provision reproduces the substance of Articles 449, 460(1), and 461 of the Louisiana Civil Code of 1870. It does not change the law.

Art. 449. Common things

Common things may not be owned by anyone. They are such as the air and the high seas that may be freely used by everyone comformably with the use for which nature has intended them.

Acts 1978, No. 728, § 1, eff. Jan. 1, 1979.

REVISION COMMENTS—1978

(a) This provision reproduces the substance of Articles 450 and 482(1) of the Louisiana Civil Code of 1870. It does not change the law.

(b) According to traditional civilian conceptions, common things are not owned by any one, not even by the state or its political subdivisions.

(c) Running water and the seashore have been taken out of the category of common things by legislation declaring that these things are owned by the state. See, e.g., R.S. 9:1101, as amended by Acts 1954, No. 443 (declaring that the waters of all bayous, rivers, lagoons, lakes, and bays "not under direct ownership of any person on August 12, 1910" are owned by the state); R.S. 49:3 (declaring that the waters and bed of the Gulf of Mexico within Louisiana boundaries are owned by the state). See also R.S. 14:58, 38:216, 56:362, 1431, 1451.

(d) Congress and the Louisiana legislature have enacted laws designed to protect the purity of the atmosphere. See Clean Air Act, 42 U.S.C. §§ 1857–1857(1) (1970); Air Control Law, R.S. 40:2201–16 (1964). Both acts establish administrative agencies charged with the duty to prevent air contaminants from reaching harmful levels. See Note, 36 La.L.Rev. 1090 (1976).

Art. 450. Public things

Public things are owned by the state or its political subdivisions in their capacity as public persons.

Public things that belong to the state are such as running waters, the waters and bottoms of natural navigable water bodies, the territorial sea, and the seashore.

Public things that may belong to political subdivisions of the state are such as streets and public squares.

Acts 1978, No. 728, § 1, eff. Jan. 1, 1979.

REVISION COMMENTS—1978

(a) The first two paragraphs of this provision reflect the definition of public things in Article 453 of the Louisiana Civil Code of 1870. The third paragraph reproduces the substance of Article 454 of the same Code. This provision does not change the law.

(b) As to the nature of public things, see City of New Orleans v. Carrollton Land Co., 131 La. 1092, 1095, 60 So. 695, 696 (1913): "Such property is out of commerce. It is dedicated to public use, and held as a public trust, for public uses"; Kline v. Parish of Ascension, 33 La. 652, 656 (1881): "The parochial authorities are mere trustees for the benefit of the inhabitants of the parish"; Mayor of New Orleans v. Metzinger, 3 Mart. (O.S.) 296, 303 (La.1814): "That public places, such as roads and streets, cannot be appropriated to private use, is one of these principles of public law which require not the support of much argument." Certain public things are inalienable and forever insusceptible of private ownership. See Const., Art. IX, §§ 3, 4 (1974). For exemption from seizure and prescription, see Const. Arts. XII, §§ 10, 13 (1974); cf. IX, § 4(B).

(c) According to civilian theory, the state and its political subdivisions have dual personality. At times they act as public persons, that is, in a sovereign capacity, and at times as private persons, that is, as private citizens or corporations. The relations in which the state and its political subdivisions figure in a sovereign capacity are governed by rules of public law, and the relations in which the state and its political subdivisions figure as private persons are governed by private law. See Yiannopoulos, Louisiana Civil Law System, Part I, p. 78 (1977).

The property of the state and its political subdivisions is known as "public property". This property consists of two categories of things: public things, namely, things that the state and its political subdivisions hold in a sovereign capacity, and private things, dealt with in Article 453 (1978). Public things may also be subdivided into two categories. The first category consists of things which according to constitutional and legislative provisions are inalienable and necessarily owned by the state or its political subdivisions. The second category consists of things which, though alienable and thus susceptible of ownership by private persons, are applied to some public purpose and are held by the state or its political subdivisions in their capacity as public persons.

According to French doctrine and jurisprudence, public property is divided into property of public domain and property of the private domain. This distinction, which corresponds to some extent to the Roman law distinction, between res publicae and res fisci, has ample foundation in the French as well as in the Louisiana Civil Code of 1870. Writers, however, are not in agreement as to which things belong to the public domain and which to the private domain, nor as to the criteria for this distinction. See Yiannopoulos, Civil Law Property, § 30 (1966). The present text has formally dispensed with the theory of the public domain. The public things are owned by the state or its political subdivisions, though this ownership may be subject to limitations not present in the case of "private things" which may also be owned by the state or its political subdivisions.

(d) Act No. 62 of 1912, now R.S. 9:5661, provides that "actions, including those by the State of Louisiana, to annul any patent issued by the state, duly signed by the governor and the register of the state land office, and of record in the state land office, are prescribed by six years, reckoning from the day of the issuance of the patent." Courts interpreting this statute have held in the past that, in the absence of any constitutional prohibition against the alienation of navigable water bottoms prior to 1921, state patents meeting the requirements of the statute are unassailable even if they purport to convey to private persons the ownership of navigable water bottoms. See California Co. v. Price, 225 La. 706, 74 So.2d 1 (1954). The legislature sought to overrule the California case by Act 727 of 1954, now R.S. 9:1107–1109. The Louisiana Supreme Court overruled California in Gulf Oil Corp. v. State Mineral Board, 317 So.2d 576 (La.1975). The alienation of navigable water bottoms by patents issued after 1921 is ineffectual both under Article IV, § 2 of the Constitution of 1921 and under Article IX, § 3 of the 1974 Constitution.

(e) The enumeration of public things is illustrative rather than exclusive. Thus, for example, drainage ditches may be "public things" under this article. See Town of Amite City v. Southern United Ice Co., 34 So.2d 60 (La.App. 1st Cir. 1948). Further, parks, cemeteries, or even open spaces might, under certain circumstances, qualify as "public things". See Town of Vinton v. Lyons, 131 La. 673, 60 So. 54 (1912); Town of Kenner v. Zito, 13 Orl.App. 465 (La.App.Orl.Cir.1916); Locke v. Lester,

78 So.2d 14 (La.App. 2d Cir. 1955); Collins v. Zander, 61 So.2d 897 (La.App.Orl.Cir.1952); Shreveport v. Walpole, 22 La.Ann. 526 (1870).

(f) The question whether a body of water is a river or a lake, and the question whether it is navigable or not, are controlled by Louisiana doctrine and jurisprudence. For literature and decisions on point, see Yiannopoulos, Civil Law Property, §§ 32, 38 (1966). The expression "natural navigable water bodies" refers to inland waters the bottoms of which belong to the state either by virtue of its inherent sovereignty or by virtue of other modes of acquisition, including expropriation. Artificial waterways located on private property for private purposes may, of course, be private things, for the same reasons that a road built on private property for private purposes may be a private thing.

(g) Running waters, the sea, and the seashore are public things by virtue of R.S. 9:1101 and 49:3; see Comments under Article 449 (1978). As to arms of the sea, see Morgan v. Negodich, 40 La.Ann. 246, 3 So. 636 (1888); Buras v. Salinovich, 154 La. 495, 97 So. 748 (1923). Cf. D'Albora v. Garcia, 144 So.2d 911 (La.App. 4th Cir. 1962). Lake Pontchartrain has been consistently regarded as an arm of the sea. See Brunning v. City of New Orleans, 165 La. 511, 115 So. 733 (1928); Burns v. Crescent Gun and Rod Club, 116 La. 1038, 41 So. 249 (1906); Zeller v. Southern Yacht Club, 34 La.Ann. 837 (1882). See also Milne v. Girodeau, 12 La. 324 (1838) (declaring that the bed of Lake Pontchartrain is insusceptible of private ownership and thus, by implication, classifying the Lake as "sea"); New Orleans Land Co. v. Board of Commissioners of Orleans Levee Dist., 171 La. 718, 132 So. 121, aff'd 51 S.Ct. 646, 283 U.S. 809, 75 L.Ed. 1427 (1931) (the bed of Lake Pontchartrain is owned by the state up to the high water mark).

Following a general trend in the United States, the Louisiana legislature has asserted, by a series of statutes, state ownership over a variety of living creatures of the land, sea, and air. See Acts 1926, No. 273; 1932, No. 68; 1918, No. 83; 1926, No. 80; 1932, No. 50; 1932, No. 67; 1918, No. 104. In a sense, these are now public things rather than res nullius. Ownership of wildlife, however, is a new concept. This form of state ownership, asserted in an effort at conservation of natural resources, confers mainly administrative advantages and stresses the idea that certain assets of society are not capable of private appropriation except under regulations that protect the general interest. See Yiannopoulos, Civil Law Property, § 38 (1966).

Art. 451.   Seashore

Seashore is the space of land over which the waters of the sea spread in the highest tide during the winter season.

Acts 1978, No. 728, § 1, eff. Jan. 1, 1979.

REVISION COMMENTS—1978

(a) This provision reproduces the substance of Article 451 of the Louisiana Civil Code of 1870. It does not change the law. Accordingly, Louisiana jurisprudence interpreting the source provision continues to be relevant.

(b) According to Louisiana decisions seashore is the space of land in the open coast that is directly overflown by the tides. See Buras v. Salinovich, 154 La. 495, 97 So. 748 (1923); Morgan v. Negodich, 40 La.Ann. 246, 3 So. 636 (1888). See also Burns v. Crescent Gun & Rod Club, 116 La. 1038, 41 So. 249 (1906). Thus, not all lands subject to tidal overflow are "seashore".

(c) For doctrinal observations concerning Article 451 of the 1870 Code, see Yiannopoulos, Civil Law Property, § 28 (1966). In Roy v. Board of Commissioners for Pontchartrain Levee District, 238 La. 926, 117 So.2d 60 (1960), the defendant levee board urged that seashore should be defined as the space of land "normally covered by the highest tides of the year." The court, though "conceding defendant's contentions to be sound," refused to accept the proposed definition because this would be a rewriting of the Civil Code provision—"a prerogative that belongs under our system of government to the legislature." 117 So.2d 60, 62.

Art. 452.   Public things and common things subject to public use

Public things and common things are subject to public use in accordance with applicable laws and regulations. Everyone has the right to fish in the rivers, ports, roadsteads, and harbors, and the right to land on the seashore, to fish, to shelter himself, to moor ships, to dry nets, and the like, provided that he does not cause injury to the property of adjoining owners.

The seashore within the limits of a municipality is subject to its police power, and the public use is governed by municipal ordinances and regulations

Acts 1978, No. 728, § 1, eff. Jan. 1, 1979.

REVISION COMMENTS—1978

This provision reproduces the substance of Article 452 of the Louisiana Civil Code of 1870 as well as the substance of the second paragraph of Article 453 of the same Code. It changes the law as it excludes the right of members of the general public to build cabins on the seashore. It does not supersede special legislation governing fishing licenses and permits. See R.S. 56:331, et seq.

Art. 453.   Private things

Private things are owned by individuals, other private persons, and by the state or its political subdivisions in their capacity as private persons.

Acts 1978, No. 728, § 1, eff. Jan. 1, 1979.

REVISION COMMENTS—1978

(a) This provision reproduces the substance of Articles 449, 458(3), 459, and 483 of the Louisiana Civil Code of 1870. Changes in terminology and structure, made in the interests of clarity and simplicity, do not effect a change in the law. As in the 1870 Code, private things form a residuary category.

(b) For the nature of private things of the state and of its political subdivisions, see, in general, City of New Orleans v. Salmen Brick and Lumber Co., 135 La. 828, 868, 66 So. 237, 251 (1914): "The character of municipal property and the nature, whether alienable or inalienable, must be determined by the purpose to which the property is dedicated." In Anderson v. Thomas, 166 La. 512, 526, 117 So. 573, 579 (1928), the Louisiana Supreme Court indicated that private things of political subdivisions, such as "public offices, police and fire stations, markets, schoolhouses . . . may be dealt with as the municipality sees fit, subject only to the restrictions imposed by the deed of acquisition or by special laws."

(c) Private property of the state or of a political subdivision is exempt from seizure. See Const.Art. XII, § 10(C). Private property of the state is exempt from prescription. See Const.Arts. IX, § 4(B), XII, § 13. Private property of a political subdivision is prescriptible. Cf. Louisiana Highway Commission v. Raxdale, 12 So.2d 631 (La.App.2d Cir. 1943).

(d) This provision does not deal with property of state agencies. For example, school property is always exempt from seizure under R.S. 20:31. But property of other state agencies may or may not be subject to the general law governing prescription. See Haas v. Board of Commissioners of Red River, Atchafalaya and Bayou Boeuf Levee District, 206 La. 378, 19 So.2d 173 (1944); Board of Commissioners of Port of New Orleans v. Toyo Kisen Kaisha, 163 La. 865, 113 So. 127 (1927).

(e) Article 486 of the Louisiana Civil Code of 1870 has been suppressed. This article has no counterpart in the French Civil Code. It derives from Book II, Title I, Article 24 of the Projet du Gouvernement. The provision reflects terminological and conceptual difficulties encountered by the codifiers in France. See Demolombe, Traité de la distinction des biens 320 (1874); 3 Planiol et Ripert, Traité pratique de droit civil français 124 (2d ed. Picard 1952).

Article 486 of the Louisiana Civil Code of 1870 has not been interpreted in any reported Louisiana decision. It contains a "general definition of things belonging to the private domain of the state, and it must be necessarily supplemented by other articles of the Civil Code and special statutes". Yiannopoulos, Civil Law Property § 38 (1966).

Art. 454.   Freedom of disposition by private persons

Owners of private things may freely dispose of them under modifications established by law.

Acts 1978, No. 728, § 1, eff. Jan. 1, 1979.

(a) The text of this provision is new. It is based on Article 484 of the Louisiana Civil Code of 1870. It does not change the law.

(b) The word "property" in Article 484 of the 1870 Code is a translation of the French biens. See 1972 Compiled Edition of the Civil Codes of Louisiana art. 484, in 16 West's L.S.A.-Code is a translation of the French modifications.

(c) The second paragraph of Article 484 of the Louisiana Civil Code of 1870 has not been reproduced because it deals with a matter of public law. Things belonging to the state, its political subdivisions, and agencies, may be disposed of in accordance with the applicable laws and regulations.

Art. 455.   Private things subject to public use

Private things may be subject to public use in accordance with law or by dedication.

Acts 1978, No. 728, § 1, eff. Jan. 1, 1978.

(a) The text of this provision is new. It is intended to pave the way for the following articles. It does not change the law.

(b) In Louisiana decisions, private things subject to public use are frequently termed "public things", whether they belong to the state, its political subdivisions, or to private persons. These things, however, are not necessarily public things in the sense of Articles 453 and 454 of the Louisiana Civil Code of 1870, nor in the sense of Article 450 (1978). They are "public" merely in the sense that they are destined or dedicated to public use (res publicae publico usui destinatae). Thus, in addition to common things and public things under Article 450 (1978) which are subject to public use by definition, private things of the state and its political subdivisions, and things belonging to private persons may be subject to public use as a result of a legal provision or dedication.

Art. 456.   Banks of navigable rivers or streams

The banks of navigable rivers or streams are private things that are subject to public use.

The bank of a navigable river or stream is the land lying between the ordinary low and the ordinary high stage of the water. Nevertheless, when there is a levee in proximity to the water, established according to law, the levee shall form the bank.

Acts 1978, No. 728, § 1, eff. Jan. 1, 1979.

(a) This article reproduces the substance of Articles 455 and 457 of the Louisiana Civil Code of 1870, as interpreted by Louisiana jurisprudence. Changes in phraseology and structure have not been intended to change the law. Accordingly, Louisiana decisions interpreting Articles 455 and 457 of the Louisiana Civil Code of 1870 continue to be relevant.

(b) Article 455(1) of the Louisiana Civil Code of 1870 declares that "everyone has a right freely to bring his vessels to land there, to make fast the same to the trees which are there planted, to unload his vessels, to deposit his goods, to dry his nets, and the like". According to well-settled Louisiana jurisprudence, which continues to be relevant, the servitude of public use under this provision is not "for the use of the public at large for all purposes" but merely for purposes that are "incidental" to the navigable character of the stream and its enjoyment as an avenue of commerce. See State v. Richardson, 140 La. 329, 72 So. 984 (1916); Lyons v. Hinckley, 12 La.Ann. 655 (1856); Chinn v. Petty, 163 So. 735 (La.App.2d Cir. 1935). The right to dry nets is practically meaningless today in most of Louisiana's navigable rivers. Vessels may be temporarily moored to the banks of navigable rivers, but there is strong doubt that this may be done "freely" as Article 455 (1870) declares. The rights of the general public to unload vessels and to deposit goods may be clearly exercised in public landings or other facilities, but it is questionable whether these rights may be exercised in all banks. Under the circumstances, it has been thought preferable to suppress the illustrations of public use contained in Article 455 of the 1870 Code. Special laws and regulations govern the extent and incidents of public use. See e.g., R.S. 34:1 et seq.

(c) According to both the 1870 Code and the 1978 revision, the banks of navigable rivers are private things which, ordinarily, belong to the riparian proprietors. According to Article 455(2) of the 1870 Code, "the ownership of the riverbanks belong to those who possess the adjacent lands". Article 456 (1978), by declaring that the banks of navigable rivers are private things, reproduces the substance of this article. It does not change the law.

(d) The definition of "bank of a river" (Article 456 (1978)) follows Louisiana decisions interpreting Article 457(1) of the Louisiana Civil Code of 1870. See Wemple v. Eastham, 150 La. 247, 90 So. 637, 638 (1922): "The land lying between the edge of the water at its ordinary low stage and the line which the edge of the water reaches at its ordinary high stage, that is the highest stage—is called bank of the stream, and belongs to the owner of the adjacent land". Conversely, the bed of the river is "the land that is covered by the water in its ordinary low stage". Ibid. See also State v. Richardson, 140 La. 329, 72 So. 984 (1916); Morgan v. Livingston, 6 Mart. (O.S.) 19 (La.1819); State v. Cockrell, 162 So.2d 361 (La.App. 1st Cir. 1964). Article 457(2) of the Louisiana Civil Code of 1870 declares: "Nevertheless on the borders of the Mississippi and other navigable streams, where there are levees, established according to law, the levee shall form the bank". This provision has been applied by Louisiana courts only as to levees located in the proximity to the water. See Mayer v. Board of Commissioners, 177 La. 1119, 150 So. 295 (1933). Following this jurisprudence, Article 456 (1978) declares that when there is a levee in proximity to the water, established according to law, the levee shall form the bank. The change in the definition of banks is relevant only insofar as use of the banks by members of the general public is concerned; the powers of public authorities to appropriate the use of the banks of navigable rivers is dealt with elsewhere. See Article 665.

(e) Louisiana decisions dealing with the scope of application of Article 509 of the Louisiana Civil Code of 1870 establish a distinction between "rivers" and "lakes". See State v. Placid Oil Co., 300 So.2d 154 (La.1974).

(f) The definition of the "bank of a river" may include, in addition to the banks of natural watercourses, artificial navigation canals. Cf. Harvey Canal & Land Imp. Co. v. Koch-Ellis Marine Contractors, 34 So.2d 66 (La.App.Orl.Cir.1948). A navigation canal constructed by public authorities on a right of way servitude or on public lands is a public thing. If the banks of a public canal are within the right of way acquired by the authorities, they are subject to public use under Article 456 (1978). If the navigation canal is built entirely on private property for private purposes, or if the banks of a public canal belong to private individuals, public use of the banks may be excluded.

Art. 457.   Roads; public or private

A road may be either public or private.

A public road is one that is subject to public use. The public may own the land on which the road is built or merely have the right to use it.

A private road is one that is not subject to public use.

Acts 1978, No. 728, § 1, eff. Jan. 1, 1979.

REVISION COMMENTS—1978

(a) The text of this provision is new. It is based on Articles 704 through 706, and 658(2) of the Louisiana Civil Code of 1870. It does not change the law.

(b) According to Louisiana law, public roads are those that are subject to public use. The public may own the land on which they are built or it may merely have a servitude. For detailed discussion, see Yiannopoulos, Civil Law Property, § 33 (1966).

Art. 458.   Works obstructing the public use

Works built without lawful permit on public things, including the sea, the seashore, and the bottom of natural navigable waters, or on the banks of navigable rivers, that obstruct the public use may be removed at the expense of the persons who built or own them at the instance of the public authorities, or of any person residing in the state.

The owner of the works may not prevent their removal by alleging prescription or possession.

Acts 1978, No. 728, § 1, eff. Jan. 1, 1979.

REVISION COMMENTS—1978

(a) This provision reproduces the substance of Article 861 of the Louisiana Civil Code of 1870. It does not change the law.

(b) For detailed discussion of this provision, and its interpretation by Louisiana courts, see Yiannopoulos, The Public Use of the Banks of Navigable Rivers in Louisiana, 31 La.L.Rev. 563, 579–585 (1971).

(c) This provision does not supersede special legislation governing the Louisiana Department of Highways.

Art. 459. Building encroaching on public way

A building that merely encroaches on a public way without preventing its use, and which cannot be removed without causing substantial damage to its owner, shall be permitted to remain. If it is demolished from any cause, the owner shall be bound to restore to the public the part of the way upon which the building stood.

Acts 1978, No. 728, § 1, eff. Jan. 1, 1979.

REVISION COMMENT—1978

This provision reproduces the substance of Article 862 of the Louisiana Civil Code of 1870. It does not change the law.

Art. 460. Construction of navigation facilities on public places by port commissions or municipalities

Port commissions of the state, or in the absence of port commissions having jurisdiction, municipalities may, within the limits of their respective jurisdictions, construct and maintain on public places, in beds of natural navigable water bodies, and on their banks or shores, works necessary for public utility, including buildings, wharves, and other facilities for the mooring of vessels and the loading or discharging of cargo and passengers.

Acts 1978, No. 728, § 1, eff. Jan. 1, 1979.

REVISION COMMENT—1978

This provision reproduces the substance of Article 863 of the Louisiana Civil Code of 1870. It does not change the law.

Art. 461. Corporeals and incorporeals

Corporeals are things that have a body, whether animate or inanimate, and can be felt or touched.

Incorporeals are things that have no body, but are comprehended by the understanding, such as the rights of inheritance, servitudes, obligations, and right of intellectual property.

Acts 1978, No. 728, § 1, eff. Jan. 1, 1979.

REVISION COMMENTS—1978

(a) This provision reproduces the substance of Article 460 of the Louisiana Civil Code of 1870. It does not change the law.

(b) According to French doctrine and jurisprudence, energies, including electricity, are classified as corporeal things. The purpose of this classification is to insure application of the rules dealing with theft to the unauthorized appropriation of energies. See 3 Planiol et Ripert, Traité pratique de droit civil français 102 (2 ed. Picard 1952). In Louisiana, energies are clearly objects which enjoy full proprietary protection under the applicable provisions of the Criminal Code. See Criminal Code,

§ 2(3), as amended by Acts 1962, No. 68, § 1, R.S. 14:2. It is thus unnecessary to resort to a fiction and to classify energies as corporeal things.

SECTION 2—IMMOVABLES

Art. 462.   Tracts of land

Tracts of land, with their component parts, are immovables.

Acts 1978, No. 728, § 1, eff. Jan. 1, 1979.

REVISION COMMENTS—1978

(a) The text of this provision is new. It is based on Article 464 of the Louisiana Civil Code of 1870 and jurisprudence interpreting it. It does not change the law.

(b) Lands, buildings, and other constructions are designated in Article 464 of the Louisiana Civil Code of 1870 as "immovable by their nature". In this revision, lands, buildings, and other constructions are simply "immovables". The change in nomenclature, made in the interests of clarification and simplification of the law, does not result in change of the law. Accordingly, Louisiana jurisprudence interpreting Article 464 of the 1870 Code continues to be relevant.

(c) Lands may be defined as portions of the surface of the earth. The ownership of land carries, by accession, the ownership of "all that is directly above and under it." C.C. art. 505 (1870).

Art. 463.   Component parts of tracts of land

Buildings, other constructions permanently attached to the ground, standing timber, and unharvested crops or ungathered fruits of trees, are component parts of a tract of land when they belong to the owner of the ground.

Acts 1978, No. 728, § 1, eff. Jan. 1, 1979.

REVISION COMMENTS—1978

(a) The text of this provision is new. It is based on Articles 464 and 465 of the Louisiana Civil Code of 1870 and jurisprudence interpreting it. It does not change the law.

(b) Classification of buildings or other constructions as component parts of a tract of land does not determine the question of ownership of buildings and other constructions. This question is determined under the rules governing acquisition of ownership by juridical act, prescription, or accession. See Prevot v. Courtney, 241 La. 313, 129 So.2d 1 (1960); Louisiana Land & Pecan Co. v. Gulf Lumber Co., 134 La. 784, 64 So. 713 (1914); Industrial Outdoor Displays Inc. v. Reuter, 162 So.2d 160 (La.App. 4th Cir. 1964); Bacque v. Darby, 69 So.2d 145 (La.App. 1st Cir. 1954); Vaughn v. Kemp, 4 La.App. 682 (2d Cir. 1926). For the classification of mobile homes, see Comment under Art. 475 (1978).

(c) The word "constructions" in Article 464 of the Louisiana Civil Code of 1870 has been interpreted in a number of judicial decisions. In Industrial Outdoor Displays v. Reuter, 162 So.2d 160 (La.App. 4th Cir. 1964), the court held that an advertising sign imbedded in concrete was a "construction", and therefore, an immovable. In the absence of foundations, a certain degree of integration with the ground is necessary. A tractor and poultry house, a canal, a cistern, a brick pit, a corn mill, and a gas tank, have been classified as immovables by nature. See Prevot v. Courtney, 241 La. 313, 129 So.2d 1 (1961); Albert Hanson Lumber Co. v. Board of State Affairs, 154 La. 988, 98 So. 552 (1924); Pohlman v. DeBouchel, 32 La.Ann. 1158 (1880); Folse v. Loreauville Sugar Factory, 156 So. 667 (La.App. 1st Cir. 1934); Bigler v. Brashear, 11 Rob. 484 (La.1845); Monroe Auto & Supply Co. v. Cole, 6 La.App. 337 (2d Cir. 1927). Likewise, railroad tracks qualify as constructions. See American Creosote Co. v. Springer, 257 La. 116, 241 So.2d 510 (1970). On the other hand, a derrick erected by a lessee for the purpose of drilling a well has been held to be a movable. Jones v. Conrad, 154 La. 860, 98 So. 397 (1924).

(d) According to this provision, standing timber is a component part of a tract of land when it belongs to the owner of the ground. The provision accords with the text of Article 465 of the Louisiana Civil Code of 1870. However, according to R.S. 9:1103, the substance of which is reproduced in Article

465 (1978), standing timber is a separate immovable when it belongs to a person other than the owner of the ground. Classification of standing timber as a component part of the ground does not determine the question of the ownership of the timber. This question is determined under the juridical act, prescription, or accession.

Trees cut down, whether carried off or not, are movables. Cf. Woodruff v. Roberts, 4 La.Ann. 127 (1840); Gillespie v. Ransom Lumber Co., 132 F.Supp. 11 (E.D.La.1955), aff'd 234 F.2d 285 (5th Cir. 1956). Trees and plants in nurseries, though destined to be transplanted, have been correctly held to be parts of the immovable. Louisiana v. Henderson, 138 So.2d 597 (La.App. 3rd Cir. 1962).

(e) According to this provision, unharvested crops and ungathered fruits of trees are component parts of a tract of land when they belong to the owner of the ground. The provision accords with the text of Article 465 of the Louisiana Civil Code of 1870. However, according to Louisiana jurisprudence codified in Article 474 (1978), unharvested crops and ungathered fruits of trees are movables by anticipation when they belong to a person other than the owner of the ground; when they are burdened with security rights or privileges they are movables by anticipation insofar as the creditor is concerned. See Citizens Bank v. Wiltz, 31 La.Ann. 244 (1879).

Crops harvested and fruits gathered are movables. Cf. Succession of Minter v. Opposition of Union Central Life Insurance Co., 180 La. 38, 156 So. 167 (1934); Alliance Trust Co. v. Gueydan Bank, 162 La. 1062, 111 So. 421 (1927).

(f) According to Article 466 of the Louisiana Civil Code of 1870, "the fruits of an immovable, gathered or produced while it is under seizure, are considered as making part thereof, and inure to the benefit of the person making the seizure." This provision is no longer needed and is not reproduced in this revision. According to well-settled jurisprudence and special legislation, the fruits of an immovable under seizure do not necessarily inure to the benefit of the seizing creditor, but are applied to the satisfaction of claims under the rules governing priorities among creditors. Cf. C.C.P. art. 1092, as amended by Acts 1962, No. 92; id. art. 2292; id. art. 2299, as amended by Acts 1961, No. 23. Moreover, according to Article 327 of the Louisiana Code of Civil Procedure "the seizure of property by the sheriff effects the seizure of the fruits and issues which it produces while under seizure. The sheriff shall collect all rents and revenue produced by the property under seizure." The matter of the status of fruits is thus dealt with elsewhere without reference to classification: gathered fruits, though movables according to the general rule, form part of the immovable property seized.

Art. 464.   Buildings and standing timber as separate immovables

Buildings and standing timber are separate immovables when they belong to a person other than the owner of the ground.

Acts 1978, No. 728, § 1, eff. Jan. 1, 1979.

REVISION COMMENTS—1978

(a) The text of this provision is new. It is based on R.S. 9:1103 and on Louisiana jurisprudence interpreting Article 464 of the Louisiana Civil Code of 1870. This provision does not change the law.

(b) According to Louisiana jurisprudence, buildings separated in ownership from the land on which they stand are distinct immovables for all purposes. See e.g., Lange v. Baranco, 32 La.Ann. 697 (1880); Keary v. Ducote, 23 La.Ann. 196 (1871); Meraux v. Andrews, 145 So.2d 104 (La.App. 4th Cir. 1962) (real actions); Buchler v. Forroux, 193 La. 445, 190 So. 640 (1939) (mortgage); David-Wood Lumber Co. v. Ins. Co. of North America, 154 So. 760 (La.App. 1st Cir. 1934) (insurance); Cloud v. Cloud, 145 So.2d 331 (La.App. 3d Cir. 1962) (homestead exemption). Cf. Augustin v. Dours, 26 La.Ann. 261 (1874) (separate execution sale); Scardino v. Maggio, 15 La.App. 444, 131 So. 217 (1st Cir. 1931); Di Crispino v. Bares, 5 Orl.App. 69 (Orl. Cir. 1908). According to the Louisiana Condominium Act, R.S. 9:1121 (1974), a unit in a condominium is a separate immovable.

(c) According to R.S. 9:1103, standing timber segregated in ownership from the land on which it stands is a separate immovable. The proposed text supersedes the statute. See Acts 1978, No. 728, § 3.

(d) Constructions permanently attached to the ground, other than buildings, are component parts of a tract of land when they belong to the owner of the ground. Article 463, supra. They are movables when they belong to another person. Article 464, following Louisiana legislation and jurisprudence, declares that only buildings and standing timber may be separate immovables.

(e) The questions whether buildings and standing timber belong to the owner of the ground or to another person is determined under the rules governing acquisition of ownership. Separate ownership may be asserted toward third persons when it is evidenced by an instrument filed for registry in the conveyance records of the parish in which the immovable is located. Art. 491, infra.

Art. 465.   Things incorporated into an immovable

Things incorporated into a tract of land, a building, or other construction, so as to become an integral part of it, such as building materials, are its component parts.

Acts 1978, No. 728, § 1, eff. Jan. 1, 1979.

REVISION COMMENTS—1978

(a) The text of this provision is new. It is based on Louisiana jurisprudence. It does not change the law.

(b) According to Louisiana jurisprudence, movables incorporated into a tract of land or a building are parts of the immovable. See Lighting Fixture Co. v. Pacific Fire Ins. Co., 176 La. 499, 146 So. 35, 59 (1932): "Some of these betterments and improvements probably, were so incorporated into the building as to be a component part of it—and hence a part of an immovable by nature. . . . Other parts . . . were probably not incorporated into the building as to become a component part of it" (concurring opinion by O'Neil, C.J.). See also Monroe Auto & Supply Co. v. Cole, 6 La.App. 337 (2d Cir. 1927).

(c) Incorporation is a question of fact to be determined by the trier of facts. It may be regarded as established when movables lose their identity or become an integral part of the immovable. Everything incorporated into a tract of land, a building, or other construction, becomes immovable without regard to ownership. Thus, things that a lessee has incorporated into an immovable become themselves immovables. Classification does not determine the question of ownership of the things. This question is determined by the rules governing acquisition of ownership by juridical act, prescription, or accession.

(d) Immobilization under this article is inoperative when the law provides otherwise. According to R.S. 9:5357, a movable that is subject to a chattel mortgage "shall be and will remain movable insofar as the mortgage upon it is concerned, and shall not pass by the sale of the immovable property to which it has been actually or fictitiously attached, whether such sale be conventional or judicial." According to R.S. 9:1106, tanks placed by a person other than the owner on a rural or urban immovable for the storage of liquefied gases or liquid fertilizers "shall remain movable property, and the ownership of such tank or tanks shall not be affected by the sale, either private or judicial, of the land on which they are placed." See Acts 1978, No. 728, § 3.

Art. 466.   Component parts of a building or other construction

Things that are attached to a building and that, according to prevailing usages, serve to complete a building of the same general type, without regard to its specific use, are its component parts. Component parts of this kind may include doors, shutters, gutters, and cabinetry, as well as plumbing, heating, cooling, electrical, and similar systems.

Things that are attached to a construction other than a building and that serve its principal use are its component parts.

Other things are component parts of a building or other construction if they are attached to such a degree that they cannot be removed without substantial damage to themselves or to the building or other construction.

Acts 1978, No. 728, § 1, eff. Jan. 1, 1979. Amended by Acts 2005, No. 301, § 1, eff. June 29, 2005; Acts 2006, No. 765, § 1; Acts 2008, No. 632, § 1, eff. July 1, 2008.

REVISION COMMENTS—1978

(a) The text of this provision is new. It is based in part on Article 469 of the Louisiana Civil Code of 1870. It changes the law.

(b) According to the first paragraph of Article 468 of the Louisiana Civil Code of 1870, things that the owner of a tract of land or a building has placed upon it for its service and improvement are "immovables by destination". This classification is no longer desirable in the light of contemporary conditions. In this revision, things that are not permanently attached to a building or other construction remain movables. However, certain movables may be immobilized by declaration.

(c) According to the second paragraph of Article 468 of the Louisiana Civil Code of 1870, things that the owner of a tract of land or a building has permanently attached to it become immovables by destination. Ownership in this respect ought to be immaterial. Accordingly, in this revision, things permanently attached to a building or other construction are immovables even if they belong to a predial lessee or other person.

(d) According to Article 467 of the Louisiana Civil Code of 1870, things that the owner of a building "has attached to or actually connected with" the building "for the use or convenience" of the building are "immovables by nature." This provision has been suppressed. Unity of ownership of the building and of the movables is no longer required; moreover, the test of use or convenience of the building is abrogated. Immobilization takes place under Article 466 when movables are permanently attached to a building or other construction.

(e) According to Article 469 of the Louisiana Civil Code of 1870, "the owner is supposed to have attached to his tenement or building forever such movables as are affixed to the same with plaster, or mortar, or such as cannot be taken off without being broken or injured, or without breaking or injuring the part of the building to which they are attached". The substance of this provisions has been reproduced. Louisiana jurisprudence interpreting Article 469, therefore, continues to be relevant.

(f) Immobilization under this article is inoperative for certain purposes specified in the law. According to R.S. 9:5357, a movable that is subject to a chattel mortgage "shall be and will remain movable insofar as the mortgage upon it is concerned, and shall not pass by the sale of the immovable property to which it has been actually or fictitiously attached, whether such sale be conventional or judicial." According to R.S. 9:1106, tanks placed by a person other than the landowner on rural or urban immovables for the storage of liquefied gases or liquid fertilizers "shall remain movable property, and the ownership of such tank or tanks shall not be affected by the sale, either private or judicial, of the land on which they are placed." See Acts 1978, No. 728, § 3.

(g) A review of Louisiana jurisprudence supports the view that the vendor's privilege is not lost merely because a movable sold becomes an immovable by destination under Articles 468 or 469 of the Civil Code. The issue of immobilization by permanent attachment under the proposed provision is likewise immaterial insofar as the vendor's privilege is concerned; whether this privilege is preserved or lost is determined on other grounds. See Yiannopoulos, Civil Law Property § 56 (1966).

(h) R.S. 9:5104 declares that "no mortgage placed on rural real estate subsequent to July 22, 1934, shall affect the livestock and implements of husbandry used in farming the property nor the machinery likewise used and not permanently attached to the soil." This provision has been repealed. See Acts 1978, No. 728, § 3.

REVISION COMMENTS—2008

(a) This Article represents a fresh start in an area of law that has been the focus of extensive academic and jurisprudential debate. Cf. Willis-Knighton Medical Center v. Caddo-Shreveport Sales and Use Tax Commission, 903 So.2d 1071 (La. 2005) and Prytania Park Hotel Ltd. v. General Star Indemnity Co., 179 F.3d 169 (5th Cir. 1999) with Equibank v. United States Internal Revenue Service, 749 F. 2d 1176 (5th Cir. 1985) and LaFleur v. Foret, 213 So.2d 141 (La.App. 3 Cir. 1968). See John A. Lovett, Another Great Debate?: The Ambiguous Relationship Between the Revised Civil Code and Pre-Revision Jurisprudence as Seen Through the Prytania Park Controversy, 48 Loy. L. J. 615 (2002); A. N. Yiannopoulos, Of Immovables, Component Parts, Societal Expectations and the Forehead of Zeus, 60 La. L. Rev. 1379 (2000); A. N. Yiannopoulos, Property § 142.5, 2 La. Civil Law Treatise (4th Ed. 2001). Prior jurisprudence remains relevant only to the extent that it employs principles consistent with those provided under this Article.

(b) The substantial damage test appearing in the third paragraph of this Article—which applies to buildings and other constructions alike—is carried forward from the prior Article without change in the law applicable to that test. If a thing is permanently attached to a building or other construction to such a degree that it cannot be removed without causing substantial damage either to itself or to the building or other construction, then the thing is a component part of the building or other construction under the third paragraph of this Article. In that case, it is irrelevant whether or not the thing satisfies the tests of either of the first two paragraphs of the Article.

(c) Even though substantial damage would not result from their removal, things attached to a building are nonetheless its component parts if they satisfy the test set forth in the first paragraph of this Article. This test finds its roots in civilian writings. See Planiol et Ripert, Traité Élémentaire de Droit Civil Français Volume I, Part II, No. 2209 (1939)(An English Translation by the Louisiana State Law Institute, 1959); Aubry and Rau, Droit Civil Français, Vol. II, No. 164 (1961), (An English Translation by the Louisiana State Law Institute; 1966).

(d) In the determination of whether things serve to complete a building of the same general type, resort is to be made to prevailing usages, a concept familiar under Civil Code Article 4 (Rev. 1987). As the term itself implies, prevailing usages are susceptible of change over time, and the first paragraph of this Article is not intended to impose rigidity in the face of evolving usage. The list of examples given in the first paragraph of the Article is merely illustrative.

(e) Completion of a building under the first paragraph is not to be viewed as a discrete and identifiable event beyond which nothing further can be done. A house that has stood for fifty years without gutters is nonetheless made more complete by their installation. Further, in order to serve to complete a building, a thing need not be of such necessity or importance that, in its absence, a construction would not be considered to be a building.

(f) In the application of the first paragraph of the Article, the specific use of a building is not to be considered, nor is any specific industrial or commercial activity that may happen to be conducted within the building. See Day v. Goff, 2 La.App. 75 (2d Cir. 1925). Cf. Showboat Star Partnership v. Slaughter, 789 So.2d 554 (La. 2001), which, in applying Civil Code Article 466 (1978) by analogy, found the relevant inquiry to encompass vessels in general rather than riverboats operated for gaming purposes. Similarly, in applying the same Article to a building used as a hospital, Willis-Knighton Medical Center v. Caddo-Shreveport Sales & Use Tax Commission, 862 So.2d 358 (La.App. 2 Cir. 2003) focused on commercial buildings in general, rather than hospitals. A lighting fixture that illuminates the interior of a commercial building, such as a hospital, serves to complete the building in its quality as a commercial building and is therefore its component part. By contrast, a nuclear camera located in a building used as a hospital, as in the Willis Knighton cases, cannot be a component part of the building under the first paragraph of this Article, because the camera does not serve to complete the building itself, though it might be useful in the operation of a hospital within the building. The nuclear camera would nonetheless constitute a component part of the building under the third paragraph of the Article if it could not be removed without substantial damage to either itself or the building.

(g) In contrast to the test that applies to buildings in the first paragraph of this Article, the test applicable to other constructions in the second paragraph focuses upon the principal use of the construction. If the thing in question furthers that principal use, it is a component part of the construction, even though it can be removed without substantial damage to itself or to the construction. Thus, valves, piping and access ladders that are attached to a water tower, and in a somewhat more oblique sense lightning rods and beacon lights installed on the water tower to protect it, further its principal use and are consequently its component parts. On the other hand, a cellular telephone antenna which is bolted atop a water tower as a convenient point of elevation but which transmits radio signals having nothing to do with the operation of the water tower itself does not further the water tower's principal use and thus does not constitute its component part under the second paragraph of this Article.

(h) The first two paragraphs of this Article require a modicum of physical attachment, though the attachment need not approach the degree necessary to satisfy the substantial damage test of the third paragraph. Attachment consisting solely of the insertion of an electrical plug into an outlet is too ephemeral and insubstantial to satisfy the requirements of this Article. See Equibank, supra. Mere placement of movables upon an immovable for its service and improvement, without physical attachment, is insufficient to cause them to become component parts of the immovable under this

Article, though they may be susceptible of immobilization by declaration made in accordance with Civil Code Article 467 (Rev. 1978). This Article does not revive the legal fiction of Civil Code Article 468 (1870), which, prior to its suppression in 1978, classified certain unattached things as immovables by destination when they were placed on a tract of land for its service and improvement.

(i) This Article applies directly both to buildings, which are always immovable, and also to other constructions that are classified as immovables on account of their permanent attachment to the ground and ownership by the owner of the ground. See C.C. Art. 463 (Rev. 1978). A construction permanently attached to the ground, other than a building, is movable when it does not belong to the owner of the ground; thus, it is not within the direct application of this Article. See C.C. Art. 475 (Rev. 1978). Even so, Civil Code Article 508 (Rev. 2008) applies the principles of this Article to the determination of whether a thing attached to such a movable construction constitutes its accessory.

Art. 467.   Immovables by declaration

The owner of an immovable may declare that machinery, appliances, and equipment owned by him and placed on the immovable, other than his private residence, for its service and improvement are deemed to be its component parts. The declaration shall be filed for registry in the conveyance records of the parish in which the immovable is located.

Acts 1978, No. 728, § 1, eff. Jan. 1, 1979.

REVISION COMMENTS—1978

(a) This provision is new. It is based in part on R.S. 9:1104 and in part on Article 468(1) of the Louisiana Civil Code of 1870.

(b) The owner of an industrial, commercial, and agricultural immovable, as well as the owner of a residential apartment complex, may declare that machinery, appliances, and equipment he has placed on the immovable for its service and improvement are its component parts. Immobilization under this provision is subject to the requirement that there be unity of ownership, that is, the owner of the immovable must also be owner of the movables, and that the movables must be placed on the immovable for its service and improvement. These requirements are the same as under Article 468(1) of the Louisiana Civil Code of 1870. Accordingly, Louisiana jurisprudence interpreting the source provision continues to be relevant. However, whereas immobilization under Article 468 of the 1870 Code was taking place by operation of law, immobilization under Article 467 (1978) takes place only by declaration of the owner. The declaration must be filed for registry in the conveyance records of the parish in which the immovable is located.

(c) Immobilization under this provision does not take place as to movables subject to chattel mortgage insofar as the mortgage creditor is concerned. See R.S. 9:5337; Article 469, Comment (f), infra.

Art. 468.   Deimmobilization

Component parts of an immovable so damaged or deteriorated that they can no longer serve the use of lands or buildings are deimmobilized.

The owner may deimmobilize the component parts of an immovable by an act translative of ownership and delivery to acquirers in good faith.

In the absence of rights of third persons, the owner may deimmobilize things by detachment or removal.

Acts 1978, No. 728, § 1, eff. Jan. 1, 1979. Amended by Acts 1979, No. 180, § 2, eff. Jan. 1, 1980.

REVISION COMMENTS—1978

(a) This provision codifies rules developed by Louisiana courts.

(b) Component parts of an immovable so damaged or deteriorated that they can no longer serve the use of lands or buildings are de-immobilized. See Folse v. Triche, 133 La. 915, 37 So. 875 (1904): "[W]hen, from any cause, a movable ceases to be of service to a tract of land, or is detached from a building or tenement of which it formed a part as an accessory, there is no longer ground for the claim that such movable appertains to the realty." See also Wakefield State Bank v. T. Fitz-Williams & Co.,

113

---

158 La. 838, 104 So. 734 (1925); Von Phul v. Caire & Graugnard, 12 Orl.App. 93 (La.App.Orl.Cir.1914). Under the circumstances, prior mortgages or other interests of third persons do not preclude de-immobilization. Ibid.

(c) The owner may de-immobilize component parts of an immovable by an act translative of ownership and delivery to acquirers in good faith. See Weil v. Lapeyre, 38 La.Ann. 303 (1886); Mechanics and Traders Ins. Co. v. Gerson, 38 La.Ann. 310 (1886); Bludworth v. Hunter, 9 Rob. 256 (La.1844); Von Phul v. Caire & Graugnard, 12 Orl.App. 93 (La.App.Orl.Cir.1914); cf. Bon Air Planting Co. v. Barringer, 142 La. 60, 76 So. 234 (1917); Chestnut v. Hammatt, 157 So.2d 915 (La.App.1st Cir. 1963). In these circumstances, prior mortgages, or other interests of third persons do not preclude de-immobilization. See Weil v. Lapeyre, supra; Mechanics and Traders Ins. Co. v. Gerson, supra; but cf. Alliance Trust Co. v. Gueydan Bank, 162 La. 1062, 111 So. 421 (1927) (mortgage creditor entitled to the value of immovables by destination that were seized and sold by general creditors of the debtor). In any case, a creditor may enjoin the sale of things forming part of the security of his mortgage. Citizens Bank v. Knapp, 22 La.Ann. 117 (1870). By way of exceptional legislation, the de-immobilization of certain home appliances covered by a real mortgage is excluded until payment of the indebtedness secured by the mortgage. R.S. 9:5121–5126. See Acts 1978, No. 728, § 3.

(d) In the absence of rights of third persons, the owner is free to de-immobilize anything. Cf. Chestnut v. Hammatt, 157 So.2d 915 (La.App.1st Cir. 1963). De-immobilization may be effected by actual detachment or removal; a mere intention to remove or detach does not suffice. See Bon Air Planting Co. v. Barringer, 142 La. 60, 76 So. 234 (1917); Maginnis v. Union Oil Co., 47 La.Ann. 1489, 18 So. 459 (1895). The execution of a chattel mortgage on previously unencumbered things has the same effect as actual detachment. Bank of White Castle v. Clerk, 181 La. 303, 159 So. 409 (1935). Upon detachment, in the absence of contrary provision of law, the things re-acquire the status of movables. Cf. Wakefield State Bank v. Fitz-Williams & Co., 158 La. 838, 104 So. 734 (1925).

Art. 469.   Transfer or encumbrance of immovable

The transfer or encumbrance of an immovable includes its component parts.

Acts 1978, No. 728, § 1, eff. Jan. 1, 1979. Amended by Acts 1979, No. 180, § 2, eff. Jan. 1, 1980.

REVISION COMMENTS—1978

(a) This provision is new. It clarifies the law.

(b) Buildings, other constructions permanently attached to the ground, standing timber, and unharvested crops or ungathered fruits of trees are component parts of a tract of land when they belong to the owner of the ground. They are not component parts of a tract of land when they belong to a person other than the owner of the ground.

Buildings and standing timber that belong to a person other than the owner of the ground are separate immovables. Art. 464, supra. Constructions permanently attached to the ground, other than buildings, that belong to a person other than the owner of the ground are movables. Art. 475, infra, in combination with Articles 463 and 464. Unharvested crops and ungathered fruits of trees are movables by anticipation when they belong to a person other than the owner of the ground. They are movables by anticipation insofar as the creditor is concerned when they are burdened with security rights or privileges. Art. 474, infra.

(c) The question whether buildings, other constructions permanently attached to the ground, standing timber, and unharvested crops or ungathered fruits of trees belong to the owner of the ground or to other persons is determined under the rules governing acquisition of ownership by juridical act, prescription, accession, and other modes by which ownership may be acquired. Separate ownership of such things may be asserted toward third persons when it is evidenced by an instrument filed for registry in the conveyance records of the parish in which the immovable is located. Art. 491, infra.

(d) Louisiana courts have classified as "constructions" under Article 464 of the Louisiana Civil Code of 1870 things having a certain size, permanence, and a degree of integration with the soil. See Yiannopoulos, Civil Law Property § 48 (1966). The same criteria apply to the classification of things as constructions under this provision.

(e) Trees cut down, whether carried off or not, are movables. Cf. Woodruff v. Roberts, 4 La.Ann. 127 (1840). Trees and plants in nurseries, though destined to be transplanted, are component parts of a tract of land when they belong to the owner of the ground. Cf. Louisiana v. Henderson, 138 So.2d 597 (La.App.3rd Cir. 1962). Crops harvested and fruits gathered are movables. Cf. Succession of Minter v. Opposition of Union Central Life Insurance Co., 180 La. 38, 156 So. 167 (1934); Alliance Trust Co. v. Gueydan Bank, 162 La. 1062, 111 So. 421 (1927).

(f) A movable subject to chattel mortgage which, under Articles 463, 465, and 466 (1978), might be regarded as a component part of an immovable, "shall remain movable, insofar as the mortgage upon it is concerned, and shall not pass by the sale of the immovable property to which it has been actually or fictitiously attached, whether such sale be conventional or judicial." R.S. 9:5357. Accordingly, the chattel mortgagee will not lose his interest in case of sale or encumbrance of the immovable on which the mortgaged movable is located. In such a case, registration is controlled by R.S. 9:5353.

(g) Article 2461 of the Louisiana Civil Code of 1870 declares that "The sale of a thing includes that of its accessories, and of whatever has been destined for its constant use, unless there be a reservation to the contrary." Likewise, the obligation of delivering a thing includes its accessories. C.C. Art. 2490 (1870). New Article 469 is to be applied in combination with these and other articles of the 1870 Code dealing with accessories. See e.g., C.C. Arts. 559, 642, as revised in 1976; id. Art. 743, as revised in 1977; id. Arts. 1636, 2465, 3040, 3250 (1870). Thus, on principle, the transfer of a thing does not only include its component parts, Article 469, but also its accessories in the absence of contrary stipulation. Under the regime of the Louisiana Civil Code of 1870, the transfer of an immovable included, specifically, its accessories that were classified as immovables by destination. In this revision, the transfer of an immovable includes its accessories though classified as movables. Article 508, infra, defines the accessories of a movable. The same definition may be applied by analogy to define the accessories of an immovable.

Art. 470. Incorporeal immovables

Rights and actions that apply to immovable things are incorporeal immovables. Immovables of this kind are such as personal servitudes established on immovables, predial servitudes, mineral rights, and petitory or possessory actions.

Acts 1978, No. 728, § 1, eff. Jan. 1, 1979.

REVISION COMMENT—1978

(a) This provision is based in part on Articles 470 and 471 of the Louisiana Civil Code of 1870, and Article 18 of the Mineral Code. It changes the law as it no longer classifies as immovable an action for the recovery of an entire succession.

(b) The enumeration of incorporeal immovables is merely illustrative. All rights and actions that have an immovable object are incorporeal immovables. Thus, the right of ownership of an immovable is an incorporeal immovable. Personal servitudes established on immovables are: usufruct, habitation, and rights of use. C.C. art. 534 (1976). Mineral servitudes, royalties, and leases are collectively referred to as "mineral rights". See Mineral Code arts. 16, and 18.

(c) The consequences of the classification of rights and actions as incorporeal immovables are determined by the courts. According to Louisiana jurisprudence, incorporeal immovables are not subject to all the rules governing immovable property. Certain legal provisions governing "immovables" or "immovable property" apply to corporeal things only. See Yiannopoulos, Civil Law Property § 63 (1966).

(d) An action for the recovery of an entire succession should not be necessarily an incorporeal immovable. Classification should instead depend on the object of the action. Thus, an action by a universal heir or legatee for the recovery of immovable property belonging to a succession should be regarded as an incorporeal immovable; conversely, an action for the recovery of movable property belonging to a succession should be regarded as an incorporeal movable.

Classification of an action for the recovery of an entire succession as an incorporeal immovable was first made in the 1825 revision. Article 22, p. 98, of the Louisiana Civil Code of 1808, corresponding with Article 526 of the Code Civil, provided: "The following are considered immovable from the object to which they apply: . . . The actions the end of which is to claim an immovable thing." The last sentence, however, was changed in Article 463 of the Louisiana Civil Code of 1870, to read: "An action for the recovery of an immovable estate or an entire succession." The redactors observed: "The reasons for the changes or additions which we have made in this article are those: . . . Actions which tend to claim a succession or a partition of it, are certainly immovable actions." 1 Louisiana Legal Archives, Projet of the Louisiana Civil Code of 1825, p. 38 (1937).

There is no reported Louisiana decision holding that an action for the recovery of an entire succession composed of movables is an incorporeal immovable. In the old case of Bonneau v. Poydras, 2 Rob. 1 (La.1842), the court refused to apply Article 463 of the 1825 Code to an heir's claim for the proceeds of a liquidated succession, declaring that the provision applies only when a universal heir or legatee claims an entire succession in kind. Article 471 of the Louisiana Civil Code (1870) was applied in Succession of Harris, 179 La. 954, 155 So. 446 (1934), involving an action by a forced heir for the recovery of a succession including both movables and immovables.

SECTION 3—MOVABLES

Art. 471.   Corporeal movables

Corporeal movables are things, whether animate or inanimate, that normally move or can be moved from one place to another.

Acts 1978, No. 728, § 1, eff. Jan. 1, 1979.

REVISION COMMENTS—1978

(a) This provision follows the conceptual framework of Articles 473 and 475 of the Louisiana Civil Code of 1870. Definition of corporeal movables is made, on principle, in accordance with notions of physical mobility.

(b) The illustrations of movables by nature conform to the illustrations of corporeal things in this revision.

(c) Corporeal movables may be immobilized under arts. 465 through 467 (1978).

Art. 472.   Building materials

Materials gathered for the erection of a new building or other construction, even though deriving from the demolition of an old one, are movables until their incorporation into the new building or after construction.

Materials separated from a building or other construction for the purpose of repair, addition, or alteration to it, with the intention of putting them back, remain immovables.

Acts 1978, No. 728, § 1, eff. Jan. 1, 1979.

REVISION COMMENTS—1978

(a) This provision reproduces the substance of Article 476 of the Louisiana Civil Code of 1870. It does not change the law.

(b) The first paragraph of this provision concerns materials collected for the erection of a new building or other construction. Such materials, by definition, are and remain movables until their incorporation. If the materials are entirely new, there should be no question as to their status; but if the materials derive from the demolition of an old building, argument might be made that they preserve their status as immovables. For this reason, and in accordance with the rules governing de-immobilization, the law clarifies the situation and declares that building materials "whether arising from the demolition of an old construction or not, are movables until their incorporation." See Beard v. Duralde, 23 La.Ann. 284 (1871).

(c) The second paragraph of this provision concerns materials separated from a building or other structure for purposes of repairs, additions, or alterations. Since argument might be made that such materials became de-immobilized, the law clarifies the situation and declares that they remain immovables. See Beard v. Duralde, 23 La.Ann. 284 (1871).

Art. 473.   Incorporeal movables

Rights, obligations, and actions that apply to a movable thing are incorporeal movables. Movables of this kind are such as bonds, annuities, and interests or shares in entities possessing juridical personality.

Interests or shares in a juridical person that owns immovables are considered as movables as long as the entity exists; upon its dissolution, the right of each individual to a share in the immovables is an immovable.

Acts 1978, No. 728, § 1, eff. Jan. 1, 1979.

REVISION COMMENTS—1978

(a) This provision reproduces in substance Article 474 of the Louisiana Civil Code of 1870. It does not change the law.

(b) The words "obligations which have for their object a specific performance, and those which from their nature, resolve themselves into damages", figuring in Article 474 of the Louisiana Civil Code of 1870, have been omitted as unnecessary. Indeed, the specific performance mentioned is directed to the recovery of a movable and is covered by the preceding illustration in the same article; and obligations which resolve themselves into damages are obligations for the recovery of money, likewise covered by the preceding illustration.

(c) The words "although these obligations are accompanied with a mortgage", figuring in Article 474 of the Louisiana Civil Code of 1870, have been omitted as unnecessary. Real mortgage, the kind of interest the redactors of the Civil Code had in mind, is a real right which, in the light of its object, ought to be classified as an incorporeal immovable by disposition of the law. The hypothecary action, available under the Louisiana Code of Civil Procedure for the enforcement of a real mortgage is likewise an incorporeal immovable; but an action on the principal debt, directed to the recovery of a sum of money, is a movable according to the illustration given in the text.

(d) The words "whether they be founded on a price in money or on the price or the condition of the alienation of an immovable", qualifying "perpetual rents and annuities" in the text of Article 474 of the Louisiana Civil Code of 1870, have been omitted as unnecessary. It ought to be clear from the unqualified formulation in the text that all perpetual rents and all annuities are movables, whether the consideration for the right to periodical payments has been money or any other thing, movable or immovable.

(e) According to settled civilian interpretation, the words "shares or interests in banks or companies of commerce, or industry or other speculations" in Article 474 of the Louisiana Civil Code of 1870 refer to shares or interests in entities possessing juridical personality. See St. Charles Land Trust v. St. Amant, 253 La. 243, 217 So.2d 385 (1969); 3 Planiol et Ripert, Traité pratique de droit civil français 118 (2d ed. Picard 1952); Rotondi, The Movable Character of Shares and Interests in Companies in the Romanesque Codes, in XXth Century Comparative and Conflicts Law 232, 238 (1961). The underlying theory is that while the entity is a going concern, the interests of individual members are distinct and distinguishable from the property of the entity. Upon dissolution of the entity, the rights of the individual members are regarded as movable or immovable depending on the nature of the remaining property of the former entity. The proposed general solution is subject to special legislation. Cf. R.S. 12:1–178 (1969) (business corporations); id. 12:201–269 (nonprofit corporations); id. 12:407–493 (special corporations).

(f) According to Louisiana jurisprudence, commercial partnerships cannot own immovable property. "If the title to real property is conveyed to or taken in the name of a commercial partnership, the ownership of that property becomes vested not in the partnership, but in the partners in their individual capacities, as joint owners thereof". Hollier v. Fontenot, 216 So.2d 842, 846 (La.App. 3rd Cir. 1968), writ refused 253 La. 868, 220 So.2d 456.

Art. 474.   Movables by anticipation

Unharvested crops and ungathered fruits of trees are movables by anticipation when they belong to a person other than the landowner. When encumbered with security rights of third persons, they are movables by anticipation insofar as the creditor is concerned.

The landowner may, by act translative of ownership or by pledge, mobilize by anticipation unharvested crops and ungathered fruits of trees that belong to him.

Acts 1978, No. 728, § 1, eff. Jan. 1, 1979.

REVISION COMMENTS—1978

(a) This provision codifies Louisiana jurisprudence and articulates principles inherent in the Louisiana Civil Code of 1870 and in special legislation. It does not change the law.

(b) According to Louisiana jurisprudence, principles inherent in the Louisiana Civil Code of 1870, and special legislation, unharvested crops and ungathered fruits of trees are movables by anticipation when they belong to a person other than the landowner or when they are encumbered with rights of third persons. See Citizens Bank v. Wiltz, 31 La.Ann. 244, 246 (1879): "The immovability of a growing crop is in the order of things temporary, for the crop passes from the state of a growing to that of a gathered one, from an immovable to a movable. The existence of a right on the growing crop is a mobilization by anticipation, a gathering as it were in advance, rendering the crop movable quoad the right acquired thereon". See also R.S. 9:4341.

(c) The landowner may mobilize by anticipation unharvested crops and ungathered fruits of trees that belong to him. In order to be effective against third persons, the act of mobilization must be recorded. See Succession of Minter v. Opposition of Union Life Ins. Co., 180 La. 38, 156 So. 167 (1934); cf. Williamson v. Richardson, 31 La.Ann. 685 (1879).

Art. 475.   Things not immovable

All things, corporeal or incorporeal, that the law does not consider as immovables, are movables.

Acts 1978, No. 728, § 1, eff. Jan. 1, 1979.

REVISION COMMENT—1978

This article reproduces the substance of Article 475 of the Louisiana Civil Code of 1870. It does not change the law. Thus, mobile homes are movables. See R.S. 32:710 (1975); cf. Osborne v. Mossler Acceptance Co., 214 La. 503, 38 So.2d 151 (1949) (mobile home subject to chattel mortgage). They may become immovables under Articles 463, 465–467 (1978) or under the Motor Vehicle Law, R.S. 32:710 (1975).

CHAPTER 2—RIGHTS IN THINGS

Art. 476.   Rights in things

One may have various rights in things:

1.   Ownership;

2.   Personal and predial servitudes; and

3.   Such other real rights as the law allows.

Acts 1978, No. 728, § 1, eff. Jan. 1, 1979.

REVISION COMMENTS—1978

(a) The text of this provision is new. It is based on Article 487 of the Louisiana Civil Code of 1870. It does not change the law.

(b) Real rights confer direct and immediate authority over a thing. They are distinguished from personal (obligatory) rights that confer merely authority over the person of a certain debtor who has assumed the obligation to allow the enjoyment of a thing by his creditor. See Yiannopoulos, Civil Law Property §§ 87, 90, 97 (1966). Legal usage in the state seems to associate the term "real right" with a right in immovable property; this, however, is not the usage in the Civil Code. According to the Civil Code real rights may exist in both movables and immovables. The right of pledge, ownership, and usufruct of immovables have all the substantive characteristics of real rights. See C.C. art. 535 (1976), Comment (b). Restricted application of the term real rights to interests in immovable property is meaningful only in the framework of the Louisiana Code of Civil Procedure; "real actions" are available only to holders of real rights in immovable property. Under this Article, as under the Louisiana Civil Code of 1870, the object of a real right may be either a movable or an immovable. Nevertheless, real rights in movables are not protected by the nominate real actions of the Code of Civil Procedure.

(c) Article 487 of the Louisiana Civil Code of 1870 corresponds with Article 543 of the French Civil Code. The provision is explained in the Exposé des Motifs by Mr. Treilhard, 11 Fenet, Recueil Complet des travaux préparatoires du Code Civil 33 (1836): "These are actually the only modifications of which ownership is susceptible in our political and social organization; there cannot be in things any other species of rights: one has either a complete and perfect ownership which includes the right to enjoy and dispose of; or one has a simple right of enjoyment without being able to dispose of the land; or finally, one has only the right to claim predial servitudes on the property of another; servitudes which cannot be established but for the use and utility of an estate; servitudes which do not entail any affirmative duties of the person; servitudes, finally, which have nothing in common with feudal tenures, destroyed forever."

(d) The question whether individuals may create new real rights or work modifications on the real rights established in the Code Civil has been a highly controversial matter in France. In the absence of a directly applicable legislative text, the prevailing view in France is that contractual freedom ought to be respected, provided that the limits of public policy are not transcended. See 3 Planiol et Ripert, Traité pratique de droit civil français 54 (2d ed. Picard 1952). Within these broad limits individuals may create new real rights by dismembering their ownership as they see fit, and work modifications on recognized real rights. The enumeration of real rights in Article 543 of the Code Civil (1870) was set aside: this enumeration is incomplete and the article has been interpreted as illustrative rather than exclusive. Cass., Feb. 13, 1845, D. 1834.1.205, S. 1834.1.206.

Question has also arisen in Louisiana as to whether the real rights established in the Civil Code may be altered and modified by contract, and whether the parties to a contract may create real rights not regulated in the Civil Code. Under the influence of French doctrine and jurisprudence, Louisiana courts have treated Article 487 of the Civil Code of 1870 as merely illustrative of permissible dismemberments of ownership. See Queensborough Land Co. v. Cazeaux, 136 La. 724, 67 So. 641 (1915). In this case, the Louisiana Supreme Court adopted the view that, in principle, the parties to a contract may create real rights "apart and beyond" those created in the Civil Code, subject to close judicial scrutiny in the general interest of the public. However, little use of this facility has been made in practice. The most important examples of real rights created by the exercise of contractual freedom in Louisiana are the mineral rights, now regulated by the Mineral Code, and building restrictions in subdivision developments. For detailed discussion, see Yiannopoulos, Real Rights: Limits of Contractual and Testamentary Freedom, 30 La.L.Rev. 44 (1969).

TITLE II—OWNERSHIP

CHAPTER 1—GENERAL PRINCIPLES

Art. 477. Ownership; content

A. Ownership is the right that confers on a person direct, immediate, and exclusive authority over a thing. The owner of a thing may use, enjoy, and dispose of it within the limits and under the conditions established by law.

B. A buyer and occupant of a residence under a bond for deed contract is the owner of the thing for purposes of the homestead exemption granted to other property owners pursuant to Article VII, Section 20(A) of the Constitution of Louisiana. The buyer under a bond for deed contract shall apply for the homestead exemption each year.

Acts 1979, No. 180, § 1, eff. Jan. 1, 1980. Amended by Acts 1995, No. 640 § 1, eff. Jan. 1, 1996.

REVISION COMMENTS—1979

(a) This provision is based on Articles 488 and 491 of the Louisiana Civil Code of 1870. It does not change the law.

(b) The definition of ownership in this article follows closely the definition in the treatise of Planiol: "Ownership is the right by virtue of which a thing is subjected perpetually and exclusively, to the acts and will of a person." 3 Planiol et Ripert, Traité pratique de droit civil français 220 (2d ed. Picard 1952).

(c) Article 489 of the Louisiana Civil Code of 1870 has been suppressed as unnecessary and confusing. This provision was first adopted in the 1825 revision. The redactors observed: "By this means the usufructuary can always be distinguished from the proprietor. Digest, book 4, Title 2. law 12." 1 Louisiana Legal Archives, Projet of the Louisiana Civil Code of 1825, 42 (1937).

(d) For corresponding provisions in modern civil codes, see Italian Civil Code Article 832: "The owner has the right to enjoy and dispose of things fully and exclusively, within the limits and with observance of the duties established by the legal order." Greek Civil Code Article 1000: "The owner of a thing may, to the extent that this does not conflict with law or rights of third persons, dispose of it as he pleases and to exclude interference by other persons." B.G.B. § 903: "The owner of a thing may, to the extent that it is not contrary to the law or the rights of third persons, deal with the thing as he pleases and exclude others from any interference." Swiss Civil Code Article 641: "The owner of a thing may freely dispose of it within the limits established by law. He has the right to revendicate it from anyone who retains it, and to enjoin any usurpation." Quebec Report on Property Article 34: "Ownership is the right to use, enjoy and dispose of things as fully as possible, within the limits and under the conditions established by law."

Art. 478. Resolutory condition; real right in favor of other person

The right of ownership may be subject to a resolutory condition, and it may be burdened with a real right in favor of another person as allowed by law. The ownership of a thing burdened with a usufruct is designated as naked ownership.

Acts 1979, No. 180, § 1, eff. Jan. 1, 1980.

REVISION COMMENTS—1979

(a) This provision is new. It is based in part on Articles 490 and 492 of the Louisiana Civil Code of 1870. It does not change the law.

(b) Under this revision ownership is no longer distinguished into perfect ownership and imperfect ownership. Ownership, however, may be subject to a resolutory condition, and it may be burdened with a real right in favor of another person as allowed by law.

(c) The ownership of a thing burdened with a usufruct is designated as naked ownership. See, e.g., Civil Code Art. 603, as revised in 1976.

(d) Article 490 of the Louisiana Civil Code of 1870 derives from the 1825 revision. The redactors observed: "This distinction between perfect and imperfect ownership has been deemed necessary in order that the subsequent provisions may be understood, which relate to the rights which each of these kinds of ownership gives rise to the owner. Pothier, de la propriété, Nos. 6 and 8." 1 Louisiana Legal Archives, Projet of the Louisiana Civil Code of 1825, p. 42 (1937). Article 492 of Louisiana Civil Code of 1870 derives from the 1825 revision. The redactors observed: "Such is the difference existing between the rights conferred by perfect and imperfect ownership. Pothier, de la propriété, Nos. 12 and 13." Louisiana Legal Archives Projet of the Louisiana Civil Code of 1825 p. 43 (1937). Modern civil codes do not draw a distinction between perfect and imperfect ownership; nor does the French Civil Code.

Art. 479.   Necessity of a person

The right of ownership may exist only in favor of a natural person or a juridical person.

Acts 1979, No. 180, § 1, eff. Jan. 1, 1980.

REVISION COMMENTS—1979

(a) This provision reproduces the substance of Article 493 of the Louisiana Civil Code of 1870. It does not change the law.

(b) There is no corresponding provision in modern civil codes or in the French Civil Code. Article 493 of the Louisiana Civil Code of 1870 derives from the 1825 revision. The redactors observed: "This additional article and the three which follow, contain rules which will be useful in their application, and which Pothier has placed at the head of his treatise on property. Pothier, treatise de la propriété, No. 15." 1 Louisiana Legal Archives, Projet of the Louisiana Civil Code of 1825, p. 43 (1937).

(c) A juridical person is a legal entity, such as a corporation or a partnership. An unincorporated association may have certain attributes of juridical personality. See Yiannopoulos, Louisiana Civil Law System 105 (1978).

Art. 480.   Co-ownership

Two or more persons may own the same thing in indivision, each having an undivided share.

Acts 1979, No. 180, § 1, eff. Jan. 1, 1980.

REVISION COMMENTS—1979

(a) This provision reproduces the substance of Article 494 of the Louisiana Civil Code of 1870. It does not change the law.

(b) Modern civil codes contain detailed provisions dealing with co-ownership. Article 480 merely states a general principle, and it is left intact. The provision derives from the 1825 revision. The redactors observed: "The right of ownership consisting, as we have defined it at the head of the title, in being owner to the exclusion of all other persons, it follows that two persons cannot be owners of the whole of the same thing, but nothing prevents them from being owners in common, for the part for which each one has therein; because of the part of one in a thing in common, is not the part of the other, and each can only dispose of his own part. Pothier, de la propriété, Nos. 16, 17." 1 Louisiana Legal Archives, Projet of the Louisiana Civil Code of 1825, p. 43 (1937).

Art. 481.   Ownership and possession distinguished

The ownership and the possession of a thing are distinct.

Ownership exists independently of any exercise of it and may not be lost by nonuse. Ownership is lost when acquisitive prescription accrues in favor of an adverse possessor.

Acts 1979, No. 180, § 1, eff. Jan. 1, 1980.

REVISION COMMENTS—1979

(a) This provision reproduces the substance of Article 496 of the Louisiana Civil Code of 1870. It does not change the law.

(b) There are no corresponding provisions in modern civil codes or in the French Civil Code. Article 496 of the Louisiana Civil Code of 1870 derives from the 1825 revision. The redactors observed: "The principle developed in this article is necessary in order to show that the right of ownership can be preserved without the exercise of any act of ownership, and without any actual possession on the part of the owner. Digest Book 41, title 2, law 22, Sec. 1, and Toullier, lois civiles, vol. 3, No. 82, p. 68." 1 Louisiana Legal Archives, Projet of the Louisiana Civil Code of 1825, p. 44 (1937).

Art. 482.   Accession

The ownership of a thing includes by accession the ownership of everything that it produces or is united with it, either naturally or artificially, in accordance with the following provisions.

Acts 1979, No. 180, § 1, eff. Jan. 1, 1980.

REVISION COMMENTS—1979

(a) This provision reproduces the substance of Article 498 of the Louisiana Civil Code of 1870. It does not change the law.

(b) Article 3, p. 102 of the Louisiana Civil Code of 1808, corresponding with Article 546 of the French Civil Code, provided: "The right of accession is a consequence of the right of ownership. The right of accession is the right which the owner of a thing has to what the thing produces, and to what unites itself to the same by a kind of accessory incorporation whether naturally or artificially." The present version of the Louisiana Civil Code of 1870 derives from the 1825 revision. See 1 Louisiana Legal Archives Projet of the Louisiana Civil Code of 1825, p. 44 (1937).

CHAPTER 2—RIGHT OF ACCESSION

SECTION 1—OWNERSHIP OF FRUITS

Art. 483.   Ownership of fruits by accession

In the absence of rights of other persons, the owner of a thing acquires the ownership of its natural and civil fruits.

Acts 1979, No. 180, § 1, eff. Jan. 1, 1980.

REVISION COMMENTS—1979

(a) This provision reproduces the substance of Article 499 of the Louisiana Civil Code of 1870. It does not change the law.

(b) The generic "fruits", and "natural" and "civil" fruits, have been defined in the framework of the institution of usufruct. See C.C. Art. 551 (1976).

(c) The phrase "in the absence of rights of other persons" has been inserted to indicate that accession does not supersede rights of other persons. For example, despite the principle of accession, the fruits of a thing may belong to a usufructuary, a possessor in good faith, or even a lessee.

Art. 484.   Young of animals

The young of animals belong to the owner of the mother of them.

Acts 1979, No. 180, § 1, eff. Jan. 1, 1980.

(a) This provision reproduces the substance of Article 500 of the Louisiana Civil Code of 1870. It does not change the law.

(b) There is no corresponding provision in the Louisiana Civil Code of 1808 or in the French Civil Code. The present version of the Louisiana Civil Code of 1870 derives from the 1825 revision. The redactors observed: "This disposition is not in our Code; it is taken from law 25, title 28, Part. 3. Partida." 1 Louisiana Legal Archives, Projet of the Louisiana Civil Code of 1825, p. 45 (1937).

Art. 485.   Fruits produced by a third person; reimbursement

When fruits that belong to the owner of a thing by accession are produced by the work of another person, or from seeds sown by him, the owner may retain them on reimbursing such person his expenses.

Acts 1979, No. 180, § 1, eff. Jan. 1, 1980.

This provision is new. It is based in part on Article 501 of the Louisiana Civil Code of 1870. It establishes the general principle that when fruits are produced by the work of another person, be he a possessor of the property or not, the owner who acquires the ownership of the fruits by accession must pay to the person who produced the fruits the cost of production.

Art. 486.   Possessor's right to fruits

A possessor in good faith acquires the ownership of fruits he has gathered. If he is evicted by the owner, he is entitled to reimbursement of expenses for fruits he was unable to gather.

A possessor in bad faith is bound to restore to the owner the fruits he has gathered, or their value, subject to his claim for reimbursement of expenses.

Acts 1979, No. 180, § 1, eff. Jan. 1, 1980.

This provision reproduces the substance of Articles 502 and 3453(1) of the Louisiana Civil Code of 1870. It does not change the law.

Art. 487.   Possessor in good faith; definition

For purposes of accession, a possessor is in good faith when he possesses by virtue of an act translative of ownership and does not know of any defects in his ownership. He ceases to be in good faith when these defects are made known to him or an action is instituted against him by the owner for the recovery of the thing.

Acts 1979, No. 180, § 1, eff. Jan. 1, 1980.

(a) This provision reproduces the substance of Article 503 of the Louisiana Civil Code of 1870. It does not change the law.

(b) For purposes of accession, a possessor is in good faith when he possesses by virtue of an act translative of ownership and does not know of its defects. An act translative of ownership is "an act sufficient in terms to transfer property", such as a sale, an exchange, or a donation. C.C. Art. 503 (1870). A possessor is not in good faith for purposes of accession when he merely believes that his author was the true owner of the thing; he must also be ignorant of the defects of his title. It is different in matters of prescription. According to Article 3451 of the Louisiana Civil Code of 1870, a possessor may be in good faith even if he possesses without any act translative of ownership. For purposes of prescription, good faith and just title are distinct requirements whereas for purposes of accession good faith depends on the existence of an act translative of ownership and ignorance of its defects. See 3 Planiol et Ripert, Traité pratique de droit civil français 184 (2d ed. Picard 1952).

(c) Louisiana courts have declared that Articles 503 and 3451 of the Louisiana Civil Code of 1870 must be applied together for the determination of the question of good faith in matters of accession as well as in matters of acquisitive prescription. Vance v. Sentell, 178 La. 749, 152 So. 513 (1934), and cases cited. This jurisprudence, though doctrinally unsound, has reached correct results. Thus one who possesses a thing without an act translative of ownership may not retain fruits and may not avail himself of the shorter prescriptive periods. The same results are properly reached by application of Article 503 in matters of accession and by application of Article 3451, in combination with Article 3483, in matters of prescription. Under this projet, as well as under a correct reading of the corresponding provisions of the Louisiana Civil Code of 1870, there are different definitions of good faith for different purposes. In matters of accession, good faith is dependent upon the existence of a just title; in matters of prescription good faith and just title are distinct requirements but both must exist for acquisition of ownership by the shorter prescriptive periods. If it were otherwise, one would be allowed to retain fruits but he could not acquire the ownership of a thing in three or ten years.

(d) According to French doctrine and jurisprudence interpreting the corresponding provision in the Code Civil, a possessor may be in good faith even though his title is null or annullable on account of defects of substance or form. Further, the title may be merely "putative". Such is the title of an apparent heir or of a legatee under an invalid or a revoked will. 3 Planiol et Ripert, Traité pratique de droit civil français 186 (2d ed. Picard 1952). A possessor is not in good faith when he merely believes that his author was the true owner of the thing; the good faith requirement contemplates that the possessor be ignorant of the defects of his title. There are, however, certain exceptions. For example, one who acquires a thing from a minor without compliance with the requisite formalities may be in good faith if he has serious reasons to believe that the minor will ratify the transaction upon reaching majority. Good faith is not excluded by an error of law or an error of fact. The possessor is always required to produce his title, but he is not required to prove his good faith, because good faith is presumed. Ibid.

(e) Article 3481 of the Louisiana Civil Code of 1870 declares that "good faith is always presumed in matters of prescription; and he who alleges bad faith in the possessor, must prove it." According to Louisiana jurisprudence the same presumption applies in matters of accession.

(f) One who possesses a thing as a successor of another may or may not possess by virtue of an act translative of ownership. A universal successor occupies the same position as his ancestor. C.C. Art. 3556(28) (1870). Thus, if the ancestor possessed by virtue of an act translative of ownership, so does the universal successor. A particular successor necessarily possesses by virtue of an act translative of ownership. Ibid.

(g) This provision may apply by analogy to one who possesses more land than his title calls for with the belief that he is owner of the excess.

Art. 488.   Products; reimbursement of expenses

Products derived from a thing as a result of diminution of its substance belong to the owner of that thing. When they are reclaimed by the owner, a possessor in good faith has the right to reimbursement of his expenses. A possessor in bad faith does not have this right.

Acts 1979, No. 180, § 1, eff. Jan. 1, 1980.

REVISION COMMENTS—1979

(a) This provision is new. It is based on Louisiana jurisprudence. It changes the law as indicated in Comment (d).

(b) According to Louisiana jurisprudence, persons engaging in timber or mineral operations in good faith are bound to account to the owner of the land but they are entitled to reimbursement of their production costs. As to timber operations, see Ball Bros. Lumber Co. v. Simms Lumber Co., 121 La. 627, 46 So. 674 (1908); Guarantee Trust & Safe Deposit Co. v. E. G. Drew Co., 107 La. 251, 31 So. 736 (1902); Gardere v. Blanton, 35 La.Ann. 811 (1883). As to mineral operations, see Huckabay v. Texas Co., 227 La. 191, 78 So.2d 829 (1955); Allies Oil Co. v. Ayers, 152 La. 19, 92 So. 720 (1922); Cooke v. Gulf Refining Co., 135 La. 609, 65 So. 758 (1914). Recovery of expenses in these circumstances is said to rest on the principle of unjust enrichment. See Scott v. Hunt Oil Co., 152 So.2d 599 (La.App. 2d Cir. 1963).

(c) Persons engaging in timber operations in bad faith are not entitled to reimbursement of production costs. See Nabors Oil and Gas Co. v. Louisiana Oil Refining Co., 151 La. 361, 91 So. 765 (1922) (minerals; reversed on other grounds); State v. F.B. Williams Cypress Co., 131 La. 62, 58 So. 1033 (1912) (timber); Comment, Measure of Damages for Unauthorized Production of Oil and Gas; the Role of Good and Bad Faith, 15 Tul.L.Rev. 291 (1941); Comment, Liability for Removal of Timber, Minerals, and Dirt, 31 La.L.Rev. 616 (1971).

(d) The jurisprudence establishing the distinctions of good faith, moral good faith but legal bad faith, and legal and moral bad faith is overruled legislatively. A possessor who removes timber, minerals, or dirt, may be either in good faith or in bad faith. His good or bad faith is determined by application of Article 487, supra. The measure of reimbursement of a possessor in good faith is the production costs.

(e) Article 488 applies to possessors, that is, persons who have physical control of an immovable with the intent to own it. It does not apply to a trespasser or other wrongdoer. The obligations of a possessor under Article 488 are independent of liability under the law of delictual obligations. Thus, a possessor is bound to restore to the owner the products of a thing under Article 488, and, in addition, he may be liable for an offense or quasi offense he may have committed.

Art. 489.   Apportionment of fruits

In the absence of other provisions, one who is entitled to the fruits of a thing from a certain time or up to a certain time acquires the ownership of natural fruits gathered during the existence of his right, and a part of the civil fruits proportionate to the duration of his right.

Acts 1979, No. 180, § 1, eff. Jan. 1, 1980.

REVISION COMMENTS—1979

(a) This provision is new. It expresses the principle inherent in Articles 555 and 556 of the Louisiana Civil Code, as revised in 1976. It does not change the law.

(b) This provision establishes a general rule for the apportionment of natural and civil fruits, in the absence of contrary provisions of law or contract.

SECTION 2—ACCESSION IN RELATION TO IMMOVABLES

Art. 490.   Accession above and below the surface

Unless otherwise provided by law, the ownership of a tract of land carries with it the ownership of everything that is directly above or under it.

The owner may make works on, above, or below the land as he pleases, and draw all the advantages that accrue from them, unless he is restrained by law or by rights of others.

Acts 1979, No. 180, § 1, eff. Jan. 1, 1980.

REVISION COMMENTS—1979

(a) This provision reproduces the substance of Article 505 of the Louisiana Civil Code of 1870. It does not change the law.

(b) The ownership of the soil carries with it everything that is directly above or under it unless otherwise provided by law. Buildings, other constructions permanently attached to the ground, timber, and unharvested crops or ungathered fruits of trees may, according to law, belong to a person other than the landowner. See C.C. Art. 463, as revised in 1978; Art. 491, infra.

Art. 491.   Buildings, other constructions, standing timber, and crops

Buildings, other constructions permanently attached to the ground, standing timber, and unharvested crops or ungathered fruits of trees may belong to a person other than the owner of the ground. Nevertheless, they are presumed to belong to the owner of the ground, unless separate ownership is evidenced by an instrument filed for registry in the conveyance records of the parish in which the immovable is located.

Acts 1979, No. 180, § 1, eff. Jan. 1, 1980.

REVISION COMMENTS—1979

(a) This provision is new. It is based on Article 506 of the Louisiana Civil Code of 1870 and the jurisprudence interpreting it.

(b) Buildings, other constructions permanently attached to the ground, standing timber, and unharvested crops or ungathered fruits of trees are component parts of a tract of land when they belong to the owner of the ground. C.C. Art. 463. Buildings and standing timber that belong to a person other than the owner of the ground are separate immovables. C.C. Art. 464. Crops and fruits belonging to a person other than the owner of the ground are movables by anticipation. C.C. Art. 474. Constructions permanently attached to the ground that belong to a person other than the owner of the ground are, by clear implication, movables. Art. 474, in combination with Arts. 463 and 464.

(c) Separate ownership of buildings, of other constructions permanently attached to the ground, of standing timber, and of unharvested crops or ungathered fruits of trees may be asserted toward third persons only if it is evidenced by an instrument filed for registry in the conveyance records of the parish in which the immovable is located. In the absence of such an instrument, third persons are entitled to assume that these things are component parts of the ground.

(d) This provision does not determine the ownership of buildings, constructions, standing timber, and crops on the land of another. The question whether these things belong to the owner of the ground or to another person is determined in accordance with the rules governing acquisition of ownership.

(e) The transfer or encumbrance of an immovable includes its component parts. Art. 469. Buildings, other constructions permanently attached to the ground, standing timber, and unharvested crops or ungathered fruits of trees are presumed to belong to the owner of the ground, that is, they are presumed to be component parts of a tract of land. The presumption is rebutted when separate ownership of such things is evidenced by an instrument filed for registry in the conveyance records of the parish in which the immovable is located. In the absence of such an instrument, third persons relying on the public records are entitled to assume that these things are component parts of the ground.

Art. 492.   Separate ownership of part of a building

Separate ownership of a part of a building, such as a floor, an apartment, or a room, may be established only by a juridical act of the owner of the entire building when and in the manner expressly authorized by law.

Acts 1979, No. 180, § 1, eff. Jan. 1, 1980.

REVISION COMMENTS—1979

(a) This provision is new. It is based on a corresponding provision of the Greek Civil Code. Separate ownership of a floor or of an apartment of a building may not be established by acquisitive prescription, by judgment in an action for partition, or by juridical act of an owner in indivision. It may only be established by a juridical act, that is, a contract or a testament, of the owner of the entire building when authorized expressly by law. If the building is owned in indivision, all co-owners must consent.

(b) A juridical act is a manifestation of will intended to have legal consequences.

Art. 493.   Ownership of improvements

Buildings, other constructions permanently attached to the ground, and plantings made on the land of another with his consent belong to him who made them. They belong to the owner of the ground when they are made without his consent.

When the owner of buildings, other constructions permanently attached to the ground, or plantings no longer has the right to keep them on the land of another, he may remove them subject to his obligation

127

to restore the property to its former condition. If he does not remove them within ninety days after written demand, the owner of the land may, after the ninetieth day from the date of mailing the written demand, appropriate ownership of the improvements by providing an additional written notice by certified mail, and upon receipt of the certified mail by the owner of the improvements, the owner of the land obtains ownership of the improvements and owes nothing to the owner of the improvements. Until such time as the owner of the land appropriates the improvements, the improvements shall remain the property of he who made them and he shall be solely responsible for any harm caused by the improvements.

When buildings, other constructions permanently attached to the ground, or plantings are made on the separate property of a spouse with community assets or with separate assets of the other spouse and when such improvements are made on community property with the separate assets of a spouse, this Article does not apply. The rights of the spouses are governed by Articles 2366, 2367, and 2367.1.

Acts 1979, No. 180, § 1, eff. Jan. 1, 1980. Amended by Acts 1984, No. 933, § 1; Acts 2003, No. 715, § 1.

REVISION COMMENTS—1979

(a) This provision is new.

(b) Buildings, other constructions permanently attached to the ground, and plantings made on the land of another with his consent, as by a lessee, a coowner, a purchaser under a contract to sell, or a precarious possessor, belong to him who made them. Such separate ownership may be asserted toward third persons when it is evidenced by an instrument filed for registry in the conveyance records of the parish in which the immovable is located. Art. 491, supra.

(c) Buildings, other constructions permanently attached to the ground, and plantings made on the land of another without his consent, as by a good or bad faith possessor, belong to the owner of the ground. The person who made them may have a claim against the owner of the ground or against third persons in accordance with Articles 493 through 497, infra.

(d) Things incorporated in, or attached to an immovable so as to become its component parts under Articles 465 and 466 belong to the owner of the immovable. These things may not be owned separately from the ground. The former owner of these things may have a claim against the owner of the immovable or against third persons in accordance with Articles 493 through 497, infra.

(e) A possessor in good faith acquires the ownership of natural fruits he has gathered. Art 486, supra.

COMMENTS TO 1984 AMENDMENT

(a) The first paragraph of this article reproduces verbatim the first paragraph of Article 493 as revised in 1979. It does not change the law.

(b) The second paragraph of this article is new. In Article 493 as adopted in 1979 there was no express provision of law that determined the rights and obligations of the owner of the improvements and the rights and obligations of the owner of the ground when their legal relationship terminated. The added paragraph fills that gap. This paragraph may apply when a lease expires, when a predial or personal servitude is extinguished, or when a precarious possessor is given notice to vacate.

(c) This article applies in the absence of other provisions of law or juridical acts. When the parties are spouses, the special provisions of Civil Code Articles 2366, 2367, and 2367.1 (Rev.1984) control, as stated in the third paragraph of this article.

(d) This article does not apply to cases of encroachment on neighboring property. Such cases are governed by Civil Code Article 670 (Rev.1977).

Art. 493.1. Ownership of component parts

Things incorporated in or attached to an immovable so as to become its component parts under Articles 465 and 466 belong to the owner of the immovable.

Added by Acts 1984, No. 933, § 1.

COMMENT

This provision redesignates the former second paragraph of Civil Code Article 493 (Rev.1979) as a new article. It does not change the law.

Art. 493.2.   Loss of ownership by accession; claims of former owner

One who has lost the ownership of a thing to the owner of an immovable may have a claim against him or against a third person in accordance with the following provisions.

Added by Acts 1984, No. 933, § 1.

COMMENT

This provision redesignates the former third paragraph of Civil Code Article 493 (Rev.1979) as a new article. It does not change the law.

Art. 494.   Constructions by landowner with materials of another

When the owner of an immovable makes on it constructions, plantings, or works with materials of another, he may retain them, regardless of his good or bad faith, on reimbursing the owner of the materials their current value and repairing the injury that he may have caused to him.

Acts 1979, No. 180, § 1, eff. Jan. 1, 1980.

REVISION COMMENTS—1979

(a) This provision is based on Article 507 of the Louisiana Civil Code of 1870. It clarifies the law.

(b) Article 507 of the Louisiana Civil Code of 1870 derives from the 1825 revision. The redactors observed: "The owner of the soil who has made use of the materials of another, whether in good or bad faith, has the right to keep them; otherwise the buildings and other works in which they have been used must be destroyed, which is contrary to the public good; for this the owner of the soil is bound to indemnify the owner of the materials not only for the value of them, but for the loss and damage the latter may have sustained by the use of them." 1 Louisiana Legal Archives, Projet of the Civil Code of 1825, p. 47 (1937).

(c) Article 507 of the Louisiana Civil Code of 1870 has been seldom applied. The remedy it provided overlapped in part with that under the law of delictual obligations and of unjust enrichment. See Civil Code Arts. 1965, 2292, 2295–2299, 2301, 2311–2314 and 2315 (1870).

(d) Application of Article 507 of the Louisiana Civil Code of 1870 presupposes that the materials have been so incorporated into an immovable as to become its component parts. See Blackman, Artificial Accession to Immovables, 28 La.L.Rev. 584, 587 (1968).

Art. 495.   Things incorporated in, or attached to, an immovable with the consent of the owner of the immovable

One who incorporates in, or attaches to, the immovable of another, with his consent, things that become component parts of the immovable under Articles 465 and 466, may, in the absence of other provisions of law or juridical acts, remove them subject to his obligation of restoring the property to its former condition.

If he does not remove them after demand, the owner of the immovable may have them removed at the expense of the person who made them or elect to keep them and pay, at his option, the current value of the materials and of the workmanship or the enhanced value of the immovable.

Acts 1979, No. 180, § 1, eff. Jan. 1, 1980.

REVISION COMMENTS—1979

(a) This provision is new. It establishes the principle that, in the absence of other provisions of law or juridical act, a person making improvements on another's immovable, with his consent, may remove them subject to the obligation of restoring the property to its former condition. If he does not remove them after demand, the owner of the immovable may have them removed at the expense of the person who made them or elect to keep them and pay either the current value of the materials and the price of workmanship or the enhanced value of the immovable, whichever is less.

(b) When improvements are made by a lessee in accordance with the terms of the lease, the rights of the parties are determined by the contract or under the law of lease. Article 495 applies only in the absence of other provisions of law or juridical act. When improvements are made by a co-owner, another co-owner of the immovable property will owe only a proportionate part of the value of the improvements or of the enhanced value of the immovable property.

(c) This provision applies to things that become component parts of an immovable under Articles 465 and 466, supra. It does not apply to buildings, other constructions permanently attached to the ground, standing timber, and unharvested crops or ungathered fruits of trees, dealt with in Articles 491, supra. Buildings, other constructions permanently attached to the ground, standing timber, and unharvested crops or ungathered fruits of trees are not component parts of a tract of land when they belong to a person other than the owner of the ground. Separate ownership of these things may be asserted toward third persons when it is evidenced by an instrument filed for registry in the conveyance records of the parish in which the immovable is located.

Art. 496. Constructions by possessor in good faith

When constructions, plantings, or works are made by a possessor in good faith, the owner of the immovable may not demand their demolition and removal. He is bound to keep them and at his option to pay to the possessor either the cost of the materials and of the workmanship, or their current value, or the enhanced value of the immovable.

Acts 1979, No. 180, § 1, eff. Jan. 1, 1980.

REVISION COMMENTS—1979

(a) This provision is based on Article 508(4) of the Louisiana Civil Code of 1870. It clarifies the law.

(b) The Louisiana Civil Code of 1870 did not directly cover the situation of works made on the land of another with materials of a third person nor does this revision. In such a case, Articles 507 and 508 of the Louisiana Civil Code of 1870 applied cumulatively. In a like manner this situation is adequately covered by Articles 493 and 494 of this revision. See 1 Planiol, Civil Law Treatise 2722 (an English Translation by the Louisiana State Law Institute 1959). The landowner had his rights under Article 508, and the owner of the materials had his rights under Article 507 vis-a-vis the landowner and the third person. See Blackman, Artificial Accession to Immovables, 28 La.L.Rev. 584, 586 (1966). The same solutions are reached under this revision.

(c) This provision applies to buildings, other constructions permanently attached to the ground, standing timber, unharvested crops or ungathered fruits or trees, and things that become component parts of an immovable under Articles 465 and 466, supra. All improvements made by a possessor in good faith on another's immovable belong to the owner of the immovable. Arts. 490 and 493, supra.

Art. 497. Constructions by bad faith possessor

When constructions, plantings, or works are made by a bad faith possessor, the owner of the immovable may keep them or he may demand their demolition and removal at the expense of the possessor, and, in addition, damages for the injury that he may have sustained. If he does not demand demolition and removal, he is bound to pay at his option either the current value of the materials and of the workmanship of the separable improvements that he has kept or the enhanced value of the immovable.

Acts 1979, No. 180, § 1, eff. Jan. 1, 1980.

REVISION COMMENTS—1979

(a) This provision is new. It is based in part on Article 508 of the Louisiana Civil Code of 1870.

(b) Article 497 applies when a building is erected on, or moved to the land of another without his consent. In this case, the ownership of the building is extinguished but its former owner may have claims under this provision.

(c) According to Louisiana jurisprudence, separable improvements are those that do not become merged with the soil and remain distinguishable as individual works, such as houses, barns, carports, and the like. Inseparable improvements are those that become permanently merged with the soil and lose their identity as separate works, such as clearing, draining, filling in, digging irrigation ditches, building levees, reservoirs, or lakes, and the like. See Willenzik, The Possessor's Right to Compensation, 31 La.L.Rev. 491, 505 (1971). In effect, separable improvements are new constructions subject to accession, while inseparable improvements are useful expenditures. In Gibson v. Hutchins & Vaughn, 12 La.Ann. 545 (1857), the Louisiana Supreme Court held that a possessor in bad faith has no right to seek compensation for "ameliorations inseparable from the soil". This holding was apparently motivated by a desire to align the Louisiana jurisprudence on this subject with that of the common law states. Id. at 548. See also Heirs of Wood v. Nichols, 33 La.Ann. 744, 751 (1881). The Supreme Court apparently reasoned that it would be unnecessary to hold the owner to an election in cases in which inseparable improvements are involved. Hence, the court established a rule that prevents the bad faith possessor from claiming compensation for inseparable improvements. The landowner does not have to demand demolition and removal of the improvements in order to avoid payment of the value of the materials and of the price of workmanship; but if the landowner used them, he may not subsequently demand that they be removed at the expense of the bad faith possessor.

(d) Although the bad faith possessor may not claim compensation from the landowner for inseparable improvements, he may set-off the value of these improvements against any claim that the landowner may have against him for the return of fruits. See Voiers v. Atkins Bros., 113 La. 303, 36 So. 974 (1903).

(e) This provision applies to buildings, other constructions permanently attached to the ground, standing timber, unharvested crops or ungathered fruits of trees, and things that become component parts of an immovable under Articles 465 and 466, supra. All improvements made by a possessor in bad faith on another's immovable belong to the owner of the immovable. Arts. 490 and 493, supra.

Art. 498.   Claims against third persons

One who has lost the ownership of a thing to the owner of an immovable may assert against third persons his rights under Articles 493, 493.1, 494, 495, 496, or 497 when they are evidenced by an instrument filed for registry in the appropriate conveyance or mortgage records of the parish in which the immovable is located.

Act 1979, No. 180, § 1, eff. Jan. 1, 1980. Amended by Acts 1984, No. 933, § 1.

REVISION COMMENT—1979

(a) This provision is new. One who lost the ownership of a thing to the owner of an immovable may assert his rights for compensation against third persons if they are evidenced by an instrument filed for registry in the appropriate conveyance or mortgage records of the parish in which the immovable is located.

(b) When a movable is incorporated in, or permanently attached to, an immovable so as to become its component part under Articles 465 and 466, supra, the ownership of the immovable includes that of the movable. Art. 493, supra. This means that, by accession, the owner of the immovable acquires the ownership of the movable. One whose ownership of the movable is extinguished may have claims against the owner of the immovable under Articles 494–497, supra. These rights may also be asserted against third persons, such as purchasers of the immovable, if the former owner of the movable has taken care to file for registry in the appropriate conveyance or mortgage records of the parish in which the immovable is located an instrument evidencing his rights. Thus, one may lease or loan to the owner of an immovable various movables, such as appliances, machinery, or equipment. These may be so incorporated in, or attached to the immovable as to be regarded as its component parts. Likewise, a predial lessee may incorporate into the immovable he has leased, or attached to it, certain machinery, equipment or appliances so as to become component parts of the immovable. The lessee may assert his rights against a transferee of the immovable if he has filed for registry an instrument in the conveyance records of the parish in which the immovable is located.

(c) Under Articles 3227 and 3229 of the Louisiana Civil Code of 1870, the vendor of movables may assert his privilege and right of dissolution, without recordation, as long as the thing sold remains in the possession of the purchaser. The rights of the vendor are extinguished when the movables sold are transferred to a third person. Article 498 does not change the law in this respect. If change is desirable, Articles 3227 and 3229 of the Civil Code should be amended to provide that a vendor of movables may preserve his privilege and right of dissolution in case of transfer or encumbrances of the movables he has sold by filing for registry an instrument in accordance with Article 498.

(d) A movable subject to a chattel mortgage which, under Articles 463, 465, and 466 (1978), might be regarded as a component part of an immovable, "shall remain movable, insofar as the mortgage upon it is concerned, and shall not pass by the sale of the immovable property to which it has been actually or fictitiously attached, whether such sale be conventional or judicial." R.S. 9:5357. Accordingly, the chattel mortgagee will not lose his interest in case of sale or encumbrance of the immovable on which the mortgaged movable is located. In such a case, registration is controlled by R.S. 9:5353.

(e) The transfer or encumbrance of an immovable includes its component parts. In the absence of a recorded instrument, the third person's or good faith possessor's rights in constructions, plantings, or works that he may have made on the land of another are lost in case of alienation of the land. See Prevot v. Courtney, 241 La. 313, 129 So.2d 211 (1961); Westwego Canal & Terminal Co. v. Pizanie, 174 La. 1068, 142 So. 691 (1932); Davis-Wood Lumber Co. v. Insurance Co., 154 So. 760 (La.App. 1st Cir. 1934); Vaughn v. Kemp, 4 La.App. 682 (2d Cir. 1926); but cf. Gregory v. Kedley, 185 So. 105 (La.App. 2d Cir. 1938). In such a case, the third person is relegated to a personal action for reimbursement from the former landowner. See Police Jury v. McDonogh, 10 La.Ann. 395 (1855); Harrison v. Faulk, 2 La. 92, 94 (1930). In order to protect his interest against any owner of the land, a person who constructs improvements should record "his title to these improvements". The Work of the Louisiana Supreme Court for the 1960–1961 Term—Civil Law Property, 22 La.L.Rev. 310, 311 (1962).

Art. 499.   Alluvion and dereliction

Accretion formed successively and imperceptibly on the bank of a river or stream, whether navigable or not, is called alluvion. The alluvion belongs to the owner of the bank, who is bound to leave public that portion of the bank which is required for the public use.

The same rule applies to dereliction formed by water receding imperceptibly from a bank of a river or stream. The owner of the land situated at the edge of the bank left dry owns the dereliction.

Acts 1979, No. 180, § 1, eff. Jan. 1, 1980.

REVISION COMMENTS—1979

(a) The first paragraph of this provision reproduces the substance of Article 509 of the Louisiana Civil Code of 1870. It does not change the law.

(b) The second paragraph of this provision reproduces the substance of the first paragraph of Article 510 of the Louisiana Civil Code of 1870, as interpreted by Louisiana jurisprudence. It does not change the law.

Art. 500.   Shore of the sea or of a lake

There is no right to alluvion or dereliction on the shore of the sea or of lakes.

Acts 1979, No. 180, § 1, eff. Jan. 1, 1980.

REVISION COMMENT—1979

This provision reproduces the substance of the last paragraph of Article 510 of the Louisiana Civil Code of 1870 as interpreted by Louisiana jurisprudence. It does not change the law.

Art. 501.   Division of alluvion

Alluvion formed in front of the property of several owners is divided equitably, taking into account the extent of the front of each property prior to the formation of the alluvion in issue. Each owner is entitled to a fair proportion of the area of the alluvion and a fair proportion of the new frontage on the river, depending on the relative values of the frontage and the acreage.

Acts 1979, No. 180, § 1, eff. Jan. 1, 1980.

REVISION COMMENTS—1979

(a) This provision is based on Article 516 of the Louisiana Civil Code, as interpreted by Louisiana jurisprudence.

(b) See Jones v. Hogue, 241 La. 407, 129 So.2d 194 (1960): "When alluvion formed in front of the estates of riparian owners is to be divided, two objects, insofar as possible, are to be attained: (1) Each owner shall receive a fair proportion of the area of the alluvion, and (2) Each should receive a fair proportion of the new frontage on the water."

Art. 502.   Sudden action of waters

If a sudden action of the waters of a river or stream carries away an identifiable piece of ground and unites it with other lands on the same or on the opposite bank, the ownership of the piece of ground so carried away is not lost. The owner may claim it within a year, or even later, if the owner of the bank with which it is united has not taken possession.

Acts 1979, No. 180, § 1, eff. Jan. 1, 1980.

REVISION COMMENT—1979

This provision reproduces the substance of Article 511 of the Louisiana Civil Code of 1870. It does not change the law.

Art. 503.   Island formed by river opening a new channel

When a river or stream, whether navigable or not, opens a new channel and surrounds riparian land making it an island, the ownership of that land is not affected.

Acts 1979, No. 180, § 1, eff. Jan. 1, 1980.

REVISION COMMENT—1979

This provision reproduces the substance of Article 517 of the Louisiana Civil Code of 1870. It does not change the law.

Art. 504.   Ownership of abandoned bed when river changes course

When a navigable river or stream abandons its bed and opens a new one, the owners of the land on which the new bed is located shall take by way of indemnification the abandoned bed, each in proportion to the quantity of land that he lost.

If the river returns to the old bed, each shall take his former land.

Acts 1979, No. 180, § 1, eff. Jan. 1, 1980.

REVISION COMMENT—1979

This provision reproduces the substance of Article 518 of the Louisiana Civil Code of 1870. It does not change the law.

Art. 505.   Islands and sandbars in navigable rivers

Islands, and sandbars that are not attached to a bank, formed in the beds of navigable rivers or streams, belong to the state.

Acts 1979, No. 180, § 1, eff. Jan. 1, 1980.

133

(a) This provision reproduces the substance of Article 512 of the Louisiana Civil Code of 1870. It does not change the law.

(b) The words "if there be no adverse title or prescription" in the source provision have not been reproduced. There cannot be adverse title to the bed of a navigable river, at least since 1921, and prescription does not run against the state.

Art. 506.   Ownership of beds of nonnavigable rivers or streams

In the absence of title or prescription, the beds of nonnavigable rivers or streams belong to the riparian owners along a line drawn in the middle of the bed.

Acts 1979, No. 180, § 1, eff. Jan. 1, 1980.

(a) This provision is new. It is based in part on Articles 513, 514 and 515 of the Louisiana Civil Code of 1870, as interpreted by Louisiana jurisprudence. It clarifies the law.

(b) According to well-settled Louisiana jurisprudence, the beds of nonnavigable rivers or streams, if not owned by anyone by virtue of title or acquisitive prescription, belong to the riparian owners. Wemple v. Eastham, 150 La. 247, 90 So. 637 (1922). Normally, each owner should take the portion of the bed between lines drawn from the extreme points of his estate in front of the river to the nearest points of the line defining the middle of the bed.

(c) Nonnavigable lakes are private things. Accordingly, they may belong to the state, a political subdivision, or a private person. Thus, swamp lands may belong to the state under grant from the United States as property of the private domain. See, e.g., Act of March 2, 1849, c. 87, 9 Stat. 352; Act of Sept. 28, 1850, c. 84, 9 Stat. 519; La.Acts 1862, No. 124.

(d) Several Louisiana decisions declare that the beds of nonnavigable waterbodies belong to the riparian landowners. See e.g., Burns v. Crescent Gun & Rod Club, 116 La. 1038, 41 So. 249 (1906); Wemple v. Eastham, 150 La. 247, 90 So. 637 (1922). These decisions actually dealt with rivers or streams. See Comment, Navigability as Applied to Lakes in Louisiana, 6 La.L.Rev. 698, 703 (1946). In R.D. Fornea v. Fornea, 324 So.2d 619 (La.App. 1st Cir.1976), writ refused, 326 So.2d 374 (La.1976), the court found that the description of the title of one of the parties included the nonnavigable lake in question. The court held that the other party's ownership extended only to the edge of the water: "Unless a clear intention to the contrary is expressed in the act of conveyance, the waterline will be regarded as the boundary where meandered water is present." See also State v. Aucoin, 206 La. 786, 20 So.2d 136 (1944). Nonnavigable lakes are subject to the law governing dry lands. Consequently, there are no riparian rights to the beds of nonnavigable lakes. See McDade v. Caplis, 154 La. 1019, 98 So. 625 (1924); Bank of Coushatta v. Yarborough, 139 La. 510, 71 So. 784 (1916); McDade v. Bossier Levee Board, 109 La. 625, 33 So. 628 (1902); R.D. Fornea, Inc. v. Fornea, supra.

SECTION 3—ACCESSION IN RELATION TO MOVABLES

Art. 507.   Accession as between movables

In the absence of other provisions of law or contract, the consequences of accession as between movables are determined according to the following rules.

Acts 1979, No. 180, § 1, eff. Jan. 1, 1980.

(a) This provision reproduces the substance of Article 520 of the Louisiana Civil Code of 1870.

(b) The source of this provision is the text of Toullier. See 2 Toullier, Droit civil français 32 (1833). There is no comment in the projet of the Louisiana Civil Code of 1825.

Art. 508.   Things principal and accessory

Things are divided into principal and accessory. For purposes of accession as between movables, an accessory is a corporeal movable that serves the use, ornament, or complement of the principal thing.

In the case of a principal thing consisting of a movable construction permanently attached to the ground, its accessories include things that would constitute its component parts under Article 466 if the construction were immovable.

Acts 1979, No. 180, § 1, eff. Jan. 1, 1980. Amended by Acts 2008, No. 632, § 1, eff. July 1, 2008.

REVISION COMMENTS—1979

(a) This provision reproduces the substance of Article 522 of the Louisiana Civil Code of 1870. It does not change the law.

(b) The second and third paragraphs of Article 522 of the Louisiana Civil Code of 1870 have not been reproduced because they contain unnecessary illustrations.

(c) Article 522 of the Louisiana Civil Code of 1870 derives from the 1825 revision. Its source is the text of Toullier. See 2 Toullier, Droit civil français 32 (1833).

(d) The words "or completion of the other" in Article 522 of the Louisiana Civil Code of 1870 ought to be translated "or complement of the other." The French word is complément.

REVISION COMMENTS—2008

A construction permanently attached to the ground, other than a building, is movable when it does not belong to the owner of the ground, even though the identical construction would be classified as immovable if it belonged to the owner of the ground. See C.C. Arts. 463 and 475 (Rev. 1978); A. N. Yiannopoulos, Property § 141, 2 La. Civil Law Treatise (4th Ed. 2001). In order to avoid an incongruity that would exist if different rules of accession were applied to such constructions depending upon the fortuity of whether or not they belong to the owner of the ground, the second paragraph of this Article adopts the principles of component parts set forth in C.C. Art. 466 (Rev. 2008), which is directly applicable only to buildings and other constructions classified as immovables. In the case of a principal thing consisting of a construction that is owned separately from the ground and is therefore movable, things that would be characterized under Civil Code Article 466 (Rev. 2008) as its component parts, if the construction were immovable, constitute its accessories under this Article.

Art. 509.   Value or bulk as a basis to determine principal thing

In case of doubt as to which is a principal thing and which is an accessory, the most valuable, or the most bulky if value is nearly equal, shall be deemed to be principal.

Acts 1979, No. 180, § 1, eff. Jan. 1, 1980.

REVISION COMMENTS—1979

(a) This provision reproduces the substance of Article 524 of the Louisiana Civil Code of 1870.

(b) Article 524 of the Louisiana Civil Code of 1870 derives from the 1825 revision. Its source is the text of Toullier. See 2 Toullier, Droit civil français 32 (1833). There is no comment in the 1823 projet.

Art. 510.   Union of a principal and an accessory thing

When two corporeal movables are united to form a whole, and one of them is an accessory of the other, the whole belongs to the owner of the principal thing. The owner of the principal thing is bound to reimburse the owner of the accessory its value. The owner of the accessory may demand that it be separated and returned to him, although the separation may cause some injury to the principal thing, if the accessory is more valuable than the principal and has been used without his knowledge.

Acts 1979, No. 180, § 1, eff. Jan. 1, 1980.

(a) This provision reproduces the substance of Articles 521 and 523 of the Louisiana Civil Code of 1870. It does not change the law.

(b) Articles 521 and 523 of the Louisiana Civil Code of 1870 derive from the 1825 revision. Their source is the text of Toullier. See 2 Toullier, Droit civil français 32 (1833). There are no comments in the 1823 projet.

Art. 511.   Ownership of new thing made with materials of another

When one uses materials of another to make a new thing, the thing belongs to the owner of the materials, regardless of whether they may be given their earlier form. The owner is bound to reimburse the value of the workmanship.

Nevertheless, when the value of the workmanship substantially exceeds that of the materials, the thing belongs to him who made it. In this case, he is bound to reimburse the owner of the materials their value.

Acts 1979, No. 180, § 1, eff. Jan. 1, 1980.

(a) This provision reproduces the substance of Articles 525 and 526 of the Louisiana Civil Code of 1870.

(b) Articles 525 and 526 of the Louisiana Civil Code of 1870 derive from the 1825 revision. Their source is the text of Toullier. See 2 Toullier, Droit civil français 33 (1833). There is no comment in the 1823 projet.

Art. 512.   Effect of bad faith

If the person who made the new thing was in bad faith, the court may award its ownership to the owner of the materials.

Acts 1979, No. 180, § 1, eff. Jan. 1, 1980.

This provision is new. It is based on Article 1062 of the Greek Civil Code.

Art. 513.   Use of materials of two owners; separation or co-ownership

When one used partly his own materials and partly the materials of another to make a new thing, unless the materials can be conveniently separated, the thing belongs to the owners of the materials in indivision. The share of one is determined in proportion to the value of his materials and of the other in proportion to the value of his materials and workmanship.

Acts 1979, No. 180, § 1, eff. Jan. 1, 1980.

(a) This provision reproduces the substance of Article 527 of the Louisiana Civil Code of 1870. It does not change the law.

(b) Article 527 of the Louisiana Civil Code of 1870 derives from the 1825 revision. Its source is the text of Toullier. See 2 Toullier, Droit civil français 33 (1833). There is no comment in the 1823 projet.

Art. 514.   Mixture of materials

When a new thing is formed by the mixture of materials of different owners, and none of them may be considered as principal, an owner who has not consented to the mixture may demand separation if it can be conveniently made.

If separation cannot be conveniently made, the thing resulting from the mixture belongs to the owners of the materials in indivision. The share of each is determined in proportion to the value of his materials.

One whose materials are far superior in value in comparison with those of any one of the others, may claim the thing resulting from the mixture. He is then bound to reimburse the others the value of their materials.

Acts 1979, No. 180, § 1, eff. Jan. 1, 1980.

REVISION COMMENTS—1979

(a) This provision reproduces the substance of Articles 528 and 529 of the Louisiana Civil Code of 1870.

(b) Articles 528 and 529 of the Louisiana Civil Code of 1870 derive from the 1825 revision. Their source is the text of Toullier. See 2 Toullier, Droit civil français 33 (1833). There is no comment in the 1823 projet.

Art. 515. Recovery of materials or value in lieu of ownership

When an owner of materials that have been used without his knowledge for the making of a new thing acquires the ownership of that thing, he may demand that, in lieu of the ownership of the new thing, materials of the same species, quantity, weight, measure and quality or their value be delivered to him.

Acts 1979, No. 180, § 1, eff. Jan. 1, 1980.

REVISION COMMENT—1979

This provision reproduces the substance of Article 531 of the Louisiana Civil Code of 1870.

Art. 516. Liability for unauthorized use of a movable

One who uses a movable of another, without his knowledge, for the making of a new thing may be liable for the payment of damages.

Acts 1979, No. 180, § 1, eff. Jan. 1, 1980.

REVISION COMMENT—1979

This provision is new. It is based on Article 532 of the Louisiana Civil Code of 1870.

CHAPTER 3—TRANSFER OF OWNERSHIP BY AGREEMENT

Art. 517. Voluntary transfer of ownership of an immovable

The ownership of an immovable is voluntarily transferred by a contract between the owner and the transferee that purports to transfer the ownership of the immovable. The transfer of ownership takes place between the parties by the effect of the agreement and is not effective against third persons until the contract is filed for registry in the conveyance records of the parish in which the immovable is located.

Acts 1979, No. 180, § 1, eff. Jan. 1, 1980. Amended by Acts 2005, No. 169, § 2, eff. July 1, 2006.

REVISION COMMENTS—1979

(a) This provision is new. It does not change the law.

(b) Immovable property may only be alienated by the owner or by persons authorized by him or by law. Article 2015 of the Louisiana Civil Code of 1870 establishes the fundamental principle that "no one can transfer a greater right than he himself has", and Article 2452 of the same Code declares that "the sale of a thing belonging to another person is null." The owner need not act in person. He may be represented by an agent, mandatory, or other person authorized to act on his behalf. A tutor or a curator of an incompetent owner may dispose of his property in accordance with the formalities and procedures established in the Louisiana Code of Civil Procedure. See C.C.P. Arts. 4301–4342 and

4554. Likewise, the transferee need not act in person. As a matter of fact, the transferee may be the beneficiary of a stipulation pour autrui. See C.C. Art. 1890.

(c) The ownership of an immovable is transferred by a contract that "purports to transfer the ownership of the property." See C.C. Art. 1919. Such a contract is often designated in Louisiana doctrine and jurisprudence as an "act translative of ownership." Examples of acts translative of ownership are sales, donations, or exchanges of property. See C.C. Art. 3485. A unilateral juridical act, such as an acknowledgement that a particular person is the true owner of an immovable, does not suffice to convey ownership. See C.C. Arts. 870 and 1919.

(d) According to Article 1920 of the Louisiana Civil Code of 1870, the contract must "be clothed with the formalities required by law". Article 2275 of the same Code requires that every transfer of immovable property "must be in writing"; however, the same article recognizes the validity of a verbal alienation, provided that the transferor "confesses it when interrogated on oath" and that "actual delivery has been made of the immovable property."

Art. 518.   Voluntary transfer of the ownership of a movable

The ownership of a movable is voluntarily transferred by a contract between the owner and the transferee that purports to transfer the ownership of the movable. Unless otherwise provided, the transfer of ownership takes place as between the parties by the effect of the agreement and against third persons when the possession of the movable is delivered to the transferee.

When possession has not been delivered, a subsequent transferee to whom possession is delivered acquires ownership provided he is in good faith. Creditors of the transferor may seize the movable while it is still in his possession.

Acts 1979, No. 180, § 1, eff. Jan. 1, 1980. Amended by Acts 1984, No. 331, § 2, eff. Jan. 1, 1985.

REVISION COMMENTS—1979

(a) This provision is new. It does not change the law.

(b) The phrase "when the possession of the movable is delivered" contemplates both actual delivery (C.C. Arts. 1539 and 2477) and constructive delivery (C.C. Art. 2478) as well as the point in time and place in which the seller performs his obligation to deliver (cf. U.C.C. Sec. 2–401(2)).

(c) According to Article 2456 of the Louisiana Civil Code of 1870, the ownership of movable property is transferred upon the consent of the parties, and according to Article 2467 of the same Code, the risk of loss is transferred to the buyer at that time. Thus, in Louisiana, the risk is placed on the buyer at an earlier point in time than under the U.C.C. However, under the U.C.C. the buyer maintains a superior rank over the seller's unsecured creditors. (U.C.C. Secs. 2–402, 502 and 716), while under the Louisiana Civil Code the creditors of the seller are preferred over the buyer until the movable property is deemed to have been delivered to the buyer. C.C. Arts. 1923, 2477 and 2478.

(d) For pertinent provisions of modern civil codes, see Greek Civil Code Article 1034: "The ownership of a movable is transferred by delivery of its possession by the owner to the transferee and agreement between them that the ownership of the movable is transferred." B.G.B. Sec. 929: "(Agreement and delivery) For the transfer of ownership of a movable thing, it is necessary that the owner of the thing deliver it to the acquirer and that both agree that the ownership be transferred. If the acquirer is in possession of the thing, the agreement on the transfer of ownership is sufficient."

(e) Article 518 reiterates the fundamental principle that a movable may be alienated only by the owner or by persons authorized by him or by law. See Comment (b) under Article 517, supra. For an exceptional provision authorizing the usufructuary to dispose of movables, see C.C. Arts. 568 and 600 (1976).

COMMENTS—1984 AMENDMENT

(f) Article 518, as amended by Acts 1984, No. 331, incorporates the principles contained in C.C. Arts. 1922 and 1923 (1870). For that reason, those Articles are repealed though without intending any change in the law. Thus, under the second paragraph of Article 518, as amended by Acts 1984, No. 331, the owner of a movable thing who remains in possession after selling it may transfer ownership of the movable to a second vendee in good faith, that is without knowledge of the first sale, if the movable is delivered to that second vendee. By the same token, creditors of the vendor of a

138

movable thing may seize it while still in the possession of the vendor. See Primeaux v. Hinds, 350 So.2d 1310 (La.App.3rd Cir.1977).

Art. 519.   Transfer of action for recovery of movable

When a movable is in the possession of a third person, the assignment of the action for the recovery of that movable suffices for the transfer of its ownership.

Acts 1979, No. 180, § 1, eff. Jan. 1, 1980.

REVISION COMMENTS—1979

(a) This provision is based on Article 2642 of the Louisiana Civil Code of 1870. It also expresses a rule that is implicit in other articles of the same Code. There are corresponding provisions in modern civil codes. See Greek Civil Code Art. 1035 and German Civil Code Sec. 931.

(b) Article 2482 of the Louisiana Civil Code declares: "When the object sold is out of the vendor's possession, he must redeem it at his cost, and deliver it to the buyer, unless it be differently agreed between the parties, or unless it evidently appears from the contract, that the buyer himself has undertaken to reclaim it." This provision is not affected. Article 519 contemplates an express assignment of the action for the recovery of a movable.

(c) Article 2642 of the Louisiana Civil Code of 1870 declares: "In the transfer of, rights or claims to a third person, the delivery takes place between the transferor and the transferee by giving of the title." Article 2643 of the same Code declares: "The transferee is only possessed, as it regards third persons, after notice has been given to the debtor of the transfer having taken place. The transferee may nevertheless become possessed by the acceptance of the transfer by the debtor in an authentic act." These provisions are not affected. The delivery of title to a movable constitutes assignment of the action for the recovery of the movable. The assignment of the action is effective toward third persons if notice has been given to them; but if the assignment is made by authentic act, notice is dispensed with.

Art. 520.   [Blank]

Art. 521.   Lost or stolen thing

One who has possession of a lost or stolen thing may not transfer its ownership to another. For purposes of this Chapter, a thing is stolen when one has taken possession of it without the consent of its owner. A thing is not stolen when the owner delivers it or transfers its ownership to another as a result of fraud.

Acts 1979, No. 180, § 1, eff. Jan. 1, 1980.

REVISION COMMENTS—1979

(a) This provision is new. It establishes an exception to Article 520, supra.

(b) In continental legal systems, theft is narrowly defined to mean misappropriation or taking of a corporeal movable, without the consent of its owner, by one who intends to make it his own. 2 Aubry et Rau, Droit civil français, § 183 at 113 (Translation by the Louisiana State Law Institute 1966). This is the same as larceny in common law jurisdictions. Thus, a thing is not stolen if the owner delivers possession to another as a result of fraud or artifice. In common law terms, theft does not include embezzlement. Under the Louisiana Criminal Code, however, theft is broadly defined by R.S. 14:67, to include taking without the consent of the owner of a movable or by fraudulent means. For civil law purposes, and particularly for the purpose of Article 521, the definition of theft is much more limited. Louisiana jurisprudence is in accord with this narrow definition of theft. Jeffrey Motor Co. v. Higgins, 230 La. 857, 89 So.2d 369 (1956): "La.R.S. 14:67 is part of the substantive criminal law of Louisiana, and the broad definition of theft for the purposes of criminal prosecution does not alter the provisions of the Civil Code of Louisiana and other statutes relating to sales and transfer of title."

(c) The U.C.C. Sec. 2–403(d) is in accord with this article. It protects the bona fide purchaser even though "the delivery was procured through fraud punishable as larcenous under the criminal law" (emphasis added). However, one who purchases from a thief with no title at all is not protected against the true owner. 7 Litvinoff, Louisiana Civil Law Treatise, Sec. 112 at 342 (1975).

(d) Payment by a check that was subsequently dishonored was originally regarded as theft. See Packard Florida Motors Co. v. Malone, 208 La. 1058, 24 So.2d 75, 77 (1945). Thus, the transferee did not acquire ownership and could not convey it to another person. Subsequent decisions, however, treated a sale based on a dishonored check as a credit sale. As a result, the transferee acquired ownership that he could further convey to third persons. See Jeffrey Motors Co. v. Higgins, 230 La. 857, 89 So.2d 369 (1956); Flatte v. Nichols, 233 La. 171, 96 So.2d 477 (1957).

Art. 522. Transfer of ownership by owner under annullable title

A transferee of a corporeal movable in good faith and for fair value retains the ownership of the thing even though the title of the transferor is annulled on account of a vice of consent.

Acts 1979, No. 180, § 1, eff. Jan. 1, 1980.

REVISION COMMENTS—1979

(a) This provision is new. It is based on Louisiana jurisprudence. It accords with solutions reached in France and under the Uniform Commercial Code.

(b) A person having a corporeal movable under an annullable title may validly transfer ownership to an acquirer in good faith. Even if the title of the transferor is annulled, the owner may not revendicate the thing in the hands of the good faith acquirer. See Yiannopoulos, Civil Law Property, § 125 (1966).

(c) In the absence of rules in the Louisiana Civil Code of 1870 dealing with the consequences of the annulment of the title of an acquirer of a movable, Louisiana courts have, at times, accorded protection to a good faith purchaser for value. Under this line of jurisprudence, an owner who transfers the ownership of a corporeal movable to a fraudulent transferee may not recover it in the hands of a subsequent acquirer of good faith who paid fair value. See Flatte v. Nichols, 233 La. 171, 96 So.2d 477 (1957); Thomas v. Mead, 8 Mart. (N.S.) 341 (La.1829) (fraud); Franklin, Security of Acquisition and Translation; La Possession Vaut Titre and Bona Fide Purchasers, 6 Tul.L.Rev. 589 (1952). The rule is based on the equitable principle that "where two innocent parties must suffer loss through the fraud of another the burden of such loss is imposed upon the one who most contributed thereto." Trumbull Chevrolet Sales Co. v. Maxwell, 142 So.2d 805, 806 (La.App.2d Cir. 1962) (dishonored check). See also Comment, Sale of Another's Movables 29 La.L.Rev. 329, 360 (1969).

(d) Article 522 accords with Sec. 2–403(1) of the Uniform Commercial Code. It would seem, however, that under the U.C.C. a person with a voidable title may transfer good title to persons of good faith only. Under Louisiana law, an owner under an annullable title may validly transfer ownership to another, whether in good or in bad faith. But if the title of the transferor is annulled, the owner may recover the movable in the hands of subsequent transferees. Such recovery is excluded under Article 522 only against an acquirer of good faith for fair value.

(e) Payment by a check that was subsequently dishonored was originally regarded as theft. See Packard Florida Motors Co. v. Malone, 208 La. 1058, 24 So.2d 75, 77 (1945). Thus, the transferee did not acquire ownership and could not convey it to another person. Subsequent decisions, however, treated a sale based on a dishonored check as a credit sale. As a result, the transferee acquired ownership that he could further convey to third persons. See Jeffrey Motors Co. v. Higgins, 230 La. 857, 89 So.2d 369 (1956); Flatte v. Nichols, 233 La. 171, 96 So.2d 477 (1957).

(f) Under Article 522, a good faith acquirer of a corporeal movable for value from one having a title vitiated by fraud is protected even if the original owner is not charged with negligence in the pursuit of his affairs.

Art. 523. Good faith; definition

An acquirer of a corporeal movable is in good faith for purposes of this Chapter unless he knows, or should have known, that the transferor was not the owner.

Acts 1979, No. 180, § 1, eff. Jan. 1, 1980.

REVISION COMMENTS—1979

(a) This provision is new. It is based in part on Article 1037 of the Greek Civil Code and Sec. 932(2) of the German Civil Code.

(b) A transferee is in good faith when he ignores, without fault on his part, that the transferor is not the owner of the movable. If the acquirer has notice of facts that would put a reasonably prudent man on inquiry, he is under duty to investigate with the view to ascertaining the true situation. If he does not do so, he cannot claim that he is a purchaser in good faith. See William Frantz & Co. v. Fink, 125 La. 1014, 52 So. 131 (1910).

Art. 524.   Recovery of lost or stolen things

The owner of a lost or stolen movable may recover it from a possessor who bought it in good faith at a public auction or from a merchant customarily selling similar things on reimbursing the purchase price.

The former owner of a lost, stolen, or abandoned movable that has been sold by authority of law may not recover it from the purchaser.

Acts 1979, No. 180, § 1, eff. Jan. 1, 1980.

REVISION COMMENTS—1979

(a) This provision reproduces the substance of Articles 3507 and 3508 of the Louisiana Civil Code of 1870. It overrules Louisiana jurisprudence interpreting Article 3507 in combination with Article 3506 of the Civil Code.

(b) In Securities Sales Co. v. Blackwell, 167 La. 667, 120 So. 45 (1928), the Louisiana Supreme Court decided that Articles 3506 and 3507 mean that "if a person possesses a movable, as owner, in good faith and by a just title, for three consecutive years without interruption, he acquires the ownership of it by prescription, unless the thing was stolen or lost, in which event he does not acquire the ownership by possessing as owner, under a just title, and in good faith, for three years. But, if the person who should so possess a thing which was stolen or lost acquired the thing at public auction or from one in the habit of selling such things, the law will not permit him to acquire the ownership by three years prescription, notwithstanding his possession for three years, under the circumstances stated, nevertheless it will require the owner, after the lapse of that time, to pay to the possessor of the thing the price that the possessor paid for it, before the owner may require the possessor to return the thing. To hold otherwise would make it more burdensome for the owner to recover a thing, before the required three years had elapsed, that had been lost or stolen, than one which had not been." This interpretation was necessary because the redactors of the Louisiana Civil Codes of 1808, 1825 and 1870 omitted a provision corresponding with Article 2279 of the French Civil Code. In this revision, a possessor may transfer the ownership of a corporeal movable to a good faith acquirer for value, unless the thing was lost or stolen. The transferee of a lost or stolen thing, whether in good or in bad faith acquires ownership by ten years prescription. C.C. Arts. 3506 and 3509. The owner of a lost or stolen thing may recover it in the hands of a good faith transferee for value prior to the accrual of the ten years prescription without any reimbursement; but if the transferee bought the thing at a public auction or from a person customarily selling similar things the owner must restore to him the purchase price.

(c) This provision applies to things lost, stolen, or abandoned. See Thompson v. Cullinane, 22 La.Ann. 586 (1870).

Art. 525.   Registered movables

The provisions of this Chapter do not apply to movables that are required by law to be registered in public records.

Acts 1979, No. 180, § 1, eff. Jan. 1, 1980.

REVISION COMMENTS—1979

(a) This provision is new. It is based in part on Articles 1156 and 1157 of the Italian Civil Code.

(b) Louisiana jurisprudence is not conclusive as to the law governing registered movables. The Vehicle Certificate of Title Law, R.S. 32:706, declares: "On and after December 15, 1950, except as provided in R.S. 32:705 and 32:712 no person buying a vehicle from the owner thereof, whether the owner be a dealer or otherwise, hereafter shall acquire a marketable title in or to said vehicle until the purchaser shall have obtained a certificate of title to said vehicle." Nevertheless, Louisiana courts have accorded protection to a good faith acquirer of a vehicle despite noncompliance with the provisions of the Vehicle Certificate of Title Law. See, e.g., Flatte v. Nichols, 233 La. 171, 96 So.2d 477 (1957); Tarver v. Tarver, 242 So.2d 374 (La.App.2d Cir. 1970); Shanks v. Callahan, 232 So.2d 306 (La.App.1st Cir. 1969); Yiannopoulos, Civil Law Property, Sec. 145 at 441 (1966). In Robinson v. Jackson, 255 So.2d 846, 848 (La.App.2d Cir. 1971), writ refused, 260 La. 700, 257 So.2d 155, the court declared that R.S. 32:701 et seq. provide "a method of registry of title to motor vehicles, but do not alter the basic provisions of La.C.C. Art. 2456, nor do they provide an exclusive manner of transferring ownership." Nevertheless, the court found that the intervenor was not the owner of the automobile that he had claimed.

(c) For the transfer of negotiable instruments, see Louisiana Commercial Law, R.S. 10:1–101.

CHAPTER 4—PROTECTION OF OWNERSHIP

Art. 526.   Recognition of ownership; recovery of the thing

The owner of a thing is entitled to recover it from anyone who possesses or detains it without right and to obtain judgment recognizing his ownership and ordering delivery of the thing to him.

Acts 1979, No. 180, § 1, eff. Jan. 1, 1980.

REVISION COMMENTS—1979

(a) This provision is new. It expresses a rule inherent in the Louisiana Civil Code of 1870 and partially expressed in the Louisiana Code of Civil Procedure and in Louisiana jurisprudence. It does not change the law.

(b) In all civil law systems, the owner of a thing may bring a revendicatory action (action en revendication) for the recognition of his ownership and for the recovery of the thing from anyone who possesses or detains it without right. 1 Planiol, Civil Law Treatise, Part 2, Sec. 2445 et seq.; Yiannopoulos, Civil Law Property Secs. 124, 125 and 126 (1968); See specifically, Greek Civil Code Arts. 1094, 1095 and B.G.B. Secs. 985 and 986.

In Louisiana, the revendicatory action for the recovery of immovable property is more specifically designated as petitory action and is governed by Articles 3651–3654 of the Louisiana Code of Civil Procedure. In addition, the owner of an immovable or of a movable may bring an action for declaratory judgment for the recognition of his ownership. See Code of Civil Procedure Articles 1871–1883. In Louisiana, the revendicatory action for the recovery of movables is an innominate real action. For Louisiana jurisprudence and doctrine, see Yiannopoulos, Civil Law Property Secs. 135 and 145 (1968); Bouchard v. Parker, 32 La.Ann. 535 (1880). The expressions revendication and action en revendication have been used in the French text of the Code of Practice of 1825. These expressions have been translated in the English texts of the two codes as "reclamation" and "action for the ownership" (or claim for restitution). See Civil Code Arts. 3453 and 3456 (1870). Cf. Code of Practice Art. 4 (1870).

(c) For the recovery of movables in kind, see Yiannopoulos, Civil Law Property Sec. 145 (1968). The plaintiff in the revendicatory action has the burden of proof of his ownership, and if he fails to carry this burden his claim is dismissed. The possessor of a corporeal movable is presumed to be its owner, though not if the thing is lost or stolen. Article 530, infra. The possessor may defend the action on the basis of any personal or real right he may have for the possession and enjoyment of the movable. He may thus claim that he is entitled to retain the movable by virtue of any contractual arrangement with the owner or by virtue of his right of usufruct or ownership of the movable. His right of ownership, in particular, may derive from a valid transfer by the owner or his agent, from acquisitive prescription, or from rules of law concerning accession. These defenses, based on the possessor's own right of ownership, may also be regarded as the consequence of the loss of the right of ownership by the original owner.

Art. 527.   Necessary expenses

The evicted possessor, whether in good or in bad faith, is entitled to recover from the owner compensation for necessary expenses incurred for the preservation of the thing and for the discharge of private or public burdens. He is not entitled to recover expenses for ordinary maintenance or repairs.

Acts 1979, No. 180, § 1, eff. Jan. 1, 1980.

REVISION COMMENTS—1979

(a) This provision is new. It is based in part on Article 2314 of the Louisiana Civil Code of 1870.

(b) According to Article 2314 of the Louisiana Civil Code of 1870, a possessor, whether in good or in bad faith, is entitled to reimbursement for necessary expenses, that is, expenses incurred for the preservation of the property. See Yiannopoulos, Civil Law Property Sec. 137 (1968); Comment, 31 La.L.Rev. 491 (1971). Recovery is based on the principle of unjust enrichment and is allowed to the full extent of the expenses incurred. See 2 Aubry et Rau, Droit civil français Sec. 219 (La.State Law Inst. Transl. 1966); 1 Planiol, Civil Law Treatise, Secs. 2456 and 2732 (La. State Law Inst. translation 1959). According to Louisiana decisions, the notion of necessary expenses includes property taxes and assessments, Dunlup v. Whitner, 157 La. 792, 69 So. 189 (1919); Gregory v. Kedley, 185 So. 105 (La.App.2nd Cir. 1938); indispensable repairs and maintenance costs, Nabors Oil and Gas Co. v. Louisiana Oil Ref. Co., 151 La. 361, 91 So. 765 (1922); Keller v. Thompson, 121 So.2d 575 (La.App.2d Cir. 1960); and insurance costs, Litton v. Litton, 36 La.Ann. 348 (1884). The costs of ordinary maintenance and repairs, however, are not necessary expenses. See Ferrier v. Mossler, 23 So.2d 341 (La.App.1st Cir. 1945); Brown v. Tauzin, 185 La. 86, 168 So. 502 (1936); Citizens' Bank of Louisiana v. Miller, 44 La.Ann. 199, 10 So. 779 (1892); Johnson v. Mattle, 6 Orl.App. 218 (1909).

(c) The rights and obligations of the possessor and of the owner with respect to constructions made by the possessor are governed by Articles 492–497, this Revision.

Art. 528.   Useful expenses

An evicted possessor in good faith is entitled to recover from the owner his useful expenses to the extent that they have enhanced the value of the thing.

Acts 1979, No. 180, § 1, eff. Jan. 1, 1980.

REVISION COMMENTS—1979

(a) This provision is new. It is based in part on Article 2314 of the Louisiana Civil Code of 1870.

(b) Useful expenses are those that, though not needed for the preservation of the property, result in enhancement of its value. See Civil Code Art. 1259 (1870). According to the French text of Article 2292 of the Louisiana Civil Code of 1825, a possessor in good faith is entitled to reimbursement of his useful expenses. However, the English text of the same article, same as Article 2314 of the Louisiana Civil Code of 1870, does not mention recovery for useful expenses because of an error in translation. See Compiled Edition of the Civil Codes of Louisiana, Art. 2314, in Volume 17 of West's LSA-Civil Code (Dainow ed. 1972). Despite the mistranslation, Louisiana Courts have allowed good faith possessors to recover their useful expenses by an expansive interpretation of Article 508 of the Louisiana Civil Code of 1870. See Pearce v. Frantum, 16 La. 414 (1840); Beard v. Morancy, 2 La.Ann. 347 (1847). Other courts have reached the same result by application of Article 3453 of the Louisiana Civil Code of 1870. See Yiannopoulos, Civil Law Property Sec. 137 (1966); Bishop v. Copeland, 222 La. 284, 62 So.2d 486 (1953); Orr v. Talley, 84 So.2d 894 (La.App.2d Cir. 1956). Article 528 corrects the error in the translation of Article 2292 of the Louisiana Civil Code of 1825 insofar as a good faith possessor is concerned and allows him to recover his useful expenses.

(c) Under a correct translation of Article 2292 of the Louisiana Civil Code of 1825 not only possessors in good faith but also possessors in bad faith would be entitled to recover useful expenses. Nevertheless, Louisiana courts have consistently denied such recovery to bad faith possessors. See Comment, 31 La.L.Rev. 491 (1971). Moreover, decisions interpreting Article 508 of the 1870 Civil Code draw a distinction between separable and inseparable improvements and refuse to award to bad faith possessors recovery for inseparable improvements. See Gibson v. Hutchins and Vaughn, 12 La.Ann. 545 (1857); Heirs of Wood v. Nicholls, 33 La.Ann. 744 (1881). A bad faith possessor, however, is allowed to offset the value of fruits he owes to the owner of the property against the value of inseparable improvements. See Voiers v. Atkins Bros., 113 La. 303, 36 So. 974 (1903). Article 528 applies to a good faith possessor only; it does not accord any rights to a bad faith possessor. Accordingly, insofar as a bad faith possessor is concerned, Louisiana decisions interpreting Articles 508 and 2314 of the 1870 Civil Code continue to be relevant.

(d) The rights and obligations of the possessor and of the owner with respect to constructions made by the possessor are governed by Articles 492–497, this Revision.

Art. 529.   Right of retention

The possessor, whether in good or in bad faith, may retain possession of the thing until he is reimbursed for expenses and improvements which he is entitled to claim.

Acts 1979, No. 180, § 1, eff. Jan. 1, 1980.

REVISION COMMENTS—1979

(a) This provision is new. It is based on Article 3453(2) of the Louisiana Civil Code of 1870 and on a line of jurisprudence according the right of retention to all possessors, whether in good or in bad faith.

(b) Possessors in good faith are clearly entitled to retain possession of the thing until reimbursed for their expenses. Civil Code Art. 3453(2); Orr v. Talley, 84 So.2d 894 (La.App.2d Cir. 1956); Pearce v. Frantum, 16 La. 423 (1840); Yiannopoulos, Civil Law Property, Sec. 137 (1968); Comment, 31 La.L.Rev. 491 (1971). Article 3453 of the 1870 Civil Code does not accord the same right to possessors in bad faith. Nevertheless, according to one line of Louisiana jurisprudence, an evicted possessor in bad faith is allowed to retain the property until reimbursed for all his expenses. See Page v. Kidd, 121 La. 1, 46 So. 35 (1908); Cloud v. Cloud, 145 So.2d 331 (La.App.3rd Cir. 1962); Levy v. Clemons, 3 So.2d 440 (La.App.2d Cir. 1941); Gregory v. Kedley, 185 So. 105 (La.App.2d Cir. 1938). Contra: Payne v. Anderson, 35 La.Ann. 979 (1883); Baldwin v. Union Ins. Co., 2 Rob. 133 (La.1842); Ferrier v. Mossler, 23 So.2d 341 (La.App.1st Cir. 1945). Article 529 expands the rule of Article 3453(2) of the Louisiana Civil Code of 1870 and allows a bad faith possessor to retain the property until he has been reimbursed for the expenses he is legally entitled to recover.

Art. 530.   Presumption of ownership of movable

The possessor of a corporeal movable is presumed to be its owner. The previous possessor of a corporeal movable is presumed to have been its owner during the period of his possession.

These presumptions do not avail against a previous possessor who was dispossessed as a result of loss or theft.

Acts 1979, No. 180, § 1, eff. Jan. 1, 1980.

REVISION COMMENT—1979

This provision is new. It is based in part on Articles 1110 and 1111 of the Greek Civil Code. It complements Articles 517–525, this Revision. On the European continent, in actions for the recovery of movable property, there is a rebuttable presumption in favor of the present possessor. Yiannopoulos, Civil Law Property, Secs. 127, 150 and 152 (1968). The presumption is generally rebutted where the claimant proves that the possession of his adversary is precarious, equivocal, clandestine, or the result of fraud. Yiannopoulos, Civil Law Property, Sec. 127 (1968).

Art. 531.   Proof of ownership of immovable

One who claims the ownership of an immovable against another in possession must prove that he has acquired ownership from a previous owner or by acquisitive prescription. If neither party is in possession, he need only prove a better title.

Acts 1979, No. 180, § 1, eff. Jan. 1, 1980.

(a) One who claims the ownership of an immovable adversely to another in possession has the burden of proof of his claim. When the defendant is in possession of the immovable property, the plaintiff discharges this burden by proving that he has acquired the ownership of the immovable he claims. When the defendant is not in possession, the plaintiff discharges this burden by proving that he has a better title than the defendant. The defendant is in possession when he and his ancestors in title have had corporeal possession for at least one year or civil possession for the same period of time preceded by corporeal possession. See Yiannopoulos, Civil Law Property § 133 (1966).

(b) Article 3653(1) of the Louisiana Code of Civil Procedure declares that the plaintiff in the petitory action, in order to recover, "must make out his title". The word "title" in this article means ownership. A plaintiff in a petitory action thus makes out his title when he proves his ownership of the immovable. Ownership of immovable property may be acquired by an unbroken chain of transfers from a previous owner or by acquisitive prescription. See Pure Oil Co. v. Skinner, 294 So.2d 797 (La.1974); Tenneco Oil Co. v. Houston, 364 So. 1056 (La.App.2d Cir. 1978). In a sense, proof of acquisition of ownership in one of these manners establishes "a title good against the world".

Art. 532.   Common author

When the titles of the parties are traced to a common author, he is presumed to be the previous owner.

Acts 1979, No. 180, § 1, eff. Jan. 1, 1980.

(a) The text of Article 3653 of the Louisiana Code of Civil Procedure seems to indicate that when defendant is in possession the plaintiff may not recover upon proof of a more ancient title from a common author because this is not proof of ownership but merely proof of a better title. See Maraist, The Work of the Louisiana Appellate Courts for the 1974–1975 Term, 36 La.L.Rev. 572 (1976); Tenneco Oil Co. v. Houston, 364 So.2d 1055 (La.App.2d Cir. 1978). Nevertheless, certain courts relying on the comment accompanying Article 3653 of the Louisiana Code of Civil Procedure and the intent of the redactors not to change the prior law, have held that a plaintiff in a petitory action is entitled to judgment recognizing his ownership against a defendant in possession upon proof of a more ancient title from a common ancestor. Article 532 follows this line of jurisprudence. It declares that when the titles of the parties are traced to a common author, he is presumed to be the previous owner. Accordingly, plaintiff may recover against another in possession upon proof that his title is the more ancient from the common ancestor. Of course, the judgment is not res judicata as to third persons.

(b) Article 532 establishes a rebuttable presumption. It does not preclude a party from proving ownership by prescription or by another chain of title. Prescription is preferable to title. Cf. C.C. Art. 794, as revised in 1978.

(c) The reference in Article 532 to "title" incorporates the recordation requirements of the public records doctrine. See C.C. Arts. 2264, 2266, and McDuffie v. Walker, 125 La. 152, 51 So. 100 (La.1909).

TITLE III—PERSONAL SERVITUDES

CHAPTER 1—KINDS OF SERVITUDES

Art. 533.   Kinds of servitudes

There are two kinds of servitudes: personal servitudes and predial servitudes.

Acts 1976, No. 103, § 1, eff. Jan. 1, 1977.

REVISION COMMENT—1976

This provision reproduces the substance of the first paragraph of Article 646 of the Louisiana Civil Code of 1870. It does not change the law.

Art. 534.   Personal servitude

A personal servitude is a charge on a thing for the benefit of a person. There are three sorts of personal servitudes: usufruct, habitation, and rights of use.

Acts 1976, No. 103, § 1, eff. Jan. 1, 1977.

REVISION COMMENTS—1976

(a) This provision is new. It is based on the second paragraph of Article 646 of the Louisiana Civil Code of 1870. It changes the law as it suppresses the personal servitude of "use" and establishes the new category of "rights of use". See Chapter 4, infra.

(b) A right of use is defined as a servitude that "confers in favor of a person a specified use of an estate less than full enjoyment." Article 639, infra.

CHAPTER 2—USUFRUCT

SECTION 1—GENERAL PRINCIPLES

Art. 535.   Usufruct

Usufruct is a real right of limited duration on the property of another. The features of the right vary with the nature of the things subject to it as consumables or nonconsumables.

Acts 1976, No. 103, § 1, eff. Jan. 1, 1977.

REVISION COMMENTS—1976

(a) This provision is new. It is based on Article 534, first paragraph, of the Louisiana Civil Code of 1870. It does not change the law.

(b) Usufruct is a real right. Cf. Civil Code art. 490, second paragraph (1870): ". . . any real right towards a third person; as a usufruct, use or servitude." Legal usage in the state seems to associate the term "real right" with a right in immovable property; this, however, is not the usage in the Civil Code. According to the Civil Code real rights may exist in both movables and immovables. The rights of pledge, ownership, use, and usufruct of movables have all the substantive characteristics of real rights. See Yiannopoulos, Civil Law Property § 91 (1966). Restricted application of the term real rights to interests in immovable property is meaningful only in the framework of the Louisiana Code of Civil Procedure: "real actions" are available only to holders of real rights in immovable property. Under Article 535, as under the Louisiana Civil Code of 1870, usufruct is a real right whether its object is a movable or an immovable. Nevertheless, the usufruct of movables, though a real right, is not protected by the nominate real actions of the Code of Civil Procedure.

(c) This provision renders unnecessary the use of the terms "perfect usufruct" and "imperfect usufruct". A usufruct of consumables is the same as an imperfect usufruct, and a usufruct of nonconsumables is the same as a perfect usufruct. See Articles 537, 538, infra.

Art. 536.   Consumable things

Consumable things are those that cannot be used without being expended or consumed, or without their substance being changed, such as money, harvested agricultural products, stocks of merchandise, foodstuffs, and beverages.

Acts 1976, No. 103, § 1, eff. Jan. 1, 1977.

REVISION COMMENTS—1976

(a) This provision is new. The definition of consumable things is based on Article 534, second paragraph of the Louisiana Civil Code of 1870. It does not change the law.

(b) A usufruct established over things that cannot be used without being expended or consumed, or without their substance being changed, is a usufruct of consumables. It is the same as an imperfect usufruct under the Louisiana Civil Code of 1870. Classification of things as consumables or nonconsumables depends on inherent characteristics, and it is normally made in accordance with objective criteria. See Yiannopoulos, Civil Law Property, § 15 (1966). Nevertheless, in the framework of the law of usufruct, parties may in the exercise of contractual and testamentary freedom treat consumable things as nonconsumables, and vice versa. See Comment (c) under Article 537, infra.

(c) In matters of usufruct, Louisiana courts have classified as consumables money, promissory notes, certificates of deposit, negotiable instruments to the bearer, bales of cotton, stocks of merchandise, and optional share accounts in a Homestead Association. See, as to money: Mariana v. Eureka Homestead Soc., 181 La. 125, 158 So. 642 (1953); Gryder v. Gryder, 37 La.Ann. 638 (1885); Succession of Bickham, 197 So. 927 (La.App. 1st Cir. 1940); Danna v. Danna, 171 So. 348 (La.App. 1st Cir. 1935); Johnson v. Bolt, 146 So. 375 (La.App.2d Cir. 1933); as to promissory notes: Succession of Block, 137 La. 302, 68 So. 618 (1915); Miguez v. Delcambre, 125 La. 176, 51 So. 108 (1910); Kahn v. Becnel, 108 La. 296, 32 So. 444 (1902); as to certificates of deposit: Vivian State Bank v. Thomason-Lewis Lumber Co., 162 La. 660, 111 So. 51 (1926); as to negotiable instruments to the bearer: Taylor v. Taylor, 189 La. 1084, 181 So. 543 (1938); Johnson v. Bolt, 146 So. 375 (La.App.2d Cir. 1933); as to bales of cotton: Succession of Hays, 33 La.Ann. 1143 (1881); as to stocks of merchandise: Succession of Trouilly, 52 La.Ann. 276, 26 So. 851 (1899); Succession of Blancand, 48 La.Ann. 578, 19 So. 683 (1885); and as to optional share accounts in a Homestead Association: Succession of Chauvin, 242 So.2d 340 (La.App. 4th Cir. 1971), cert. on this issue denied, 257 La. 862, 244 So.2d 612 (1971).

Art. 537.   Nonconsumable things

Nonconsumable things are those that may be enjoyed without alteration of their substance, although their substance may be diminished or deteriorated naturally by time or by the use to which they are applied, such as lands, houses, shares of stock, animals, furniture, and vehicles.

Acts 1976, No. 103, § 1, eff. Jan. 1, 1977.

REVISION COMMENTS—1976

(a) This provision is new. The definition of nonconsumable things is based on Article 534, first paragraph of the Louisiana Civil Code of 1870. It does not change the law.

(b) A usufruct established over things that are susceptible of enjoyment without alteration of their substance, although their substance may diminish, deteriorate, or depreciate naturally or by use, is a usufruct of nonconsumables. It is the same as a perfect usufruct under the Louisiana Civil Code of 1870. See 3 Planiol et Ripert, Traité pratique de droit civil français 61 (2d ed. Picard 1952); Yiannopoulos, Personal Servitudes § 3 (1968).

(c) Parties may, in the exercise of contractual and testamentary freedom, treat as consumables things that are susceptible of enjoyment without alteration of their substance. Thus, parties may subject consumables to the rules governing usufruct of nonconsumables. See 3 Planiol et Ripert, Traité pratique de droit civil français 800 (2d ed. Picard 1952); 5 Baudry-Lacantinerie, Traité théorique et pratique de droit civil 410 (2d ed. Chauveau 1899).

(d) According to Louisiana jurisprudence, shares of stock are nonconsumables. Leury v. Mayer, 122 La. 486, 47 So. 839 (1908); Succession of Heckert, 160 So.2d 375 (La.App. 4th Cir. 1964). Optional share accounts in a Homestead Association, however, have been held to be money, and, therefore, subject to the rules governing usufruct of consumables. Succession of Chauvin, 242 So.2d 340 (La.App.4th Cir. 1971), cert. on this issue denied, 257 La. 862, 244 So.2d 612 (1971).

Art. 538.   Usufruct of consumable things

If the things subject to the usufruct are consumables, the usufructuary becomes owner of them. He may consume, alienate, or encumber them as he sees fit. At the termination of the usufruct he is bound either to pay to the naked owner the value that the things had at the commencement of the usufruct or to deliver to him things of the same quantity and quality.

Acts 1976, No. 103, § 1, eff. Jan. 1, 1977. Amended by Acts 2010, No. 881, § 1, eff. July 2, 2010.

REVISION COMMENTS—1976

(a) This provision is new. It does not change the law. The first sentence is based on Article 536 of the Louisiana Civil Code of 1870. The second sentence reproduces the substance of Article 549 of the same Code.

(b) The usufruct of consumables is a real right that may be established for a limited duration only. The usufructuary acquires the ownership of the property subject to the usufruct, and, therefore, he is free to dispose of it as he sees fit, subject to certain obligations prescribed by law. The ownership of the usufructuary does not terminate with the usufruct; upon termination of the right, the usufructuary or his heirs, as the case may be, are merely under obligation to account to the naked owner. The notion of usufruct of consumables accords substantially with similar notions in modern civil codes, as it derives from a common reservoir of civilian doctrine and jurisprudence. See B.G.B. § 1067; Greek Civil Code art. 1174; 3 Planiol et Ripert, Traité pratique de droit civil français 756 (2d ed. Picard 1952).

(c) Article 549 of the Louisiana Civil Code of 1870 declares that: "If the usufruct includes things, which can not be used without being expended or consumed, or without their substance being changed, the usufructuary has a right to dispose of them at his pleasure, but under the obligation of returning the same quantity, quality and value to the owner, or their estimated price, at the expiration of the usufruct". While the corresponding article in the French Civil Code has given rise to divergent interpretations, Louisiana courts have consistently charged the usufructuary with the obligation to restore the value that the things had at the commencement of the usufruct. See Succession of Trouilly, 52 La.Ann. 276, 26 So. 851 (1899); Succession of Blancand, 48 La.Ann. 578, 19 So. 683 (1896); Succession of Hays, 33 La.Ann. 1143 (1881); cf. In re Tutorship of Jones, 41 La.Ann. 620 (1889). Article 538 codifies this interpretation of Article 549.

REVISION COMMENTS—2010

This article reproduces and clarifies the substance of Article 538. It is not intended to change the law.

Art. 539.   Usufruct of nonconsumable things

If the things subject to the usufruct are nonconsumables, the usufructuary has the right to possess them and to derive the utility, profits, and advantages that they may produce, under the obligation of preserving their substance.

He is bound to use them as a prudent administrator and to deliver them to the naked owner at the termination of the usufruct.

Acts 1976, No. 103, § 1, eff. Jan. 1, 1977.

REVISION COMMENTS—1976

(a) This provision is new. It is based on Articles 533 and 535 of the Louisiana Civil Code of 1870. It does not change the law.

(b) Usufruct of nonconsumables is a real right that may be established for a limited duration only, under the obligation of preserving the substance of the thing. This definition accords with provisions in modern civil codes, as it derives from a common reservoir of civilian doctrine and jurisprudence. See B.G.B. § 1030; Greek Civil Code art. 1142; 3 Planiol et Ripert, Traité pratique de droit civil français 745 (2d ed. Picard 1952); Paul D. 7.1.1., usufructus est jus alienis rebus utendi fruendi salva rerum substantia.

(c) The grantor of the usufruct may relieve the usufructuary of the obligation to preserve the substance of the property subject to the usufruct. For example, the grantor may confer on the usufructuary authority to sell the property. In such a case, the usufruct of nonconsumables may be converted into a usufruct of consumables at the option of the usufructuary, with the usufructuary's right of enjoyment attaching to the proceeds of the sale. Heirs of Mitchel v. Knox, 34 La.Ann. 399 (1882).

Art. 540.   Nature of usufruct

Usufruct is an incorporeal thing. It is movable or immovable according to the nature of the thing upon which the right exists.

Acts 1976, No. 103, § 1, eff. Jan. 1, 1977.

REVISION COMMENTS—1976

(a) This provision reproduces the substance of Article 537 of the Louisiana Civil Code of 1870. It does not change the law.

(b) The usufruct of immovable property is an incorporeal immovable, and the usufruct of movable property an incorporeal movable.

Art. 541.   Divisibility of usufruct

Usufruct is susceptible to division, because its purpose is the enjoyment of advantages that are themselves divisible. It may be conferred on several persons in divided or undivided shares, and it may be partitioned among the usufructuaries.

Acts 1976, No. 103, § 1, eff. Jan. 1, 1977.

REVISION COMMENTS—1976

(a) This provision reproduces the substance of Articles 538 and 539 of the Louisiana Civil Code of 1870. It does not change the law.

(b) When a usufruct is conferred jointly on two or more persons, it is frequently a matter of contractual or testamentary interpretation to determine whether the grant is in divided or undivided portions. The grant of a usufruct in divided portions involves the creation of as many distinct rights of enjoyment as there are portions. Thus, if a usufruct is conferred on a number of beneficiaries in divided portions, the termination of the interest of each beneficiary benefits the naked owner. See Samuels v. Brownlee, 36 La.Ann. 228 (1884). The grant of a usufruct in undivided portions, on the other hand, involves the creation of a single right, which is apportioned among the beneficiaries and persists until the termination of the last interest. Thus, in the absence of an express provision to the contrary, the termination of one usufructuary's interest results in the accrual of that interest in favor of the remaining usufructuaries. Article 547, infra.

(c) When a usufruct is conferred in undivided portions, the state of indivision may terminate at any time by partition in kind or by licitation upon the demand of any of the cousufructuaries. See C.C. art. 1309 (1870): "[U]sufructuaries of the same estate can institute among themselves the action of partition"; Comment, 8 Tul.L.Rev. 574 (1934). Article 538 of the Louisiana Civil Code of 1870 seems to assume that a usufruct may always be partitioned in kind, "because the object of this right is the receiving the fruits of the thing, which are corporeal and divisible." Usufruct, however, may be established on things which do not produce fruits, but merely advantages of use, as jewelry and automobiles. In these cases, apportionment of the advantages of use, or partition of the enjoyment by licitation, ought to be the appropriate remedies.

Art. 542.   Divisibility of naked ownership

The naked ownership may be partitioned subject to the rights of the usufructuary.

Acts 1976, No. 103, § 1, eff. Jan. 1, 1977.

REVISION COMMENTS—1976

(a) This provision clarifies the applicability of Articles 1289 and 1308 of the Louisiana Civil Code of 1870 to the naked owners of property subject to usufruct. It does not change the law.

(b) When the naked ownership of a thing is held by several persons in undivided shares and the usufruct by another person or persons, partition of the naked ownership in kind or by licitation may be demanded by any of the naked owners. See Smith v. Nelson, 121 La. 170, 46 So. 200 (1908); Succession of Glancy, 108 La. 414, 32 So. 356 (1902); Byrnes v. Byrnes, 115 La. 275, 38 So. 991 (1905); Day v. Collins, 5 La.Ann. 589 (1850). This partition of the naked ownership does not affect adversely the interests of the usufructuaries, who continue to enjoy the things as if no change of ownership took place. See Kaffie v. Wilson, 130 La. 350, 57 So. 1001 (1911).

(c) When several persons acquire an undivided interest in usufruct and an undivided interest in naked ownership; when the sole naked owner has also an individual interest in usufruct; or when the sole usufructuary has also an undivided interest in the naked ownership, partition merely of the right of enjoyment or of the naked ownership in kind or by licitation has long been recognized in France. See 4 Planiol et Ripert, Traité pratique de droit civil français 675 (2d ed. Maury and Vialleton 1956). In Louisiana, courts and litigants have failed to distinguish clearly between partition of the elements held in common (right of enjoyment or naked ownership) and partition of the property free of the usufruct. Thus, while no case holds squarely that partition of the elements held in common cannot be forced as between naked owners or between usufructuaries, it seems to be assumed, on the authority of cases involving the distinguishable situation of sale of the entire property free of the usufruct, that such partition is excluded. Actually, the assumption rests on dicta which indicate that the naked ownership may not be partitioned by licitation if one of the coowners has also an undivided interest in usufruct. Cf. Smith v. Nelson, 121 La. 170, 46 So. 200 (1908). But see Day v. Collins, 5 La.Ann. 588 (1850) (community partitioned notwithstanding the existence of survivor's usufruct). Under this draft, partition of the common elements is always permissible.

(d) This provision contemplates the existence of several naked owners none of whom has an interest in usufruct or in full ownership. Thus, there can be no partition under this provision when a person has the full ownership of an undivided share.

Art. 543.   Partition of the property in kind or by licitation

When property is held in indivision, a person having a share in full ownership may demand partition of the property in kind or by licitation, even though there may be other shares in naked ownership and usufruct.

A person having a share in naked ownership only or in usufruct only does not have this right, unless a naked owner of an undivided share and a usufructuary of that share jointly demand partition in kind or by licitation, in which event their combined shares shall be deemed to constitute a share in full ownership.

Acts 1976, No. 103, § 1, eff. Jan. 1, 1977. Amended by Acts 1983, No. 535, § 1.

REVISION COMMENTS—1976

(a) The first sentence of this article allows partition of the property in kind, that is, free of the usufruct, at the demand of a person to the extent that he holds undivided interests in usufruct and in ownership. There is no contrary holding in Louisiana jurisprudence. In the leading case of Nelson v. Smith, 121 La. 170, 171, 46 So. 200, 201 (1908), the question was left open: "We may remark, in conclusion, that, it having been conceded that the property here in question is not susceptible of division in kind, we have not felt called upon to express an opinion upon the question." In France, commentators and jurisprudence are in agreement that property susceptible of division in kind may be so partitioned, when the same person holds undivided interests in usufruct and in ownership. As a result of such a partition, the person holding undivided interests in both usufruct and ownership may acquire perfect ownership over certain individually determined things. See 3 Planiol et Ripert, Traité pratique de droit civil français 758 (2d ed. Picard 1952). This question has been resolved in favor of the availability of partition in kind in appropriate circumstances.

(b) The second sentence of this article excludes partition of the entire property by licitation even though there is a person who is both a usufructuary and a naked owner. It restates a rule established by Louisiana jurisprudence and does not change the law. Smith v. Nelson, 121 La. 170, 46 So. 200 (1908); Succession of Glancey, 112 La. 430, 36 So. 483 (1904); Fricke v. Stafford, 159 So.2d 52 (La.App.1st Cir. 1963).

(c) In the absence of elements held in common, partition in kind or by licitation amont naked owners and usufructuaries is excluded. Smith v. Nelson, 121 La. 170, 46 So. 200 (1908); 2 Aubry et Rau, Droit civil francais 639 (7th ed. Esmein 1961). These persons do not hold the same type of interest by undivided shares, i.e., they do not possess rights of the same nature over the same object. Partition upon demand of the usufructuary would constitute, in effect, denial of ultimate perfect ownership; partition upon demand of the naked owner would result in termination of the usufruct or in its transfer to the proceeds of the sale of the property.

(d) This provision is applicable to the usufruct of the surviving spouse under Article 916 of the Louisiana Civil Code of 1870. Determination of the question whether the property is susceptible to division in kind is made in all cases in accordance with Articles 1339 and 1340 of the Louisiana Civil Code of 1870.

COMMENTS—1983

(a) This Article amends and reenacts C.C. Art. 543 (rev.1976). Its purpose is to change the law governing partition of property held in indivision, in full ownership, in usufruct, and in naked ownership, and of property held in indivision, in usufruct and in naked ownership.

(b) Partition in kind is available, in accordance with the general law, only when the property is susceptible to such partitioning. C.C. Arts. 1339, 1340 (1870).

(c) The first sentence of this Article allows partitioning in kind, if the property is susceptible to such a partitioning, as well as partition by licitation, at the demand of a person who has an undivided share in full ownership. Such a person may bring an action for partition of the property held in common against persons holding shares in usufruct, in naked ownership, or in full ownership. For example, a surviving spouse in community under C.C. Art. 890 (rev.1981) may bring an action for partition of the property, in kind or by licitation, against children holding undivided shares in naked ownership. The rule accords with the rationale of Smith v. Nelson, 121 La. 170, 46 So. 200 (La.1908) and the holding of Devillier v. Devillier, 371 So.2d 1230 (La.App. 3rd Cir.1979).

When a person has a share in naked ownership and a share in usufruct over the same thing, confusion takes place. C.C. Art. 622 (rev.1976). In such a case, an action for partition lies under the first sentence of Article 543.

(d) The second sentence of this Article excludes partition, whether in kind or by licitation, at the demand of a person holding a share in naked ownership only or in usufruct only. For example, children holding an interest in naked ownership under C.C. Art. 890 (rev.1981) may not demand partition of the property against the surviving spouse. This accords with the rationale of Smith v. Nelson, 121 La. 170, 46 So. 200 (La.1908) and Devillier v. Devillier, 371 So.2d 1230 (La.App. 3rd Cir.1979). A person holding a share in naked ownership only or in usufruct only may not compel a person holding a share in full ownership to dismember his title. Such a person may only demand partition of the naked ownership against naked owners (C.C. Art. 541 (rev.1976)) or of the usufruct against usufructuaries (C.C. Art. 542 (rev.1976)).

(e) The second sentence of this Article allows partition upon joint demand of a usufructuary and a naked owner whose share is burdened with that usufruct. In such a case, the shares of the naked owner and of the usufructuary shall be deemed to constitute a share in full ownership as if confusion had taken place.

(f) See R.S. 9:1201 regarding rights and obligations burdened with a usufruct.

Art. 544.   Methods of establishing usufruct; things susceptible of usufruct

Usufruct may by established by a juridical act either inter vivos or mortis causa, or by operation of law. The usufruct created by juridical act is called conventional; the usufruct created by operation of law is called legal.

Usufruct may be established on all kinds of things, movable or immovable, corporeal or incorporeal.

Acts 1976, No. 103, § 1, eff. Jan. 1, 1977.

REVISION COMMENTS—1976

(a) This provision reproduces the substance of Articles 540 and 541 of the Louisiana Civil Code of 1870. It does not change the law.

(b) Conventional usufructs are of two kinds: either contractual, created by inter vivos juridical act, or testamentary, created by mortis causa juridical act. Legal usufructs may be of various kinds. In Louisiana, parents have, during marriage, the enjoyment of the property of their minor children; the surviving spouse has the usufruct of one-half of the community property inherited by issue of the marriage; a widow or widower may have the so-called marital portion in usufruct; and a widow in necessitous circumstances may have in usufruct up to one thousand dollars from the succession of her husband.

(c) Neither the Louisiana Civil Code nor the French Civil Code provides expressly for the creation of usufruct by acquisitive prescription; nevertheless, this additional method for the creation of usufruct is, according to doctrine, implicitly recognized in the two Codes. See 3 Planiol et Ripert, Traité pratique de droit civil français 766 (2d ed. Picard 1952); 2 Aubry et Rau, Droit civil français 640 (7th ed. Esmein 1961). Both the German and the Greek Civil Codes declare expressly that usufruct may be acquired by acquisitive prescription. See B.G.B. §§ 900(2), 1033; Greek Civil Code art. 1143. A usufruct that has been created by prescription is subject to the rules governing conventional usufruct. See Yiannopoulos, Personal Servitudes § 618 (1968).

(d) Usufruct may bear on copyrights, claims or, leases, partnerships, business enterprises, and on another usufruct. Generally, any corporeal or incorporeal which is capable of producing an economic advantage may become the object of usufruct. See 3 Planiol et Ripert, Traité pratique de droit civil français 755 (2d ed. Picard 1952); Yiannopoulos, Civil Law Property §§ 4, 47 (1966).

Art. 545. Modifications of usufruct

Usufruct may be established for a term or under a condition, and subject to any modification consistent with the nature of usufruct.

The rights and obligations of the usufructuary and of the naked owner may be modified by agreement unless modification is prohibited by law or by the grantor in the act establishing the usufruct.

Acts 1976, No. 103, § 1, eff. Jan. 1, 1977.

REVISION COMMENTS—1976

(a) This provision reproduces the substance of Articles 542 and 569, third paragraph of the Louisiana Civil Code of 1870.

(b) In spite of the unqualified declaration in Article 542, second sentence, of the Louisiana Civil Code of 1870, freedom of the will obtains only as to modifications which do not contravene public policy or prohibitory laws. It is only within these broad limits that contractual and testamentary freedom is recognized in Louisiana. See C.C. arts. 11, 12, 709, 2013 (C.C., 1870). Thus, usufruct may be created for a term or under condition, but it may not be created for a period exceeding the lifetime of an individual usufructuary, i.e., as a heritable right. The grantor of the usufruct may, however, create successive rights of enjoyment or establish testamentary usufructs "in favor of several persons jointly, and revertible from one person to the other, not terminating until the death of the last survivor." Succession of Fournet, 195 So.2d 333, 335 (La.App. 3d Cir. 1967). He may accord to the usufructuary power of disposition over the things subject to imperfect usufruct. Heirs of Mitchel v. Knox, 35 La.Ann. 399 (1882). The grantor may also relieve the usufructuary of consumable things of the obligation to account for their value to the naked owner. In re Courtin, 144 La. 971, 81 So. 457 (1919). Further, the grantor may confine the enjoyment to certain designated advantages of use. Gibson v. Zylks, 186 La. 1043, 173 So. 757 (1919).

(c) The grantor may not deprive the usufructuary of the administration of the property subject to the usufruct. Succession of Ward, 110 La. 75, 34 So. 135 (1903); Succession of Stephens, 45 La.Ann. 962, 13 So. 197 (1893). In the framework of the law of trusts, however, the property subject to usufruct may be placed under the administration of the trustee. See La.R.S. 9:1771; cf. Oppenheim, Limitation and Uses of Louisiana Trusts, 27 Tul.L.Rev. 41, 50 (1952).

Art. 546.   Usufruct in favor of successive usufructuaries

Usufruct may be established in favor of successive usufructuaries.

Acts 1976, No. 103, § 1, eff. Jan. 1, 1977.

REVISION COMMENTS—1976

(a) This provision is new. It articulates a rule implied in Article 609 of the Civil Code of 1870 and codifies Louisiana jurisprudence. It does not change the law.

(b) There is sufficient statutory basis to sustain the establishment of successive usufructs in Louisiana. The Civil Code affirms expressly the validity of a testamentary usufruct to one legatee and the naked ownership to another, the divisibility of usufruct is recognized, and successive usufructs are permitted by clear implication. C.C. arts. 1522, 538, 609 (1870). Accordingly, Louisiana courts have rightly upheld the validity of juridical acts creating successive usufructs. See Succession of Fournet, 195 So.2d 333 (La.App.3rd Cir. 1967); Succession of Buissiere, 41 La.Ann. 217, 5 So. 668 (1889); McCalop v. Stewart, 11 La.Ann. 106 (1866); cf. Fricke v. Stafford, 159 So.2d 52 (La.App. 1st Cir. 1963).

(c) According to Article 611, infra, "if the usufructuary is charged to restore or transfer the usufruct to another person, his right to the usufruct terminates when the time of delivery arrives". Article 611 may thus determine the commencement or termination of a successive usufruct.

Art. 547.   Usufruct in favor of several usufructuaries

When the usufruct is established in favor of several usufructuaries, the termination of the interest of one usufructuary inures to the benefit of those remaining, unless the grantor has expressly provided otherwise.

Acts 1976, No. 103, § 1, eff. Jan. 1, 1977.

REVISION COMMENTS—1976

(a) This provision is new. It changes the law as indicated in Comment (b), below.

(b) According to Louisiana jurisprudence, the question whether the termination of the interest of a co-usufructuary benefits the naked owner or accrues in favor of remaining cousufructuaries is a matter of contractual or testamentary interpretation. In the absence of express provision, courts used to search for an implied or presumed intent. See Samuels v. Brownlee, 36 La.Ann. 228 (1884) (implied intent that the termination of the interest of one usufructuary should benefit the naked owner); Arcenaux v. Bernard, 10 La. 246 (1836) (implied intent that the termination of the interest of one usufructuary should accrue in favor of the remaining). The provision dispenses with the necessity of interpretation and search for the implied intent of the grantor.

In the absence of an express provision to the contrary, the termination of one usufructuary's interest results in the accrual of that interest in favor of the remaining usufructuaries.

(c) This provision does not affect the rule of Article 1708 of the Civil Code of 1870. According to Article 1708, a legacy of usufruct made to several persons without designation of shares qualifies as a conjoint legacy. The failure of the disposition in favor of a co-legatee of the usufruct benefits the remaining colegatees of the usufruct.

(d) This provision contemplates the creation of a single right of usufruct. Thus, Article 547 does not apply when the grantor intended to establish distinct rights of usufruct in favor of several persons.

Art. 548.   Existence of usufructuaries

When the usufruct is established by an act inter vivos, the usufructuary must exist or be conceived at the time of the execution of the instrument. When the usufruct is established by an act mortis causa, the usufructuary must exist or be conceived at the time of the death of the testator.

Acts 1976, No. 103, § 1, eff. Jan. 1, 1977.

(a) This provision is new. It articulates a principle inherent in Articles 493 and 1482 of the Louisiana Civil Code of 1870. It does not change the law.

(b) This provision accords with the rules adopted in Sections 1821 through 1822 of the Louisiana Trust Code.

Art. 549.   Capacity to receive usufruct

Usufruct may be established in favor of a natural person or a juridical person.

Acts 1976, No. 103, § 1, eff. Jan. 1, 1977. Amended by Acts 2010, No. 881, § 1, eff. July 2, 2010.

REVISION COMMENT—1976

This provision reproduces the substance of Article 543 of the Louisiana Civil Code of 1870. It does not change the law.

REVISION COMMENTS—2010

This article is based on Article 549 as revised in 1976. It is not intended to change the law. The change in language is intended to make the article more technically accurate and consistent with the definition of "person" in Article 24, which provides that there are two kinds of persons—natural and juridical. Under this article, usufruct may be established in favor of either kind of person, but it may not be established in favor of something that is not a person, for example, a trust, which is a "relationship", not an entity. See La. R.S. 9:1731 and comments to Article 608, infra. A usufruct may be held in trust. See La. R.S. 9:1771, and comment (c) thereto.

SECTION 2—RIGHTS OF THE USUFRUCTUARY

Art. 550.   Right to all fruits

The usufructuary is entitled to the fruits of the thing subject to usufruct according to the following articles.

Acts 1976, No. 103, § 1, eff. Jan. 1, 1977.

REVISION COMMENT—1976

This provision reproduces the substance of Article 544 of the Louisiana Civil Code of 1870. It does not change the law.

Art. 551.   Kinds of fruits

Fruits are things that are produced by or derived from another thing without diminution of its substance.

There are two kinds of fruits; natural fruits and civil fruits.

Natural fruits are products of the earth or of animals.

Civil fruits are revenues derived from a thing by operation of law or by reason of a juridical act, such as rentals, interest, and certain corporate distributions.

Acts 1976, No. 103, § 1, eff. Jan. 1, 1977.

REVISION COMMENTS—1976

(a) The definition of fruits in the first paragraph accords with doctrine, the theory underlying several articles of the Louisiana Civil Code of 1870, and Louisiana jurisprudence in the fields of usufruct, good or bad faith possession, and state severance tax. See, e.g., Gueno v. Medlenka, 238 La. 1081, 117 So.2d 817 (1960); Wright Imperial Oil & Gas Products Co., 177 La. 482, 148 So. 685 (1933); Harang v. Bowie Lumber Co., 145 La. 96, 81 So. 769 (1919); Elder v. Ellerbe, 135 La. 99, 66 So. 337 (1914).

(b) Trees are born and reborn of the soil, but they are ordinarily considered to be capital assets rather than fruits on account of their slow growth and high value. See Harang v. Bowie Lumber Co., 145 La. 96, 81 So. 769 (1919). However, trees in a tree farm or in a regularly exploited forest may be regarded as fruits, because they are produced according to the destination of the property and without diminution of its substance. See Yiannopoulos, Personal Servitudes § 27 (1968).

(c) Mineral substances extracted from the ground and the proceeds of mineral rights are not fruits, because their production results in depletion of the property. See Gueno v. Medlenka, 238 La. 1081, 117 So.2d 817 (1960). Nevertheless, mineral substances extracted from the ground, the proceeds of mineral rights, and the revenues of regularly exploited mines or quarries may, by virtue of exceptional provisions, belong to the usufructuary or they may fall into the community of acquets and gains. Mineral Code arts. 188–196; See Yiannopoulos, Personal Servitudes § 28 (1968).

(d) The definition applies to both natural and civil fruits. For the status of corporate distributions as fruits, see comments under Article 552, infra.

(e) Article 545 of the Louisiana Civil Code of 1870 seems to establish three categories of fruits, namely, natural fruits, fruits of industry, and civil fruits. Actually, fruits of industry differ from natural fruits only in that they are the result of industry whereas natural fruits are the spontaneous product of the earth. Since the rules governing natural fruits and fruits of industry are the same, the two categories have been combined into one in this article. This article changes slightly the conceptual framework of the Louisiana Civil Code of 1870, but it does not change the law.

(f) The third paragraph of this article combines the categories of natural fruits and fruits of industry into a single category, but it does not change the law. The word earth includes the land, waters, and the atmospheric air. The word animals includes living creatures of the air, sea, and land.

(g) The definition of civil fruits in the fourth paragraph represents a slight change in the language of Article 545 of the Civil Code of 1870 but does not change the substantive law.

(h) In the fields of community property and state income taxation, the Louisiana Supreme Court has held that mineral royalties are civil fruits falling into the community of acquets and gains. See Milling v. Collector of Revenue, 200 La. 773, 57 So.2d 679 (1952). Under the proposed definition of fruits, however, mineral substances extracted from the ground and the proceeds of mineral rights are not fruits, because their production results in depletion of the property. They may fall into the community of acquets and gains by virtue of directly applicable provisions rather than as the result of their classification as fruits. See C.C. art. 2402 (1870).

Art. 552.　　Corporate distributions

A cash dividend declared during the existence of the usufruct belongs to the usufructuary. A liquidation dividend or a stock redemption payment belongs to the naked owner subject to the usufruct.

Stock dividends and stock splits declared during the existence of the usufruct belong to the naked owner subject to the usufruct.

A stock warrant and a subscription right declared during the existence of the usufruct belong to the naked owner free of the usufruct.

Acts 1976, No. 103, § 1, eff. Jan. 1, 1977.

REVISION COMMENTS—1976

(a) According to Louisiana jurisprudence, cash dividends other than liquidation payments are treated as fruits which belong to the usufructuary. See Succession of Wengert, 180 La. 483, 156 So. 473 (1934); Leury v. Mayer, 122 La. 486, 47 So. 839 (1908); Succession of Stewart, 100 So.2d 228 (La.App.2d Cir. 1958). In Leury v. Mayer, supra, the court held that cash dividends "declared" up to the date of the termination of the usufruct belong to the usufructuary.

(b) Louisiana courts have dealt with cases involving liquidation dividends. See Succession of Dielmann, 119 La. 101, 43 So. 972 (1907); Succession of Stewart, 100 So.2d 228 (La.App.2d Cir. 1958). These cases hold that liquidation dividends belong to the naked owner subject to the enjoyment of the usufructuary. The rule is susceptible of generalization as to other capital payments. Accordingly, the second sentence of the proposed text makes it clear that liquidation payments and stock redemption payments belong to the naked owner subject to the enjoyment of the usufructuary. This means that, upon termination of the usufruct, the usufructuary or his heirs will be under obligation to return to the naked owner the value received.

(c) According to the second paragraph of this article, stock dividends and stock splits, whether representing a dilution of the corporate capital or capitalization of profits, are not fruits; these belong to the naked owner. Nevertheless, the usufructuary's right of enjoyment attaches to these dividends for the period of the usufruct. This means that upon termination of the enjoyment, the usufructuary or his heirs shall be under obligation to return to the naked owner the stock received. There are no Louisiana decisions dealing directly with the rights of the usufructuary to stock splits and stock dividends. However, guidelines may be derived from cases considering the nature of these operations for purposes of taxation and community property. In these two fields, when stock has been split and a greater number of new shares issued in the place of the old, it has been determined that the new shares are capital rather than income or fruits. See Succession of Hemenway, 228 La. 572, 83 So.2d 377 (1955). Likewise, when the corporation, instead of making a cash distribution from surplus, capitalizes profits and issues stock dividends, the Louisiana Supreme Court has held that the new shares are a capital asset rather than income. Daigre v. Daigre, 228 La. 682, 83 So.2d 900 (1955). This is in line with most tax cases which have held that a stock dividend is not taxable under the federal internal revenue legislation. See Eisner v. Macomber, 252 U.S. 189, 40 S.Ct. 189, 64 L.Ed. 521 (1920).

(d) Stock dividends representing distribution of shares of a different character in the same corporation or shares of another corporation are treated as income by federal courts. See, e.g., Koshland v. Helvering, 298 U.S. 441, 56 S.Ct. 767, 80 L.Ed. 1268 (1936); Peabody v. Eisner, 247 U.S. 347, 38 S.Ct. 546, 62 L.Ed. 1152 (1918). Nevertheless, in the framework of the law of usufruct, these dividends are not fruits; they belong to the naked owner subject to the enjoyment of the usufructuary.

(e) According to the third paragraph of this article, stock warrants and subscription rights attributed to shares of stock belong to the naked owner free of the enjoyment of the usufructuary. Like voting rights, these are not fruits, nor increase of the stock, but powers inherent in the naked ownership of shares. Cf. 3 Planiol et Ripert, Traité pratique de droit civil français 786 (2d ed. Picard 1952).

Art. 553.   Voting of shares of stock and other rights

The usufructuary has the right to vote shares of stock in corporations and to vote or exercise similar rights with respect to interests in other juridical persons, unless otherwise provided.

Acts 1976, No. 103, § 1, eff. Jan. 1, 1977. Amended by Acts 2010, No. 881, § 1, eff. July 2, 2010.

REVISION COMMENTS—1976

(a) This provision is new. It fills a gap in the existing law.

(b) According to Louisiana jurisprudence, shares of stock are subject to the rules governing usufruct of nonconsumables. Leury v. Mayer, 122 La. 486, 47 So. 839 (1908); Succession of Heckert, 150 So. 375 (La.App.4th Cir. 1964). Optional share accounts in a Homestead Association, however, have been held to be money, and, therefore, subject to the rules governing usufruct of consumables. Succession of Chauvin, 242 So.2d 340 (La.App.4th Cir. 1971), cert. on this issue denied, 257 La. 862, 244 So.2d 612 (1971).

(c) According to French doctrine and jurisprudence, the right to vote belongs to the naked owner. This right is not a fruit, but a power inherent in the naked ownership of shares. See 3 Planiol et Ripert, Traité pratique de droit civil français 786 (2d ed. Picard 1952). Article 1177 of the Greek Civil Code, however, declares that, in the absence of contrary provision, the usufructuary is entitled to participate (and vote) in stockholder meetings. Article 553 adopts the Greek solution. From the doctrinal point of view, the right to vote shares of stock may not be a part of the enjoyment; nevertheless, it is a desirable practical solution to attribute to the usufructuary the right to vote shares of stock. In effect, this provision attributes to the grantor of the usufruct a presumptive intent to confer on the usufructuary power to vote shares of stock. The solution also accords with the policy underlying the institution of legal usufruct.

This article is based on Article 553. It is not intended to change the law. This article expands the rule to allow the usufructuary to exercise rights similar to voting rights in juridical persons that are not corporations, such as limited liability companies.

By way of illustration, this article is intended to allow the usufructuary to exercise management rights of members of limited liability companies. See R.S. 12:1311 et seq. As a member of an LLC, the usufructuary would have the same powers and responsibilities as other members, including fiduciary duties. See R.S. 12:1314, relative to duties of members and managers of a limited liability company.

Art. 554. Commencement of the right to fruits

The usufructuary's right to fruits commences on the effective date of the usufruct.

Acts 1976, No. 103, § 1, eff. Jan. 1, 1977.

REVISION COMMENT—1976

Article 566 of the Louisiana Civil Code of 1870 seems to indicate that the usufructuary's right to obtain fruits commences, in all cases, "from the moment that the usufruct has accrued." In reality, this rule applies merely to legal usufructs and to contractual usufructs in the absence of contrary party agreement. In cases of testamentary usufructs, the commencement of the usufructuary's right to fruits is determined in the light of Articles 1608 and 1626 of the Louisiana Civil Code of 1870. Article 554 does not change the law.

Art. 555. Nonapportionment of natural fruits

The usufructuary acquires the ownership of natural fruits severed during the existence of the usufruct. Natural fruits not severed at the end of the usufruct belong to the naked owner.

Acts 1976, No. 103, § 1, eff. Jan. 1, 1977.

REVISION COMMENTS—1976

(a) This provision embodies principles underlying Articles 465, 546, 547, and 567 of the Louisiana Civil Code of 1870. It has been drafted in the light of civilian doctrine.

(b) French doctrine and jurisprudence, relying on traditional civilian sources and drawing arguments from Articles 520 and 585 of the Code Civil, decide that the usufructuary acquires the ownership of natural fruits upon their actual separation and without the necessity of taking possession. Strict adherence to the corresponding texts of Articles 465 and 546 of the Louisiana Civil Code of 1870 should produce the same result as in France. It has been thought to be preferable, however, to articulate the principle in the above provision.

(c) According to French doctrine and jurisprudence, the usufructuary is entitled to natural fruits severed during the existence of the usufruct. Fruits that have not been severed at the end of the usufruct, even on account of irresistible force, belong to the naked owner. But the usufructuary is entitled to the value of the fruits he was unable to collect because of the acts of the owner or because of disputes as to ownership. See 2 Aubry et Rau, Droit civil français 655 (7th ed. Esmein 1961). The issue has not arisen in Louisiana jurisprudence. It would seem that the solutions reached in France are well founded.

Art. 556. Apportionment of civil fruits

The usufructuary acquires the ownership of civil fruits accruing during the existence of the usufruct.

Civil fruits accrue day by day and the usufructuary is entitled to them regardless of when they are received.

Acts 1976, No. 103, § 1, eff. Jan. 1, 1977.

REVISION COMMENTS—1976

(a) This provision reproduces the substance of Articles 546 and 547 of the Louisiana Civil Code of 1870. It does not change the law.

(b) According to traditional civilian ideas, maintained in modern civil codes, civil fruits accrue by virtue of an obligation; hence, the usufructuary acquires a "claim" for civil fruits rather than the "ownership" thereof. The creation of the usufruct operates as an assignment of a credit and the usufructuary is entitled to demand payment from the obligor.

In Louisiana and in France, no clear distinction is made between the usufructuary's claim for the payment of civil fruits against the obligor and the usufructuary's or the naked owner's claim for apportionment of civil fruits. Commentators, relying on Article 586 of the Code Civil which corresponds to Article 547 of the Louisiana Civil Code of 1870, declare cryptically that civil fruits are acquired by the usufructuary day by day. One might thus conclude that the usufructuary is merely entitled to claim from the debtor of the obligation the part of the civil fruits to which he is entitled and no more. It is submitted, however, that Articles 586 of the Code Civil and 547 of the Louisiana Civil Code of 1870 refer exclusively to the relations between the usufructuary and the naked owner and establish claims for the apportionment of fruits between these persons. In the light of civilian tradition and contemporary analysis, the usufructuary acquires upon the creation of the usufruct, both in Louisiana and in France, a claim for the payment of all exigible civil fruits against the obligor. Naturally, after payment to the usufructuary, the naked owner may have a claim against him for apportionment; and, if the naked owner has received civil fruits in advance or from an obligor who had no knowledge of the usufruct, the usufructuary may have a claim against the naked owner for apportionment. These solutions are expressly sanctioned in modern civil codes and have been adopted in this revision.

(c) According to Louisiana and French jurisprudence, the usufructuary has a claim to civil fruits accruing during the years of commencement or termination of the usufruct in proportion to the days of his enjoyment. Payment during the existence of the usufruct is not required. See Gaspard v. Coco, 116 La. 1096, 41 So.2d 326 (1906).

(d) Corporate distributions declared during the existence of the usufruct may belong to the usufructuary or to the naked owner in accordance with the rules established in Article 552, supra.

Art. 557.   Possession and use of the things

The usufructuary takes the things in the state in which they are at the commencement of the usufruct.

Acts 1976, No. 103, § 1, eff. Jan. 1, 1977.

REVISION COMMENTS—1976

(a) This provision reproduces ideas embodied in Articles 535, 551 (first paragraph), 557 (first sentence) and 599 of the Louisiana Civil Code of 1870. It does not change the law.

(b) The usufructuary may not compel the naked owner to make repairs needed at the commencement of the usufruct. Article 557, following Article 557 of the 1870 Code, declares that "the usufructuary takes the things in the state in which they are."

(c) It might be preferable to state that the usufructuary is entitled to use the thing "as the owner himself", subject to exceptions established by law. However, in deference to changes adopted in the 1825 revision and allowed to remain in Article 533 of the 1870 Code, the usufructuary is merely accorded the right to use the things as a prudent administrator. See Projet of the Civil Code of 1825, 1 La.Legal Archives p. 48 (1937).

(d) The right of the usufructuary to take possession of the things may be predicated upon discharge of his obligations to make an inventory and to give security. See Articles 570 and 575, infra.

(e) Article 565 of the Louisiana Civil Code of 1870 declares that "the usufructuary is bound to suffer the servitude which existed on the land of which he has the usufruct, at the time his right commenced." This provision has not been reproduced, because it is an application of the principle that the usufructuary "takes the things in the state in which they are." Moreover, Article 565 (C.C., 1870) states the obvious proposition that persons who acquired real rights on the things prior to the commencement of the usufruct have claims superior to those of the usufructuary. Cf. Yiannopoulos, Civil Law Property § 88 (1966).

Art. 558.   Improvements and alterations

The usufructuary may make improvements and alterations on the property subject to the usufruct at his cost and with the written consent of the naked owner. If the naked owner fails or refuses to give his consent, the usufructuary may, after notice to the naked owner and with the approval of the court, make at his cost those improvements and alterations that a prudent administrator would make.

Acts 1976, No. 103, § 1, eff. Jan. 1, 1977. Amended by Acts 2010, No. 881, § 1, eff. July 2, 2010.

REVISION COMMENTS—1976

(a) This provision suppresses most of the detailed rules of Articles 568 and 569 of the Louisiana Civil Code of 1870. It changes the law as it allows the usufructuary to make at his cost, after notice to the owner and with the approval of the proper court, those improvements and alterations that a prudent administrator would make. The change is desirable in the light of modern conditions.

(b) The substance of the third paragraph of Article 569 of the Louisiana Civil Code of 1870 is reproduced in Article 545, supra.

REVISION COMMENTS—2010

This article reproduces the substance of Civil Code Article 558. It is not intended to change the law.

Art. 559.   Accessories

The right of usufruct extends to the accessories of the thing at the commencement of the usufruct.

Acts 1976, No. 103, § 1, eff. Jan. 1, 1977.

REVISION COMMENTS—1976

(a) This provision articulates a principle inherent in the Louisiana Civil Code of 1870. It does not change the law. Cf. C.C. arts. 548, 553, 554, 1636, 2490 (C.C., 1870); Peters v. Fonville, 70 So.2d 209 (La.App. 2d Cir. 1954); 3 Planiol et Ripert, Traité pratique de droit civil français 769 (2d ed. Picard 1952).

(b) Accessories are defined in Article 522 of the Louisiana Civil Code of 1870 as things which are for the "use, ornament or completion" of the principal thing. Cf. Yiannopoulous, Civil Law Property § 19 (1966).

(c) Article 548 of the Louisiana Civil Code of 1870 declares: "The usufruct of a house carries with it the enjoyment of the house, of the profits which it may bring, and indeed of such furniture as is permanently fixed therein, even should the title by which the usufruct is established make no mention of the same." This provision has not been reproduced because it is merely an illustration of the principle that Article 559 has articulated.

Art. 560.   Trees, stones, and other materials

The usufructuary may cut trees growing on the land of which he has the usufruct and take stones, sand, and other materials from it, but only for his use or for the improvement or cultivation of the land.

Acts 1976, No. 103, § 1, eff. Jan. 1, 1977.

REVISION COMMENTS—1976

(a) This article reproduces the substance of Article 551, second paragraph, Louisiana Civil Code of 1870. It does not change the law.

(b) For the usufructuary's right to continue the timber operations of the owner, and to treat as fruits the products of a regularly exploited forest, see Article 562, infra; Yiannopoulos, Personal Servitudes § 27 (1968).

Art. 561. Mines and quarries

The rights of the usufructuary and of the naked owner in mines and quarries are governed by the Mineral Code.

Acts 1976, No. 103, § 1, eff. Jan. 1, 1977.

REVISION COMMENTS—1976

(a) The Mineral Code applies to all minerals and deals comprehensively with the rights and obligations of the usufructuary and of the naked owner in mines and quarries. The Mineral Code is a specialized extension of the Civil Code. The Civil Code or other laws are applicable when the Mineral Code "does not expressly or impliedly provide for a particular situation." See Mineral Code art. 2.

(b) Article 190 of the Mineral Code maintains the "open mine" doctrine and determines its application. The doctrine applies to legal usufructs and to conventional usufructs when the title does not contain an express provision concerning the use and enjoyment of minerals.

(c) Article 191 of the Mineral Code defines what constitutes a mine or quarry actually worked at the time of the creation of the usufruct for purposes of oil and gas production only. Courts will have the task of working out rules for other types of mining. For purposes of oil and gas, there is an open mine, namely, a mine or quarry actually worked at the time of the creation of the usufruct, "if . . . minerals are being produced from the land or other land unitized therewith, or if there is present on the land or other land unitized therewith a well shown by surface production test to be capable of producing in paying quantities." In such a case, the usufructuary is "entitled to the use and enjoyment of the landowner's rights in minerals as to all pools penetrated by the well or wells in question."

Art. 562. Usufruct of timberlands

When the usufruct includes timberlands, the usufructuary is bound to manage them as a prudent administrator. The proceeds of timber operations that are derived from proper management of timberlands belong to the usufructuary.

Acts 1976, No. 103, § 1, eff. Jan. 1, 1977.

REVISION COMMENTS—1976

(a) This article is new. It establishes the duty of the usufructuary to manage timberlands as a prudent administrator and his right to the proceeds of certain timber operations.

(b) Contractual or testamentary provisions may determine the rights and obligations of the usufructuary and of the naked owner insofar as timberlands are concerned. In the absence of such provisions, and in the more prevalent case of legal usufruct, the usufructuary is bound to manage timberlands as a prudent administrator and is entitled to the proceeds of timber operations that derive from a proper management of timberlands. These solutions are dictated by considerations of social and economic utility as well as concern for the interests of both the usufructuary and the naked owner. Society has an interest in the continuous productivity of timberlands, the naked owner has an interest in the maintenance of crafts and skills organized around timber exploitation, and the usufructuary has an interest in the security of a regular income.

(c) Timber may be defined as trees which, if cut, would produce lumber for building or manufacturing purposes. This includes any trees that could be cut for economic gain, such as pulp wood, pines, hardwoods or building lumber. This would be equivalent to the definition of "merchantable timber" as used in Louisiana law.

(d) Timber operations by the usufructuary should not deplete the substance of the land. Modern techniques of regulated felling insure continuous production of timber and improvement of its quality. The interests of the naked owner are protected by the prohibition of waste and by the obligations of the usufructuary to act as a prudent administrator and to preserve the substance of the property subject to the usufruct.

Art. 563.   Alluvion

The usufruct extends to the increase to the land caused by alluvion or dereliction.

Acts 1976, No. 103, § 1, eff. Jan. 1, 1977.

REVISION COMMENTS—1976

(a) This article reproduces the substance of Article 553, first sentence of the Louisiana Civil Code of 1870. It changes the law as it extends the right of the usufructuary to land formed in a river.

(b) The first sentence of Article 553 of the Louisiana Civil Code of 1870 also declares that the usufructuary "has no right to islands formed in a stream not navigable opposite the land; they belong to the riparian proprietors, as is prescribed in the title; Of Things." This part of the first sentence has been suppressed because the navigability or nonnavigability of the river is immaterial for the rights of the usufructuary. If the river is navigable, the islands formed in the bed belong to the state. C.C. art. 512 (1870). If the river is nonnavigable, the island formed in the bed belong to the riparian proprietors, subject to the enjoyment of the usufructuary.

Art. 564.   Treasure

The usufructuary has no right to the enjoyment of a treasure found in the property of which he has the usufruct. If the usufructuary has found the treasure, he is entitled to keep one-half of it as finder.

Acts 1976, No. 103, § 1, eff. Jan. 1, 1977.

REVISION COMMENT—1976

This article reproduces the substance of Article 553, second paragraph, of the Louisiana Civil Code of 1870. It does not change the law.

Art. 565.   Predial servitudes

The usufructuary has a right to the enjoyment of predial servitudes due to the estate of which he has the usufruct. When the estate is enclosed within other lands belonging to the grantor of the usufruct, the usufructuary is entitled to a gratuitous right of passage.

Acts 1976, No. 103, § 1, eff. Jan. 1, 1977.

REVISION COMMENT—1976

This article reproduces the substance of Article 554 of the Louisiana Civil Code of 1870. It does not change the law.

Art. 566.   Actions

The usufructuary may institute against the naked owner or third persons all actions that are necessary to insure the possession, enjoyment, and preservation of his right.

Acts 1976, No. 103, § 1, eff. Jan. 1, 1977.

REVISION COMMENTS—1976

(a) This article reproduces the substance of Article 556 of the Louisiana Civil Code of 1870. It does not change the law.

(b) The usufruct of immovable property, being an incorporeal immovable, is protected by several innominate real actions as well as by three nominate real actions: the petitory action, the possessory action, and the action of boundary. See C.C.P. art. 3651; Messick v. Mayer, 52 La.Ann. 1161, 27 So. 815 (1900) (petitory action); C.C.P. art. 3655; Preston v. Zabrisky, 2 La. 226 (1813); Bagents v. Crowell Long Leaf Lumber Co., 20 So.2d 641 (La.App.1st Cir. 1945) (possessory action); C.C. art. 830 (boundary action).

(c) In addition to the real actions, the usufructuary may bring all the appropriate personal actions for the protection of his interests. Thus, in case of wrongful interference with his enjoyment, he may sue for damages under the law of delictual obligations without the concurrence of the naked owner. See Miller v. Colonial Pipeline Co., 173 So.2d 840 (La.App. 3d Cir. 1965); New Orleans v. Wire, 20 La.Ann. 500 (1868). If the usufruct bears on a credit, on its maturity the usufructuary is entitled to bring an action for payment. See 2 Aubry et Rau, Droit civil français 671 (7th ed. Esmein 1961); cf. Succession of Block, 137 La. 302, 68 So. 618 (1915); Kahn v. Becnel, 108 La. 296, 32 So. 444 (1902).

(d) In actions brought by the usufructuary against third persons for damage to, or destruction of, the property subject to the usufruct, the naked owner may be a necessary or even an indispensable party under Articles 641 and 642 of the Louisiana Code of Civil Procedure. Cf. Tennessee Gas Transmission Co. v. Drouen, 239 La. 467, 118 So.2d 889 (1960). But if, for any reason, the naked owner does not wish to prosecute his claim, the usufructuary is allowed to proceed alone and recover damages representing injuries to the right of enjoyment. See Miller v. Colonial Pipeline Co., 173 So.2d 840 (La.App. 3d Cir. 1965). In cases involving damage to property subject to the usufruct of the surviving spouse, however, the usufructuary is not only allowed to sue in his own name but also to recover full indemnity and to enjoy it for the period of the usufruct. Barry v. U.S. Fidelity & Guaranty Co., 236 So.2d 229 (La.App. 3d Cir. 1970).

Art. 567.   Contracts affecting the usufructuary's liability

The usufructuary may lease, alienate, or encumber his right. All such contracts cease of right at the end of the usufruct.

If the usufructuary leases, alienates, or encumbers his right, he is responsible to the naked owner for the abuse that the person with whom he has contracted makes of the property.

Acts 1976, No. 103, § 1, eff. Jan. 1, 1977. Amended by Acts 2010, No. 881, § 1, eff. July 2, 2010.

REVISION COMMENTS—1976

(a) This article reproduces the substance of Articles 555 and 561 of the Louisiana Civil Code of 1870. It does not change the law.

(b) The alienation of the usufruct is clearly an act of disposition of the right of enjoyment rather than of the property subject to usufruct. The usufructuary, being entitled to enjoyment, ought to have, on principle, the right to dispose of it as he pleases. Thus, in the absence of a prohibition in the act creating the usufruct, the usufructuary may transfer "his right" to another person. The transferee becomes himself usufructuary, i.e., the holder of a real right of enjoyment, vis-a-vis the transferor, the naked owner, and third persons. However, the original usufructuary remains bound toward the naked owner for any violations of duty by the transferee of the usufruct. C.C. art. 561 (1870). And the usufruct terminates upon the death of the original usufructuary rather than upon the death of the transferee. See 2 Aubry et Rau, Droit civil français 670 (7th ed. Esmein 1961).

(c) Since usufruct is transferable, it follows that in the absence of contrary provision, the usufructuary may mortgage his right of enjoyment over immovables and pledge his right of enjoyment over movables. C.C. art. 3289; cf. La.R.S. 9:4321.

(d) For the validity and effect of leases made by the usufructuary, see C.C. art. 2730 (1870); Sparks v. Dan Cohen Co., 187 La. 830, 175 So. 590 (1937); Yiannopoulos, Personal Servitudes § 40 (1968).

REVISION COMMENTS—2010

(a) This article reproduces the substance of Civil Code Article 567. It is intended to clarify the law regarding the usufructuary's liability in cases where the usufructuary leases, alienates, or encumbers his right.

(b) There is a significant distinction between the usufructuary's leasing, alienating or encumbering his right, and disposing of the thing itself. The right to dispose of the thing may be granted pursuant to the provisions of Article 568. Article 567 covers the situation where the usufructuary has not been granted the power to dispose of the property, as in the case of an Article 890 usufruct arising from intestacy. Also, even if granted the power to dispose of the property, the usufructuary may choose simply to deal with his right and not to dispose of the property itself, in which case Article 567 would govern.

(c) This Article clarifies that the liability of the usufructuary is to the naked owner, which is appropriate as a corollary to the usufructuary's duty to act as a prudent administrator.

Art. 568.   Disposition of nonconsumable things

The usufructuary may not dispose of nonconsumable things unless the right to do so has been expressly granted to him. Nevertheless, he may dispose of corporeal movables that are gradually and substantially impaired by use, wear, or decay, such as equipment, appliances, and vehicles, provided that he acts as a prudent administrator.

The right to dispose of a nonconsumable thing includes the rights to lease, alienate, and encumber the thing. It does not include the right to alienate by donation inter vivos, unless that right is expressly granted.

Acts 1976, No. 103, § 1, eff. Jan. 1, 1977. Amended by Acts 1986, No. 203, § 1; Acts 2010, No. 881, § 1, eff. July 2, 2010.

REVISION COMMENTS—1976

(a) The first sentence of this provision does not change the law. According to a Louisiana decision, the grantor may expressly grant to the usufructuary the right to dispose of nonconsumable things subject to the usufruct, in which case the usufruct of nonconsumables may be converted into a usufruct of consumables at the option of the usufructuary. Heirs of Michel v. Knox, 34 La.Ann. 399 (1882). The usufructuary and the naked owner may jointly dispose of nonconsumable things subject to usufruct unless this is prohibited by law or by the grantor of the usufruct.

(b) The second sentence of this provision changes the law as it allows disposition of nonconsumable things subject to usufruct, if they are gradually and substantially impaired by wear and decay. Upon disposition of the things within the limits of this provision, the usufruct of nonconsumables is converted into a usufruct of money, and the usufructuary is under obligation to deliver to the naked owner at the end of the usufruct the value that the things had at the time of disposition.

(c) The right of the usufructuary to dispose of things under the second sentence of this provision is not absolute. Its exercise depends upon the conditions that the things "are gradually and substantially impaired by wear and decay" and that the usufructuary acts in this respect "as a prudent administrator."

REVISION COMMENTS—2010

(a) This article reproduces the substance of Civil Code Article 568. It is intended to clarify the rights and obligations of the usufructuary who has a power of disposition over nonconsumable things.

(b) Paragraph one restates the rule that, except for things subject to wear and tear, the usufructuary may not dispose of nonconsumables, unless the right to do so has been expressly granted to him. Paragraph two introduces an important clarification by defining the right to dispose to include the rights to "lease, alienate, and encumber" the thing. Under this article, it is now clear that a usufructuary who has the right to dispose may not only alienate the thing by sale, exchange, or giving in payment, but may also encumber the thing by mortgage or otherwise.

(c) While the ability to donate is now clearly recognized as part of the power to dispose, paragraph two makes it clear that the power to donate must be expressly granted to the usufructuary.

Art. 568.1.   Donation and alienation

If a thing subject to the usufruct is donated inter vivos by the usufructuary, he is obligated to pay to the naked owner at the termination of the usufruct the value of the thing as of the time of the donation. If a thing subject to the usufruct is otherwise alienated by the usufructuary, the usufruct attaches to any money or other property received by the usufructuary. The property received shall be classified as consumable or nonconsumable in accordance with the provisions of this Title, and the usufruct shall be governed by those provisions subject to the terms of the act establishing the original usufruct. If, at the time of the alienation, the value of the property received by the usufructuary is less than the value of the thing alienated, the usufructuary is bound to pay the difference to the naked owner at the termination of the usufruct.

Added by Acts 2010, No. 881, § 1, eff. July 2, 2010.

COMMENTS—2010

(a) If the property received by the usufructuary is consumable, then under the provisions of this Title, the usufructuary will be bound to pay to the naked owner at the termination of the usufruct the value of the consumables that he received, and under the regular provisions governing usufruct the usufructuary will become the "owner" of the consumable property. See Civil Code Article 538. This will leave open the question of whether he may have sold the property for too low a price, and he is always subject to the obligation of acting as a prudent administrator. See Civil Code Article 576 and revision comment (b). If the usufructuary receives property that is nonconsumable, the usufruct will always attach to it and the usufructuary will be bound to deliver the thing received to the naked owner at the termination of the usufruct. See Civil Code Article 539.

(b) The provisions expressed in comment (a) are the provisions to which Article 568.1 refers when it states that the usufruct "shall be governed by those provisions." This Article expressly refers to the act establishing the original usufruct, because if that act granted authority to dispose of nonconsumables, that grant would be a continuing grant of authority and would apply to the new nonconsumables that have been received.

REVISION COMMENTS—2010

(a) This article provides rules governing the alienation by the usufructuary of things subject to the usufruct. It clarifies the law in part in that there is no authority under prior law authorizing the usufructuary to donate things subject to the usufruct.

(b) A donation is an alienation, but under this article an exception is carved out for donations. The usufructuary is not entitled to donate nonconsumable things subject to the usufruct unless this right has been expressly granted to him. If the right to donate has been expressly granted, then the usufructuary may donate things by inter vivos transfer and is obligated to account to the naked owner at the termination of the usufruct for the value that the things donated had at the time of the gratuitous transfer.

(c) If the property is alienated other than by donation, the property received in return by the usufructuary will also be held in usufruct. If the property received thereby is consumable, the provisions of Article 538 apply, and if it is nonconsumable the provisions of Article 539 apply, provided, however, that any provision in the act granting authority to dispose of nonconsumables will apply equally to the nonconsumables that are thereby received.

(d) This Article expressly refers to the act "establishing the original usufruct", because, if that act granted authority to dispose of nonconsumables, that grant would be a continuing grant of authority and would apply to the new nonconsumables that have been received.

Art. 568.2. Right to lease

The right to dispose of a nonconsumable thing includes the right to lease the thing for a term that extends beyond the termination of the usufruct. If, at the termination of the usufruct, the thing remains subject to the lease, the usufructuary is accountable to the naked owner for any diminution in the value of the thing at that time attributable to the lease.

Added by Acts 2010, No. 881, § 1, eff. July 2, 2010.

REVISION COMMENTS—2010

(a) This article allows a usufructuary with the right to dispose the authority to lease things subject to the usufruct for a term that goes beyond the existence of the usufruct. Otherwise, without the power to dispose of nonconsumables, the usufructuary may lease the property subject to the usufruct, but, unless confirmed or ratified by the naked owner, any such lease will terminate at the end of the usufruct, regardless of the length of the term conventionally agreed by the usufructuary and the lessee. See Civil Code Article 567 (1976); Yiannopoulos, Personal Servitudes, 3 Louisiana Civil Law Treatise (4th ed. 2000), at 188–189. See also Civil Code Article 2716, which provides: "A lease granted by a usufructuary terminates upon the termination of the usufruct. The lessor is liable to the lessee for any loss caused by such termination, if the lessor failed to disclose his status as a usufructuary." It is important to note that the usufructuary's right to lease for a term beyond the term of the usufruct only obtains when the usufructuary has been granted the power to dispose of the thing. There is a significant distinction between the usufructuary's "leasing, alienating, or encumbering" his right and disposing of the thing itself. See the discussion in comment to Article 567, supra.

(b) Even though he may have been granted the power to lease a thing for a term that extends beyond his lifetime, a usufructuary should be wary in granting such a lease. He may have the power to do so, but he is not released from liability to the naked owner if, at the termination of the usufruct, the existence of the lease diminishes the value of the thing. The article provides that the usufructuary is "accountable" to the naked owner for any diminution in the value of the thing attributable to the existence of the lease when the usufruct terminates. The lessee is protected against a premature termination of the lease, but the usufructuary remains exposed to potential liability. Consequently, a usufructuary contemplating the grant of a lease that may extend beyond the usufructuary's life should be cautious in the terms and conditions of the lease that he grants.

Art. 568.3. Requirement to remove encumbrance

If, at the termination of the usufruct, the thing subject to the usufruct is burdened by an encumbrance established by the usufructuary to secure an obligation, the usufructuary is bound to remove the encumbrance.

Added by Acts 2010, No. 881, § 1, eff. July 2, 2010.

REVISION COMMENTS—2010

(a) This article is intended to address the situation in which a usufructuary with a right to dispose has elected to encumber a nonconsumable thing subject to the usufruct to secure a debt. The article does not itself automatically remove the encumbrance by operation of law; it obligates the usufructuary to remove the encumbrance at the time the usufruct terminates.

(b) There is no simple rule to fit all cases. For example, a usufructuary who encumbers property to discharge or pay off a pre-existing debt of the grantor will be entitled to reimbursement from the naked owner for paying off that debt, and that right will be an offset against the amount needed to pay to remove the new encumbrance. Also, a usufructuary and naked owner may agree on a different resolution that may be fair and appropriate given all circumstances. For example, it may be advantageous to leave the encumbrance in place. In the absence of such an agreement, this Article establishes the base-line rule or starting point, which is that the encumbrance must be removed. The rule is not onerous because the usufructuary will have received the proceeds of the encumbrance, directly or indirectly, which he may have spent or used to improve the property for which he may receive reimbursement. Also there may be incidental tax benefits for the usufructuary, such as the ability to deduct depreciation on improvements made with those proceeds.

Art. 569.   Duties with regard to things gradually or totally impaired

If the usufructuary has not disposed of corporeal movables that are by their nature impaired by use, wear, or decay, he is bound to deliver them to the owner in the state in which they may be at the end of the usufruct.

The usufructuary is relieved of this obligation if the things are entirely worn out by normal use, wear, or decay.

Acts 1976, No. 103, § 1, eff. Jan. 1, 1977. Amended by Acts 2010, No. 881, § 1, eff. July 2, 2010.

REVISION COMMENT—1976

This provision reproduces the substance of Article 550 of the Louisiana Civil Code of 1870 subject to an important modification. Under Article 550 of the 1870 Code the usufructuary does not have the right to dispose of things that are gradually and substantially impaired by use, wear, or decay. Under Article 568, however, the usufructuary has this right and Article 569 applies only if the usufructuary keeps the things that are gradually impaired by use, wear, or decay.

REVISION COMMENTS—2010

This Article reproduces the substance of Article 569 of the Louisiana Civil Code. It is not intended to change the law.

SECTION 3—OBLIGATIONS OF THE USUFRUCTUARY

Art. 570.   Inventory

The usufructuary shall cause an inventory to be made of the property subject to the usufruct. In the absence of an inventory the naked owner may prevent the usufructuary's entry into possession of the property.

The inventory shall be made in accordance with the rules established in Articles 3131 through 3137 of the Code of Civil Procedure.

Acts 1976, No. 103, § 1, eff. Jan. 1, 1977.

REVISION COMMENTS—1976

(a) The first paragraph of this provision, following Article 557 of the Louisiana Civil Code of 1870, establishes the obligation of the usufructuary to make an inventory. It does not change the law.

(b) Neither the Louisiana nor the French Civil Code deals with the question of who is responsible for the expenses of the inventory. According to French doctrine and jurisprudence, which should also be relevant for Louisiana, the usufructuary must bear these expenses because the law imposes on him the obligation to make an inventory. Of course, the grantor may relieve the usufructuary of the expenses involved in the making of the inventory. See Breaux v. Carmouche, 15 La.Ann. 588 (1860). The naked owner, if he so wishes, may renounce his right to demand the confection of an inventory.

(c) If the usufructuary does not discharge his obligation to make an inventory, the naked owner may object to the usufructuary's entry into possession of the property. The second sentence of the article thus reproduces the rule established in Article 557 of the 1870 Code. If, for any reason, the things are in the possession of the usufructuary, the naked owner preserves the right to demand the confection of an inventory at any time during the existence of the usufruct. See Succession of Viaud, 11 La.Ann. 297 (1856). Further, in case of nonfulfillment of the obligation of the usufructuary to make an inventory, the naked owner should be able to prove his claims by all means of evidence, and the usufructuary should be held to strict accounting as a spoliator. See Tujague v. Courtiade, 140 La. 779, 73 So. 862 (1917).

(d) Ordinarily, the nonfulfillment of the usufructuary's obligation to make an inventory does not result in loss of the enjoyment or in loss of the right to fruits since the creation of the usufruct. See Succession of Viaud, 11 La.Ann. 297 (1856); 3 Planiol et Ripert, Traité pratique de droit civil français 808 (2d ed. Picard 1852). By way of exception to the rule, however, Article 3350 of the Louisiana Civil Code of 1870 provides that parents do not acquire the enjoyment of the property of their minor children without the confection of an inventory. Cf. Succession of Landier, 51 La.Ann. 968, 25 So. 938 (1899).

(e) The surviving spouse in community, as any other usufructuary, is under obligation to make an inventory. Saloy v. Chexnaidre, 14 La.Ann. 567 (1859). Unlike parents having the enjoyment of the property of minor children, however, the surviving spouse in community is not deprived of his enjoyment over property inherited by issue of the marriage in case of nonfulfillment of his obligation to make an inventory. See Burdin v. Burdin, 171 La. 7, 129 So. 651 (1930); Thomas v. Blair, 111 La. 678, 35 So. 811 (1903). And if the survivor is not in possession of the property subject to usufruct, the naked owners may refuse to deliver the property until the inventory is made. See Succession of Landier, 51 La.Ann. 968, 25 So. 938 (1899).

(f) The second paragraph of this provision changes the law as it declares that the inventory shall be made in accordance with the rules established in Articles 3131 through 3137 of the Code of Civil Procedure and suppresses the substantially different provisions of Article 557 of the Louisiana Civil Code of 1870. Application of the rules of the Code of Civil Procedure affords adequate protection to the interests of the naked owner, and there is no reason for the adoption of additional safeguards in the Civil Code.

(g) The naked owner may be notified to appear at the confection of the inventory. If the naked owner is an absentee, a nonresident, or an incompetent, and if he has no representative, the usufructuary may demand the appointment of an attorney to represent the naked owner in accordance with the rules established in Articles 5091 through 5098 of the Code of Civil Procedure.

(h) A descriptive list may be used in lieu of inventory. See La. Code Civ.P. art. 3136.

Art. 571.   Security

The usufructuary shall give security that he will use the property subject to the usufruct as a prudent administrator and that he will faithfully fulfill all the obligations imposed on him by law or by the act that established the usufruct unless security is dispensed with. If security is required, the court may order that it be provided in accordance with law.

Acts 1976, No. 103, § 1, eff. Jan. 1, 1977. Amended by Acts 2004, No. 158, § 1.

REVISION COMMENT—1976

This provision reproduces the substance of Article 558 of the Louisiana Civil Code of 1870. It does not change the law.

Art. 572.   Amount of security

The security shall be in the amount of the total value of the property subject to the usufruct.

The court may increase or reduce the amount of the security, on proper showing, but the amount shall not be less than the value of the movables subject to the usufruct.

Acts 1976, No. 103, § 1, eff. Jan. 1, 1977.

REVISION COMMENTS—1976

(a) This provision changes the law as it follows principles adopted in Article 3151 of the Code of Civil Procedure and suppresses the provisions of Articles 559 and 562 of the Louisiana Civil Code of 1870.

(b) Article 562 of the Louisiana Civil Code of 1870 provides that "the usufructuary may for the security required of him by law, give a special mortgage on immovable property of sufficient value and unincumbered, lying within the State". This article, read in combination with Article 558 of the same Code, seems to indicate that the required security may be of many kinds, one of which is a special mortgage. In reality, however, "security" in both Articles 558 and 562 ought to read "surety", and the correct interpretation is that the required surety may be replaced, at the option of the usufructuary, by a special mortgage. See Yiannopoulos, Personal Servitudes § 59 (1968). The rules adopted impose no limitations on the kinds of security that the usufructuary may furnish.

Art. 573.   Dispensation of security

A.   Security is dispensed with when any of the following occur:

(1) A person has a legal usufruct under Article 223 or 3252.

(2) A surviving spouse has a legal usufruct under Article 890 unless the naked owner is not a child of the usufructuary or if the naked owner is a child of the usufructuary and is also a forced heir of the decedent, the naked owner may obtain security but only to the extent of his legitime.

(3) A parent has a legal usufruct under Article 891 unless the naked owner is not a child of the usufructuary.

(4) A surviving spouse has a legal usufruct under Article 2434 unless the naked owner is a child of the decedent but not a child of the usufructuary.

B.   A seller or donor of property under reservation of usufruct is not required to give security.

Acts 1976, No. 103, § 1, eff. Jan. 1, 1977. Amended by Acts 2004, No. 158, § 1; Acts 2010, No. 881, § 1, eff. July 2, 2010.

REVISION COMMENTS—1976

(a) This provision reproduces the substance of Articles 559, second paragraph, and 560 of the Louisiana Civil Code of 1870.

(b) The dispensation of security by the grantor need not be express, but must be clearly implied from the testamentary dispositions or contractual provisions. See Maguire v. Maguire, 110 La. 279, 34 So. 443 (1903). See also Succession of Carlisi, 217 La. 675, 47 So.2d 42 (1950); Succession of Steele, 23 La.Ann. 734 (1870); Succession of Cardona, 14 La.Ann. 356 (1859). Further, the usufructuary may be relieved of the obligation to furnish security if the naked owner renounces his right to demand security. If the naked owner has neglected to demand security at the commencement of the usufruct, he does not forfeit his right and is entitled to demand security at any time during the existence of the usufruct. See 3 Planiol et Ripert, Traité pratique de droit civil français 809 (2d ed. Picard 1952).

(c) Article 560 of the Louisiana Civil Code of 1870 declares that "neither the father nor mother, having the legal usufruct of the estate of their children . . . is required to give this security". Louisiana courts have extended this dispensation of security to parents having any kind of legal usufruct over the property of their children. Thus, the surviving spouse having the usufruct of the deceased's share in the community inherited by issue of the marriage, the surviving spouse having the legal usufruct of the marital portion inherited by issue of the marriage with the deceased, and the necessitous widow having the legal usufruct of the amount of one thousand dollars attributed in naked ownership to children of the marriage need not give security. See Canal Bank & Trust Co. v. Liuzza, 175 La. 53, 143 So. 2 (1932); Succession of Dielmann, 119 La. 101, 43 So. 972 (1907); Succession of Glancey, 114 La. 1051, 38 So. 826 (1905) (surviving spouse in community); Taylor v. Taylor, 189 La. 1084, 181 So. 543 (1938) (usufruct of marital portion); Succession of White, 29 La.Ann. 792 (1877) (necessitous widow). Article 573 codifies this jurisprudence.

REVISION COMMENTS—2010

This article reproduces the substance of Civil Code Article 573. It is not intended to change the law. As revised, the article does not expressly provide that security is "dispensed by operation of law," because such a statement is unnecessary.

Art. 574.   Delay in giving security

A delay in giving security does not deprive the usufructuary of the fruits derived from the property since the commencement of the usufruct.

Acts 1976, No. 103, § 1, eff. Jan. 1, 1977. Amended by Acts 2010, No. 881, § 1, eff. July 2, 2010.

REVISION COMMENTS—1976

(a) This provision reproduces the substance of Article 566 of the Louisiana Civil Code of 1870. It does not change the law.

(b) It might be argued that, according to Article 566 of the Louisiana Civil Code of 1870, the usufructuary may claim the fruits produced since the commencement of the usufruct after he has fulfilled his obligation to furnish security. This interpretation, however, would involve an unnecessary hardship. Security is required for the protection of the naked owner when the things are in the possession of the usufructuary. When the things are in the possession of the naked owner, as it happens in cases covered by Article 566 (C.C., 1870), the interests of the naked owner are safe, and the usufructuary ought to be entitled to the fruits. Indeed, if the usufructuary is entitled to the fruits under the terms of Article 563 (C.C., 1870), namely, when he does not give security and possession of the property is in the hands of third persons, he ought a fortiori to be entitled to fruits when the property is in the hands of the naked owner. See Succession of Weller, 107 La. 466, 31 So. 883 (1902).

(c) If the usufructuary delays to give security, the naked owner in Louisiana and in France is entitled to refuse delivery of the property. See Samuels v. Brownlee, 36 La.Ann. 228 (1884); Westholz v. Retaud, 18 La.Ann. 285 (1866); 3 Planiol et Ripert, Traité pratique de droit civil français 809 (2d ed. Picard 1952).

REVISION COMMENTS—2010

This article reproduces the substance of Civil Code Article 574 with a minor grammatical change. It is not intended to change the law.

Art. 575.   Failure to give security

If the usufructuary does not give security, the court may order that the property be delivered to an administrator appointed in accordance with Articles 3111 through 3113 of the Code of Civil Procedure for administration on behalf of the usufructuary. The administration terminates if the usufructuary gives security.

Acts 1976, No. 103, § 1, eff. Jan. 1, 1977. Amended by Acts 2010, No. 881, § 1, eff. July 2, 2010.

REVISION COMMENTS—1976

(a) This provision reproduces principles adopted in Article 1160 of the Greek Civil Code and Section 1052 of the German Civil Code. It changes the law as it suppresses the provisions of Articles 563 and 564 of the Louisiana Civil Code of 1870. The change is considered desirable in the light of modern conditions.

(b) The naked owner may, of course, be a "qualified person" under Article 3111 of the Code of Civil Procedure.

REVISION COMMENTS—2010

This article reproduces the substance of Civil Code Article 575. It is not intended to change the law.

Art. 576.   Standard of care

The usufructuary is answerable for losses resulting from his fraud, default, or neglect.

Acts 1976, No. 103, § 1, eff. Jan. 1, 1977.

REVISION COMMENTS—1976

(a) This provision reproduces the substance of Article 567 of the Louisiana Civil Code of 1870. It does not change the law.

(b) The expressions "prudent owner" and "prudent administrator" in the Louisiana Civil Code of 1870, and the corresponding bon père de famille in the French Civil Code, reflect the notion of homo diligens et studiosus paterfamilias of the Roman law. Thus, the usufructuary is liable even for slight fault, namely, he must exercise the diligence that an attentive and careful man exercises in the management of his own affairs. See C.C. art. 3556(13) (1870): "The slight fault is that want of care which a prudent man usually takes of his business." The usufructuary is a fortiori liable for fraud and gross fault. Ibid. The second paragraph of Article 567 of the Louisiana Civil Code of 1870 declares that the usufructuary is "answerable for such losses as proceed from his fraud, default or neglect." According to Article 2315 of the Civil Code of 1870, the usufructuary, as any other person, is answerable for losses that result from any fault on his part.

(c) For Louisiana jurisprudence, see Bell v. Saunders, 139 La. 1037, 72 So. 727 (1916) (the usufructuary is bound "to take the same care of the property of which he enjoys the usufruct as though it were his own"); cf. Succession of Benoit, 196 La. 509, 199 So. 625 (1941) (a prudent administrator is not responsible for the decline of rental income attributed to the general decline of the economy); Mehle v. Bensel, 39 La.Ann. 680, 2 So. 201 (1887) (Syllabus).

(d) With respect to the obligation to take insurance, see Yiannopoulos, Personal Servitudes § 62 (1968).

Art. 577.   Liability for repairs

The usufructuary is responsible for ordinary maintenance and repairs for keeping the property subject to the usufruct in good order, whether the need for these repairs arises from accident or force majeure, the normal use of things, or his fault or neglect.

The naked owner is responsible for extraordinary repairs, unless they have become necessary as a result of the usufructuary's fault or neglect in which case the usufructuary is bound to make them at his cost.

Acts 1976, No. 103, § 1, eff. Jan. 1, 1977. Amended by Acts 1979, No. 157, § 1; Acts 2010, No. 881, § 1, eff. July 2, 2010.

REVISION COMMENTS—1976

(a) This provision reproduces the substance of Article 571 of the Louisiana Civil Code of 1870. It does not change the law.

(b) The words "indispensably necessary" in Article 571 of the 1870 Code ought to read "maintenance" repairs. The French text of Article 565 of the 1825 Code reads "réparations d' entretien." This article corrects the mistranslation.

(c) According to Louisiana jurisprudence, the notion of ordinary repairs includes "an awning that had been permitted to decay" and "a woodshed that had been torn down". Mehle v. Bensel, 39 La.Ann. 680, 2 So. 201 (1887); cf. Pendegast v. Schawtz, 30 La.Ann. 590 (1878).

(d) The responsibility of the usufructuary for maintenance and ordinary repairs exists from the time the usufruct was acquired by him. Cf. Articles 580, 581, infra.

(e) The words "a result" in the second paragraph were inadvertently omitted from the Article in 1976. The Article was amended in 1979 to reinsert these words.

REVISION COMMENTS—2010

(a) This article adds the term "force majeure" as one of the causes of a need for repairs for which the usufructuary is responsible. In that sense it clarifies the law. Under the 1976 revision of Article 577 the usufructuary must make ordinary repairs if the need for repairs arises from "accident, from the normal use of the things, or from his fraud or neglect," but the term force majeure was not included in that list as a cause of the need for ordinary repairs for which the usufructuary is responsible. The source articles in the 1870 Code to this and other articles that employed the term "accident", including the use of the general word "accident" in 1976, indicate that the term "accident" has always incorporated the concept of force majeure. See also Comment (e) to Article 613, which confirms this view by suggesting that "accident means 'irresistible force' (force majeure) or fortuitous event (cas fortuit)". The new article adds the term expressly to remove any doubt.

(b) Under this revision, the obligation to make ordinary repairs also includes those ordinary repairs made necessary by force majeure events, including hurricanes. This is consistent with the usufructuary's obligation to enjoy the things subject to the usufruct as a prudent administrator. See Civil Code Article 539. See also, generally, Yiannopoulos, Personal Servitudes, 3 Louisiana Civil Law Treatise (4th ed. 2000), at 256–258.

Art. 578. Ordinary and extraordinary repairs

Extraordinary repairs are those for the reconstruction of the whole or of a substantial part of the property subject to the usufruct. All others are ordinary repairs.

Acts 1976, No. 103, § 1, eff. Jan. 1, 1977.

REVISION COMMENTS—1976

(a) This provision changes the law as it replaces the exclusive enumeration of Article 572 of the 1870 Code with a broad definition of extraordinary repairs that is relevant for both movables and immovables. Repairs which under Article 572 (C.C., 1870) were classified as extraordinary continue to be so, but, in addition, the notion of extraordinary repairs has been expanded to include certain repairs that should be regarded as extraordinary by virtue of an expansive interpretation.

(b) According to French doctrine and jurisprudence, repairs to principal walls, vaults, and beams are extraordinary even if they involve only partial reconstruction. On the contrary, repairs to the roof, to a levee, and repairs to dikes, supporting walls, and walls of enclosure are extraordinary only if they involve complete or nearly complete reconstruction. See 2 Aubry et Rau, Droit civil français 676 (7th ed. Esmein 1961).

(c) "Ordinary repairs" is a residual category established by the process of exclusion. The usufructuary is not bound to make repairs needed at the time of the creation of the usufruct. These repairs, and attending expenses, are charged to the naked owner. The usufructuary is thus responsible only for repairs the need for which arose after the commencement of the usufruct. See Article 577, second paragraph, supra.

Art. 579.   Rights of action for repairs

During the existence of the usufruct, the naked owner may compel the usufructuary to make the repairs for which the usufructuary is responsible.

The usufructuary may not compel the naked owner to make the extraordinary repairs for which the owner is responsible. If the naked owner refuses to make them, the usufructuary may do so, and he shall be reimbursed without interest by the naked owner at the end of the usufruct.

Acts 1976, No. 103, § 1, eff. Jan. 1, 1977.

REVISION COMMENTS—1976

(a) This provision reproduces the substance of Articles 573 and 576 of the 1870 Code. It does not change the law.

(b) Expenses for extraordinary repairs incurred by the usufructuary in accordance with the second paragraph of this Article, are not included among the improvements that the usufructuary is bound to abandon to the owner at the end of the usufruct.

Art. 580.   Reimbursement for necessary repairs

If, after the usufruct commences and before the usufructuary is put in possession, the naked owner incurs necessary expenses or makes repairs for which the usufructuary is responsible, the naked owner has the right to claim the cost from the usufructuary and may retain the possession of the things subject to the usufruct until he is paid.

Acts 1976, No. 103, § 1, eff. Jan. 1, 1977. Amended by Acts 2010, No. 881, § 1, eff. July 2, 2010.

REVISION COMMENTS—1976

(a) This article reproduces the substance of Article 574 of the Louisiana Civil Code of 1870. It does not change the law.

(b) Since ordinary repairs are charges of the enjoyment, the usufructuary is not bound to make repairs already needed at the time of the creation of the usufruct. These repairs and the attending expenses are charged to the naked owner. The usufructuary is thus responsible for repairs the need for which arose after the commencement of the usufruct. Article 580 indicates that the usufructuary is responsible for the expenses of repairs made by the naked owner prior to the delivery of possession when the need for repairs arises after the commencement of the usufruct. See Yiannopoulos, Personal Servitudes § 66 (1968).

REVISION COMMENTS—2010

This article reproduces the substance of Civil Code Article 580. It is not intended to change the law.

Art. 581.   Liability for necessary expenses

The usufructuary is answerable for all expenses that become necessary for the preservation and use of the property after the commencement of the usufruct.

Acts 1976, No. 103, § 1, eff. Jan. 1, 1977. Amended by Acts 2010, No. 881, § 1, eff. July 2, 2010.

REVISION COMMENTS—1976

(a) This provision reproduces the substance of Article 570 of the Louisiana Civil Code of 1870. It does not change the law.

(b) "Working of the estates" in Article 570 of the 1870 Code ought to read "exploitation of the things". The French text of Article 564 of the 1825 Code reads "à l'exploitation des biens." The expression "use of the property" in Article 581 has the same meaning as "exploitation of the things".

(c) This provision deals with the liability of the usufructuary for expenses other than the cost of ordinary maintenance and repairs. The need for ordinary maintenance and repairs, and the corresponding liability of the usufructuary, are matters determined in the light of the obligation of the usufructuary "for losses resulting from his fraud, default, or neglect." Article 576, supra.

REVISION COMMENTS—2010

This article reproduces the substance of Civil Code Article 581. It is not intended to change the law.

Art. 582.   Abandonment of usufruct

The usufructuary may release himself from the obligation to make repairs by abandoning the usufruct or, with the approval of the court, a portion thereof, even if the owner has instituted suit to compel him to make repairs or bear the expenses of them, and even if the usufructuary has been cast in judgment.

He may not release himself from the charges of the enjoyment during the period of his possession, nor from accountability for the damages that he, or persons for whom he is responsible, may have caused.

Acts 1976, No. 103, § 1, eff. Jan. 1, 1977.

REVISION COMMENTS—1976

(a) This provision reproduces the substance of Article 575 of the Louisiana Civil Code of 1870. It does not change the law.

(b) A Louisiana court interpreting Article 575 of the 1870 Code has held that the usufructuary is entitled to abandon his entire enjoyment; he may not abandon merely a part of his enjoyment bearing on things that are particularly burdensome for the usufructuary to hold. Judice v. Provost, 18 La.Ann. 601 (1866). Under Article 582, the usufructuary may abandon, with the approval of the court, a portion of the property subject to the usufruct. The usufructuary has this right because, in principle, usufruct is divisible. Article 541, supra. As to the right of the usufructuary to abandon his entire enjoyment at any time, see Succession of Dougart, 30 La.Ann. 268 (1878).

(c) The usufructuary "may not release himself from the charges of the enjoyment during the period of his possession". This means that the usufructuary is bound to make all the ordinary maintenance repairs the need for which arises from the commencement of the usufruct until abandonment, and to pay all annual and extraordinary charges in proportion to the duration of his enjoyment. See Articles 577, 584, 585. The usufructuary may not avoid these obligations by returning to the naked owner the fruits produced by the property since the commencement of the usufruct and until the time of the abandonment. The abandonment of the usufruct is not retroactive but prospective. The usufructuary is bound for the charges of the enjoyment incurred during the period of his possession, and, correspondingly, he is entitled to keep the fruits accrued since the commencement of the usufruct and until its abandonment. See 3 Planiol et Ripert, Traité pratique de droit civil français 820 (2d ed. Picard 1952).

Art. 583.   Ruin from accident, force majeure, or age

Neither the usufructuary nor the naked owner is bound to restore property that has been totally destroyed through accident, force majeure, or age.

If the naked owner elects to restore the property or to make extraordinary repairs, he shall do so within a reasonable time and in the manner least inconvenient and onerous for the usufructuary.

Acts 1976, No. 103, § 1, eff. Jan. 1, 1977. Amended by Acts 2010, No. 881, § 1, eff. July 2, 2010.

REVISION COMMENTS—1976

(a) This provision reproduces the substance of Article 577 of the Louisiana Civil Code of 1870. It does not change the law.

(b) The words "ordinary repairs" in Article 577(1) of the 1870 Code ought to read "extraordinary repairs". 3 La.Legal Archives, Compiled Edition of the Civil Codes of Louisiana 334 (1937). The intent of the redactors was that, in case of partial destruction of the property through accident or decay, the naked owner should be bound to make extraordinary repairs. It is hardly imaginable that the redactors intended to classify all repairs for the restoration of partially destroyed property as "extraordinary" repairs at the charge of the naked owner. This article makes it clear that in case of partial destruction of the property through accident or decay the duties of the naked owner and of the usufructuary are determined by application of the rules governing repairs. Thus, the usufructuary will be bound to make ordinary repairs and the naked owner will be bound to make extraordinary repairs.

(c) If property has been partially or totally destroyed through the fault of the usufructuary or as a result of neglect of upkeep, the usufructuary is bound to repair the damage. See Articles 576, 577, supra; 3 Planiol et Ripert, Traité pratique de droit civil français 319 (2d ed. Picard 1952). If property is destroyed through the fault of a third person, the usufruct attaches to the claim of damages due by the wrongdoer. See Article 614, infra.

REVISION COMMENTS—2010

This article clarifies the law by making clear that "force majeure" is one of the causes of destruction of property for which the usufructuary is not responsible. Under article 583, as revised in 1976, the owner is not obligated to restore the property when the same is destroyed "through accident or because of age". See, generally, Yiannopoulos, Personal Servitudes, 3 Louisiana Civil Law Treatise (4th ed. 2000), at 273.

Art. 584.   Periodic charges

The usufructuary is bound to pay the periodic charges, such as property taxes, that may be imposed, during his enjoyment of the usufruct.

Acts 1976, No. 103, § 1, eff. Jan. 1, 1977. Amended by Acts 2010, No. 881, § 1, eff. July 2, 2010.

REVISION COMMENTS—1976

(a) This provision reproduces the substance of Article 578 of the Louisiana Civil Code of 1870. It does not change the law.

(b) Reference to "ground rents" has been omitted because this institution has fallen into disuse. Reference to charges for the repair of "roads, bridges, ditches, levees and the like" has also been omitted because these are included in the notion of "taxes".

(c) The usufructuary owes the annual taxes on the property subject to his usufruct, but he is not a "property taxpayer" within the meaning of election laws. Accordingly, the right to vote belongs to the naked owner. Endom v. City of Monroe, 112 La. 779, 36 So. 681 (1904). The liability for the payment of annual charges gives rise to a personal obligation of the usufructuary toward the public authorities. Accordingly, public authorities may seize and sell the entire property of the usufructuary for the satisfaction of their claims. See Leadman v. First Natl. Bank of Shreveport, 184 La. 715, 167 So. 200 (1936); Mehle v. Bensel, 39 La.Ann. 680, 2 So. 201 (1887); Pendegast v. Schawtz, 30 La.Ann. 590 (1878); Gilmer v. Stinson, 197 So. 299 (La.App.2d Cir. 1940).

(d) Annual public charges, though payable by the usufructuary, are assessed on the things subject to the usufruct. Accordingly if the usufructuary fails to pay annual charges, the public authorities may seize and sell, in addition to the usufructuary's own property, the things subject to the usufruct. Louisiana decisions declare that a tax sale is indeed valid if the registered owner has been given notice of the proceedings and of the tax debts. See Gilmer v. Stinson, 197 So. 299 (La.App.2d Cir. 1940); Spikes v. O'Neal, 193 So. 487 (La.App.1st Cir. 1940). But see Milburn v. Proctor Trust Co., 32 F.Supp. 635 (W.D.La.1940), affirmed 122 F.2d 569 (1941), cert. den. 314 U.S. 698 (1942), holding that the property subject to the usufruct may not be seized and sold if the usufructuary fails to pay taxes.

(e) The naked owner, in order to avoid a tax sale of his property, may pay the taxes due by the usufructuary and bring against him an action for reimbursement. In this respect Articles 579 and 580, supra, apply by analogy. If the naked owner is unable to make payment and the property is sold at a tax sale, the usufructuary is liable to pay damages.

(f) The usufructuary is bound to pay the annual charges "during his enjoyment". Thus, if at the commencement or at the end of the usufruct the usufructuary had the enjoyment of the things for less than a year, the taxes and charges due for that year must be apportioned between the usufructuary and the naked owner. In this respect, the rules governing apportionment of civil fruits ought to apply by analogy. The charges are divided into 365 or 366 equal parts. The usufructuary pays as many parts as he had days of enjoyment. See 3 Planiol et Ripert, Traité pratique de droit civil français 828 (2d ed. Picard 1952).

REVISION COMMENTS—2010

This article amends the language of Civil Code Article 584 in order to make it more technically accurate. The intent of this revision is to clarify the law, by providing that the usufructuary is liable for "periodic" charges, and not just annual ones. In addition, the article provides that the liability of the usufructuary for charges includes those that may be imposed during the existence of the usufruct, in order to make it clear that the usufructuary is liable for charges that are imposed after the usufruct commences, even if the charges had not been imposed at the commencement of the usufruct.

Art. 585.   Extraordinary charges

The usufructuary is bound to pay the extraordinary charges that may be imposed, during the existence of the usufruct, on the property subject to it. If these charges are of a nature to augment the value of the property subject to the usufruct, the naked owner shall reimburse the usufructuary at the end of the usufruct only for the capital expended.

Acts 1976, No. 103, § 1, eff. Jan. 1, 1977.

REVISION COMMENTS—1976

(a) This provision reproduces the substance of Article 579 of the Louisiana Civil Code of 1870. It does not change the law.

(b) Paving assessment are extraordinary charges payable by the usufructuary but recoverable from the naked owner, without interest, at the end of the usufruct. See 1 La.Legal Archives, Project of the Civil Code of 1825, art. 34, p. 57 (1937): "Some of these [extraordinary charges] augment the value of the property subject to usufruct, as the construction of banquets in cities." Cf. Coleman v. Poydras Asylum, 17 La.Ann. 325 (1865) (usufructuaries are "true and direct" debtors of paving assessments). Accordingly, suits for paving assessments may not be brought against the naked owners. Ibid. See also City of New Orleans v. Wire, 20 La.Ann. 500 (1868) (paving assessment is a personal debt of the usufructuary widow rather than a debt of the succession); Perez v. Guitard, 14 Orl.App. 191 (La.App.Orl.Cir.1916).

Art. 586.   Liability for debts; usufruct inter vivos

When the usufruct is established inter vivos, the usufructuary is not liable for debts of the grantor, but if the debt is secured by an encumbrance of the thing subject to the usufruct, the thing may be sold for the payment of the debt.

Acts 1976, No. 103, § 1, eff. Jan. 1, 1977. Amended by Acts 2010, No. 881, § 1, eff. July 2, 2010.

REVISION COMMENTS—1976

(a) This provision is new. It articulates concepts inherent in Articles 582 and 3556(28) of the Louisiana Civil Code of 1870. It does not change the law.

(b) According to Articles 582 and 3556(28) of the Louisiana Civil Code of 1870, if the usufruct is established inter vivos, the usufructuary is a particular successor of the grantor. As a particular successor, the usufructuary is not responsible for the debts of the grantor.

(c) If the property subject to the usufruct is burdened with a preexisting mortgage, pledge, or privilege, the usufructuary has the right to discharge the indebtedness. If the usufructuary discharges the indebtedness, he has a claim for reimbursement for the capital he has expended, that is, without interest.

(d) If the usufruct is gratuitous, action for reimbursement shall lie against the naked owner at the end of the usufruct, subject to the provisions contained in the title: Of donations inter vivos and mortis causa. If the usufruct is onerous, action may be brought at any time; defendant shall be the grantor of the usufruct, subject to the provisions contained in the title: Sale.

REVISION COMMENTS—2010

This article restates the principle that a usufructuary of an inter vivos usufruct is not liable for the debts of the grantor. It is intended to clarify the rule of prior law to the effect that if the property subject to the usufruct is subject to an encumbrance that secures a debt, the thing may be sold for the payment of the debt. It is not intended to change the law.

Art. 587.   Liability for debts; usufruct established mortis causa

When the usufruct is established mortis causa, the usufructuary is not liable for estate debts, but the property subject to the usufruct may be sold for the payment of estate debts, in accordance with the rules provided for the payment of the debt of an estate in Book III of this Code.

Acts 1976, No. 103, § 1, eff. Jan. 1, 1977. Amended by Acts 2010, No. 881, § 1, eff. July 2, 2010.

REVISION COMMENTS—1976

(a) This provision articulates concepts inherent in Articles 581, 583 through 587 of the Louisiana Civil Code of 1870. It does not change the law.

(b) According to the Louisiana and French Civil Codes, usufruct may be universal, under universal title, or under particular title. The usufruct of an entire patrimony is universal. C.C. art. 585 (1870). The usufruct of a fraction of a patrimony is under universal title. C.C. art. 586 (1870). The usufruct of individually determined things is under particular title. C.C. art. 581 (1870). See also id. art. 3556(28); Cecile v. Lacoste, 8 La.Ann. 142 (1853). When, however, the usufruct is granted over individually determined things but in fact exhausts the patrimony of the grantor, the usufruct is in reality universal. Accordingly, the usufructuary incurs the obligations of a universal usufructuary. See Succession of Sinot, 3 La.Ann. 175 (1848); 3 Planiol et Ripert, Traité pratique de droit civil français 757 (2d ed. Picard 1952).

(c) The classification of usufructs as universal, under universal title, and under particular title should not be confused with the classification of legacies as universal, under universal title, and under particular title, nor with the related question whether the usufructuary is a universal or a particular successor of the grantor of the usufruct. See Yiannopoulos, Personal Servitudes § 7 (1968). According to an early Louisiana decision, the legacy of a usufruct is always a legacy under particular title. Succession of Dougart, 30 La.Ann. 268 (1878). According to modern French doctrine and jurisprudence, however, the legacy of a universal usufruct or of a usufruct under universal title ought to qualify as a legacy under universal title. See 11 Aubry et Rau, Droit civil français 344 n. 7, 348 (7th ed. Esmein 1956).

REVISION COMMENTS—2010

(a) Under current law, a legacy of a usufruct is a particular legacy. See La Civil Code Art. 1587 and revision comment (b) to that article. Thus, the classifications of "usufruct under universal title", "universal usufruct", and "usufruct under particular title" have been eliminated. Formerly it was necessary to have a separate article for usufructs under particular title (Civil Code Article 588, as revised in 1976), but such an article is no longer needed.

(b) This Article was also thought to be necessary because, after the adoption of the usufruct law in 1976, the law of successions was revised and a complete chapter on payment of estate debts was added, with a new classification of debts as being estate debts, which debts are in turn subdivided into debts of the decedent and administration expenses. See Civil Code Article 1415 as amended by Act 1421 of 1997. These new terms of art, the concepts they represent, and the manner in which they operate, necessitated changes in the language of the article to appropriately incorporate them into this new Article. Under the new rules for payment of estate debts, a successor is personally liable only "to the extent of the value of the property received by him". See Civil Code Article 1416. The liability is in rem in the sense that the property may be sold in order to pay an estate debt, and the allocation of the liability to property depends on the application of the rules in the chapter on payment of estate debts. This Article removes the archaic references to classifications that existed in 1976, but no longer exist, and properly coordinates the mortis causa usufructuary's liability for debts with the newer rules regarding payment of estate debts.

Art. 588. Discharge of debt on encumbered property; usufruct established inter vivos

When property subject to a usufruct established inter vivos is encumbered to secure a debt before the commencement of the usufruct, the usufructuary may advance the funds needed to discharge the indebtedness. If he does so, the naked owner shall reimburse the usufructuary, without interest, at the termination of the usufruct, for the principal of the debt the usufructuary has discharged, and for any interest the usufructuary has paid that had accrued on the debt before the commencement of the usufruct.

Acts 1976, No. 103, § 1, eff. Jan. 1, 1977. Amended by Acts 2010, No. 881, § 1, eff. July 2, 20

REVISION COMMENTS—1976

(a) This provision reproduces the substance of Article 581 of the Louisiana Civil Code of 1870. It does not change the law.

(b) In the light of the proposed text, the legatee of usufruct under particular title is not liable for the debts of the succession. These debts must be paid by the universal successor of the grantor, be he the naked owner or a third person.

(c) If the property subject to the usufruct is burdened with a mortgage, pledge, or privilege, the usufructuary may discharge the indebtedness. If he does so, he may claim reimbursement from the naked owner at the end of the usufruct only for the capital he has expended, subject to the provisions contained in the title: Of donations inter vivos and mortis causa.

(d) Article 1638 of the Louisiana Civil Code of 1870 declares that: "If prior to the testament or subsequently, the thing has been mortgaged by the testator for his own debt or for that of another, or if it be burdened with an usufruct, he who is to pay the legacy is not bound to discharge the thing bequeathed of the incumbrance, unless he be required to do it by an express disposition of the testator." Cf. Succession of Waterman, 298 So.2d 731 (La. 1974). In this case, the court held that testator's direction concerning payment of all his just debts was an express disposition under Article 1638 of the Civil Code; hence, the court ordered that a mortgage debt be paid from residuary assets. Article 1638 applies to the relations between a particular legatee of an immovable encumbered with mortgage or usufruct and the universal successor of the testator. Article 588 applies to the relations between the particular legatee of the usufruct of a mortgaged immovable and the naked owner of the same immovable, be he a particular or a universal successor of the testator.

REVISION COMMENTS—2010

(a) This article simplifies the language of the source provision, which enumerated the kinds of encumbrances with which the usufruct could be burdened at the time of the commencement of the usufruct. Under this article, the usufructuary of an inter vivos usufruct who advances the funds necessary for the discharge of an encumbrance existing on the property at the time of the commencement of the usufruct is entitled to recover not only the amount of the principal of the debt he has discharged, but also any interest paid by him that had accrued on the debt prior to the commencement of the usufruct. Under the source provision, the usufructuary was entitled to obtain reimbursement "only for the capital he has expended".

(b) As under prior law, the usufructuary of an inter vivos usufruct is not personally liable for obligations burdening the property at the commencement of the usufruct. As stated by one authority: "if the usufruct is established by inter vivos juridical act, the usufructuary is not bound to discharge secured obligations burdening the property subject to the usufruct". Yiannopoulos, Personal Servitudes, 3 Louisiana Civil Law Treatise (4th ed. 2000) at 287.

Art. 589. Discharge of debt on encumbered property by mortis causa usufructuary

If the usufructuary of a usufruct established mortis causa advances funds to discharge an estate debt charged to the property subject to the usufruct, the naked owner shall reimburse the usufructuary, without interest, at the termination of the usufruct, but only to the extent of the principal of the debt he has discharged and for any interest he has paid that had accrued on the debt before the commencement of the usufruct.

Acts 1976, No. 103, § 1, eff. Jan. 1, 1977. Amended by Acts 2010, No. 881, § 1, eff. July 2, 2010.

REVISION COMMENTS—1976

(a) This provision reproduces the substance of Article 583 of the Louisiana Civil Code of 1870. It does not change the law.

(b) For the proposition that the usufructuary is not personally liable for the debts of the succession, see Succession of Weller, 107 La. 406, 31 So. 883 (1903). The fruits that the usufructuary has collected since the creation of the usufruct are his property; accordingly, creditors of the succession may not demand that the usufructuary should apply his fruits to the payment of debts. Boyle v. Sibley, 22 La.Ann. 446 (1870).

(c) With respect to the payment of the debts of the succession neither the universal usufructuary nor the usufructuary under universal title assumes the obligations of a universal successor of the grantor. See Godwin v. Neustadtl, 47 La.Ann. 841, 17 So. 471 (1895); cf. Long v. Dickerson, 127 La. 341, 53 So. 598 (1910). In effect, however, the legacy of a universal usufruct or of a usufruct under universal title is subordinated to the payment of the debts of the succession. The universal usufructuary as well as the usufructuary under universal title, though neither personally bound nor directly liable toward creditors of the succession for the payment of debts, must contribute, along with the universal successors, for the payment of these debts. In principle, the universal successors of the testator are bound for the payment of the capital whereas the contribution of the usufructuaries consists in their liability toward the successors for the payment of interest. See Articles 591 and 592, infra.

(d) The debts of the succession to which Articles 589 through 592 refer are personal as well as secured debts of the deceased: Haight v. Johnson, 131 La. 781, 60 So. 248 (1912); Martin Davie & Co. v. Carville, 110 La. 862, 34 So. 807 (1903); particular legacies: Le Goaster v. Lafon Asylum, 155 La. 158, 99 So. 22 (1924); Succession of Moore, 42 La.Ann. 332, 7 So. 651 (1890); cf. Fink v. Delmore, 192 La. 317, 188 So. 15 (1939); and administration charges, if the estate of the deceased is under administration. Cf. Succession of Ratcliff, 212 La. 563, 33 So.2d 114 (1947). Legacies of an annuity or of alimony are to be acquitted wholly by the universal usufructuary; and, if the usufruct is under universal title, by the usufructuary under that title in proportion to his enjoyment, without right of reimbursement. See Article 593, infra.

(e) This provision applies to the legal usufruct of the surviving spouse. See comment (c) under Article 591, infra.

REVISION COMMENTS—2010

(a) This article contemplates a situation in which an estate debt has been charged against property that is subject to a mortis causa usufruct under the rules regulating the liability of successors for payment of estate debts. See Civil Code Articles 1421–1427. It allows the usufructuary who advances funds to discharge such a debt to obtain reimbursement from the naked owner for the principal of the debt discharged and for payments of interest that had accrued prior to the commencement of the usufruct.

(b) Under this article, the mortis causa usufructuary who advances funds to pay an encumbrance burdening the property at the time of commencement of the usufruct has the same rights as an inter vivos usufructuary who pays such a mortgage. See comments (a) and (b) to Article 588 of this revision.

(c) Article 589 previously provided that, while neither the "universal usufructuary" nor the "usufructuary under universal title" was liable for the payment of the estate debts, the property subject to the usufruct could be "seized and sold for the payment of succession debts." The classifications of "universal usufructuary" and "usufructuary under universal title" have been eliminated, but the rule that property subject to the usufruct may be sold to pay estate debts has been retained. See revised Article 587 and revision comments (a) and (b) to that article, supra

(d) The sources of this article are former Civil Code Articles 588, 590, 591 and 592. Former Article 591 provided that a "universal usufructuary" was required to advance the funds necessary to pay all of the debts of the succession and the usufructuary "under universal title" was required to contribute to the payment of the debts of the succession also in proportion to the value of the property

178

subject to the usufruct. The classifications have been eliminated, and the mandatory language of former Article 591 is not included in this article.

Art. 590.   Encumbered property; discharge of debt on encumbered property by naked owner

If the usufructuary fails or refuses to advance the funds needed to discharge a debt secured by property subject to the usufruct, or an estate debt that is charged to the property subject to the usufruct, the naked owner may advance the funds needed. If he does so, the naked owner may demand that the usufructuary pay him interest during the period of the usufruct. If the naked owner does not advance the funds, he may demand that all or part of the property be sold as needed to discharge the debt.

Acts 1976, No. 103, § 1, eff. Jan. 1, 1977. Amended by Acts 2010, No. 881, § 1, eff. July 2, 2010.

REVISION COMMENTS—1976

(a) This provision reproduces the substance of Article 584 of the Louisiana Civil Code of 1870. It does not change the law.

(b) This provision applies specifically to universal usufructs and usufructs under universal title that have been created mortis causa. The usufruct of an entire succession is universal. C.C. art. 585 (1870). The usufruct of a fraction of a succession is under universal title. C.C. art. 586 (1870). The classification of usufructs as universal or under universal title should not be confused with the classification of legacies as universal or under universal title. See Yiannopoulos, Personal Servitudes § 7 (1968). According to an early Louisiana decision, all legacies of usufruct are legacies under particular title. Succession of Dougart, 30 La.Ann. 268 (1878). According to modern French doctrine and jurisprudence, however, the legacy of a universal usufruct or of a usufruct under universal title ought to qualify as a legacy under universal title. See 11 Aubry et Rau, Droit civil français 344 n. 7, 348 (7th ed. Esmein 1956).

(c) This provision does not apply to particular legacies of usufruct. Particular legacies of usufruct are, of course, subordinated to payment of the debts of the succession. But the particular legatee of the usufruct is not bound to contribute to the payment of the debts of the succession out of the property subject to his usufruct. In this respect, his position is different from that of the universal usufructuary or usufructuary under universal title.

(d) For the sale of succession property for the discharge of the debts of the succession, see Succession of Russell, 208 La. 213, 23 So.2d 50 (1945); Succession of Singer, 208 La. 463, 23 So.2d 184 (1945). If property of the succession is sold, the usufruct attaches to any such residue remaining after the payment of debts. Ibid.

(e) In the absence of contrary provision, federal estate taxes and the Louisiana Estate Transfer Act tax are to be paid by the naked owner out of the entire estate. See Yiannopoulos, Personal Servitudes § 17 (1968). The Louisiana inheritance tax is to be paid by the naked owner and by the usufructuary in proportion to the value of their respective interests. See Succession of Baker, 129 La. 74, 55 So. 714 (1911); Succession of Eisman, 170 So.2d 913 (La.App. 4th Cir. 1965).

REVISION COMMENTS—2010

This article addresses the situation in which property subject to a usufruct is encumbered to secure a debt at the commencement of the usufruct and the usufructuary fails to advance the funds necessary for the discharge of the mortgage or other encumbrance. In such a situation, the naked owner may either (1) advance the funds and demand that the usufructuary pay him interest on the capital expenditures, or (2) sell the property, in whole or in part, "as needed to discharge the debt". The provisions of this article apply to both an inter vivos usufruct and to a mortis causa usufruct.

Art. 591.   Continuation of usufruct after sale of property

If property subject to the usufruct is sold to pay an estate debt, or a debt of the grantor, the usufruct attaches to any proceeds of the sale of the property that remain after payment of the debt.

Acts 1976, No. 103, § 1, eff. Jan. 1, 1977. Amended by Acts 2010, No. 881, § 1, eff. July 2, 2010.

REVISION COMMENTS—1976

(a) This provision combines ideas expressed in Articles 585, 586, and 587, first paragraph, of the Louisiana Civil Code of 1870. It does not change the law.

(b) The universal usufructuary having the enjoyment of the entire estate, must contribute to the payment of the sum total of the debts of the succession. The usufructuary under universal title, having merely the enjoyment of a fraction of the estate, must contribute with the universal successor to the payment of the corresponding fraction of the debts of the succession. The contribution of the usufructuary under universal title is fixed in proportion to the value of the property subject to the usufruct and of that remaining to the universal successor.

(c) A literal interpretation of Articles 585 through 587 of the Louisiana Civil Code of 1870 might lead to the conclusion that these articles apply only to legacies of usufruct, whether universal or under universal title. Louisiana courts however, have held correctly that these articles apply as well to the legal usufruct of the surviving spouse. See Long v. Dickerson, 127 La. 341, 53 So. 598 (1910); Haight v. Johnson, 131 La. 781, 60 So. 248 (1912); Succession of Bringier, 4 La.Ann. 389 (1848). Indeed, the usufruct of the surviving spouse in community is under universal title, created mortis causa by operation of law. Article 591 is applicable to all usufructs created mortis causa. In this respect, it codifies Louisiana jurisprudence.

(d) This provision deals merely with the obligations of the usufructuary to advance sums for the payment of the debts of the succession; the usufructuary's right of reimbursement at the end of the usufruct is dealt with in the following article.

REVISION COMMENTS—2010

This article is intended to address the situation in which property subject to the usufruct is sold to pay an estate debt or a debt of the grantor of the usufruct and there are proceeds remaining after payment of the debt or debts involved. This article fills a gap that existed under prior law where such a situation was not addressed. It is not intended to change the law.

Art. 592.   Multiple usufructuaries; contribution to payment of estate debts

If there is more than one usufructuary of the same property, each contributes to the payment of estate debts that are charged to the property in proportion to his enjoyment of the property. If one or more of the usufructuaries fails to advance his share, those of them who advance the funds shall have the right to recover the funds they advance from those who do not advance their shares.

Acts 1976, No. 103, § 1, eff. Jan. 1, 1977. Amended by Acts 2010, No. 881, § 1, eff. July 2, 2010.

REVISION COMMENTS—1976

(a) This provision combines ideas expressed in Articles 585 and 587, second paragraph, of the Louisiana Civil Code of 1870. It does not change the law.

(b) The usufructuary may prevent the sale of the property by advancing the requisite funds for the discharge of the debts of the succession. If he does so, the capital shall be returned to him without interest at the end of the usufruct. If the usufructuary is unwilling or unable to make this advance, the universal successor has the choice of making the advance himself, in which case the usufructuary shall pay him interest during the period of the usufruct, or of selling a part of the property sufficient to raise the requisite funds for the payment of the debts of the succession. For Louisiana jurisprudence, see Le Goaster v. Lafon Asylum, 155 La. 158, 99 So. 22 (1924); Long v. Dickerson, 127 La. 341, 53 So. 598 (1910); Succession of Weller, 197 La. 466, 31 So. 883 (1902); Newman v. Cooper, 40 La.Ann. 397, 23 So. 116 (1878); Succession of Pratt, 12 La.Ann. 457 (1857); Succession of Bringier, 4 La.Ann. 389 (1848).

(c) A literal interpretation of Articles 585 and 587 of the 1870 Code might lead to the conclusion that the usufructuary is merely entitled to advance the capital needed for the discharge of the debts and that his obligation to pay interest arises only if the heir advances the sums needed. Louisiana courts, however, have interpreted these articles broadly and have rightly held that the usufructuary is entitled to make arrangements with the creditors for an extension of the maturity date of a debt and for payment of interest without any repayment of capital. See Haight v. Johnson, 131 La. 781, 60 So. 248 (1912); Long v. Dickerson, 127 La. 341, 53 So. 598 (1910); Moniotte v. Lieux, 41 La.Ann. 528,

6 So. 817 (1889); Saloy v. Chexnaidre, 14 La.Ann. 567 (1859). In these circumstances, the heirs may not validly claim that the debt has been extinguished by liberative prescription, because the usufructuary acts in a representative capacity. Haight v. Johnson, supra. In any case, the usufructuary may not retain the property burdened, leave the debts unpaid, and return it to the heirs with the additional burden of accrued interest. See Succession of Fitzwilliams, 3 La.Ann. 489 (1848). This jurisprudence continues to be relevant.

REVISION COMMENTS—2010

(a) This article is new. It is intended to fill a gap that existed under prior law regarding contribution to the payment of debts charged to the property in the rare situation when there are multiple usufructuaries, and one of them fails to pay his share of the debt.

(b) The remedy of a usufructuary who pays his share, and who wants to avoid having the property seized and sold for non-payment of a debt for which the property is liable because another usufructuary fails to pay his share, is to pay the share of the non-paying usufructuary, file suit against the usufructuary, obtain a judgment against the non-paying usufructuary, then seize the usufruct of the non-paying usufructuary and have it sold in order to recover the funds he advanced. Although that approach may be cumbersome, it serves a double purpose: it affords a remedy to usufructuaries to enable them to protect their interest and not lose the property, and in another sense it protects a non-paying usufructuary against possible collusion by making it clear that he must receive notice and be given an opportunity to pay the share he has not paid rather than have his share automatically forfeited. The article protects all of the usufructuaries, so that they do not lose their usufruct unfairly. The most likely situation in which to have multiple usufructuaries is the intestate usufruct of surviving parents over property inherited by them in usufruct when their child dies intestate and is survived by a sibling who inherits the naked ownership. La. Civil Code article 891.

(c) The focus of Article 592 is a joint usufruct where more than one person enjoys a usufruct of the same property at the same time. Arguably, in the situation of a successive usufruct under Louisiana Civil Code Article 546, where A has the usufruct of the entire property and at the termination of A's usufruct, B is the successive usufructuary, there are "multiple" usufructuaries, but Article 592 refers to each usufructuary contributing to the payment of debts "in proportion to his enjoyment" of the property. A successive usufructuary is not yet entitled to "enjoyment" of the property, so Article 592 does not apply to that situation. If, in the example, A fails to pay, B can protect his successive usufructuary interest by paying the creditor and being subrogated to the creditor's rights.

Art. 593.   Discharge of legacy of annuity

Unless there is a governing testamentary disposition, the legacy of an annuity that is chargeable to property subject to a usufruct is payable first from the fruits and products of the property subject to the usufruct and then from the property itself.

Acts 1976, No. 103, § 1, eff. Jan. 1, 1977. Amended by Acts 1990, No. 706, § 1; Acts 2010, No. 881, § 1, eff. July 2, 2010.

REVISION COMMENTS—1976

(a) This provision reproduces the substance of Article 580 of the Louisiana Civil Code of 1870. It does not change the law.

(b) This provision establishes an exception to the rules contained in Articles 589 through 592, supra, as it imposes on the legatee of a universal usufruct or of a usufruct under universal title a direct obligation to discharge a legacy of annuity or alimony.

COMMENTS—1990

(a) Article 593 of the Louisiana Civil Code, as revised by Acts 1976, No. 103, § 1, provided: "The legacy of an annuity or alimony must be acquitted wholly by the universal heir or by the legatee of a universal usufruct. If the legacy of the usufruct is under universal title, it must be acquitted by the usufructuary in proportion to his enjoyment." Literally, this article seemed to say that if a testator made a legacy of an annuity or alimony, this legacy must be paid either by the universal heir of the testator or by the legatee of a universal usufruct. However, the article did not specify the circumstances in which each of the two would be liable for the discharge of the legacy of an annuity or alimony, and the article was not susceptible of literal application. See Yiannopoulos, Personal Servitudes, § 143 (3d ed. 1989):

"The correct interpretation of Article 593 is that a legacy of an annuity or alimony must be discharged by the universal usufructuary, be he a universal heir of the testator or the legatee of a universal usufruct. Article 593 reproduces the substance of Article 580 of the Louisiana Civil Code of 1870; it was not intended to change the law."

(b) Article 593 of the Civil Code, as amended by Acts 1990, No. 706, is intended to clarify its meaning and to give it the same meaning as the corresponding provisions of the 1870 Code.

REVISION COMMENTS—2010

This article changes the law by providing that a legacy of an annuity chargeable to property that is subject to a usufruct is to be paid according to the order of payment set forth in the article: that is, first from the fruits and products of the property and then from the property itself. Under prior law, the article indicated who was to be the payor of the annuity—that is, either the "universal usufructuary" or the "usufructuary under universal title". In this revision, the distinctions between universal usufructuaries and usufructuaries under universal title under prior law have been eliminated; the categories themselves no longer exist.

Art. 594.   Court costs; expenses of litigation

Court costs in actions concerning the property subject to the usufruct are taxed in accordance with the rules of the Code of Civil Procedure. Expenses of litigation other than court costs are apportioned between usufructuaries and naked owners in accordance with the following Articles.

Acts 1976, No. 103, § 1, eff. Jan. 1, 1977. Amended by Acts 2010, No. 881, § 1, eff. July 2, 2010.

REVISION COMMENT—1976

This provision does not change the law. Article 588 of the Civil Code of 1870, to the extent that it concerns costs taxed by the court, has been impliedly repealed by the Code of Civil Procedure. According to Louisiana jurisprudence court costs are consistently taxed without reference to Article 588 of the Civil Code of 1870. See, e.g., Succession of Ramp, 252 La. 660, 212 So.2d 419 (1968); Giroir v. Dumesnil, 248 La. 1037, 184 So.2d 1 (1966); Barry v. United States Fidelity and Guaranty Co., 236 So.2d 229 (La.App.3rd Cir. 1970); Succession of Michel, 216 So.2d 597 (La.App.4th Cir. 1969); Taylor v. Spencer, 225 So.2d 98 (La.App.2d Cir. 1969); Succession of Young, 205 So.2d 791 (La.App.1st Cir. 1968); Succession of Daste, 210 So.2d 521 (La.App.4th Cir. 1968); Theriot v. Terrebonne, 195 So.2d 740 (La.App.1st Cir. 1967); Succession of Johnson, 184 So.2d 70 (La.App.4th Cir. 1966); Succession of Grubbs, 182 So.2d 203 (La.App.2d Cir. 1966).

REVISION COMMENT—2010

This article reproduces the substance of Article 594. It is not intended to change the law.

Art. 595.   Expenses of litigation; legal usufruct

Parents who have a legal usufruct of the property of their children are bound for expenses of litigation concerning that property, in the same manner as if they were owners of it; but reimbursement may be ordered by the court at the termination of the usufruct in cases in which inequity might otherwise result.

Acts 1976, No. 103, § 1, eff. Jan. 1, 1977.

REVISION COMMENTS—1976

(a) The first sentence of this provision reproduces the substance of Article 589 of the Louisiana Civil Code of 1870. It does not change the law. The second sentence is new. It changes the law in the light of equitable considerations.

(b) Application of this provision is subject to two conditions: there must be property subject to legal usufruct and the litigation must be one "concerning that property". According to the Louisiana Supreme Court, a child's cause of action for personal injuries constitutes "property" and an action brought by a father having parental enjoyment for the recovery of damages suffered by the child as a result of personal injuries is an action "concerning that property". Heyse v. Fidelity & Casualty Co., 255 La. 127, 229 So.2d 724 (1969).

(c) Since the legal usufructuary is bound to bear the expenses of litigation, he cannot proceed in forma pauperis under Articles 5181 and 5182 of the Code of Civil Procedure, unless, of course, he is himself impecunious. Heyse v. Fidelity & Casualty Co., 255 La. 127, 229 So.2d 724 (1969).

Art. 596. Expenses of litigation; conventional usufruct

Conventional usufructuaries are bound for expenses of litigation with third persons concerning the enjoyment of the property. Expenses of litigation with third persons concerning both the enjoyment and the ownership are divided equitably between the usufructuary and the naked owner. Expenses of litigation between the usufructuary and the naked owner are borne by the person who has incurred them.

Acts 1976, No. 103, § 1, eff. Jan. 1, 1977.

REVISION COMMENTS—1976

(a) The first sentence of this article reproduces the substance of Article 588(1) of the Louisiana Civil Code of 1870 and does not change the law. The second sentence articulates an equitable solution suggested by Article 588 of the 1870 Code. The third sentence changes the law as it suppresses Article 588, second paragraph, of the Louisiana Civil Code of 1870 and establishes the rule that expenses of litigation between the usufructuary and the naked owner are borne by the person who has incurred them.

(b) This provision gives rise to an argument a contrario that expenses incurred in litigation with third persons for the protection of the interests of the naked owner are to be borne by the naked owner. See Yiannopoulos, Personal Servitudes § 52 (1968).

(c) According to French doctrine and jurisprudence, Article 613 of the Code Civil, corresponding with Article 588 of the Louisiana Civil Code of 1870, refers to gratuitous usufructs only. See 3 Planiol et Ripert, Traité pratique de droit civil français 829 (2d ed. Picard 1952). Indeed, if the usufruct is created by onerous title, expenses of litigation incurred by the usufructuary in lawsuits concerning his enjoyment ought to be covered by the warranty of the vendor in accordance with the general rules of sales. If a lawsuit concerns both the enjoyment and the naked ownership, a distinction is made by French commentators according to whether the lawsuit is won or lost. If won, expenses which cannot be recovered from the losing party should be borne by the person who incurred them, be he the usufructuary or the naked owner. If the lawsuit is lost, the usufructuary and the naked owner should share equally the costs of the judgment given to the adversary. See 3 Planiol et Ripert, supra.

Art. 597. Liability of the usufructuary for servitudes

The usufructuary who loses a predial servitude by nonuse or who permits a servitude to be acquired on the property by prescription is responsible to the naked owner.

Acts 1976, No. 103, § 1, eff. Jan. 1, 1977.

REVISION COMMENTS—1976

(a) This provision reproduces the substance of Article 590 of the Louisiana Civil Code of 1870. It does not change the law.

(b) On principle, the usufructuary does not have legal power of alienation or encumbrance over things subject to usufruct of non-consumables. Thus, the usufructuary, in the absence of contrary provision, may not sell, mortgage, or generally burden with a real right non-consumable things subject to usufruct; nor may he validly renounce a servitude in favor of the property subject to the usufruct. And, if the usufructuary loses by the effect of liberative prescription a servitude belonging to the property or allows a third person to acquire a servitude by acquisitive prescription, he is civilly responsible to the naked owner. See Yiannopoulos, Personal Servitudes §§ 46, 62 (1968).

Art. 598.   Duty to give information to owner

If, during the existence of the usufruct, a third person encroaches on the immovable property or violates in any other way the rights of the naked owner, the usufructuary must inform the naked owner. When he fails to do so, he shall be answerable for the damages that the naked owner may suffer.

Acts 1976, No. 103, § 1, eff. Jan. 1, 1977.

REVISION COMMENT—1976

This provision reproduces the substance of Article 591 of the Louisiana Civil Code of 1870. It does not change the law.

Art. 599.   Usufruct of a herd of animals

When the usufruct includes a herd of animals, the usufructuary is bound to use it as a prudent administrator and, from the increase of the herd, replace animals that die. If the entire herd perishes without the fault of the usufructuary, the loss is borne by the naked owner.

Acts 1976, No. 103, § 1, eff. Jan. 1, 1977.

REVISION COMMENTS—1976

(a) This provision is based on Article 593 of the Louisiana Civil Code of 1870. It changes the law as it relieves the usufructuary of the obligation to deliver to the naked owner the hides of dead animals or their value.

(b) According to Article 592 of the Louisiana Civil Code of 1870, "[i]f the usufruct consists of only one head of cattle, which dies without any neglect on the part of the usufructuary, he is not bound to return another, or to pay the estimated value of the same." This provision has been suppressed as unnecessary. According to general principle, if the animal dies as a result of the fault of the usufructuary, the usufructuary is bound to compensate the owner. If the animal dies without the fault of the usufructuary, res perit domino.

(c) According to Article 537, animals are nonconsumables. The usufructuary has the right to enjoy them and to derive the utility, profits, and advantages that they may produce, under the obligation of preserving their substance. In accordance with the principle of the first sentence of Article 568, the usufructuary has the right to dispose of animals only if this right has been expressly granted to him by law or by the grantor of the usufruct. Animals are not subject to the second sentence of Article 568. Thus, the usufructuary of individual animals may dispose of them only with the consent of the naked owner, unless, of course, this right has been granted to him by the grantor of the usufruct. The usufructuary of a herd of animals, however, may dispose of individual animals of the herd under the terms of the first paragraph of Article 600. He may also dispose of the herd or of a substantial part thereof under the terms of the second paragraph of Article 600.

(d) According to the first paragraph of Article 593 of the Louisiana Civil Code of 1870, "[i]f a whole herd of cattle subject to the usufruct dies owing to some accident or disease, without any neglect on the part of the usufructuary, he is bound only to return the owner the hides of such cattle, or the value of such hides". The underscored language of this provision is suppressed. According to general principle, if the entire herd perishes without the fault of the usufructuary, res perit domino.

According to the second paragraph of Article 593, "[i]f the whole herd does not die, the usufructuary is bound to make good the number of dead out of the new born cattle, as far as they go." The usufructuary is bound to use the herd as a prudent administrator, and, normally, this means that he must replace animals that die out of the increase of the herd.

Art. 600.   Disposition of animals

The usufructuary may dispose of individual animals of the herd, subject to the obligation to deliver to the naked owner at the end of the usufruct the value that the animals had at the time of disposition.

The usufructuary may also dispose of the herd or of a substantial part thereof, provided that he acts as a prudent administrator. In such a case, the proceeds are subject to the provisions of Article 618.

Acts 1976, No. 103, § 1, eff. Jan. 1, 1977.

REVISION COMMENT—1976

This provision is new. It changes the law in the interest of simplicity and in order to achieve correspondence with actual practices.

Art. 601.   Removal of improvements

The usufructuary may remove all improvements he has made, subject to the obligation of restoring the property to its former condition. He may not claim reimbursement from the owner for improvements that he does not remove or that cannot be removed.

Acts 1976, No. 103, § 1, eff. Jan. 1, 1977. Amended by Acts 2010, No. 881, § 1, eff. July 2, 2010.

REVISION COMMENTS—1976

(a) The first sentence of this provision changes the law as it suppresses Articles 569, second paragraph, and 594, second paragraph of the Louisiana Civil Code of 1870. The second sentence reproduces the substance of Article 594, first paragraph, of the Louisiana Civil Code of 1870. The change, made in the light of contemporary conditions, reflects solutions adopted in Germany and in Greece.

(b) The purpose of Articles 569, second paragraph, and 594, first and second paragraphs, of the Louisiana Civil Code of 1870 is to exclude litigation between the usufructuary and the naked owner. See 3 Planiol et Ripert, Traité pratique de droit civil français 855 (2d ed. Picard 1952). Adoption of the opposite solution in modern civil codes, however, has not resulted in increased litigation. Moreover, since the usufructuary may make all improvements that a prudent administrator would do (Article 558, supra), he ought to be entitled to remove the same, subject to his obligation of restoring the property to its former condition.

(c) The second sentence of this provision makes it clear that the usufructuary may not claim from the owner compensation for improvements that cannot be removed. The contrary solution would impose on the owner the burden of onerous restitutions for works that he may not wish to have on his property. See 3 Planiol et Ripert, Traité pratique de droit civil français 855 (2d ed. Picard 1952).

REVISION COMMENTS—2010

This article reproduces the substance of Article 601. It is not intended to change the law.

Art. 602.   Set off against damages

The usufructuary may set off against damages due to the owner for the destruction or deterioration of the property subject to the usufruct the value of improvements that cannot be removed, provided they were made in accordance with Article 558.

Acts 1976, No. 103, § 1, eff. Jan. 1, 1977.

REVISION COMMENT—1976

This article changes the law as it makes setoff subject to two conditions: (1) the improvements must be inseparable; and (2) the improvements must be made in accordance with Article 558.

SECTION 4—RIGHTS AND OBLIGATIONS
OF THE NAKED OWNER

Art. 603.   Disposition of the naked ownership; alienation or encumbrance of the property

The naked owner may dispose of the naked ownership, but he cannot thereby affect the usufruct.

Acts 1976, No. 103, § 1, eff. Jan. 1, 1977. Amended by Acts 2010, No. 881, § 1, eff. July 2, 2010.

REVISION COMMENT—1976

This provision reproduces the substance of Article 605 of the Louisiana Civil Code of 1870. It does not change the law.

REVISION COMMENTS—2010

This article is intended to remove a potential inconsistency that existed under prior law in situations where the usufructuary was given the right to dispose of nonconsumable things subject to the usufruct. See Civil Code Article 568.

Under prior law, if a usufructuary had the power to dispose of a nonconsumable, this article potentially permitted two persons to dispose of the property: the naked owner (Article 603) and the usufructuary (Article 568). That situation could create serious title uncertainties, particularly if both the usufructuary and the naked owner attempted to sell the same immovable to different buyers. This revision of Article 603 is intended to resolve the problem by removing the language that allowed the naked owner to alienate or encumber the property itself subject to the usufruct. He may, of course, alienate or encumber his right of naked ownership, but not the thing itself.

Art. 604.   Servitudes

The naked owner may establish real rights on the property subject to the usufruct, provided that they may be exercised without impairing the usufructuary's rights.

Acts 1976, No. 103, § 1, eff. Jan. 1, 1977. Amended by Acts 2010, No. 881, § 1, eff. July 2, 2010.

REVISION COMMENTS—1976

(a) This provision reproduces the substance of Article 602 of the Louisiana Civil Code of 1870. It does not change the law.

(b) For the right of the naked owner to grant mineral rights on the property subject to usufruct, see Mineral Code arts. 195 and 196.

REVISION COMMENTS—2010

This article clarifies the law and makes the provisions thereof more technically accurate. There is no intent to change the law.

Art. 605.   Toleration of the enjoyment

The naked owner must not interfere with the rights of the usufructuary.

Acts 1976, No. 103, § 1, eff. Jan. 1, 1977.

REVISION COMMENTS—1976

(a) This provision reproduces the substance of Articles 600, 601 (second paragraph), and 603 of the Louisiana Civil Code of 1870. It does not change the law.

(b) Article 601, second paragraph, of the Louisiana Civil Code of 1870 declares that the naked owner may not "cut down any trees of a wood". The exact language has not been reproduced because the cutting of trees may or may not constitute interference with the rights of the usufructuary. See Article 562, supra. According to French doctrine and jurisprudence, if the usufruct includes timberlands not previously exploited, the naked owner may not begin timber operations for commercial purposes. He may, however, remove dead trunks and cut down trees in order to obtain lumber for extraordinary repairs. See 3 Planiol et Ripert, Traité pratique de droit civil français 835 (2d ed. Picard 1952).

Art. 606.   Improvements

The naked owner may not make alterations or improvements on the property subject to the usufruct.

Acts 1976, No. 103, § 1, eff. Jan. 1, 1977.

REVISION COMMENTS—1976

(a) This provision reproduces the substance of Article 601 of the Louisiana Civil Code of 1870. It does not change the law.

(b) This provision declares that the naked owner may not make improvements on the property subject to the usufruct. According to Article 583, the naked owner has the right to restore the property and to make extraordinary repairs, but within a reasonable time and in the manner the least inconvenient and onerous for the usufructuary.

SECTION 5—TERMINATION OF THE USUFRUCT

Art. 607.   Death of the usufructuary

The right of usufruct expires upon the death of the usufructuary.

Acts 1976, No. 103, § 1, eff. Jan. 1, 1977.

REVISION COMMENTS—1976

(a) This provision reproduces the substance of Article 606 of the Louisiana Civil Code of 1870. It does not change the law.

(b) This is a rule of public policy. The dismemberment of ownership into usufruct and naked ownership, though a useful device, may not be made to extend over a period of time longer than the life of the usufructuary. Thus, freedom of contracting or disposing is limited in the general interest, and any clause purporting to create a heritable right of usufruct is null and void.

(c) The rule that usufruct is only for life and nontransmissible to heirs does not necessarily exclude the creation of a single usufruct with right of survivorship of cousufructuaries or of successive usufructs. If a single usufruct is conferred on a number of usufructuaries by undivided shares, the share of a deceased usufructuary accrues in favor of the survivors. See Articles 546, 547, supra; Succession of Fournet, 195 So.2d 333, 335 (La.App.3rd Cir. 1967); Samuels v. Brownlee, 36 La.App. 228 (1884); Arceneaux v. Bernard, 10 La. 246 (1836).

(d) Successive usufructs are not prohibited substitutions. They are subject to the limitations that in contractual successive usufructs all usufructuaries must exist or at least be conceived at the time of the creation of the usufruct and in testamentary successive usufructs that all usufructuaries must exist or at least be conceived at the time of the testator's death. See Article 548, supra; 2 Aubry et Rau, Droit civil français 641 (7th ed. Esmein 1961). The creation of successive usufructs therefore does not violate the rule that usufruct is for life. The duration of the dismemberment of ownership is the same as if the grantor had created one usufruct in favor of the last usufructuary. See Article 546, supra; 3 Planiol et Ripert, Traité pratique de droit civil français 840 (2d ed. Picard 1952).

Art. 608.   Dissolution of juridical person; thirty year limitation

A usufruct established in favor of a juridical person terminates if the juridical person is dissolved or liquidated, but not if the juridical person is converted, merged or consolidated into a successor juridical person. In any event, a usufruct in favor of a juridical person shall terminate upon the lapse of thirty years from the date of the commencement of the usufruct. This Article shall not apply to a juridical person in its capacity as the trustee of a trust.

Acts 1976, No. 103, § 1, eff. Jan. 1, 1977. Amended by Acts 2010, No. 881, § 1, eff. July 2, 2010.

REVISION COMMENTS—1976

(a) This provision reproduces the substance of Article 612 of the Louisiana Civil Code of 1870. It does not change the law.

(b) A legal entity is one that possesses legal personality, namely, the capacity to have rights and obligations. Persons are distinguished into natural persons and juristic persons, such as corporations and partnerships. For the incidents and effects of legal personality, see Yiannopoulos, Louisiana Civil Law System-Part I §§ 49, 53–57 (1971).

COMMENT—2010

The last sentence explains that a trust is not itself a juridical person and therefore the Article does not apply to it. A trust is a "relationship." La. R.S. 9:1731. Nevertheless, the trustee may be a corporate or institutional trustee which a juridical person and it is intended this article not affect the trust in that event.

REVISION COMMENTS—2010

(a) This article retains the rule that a usufruct in favor of a juridical person terminates thirty years from the commencement thereof; but it clarifies the law by providing that a usufruct in favor of a juridical person does not terminate if the juridical person undergoes a structural transformation, such as a merger or a consolidation.

(b) The last sentence comports with the fact that a trust is not itself a juridical person and therefore the Article does not apply to it. A trust is a "relationship." La. R.S. 9:1731. Technically, however, title to property owned by the trust is placed in the name of the trustee, but in his representative capacity. The trustee may be a corporate or institutional trustee which is a juridical person, and it is intended this article not affect the trust in that event.

Art. 609.   Termination of legacy of revenues

A legacy of revenues from specified property is a kind of usufruct and terminates upon death of the legatee unless a shorter period has been expressly stipulated.

Acts 1976, No. 103, § 1, eff. Jan. 1, 1977.

REVISION COMMENTS—1976

(a) This provision does not change the law. It reproduces the substance of the first paragraph of Article 607 of the Louisiana Civil Code of 1870; the second paragraph has not been reproduced because it contains an unnecessary illustration.

(b) Under this provision, a legacy of revenues from specified property is a real right in the nature of usufruct. This right terminates at the death of the legatee unless a shorter period has been expressly stipulated.

(c) A legacy of revenues gives rise to the question whether the testator intended to grant a usufruct, a limited real right in the nature of usufruct, or merely a personal right. A legacy that exhausts the utility of certain specified things, whose possession and administration is entrusted to the legatee, is a usufruct. See Yiannopoulos, Personal Servitudes § 14 (1968). A legacy of revenues intended as a charge on specified property whose possession and administration is not entrusted to the legatee is a real right in the nature of usufruct. If, however, the revenues are to be derived from an unliquidated succession or from unspecified property, the legacy establishes merely a personal right in favor of the legatee; it is a debt of the succession to be discharged by the personal representative of the deceased, his heirs, or his universal legatee. Cf. C.C. arts. 1626, 1633; In re Courtin, 144 La. 971, 81 So. 457 (1919); Succession of Ward, 110 La. 75, 34 So. 135 (1903); Orleans v. Baltimore, 13 La.Ann. 162 (1858).

(d) Louisiana courts have declared that the intention of the legislature "was, not to make such bequests as these 'annuities' usufructs in reality, for there is no transfer of possession to the usufructuary, but to make them quasi-usufructs, only for the purpose of limiting their duration." New Orleans v. Baltimore, 13 La.Ann. 162 (1858) (decided under the corresponding Article 602 of the 1825 Code). See also Succession of Ward, 110 La. 75, 34 So. 135 (1903). This correct interpretation that a legacy of revenues does not necessarily establish a real right of enjoyment in favor of the legatee was followed in Peyton v. Hammonds, 125 So.2d 491 (La.App.2d Cir. 1960).

Art. 610.   Usufruct for a term or under condition

A usufruct established for a term or subject to a condition terminates upon the expiration of the term or the happening of the condition.

Acts 1976, No. 103, § 1, eff. Jan. 1, 1977.

(a) This provision reproduces the part of Article 608 of the Louisiana Civil Code of 1870 concerning termination of usufruct. It does not change the law.

(b) According to Article 545, usufruct may be established for a term or under condition. If the usufruct is established under a term or suspensive condition, the right commences upon the lapse of the term or the happening of the condition. According to Article 610, if the usufruct is established under a resolutory term or condition, the right terminates upon the expiration of the term or the happening of the condition.

Art. 611.   Term; transfer of usufruct to another person

When the usufructuary is charged to restore or transfer the usufruct to another person, his right terminates when the time for restitution or delivery arrives.

Acts 1976, No. 103, § 1, eff. Jan. 1, 1977.

REVISION COMMENTS—1976

(a) This provision reproduces the substance of Article 609 of the Louisiana Civil Code of 1870. It does not change the law.

(b) This provision may be dispensable insofar as it states the obvious, that the right to the usufruct terminates when the time of delivery to another person arrives. It is maintained, however, for two reasons: (1) this article sanctions the validity of successive usufructs by clear implication; and (2) this article indicates that the right to a successive usufruct commences when the time of delivery arrives, even if the property has not yet been delivered to a successive usufructuary.

Art. 612.   Term; third person reaching a certain age

A usufruct granted until a third person reaches a certain age is a usufruct for a term. If the third person dies, the usufruct continues until the date the deceased would have reached the designated age.

Acts 1976, No. 103, § 1, eff. Jan. 1, 1977.

REVISION COMMENTS—1976

(a) This provision reproduces the substance of Article 610 of the Louisiana Civil Code of 1870. It does not change the law.

(b) According to French doctrine and jurisprudence a usufruct granted until a third person reaches a certain age is a usufruct for a term. If the third person dies, the usufruct continues until the date the deceased would have reached the designated age. The result may be avoided by contrary stipulations or inferences tending to establish the actual intention of the parties. For example, the usufruct granted to a parent until a child reaches a certain age, for the purpose of providing means of education, terminates at the death of the child. See 3 Planiol et Ripert, Traité de droit civil français 841 (2d ed. Picard 1952).

Art. 613.   Loss, extinction, or destruction of property

The usufruct of nonconsumables terminates by the permanent and total loss, extinction, or destruction through accident, force majeure or decay of the property subject to the usufruct.

Acts 1976, No. 103, § 1, eff. Jan. 1, 1977. Amended by Acts 2010, No. 881, § 1, eff. July 2, 2010.

REVISION COMMENTS—1976

(a) This provision reproduces the substance of Articles 613 and 614 of the Louisiana Civil Code of 1870. It does not change the law.

(b) According to Article 613, first paragraph, of the Louisiana Civil Code of 1870, and partly corresponding Article 617(6) of the French Civil Code, usufruct expires before the death of the usufructuary "by the loss, extinction, or destruction of the thing subject to the usufruct." Obviously, this article contemplates usufruct of nonconsumable things. By way of illustration, Article 613(2) of the 1870 Louisiana Code declares that "the usufruct, which is established upon a building, expires, if the building is destroyed by fire or any other accident, or if it falls down through the decay of years". The provision has not been reproduced because it contains an unnecessary explanation.

(c) The usufruct terminates only if the loss is permanent. Article 615 of the Louisiana Civil Code of 1870 declares that "the usufruct of a field or lot is extinguished, if one or the other be so covered with water by inundation that it becomes changed into a pond or swamp. But the usufruct revives if the inundation ceases, and the waters, on retiring, leave the land uncovered and in its former condition." Accord: 2 Aubry et Rau, Droit civil français 694 (7th ed. Esmein 1961).

(d) The usufruct terminates only if the loss is total. Thus, if the usufruct is established simply on a building, and this building is destroyed completely, the usufruct terminates. C.C. art. 613(2) (1870); Cf. French C.C. art. 624(1); 3 Planiol et Ripert, Traité pratique de droit civil français 842 (2d ed. Picard 1952). In this case, "the usufructuary would not even have the usufruct of the materials of the building, nor of the place in which it stood". C.C. art. 613 (1870), third paragraph. If the loss is only partial, the usufruct continues and is exercised on whatever remains of the thing. C.C. art. 614 (1870). Thus, if the usufruct is established "upon an estate of which the building is a part, the usufructuary shall enjoy both the soil and the materials". C.C. art. 613 (1870), third paragraph. Article 614 (C.C., 1870) and the second and third sentences of Articles 615 (C.C., 1870) have not been reproduced because they contain unnecessary explanations.

(e) The loss of the thing entails termination of the usufruct only if it is the result of an accident. Cf. C.C. art. 613 (1870), second paragraph, ". . . or any other accident . . ."; id. art. 615 (1870), ". . . when it undergoes from accident . . ."; 3 Planiol et Ripert, Traité pratique de droit civil français 841 (2d ed. Picard 1952). In this respect, accident means "irresistible force" (force majeure) or fortuitous event (cas fortuit). See Barry v. United States Fidelity & Guaranty Co., 236 So.2d 229 (La.App.3d Cir. 1970). If the loss is attributed to the fault of the usufructuary or of the naked owner, the usufruct continues to exist and the consequences of the loss are determined under the general rules of delictual obligations or under the provisions governing the respective obligations of the usufructuary and of the naked owner. See 2 Aubry et Rau, Droit civil français 694 (7th ed. Esmein 1961); 5 Baudry-Lacantinerie, Traité théorique et pratique de droit civil 485 (2nd ed. Chauveau, 1899). If the loss is attributed to the fault of a third person, the usufruct attaches to the claim for damages due by the wrongdoer. Barry v. United States Fidelity & Guaranty Co., supra; 2 Aubry et Rau, supra; Article 614, infra.

REVISION COMMENTS—2010

This article clarifies the law in part by adding the term "force majeure" as one of the causes of permanent and total loss of a thing as a result of which a usufruct of nonconsumables terminates. See Revision Comments to Article 577, infra.

Art. 614.　　Fault of a third person

When any loss, extinction, or destruction of property subject to usufruct is attributable to the fault of a third person, the usufruct does not terminate but attaches to any claim for damages and the proceeds therefrom.

Acts 1976, No. 103, § 1, eff. Jan. 1, 1977.

REVISION COMMENT—1976

This provision is new. It articulates precepts developed by doctrine and jurisprudence on the basis of Articles 613 through 615 of the Louisiana Civil Code of 1870. It does not change the law. See Barry v. United States Fidelity & Guaranty Co., 236 So.2d 229 (La.App.3rd Cir. 1970); Yiannopoulos, Personal Servitudes § 87 (1968); 2 Aubry et Rau, Droit civil français 694 (7th ed. Esmein 1961).

Art. 615.　　Change of the form of property

When property subject to usufruct changes form without an act of the usufructuary, the usufruct does not terminate even though the property may no longer serve the use for which it was originally destined.

When property subject to usufruct is converted into money or other property without an act of the usufructuary, as in a case of expropriation of an immovable or liquidation of a corporation, the usufruct terminates as to the property converted and attaches to the money or other property received by the usufructuary.

Acts 1976, No. 103, § 1, eff. Jan. 1, 1977. Amended by Acts 2010, No. 881, § 1, eff. July 2, 2010.

REVISION COMMENTS—1976

(a) This provision is new. It abrogates Article 615, second sentence, of the Louisiana Civil Code of 1870 which declares that "the usufruct of a field or lot is extinguished, if one or the other be so covered with water by inundation that it becomes changed into a pond or swamp". There is no reason why the usufruct should terminate if the usufructuary may still derive some utility from the property. Inundation may destroy the original destination of the land, but the usufructuary may apply the land to new uses.

(b) According to Louisiana jurisprudence, when shares of stock are converted into money without any act of the usufructuary, as a result of redemption by the corporation or liquidation of its capital, the right of the usufructuary attaches to the proceeds. Succession of Dielmann, 119 La. 101, 43 So. 972 (1907). Further, when property is expropriated for public utility, the proceeds "belong to the naked owner, subject however to the rights of the usufructuary". State through Department of Highways v. Costello, 158 So.2d 850 (La.App.4th Cir. 1963).

(c) If property is converted into money, the usufructuary becomes owner of it. At the termination of the usufruct, the usufructuary will be bound to restore to the naked owner the value that the property had at the time of disposition. If property is converted into other property, the usufructuary may continue having its enjoyment or he may acquire ownership of it, depending on the nature of the things that the usufructuary has received as consumables or nonconsumables.

(d) This provision is inapplicable to cases in which property subject to usufruct is converted into money with the participation of the usufructuary. The matter is governed by Article 616, infra.

REVISION COMMENTS—2010

(a) This article addresses the situation in which property subject to a usufruct undergoes change in form without an act of the usufructuary, or is converted into other property.

(b) Paragraph one involves a situation in which the thing subject to the usufruct changes form without an act on the part of the usufructuary. The change in form may result in the thing no longer being capable of serving the use for which the usufruct was granted, as where the usufruct of a lot becomes flooded and turns into a pond. Under this revision, as under prior law, a mere change in the form of the property does not terminate the usufruct. As provided in comment "a" of the 1976 version: "Inundation may destroy the original destination of the land, but the usufructuary may apply the land to new uses". As stated by one authority: "There is no reason why the usufruct should terminate if the usufructuary may still derive some utility from the property." Yiannopoulos, Personal Servitude, 3 Louisiana Civil Law Treatise (4th ed. 2000) at 326.

(c) The second paragraph covers not only a conversion of the property into money, as when there is a sale or an expropriation of an immovable or liquidation of a corporation, but when it is converted into other property, which may occur if there is an exchange or if there is a liquidation of the corporation and the usufructuary receives property that formerly belonged to the corporation that is then distributed to the usufructuary. The rules for changing form without an act of the usufructuary provide that the usufruct simply continues on the property in its changed form, but the second paragraph provides that the usufruct terminates as to the property converted and attaches to the money or the other property that may be received by the usufructuary. Thus, there are different rules and different remedies for the two different situations. This revision is not intended to change the law. Although the language in Article 615 has been changed from "does not terminate" to "terminates as to the property," the intent is to clarify that once property is converted, the usufruct is transferred from a usufruct over the original object or property to a usufruct over the new object or property.

Art. 616.   Sale or exchange of the property; taxes

When property subject to usufruct is sold or exchanged, whether in an action for partition or by agreement between the usufructuary and the naked owner or by a usufructuary who has the power to dispose of nonconsumable property, the usufruct terminates as to the nonconsumable property sold or exchanged, but as provided in Article 568.1, the usufruct attaches to the money or other property received by the usufructuary, unless the parties agree otherwise. Any tax or expense incurred as the result of the sale or exchange of property subject to usufruct shall be paid from the proceeds of the sale or exchange, and shall be deducted from the amount due by the usufructuary to the naked owner at the termination of the usufruct.

Acts 1976, No. 103, § 1, eff. Jan. 1, 1977. Amended by Acts 1983, No. 535, § 1; Acts 2010, No. 881, § 1, eff. July 2, 2010.

COMMENTS—1976 REVISION

(a) This provision is new. It clarifies the law.

(b) This article is applicable to cases in which property subject to usufruct is converted into money or other property with the participation of the usufructuary. For example, the naked owner and the usufructuary may agree to sell property to a third person free of the usufruct. The transaction involves a simultaneous sale of the naked ownership and of the usufruct for a single price. The usufructuary and the naked owner may agree that the usufructuary shall have the enjoyment of the entire price for the period of the usufruct or that the price shall be apportioned between them in any manner that they see fit. In the absence of agreement concerning apportionment of the price, French doctrine and jurisprudence suggest that the price is apportioned between the naked owner and the usufructuary in proportion to the value of their respective interests. See 3 Planiol et Ripert, Traité pratique de droit civil français 830 (2d ed. Picard 1952). Two Louisiana decisions bear on this point. In Bauman v. George, 154 La. 680, 98 So. 85 (1923), the usufructuary sued for partition of the property, and the court apportioned the proceeds of the judicial sale "among the owners in accordance with their respective interests" on the theory that the usufructuary had renounced the usufruct. In Succession of Block, 137 La. 302, 68 So. 618 (1915), property was sold free of the usufruct by agreement between the naked owner and the usufructuary. The usufructuary retained the proceeds, perhaps by agreement with the naked owner. After the death of the usufructuary and of the naked owner, an heir of the naked owner brought action claiming his portion of the proceeds with interest from the death of the usufructuary. The court granted the demand, declaring that the naked owner "owned the proceeds of the sale" and that the usufructuary's "estate must account for the same to the plaintiff". In the course of the same opinion, however, the court declared that "the usufruct of the money and notes representing the proceeds of the sale being imperfect, they became the property of the usufructuary". The decision is thus inconclusive as to the disposition of the proceeds of the sale. Article 616 clarifies the law as it determines that in the absence of other agreement the usufruct attaches to the proceeds of the sale.

COMMENTS—1983

(c) The 1983 amendment was necessary because of the amendment of Article 543. Since property subject to usufruct may now be subjected to partition by licitation, provision is made for the disposition of the proceeds. Parties are free to provide for the distribution of the proceeds. In the absence of such a provision, the usufruct attaches to the proceeds of the sale. The naked owner is entitled to demand security under C.C. Arts. 571–575 and 890 (Rev.1976) or safe investment of the funds under C.C. Art. 618 (Rev.1976).

REVISION COMMENTS—2010

(d) This article combines the provisions of Articles 568 and 616, as revised in 1976, relative to certain effects of a sale of property subject to the usufruct. Under this article, when property subject to the usufruct is sold or exchanged, whether in an action for partition or by agreement between the usufructuary and the naked owner, or by a usufructuary with a power of disposition, the usufruct attaches to the money or other property received by the usufructuary as a result of the sale or exchange. This article changes the law in part, by making this rule applicable to exchange transactions. In addition, this article clarifies the law by providing that if property is acquired as a result of the exchange or sale of property subject to the usufruct, the usufruct attaches not only to money received but also to any property acquired as a result of the sale or exchange.

(e) Under prior law, when the usufructuary who had been expressly given the power to dispose of nonconsumables sold the property and a tax was owed as a result of the sale, Article 568 provided that such a tax was payable from the proceeds of the sale. This provision has been moved to Article 616 and expanded to include other expenses as well as taxes and to cover other situations in which property subject to a usufruct is sold or exchanged, whether in an action for partition or by agreement

192

between the usufructuary and the naked owner. The new article also clarifies that the amount due by the usufructuary to the naked owner at the termination of the usufruct is reduced by the amount of tax paid and the expenses incurred. An example of expenses would be closing costs or broker's fees that may be incurred in the sale of the property. The new article recognizes that the usufructuary should be given credit for those taxes and expenses and should not be obligated to pay the naked owner for them, since they have reduced the net amount received by the usufructuary.

Art. 617.   Proceeds of insurance

When proceeds of insurance are due on account of loss, extinction, or destruction of property subject to usufruct, the usufruct attaches to the proceeds. If the usufructuary or the naked owner has separately insured his interest only, the proceeds belong to the insured party.

Acts 1976, No. 103, § 1, eff. Jan. 1, 1977.

REVISION COMMENTS—1976

(a) This provision is new. It clarifies the law.

(b) If the property subject to the usufruct has been insured by the usufructuary or by the naked owner, questions may arise whether the proceeds ought to be apportioned in the light of the respective losses of the parties, whether the insured party ought to receive the entire proceeds, or whether the usufruct ought to attach to the proceeds. According to Article 617, the usufruct attaches to the proceeds. If the usufructuary or the naked owner has separately insured his interest only, the proceeds belong to the insured party.

Art. 618.   Security for proceeds

In cases governed by Articles 614, 615, 616, and the first sentence of Article 617, the naked owner may demand, within one year from receipt of the proceeds by the usufructuary that the usufructuary give security for the proceeds. If such a demand is made, and the parties cannot agree, the nature of the security shall be determined by the court. This Article does not apply to corporeal movables referred to in the second sentence of Article 568, or to property disposed of by the usufructuary pursuant to the power to dispose of nonconsumables if the grantor of the usufruct has dispensed with the security.

Acts 1976, No. 103, § 1, eff. Jan. 1, 1977. Amended by Acts 2010, No. 881, § 1, eff. July 2, 2010.

REVISION COMMENTS—1976

(a) This article is new. It changes the law as it gives to the naked owner the right to demand investment of money in cases in which a usufruct of nonconsumables is converted into a usufruct of money. The usufructuary should acquire the ownership of the money. Nevertheless, due regard for the interest of the naked owner requires that the money be safely invested. It has been thought that safe investment is preferable to a possible requirement of security.

(b) The Louisiana Code of Civil Procedure provides for the investment of funds in succession and tutorship proceedings. See C.C.P. arts. 3223, 4269, 4270, 4271; R.S. 9:2127.

REVISION COMMENTS—2010

This article changes the law in part by providing that in situations where there has been a loss or destruction of the property, a change in the form of, or a sale or exchange of property subject to the usufruct, and the usufruct now attaches to the sum of money or other property attributable to the property originally subject to the usufruct, the naked owner may demand that the usufructuary give security for the proceeds. Under prior law, the naked owner's remedy was limited to requesting that the money received by the usufructuary be safely invested, subject to the rights of the usufructuary. Such a remedy was determined to be impractical. When the usufruct is transformed from a usufruct of a nonconsumable to a usufruct of consumable property, the usufructuary becomes the owner under Louisiana Civil Code article 538. It is believed that the new rule provides a more practical and more appropriate remedy, namely requiring the usufructuary to furnish security.

Art. 619.   Changes made by the testator

A usufruct by donation mortis causa is not considered revoked merely because the testator has made changes in the property after the date of his testament. The effect of the legacy is determined by application of the rules contained in the Title: Of donations inter vivos and mortis causa.

Acts 1976, No. 103, § 1, eff. Jan. 1, 1977. Amended by Acts 2010, No. 881, § 1, eff. July 2, 2010.

REVISION COMMENTS—1976

(a) This provision reproduces the substance of Article 616 of the Louisiana Civil Code of 1870. It does not change the law.

(b) According to this provision, changes made by the testator to the form or substance of a thing bequeathed in usufruct do not by themselves result in revocation of the legacy. These changes, however, may be indicative of the testator's intention to revoke. Accordingly, the situation is controlled by the rules of interpretation relative to the revocation of legacies.

REVISION COMMENTS—2010

This article substitutes the term "testament" for "will" in the first sentence. There is no change in the law.

Art. 620.   Sale of the property or of the usufruct

Usufruct terminates by the enforcement of an encumbrance established upon the property prior to the creation of the usufruct to secure a debt. The usufructuary may have an action against the grantor of the usufruct or against the naked owner under the provisions established in Section 3 of this Chapter.

The judicial sale of the usufruct by creditors of the usufructuary deprives the usufructuary of his enjoyment of the property but does not terminate the usufruct.

Acts 1976, No. 103, § 1, eff. Jan. 1, 1977. Amended by Acts 2010, No. 881, § 1, eff. July 2, 2010.

REVISION COMMENTS—1976

(a) This provision reproduces the substance of Article 617 of the Louisiana Civil Code of 1870. It does not change the law.

(b) The provisions of this article are applications of the principle that no one may dispose of a greater right than one has. Thus, the naked owner may merely dispose of the naked ownership and the usufructuary may merely dispose of the usufruct. Further, the provisions of this article are applications of the principle that real rights are subject to temporal priority: prior tempore, potior jure. Thus, a prior mortgage takes precedence over a subsequent usufruct; a prior usufruct takes precedence over a subsequent mortgage. In the case of rights affecting immovable property, temporal priority is, of course, determined in the light of the rules of registry.

(c) The action that the usufructuary may have against the grantor of the usufruct or against the naked owner on account of the enforcement of a mortgage burdening the property subject to the usufruct is governed by Articles 586 and 588, supra.

(d) According to the third paragraph of this article, the judicial sale of the usufruct by creditors of the usufructuary is not a cause of termination of the usufruct. The purchaser of the usufruct becomes usufructuary but the original usufructuary remains bound toward the naked owner for any violations of duty by the purchaser of the usufruct. Cf. C.C. art. 561 (1870). The usufruct terminates upon the death of the original usufructuary rather than upon the death of the purchaser of the usufruct. See 2 Aubry et Rau, Droit civil français 670 (7th ed. Esmein 1961); 2 Colin, Capitant et Julliot de la Morandiére, Traité de droit civil 162 (1959).

REVISION COMMENTS—2010

The elimination of Paragraph two of Article 620 is not intended to effect a change in the law. The subject is already covered in Article 603.

Art. 621.   Prescription of nonuse

A usufruct terminates by the prescription of nonuse if neither the usufructuary nor any other person acting in his name exercises the right during a period of ten years. This applies whether the usufruct has been constituted on an entire estate or on a divided or undivided part of an estate.

Acts 1976, No. 103, § 1, eff. Jan. 1, 1977.

REVISION COMMENTS—1976

(a) This provision reproduces the substance of Article 618 of the Louisiana Civil Code of 1870. It does not change the law.

(b) Use of the property by the naked owner with the permission of the usufructuary constitutes use in the "name" of the usufructuary. See Theriot v. Terrebonne, 195 So.2d 740 (La.App.1st Cir. 1967).

Art. 622.   Confusion of usufruct and naked ownership

A usufruct terminates by confusion when the usufruct and the naked ownership are united in the same person.

The usufruct does not terminate if the title by which the usufruct and the naked ownership were united is annulled for some previously existing defect or some vice inherent in the act.

Acts 1976, No. 103, § 1, eff. Jan. 1, 1977.

REVISION COMMENTS—1976

(a) This provision is based on Articles 619 and 620 of the Louisiana Civil Code of 1870. It improves the law.

(b) Much of the language of Article 619 (C.C., 1870) has been suppressed because it is doctrinal and unnecessary. It is a broadly accepted principle of civil law that no one can have a servitude on his own property: neminem res sua servit. C.C. art. 649 (1870). Further, by definition, usufruct is a real right of enjoyment burdening the property of another person. C.C. art. 533 (1870). The principle of confusion of rights is firmly embedded in the Civil Code. See C.C. arts. 805 through 812 (1870); id. arts. 2217 and 2218. Article 622 is an application of the principle.

(c) Much of the language of Article 620 (C.C., 1870) has been suppressed because it is doctrinal and unnecessary. This article contemplates acquisition of the naked ownership by the usufructuary, but it ought to be equally applicable to cases in which the usufruct is acquired by the naked owner. In Article 622, the rule is made expressly applicable to both the usufructuary and the naked owner. Usufruct terminates by confusion when the naked ownership and the enjoyment are united in the same person, unless the act by which the usufruct was acquired by the naked owner, or the naked ownership was acquired by the usufructuary, is annulled. According to well-established principle, the annulment operates retroactively and prevents confusion.

(d) According to civilian doctrine, the termination of the usufruct under this provision does not extinguish real security rights in favor of the creditors of the usufructuary. These creditors may exercise their right to follow the property in the hands of any possessor and may obtain preferential treatment in spite of the confusion of rights in the persons of the usufructuary or of the naked owner. See 2 Aubry et Rau, Droit civil français 697 (7th ed. Esmein 1961); 3 Planiol et Ripert, Traité pratique de droit civil français 850 (2d ed. Picard 1952).

Art. 623.   Abuse of the enjoyment; consequences

The usufruct may be terminated by the naked owner if the usufructuary commits waste, alienates things without authority, neglects to make ordinary repairs, or abuses his enjoyment in any other manner.

Acts 1976, No. 103, § 1, eff. Jan. 1, 1977. Amended by Acts 2010, No. 881, § 1, eff. July 2, 2010.

REVISION COMMENTS—1976

(a) This provision reproduces the substance of the first paragraph of Article 621 of the Louisiana Civil Code of 1870. It does not change the law.

(b) If the usufructuary abuses his enjoyment, the usufruct may terminate in part or in whole. See 3 Planiol et Ripert, Traité pratique de droit civil français 848 (2d ed. Picard 1952). This is because usufruct is a divisible right. C.C. art. 538 (1870). In Magee v. Gatlin, 51 So.2d 154 (La.App.1st Cir. 1951), the court erroneously assumed that Article 621 of the Civil Code of 1870 contemplates termination "of the whole usufruct, and . . . not . . . merely a part thereof".

(c) Abuse of the enjoyment is any serious violation of the obligation of the usufructuary to preserve the substance of nonconsumable things. See 2 Aubry et Rau, Droit civil français 698 (7th ed. Esmein 1961); Francez v. Francez, 152 La. 666, 94 So. 203 (1922); Mehle v. Bensel, 39 La.Ann. 680 (1887); Dickson v. Dickson, 33 La.Ann. 1370 (1881); Thomas v. Thomas, 73 So.2d 482 (La.App.2d Cir. 1954). Violation of the usufructuary's obligation to make an inventory is not "an act of waste or abuse" under this provision. Gryder's Heirs v. Gryder, 37 La.Ann. 638, 640 (1885); Burdin v. Burdin, 171 La. 7, 129 So. 651 (1930); Thomas v. Blair, 11 La. 678, 35 So. 811 (1903); Succession of Viaud, 11 La.Ann. 297 (1856).

(d) Unauthorized alienation by the usufructuary of property is an abuse of the enjoyment. See 2 Aubry et Rau, Droit civil français 698 n. 29 (7th ed. Esmein 1961); Ogden v. Leland University, 49 La.Ann. 190, 21 So. 685 (1906); Gryder's Heirs v. Gryder, 37 La.Ann. 638 (1885); cf. Thomas v. Thomas, 73 So.2d 482 (La.App.2d Cir. 1954). The naked owner may set aside the sale and reclaim the property sold in the hands of any acquirers, even bona fide purchasers. See Miller v. Blackwell, 142 La. 571, 77 So. 285 (1918); Succession of Franklin, 13 La.App. 289, 127 So. 767 (1930); Ogden v. Leland University, supra; cf. Leury v. Mayer, 122 La. 486, 47 So. 839 (1908).

(e) In Magee v. Gatlin, 51 So.2d 154 (La.App.1st Cir. 1951), the surviving widow and usufructuary of the deceased spouse's share in the community sold two automobiles belonging to the former community. Children of the marriage brought action against the usufructuary claiming that the usufruct over the automobiles had terminated by waste and demanding their shares of the price realized by the widow. The court dismissed the action on the ground that the usufruct had not terminated, and, therefore the usufructuary could not be sued for accounting. Deviating from a long line of Louisiana decisions, the court declared that "the mere fact that the property was sold, without any allegation to show waste, abuse, or mismanagement on the part of the usufructuary would not show sufficient right of cause of action as to terminate the usufruct". Article 568 has adopted the rule of this case as it applies to automobiles and generally to things that are gradually and substantially impaired by wear and decay. Article 623 overrules the Magee case, supra, in all other respects.

REVISION COMMENTS—2010

This article amends the title of Article 623 and makes a minor grammatical change in the text without changing the law.

Art. 624.   Security to prevent termination

In the cases covered by the preceding Article, the court may decree termination of the usufruct or decree that the property be delivered to the naked owner on the condition that he shall pay to the usufructuary a reasonable annuity until the end of the usufruct. The amount of the annuity shall be based on the value of the usufruct.

The usufructuary may prevent termination of the usufruct or delivery of the property to the naked owner by giving security to insure that he will take appropriate corrective measures within a period fixed by the court.

Acts 1976, No. 103, § 1, eff. Jan. 1, 1977. Amended by Acts 2010, No. 881, § 1, eff. July 2, 2010.

REVISION COMMENTS—1976

(a) This provision is based on Articles 621(2) and 622 of the Louisiana Civil Code of 1870. It changes the law as indicated in the following comments.

(b) The first sentence of the first paragraph of Article 624 makes no change in the law. The second sentence of the first paragraph changes the law as it declares that the value of the annuity is determined in the light of the value of the usufruct rather than in the light of the value of the property subject to usufruct. This is an equitable solution designed to balance the gain realized by the naked owner and the loss suffered by the usufructuary.

(c) The second paragraph of Article 624 broadens the scope of Article 622 of the Louisiana Civil Code of 1870. According to Article 622 (C.C. 1870), the usufructuary may prevent delivery of the property to the naked owner "in case of damages committed by the former on the property subject to the usufruct, by offering to make the necessary repairs, and giving a sufficient security that he will make them within a certain fixed time". Under Article 624, the usufructuary may prevent both termination of the usufruct and delivery of the property to the naked owner.

REVISION COMMENTS—2010

This article amends the title of Article 624 and makes a minor grammatical change in the text without changing the law.

Art. 625.   Intervention by creditors of the usufructuary

A creditor of the usufructuary may intervene and may prevent termination of the usufruct and delivery of the property to the naked owner by offering to repair the damages caused by the usufructuary and by giving security for the future.

Acts 1976, No. 103, § 1, eff. Jan. 1, 1977. Amended by Acts 2010, No. 881, § 1, eff. July 2, 2010.

REVISION COMMENT—1976

This provision reproduces the substance of Article 623 of the Louisiana Civil Code of 1870. It does not change the law.

REVISION COMMENT—2010

This article reproduces the substance of Article 625. It is not intended to change the law.

Art. 626.   Renunciation; rights of creditors

A usufruct terminates by an express written renunciation.

A creditor of the usufructuary may cause to be annulled a renunciation made to his prejudice.

Arts 1976, No. 103, § 1, eff. Jan. 1, 1977.

REVISION COMMENTS—1976

(a) This provision reproduces the substance of Article 624 of the Louisiana Civil Code of 1870. It does not change the law.

(b) According to a fundamental principle of the civil law, creditors may exercise all the rights and actions of their debtor that are not qualified as strictly personal. See C.C. arts. 1889–1992 (1870); Belcher and Creswell v. Johnson, 114 La. 640, 38 So. 481 (1905); Yiannopoulos, Civil Law Property § 78 (1966). The part of Article 624 that declares "and they are permitted to exercise all the rights of their debtor in this respect", is unnecessary and has been suppressed.

(c) A Louisiana court interpreting Article 575 of the 1870 Code has held that the usufructuary is entitled to abandon his entire enjoyment; he may not abandon merely a part of his enjoyment bearing on things that are particularly burdensome for the usufructuary to hold. Judice v. Provost, 18 La.Ann. 601 (1866); cf. Bauman v. George, 154 La. 680, 98 So. 85 (1923). Article 582, however, provides that: "The usufructuary may release himself from the obligation to make repairs by abandoning the usufruct or, with the approval of the court, a portion thereof, even if the owner has instituted suit to compel him to make repairs or bear the expense of them, and even if the usufructuary has been cast in judgment". Article 626 must be interpreted in combination with Article 582; hence the usufructuary may renounce the whole of the usufruct unilaterally or a part thereof with the approval of the court.

(d) According to Louisiana jurisprudence, usufruct terminates only by express renunciation. Succession of Singer, 208 La. 463, 23 So.2d 184 (1945). Occasionally, however, courts have erroneously concluded that certain acts of the usufructuary result in renunciation of the usufruct. See

Bauman v. George, 154 La. 680, 98 So. 85 (1923) (suit for partition by the usufructuary and co-owner of the property allowed on the assumption that the usufructuary had, in effect, renounced the usufruct since the demand for partition was made "without reservation of her usufruct, and without any claim of right to the entire proceeds"); cf. Lasyone v. Emerson, 220 La. 951, 57 So.2d 906 (1952) (waiver of usufruct by plaintiff in a partition suit); Ogden v. Leland University, 49 La.Ann. 190 (1896) (unauthorized sale of things by the usufructuary regarded as renunciation of the enjoyment).

(e) If the usufructuary merely consents to the sale of the things free of his enjoyment, he does not thereby renounce his usufruct. The transaction involves, ordinarily, a simultaneous sale of the naked ownership and of the usufruct to the third purchaser for a single price. The usufructuary and the naked owner may agree that the usufructuary shall have the enjoyment of the entire price for the period of the usufruct; but, even in the absence of agreement, the usufruct attaches to the proceeds of the sale. Article 616, supra.

(f) The sale of the effects of a succession, made by the usufructuary as executor of the will of the grantor of the usufruct or as administrator of the succession, for the purpose of obtaining cash needed for the satisfaction of debts, is not a renunciation of the enjoyment. In this case, the usufruct attaches to any residue remaining after the payment of debts. See Succession of Russell, 208 La. 213, 23 So.2d 50 (1945); Succession of Singer, 208 La. 463, 23 So.2d 184 (1945).

(g) The part of Article 624 (C.C., 1870) allowing the creditor of the usufructuary to annul a renunciation of the usufruct "whether it be accompanied with fraud or not" has been suppressed as unnecessary. See Comment (b), supra.

Art. 627.   Right of retention

Upon termination of the usufruct, the usufructuary or his heirs have the right to retain possession of the property until reimbursed for all expenses and advances for which they have recourse against the owner or his heirs.

Acts 1976, No. 103, § 1, eff. Jan. 1, 1977.

REVISION COMMENTS—1976

(a) This provision reproduces the substance of the second paragraph of Article 625 of the Louisiana Civil Code of 1870. It does not change the law.

(b) Article 625 (C.C., 1870), first paragraph, has not been reproduced because it states the obvious. Moreover, Article 625 (C.C., 1870), first paragraph, is analytically inaccurate. It is only upon termination of a usufruct of nonconsumables for a cause other than the permanent and total destruction of the property that the usufruct "returns and becomes again incorporated with the ownership." This reintegration of ownership ordinarily incurs in favor of the naked owner who "begins to enter into a full and entire ownership of the thing." However, it may also incur in favor of the usufructuary or in favor of a third person who has acquired the ownership of the property by acquisitive prescription.

(c) The usufructuary or his heirs have by law recourse against the owner for expenses and advances made by them to discharge obligations of the naked owner. The expenses and advances contemplated by this article thus include the costs of extraordinary repairs unless made necessary by the fault of the usufructuary, extraordinary charges of a nature to augment the value of the property, and advances made by a universal usufructuary or usufructuary under universal title in order to discharge debts of the grantor of the usufruct. See Le Goaster v. LeFon Asylum, 155 La. 158, 99 So. 22 (1924).

(d) Under this provision, the usufructuary continues to possess the property in the same manner as if the usufruct had not terminated. The right of retention does not qualify the usufructuary or his heirs as possessors for all purposes. As of the termination of the usufruct, the fruits of the property belong to the owner.

Art. 628.   Consequences of termination; usufruct of nonconsumables

Upon termination of a usufruct of nonconsumables for a cause other than total and permanent destruction of the property, full ownership is restored. The usufructuary or his heirs are bound to deliver the property to the owner with its accessories and fruits produced since the termination of the usufruct.

If property has been lost or deteriorated through the fault of the usufructuary, the owner is entitled to the value the property otherwise would have had at the termination of the usufruct.

Acts 1976, No. 103, § 1, eff. Jan. 1, 1977.

REVISION COMMENTS—1976

(a) This provision is new. It articulates rules inherent in Articles 625 (first paragraph), 535, and 567 (second paragraph) of the Louisiana Civil Code of 1870. It does not change the law.

(b) Upon termination of the usufruct, full ownership is ordinarily vested in the naked owner. However, full ownership may also be vested in the usufructuary as a result of confusion or in a third person who has acquired the ownership of the property by acquisitive prescription.

(c) Upon termination of the usufruct, the right of the usufructuary ceases to exist and the owner enjoys all the prerogatives of full ownership, including the right to the fruits of the property. The usufructuary, however, is entitled to keep the property until he is fully reimbursed for advances and expenses. Article 627, supra.

(d) The second paragraph of the provision reproduces the substance of Article 567 (second paragraph) of the Louisiana Civil Code of 1870 and prescribes the applicable measure of recovery under the law of usufruct. In addition, the usufructuary may be liable to the owner under the law of delictual obligations.

Art. 629.   Consequences of termination; usufruct of consumables

At the termination of a usufruct of consumables, the usufructuary is bound to deliver to the owner things of the same quantity and quality or the value they had at the commencement of the usufruct.

Acts 1976, No. 103, § 1, eff. Jan. 1, 1977.

REVISION COMMENTS—1976

(a) This provision is new. It is based on Louisiana jurisprudence interpreting Article 549 of the Civil Code of 1870. It does not change the law.

(b) For Louisiana jurisprudence, see Succession of Trouilly, 52 La.Ann. 276 (1899); Succession of Blanchard, 48 La.Ann. 578 (1896); Succession of Hayes, 33 La.Ann. 1143 (1881); cf. Tutorship of Jones, 41 La.Ann. 620 (1889).

CHAPTER 3—HABITATION

Art. 630.   Habitation

Habitation is the nontransferable real right of a natural person to dwell in the house of another.

Acts 1976, No. 103, § 1, eff. Jan. 1, 1977.

REVISION COMMENTS—1976

(a) This provision reproduces the substance of Article 627 of the Louisiana Civil Code of 1870. It does not change the law.

(b) Habitation is a personal servitude, namely, a charge on property in favor of a person, akin to usufruct. As a personal servitude, habitation is a dismemberment of ownership and a real right. Habitation is also similar to predial servitudes in that it is a charge on an immovable which does not exhaust the utility of the property.

(c) Habitation is a nontransferable real right. C.C. art. 643 (1870); Article 637, infra. Habitation may be established in favor of natural persons only. There is no provision like that of Article 543

(C.C., 1870), which indicates that usufruct "may be granted to all such as may be possessed of an estate, even to communities or corporations." Cf. 3 Planiol et Ripert, Traité pratique de droit civil français 861 (2d ed. Picard 1952).

(d) Article 627 of the 1870 Code speaks of "dwelling gratuitously" in a house, but this refers to the obvious, namely, that the beneficiary of the right of habitation owes no rental to the owner. Most Louisiana decisions dealing with the right of habitation involve onerous transactions. See Chenevert v. Lemoine, 52 La.Ann. 586 (1900); Louis v. Garrison, 64 So.2d 254 (La.App.Orl.Cir.1953); Barrett v. Barrett, 5 So.2d 381 (La.App.2d Cir. 1941); Landry v. Hawkins, 156 So. 795 (La.App. 1st Cir. 1934). Under Article 630, habitation may be created by onerous or gratuitous title.

Art. 631.　　Establishment and extinction

The right of habitation is established and extinguished in the same manner as the right of usufruct.

Acts 1976, No. 103, § 1, eff. Jan. 1, 1977.

REVISION COMMENTS—1976

(a) This provision reproduces the substance of Article 628 of the Louisiana Civil Code of 1870 as it relates to habitation. It does not change the law.

(b) Since the right of habitation is never created by operation of law, this provision refers, by necessity, to establishment by juridical act. The establishment of the right of habitation by contract or by will is subject to the general rules concerning the substance and form of juridical acts. Thus, since the object of the right is immovable property, the law requires a written instrument, which, in order to be effective against third persons, must be recorded. Formal, precise language is not required. See Chenevert v. Lemoine, 52 La.Ann. 586 (1900); Louis v. Garrison, 64 So.2d 906 (1952); Landry v. Hawkins, 156 So. 795 (La.App. 1st Cir. 1934).

(c) Habitation may be established on houses only; since the object of the right is an immovable, habitation is an incorporeal immovable. Cf. Article 540, supra.

(d) According to Article 629 of the Louisiana Civil Code of 1870 the person having the habitation is bound to make an inventory and to give security in the same manner as the usufructuary. The provision has been suppressed. Thus, the person having the habitation will be bound to make an inventory and to give security only if such obligations are imposed on him by juridical act.

Art. 632.　　Regulation by title

The right of habitation is regulated by the title that establishes it. If the title is silent as to the extent of habitation, the right is regulated in accordance with Articles 633 through 635.

Acts 1976, No. 103, § 1, eff. Jan. 1, 1977.

REVISION COMMENTS—1976

(a) This provision reproduces the substance of the first paragraph of Article 631 and Article 632 of the Louisiana Civil Code of 1870 as they relate to habitation. It does not change the law.

(b) The second paragraph of Article 631 of the 1870 Code has not been reproduced because it is purely didactic. Indeed, if an agreement exceeds the limits of the rules governing habitation, the agreement creates another right. Thus a right to receive the fruits of a house and to sell and dispose of them freely, would be a right of usufruct, and all the laws concerning usufruct would be applicable to it.

Art. 633.　　Persons residing in the house

A person having the right of habitation may reside in the house with his family, although not married at the time the right was granted to him.

Acts 1976, No. 103, § 1, eff. Jan. 1, 1977.

(a) This provision reproduces the substance of Article 640 of the Louisiana Civil Code of 1870. It does not change the law.

(b) Article 642 of the Louisiana Civil Code of 1870 defining the word "family" for purposes of habitation is suppressed. Accordingly, the word "family" will be interpreted in the light of Article 3556(12) of the Civil Code of 1870.

Art. 634.   Extent of right of habitation

A person having the right of habitation is entitled to the exclusive use of the house or of the part assigned to him, and, provided that he resides therein, he may receive friends, guests, and boarders.

Acts 1976, No. 103, § 1, eff. Jan. 1, 1977.

(a) This provision reproduces the substance of the second paragraph of Article 641 of the Louisiana Civil Code of 1870. It changes the law.

(b) When the title is silent, the extent of the right of habitation is to be determined in accordance with the rules governing contractual or testamentary interpretation. Article 641(1) of the 1870 Code restricted the right of habitation to what was necessary for the needs of the person having the right and those of his family. Under Article 634, however, the person having the right of habitation is entitled to the exclusive use of the house or of the part assigned to him. A restriction to what is necessary may now be inferred only from the title.

Art. 635.   Degree of care; duty to restore the property

A person having the right of habitation is bound to use the property as a prudent administrator and at the expiration of his right to deliver it to the owner in the condition in which he received it, ordinary wear and tear excepted.

Acts 1976, No. 103, § 1, eff. Jan. 1, 1977.

This provision reproduces the substance of Article 644 of the Louisiana Civil Code of 1870 as it relates to habitation. It does not change the law.

Art. 636.   Taxes, repairs, and other charges

When the person having the right of habitation occupies the entire house, he is liable for ordinary repairs, for the payment of taxes, and for other annual charges in the same manner as the usufructuary.

When the person having the right of habitation occupies only a part of the house, he is liable for ordinary repairs to the part he occupies and for all other expenses and charges in proportion to his enjoyment.

Acts 1976, No. 103, § 1, eff. Jan. 1, 1977.

This provision reproduces the substance of Article 645 of the Louisiana Civil Code of 1870 as it relates to habitation. It does not change the law.

Art. 637.   Nontransferable and nonheritable right

The right of habitation is neither transferable nor heritable. It may not be alienated, let, or encumbered.

Acts 1976, No. 103, § 1, eff. Jan. 1, 1977.

This provision reproduces the substance of Articles 638 and 643 of the Louisiana Civil Code of 1870. It does not change the law.

Art. 638.   Duration of habitation

The right of habitation terminates at the death of the person having it unless a shorter period is stipulated.

Acts 1976, No. 103, § 1, eff. Jan. 1, 1977.

REVISION COMMENTS—1976

(a) This provision reproduces the substance of Article 639 of the Louisiana Civil Code of 1870 as it relates to habitation. It does not change the law.

(b) Article 639 of the 1870 Code speaks of "use" only. However, the rule concerning the duration of use is also applicable to habitation. C.C. art. 635 (1870). Article 638 is expressly applicable to habitation.

CHAPTER 4—RIGHTS OF USE

Art. 639.   Right of use

The personal servitude of right of use confers in favor of a person a specified use of an estate less than full enjoyment.

Acts 1976, No. 103, § 1, eff. Jan. 1, 1977.

REVISION COMMENTS—1976

(a) This provision is new. In accordance with corresponding provisions in modern civil codes, it authorizes charges on an estate in favor of a person.

(b) The personal servitude of right of use confers advantages less than full enjoyment of an estate. In this respect, it resembles a predial servitude. If a juridical act confers advantages that exhaust the utility of the property, it establishes a usufruct rather than a right of use.

(c) In the framework of the German and Greek Civil Codes, real rights that confer on a person limited advantages of use or enjoyment over an immovable belonging to another person are termed "limited personal servitudes". They constitute an intermediary category between personal and predial servitudes. Like usufruct and habitation, they are charges on things in favor of a person rather than an estate; like predial servitudes, they are necessarily charges on an immovable belonging to another person and are confined to certain advantages of use or enjoyment. Thus, they are both "personal" and "limited". For detailed discussion, see Yiannopoulos, Personal Servitudes §§ 123, 124 (1968).

(d) The question of the freedom of parties to create personal servitudes other than usufruct, use, or habitation has been raised in a number of Louisiana cases. In a landmark decision, Frost-Johnson Lumber Co. v. Salling's Heirs, 150 La. 756, 864, 91 So. 207, 245 (1902), the Louisiana Supreme Court declared that "we cannot say that the law clearly prohibits the creation of a servitude upon lands in favor of a person and his heirs. And hence the intention of the parties should govern in such matters". In Mallet v. Thibault, 212 La. 79, 31 So.2d 601, 604 (1947), a servitude of passage was held to be a personal servitude. "We are not unmindful", the court declared, "of Article 709 of the Code which seems to forbid conventional establishment of a servitude in favor of a person. However, that article cannot be reconciled with Articles 757 and 758 which are contained in Section 2 of Chapter 4 of Title IV dealing with the establishment of servitudes and which provide directly to the contrary. . . . Thus the creation of personal servitude by convention will be approved, provided, of course, that it does not contravene the public order". For another case in which a right of passage was established as a servitude in favor of a person, see Simoneaux v. Lebermuth & Israel Planting Co., 155 La. 689, 99 So. 531 (1924).

Art. 640.   Content of the servitude

The right of use may confer only an advantage that may be established by a predial servitude.

Acts 1976, No. 103, § 1, eff. Jan. 1, 1977.

REVISION COMMENTS—1976

(a) This provision is new. In accordance with modern civil codes, it prescribes the limits of contractual freedom to create rights of use. It is only advantages that may become the object of a predial servitude that may also be stipulated in the form of a right of use servitude.

(b) The rights of passage, of aqueduct, or of light and view, may thus be stipulated in favor of a person rather than an estate. Further, fishing or hunting rights and the taking of certain fruits or products from an estate may likewise be stipulated in the form of a right of use servitude.

Art. 641.   Persons having the servitude

A right of use may be established in favor of a natural person or a legal entity.

Acts 1976, No. 103, § 1, eff. Jan. 1, 1977.

REVISION COMMENT—1976

This provision is new. In accordance with modern civil codes and judicial practice in France, it permits the creation of rights of use servitudes in favor of natural persons as well as legal entities.

Art. 642.   Extent of the servitude

A right of use includes the rights contemplated or necessary to enjoyment at the time of its creation as well as rights that may later become necessary, provided that a greater burden is not imposed on the property unless otherwise stipulated in the title.

Acts 1976, No. 103, § 1, eff. Jan. 1, 1977.

REVISION COMMENT—1976

This provision is new. It is based on corresponding provisions in the German and Greek Civil Codes.

Art. 643.   Transferable right

The right of use is transferable unless prohibited by law or contract.

Acts 1976, No. 103, § 1, eff. Jan. 1, 1977.

REVISION COMMENTS—1976

(a) This provision is new. It differs from corresponding provisions of the German and Greek Civil Codes, according to which a limited personal servitude is a nontransferable right unless the contrary has been stipulated.

(b) In Simoneaux v. Lebermuth & Israel Planting Co., 155 La. 689, 99 So. 531 (1924), plaintiff had granted to defendant a right of way over her property for the construction of a railway needed for the transportation of crops to defendant's refinery. Years later, the defendant sold both the refinery and the right of way to a third person. Plaintiff sued to annul the grant on the ground that it was a personal servitude in favor of the defendant which could not be transferred by sale or otherwise. The court declared that "the right granted whether it be considered a real or a personal servitude, may be sold. . . . If the right granted by considered a personal servitude, we think that its sale is authorized by Article 2449 of the Civil Code. . . . There is nothing in Article 758 (1870), cited by plaintiff, that provides to the contrary, directly or indirectly. All the article provides is that, unless the contrary be expressly stipulated, a servitude personal to the individual expires with him. If the servitude in contest be considered personal, it can be so considered only in the sense that it is not predial, or in favor of an estate. It cannot be considered personal in the sense of being nonheritable or nontransferable. It is only to personal servitudes that are nonheritable or nontransferable that Article 758 refers".

Art. 644.   Heritable right

A right of use is not extinguished at the death of the natural person or at the dissolution of any other entity having the right unless the contrary is provided by law or contract.

Acts 1976, No. 103, § 1, eff. Jan. 1, 1977.

REVISION COMMENT—1976

This provision is new. It differs from corresponding provisions of the German and Greek Civil Codes, according to which a limited personal servitude is a nonheritable right unless the contrary has been stipulated.

Art. 645.   Regulation of the servitude

A right of use is regulated by application of the rules governing usufruct and predial servitudes to the extent that their application is compatible with the rules governing a right of use servitude.

Acts 1976, No. 103, § 1, eff. Jan. 1, 1977.

REVISION COMMENTS—1976

(a) This provision is new. It is based on corresponding provisions of the German and Greek Civil Codes.

(b) A number of Louisiana statutes provide for the creation of "servitudes" other than usufruct, use, or habitation, in favor of public utilities or governmental agencies. See, in general, R.S. 19:2; 2:82; 12:428; 38:2334; 45:64; and 48:833. These so called servitudes are not predial servitudes because they are not charges on an estate in favor of another estate. They should be classified as rights of use under Article 639—real rights of enjoyment in favor of a person governed by the rules of the Civil Code pertaining to both predial and personal servitudes. Cf. Rock Island, A. & L.R.R. v. Gournay, 205 La. 164, 17 So.2d 21 (1944) (railroad right of way); Tate v. Ville Platte, 44 So.2d 360 (La.App. 1st Cir. 1950) (pipeline servitude in favor of town); Arkansas Louisiana Gas Co. v. Cutrer, 30 So.2d 864 (La.App.2d Cir. 1947) (pipeline servitude).

TITLE IV—PREDIAL SERVITUDES

CHAPTER 1—GENERAL PRINCIPLES

Art. 646.   Predial servitude; definition

A predial servitude is a charge on a servient estate for the benefit of a dominant estate.

The two estates must belong to different owners.

Acts 1977, No. 514, § 1, eff. Jan. 1, 1978.

REVISION COMMENTS—1977

(a) This provision reproduces the substance of Articles 646, 647, 648, and 649 of the Louisiana Civil Code of 1870. It does not change the law.

(b) The definition indicates that predial servitudes are real rights burdening immovables that the creation of these rights requires the existence of two distinct immovables, belonging to different owners and that these rights are for the benefit of an immovable rather than a person. The word "estate" is a translation of héritage, occurring in the French text of the Louisiana Civil Codes of 1808 and 1825 as well as in the French Civil Code. In Louisiana, the word "estate" in Article 647 means, as in France, a distinct corporeal immovable. This is made clear by Article 710 of the Louisiana Civil Code of 1870 which indicates that predial servitudes may be established on, or in favor of, tracts of land and buildings. In 1870 these were the only immovables susceptible of servitudes.

Constructions other than buildings, though classified as immovables by nature under Article 464 of the Civil Code, are not susceptible of predial servitudes; the same is true of immovables by destination and incorporeal immovables. Timber estates and individual apartments, however, qualify today by virtue of special legislation as distinct corporeal immovables; hence, it ought to be clear that predial servitudes may be established on, or in favor of, timber estates and individual apartments. See Acts 1974, No. 502, now R.S. 9:1121–1142; Kavanaugh v. Frost-Johnson Lumber Co., 149 La. 972, 90 So. 275 (1921); Walker v. Simmons, 155 So.2d 234 (La.App. 3rd Cir. 1963) (servitude of passage in favor of timber estate). See also Yiannopoulos, Predial Servitudes; General Principles: Louisiana and Comparative Law, 29 La.L.Rev. 1 (1968).

(c) Language in the Louisiana and French Civil Codes indicates that predial servitudes are due to an estate rather than the owner of an estate. This apparent personification of the dominant estate has its roots in Roman sources. According to modern analysis, however, things cannot have rights; rights belong to persons only. Therefore, legislative declarations in Louisiana and in France that predial servitudes are due to an estate must be taken as metaphors; they merely mean that predial servitudes are not attached to a particular person but that they are due to anyone who happens to be owner of the dominant estate. The German and Greek Civil Codes provide expressly that predial servitudes are due to the owner of the dominant estate. B.G.B. § 1018; Greek C.C. art. 1118.

(d) In the civilian literature, the estate burdened with a predial servitude is designated as "servient"; the estate in whose favor (or in whose owner's favor) the servitude is established is designated as "dominant". In France, the redactors of the Civil Code have avoided these expressions in an effort to wipe out the memory of reprobated feudal tenures. The redactors of the Louisiana Civil Code of 1870, perhaps unnecessarily, likewise avoided reference to the "servient" or "dominant" estate. Feudal tenures, however, have never had a place in Louisiana property law. Xigues v. Bujac, 7 La.Ann. 498 (1852). The words "servient" and "dominant" estates are consistently used in judicial decisions and in headings of the annotated edition of the Louisiana Civil Code of 1870. Accordingly, for the sake of brevity, these words rather than descriptive expressions are used in this revision.

(e) A servitude may not be imposed on an estate in its own favor. Efner v. Ketteringham, 41 So.2d 130 (La.App. 2d Cir. 1949). Nor may a servitude be imposed on a person in favor of an estate. If a servitude is imposed on an estate in favor of a person rather than of another estate it is not a predial servitude but a personal servitude of right of use. C.C. arts. 639–645 (1977).

(f) The second paragraph of Article 646 is an application of the maxim nemini res sua servit (no one has a right of servitude in his own property). The maxim refers to situations in which two estates belong in their entirety to the same owner. Thus, the co-owner of an estate owned in indivision may have a right of servitude on an estate of which he is the sole owner; and, conversely, the sole owner of an estate may have a right of servitude on an estate in which he has an undivided interest. See C.C.art. 805(2); 3 Planiol et Ripert, Traité pratique de droit civil français 871 (2d ed. Picard 1952).

Art. 647. Benefit to dominant estate

There must be a benefit to the dominant estate. The benefit need not exist at the time the servitude is created; a possible convenience or a future advantage suffices to support a servitude.

There is no predial servitude if the charge imposed cannot be reasonably expected to benefit the dominant estate.

Acts 1977, No. 514, § 1, eff. Jan. 1, 1978.

REVISION COMMENTS—1977

(a) This provision reproduces the substance of Article 650 of the Louisiana Civil Code of 1870. The second paragraph changes the law as it declares that a predial servitude does not exist when the charge imposed cannot be reasonably expected to benefit the dominant estate.

(b) The principle of utility, expressed in the adage servitus utilis esse debet, sets the outer limits of party autonomy in the field of predial servitudes. The law will allow contractual or testamentary freedom to the extent that a servitude may serve a useful purpose; unreasonable whims of parties, serving no socially useful purpose, may not give rise to predial servitudes. See Parish v. Municipality No. 2, 8 La.Ann. 145 (1853). The benefit to be derived from the servitude need not be economic; it may be merely esthetic. See 3 Planiol et Ripert, Traité pratique de droit civil français 871 (2d ed. Picard 1952).

(c) The benefit of the servitude must derive from the servient estate and must be attributed to the person who, at any given time, happens to be owner of the dominant estate. 3 Plainol et Ripert, Traité pratique de droit civil français 921 (2d ed. Picard 1952). If the benefit is attributed to a designated person, the servitude is personal rather than predial. For example, a servitude for the benefit of a named owner of an estate for the enjoyment of a swimming pool or of a tennis court in another estate is a personal servitude of right of use, but the same stipulation for the benefit of an estate, or any owner of that estate, gives rise to a predial servitude. In Greco v. Frigerio, 3 La.App. 649, 651 (Orl. Cir.1926), question arose whether a servitude for the maintenance of a bathroom was personal or predial. The court declared that the servitude was "so obviously advantageous to the property possessing the bathroom as to permit of little discussion. The fact that bathing is a personal habit cannot affect the situation". Indeed, the utility of the servitude was attributed to any person who happened to be owner of the dominant estate rather than a named owner.

Art. 648. Contiguity or proximity of the estates

Neither contiguity nor proximity of the two estates is necessary for the existence of a predial servitude. It suffices that the two estates be so located as to allow one to derive some benefit from the charge on the other.

Acts 1977, No. 514, § 1, eff. Jan. 1, 1978.

REVISION COMMENT—1977

This provision reproduces the substance of Article 651 of the Louisiana Civil Code of 1870. It does not change the law.

Art. 649. Nature; incorporeal immovable

A predial servitude is an incorporeal immovable.

Acts 1977, No. 514, § 1, eff. Jan. 1, 1978.

REVISION COMMENTS—1977

(a) This provision reproduces the substance of Article 652 of the Louisiana Civil Code of 1870. It does not change the law.

(b) In Louisiana and in France, predial servitudes are immovable real rights, namely, incorporeal immovables, governed in principle by rules applicable to immovable property. See Yiannopoulos, Civil Law Property §§ 60–63 (1966).

(c) The idea that a predial servitude is an accessory of the dominant estate is expressed in Article 650, infra.

Art. 650.   Inseparability of servitude

A.   A predial servitude is inseparable from the dominant estate and passes with it. The right of using the servitude cannot be alienated, leased, or encumbered separately from the dominant estate.

B.   The predial servitude continues as a charge on the servient estate when ownership changes.

Acts 1977, No. 514, § 1, eff. Jan. 1, 1978. Amended by Acts 2004, No. 821, § 2, eff. Jan. 1, 2005.

REVISION COMMENTS—1977

(a) This provision reproduces the substance of Articles 653 and 654 of the Louisiana Civil Code of 1870. It does not change the law.

(b) Predial servitudes, according to the Romanist tradition, are inherent qualities of estates: praediis inhaerent. Digest 50.16.86. They may not exist independently of the dominant or of the servient estate. Once they are created, predial servitudes may not be alienated or seized separately from the dominant estate to which they belong. On the contrary, any alienation, seizure, or encumbrance of the dominant estate includes predial servitudes established for its benefit: ambulant cum dominio. Conversely, an alienation, seizure, or encumbrance of the servient estate is made subject to existing rights of servitudes.

(c) Changes in the ownership of the two estates are immaterial. The person who happens to be the owner of the servient estate is bound to suffer the exercise of the right of servitude by the person who happens to be owner of the dominant estate. This follows from the nature of predial servitudes as real rights which give rise to real obligations. C.C. arts. 2012, 2015. Any alienation, seizure, or encumbrance of the dominant estate includes predial servitudes established in its favor, because predial servitudes ambulant cum dominio. 3 Planiol et Ripert, Traité pratique de droit civil français 872 (& d ed. Picard 1952); cf. Coguenhem v. Trosclair, 137 La. 985, 991, 69 So. 800, 802 (1915): "The servitude is part and parcel of the estate to which it is due, and, as such, accompanies it when the latter is mortgaged or sold. It passes with the estate". Conversely, an alienation, seizure, or encumbrance of the servient estate is made subject to existing rights of servitudes.

REVISION COMMENTS—2004

This Article is amended by adding the word "leased" to the second sentence of the Article. This amendment does not change the law. Rather, it transfers to this Article the content of Article 2680 of the Civil Code of 1870, which provided that "[a] right of servitude can not be leased separately from the property to which it is annexed."

Art. 651.   Obligations of the owner of the servient estate

The owner of the servient estate is not required to do anything. His obligation is to abstain from doing something on his estate or to permit something to be done on it. He may be required by convention or by law to keep his estate in suitable condition for the exercise of the servitude due to the dominant estate. A servitude may not impose upon the owner of the servient estate or his successors the obligation to pay a fee or other charge on the occasion of an alienation, lease, or encumbrance of the servient estate.

Acts 1977, No. 514, § 1, eff. Jan. 1, 1978. Amended by Acts 2010, No. 938, § 2, eff. July 2, 2010.

REVISION COMMENTS—1977

(a) This provision reproduces the substance of Article 655 of the Louisiana Civil Code of 1870. It does not change the law.

(b) In principle, predial servitudes may not involve affirmative duties for the owner of the servient estate. This is a rule of public policy that may not be derogated from by juridical act, unless the law provides otherwise. For the limits of contractual or testamentary freedom in the field of property law, see Succession of Franklin, 7 La.Ann. 395 (1852); Yiannopoulos, Civil Law Property §§ 87, 96 (1966). The principle that servitudes may not involve affirmative duties for the owner of the servient estate admits exception as to certain incidental duties necessary for the exercise of the servitude. Thus, parties may stipulate that the owner of the servient estate shall be charged with the duty to keep his estate fit for the purposes of the servitude. See 4 Huc, Commentaire théorique et pratique de Code Civil 495–96, 533 (1893). At least in connection with natural and legal servitudes, the law implies that the owner of the servient estate is charged with the duty to keep his estate fit for the purposes of the servitude. See Wild v. LeBlanc, 191 So.2d 146 (La.App.3rd Cir. 1966); cf. Brown v. Blankenship, 28 So.2d 496 (La.App.2d Cir. 1946). Parties may also stipulate that the owner of the servient estate shall maintain in good state of repair certain works necessary for the use and preservation of the servitude. If the exercise of the servitudes requires certain structures, the owner of the dominant estate must keep these structures fit at his expense, unless the contrary is stipulated. All these incidental affirmative duties of the owner of the servient estate qualify as land charges or real obligations. See C.C. art. 1997(3).

(c) The owner of the servient estate may bind himself by a personal obligation to perform certain affirmative duties in connection with a predial servitude. These obligations may be heritable, but they are not transferred to successors by particular title without express stipulation to that effect. Cf. C.C. art. 3556(28).

(d) Predial servitudes involving toleration of certain activities on the servient estate may be for the use of that estate for certain purposes, for example, in connection with rights of way, aqueducts, or support of structures; or they may be for the taking of certain materials, as earth, stones, water, or wood. The taking of mineral substances, however, ordinarily forms the objects of rights other than predial servitudes. In Louisiana, servitudes for the taking of minerals, as oil and gas, are sui generis real rights rather than predial servitudes. Mineral Code art. 18.

(e) Servitudes involving prohibition of certain material acts may exclude, for example, the erection of a building on a vacant lot or the use of the servient estate as a pasture or as an industrial establishment. In Louisiana, restraints on the use of property may be veritable predial servitudes or sui generis real rights in the nature of building restrictions. See Yiannopoulos, Civil Law Property § 104 (1966).

(f) Predial servitudes may exclude certain rights that the owner of the servient estate would be entitled to exercise by virtue of his ownership. For example, the owner of the servient estate may be deprived of his right to drain waters into an estate situated below or of his right to diffuse reasonable quantities of smoke, heat, or noise. Conversely, the owner of the servient estate may be bound to tolerate an excessive emission of smoke, heat, or noise from the dominant estate, which, without the servitude, he would be entitled to suppress. See Ellis v. Blanchard, 45 So.2d 100 (La.App.2d Cir. 1950). Predial servitudes, however, may not exclude the performance of juridical acts affecting the servient estate; thus, a prohibition of alienation or partition may not form the content of a predial servitude. In the context of a subdivision, certain restrictions on the alienability of property may constitute valid sui generis real rights in the nature of building restrictions. See Queensborough Land Co. v. Cazeaux, 136 La. 724, 67 So. 641 (1915). Yiannopoulos, Predial Servitudes; General Principles, 29 La.L.Rev. 1, 6 (1968).

Art. 652.   Indivisibility of servitude

A predial servitude is indivisible. An estate cannot have upon another estate part of a right of way, or of view, or of any other servitude, nor can an estate be charged with a part of a servitude.

The use of a servitude may be limited to certain days or hours; when limited, it is still an entire right. A servitude is due to the whole of the dominant estate and to all parts of it; if this estate is divided, every acquirer of a part has the right of using the servitude in its entirety.

Acts 1977, No. 514, § 1, eff. Jan. 1, 1978.

REVISION COMMENTS—1977

(a) This provision reproduces the substance of Article 656 of the Louisiana Civil Code of 1870. It does not change the law.

(b) The principle of indivisibility of predial servitudes carries significant practical consequences. For example, it follows from the principle of indivisibility that no predial servitude may be established on, or in favor of, an undivided part of an estate. 3 Planiol et Ripert, Traité pratique de droit civil français 873 (2d ed. Picard 1952). The creation of a predial servitude on an estate owned in indivision by several co-owners requires the consent of all; and the release of a servitude in favor of an estate owned in indivision requires the consent of all the co-owners.

(c) If the dominant estate is divided into parts, the principle of indivisibility requires that every acquirer of a part shall have the right of using the servitude in its entirety. Nevertheless, the division of the dominant estate may not result in the placing of an additional burden on the servient estate. Article 747, infra. Each acquirer of a part is entitled to use the servitude in its entirety but the use made by all of the acquirers may not exceed the limits of the use previously made. For example, if the servitude was one of right of way, all acquirers of parts of the dominant estate are bound to exercise the right through the same place. Neither the Louisiana Civil Code of 1870 nor the French Civil Code provides expressly for the consequences of the division of the servient estate. Nevertheless, on principle as well as in the light of a proper interpretation of pertinent provisions in the two codes, it is clear that the division of the servient estate does not affect adversely the interests of the owner of the dominant estate. Insofar as these interests are concerned, the servitude remains the same. See Yiannopoulos, Predial Servitudes; General Principles, 29 La.L.Rev. 1, 27 (1968).

Art. 653.   Division of advantages

The advantages resulting from a predial servitude may be divided, if they are susceptible of division.

Acts 1977, No. 514, § 1, eff. Jan. 1, 1978.

REVISION COMMENTS—1977

(a) This provision reproduces the substance of Article 657 of the Louisiana Civil Code of 1870. It does not change the law.

(b) The principle of indivisibility of predial servitudes does not exclude division of the advantages resulting from predial servitudes provided, of course, that these advantages are susceptible of division. Thus, if a servitude for the pasturage of one hundred head of cattle exists in favor of an estate belonging to two owners, each of them may be attributed the right to send to pasture fifty animals.

(c) Limitations of the use of the servitude do not constitute division of the servitude or of the advantages of the servitude. Thus, the limitation of the use to certain days or hours is an entire right rather than a part of a right. Article 652, supra.

Art. 654.   Kinds of predial servitudes

Predial servitudes may be natural, legal, and voluntary or conventional. Natural servitudes arise from the natural situation of estates; legal servitudes are imposed by law; and voluntary or conventional servitudes are established by juridical act, prescription, or destination of the owner.

Acts 1977, No. 514, § 1, eff. Jan. 1, 1978.

REVISION COMMENTS—1977

(a) This provision reproduces the substance of Article 659 of the Louisiana Civil Code of 1870. It does not change the law.

(b) Article 659 of the Louisiana Civil Code of 1870 speaks of servitudes arising from "contract between the respective owners", but this is only an example of the methods available for the creation of conventional servitudes. Elsewhere conventional servitudes are designated as "voluntary" or as arising "from an act of man", and Article 743 declares to the point that "servitudes are established by all acts by which property can be transferred". Hence, there should be no doubt that conventional servitudes may arise from contracts as well as from unilateral juridical acts. Cf. McGuffy v. Weil, 240 La. 758, 765, 125 So.2d 154, 157 (1960).

(c) This tripartite division of servitudes has been subjected to vivid criticism in France. In the first place, critics have observed that the division of servitudes into natural and legal is arbitrary;

both kinds of servitudes are legal in the sense that they arise by operation of law and are imposed by directly applicable provisions of legislative texts. Predial servitudes like personal servitudes, should thus be divided into legal and conventional. This criticism has been answered by the observation that natural servitudes are not, strictly speaking, imposed by the law; the law merely takes cognizance of certain natural situations of fact. In contrast, legal servitudes are creatures of the law and are imposed in the light of considerations of policy. See 6 Baudry-Lacantinerie, Traité théorique et pratique de droit civil No. 534 (3rd ed. Chauveau 1905).

(d) Critics have observed that, from the viewpoint of accurate analysis, natural and legal servitudes involve limitations on the content of ownership rather than veritable servitudes. See 2 Aubry et Rau, Droit civil français 280–323 (7th ed. Esmein 1961). Indeed, it is often impossible to determine which is the dominant estate, in whose favor a legal servitude is established, and which is the servient estate owing the servitude. And, in practice, the word servitude is ordinarily reserved for conventional servitudes; thus, the vendor of an immovable may well declare that his immovable is free of servitudes although it may be burdened with natural or legal servitudes. Cf. Lallande v. Wentz, 18 La.Ann.289 (1866). This criticism is "difficult to answer". 6 Baudry-Lacantinerie, Traité théorique et pratique de droit civil No. 535 (3rded. Chauveau 1905). In modern civil codes, the concepts of natural and legal servitudes have thus given way to the idea of limitations on the content of ownership. See B.G.B. §§ 903–924; Greek C.C. arts. 999–1032. It seems that the redactors of the French Civil Code grouped together natural, legal, and conventional servitudes as a matter of convenience. As servitudes, limitations on the right of ownership could be, on principle, subject to the detailed rules governing conventional servitudes. In deference to the tradition, and in the light of practical considerations, the tripartite division of servitudes is maintained in this revision.

CHAPTER 2—NATURAL SERVITUDES

Art. 655.   Natural drainage

An estate situated below is bound to receive the surface waters that flow naturally from an estate situated above unless an act of man has created the flow.

Acts 1977, No. 514, § 1, eff. Jan. 1, 1978.

REVISION COMMENTS—1977

(a) This provision reproduces the substance of the first paragraph of Article 660 of the Louisiana Civil Code of 1870. It does not change the law. Louisiana jurisprudence interpreting Article 660 continues to be relevant.

(b) Article 660(1) of the 1870 Code declares that "[i]t is a servitude due by the estate situated below to receive the waters which run naturally from the estate situated above, provided the industry of man has not been used to create that servitude" (emphasis added). Note error in English translation of French text; "been used to create that servitude" should be "contributed to the flow". See art. 660, 1972 Compiled Edition of the Civil Codes of Louisiana (16 West's LSA-Civil Code, Dainow ed. 1973). The proposed provision follows the French text of the original article.

(c) According to a Louisiana decision, Civil Code Articles 660 and 661 of the 1870 Code do not apply to subterranean waters. Adams v. Grigsby, 152 So.2d 619 (La.App.2d Cir.), writ refused 244 La. 662, 153 So.2d 880 (1963).

Art. 656.   Obligations of the owners

The owner of the servient estate may not do anything to prevent the flow of the water. The owner of the dominant estate may not do anything to render the servitude more burdensome.

Acts 1977, No. 514, § 1, eff. Jan. 1, 1978.

REVISION COMMENT—1977

This provision reproduces the substance of the second and third paragraphs of Article 660 of the Louisiana Civil Code of 1870. It does not change the law. Louisiana jurisprudence interpreting Article 660 of the 1870 Code remains relevant.

Art. 657.   Estate bordering on running water

The owner of an estate bordering on running water may use it as it runs for the purpose of watering his estate or for other purposes.

Acts 1977, No. 514, § 1, eff. Jan. 1, 1978.

REVISION COMMENT—1977

This provision reproduces the substance of the first paragraph of Article 661 of the Louisiana Civil Code of 1870. It does not change the law. Louisiana jurisprudence interpreting the source provision continues to be relevant.

Art. 658.   Estate through which water runs

The owner of an estate through which water runs, whether it originates there or passes from lands above, may make use of it while it runs over his lands. He cannot stop it or give it another direction and is bound to return it to its ordinary channel where it leaves his estate.

Acts 1977, No. 514, § 1, eff. Jan. 1, 1978.

REVISION COMMENTS—1977

(a) This provision reproduces the substance of the second paragraph of Article 661 of the Louisiana Civil Code of 1870. It does not change the law. Louisiana jurisprudence interpreting the source provision continues to be relevant.

(b) R.S. 38:218 declares: "No person diverting or impeding the course of water from a natural drain shall fail to return the water to its natural course before it leaves his estate without any undue retardation of the flow of water outside of his enclosure thereby injuring an adjacent estate."

CHAPTER 3—LEGAL SERVITUDES

SECTION 1—LIMITATIONS OF OWNERSHIP

Art. 659.   Legal servitudes; notion

Legal servitudes are limitations on ownership established by law for the benefit of the general public or for the benefit of particular persons.

Acts 1977, No. 514, § 1, eff. Jan. 1, 1978.

REVISION COMMENTS—1977

(a) This provision is new. It is based on Article 664 of the Louisiana Civil Code of 1870. It does not change the law.

(b) For the nature of legal servitudes as limitations on ownership, see Yiannopoulos, Predial Servitudes; General Principles: Louisiana and Comparative Law, 29 La.L.Rev. 1, 43 (1968); 2 Aubry et Rau, Droit civil français 280–323 (7th ed. Esmein 1961).

Art. 660.   Keeping buildings in repair

The owner is bound to keep his buildings in repair so that neither their fall nor that of any part of their materials may cause damage to a neighbor or to a passerby. However, he is answerable for damages only upon a showing that he knew or, in the exercise of reasonable care, should have known of the vice or defect which caused the damage, that the damage could have been prevented by the exercise of reasonable care, and that he failed to exercise such reasonable care. Nothing in this Article shall preclude the court from the application of the doctrine of res ipsa loquitur in an appropriate case.

Acts 1977, No. 514, § 1, eff. Jan. 1, 1978. Amended by Acts 1996, 1st Ex.Sess., No. 1, § 1, eff. April 16, 1996.

REVISION COMMENTS—1977

(a) This provision is new. It is based on Article 670 of the Louisiana Civil Code of 1870 and Louisiana jurisprudence interpreting it.

(b) According to Louisiana jurisprudence, Article 670 of the Louisiana Civil Code of 1870 establishes responsibility without regard to negligence. See Cothern v. La Rocca, 255 La. 673, 232 So.2d 473 (1970); Crawford v. Wheless, 265 So.2d 661 (La.App.2d Cir. 1972). Cf. Comment, Article 2322 and the Liability of the Owner of an Immovable, 42 Tul.L.Rev. 178 (1967); Davis, Liability of an Owner to Third Persons Injured by Structural Defects, 29 La.L.Rev. 626 (1969).

Art. 661.　　Building in danger of falling

When a building or other construction is in danger of falling a neighbor has a right of action to compel the owner to have it properly supported or demolished. When the danger is imminent the court may authorize the neighbor to do the necessary work for which he shall be reimbursed by the owner.

Acts 1977, No. 514, § 1, eff. Jan. 1, 1978.

REVISION COMMENT—1977

This provision is new. It is based on Article 671 of the Louisiana Civil Code of 1870.

Art. 662.　　Building near a wall

One who builds near a wall, whether common or not, is bound to take all necessary precautions to protect his neighbor against injury.

Acts 1977, No. 514, § 1, eff. Jan. 1, 1978.

REVISION COMMENT—1977

This provision is new. It expresses the principle underlying the detailed rules of Articles 692–695 of the Louisiana Civil Code of 1870. It changes the law as it allows flexibility in the determination of the appropriate measures for the protection of the interests of a neighbor.

Art. 663.　　Projections over boundary

A landowner may not build projections beyond the boundary of his estate.

Acts 1977, No. 514, § 1, eff. Jan. 1, 1978.

REVISION COMMENT—1977

This provision reproduces the substance of Article 697 of the Louisiana Civil Code of 1870. It does not change the law.

Art. 664.　　Rain drip from roof

A landowner is bound to fix his roof so that rainwater does not fall on the ground of his neighbor.

Acts 1977, No. 514, § 1, eff. Jan. 1, 1978.

REVISION COMMENT—1977

This provision reproduces the substance of Articles 698 and 713, first paragraph, of the Louisiana Civil Code of 1870. It does not change the law.

Art. 665.　　Legal public servitudes

Servitudes imposed for the public or common utility relate to the space which is to be left for the public use by the adjacent proprietors on the shores of navigable rivers and for the making and repairing of levees, roads, and other public or common works. Such servitudes also exist on property necessary for the building of levees and other water control structures on the alignment approved by the U.S. Army Corps of Engineers as provided by law, including the repairing of hurricane protection levees.

All that relates to this kind of servitude is determined by laws or particular regulations.

Amended by Acts 2006, No. 776, § 1.

Art. 666. River road; substitution if destroyed or impassable

He who from his title as owner is bound to give a public road on the border of a river or stream, must furnish another without any compensation, if the first be destroyed or carried away.

And if the road be so injured or inundated by the water, without being carried away, that it becomes impassable, the owner is obliged to give the public a passage on his lands, as near as possible to the public road, without recompense therefor.

Art. 667. Limitations on use of property

Although a proprietor may do with his estate whatever he pleases, still he cannot make any work on it, which may deprive his neighbor of the liberty of enjoying his own, or which may be the cause of any damage to him. However, if the work he makes on his estate deprives his neighbor of enjoyment or causes damage to him, he is answerable for damages only upon a showing that he knew or, in the exercise of reasonable care, should have known that his works would cause damage, that the damage could have been prevented by the exercise of reasonable care, and that he failed to exercise such reasonable care. Nothing in this Article shall preclude the court from the application of the doctrine of res ipsa loquitur in an appropriate case. Nonetheless, the proprietor is answerable for damages without regard to his knowledge or his exercise of reasonable care, if the damage is caused by an ultrahazardous activity. An ultrahazardous activity as used in this Article is strictly limited to pile driving or blasting with explosives.

Amended by Acts 1996, 1st Ex.Sess., No. 1, § 1, eff. April 16, 1996.

Art. 668. Inconvenience to neighbor

Although one be not at liberty to make any work by which his neighbor's buildings may be damaged, yet every one has the liberty of doing on his own ground whatsoever he pleases, although it should occasion some inconvenience to his neighbor.

Thus he who is not subject to any servitude originating from a particular agreement in that respect, may raise his house as high as he pleases, although by such elevation he should darken the lights of his neighbors's [neighbor's] house, because this act occasions only an inconvenience, but not a real damage.

Art. 669. Regulation of inconvenience

If the works or materials for any manufactory or other operation, cause an inconvenience to those in the same or in the neighboring houses, by diffusing smoke or nauseous smell, and there be no servitude established by which they are regulated, their sufferance must be determined by the rules of the police, or the customs of the place.

Art. 670. Encroaching building

When a landowner constructs in good faith a building that encroaches on an adjacent estate and the owner of that estate does not complain within a reasonable time after he knew or should have known of the encroachment, or in any event complains only after the construction is substantially completed the court may allow the building to remain. The owner of the building acquires a predial servitude on the land occupied by the building upon payment of compensation for the value of the servitude taken and for any other damage that the neighbor has suffered.

Acts 1977, No. 514, § 1, eff. Jan. 1, 1978.

REVISION COMMENTS—1977

(a) This provision is new. It reflects solutions reached by continental civil codes and Louisiana jurisprudence. It clarifies the law.

(b) Article 508 of the Louisiana Civil Code of 1870 deals with constructions made by a possessor, in good or in bad faith, on the land of another. It does not deal with constructions that merely encroach on the land of another. See Gordon v. Fahrenberg & Penn, 26 La.Ann. 366, 367 (1874).

According to well-settled Louisiana jurisprudence, one who encroaches on the land of another in bad faith, that is, knowingly, is bound to remove the encroachments and pay damages. Esnard v. Cangelosi, 200 La. 703, 8 So.2d 673 (1942); Barker v. Houssiere-Latreille Oil Co., 160 La. 52, 106 So. 672 (1925); Gordon v. Fahrenberg & Penn, 26 La.Ann. 366 (1874). The damage suffered by the landowner may be measured by the fair rental value of the occupied strip of land for the period of the occupancy. Dupuy Storage and Forwarding Corporation v. Cowan, 216 So.2d 610 (La.App.4th Cir. 1968).

(c) Question arises as to the legal situation when one encroaches on the land of another in good faith. In Esnard v. Cangelosi, 200 La. 703, 722, 8 So.2d 673, 679 (1942), involving an encroachment in bad faith, the court declared by way of dictum that "we find no warrant to introduce into the jurisprudence of this state the doctrine of 'Balancing of Equities in Trespass Cases,' where, as in this case, under the provisions of Article 508 of the Civil Code the plaintiff has a clear and legal right to demand the demolition and removal from the premises of the encroaching wall." There are cases, however, in which an encroaching wall, built in good faith and with the acquiescence of the adjoining landowner, was allowed to remain. In Pokorny v. Pratt, 110 La. 609, 34 So. 706 (1903), the court found that the landowner had acquiesced and, on procedural grounds, plaintiff was allowed to press a claim for damages only. In Morehead v. Smith, 225 So.2d 729 (La.App.2d Cir. 1969), the building of the defendant was substantially completed when plaintiff learned of the encroachment and advised defendant thereof. The court declared that a "judgment ordering demolition of a structure is a harsh remedy and should be granted only in an exceptional case and in strict compliance with law". Ibid. at 734–735. The court further found that the first three paragraphs of Article 508 were inapplicable, and that the last did not provide for the kind of relief that plaintiff had requested. Indeed, the demand was for the demolition of the building, and, in the alternative, for damages for the value of the land taken by the encroachment, as if it were a forced sale. The court, therefore, considered the matter as a demand in equity under Article 21 of the Civil Code. After determining that removal of the building would result in great loss to the defendant, and that this would be an inequitable solution, the court granted plaintiff's alternative demand for a forced sale of the land taken.

Art. 671.   Destruction of private property to arrest fire

Governing bodies of parishes and municipalities are authorized to adopt regulations determining the mode of proceeding to prevent the spread of fire by the destruction of buildings.

When private property is so destroyed in order to combat a conflagration, the owner shall be indemnified by the political subdivision for his actual loss.

Acts 1977, No. 514, § 1, eff. Jan. 1, 1978.

REVISION COMMENT—1977

This provision is new. It is based on Article 672 of the Louisiana Civil Code of 1870. It changes the law as it broadens the right to indemnification for the destruction of private property.

Art. 672.   Other legal servitudes

Other legal servitudes relate to common enclosures, such as common walls, fences and ditches, and to the right of passage for the benefit of enclosed estates.

Acts 1977, No. 514, § 1, eff. Jan. 1, 1978.

REVISION COMMENT—1977

This provision is new. It is based on Article 674 of the Louisiana Civil Code of 1870.

SECTION 2—COMMON ENCLOSURES

Art. 673.   Common wall servitude

A landowner who builds first may rest one-half of a partition wall on the land of his neighbor, provided that he uses solid masonry at least as high as the first story and that the width of the wall does not exceed eighteen inches, not including the plastering which may not be more than three inches in thickness.

Acts 1977, No. 514, § 1, eff. Jan. 1, 1978.

REVISION COMMENTS—1977

(a) This provision reproduces the substance of Article 675 of the Louisiana Civil Code of 1870. It does not change the law.

(b) This provision applies only to the extent that it does not conflict with municipal ordinances enacted under the authority of R.S. 33:4751. See Yiannopoulos, Common Walls, Fences and Ditches: Louisiana and Comparative Law, 35 La.L.Rev. 1249, 1299 (1975).

(c) The purpose of this provision is "to promote the enclosure of lots, with stone or brick walls, as much as possible." Larche v. Jackson, 9 Mart. (O.S.) 724, 726 (La.1821). The provision establishes a rule of public policy as it is designed to conserve land, labor, and materials, and to "encourage the improvement of urban property." Lavergne v. Lacoste, 26 La.Ann. 507, 510 (1874). A landowner need not wait for his adjoining neighbor to build a wall at the property line in order to make this wall common; he may build first and locate one-half of his wall on the land of his neighbor. In this light, Article 673 involves a logical extension of the policy embodied in Article 676, infra; at the same time, it encourages building with fire resistant materials.

(d) The person exercising the right under Article 673 must be the first to build. One does not have the right to build a wall under this provision if his neighbor has already taken advantage of it and has built a partition wall of the type contemplated. But one has the right to build a wall under this provision if his neighbor has merely built a fence or a wooden wall on or at the property line. See Bellino v. Abraham, 15 La.App. 537, 132 So. 373 (2d Cir. 1931); Bryant v. Sholars, 104 La. 786, 29 So. 350 (1901). Likewise, the existence of a house or of a brick or stone wall more than nine inches away from the boundary does not preclude the exercise of the right granted to a neighbor by Article 673. If the brick or stone wall is within the nine inch servitude, exercise of the right under Article 673 is excluded. See Carrigan v. De Neufbourg, 3 La.Ann. 440 (1848); Larche v. Jackson, 9 Mart. (O.S.) 724, 726 (La.1821). See also Crocker v. Blanc, 2 La. 531, 532 (1831).

No more than one-half of the wall may rest on the land of the neighbor. If more than one-half of the thickness of the wall is taken from the land of the neighbor, the wall encroaches to that extent, and the neighbor is entitled to the remedies that the law provides against encroachment.

(e) The right under Article 673 is given to one who builds a wall with "solid masonry at least as high as the first story." According to French doctrine and jurisprudence, the word "wall" refers to a masonry work made of materials bonded with plaster, lime, or cement. Rennes, Feb. 29, 1904, S. 1904.2.186, D. 1904.2.326; 2 Aubry et Rau, Droit civil français 564 (7th ed. Esmein 1961). It has been held in France that any form of solid construction satisfies the requirements of Article 661 of the Napoleonic Code, which corresponds with Article 684 of the Louisiana Civil Code of 1870, even if the materials were unknown at the time of the redaction of the Code. Thus, the use of reinforced concrete is allowed. See Capitant, La mitoyenneté et les nouveaux matéraux de construction, D.H.1929, Chr. 81; Delage, Questions soulevées en matière de mitoyenneté par la construction moderne (Thesis, Paris 1929).

The thickness of the wall may not exceed eighteen inches, not including the plastering. The foundation of this wall, however, under the land of each neighbor, may extend as far as it is necessary for solid construction. Heine v. Merrick, 41 La.Ann. 194, 5 So. 760 (1889).

(f) Exercise of the right given by Article 673 does not require the consent of the neighbor. If the neighbor objects, entry into his land may be secured by injunction. Heine v. Merrick, 41 La.Ann. 194, 5 So. 760 (1889). A wall built under Article 673, without the neighbor's contribution, is a private wall; it belongs to the neighbor who built it, but it may become one in common at any time by application of Article 674, infra.

Art. 674.   Contribution by neighbor

The wall thus raised becomes common if the neighbor is willing to contribute one-half of its cost. If the neighbor refuses to contribute, he preserves the right to make the wall common in whole or in part, at

215

any time, by paying to the owner one-half of the current value of the wall, or of the part that he wishes to make common.

Acts 1977, No. 514, § 1, eff. Jan. 1, 1978.

REVISION COMMENTS—1977

(a) This provision is based on Article 676 of the Louisiana Civil Code of 1870. It changes the law as it specifies that the neighbor who refuses to contribute to the raising of the wall may make the wall common at any time by paying one-half of the current value of the wall.

(b) A private wall that a neighbor has built on the boundary in compliance with Article 673, supra, may become common by application of Article 674. If the person who built first did not take advantage of the legal servitude established by Article 673 but located the wall on his own land at the boundary, the wall that he built may become common by virtue of the legal servitude established by Article 676, infra.

(c) A landowner who wishes to use an adjoining wall belonging to his neighbor should first obtain the owner's permission or demand that the wall be made common. See Faisans v. Lovie, 1 McGloin 113 (La.App. Orl.Cir.1881). One who has not contributed to the raising of the wall "has no right, without the owner's consent, to make any use thereof whatever; and the most simple structure, leaning against or attached to the wall, is a violation of the right of the owner." Ibid. at 116. The owner of the wall may protect his ownership against unauthorized interference by all procedural means, including injunctions and personal as well as real actions. Yiannopoulos, Common Walls, Fences and Ditches: Louisiana and Comparative Law, 35 La.L.Rev. 1249 (1975).

(d) The owner of the wall is entitled to demand reimbursement if his neighbor, or a person acting under him, such as a lessee, makes any use at all of the wall, or if he derives from it an advantage of use other than what is "merely a natural or necessary consequence or incident of the proximity of the wall, provided the benefit or advantage is not the result of any act on his part." Olsen v. Tung, 179 La. 760, 773, 155 So. 16, 20 (1934). The neighbor may thus render himself liable to the owner of the wall without making full use of the rights accorded to the co-owner of a wall.

(e) Under the Louisiana Civil Code of 1870, the amount of reimbursement due the owner of the wall, that is, the price for the acquisition of the co-ownership, varies according to whether the wall is built on the land of the neighbor at the property line or on the boundary. In this revision, the measure of reimbursement is the current value of the wall, whether co-ownership is claimed under Article 674 or under Article 676.

Art. 675.　　Presumption of common wall

A wall that separates adjoining buildings and is partly on one estate and partly on another is presumed to be common up to the highest part of the lower building unless there is proof to the contrary.

Acts 1977, No. 514, § 1, eff. Jan. 1, 1978.

REVISION COMMENTS—1977

(a) This provision is based on Article 677 of the Louisiana Civil Code of 1870. It does not change the law.

(b) According to well-settled jurisprudence in Louisiana and in France, the presumption of co-ownership applies in the absence of other evidence to walls straddling the boundary that separates two buildings. See Weill v. Baker, Sloo, & Co., 39 La.Ann. 1102, 3 So. 361 (1887); Fisk v. Haber, 7 La.Ann. 652 (1852). Thus if the wall is located on one side of the boundary, the presumption does not apply, even if the foundation of the wall extends into the land of the neighbor. See Olsen v. Tung, 179 La. 760, 155 So. 16 (1934); Murrell v. Fowler, 3 La.Ann. 165 (1848). In cases to which the presumption applies, the entire wall is presumed to be common if the adjoining buildings are of the same height; if one building is higher than the other, the wall is presumed to be common up to the highest part of the lower building. See Civ., Feb. 22, 1932, Gaz. Pal. 1932.1.909; Weill v. Baker, Sloo, & Co., supra. The presumption of co-ownership applies also to walls on the boundary that separate yards or gardens, and to walls that separate fields. See Cordill v. Israel, 130 La. 138, 141, 57 So. 778, 780 (1912); 3 Planiol et Ripert, Traité pratique de droit civil français 298 (2d ed. Picard 1952);

Yiannopoulos, Common Walls, Fences, and Ditches, Louisiana and Comparative Law, 35 La.L.Rev. 1249 (1975).

(c) The presumption of co-ownership is based on the assumptions that neighbors have a common interest in the enclosure of their estates and that each one derives some utility from the wall. When these assumptions are contradicted by the factual situation the presumption of co-ownership has no application. In determining the question whether the presumption applies, courts take into account not only the contemporary situation of the premises but also their situation at the time the wall was erected. Thus, if there is evidence that one of the adjoining buildings was erected after the construction of the wall, the owner of that building may not avail himself of the presumption of co-ownership. See Cordill v. Israel, 130 La. 138, 57 So. 778 (1912); Oldstein v. Firemen's Bldg. Ass'n, 44 La.Ann. 492, 10 So. 928 (1892); Req., July 10, 1865, D. 1865.1.483; Civ., Oct. 24, 1951, D. 1951.772. If the contemporary situation has existed for over thirty years, evidence as to the original situation becomes immaterial. 2 Aubry et Rau, Droit civil français 567 (7th ed. Esmein 1961).

(d) A wall separating a building from a yard or from a garden is not presumed to be common. Olsen v. Tung, 179 La. 760, 155 So. 16 (1934). Such a wall is considered to have been constructed by the owner of the building, because it is improbable that the owner of the yard or garden would have contributed anything for the erection of a wall designed to support his neighbor's building. Canal Villere Realty Co. v. S. Gumble Realty & Securities Co., 1 La.App. 123 (Orl. Cir.1924). The same is true of all cases in which, under the circumstances, only one of the neighbors had an interest in the erection of a supporting wall. See Req., April 25, 1888, D. 1889.1.262, S. 1888.1.380; Req. Feb. 13, 1939, Gaz. Pal. 1939.1.709.

Art. 676. Adjoining wall

When a solid masonry wall adjoins another estate, the neighbor has a right to make it a common wall, in whole or in part, by paying to its owner one-half of the current value of the wall, or of the part that he wishes to make common, and one-half of the value of the soil on which the wall is built.

Acts 1977, No. 514, § 1, eff. Jan. 1, 1978.

REVISION COMMENTS—1977

(a) This provision is based on Article 684 of the Louisiana Civil Code of 1870. It changes the law in two respects: (1) it deletes the proviso at the end of the source provision, and (2) it specifies that the landowner who wishes to make an adjoining wall common is bound to pay one-half of the current value of the wall or of the part that he wishes to make common.

(b) The proviso "if the person who has built the wall has laid the foundation entirely upon his own estate" is suppressed. In Heine v. Merrick, 41 La.Ann. 194, 204, 5 So. 760, 765 (1889), the Louisiana Supreme Court declared: "That proviso has already been characterized as an obvious mistranslation of Article 661 of the French Code, which it was intended to reproduce, and has been practically nullified by this court. Murrell v. Fowler, 3 La.Ann. [165 (1848)]. It is indeed so absurd and so incongruous that it is difficult to see how any other view could be taken of it."

(c) The right that Article 676 confers on an adjoining neighbor applies to walls exclusively. 2 Aubry et Rau, Droit civil français 564 (7th ed. Esmein 1961). Other types of enclosures may be held in common by virtue of agreements or by application of the presumptions of Articles 685 and 686.

The walls that Article 676 contemplates are of the same nature as those built under Article 673, namely, walls of solid masonry. Bryant v. Sholars, 104 La. 786, 794, 29 So. 350, 354 (1901). French jurisprudence and doctrine interpreting the corresponding provision of Article 661 of the Code Civil are in accord. 3 Planiol et Ripert, Traité pratique de droit civil français 307 (2d ed. Picard 1952).

(d) All walls built with solid masonry, such as bricks or stones, are susceptible of becoming common, whether they are located in towns or in the country, and whether they separate houses, yards, or gardens. According to French doctrine and jurisprudence, which ought to be relevant for Louisiana, acquisition of the co-ownership of a wall is excluded in two situations only: when a wall belongs to the public domain, because the property of the public domain is inalienable; and when the owner of the wall enjoys servitudes of light and view on adjoining property, because a regime of co-ownership of the wall would be incompatible with these real rights. See Yiannopoulos, Common Walls, Fences and Ditches: Louisiana and Comparative Law, 35 La.L.Rev. 1249 (1975).

(e) Article 676 presupposes an "adjoining" wall, namely, a wall located along its entire length at the boundary line. If a wall is removed, even a fraction of an inch, from the boundary, Article 676 would exclude the possibility that this wall may ever become common. Moreover, the existence of this wall would exclude application of Article 673 because the premises would be surrounded by a wall. Thus, for all practical purposes, the common wall servitude is limited to the two situations provided for expressly in the Code, namely, when neighboring estates are not surrounded by walls or when there is a wall at or on the property line. See Jamison & McIntosh v. Duncan, 12 La.Ann. 785 (1857). The existence of a wall near the property line effectively precludes the creation of a partition wall as a common enclosure.

Art. 677.   Rights and obligations of co-owners

In the absence of a written agreement or controlling local ordinance the rights and obligations of the co-owners of a common wall, fence, or ditch are determined in accordance with the following provisions.

Acts 1977, No. 514, § 1, eff. Jan. 1, 1978.

REVISION COMMENT—1977

This provision is new. Its purpose is to indicate that the following provisions are applicable only in the absence of agreement among the co-owners of a common wall.

Art. 678.   Cost of repairs

Necessary repairs to a common wall, including partial rebuilding, are to be made at the expense of those who own it in proportion to their interests.

Acts 1977, No. 514, § 1, eff. Jan. 1, 1978.

REVISION COMMENT—1977

This provision is new. It is based on Article 678 of the Louisiana Civil Code of 1870. It changes the law as it limits the notion of repairs to partial rebuilding. "Building" in Article 678 of the Civil Code ought to real "rebuilding". See art. 678, p. 416, 1972 Compiled Edition of the Civil Codes of Louisiana, (16 West's LSA-Civil Code, Dainow ed., 1973). Under the new provision, there is no obligation to rebuild a completely destroyed common wall.

Art. 679.   Abandonment of common wall

The co-owner of a common wall may be relieved of the obligation to contribute to the cost of repairs by abandoning in writing his right to use it, if no construction of his is actually supported by the common wall.

Acts 1977, No. 514, § 1, eff. Jan. 1, 1978.

REVISION COMMENTS—1977

(a) This provision is new. It is based on Article 679 of the Louisiana Civil Code of 1870.

(b) If a common wall is totally destroyed, there is no obligation to rebuild it. Article 678, comment, supra.

Art. 680.   Rights in common walls

The co-owner of a common wall may use it as he sees fit, provided that he does not impair its structural integrity or infringe on the rights of his neighbor.

Acts 1977, No. 514, § 1, eff. Jan. 1, 1978.

REVISION COMMENT—1977

This provision is new. It expresses the principle underlying the detailed rules contained in Articles 680 and 685 of the Louisiana Civil Code of 1870. It changes the law as it determines rights in a common wall in the light of a general principle rather than casuistry.

Art. 681.   Opening in common wall

The co-owner of a common wall may not make any opening in the wall without the consent of his neighbor.

Acts 1977, No. 514, § 1, eff. Jan. 1, 1978.

REVISION COMMENT—1977

This provision reproduces the substance of Article 696 of the Louisiana Civil Code of 1870. It does not change the law.

Art. 682.   Raising the height of common wall

A co-owner may raise the height of a common wall at his expense provided the wall can support the additional weight. In such a case, he alone is responsible for the maintenance and repair of the raised part.

Acts 1977, No. 514, § 1, eff. Jan. 1, 1978.

REVISION COMMENTS—1977

(a) This provision reproduces the substance of Article 681 of the Louisiana Civil Code of 1870. It changes the law as it limits the right to raise a common wall only in cases in which the existing wall "can support the additional weight of raising it".

(b) Article 682 of the Louisiana Civil Code of 1870 is abrogated for the future. Thus, the co-owner of a common wall under the new regime will not have the right to demolish it and rebuild it to the desired height, unless, of course, such right is established by agreement.

Art. 683.   Neighbor's right to make the raised part common

The neighbor who does not contribute to the raising of the common wall may at any time cause the raised part to become common by paying to its owner one-half of its current value.

Acts 1977, No. 514, § 1, eff. Jan. 1, 1978.

REVISION COMMENTS—1977

(a) This provision is new; it is based on Article 683 of the Louisiana Civil Code of 1870. It changes the law as it determines that the neighbor must pay one-half of the present value of the raised part rather than one-half of the expense of raising the wall.

(b) The current value of the wall is its construction cost less depreciation or plus appreciation.

Art. 684.   Enclosures

A landowner has the right to enclose his land.

Acts 1977, No. 514, § 1, eff. Jan. 1, 1978.

REVISION COMMENT—1977

This provision reproduces the substance of Article 662 of the Louisiana Civil Code of 1870. It does not change the law.

Art. 685.   Common fences

A fence on a boundary is presumed to be common unless there is proof to the contrary.

When adjoining lands are enclosed, a landowner may compel his neighbors to contribute to the expense of making and repairing common fences by which the respective lands are separated.

When adjoining lands are not enclosed, a landowner may compel his neighbors to contribute to the expense of making and repairing common fences only as prescribed by local ordinances.

Acts 1977, No. 514, § 1, eff. Jan. 1, 1978.

REVISION COMMENTS—1977

(a) This provision is new. It abrogates for the future Articles 686, 687, and 688 of the Louisiana Civil Code of 1870. It changes the law.

(b) Under this provision, there is no longer distinction between rural and urban enclosures. The only pertinent distinction is between enclosed and unenclosed lands. If lands are enclosed, a landowner may compel his neighbors to contribute to the expense of making and repairing of common fences that separate the respective lands. If lands are not enclosed, a landowner has this right only as prescribed by local ordinances or police regulations.

Art. 686.   Common ditches

A ditch between two estates is presumed to be common unless there be proof to the contrary.

Adjoining owners are responsible for the maintenance of a common ditch.

Acts 1977, No. 514, § 1, eff. Jan. 1, 1978.

REVISION COMMENT—1977

This provision reproduces the substance of Articles 689 and 690 of the Louisiana Civil Code of 1870. It does not change the law.

Art. 687.   Trees, bushes, and plants on the boundary

Trees, bushes, and plants on the boundary are presumed to be common unless there be proof to the contrary.

An adjoining owner has the right to demand the removal of trees, bushes, or plants on the boundary that interfere with the enjoyment of his estate, but he must bear the expense of removal.

Acts 1977, No. 514, § 1, eff. Jan. 1, 1978.

REVISION COMMENTS—1977

(a) This provision is new. It establishes a presumption that trees, bushes, and plants on the boundary are common.

(b) Under the second sentence of this provision, a neighbor has the right to demand that trees, bushes, or plants on the boundary line that interfere with the enjoyment of his estate be cut at his expense even if they are not common.

Art. 688.   Branches or roots of trees, bushes, or plants on neighboring property

A landowner has the right to demand that the branches or roots of a neighbor's trees, bushes, or plants, that extend over or into his property be trimmed at the expense of the neighbor.

A landowner does not have this right if the roots or branches do not interfere with the enjoyment of his property.

Acts 1977, No. 514, § 1, eff. Jan. 1, 1978.

REVISION COMMENT—1977

This provision is new. It is based on Article 691 of the Louisiana Civil Code of 1870 and corresponding provisions of modern civil codes.

SECTION 3—RIGHT OF PASSAGE

Art. 689.   Enclosed estate; right of passage

The owner of an estate that has no access to a public road or utility may claim a right of passage over neighboring property to the nearest public road or utility. He is bound to compensate his neighbor for the right of passage acquired and to indemnify his neighbor for the damage he may occasion.

New or additional maintenance burdens imposed upon the servient estate or intervening lands resulting from the utility servitude shall be the responsibility of the owner of the dominant estate.

Acts 1977, No. 514, § 1, eff. Jan. 1, 1978. Amended by Acts 2012, No. 739, § 1.

REVISION COMMENT—1977

This provision is based on Article 699 of the Louisiana Civil Code of 1870. It changes the law as it declares that an estate is enclosed if it does not have access to a public road, even though it has access to a railway or tramway.

Art. 690.   Extent of passage

The right of passage for the benefit of an enclosed estate shall be suitable for the kind of traffic or utility that is reasonably necessary for the use of that estate.

Acts 1977, No. 514, § 1, eff. Jan. 1, 1978. Amended by Acts 2012, No. 739, § 1.

REVISION COMMENT—1977

This provision reproduces the substance of Article 702 of the Louisiana Civil Code of 1870. It does not change the law.

Art. 691.   Constructions

The owner of the enclosed estate may construct on the right-of-way the type of road, utility, or railroad reasonably necessary for the exercise of the servitude.

The utility crossing shall be constructed in compliance with all appropriate and applicable federal and state standards so as to mitigate all hazards posed by the passage and the particular conditions of the servient estate and intervening lands.

Acts 1977, No. 514, § 1, eff. Jan. 1, 1978. Amended by Acts 2012, No. 739, § 1.

REVISION COMMENT—1977

This provision is new. It is partly based on Article 699 of the Louisiana Civil Code of 1870.

Art. 692.   Location of passage

The owner of the enclosed estate may not demand the right of passage or the right-of-way for the utility anywhere he chooses. The passage generally shall be taken along the shortest route from the enclosed estate to the public road or utility at the location least injurious to the intervening lands.

The location of the utility right-of-way shall coincide with the location of the servitude of passage unless an alternate location providing access to the nearest utility is least injurious to the servient estate and intervening lands. The court shall evaluate and determine that the location of the servitude of passage or utility shall not affect the safety of the operations or significantly interfere with the operations of the owner of the servient estate or intervening lands prior to the granting of the servitude of passage or utility.

Acts 1977, No. 514, § 1, eff. Jan. 1, 1978. Amended by Acts 2012, No. 739, § 1.

REVISION COMMENT—1977

This provision reproduces the substance of Article 700 of the Louisiana Civil Code of 1870. It does not change the law.

Art. 693. Enclosed estate; voluntary act

If an estate becomes enclosed as a result of a voluntary act or omission of its owner, the neighbors are not bound to furnish a passage to him or his successors.

Acts 1977, No. 514, § 1, eff. Jan. 1, 1978.

REVISION COMMENT—1977

This provision is new. It is based on Article 1014 of the Greek Civil Code. It does not change the law. Cf. Rockholt v. Keaty, 256 La. 629, 237 So.2d 663 (1970).

Art. 694. Enclosed estate; voluntary alienation or partition

When in the case of partition, or a voluntary alienation of an estate or of a part thereof, property alienated or partitioned becomes enclosed, passage shall be furnished gratuitously by the owner of the land on which the passage was previously exercised, even if it is not the shortest route to the public road or utility, and even if the act of alienation or partition does not mention a servitude of passage.

Acts 1977, No. 514, § 1, eff. Jan. 1, 1978. Amended by Acts 2012, No. 739, § 1.

REVISION COMMENT—1977

This provision reproduces the substance of Article 701 of the Louisiana Civil Code of 1870. It does not change the law.

Art. 695. Relocation of servitude

The owner of the enclosed estate has no right to the relocation of this servitude after it is fixed. The owner of the servient estate has the right to demand relocation of the servitude to a more convenient place at his own expense, provided that it affords the same facility to the owner of the enclosed estate.

Acts 1977, No. 514, § 1, eff. Jan. 1, 1978.

REVISION COMMENT—1977

This provision reproduces the substance of Article 703 of the Louisiana Civil Code of 1870. It changes the law as it makes relocation of the passage more burdensome for the owner of the servient estate. The owner of the enclosed estate may, of course, demand relocation of the servitude when the existing passage no longer affords access to the public road or when the access it affords is not suitable for the kind of traffic that is reasonably necessary for the use of the enclosed estate. See Articles 689 and 690, supra.

Art. 696. Prescriptibility of action for indemnity

The right for indemnity against the owner of the enclosed estate may be lost by prescription. The accrual of this prescription has no effect on the right of passage.

Acts 1977, No. 514, § 1, eff. Jan. 1, 1978.

REVISION COMMENT—1977

This provision reproduces the substance of Article 708 of the Louisiana Civil Code of 1870. It does not change the law.

Art. 696.1. Utility

As used in this Section, a utility is a service such as electricity, water, sewer, gas, telephone, cable television, and other commonly used power and communication networks required for the operation of an ordinary household or business.

Added by Acts 2012, No. 739, § 1.

CHAPTER 4—CONVENTIONAL OR VOLUNTARY SERVITUDES

SECTION 1—KINDS OF CONVENTIONAL SERVITUDES

Art. 697.   Right to establish predial servitudes; limitations

Predial servitudes may be established by an owner on his estate or acquired for its benefit.

The use and extent of such servitudes are regulated by the title by which they are created, and, in the absence of such regulation, by the following rules.

Acts 1977, No. 514, § 1, eff. Jan. 1, 1978.

REVISION COMMENTS—1977

(a) This provision reproduces the substance of Article 709 of the Louisiana Civil Code of 1870. It does not change the law.

(b) Owners have the right to establish on their estate, or to acquire for the benefit of their estate, such predial servitudes as they deem proper. This freedom, however, is tempered by rules of public policy enacted in the general interest. C.C. art. 11. Apart from general limitations, the creation of predial servitudes by juridical act is subject to special rules that are largely insusceptible of modification by agreement. These rules, limiting contractual and testamentary freedom, are designed to effect a balance between individual demands for the recognition of modifications of property rights to suit individual needs and social demands for the preservation of a relatively simple system of unencumbered property. See Yiannopoulos, Real Rights: Limits of Contractual and Testamentary Freedom, 30 La.L.Rev. 44 (1969).

(c) Article 709 of the Louisiana Civil Code of 1870, corresponding with Article 686 of the Code Civil, declares that owners have the right to establish such servitudes as they deem proper, provided that "services be not imposed on a person." This provision has not been reproduced in Article 697 because it is apparent from the definition and the essential features of predial servitudes, Articles 646 and 647, supra, that these rights may not involve charges on a person in favor of an estate. Moreover, Article 651, supra, excludes, on principle, the imposition of affirmative duties on the owner of the servient estate. The redactors of the Civil Code felt compelled to spell out the rule that services may not be imposed on a person as a further insurance against the resurrection of feudal tenures. The redactors of the Louisiana Civil Codes of 1808, 1825, and 1870, however, had no compelling reason to follow verbatim the text of Article 686 of the Code Civil, because feudal tenures have never had a place in Louisiana property law. Xigues v. Bujac, 7 La.Ann. 498, 504 (1852).

(d) Article 709 of the Louisiana Civil Code of 1870 declares that services may not be imposed in favor of a person. This language has not been reproduced in Article 697 because it is apparent from the definition and the essential features of predial servitudes, Articles 646 and 647, supra, that these rights may not involve charges on an estate in favor of a person. A charge on an estate in favor of a person is a personal servitude. See C.C. art. 534 (1977).

(e) Article 709 of the Louisiana Civil Code of 1870 declares that servitudes may "imply nothing contrary to public order". This language has not been reproduced in Article 697 because contractual and testamentary freedom in derogation of rules of public order is excluded by Article 11 of the Louisiana Civil Code of 1870.

Art. 698.   Property susceptible of servitudes

Predial servitudes are established on, or for the benefit of, distinct corporeal immovables.

Acts 1977, No. 514, § 1, eff. Jan. 1, 1978.

REVISION COMMENTS—1977

(a) This provision is new. It is based on Article 710 of the Louisiana Civil Code of 1870. It does not change the law.

(b) A predial servitude is a charge on an estate for the benefit of an estate belonging to another owner. Article 646, supra. The word "estate" in Article 647 of the Louisiana Civil Code of 1870 and in Article 646, supra, means a distinct corporeal immovable. It corresponds with the word héritage in the French Civil Code and in the French text of the Louisiana Civil Code of 1825. The only immovables susceptible of servitudes under the Louisiana Civil Code of 1870 are tracts of land and buildings. C.C. art. 710 (1870). Constructions other than buildings, though classified as immovables by nature under Article 464 of the Civil Code of 1870, are not susceptible of predial servitudes; the same is true of immovables by destination and incorporeal immovables.

(c) Timber estates and individual apartments in a condominium development qualify today by virtue of special legislation as distinct corporeal immovables. Hence, it ought to be clear that predial servitudes may be established on, or for the benefit of, timber estates and individual apartments in a condominium development. See Acts 1974, No. 502, R.S. 9:1121 et seq.; Kavanaugh v. Frost-Johnson Lumber Co., 149 La. 972, 90 So. 275 (1921); Walker v. Simmons, 155 So.2d 234 (La.App. 3rd Cir. 1963) (servitude of passage in favor of timber estate).

(d) The division of servitudes into urban and rural is suppressed. This distinction has mostly historical significance; it has been suppressed in all modern civil codes.

Art. 699.   Examples of predial servitudes

The following are examples of predial servitudes:

Rights of support, projection, drip, drain, or of preventing drain, those of view, of light, or of preventing view or light from being obstructed, of raising buildings or walls, or of preventing them from being raised, of passage, of drawing water, of aqueduct, of watering animals, and of pasturage.

Acts 1977, No. 514, § 1, eff. Jan. 1, 1978.

REVISION COMMENT—1977

This provision reproduces the substance of Articles 711 and 721–726 of the Louisiana Civil Code of 1870. It does not change the law.

Art. 700.   Servitude of support

The servitude of support is the right by which buildings or other constructions of the dominant estate are permitted to rest on a wall of the servient estate.

Unless the title provides otherwise, the owner of the servient estate is bound to keep the wall fit for the exercise of the servitude, but he may be relieved of this charge by abandoning the wall.

Acts 1977, No. 514, § 1, eff. Jan. 1, 1978.

REVISION COMMENT—1977

This provision reproduces the substance of the first two paragraphs of Article 712 of the Louisiana Civil Code of 1870. It does not change the law.

Art. 701.   Servitude of view

The servitude of view is the right by which the owner of the dominant estate enjoys a view; this includes the right to prevent the raising of constructions on the servient estate that would obstruct the view.

Acts 1977, No. 514, § 1, eff. Jan. 1, 1978.

REVISION COMMENTS—1977

(a) This provision reproduces the part of Article 716 of the Louisiana Civil Code of 1870 dealing with the servitude of view. It does not change the law.

(b) Article 715(1) of the Louisiana Civil Code of 1870 provides: "We understand by view every opening which may, more or less, facilitate the means of looking out of a building". This provision has not been reproduced as unnecessary. There is no reason to limit view to an opening for the looking out from a building.

Art. 702. Prohibition of view

The servitude of prohibition of view is the right of the owner of the dominant estate to prevent or limit openings of view on the servient estate.

Acts 1977, No. 514, § 1, eff. Jan. 1, 1978.

REVISION COMMENT—1977

This provision reproduces the part of Article 716 of the Louisiana Civil Code of 1870 dealing with the servitude of prohibition of view. It does not change the law.

Art. 703. Servitude of light

The servitude of light is the right by which the owner of the dominant estate is entitled to make openings in a common wall for the admission of light; this includes the right to prevent the neighbor from making an obstruction.

Acts 1977, No. 514, § 1, eff. Jan. 1, 1978.

REVISION COMMENTS—1977

(a) This provision reproduces the part of Article 717 of the Louisiana Civil Code of 1870 dealing with the servitude of light. It does not change the law.

(b) Article 715(2) of the Louisiana Civil Code of 1870 provides: "Lights are those openings which are made rather for the admission of light than to look out of." This provision has not been reproduced as unnecessary. There should be no doubt that light is an opening for the admission of light into a building rather than looking out from it.

Art. 704. Prohibition of light

The servitude of prohibition of light is the right of the owner of the dominant estate to prevent his neighbor from making an opening in his own wall for the admission of light or that limits him to certain lights only.

Acts 1977, No. 514, § 1, eff. Jan. 1, 1978.

REVISION COMMENT—1977

This provision reproduces the part of Article 717 of the Louisiana Civil Code of 1870 dealing with the prohibition of light. It does not change the law.

Art. 705. Servitude of passage

The servitude of passage is the right for the benefit of the dominant estate whereby persons, animals, utilities, or vehicles are permitted to pass through the servient estate. Unless the title provides otherwise, the extent of the right and the mode of its exercise shall be suitable for the kind of traffic or utility necessary for the reasonable use of the dominant estate.

Acts 1977, No. 514, § 1, eff. Jan. 1, 1978. Amended by Acts 2012, No. 739, § 1.

REVISION COMMENTS—1977

(a) This provision is new. It is based in part on Articles 719 and 722 of the Louisiana Civil Code of 1870. It changes the law in certain important respects.

(b) There is no longer distinction between urban and rural passage; the servitude is perpetual unless the title provides otherwise. Moreover, the extent of the right is the same in cities and in the country; it is determined by the title creating the servitude.

Art. 706. Servitudes; affirmative or negative

Predial servitudes are either affirmative or negative.

Affirmative servitudes are those that give the right to the owner of the dominant estate to do a certain thing on the servient estate. Such are the servitudes of right of way, drain, and support.

Negative servitudes are those that impose on the owner of the servient estate the duty to abstain from doing something on his estate. Such are the servitudes of prohibition of building and of the use of an estate as a commercial or industrial establishment.

Acts 1977, No. 514, § 1, eff. Jan. 1, 1978.

REVISION COMMENTS—1977

(a) This provision is new. It articulates a division of servitudes inherent in the Louisiana Civil Code of 1870. It does not change the law.

(b) See 3 Planiol et Ripert, Traité pratique de droit civil français 875 (2d ed. Picard 1952): "Certain servitudes authorize the owner of the dominant estate to do directly certain acts of enjoyment on the servient estate: passage, drawing of water; these are affirmative servitudes that confer on an owner of another estate a part of the advantages resulting from the ownership of land. On the contrary, there are servitudes that tend to paralyze, in a certain measure, the rights of the owner of the servient estate, by either withdrawing from him a part of the use of his estate, or by preventing him from exercising a right forming part of his ownership: these are negative servitudes, such as the prohibition of building." See also Yiannopoulos, Predial Servitudes; General Principles, 29 La.L.Rev. 1, 6–8, 30–31 (1968): "Servitudes which confer on the owner of the dominant estate the right to take certain materials from the servient estate or to use this estate for certain purposes are termed affirmative servitudes. Servitudes which deprive the owner of the servient estate of certain prerogatives of his ownership, i.e., prohibit certain material acts or the exercise of certain rights, are termed negative servitudes." Negative servitudes are always continuous and nonapparent under the regime of the 1870 Code. Ibid.

(c) The distinction of servitudes into continuous and discontinuous has been suppressed in this revision. However, the distinction of servitudes into apparent and nonapparent has been maintained. See Article 707, infra. The distinction of servitudes into affirmative and negative is significant in the light of Article 754, infra.

Art. 707.   Servitudes; apparent or nonapparent

Predial servitudes are either apparent or nonapparent. Apparent servitudes are those that are perceivable by exterior signs, works, or constructions; such as a roadway, a window in a common wall, or an aqueduct.

Nonapparent servitudes are those that have no exterior sign of their existence; such as the prohibition of building on an estate or of building above a particular height.

Acts 1977, No. 514, § 1, eff. Jan. 1, 1978.

REVISION COMMENT—1977

This provision reproduces the substance of Article 728 of the Louisiana Civil Code of 1870. It does not change the law.

SECTION 2—ESTABLISHMENT OF PREDIAL SERVITUDES BY TITLE

Art. 708.   Establishment of predial servitude

The establishment of a predial servitude by title is an alienation of a part of the property to which the laws governing alienation of immovables apply.

Acts 1977, No. 514, § 1, eff. Jan. 1, 1978.

REVISION COMMENTS—1977

(a) This provision is new. It states the principle that the establishment of a predial servitude is an alienation of a part of the property. Thus, the laws governing alienation of immovable property apply to the establishment of a predial servitude.

(b) Article 729 of the Louisiana Civil Code of 1870 declares: "The right of imposing a servitude permanently on an estate belongs to the owner alone." The provision has not been reproduced as unnecessary. In accordance with the principle that "no one can transfer a greater right than he himself has" (C.C. art. 2015), the person granting a predial servitude must be the owner of the servient estate or must act under the authority of the owner. The owner need not act in person; he may be represented by a qualified mandatary or other representative. A predial servitude granted without the authority of the owner is invalid; the owner may object to its exercise and may demand damages for the unlawful entry into his property.

(c) Article 731 of the Louisiana Civil Code of 1870 has not been reproduced as unnecessary. Since the establishment of a predial servitude by title involves the execution of a juridical act, the grantor must be competent. Incompetents, such as minors and interdicts, may establish predial servitudes on their estates according to the rules prescribed for the alienation of their property. Detailed provisions in the Louisiana Code of Civil Procedure and in the Revised Statutes deal specifically with the alienation of the property of minors and interdicts by tutors and curators. See Code of Civil Procedure arts. 4301–4363; cf. id. arts. 4271, 4554; R.S. 9:711–713.

(d) The establishment of a predial servitude by juridical act is an alienation of a part of the property; hence, it is subject to the requirements governing the validity and effect of acts of disposition. Cf. 3 Planiol et Ripert, Traité pratique de droit civil français 928 (2d ed. Picard 1952). These are acts which tend to divest the owner of his interest, to deprive him, in part or in whole, of a real or a personal right. See Yiannopoulos, Predial Servitudes; Creation by Title, 45 Tul.L.Rev. 459, 461 (1971). The substantive requirements governing the validity and effect of acts of disposition vary with the qualification of a particular act as onerous or gratuitous. See, e.g., C.C. arts. 1467, 1470, 1519, 1536, 2404.

Art. 709.   Mandatary

A mandatary may establish a predial servitude if he has an express and special power to do so.

Acts 1977, No. 514, § 1, eff. Jan. 1, 1978.

REVISION COMMENTS—1977

(a) This provision reproduces the substance of Article 733 of the Louisiana Civil Code of 1870. It does not change the law.

(b) The words "attorney in fact" in Article 733 is a translation of the French "un fondé de procuration". The source of the original provision is Pardessus, Traité des servitudes 424 (1817). See 1 La.Legal Archives, Projet of the Louisiana Civil Code of 1825, p. 79 (1937). According to this provision, the conventional representative of the owner must have express and special authority to establish a predial servitude.

(c) Article 734 of the Louisiana Civil Code of 1870 has not been reproduced as unnecessary. Business corporations as well as nonprofit corporations possess juridical personality and have capacity to enter into juridical acts, subject to limitations imposed by law or by their acts of incorporation. See La.Business Corporation Law, R.S. 12:41A and B(4); La.Nonprofit Corporation Law, R.S. 12:207A and B(4). They may thus establish predial servitudes on their estates. Unincorporated associations possess certain incidents of juridical personality in Louisiana and are entitled to own immovable property. See C.C. art. 446. According to the jurisprudence, they may alienate their property either in accordance with their constitutions and bylaws or by acts signed by all the members of the association. See Carpenters and Joiners Local 1846 v. Stephens Broadcasting Co., 214 La. 928, 39 So.2d 422 (1949). Cf. Burke v. Wall, 29 La.Ann. 38 (1877). In this case, the court held that a church congregation had actually clothed priests with authority to create servitudes for the convenience of the owners of burial plots in a cemetery.

Art. 710. Naked owner

The naked owner may establish a predial servitude that does not infringe on the rights of the usufructuary or that is to take effect at the termination of the usufruct. The consent of the usufructuary is required for the establishment of any other predial servitude.

Acts 1977, No. 514, § 1, eff. Jan. 1, 1978.

REVISION COMMENTS—1977

(a) This provision reproduces the substance of Article 730 of the Louisiana Civil Code of 1870. It does not change the law.

(b) For the establishment of mineral servitudes by the naked owner, see Mineral Code arts. 195, 196.

Art. 711. Usufructuary

The usufructuary may not establish on the estate of which he has the usufruct any charges in the nature of predial servitudes.

Acts 1977, No. 514, § 1, eff. Jan. 1, 1978.

REVISION COMMENTS—1977

(a) This provision reproduces the substance of Article 737 of the Louisiana Civil Code of 1870. It does not change the law.

(b) As a general rule, administrators of another's property have no power of alienation; hence, they may not burden the property with predial servitudes. See 6 Baudry-Lacantinerie, Traité théorique et pratique de droit civil 826 (3rd ed. Chauveau 1905). Thus a negotiorum gestor does not have the power to establish predial servitudes. Ibid.; Grenoble, July 1, 1902, Gaz. Pal. 1902.2.506. Since the French Civil Code has no provision corresponding with Article 737 of the Louisiana Civil Code of 1870, French commentators are divided on the question whether the usufructuary may create real charges in the nature of predial servitudes for the duration of his enjoyment. According to one view, the usufructuary may not impose predial servitudes, even for the period of the usufruct, because predial servitudes are dismemberments of the right of ownership and not merely of the enjoyment. The usufructuary may thus convey only a personal right. 6 Baudry-Lacantinerie, supra. According to another view, however, the usufructuary may validly impose charges in the nature of predial servitudes, which, of course, cease of right at the end of the usufruct. See 3 Aubry et Rau, Droit civil français 102 (6th ed. Bartin 1938); 12 Demolombe, Traité des servitudes 229 (1876).

(c) For the creation of mineral rights by the usufructuary, see Mineral Code arts. 26, 84, 118, 192.

Art. 712. Owner for a term or under condition

A person having ownership subject to a term or the happening of a condition may establish a predial servitude, but it ceases with his right.

Acts 1977, No. 514, § 1, eff. Jan. 1, 1978.

REVISION COMMENTS—1977

(a) This provision reproduces the substance of the first sentence of Article 736 of the Louisiana Civil Code of 1870. It does not change the law.

(b) The second sentence of Article 736 has not been reproduced as unnecessary. Prior to resolution of the right of the grantor an action for the cancellation of the servitude may not be instituted; hence, prescription does not run.

Art. 713. Purchaser with reservation of redemption

A purchaser under a reserved right of redemption may establish a predial servitude on the property, but it ceases if the seller exercises his right of redemption.

Acts 1977, No. 514, § 1, eff. Jan. 1, 1978.

REVISION COMMENTS—1977

(a) This provision reproduces the substance of Article 735 of the Louisiana Civil Code of 1870. It does not change the law.

(b) One whose ownership is limited by a term or condition may grant a predial servitude only for the duration of his ownership. See Article 712, supra. As an application of this principle, the purchaser with reservation of redemption may establish predial servitudes on the property he has acquired; but these cease if the seller exercises his right of redemption. See Zeigler v. His Creditors, 49 La.Ann. 144, 21 So. 666 (1896).

Art. 714.   Co-owner; servitude on entire estate

A predial servitude on an estate owned in indivision may be established only with the consent of all the co-owners.

When a co-owner purports to establish a servitude on the entire estate, the contract is not null; but, its execution is suspended until the consent of all co-owners is obtained.

Acts 1977, No. 514, § 1, eff. Jan. 1, 1978.

REVISION COMMENTS—1977

(a) This provision reproduces the substance of Article 738 of the Louisiana Civil Code of 1870. It does not change the law.

(b) The creation of a predial servitude is an alienation of a part of the servient estate. Accordingly, a predial servitude on an entire estate owned in indivision must be established with the consent of all the co-owners. See Yiannopoulos, Predial Servitudes; Creation by Title, 45 Tul.L.Rev. 459, 465 (1971). Nevertheless, the act by which one of the co-owners establishes a predial servitude on the entire estate owned in indivision is not null; execution of the contract is merely suspended until the consent of all the co-owners is obtained. See Greater Baton Rouge Port Commission v. Morley, 232 La. 87, 93 So.2d 912 (1957). It has been held by one court that the consent of the co-owners may be obtained by acquiescence. Superior Oil Producing Co. v. Leckelt, 189 La. 972, 181 So. 462 (1938).

(c) In proceedings for the expropriation of a servitude for public utility all the co-owners must be made parties. Exception, however, may be made as to co-owners who have reached an amicable agreement with the expropriating authority. See Greater Baton Rouge Port Commission v. Morley, 232 La. 87, 93 So.2d 912 (1957).

(d) Predial servitudes granted by all the co-owners, whether by a single act or by separate acts, burden the land and follow it in the hands of any acquirer. These servitudes may be clearly exercised while the state of indivision lasts and are unaffected by the partition of the servient estate. If the partition is made by licitation, the acquirer purchases subject to the pre-existing servitudes. If he is unaware of the existence of predial servitudes, he is entitled to consider the title as not merchantable and to reclaim his deposit. Goodwin v. Sanders, 231 So.2d 727 (La.App. 4th Cir. 1970). If the partition is made in kind, each divided part may be burdened by the pre-existing servitudes in accordance with the rules governing division of the servient estate. See Yiannopoulos, Predial Servitudes; General Principles, 29 La.L.Rev. 1, 29 (1968).

Art. 715.   Exercise of the servitude

A co-owner who has consented to the establishment of a predial servitude on the entire estate owned in indivision may not prevent its exercise on the ground that the consent of his co-owner has not been obtained.

If he becomes owner of the whole estate by any means which terminates the indivision, the predial servitude to which he has consented burdens his property.

Acts 1977, No. 514, § 1, eff. Jan. 1, 1978.

REVISION COMMENTS—1977

(a) This provision reproduces the substance of Article 739 of the Louisiana Civil Code of 1870. It does not change the law.

(b) According to Article 714, the execution of the contract establishing a predial servitude on the entire estate owned in indivision is suspended until the consent of all the co-owners is given. According to Article 715, the contract is executed, without the consent of all the co-owners, if the grantor of the servitude becomes owner of the whole of the estate held in common. The grantor may not prevent execution of the contract on the ground that the consent of another co-owner has not been given. The original provision derives from the text of Toullier. See 2 Toullier, Droit civil français 163 (1833).

(c) The second paragraph of Article 739 of the Louisiana Civil Code of 1870 ought to read: "If he becomes owner of the whole estate, by any means whatever, he is bound to permit the exercise of the servitude to which he has before consented." See art. 739, 1972 Compiled Edition of the Civil Codes of Louisiana (16 West's LSA-Civil Code, Dainow ed. 1973). This provision furnishes a foundation for the so-called after-acquired property doctrine. See Comment, The After-Acquired Title Doctrine in Louisiana Mineral Law 27 La.L.Rev. 576 (1967).

Art. 716.   Servitude on undivided part

When a co-owner has consented to the establishment of a predial servitude on his undivided part only, the consent of the other co-owners is not required, but the exercise of the servitude is suspended until his divided part is determined at the termination of the state of indivision.

Acts 1977, No. 514, § 1, eff. Jan. 1, 1978.

REVISION COMMENTS—1977

(a) This provision is new. It is based in part on Article 740 of the Louisiana Civil Code of 1870. It changes the law as it withdraws from the acquirer of the servitude the right to compel partition of the property.

(b) In Louisiana and in France, a co-owner may freely burden his own undivided part of the estate held in common with a predial servitude. But, since predial servitudes are indivisible, the execution of the contract is suspended until termination of the state of indivision and acquisition of a divided part or of the entire estate by the grantor or by his successors. See 3 Aubry et Rau, Droit civil français 102 (6th ed. Bartin 1938); 6 Baudry-Lacantinerie, Traité théorique et pratique de droit civil 826 (3rd ed. Chauveau 1905).

Art. 717.   Partition in kind

If the estate owned in indivision is partitioned in kind, the servitude established by a co-owner on his undivided part burdens only the part allotted to him.

Acts 1977, No. 514, § 1, eff. Jan. 1, 1978.

REVISION COMMENTS—1977

(a) This provision is new. It is based in part on Article 740 of the Louisiana Civil Code of 1870. It does not change the law.

(b) If the estate is partitioned in kind, the predial servitude attaches to the part allotted to the grantor. All other parts remain free of the burden. See Pardessus, Traité des servitudes 433 (1817).

Art. 718.   Partition by licitation

If the estate is partitioned by licitation and the co-owner who consented to the establishment of the predial servitude acquires the ownership of the whole, the servitude burdens the entire estate as if the co-owner had always been sole owner. If the entire estate is adjudicated to any other person the right granted by the co-owner is extinguished.

Acts 1977, No. 514, § 1, eff. Jan. 1, 1978.

(a) This provision reproduces the substance of the original Article 741 of the Louisiana Civil Code of 1870. It changes the law only to the extent that it suppresses the obligation of the grantor of the servitude to return the price.

(b) Under Article 716, the acquirer of a predial servitude on an undivided part of an estate owned in indivision acquires a conditional right, namely, a predial servitude subject to the condition that the grantor or his successor will acquire the ownership of the entire estate or of a divided part of it. If the condition is fulfilled, the right becomes absolute. See Pardessus, Traité des servitudes 437 (1817).

Art. 719.   Successor of the co-owner

Except as provided in Article 718, the successor of the co-owner who has consented to the establishment of a predial servitude, whether on the entire estate owned in indivision or on his undivided part only, occupies the same position as his ancestor. If he becomes owner of a divided part of the estate the servitude burdens that part, and if he becomes owner of the whole the servitude burdens the entire estate.

Acts 1977, No. 514, § 1, eff. Jan. 1, 1978.

(a) This provision is a logical extension of the rule contained in Article 742 of the Louisiana Civil Code of 1870. It changes the law as it expands the scope of the source provision.

(b) According to the letter of Article 742 of the Louisiana Civil Code of 1870, the particular successor of a co-owner who established a predial servitude is bound to tolerate the charge only if he acquires the ownership of the entire estate by licitation. Under Article 719, the successor of the co-owner is bound to tolerate the servitude if he acquires, by any means, the ownership of a divided part or of the entire estate. For the doctrinal basis of the provision, see Pardessus, Traité des servitudes 437 (1817).

(c) Articles 714 through 719 are intended to cover all cases in which the co-owner of an estate grants a predial servitude on it or on his undivided part and subsequently acquires the ownership of the entire estate or of a divided part of it whether by licitation or by other transactions. Thus, if the grantor of the servitude on the estate owned in indivision acquires the ownership of the entire estate by licitation, sale, donation, or exchange, the servitude that he has granted attaches to the whole. Article 715. If he acquires only a divided part of the estate, by whatever means, this part only is burdened with the servitude. Article 718 and analogy therefrom. If the grantor of the servitude conveys his undivided part to another person, the transferee incurs the same liabilities as the transferor. Article 719. If a divided part is acquired by a third person who is not a successor of the grantor, the servitude is extinguished as to this part. And if the entire estate is acquired by a third person who is not a successor of the grantor, the servitude is extinguished for the whole. Article 718.

Art. 720.   Additional servitudes

The owner of the servient estate may establish thereon additional servitudes, provided they do not affect adversely the rights of the owner of the dominant estate.

Acts 1977, No. 514, § 1, eff. Jan. 1, 1978.

(a) This provision reproduces the substance of Article 749 of the Louisiana Civil Code of 1870. It does not change the law.

(b) According to this provision, if the estate is already encumbered with a predial servitude, the owner's right to grant additional servitudes is limited to those that do not affect the rights of the owner of the dominant estate who acquired the first. Proper application of this provision ought to lead to the conclusion that no servitude may be validly created to the prejudice of a pre-existing predial servitude. The acquirer of the servitude may have contractual remedies against the grantor but no real right on the property.

(c) For cases in which the acquirer of the additional servitude to the prejudice of a pre-existing servitude on the same property is a public body having power of expropriation, see Arkansas Louisiana Gas Co. v. Louisiana Department of Highways, 104 So.2d 204 (La.App. 2d Cir. 1958) (recovery of cost of relocation of pipe line from the Department of Highways); Louisiana Power and Light Co. v. Dileo, 79 So.2d 150 (La.App. 1st Cir. 1955) (cost of relocation of poles borne by the utility company). For discussion and critique, see Yiannopoulos, Predial Servitudes; Creation by Title, 45 Tul.L.Rev. 459, 473–474 (1971).

Art. 721.　　Servitude on mortgaged property

A predial servitude may be established on mortgaged property. If the servitude diminishes the value of the estate to the substantial detriment of the mortgagee, he may demand immediate payment of the debt.

If there is a sale for the enforcement of the mortgage the property is sold free of all servitudes established after the mortgage. In such a case, the acquirer of the servitude has an action for the restitution of its value against the owner who established it.

Acts 1977, No. 514, § 1, eff. Jan. 1, 1978.

REVISION COMMENTS—1977

(a) This provision reproduces the substance of Article 750 of the Louisiana Civil Code of 1870. It does not change the law.

(b) If an estate is mortgaged, the owner may grant predial servitudes; but, if these diminish the value of the estate to the detriment of the mortgage creditor, he has the right to have the estate sold free of all servitudes established after the creation of the mortgage. See 3 Planiol et Ripert, Traité pratique de droit civil francais 929 (2d ed. Picard 1952); 6 Baudry-Lacantinerie, Traité théorique et pratique de droit civil 827 (3rd ed. Chauveau 1905). The owner of the dominant estate, however, should have the right to preserve his servitude by paying to the mortgage creditor the full amount of the debt. See 3 Aubry et Rau, Droit civil francais 103 (6th ed. Bartin 1938).

Art. 722.　　Modes of establishment

Predial servitudes are established by all acts by which immovables may be transferred. Delivery of the act of transfer or use of the right by the owner of the dominant estate constitutes tradition.

Acts 1977, No. 514, § 1, eff. Jan. 1, 1978.

REVISION COMMENTS—1977

(a) This provision reproduces the substance of Article 743 of the Louisiana Civil Code of 1870. It does not change the law.

(b) Predial servitudes may be created by testament as well as by means of any contract translative of ownership, as a sale, an exchange, or a donation. See 3 Planiol et Ripert, Traité pratique de droit civil français 928 (2d ed. Picard 1952). For the proposition that servitudes must be established by acts translative of ownership and that agreements establishing personal obligations among coowners are not sufficient to give rise to predial servitudes, see Kelly v. Pippitone, 12 La.App. 635, 126 So. 79 (Orl.Cir.1930). Predial servitudes may also be established by voluntary or by judicial partition. See Talbot v. Kern, 62 So.2d 548 (La.App.1st Cir. 1952); Ronaldson v. Vicknair, 185 So. 52 (La.App.1st Cir. 1938). The establishment of predial servitudes by juridical act is subject to the formal and substantive requirement governing transfer of immovable property.

(c) Since the legacy of a predial servitude is not a universal legacy, the legatee of the servitude has no seizin, and, technically, must demand delivery of quasi-possession from the heirs, universal legatees, or the executors of the will. See C.C. arts. 1609, 1613, 1630. According to Article 722, the use of the right by the legatee of the servitude constitutes delivery. Under Article 3062 of the Louisiana Code of Civil Procedure, the judgment of possession constitutes prima facie evidence of the legatee's right of quasi-possession.

Art. 723.   Servitudes on public things

Predial servitudes may be established on public things, including property of the state, its agencies and political subdivisions.

Acts 1977, No. 514, § 1, eff. Jan. 1, 1978.

REVISION COMMENTS—1977

(a) This provision reproduces the substance of Article 744 of the Louisiana Civil Code of 1870. It does not change the law.

(b) Predial servitudes on property of the state may not be acquired by prescription; they must be established by title. See Const. Art. 12, § 13; C.C. art. 861; cf. Yiannopoulos, Civil Law Property § 36 (1966); Yiannopoulos, Predial Servitudes; General Principles, 29 La.L.Rev. 1, 18–22 (1968).

(c) Article 744 of the Louisiana Civil Code of 1870 corresponds with Article 740 of the Louisiana Civil Code of 1825 which reads: "Les servitudes peuvent être établies sur toutes les choses susceptibles de propriété; elles peuvent même l'être sur le domaine public, et sur les biens communaux des villes et autres lieux incorporés." According to the redactors, the source of this provision is: "Pardessus, Traité des servitudes. No. 47, p. 67." 1 La. Legal Archives Projet of the Louisiana Civil Code of 1825, p. 81 (1937). It appears, however, that Pardessus has been misunderstood. He was stating that predial servitudes may be established on all things susceptible of private ownership, including things of the private domain of the state and of its political subdivision. See Pardessus, Traité des servitudes 67 (1817): "Tous les immeubles susceptibles de propriété privée, quel que soit celui à qui ils appartiennent, peuvent être grevés de Servitudes. Sous ce titre, nous ne comprenons pas seulement les biens des particuliers, mais encore ceux qui appartiennent à l'Etat, aux communes ou à des etablissemens publics ou communaux."

Article 723 follows the text of Article 740 of the Louisiana Civil Code of 1825 rather than the text of Pardessus. This accords with well-settled contemporary French doctrine and jurisprudence, according to which servitudes like rights may be established on immovable property of the public domain. See Yiannopoulos, Predial Servitudes; General Principles, 29 La.L.Rev. 1, 21 (1968); 3 Planiol et Ripert, Traité pratique de droit civil français 150 (2d ed. Picard 1952).

Art. 724.   Multiple dominant or servient estates

A predial servitude may be established on several estates for the benefit of one estate. One estate may be subjected to a servitude for the benefit of several estates.

Acts 1977, No. 514, § 1, eff. Jan. 1, 1978.

REVISION COMMENT—1977

This provision reproduces the substance of Article 745 of the Louisiana Civil Code of 1870. It does not change the law.

Art. 725.   Reciprocal servitudes

The title that establishes a servitude for the benefit of the dominant estate may also establish a servitude on the dominant estate for the benefit of the servient estate.

Acts 1977, No. 514, § 1, eff. Jan. 1, 1978.

REVISION COMMENTS—1977

(a) This provision reproduces the substance of the first paragraph of Article 746 of the Louisiana Civil Code of 1870. It does not change the law.

(b) The second paragraph of Article 746 of the Louisiana Civil Code of 1870 has not been reproduced. It is self-evident and unnecessary.

Art. 726.   Servitude on after-acquired property

Parties may agree to establish a predial servitude on, or for the benefit of, an estate of which one is not then the owner. If the ownership is acquired, the servitude is established.

Parties may agree that a building not yet built will be subjected to a servitude or that it will have the benefit of a servitude when it is built.

Acts 1977, No. 514, § 1, eff. Jan. 1, 1978.

REVISION COMMENT—1977

This provision reproduces the substance of Article 747 of the Louisiana Civil Code of 1870.

Art. 727.   Servitude on part of an estate

A predial servitude may be established on a certain part of an estate, if that part is sufficiently described.

Acts 1977, No. 514, § 1, eff. Jan. 1, 1978.

REVISION COMMENTS—1977

(a) This provision reproduces the substance of Article 748 of the Louisiana Civil Code of 1870. It does not change the law.

(b) The "release" of a servitude is a matter of termination, dealt with infra. For this reason, the word "released", figuring in the source provision, has not been reproduced.

Art. 728.   Limitation of use

The use of a predial servitude may be limited to certain times. Thus, the rights of drawing water and of passage may be confined to designated hours.

Acts 1977, No. 514, § 1, eff. Jan. 1, 1978.

REVISION COMMENT—1977

This provision reproduces the substance of Article 751 of the Louisiana Civil Code of 1870. It does not change the law.

Art. 729.   Conventional alteration of legal or natural servitude

Legal and natural servitudes may be altered by agreement of the parties if the public interest is not affected adversely.

Acts 1977, No. 514, § 1, eff. Jan. 1, 1978.

REVISION COMMENT—1977

This provision reproduces the substance of Article 752 of the Louisiana Civil Code of 1870. It does not change the law.

Art. 730.   Interpretation of servitude

Doubt as to the existence, extent, or manner of exercise of a predial servitude shall be resolved in favor of the servient estate.

Acts 1977, No. 514, § 1, eff. Jan. 1, 1978.

REVISION COMMENTS—1977

(a) This provision reproduces the substance of Article 753 of the Louisiana Civil Code of 1870. It does not change the law.

(b) It is a cardinal rule of interpretation that, in case of doubt, instruments purporting to establish predial servitudes are always interpreted in favor of the owner of the property to be affected. The rule incorporates into Louisiana law the civilian principle that any doubt as to the free use of immovable property must be resolved in favorem libertatis. See Domat, Les lois civiles dans leur ordre naturel, 1 Oeuvres de Domat 329 (ed. Remy 1828); 2 Toullier, Droit civil français 192 (1833). The Louisiana Supreme Court has repeatedly declared that "servitudes are restraints on the free disposal and use of property, and are not, on that account, entitled to be viewed with favor by the law." Parish v. Municipality No. 2, 8 La.Ann. 145, 147 (1853), cited with approval in Buras Ice Factory, Inc. v. Department of Highways, 235 La. 158, 103 So.2d 74 (1958). See also McGuffy v. Weil, 240 La. 758, 767, 125 So.2d 154, 158 (1960): "any doubt as to the interpretation of a servitude encumbering property must be resolved in favor of the property owner". The rule that the proper interpretation of an ambiguous instrument is that which least restricts the ownership of the land has been applied by Louisiana courts in a variety of contexts. See, e.g., Whitehall Oil Co. v. Heard, 197 So.2d 672 (La.App.3rd Cir.), writ refused 250 La. 924, 199 So.2d 923 (1967) (determination of the question whether a landowner created a single servitude over contiguous tracts or a series of multiple interests).

(c) "Servitudes claimed under titles, are never sustained by implication—the title creating them must be express, as to their nature and extent, as well as to the estate to which they are due." Parish v. Municipality No. 2, 8 La.Ann. 145, 147 (1853), cited with approval in Buras Ice Factory, Inc. v. Department of Highways, 235 La. 158, 103 So.2d 74 (1958).

Art. 731.   Charge expressly for the benefit of an estate

A charge established on an estate expressly for the benefit of another estate is a predial servitude although it is not so designated.

Acts 1977, No. 514, § 1, eff. Jan. 1, 1978.

REVISION COMMENTS—1977

(a) This provision reproduces the substance of Article 754 of the Louisiana Civil Code of 1870. It does not change the law.

(b) When contracting parties do not specify in their agreements the kind of right they intended to create question may arise as to whether they intended to establish a predial servitude, a personal servitude, or merely a personal obligation. This question is resolved in Louisiana by application of Articles 754–758 of the Civil Code of 1870, which furnish rules of interpretation as to the kinds of rights created by juridical acts. Articles 730 through 734 of this revision deal with the same matter.

(c) According to this provision, when a right of passage is expressly reserved "for the benefit and advantage of the property", a predial servitude is clearly established. Theriot v. Consolidated Companies, 160 La. 459, 107 So. 305 (1926). But when the act establishing the servitude either does not declare that the right is given for the benefit of an estate or declares that the right is given to the owner of an estate, determination of the question whether the parties intended to create a predial servitude or another right is made by application of Articles 732 through 734, infra.

Art. 732.   Interpretation in the absence of express declaration

When the act does not declare expressly that the right granted is for the benefit of an estate or for the benefit of a particular person, the nature of the right is determined in accordance with the following rules.

Acts 1977, No. 514, § 1, eff. Jan. 1, 1978.

REVISION COMMENT—1977

This provision reproduces the substance of Article 755 of the Louisiana Civil Code of 1870. It does not change the law.

Art. 733.   Interpretation; benefit of dominant estate

When the right granted be of a nature to confer an advantage on an estate, it is presumed to be a predial servitude.

Acts 1977, No. 514, § 1, eff. Jan. 1, 1978.

REVISION COMMENTS—1977

(a) This provision reproduces the substance of the first paragraph of Article 756 of the Louisiana Civil Code of 1870. It does not change the law. The second paragraph has not been reproduced as containing an unnecessary explanation.

(b) The question whether an instrument created a predial servitude or merely a personal obligation was raised in Burgas v. Stoutz, 174 La. 586, 141 So. 67 (1932). In this case, an act of sale stipulated that "the purchaser, its successors and assigns, shall have the privilege of using the paved driveway in the rear" of the vendor's property. The act had been recorded, but the words "its successors and assigns" were omitted from the public records. A subsequent purchaser of the vendor's property, relying in part on the omission of these words, argued that the recorded act had established merely a personal obligation. The court held that the act of sale, as recorded, established a predial servitude because the right of passage was of real utility to the property. The court bolstered its conclusion by the observation that the right of passage was not given to a named individual but to "the purchaser" thereby "connecting the servitude with the property as a real advantage to it, and not merely as a matter of convenience to a particular person and terminating with him." See also Charles M. Gillis & Co. v. Nelson & Donalson, 16 La.Ann. 275, 279 (1861), (irrigation servitude; the court declared that "the contract does not appear to us to be personal, for its object could only be for the advantage of the respective tracts of land"). For cases involving the creation of personal rights in favor of named persons rather than predial servitudes, see Declouet v. Borel, 15 La.Ann. 606 (1860); Martin v. Louisiana Public Utilities Co., 13 La.App. 181, 127 So. 470 (1930); Kelly v. Pippitone, 12 La.App. 625, 126 So. 79 (1st Cir. 1930).

(c) The question whether property is burdened with a predial servitude or is used by virtue of a personal right may also arise in the absence of a title. In Levet v. Lapeyrollerie, 39 La.Ann. 210, 1 So. 672 (1887), contention was made that a right of drain was a predial servitude that had been acquired by prescription rather than a personal right established in favor of a dissolved partnership. The court found that the right of drain in question had been established for the benefit of a tract of land because it was "of such advantage to it, that, without it, the tract could not be successfully cultivated." On the basis of this finding, the court held that the claimant of the servitude was entitled to the full benefit of the presumption of Article 756 of the Civil Code and rendered judgment recognizing the predial servitude. See also Greco v. Frigerio, 3 La.App. 649 (Orl.Cir.1926) (bathroom servitude; held, a predial servitude for the benefit of the dominant estate rather than a personal right for the convenience of the owner).

Art. 734.   Interpretation; convenience of a person

When the right granted is merely for the convenience of a person, it is not considered to be a predial servitude, unless it is acquired by a person as owner of an estate for himself, his heirs and assigns.

Acts 1977, No. 514, § 1, eff. Jan. 1, 1978.

REVISION COMMENTS—1977

(a) This provision reproduces the substance of the first paragraph of Article 757 of the Louisiana Civil Code of 1870. It does not change the law.

(b) Instruments do not only raise the question whether contracting parties intended to create a predial servitude or a personal obligation; they also raise the question whether contracting parties intended to create a predial servitude or a right of use, namely, a charge on an estate in favor of a person. The expression "personal to the individual" in Articles 757 and 758 of the Louisiana Civil Code of 1870 does not mean that if a right is not a predial servitude it is necessarily a personal obligation binding only on the parties to the agreement. The right may also be a right of use servitude, that is, a charge on an immovable in favor of a person, that may be a heritable and transferable right. See Yiannopoulos, Personal Servitudes §§ 118, 122 (1968).

(c) For instruments creating rights of use, see Simoneaux v. Lebermuth & Israel Planting Co., 155 La. 689, 99 So. 531 (1924) (right of passage); Brown v. Terry, 103 So.2d 541 (La.App.1st Cir. 1958). In this case, a stipulation in an act of sale created a right of passage in favor of the purchaser and provided that the "servitude shall remain in effect only so long as [vendee] shall be the record owner." In Mallet v. Thibault, 212 La. 79, 89–90, 31 So.2d 601, 604 (1947), the Louisiana Supreme Court clearly recognized the validity of rights of use as personal servitudes, and found that a servitude of passage had been established in favor of a person. "We are not unmindful," the court declared, "of Article 709 of the Code which seems to forbid conventional establishment of a servitude in favor of a person. However, that article cannot be reconciled with Articles 757 and 758 which are contained in Section 2 of Chapter 4 of Title IV dealing with the establishment of servitudes and which provide directly to the contrary. . . . Thus, the creation of a personal servitude by convention will be approved, provided, of course, that it does not contravene the public order."

SECTION 3—ACQUISITION OF CONVENTIONAL SERVITUDES FOR THE DOMINANT ESTATE

Art. 735.   Persons acquiring servitude

A predial servitude may be acquired for the benefit of the dominant estate by the owner of that estate or by any other person acting in his name or in his behalf.

Acts 1977, No. 514, § 1, eff. Jan. 1, 1978.

REVISION COMMENTS—1977

(a) This provision is new. It expresses the principle underlying Articles 759, 762, and 764 of the Louisiana Civil Code of 1870. Thus, a predial servitude may be acquired for the benefit of the dominant estate by a possessor in good or in bad faith, an authorized or unauthorized mandatary, a manager of affairs, a person making a stipulation pour autrui, a co-owner, a usufructuary, and a tutor or a curator.

(b) Articles 759–764 of the Louisiana Civil Code of 1870 deal with the question of capacity for the acquisition of predial servitudes for the dominant estate. While these articles contemplate, primarily, acquisition of predial servitudes by contract, they are susceptible of application to all modes of acquisition, including prescription and destination of the owner. On principle, one who may establish a predial servitude may also acquire such a servitude. But, in contrast with the grantor of the predial servitude, who must be competent and owner of the servient estate with power of alienation, the acquirer of the servitude need not be a competent person nor owner of the dominant estate.

(c) Servitudes may be acquired for the benefit of an estate by a possessor, whether in good or in bad faith, by a mandatary, whether acting within the scope of his mandate or not, by a negotiorum gestor, and even by a person who does not act in the name of the owner but makes a stipulation pour autrui. See 3 Aubry et Rau, Droit civil français 104 (6th ed. Bartin 1938); 3 Planiol et Ripert, Traité pratique de droit civil français 928 (2d ed. Picard 1952); 12 Demolombe, Traité des servitudes 255 (1855). In all cases, if the servitude is acquired by onerous title, the owner, whether he is competent or incompetent, may annul the contract or refuse to execute it by renouncing the servitude. The same faculty, however, is not accorded to the grantor of the servitude; he may not revoke the servitudes he has granted on the ground that they are onerous or that the owner was not a party to the contract, because it is not to the person but to the estate that they are granted. Article 738, infra.

(d) Tutors, curators, and other administrators, may acquire predial servitudes in favor of the property of persons under their control. The source provision does not mention the necessity of compliance with any formalities. It would seem, however, that the provision contemplates, primarily, acquisition of predial servitudes by gratuitous title or by prescription. If servitudes are acquired by onerous title, tutors and curators ought to comply with the formalities governing acquisition of property for minors and interdicts. Simple administrators do not have power of disposition; hence, any onerous engagement they have undertaken in connection with the acquisition of a servitude ought to be regarded as their own personal obligation.

(e) Under this provision, a coowner may acquire a predial servitude in favor of an estate owned in indivision, but the remaining co-owners may refuse to avail themselves of the servitude. This faculty exists in favor of the nonconsenting co-owners only; the grantor of the servitude may not refuse to recognize the servitude merely on the ground that the remaining co-owners have not consented. Of course, if the remaining co-owners refuse to be bound by the terms of a reciprocal contract, the grantor may sue the co-owner with whom he has contracted for rescission and damages.

See 3 Aubry et Rau, Droit civil français 104 (6th ed. Bartin 1938); Pardessus, Traité des servitudes 444 (1817).

Under this provision, a co-owner acquires a predial servitude for the benefit of the estate owned in indivision. If a coowner wishes to acquire a servitude under the condition that he should become owner of a divided part or of the entire estate following partition, he should make a declaration to that effect. See Pardessus, Traité des servitudes 448 (1817). For the proposition that a predial servitude may not be established in favor of an undivided part of an estate while the state of indivision lasts, see 3 Planiol et Ripert, Traité pratique de droit civil français 873 (2d ed. Picard 1952).

(f) The usufructuary, as administrator of the property subject to his enjoyment, may acquire predial servitudes for the owner. Under Article 764 of the Louisiana Civil Code of 1870, the usufructuary must declare that he acts for the owner or that the servitude is established in favor of all subsequent possessors of the property. This provision is a codification of the views expressed by Toullier and Pardessus. See 1 La. Legal Archives, Projet of the Louisiana Civil Code of 1825, p. 85 (1937). In the absence of a provision in the Code Civil corresponding with Article 1764 of the Louisiana Civil Code of 1870, the majority view of commentators in France is that the usufructuary is presumed to have acquired a predial servitude in favor of the estate he enjoys, unless there is a declaration to the contrary or unless the acquisition of the usufruct is by gratuitous title. See 3 Aubry et Rau, Droit civil francais 104 (6th ed. Bartin 1938); 12 Demolombe, Traité des servitudes 255 (1855). This view is adopted in the present revision.

If the usufructuary acts merely in his own interest the predial servitude that he has acquired terminates with the usufruct. Servitudes acquired by the usufructuary by means of acquisitive prescription, however, ought to accrue to the benefit of the estate. Pardessus, Traité des servitudes 441 (1817).

Art. 736.   Capacity to acquire servitude

An incompetent may acquire a predial servitude for the benefit of his estate without the assistance of the administrator of his patrimony or of his tutor or curator.

Acts 1977, No. 514, § 1, eff. Jan. 1, 1978.

REVISION COMMENTS—1977

(a) This provision is based on Article 759 of the Louisiana Civil Code of 1870. It does not change the law.

(b) Incompetents, as unemancipated minors and interdicts, may validly acquire predial servitudes in favor of their estates without the consent of their tutors or curators, because the acquisition of a predial servitude normally enhances the value and utility of the dominant estate. The provision establishes an exception from the general rules of the Civil Code that require the consent of tutors or curators for contracts made by unemancipated minors or interdicts. C.C. arts. 31, 401, 1784, 1785(6). Whether the acquisition of the servitude is made by onerous or by gratuitous act, the incompetents acquire a present right in favor of their estates rather than merely the faculty to enforce the grant upon termination of their disability. But, if the incompetents find the contract onerous, they may renounce the servitude. Article 737, infra.

Art. 737.   Renunciation of servitude by owner of dominant estate

The owner of the dominant estate may renounce the contract by which a predial servitude was acquired for the benefit of his estate, if he finds the contract onerous, and if the contract was made without his authority or while he was incompetent.

Acts 1977, No. 514, § 1, eff. Jan. 1, 1978.

REVISION COMMENTS—1977

(a) This provision reproduces the substance of Article 761 of the Louisiana Civil Code of 1870. It changes the law as indicated in Comment (c).

(b) If the owner renounces a contract made on his behalf, the grantor of the servitude may have recourse against the person he has contracted with for damages resulting from nonperformance. See Pardessus, Traité des servitudes 440 (1817).

(c) According to Article 763 of the Louisiana Civil Code of 1870, a co-owner may refuse to avail himself of a servitude acquired by another co-owner for the estate held in indivision on the ground that the acquisition of the servitude involves a change in the condition of the common estate that requires his consent rather than a mere act of administration. Under this revision, a co-owner, like any other owner, may renounce the servitude, if he finds the contract onerous, and if the contract was made without his authority.

Art. 738.   No revocation by grantor

The grantor may not revoke the servitude on the ground that the person who acquired it for the benefit of the dominant estate was not the owner, that he was incompetent, or that he lacked authority.

Acts 1977, No. 514, § 1, eff. Jan. 1, 1978.

REVISION COMMENTS—1977

(a) This provision is based on Articles 760 and 763 of the Louisiana Civil Code of 1870. It changes the law in certain respects.

(b) The person who established the servitude on the servient estate may not revoke it on the ground that the acquirer of the servitude was not owner of the dominant estate, that he was incompetent, or that he lacked authority, because he is presumed to have granted the servitude for the benefit of an estate rather than a person.

Art. 739.   Acquisition by title only

Nonapparent servitudes may be acquired by title only, including a declaration of destination under Article 741.

Acts 1977, No. 514, § 1, eff. Jan. 1, 1978. Amended by Acts 1978, No. 479, § 1.

REVISION COMMENTS—1977

(a) This provision is new. It is based on Article 766, first paragraph, of the Louisiana Civil Code of 1870. Nonapparent servitudes, as under the regime of the 1870 Code, may not be acquired by prescription or by destination of the owner.

(b) Since nonapparent servitudes must be established by title, it follows that such servitudes may not be established by immemorial possession. Immemorial possession, according to Romanist sources, "Is that which no man living has seen the beginning, and the existence of which he has learned from his elders." C.C. art. 766(3). The definition derives from the text of Toullier. See 1 La.Legal Archives, Projet of the Louisiana Civil Code of 1825, p. 85 (1937).

(c) Article 770 of the Louisiana Civil Code of 1870 is abrogated as obsolete and unnecessary.

Art. 740.   Modes of acquisition of servitudes

Apparent servitudes may be acquired by title, by destination of the owner, or by acquisitive prescription.

Acts 1977, No. 514, § 1, eff. Jan. 1, 1978.

REVISION COMMENTS—1977

(a) This provision is new. Under the 1870 Code, it is continuous and apparent servitudes that may be acquired by title, by destination of the owner, or by acquisitive prescription. Under Article 756, apparent servitudes may be acquired by prescription or by destination of the owner, even though they might be considered discontinuous under the regime of the 1870 Code and thus insusceptible of such modes of acquisition. A right of way servitude exercised by means of a railroad track or a paved roadway may be acquired by prescription and by destination of the owner.

The provision is not retroactive. Thus, the quasi-possession of a servitude that would be discontinuous under the prior law does not give rise to prescriptive rights except from the effective date of the new legislation. Prescription, however, commenced prior to the effective date of the new legislation for the acquisition of a servitude that would be continuous and apparent under the prior law continues to run. Upon accrual of the prescription, the right acquired will be that of an apparent servitude under the new legislation.

(b) While the word "title" has many meanings, it is used in the source provision synonymously with juridical act; it includes a contract, a testament or other act such as sale by expropriation intended to create a predial servitude and is not limited to an instrument in writing. See McGuffy v. Weil, 240 La. 758, 765, 125 So.2d 154, 157 (1960): "The plaintiff attempts to equate 'title' as used in the article [766] with the deed, or act of sale, by which the servient estate is acquired. He contends that, in order to create the servitude, the restriction must be incorporated in the deed conveying the land. Such a narrow construction, necessarily, does violence to the codal provision. . . . The conclusion is inescapable that 'title' as used in Article 766 refers to the method by which the servitude may be acquired and does not relate exclusively to the conveyance of the servient estate. It is a generic term which embraces any juridical act." See, also, Yiannopoulos, Predial Servitudes; Creation by Title, 45 Tul.L.Rev. 459, 460 (1971).

(c) Article 659 of the Louisiana Civil Code of 1870 speaks of servitudes "arising from contract between the respective owners", but this is merely an example. See Article 655, supra; 6 Baudry-Lacantinerie, Traité théorique et pratique de droit civil 534 (3rd ed. Chauveau 1905). Article 743 of the same Code declares that "servitudes are established by all acts by which property can be transferred." Hence there should be no doubt that conventional servitudes may be established by contract as well as by testament.

(d) The second sentence of Article 765 of the Louisiana Civil Code is abrogated as obsolete and unnecessary. For several reasons, and perhaps mostly due to the development of the law governing dedication to public use, the second sentence of Article 765 has never been applied by appellate courts. In cases in which Article 765 was invoked to establish public interests, its application was avoided by a statement that roads and streets within the limits of a municipality were outside the scope of this article. See, e.g., Bomar v. City of Baton Rouge, 162 La. 342, 110 So. 497 (1926). In another case application of Article 765 was avoided by a finding that ten years had not elapsed from the date the road was declared public by the police jury. Landry v. Gulf States Utilities Co., 166 La. 1069, 118 So. 142 (1928).

(e) The modes of acquisition of servitudes under the Civil Code are not exclusive of other modes of acquisition to the same extent as heretofore recognized under the law. See e.g., Lake v. Louisiana Power & Light Company, 330 So.2d 914 (La.1976), and R.S. 19:14.

Art. 741.   Destination of the owner

Destination of the owner is a relationship established between two estates owned by the same owner that would be a predial servitude if the estates belonged to different owners.

When the two estates cease to belong to the same owner, unless there is express provision to the contrary, an apparent servitude comes into existence of right and a nonapparent servitude comes into existence if the owner has previously filed for registry in the conveyance records of the parish in which the immovable is located a formal declaration establishing the destination.

Acts 1977, No. 514, § 1, eff. Jan. 1, 1978. Amended by Acts 1978, No. 479, § 1.

REVISION COMMENTS—1977

(a) This provision is new. It is based on Articles 649, 767, 768, and 769 of the Louisiana Civil Code of 1870. An apparent servitude may be acquired by destination of the owner under Article 741, even though it might be regarded as discontinuous under the regime of the 1870 Code.

(b) The text of Article 768 of the Louisiana Civil Code of 1870 has not been reproduced because it relates to matters of proof. It should be evident that there is no destination under Article 741 unless there is proof that the two estates belonged to the same owner, and that it was he who established the relationship giving rise to the servitude.

Art. 742. Acquisitive prescription

The laws governing acquisitive prescription of immovable property apply to apparent servitudes. An apparent servitude may be acquired by peaceable and uninterrupted possession of the right for ten years in good faith and by just title; it may also be acquired by uninterrupted possession for thirty years without title or good faith.

Acts 1977, No. 514, § 1, eff. Jan. 1, 1978.

REVISION COMMENTS—1977

(a) This provision is new. It is based on a combined reading of Articles 765, first sentence, and 3504 of the Louisiana Civil Code of 1870. It legislatively overrules contrary jurisprudence.

(b) The interrelation of Articles 765 and 3504 of the Louisiana Civil Code of 1870 is an unresolved matter. See Comment, Acquisitive Prescription of Servitudes, 15 La.L.Rev. 777 (1955). Early Louisiana decisions seem to suggest that Article 765 requires good faith and just title for the completion of the acquisitive prescription of ten years. See Kennedy v. Succession of McCollam, 34 La.Ann. 568 (1882). Scores of subsequent decisions, however, have held that particular parties acquired, without just title or good faith, continuous and apparent servitudes by the prescription of ten years under Article 765 of the Louisiana Civil Code. See, e.g., Levet v. Lapeyrollerie, 39 La.App. 210, 1 So. 672 (1887); Johnson v. Wills, 220 So.2d 134 (La.App.3rd Cir.), application denied 254 La. 132, 222 So.2d 883 (1969); Wild v. LeBlanc, 191 So.2d 146 (La.App.3rd Cir. 1966); Acadia-Vermilion Rice Irrigating Co. v. Broussard, 175 So.2d 856 (La.App.3rd Cir. 1965); Hale v. Hulin, 130 So.2d 519 (La.App.3rd Cir. 1961). It was in part the desire of the Louisiana Supreme Court to resolve this issue that prompted the grant of certiorari in Poole v. Guste, 261 La. 1110, 262 So.2d 339 (1972). This question, however, was not raised under the facts and pleadings, and the court did not have the opportunity to determine the issue.

(c) Just title for the purpose of acquisitive prescription of ownership is defined in Article 3484 of the Louisiana Civil Code of 1870: "By the term just title, in cases of prescription, we do not understand that which the possessor may have derived from the true owner, for then no true prescription would be necessary, but a title which the possessor may have received from any person whom he honestly believed to be the real owner, provided the title were such as to transfer the ownership of the property." By analogy, for the acquisition of a predial servitude by 10 years possession, the possessor must have a just title, namely, a title that would have established the servitude if it had been granted by the true owner. For the meaning of title, see Comment (b) under Article 740, supra.

(d) Good faith for the purpose of acquisitive prescription of ownership is defined in Article 3451 of the Louisiana Civil Code of 1870: "The possessor in good faith is he who has just reason to believe himself the master of the thing which he possesses, although he may not be in fact; as happens to him who buys a thing which he supposes to belong to the person selling it to him, but which, in fact, belongs to another." See also C.C. art. 503. By analogy, for the acquisition of a predial servitude by 10 years possession, the possessor must be in good faith, namely, he must honestly believe that he is entitled to the right he exercises as a servitude. Of course, good faith is always presumed. C.C. art. 3481.

(e) For legislative technique in modern codifications, see e.g., Italian Civil Code art. 1158: "Ownership and other real rights in immovable property are acquired by continuous possession of twenty years." Article 1159: "A person who, in good faith, acquires an immovable from another person who is not the owner thereof, such purchase being based on a title sufficient for the transfer of the property and duly entered in the register, shall accomplish the acquisition of the immovable, in his own favor, after ten years from the entry of such title. The same provision is applicable in the case of acquisition of other real rights in immovable property." Greek Civil Code art. 1041: "One who possesses as owner, in good faith, and by just title, a movable thing for three years, and an immovable for ten years, acquires its ownership." Article 1045: "One who possesses as owner a movable or an immovable thing for twenty years acquires its ownership". Article 1121: "A predial servitude is acquired by juridical act or by prescription. The provisions governing acquisitive prescription of immovable property and conventional transfer apply by analogy to the acquisition of predial servitudes."

Art. 743.   Accessory rights

Rights that are necessary for the use of a servitude are acquired at the time the servitude is established. They are to be exercised in a way least inconvenient for the servient estate.

Acts 1977, No. 514, § 1, eff. Jan. 1, 1978.

REVISION COMMENTS—1977

(a) This provision reproduces the substance of Article 771 of the Louisiana Civil Code of 1870. It does not change the law.

(b) Under this provision, rights that are presumed to be accessory to the servitude must be used in the least inconvenient way for the servient estate. Thus, an accessorial right of passage must be used in the most direct, shortest, and least inconvenient way for the servient estate.

SECTION 4—RIGHTS OF THE OWNER
OF THE DOMINANT ESTATE

Art. 744.   Necessary works; cost of repairs

The owner of the dominant estate has the right to make at his expense all the works that are necessary for the use and preservation of the servitude.

Acts 1977, No. 514, § 1, eff. Jan. 1, 1978.

REVISION COMMENTS—1977

(a) This provision reproduces the substance of Articles 772 and 773 of the Louisiana Civil Code of 1870. It does not change the law.

(b) The act establishing the servitude may provide that works necessary for the use and preservation of the servitude shall be made at the expense of the owner of the servient estate. Articles 651, 700, supra.

Art. 745.   Right to enter into the servient estate

The owner of the dominant estate has the right to enter with his workmen and equipment into the part of the servient estate that is needed for the construction or repair of works required for the use and preservation of the servitude. He may deposit materials to be used for the works and the debris that may result, under the obligation of causing the least possible damage and of removing them as soon as possible.

Acts 1977, No. 514, § 1, eff. Jan. 1, 1978.

REVISION COMMENT—1977

This provision reproduces the substance of Article 774 of the Louisiana Civil Code of 1870. It does not change the law.

Art. 746.   Exoneration from responsibility by abandonment of the servient estate

If the act establishing the servitude binds the owner of the servient estate to make the necessary works at his own expense, he may exonerate himself by abandoning the servient estate or the part of it on which the servitude is granted to the owner of the dominant estate.

Acts 1977, No. 514, § 1, eff. Jan. 1, 1978.

REVISION COMMENTS—1977

(a) This provision reproduces the substance of Article 775 of the Louisiana Civil Code of 1870. It does not change the law.

(b) The act establishing the servitude may bind the owner of the servient estate to make the necessary works at his own expense in derogation from the principle that predial servitudes may not involve affirmative duties. This derogation is allowed because the obligations assumed by the owner of the servient estate are merely accessorial. See 3 Planiol et Ripert, Traité pratique de droit civil français 959 (2d ed. Picard 1952). This obligation is propter rem, that is, a real obligation that follows the immovable in the hands of every successor. The owner of the servient estate may exonerate himself from this responsibility by abandoning to the owner of the dominant estate the part of the estate that is burdened with the servitude. C.C. art. 2012(4). Of course, exoneration is excluded if the owner of the servient estate assumed a personal obligation to make the necessary works at his expense.

Art. 747.   Division of dominant estate

If the dominant estate is divided, the servitude remains due to each part, provided that no additional burden is imposed on the servient estate. Thus, in case of a right of passage, all the owners are bound to exercise that right through the same place.

Acts 1977, No. 514, § 1, eff. Jan. 1, 1978.

REVISION COMMENT—1977

This provision reproduces the substance of Article 776 of the Louisiana Civil Code of 1870. It does not change the law.

Art. 748.   Noninterference by the owner of servient estate

The owner of the servient estate may do nothing tending to diminish or make more inconvenient the use of the servitude.

If the original location has become more burdensome for the owner of the servient estate, or if it prevents him from making useful improvements on his estate, he may provide another equally convenient location for the exercise of the servitude which the owner of the dominant estate is bound to accept. All expenses of relocation are borne by the owner of the servient estate.

Acts 1977, No. 514, § 1, eff. Jan. 1, 1978.

REVISION COMMENT—1977

This provision is new. It is based on Article 777 of the Louisiana Civil Code of 1870.

Art. 749.   Extent and manner of use of servitude when title is silent

If the title is silent as to the extent and manner of use of the servitude, the intention of the parties is to be determined in the light of its purpose.

Acts 1977, No. 514, § 1, eff. Jan. 1, 1978.

REVISION COMMENT—1977

This provision is new. It is based on Article 780 of the Louisiana Civil Code of 1870. It changes the law as it establishes a broad principle according to which the extent and manner of use of the servitude is determined.

Art. 750.   Location of servitude when the title is silent

If the title does not specify the location of the servitude, the owner of the servient estate shall designate the location.

Acts 1977, No. 514, § 1, eff. Jan. 1, 1978.

REVISION COMMENT—1977

This provision reproduces the substance of Article 779 of the Louisiana Civil Code of 1870. It does not change the law.

SECTION 5—EXTINCTION OF PREDIAL SERVITUDES

Art. 751.   Destruction of dominant or of servient estate

A predial servitude is extinguished by the permanent and total destruction of the dominant estate or of the part of the servient estate burdened with the servitude.

Acts 1977, No. 514, § 1, eff. Jan. 1, 1978.

REVISION COMMENTS—1977

(a) This provision reproduces the substance of Articles 783(1) and 784 of the Louisiana Civil Code of 1870. It does not change the law.

(b) A predial servitude is extinguished by the permanent and total destruction of the dominant estate. If the destruction is merely temporary, as in the case of a temporary inundation, the servitude is not extinguished; there is merely a material obstacle to the exercise of the servitude. See 3 Planiol et Ripert, Traité pratique de droit civil français 974 (2d ed. Picard 1952): "When there is impossibility of use, Article 703 says that 'servitudes cease', and Article 704 adds that 'they revive when things are reestablished so that they may again be used. . . .'" The expressions cease and revive are inexact, and the law erroneously includes impossibility of use among the causes that extinguish the servitudes. Whenever there is impossibility of use there is a material obstacle which prevents the exercise of the servitude. However, the right subsists and may be used again if things are reestablished. Strictly speaking, the servitude does not revive; it continues to exist. Its exercise alone has ceased."

(c) A predial servitude is extinguished by the total destruction of the dominant estate. If the destruction is partial, the servitude continues to exist for the benefit of the remaining part by virtue of the principle of indivisibility. See Article 652, supra.

(d) A predial servitude is extinguished by the permanent and total destruction of the part of the servient estate burdened with the servitude. The destruction of the part of the servient estate that is not burdened with the servitude is immaterial.

Art. 752.   Reestablishment of things

If the exercise of the servitude becomes impossible because the things necessary for its exercise have undergone such a change that the servitude can no longer be used, the servitude is not extinguished; it resumes its effect when things are reestablished so that they may again be used, unless prescription has accrued.

Acts 1977, No. 514, § 1, eff. Jan. 1, 1978.

REVISION COMMENTS—1977

(a) This provision reproduces the substance of Articles 785 and 786 of the Louisiana Civil Code of 1870. It does not change the law.

(b) A change in the condition of things subject to the servitude may constitute a material obstacle preventing its exercise. In such a case, the running of prescription may be suspended for a period of ten years in accordance with Article 755.

(c) Thus, the destruction of a building, on the servient or on the dominant estate, does not entail extinction of a predial servitude established on it or for its benefit; if it is rebuilt prior to the accrual of prescription, the servitudes appertaining to the old exist on the new building.

Art. 753.   Prescription for nonuse

A predial servitude is extinguished by nonuse for ten years.

Acts 1977, No. 514, § 1, eff. Jan. 1, 1978.

REVISION COMMENT—1977

This provision reproduces the substance of Article 789 of the Louisiana Civil Code of 1870. It does not change the law.

244

Art. 754.   Commencement of nonuse

Prescription of nonuse begins to run for affirmative servitudes from the date of their last use, and for negative servitudes from the date of the occurrence of an event contrary to the servitude.

An event contrary to the servitude is such as the destruction of works necessary for its exercise or the construction of works that prevent its exercise.

Acts 1977, No. 514, § 1, eff. Jan. 1, 1978.

REVISION COMMENTS—1977

(a) This provision is new. It is based in part on Articles 790 and 791 of the Louisiana Civil Code of 1870. It changes the law.

(b) Under the Article 754, prescription for nonuse begins to run for affirmative servitudes from the date of their last use. Under the regime of the 1870 Code, prescription for nonuse begins to run for discontinuous servitudes, whether affirmative or negative, from the date of the last use.

(c) Under Article 754, prescription begins to run for negative servitudes from the date an event contrary to the servitude occurs. Under the regime of the 1870 Code, prescription for nonuse from the date an event contrary to the servitude occurs is material for continuous servitudes, whether affirmative or negative.

Art. 755.   Obstacle to servitude

If the owner of the dominant estate is prevented from using the servitude by an obstacle that he can neither prevent nor remove, the prescription of nonuse is suspended on that account for a period of up to ten years.

Acts 1977, No. 514, § 1, eff. Jan. 1, 1978.

REVISION COMMENTS—1977

(a) This provision is new. It is based in part on Article 792 of the Louisiana Civil Code of 1870. It changes the law as it declares that the maximum period of suspension on account of an obstacle is ten years.

(b) The existence of an obstacle under Article 792 of the Louisiana Civil Code of 1870 is a cause of suspension rather than interruption of prescription. See C.C. arts. 3516, 3521. The same is true under Article 755. Prescription of nonuse, however, begins to run ten years from the date the obstacle arose.

(c) Article 59 of the Mineral Code declares: "If the owner of a mineral servitude is prevented from using it by an obstacle that he can neither prevent nor remove, the prescription of nonuse does not run as long as the obstacle remains".

Art. 756.   Failure to rebuild dominant or servient estate

If the servitude cannot be exercised on account of the destruction of a building or other construction that belongs to the owner of the dominant estate, prescription is not suspended. If the building or other construction belongs to the owner of the servient estate, the preceding article applies.

Acts 1977, No. 514, § 1, eff. Jan. 1, 1978.

REVISION COMMENTS—1977

(a) This provision is new; it is based in part on Articles 787 and 788 of the Louisiana Civil Code of 1870. It changes the law as it contemplates suspension of prescription for a maximum period of ten years.

(b) This provision illustrates application of the obstacle doctrine that is established in the preceding article. If the building or other construction that is destroyed belongs to the owner of the dominant estate, the servitude may be extinguished by prescription prior to rebuilding because "it depended on him alone, by rebuilding his house to revive the servitude it enjoyed." C.C. art. 787 (1870). If the building or other construction that has been destroyed belongs to the owner of the servient estate, prescription does not run for a period of ten years because "he to whom the servitude was due had not the power to compel the other to rebuild the house or edifice thus destroyed." C.C. art. 788 (1870).

(c) If the owner of the dominant estate has the right to compel the rebuilding of the servient estate, prescription runs. The owner of the dominant estate, however, may cause an interruption of the prescription by filing suit. C.C. art. 3518.

Art. 757. Sufficiency of acts by third persons

A predial servitude is preserved by the use made of it by anyone, even a stranger, if it is used as appertaining to the dominant estate.

Acts 1977, No. 514, § 1, eff. Jan. 1, 1978.

REVISION COMMENTS—1977

(a) This provision reproduces the substance of Articles 793 and 794 of the Louisiana Civil Code of 1870. It does not change the law.

(b) Thus, the servitude is preserved by the use made of it by one who possesses the dominant estate in bad faith. But if any one passes over the land of another considering the way as public, or as belonging to another estate, the owner of the dominant estate may not avail himself of the use thus made of the servitude in order to prevent the running of the prescription. C.C. art. 794(1), (2) (1870).

(c) In order to preserve a predial servitude and prevent prescription from running against it, it is not necessary that the servitude be exercised personally by the owner of the dominant estate or by a person who uses his rights or who represents him directly, as a usufructuary, a lessee, or a mandatary. It suffices that the servitude be exercised by employees of the owner, his friends, or visitors. C.C. art. 793 (1870).

Art. 758. Imprescriptibility of natural servitudes

The prescription of nonuse does not run against natural servitudes.

Acts 1977, No. 514, § 1, eff. Jan. 1, 1978.

REVISION COMMENT—1977

This provision reproduces the substance of Article 795 of the Louisiana Civil Code of 1870. It does not change the law.

Art. 759. Partial use

A partial use of the servitude constitutes use of the whole.

Acts 1977, No. 514, § 1, eff. Jan. 1, 1978.

REVISION COMMENTS—1977

(a) This provision is new. It is in part based on Article 1075 of the Italian Civil Code. It changes the law but accords in part with Louisiana jurisprudence.

(b) Article 798 of the Louisiana Civil Code of 1870 has no counterpart in the French Civil Code. It was first adopted in the 1825 revision. It has been taken verbatim from the text of Toullier. See 2 Toullier, Droit civil français 206 (1833). In context, it is abundantly clear that Toullier speaks of the mode of exercise of servitudes rather than the different problem of the partial use of the area subject to the servitude. Further, Toullier makes it clear that the prescription of the mode of exercise of the servitude is pertinent only if the title of a discontinuous servitude contains limitations as to its mode of exercise. If there are no limitations in the title, there is no question of prescription of the mode of exercise.

(c) According to Louisiana jurisprudence, Article 798 of the Louisiana Civil Code of 1870 does not apply to cases in which there has been partial use of the area subject to a continuous servitude. Since servitudes are indivisible, use of any part of a continuous tract of land under a servitude preserves the servitude over the entire land. Prescription begins to run against a continuous servitude from the date contrary works are constructed. Armstrong v. Red River, Atchafalaya & Bayou Bouef Levee Board, 278 So.2d 496 (La.1973); cf. Hanks v. Gulf States Utilities Co., 253 La. 946, 221 So. 249 (1969). For analysis, see The Work of the Louisiana Appellate Courts for the 1971– 72 Term—Property, 33 La.L.Rev. 172, 191–197 (1973). The author concluded: "Articles 796–797 of the Civil Code were intended to apply, and do apply, to discontinuous servitudes in cases in which the exercise of the servitude is subject to limitations contained in the title. These articles have no application to continuous servitudes or to discontinuous servitudes in the absence of limitations in the title. Louisiana courts ought to apply these articles as exceptional provisions that are not susceptible of extension by analogy."

Art. 760.   More extensive use than title

A more extensive use of the servitude than that granted by the title does not result in the acquisition of additional rights for the dominant estate unless it be by acquisitive prescription.

Acts 1977, No. 514, § 1, eff. Jan. 1, 1978.

REVISION COMMENT—1977

This provision is new. It is based in part on Article 797 of the Louisiana Civil Code of 1870. It changes the law as it allows acquisition by prescription of an apparent servitude, even though it might be considered as discontinuous under the 1870 Code.

Art. 761.   Use of accessory right

The use of a right that is only accessory to the servitude is not use of the servitude.

Acts 1977, No. 514, § 1, eff. Jan. 1, 1978.

REVISION COMMENTS—1977

(a) This provision reproduces the substance of Article 799 of the Louisiana Civil Code of 1870. It does not change the law.

(b) Thus, if one who has the servitude of drawing water from the well of his neighbor passes over the servient estate and goes to the well without drawing any water during the period required for prescription, he will lose the servitude because the passage is merely accessory to the right of drawing water. C.C. art. 799(2) (1870).

Art. 762.   Use by co-owner

If the dominant estate is owned in indivision, the use that a co-owner makes of the servitude prevents the running of prescription as to all.

If the dominant estate is partitioned, the use of the servitude by each owner preserves it for his estate only.

Acts 1977, No. 514, § 1, eff. Jan. 1, 1978.

REVISION COMMENTS—1977

(a) This provision reproduces the substance of Articles 801 and 803 of the Louisiana Civil Code of 1870. It does not change the law.

(b) Article 803(2) of the Louisiana Civil Code of 1870 provides: "If a servitude be due to several persons, but on different days, as the right of drawing water, he who does not exercise his right, loses it, and the estate subject to the servitude becomes free from it, as respects him." This provision has not been reproduced as containing an unnecessary illustration. If a predial servitude is due to several estates, but on different days, there are, in effect, as many servitudes as there are dominant estates. Use of the servitude by the owner of one estate does not preserve the servitude for the other estates.

Art. 763.   Minority or other disability

The prescription of nonuse is not suspended by the minority or other disability of the owner of the dominant estate.

Acts 1977, No. 514, § 1, eff. Jan. 1, 1978.

REVISION COMMENTS—1977

(a) This provision is new. It accords with the policy underlying Article 58 of the Mineral Code, and Articles 3541 and 3478 of the Louisiana Civil Code of 1870.

(b) According to Article 3541 of the Louisiana Civil Code of 1870, as amended in 1958, the liberative prescription of one and three years as well as the prescription of thirty years, whether acquisitive or liberative, runs against "married women, minors, and interdicted persons". According to Article 3478 of the same code the ten year acquisitive prescription runs against "interdicts, married women, absentees and all others now excepted by law; and as to minors this prescription shall accrue and apply in nineteen years from the date of the birth of said minor; provided that this prescription once it has begun to run against a party shall not be interrupted in favor of any minor heirs of said party." Finally, Article 58 of the Mineral Code declares that "The prescription of nonuse is not suspended by the minority or other legal disability of the owner of a mineral servitude."

Art. 764.   Burden of proof of use

When the prescription of nonuse is pleaded, the owner of the dominant estate has the burden of proving that he or some other person has made use of the servitude as appertaining to his estate during the period of time required for the accrual of the prescription.

Acts 1977, No. 514, § 1, eff. Jan. 1, 1978.

REVISION COMMENT—1977

This provision reproduces the substance of Article 804 of the Louisiana Civil Code of 1870. It does not change the law.

Art. 765.   Confusion

A predial servitude is extinguished when the dominant and the servient estates are acquired in their entirety by the same person.

Acts 1977, No. 514, § 1, eff. Jan. 1, 1978.

REVISION COMMENTS—1977

(a) This provision reproduces the substance of Article 805 of the Louisiana Civil Code of 1870. It does not change the law.

(b) Article 805(2) of the Louisiana Civil Code of 1870 indicates that if the owner of one estate acquires only a part of the other estate or in indivision with another person, confusion does not take place. The provision has not been reproduced as containing an unnecessary illustration.

Art. 766.   Resolutory condition

When the union of the two estates is made under resolutory condition, or if it cease by legal eviction, the servitude is suspended and not extinguished.

Acts 1977, No. 514, § 1, eff. Jan. 1, 1978.

REVISION COMMENTS—1977

(a) The provision reproduces the substance of the first paragraph of Article 806 of the Louisiana Civil Code of 1870. It does not change the law.

(b) The second paragraph of Article 806 of the Louisiana Civil Code of 1870 has not been reproduced as containing an unnecessary illustration. There should be no doubt that upon exercise of the right of redemption, the happening of a resolutory condition, or the relinquishment of a mortgaged estate by a third person, servitudes resume their effect.

Art. 767. Acceptance of succession; confusion

Until a successor has formally or informally accepted a succession, confusion does not take place. If the successor renounces the succession, the servitudes continue to exist.

Acts 1977, No. 514, § 1, eff. Jan. 1, 1978. Amended by Acts 2001, No. 572, § 1.

REVISION COMMENT—1977

This provision is new. It is based on Article 810 of the Louisiana Civil Code of 1870. It clarifies the law.

REVISION COMMENT—2001

Under the law of predial servitudes, when a dominant estate and a servient estate are acquired by the same person, a predial servitude is extinguished by confusion. C.C. Art. 765 (Rev. 1977). When such acquisition is by inheritance, a problem arises because of the uncertainty in knowing whether the successor will accept or renounce the inheritance. The servitude would be extinguished by confusion if the successor accepted the inheritance, but the servitude should not be extinguished when the successor ultimately renounces the inheritance. That is the fundamental principle underlying Article 767 (Rev. 2001). The language of former Article 767 (Rev. 1977), however, was inappropriate, not only because it referred to "benefit of inventory," which no longer exists, but because it improperly referred to the "period of deliberation" for accepting a succession with benefit of inventory, and no such period of time existed even under prior law. The 2001 amendment to this Article is consistent with the new successions law and properly preserves the underlying rationale of Article 767 regarding servitudes.

Art. 768. Confusion; separate and community property

Confusion does not take place between separate property and community property of the spouses. Thus, if the servient estate belongs to one of the spouses and the dominant estate is acquired as a community asset, the servitude continues to exist.

Acts 1977, No. 514, § 1, eff. Jan. 1, 1978.

REVISION COMMENT—1977

This provision reproduces the substance of Article 811 of the Louisiana Civil Code of 1870. It does not change the law.

Art. 769. Irrevocability of extinction by confusion

A servitude that has been extinguished by confusion may be reestablished only in the manner by which a servitude may be created.

Acts 1977, No. 514, § 1, eff. Jan. 1, 1978.

REVISION COMMENT—1977

This provision reproduces the substance of Article 812 of the Louisiana Civil Code of 1870. It does not change the law.

Art. 770. Abandonment of servient estate

A predial servitude is extinguished by the abandonment of the servient estate, or of the part on which the servitude is exercised. It must be evidenced by a written act. The owner of the dominant estate is bound to accept it and confusion takes place.

Acts 1977, No. 514, § 1, eff. Jan. 1, 1978.

REVISION COMMENTS—1977

(a) This provision reproduces the substance of Articles 813, 814, and 815 of the Louisiana Civil Code of 1870. It does not change the law.

(b) Article 815 of the Louisiana Civil Code of 1870 provides that if a landowner is bound to support a building or the beams of his neighbor on a part of his wall, and to make the necessary repairs for the maintenance of the wall in a condition suitable for the exercise of the servitude, he may discharge himself from these obligations by abandoning to the owner of the dominant estate the part of the wall on which the servitude is exercised. The provision has not been reproduced as containing an unnecessary illustration.

(c) For the necessity of a written act, see Hereford v. Police Jury, 4 La.Ann. 172 (1849).

Art. 771.   Renunciation of servitude

A predial servitude is extinguished by an express and written renunciation by the owner of the dominant estate.

Acts 1977, No. 514, § 1, eff. Jan. 1, 1978.

REVISION COMMENTS—1977

(a) This provision is new. It is based on Arts. 783(5), 816 and 817 of the Louisiana Civil Code of 1870. It changes the law as it suppresses the rule that the renunciation may be tacit.

(b) Article 817(1) of the Louisiana Civil Code of 1870 declares that the renunciation is confined to what is clearly expressed in the act containing it, because one is not presumed to have renounced his right. The provision has not been reproduced as containing an obvious rule of interpretation and an unnecessary explanation.

(c) Article 817(2) of the Louisiana Civil Code of 1870 declares that the owner who makes an express renunciation must have capacity to dispose of immovables, because the renunciation of a predial servitude is an alienation of immovable property. The provision has not been reproduced as unnecessary.

Art. 772.   Renunciation by owner

A renunciation of a servitude by a co-owner of the dominant estate does not discharge the servient estate, but deprives him of the right to use the servitude.

Acts 1977, No. 514, § 1, eff. Jan. 1, 1978.

REVISION COMMENT—1977

This provision reproduces the substance of Article 818 of the Louisiana Civil Code of 1870. It does not change the law.

Art. 773.   Expiration of time or happening of condition

A predial servitude established for a term or under a resolutory condition is extinguished upon the expiration of the term or the happening of the condition.

Acts 1977, No. 514, § 1, eff. Jan. 1, 1978.

REVISION COMMENT—1977

This provision reproduces the substance of Article 821 of the Louisiana Civil Code of 1870. It does not change the law.

Art. 774.   Dissolution of the right of the grantor

A predial servitude is extinguished by the dissolution of the right of the person who established it.

Acts 1977, No. 514, § 1, eff. Jan. 1, 1978.

REVISION COMMENTS—1977

(a) This provision reproduces the substance of Article 783(7) of the Louisiana Civil Code of 1870. It does not change the law.

(b) Article 822 of the Louisiana Civil Code of 1870 declares that if one establishes a servitude on an estate on which he has only a right subject to a condition or defeasible at a certain time or in certain cases, or subject to rescission, the servitude that he has established is extinguished with his right. It is the same if his title to the servient estate is annulled by reason of some preexisting defect inherent in the act. The provision has not been reproduced as containing unnecessary explanations.

(c) On principle, predial servitudes are extinguished when the title of the grantor is subsequently declared nonexistent or is annulled for defects. According to Louisiana substantive law, the declaration of nullity clearly results in the cancellation of all real rights granted by the person whose title is annulled. See C.C. art. 736; Article 712, supra.

(d) Cf. Mineral Code Article 27(5). In Jefferson v. Childers, 189 La. 46, 179 So. 30 (1937), the court declared that the grant of a mineral right by the record owner whose title is subsequently annulled for want of consideration was valid and binding on the true owner. The court held the property may not be recovered to the detriment of "a third person who relied upon the public records"; it may only be recovered "subject to transactions" between the apparent owner and third persons acting in good faith. The result, applies the parol evidence exclusionary rule making an authentic act "full proof of the agreement contained in it, against the contracting parties and their heirs or assigns, unless it be declared and proved a forgery." C.C. art. 2236. The parol evidence rule, not the public records doctrine, enables third persons to rely on the essential recitals of recorded acts. See Yiannopoulos, Predial Servitudes; Creation by Title, 45 Tul.L.Rev. 459, 491 (1971).

TITLE V—BUILDING RESTRICTIONS

Art. 775.   Building restrictions

Building restrictions are charges imposed by the owner of an immovable in pursuance of a general plan governing building standards, specified uses, and improvements. The plan must be feasible and capable of being preserved.

Acts 1977, No. 170, § 1, eff. Jan. 1, 1978.

REVISION COMMENTS—1977

(a) This provision is new. It codifies Louisiana jurisprudence. It does not change the law.

(b) The law of building restrictions is a creature of Louisiana jurisprudence. See Queensborough Land Co. v. Cazeaux, 136 La. 724, 67 So. 641 (1915). In this revision, building restrictions may merely involve restraints on the use of immovables. Restraints on alienation, to the extent that they may be valid under Louisiana law, are not affected by this revision.

(c) The creation of building restrictions as sui generis real rights is subject to the requirement that there be a general plan that is feasible and capable of being preserved. See Gerde v. Simonson Investments, Inc., 251 La. 893, 207 So.2d 360 (1968); Salerno v. DeLucca, 211 La. 659, 30 So.2d 678 (1947); Yiannopoulos, Real Rights: Limits of Contractual and Testamentary Freedom, 30 La.L.Rev. 44, 59–75 (1969). In the absence of a general plan, however, the building restrictions may constitute veritable predial servitudes. See McGuffy v. Weil, 240 La. 758, 125 So.2d 154 (1960). When restrictions are imposed by stipulations inserted in individual acts of sale, care should be taken to impose uniform restrictions on most, if not all, individual lots in the subdivision. Omission to make the restrictions uniform or to insert them in a substantial number of sales may be taken to indicate absence of a general development plan. In these circumstances, the stipulations establishing the restrictions may create personal obligations rather than sui generis real rights.

(d) Building restrictions constitute the most important category of restraints on the use or disposition of immovables from the viewpoints of urban and suburban developments in Louisiana. They have been defined as limitations "inserted in deeds in pursuance of a general plan devised by the ancestor in title to maintain certain building standards and uniform improvements. . . ." Salerno v. DeLucca, 211 La. 659, 30 So.2d 678, 679–680 (1947). The requirements of an ancestor in title and of a general development plan are essential features of building restrictions as sui generis real rights. Unlike predial servitudes under the Civil Code, building restrictions may involve certain affirmative duties and may exclude the performance of certain juridical acts; moreover, building restrictions may be imposed even in the absence of a dominant estate.

(e) According to firmly established Louisiana jurisprudence, building restrictions constitute real rights only in the framework of subdivision planning. They must be imposed, at least by implication, in favor of lots in a subdivision in accordance with a general development plan. If the restrictions are imposed on individual lots without regard to a general development plan, they may constitute veritable predial servitudes, provided, of course, that the requirements for the creation of predial servitudes are met. See McGuffy v. Weil, 240 La. 758, 125 So.2d 154 (1960) (restriction of commercial usage imposed on a single lot in favor of another lot). If the requirements for the creation of predial servitudes are not met, the restrictions may only be personal obligations. See Leonard v. Lavigne, 245 La. 1004, 162 So.2d 341 (1964); Cambais v. Douglas, 167 La. 791, 120 So. 369 (1929); LeBlanc v. Palmisano, 43 So.2d 263 (La.App.Orl.Cir.1949). But see Tucker v. Woodside, 53 So.2d 503 (La.App.1st Cir., 1951), criticized in Yiannopoulos, Civil Law Property § 114 (1966). This isolated decision, deviating from well-established principles of property law, should be regarded as confined to its own facts.

Art. 776.   Establishment

Building restrictions may be established only by juridical act executed by the owner of an immovable or by all the owners of the affected immovables. Once established, building restrictions may be amended or terminated as provided in this Title.

Acts 1977, No. 170, § 1, eff. Jan. 1, 1978. Amended by Acts 1999, No. 309, § 1, eff. June 16, 1999.

REVISION COMMENTS—1977

(a) This provision is new. It codifies Louisiana jurisprudence. It does not change the law.

(b) Building restrictions are ordinarily created by developers of land who intend to subdivide their property into individual lots destined to residential, commercial, or industrial uses. After the establishment of a subdivision, however, landowners may occasionally enter into agreements designed to restrict the use of their property. Unlike restrictions created by developers of land, which do not qualify as veritable servitudes due to the absence of a dominant estate, restrictions imposed by landowners after the creation of a subdivision may qualify either as predial servitudes or as sui generis real rights. Outside of subdivision planning, agreements among landowners imposing restrictions on individual lots in favor of other lots may give rise to veritable predial servitudes. See C.C. arts. 646, 697; McGuffy v. Weil, 240 La. 758, 125 So.2d 154 (1960) (restriction affecting a single lot). The Civil Code specifically permits the creation of a servitude on one estate in favor of several estates or of servitudes on several estates in favor of one estate. Agreements among landowners imposing restrictions on their property in the framework of subdivision planning constitute building restrictions, i.e., sui generis real rights, rather than predial servitudes. See Gerde v. Simonson Investments, Inc., 251 La. 893, 207 So.2d 360 (1968); cf. Pizzolato v. Cataldo, 202 La. 675, 12 So.2d 677 (1943). Since the rules governing building restrictions as sui generis real rights differ in certain particulars from the rules governing predial servitudes, question may arise as to the precise nature of the rights created by the agreement among landowners. This is a matter of contractual interpretation, resolved in the light of the facts of each case and in accordance with the intention of the parties.

(c) By analogy to non-apparent servitudes, building restrictions must be created by title which, in order to be effective against third persons, must be recorded. In this respect, title means any juridical act: hence, restrictions may validly be established by declarations of intent made in the act of sale to the present owner, to an ancestor or in a separate document. By virtue of the public records doctrine, an acquirer of immovable property burdened with recorded restrictions is presumed to have notice. The restrictions need not appear in the act by which the present owner acquired the property nor in his chain of title; it suffices that the restrictions were recorded in some form at the time the original subdivider conveyed the property to the ancestor of the present owner. In the absence of recorded restrictions at the time of the first sale by the subdivider, the property is transferred free from any restrictions. If, after the first sale, the subdivider imposes blanket restrictions by a recorded declaration of intent, the successors of the original acquirer are not bound by these restrictions. See McGuffy v. Weil, 240 La. 758, 125 So.2d 154 (1960); Anderson v. Courtney, 190 So.2d 493 (La.App.1st Cir. 1966); Clark v. Reed, 122 So.2d 344 (La.App.2d Cir. 1960).

Art. 777.   Nature and regulation

Building restrictions are incorporeal immovables and real rights likened to predial servitudes. They are regulated by application of the rules governing predial servitudes to the extent that their application is compatible with the nature of building restrictions.

Acts 1977, No. 170, § 1, eff. Jan. 1, 1978.

REVISION COMMENTS—1977

(a) This provision is new. It codifies Louisiana jurisprudence. It does not change the law.

(b) Certain types of restraints on the use of immovables may be stipulated as predial servitudes, provided that the essential requirements for the creation of predial servitudes are met. Thus, an estate may be charged in favor of another estate with restrictions pertaining to the height of buildings, building set offs from property lines, and the exclusion of commercial or industrial uses. But restraints involving affirmative acts, as those concerning the type and value of buildings to be erected, may not properly form the object of predial servitudes. Nevertheless, landowners who acquired or alienated property in reliance upon restrictions that may not give rise to predial servitudes may have a legitimate interest in the enforcement of these restrictions against any violator.

(c) A restraint on the use of an immovable imposed in favor of another immovable should be qualified as a predial servitude; a similar restraint established in favor of a person might be qualified as a limited personal servitude, that is, a right of use servitude. Restraints on the use of immovables that may qualify as servitudes are enforceable against anyone as charges on the land. In contrast, personal obligations are enforceable against the original obligor and his universal successors, i.e., heirs, universal legatees, or legatees under universal title. They are not enforceable against particular successors, i.e., buyers, donees, or legatees of particular things, unless expressly assumed. See C.C. art. 3556(28); Cambias v. Douglas, 167 La. 791, 120 So. 369 (1929); Yiannopoulos, Civil Law Property §§ 104, 113 (1966).

Restrictions imposed by subdivider prior to the creation of a subdivision do not qualify as predial servitudes because the requirement of two estates is not met. See C.C. art. 646 (1977). After the first lot is sold, however, restrictions involving passive duties may certainly constitute veritable predial servitudes.

(d) The matter of classification of building restrictions has given rise to analytical difficulties in Louisiana. Preferably, building restrictions that may not qualify as predial servitudes under the Louisiana Civil Code should be classified as sui generis real rights akin to predial servitudes. Thus, they should be governed by the general rules applicable to predial servitudes, subject to certain modifications concerning the creation, enforcement or termination of building restrictions.

Art. 778. Affirmative duties

Building restrictions may impose on owners of immovables affirmative duties that are reasonable and necessary for the maintenance of the general plan. Building restrictions may not impose upon the owner of an immovable or his successors the obligation to pay a fee or other charge on the occasion of an alienation, lease or encumbrance of the immovable.

Acts 1977, No. 170, § 1, eff. Jan. 1, 1978. Amended by Acts 2010, No. 938, § 2, eff. July 2, 2010.

REVISION COMMENTS—1977

(a) This provision is new. It codifies Louisiana jurisprudence. It does not change the law.

(b) Cf. Queensborough Land Co. v. Cazeaux, 136 La. 724, 729, 67 So. 641, 643 (1915): "The question of how far such a condition will be sustained is one dependent very much upon the facts of each particular case. If the condition is founded upon no substantial reason but merely in caprice, and is of a character to tie up property to the detriment of the public interest, it will not be sustained; otherwise, it will."

Art. 779. Injunctive relief

Building restrictions may be enforced by mandatory and prohibitory injunctions without regard to the limitations of Article 3601 of the Code of Civil Procedure.

Acts 1977, No. 170, § 1, eff. Jan. 1, 1978.

REVISION COMMENTS—1977

(a) This provision is new. It corresponds with Article 654, this revision. It does not change the law.

(b) Actions for the protection and enforcement of building restrictions may be brought against any violator by the persons entitled to these property rights. Willis v. New Orleans East Unit of Jehovah's Witnesses, Inc., 156 So.2d 310, 313 (La.App.4th Cir. 1963). Quite apart from property theory the building restrictions imposed by a subdivider may constitute a tacit stipulation pour autrui in favor of the purchasers of individual lots. Queensborough Land Co. v. Cazeaux, 136 La. 724, 737, 67 So. 641, 646 (1915). Accordingly, landowners in a subdivision may have recourse to both contractual and property actions.

(c) A decision of the Louisiana Supreme Court, based mostly on common law authorities, might be taken to indicate that actions for the protection and enforcement of building restrictions may be brought only by landowners in the immediate vicinity of the alleged violation. Guyton v. Yancey, 240 La. 794, 125 So.2d 365 (1960); Comment, Building Restrictions in Louisiana, 21 La.L.Rev. 468 (1961).

However, every landowner in a subdivision is adversely affected by violations and has a substantive right as well as procedural standing to bring action. Persons whose property is located outside the restricted area may not sue for the enforcement of building restrictions as sui generis real rights; these persons, however, may have claims for the enforcement of limitations on use as personal obligations. Dicta in a number of Louisiana decisions might be taken to indicate that landowners whose property is free of restrictions may not bring actions to set aside violations on restricted property in the subdivision. However, restrictions may be imposed in favor of any lot in a subdivision without the necessity of mutuality of obligations. Hence, depending on the particular plan of a subdivision, owners of unrestricted property may have "a real and actual interest" in the enforcement of restrictions as real rights. C.C.P. art. 681; cf. Salerno v. DeLucca, 211 La. 659, 30 So.2d 678 (1947), involving reservation of certain lots in the subdivision "for business purposes for the convenience of the lot owners."

(d) Building restrictions are ordinarily enforced by actions for injunction brought by the original subdivider or by landowners in a subdivision. Violators may thus be forced to cease activities in contravention of the restrictions or to remove objectionable structures. Gerde v. Simonson Investments, Inc., 251 La. 893, 207 So.2d 360 (1968); Salerno v. DeLucca, 211 La. 659, 30 So.2d 678 (1947). Apart from the injunctive process, however, violators of building restrictions may be sued for damages; and, in case the building restrictions form part of a contract that has been violated, proper parties may have recourse to contractual remedies under the law of conventional obligations. Queensborough Land Co. v. Cazeaux, 136 La. 724, 737, 67 So. 641, 646 (1915). Moreover, if the violation of a restriction fulfills the elements of delictual responsibility for damage to property, if it constitutes an unreasonable use of property, or if it amounts to a disturbance of possession, landowners may demand protection of their property rights under the general law. C.C. arts. 667, 669 (1870); cf. Roche v. St. Romain, 51 So.2d 666 (La.App.Orl.Cir.1951); Talbot v. Stiles, 189 So. 469 (La.App.2d Cir. 1939). See also, C.C. arts. 3454 and 3455; C.C.P. art. 3656; Yiannopoulos, Civil Law Property § 138 (1966).

Art. 780.   Amendment and termination of building restrictions

Building restrictions may be amended, whether such amendment lessens or increases a restriction, or may terminate or be terminated, as provided in the act that establishes them. In the absence of such provision, building restrictions may be amended or terminated for the whole or a part of the restricted area by agreement of owners representing more than one-half of the land area affected by the restrictions, excluding streets and street rights-of-way, if the restrictions have been in effect for at least fifteen years, or by agreement of both owners representing two-thirds of the land area affected and two-thirds of the owners of the land affected by the restrictions, excluding streets and street rights-of-way, if the restrictions have been in effect for more than ten years.

Acts 1977, No. 170, § 1, eff. Jan. 1, 1978. Amended by Acts 1980, No. 310, § 1; Acts 1983, No. 129, § 1; Acts 1999, No. 309, § 1, eff. June 16, 1999.

REVISION COMMENTS—1977

(a) This provision reproduces the substance of R.S. 9:5622, repealed by Acts 1977, No. 170, § 8, effective January 1, 1978. It does not change the law.

(b) Building restrictions may terminate according to terms prescribed in the act that created them. In addition, since building restrictions are likened to predial servitudes, the methods provided in the Louisiana Civil Code of 1870 for the extinction of predial servitudes may be applied by analogy, to the extent that application of these methods is compatible with the notion and function of building restrictions. See C.C. arts. 771–774, this revision; Gerde v. Simonson Investments, Inc., 251 La. 893, 900, 207 So.2d 360, 363 (1968). The ten-year prescription of non-use has been superseded by special legislation establishing a two-year prescriptive period. See Article 781, infra.

Persons imposing building restrictions may, in the exercise of their freedom of will, prescribe rules for termination, provided, of course, that these rules imply nothing contrary to the public order. Thus, provision may be made for termination of the restrictions upon the lapse of a period of time or upon the happening of an event; moreover, provision may be made for termination of the restrictions by agreement among the landowners in whose favor the restrictions are imposed and for the procedures by which this consent is to be obtained. Gerde v. Simonson Investments, Inc., 251 La. 893, 207 So.2d 360 (1968). In the absence of pertinent provisions in the act that imposed the restrictions, landowners representing more than one-half of the land area affected by the restrictions have the right to terminate by agreement restrictions that have been in effect for at least fifteen years. This agreement, in order to affect third persons, must be recorded in the conveyance records of the parish in which the land is located.

Art. 781.   Termination; liberative prescription

No action for injunction or for damages on account of the violation of a building restriction may be brought after two years from the commencement of a noticeable violation. After the lapse of this period, the immovable on which the violation occurred is freed of the restriction that has been violated.

Acts 1977, No. 170, § 1, eff. Jan. 1, 1978.

Revision Comments—1977

(a) This provision is new. It is based on R.S. 9:5622, repealed by Acts 1977, No. 170, § 8, effective January 1, 1978. It does not change the law.

(b) Actions to enjoin or to obtain damages for any violation of building restrictions are subject to a two-year liberative prescription that begins to run upon the commission of a violation. This prescription does not merely bar actions for the enforcement of building restrictions as sui generis real rights; it extinguishes the real right itself in the same way that the prescription of nonuse extinguishes the right of a servitude. Accordingly, any action based on principles of property law would become without object after the completion of the two-year prescriptive period.

(c) Upon completion of the prescription, the restriction is treated as if it never existed on that particular piece of land. See Edwards v. Wiseman, 198 La. 382, 3 So.2d 661 (1941). Determination of the restriction that has been violated is a matter of statutory as well as contractual interpretation. In case restrictions exclude the use of the property for commercial purposes, question may arise whether activities in violation of the restrictions free the property from any limitations relating to commercial use or only from limitations relating to the particular use that has been practiced. Louisiana courts have held that when an owner uses his property for commercial purposes contrary to restrictions during a period in excess of two years, the property is free from any limitation pertaining to commercial activities; the landowner is thus entitled to enlarge his business, and even to conduct a business of a different nature. Chexnayder v. Rogers, 95 So.2d 381 (La.App.Orl.Cir.1957).

(d) Prescription of one type of restriction on a particular lot does not free that lot from other restrictions nor other lots from restrictions of the type that has been violated, unless, of course, there has been a general abandonment of the restrictive plan or of particular restrictions. See Edwards v. Wiseman, 198 La. 382, 3 So.2d 661 (1941); Olivier v. Berggren, 136 So.2d 325 (La.App.4th Cir.1962); Sherrouse Realty Co. v. Marine, 46 So.2d 156 (La.App.2d Cir. 1950).

Art. 782.   Abandonment of plan or of restriction

Building restrictions terminate by abandonment of the whole plan or by a general abandonment of a particular restriction. When the entire plan is abandoned the affected area is freed of all restrictions; when a particular restriction is abandoned, the affected area is freed of that restriction only.

Acts 1977, No. 170, § 1, eff. Jan. 1, 1978.

REVISION COMMENTS—1977

(a) This provision is new. It codifies Louisiana jurisprudence. It does not change the law.

(b) According to Louisiana decisions building restrictions terminate by abandonment of the entire restrictive plan or by a general abandonment of a particular restriction. See Guyton v. Yancey, 240 La. 794, 125 So.2d 365 (1960); Alfortish v. Wagner, 200 La. 198, 7 So.2d 708 (1942); Edwards v. Wiseman, 198 La. 382, 3 So.2d 661 (1941). Abandonment of the entire restrictive plan is ordinarily predicated on a great number of violations of all or most restrictions. Upon abandonment of the entire plan all restrictions fall, and the use of the property is free for all purposes. Abandonment of a particular restriction is predicated on a sufficient number of violations of that restriction in relation to the number of lots affected by it. Thus, if a restriction requires that a building should face a certain street, or should be erected a number of feet from the property line, only violations on property subject to the same restrictions are considered in determining the question of abandonment. When the violations are sufficient in number to warrant the conclusion that a particular restriction has been abandoned, the property is freed of that restriction only. Thus, a change in the neighborhood from residential to commercial does not affect restrictions relating to the setback from property lines. See Alfortish v. Wagner, 200 La. 198, 7 So.2d 708 (1942).

(c) Zoning ordinances neither terminate nor supersede existing building restrictions. See C.C. art. 1945: ". . . [N]o general or special legislative act can be so construed as to avoid or modify a legal contract previously made." See also Alfortish v. Wagner, 200 La. 198, 7 So.2d 708 (1942); Olivier v. Berggren, 136 So.2d 325 (La.App.4th Cir. 1962). For example, the zoning of a restricted residential area as commercial does not prevent the enforcement of existing restrictions; it may merely give rise to an inference that the general plan has been abandoned in the area. Zoning ordinances affecting previously unrestricted areas involve a valid exercise of police power and exclude the freedom of landowners to establish building restrictions that are incompatible with the public acts. See Ransome v. Police Jury of Parish of Jefferson, 216 La. 994, 45 So.2d 601 (1950).

(d) Multiple violations of particular restrictions may, of course, constitute an abandonment of the entire plan.

Art. 783.   Matters of interpretation and application

Doubt as to the existence, validity, or extent of building restrictions is resolved in favor of the unrestricted use of the immovable. The provisions of the Louisiana Condominium Act, the Louisiana Timesharing Act, and the Louisiana Homeowners Association Act shall supersede any and all provisions of this Title in the event of a conflict.

Acts 1977, No. 170, § 1, eff. Jan. 1, 1978. Amended by Acts 1999, No. 309, § 1, eff. June 16, 1999.

REVISION COMMENTS—1977

(a) This provision is new. It codifies Louisiana jurisprudence. It does not change the law.

(b) According to well-settled Louisiana jurisprudence, documents establishing building restrictions are subject to strict interpretation. Any doubt as to the existence, validity, or extent of building restrictions must be resolved, therefore, in favor of the unrestricted use of the property. Thus, when there was doubt as to the intent of a person to impose restrictions, or as to the existence of a general plan, the doubt was resolved in favor of the owner whose property was allegedly restricted. See Fatjo v. Mayer, 247 La. 327, 170 So.2d 859 (1965); Leonard v. Lavigne, 245 La. 1004, 162 So.2d 341 (1964); McGuffy v. Weil, 240 La. 758, 125 So.2d 154 (1960); Salerno v. DeLucca, 211 La. 659, 30 So.2d 678 (1947); Herzberg v. Harrison, 102 So.2d 554 (La.App.1st Cir. 1958).

(c) Apart from the rule of strict interpretation, documents establishing building restrictions are subject to the general rules of the Louisiana Civil Code of 1870 governing the interpretation of juridical acts. Words used are to be understood in the common and usual signification; terms of art or technical phrases are to be interpreted according to their received meaning. Accordingly, if the document provides that the property shall be used for residential purposes only, churches may not be erected; if commercial establishments are excluded, the erection of an advertising billboard sign violates the restriction; and if the document requires that only single residences be erected, multiple dwellings or apartment houses are forbidden. See Yiannopoulos, Real Rights: Limits of Contractual and Testamentary Freedom, 30 La.L.Rev. 44, 73–79 (1969).

TITLE VI—BOUNDARIES

CHAPTER 1—GENERAL PRINCIPLES

Art. 784.   Boundary; marker

A boundary is the line of separation between contiguous lands. A boundary marker is a natural or artificial object that marks on the ground the line of separation of contiguous lands.

Acts 1977, No. 169, § 1, eff. Jan. 1, 1978.

REVISION COMMENTS—1977

(a) This provision is based on Article 826 of the Louisiana Civil Code of 1870. It does not change the law.

(b) The words "boundary" and "bounds" are used loosely in the English text of the Louisiana Civil Code of 1870. In the corresponding French text, however, the word bornes (bounds) refers consistently to boundary markers. The process of fixing and marking the boundary is referred to as bornage. See Lemoin v. Moncla, 9 La.Ann. 515 (1854). In this revision, clear distinction is made between a boundary, which is the line of division between contiguous lands, and markers designating the boundary on the ground.

Art. 785.   Fixing of the boundary

The fixing of the boundary may involve determination of the line of separation between contiguous lands, if it is uncertain or disputed; it may also involve the placement of markers on the ground, if markers were never placed, were wrongly placed, or are no longer to be seen.

The boundary is fixed in accordance with the following rules.

Acts 1977, No. 169, § 1, eff. Jan. 1, 1978.

REVISION COMMENT—1977

This provision reproduces the substance of Article 823 of the Louisiana Civil Code of 1870. It does not change the law.

Art. 786.   Persons who may compel fixing of boundary

The boundary may be fixed upon the demand of an owner or of one who possesses as owner. It may also be fixed upon the demand of a usufructuary but it is not binding upon the naked owner unless he has been made a party to the proceeding.

Acts 1977, No. 169, § 1, eff. Jan. 1, 1978.

REVISION COMMENTS—1977

(a) This provision is based on Articles 823, 829, and 830 of the Louisiana Civil Code of 1870. It does not change the law.

(b) Article 827 of the Louisiana Civil Code of 1870 has not been reproduced as unnecessary.

Art. 787.   Lessee may compel lessor

When necessary to protect his interest, a lessee may compel the lessor to fix the boundary of the land subject to the lease.

Acts 1977, No. 169, § 1, eff. Jan. 1, 1978.

REVISION COMMENT—1977

This provision is based on Article 831 of the Louisiana Civil Code of 1870. It changes the law as it limits the right of the lessee to compel the lessor to fix the boundary of the land subject to the lease "when necessary to protect his interest."

Art. 788.   Imprescriptibility of the right

The right to compel the fixing of the boundary between contiguous lands is imprescriptible.

Acts 1977, No. 169, § 1, eff. Jan. 1, 1978.

REVISION COMMENTS—1977

(a) This provision reproduces the substance of Articles 824 and 825 of the Louisiana Civil Code of 1870. It does not change the law.

(b) The boundary action derives from the same source as the action for partition. For the same reasons that no one is bound to hold an estate in indivision, no one is bound to leave the limits of contiguous estates undetermined. Article 824 of the Louisiana Civil Code of 1870 contains a doctrinal explanation and has not been reproduced.

(c) Liberative prescription does not run against the boundary action. This means that the action may not be dismissed merely on the basis of a peremptory exception of liberative prescription. As one is always permitted to bring an action for partition, likewise one is always permitted to demand that the limits of his property be ascertained.

(d) Article 828 of the Louisiana Civil Code of 1870 has not been reproduced as unnecessary.

Art. 789.   Fixing of boundary judicially or extrajudicially

The boundary may be fixed judicially or extrajudicially. It is fixed extrajudicially when the parties, by written agreement, determine the line of separation between their lands with or without reference to markers on the ground.

Acts 1977, No. 169, § 1, eff. Jan. 1, 1978.

REVISION COMMENTS—1977

(a) This provision is new. It changes the law.

(b) Under this provision, the boundary may be fixed extrajudicially even if one of the adjoining owners is an incompetent. There is no reason why the tutor or curator should not be given authority by the court to proceed to an extrajudicial fixing of the boundary of a minor's or interdict's property.

(c) Owners of contiguous lands may enter into a written agreement designating in it a boundary or line of division between their lands. When recorded, this agreement may be asserted against third persons in the same way as any other agreement affecting immovable property. The effect of such an agreement is to convey ownership to each party up to the designated line. It may, of course, be annulled on account of error or other vices of consent under the applicable provisions of the Civil Code. Such an agreement creates a new boundary. Owners of contiguous lands, however, may also enter into a written agreement designating the boundary between their lands with reference to markers on the ground. They may utilize fences, natural monuments, or other boundary markers.

(d) Articles 834 through 837 of the Louisiana Civil Code of 1870, containing detailed provisions dealing with the duties of the surveyor and surveying procedures have not been reproduced in this revision; they have been replaced by a single provision in the Code of Civil Procedure declaring that the surveyor will fix and mark the boundary on the ground in accordance "with the prevailing standards and practices of his profession." See C.C.P. art. 3692 (1977) infra.

(e) Article 838 has not been reproduced. According to its first sentence, a landowner is forbidden to mark his boundary without notice to the neighbor to be present; according to its second sentence, the operation has no effect in the absence of notice and the contiguous neighbor may have an action for damages that he may have sustained. As a result of the suppression of this article, a landowner may freely mark his boundary; but there should be no doubt that such a marking does not constitute an extrajudicial fixing of the boundary. See Article 789. Moreover, there should be no doubt that the placement of boundary markers by a landowner may constitute a disturbance of possession under Article 3455 of the Civil Code or a wrongful act under Article 2315.

Article 839 has not been reproduced. This article established the notion of a provisional fixing of the boundary by the placement of boundary markers after notice to the owner of contiguous lands to be present and without opposition by him. As a result of the suppression of this provision, there is no longer room for the notion of provisional fixing of boundary. Whether the owner of contiguous lands has been notified to be present or not, and whether there has been opposition or not, the placement of boundary markers by a landowner does not constitute fixing of the boundary.

Articles 840, 841, and 842, have not been reproduced as unnecessary. Article 840 provides for venue; the matter is covered by Article 80 of the Code of Civil Procedure. Article 841 provides for the appointment of a surveyor by the court; the matter is covered by Article 3692 of the Code of Civil Procedure. And finally, Article 842 provides for continuation of a boundary action in case of partition or alienation of one of the contiguous lands; the matter is covered by the rules of the Code of Civil Procedure concerning substitution of parties.

Art. 790.   Costs

When the boundary is fixed extrajudicially costs are divided equally between the adjoining owners in the absence of contrary agreement. When the boundary is fixed judicially court costs are taxed in accordance with the rules of the Code of Civil Procedure. Expenses of litigation not taxed as court costs are borne by the person who has incurred them.

Acts 1977, No. 169, § 1, eff. Jan. 1, 1978.

REVISION COMMENTS—1977

(a) This provision is based on Article 663 of the Louisiana Civil Code of 1870. It does not change the law.

(b) According to well settled Louisiana jurisprudence, costs incurred in fixing boundaries are divided equally between the adjoining proprietors by application of Article 663 of the Louisiana Civil Code of 1870 only when there is an amicable settlement. In case of litigation, costs are apportioned equitably. Thus, the costs may be borne by a defendant who unjustifiably refused to cooperate with plaintiff toward an amicable settlement: Authement v. Theriot, 292 So.2d 319 (La.App. 1st Cir. 1974); Arnaud v. Barber, 225 So.2d 656 (La.App. 3d Cir. 1969); Miley v. Walker, 159 So.2d 38 (La.App. 1st Cir. 1964); Lirette v. Duplantis, 65 So.2d 639 (La.App. 1st Cir. 1953). The costs may also be borne by an unsuccessful plaintiff: Savoie v. Savoy, 262 So.2d 582 (La.App. 3d Cir. 1972); or they may be equally divided between the parties: Girard v. Donlon, 127 So.2d 761 (La.App. 3d Cir. 1961); Sharpless v. Adkins, 22 So.2d 692 (La.App. 2d Cir. 1945). Cf. 2 Toullier, Droit civil français 50 (1833).

Art. 791.   Liability for unauthorized removal of markers

When the boundary has been marked judicially or extrajudicially, one who removes boundary markers without court authority is liable for damages. He may also be compelled to restore the markers to their previous location.

Acts 1977, No. 169, § 1, eff. Jan. 1, 1978.

REVISION COMMENT—1977

This provision reproduces the substance of Article 855 of the Louisiana Civil Code of 1870. It does not change the law.

CHAPTER 2—EFFECT OF TITLES, PRESCRIPTION, OR POSSESSION

Art. 792.   Fixing of boundary according to ownership or possession

The court shall fix the boundary according to the ownership of the parties; if neither party proves ownership, the boundary shall be fixed according to limits established by possession.

Acts 1977, No. 169, § 1, eff. Jan. 1, 1978.

REVISION COMMENTS—1977

(a) This provision is based on Article 845 of the Louisiana Civil Code of 1870. It does not change the law.

(b) According to Article 786, supra, the boundary action may be brought by one who possesses as owner against the possessor of adjoining lands. If the parties do not set up titles or rights under acquisitive prescription, the boundary is fixed along the lines established by possession.

(c) Prior to 1960, Louisiana courts had held that questions of title and ownership could not be determined in an action of boundary. This jurisprudence has been overruled legislatively by Article 3693 of the Louisiana Code of Civil Procedure. See Ledoux v. Waterbury, 292 So.2d 485 (La.1974).

(d) Articles 843 and 844 of the Louisiana Civil Code of 1870 have not been reproduced as unnecessary.

Art. 793. Determination of ownership according to titles

When both parties rely on titles only, the boundary shall be fixed according to titles. When the parties trace their titles to a common author preference shall be given to the more ancient title.

Acts 1977, No. 169, § 1, eff. Jan. 1, 1978.

REVISION COMMENTS—1977

(a) This provision is based on Articles 845, 846, 847, and 848 of the Louisiana Civil Code of 1870. It does not change the law.

(b) Articles 849, 850, 851 of the Louisiana Civil Code of 1870 have not been reproduced as unnecessary.

(c) The reference in Article 793 to "title" incorporates the recordation requirements of the public records doctrine. See C.C. arts. 2264, 2266, and McDuffie v. Walker, 125 La. 152, 51 So. 100 (La.1909).

Art. 794. Determination of ownership according to prescription

When a party proves acquisitive prescription, the boundary shall be fixed according to limits established by prescription rather than titles. If a party and his ancestors in title possessed for thirty years without interruption, within visible bounds, more land than their title called for, the boundary shall be fixed along these bounds.

Acts 1977, No. 169, § 1, eff. Jan. 1, 1978.

REVISION COMMENTS—1977

(a) This provision is based on Article 852 of the Louisiana Civil Code of 1870. It does not change the law. Articles 846, 847, and 851 of the Louisiana Civil Code of 1870 indicate that acquisitive prescription takes precedence over claims based on titles. The first sentence of Article 794 is an expedient for the avoidance of repetitious statements.

(b) According to Louisiana jurisprudence, prescription accrues under Article 852 of the Civil Code even if there is no juridical link among the possessors. Opdenwyer v. Brown, 155 La. 617, 99 So. 482 (1924); Ponder v. Fussell, 180 So.2d 413 (La.App.1st Cir. 1965).

(c) According to Article 3693 of the Louisiana Code of Civil Procedure, "Title prescriptions may be pled in boundary actions, and boundary prescriptions in title suits." Ledoux v. Waterbury, 292 So.2d 485 (La.1974).

Art. 795. Effect of boundary agreement

When the boundary is fixed extrajudicially, the agreement of the parties has the effect of a compromise.

Acts 1977, No. 169, § 1, eff. Jan. 1, 1978.

(a) This provision is new. It changes the law as it suppresses Article 853 of the Louisiana Civil Code of 1870.

(b) The boundary is fixed extrajudicially when parties determine, by written agreement, the line of separation between contiguous lands with or without reference to markers on the ground. Article 789, supra. Thus, owners of contiguous lands may determine the line of separation on paper and then proceed to have it marked on the ground; or they may mark the boundary on the ground and then determine the line of separation with reference to the markers. In either case, the agreement is an act translative of ownership and has the effect of a compromise. Ownership is conveyed, respectively, up to the line fixed by the agreement. If the parties or the surveyor committed an error in the location of the line of separation, or the markers, or both, the error may be rectified by the court unless the agreement is no longer assailable as a result of the ten year liberative prescription. The fixing of the boundary does not preclude the running of acquisitive prescription in favor of an adverse possessor. For example, one of the owners of contiguous lands may disregard the boundary agreement and possess within visible bounds without interruption for thirty years. In such a case, prescription takes precedence over the boundary agreement.

(c) When parties merely determine on paper the line of separation between contiguous lands, either of them may subsequently demand that the line be marked on the ground in accordance with the agreement. If markers are wrongly placed, that is, not in accordance with the previous agreement, the error may be rectified by the court unless the thirty year acquisitive prescription has accrued in favor of a neighbor. See Article 796, infra. In such a case, liberative prescription is immaterial because the placement of markers on the ground is not a contract. But when the owners of contiguous lands agree again that the markers, as placed, shall constitute the boundary, their agreement has the effect of a compromise. Accordingly, the error may be rectified by the court unless the agreement is no longer assailable as a result of the ten year liberative prescription. See Article 795.

(d) The action to rectify the boundary lies only when it has been fixed extrajudicially; "for if judicially fixed, the question of boundaries is then merged in the judgment, and becomes res judicata; which judgment, like any other, cannot be attacked for error but only for fraud, and then only within one year." Opdenwyer v. Brown, 155 La. 617, 99 So. 482 (1924). See also Brownson v. Richard, 11 La. 414 (1837).

(e) Article 853 of the Louisiana Civil Code of 1870 has been interpreted by three lines of decisions. According to the first, the ten year prescription applies even in the absence of a survey made by a surveyor if the parties placed visible bounds and actively acquiesced for many years. Morris v. Prutsman, 7 La.App. 404 (La.App.1st Cir. 1928); cf. Opdenwyer v. Brown, 155 La. 617, 99 So. 482 (1924) (dicta). According to the second line, the ten year prescription applies when the lines are fixed by a survey even though the surveyor did not comply with all requisite formalities, provided the parties actively acquiesced in the boundary for the requisite period of time. La Calle v. Chapman, 174 So.2d 668 (La.App. 3rd Cir. 1965); cf. Sessum v. Hemperley, 233 La. 444, 96 So.2d 832 (1957) (dicta). Finally, it has been held that the ten year prescription is available only when the lines are fixed by a survey conducted in accordance with all the requisite formalities. Fiorello v. Knecht, 334 So.2d 761 (La.App. 4th Cir. 1976); Harvey v. Havard, 225 So.2d 615 (La.App.1st Cir. 1969); cf. Pan American Prod. Co. v. Robichaux, 200 La. 666, 8 So.2d 635 (1942).

In this revision, Article 853 of the Louisiana Civil Code of 1870 has been suppressed. There is no longer ten year acquisitive prescription by possession under an erroneous or formally defective survey. If the survey has become part of the agreement of the parties, the error of the surveyor in the location of the line of separation is the error of the parties. This error may be rectified unless the ten year liberative prescription has accrued. If the survey has not become a part of the agreement of the parties, the error of the surveyor is immaterial insofar as ten year acquisitive prescription is concerned.

Art. 796.   Error in the location of markers; rectification

When visible markers have been erroneously placed by one of the contiguous owners alone, or not in accordance with a written agreement fixing the boundary, the error may be rectified by the court unless a contiguous owner has acquired ownership up to the visible bounds by thirty years possession.

Acts 1977, No. 169, § 1, eff. Jan. 1, 1978.

REVISION COMMENTS—1977

(a) This provision is based on Article 852 of the Louisiana Civil Code of 1870. It does not change the law.

(b) Under this provision, an action for the correction of the boundary may be brought more than ten years after the location of boundary markers. There is no ten year liberative prescription running because the acquiescence in the location of the bounds does not constitute a contract. Cf. Pan American Prod. Co. v. Robichaux, 200 La. 666, 8 So.2d 635 (1942).

(c) Article 854 of the Louisiana Civil Code of 1870 has not been reproduced as unnecessary.

(d) When markers are placed by one of the contiguous owners alone, or by two contiguous owners without a written agreement, the boundary is not fixed. A demand for a judicial or extrajudicial fixing of the boundary may, therefore, be proper. If one of the contiguous owners has possessed, however, within visible bounds without interruption for thirty years, the boundary shall be fixed according to lines established by prescription. See Article 794, supra. In this revision, the mere passive failure of a contiguous owner to object to the location of a fence or other marker, or the informal acquiescence by the contiguous owners to a jointly erected fence, does not constitute a fixing of the boundary.

(e) When parties merely determine on paper the line of separation between contiguous lands, and markers are subsequently placed on the ground not in accordance with the agreement, the error may be rectified by the court unless a contiguous owner has acquired ownership up to the visible bounds by thirty years' possession. The words "or not in accordance with a written agreement fixing the boundary" necessarily contemplate a fixing of the boundary on paper, that is, without reference to markers on the ground.

TITLE VII—OWNERSHIP IN INDIVISION

Art. 797.   Ownership in indivision; definition

Ownership of the same thing by two or more persons is ownership in indivision. In the absence of other provisions of law or juridical act, the shares of all co-owners are presumed to be equal.

Added by Acts 1990, No. 990, § 1, eff. Jan. 1, 1991.

REVISION COMMENTS—1990

(a) This provision is new. It expresses the premise underlying Civil Code Article 480 (Rev.1979). There are corresponding provisions in modern civil codes. See, e.g., Greek Civil Code Art. 785; Swiss Civil Code Art. 646; Italian Civil Code Art. 1101.

(b) For community property as a distinct species of co-ownership, see C.C. Art. 2336 (Rev.1979), Comment (a); Spaht, Developments in the Law, Matrimonial Regimes, 48 La.L.Rev. 371, 375–76 (1987).

(c) For co-ownership under the Louisiana Condominium Act, see R.S. 9:1121.101–1124.115. For time-sharing, see R.S. 9:1131.1–1131.30.

(d) Ownership in indivision is the only type of co-ownership that Louisiana law recognizes. See La. Civil Code Art. 480 (Rev.1979); State v. Executors of McDonogh, 8 La.Ann. 171, 251 (1853): "The general idea of property under the Roman law, and under our system, is that of simple, uniform and absolute dominion. The subordinate exceptions of use, usufruct, and servitudes are abundantly sufficient to meet all the wants of civilization, and there is no warrant of law, no reason of policy, for the introduction of any other." Joint tenures and the common law doctrine of estates are not recognized in Louisiana. See Succession of Grigsby, 219 So.2d 832 (La.App. 2d Cir.1969), writ refused 254 La. 10; 222 So.2d 65 (La.1969); Yiannopoulos, Civil Law Property § 148 (2d ed. 1980); Harrell, "Problems Created by Co-ownership in Louisiana," in 32 Institute on Mineral Law 381, 382–384 (1985).

Art. 798.   Right to fruits and products

Co-owners share the fruits and products of the thing held in indivision in proportion to their ownership.

When fruits or products are produced by a co-owner, other co-owners are entitled to their shares of the fruits or products after deduction of the costs of production.

Added by Acts 1990, No. 990, § 1, eff. Jan. 1, 1991.

REVISION COMMENTS—1990

(a) This provision is new. It expresses principles inherent in the Louisiana Civil Code of 1870.

(b) Fruits defined in Civil Code Articles 551 and 552 (Rev.1976). They are things that are produced by or derived from another thing without diminution of its substance. In contrast, products are things that are produced by or derived from a thing as a result of the diminution of its substance. See Civil Code Art. 488 (Rev.1979); Yiannopoulos, Civil Law Property §§ 24, 28 (2d ed. 1980). For a discussion of fruits and products in the framework of community property legislation, see Civil Code Arts. 2338, 2339 (Rev.1979).

(c) The second paragraph of this Article is a specification of the principles expressed in Civil Code Articles 485 and 488 (Rev. 1979). A co-owner does not have the right to claim compensation for his own labor or services. Nevertheless, he may be entitled to such compensation under the law of unjust enrichment.

Art. 799.   Liability of a co-owner

A co-owner is liable to his co-owner for any damage to the thing held in indivision caused by his fault.

Added by Acts 1990, No. 990, § 1, eff. Jan. 1, 1991.

This provision is new. It expresses a principle inherent in the Louisiana Civil Code of 1870. Cf. C.C. Arts. 576 (Rev.1976) and 2315 (1870).

Art. 800.   Preservation of the thing

A co-owner may without the concurrence of any other co-owner take necessary steps for the preservation of the thing that is held in indivision.

Added by Acts 1990, No. 990, § 1, eff. Jan. 1, 1991.

This provision is new. It expresses the principle that necessary steps for the preservation of the thing held in indivision may be taken by any of the co-owners acting alone. This is not unauthorized management of the affairs of another under Civil Code Article 2295 (1870). For the distinction between conservatory acts, acts of administration, and acts of disposition, see Yiannopoulos, Personal Servitudes § 37 (2d ed. 1978); Baudry-Lacantinerie, Traite Theorique et pratique de droit civil, III Supplement by Bonnecase 630–686 (1926).

Art. 801.   Use and management by agreement

The use and management of the thing held in indivision is determined by agreement of all the co-owners.

Added by Acts 1990, No. 990, § 1, eff. Jan. 1, 1991.

This provision is new. It expresses, however, a principle that is inherent in the Louisiana Civil Code of 1870.

Art. 802.   Right to use the thing

Except as otherwise provided in Article 801, a co-owner is entitled to use the thing held in indivision according to its destination, but he cannot prevent another co-owner from making such use of it. As against third persons, a co-owner has the right to use and enjoy the thing as if he were the sole owner.

Added by Acts 1990, No. 990, § 1, eff. Jan. 1, 1991.

(a) This provision is new. It expresses principles inherent in the Louisiana Civil Code of 1870.

(b) For the use of the family residence and of community movables and immovables after the filing of a petition for separation of divorce, see R.S. 9:308.

(c) Civil Code Article 477 (Rev.1979) declares that ownership confers direct, immediate, and exclusive authority over a thing and that the owner "may use, enjoy, and dispose of it within the limits and under the conditions established by law." Articles 800, 801, and 802 (supra) work modifications on the terms of Civil Code Article 477 (Rev.1979) in the light of the interests of all the co-owners. Thus a co-owner has neither a right to exclusive use nor a right to dispose of the thing without the consent of his co-owners. However, as against third persons, a co-owner has the right to use and enjoy the thing as if he were its sole owner. For example, a co-owner may alone take all the necessary steps for the preservation of the property, including the institution of suits against trespassers or usurpers.

Art. 803.   Use and management of the thing in the absence of agreement

When the mode of use and management of the thing held in indivision is not determined by an agreement of all the co-owners and partition is not available, a court, upon petition by a co-owner, may determine the use and management.

Added by Acts 1990, No. 990, § 1, eff. Jan. 1, 1991.

REVISION COMMENTS—1990

(a) This provision is new. It changes the law as it authorizes the court to determine the most suitable mode of use and management of the thing held in indivision when partition is not available, and the mode of use and management is not determined by an agreement of all co-owners.

(b) Since under R.S. 9:1112 and 9:1702, the state of indivision may last up to fifteen years, this Article will have a useful function.

Art. 804. Substantial alterations or improvements

Substantial alterations or substantial improvements to the thing held in indivision may be undertaken only with the consent of all the co-owners.

When a co-owner makes substantial alterations or substantial improvements consistent with the use of the property, though without the express or implied consent of his co-owners, the rights of the parties shall be determined by Article 496. When a co-owner makes substantial alterations or substantial improvements inconsistent with the use of the property or in spite of the objections of his co-owners, the rights of the parties shall be determined by Article 497.

Added by Acts 1990, No. 990, § 1, eff. Jan. 1, 1991.

REVISION COMMENT—1990

The first paragraph of this provision is new. It expresses a principle inherent in the Louisiana Civil Code of 1870.

Art. 805. Disposition of undivided share

A co-owner may freely lease, alienate, or encumber his share of the thing held in indivision. The consent of all the co-owners is required for the lease, alienation, or encumbrance of the entire thing held in indivision.

Added by Acts 1990, No. 990, § 1, eff. Jan. 1, 1991.

REVISION COMMENT—1990

This provision is new. It expresses a principle inherent in the Louisiana Civil Code of 1870.

Art. 806. Expenses of maintenance and management

A co-owner who on account of the thing held in indivision has incurred necessary expenses, expenses for ordinary maintenance and repairs, or necessary management expenses paid to a third person, is entitled to reimbursement from the other co-owners in proportion to their shares.

If the co-owner who incurred the expenses had the enjoyment of the thing held in indivision, his reimbursement shall be reduced in proportion to the value of the enjoyment.

Added by Acts 1990, No. 990, § 1, eff. Jan. 1, 1991.

REVISION COMMENTS—1990

(a) This provision is new. It expresses principles inherent in the Louisiana Civil Code of 1870.

(b) Under this provision, a co-owner is responsible to his co-owners for his share of necessary expenses. For the definition of such expenses, and their distinction from useful and luxurious expenses, see La. Civil Code Art. 527 and 528 (Rev.1979), and 2314 Repealed 1979; Yiannopoulos, Civil Law Property § 197 (2d ed. 1980).

(c) Under this provision, a co-owner is responsible to his co-owners for his share of necessary management expenses paid to a third person. A co-owner is not allowed to receive anything for his own management of the thing that is held in indivision unless he is entitled to such a recovery under a management plan adopted by agreement of all the co-owners, by judgment, or under the law of unjust enrichment.

Art. 807.   Right to partition; exclusion by agreement

No one may be compelled to hold a thing in indivision with another unless the contrary has been provided by law or juridical act.

Any co-owner has a right to demand partition of a thing held in indivision. Partition may be excluded by agreement for up to fifteen years, or for such other period as provided in R.S. 9:1702 or other specific law.

Added by Acts 1990, No. 990, § 1, eff. Jan. 1, 1991. Amended by Acts 1991, No. 349, § 1.

REVISION COMMENT—1990

This provision is new. It restates, however, rules contained in Civil Code Articles 1289 and 1303 (1870).

Art. 808.   Partition excluded

Partition of a thing held in indivision is excluded when its use is indispensable for the enjoyment of another thing owned by one or more of the co-owners.

Added by Acts 1990, No. 990, § 1, eff. Jan. 1, 1991.

REVISION COMMENT—1990

This provision is new. It is based on Article 1303 of the Louisiana Civil Code of 1870.

Art. 809.   Judicial and extrajudicial partition

The mode of partition may be determined by agreement of all the co-owners. In the absence of such an agreement, a co-owner may demand judicial partition.

Added by Acts 1990, No. 990, § 1, eff. Jan. 1, 1991.

REVISION COMMENTS—1990

(a) This provision is new. However, it is based on Articles 1294, 1322, and 1323 of the Louisiana Civil Code of 1870. It does not change the law.

(b) The word "mode" in this provision means the form, kind, or incidents of partition. This word must be given a broad interpretation.

Art. 810.   Partition in kind

The court shall decree partition in kind when the thing held in indivision is susceptible to division into as many lots of nearly equal value as there are shares and the aggregate value of all lots is not significantly lower than the value of the property in the state of indivision.

Added by Acts 1990, No. 990, § 1, eff. Jan. 1, 1991.

REVISION COMMENT—1990

This provision restates the principle of Article 1340 of the Louisiana Civil Code of 1870. It does not change the law. See Yiannopoulos, Civil Law Property § 20 (2d ed. 1980).

Art. 811.   Partition by licitation or by private sale

When the thing held in indivision is not susceptible to partition in kind, the court shall decree a partition by licitation or by private sale and the proceeds shall be distributed to the co-owners in proportion to their shares.

Added by Acts 1990, No. 990, § 1, eff. Jan. 1, 1991.

REVISION COMMENTS—1990

(a) This provision is new. Its purpose is to clarify the law.

(b) Partition by licitation is a sale of a thing held in indivision, with the proceeds of the sale divided among the co-owners in proportion to their shares. If the sale of the thing to a third person is excluded by previous agreement, an auction is conducted among the co-owners.

Art. 812.   Effect of partition on real rights

When a thing held in indivision is partitioned in kind or by licitation, a real right burdening the thing is not affected.

Added by Acts 1990, No. 990, § 1, eff. Jan. 1, 1991.

REVISION COMMENTS—1990

(a) This provision is new. It expresses a principle inherent in the Louisiana Civil Code of 1870. Cf. La.Civil Code Art. 542 (Rev.1976).

(b) When a thing held in indivision is burdened with a real right, such as a personal servitude, a predial servitude, or a mortgage, a partition, whether in kind or by licitation, is without effect on the real right. Despite the partition, the real right continues to exist and to burden the property. A residential or predial lease is a personal right according to Louisiana jurisprudence. However, if properly recorded, such a lease may function as a real right and may be asserted against third persons. See Yiannopoulos, Civil Law Property § 158 (2d ed. 1980).

(c) When the share of a co-owner is burdened with a right of a third person, questions may arise as to the effect of a partition on that right. Since the share of a co-owner in a thing held in indivision is an incorporeal, movable or immovable, such a share cannot be burdened with a predial servitude or a conventional mortgage. See La.Civil Code Arts. 698 (Rev.1977) and 3289(1) (1870). However, a share in a thing held in indivision may be burdened with a mortgage in accordance with special legislation. See La.Civil Code Art. 2389(5) (1870). It may also be burdened with a usufruct or a pledge. Finally, liens and privileges may attach to the share of a co-owner rather than the thing held in indivision. In all cases, the partition of the thing held in indivision is without effect on real rights burdening the share of a co-owner. See Article 813, infra.

(d) A real right is a dismemberment of ownership, such as a usufruct, a predial servitude, a right of use servitude, or a real mortgage. See Yiannopoulos, Civil Law Property § 134 (2d. ed. 1980).

Art. 813.   Partition in kind

When a thing is partitioned in kind, a real right that burdens the share of a co-owner attaches to the part of the thing allotted to him.

Added by Acts 1990, No. 990, § 1, eff. Jan. 1, 1991.

REVISION COMMENTS—1990

(a) This provision is new. It is based on Articles 1338 and 1383 of the Louisiana Civil Code of 1870.

(b) When a thing burdened with a real right is partitioned, whether in kind or by licitation, and whether judicially or extrajudicially, the partition is without effect on the real right. See Article 812, supra. Article 813 contemplates the situation of a real right burdening the share of a co-owner rather than the thing held in indivision. In such a case, if the thing is partitioned in kind, the real right attaches to the part allotted to the co-owner whose share was burdened with such a right.

Art. 814.   Rescission of partition for lesion

An extrajudicial partition may be rescinded on account of lesion if the value of the part received by a co-owner is less by more than one-fourth of the fair market value of the portion he should have received.

Added by Acts 1990, No. 990, § 1, eff. Jan. 1, 1991.

REVISION COMMENTS—1990

(a) This provision reproduces the substance of Article 1398 of the Louisiana Civil Code of 1870. It does not change the law.

(b) This provision establishes a co-owner's right to the rescission of an extrajudicial partition in case the value of the part received by him is less by more than one-fourth of the fair market value of the portion he should have received. For the rest, rules governing rescission of a sale on account of lesion apply. See C.C. Arts. 2589–2600 (1870).

Art. 815.   Partition by licitation

When a thing is partitioned by licitation, a mortgage, lien, or privilege that burdens the share of a co-owner attaches to his share of the proceeds of the sale.

Added by Acts 1990, No. 990, § 1, eff. Jan. 1, 1991.

REVISION COMMENTS—1990

(a) The provision is new. It is based on Article 1338 of the Louisiana Civil Code of 1870. But cf. R.S. 9:5031, 5251.

(b) This provision does not apply when a co-owner has consented to the establishment of a predial servitude on his undivided share or on the entire estate. In such a case, upon partition by licitation, the right granted by a co-owner may be extinguished or it may burden the whole of the estate. See La.Civil Code Art. 718 (Rev.1977).

Art. 816.   Partition in kind; warranty

When a thing is partitioned in kind, each co-owner incurs the warranty of a vendor toward his co-owners to the extent of his share.

Added by Acts 1990, No. 990, § 1, eff. Jan. 1, 1991.

REVISION COMMENT—1990

This provision is new. It is based on Articles 1384, 1385, and 2501 of the Louisiana Civil Code of 1870.

Art. 817.   Imprescriptibility of action

The action for partition is imprescriptible.

Added by Acts 1990, No. 990, § 1, eff. Jan. 1, 1991.

REVISION COMMENT—1990

This provision reproduces the substance of Article 1304 of the Louisiana Civil Code of 1870. It does not change the law.

Art. 818.   Other rights held in indivision

The provisions governing co-ownership apply to other rights held in indivision to the extent compatible with the nature of those rights.

Added by Acts 1990, No. 990, § 1, eff. Jan. 1, 1991.

REVISION COMMENT—1990

Not only ownership but other real rights as well as possession may be held in indivision. For example, the right of usufruct may belong to several usufructuaries and a predial servitude may be established in favor of several estates belonging to several owners. In such a case, the provisions governing co-ownership will apply to the right held in indivision to the extent that their application is compatible with the nature of that right. Of course, provisions dealing directly with the usufruct held in common will take precedence as special law. Cf. C.C. Arts. 541–543 (Rev.1976). For servitudes established by a co-owner, see C.C. Arts. 714–719 (Rev.1977); Yiannopoulos, Predial Servitudes § 116 (1983).

Arts. 819 to 869.   [Blank]

BOOK III—OF THE DIFFERENT MODES OF ACQUIRING THE OWNERSHIP OF THINGS

PRELIMINARY TITLE— GENERAL DISPOSITIONS

Art. 870.   Modes of acquiring ownership

A.   The ownership of things or property is acquired by succession either testate or intestate, by the effect of obligations, and by the operation of law.

B.   Testate and intestate succession rights, including the right to claim as a forced heir, are governed by the law in effect on the date of the decedent's death.

Acts 1981, No. 919, § 1, eff. Jan. 1, 1982. Amended by Acts 2001, No. 560, § 1, eff. June 22, 2001.

REVISION COMMENT—1981

This provision is based on Article 870 of the Louisiana Civil Code of 1870. It simply reflects that the category of irregular successions is eliminated in this revision, and describes the process by which one acquires ownership as either testate or intestate succession. It makes no substantive change in the law.

TITLE I—OF SUCCESSIONS

CHAPTER 1—OF THE DIFFERENT SORTS OF SUCCESSIONS AND SUCCESSORS

Art. 871. Meaning of succession

Succession is the transmission of the estate of the deceased to his successors. The successors thus have the right to take possession of the estate of the deceased after complying with applicable provisions of law.

Acts 1981, No. 919, § 1, eff. Jan. 1, 1982.

REVISION COMMENT—1981

This provision combines two of the meanings of "succession" in the Civil Code of 1870. It is intended to establish that the word "succession" means the process by which heirs and legatees succeed to the property of the deceased. Since the property is transmitted immediately upon death to the proper successors, it follows that they have a right to possession after complying with appropriate procedural requisites. This revision, together with the next article, is intended to eliminate the meaning of "succession" which describes the "estate" of the deceased as if it were a separate legal entity.

Art. 872. Meaning of estate

The estate of a deceased means the property, rights, and obligations that a person leaves after his death, whether the property exceeds the charges or the charges exceed the property, or whether he has only left charges without any property. The estate includes not only the rights and obligations of the deceased as they exist at the time of death, but all that has accrued thereto since death, and the new charges to which it becomes subject.

Acts 1981, No. 919, § 1, eff. Jan. 1, 1982.

REVISION COMMENT—1981

This provision combines two articles of the Civil Code of 1870 without substantive change. It permits reference to the "estate" of the deceased as defined, but grants no separate legal existence to such an entity.

Art. 873. Kinds of succession

There are two kinds of succession: testate and intestate.

Acts 1981, No. 919, § 1, eff. Jan. 1, 1982.

REVISION COMMENTS—1981

(a) The use of the singular of "succession" in this article is intentional. A person succeeds to the right of the deceased in a particular portion of his patrimony, either due to testate or intestate rights. The "estate" itself might be neither wholly "testate" nor wholly "intestate."

(b) The general revision of the intestate succession articles makes the distinction between legal and irregular successions contained in Article 875 of the Civil Code of 1870 obsolete.

Art. 874. Testate succession

Testate succession results from the will of the deceased, contained in a testament executed in a form prescribed by law. This kind of succession is covered under the Title: Of donations inter vivos and mortis causa.

Acts 1981, No. 919, § 1, eff. Jan. 1, 1982.

(a) This is a revision of Article 876 of the Civil Code of 1870 without substantive change.

(b) The institution of an heir, known to the Roman law, was the rough equivalent of establishing a universal legatee. The position of succession representative and the procedure for administering succession under the Code of Civil Procedure have limited the importance of "institution of heir" to the point that there is little reason to continue its use. The term is accordingly suppressed in this revision.

Art. 875.   Intestate succession

Intestate succession results from provisions of law in favor of certain persons, in default of testate successors. Intestate succession is the subject of the present title.

Acts 1981, No. 919, § 1, eff. Jan. 1, 1982.

(a) This is a revision of Articles 877 and 878 of the Civil Code of 1870 without substantive change.

(b) The word "successors" replaces "heirs either legal or instituted by testament". "Successors" is a broader term which will include both heirs and legatees. "Successor" was also used in the Civil Code of 1870 in Article 884, as a translation of the French word successeur.

Art. 876.   Kinds of successors

There are two kinds of successors corresponding to the two kinds of succession described in the preceding articles:

Testate successors, also called legatees.

Intestate successors, also called heirs.

Acts 1981, No. 919, § 1, eff. Jan. 1, 1982.

(a) This is a parallel provision to the article dividing rights of succession into testate and intestate. It replaces Article 879 of the Civil Code of 1870, which established three types of heirs.

(b) Articles 880, 884 and 885 of the Civil Code of 1870 are repealed without the enactment of any similar provisions.

Article 880 appeared to serve no purpose. It had no counterpart in either the Code Napoleon or the Digest of 1808. It also has no counterpart in the draft of the Quebec Civil Code. It appears that the article was only cited in two Louisiana cases. In Succession of Farley, 205 La. 972, 18 So.2d 586 (1944), the article was cited only in passing, and then for the purpose of showing that certain defendants had no interest as "heirs" of a living person to object to the form of an authentic act. They were only "presumptive heirs".

In Crawford v. Puckett, 14 La.Ann. 639 (1859), certain property had been given to "the heirs of William George." George was living at the time, and apparently also had one minor child at the time. Subsequently, George sold the property to defendant. Plaintiff, on behalf of all the minor children of George (some born since the gift), sued defendant to recover the property. The court held that although nemo est hoeres viventis (no one is heir to a living person), Article 880 required that the gift be interpreted as made to the living minor child of George. It thus concluded that the sale by George was invalid. Such a gift may still present problems, but they can be solved in articles on interpretation of legacies. Article 880 need not be retained to solve this type of problem. The concept of "nearest in degree" is retained in Article 899, infra.

Article 884 of the Civil Code of 1870 contained the concept of "instituted heir," which is suppressed in this revision.

Article 885 of the Civil Code of 1870 was clearly inaccurate, in light of the differing treatments given to separate and community property. At the time it was written, the article was correct, since prior to 1844 there were no special rules for former community property. See Acts 1844, No. 152, RCC (1870), Arts. 915, 916.

Arts. 877 to 879.   [Blank]

CHAPTER 2—OF INTESTATE SUCCESSION

Art. 880.   Intestate succession

In the absence of valid testamentary disposition, the undisposed property of the deceased devolves by operation of law in favor of his descendants, ascendants, and collaterals, by blood or by adoption, and in favor of his spouse not judicially separated from him, in the order provided in and according to the following articles.

Acts 1981, No. 919, § 1, eff. Jan. 1, 1982.

REVISION COMMENTS—1981

(a) This is a revision of Articles 886 and 887 of the Civil Code of 1870. It reflects the deletion of the concept of institution of heir.

(b) The heirs succeed even when there is a valid testament to any portion of the property not disposed of by the testament, due to caducity of a legacy or simple omission, for example.

(c) Once a relationship is proven by blood or adoption, the succession rights of such a relative are established without reference to the legitimacy of that relationship.

(d) Under this article the spouse is simply an intestate successor, not an "irregular" heir as under the Civil Code of 1870.

Art. 881.   Representation: effect

Representation is a fiction of the law, the effect of which is to put the representative in the place, degree, and rights of the person represented.

Acts 1981, No. 919, § 1, eff. Jan. 1, 1982.

REVISION COMMENT—1981

This is a reenactment of Article 894 of the Civil Code of 1870 without change.

Art. 882.   Representation in direct line of descendants

Representation takes place ad infinitum in the direct line of descendants. It is permitted in all cases, whether the children of the deceased concur with the descendants of the predeceased child, or whether, all the children having died before him, the descendants of the children be in equal or unequal degrees of relationship to the deceased. For purposes of forced heirship, representation takes place only as provided in Article 1493.

Acts 1981, No. 919, § 1, eff. Jan. 1, 1982. Amended by Acts 1990, No. 147, § 1, eff. July 1, 1990; Acts 1995, No. 1180, § 1, eff. Jan. 1, 1996.

REVISION COMMENT—1981

This is a reenactment of Article 895 of the Civil Code of 1870 without substantive change.

Art. 883.   Representation of ascendants not permissible

Representation does not take place in favor of the ascendants, the nearest relation in any degree always excluding those of a more remote degree.

Acts 1981, No. 919, § 1, eff. Jan. 1, 1982.

REVISION COMMENT—1981

This is a reenactment of Article 896 of the Civil Code of 1870 without substantive change.

Art. 884.   Representation in collateral line

In the collateral line, representation is permitted in favor of the children and descendants of the brothers and sisters of the deceased, whether they succeed in concurrence with their uncles and aunts, or whether, the brothers and sisters of the deceased having died, their descendants succeed in equal or unequal degrees.

Acts 1981, No. 919, § 1, eff. Jan. 1, 1982.

REVISION COMMENT—1981

This is a reenactment of Article 897 of the Civil Code of 1870 without substantive change.

Art. 885.   Basis of partition in cases of representation

In all cases in which representation is permitted, the partition is made by roots; if one root has produced several branches, the subdivision is also made by roots in each branch, and the members of the same branch take by heads.

Acts 1981, No. 919, § 1, eff. Jan. 1, 1982.

REVISION COMMENT—1981

This is a reenactment of Article 898 of the Civil Code of 1870 without substantive change.

Art. 886.   Representation of deceased persons only

Only deceased persons may be represented.

Acts 1981, No. 919, § 1, eff. Jan. 1, 1982.

REVISION COMMENT—1981

This is a reenactment of Article 899 of the Civil Code of 1870 without substantive change.

Art. 887.   Representation of decedent whose succession was renounced

One who has renounced his right to succeed to another may still enjoy the right of representation with respect to that other.

Acts 1981, No. 919, § 1, eff. Jan. 1, 1982.

REVISION COMMENT—1981

This is a reenactment of Article 900 of the Civil Code of 1870 without substantive change.

Art. 888.   Succession rights of descendants

Descendants succeed to the property of their ascendants. They take in equal portions and by heads if they are in the same degree. They take by roots if all or some of them succeed by representation.

Acts 1981, No. 919, § 1, eff. Jan. 1, 1982.

REVISION COMMENT—1981

This provision deletes the word "legitimate" from Article 902 of the Civil Code of 1870. The definition of "children" in Article 3556(8) [redesignated as Article 3506 in 1991], infra, carries out the same concept. The intent of this article is that the children's rights extend to all property, both community and separate, as was the case under the Civil Code of 1870.

Art. 889.   Devolution of community property

If the deceased leaves no descendants, his surviving spouse succeeds to his share of the community property.

Acts 1981, No. 919, § 1, eff. Jan. 1, 1982.

REVISION COMMENTS—1981

(a) This provision revises Article 915 of the Civil Code of 1870 and changes the law with respect to the disposition of community property. It deletes the word "legitimate" which had been added by Acts 1979, No. 607. Moreover, it deletes the former division of the deceased's share of the community, if there were no descendants, between the surviving parent or parents and the surviving spouse. Now, in the absence of descendants, the surviving spouse succeeds to the deceased's share of the community, to the exclusion of a surviving parent or parents.

(b) This provision also deletes reference to the surviving spouse as a "legal heir," who did not have to follow the requirements for the placing of irregular heirs in possession under the Civil Code of 1870. The category of legal heir and the procedure for placing irregular heirs in possession have both been suppressed in this revision.

Art. 890. Usufruct of surviving spouse

If the deceased spouse is survived by descendants, the surviving spouse shall have a usufruct over the decedent's share of the community property to the extent that the decedent has not disposed of it by testament. This usufruct terminates when the surviving spouse dies or remarries, whichever occurs first.

Acts 1996, 1st Ex.Sess., No. 77, § 1.

REVISION COMMENTS—1996

(a) This Article represents a policy decision to separate the multiple provisions of Article 890 of the Louisiana Civil Code, as it stood prior to the revision, and, in a more conceptually consistent approach, to use separate code articles to cover the different concepts. Like its predecessor (Civil Code Article 916 of the Code of 1870), Article 890 is located in the section of the Civil Code that deals with intestate succession. To the extent that the article provides a usufruct to a surviving spouse over community property inherited by descendants of the decedent, the article is appropriately placed. Over the years, however, amendments to the article (and its predecessor) have unduly complicated the article by expanding its application to matters of testate succession, such as authorizing a testator to grant a usufruct of separate property. Consequently, for reasons of stylistic purity and conceptual consistency, revised Article 890 deals only with a usufruct of the surviving spouse that arises by virtue of intestacy. A separate article covers issues of testacy, such as the ability of a testator to grant a usufruct over separate property, as well as other authorized impingements on the legitime. See Article 1499, infra.

(b) Since this usufruct arises by operation of law, it is a legal usufruct under C.C. Article 544. Although C.C. Article 573 provides that a legal usufructuary is not required to give security, C.C. Article 1514, infra, provides an exception to that rule.

Art. 890.1. [Blank]

Art. 891. Devolution of separate property; parents and brothers and sisters

If the deceased leaves no descendants but is survived by a father, mother, or both, and by a brother or sister, or both, or descendants from them, the brothers and sisters or their descendants succeed to the separate property of the deceased subject to a usufruct in favor of the surviving parent or parents. If both parents survive the deceased, the usufruct shall be joint and successive.

Acts 1981, No. 919, § 1, eff. Jan. 1, 1982. Amended by Acts 2004, No. 26, § 1.

REVISION COMMENT—1981

This provision changes the law. When the deceased is survived by brothers or sisters, or both, or their descendants, and by a parent or parents, the separate property is not divided between the siblings and the parents as under the Civil Code of 1870. Rather, the surviving parent receives a usufruct over this property, while naked ownership passes to the deceased's siblings, or to their descendants. If both parents survive the deceased they receive this usufruct in indivision. If one parent subsequently predeceases the other, the entire usufruct accrues to the survivor, and the siblings or their descendants continue to have only a naked ownership interest in the property.

Art. 892. Devolution of separate property in absence of parents or in absence of brothers and sisters

If the deceased leaves neither descendants nor parents, his brothers or sisters or descendants from them succeed to his separate property in full ownership to the exclusion of other ascendants and other collaterals.

If the deceased leaves neither descendants nor brothers or sisters, nor descendants from them, his parent or parents succeed to the separate property to the exclusion of other ascendants and other collaterals.

Acts 1981, No. 919, § 1, eff. Jan. 1, 1982.

REVISION COMMENT—1981

This provision completes the revision with reference to intestate rights of parents and siblings. In the absence of one group, the other succeeds to the exclusion of other heirs.

Art. 893. Brothers and sisters related by half-blood

The property that devolves to the brothers or sisters is divided among them equally, if they are all born of the same parents. If they are born of different unions, it is equally divided between the paternal and maternal lines of the deceased: brothers or sisters fully related by blood take in both lines and those related by half-blood take each in his own line. If there are brothers or sisters on one side only, they take the entirety to the exclusion of all relations in the other line.

Acts 1981, No. 919, § 1, eff. Jan. 1, 1982.

REVISION COMMENTS—1981

(a) This is a revision of Article 913 of the Civil Code of 1870 which changes the article to provide for the rights of "illegitimate" siblings. If one may not distinguish between proven biological children as to inheritance rights, then all siblings born of the same set of parents should share equally. If there are siblings who only have one parent in common with the deceased, they should share only in the appropriate parental line, as was the law under the Civil Code of 1870.

(b) This article does not alter the provisions of the Civil Code of 1870 with reference to division among siblings of the full blood and those of the half-blood. Specifically, it does not provide that "half-blood" siblings take only a "half share".

Art. 894. Separate property; rights of surviving spouse

If the deceased leaves neither descendants, nor parents, nor brothers, sisters, or descendants from them, his spouse not judicially separated from him shall succeed to his separate property to the exclusion of other ascendants and other collaterals.

Acts 1981, No. 919, § 1, eff. Jan. 1, 1982.

REVISION COMMENT—1981

This provision changes the law by elevating the surviving spouse not judicially separated from the deceased to a point in intestate succession above ascendants and collaterals, but behind parents and siblings, or their descendants.

Art. 895. Separate property; rights of other ascendants

If a deceased leaves neither descendants, nor brothers, sisters, or descendants from them, nor parents, nor spouse not judicially separated, his other ascendants succeed to his separate property. If the ascendants in the paternal and maternal lines are in the same degree, the property is divided into two equal shares, one of which goes to the ascendants on the paternal side, and the other to the ascendants on the maternal side, whether the number of ascendants on each side be equal or not. In this case, the ascendants in each line inherit by heads.

If there is in the nearest degree but one ascendant in the two lines, such ascendant excludes ascendants of a more remote degree.

Acts 1981, No. 919, § 1, eff. Jan. 1, 1982.

REVISION COMMENT—1981

This is a revision of Articles 905, 906 and 907 of the Civil Code of 1870 without substantive change, except to reflect the placing of the surviving spouse ahead of ascendants other than parents, and of collaterals. See Article 894 in this revision.

Art. 896.   Separate property; rights of other collaterals

If the deceased leaves neither descendants, nor brothers, sisters, or descendants from them, nor parents, nor spouse not judicially separated, nor other ascendants, his other collaterals succeed to his separate property. Among the collateral relations, the nearest in degree excludes all the others. If there are several in the same degree, they take equally and by heads.

Acts 1981, No. 919, § 1, eff. Jan. 1, 1982.

REVISION COMMENT—1981

This is a revision of Article 914 of the Civil Code of 1870 without substantive change, except to reflect the increased rights of the surviving spouse under Article 894 of this revision.

Art. 897.   Ascendant's right to inherit immovables donated to descendant

Ascendants, to the exclusion of all others, inherit the immovables given by them to their children or their descendants of a more remote degree who died without posterity, when these objects are found in the succession.

If these objects have been alienated, and the price is yet due in whole or in part, the ascendants have the right to receive the price. They also succeed to the right of reversion on the happening of any event which the child or descendant may have inserted as a condition in his favor in disposing of those objects.

Acts 1981, No. 919, § 1, eff. Jan. 1, 1982.

REVISION COMMENT—1981

This is a revision of Article 908 of the Civil Code of 1870 without substantive change.

Art. 898.   Reversion of property subject to encumbrances and succession debts

Ascendants inheriting the things mentioned in the preceding article, which they have given their children or descendants who die without issue, take them subject to all the mortgages which the donee may have imposed on them during his life.

Also ascendants exercising the right of reversion are bound to contribute to the payment of the debts of the succession, in proportion to the value of the objects given.

Acts 1981, No. 919, § 1, eff. Jan. 1, 1982.

REVISION COMMENT—1981

This is a revision of Article 910 of the Civil Code of 1870 without substantive change.

Art. 899.   Nearest in degree among more remote relations

Among the successors in each class the nearest relation to the deceased, according to the following articles, is called to succeed.

Acts 1981, No. 919, § 1, eff. Jan. 1, 1982.

REVISION COMMENT—1981

This is a revision of Article 888 of the Civil Code of 1870 without substantive change.

Art. 900. Degrees of relationship

The propinquity of consanguinity is established by the number of generations, and each generation is called a degree.

Acts 1981, No. 919, § 1, eff. Jan. 1, 1982.

Art. 901. Direct and collateral relationship

The series of degrees forms the line. The direct line is the series of degrees between persons who descend one from another. The collateral line is the series of degrees between persons who do not descend one from another, but who descend from a common ancestor.

In the direct line, the number of degrees is equal to the number of generations between the heir and the deceased. In the collateral line, the number of degrees is equal to the number of generations between the heir and the common ancestor, plus the number of generations between the common ancestor and the deceased.

Acts 1981, No. 919, § 1, eff. Jan. 1, 1982.

REVISION COMMENT—1981

This is a revision of Articles 890, 891 and 892 of the Civil Code of 1870 without substantive change.

CHAPTER 3—OF THE RIGHTS OF THE STATE

Art. 902. Rights of the state

In default of blood, adopted relations, or a spouse not judicially separated, the estate of the deceased belongs to the state.

Acts 1981, No. 919, § 1, eff. Jan. 1, 1982.

REVISION COMMENT—1981

This is a revision of Article 929 of the Civil Code of 1870 without substantive change. The State should not be considered an "heir" but rather an entity which may take the property only in default of heirs.

Arts. 903 to 933. [Blank]

CHAPTER 4—COMMENCEMENT OF SUCCESSION

Art. 934. Commencement of succession

Succession occurs at the death of a person.

Acts 1997, No. 1421, § 1, eff. July 1, 1999.

REVISION COMMENTS—1997

(a) The word "death" as used in this Article is intended to include both physical death and death established by presumption under Article 54 of the Louisiana Civil Code. See also R.S. 9:1441–1443.

(b) This Article is not intended to affect the definition of death contained in Louisiana Revised Statutes 9:111.

(c) This revision does not reproduce the provisions of Civil Code Articles 1644 through 1647 (1870), which were the vestiges of a much larger section of the Civil Code that had been transplanted to the Code of Civil Procedure in 1960. No substantive change is intended by this omission, however. Almost the entirety of those articles was duplicative of the material now in the Code of Civil Procedure. See Code of Civil Procedure Articles 2811–2903. Those procedural provisions (and the deleted Civil Code provisions) provide, in essence, that, upon sufficient proof of death or of circumstances under which death is presumed, a document purporting to be a testament of the deceased may be presented to a court of competent jurisdiction, and shall be probated in accordance with the procedures stated in those Articles.

(d) Under Civil Code Articles 54 and 55 a testament may be probated without proof of death when the testator "has been an absent person for five years" and the declaration of death called for under that circumstance has been rendered by a court of competent jurisdiction. See also C.C. Art. 30.

(e) With respect to the prescription of the right to present a testament for probate, see R.S. 9:5643.

Art. 935.   Acquisition of ownership; seizin

Immediately at the death of the decedent, universal successors acquire ownership of the estate and particular successors acquire ownership of the things bequeathed to them.

Prior to the qualification of a succession representative only a universal successor may represent the decedent with respect to the heritable rights and obligations of the decedent.

Acts 1997, No. 1421, § 1, eff. July 1, 1999.

REVISION COMMENTS—1997

(a) The first sentence of this article is consistent with Baten v. Taylor, 386 So.2d 333 (La. 1978), in which the Supreme Court noted that ownership was distinct from seizin, and that even particular legatees, who did not have seizin, had ownership from the date of the decedent's death. See also Tulane University of Louisiana v. Board of Assessors, 40 So. 445 (La. 1905). See also La. Civil Code Article 477 on ownership, and La. Civil Code Article 448, et seq., concerning "things."

(b) The Civil Code articles on seizin were taken from French doctrine and not from the Code Napoleon, and were repetitious and didactic. La. Civil Code Articles 940–945 (1870). In most respects, the theory of seizin is retained, but it is modernized as mentioned in comment (c), infra, and to take account of the authority of the succession representative in administered successions. Essentially, the succession representative has seizin. La. Code Civil Pro. Article 3211. While an estate is under administration, the universal successors may not exercise the rights of the deceased, such as the right to alienate or encumber the property of the deceased, without first terminating the administration. A successor may, however, alienate or encumber his own interest in the estate even while the estate is under administration. See Succession of Cutrer v. Curtis, 341 So.2d 1209 (La.App. 1st Cir. 1976).

(c) Under previous law, only universal successors had seizin, an attribute of which is possession, but under Article 936, possession is now transferred to particular legatees as well as universal successors.

(d) As under previous law, the decedent's possession is transmitted to the universal successors with all of its defects as well as its advantages. La. Civil Code Article 943 (1870). They may institute all actions that the decedent could have brought unless the estate is under administration, in which case the succession representative is the proper party plaintiff or defendant and the successors need not be joined. La. Code Civil Proc. Articles 685, 734.

(e) Article 954 provides for the effect of acceptance or renunciation to be retroactive, making it unnecessary to retain Civil Code Articles 947–948 (1870). No change in the law is intended by their elimination.

(f) Civil Code Article 949 (1870) is obsolete because of the elimination of irregular successors and therefore has been deleted.

(g) Articles 936–938 (1870), which contained the commorientes presumptions, are repealed. Under this revision, when there is a common disaster involving two persons who were entitled to inherit from each other, and it cannot be proven which of the two decedents survived, by application of Civil Code Article 31 (1870), the estate of each decedent devolves as if that decedent survived the other decedent by application of Civil Code Article 31 (1870).

(h) "Universal Successors" is a term of art defined in Article 3506(28) to include heirs by intestacy and general and universal legatees.

Art. 936.   Continuation of the possession of decedent

The possession of the decedent is transferred to his successors, whether testate or intestate, and if testate, whether particular, general, or universal legatees.

A universal successor continues the possession of the decedent with all its advantages and defects, and with no alteration in the nature of the possession.

A particular successor may commence a new possession for purposes of acquisitive prescription.

Acts 1997, No. 1421, § 1, eff. July 1, 1999.

REVISION COMMENTS—1997

(a) The transfer of possession that occurs under this Article is consistent with the provisions of Civil Code Article 3441. See Civil Code Article 3441 and the Comments thereunder; see also Civil Code Article 3442. The possession of the successor has the same attributes as the possession of the deceased.

(b) Civil Code Article 1607 (1870) distinguishes between forced heirs and universal legatees, and provides that as between the two, the forced heirs are the ones entitled to enjoy the possession of the decedent. The revision alters that distinction and recognizes that all successors have rights that vest at the moment of death of the decedent. C.C. Art. 935.

(c) See Article 3506(28) for the distinction between universal successors and particular successors.

Art. 937.   Transmission of rights of successor

The rights of a successor are transmitted to his own successors at his death, whether or not he accepted the rights, and whether or not he knew that the rights accrued to him.

Acts 1997, No. 1421, § 1, eff. July 1, 1999.

REVISION COMMENTS—1997

This Article reproduces the substance of Article 944 of the Louisiana Civil Code of 1870. It does not change the law.

Art. 938.   Exercise of succession rights

A.   Prior to the qualification of a succession representative, a successor may exercise rights of ownership with respect to his interests in a thing of the estate as well as his interest in the estate as a whole.

B.   If a successor exercises his rights of ownership after the qualification of a succession representative, the effect of that exercise is subordinate to the administration of the estate.

Acts 1997, No. 1421, § 1, eff. July 1, 1999. Amended by Acts 2001, No. 556, § 1, eff. June 22, 2001.

REVISION COMMENTS—1997

(a) This Article recognizes the ownership of estate property enjoyed by a successor prior to a formal judgment of possession, and affords a basis for his binding acts with respect to his own interest. A person dealing with a successor may acquire such title or interest as the successor has; in particular, the rights of creditors may supersede that of a purchaser from the successor if timely asserted. This principle is consistent with Civil Code Articles 2513 and 2650, which provide, in essence, that when a successor acts with respect to his right in an estate, he can do so with binding effect only as to his right as it may eventually be determined. He does not warrant title to a particular asset or portion of an asset, but only "his right as an heir." C.C. Art. 2650 (1870).

(b) There is a delicate balance between vesting rights in the successor on the one hand, and protecting the rights of creditors and correlating the rule with the role of the succession representative on the other hand, particularly when an administration is required. If the succession representative sells Blackacre in order to pay debts, the judgment of possession obviously could not put any successor in possession of Blackacre. By the same token, in a testate succession, if the testament leaves Blackacre to A, and the succession representative sells Blackacre, A's rights attach to the proceeds, and no other successor would be able to dispose of Blackacre either prior to qualification of a succession representative or during administration.

This revision preserves the important functional distinction that has been made in prior law with reference to acts prior to and acts subsequent to qualification of a succession representative.

(c) It is clear from provisions of the Code of Civil Procedure (Articles 426 and 427) that a successor who accepts his succession rights is also a proper party plaintiff or defendant.

(d) Under Article 3211 of the Code of Civil Procedure a succession representative is deemed to have possession of all property of the succession and is obligated to enforce all obligations in its favor. When such a representative has been qualified, the acts of a successor are clearly subordinate to the power and authority of the succession representative conferred by Code of Civil Procedure Article 3211 and the other articles of the Code of Civil Procedure with respect to the rights, duties and obligations of the succession representative.

(e) As to appointment of an attorney for absentee successors, see Article 3171 et seq. of the Code of Civil Procedure.

(f) A successor who acts with respect to his own interest during administration of the estate does not have to comply with the same procedural formalities that are required of a succession representative, such as, in the case of a sale of immovable property, the requirements of advertisement and court approval. His actions are, however, subject to the administrative powers of the succession representative.

(g) Upon qualification, a succession representative is the proper party to exercise rights of ownership in the assets of the deceased, to sue to enforce a right of the deceased, and to be sued to enforce an obligation of the deceased. See Articles 685, 734, and 3211 of the Code of Civil Procedure. Though the representative has the authority to act with court approval with respect to the assets of the deceased, a successor retains the right to act with respect to his own interest in an asset or in the entire estate, such as it ultimately may appear.

CHAPTER 5—LOSS OF SUCCESSION RIGHTS

Art. 939.   Existence of successor

A successor must exist at the death of the decedent.

Acts 1997, No. 1421, § 1, eff. July 1, 1999.

REVISION COMMENTS—1997

This article reproduces the substance of Article 953 of the Louisiana Civil Code of 1870. It does not change the law.

Art. 940.   Same; unborn child

An unborn child conceived at the death of the decedent and thereafter born alive shall be considered to exist at the death of the decedent.

Acts 1997, No. 1421, § 1, eff. July 1, 1999.

REVISION COMMENTS—1997

This article reproduces the substance of the first paragraph of Article 954 of the Louisiana Civil Code of 1870. It is consistent with Civil Code Article 26 (1870). See also, Civil Code Article 1474 (1870), adopted in 1991.

Art. 941.   Declaration of unworthiness

A successor shall be declared unworthy if he is convicted of a crime involving the intentional killing, or attempted killing, of the decedent or is judicially determined to have participated in the intentional, unjustified killing, or attempted killing, of the decedent. An action to declare a successor unworthy shall be brought in the succession proceedings of the decedent.

An executive pardon or pardon by operation of law does not affect the unworthiness of a successor.

Acts 1997, No. 1421, § 1, eff. July 1, 1999.

REVISION COMMENTS—1997

(a) This article reproduces the substance of Articles 964 and 966 of the Civil Code of 1870, but it deletes the second and third provisions of Article 966, which are deleted as archaic. The article uses the term "unworthy," which is used in the source provisions. The functional aspect of the provisions is to divest a successor of rights for cause, and the articles of this chapter set out the grounds that establish such cause.

(b) The requirement that a court pronounce "unworthiness" found in Article 967 of the Civil Code of 1870 is reflected in the basic concept of this Article. Although French law is to the contrary, Louisiana has always required judicial pronouncement. This Article continues that requirement.

(c) Civil Code Article 965 (1870) has not been reproduced because its provisions appear to be unnecessary in light of the definitions of incapacity and the grounds for unworthiness provided in the revised Articles. It should be clear that a person who lacks capacity to be a successor has never been a successor, while the person who is declared unworthy clearly has the capacity to be a successor but loses that right and is judicially divested of the right to inherit because of certain conduct on his part.

(d) This Article restates the prior law as to the procedure for declaring a successor unworthy without substantive change, except in one major respect. Rather than envisioning a separate civil proceeding, the Article requires that the declaration be a part of the succession proceeding itself. Requiring that the action be a part of the succession proceeding is consistent with the reconciliation provisions in Article 943 and reflects the common understanding that such an action is not permitted during the lifetime of the ancestor because he might reconcile with the offending successor at any time up to the moment of his death. It is also consistent with the provisions of Article 81 of the Code of Civil Procedure.

(e) The articles on unworthiness do not apply to a judgment of possession that merely declines to recognize a person as a successor. In that instance, the person never was a successor. Unworthiness necessarily implies that the person divested is a successor and those rights are stripped from him. For example, if there were a challenge between an alleged heir who claimed to be in the fourth degree and another heir who claimed to be in the fifth degree, and the heir in the fifth degree prevailed because the heir claiming in the fourth degree could not prove his relationship, then the losing claimant would not be "unworthy" of succession rights: he was never an heir to start with, and the court simply declines to recognize him as a successor.

(f) This article intentionally uses the phrase "judicially determined" to continue the provisions of Civil Code Article 966 (1870) that if the successor is not convicted but is judicially determined to have participated in the intentional unjustified killing or attempted killing of a deceased, he should be declared unworthy. The determination may be made by the court having jurisdiction of the succession proceedings itself or by any other court of competent jurisdiction that makes the determination.

(g) Article 966(1) of the Louisiana Civil Code (1870) contains a provision that: "An executive pardon does not restore the right to succeed." The concept that an executive pardon does not exonerate unworthy behavior is retained, but its application has been expanded and at the same time made more precise. The new article refers not only to an executive pardon but any other pardon that arises by operation of law. The change is appropriate because under the Louisiana Constitution, an executive pardon is no longer the only way a felon can be pardoned. There are pardons for first time offenders that arise by operation of law. See, La. Const. Art. 4, Section 5(E). Furthermore, the brief statement that a pardon "does not restore the right to succeed" is too limited in its application, and is inadequate in dealing with the effects of a declaration of unworthiness. For example, a declaration of unworthiness not only deprives the successor of the inheritance rights, either by testacy or intestacy, but also precludes the successor from serving as an executor, administrator, trustee or other fiduciary. See, C.C. Art. 945, infra. Unworthiness also requires the return of property over which the successor took possession. Id. Furthermore, the verb "restore" would be inaccurate in the case of a pardon granted before the successor has been judicially declared unworthy. Whether the pardon occurs before or after the judicial declaration of unworthiness is irrelevant. For that reason, the revision provides that the granting of a pardon does not "affect" the unworthiness, which means that it does not prevent or stop the rendering of a declaration, and it does not nullify the effects of a declaration that has already been rendered. The use of the mandatory "shall" in the first sentence of Article 941 means that when the conditions are met, the judge is obligated to declare a successor unworthy. A pardon does not preclude the rendering of such a declaration, nor does it in any way alter the effects of such a declaration if the declaration has already been rendered.

Art. 942.   Persons who may bring action

A.   An action to declare a successor unworthy may be brought only by a person who would succeed in place of or in concurrence with the successor to be declared unworthy, or by one who claims through such a person.

B.   When a person who may bring the action is a minor or an interdict, the court, on its own motion, or on the motion of any family member, may appoint an attorney to represent the minor or interdict for purposes of investigating and pursuing an action to declare a successor unworthy.

Acts 1997, No. 1421, § 1, eff. July 1, 1999. Amended by Acts 2001, No. 824, § 1.

REVISION COMMENTS—1997

A person who successfully brings an action to declare a successor unworthy must be someone who is entitled to the share that would have fallen to the successor whose rights are divested. This Article includes the phrase "one who claims through such a person" specifically to cover the case of a right that is transmitted through a deceased successor pursuant to the rules of Civil Code Article 937, supra.

REVISION COMMENTS—2001

(a) Under this amendment, if the person who would have the right to bring an action to declare a successor unworthy is either a minor or an interdict, the court can appoint an attorney to represent that person for purposes of investigating whether there may be a cause of action to declare a successor unworthy, and if so, to pursue the cause of action. It is important for the court to have the opportunity to appoint an attorney where the person who might inherit is interdicted, since there is a strong possibility that, if that is the case, the unworthy successor himself may be the curator for the interdict.

(b) This amendment authorizes the court to appoint an attorney either on the court's own motion or on the motion of any "family member." The term "family member" is not defined, because the area should be kept intentionally broad to enable anyone reasonably related to the family to step forward and raise the issue. One purpose of the concept of unworthiness is to prevent a malefactor, such as a murderer, from profiting from his misdeed. Even if someone may not be, technically speaking, a "family" member, the fact that the issue would be raised to the court may be important, and the amendment authorizes the court "on its own motion" to appoint an attorney at law.

Art. 943.   Reconciliation or forgiveness

A successor shall not be declared unworthy if he proves reconciliation with or forgiveness by the decedent.

Acts 1997, No. 1421, § 1, eff. July 1, 1999.

REVISION COMMENTS—1997

This Article clarifies prior law. It does not preserve the presumption of forgiveness in Civil Code Article 975 (1870). The measure of sufficient conduct to conclude that reconciliation has occurred or that forgiveness has occurred has been intentionally left to the courts. Obviously the decedent himself may remove the possibility of a declaration of unworthiness by the acts of reconciliation or forgiveness, although it should be noted that even a formal executive pardon does not have the same effect. See Civil Code Article 941.

Art. 944. Prescription

An action to declare a successor unworthy is subject to a liberative prescription of five years from the death of the decedent as to intestate successors and five years from the probate of the will as to testate successors.

Acts 1997, No. 1421, § 1, eff. July 1, 1999.

REVISION COMMENTS—1997

(a) The prescriptive period for an action to declare an intestate successor unworthy under prior law is unclear. It may be that of a personal action not otherwise provided for in the Civil Code, subject to a ten-year prescriptive period under Civil Code Article 3499, or it may be subject to the thirty-year prescriptive period for actions for "recognition of a right of inheritance and recovery of the whole or a part of a succession" under Civil Code Article 3502. This Article establishes a period considerably shorter than either of those alternatives and is more in keeping with improved communications and modern succession procedure.

(b) As to interruption of the prescriptive period, see Civil Code Articles 3462 et seq.

(c) As regards the date of death of the decedent, see Civil Code Article 54 (presumed death after five years' absence) and La. R.S. 9:1441 through 9:1443 (presumption of death of military personnel).

(d) In connection with the subject matter of this article, see also Article 3497 of the Civil Code.

(e) Prescription under this article is not suspended in favor of minors during minority. See Louisiana Civil Code Article 3468.

Art. 945. Effects of declaration of unworthiness

A judicial declaration that a person is unworthy has the following consequences:

(1) The successor is deprived of his right to the succession to which he had been called.

(2) If the successor has possession of any property of the decedent, he must return it, along with all fruits and products he has derived from it. He must also account for an impairment in value caused by his encumbering it or failing to preserve it as a prudent administrator.

(3) If the successor no longer has possession because of a transfer or other loss of possession due to his fault, he must account for the value of the property at the time of the transfer or other loss of possession, along with all fruits and products he has derived from it.

He must also account for any impairment in value caused by his encumbering the property or failing to preserve it as a prudent administrator before he lost possession.

(4) If the successor has alienated, encumbered, or leased the property by onerous title, and there is no fraud on the part of the other party, the validity of the transaction is not affected by the declaration of unworthiness. But if he has donated the property and it remains in the hands of the donee or the donee's successors by gratuitous title, the donation may be annulled.

(5) The successor shall not serve as an executor, trustee, attorney or other fiduciary pursuant to a designation as such in the testament or any codicils thereto. Neither shall he serve as administrator, attorney, or other fiduciary in an intestate succession.

Acts 1997, No. 1421, § 1, eff. July 1, 1999.

REVISION COMMENTS—1997

(a) This article sets forth comprehensively the various civil effects of a declaration of unworthiness. It begins with the principal effect, which is that the successor is deprived of the right to succeed, that is, that he is judicially divested of his right to inherit any of the property left by the decedent. The effect, spelled out in Section (1), is modeled on existing language of the Code to the effect that the successor is deprived "of the succession to which he is called." C.C. Art. 966. The new language implements that same effect, in more modern terminology. Deprivation of the right to inherit property of the decedent follows whether the decedent has died testate or intestate. Accordingly, there are corresponding provisions elsewhere in the revisions specifically enunciating the rule that a declaration of unworthiness results in the lapse of a legacy to the successor. C.C. Art. 1589. And C.C. Art. 1500 of the Civil Code of 1870, as amended by Act 77 of the Special Session of 1996, provides that if the successor is a forced heir, he is deprived of his right to claim as a forced heir. See C.C. Art. 1500 (1870).

(b) Parts (2) and (3) of this Article restate with some changes the provisions of Articles 969, 970, and 971 of the Civil Code of 1870 relative to the consequences of a declaration of unworthiness with respect to property already in the possession of the later-divested heir and the validity of transfers or encumbrances that he may have made. If the declaration has preceded a judgment of possession in the succession proceedings, it is unlikely that these provisions would be needed. But in the unusual situation in which the action to declare a successor unworthy takes place after a judgment of possession had been rendered, they would be needed. The concept of the predecessor Articles is broadened to extend to all forms of transfer by the later-divested successor.

(c) A successor may no longer have possession for a number of reasons. He may have alienated the property by onerous title. He may have sold or exchanged it for less than its fair market value. He may have entered into a giving in payment with respect to the property. It may have been destroyed in his hands, or may have been stolen from him. In all such instances, Parts (3) and (4) of this Article apply.

(d) Under this Article, loss of possession other than transfer includes destruction or theft.

(e) Under this Article, an alienation, encumbrance, or lease of the successor's interest in the property includes exchange.

(f) If those persons who seek a declaration of unworthiness are concerned about the conduct of the successor with reference to property during the pendency of the litigation, they may protect their interest in immovable property by filing a notice of lis pendens under Article 3751 et seq. of the Code of Civil Procedure and their interest in movable property by securing a writ of sequestration under Articles 3501 et seq. of the Code of Civil Procedure.

(g) Part 5 of this article prohibits the successor from serving in a fiduciary capacity, and the language in that regard is modeled closely on Article 1481 which imposes the same result when there has been fraud, duress, or undue influence in connection with a donation.

Art. 946.   Devolution of succession rights of successor declared unworthy

A.   If the decedent died intestate, when a successor is declared unworthy his succession rights devolve as if he had predeceased the decedent; but if the decedent died testate, then the succession rights devolve in accordance with the provisions for testamentary accretion as if the unworthy successor had predeceased the testator.

B.   When the succession rights devolve upon a child of the successor who is declared unworthy, the unworthy successor and the other parent of the child cannot claim a legal usufruct upon the property inherited by their child.

Acts 1997, No. 1421, § 1, eff. July 1, 1999. Amended by Acts 2001, No. 824, § 1.

REVISION COMMENTS—1997

(a) This Article is new and definitely changes the law. In an intestate succession, the Article protects the innocent descendants of a successor whose rights are judicially divested for unworthiness. It changes the law by permitting the descendants of a person whose rights have been divested to inherit even when their degree of relationship would not otherwise permit them to do so. It establishes an exception to the normal rule of representation, which is that only deceased persons may be represented (see Civil Code Article 886 (1870)). It permits the children who could have represented the successor now judicially divested of his rights to succeed despite the cause for which their ancestor's rights are divested and despite his having survived the decedent. Civil Code Article 973 (1870) permits such children to take only in their own right. Thus they would be excluded by a first-degree descendant in the absence of this Article.

(b) An example of the application of this Article is as follows: The decedent is survived by two sons, A and B. A has participated in the intentional murder of the decedent, but A has a son, C, who is totally innocent and blameless in the affair. In the absence of the provisions contained in this

Article, when A is declared unworthy, his one-half interest in the estate is inherited entirely and exclusively by his surviving brother, B, and the innocent grandchild C inherits nothing. Under the provisions of this Article, C would inherit ahead of A's co-heirs of the same degree.

(c) In a testate succession, the testament may provide for the devolution of the property by a vulgar substitution. Under the provisions of Article 1589, a declaration of unworthiness causes the legacy to lapse, and in that case the devolution of the property may be governed by the provisions of the testament.

(d) The second paragraph of this article preserves the provisions of Civil Code Article 973 (1870) that prohibit an unworthy parent from obtaining the usufruct of his child's inheritance. The paragraph clarifies another aspect of that problem and removes any question whether the other parent, who may be blameless, would have a usufruct over the inherited property under Civil Code Article 223 (1870), and expressly provides that the other parent does not have such a usufruct, either.

CHAPTER 6—ACCEPTANCE AND RENUNCIATION OF SUCCESSIONS

SECTION 1—GENERAL PRINCIPLES

Art. 947.   Right of successor to accept or renounce

A successor is not obligated to accept rights to succeed. He may accept some of those rights and renounce others.

Acts 1997, No. 1421, § 1, eff. July 1, 1999.

REVISION COMMENTS—1997

(a) This article is based on the provisions of Articles 977, 986, and 1018 of the Louisiana Civil Code (1870). It does not change the law. It enunciates the principle that a successor does not have to accept in toto, but may selectively accept part and renounce part. The ability to partially accept or renounce applies to both testate successions and intestate successions, and applies even to a particular legatee, who may accept all or part of the particular legacy to him. If he is the recipient of two particular legacies, he may accept one particular bequest and renounce another particular bequest. This principle was most likely intended by Act No. 249 of 1981, which amended Civil Code Article 986 (1870), but the specific language of Civil Code Article 986 (1870) is not so clear. The Article refers only to "he who has the power of accepting the entire succession. . . ." The new article clarifies the matter by using language that is sufficiently broad to cover all such instances.

(b) Obviously the rules in this Chapter governing acceptance apply to a partial acceptance as well as to a full acceptance.

Art. 948.   Minor successor deemed to accept

A successor who is a minor is deemed to accept rights to succeed, but his legal representative may renounce on behalf of the minor when expressly authorized by the court.

Acts 1997, No. 1421, § 1, eff. July 1, 1999.

REVISION COMMENTS—1997

(a) This Article reproduces the substance of the second paragraph of Civil Code Article 977 (1870) without changing the law, but it adds an important new right by authorizing a legal representative of a minor to renounce an inheritance when expressly authorized to do so by the court. Such a renunciation could be a matter of significant tax import under the federal tax rules regarding disclaimers. A minor's rights should not, however, be renounced except under scrutiny, and the provision is made that the minor's representative must have express authorization by the court.

(b) The word "deemed" is intentionally used as a term of art to establish a stronger rule than a mere rebuttable presumption. As such, it is conclusive and thus irrebuttable.

Art. 949.   Death of decedent as prerequisite to acceptance or renunciation

A person may not accept or renounce rights to succeed before the death of the decedent.

Acts 1997, No. 1421, § 1, eff. July 1, 1999.

REVISION COMMENTS—1997

This Article reproduces the substance of Articles 978 and 979 of the Louisiana Civil Code (1870). It does not change the law. It states an important rule of public policy that until the person who is to be succeeded has died the presumptive successors cannot act with reference to his succession. See also Article 951 of the Civil Code regarding a premature acceptance.

Art. 950.   Knowledge required of successor as prerequisite to acceptance or renunciation

An acceptance or renunciation is valid only if the successor knows of the death of the person to be succeeded and knows that he has rights as a successor. It is not necessary that he know the extent of those rights or the nature of his relationship to the decedent.

Acts 1997, No. 1421, § 1, eff. July 1, 1999.

REVISION COMMENTS—1997

This Article reproduces the substance of Articles 980 and 983 of the Louisiana Civil Code (1870), but the language of the source Articles is awkward, and the revision intends to clarify these provisions. It clarifies the predicate needed to validate an acceptance or renunciation. The predicate is made conjunctive so that the successor must (1) know of the death of the person to be succeeded, and (2) know that he has rights as a successor. If the successor merely knows of the death of a person but does not know of his own rights as a successor, an acceptance or renunciation would be premature. The second sentence clarifies that it is not necessary that the successor know the extent of the inheritance rights, or even that the successor know the exact nature of his relationship to the decedent, so long as he knows that the person has died and he knows that he has rights. Even if he believes the rights to be more extensive or less extensive than they actually are, it is the conjunction of the knowledge of death and the knowledge of rights that satisfies the predicate and validates an acceptance or renunciation.

Art. 951.   Nullity of premature acceptance or renunciation

A premature acceptance or renunciation is absolutely null.

Acts 1997, No. 1421, § 1, eff. July 1, 1999.

REVISION COMMENTS—1997

This Article reproduces the substance of Article 984 of the Louisiana Civil Code (1870). It does not change the law. There is no reason to preserve the archaic language of the source article. The use of the word "premature" ties in with the immediately preceding article, and refers to an acceptance that has been made either before the successor knows of the death of the person, or before he knows that he has rights as a successor, or before the person to be succeeded has in fact died. It is believed unnecessary to detail all of the different ways in which an acceptance or renunciation might be premature. It is also unnecessary to keep the prior language that the acceptance or rejection could produce no effect, or to keep language stating the obvious, that the heir could later validly accept or renounce.

Art. 952.   Probate or annulment of testament after acceptance or renunciation of succession

An acceptance or renunciation of rights to succeed by intestacy is null if a testament is subsequently probated or given the effect of probate. An acceptance or renunciation of rights to succeed in a testate succession is null if the probate of the testament is subsequently annulled or the rights are altered, amended, or revoked by a subsequent testament or codicil.

Acts 1997, No. 1421, § 1, eff. July 1, 1999. Amended by Acts 2001, No. 824, § 1.

REVISION COMMENTS—1997

(a) This Article is intentionally divided into two parts, to cover separately the situations in testate and intestate successions. Where the successor believes that the rights to succeed that are involved arise by intestacy, the operative fact that would nullify his acceptance or renunciation is the probate of a will. Present law refers to "discovery" of a will, but this Article uses the concept of probate of a will, which assumes that the newly discovered will is valid. It would be inappropriate to nullify an acceptance or renunciation if an instrument that purported to be a will was discovered but was without effect. Of course, the testament must be a testament of the decedent whose estate is at issue.

(b) The second sentence of this Article covers the situation involved in a testate succession and consequently by definition there must be a testament that has been probated. The sentence refers to annulling the probate of that testament. The situation might arise either because a subsequent testament is discovered and it supersedes the one that was originally probated, or the probate of the testament may be nullified because of form, that is, lack of authenticity, or as the result of a challenge such as the testator's lack of capacity. In either event the critical point is that there is a definite change in circumstances from those under which the original acceptance or renunciation was made. Further, the probate may not be annulled, but the rights may be altered by the subsequent discovery of a codicil or of a testament that does not revoke the earlier testament and merely supersedes it in part.

(c) The source provisions, Civil Code Articles 981 and 982 (1870) apply only to intestate successors, but this Article intentionally covers both testate and intestate successions. As noted above, the language of the source provisions refers to "discovery" of a will, and this Article clarifies that the mere discovery of the will may not be sufficient to bring the provisions of the article into operation, because a will might be discovered that would not be a valid will. Whether the Article becomes operative because of the discovery of a valid will, where the decedent was believed to have died intestate, or because of the discovery of a second or subsequent testament, or because the originally probated will is annulled and an earlier will is revived or the estate then devolves by intestacy, in all of these situations the provisions that ultimately govern may be similar or even the same provisions that the successor accepted or renounced earlier. Even with intestacy, for example, the probate of a testament may be essentially meaningless, if the discovered testament simply disposes of the estate in accordance with the laws of intestacy. Nevertheless, it makes no difference to the applicability of this Article whether the resulting situation involves a disposition of all or part of the property of the estate in a manner that is different from the disposition originally accepted or renounced: the acceptance or renunciation is annulled, and the successor who accepted or renounced has the opportunity to reconsider whether he wishes to succeed to any portion of the estate.

Art. 953. Legacy subject to a suspensive condition

A legacy that is subject to a suspensive condition may be accepted or renounced either before or after the fulfillment of the condition.

Acts 1997, No. 1421, § 1, eff. July 1, 1999.

REVISION COMMENTS—1997

(a) This Article is fundamentally new and changes the law. The Article reverses the rule of Civil Code Article 985 (1870) by permitting a legacy under a suspensive condition to be accepted or renounced prior to fulfillment of the condition, instead of prohibiting acceptance or renunciation during that period. There is no reason of public policy nor any pragmatic reason to prohibit such renunciation or acceptance of a legacy under a suspensive condition. Thus, it is appropriate to permit a legatee to accept such a legacy pending the fulfillment of the condition.

(b) This Article addresses only legacies on a suspensive condition, because it is unnecessary to address legacies that are subject to a resolutory condition. A legacy subject to a resolutory condition may be accepted like any other legacy, prior to fulfillment of the condition, and becomes nugatory once the condition has occurred. See Civil Code Articles 1767–1776, inclusive, regarding conditional obligations.

Art. 954.   Retroactive effects of acceptance and renunciation

To the extent that he accepts rights to succeed, a successor is considered as having succeeded to those rights at the moment of death of the decedent. To the extent that a successor renounces rights to succeed, he is considered never to have had them.

Acts 1997, No. 1421, § 1, eff. July 1, 1999.

REVISION COMMENTS—1997

(a) This Article is a corollary of the salutary rule of "Le Mort Saisit Le Vif," by which rights are always considered to flow and vest as of the moment of death. C.C. Art. 935. Obviously the treatment is theoretical and fictitious. Since an acceptance may be made months or years later, it is the fictitious relation-back to the moment of death that is important in terms of vesting of rights. The same rules apply for renunciation, so that if successor "A" renounces three months after the decedent has died, the renunciation relates back to the moment of death, and the acceptance by successor "B" also relates back to the moment of death. This relation-back has always been the law of Louisiana, and Article 954 does not represent a substantive change in the law.

(b) This Article twice contains the phrase, "to the extent," which is intended to refer to the newly-clarified right of a successor to accept or renounce part of a succession. C.C. Art. 947. If the successor accepts part and renounces part, then "to the extent" that he has accepted part, that acceptance relates back to the moment of death, and "to the extent" that he has renounced part, that renunciation relates back to the moment of death. This approach is consistent with Articles 935 and 947, and the revision as a whole.

(c) This Article applies not only to the initial rights that flow from the decedent but also to rights that may come by virtue of accretion. An acceptance of part that accretes through renunciation of other successors will have the same retroactive effect and relate back to the moment of death.

Art. 955.   [Blank]

Art. 956.   Claims of successor who is a creditor of the estate

A successor may assert a claim that he has as a creditor of the estate whether he accepts or renounces his succession rights.

Acts 1997, No. 1421, § 1, eff. July 1, 1999.

REVISION COMMENTS—1997

This Article represents a clarification of the law, and is not intended to change the law. Civil Code Article 1059 (1870) refers to an heir preserving rights as a creditor when he renounces his rights as an heir, and Article 1058 addresses the issue of the successor's rights when he accepts with benefit of inventory. Except to the extent that rights may be extinguished by confusion, a successor who is a creditor of the estate should have the right to pursue his claims as a creditor. See Civil Code Article 1903 (1870). The roles of successor and creditor may be different, and when they are, the successor is not precluded from asserting his right as a creditor. See, e.g., Article 1616, infra.

SECTION 2—ACCEPTANCE

Art. 957.   Formal or informal acceptance

Acceptance may be either formal or informal. It is formal when the successor expressly accepts in writing or assumes the quality of successor in a judicial proceeding. It is informal when the successor does some act that clearly implies his intention to accept.

Acts 1997, No. 1421, § 1, eff. July 1, 1999.

REVISION COMMENTS—1997

(a) This Article reproduces the substance of Articles 988, 989, and 990 of the Louisiana Civil Code (1870). It does not change the law. There is a change of terminology, making acceptance either "formal" or "informal," instead of "tacit" or "express." The changes are not intended to change the law but merely to clarify it.

(b) Even in the absence of either formal or informal acceptance there is, nonetheless, a presumption that all successors accept their rights. See Article 962. That presumption will simplify matters in many areas, as, for example, prescription of the right to accept under former Civil Code Article 1030 (1870). The consequences of acceptance under this revision are consistent with the changes that were intended to be brought about by the adoption of R.S. 9:1421 in 1986. They do not carry with them the specter of unlimited personal liability that stalked successors who considered unconditional acceptance under prior law. Under this revision a successor cannot be personally liable for more than the value of property he actually receives, so the presumption of acceptance or indeed the act of acceptance does not carry dire or baleful consequences with it as before.

Art. 958.   Informal acceptance; use or disposition of property

Acts of the successor concerning property that he does not know belongs to the estate do not imply an intention to accept.

Acts 1997, No. 1421, § 1, eff. July 1, 1999.

REVISION COMMENTS—1997

(a) This Article does not change the law but merely restates it in clearer fashion. If the successor disposes of property that does not actually belong to the estate, then he is not implying an intention to accept, and the Article does not apply. If he disposes of property that does belong to the estate, then the Article requires that he know that it belongs to the estate before the inference of an intention to accept may be made.

(b) Inasmuch as there is a presumption of acceptance under this revision, the importance of tacit as well as express acceptance is that such actions in effect ratify the presumption and preclude renunciation.

Art. 959.   Informal acceptance; act of ownership

An act of ownership that can be done only as a successor implies acceptance, but an act that is merely administrative, custodial, or preservative does not imply acceptance.

Acts 1997, No. 1421, § 1, eff. July 1, 1999.

REVISION COMMENTS—1997

(a) This Article is based on Articles 994–997, 999–1002 of the Louisiana Civil Code (1870). It does not change the law, but intentionally revises the language to clarify the provisions of prior law. Its new terminology is more consistent with modern usage and is clearer as to the kinds of acts that do not imply acceptance. For example, the use of the word "custodial" should help differentiate the kinds of acts that one may do as an owner as opposed to acts one may do as a custodian who holds property for someone else.

(b) Obviously if the successor disposes of property in a capacity different from that of successor, as, for example, if he is the executor or administrator of the estate, there should not be an implication of acceptance as a successor.

(c) Practical problems in this area involve situations such as those where the successor is sued and fails to defend himself, or takes care of the burial of the decedent, or pays funeral expenses. Clearly if the successor is sued in his capacity as a successor, he should respond by affirming or denying that capacity. That issue should be resolved based on the activity in the lawsuit itself. With regard to taking care of a burial or paying funeral expenses, these would appear to be nothing more than acts of piety or reverence that do not constitute acts of ownership with reference to property of the decedent. On the other hand, making a donation, a sale, or an assignment of rights that the successor receives, whether they are transferred to a stranger or to co-heirs, ought to be considered an acceptance. The courts are given latitude to determine under particular circumstances whether or not a given act constitutes "an act of ownership". See C.C. Arts 1000–1002 (1870).

Art. 960.   Donative renunciation deemed acceptance

A renunciation shall be deemed to be an acceptance to the extent that it causes the renounced rights to devolve in a manner other than that provided by law or by the testament if the decedent died testate.

Acts 1997, No. 1421, § 1, eff. July 1, 1999.

REVISION COMMENTS—1997

This Article codifies the jurisprudence under prior law and further amplifies it by considering issues not addressed in the jurisprudence. In the case of Aurienne v. Mount Olivet, 153 La. 451, 96 So. 29 (1922), the Louisiana Supreme Court upheld a renunciation as a true renunciation and not a donation, when the renouncing successors renounced rights in such a way that they devolved in favor of the person who was legally entitled to succeed to them under succession law. In deciding the case, the court pointed to the principle that when a person renounces succession rights in favor of another person in a manner other than that provided by law, the renunciation is not a true renunciation, but in fact constitutes an acceptance of the rights coupled with a donation to the third person in whose favor the rights are renounced. For such an act to be a true renunciation, the successor must merely renounce, leaving the renounced rights to devolve on those who would be legally entitled to succeed to them under the provisions of the testament or under the succession law. One additional aspect of this problem is that to the extent that such a renunciation-qua-acceptance disposes of incorporeal rights, it constitutes a donation and therefore must be in authentic form. The unfortunate consequence if the "renunciation" were not in authentic form would be that the acceptance would be valid but the donation over to the third party would be invalid. Although a renunciation must be express and in writing, it is not required to be in notarial form. See La. Civil Code Article 963. The failure to make it in notarial form, therefore, could be a serious problem if it is a donative renunciation.

The renunciation-qua-acceptance is only treated as an acceptance to the extent that the renunciation-over in favor of the third person is different from the manner in which the rights would devolve otherwise. If the successor renounces in favor of "A," but "A" would have received the property if the successor had merely renounced, then the renunciation should be treated as a renunciation and not as a renunciation-qua-acceptance.

Art. 961.   Effect of acceptance

Acceptance obligates the successor to pay estate debts in accordance with the provisions of this Title and other applicable laws.

Acts 1997, No. 1421, eff. July 1, 1999.

REVISION COMMENTS—1997

(a) Although on its face this Article appears to state very little, in reality there is a great deal of substance implicit in it. The statement that the successor must pay debts "in accordance with the rules of this Title," brings into play other Articles of this revision that deal with payment of debts of the decedent and administrative expenses and the limitation of liability that the revision provides. See Civil Code Articles 1415–29.

(b) Because this revision provides for a limitation of the liability of accepting successors for estate debts, R.S. 9:1421 (by which all successors are deemed to accept with benefit of inventory where an inventory or descriptive list has been executed) is no longer necessary and it is, therefore, repealed as part of this revision.

(c) See Article 1415, infra, for a definition of "estate debts," which includes both debts of the decedent and administrative expenses.

(d) The reference to "other applicable law" is intended to include such rules as those in the Estate Tax Apportionment Law. See La. R.S. 9:2431, et seq.

Art. 962.   Presumption of acceptance

In the absence of a renunciation, a successor is presumed to accept succession rights. Nonetheless, for good cause the successor may be compelled to accept or renounce.

Acts 1997, No. 1421, § 1, eff. July 1, 1999.

REVISION COMMENTS—1997

(a) It should be noted first that the concept of this Article is very close to that of Article 1014 (1870); namely that the person who is called to the succession, being seized thereof in right, is considered the heir as long as he does not renounce. Under this revision, where acceptance does not carry with it unlimited personal liability, all successors are presumed to accept. Nonetheless, a successor may renounce, and unless there is a formal or informal acceptance, which would preclude such renunciation, the successor will have the right to renounce even though he has been presumed to accept. This is a substantial change in the law, but it is consistent with the new rules regarding limited liability for accepting successors.

(b) The second sentence of this Article codifies a principle that has been unclear, but which many persons thought was implicit in the prior law, although a recent case has held to the contrary. See In re Succession of Bradford, 567 So.2d 751 (La.App. 2 Cir. 1990), holding that a court did not have authority to order one of four sisters to accept or renounce the succession, thereby preventing the signing of a Judgment of Possession placing all sisters into possession without administration. In the course of administration of a succession, the succession representative may need to compel a decision by a successor. If the succession representative wants to place the successors in possession of the assets of the estate, a mere presumption of acceptance is not sufficient. In that instance there would be good cause for the representative to compel a successor to either accept or renounce, and the second sentence of this Article would authorize such an action. The phrase "for good cause" should cover many kinds of cases. The example given above of a succession representative who needs to terminate the administration and place the successors in possession would clearly be a good cause for compelling a response by a successor. On the other hand, the successor who has been asked to accept or renounce may have good cause for further delay, as for example if the extent of the assets and liabilities of the estate has not been determined. The "good cause" language would permit persons seeking to compel an election between acceptance and renunciation to do so in appropriate circumstances, but it should also protect the successor who reasonably needs a longer time in which to deliberate, and for that reason the permissive "may" is used in the sentence. This language is intended to grant a court discretion to allow the successor the time needed to deliberate in appropriate circumstances.

(c) Article 962 intentionally does not provide who has the right to compel the successor to accept or renounce. It is purposefully unrestricted in that regard so that any interested party, such as a succession representative, or another heir, or legatee, or even a creditor, will have the right to compel the successor to accept or renounce in appropriate circumstances. Obviously a court should not permit a person to maintain the action unless that person is an "interested party", and even then the interested party who seeks to compel the successor to accept or renounce should have "good cause" to do so.

SECTION 3—RENUNCIATION

Art. 963.　Requirement of formality

Renunciation must be express and in writing.

Acts 1997, No. 1421, § 1, eff. July 1, 1999.

REVISION COMMENTS—1997

(a) This Article provides a simpler statement of the rules that are contained in Articles 1015 and 1017 of the Louisiana Civil Code of 1870. It changes the law by requiring only that a renunciation be in writing, rather than in authentic form, as was required by Article 1017 of the Civil Code of 1870. Informal renunciation is not permitted.

(b) The provisions of Article 1016 of the Louisiana Civil Code (1870) have not been reproduced, and to that extent, the new law does intend a change. Article 1016 (1870) provides that "a succession can neither be accepted nor rejected conditionally." With the changes in the law that affect the consequences of acceptance or renunciation as the revision does, there is no reason to prohibit conditional acceptances or conditional renunciations.

(c) The provisions of Article 1014 of the Louisiana Civil Code (1870) have been deleted as unnecessary, but the content of Civil Code Article 1014 (1870) is consistent with the approach of this revision to presume that successors accept the succession until they have formally renounced. See Article 962.

(d) The language of this Article is modeled on Civil Code Article 3038 (1870), pertaining to the formal requirements of suretyship.

Art. 964.   Accretion upon renunciation in intestate successions

The rights of an intestate successor who renounces accrete to those persons who would have succeeded to them if the successor had predeceased the decedent.

Acts 1997, No. 1421, § 1, eff. July 1, 1999.

REVISION COMMENTS—1997

(a) This Article represents a very substantial change in the law. Under Article 1022 of the Civil Code of 1870, the portion of an heir who renounces goes to his coheirs of the same degree, and if there are none, then it goes to those in the next degree. That approach often produced unfortunate results, and was considered to be inappropriate. The new approach is to treat renounced rights as if the successor who renounces had predeceased the decedent, which produces a result similar to representation of the successor by his descendants. More often than not, the intended result of such a renunciation is in fact for the successor's descendants to take by virtue of the renunciation.

(b) By way of illustration, if a decedent is survived by two children, "A" and "B," and "A" has a child "C," and "A" renounces, then under prior law (specifically Civil Code Article 1022 (1870)) the portion renounced goes to "A's" co-heir "B," who is a co-heir in the same degree. "A's" child "C" would inherit nothing. By contrast, under this Article, when "A" renounces, the rights accrete to those persons who would have represented "A" if he had predeceased the decedent, which means that "C" would inherit the full set of rights renounced by "A."

(c) Intestate successors to whom a portion accretes by renunciation share the accretion in the same proportion that they do the inheritance. That is the substance of Article 1027 of the Civil Code of 1870, but it is unnecessary to codify the principle in this revision. For example, if a decedent is survived by three children, "A," "B," and "C," and "B" renounces, but "B" has no descendants, then it is obvious that the share of "B" will be divided evenly between "A" and "C." If "C" subsequently renounces and has no descendants then his inheritance devolves on "A" and "B," equally. "B's" renunciation of his original inheritance would not preclude him from accepting what might come to him by accretion by virtue of "C's" renunciation. See Civil Code Article 966.

Art. 965.   Accretion upon renunciation in testate successions

In the absence of a governing testamentary disposition, the rights of a testate successor who renounces accrete to those persons who would have succeeded to them if the legatee had predeceased the decedent.

Acts 1997, No. 1421, § 1, eff. July 1, 1999. Amended by Acts 2001, No. 824, § 1.

REVISION COMMENTS—1997

(a) Accretion in a testate succession must be treated different from accretion in intestacy. In the first place, the testament itself may govern to whom the rights accrete in the event of a renunciation, and sophisticated lawyers commonly place such provisions in wills. If the testament specifies what happens in the event of renunciation, then the successor who renounces is bound by the provisions of the testament. If the successor wants to achieve a different result, he must accept the bequest and then make a donation to the person or persons whom he intends to favor.

(b) Renunciation causes a legacy to lapse under Civil Code Article 1589. Unlike the other events enumerated in Article 1589 that cause a legacy to lapse, however, renunciation is a voluntary act of the legatee. For that reason, among others, renunciation is treated differently than the other events. In addition, it is hoped that the new rule will provide some useful opportunities for estate planning that do not now exist. See Revision Comment (h) to C.C. Art. 1593, infra.

(c) The special rules regarding lapsed legacies and particularly accretion among joint legatees are located in Title II, Chapter 6, Section 2: "Testamentary Dispositions." See, for example, Civil Code Article 1593, and Revision Comments to it.

Art. 966.   Acceptance or renunciation of accretion

A person to whom succession rights accrete may accept or renounce all or part of the accretion. The acceptance or renunciation of the accretion need not be consistent with his acceptance or renunciation of other succession rights.

Acts 1997, No. 1421, § 1, eff. July 1, 1999.

REVISION COMMENTS—1997

This Article represents a change in the law that existed before 1986 but conforms to the amendment of Civil Code Article 1024 made by Act 239 of 1986. The revision attempts to further clarify Article 1024, broadening its scope. Following the 1986 amendment, Article 1024 comprehended only the situation of accretion that may be renounced after one has accepted because, under prior law, specifically Civil Code Article 1026 (1870), accretion only operates in favor of heirs who have accepted. Thus, a successor must accept the initial inheritance, but he may thereafter renounce the accretion. The revision broadens the scope of choices by permitting an heir who has renounced the original inheritance to accept what may come to him by accretion, or conversely, to accept the initial inheritance and renounce the accretion. A successor may accept both, or renounce both, or accept one and renounce the other. This flexibility is conveyed by the statement contained in this Article that acceptance or renunciation with reference to accretion "need not be consistent with" acceptance or renunciation of the original inheritance. The policy reasons that underlay requiring an initial acceptance no longer exist with the new revision.

SECTION 4—ACCEPTANCE OF SUCCESSION BY CREDITORS

Art. 967.   Acceptance of succession by creditor

A creditor of a successor may, with judicial authorization, accept succession rights in the successor's name if the successor has renounced them in whole or in part to the prejudice of his creditor's rights. In such a case, the renunciation may be annulled in favor of the creditor to the extent of his claim against the successor, but it remains effective against the successor.

Acts 1997, No. 1421, § 1, eff. July 1, 1999.

REVISION COMMENTS—1997

(a) This Article clarifies the prior rules and uses simpler terminology. As in prior law, judicial authorization for an acceptance by a creditor in the name of a successor is required, and that principle is set forth in the Article. There is no need to set forth specific procedures for obtaining such judicial authorization, since that matter should be determined in the succession proceedings themselves, and the request for authorization obviously should be made in the succession proceedings. The consequences of a creditor's acceptance are definitely limited, because of the nature of this revision's provision for limited personal liability of successors. A creditor who accepts succession rights in the name of his debtor can only accept those rights under the same conditions as the successor himself. As a result, it is implicit that the acceptance does not render the creditor liable for debts or administrative expenses of the estate, except to the value of the effects of the estate that may be received by the creditor.

One problem that perhaps should be addressed is the ranking among the creditors. If there are three creditors but only one accepts, then that one may receive payment in full of his claim whereas the other two creditors receive nothing. Since no single rule could be designed to cover all instances, and the problem has not been a serious one for the last hundred and seventy years, it was concluded that the effects of such acceptances ought to be viewed on an ad hoc basis. The creditor who accepts may or may not actually receive the inheritance, and indeed the proper results may be instead that the inheritance is seized and sold at a public auction, with the proceeds then distributed by the Sheriff. If there are sufficient assets in the inheritance to pay all creditors, then the questions of ranking and procedure are irrelevant. If there are not sufficient assets, then the court should be able to fashion an appropriate remedy under the general law.

(b) The requirement of judicial authorization is based on Articles 1071–1072 of the Louisiana Civil Code (1870) and is not a change in the law.

Arts. 968 to 1074.   [Blank]

CHAPTER 7—OF THE SEALS, AND OF THE AFFIXING AND RAISING OF THE SAME [REPEALED]

CHAPTER 8—OF THE ADMINISTRATION OF VACANT AND INTESTATE SUCCESSIONS

SECTION 1—GENERAL DISPOSITIONS

Art. 1095.   Vacant succession, definition

A succession is called vacant when no one claims it, or when all the heirs are unknown, or when all the known heirs to it have renounced it.

Art. 1096.   Intestate succession, definition

A succession is called intestate when the deceased has left no will, or when his will has been revoked or annulled as irregular.

Therefore the heirs to whom a succession has fallen by the effects of law only, are called heirs ab intestato.

Art. 1097.   Vacant succession; administration by administrators

Vacant successions are administered by legal representatives known as administrators of vacant successions.

Amended by Acts 1960, No. 30, § 1, eff. Jan. 1, 1961.

Arts. 1098 to 1099.   [Blank]

Art. 1100.   Liability for unauthorized possession of vacant succession

In case any person shall take possession of a vacant succession, or a part thereof, without being duly authorized to that effect, with the intent of converting the same to his own use, he shall be liable to pay all the debts of the said estate, exclusive of the damages to be claimed by the parties who may have suffered thereby.

SECTION 2—OF THE INVENTORY OF VACANT AND INTESTATE SUCCESSIONS SUBJECT TO ADMINISTRATION [REPEALED]

Arts. 1101 to 1112.   [Blank]

SECTION 3—OF THE APPOINTMENT OF CURATORS TO SUCCESSIONS, AND OF THE SECURITY THEY ARE BOUND TO GIVE [REPEALED]

Arts. 1113 to 1132. [Blank]

SECTION 4—OF THE DUTIES AND POWERS OF CURATORS OF VACANT SUCCESSIONS AND OF ABSENT HEIRS

Arts. 1133 to 1147. [Blank]

Art. 1148.   Interest on succession funds; liability for private use

A curator of a vacant succession or of absent heirs, owes no interest on the sums of money in his hands belonging to the succession which he administers, but he is forbidden from using them on his private account, under the pain of dismissal and responsibility for all damages caused thereby.

Arts. 1149 to 1157. [Blank]

SECTION 5—OF THE CAUSES FOR WHICH A CURATOR MAY BE DISMISSED OR SUPERSEDED [REPEALED]

Arts. 1158 to 1161. [Blank]

SECTION 6—OF THE SALE OF THE EFFECTS AND OF THE SETTLEMENT OF SUCCESSIONS ADMINISTERED BY CURATORS

Arts. 1162 to 1170. [Blank]

Art. 1171.   Persons authorized to make sale

Representatives of successions shall have the right to cause sales of the property administered by them to be made either by the sheriff or an auctioneer, or to make it themselves; but in the event of making the sales themselves, they shall receive no commission therefor.

Arts. 1172 to 1187. [Blank]

Art. 1188.   Unpaid new creditors' action against paid creditors; prescription

If, after the creditors of the succession have been paid by the curator, in conformity with the dispositions of the preceding articles, creditors present themselves, who have not made themselves known before, and if there does not remain in the hands of the curator a sum sufficient to pay what is due them, in whole or in part, these creditors have an action against those who have been paid, to compel them to refund the proportion they are bound to contribute, in order to give the new creditors a part equal to that which they would have received, had they presented themselves at the time of the payment of the debts of the succession.

But this action on the part of the creditors who have not been paid, against the creditors who have been, is prescribed by the lapse of three years, counting from the date of the order or judgment, in virtue of which the payment has been made.

In all these cases, the creditors who have thus presented themselves can in no manner disturb the curator on account of the payments he has made under the authorization of the judge, as before stated.

Arts. 1189 to 1190. [Blank]

SECTION 7—OF THE ACCOUNT TO BE RENDERED BY THE CURATORS AND THE COMMISSION DUE TO THEM

Art. 1191.   [Blank]

Art. 1192.   Termination of curator's duties on appearance of heirs

The duties of the curators cease when the heirs, or other persons having a right to the succession administered by them, present themselves or send their powers of attorney to claim the succession, and furnish security if required by law.

Amended by Acts 1981, No. 254, § 1.

COMMENT

The 1981 amendment to this article deleted reference to C.C. Art. 1012 which was repealed by Acts 1960, No. 30. The words "and furnish security if required by law" call attention to the duty of the heirs to furnish security if required by law. See C.C.P. Arts. 3007 and 3034.

Arts. 1193 to 1209. [Blank]

SECTION 8—OF THE APPOINTMENT OF COUNSEL OF ABSENT HEIRS, AND OF THEIR DUTIES [REPEALED]

Arts. 1210 to 1219. [Blank]

CHAPTER 9—OF THE SUCCESSIONS OF PERSONS DOMICILED OUT OF THE STATE, AND OF THE TAX DUE BY FOREIGN HEIRS, LEGATEES, AND DONEES [REPEALED]

SECTION 1—OF THE SUCCESSIONS OF PERSONS DOMICILED OUT OF THE STATE [REPEALED]

Art. 1220.   [Blank]

SECTION 2—OF THE TAX DUE BY FOREIGN HEIRS, LEGATEES, AND DONEES [REPEALED]

Arts. 1221 to 1223. [Blank]

CHAPTER 10—OF SUCCESSIONS ADMINISTERED BY SYNDICES [REPEALED]

Arts. 1224 to 1226. [Blank]

CHAPTER 11—OF COLLATION

SECTION 1—WHAT COLLATION IS, AND BY WHOM IT IS DUE

Art. 1227.　Collation, definition

The collation of goods is the supposed or real return to the mass of the succession which an heir makes of property which he received in advance of his share or otherwise, in order that such property may be divided together with the other effects of the succession.

Art. 1228.　Collation by descendants

A.　Children or grandchildren, coming to the succession of their fathers, mothers, or other ascendants, must collate what they have received from them by donation inter vivos, directly or indirectly, and they cannot claim the legacies made to them by such ascendants unless the donations and legacies have been made to them expressly as an advantage over their coheirs and besides their portion.

B.　This rule takes place whether the children or their descendants succeed to their ascendants as legal or as testamentary heirs.

Amended by Acts 2001, No. 572, § 1.

Art. 1229.　Reasons for collation

The obligation of collating is founded on the equality which must be naturally observed between children and other lawful descendants, who divide among them the succession of their father, mother and other ascendants; and also on the presumption that what was given or bequeathed to children by their ascendants was so disposed of in advance of what they might one day expect from their succession.

Art. 1230.　Presumption in favor of collation

Collation must take place, whether the donor has formerly [formally] ordered it, or has remained silent on the subject; for collation is always presumed, where it has not been expressly forbidden.

Art. 1231.　Express exclusion of collation; extra portion

But things given or bequeathed to children or other descendants by their ascendants, shall not be collated, if the donor has formally expressed his will that what he thus gave was an advantage or extra part, unless the value of the object given exceed the disposable portion, in which case the excess is subject to collation.

Art. 1232.　Method of declaring dispensation from collation

The declaration that the gift or legacy is made as an advantage or extra portion may be made in the instrument where such disposition is contained, or afterwards by an act passed before a notary and two witnesses, or in the donor's last will and testament. Unless expressly stated to the contrary, a declaration of dispensation from collation made in the last will and testament of the donor shall be effective as a dispensation from collating donations made both before and after execution of said testament.

Amended by Acts 1986, No. 246, § 1.

Art. 1233.　Sufficiency of declaration

The declaration that the gift or legacy is intended as an advantage or extra portion, may be made in other equivalent terms, provided they indicate, in an unequivocal manner, that such was the will of the donor.

Art. 1234. Reduction of donations exceeding disposable portion; calculation of legitime

If, upon calculation of the value of advantages thus given, and of the other effects remaining in the succession, such remaining part should prove insufficient to give to the other children their legitimate portion, the donee would then be obliged to collate the sum by him received, as far as necessary to complete such portion, though he would wish to keep the donation, and renounce the inheritance; and in this calculation of the legitimate portion, the property given or bequeathed by the ascendants, not only to their children, but even to all other persons, whether relations or strangers, must be included.

Art. 1235. Persons entitled to demand collation

The right to demand collation is confined to descendants of the first degree who qualify as forced heirs, and only applies with respect to gifts made within the three years prior to the decedent's death, and valued as of the date of the gift. Any provision of the Civil Code to the contrary is hereby repealed.

Acts 1996, 1st Ex.Sess., No. 77, § 1.

REVISION COMMENTS—1996

(a) The amendment of Article 1235 significantly reduces the scope and application of collation by limiting it to descendants of the first degree who qualify as forced heirs. This amendment correlates the rules of collation with the new rules of forced heirship and is expressly designed to constrict the application of collation and make it more consistent with the new law regarding forced heirship.

(b) The amendment further simplifies the application of collation by limiting its range: even when the child qualifies as a forced heir, and has a right to demand collation because the inter vivos gifts have not been exempted from collation, his claim is now limited to those gifts that have been made within three years of the decedent's death, valued at the time of the gift. The new rule there by eliminates the inclusion of more remote gifts, and also makes it easier to determine the value of those that are included.

(c) Under this article, if a child has attained the age of 24 and is not otherwise disabled, he is not permitted to demand collation; nor is a grandchild permitted to demand it, even if he qualifies as a forced heir. Collation is a presumption of the law that a parent wants to treat all of his children equally, but it is not required, as is forced heirship, and the donor may dispense with it. The rules on collation did not coordinate with the new law on forced heirship by which only children who are "23 years of age or younger" are forced heirs, because, without amendment, collation would apply to all children, regardless of age. The amendment of Civil Code Article 1235 avoids the situation where an older child might have no claim as a forced heir but, because of the inadvertent failure of his parent to exempt inter vivos gifts from collation, the older child might nonetheless assert a claim against his siblings, even those who are forced heirs, to equalize the gifts. An unusual spin on this situation appeared in Succession of Del Buno, 665 So.2d 172 (La.App. 1st Cir. 1995) in which the forced heir was disinherited by his parent, but the parent had not expressly dispensed with collation. The Court of Appeal remanded the case to a lower court to determine whether the heir was precluded from asserting collation in that circumstance.

(d) This provision repeals the rule that permitted a child to demand collation with regard to gifts that had been made many years previously, and intentionally adopts rules that are parallel to the new forced heirship rules, which now limit the "fictitious collation" for purposes of calculating the "active mass" to gifts that were made within three years, and which now require that the gifts be valued at the time of the gift. See Article 1505 (A). The valuation rules for collation purposes were also different from the rules for valuation of gifts for forced heirship purposes: collation previously required that immovables be valued as of the date of death, not the date of gift, but that movables be valued at the date of the gift. Article 1235 now makes the collation and forced heirship rules more consistent with each other, especially as to scope and valuation.

Art. 1236. [Blank]

Art. 1237. Renouncing heir's right to donations not exceeding disposable portion

If children, or other lawful descendants holding property or legacies subject to be collated, should renounce the succession of the ascendant, from whom they have received such property, they may retain the gift, or claim the legacy to them made, without being subject to any collation.

If, however, the remaining amount of the inheritance should not be sufficient for the legitimate portion of the other children, including in the succession of the deceased the property which the person renouncing would have collated, had he become heir, he shall then be obliged to collate up to the sum necessary to complete such legitimate portion.

Art. 1238. Grandchildren; collation of donations made by grandparent after death of parent

A.　To make descendants liable to collation, as prescribed in the preceding Articles, they must appear in the quality of heirs to the succession of the ascendants from whom they immediately have received the gift or legacy.

B.　Therefore, grandchildren, to whom a gift was made or a legacy left by their grandfather or grandmother, after the death of their father or mother, are obliged to collate, when they are called to the inheritance of the grandfather or grandmother, jointly with the other grandchildren, or by representation with their uncles or aunts, brothers or sisters of their father or mother, because it is presumed that their grandfather or grandmother had intended to make the gift, or leave the legacy by anticipation.

Amended by Acts 1990, No. 147, § 1, eff. July 1, 1990; Acts 1995, No. 1180, § 1, eff. Jan. 1, 1996.

Art. 1239. Grandchildren; right to donations made by grandparent during life of parent

A.　But gifts made or legacies left to a grandchild by his grandfather or grandmother during the life of his father, are always reputed to be exempt from collation.

B.　The father, inheriting from the grandfather, is not liable to collate the gifts or legacies left to his child.

Amended by Acts 1990, No. 147, § 1, eff. July 1, 1990; Acts 1995, No. 1180, § 1, eff. Jan. 1, 1996.

Art. 1240. Grandchildren; collation of donations made by grandparent to parent

In like manner, the grandchild, when inheriting in his own right from the grandfather or grandmother, is not obliged to refund the gifts made to his father, even though he should have accepted the succession; but if the grandchild comes in only by right of representation, he must collate what had been given to his father, even though he should have renounced his inheritance.

Art. 1241. Collation by great grandchildren and more remote descendants

What has been said in the three preceding articles, of grandchildren inheriting from their grandfather or grandmother, must be understood of the great-grandchildren and other lawful descendants called to inherit from their ascendants, either in their own name or by right of representation.

SECTION 2—TO WHOM THE COLLATION IS DUE, AND WHAT THINGS ARE SUBJECT TO IT

Art. 1242. Collation; succession of donor

The collation is made only to the succession of the donor.

Amended by Acts 1980, No. 565, § 4.

Art. 1243. Expenditures subject to collation

Collation is due for what has been expended by the father and mother to procure an establishment of their descendant coming to their succession, or for the payment of his debts.

Amended by Acts 1979, No. 711, § 1, eff. Jan. 1, 1980; Acts 2004, No. 26, § 1.

Art. 1244. Expenditures not subject to collation

Neither the expenses of board, support, education and apprenticeship are subject to collation, nor are marriage presents which do not exceed the disposable portion.

Art. 1245. Manual gifts

The same rule is established with respect to things given by a father, mother or other ascendant, by their own hands, to one of their children for his pleasure or other use.

Art. 1246. Profits from contracts with ascendant

The heir is not bound to collate the profits he has made from contracts made with his ascendant to whom he succeeds unless the contracts, at the time of their being made, gave the heir some indirect advantage.

Art. 1247. Share of partnership with ascendant

Also no collation is due for a partnership made without fraud with the deceased, if the conditions of the partnership are proved by an authentic act.

Art. 1248. Advantages other than donation

The advantage which a father bestows upon his son, though in any other manner than by donation or legacy, is likewise subject to collation. Thus, when a father has sold a thing to his son at a very low price, or has paid for him the price of some purchase, for [or] has spent money to improve his son's estate, all that is subject to collation.

Art. 1249. Wages for services to ascendant

The obligation of collation does not exclude the child or descendant coming to the succession of his father, mother or other ascendant, from claiming wages which may be due to him for having administered the property of the ascendant, or for other services.

Art. 1250. Immovables destroyed while in possession of donee

Immovable property, given by a father, mother or other ascendant, to one of their children or descendants, and which has been destroyed by accident, while in the possession of the donee and without his fault, previous to the opening of the succession, is not subject to collation.

If, on the contrary, it is by the fault or negligence of the donee that the immovable property has been destroyed, he is bound to collate to the amount of the value which the property would have had at the time of the opening of the succession.

SECTION 3—HOW COLLATIONS ARE MADE

Art. 1251. Methods of making collations

Collations are made in kind or by taking less.

Art. 1252.   Collation in kind, definition

The collation is made in kind, when the thing which has been given, is delivered up by the donee to be united to the mass of the succession.

Art. 1253.   Collation by taking less, definition

The collation is made by taking less, when the donee diminishes the portion he inherits, in proportion to the value of the object he has received, and takes so much less from the surplus of the effects as is explained in the chapter which treats of partitions.

Art. 1254.   Movables or immovable

In the execution of the collation it must first be considered whether the things subject to it are movables or immovables.

Art. 1255.   Collation of immovable

If an immovable has been given, and the donee hath it in his possession at the time of the partition, he has the choice to make the collation in kind or by taking less, unless the donor has imposed on him the condition of making the collation in kind, in which case it can not be made in any other manner than that prescribed by the donor, unless it be with the consent of the other heirs who must be all of age, present or represented in this State.

Art. 1256.   Immovables collated in kind; reimbursement for improvements

The donee who collates in kind an immovable, which has been given to him, must be reimbursed by his coheirs for the expenses which have improved the estate, in proportion to the increase of value which it has received thereby.

Art. 1257.   Immovables collated in kind; allowance for expenses of preservation

The coheirs are bound to allow to the donee the necessary expenses which he has incurred for the preservation of the estate, though they may not have augmented its value.

Art. 1258.   Immovables collated in kind; removal by donee of works erected for his pleasure

As to works made on the estate for the mere pleasure of the donee, no reimbursement is due to him for them; he has, however, the right to take them away, if he can do it without injuring the estate, and leave things in the same situation they were at the time of the donation.

Art. 1259.   Kinds of expenses made on immovable property

Expenses made on immovable property are distinguished by three kinds: necessary, useful, and those for mere pleasure.

Necessary expenses are those which are indispensable to the preservation of the thing.

Useful expenses are those which increase the value of the immovable property, but without which the estate can be preserved.

Expenses for mere pleasure are those which are only made for the accommodation or convenience of the owner or possessor of the estate, and which do not increase its value.

Art. 1260.   Deterioration and damage to immovable, liability of donee

The donee, who collates in kind the immovable property given to him, is accountable for the deteriorations and damage which have diminished its value, when caused by his fault or negligence.

Art. 1261.   Destruction of immovable after election to collate in kind

If within the time and in the form prescribed in the chapter which treats of partitions, the donee has made his election to collate in kind the immovable property which has been given to him, and it is afterwards destroyed, without the act or fault of the donee, the loss is borne by the succession, and the donee shall not be bound to collate the value of the property.

Art. 1262.   Partial destruction of immovable after election to collate in kind

If the immovable property be only destroyed in part, it shall be collated in the state in which it is.

Art. 1263.   Destruction of immovable after election to collate by taking less

But if the immovable property is destroyed after the donee has declared that he wishes to collate by taking less, the loss is his, and he is bound to take less from the succession, in the same manner as if the property had not been destroyed.

Art. 1264.   Creditors' rights on immovable collated in kind

When the collation is made in kind, the effects are united to the mass of the succession as they may be burdened with real rights created by operation of law or by onerous title. In such a case, the donee is accountable for the resulting diminution of the value of the immovable.

Amended by Acts 1981, No. 739, § 1.

Art. 1265.   Preservation of creditor's mortgage rights after partition

In the case mentioned in the preceding article, if the property mortgaged, which has been collated in kind, falls by the partition to the donee, the mortgage continues to exist thereon as if it had never been collated; but if the donee receives for his portion other movables or immovables of the succession, the creditor shall have a privilege for the amount of his mortgage on the property which has thus fallen to his debtor by the partition.

Art. 1266.   Immovables in excess of disposable portion; collation in kind

When the gift of immovable property, made to a lawful child or descendant, exceeds the portion which the ascendant could legally dispose of, the donee may make the collation of this excess in kind, if such excess can be separated conveniently.

Art. 1267.   Immovables in excess of disposable portion; collation by taking less

If, on the contrary, the retrenchment of the excess over and above the disposable portion can not conveniently be made, the donee is bound to collate the excess by taking less, as is hereafter prescribed for the cases in which the collation is made of immovable property given him otherwise than as advantage or extra portion.

Art. 1268.   Collation in kind; retention of immovable until reimbursement of expenses

The donee, who makes the collation in kind of the immovable property given to him, may keep possession of the same until the final reimbursement of the sums to him due for the necessary and useful expenses which he has made thereon, after deducting the amount of the damage the estate has suffered through his fault or neglect, as is before provided.

Art. 1269.   Collation by taking less; valuation of immovable

When the donee has elected to collate the immovable property given him by taking less on the part which comes to him from the succession, the collation must be made according to the value which the immovable property had at the opening of the succession, a deduction being made for the expenses incurred thereon, in conformity with what has been heretofore prescribed.

Art. 1270.   Voluntary alienation or negligent loss of immovables subject to collation

If the donee has voluntarily alienated the immovable property which has been given him, or if he has permitted it to be seized and sold for the payment of his debts, or if it has been destroyed by his fault or negligence, he shall not be the less bound to make the collation of it, according to the value which the immovable would have had at the time of the opening of the succession, deducting expenses, as is provided in the foregoing Article.

Amended by Acts 1981, No. 739, § 1.

Art. 1271.   Forced alienation of immovables subject to collation

But if the donee has been forced to alienate the immovable property, he shall be obliged to collate by taking less the price he has received from this sale and no more.

As, for example, if the donee shall be obliged to submit to a sale of the immovable for some object of public utility, or to discharge a mortgage imposed by the donor, or because the immovable was held in common with another person who has prayed for the sale in order to obtain a partition of it.

Art. 1272.   Sale by donee and subsequent destruction of immovable subject to collation

If the immovable property which has been given has been sold by the donee, and afterwards is destroyed by accident in the possession of the purchaser, the donee shall only be obliged to collate by taking less the price he received for the sale.

Art. 1273.   Collation by taking less; coheirs' election of collation by sale or in kind

When the collation is made by taking less, the coheirs to whom the collation is due have a right to require a sale of the property remaining to the succession, in order to be paid from the proceeds of this sale, not only the collation which is due to them, but the part which comes to them from the surplus of these proceeds, unless they prefer to pay themselves the amount of the collation due to them by taking such movables and immovables of the succession as they may choose, according to the appraisement in the inventory, or the appraisement which serves as a basis to the partition.

Art. 1274.   Failure of coheirs to make timely election

If the coheirs to whom the collation is made by taking less, wish that the effects of the succession be sold, in order that they may be paid what is due them, they are bound to decide thereon in three days from their being notified of the motion of the donee to that effect, before the judge of the partition, otherwise they shall be deprived of this right, and shall be considered as having consented to receive payment of the collation due them in effects and property of the succession, or otherwise from the hands of the donee.

Art. 1275.   Payment of collation by sale of succession effects

When the coheirs, thus notified, require the sale of the effects of the succession to pay themselves the collation due them, the sale shall be made at public auction, in the same manner as when it is necessary to sell property held in common, in order to effect a partition.

Art. 1276.   Payment of collation with property of succession

If, on the contrary, the coheirs to whom the collation is due prefer to be paid the amount thereof in property and effects of the succession, or are divested of their right to require the sale of these effects, they shall be paid the amount of the collation in movables, immovables and other effects of the succession, in the same manner as is prescribed in the chapter which treats of partitions.

But in no case will these heirs be obliged to receive in payment of the succession.

Art. 1277. Payment of collation by donee where succession effects insufficient

If there are no effects in the succession, or not sufficient to satisfy the heirs to whom the collation is due, the amount of the collation, or the balance due on it, shall be paid them by the heir who owes the collation.

Art. 1278. Time and security for payment

This heir shall have one year to pay the sum thus by him due, if he furnish his coheirs with his obligation payable at that time, with eight per cent. interest, and give a special mortgage to secure the payment thereof, either on the immovable property subject to the collation, if it is in his possession, or in want thereof, on some other immovable property which may suit the coheirs.

Art. 1279. Rights of coheirs against defaulting heir; foreclosure of special mortgage

If the heir, who has been allowed to furnish his obligation as mentioned in the preceding article, fails to fulfill his engagement at the expiration of the year granted to him, the heirs, in whose favor this obligation has been made, or their representatives, have a right to cause the property mortgaged to them to be seized and sold, without any appraisement, and at the price offered at the first exposure for sale.

Art. 1280. Privilege of seizing coheirs on proceeds of mortgage sale

If the property thus seized and sold is the same which was subject to the collation, the coheirs seizing, or their representatives, shall be paid the amount of their debt due for the collation, by privilege and in preference to all the creditors of the donee, even to those to whom he may have mortgaged the property for his own debts or engagements, previous to the opening of the succession, saving to these mortgage creditors their recourse against other property of the donee.

Art. 1281. Alienation of immovable by donee by onerous title; creation of real right in immovable by donee or operation of law

(a) If the donee who owes the collation has alienated by onerous title the immovable given to him, the coheirs shall not have the right to claim the immovable in the hands of the transferee.

(b) If the donee who owes the collation has created a real right by onerous title in the immovable given to him or such right has been created by operation of law since the donee received the immovable, the coheirs may claim the immovable in the hands of the donee but subject to such real right as has been created. In such a case, the donee and his successors by gratuitous title are accountable for the resulting diminution of the value of the property.

Amended by Acts 1981, No. 739, § 1; Acts 1984, No. 869, § 1.

Art. 1282. Purchaser's retention of immovable upon payment of collations

The third purchaser or possessor of the real estate subject to collation may avoid the effect of the action of revendication, by paying to the coheirs of the donee, to whom the collation is due, to wit: the excess of the value of the property above the disposable portion, if the donation has been made as an advantage or extra portion, or the whole of the value thereof, if the donation has been made without this provision, by fulfilling in this respect all the obligations by which the donee himself was bound towards the coheirs.

Art. 1283. Collation of movables

When movables have been given, the donee is not permitted to collate them in kind; he is bound to collate for them by taking less, according to their appraised value at the time of the donation, if there be any annexed to the donation. In default thereof, recourse may be had to other evidence to establish the value of these movables at the time of the donation.

Art. 1284. Donation of movables as absolute transfer of rights

Therefore the donation of movables contains an absolute transfer of the rights of the donor to the donee in the movables thus given.

Art. 1285. Collation of money

The collation of money may be made in money or by taking less, at the choice of the donee who is bound to decide thereon, in the same manner as is prescribed for the collation of immovable property.

Art. 1286. Collation of movables or money by taking less; payment in money

If it be movables or money, of which the donee wishes to make the collation by taking less, he has the right of compelling his coheirs to pay themselves the collation due to them in money, and not otherwise, if there be sufficient in the succession to make these payments with.

Art. 1287. Collation of movables or money by taking less; payment in succession effects

But if there is not sufficient money in the succession to pay such heirs the collation due to them, they shall pay themselves by taking an equivalent in the other movables or immovables of the succession, as is directed with respect to the collation of immovable property.

Art. 1288. Payment of collation by donee where succession effects insufficient

In case there be no property or effects in the succession to satisfy the collations due for movables or money given, the donee shall have, for the payment of the sum due to his coheirs, the same terms of payment as are given for the payment of the amount of collations of immovable property, and under the same conditions as are before prescribed.

CHAPTER 12—OF THE PARTITION OF SUCCESSION

SECTION 1—OF THE NATURE OF PARTITION, AND OF ITS SEVERAL KINDS

Art. 1289. [Blank]

Art. 1290. Extent and application of rules; venue of action

All the rules, established in the present chapter, with the exception of that which relates to the collations, are applicable to partitions between coproprietors of the same thing when among the coproprietors any are absent, minors, or interdicted, or when the coproprietors of age and present can not agree on the partition and on the manner of making it.

But in these kinds of partitions the action must be brought before the judge of the place where the property to be divided is situated, wherever the parties interested may be domiciliated.

Art. 1291. Venue of action where property partly in different parishes

Whenever two or more persons shall be coproprietors of one continuous tract of land situated partly in different parishes, any one or more of the coproprietors may institute an action for partition of the whole of the tract in any one of such parishes.

Art. 1292. Undivided ownership rights until partition

When a person, at his decease, leaves several heirs, each of them becomes an undivided proprietor of the effects of the succession, for the part or portion coming to him, which forms among the heirs a community of property, as long as it remains undivided.

Art. 1293. Partition of a succession, definition

The partition of a succession is the division of the effects, of which the succession is composed, among all the coheirs, according to their respective rights.

Art. 1294. [Blank]

Art. 1295. Definitive and provisional partitions, definitions

Every partition is either definitive or provisional: Definitive partition is that which is made in a permanent and irrevocable manner;

Provisional partition is that which is made provisionally, either of certain things before the rest can be divided, or even of everything that is to be divided, when the parties are not in a situation to make an irrevocable partition.

Art. 1296. Definitive and provisional partitions, distinguished

By definitive partition is also understood the judicial partition, made according to law; and by provisional partition, that in which the formalities prescribed by law have not been observed, or that by which the parties are not definitively bound.

Art. 1297. Stipulations against partition

It can not be stipulated that there never shall be a partition of a succession or of a thing held in common. Such a stipulation would be null and of no effect.

Art. 1298. [Blank]

Art. 1299. Perpetual prohibition against partition by donor

A donor or testator can not order that the effects given or bequeathed by him to two or more persons in common, shall never be divided, and such a prohibition would be considered as if it were not made.

Art. 1300. Limited or conditional prohibition against partition by donor

But a donor or testator can order that the effects given or bequeathed by him, be not divided for a certain time, or until the happening of a certain condition.

But if the time fixed exceed five years, or if the condition do not happen within that term, from the day of the donation or of the opening of the succession, the judge, at the expiration of this term of five years, may order the partition, if it is proved to him that the coheirs can not agree among themselves, or differ as to the administration of the common effects.

Art. 1301. Testator's right to prohibit partition during minority of heirs

If the father or other ascendant orders by his will that no partition shall be made among his minor children or minor grandchildren inheriting from him, during the time of their minority, this prohibition must be observed, until one of the children or grandchildren comes of age, and demands the partition.

Art. 1302. Testamentary partition

There is no occasion for partition, if the deceased has regulated it between his lawful heirs, or strangers, or if the deceased has expressly delegated the authority to his executor to allocate specific assets to satisfy a legacy expressed in terms of a quantum or value; and in such case the judge must follow the will of the testator or his executor.

The same thing takes place when the testator has expressly assigned specific assets of his estate, or delegated the authority to assign specific assets of his estate, in satisfaction of the forced portion of his children.

Amended by Acts 1982, No. 448, § 1, eff. July 21, 1982.

Arts. 1303 to 1304. [Blank]

Art. 1305. Prescription where possession is separate

When one of the heirs has enjoyed the whole or part of the succession separately, or all the coheirs have possessed separately each a portion of the hereditary effects, he or they who have thus separately possessed, can successfully oppose the suit for a partition of the effects of the succession, if their possession has continued thirty years without interruption.

Art. 1306. Prescription where one heir possesses separately and others possess in common

If there be but one of the heirs who has separately enjoyed a portion of the effects of the succession during thirty years, and all the other heirs have possessed the residue of the effects of the succession in common, the action of partition among the latter will always subsist.

SECTION 2—AMONG WHAT PERSONS
PARTITION CAN BE SUED FOR

Art. 1307. Partition between heirs and legatees

A partition may be sued for by any heirs, testamentary or ab intestato.

It can also be sued for by any universal legatee or legatee under an universal title, and even by a particular legatee, when a thing has been bequeathed to him in common with one or more persons.

Art. 1308. Partition between owners in common

The action of partition will not only lie between co-heirs and co-legatees, but between all persons who hold property in common, from whatever cause they may hold in common.

Amended by Acts 1871, No. 87.

Art. 1309. Partition between possessors in common

It is not indispensable to be owner in common in order to be able to support the action of partition; possession alone, when it is lawful and proceeds from a just title, will support it.

Thus, usufructuaries of the same estate can institute among themselves the action of partition.

Art. 1310.   Nature of possession required

But the possession, necessary to support this action, must be in the names of the persons enjoying it, and for themselves; it can not be instituted by those who possess in the name of another, as tenants and depositaries.

Art. 1311.   Action maintainable by one or more co-owners

Partitions can be sued for not only by the majority of the heirs, but by each of them, so that one heir alone can force all the rest to a partition at his instance.

Art. 1312.   Partition suits by tutors and curators

Tutors of minors, and curators of persons interdicted have the right to institute in their names suits for the partition of the effects of successions, whether movable or immovable, falling to minors or persons interdicted, provided they are specially authorized by the judge on the advice of the family meeting.

Art. 1313.   Partition suits by emancipated minors

Minors who are emancipated to enable them to administer their estate can, with the same authorization and with the assistance of their curators ad lites, sue for the partition of property in which they are interested.

Art. 1314.   Defense of suits by tutors, curators and emancipated minors

But the authorization of the judge is not necessary to enable tutors or curators of minors or persons interdicted or minors emancipated, to answer suits for partition brought against them.

Art. 1315.   Partition suits by curators of absent heirs

With regard to the absent coheirs, the curators who have been appointed to them, or the relations who have been put into possession of their effects, can sue or be sued for a partition as representing in every respect the absent heirs.

Arts. 1316 to 1317. [Blank]

Art. 1318.   Partition by or against heir or successor of co-owner

Not only the coheir himself, but the heirs of that coheir, and any other successor can compel a partition of the estate, and be themselves compelled to make it.

Art. 1319.   Retrocession repealed

The right given by the ancient laws to the heirs of a deceased person, to compel the assignee or purchaser of a portion of the succession sold by their coheirs to retrocede it to them for the price paid for it, is repealed.

Art. 1320.   Ownership as basis for action of partition

It is not necessary, to support the action of partition, that the coheirs, or the party commencing it, should be in actual possession of the succession or of the thing to be divided; for among coheirs and coproprietors, it is not the possession but the ownership, which is the basis of the action.

Art. 1321. Separate possession of one co-owner, partition before prescription

It follows from the provisions of the preceding article that the partition can be demanded, even though one of the heirs should have enjoyed some part of the estate separately, if there has been no act of partition, nor possession sufficient to acquire prescription.

SECTION 3—IN WHAT MANNER THE JUDICIAL PARTITION IS MADE

Arts. 1322 to 1324. [Blank]

Art. 1325. Inventory within one year of partition suit

The public inventory, which may have been made by the parties interested at a time not exceeding one year previous to the suit for a partition, shall serve as the basis of the partition, unless one of the heirs demands a new appraisement, and proves that the effects mentioned in the inventory have not been estimated at their just price, or at the value they have acquired since the date of this act.

Art. 1326. New appraisement

In this case the judge is bound to order a new appraisement of the effects to be divided, which shall be made by experts appointed by him to that effect, and duly sworn by the officer who is appointed to make the proces verbal of the appraisement.

Art. 1327. [Blank]

Art. 1328. Summary proceeding for action of partition

The judge, before whom the action of partition is brought, is bound to pronounce thereon in a summary manner, by which is always meant with the least possible delay and in preference to the ordinary suits pending before him.

Art. 1329. Parties plaintiff and defendant

The suit for partition ought to be instituted by the heir who wishes the division; the coheirs or their representatives must be cited, in order that the partition may be ordered, and the form thereof determined, if there should be any dispute in this respect.

Art. 1330. Plaintiff's admission of defendant's heirship

He who sues another for a partition of the effects of a succession, confesses thereby that the person against whom the suit is brought is an heir.

Art. 1331. Collation in action of partition; time for deliberating

If a partition is to be made among the children or descendants of the deceased, and one of the heirs alleges that his coheir is bound to collate an immovable, which has been given him by the deceased, and requires that his coheir should decide on the manner in which he wishes to make this collation, the judge, if it be proved that the coheir is bound to collate the property, shall order that the donee decide thereon, within a term to be fixed by the judge, which can not exceed three days from the day on which the order has been notified to him, if he or his representative is found in the place.

Art. 1332.   Election to collate in kind

If the donee, who is bound to collate an immovable given xhim by the deceased, declare within the term fixed, as aforesaid, that he will return it in kind, the property, from that instant, becomes united to the other effects of the succession which is to be divided.

Art. 1333.   Election to collate by taking less; failure to elect

But if the donee declare that he will not return the immovable property which has been given him, but will take his share in the effects of the succession, after deducting the value of such immovable property, or if he permits the term, granted to him to make his decision, to expire, without deciding on the manner in which he will make his collation, he shall lose the right of returning this property in kind.

Art. 1334.   Appraisement of property to be collated

Whether the donee has decided that he will collate in kind or by taking less, the coheirs, to whom the collation is due, have the right, as soon as the donee has decided thereon, to require and obtain an order that the property subject to the collation be appraised, as is prescribed in the following section, in order that it may be included among the effects to be divided for the sum at which it is appraised.

Art. 1335.   Matters incidental to partition; procedure

All points, arising before the judge having cognizance of the suit for partition, on the manner of making the collation or other operations relating to the partition, being merely incidental to the suit, shall be decided on the simple motion of the party interested in having them decided, the same being duly notified to the other heirs or their attorneys, and a reasonable time being granted to answer thereto.

Art. 1336.   Judicial regulation of mode of partition

The judge who decides on a suit for a partition and on the mode of effecting it, has a right to regulate this mode as may appear to him most convenient and most advantageous for the general interest of the coheirs, in conformity, nevertheless, with the following provisions.

Art. 1337.   Partition in kind; sale of movables to pay debts

Each of the coheirs may demand in kind his share of the movables and immovables of the succession; but if there are creditors who have made any seizure or opposition, or if a majority of the coheirs are of opinion that the sale is necessary in order to satisfy the debts and charges of the succession, the movables shall be sold at public auction, after the usual advertisements.

Arts. 1338 to 1340.   [Blank]

Art. 1341.   Terms of sale of succession effects where all heirs are absent or minors

When the effects of a succession are to be sold, in order to effect a partition, if all the heirs of the deceased are absent, minors or interdicted, the judge may, at the instance of the tutors and curators of these heirs, and on the advice of the family meeting of those of the heirs who are minors or interdicted, order the sale to be made on certain terms of credit and on proper security, unless the payments of the debts of the succession require that the sale be made for cash.

Art. 1342.   Terms of sale of succession effects where heirs present demand sale for cash

If there be, among the heirs of the deceased, any who are of age and present, and who demand that the sale be made for cash, it shall be made for cash, for a sufficient sum to cover the portion coming to them, and on a credit for the balance, on the terms prescribed by the other heirs.

But on the partition of the proceeds of the sale, the whole amount shall be reduced to its cash value, by deducting from the whole sum to be paid, eight per cent. per annum, and those heirs who require their portion in cash, shall receive it on the whole amount thus reduced.

Art. 1343. Partition sale; coheir's right to purchase hereditary portion

Any coheir of age, at the sale of the hereditary effects, can become a purchaser to the amount of the portion owing to him from the succession, and he is not obliged to pay the surplus of the purchase money over the portion coming to him, until this portion has been definitely fixed by a partition.

Art. 1344. Partition sale; purchase of minor's hereditary portion by tutor or curator

The minor coheirs may also become purchasers of the hereditary effects, by the intervention of their tutors or curators, or by their assistance, if they have been specially authorized thereto by the judge, with the advice of the family meeting.

Art. 1345. Reference to recorder or notary for continuation of proceedings

When the judge has ordered the partition, and regulated the manner in which it shall be made, as well as the collations, if the case require it, he shall refer the parties to the recorder of the parish or a notary appointed by him to continue the judicial partition to be made between them.

Art. 1346. Amicable continuation of proceedings by heirs

If the heirs who have instituted the suit for partition be of age and present, and the judge has fixed the mode of making it, whether in kind or otherwise, nothing shall prevent the heirs from continuing their partition amicably and in the manner they think proper.

SECTION 4—HOW THE RECORDER OF THE PARISH OR THE NOTARY IS BOUND TO PROCEED IN THE JUDICIAL PARTITION

Art. 1347. Notice to parties

The officer appointed to make the partition is bound, within fifteen days at farthest from the notice of his appointment, to notify the heirs or their representatives, in writing, of the day, hour, and place in which he is to commence his work, sufficient time previous thereto, to enable them to attend, if they think proper.

Art. 1348. Continuances of proceedings

As the business of partitions sometimes requires several days, the officer may divide his procès verbal, and make as many vacations or sittings as he thinks proper.

Amended by Acts 1960, No. 30, § 1, eff. Jan. 1, 1961.

Art. 1349. Settlement of accounts due by heirs to succession

On the day appointed for the partition, the officer shall begin by settling the accounts, which each of the heirs may owe to the succession.

Art. 1350. Items included in accounts

The officer shall include in these accounts:

1.   The sums which each of the coheirs owes to the deceased;

2.   Those which each of the coheirs may have received or disbursed on account of the succession, whether for the payment of debts or for necessary and useful expenses on the effects of the succession;

3.   Those which each of the coheirs may owe by reason of damages or injury, which have been caused by his fault to the effects of the succession.

Art. 1351.   Deduction of donations not subject to collation

The accounts being thus settled, the officer must deduct from the effects of the succession the things which have been bequeathed by the deceased, either to any of the coheirs beyond his portion when the collation is dispensed with, or to any other persons, as these things ought not be included in the mass of the effects to be divided.

Art. 1352.   Court order as to mode of collation exhibited to officer

If the partition is to be made between children or descendants inheriting from their father, mother or other ascendant, and a collation is to be made, the officer shall cause the decree of the judge to be exhibited to him, by which it is decided whether the collation is to be made in kind, or by taking less.

Amended by Acts 2004, No. 26, § 1.

Art. 1353.   Inclusion of property collated in kind

If the collation is to be made in kind, the officer is bound to include the property collated in the number of the effects of the succession, for its estimated value, which shall have been fixed by experts appointed by the judge, as is said heretofore.

Art. 1354.   Inclusion of value of property collated by taking less

If, on the contrary, the collation is to be made by taking less, the officer shall add to the credit of the estate the sum due by the heir who is bound to make the collation, according to the appraisement which shall have been made by experts appointed by the judge, separately from the other articles of the succession, in order that the other heirs may have a sum of money or some object equal to the estimated value of the property subject to collation.

Art. 1355.   Formation of active mass

The officers [officer] shall then proceed to the formation of the active mass of the succession.

Art. 1356.   Composition of active mass

This active mass shall be composed:

1.   Of all the movables and immovables of the succession, which have not been sold, mention being made of their value, as stated in the inventory of the effects of the succession, or in the new appraisement which may have been made by experts appointed by the judge;

2.   Of the price of the movables and immovables, which have been sold to effect the partition;

3.   Of all the objects collated by the heirs, whether in kind or by taking less, in proportion to the appraised value given to them by the experts appointed by the judge;

4.   Of all the sums, which the heirs may owe to the succession, according to the settled account;

5.   Of all the debts due to the succession by other persons.

Art. 1357.   Deductions from active mass

The active mass of the succession being thus formed, if there be no collation, or if the collations are made in kind, the officer proceeds to the deductions to be made from the mass, in order to ascertain the balance to be divided.

Art. 1358.   Deductions, definition

By deduction is understood a portion or thing which an heir has a right to take from the mass of the succession before any partition takes place.

Art. 1359.   Deductions allowed

The deductions, which are to be made before the partition of a succession, consist:

    1.   Of the sums due to one or more of the heirs for a debt due them by the deceased, or advance [advances] made to the succession, or expenses on its effects, according to the account settled among the heirs;

    2.   Of the amount owing to the heirs to whom a collation is due, when the collation is made by taking less, in order that the heirs may receive a portion equal to the amount of the collation which is due;

    3.   Of the privileged debts due or paid on account of the succession, which have been incurred since the death of the deceased, or in order to effect the partition.

Art. 1360.   Deductions in absence of collation or when collation is in kind

When the collations have been made in kind, or when there is none to be made, the deductions are taken from the active mass of the succession, and the balance remaining forms the mass to be divided.

Art. 1361.   Deductions, when collation is by taking less

But when the collation is made fictitiously and by taking less, the officer having formed the active mass of the succession, including the collation, deducts the sum at which the property collated is estimated, and on the mass thus reduced the deduction is made.

Art. 1362.   Coheir's right to take succession effects in payment of collation

When the deduction which is to be made in favor of the heir to whom the collation is due, has been ascertained and established, according to the preceding article, if there be among the effects of the succession any movables or immovables, which this heir wishes to take at the estimated value in payment of the amount of the collation due to him, he can take them at his choice, and the officer shall give them to him.

Art. 1363.   Disagreement among heirs entitled to receive collation in property

If there be two or more heirs, who have a right to receive the collation due to them in the property and effects of the succession, and they can not agree on the partition of the effects which they have thus chosen, the officer shall appoint experts to form allotments of these effects, for which the parties entitled to the collation shall draw lots, in the same manner as is hereafter prescribed for the formation and drawing of the lots of the definitive partition.

Art. 1364.   Division into lots according to number of heirs or roots

When the deductions have been made, and those to whom the collations were due have received them, as is said in the preceding article, the officer divides what remains into as many equal lots as there are heirs, or roots entitled to a share.

No subdivision of the lots thus formed need be made between the individual coproprietors claiming under the same root.

A partition thus made, even without a subdivision being made of the lots to which each root may be entitled, shall be a definitive partition.

Amended by Acts 1938, No. 407.

Art. 1365.   Equality in formation of lots

In the formation and composition of the lots, care must be taken to avoid as much as possible the cantling of tenements, and not to separate what is necessary for the same cultivation. And there ought to be included, if possible, in each lot, the same quantity of movables, immovables, rights and of the same nature and value.

Art. 1366.   Equalization by money when one lot more valuable than others

When the lots are of unequal value, such inequality is compensated by means of a return of money, which the coheir, having a lot of more value than the other, pays to his coheirs.

Art. 1367.   Formation of lots by experts

The lots are formed by experts chosen for that purpose and sworn by the officer charged with the partition, and are afterwards drawn for by the coheirs.

Arts. 1368 to 1369.   [Blank]

Art. 1370.   Subdivision among coheirs of same root

The rules established for the division of estates to be partitioned, are equally applicable to the subdivisions to be made between the individual coproprietors claiming under the same root.

Art. 1371.   Coheirs' proportionate liability for succession debts

No partition is made of the passive debts of the succession; each heir remains bound for the part he takes in the succession, but in order to equalize the shares, those heirs who take the largest allotments may be charged with the payment of a larger portion of the debts.

Art. 1372.   Observance of formalities

Partitions, made agreeably to the above rules by tutors or curators of minors, or by curators of interdicted or absent persons, are definitive; but they are only provisional, if the rules have not been observed.

Art. 1373.   Provisional partitions; persons authorized to demand new partition

When the partition is only provisional, absent persons, minors, and persons interdicted may, if they find themselves injured thereby, demand that another be made, as provided by the section relative to the rescission of partitions.

A minor may institute this action, even before he attains the age of majority.

Amended by Acts 1979, No. 711, § 1, eff. Jan. 1, 1980; Acts 1991, No. 107, § 1.

Arts. 1374 to 1377.   [Blank]

Art. 1378.   Errors of form, effect

The form in which the officer is directed to make the act of partition, as is above described, is not a matter of such strict law that nullity results from the act, in case of this officer making any change in the form; provided all the provisions of the law relating to the formation of the accounts between the parties, the deductions, the composition of the mass of the succession, the appointment and oaths of the experts and the making and drawing of the lots, have been observed in the partition, and the parties interested therein, or their representatives, have been duly notified to be present at the same.

Art. 1379.   Delivery of property and title papers after partition

After the partition, delivery must be made to each of the coheirs, of the title papers of the objects fallen to his share.

The title papers of a divided property remain in the possession of the heir who has the most considerable part of it, under the obligation of producing them, when required by the coproprietors of the other part of the property.

Titles common to the whole inheritance shall be delivered to the person chosen by all the heirs to be the depositary of them, on condition of producing them as often as required. If they should not agree on that choice, such deposit shall be made by the order of the judge.

Art. 1380.   Subsequent discovery of property, amendment of partition

If, after the partition, a discovery should be made of some property not included in it, the partition must be amended or made over again, either in totality, or of the discovered property alone.

Art. 1381.   [Blank]

SECTION 5—OF THE EFFECT OF PARTITION

Art. 1382.   Partition compared to exchange

Partition is a sort of exchange, which the coheirs make among themselves, one giving up his right in the thing which he abandons for the right of the other in the thing he takes.

Art. 1383.   [Blank]

SECTION 6—OF THE WARRANTY OF PARTITION

Art. 1384.   Reciprocal warranty against disturbance or eviction

The coheirs remain respectively bound to warrant, one to the other, the property falling to each of their shares against the disturbance and eviction which they may suffer, when the disturbance or eviction proceeds from a cause anterior to the partition.

Art. 1385.   Exclusion of warranty

The warranty does not take place, if the kind of eviction suffered has been excepted by a particular and express clause of the act; but it can not be stipulated in a partition, by a general clause that there shall be no warranty among the coheirs for any kind of disturbance whatever.

Art. 1386.   Eviction through fault of coheir

The warranty ceases, if it be by the fault of the coheir, that he has suffered the eviction.

Art. 1387.   Proportionate liability of coheirs

Each of the coheirs is personally bound in proportion to his hereditary share, to indemnify his coheir for the loss which the eviction has caused him.

Art. 1388.   Amount of indemnity

But the indemnity is only for the sum for which the object has been given by the partition to the heir who has suffered the eviction, and for the proportion which each of the heirs is bound to contribute, the amount of his own portion being extinguished by confusion; and the heir in this case has no right to claim remuneration from his coheirs for any damages which he may have suffered by the eviction.

Art. 1389.   Liability of coheirs for portion of insolvent coheir

If one of the coheirs happens to be insolvent, the portion, for which he is bound, must be divided equally between the one who is guaranteed and the other coheirs who are solvent.

Art. 1390.   Scope of warranty as to corporeal and incorporeal things

Warranty between coheirs has two different effects, according to the two kinds of property which may exist in the succession:

One composed of things which corporeally exist, whether they be movable or immovable, with regard to which warranty goes no farther than assuring them to belong to the succession.

The other kind consists of active debts and other rights, and with respect to these, they are not only guaranteed as belonging to the succession, but also as being such as they appear to be; that is to say, as being really due to the succession, and due by debtors solvent at the time of the partition, and who shall be so when the debt becomes payable, if it be not then due.

Art. 1391.   Warranties always implied

The warranties mentioned in the preceding article exist of right, so that they are always implied, and the heirs are bound to them, though no mention be made thereof in the partition.

Art. 1392.   Warranty of solvency of debtor of rent charge, prescription

The warranty of the solvency of the debtor of a rent charge can not be claimed after the lapse of five years from the partition.

Art. 1393.   Subsequent deterioration or destruction of property

Where, after the partition, the thing decays by its nature, or perishes by accident, such loss gives rise to no action of warranty.

Art. 1394.   New debts or charges

If, since the partition, debts or charges before unknown, are discovered, such new charges, whatever they may be, shall be supported by all the heirs, and they shall mutually guarantee each other.

Art. 1395.   Tacit mortgage abolished

The tacit mortgage which resulted from the partition for the execution of all the obligations contained therein, no longer exists; but the heirs may stipulate a special mortgage.

Art. 1396.   Prescription of action of warranty

The action of warranty among coheirs is prescribed by five years, and the time commences to run, to wit: for the property included in the partition, from the day of the eviction; and for debts, from the day that the insolvency of the debtor is established by the discussion of his effects.

SECTION 7—OF THE RESCISSION OF PARTITION

Arts. 1397 to 1398. [Blank]

Art. 1399. Definitive partitions involving minors, interdicts, or absent persons

When partitions, in which minors, persons interdicted, or absent persons are interested, have been made with all the formalities prescribed by law for judicial partitions, they can not be rescinded for any other causes than those which would authorize the rescission of partitions made by persons of age and present.

Amended by Acts 1991, No. 107, § 1.

Art. 1400. Provisional partitions involving minors, interdicts, or absent persons

But if these formalities have not been fulfilled, as the partition is only considered as provisional, it is not necessary to sue for the rescission of it, but a new partition may be demanded for the least lesion, which the minor, person interdicted, or absent person, may have suffered.

Amended by Acts 1991, No. 107, § 1.

Art. 1401. Omission of succession effects not cause for rescission

The mere omission of a thing, belonging to the succession, is not ground for rescission, but simply for a supplementary partition.

Art. 1402. Rescission of transactions effecting partition

The action of the rescission mentioned in the foregoing articles takes place in the cases prescribed by law, not only against all acts bearing the title of partition, but even against all those which tend to the division of property between coheirs, whether such acts be called sales, exchanges, compromises, or by any other name.

Art. 1403. Rescission inadmissible after compromise

But, after the partition, or the act operating the same effect, the action of rescission can no longer be admitted against a compromise made to put an end to disputes arising in consequence of the first act, although there should be no suit commenced on the subject.

Art. 1404. Rescission inadmissible against sale of succession rights

The action of rescission is not admitted against a sale of successive rights, made without fraud to one of the heirs and at his risk by the other coheirs or any of them.

Art. 1405. Sale of succession rights to coheir at risk of vendor, rescission inadmissible

The sale of successive rights by one heir to his coheir is not subject to rescission, if the purchaser has run no risk; as, for example, if the vendor remains bound for the payment of the debts.

Art. 1406. Sale to coheir of immovable rights only, rescission for lesion

In order that the purchaser be not liable to this action, it is besides necessary that the vendor should have ceded to him all his successive rights, that is, all the rights he had in the succession. If he has only sold his part in the immovables to be divided, this sale shall be subject to rescission for lesion beyond a fourth.

Art. 1407.   Facts required to obtain rescission for lesion

This sale shall be subject to rescission, if it be proved that, at the time it was made, the purchaser alone knew the value of the succession, and permitted the vendor to remain in ignorance of it.

Art. 1408.   Termination of partition suit by defendant's tender

The defendant in the suit for rescission may stop its course and prevent a new partition, by offering and giving to the plaintiff the supplement of his hereditary portion, either in money or in kind, provided the rescission is not demanded for cause of violence or fraud.

Art. 1409.   Amount of tender

When the defendant is admitted to prevent a new partition, as is said in the preceding article, if he furnishes the supplement in money, it must be with interest from the day of the institution of the suit; if he furnishes it in effects, he is bound to restore the fruits from the same day.

Art. 1410.   Rescission for fraud or violence inadmissible after alienation

The coheir who has alienated his share or part of it, is no longer admitted to bring the action of rescission for fraud or violence, if the alienation he has made was posterior to the discovery of the fraud, or to the cessation of the violence.

Art. 1411.   Rescission inadmissible against partition regulated by father

If the partition has been regulated by the father among his children, no restitution can take place, even in favor of minors, when, by such partition, one or more of the heirs have received more than the others, unless that overplus should exceed the portion which the father had a right to dispose of.

Art. 1412.   Rescission in favor of minor effective for all parties

The minor who obtains relief against a partition, relieves those of full age; for the partition can not subsist for one, and be annulled for another.

Art. 1413.   Prescription of action of rescission

Suits for the rescission of partitions are prescribed by the lapse of five years from the date thereof, and in case of error and fraud, from the day in which they are discovered.

Art. 1414.   Prescription against minors after judicial partition

This prescription, in case of lesion, runs against minors as well as against persons of age, when the partition has been made judicially and with all the forms prescribed by law.

CHAPTER 13—PAYMENT OF THE DEBTS OF AN ESTATE

SECTION 1—GENERAL DISPOSITIONS INTRODUCTION

Art. 1415.   Estate debts; administrative expenses

Estate debts are debts of the decedent and administration expenses. Debts of the decedent are obligations of the decedent or those that arise as a result of his death, such as the cost of his funeral and burial. Administration expenses are obligations incurred in the collection, preservation, management, and distribution of the estate of the decedent.

Acts 1997, No. 1421, § 1, eff. July 1, 1999.

REVISION COMMENTS—1997

The basic function of this article is to define, and as such it makes three important categorical distinctions. First, it classifies "estate debts" as including not only debts of the decedent but also administration expenses. The broad inclusion of both categories of debts and expenses is very important in this revision. The second category, "debts of the decedent," would necessarily refer to obligations that were incurred by or for the decedent during his lifetime, but the article defines it also to encompass expenses that arise out of one's death such as funeral and burial expenses. The third category, "administration expenses", is broadly defined to include expenses that are incurred after death in preserving, safeguarding, and operating the property of the estate, such as repairs, costs of maintenance and upkeep, interest attributable to a debt, and custodial fees.

SECTION 2—RIGHTS OF CREDITORS

Art. 1416.   Liability of universal successors to creditors

A.   Universal successors are liable to creditors for the payment of the estate debts in proportion to the part which each has in the succession, but each is liable only to the extent of the value of the property received by him, valued as of the time of receipt.

B.   A creditor has no action for payment of an estate debt against a universal successor who has not received property of the estate.

Acts 1997, No. 1421, § 1, eff. July 1, 1999. Amended by Acts 2001, No. 824, § 1.

REVISION COMMENTS—1997

(a) This Article is consistent with prior law regarding responsibility of successors for debts and expenses. The term "universal successors" is a term of art that includes intestate successors as well as general legatees and universal legatees, but it does not include successors who inherit particular legacies, who are called "particular successors." See Louisiana Civil Code Article 3506(28). As in prior law, this article does not place the responsibility for payment of estate debts on particular legatees, although the testator himself or other rules of law may do so, as, for example, with a particular legacy of encumbered property under Civil Code Article 1422. The liability among the universal successors is joint not solidary, and in any event a successor's personal liability is limited to the extent of the value of the property, and its fruits and products, received by him, valued as of the time of receipt.

(b) This Article implements the policy of limited liability of successors intended by Louisiana Revised Statutes 9:1421, which was adopted in 1986, and in that sense is not new. The 1986 statute, however, while well-intended, contains some ambiguities and, equally important, other articles of the Louisiana Civil Code, as well as appropriate articles of the Code of Civil Procedure, were not revised to coordinate with R.S. 9:1421. The new Article simplifies the operation of the policy that is intended by R.S. 9:1421 and makes appropriate changes elsewhere that are needed to coordinate with it.

(c) The provisions of Articles 1417–1420, inclusive, of the Civil Code of 1870 have been deleted as unnecessary.

(d) This Article is consistent with Civil Code Article 872, which defines "estate" as meaning "the property, rights and obligations that a person leaves after his death, whether the property exceeds the charges or the charges exceed the property, or whether he has only left charges without any property." The second sentence of Article 872 recognizes the possibility of accrual of additional liability for debts, as, for example, those debts that bear interest after the decedent's death, and further recognizes that administrative expenses of the estate may be different from debts of the estate itself. The revision recognizes these important distinctions and the new rules on payment of debts coordinate with them.

Art. 1417.   [Blank]

Art. 1418.   Successors who are creditors, order of preference

Successors who are creditors of the estate are paid in the same order of preference as other creditors.

Acts 1997, No. 1421, § 1, eff. July 1, 1999.

REVISION COMMENTS—1997

The principle enunciated by this article is straightforward and follows the general law of the State of Louisiana. If a creditor of the estate is secured, for example, by a mortgage on the land or by a Chapter 9 security interest in shares of stock, then the creditor will be paid in accordance with the preference and priority of his security right. If the creditor is unsecured, then in accordance with Article 3183 of the Louisiana Civil Code, the creditor must share pro rata with the other unsecured creditors. The important principle set forth in this Article is that the fact that the creditor is also a successor does not enhance or diminish the rights that he may have as a creditor. A different rule was adopted in the partnership law, providing that a partner who is an unsecured creditor of the partnership ranks behind unsecured creditors who are not partners. Louisiana Civil Code Article 2833 sets forth a comprehensive hierarchy for creditors of a partnership, but the same kinds of distinction are not made for creditors of an estate.

Art. 1419.   Rights of pursuit of creditor

When there is an administration and a creditor asserts and establishes his claim after payment has been made to other creditors or distribution of the estate in whole or in part has been made to successors pursuant to a court order, the claim of the creditor must be satisfied in the following order: first, from the assets remaining under administration in the estate; next, from the successors to whom distribution has been made; and then from unsecured creditors who received payments, in proportion to the amounts received by them, but in this event the creditor may not recover more than his share.

Acts 1997, No. 1421, § 1, eff. July 1, 1999.

REVISION COMMENTS—1997

(a) This article modernizes the provisions of Articles 1067 and 1068 of the Civil Code of 1870. It does not change the basic thrust of prior law where new creditors appear after distribution has been made. The article continues the rule that such a "new" creditor should first annul distributions that have been made to the successors, and only if there is still insufficient property to satisfy his claim would the creditor then pursue the other unsecured creditors who have been paid. That same scheme of priority applies under Articles 1067 and 1068 (1870).

(b) This article is worded so that it applies to administered estates only.

(c) There should be no doubt that the liability of unsecured creditors who have been paid to pay the new creditor is joint and not solidary. Because of the basic principle that unsecured creditors shall be paid ratably, a calculation would have to be made of the pro rata share of the new creditor, but a corollary of that determination is the determination of the ratable share of all of the other unsecured creditors. An unsecured creditor who has previously been paid more than his ratable share could be compelled to restore the differential, but an unsecured creditor who had been paid less than his ratable share would not be forced to pay at all.

(d) The article does not include the express protection of prior law for the succession representative who pays pursuant to law. The latter statement appears to be unnecessary: a creditor would have no right of action against a succession representative who has made payments pursuant to law, but he may have such a claim against a succession representative who fails to obtain authority to make payments. In any event, the claim will exist against the other creditors who have been paid or the successors who have received distributions, but there would be no cause of action against an executor or administrator personally unless he failed to comply with lawful requirements.

SECTION 3—RESPONSIBILITY OF SUCCESSORS AMONG THEMSELVES

Art. 1420. Regulation of payment of debts by testament or by agreement among successors

The provisions of this Section pertaining to responsibility of the successors among themselves for estate debts do not prevent that responsibility from being otherwise regulated by the testament or by agreement of the successors. Nevertheless, the rights of creditors of the estate cannot be impaired by the testament or by agreement among the successors.

Acts 1997, No. 1421, § 1, eff. July 1, 1999.

REVISION COMMENTS—1997

This Article recognizes that the testator may, in the testament, make provisions for payment of debts, but also that the successors themselves may agree on apportionment of the payment of the debts. In doing so, the article takes cognizance of and states general principles of freedom of testation and freedom of contract. Nonetheless, neither the testator nor the successors have total freedom in that regard. The second sentence preserves the rule of Article 1416 of the Louisiana Civil Code of 1870 to the effect that neither a testator, nor the heirs, can alter rules regarding payment of debts in a way that affects the ability of creditors of the estate to be paid. But when there is no problem of public policy, the testator's wishes should control. For example, a testator who wants a legacy to be free of any obligation to bear its share of administrative expenses may so provide in his will, but that provision cannot override the mandatory rule that protects the rights of creditors.

Art. 1421. Estate debts, charged

Unless otherwise provided by the testament, by agreement of the successors, or by law, estate debts are charged against the property of the estate and its fruits and products in accordance with the following articles.

Acts 1997, No. 1421, § 1, eff. July 1, 1999.

REVISION COMMENTS—1997

The preceding article acknowledges that the method of charging debts and allocating responsibility may be determined by the testator or the successors themselves, who may allocate responsibility for payment of estate debts by agreement. In the absence of any such testamentary or conventional allocation, estate debts are charged both to the property of the estate and to its fruits and products, and this article is essentially a preamble or threshold article that serves as a springboard for the rules that follow. The article itself does not set forth a new rule. Accepting the general principle that both the property of the estate and the fruits and products of the property are chargeable with responsibility to pay estate debts, it sets the stage for the articles that follow. Of the rules enunciated in the succeeding articles, some are new, and others are mere clarifications of prior law, or in other words, expressions of what is generally believed to be prior law.

Art. 1422. Debts attributable to identifiable or encumbered property

Estate debts that are attributable to identifiable property or to the production of its fruits or products are charged to that property and its fruits and products. Also, when the decedent has encumbered property to secure a debt, the debt is presumptively charged to that property and its fruits and products. The presumption may be rebutted, by a preponderance of the evidence that the secured debt is not attributable to the encumbered property.

Acts 1997, No. 1421, § 1, eff. July 1, 1999.

REVISION COMMENTS—1997

(a) This article contains many important rules. The first sentence sets forth the principle that when an estate debt is attributable to identifiable property, or to the production of fruits or products of that property, the debt is charged to that property and its fruits and products. The simplest illustration would be a farm as to which expenses are incurred for fertilizer, pesticide or repairs to farm machinery. Those debts are administration expenses that would clearly be attributable to identifiable property, namely the farm, and to the production of fruits or products of the farm. If the farm is the object of a particular legacy, it would not customarily be charged with an estate debt, but under this article, those expenses would be allocable to the farm itself and not to other legacies. Similarly, repairs to a house would be attributable to that house. Owner's insurance with regard to rental property would be an estate debt attributable to identifiable property, namely the rental property itself, so that the insurance expense would be charged to that property and as an administration expense it would first be charged to the rents received.

(b) The second sentence of the article allocates primary responsibility for an encumbrance to the property that is encumbered. This rule is relatively simple in the case of an ordinary conventional mortgage, such as a homestead loan to purchase a home. The rule is less clear when a collateral mortgage or a mortgage to secure future advances is used by which the decedent has encumbered the property to raise funds that were or may be used for other purposes than the acquisition or preservation of that property. For example, a landowner grants a mortgage to secure future advances on Blackacre and uses it to secure a line of credit for a business that is unrelated to the property. For that reason, the article carefully states that a debt is "presumptively" charged to the encumbered property and its fruits and products. As a presumption only, the rule is not inflexible. Evidence may be introduced to overcome the presumption, and the debt may be charged differently. By way of illustration, if the decedent pledged shares of stock in a corporation to borrow money to purchase an automobile, then the debt may not be allocable to the stock, but it is presumed to be attributable to the stock which is the encumbered property, and the burden of proof is, of course, on the challenger, to show otherwise. To remove any doubt as to the standard of proof required to overcome the presumption, the article states that it must be overcome by a "preponderance of the evidence."

(c) Under prior law, the general rule in Louisiana was that a legacy of encumbered property carries the encumbrance with it to the legatee in the absence of a clear expression of intent to leave the property free and clear of the encumbrance. See Article 1638, Louisiana Civil Code (1870). There has been some interesting jurisprudence with reference to allocation of debts and whether or not a testator intends for the debt to be discharged by the executor. In Succession of Waterman, 298 So.2d 731 (La. 1974), the Louisiana Supreme Court held that the declaration by the testator that all of his "just debts" should be paid led to the conclusion that a particular legacy of Blackacre that was encumbered by a mortgage was to be delivered to the legatee free and clear of the encumbrance.

(d) The provisions of this article are, of course, exceptions to the rules set forth in the following articles with reference to charging debts ratably to the property that is the object of general and universal legacies.

Art. 1423. Decedent's debts charged ratably

Debts of the decedent are charged ratably to property that is the object of general or universal legacies and to property that devolves by intestacy, valued as of the date of death. When such property does not suffice, the debts remaining are charged in the following order:

(1) Ratably to the fruits and products of property that is the object of general or universal legacies and of property that devolves by intestacy; and

(2) Ratably to the fruits and products of property that is the object of particular legacies, and then ratably to such property.

Acts 1997, No. 1421, § 1, eff. July 1, 1999.

REVISION COMMENTS—1997

(a) This article sets forth the important general principle that "debts of the decedent" are charged ratably to general and universal legacies.

(b) As a general rule, particular legacies are not charged with the responsibility of paying estate debts, whether the debts are debts of the decedent or administration expenses. There are exceptions to that rule, of course, under the provisions of Article 1422, where an estate debt is allocable to identifiable property or property that is encumbered. For that reason, the article states that the decedent's debts are charged ratably to all of the property that devolves as general legacies, universal legacies, or by intestacy. There is no preference between a general legacy and a universal legacy, because by definition a testament cannot contain both kinds of legacies. There is a preference between a particular legacy, on the one hand, and general and universal legacies on the other hand, as in prior law. See C.C. Article 1600, but note also Article 1422 regarding debts identified with property.

Art. 1424.   Administration expenses, how charged

Administration expenses are charged ratably to the fruits and products of property that is the object of the general or universal legacies and property that devolves by intestacy. When the fruits and products do not suffice to discharge the administration expenses, the remaining expenses are charged first to the property itself, next to the fruits and products of property that is the object of particular legacies, and then to the property itself.

Acts 1997, No. 1421, § 1, eff. July 1, 1999.

REVISION COMMENTS—1997

(a) Consistent with the provisions of Article 1423, which refers to debts of the decedent, this article sets forth the identical principle for administration expenses, namely that they are not charged to particular legacies but ratably to the fruits and products of general or universal legacies and the property that passes by intestacy. The basic distinction between Articles 1423 and 1424 is that Article 1423 refers to "debts of the decedent" and Article 1424 refers to "administration expenses." Debts of the decedent are charged to the property of the estate, but administration expenses are charged to the fruits and products of the property. If the fruits and products are insufficient, then the administration expenses are charged to the property itself. The creditors are entitled, of course, to be paid out of either source, and if the property that is the object of general or universal legacies is not sufficient, either by virtue of its fruits and products or of the property itself, then the administration expenses are charged to the fruits and products of the particular legacies, and if that resource, too, is not sufficient, then they are charged to the property that is the object of the particular legacy itself. In all instances, where there are several items of property among which the charge may be allocated, the charge is made ratably.

(b) This article, in conjunction with Article 1423, attempts to set forth a priority, allocating the decedent's debts to property of the estate and administration expenses to revenues of the estate, then further breaking down those categories so that particular legacies do not bear any responsibility for these expenses unless they fall within one of the recognized exceptions, such as being encumbered to secure a debt or having a debt attributable to the object of the particular legacy as identifiable property.

(c) In most instances professional fees such as the fees of the attorney who handles the estate, or accounting fees, or the compensation paid to the executor are incurred in part for administration purposes and in part as a result of the death of the decedent, so that they should be allocated partially to principal and partially to income. No hard and fast rule can be developed, and Civil Code Article 1426 authorizes a succession representative or the heirs to allocate such fees between debts of the estate and administration expenses in accordance with what is reasonable and equitable in view of the interests of the various successors. See Civil Code Article 1426, second paragraph.

Art. 1425.   Liability of successors for contribution or reimbursement

A successor who has not received property of the estate or its fruits and products, is not liable for contribution or reimbursement. A successor who has received property of the estate, or any of its fruits or products is not liable for contribution or reimbursement for an amount greater than the value of the property or fruits or products, received by him, valued as of the time of receipt.

Acts 1997, No. 1421, § 1, eff. July 1, 1999.

REVISION COMMENTS—1997

This article is a corollary to Article 1416, which announces a rule of limited liability for successors. As the Comments to that article reflect, the liability of successors is limited to the value of property received by the successor, valued at the time of receipt. The instant article coordinates with that rule by insulating the successor from aggregate liability greater than that limitation whether it is to creditors or to other successors by way of contribution or reimbursement.

Art. 1426. Classification of receipts and expenditures in absence of controlling dispositions

In the absence of an express testamentary provision or applicable provision of law, receipts and expenditures are allocated in accordance with what is reasonable and equitable in view of the interests of the successors who are entitled to the fruits and products as well as the interests of the successors who are entitled to ownership of the property, and in view of the manner in which persons of ordinary prudence, discretion, and intelligence would act in the management of their own affairs.

The compensation of the succession representative and professional fees incurred after death, such as legal, accounting and appraisal fees, shall be allocated between debts of the decedent and administration expenses in accordance with the provisions of this Article.

Acts 1997, No. 1421, § 1, eff. July 1, 1999.

REVISION COMMENTS—1997

(a) The concepts set forth in this article are not new. The article is modeled closely on the provisions of Louisiana Revised Statutes 9:2142 and 9:2143, which are located in the Trust Code. The principles that it enunciates are general principles, and the Comments to the Trust Code articles should be equally applicable to this article. No hard and fast rule can serve to determine how each and every receipt or expenditure should be classified, and for that reason the article refers to "what is reasonable and equitable" and further references the interest of successors who are entitled to fruits and products (such as usufructuaries or income interests in trust) as well as those entitled to ownership of property (such as naked owners and principal beneficiaries in trust). The article also incorporates the well-known and universally accepted principle that the rules should be viewed the way that persons of "ordinary prudence, discretion and intelligence would act in the management of their own affairs."

(b) See Comment (c) to Article 1424.

Art. 1427. Reporting and deducting as authorized by tax law

Notwithstanding the provisions of this Chapter, for tax purposes the succession representative, or the successors if there is no representative, may report receipts and deduct expenditures as authorized by the tax law.

Acts 1997, No. 1421, § 1, eff. July 1, 1999.

REVISION COMMENTS—1997

This article is intended to re-assure executors and administrators, as well as their tax advisors, that for tax purposes they are not required to slavishly adhere to the rules set forth in this revision if they produce adverse tax consequences. The articles are intended to furnish guidelines to assist succession representatives and their professional advisors, as well as the courts. As such, they provide rules where the law has previously been silent or may be unclear, but there is no intent to preclude or foreclose appropriate tax elections under state or federal income tax law or Louisiana inheritance or federal estate tax law. For example, many expenses are recognized by the federal government as deductible on either the estate tax return, Form 706, which would be more as a debt of the decedent, or on a fiduciary income tax return, which is more as an administration expense. The fact that an expense may be a "debt of the decedent" for Louisiana civil law purposes should not impair the ability of the succession representative to claim that expense as an administration expense if permitted by federal or state tax law. That being the case, the principle set forth in this article is intended to clarify that the succession representative may properly elect either deduction and make the decision based on what is perceived to be the best interest of the estate without any impediment as a result of these articles. The articles on payment of debts are intended to be helpful to serve as useful and practical guidelines, as well as rules of law. They do not compel adverse tax consequences.

Art. 1428. Rights and obligations of usufructuary not superseded

This Chapter does not supersede the provisions of this Code governing the rights and obligations of a usufructuary with respect to payment of estate debts.

Acts 1997, No. 1421, § 1, eff. July 1, 1999.

REVISION COMMENTS—1997

This article precludes any claim that the new articles on payment of debts supersede the provisions of the Civil Code with regard to the rights and obligations of a usufructuary. Indeed, the primary function of this article is to clarify that the provisions of this section dealing with the payment of debts do not displace or over-ride the allocation of responsibility for the payment of those debts as between the usufructuary and the naked owner. Under the new scheme of limited liability of successors, estate debts are charged to property, and its fruits and products, and not to successors personally. Successors are personally liable to creditors, only to the extent that they take possession of property of the estate, or its fruits and products. The new scheme of limited liability of successors for estate debts, allocates responsibility for payment of a debt to property itself, and there is no intention to alter, modify, or tacitly repeal, any of the provisions in the law of usufruct with regard to the responsibility of the usufructuary for payment of debts. When an estate debt is allocated to Blackacre, then, as between the usufructuary, who has the usufruct of Blackacre, and the naked owner, who owns the naked ownership of Blackacre, the responsibility is determined by the provisions of the Civil Code that deal with the law of usufruct. The responsibility of the underlying property against which the debt is charged is governed by the section of the Code dealing with payment of the debts, but as between the usufructuary and the naked owner with regard to the payment of those debts, the allocation and placement of responsibility is determined by the section of the Civil Code on the law of usufruct. These new articles do not relieve a usufructuary of the responsibility properly placed upon usufructuaries under the provisions of the Civil Code elsewhere.

Art. 1429. Rights and obligations of income interest in trust not superseded

This Chapter does not supersede the provisions of the Trust Code governing the rights and obligations of an income interest in trust with respect to payment of estate debts.

Acts 1997, No. 1421, § 1, eff. July 1, 1999.

REVISION COMMENTS—1997

The comments to Article 1428 apply with equal force to this article.

Arts. 1430 to 1466. [Blank]

TITLE II—DONATIONS

CHAPTER 1—GENERAL DISPOSITIONS

Art. 1467. Methods of acquiring or disposing gratuitously

Property can neither be acquired nor disposed of gratuitously except by donations inter vivos or mortis causa, made in one of the forms hereafter established.

Acts 2008, No. 204, § 1, eff. Jan. 1, 2009.

REVISION COMMENT—2008

This Article reproduces the substance of Civil Code Article 1467 (1870). It is not intended to change the law.

Art. 1468. Donations inter vivos; definition

A donation inter vivos is a contract by which a person, called the donor, gratuitously divests himself, at present and irrevocably, of the thing given in favor of another, called the donee, who accepts it.

Acts 2008, No. 204, § 1, eff. Jan. 1, 2009.

REVISION COMMENTS—2008

(a) This Article reproduces the substance of Civil Code Article 1468 (1870). It is not intended to change the law.

(b) A donation inter vivos must be accepted during the donor's lifetime. See Article 1544.

(c) In this draft, the word "thing" refers to the object of the donation rather than to "a" thing as such. Thus, the "thing given" may be a corporeal movable or immovable thing or an incorporeal, such as a real right, an obligation, etc.

(d) See Article 1551 which states that a donation transfers ownership when the donation is accepted. See also Article 2439, regarding sale and transfer of ownership, which states that a sale ". . . transfers ownership of a thing."

Art. 1469. Donation mortis causa; definition

A donation mortis causa is an act to take effect at the death of the donor by which he disposes of the whole or a part of his property. A donation mortis causa is revocable during the lifetime of the donor.

Acts 2008, No. 204, § 1, eff. Jan. 1, 2009.

REVISION COMMENT—2008

This Article reproduces the substance of former Civil Code Article 1469 (1870). It is not intended to change the law.

CHAPTER 2—OF THE CAPACITY NECESSARY FOR DISPOSING OR RECEIVING BY DONATION INTER VIVOS OR MORTIS CAUSA

Art. 1470. Persons capable of giving or receiving

All persons have capacity to make and receive donations inter vivos and mortis causa, except as expressly provided by law.

Acts 1991, No. 363, § 1.

(a) This Article modernizes the language of the source Article without changing the law. The distinction between absolute and relative incapacities contained in prior Article 1471 of the Civil Code of 1870 has been removed as unnecessary.

(b) As a general rule of statutory drafting and of statutory construction, special legislation prevails over general legislation. Thus, the adoption of the new Civil Code Articles of this revision should not be construed in any way as intending to repeal special provisions of law that are contained elsewhere either in the Civil Code or in the Louisiana Revised Statutes. For example, despite the rules regarding capacity to donate inter vivos, there is special legislation whereby a person who technically lacks capacity and has been interdicted may nonetheless make donations through his curator. La.R.S. 9:1022–1023. Similarly, under Civil Code Article 3027, a power of attorney granted when the principal has capacity is not terminated by the principal's incapacity. C.C. Art. 3027(B). The fact that this revision has been adopted later than La.R.S. 9:1022–1023 or the amendment to Civil Code Article 3027 by Act No. 303 of 1981 that added Paragraph B should in no way give rise to the construction that either of those provisions is expressly or impliedly overruled. There is no intent to repeal special legislation that serves as an exception to these rules.

(c) With regard to capacity to make donations, there are requirements beyond merely being in existence. Age is one requirement and mental condition is another. With regard, however, to capacity to receive, being in existence is the only requirement. See Comments to Art. 1475, infra. Thus, it is necessary for natural persons to be in being in order to receive donations, and that determination may be made by reference to Civil Code Article 1472. There is a special rule, moreover, for an unborn child, and that matter is governed by Article 1474 of this revision. The time when such existence must be determined is governed by Article 1472 of this revision.

Art. 1471.   Capacity to give, time for existence

Capacity to donate inter vivos must exist at the time the donor makes the donation. Capacity to donate mortis causa must exist at the time the testator executes the testament.

Acts 1991, No. 363, § 1.

(a) This Article determines the time at which capacity to donate inter vivos or mortis causa must be determined. The source Article (C.C. Art. 1472 (1870)) referred only to capacity to donate inter vivos, and the principle contained in it is retained here for such donations. The timing for determination of capacity to donate mortis causa is also consistent with prior law.

(b) The first sentence of this Article purposefully states with regard to an inter vivos donation that capacity must exist when the donor "makes the donation." This language is carefully chosen to refer to the time when the donor acts, rather than the time when the donee accepts the donation. It would have been inappropriate for this sentence to refer to the time of the donor's "executing" an act of donation, as the second sentence of the article does to "executing" the testament. That is so because donations inter vivos may be made in different forms, and in some instances an "act" is not required. The donation of a corporeal movable, for example, may be made manually, so that there is no need for a written "act" of donation. For the inter vivos donation of an immovable, on the other hand, an authentic "act" is required. Capacity to donate must exist at the time the donor executes the "act" of donation in such a case. In general, one must be careful not to confuse the time of donating with the time of accepting. In the case of a manual donation, by the nature of the donation, there is customarily delivery and acceptance at the same time, but with a donation that requires an authentic act, such as the donation of an immovable or the donation of an incorporeal under Civil Code Article 1536, there may be a time lag between the time when the donor executes the act of donation and the time when the donee accepts the donation, which the donee may do by a subsequent act. Thus, the determination of capacity of the donor is as of when he "makes" the donation, and if he subsequently becomes incapacitated before the donee accepts, that will not prevent the donation from being effective. The death of the donor prior to acceptance, however, would prevent the donation from being completed by acceptance, as would, of course, the death of the donee prior to acceptance. See C.C. Arts. 1540, 1543 (1870). If an acceptance has been timely made, (i.e., before the death of either the donor or the donee), however, then it will not matter if the donor lacked capacity at the time the donation was accepted, provided that he had capacity at the time he made the donation. See also Comments to Arts. 1470, supra, 1475, infra.

Art. 1472.   Capacity to receive, time for existence

Capacity to receive a donation inter vivos must exist at the time the donee accepts the donation. Capacity to receive a donation mortis causa must exist at the time of death of the testator.

Acts 1991, No. 363, § 1.

REVISION COMMENT—1991

This Article does not change the law, but merely restates the prior rule in simpler form. It is not intended to and should not in any way impair the ability of a testator to make a charitable bequest that is contingent upon the creation of a charitable trust. The charitable trust law permits gifts and bequests to trustees of "educational, charitable, or literary institutions existing at the time of the donation or thereafter to be founded . . . without designating the particular purpose to be fostered. . . ." La.R.S. 9:2271. See also Comment (b) to Article 1470, regarding special legislation.

Art. 1473.   Capacity to receive conditional donation, time for existence

When a donation depends on fulfillment of a suspensive condition, the donee must have capacity to receive at the time the condition is fulfilled.

Acts 1991, No. 363, § 1.

REVISION COMMENT—1991

This Article does not change the law, but it does clarify that the kind of condition to which the rule applies is a suspensive condition. The source Article (C.C. Art. 1474 (1870)) was silent on this issue but the rule of the Article can reasonably apply only to a suspensive condition—that is, one as a result of which the donation has not yet been completed. See, C.C. Art. 1767 (Rev. 1984). Otherwise, this Article does not change the law.

Art. 1474.   Unborn children, capacity to receive

To be capable of receiving by donation inter vivos, an unborn child must be in utero at the time the donation is made. To be capable of receiving by donation mortis causa, an unborn child must be in utero at the time of the death of the testator. In either case, the donation has effect only if the child is born alive.

Acts 1991, No. 363, § 1.

REVISION COMMENT—1991

This Article modernizes the language of the source Article (C.C. Art. 1482 (1870)) without changing the law. It does, however, clarify the law in light of modern scientific developments, in that under this Article an unfertilized human ovum, or even a fertilized human embryo, is not capable of receiving a donation unless it has been implanted in the womb prior to the time the donation inter vivos is made or the testator dies. To the extent of any conflict between this Article and R.S. 9:133, the provisions of this Article shall prevail.

Art. 1475.   Nullity of donation to person incapable of receiving

A donation in favor of a person who is incapable of receiving is null.

Acts 1991, No. 363, § 1.

REVISION COMMENTS—1991

(a) This Article is new but does not change the law. The provisions contained in the second clause and second sentence of prior Civil Code Article 1491 have been suppressed as unnecessary. Those provisions specifically prohibited donations to persons who were incapable which were disguised as contracts or as donations to persons who were interposed. At the time former Article 1491 was originally adopted, there were other requirements for capacity to receive in addition to being in existence. For example, until recently there was a prohibition against leaving immovable property to a person with whom one had lived in open concubinage. Similarly, until the adoption of this revision there was a prohibition against bequests to doctors and ministers who had treated a decedent in his last illness. In light of this revision and other recent developments in the law, as a result of which there is no capacity requirement to receive other than the requirement that one be in existence, it is not necessary to retain all of the provisions of former Civil Code Article 1491. Nonetheless, a person might still attempt to make a donation to unborn children or grandchildren who had not yet been conceived, and, except as expressly provided in the class trust provisions of the Trust Code, such a gift would be null under this Article. On the other hand, a gift to a grandchild where the donor's child had conceived but had not yet given birth to the child would be covered by the provisions of Article 1474, supra on unborn children.

(b) The use of the word "person" in this Article is intentional, although there is a certain contradiction inherent in its use here because to be legally a "person" one must be in existence, or at least conceived and later born alive, and if one is those things one is in fact normally capable of receiving a donation. Clearly the word as used in this Article actually refers to a purported person; that is, it refers to the donor's designation of the donee as a person. In fact there is no such person, but the article means a designated "person".

Art. 1476.   Minors; incapacity to make donations, exceptions

A minor under the age of sixteen years does not have capacity to make a donation either inter vivos or mortis causa, except in favor of his spouse or children.

A minor who has attained the age of sixteen years has capacity to make a donation, but only mortis causa. He may make a donation inter vivos in favor of his spouse or children.

Acts 1991, No. 363, § 1.

REVISION COMMENT—1991

(a) This Article reproduces the substance of Articles 1476 and 1477 of the Civil Code of 1870. It changes the law in part, in that it allows a minor who has attained the age of 16 years to make a donation inter vivos in favor of his spouse and children.

(b) This Article recognizes that there is a significant difference between execution of a will and the making of an inter vivos donation, in terms of the considerations that should govern a minor's ability to make such dispositions. The testament is subject to more strict formalities and does not dispose of the minor's property until a later date, namely the date of his death, in contrast with a donation inter vivos, by which the minor presently and irrevocably disposes of property. For that reason, a distinction between the ability to execute a will and the ability to make an inter vivos donation is recognized, but in each case for obvious policy reasons an exception is made in favor of a spouse and children.

Art. 1477.   Capacity to donate, mental condition of donor

To have capacity to make a donation inter vivos or mortis causa, a person must also be able to comprehend generally the nature and consequences of the disposition that he is making.

Acts 1991, No. 363, § 1.

REVISION COMMENTS—1991

(a) This Article is new and is intended to change the law. It purposefully rejects the phrase "of sound mind" in order to avoid the jurisprudence regarding the usage of that phrase in former Civil Code Article 1475, and it sets forth criteria that are intentionally not limited to the prior jurisprudence. One reason for selecting a new test and rejecting the phrase "of sound mind" is specifically to overrule cases such as Succession of Buvens, 241 So.2d 89 (3 Cir., 1970), writs den., 257 La. 459, 242 So.2d 578 (La.1971), which held in the case of a 40 year old retarded person with the mental age of 9 that there was no requirement of minimum mental condition to execute a will, and that chronological age was the sole criterion. See also Succession of Brugier, 83 So. 366 (La.1919), involving a 73 year old with the mental age of a 10 to 12 year old. Under the new rule, mental retardation alone will not necessarily mean, that a person lacks donative capacity, but it will certainly be a factor to consider. If the extent of retardation is such that the individual cannot comprehend generally the nature and consequences of the disposition that he is making, then that individual will lack donative capacity.

(b) Although new for Louisiana, the test given in this Article did not spring ex nihil. In many respects it is derived from the common-law test for testamentary (donative) capacity that requires a person to be able to understand in a general way the nature and extent of his property, and his relationship to the persons who are considered to be the natural objects of his bounty, and the consequences of the disposition that he is making. In other words, at commonlaw to be competent to make a will, a person must have a general and approximate understanding of the nature and extent of his assets to be disposed of, and he must know what it means to make a will. The definition of donative capacity that is used today in most common-law jurisdictions (with slight variations from state to state) originated in an 1870 decision in England in Banks v. Goodfellow, L.R. 5 Q.G. 549 (1870), written by Lord Chief Justice Cockburn. The definition has been characterized as an "excellent but somewhat loose principle" with "somewhat broad and ambiguous criteria" by a noted Louisiana psychiatrist, Dr. Gene Usdin. See Usdin, "The Psychiatrist and Testamentary Capacity", 32 Tul.L.Rev. 89, 91 (1957). Nonetheless, despite some lack of precision, the definition of donative capacity appears to have worked well where adopted.

(c) Like the common-law formulation, that given in this Article focuses upon the donor's being "able to comprehend", rather than requiring actual comprehension of the donation. The donor who is capable of understanding has donative capacity even though he may not actually understand the exact instrument that he executes. See also comment (e) infra. The focus under this new test in Louisiana is thus not on the accuracy of the understanding but the ability to understand.

(d) As used in this Article the reference to the "nature" of the disposition means that the donor must be capable of understanding that he is making a gratuitous transfer of property that he owns to someone else who will become the owner of it, without recompense. "Consequences" obviously connotes more than mere transfer without recompense, however. One consequence of a donation, for example, is that the donor no longer owns the property, may no longer enjoy it, and that it no longer forms part of his patrimony. It enhances the patrimony of the donee, and perhaps the donee may receive more property from the donor than someone else may receive. Also the consequences of a donation are different from the consequences of a sale, or a lease, or a mortgage. There are immediate consequences and remote consequences, and it is hoped that courts will be practical in their interpretation of the word. Like the proverbial ripples from a rock thrown in a pond, the consequences could extend to a range so removed as to be insignificant.

(e) Two most important words in the new Article are "able" and "generally". Many wills and inter vivos donations contain highly technical and sophisticated language that the average lay person is not likely to understand. The donor may not grasp sophisticated tax formulae, nor should he be expected to understand them precisely. Use of the word "generally" in the Article is intended to remove any doubt in this regard: The donor is not required to understand technical terminology of the donation or testament. As one commentator observed, "testamentary capacity is the capacity to make a will, not to make the particular one offered for probate." Usdin, "The Psychiatrist and Testamentary Capacity", 32 Tul.L.Rev. 89, 92 (1957); Reichenbach v. Ruddach, 127 Pa. 564, 18 A. 432 (1889).

(f) Cases involving challenges to capacity are fact-intensive. The courts will look both to objective and subjective indicia. Illness, old age, delusions, sedation, etc. may not establish lack of capacity but may be important evidentiary factors. If illness has impaired the donor's mind and rendered him unable to understand, then that evidentiary fact will establish that he does not have donative capacity. Outrageous behavior by an individual may or may not be indicative of lack of ability to understand. Some outrageous behavior may be nothing more than a personality quirk, while other outrageous behavior may manifest serious mental disturbance. Each case is unique. Heavy sedation should be a strong factor to consider, since the sedative effects of the drug may impair the ability of the person to comprehend the nature and consequences of his act.

The courts will look to the medical evidence that is available, such as the medical records and the testimony of treating doctors, and to other expert testimony, and to the testimony of lay witnesses. Clearly, no quick litmus-paper test exists to apply to the evaluation of mental capacity in all cases.

Art. 1478. Nullity of donation procured by fraud or duress

A donation inter vivos or mortis causa shall be declared null upon proof that it is the product of fraud or duress.

Acts 1991, No. 363, § 1.

REVISION COMMENT—1991

This Article does not change the law, but it does elevate to Civil Code status principles that have long been recognized in Louisiana succession law.

Art. 1479. Nullity of donation procured through undue influence

A donation inter vivos or mortis causa shall be declared null upon proof that it is the product of influence by the donee or another person that so impaired the volition of the donor as to substitute the volition of the donee or other person for the volition of the donor.

Acts 1991, No. 363, § 1.

REVISION COMMENTS—1991

(a) This Article is new. The repeal at the 1990 legislative session of former Civil Code Article 1492, which prohibited admission of proof of a disposition having been made "through hatred, anger, suggestion or captation", prompted this Article, because of the uncertainty as to the effect of repealing the prohibition on admission of such proof.

(b) This Article, like the preceding Article, presumes a donor who has capacity. Obviously, if a donor lacks capacity, then the entire donation or will is invalid for that reason alone, and issues of fraud and undue influence are irrelevant. This Article intentionally does not use the word "undue" to describe the influence (although the word is intentionally used in the title of the Article and in two later Articles that refer to this Article), but instead defines the influence as being of such a nature that it destroys the free agency of the donor.

No single definition of "undue influence" has been found acceptable in all of the relevant legal writings. The common-law rules concerning "undue influence", fraud, and duress are derived almost entirely from case law rather than statutes. Any number of definitions exist in court opinions and in instructions to juries, but the law clearly deals largely with subjective elements, making the term "undue influence" therefore very difficult to define. In the case law, the objective aspects of undue influence are generally veiled in secrecy, and the proof of undue influence is either largely or entirely circumstantial. By referring to "influence" that impaired the volition of the donor, this Article attempts to indicate that the character of the gift or testamentary disposition itself is not determinative of the issue, although it may nonetheless be evidence on the issue. Moreover, everyone is more or less swayed by associations with other persons, so this Article attempts to describe the kind of influence that would cause the invalidity of a gift or disposition. Physical coercion and duress clearly fall within the proscription of the previous Article. The more subtle influences, such as creating resentment toward a natural object of a testator's bounty by false statements, may constitute the kind of influence that is reprobated by this Article, but will still call for evaluation by the trier of fact. Since the ways of influencing another person are infinite, the definition given in this Article is used in an attempt to place a limit on the kind of influence that is deemed offensive. Mere advice, or persuasion, or kindness and assistance, should not constitute influence that would destroy the free agency of a donor and substitute someone else's volition for his own.

(c) The Article intentionally defines the influence as being that of the donee or some other person in order to avoid a challenge based solely on the workings of the donor's own mind without pressure from someone else. It seems obvious that the influence has to be exercised with the object of procuring a particular gift or bequest. While the influence may be exerted by the donee himself, the Article covers the situation where the donee takes no part in the activities (and may even be ignorant of them), so long as some person does exercise control over the donor, presumably one who is interested in the fortunes of the donee.

(d) It is implicit in this Article that the influence must be operative at the time of the execution of the inter vivos donation or testament. Obviously, it should not be necessary that the acts themselves be done at that time, or that the person exercising the pressure be present then.

(e) Clearly, a court should distinguish between a willful deception by a donee or successor as to the character or contents of the instrument (or as to certain facts that are material to the disposition), and an innocent misrepresentation, which would not invalidate a gift or testamentary disposition. There is no intent to create a right to challenge donations based on mistake alone.

Art. 1480. Nullity due to fraud, duress, or undue influence; severability of valid provision

When a donation inter vivos or mortis causa is declared null because of undue influence or because of fraud or duress, it is not necessary that the entire act of donation or testament be nullified. If any provision contained in it is not the product of such means, that provision shall be given effect, unless it is otherwise invalid.

Acts 1991, No. 363, § 1.

REVISION COMMENTS—1991

(a) This Article adopts the doctrine of partial invalidity, which is new in this context, but it is not uncommon for one bequest in a will to be invalidated without invalidating the entire will. See e.g., C.C. Art. 1520 (1870); Succession of Walters, 261 La. 59, 259 So.2d 12 (1972).

(b) Obviously, the task of determining what parts of a will or an inter vivos gift are tainted by the elements discussed above and what parts are not tainted is essentially subjective. Nonetheless, the fundamental idea is not to do violence to the donor's intention and invalidate the entire instrument unless that is the only acceptable result. Accordingly, this Article uses the mandatory "shall" with reference to upholding an untainted provision. Although the determination of whether a provision is tainted or not is subjective, use of the mandatory "shall" is intended to indicate to the courts that in cases of doubt a provision should be upheld. The mandatory "shall" is intended to indicate stronger public policy than the use of the permissive "may" would indicate.

Art. 1481. Fiduciary appointment, termination

Any person who, whether alone or with others, commits fraud or exercises duress or unduly influences a donor within the meaning of the preceding Articles, or whose appointment is procured by such means, shall not be permitted to serve or continue to serve as an executor, trustee, attorney or other fiduciary pursuant to a designation as such in the act of donation or the testament or any amendments or codicils thereto.

Acts 1991, No. 363, § 1.

REVISION COMMENT—1991

(a) This Article is new. Because the other Articles of this Chapter speak only of "donations", and the designation of a fiduciary, such as an executor, trustee, or tutor, is not a donation but is nonetheless normally included in a testament or a trust provision, this Article closes a gap that might otherwise exist. The same principles that apply to upholding or invalidating donations should apply to such appointive provisions as these in acts of donation or testaments.

(b) This Article expressly refers to the person's being "determined" to have done something so that there is a definite implication of a judicial finding having been made. This Article also expressly refers to the appointed person's having acted "alone or with others," because the person may not have been the sole perpetrator of the offense. Also, the Article refers not only to "serving" but also to "continuing to serve", because it may well be that the testament has been probated and the named person is serving at the time the determination of wrongdoing is made. In such a case the Article does not jeopardize the validity of acts that were taken during the person's service in that representative capacity. By the same token the words "or any amendments or codicils thereto" are included because a codicil might only make a designation of an executor, and therefore by itself would not be a "donation" subject to the preceding Articles of this Chapter. Such a codicil should not be enforced if tainted with fraud, duress, or undue influence as contemplated in this Article.

Art. 1482.   Proof of incapacity to donate

A.   A person who challenges the capacity of a donor must prove by clear and convincing evidence that the donor lacked capacity at the time the donor made the donation inter vivos or executed the testament.

B.   A full interdict lacks capacity to make or revoke a donation inter vivos or disposition mortis causa.

C.   A limited interdict, with respect to property under the authority of the curator, lacks capacity to make or revoke a donation inter vivos and is presumed to lack capacity to make or revoke a disposition mortis causa. With respect to his other property, the limited interdict is presumed to have capacity to make or revoke a donation inter vivos or disposition mortis causa. These presumptions may be rebutted by a preponderance of the evidence.

Acts 1991, No. 363, § 1. Amended by Acts 2003, No. 1008, § 1.

REVISION COMMENTS—1991

(a) This Article is new. It codifies prior jurisprudential law in part, and also introduces new law in part. The burden of proof for overcoming the presumption of testamentary capacity under prior law was jurisprudentially changed in 1984 from the stringent criminal law standard of "beyond a reasonable doubt", to the more relaxed but nonetheless difficult standard of "clear and convincing" evidence. Succession of Lyons, 452 So.2d 1161 (La.1984). That decision is codified in this Article, but an exception is made for persons judicially declared to be mentally infirm.

(b) The term "mentally infirm" is intentionally employed in this Article in order to include only judicial determinations, such as interdiction, that are based on mental impairment (e.g., interdiction for "imbecility, insanity or madness" under Civil Code Article 389; continuing tutorship on grounds of mental retardation under Civil Code Article 355; civil commitment under R.S. 28:50 et seq.), and to exclude determinations based on physical handicap (e.g., interdiction for physical infirmity under Civil Code Article 422). The phrase "judicially declared" is used in the same Article to require a judicial determination of mental infirmity in order for the presumption of capacity to be removed. In the event of such a judicial declaration, there is not merely a shifting of the burden of proof, but because of that judicial declaration there is also a presumption that the donor lacked capacity, and the burden of proof itself shifts to the proponent of the will or donation to overcome that presumption, and he must do so pursuant to the rigorous standard of "clear and convincing" evidence. A simple example might be the situation of a person who is under continuing tutorship on grounds of mental retardation under Civil Code Article 355. The presumption is that such a person lacks capacity, but if the proponent of the donation could establish by "clear and convincing evidence" that the extent of retardation was moderate and that in fact the person had the ability to comprehend generally the nature and consequences of his act, then he would overcome that presumption and meet his burden of proof, and a donation inter vivos or testament by the person could be upheld.

(c) The standard of proof "clear and convincing evidence" that is employed in this Article and the next Article is well recognized in several contexts. Proof by "clear and convincing" evidence requires more than "a preponderance of the evidence", the traditional measure of persuasion, but less than "beyond a reasonable doubt", the stringent criminal standard. Succession of Bartie, 472 So.2d 578 (La.1985); Succession of Lyons, 452 So.2d 1161 (La.1984). Proof by "a preponderance of the evidence" requires that the evidence, taken as a whole, show that the fact sought to be proved is more probable than not. Prestenbach v. Sentry Ins. Co., 340 So.2d 1331 (La.1976). To prove a matter by "clear and convincing" evidence means to demonstrate that the existence of a disputed fact is highly probable, that is, much more probable than its nonexistence. Louisiana State Bar Association v. Edwins, 329 So.2d 437 (La.1976); Succession of Sanders, 485 So.2d 126 (La.App. 2d Cir.1986), writ denied, 487 So.2d 443 (La.1986).

The stricter standard, persuasion by "clear and convincing" evidence, is usually applied "where there is thought to be special danger of deception, or where the court considers that the particular type of claim should be disfavored on policy grounds." McCormick on Evidence, Sec. 340(b) (2d ed. 1972). See also Succession of Lyons, supra. Hence, by amending Civil Code Article 209 in 1982, to require illegitimates to prove filiation to a deceased alleged parent by clear and convincing evidence, the Louisiana Legislature furthered a public policy to protect individuals and their families from

336

potentially spurious claims brought at a time when the putative father cannot defend himself against paternity allegations. Spaht, "Developments in the Law, 1981–1982–Persons", 43 La.L.Rev. 535 (1982). See also, e.g., Mills v. Habluetzel, 456 U.S. 91, 102 S.Ct. 1549, 71 L.Ed.2d 770 (1982); Trimble v. Gordon, 430 U.S. 762, 97 S.Ct. 1459, 52 L.Ed.2d 31 (1977) (both recognizing a legitimate state interest in preventing fraudulent assertions). Thus, the distinction employed in this Article and the next presently exists with regard to proof of filiation under Civil Code Article 209, where the lesser standard of proof is required when the child alleges filiation against a parent who is living, and the more difficult standard where the alleged parent is deceased.

Art. 1483.   Proof of fraud, duress, or undue influence

A person who challenges a donation because of fraud, duress, or undue influence, must prove it by clear and convincing evidence. However, if, at the time the donation was made or the testament executed, a relationship of confidence existed between the donor and the wrongdoer and the wrongdoer was not then related to the donor by affinity, consanguinity or adoption, the person who challenges the donation need only prove the fraud, duress, or undue influence by a preponderance of the evidence.

Acts 1991, No. 363, § 1.

REVISION COMMENTS—1991

(a) This Article is new. It codifies prior jurisprudential law in part, and introduces new law in part.

(b) To discourage litigation, Article 1482, supra, requires that any challenge to donative capacity be proved by clear and convincing evidence, i.e., proof by a more difficult and rigorous standard than a mere preponderance of the evidence. Similarly and consistent with that decision, if capacity exists, then in order not to encourage litigation over undue influence, the stricter standard should also have to be satisfied to establish that such undue influence occurred. A single exception to requiring such strict proof in undue influence cases is made by this Article for the situation where a confidential relationship existed between the testator and the person who influenced him. As with rescission of contracts, a less difficult burden of proof should be required in such instances. See, e.g., C.C. Art. 1954 (Rev.1984).

(c) Under the second sentence of this Article the existence of a confidential relationship, such as doctor/patient, attorney/client, nurse/patient, or pastor/parishioner, will affect the burden of proof by lessening the requirement to overcome the presumption in favor of the validity of disposition. The Article does not lower the standard of proof where a challenge is made against a confidante who is related to the donor by marriage, blood, or adoption ("affinity, consanguinity or adoption") because in many instances the most likely persons who would be involved would be a spouse or child. In those instances the nature of the evidence required to prove undue influence remains "clear and convincing evidence." The standard is relaxed only where "the relationship of confidence" is more truly professional, such as that between doctor and his patient or a minister and his parishioner, and the person with whom the relationship exists is not a member of the donor's family. In light of the new rule stated in the last sentence of this Article, Article 1489 of the Civil Code of 1870, which contained a blanket prohibition against donations to doctors and ministers who attended the donor during the last illness, has been repealed, and needs no counterpart in the revision. Former Article 1489 had limited practical utility. The new Article should afford the courts ample grounds on which to invalidate dispositions such as those in Succession of Mayeux, 339 So.2d 1236 (3d Cir.1976), and will lessen the possibility of tortured reasoning as in Coleman v. Winsey, 183 So.2d 118 (1st Cir.1965) writ denied 184 So.2d 25 (La.1966), and its progeny. See also Bunge Corp. v. GATX Corp., 557 So.2d 1376 (La.1990), where the court stated: "The confidential relationship is not restricted to any specific association of the parties. While the most frequent illustrations are those of trustee and beneficiary, attorney and client, parent and child, or husband and wife, the term also embraces partners and co-partners, principal and agent, master and servant, physician and patient, 'and generally all persons who are associated by any relation of trust and confidence.' Appeal of Darlington, 147 Pa. 624, 23 A. 1046, 1047 (1892)." 557 So.2d at 1384, footnote 4.

(d) The second sentence of this Article does not require that the malefactor have been physically present at the time that the challenged donation was made or testament executed. It merely refers to a relationship of confidence existing between the parties at the time the gift was made or testament executed. It is the existence of such a relationship alone that lessens the standard of proof that is

337

required to prove fraud, duress, or undue influence. There is no language in the Article, and there was no intention on the part of the redactors, to require physical presence of the malefactor.

Art. 1484. Interpretation of revocation or modification

The rules contained in the foregoing articles also apply to the revocation of a legacy or testament, to the modification of a testamentary provision, and to any other modification of succession rights.

Added by Acts 2001, No. 560, § 1, eff. June 22, 2001.

Arts. 1485 to 1492. [Blank]

CHAPTER 3—THE DISPOSABLE PORTION AND ITS REDUCTION IN CASE OF EXCESS

Art. 1493. Forced heirs; representation of forced heirs

A.   Forced heirs are descendants of the first degree who, at the time of the death of the decedent, are twenty-three years of age or younger or descendants of the first degree of any age who, because of mental incapacity or physical infirmity, are permanently incapable of taking care of their persons or administering their estates at the time of the death of the decedent.

B.   When a descendant of the first degree predeceases the decedent, representation takes place for purposes of forced heirship only if the descendant of the first degree would have been twenty-three years of age or younger at the time of the decedent's death.

C.   However, when a descendant of the first degree predeceases the decedent, representation takes place in favor of any child of the descendant of the first degree, if the child of the descendant of the first degree, because of mental incapacity or physical infirmity, is permanently incapable of taking care of his or her person or administering his or her estate at the time of the decedent's death, regardless of the age of the descendant of the first degree at the time of the decedent's death.

D.   For purposes of this Article, a person is twenty-three years of age or younger until he attains the age of twenty-four years.

E.   For purposes of this Article "permanently incapable of taking care of their persons or administering their estates at the time of the death of the decedent" shall include descendants who, at the time of death of the decedent, have, according to medical documentation, an inherited, incurable disease or condition that may render them incapable of caring for their persons or administering their estates in the future.

Acts 1996, 1st Ex.Sess., No. 77, § 1. Amended by Acts 2003, No. 1207, § 2.

REVISION COMMENTS—1996

(a) Article 1493 is the threshold Article of the forced heirship revision. Paragraph A defines forced heirs and limits them to children, i.e. "descendants of the first degree." Paragraph B provides for representation of a predeceased child in a very limited instance to be consistent with the legislative policy expressed in the enabling legislation. Paragraph C provides for representation of a predeceased child of any age in favor of children of the predeceased child that, because of mental incapacity or physical infirmity, are permanently incapable of taking care of their persons or estates. Paragraph D makes clear that the language "twenty-three years of age or younger" in Article XII, Section 5(B) of the Louisiana Constitution, as amended in October, 1995, means that the child has "not attained the age of twenty-four years." Act 147 of 1990 used the language "attained the age of twenty-three years" to clarify the exact age, but neither the amendment of Article XII, Section 5, nor the implementing legislation uses that language. Instead, both refer to descendants of the first degree "twenty-three years of age or younger." The assumption seems warranted that the Legislature meant that until the descendant of the first degree "attains" the age of twenty-four years he is "twenty-three years of age or younger" and therefore will be a forced heir.

(b) Article XII, Section 5 of the Constitution requires the Legislature to enact legislation making all descendants of the first degree who are "twenty-three years of age or younger" forced heirs.

Indisputably, a child who has not yet reached his twenty-third birthday is "twenty-three years of age or younger." Some scholars have raised the question, however, whether, after reaching that birthday, and prior to reaching his twenty-fourth birthday, he is still "twenty-three years of age or younger." Arguably, a child who has reached his twenty-third birthday and is not midway into the year is twenty-three and one-half years of age and therefore not "twenty-three years of age or younger."

Act 147 of 1990 used different language in determining the age at which a child no longer was a forced heir. Act 147 provided that a descendant of the first degree was a forced heir until he had "attained the age of twenty-three years." That language is not used in Article XII, Section 5 of the Constitution, although, ironically, it is used in the second paragraph of Article 1493 of the enabling legislation which provides for grandchildren to represent a predeceased parent who would not have "attained the age of twenty-three years."

In order to avoid a constitutional issue in the very threshold definition of forced heirs, this Article contains the exact language of Article XII, Section 5 of the Constitution itself. The redactors believe, however, that the common sense meaning of "twenty-three years of age or younger" is that the child has not yet attained his twenty-fourth birthday and therefore that, throughout the child's twenty-third year he is still "twenty-three years of age." To assist the courts if this becomes an issue, this Article contains language to that effect in the third sentence. That statement in the third sentence should not jeopardize the constitutionality of the first and second sentences which, by using the exact same language that the Constitution uses, must of necessity be constitutional.

(c) Article XII, Section 5, of the Louisiana Constitution, as amended in 1995, requires the Legislature to provide implementing legislation to the effect that all children who are "twenty-three years of age or younger" are forced heirs, but it also permits the Legislature to provide that descendants of any age who, "because of physical incapacity or mental infirmity, are incapable of taking care of their persons or administering their estates" are also forced heirs. Utilizing that authorization, Article 1493(A) makes provision for such children to be forced heirs.

The origin of the double disjunctive "either/or" approach to incapacity or infirmity may be found in Act 147 of 1990 and its predecessor, Act 788 of 1989, which provided that descendants of any age who were "subject to interdiction" were forced heirs. The phrase "subject to interdiction" in Act 788 was considered to be unclear, among other reasons, because it did not differentiate between the two different kinds of interdiction, namely, the full interdiction in Civil Code articles 389 and 422, and the limited interdiction in Civil Code article 389.1. A decision was made to change the terminology and employ the terms found in the concept of limited interdiction, rather than the full interdiction. The new language was used in Act 147 of 1990, which provided that a child of any age would qualify as a forced heir if he were either incapable of taking care of his person or incapable of administering his estate, and which further made the exception applicable whether the incapacity was either physical or mental. That identical approach is followed in the amendment to Article XII, Section 5, of the Constitution that was adopted in 1995. The drafters of Act 147 of 1990 contemplated that the guidelines that the courts would use in interpreting and enforcing the incapacity or infirmity provisions were the jurisprudence under Civil Code Article 389.1 concerning limited interdiction.

Nevertheless, concern has been expressed regarding a possible lack of precision in the double disjunctive "either/or" approach, and also concerning difficulties involved in taking criteria that may work to determine when appointment of a curator is needed and applying them in a different context, namely inheritance rights. Concern was expressed, too, that the broad scope of the terms might encourage spurious claims for relatively minor incapacities or infirmities, and also concerning the uncertainty whether a temporary, albeit severe, incapacity or infirmity might qualify a child as a forced heir. Article 1493(A) clarifies the law in several respects and should help reduce unwarranted or inappropriate claims. For one thing, the Article specifies that the time at which the incapacity or infirmity is determined to be relevant is at the donor's death, which was always intended but may not have been fully clear in the earlier legislation. More important, the Legislature added the word "permanently" before the word "incapable" for the express purpose of emphasizing that a temporary incapacity or infirmity, even if severe, should not apply. Although the jurisprudence on limited interdiction may be helpful, the new rule expressed in this Article is intentionally different and more restrictive than the standard for interdiction because of the use of the word "permanently" to describe the nature of the incapacity or infirmity.

The Legislature also requested that these Comments note that as a factual matter a person can be permanently incapable or infirm but on occasion have a temporary remission. It is not intended to be the policy of the Article that a mere temporary remission at the time of the decedent's death would disqualify an heir from being classified as "permanently" incapable or infirm within the new definition, provided that the condition is otherwise permanent.

(d) This Article provides for representation of a predeceased child by his children. Article XII, Section 5 states emphatically that "except as provided in Paragraph B," forced heirship is abolished. Paragraph B nowhere provides for grandchildren to be forced heirs. Nonetheless, representation of a deceased parent is a fiction of the law of long standing and general acceptance, and it is certainly reasonable to accept the distinction that a grandchild who represents a deceased child is not a forced heir in his own right but standing in "the place and degree" of a child who would have been a forced heir if he were still alive.

(e) Paragraph C of this Article is new. It expands the narrow rule regarding the ability of a grandchild to represent a predeceased parent that is set forth in Paragraph B by extending the right of representation to disabled grandchildren of any age. Paragraph B requires that a predeceased parent not have attained the age of twenty-four by the time of the decedent's death for the grandchild to be able to represent him. Paragraph C, on the other hand, permits representation irrespective of the age of the predeceased parent, if the grandchild is disabled at the time of the death of the decedent. The nature of the disability of the grandchild that is required for him to qualify as a forced heir under Paragraph C is the identical kind of disability that is required for a child to qualify as a forced heir, namely, the grandchild must be severely disabled. See the discussion in Comment (c) above. It should be noted that a grandchild of any age who is disabled does not qualify as a forced heir unless the grandchild's parent predeceases the grandparent. Representation of a living person is not permitted, and Paragraph C is consistent with that requirement.

Art. 1494. Forced heir entitled to legitime; exception

A forced heir may not be deprived of the portion of the decedent's estate reserved to him by law, called the legitime, unless the decedent has just cause to disinherit him.

Acts 1996, 1st Ex.Sess., No. 77, § 1.

REVISION COMMENTS—1996

(a) This Article sets forth the principal effect of being a forced heir, namely that a portion of the parent's estate is "forced", that is, reserved for the child unless there is "just cause" for disinherison. The precise terms used elsewhere in the Code are used here to coordinate with those provisions. Of course, the law itself sets forth in the rules of unworthiness just causes for the forced heir to lose his rights. See Civil Code Article 1500.

(b) The legitime of a child is determined by dividing the forced portion by the number of qualified children living or represented at the death of the decedent. When descendants other than the child himself are involved, the legitime of these more remote descendants is determined by reference to the child they represent. Thus, when a predeceased child is represented by his descendants, the legitime of each descendant is determined by dividing the legitime of the child who is being represented among the descendants who represent him.

Art. 1495. Amount of forced portion and disposable portion

Donations inter vivos and mortis causa may not exceed three-fourths of the property of the donor if he leaves, at his death, one forced heir, and one-half if he leaves, at his death, two or more forced heirs. The portion reserved for the forced heirs is called the forced portion and the remainder is called the disposable portion.

Nevertheless, if the fraction that would otherwise be used to calculate the legitime is greater than the fraction of the decedent's estate to which the forced heir would succeed by intestacy, then the legitime shall be calculated by using the fraction of an intestate successor.

Acts 1996, 1st Ex.Sess., No. 77, § 1.

REVISION COMMENTS—1996

(a) The first paragraph of this Article follows Article 1494 logically by setting forth the amount of the reserved portions, namely one-fourth or one-half, depending on the number of forced heirs.

(b) The second paragraph of this Article resolves an issue that might otherwise be unclear and left to the courts for resolution. In certain instances the fraction to determine the share of the decedent's estate that a child would inherit by intestacy would be less than the fraction used to calculate his legitime, as, for example, when a parent has five competent children, four of whom are twenty-four or older and one of whom qualifies as a forced heir because he is twenty-three or younger. In such a case the percentage used to calculate the forced portion under Article 1495 would be twenty-five percent, but the intestate share under Article 888 would be only twenty percent.

(c) This Article reduces the amount that the forced heir may recover but does not eliminate the right of the forced heir to calculate his legitime in accordance with the formula of Civil Code Article 1505 by adding in the value of inter vivos donations to calculate the portion. Thus, the forced heir may receive a greater share than the actual intestate share, which is twenty percent of the probate estate, but not as large a share as he otherwise would be entitled to claim, namely twenty-five percent of the result of the Article 1505 calculation. This proposed resolution is similar to the one adopted by the Louisiana Supreme Court as to parental forced heirship in Succession of Greenlaw, 145 La. 255, 86 So. 786 (1920), later codified in Civil Code Article 1494 in 1956. The solution in the Greenlaw case was to make the lower, intestate portion become the forced portion, in much the same manner as under this Article.

Art. 1496. Permissible burdens on legitime

No charges, conditions, or burdens may be imposed on the legitime except those expressly authorized by law, such as a usufruct in favor of a surviving spouse or the placing of the legitime in trust.

Acts 1996, 1st Ex.Sess., No. 77, § 1.

REVISION COMMENT—1996

This Article reproduces the substance of Article 1710 of the Louisiana Civil Code (1870). It retains the fundamental principle of prior law, that a forced heir is entitled to his legitime in full ownership. Despite that general principle, however, there are well-recognized impingements on the legitime that are permitted. The two most prominent exceptions to the general rule are the usufruct of a surviving spouse, in Civil Code Articles 890 and 1499, and the ability of the testator to place the legitime in trust, in La. R.S. 9:1841 et seq. and La. Constitution, Article XII, Section 5. Another example of a condition that may be imposed on the legitime is the short-term survivorship provision presently authorized by Civil Code Article 1521.

Art. 1497. Disposable portion in absence of forced heirs

If there is no forced heir, donations inter vivos and mortis causa may be made to the whole amount of the property of the donor, saving the reservation made hereafter.

Acts 1996, 1st Ex.Sess., No. 77, § 1.

REVISION COMMENT—1996

This Article reproduces the substance of existing Article 1496. It does not change the law. The "reservation made hereafter" refers to the prohibition on donations omnium bonorum in Civil Code Article 1498.

Art. 1498. Nullity of donation inter vivos of entire patrimony

The donation inter vivos shall in no case divest the donor of all his property; he must reserve to himself enough for subsistence. If he does not do so, a donation of a movable is null for the whole, and a donation of an immovable is null for the whole unless the donee has alienated the immovable by onerous title, in which case the donation of such immovable shall not be declared null on the ground that the donor did not reserve to himself enough for his subsistence, but the donee is bound to return the value that the immovable had at the time that the donee received it. If the donee has created a real right by onerous title in the immovable given to him, or such right has been created by operation of law since the donee received the immovable, the donation is null for the whole and the donor may claim the immovable in the hands of the donee, but the property remains subject to the real right that has been created. In such a case, the donee and his successors by gratuitous title are accountable for the resulting diminution of the value of the property.

Acts 1996, 1st Ex.Sess., No. 77, § 1.

REVISION COMMENT—1996

This Article shortens slightly but essentially reproduces the substance of Article 1497 of the Louisiana Civil Code (1870).

Art. 1499.　Usufruct to surviving spouse

The decedent may grant a usufruct to the surviving spouse over all or part of his property, including the forced portion, and may grant the usufructuary the power to dispose of nonconsumables as provided in the law of usufruct. The usufruct shall be for life unless expressly designated for a shorter period, and shall not require security except as expressly declared by the decedent or as permitted when the legitime is affected.

A usufruct over the legitime in favor of the surviving spouse is a permissible burden that does not impinge upon the legitime, whether it affects community property or separate property, whether it is for life or a shorter period, whether or not the forced heir is a descendant of the surviving spouse, and whether or not the usufructuary has the power to dispose of nonconsumables.

Acts 1996, 1st Ex.Sess., No. 77, § 1. Amended by Acts 2003, No. 548, § 1.

REVISION COMMENTS—1996

(a) This Article is part of the effort to bifurcate the multiple provisions of former Civil Code Article 890, some of which dealt with testate succession and some of which dealt with intestate succession. See Revision Comments—1996 to Article 890, supra. The Article makes clear that a usufruct over separate property in favor of a surviving spouse does not constitute an impingement on the legitime. In Succession of Suggs, 612 So.2d 297 (La.App. 5th Cir. 1992) it was held that a usufruct to a second spouse over separate property comprising the forced portion was not permitted. The repeal of former Civil Code Article 1752 in 1995 effectively overruled Suggs by removing its only theoretical support. This Article leaves no doubt that under any circumstances, whether by clarification or by overruling, a usufruct in favor of a surviving spouse may be imposed over the legitime, whether the legitime is community property or separate property, and whether or not the spouse is a parent of the forced heir.

(b) This Article also clarifies an issue that has not yet been resolved in the courts, which is whether the testator may grant the usufructuary the power to dispose of nonconsumables as provided in the law regarding usufruct in Civil Code Article 568. There is disagreement among scholars as to whether the grant of such authoritywould constitute an impingement on the legitime. To remove any doubt and to establish that the grant of that right would not constitute an impingement, the Article expressly so provides.

(c) This Article does not supersede the provisions of the Louisiana Trust Code that protect a forced heir whose legitime has been placed in trust. See La. R.S. 9:1841 et seq.

(d) This Article legislatively overrules the case of Succession of B. J. Chauvin, 257 So.2d 422 (La. 1972) which held that when the will "merely confirmed" the legal usufruct to a surviving spouse over community property without specifying that it was for life, the usufruct was not a lifetime usufruct. See also Darby v. Rozas, 580 So.2d 984 (La.App. 3d Cir. 1991), which involved a grant of a usufruct over separate property, but which was settled while an application for writs to the Louisiana Supreme Court was pending. There is a transitional provision that continues this rule for testaments executed prior to the effective date of this Act.

Art. 1500.　Forced portion in cases of judicial divestment, disinherison, or renunciation of succession rights

When a forced heir renounces his legitime, is declared unworthy, or is disinherited, his legitime becomes disposable and the forced portion is reduced accordingly. The legitime of each remaining forced heir is not affected.

Acts 1996, 1st Ex.Sess., No. 77, § 1.

REVISION COMMENT—1996

This Article changes the law in part by providing that when a forced heir renounces his legitime, the decedent's forced portion is determined by the number of other forced heirs of the decedent living or represented. This changes the law as to the effects of renunciation and makes the effects of disinherison, renunciation and unworthiness consistent with each other instead of producing different results as provided under prior law in the second paragraph of Article 1498 (1995).

Art. 1501.   [Blank]

Art. 1502.   Inability to satisfy legitime by usufruct or income interest in trust only

Nevertheless, the legitime may not be satisfied in whole or in part by a usufruct or an income interest in trust. When a forced heir is both income and principal beneficiary of the same interest in trust, however, that interest shall be deemed a full ownership interest for purposes of satisfying the legitime if the trust conforms to the provisions of the Louisiana Trust Code governing the legitime in trust.

Acts 1996, 1st Ex.Sess., No. 77, § 1.

REVISION COMMENTS—1996

(a) This Article is consistent with Succession of Williams, 184 So.2d 70 (La.App. 4th Cir. 1966), which held that a child's forced portion may not be satisfied by a bequest to him of a usufruct.

(b) When the forced heir is both the income beneficiary and the principal beneficiary of the same interest in trust, those combined interests should be treated as the equivalent of full ownership for purposes of satisfying the legitime, provided, of course, that the trust conforms to the provisions of the Louisiana Trust Code governing the legitime in trust. To remove any doubt as to that result the Article expressly states that an income interest and a principal interest combined should be treated as the equivalent of full ownership for legitime purposes, but it virtually goes without saying that would be the case even in the absence of such a provision. A parallel concept is found in Civil Code Article 543 that permits a usufruct and naked ownership to be treated as a full ownership for purposes of provoking a partition.

(c) The word "nevertheless" is intended to make certain that the provisions of this Article modify and limit the provisions of Article 1501.

Art. 1503.   Reduction of excessive donations

A donation, inter vivos or mortis causa, that impinges upon the legitime of a forced heir is not null but is merely reducible to the extent necessary to eliminate the impingement.

Acts 1996, 1st Ex.Sess., No. 77, § 1.

REVISION COMMENTS—1996

(a) This Article reproduces the substance of the first paragraph of Article 1502 of the Civil Code of 1870. It changes the law in part by eliminating the rule set forth in the second paragraph of Article 1502, to the effect that if each presumptive heir receives the same value of property during a calendar year the donation is not subject to reduction. There is no need for such a provision in light of the adoption of a three year cut off period as provided in La.R.S. 9:2372, as adopted by Act 402 of 1995, and Article 1505(A) of this revision. Under La.R.S. 9:2372 there is a three year cut off on including gifts in the calculation of the "active mass" to determine the forced portion as well as to be subject to the action to reduce. Section 2 of Act 402 may have been unnecessarily restrictive, in limiting the application of that act to donations made on and after January 1, 1996, and this revision contains a provision to make it more effective. Under Article 1505(A) of this revision whether gifts are of an equal value or not in the same year, if they were given three or more years before the decedent dies, they would not be included under any circumstances.

(b) Under this Article, if the husband's will leaves all to his wife and there is a forced heir who is entitled to one-fourth, the legacy to the wife is reduced to the disposable portion in full ownership and a usufruct for life, with the power to dispose of nonconsumables, over the forced portion, since that usufruct could have been left to her expressly under Article 1499. This is the maximum extent to which reduction is needed to eliminate the excess that impinges upon the legitime, since the decedent could legally have made such a bequest to his surviving spouse. No further reduction is necessary or appropriate.

Art. 1504.   Reduction of donations, exclusive right of forced heirs

An action to reduce excessive donations may be brought only after the death of the donor, and then only by a forced heir, the heirs or legatees of a forced heir, or an assignee of any of them who has an express conventional assignment, made after the death of the decedent, of the right to bring the action.

Acts 1996, 1st Ex.Sess., No. 77, § 1.

REVISION COMMENT—1996

This Article reproduces the substance of Article 1504 of the Louisiana Civil Code (1870). It changes the law in part by requiring an "express conventional assignment" for an assignee to be entitled to assert the personal action of the forced heir. The word "assignee" clearly includes a creditor as well as a donee or vendee. There is some possible conflict in the jurisprudence because of the earlier case of Succession of Henican, 248 So.2d 385 (La.App. 4th Cir. 1971), which held that a bank as an unsecured creditor of a forced heir could not compel the forced heir to assert his rights as a forced heir because those rights were strictly personal. A later case, Succession of Hurd, 489 So.2d 1029 (La.App. 1st Cir. 1986), held that because of the supremacy of federal law over state law a trustee in bankruptcy could assert the personal right of the bankrupt to demand collation, which, like the right of the forced heir to assert an action to reduce, is also a personal right. To the extent possible, the Article clarifies that a creditor should not have the right to assert an action to reduce unless the creditor has an express conventional assignment. The rule is consistent with Henican in every context other than a bankruptcy context and, it is hoped, the rule will be held to apply even in that context.

Art. 1505.   Calculation of disposable portion on mass of succession

A.   To determine the reduction to which the donations, either inter vivos or mortis causa, are subject, an aggregate is formed of all property belonging to the donor or testator at the time of his death; to that is fictitiously added the property disposed of by donation inter vivos within three years of the date of the donor's death, according to its value at the time of the donation.

B.   The sums due by the estate are deducted from this aggregate amount, and the disposable quantum is calculated on the balance, taking into consideration the number of forced heirs.

C.   Neither the premiums paid for insurance on the life of the donor nor the proceeds paid pursuant to such coverage shall be included in the above calculation. Moreover, the value of such proceeds at the donor's death payable to a forced heir, or for his benefit, shall be deemed applied and credited in satisfaction of his forced share.

D.   Employer and employee contributions under any plan of deferred compensation adopted by any public or governmental employer or any plan qualified under Sections 401 or 408 of the Internal Revenue Code, and any benefits payable by reason of death, disability, retirement, or termination of employment under any such plans, shall not be included in the above calculation, nor shall any of such contributions or benefits be subject to the claims of forced heirs. However, the value of such benefits paid or payable to a forced heir, or for the benefit of a forced heir, shall be deemed applied and credited in satisfaction of his forced share.

Acts 1996, 1st Ex.Sess., No. 77, § 1.

REVISION COMMENTS—1996

(a) Civil Code Article 1505(A) has been modified slightly to coordinate with La.R.S. 9:2372 as adopted by act 402 of 1995, and to change the date of valuation.

(b) Act 402 may have tacitly repealed previous R.S. 9:2372 which provided an exemption to gifts to charitable organizations made more than three years before the donor died, so that curative legislation is truly needed. See Louisiana Civil Code Article 8, which provides that a law may be repealed by implication "when the new law contains provisions that are contrary to, or irreconcilable with, those of the former law." Under Paragraph (A) of this Article, all donations made more than three years prior to the decedent's death are exempt from the calculation of the "active mass." Article 1508 of this revision exempts such gifts from the action of reduction.

(c) The provisions of Civil Code Article 1505(B), (C), and (D) have not been changed.

(d) See Civil Code Articles 1510 and 1511 which may also apply to the calculation of the "active mass" when the inter vivos donations are remunerative or onerous.

Art. 1506.   [Blank]

Art. 1507.   Reduction of legacies before donations inter vivos, order of reduction

Donations inter vivos may not be reduced until the value of all the property comprised in donations mortis causa is exhausted. The testator may expressly declare in the testament that a legacy shall be paid in preference to others, in which case the preferred legacy shall not be reduced until the other legacies are exhausted.

Acts 1996, 1st Ex.Sess., No. 77, § 1.

REVISION COMMENT—1996

This Article retains the first sentence of Civil Code Article 1507 (1870), and restates the concept in Civil Code Article 1635 (1870) that the testator can assign preference in the reduction of legacies.

Art. 1508.   Reduction of donations inter vivos

When the property of the estate is not sufficient to satisfy the forced portion, a forced heir may recover the amount needed to satisfy his legitime from the donees of inter vivos donations made within three years of the date of the decedent's death, beginning with the most recent donation and proceeding successively to the most remote.

Acts 1996, 1st Ex.Sess., No. 77, § 1.

REVISION COMMENTS—1996

(a) This Article is based on the provision of Articles 1507, 1511, and 1634 of the Louisiana Civil Code (1870). It changes the law in part by limiting the forced heir's right to reduce excessive donations to those made within the three years preceding the decedent's death. See La.R.S. 9:2372, adopted by Act 402 of 1995.

(b) This Article coordinates with Article 1506 of this revision, making a consistent rule for excluding certain inter vivos gifts from the calculation of the "active mass" and in exempting them from the action to reduce.

Art. 1509.   Insolvency of a donee

When a donee from whom recovery is due is insolvent, the forced heir may claim his legitime from the donee of the next preceding donation and so on to the donee of the most remote donation. A donee who pays the share of an insolvent donee is subrogated to the rights of the forced heir against the insolvent donee.

Acts 1996, 1st Ex.Sess., No. 77, § 1.

REVISION COMMENT—1996

This Article reproduces the substance of Article 1508 of the Louisiana Civil Code (1870). It does not change the law. It is intended to clarify the law by expressly recognizing that a donee who pays the share of an insolvent donee is subrogated to the rights that the forced heir would have had against the insolvent donee. As a practical matter, in all such instances the likelihood of recovery will be negligible since the predicate is that the first donee is insolvent, but for those few cases where this may occur, the more ancient donee who has been forced to pay should have no difficulty in establishing his legal right of subrogation.

Art. 1510.   Remunerative donations, extent of reduction

The value of a remunerative donation is not included in the calculation of the forced portion, and the donation may not be reduced, unless the value of the remunerated services is less than two-thirds the value of the property donated at the time of the donation, in which event the gratuitous portion is included in the calculation and is subject to reduction.

Acts 1996, 1st Ex.Sess., No. 77, § 1.

REVISION COMMENT—1996

This Article reproduces the substance of Article 1513 of the Louisiana Civil Code. It changes the law, but it clarifies some ambiguities existing under prior law and it simplifies the formula to determine the value to be included in the calculation. Its provisions are similar to those of Civil Code Article 1526.

Art. 1511.   Onerous donation, extent of reduction

The value of an onerous donation is not included in the calculation of the forced portion, and the donation may not be reduced, unless the value of the charges is less than two-thirds the value of the property donated at the time of the donation, in which event the gratuitous portion is included in the calculation and is subject to reduction.

Acts 1996, 1st Ex.Sess., No. 77, § 1.

REVISION COMMENT—1996

This Article reproduces the substance of Article 1514 of the Louisiana Civil Code (1870). It clarifies the law as to the formula to apply, and it further clarifies the law by providing that where a donation is both onerous and gratuitous it can only be reduced to the extent that it is purely gratuitous. Its provisions are similar to those of Civil Code Article 1526.

Art. 1512.   Retention of fruits and products of donation by donee until demand for reduction

The fruits and products of property donated inter vivos belong to the donee except for those that accrue after written demand for reduction is made on him.

Acts 1996, 1st Ex.Sess., No. 77, § 1.

REVISION COMMENTS—1996

(a) This Article changes the law by providing that the donee is to restore fruits only from the time of demand in all cases. Under Article 1515 of the Louisiana Civil Code (1870), the donee restored fruits from the day of the donor's death if the demand for reduction was made within one year of the death of the donor.

(b) Under Article 1504 of the Civil Code, the demand for reduction cannot be made until after the donor has died. Therefore, the donee owns, and therefore is clearly entitled to keep all of the fruits and products that accrue before the donor's death as well as those received after death and before demand. The "demand" contemplated by this Article is not necessarily a judicial demand, as in an action to reduce excessive donations, but a written demand of any kind.

Art. 1513.   Reduction in kind when property is owned by the donee or successors by gratuitous title; effects of alienation by donee

The action for reduction of excessive donations may be brought only against the donee or his successors by gratuitous title in accordance with the order of their donations, beginning with the most recent donation. When the donated property is still owned by the donee or the successors, reduction takes place in kind or by contribution to the payment of the legitime, at the election of the donee or the successors, who are accountable for any diminution in the value of the property attributable to their fault or neglect and for any charges or encumbrances imposed upon the property after the donation.

When the property given is no longer owned by the donee or his successors by gratuitous title, the donee and the successors must contribute to the payment of the legitime. A donee or his successor who contributes to payment of the legitime is required to do so only to the extent of the value of the donated property at the time the donee received it.

Acts 1996, 1st Ex.Sess., No. 77, § 1.

REVISION COMMENT—1996

This Article combines the substance of Articles 1516 through 1518 of the Louisiana Civil Code (1870). It changes the law in part by using the date of gift value for purposes of determining the amount of liability of the donee. Under prior law, the date of death valuation is used.

Art. 1514. Usufruct of surviving spouse affecting legitime; security

A forced heir may request security when a usufruct in favor of a surviving spouse affects his legitime and he is not a child of the surviving spouse. A forced heir may also request security to the extent that a surviving spouse's usufruct over the legitime affects separate property. The court may order the execution of notes, mortgages, or other documents as it deems necessary, or may impose a mortgage or lien on either community or separate property, movable or immovable, as security.

Acts 1996, 1st Ex.Sess., No. 77, § 1. Amended by Acts 2003, No. 1207, § 2.

REVISION COMMENT—1996

(a) The first sentence of this Article makes a limited exception to the rule that a legal usufructuary is not required to give security. See Civil Code Article 573.

(b) This Article allows the forced heir to request security in instances where the testator leaves the surviving spouse a usufruct that affects his legitime, and the forced heir is not a child of the surviving spouse. A forced heir may also request security to the extent the usufruct affects legitime composed of the decedent's separate property, and in that instance the security may be required even if the usufructuary is the parent of the forced heir.

(c) This Article essentially reenacts the provisions of the last paragraph of Civil Code Article 890, which was originally adopted in 1981 and was amended periodically thereafter. Article 890 expanded the law by which its predecessor Article 916 (1870) granted a usufruct to a surviving spouse that would terminate upon the death or remarriage of the surviving spouse, but only as to community property inherited by issue of the marriage. Civil Code Article 916 did not authorize a usufruct over community property that was inherited by children of a prior marriage or by illegitimate children, nor did it authorize a usufruct over separate property. When the law was expanded to permit a testator to grant such a usufruct to a surviving spouse, the last paragraph of Civil Code Article 890 was also added to authorize the naked owner in those instances to request security. In the absence of such an authorization, the usufruct of the surviving spouse would be a "legal" usufruct and security would not have been acquired. See Civil Code Article 573. The legislature made a policy decision that children of a prior marriage and illegitimate children are entitled to greater protection than are children of the marriage, or, in other words, to treat a surviving spouse who is the parent of the naked owner different from a surviving spouse who is not the parent of the naked owner. This Article continues that policy, but the language has been revised slightly and the provision itself has been appropriately moved to a different section of the Civil Code. Civil Code Article 1499 of this revision expressly authorizes a decedent to grant a surviving spouse a usufruct over all or part of his property, including the forced portion, and to grant the usufructuary the power to dispose of nonconsumables. This Article continues in place the rule that where the usufruct affects the legitime of a forced heir who is not a child of the usufructuary, then that child "may" request security. Where the usufruct applies to separate property, however, it matters whether the separate property forms part of the legitime but not whether the naked owner is a child of the surviving parent who is the usufructuary. This Article permits a naked owner, even one who is a child of the surviving spouse, to request security whenever the naked ownership comprising the legitime consists of separate property.

347

(d) There are no reported cases under the predecessor Article, Civil Code Article 890 (1981) interpreting the nature of the duty or obligation of the court to impose security when a naked owner requests it, or the extent of the security, or even the nature of the security. If one parses the sentence, it is apparent that the requirement of "security" is not automatic; the naked owner must first make a request for security to be required. And the very word "security" itself is susceptible of several different meanings. There are many forms of security, such as a surety bond, a legal or conventional mortgage, and perhaps, in a more colloquial sense, a designation of the nature of an investment. An example of that latter kind of provision is found in Civil Code Article 618, which applies when, for example, a usufruct of a nonconsumable is transformed into a usufruct of a consumable and the naked owner and the usufructuary are unable to agree on the investment of the proceeds within one year of the transformation of the property. In that case, Civil Code Article 618 authorizes the court to determine the nature of the investment. It is hoped that courts will not inflexibly apply the rule of this Article to require a usufructuary to post bond every time a naked owner requests security, but will consider all of the circumstances of the situation, such as the nature of the property that comprises the legitime, and whether the property is movable or immovable, consumable or nonconsumable, and what practical controls exist or may be used to protect the right of the naked owner without infringing on the rights of the usufructuary, or if so, by infringing in the least restrictive manner possible.

(e) It should be noted that since the testator can alienate the disposable portion in full ownership there is no reason to require a bond when he has donated something less than that, namely, a usufruct only.

Arts. 1515 to 1518. [Blank]

CHAPTER 4—OF DISPOSITIONS REPROBATED BY LAW IN DONATIONS INTER VIVOS AND MORTIS CAUSA

Art. 1519. Impossible, illegal or immoral conditions

In all dispositions inter vivos and mortis causa impossible conditions, those which are contrary to the laws or to morals, are reputed not written.

Art. 1520. Prohibited substitutions, definitions

A disposition that is not in trust by which a thing is donated in full ownership to a first donee, called the institute, with a charge to preserve the thing and deliver it to a second donee, called the substitute, at the death of the institute, is null with regard to both the institute and the substitute.

Acts 2001, No. 825, § 1.

REVISION COMMENTS—2001

(a) Under this Article, a disposition is null as a prohibited substitution only if the following requirements are met: 1) The act involves a double disposition of the thing in full ownership; and 2) The first donee is charged to preserve the thing for his lifetime and at his death transmit it to another person designated by the donor. Thus, the definition requires that the original donation establish a successive order that deprives the first donee of the power of testation; i.e., it causes the property to leave the estate of the first person at his death and at that time enter the patrimony of the second donee.

(b) Under this Article, a charge to preserve property but no charge to deliver at death, so that the property may be delivered by the first donee to the second donee before that time, is not a substitution and is not prohibited.

(c) Under this Article, the classical substitution called the "substitutio de eo quod supererit", or as it is sometimes called the "substitutio de residuo", where the donee has no charge to preserve is not prohibited. Thus, if there is delivery to a first donee who is to deliver it to a second donee, but the first donee is not obligated to preserve the thing, there is no prohibited substitution. The key is that with the "substitutio de residuo" there is no charge to preserve the thing, and the donee who would otherwise be the institute is free to alienate or encumber the property as he pleases. Although technically the "substitutio de residuo" is a substitution, it is noteworthy that there were many kinds of substitutions in Roman law that were permitted, such as the pupillary substitution and the exemplary substitution. The classic "prohibited substitution" was the fideicommissary substitution, which was called, in French, the "substitution fidéicommissaire." A translation error of the French name into English in Article 1520 resulted in Louisiana inappropriately and awkwardly prohibiting both fidei commisa and substitutions, when in reality it was only the fideicommissary substitution that was to have been prohibited.

Art. 1521. Vulgar substitutions

The disposition by which a third person is called to take a gift or legacy in case the donee or legatee does not take it is not a prohibited substitution. A testator may impose as a valid suspensive condition that the legatee or a trust beneficiary must survive the testator for a stipulated period, which period shall not exceed six months after the testator's death, in default of which a third person is called to take the legacy. In such a case, the right of the legatee or trust beneficiary is in suspense until the survivorship as required is determined. If the legatee or trust beneficiary survives as required, he is considered as having succeeded to the deceased from the moment of his death. If he does not survive as required, he is considered as never having received it, and the third person who is called to take the bequest in default of his survival is considered as having succeeded to the deceased from the moment of his death. A survivorship condition as to the legitime of a forced heir shall only be valid if the forced heir dies without descendants, or if he dies with descendants and neither the forced heir nor the descendants survive the stipulated time.

Acts 2001, No. 825, § 1.

REVISION COMMENTS—2001

(a) This Article provides a revision of the "vulgar substitution" Article and extends the suspensive condition period for survivorship from ninety days to six months. Six months should be a reasonable time for the condition to be suspended, because every state in America permits a six month time period for short-term survivorship; the Louisiana Insurance Code permits a six month time period; and the Internal Revenue Code with regard to the marital deduction also permits a six month delay.

(b) Under this Article, the provision regarding the legitime of a forced heir is preserved with the double requirement that, to be effective, the forced heir must die without descendants, or, if there are descendants, then both the forced heir and the descendants would have to die within the time frame.

Art. 1522. Separate donations of usufruct and naked ownership

The same shall be observed as to the disposition inter vivos or mortis causa, by which the usufruct is given to one, and the naked ownership to another.

CHAPTER 5—DONATIONS INTER VIVOS

SECTION 1—GENERAL DISPOSITIONS

Arts. 1523 to 1525. [Blank]

Art. 1526. Onerous donation

The rules peculiar to donations inter vivos do not apply to a donation that is burdened with an obligation imposed on the donee that results in a material advantage to the donor, unless at the time of the donation the cost of performing the obligation is less than two-thirds of the value of the thing donated.

Acts 2008, No. 204, § 1, eff. Jan. 1, 2009.

REVISION COMMENT—2008

This Article is based on the provisions of Article 1511 and former Articles 1524 and 1526 of the Louisiana Civil Code (1870). It is not intended to change the law.

Art. 1527.   Remunerative donations

The rules peculiar to donations inter vivos do not apply to a donation that is made to recompense for services rendered that are susceptible of being measured in money unless at the time of the donation the value of the services is less than two-thirds of the value of the thing donated.

Acts 2008, No. 204, § 1, eff. Jan. 1, 2009.

REVISION COMMENT—2008

This Article is based on the provisions of former Articles 1525 and 1526, and Article 1510, of the Louisiana Civil Code (1870). It is not intended to change the law.

Art. 1528.   Charges or conditions imposed by donor

The donor may impose on the donee any charges or conditions he pleases, provided they contain nothing contrary to law or good morals.

Acts 2008, No. 204, § 1, eff. Jan. 1, 2009.

REVISION COMMENT—2008

This Article reproduces the text of former Civil Code Article 1527 (1870) verbatim. It is not intended to change the law. The imposition of a condition on a donation does not necessarily make the donation onerous. See Article 1526.

Art. 1529.   Donation of future property; nullity

A donation inter vivos can have as its object only present property of the donor. If it includes future property, it shall be null with regard to that property.

Acts 2008, No. 204, § 1, eff. Jan. 1, 2009.

REVISION COMMENT—2008

This Article reproduces the substance of former Civil Code Article 1528 (1870). It is not intended to change the law. However, see Article 1738.

Art. 1530.   Donation conditional on will of donor; nullity

A donation inter vivos is null when it is made on a condition the fulfillment of which depends solely on the will of the donor.

Acts 2008, No. 204, § 1, eff. Jan. 1, 2009.

REVISION COMMENT—2008

This Article reproduces the substance of former Civil Code Article 1529 (1870). It is not intended to change the law.

Art. 1531.   Donation conditional on payment of future or unexpressed debts and charges; nullity

A donation is also null if it is burdened with an obligation imposed on the donee to pay debts and charges other than those that exist at the time of the donation, unless the debts and charges are expressed in the act of donation.

Acts 2008, No. 204, § 1, eff. Jan. 1, 2009.

REVISION COMMENTS—2008

(a) This Article reproduces the substance of former Civil Code Article 1530 (1870). It is not intended to change the law. This draft is very close to the text of the former Article, but the clause referring to the "act that was to be annexed to it" has been removed.

(b) The obligation imposed on the donee under this Article must not otherwise be prohibited, and the discharge of the debts and charges must be permissible under the law of obligations.

Art. 1532.   Stipulation for right of return to donor

The donor may stipulate the right of return of the thing given, either in the case of his surviving the donee only, or in the case of his surviving the donee and the descendants of the donee.

The right may be stipulated only for the advantage of the donor.

Acts 2008, No. 204, § 1, eff. Jan. 1, 2009.

REVISION COMMENT—2008

This Article reproduces the substance of former Civil Code Article 1534 (1870). It is not intended to change the law.

Art. 1533.   Right of return; effect

The effect of the right of return is that the thing donated returns to the donor free of any alienation, lease, or encumbrance made by the donee or his successors after the donation.

The right of return shall not apply, however, to a good faith transferee for value of the thing donated. In such a case, the donee and his successors by gratuitous title are, nevertheless, accountable for the loss sustained by the donor.

Acts 2008, No. 204, § 1, eff. Jan. 1, 2009.

REVISION COMMENTS—2008

(a) This Article is based on former Civil Code Article 1535 (1870). It may change the law in instances in which the thing donated has been transferred to a good faith transferee for value. See Comment (b).

(b) The second paragraph addresses the situation in which the thing donated has been transferred to a good faith transferee for value, in which case the good faith transferee need not return the thing but the donee "and his successors by gratuitous title" are accountable for the loss sustained by the donor. The word "his" restricts the application to a chain of gratuitous donees from the donor, so that it does not apply to a gratuitous transferee from a transferee for value. The words "and his successors by gratuitous title" are designed to cover the situation in which the first donee donates the thing by gratuitous title to a second donee who then transfers it to a good faith transferee for value. In that instance, the donee and his successors by gratuitous title would be accountable to the donor, but the transferee for value would not be.

Arts. 1534 to 1540.   [Blank]

SECTION 2—OF THE FORM OF DONATIONS INTER VIVOS

Art. 1541.   Form required for donations

A donation inter vivos shall be made by authentic act under the penalty of absolute nullity, unless otherwise expressly permitted by law.

Acts 2008, No. 204, § 1, eff. Jan. 1, 2009.

REVISION COMMENTS—2008

(a) This Article reproduces the substance of former Civil Code Article 1536 (1870). It is not intended to change the law.

(b) Donations of both immovable and movable property must be made by notarial act unless a particular exception applies. There are numerous exceptions to this Article including Article 1543 (manual gift) and Article 1550 (stock certificates and negotiable instruments).

Art. 1542. Identification of donor, donee, and the thing donated required

The act of donation shall identify the donor and the donee and describe the thing donated. These requirements are satisfied if the identities and description are contained in the act of donation or are reasonably ascertainable from information contained in it, as clarified by extrinsic evidence, if necessary.

Acts 2008, No. 204, § 1, eff. Jan. 1, 2009.

REVISION COMMENT—2008

This Article is based on the provisions of former Civil Code Article 1538 (1870). It is not intended to change the law but it clarifies essential requirements of an act of donation. The concept of reasonable ascertainability follows the language of the provisions of Article 1575 regarding the necessity to date an olographic will.

Art. 1543. Manual gift

The donation inter vivos of a corporeal movable may also be made by delivery of the thing to the donee without any other formality.

Acts 2008, No. 204, § 1, eff. Jan. 1, 2009.

REVISION COMMENTS—2008

(a) This Article reproduces the substance of former Civil Code Article 1539 (1870). There is a change in language from former Article 1539, which referred to the "manual gift," and refers to it as the "giving of corporeal movable effects, accompanied by a real delivery," which is specified as not being "subject to any formality."

(b) The word "also" is purposefully used in this Article to make clear that the donation of a corporeal movable does not always require delivery to be effective. If the donation is made by authentic act, physical delivery to the donee is not necessary. See also Article 2477 which lists the methods of making delivery of things subject to the contract of sale.

(c) This Article refers only to the donation itself; it does not state how the donation may be accepted. See also Article 1544, regarding acceptance of donations.

Art. 1544. Donation effective from time of acceptance

A donation inter vivos is without effect until it is accepted by the donee. The acceptance shall be made during the lifetime of the donor.

The acceptance of a donation may be made in the act of donation or subsequently in writing.

When the donee is put into corporeal possession of a movable by the donor, possession by the donee also constitutes acceptance of the donation.

Acts 2008, No. 204, § 1, eff. Jan. 1, 2009.

REVISION COMMENTS—2008

(a) The concept of this Article is derived from former Civil Code Article 1540 (1870). In Tweedel v. Brasseaux, 433 So.2d 133, 139 (La. 1983), the Supreme Court upheld an acceptance signed prior to the signing of the act of donation. According to the Court: "[T]he minor discrepancy [in the dates] was known to all parties at the time. The fact that the donees' signatures were affixed the preceding day is of little significance. There is no legal provision or jurisprudence which reprobates the idea of donees signing an acceptance immediately prior to a donation. Acceptance in precise terms in the same act as a donation is valid, even though signed prior to the time the act is signed by the donors." This Article is not intended to change the result in Tweedel.

(b) See also Civil Code Articles 3421 and 3424 regarding possession.

Art. 1545. Acceptance in person or by mandatary

The donee may accept a donation personally or by a mandatary having power to accept a donation for him.

Acts 2008, No. 204, § 1, eff. Jan. 1, 2009.

REVISION COMMENT—2008

This Article is based on former Civil Code Article 1542 (1870). It is not intended to change the law.

Art. 1546. Acceptance during lifetime of donee

The acceptance shall be made during the lifetime of the donee. If the donee dies without having accepted the donation, his successors may not accept for him.

Acts 2008, No. 204, § 1, eff. Jan. 1, 2009.

REVISION COMMENT—2008

This Article reproduces the substance of former Civil Code Article 1544 (1870). It is not intended to change the law.

Art. 1547. Acceptance by creditor prohibited

If the donee refuses or neglects to accept the donation, his creditors may not accept for him.

Acts 2008, No. 204, § 1, eff. Jan. 1, 2009.

REVISION COMMENT—2008

This Article is based on former Civil Code Article 1543 (1870). It is not intended to change the law.

Art. 1548. Unemancipated minor; persons authorized to accept

A donation made to an unemancipated minor may be accepted by a parent or other ascendant of the minor or by his tutor, even if the person who accepts is also the donor.

Acts 2008, No. 204, § 1, eff. Jan. 1, 2009.

REVISION COMMENTS—2008

(a) This Article is based on former Civil Code Article 1546 (1870). It is not intended to change the law.

(b) If the parent is not the child's tutor, it is permissible for either the tutor or the parent to accept. This Article expressly permits the donor to accept the donation if he is authorized to accept on behalf of the minor.

Art. 1549. Thing acquired subject to existing charges

The donee acquires the thing donated subject to all of its charges, even those that the donor has imposed between the time of the donation and the time of the acceptance.

Acts 2008, No. 204, § 1, eff. Jan. 1, 2009.

REVISION COMMENT—2008

This Article reproduces the substance of former Civil Code Article 1551 (1870). It is not intended to change the law.

Art. 1550. Form for donation of certain incorporeal movables

The donation or the acceptance of a donation of an incorporeal movable of the kind that is evidenced by a certificate, document, instrument, or other writing, and that is transferable by endorsement or delivery, may be made by authentic act or by compliance with the requirements otherwise applicable to the transfer of that particular kind of incorporeal movable.

In addition, an incorporeal movable that is investment property, as that term is defined in Chapter 9 of the Louisiana Commercial Laws, may also be donated by a writing signed by the donor that evidences donative intent and directs the transfer of the property to the donee or his account or for his benefit. Completion of the transfer to the donee or his account or for his benefit shall constitute acceptance of the donation.

Acts 2008, No. 204, § 1, eff. Jan. 1, 2009.

REVISION COMMENTS—2008

(a) This Article is new. It is based in part on the provisions of former Civil Code Article 1536 (1870).

(b) In this Article, the words "for his benefit" are included to cover situations when the transfer may not be directly to the donee's account, but would be used to pay something for his benefit, as for example, if the transfer is made to a bank to pay off a child's debt. The same phrase is used in Article 1505 concerning life insurance and retirement benefits.

(c) Under Louisiana property law a check or promissory note is classified as an incorporeal movable. La. Civ. Co. Art. 473. See Succession of Franklin, 968 So.2d 811, No. 42,496 (La.App. Cir. 10/17/07). The transfer of such an instrument, whether negotiable or non-negotiable, may be governed by Chapter 9 of the Louisiana Commercial Laws. A donation of such property may be by, but does not necessarily require, an authentic act.

There is an important distinction, however, between a donation of the check itself, which is an incorporeal movable, and the donation of the money or funds represented by the check. If A writes a check to B, and B endorses and delivers the check to C, the transfer to C is complete upon B's negotiation of the check to C. On the other hand, if A intends to make a gift to B of cash, and writes his personal check to B, but B does not cash the check before A dies, or B dies before cashing it, there is not a completed gift of the funds in the bank account.

At all times, donative intent is required, but assuming donative intent, this Article does not change the rule that an attempted donation of cash by use of a personal check does not constitute a completed gift unless and until the check is cashed. R.S. 10:3–203(a) provides that "an instrument is transferred when it is delivered by a person other than its issuer for the purpose of giving to the person receiving delivery the right to enforce the instrument." Thus, R.S. 10:3–105(c) provides that an issuer is a "maker or drawer of an instrument." Thus, R.S. 10:3–203(a) does not apply to the situation in which A gives his personal check to B intending to make a donation of the cash in A's checking account, because A is an "issuer" of his own personal checks, and therefore R.S. 10:3–203(a) does not apply.

Art. 1551. Effects of acceptance

A donation is effective upon acceptance. When the donation is effective, the ownership or other real right in the thing given is transferred to the donee.

Acts 2008, No. 204, § 1, eff. Jan. 1, 2009.

REVISION COMMENT—2008

(a) This Article is based on the provisions of former Civil Code Article 1550 (1870). It is not intended to change the law.

(b) Under this Article delivery is not required if the acceptance is made by a means other than corporeal possession. See for example Article 1541. See also Article 1544, to the effect that if the donee is put into corporeal possession of a movable by the donor, possession by the donee also constitutes acceptance of the donation.

(c) This Article makes reference to the transfer of a "real right" to make it clear that the object of a donative transfer may involve not only ownership of a thing, but other real rights as well. Thus, for instance, under this Article a right of usufruct given by inter vivos act is transferred to the donee when the donation becomes effective. See also Comment (c) to Article 1468, explaining that the thing given by donation may be a real right.

(d) This Article states that a donation transfers ownership when the donation is accepted. See also Article 2439, regarding sale and transfer of ownership, which states that a sale "... transfers ownership of a thing."

Arts. 1552 to 1555. [Blank]

SECTION 3—EXCEPTIONS TO THE RULE OF THE IRREVOCABILITY OF DONATIONS INTER VIVOS

Art. 1556. Causes for revocation or dissolution

A donation inter vivos may be revoked because of ingratitude of the donee or dissolved for the nonfulfillment of a suspensive condition or the occurrence of a resolutory condition. A donation may also be dissolved for the nonperformance of other conditions or charges.

Acts 2008, No. 204, § 1, eff. Jan. 1, 2009.

REVISION COMMENTS—2008

(a) This Article is based on the provisions of former Article 1559 of the Louisiana Civil Code (1870). It clarifies the law and the text is made more technically accurate.

(b) The language of this Article is intended to coordinate with Civil Code Article 1767 on conditional obligations.

(c) The fourth "cause" or ground for revocation or dissolution under the source Article, the legal or conventional return, has been eliminated as technically incorrect. The return could be a consequence, but it is never a ground for revocation.

Art. 1557. Revocation for ingratitude

Revocation on account of ingratitude may take place only in the following cases:

(1) If the donee has attempted to take the life of the donor; or

(2) If he has been guilty towards him of cruel treatment, crimes, or grievous injuries.

Acts 2008, No. 204, § 1, eff. Jan. 1, 2009.

REVISION COMMENTS—2008

(a) This Article is based on the provisions of former Article 1560 of the Louisiana Civil Code (1870). It changes the law in part by eliminating the third ground for revoking a donation for ingratitude, refusing the donor food when in distress.

(b) This Article preserves "cruel treatment" as a ground for revocation. Of the three causes listed in former Article 1560 (1870) as grounds for revocation for ingratitude, "grievous injuries" is by far the most litigated one. In general, "grievous injuries" sufficient to revoke a donation has been defined as any act "naturally offensive" to the donor. Perry v. Perry, 507 So.2d 881 (La.App. 4 Cir. 1987).

(c) Under this Article, an act of the donee that is offensive to the donor is not to be considered a ground for revocation of a donation unless the offense is serious. The jurisprudence has held that cruel treatment or grievous injury sufficient to revoke a donation may include adultery by a spouse; filing suit against a parent falsely alleging criminal activity; and slandering the memory of the donor. See, for example, Perry v. Perry, 507 So.2d 881 (La.App. 4 Cir. 1987); Spruiell v. Ludwig, 568 So.2d 133 (La.App. 5 Cir. 1990); Sanders v. Sanders, 768 So.2d 739 (La.App. 2 Cir. 2000).

Art. 1558. Revocation for ingratitude; prescription, parties

An action of revocation for ingratitude shall be brought within one year from the day the donor knew or should have known of the act of ingratitude.

If the donor dies before the expiration of that time, the action for revocation may be brought by the successors of the donor, but only within the time remaining, or if the donor died without knowing or having reason to know of the act, then within one year of the death of the donor.

If the action has already been brought by the donor, his successors may pursue it.

If the donee is deceased, the action for revocation may be brought against his successors.

Acts 2008, No. 204, § 1, eff. Jan. 1, 2009.

REVISION COMMENTS—2008

(a) This Article changes the law in part by providing that an action for revocation must be brought within one year from the day the donor knew or should have known of the act of ingratitude, if that day occurs prior to the time he actually knew. Under former Article 1561 (1870), an action for revocation must be brought one year from the day of the act of ingratitude or from the day that the act was made known to the donor.

(b) As under the source Article, in instances in which the action for revocation has not prescribed prior to the donor's death the second paragraph allows the donor's heirs and other successors to bring the suit for revocation, but it does not extend the time for them to bring the action. It must be brought within the same time period, unless the donor died without knowing or having reason to know of the act, in which case it must be brought within one year of the donor's death.

(c) This Article is not intended to amend the provisions of Articles 428 and 801 of the Code of Civil Procedure which remain in full force and effect.

(d) Under this Article, an action for revocation can be brought against the donee's successors only when the donee is deceased.

(e) For the definition of "successor", see Civil Code Article 3506(28).

Art. 1559. Revocation for ingratitude, effect on alienations, leases, or encumbrances

Revocation for ingratitude does not affect an alienation, lease, or encumbrance made by the donee prior to the filing of the action to revoke. When an alienation, lease, or encumbrance is made after the filing of the action and the thing given is movable, the alienation, lease, or encumbrance is effective against the donor only when it is an onerous transaction made in good faith by the transferee, lessee, or creditor. When an alienation, lease, or encumbrance is made after the filing of the action and the thing given is immovable, the effect of the action to revoke is governed by the law of registry.

Acts 2008, No. 204, § 1, eff. Jan. 1, 2009.

REVISION COMMENTS—2008

(a) This Article amends the language but preserves the substance of former Article 1562 of the Civil Code of 1870. It is not intended to change the law.

(b) A donor who files an action to revoke a donation of an immovable should file a notice of lis pendens in the public records in order to affect third parties. It is intended that a third party in good faith can rely on the absence of a notice of lis pendens in the public records. See Civil Code Article 3338. As stated in Ducote v. McCrossa, 675 So.2d 817, 818 (La.App. 4 Cir. 1996): "The recordation of the notice of lis pendens makes the outcome of the suit as to which notice is given binding on third parties and that is the only purpose of the notice of lis pendens."

(c) Under this Article, any notice of lis pendens must comply with the requirements of the Code of Civil Procedure. C.C.P. Arts. 3751–3753.

(d) This Article is intended to protect good faith transferees only. It does not protect sham or fraudulent transactions, nor does it protect individuals who have acted in bad faith. In cases involving immovable property, the principles of recordation apply. See Article 2021.

Art. 1560. Revocation for ingratitude, restoration

In case of revocation for ingratitude, the donee shall return the thing given. If he is not able to return the thing itself, then the donee shall restore the value of the thing donated, measured as of the time the action to revoke is filed.

Acts 2008, No. 204, § 1, eff. Jan. 1, 2009.

REVISION COMMENTS—2008

(a) This Article clarifies the law by expressly providing that, as a general rule, in cases when the donation is revoked for ingratitude the donee must return the thing in kind. Thus, the donee is not entitled to retain the thing and simply return the value thereof to the donor, unless the donor consents to this.

(b) Where ingratitude is concerned, this Article provides that the donee shall return the thing given, but, if he is not able to return it, then he shall restore the value of the thing donated, measured as of the time the action to revoke is filed. That rule is modified by a new Article 1567, which supplements this Article, and applies to both an action to revoke for ingratitude and an action to dissolve for nonperformance of a condition.

(c) When a donation is revoked or dissolved, the donee must also return the fruits and products of the thing donated. See Article 1566.

Art. 1561. [Blank]

Art. 1562. Dissolution for nonfulfillment of suspensive condition or for occurrence of resolutory condition

If a donation is subject to a suspensive condition, the donation is dissolved of right when the condition can no longer be fulfilled.

If a donation is subject to a resolutory condition, the occurrence of the condition does not of right operate a dissolution of the donation. It may be dissolved only by consent of the parties or by judicial decree.

Acts 2008, No. 204, § 1, eff. Jan. 1, 2009.

REVISION COMMENTS—2008

(a) This Article is based on the provisions of former Article 1565 and current Article 1773 of the Louisiana Civil Code. It is not intended to change the law.

(b) Under this Article, when the suspensive condition can no longer be fulfilled, the donation is dissolved by operation of law without necessity of instituting an action for dissolution.

Art. 1563. Nonfulfillment of conditions or nonperformance of charges that donee can perform or prevent

If a donation is made on a condition that the donee has the power to perform or prevent, or depends on the performance of a charge by the donee, the nonfulfillment of the condition or the nonperformance of the charge does not, of right, operate a dissolution of the donation. It may be dissolved only by consent of the parties or by judicial decree.

Acts 2008, No. 204, § 1, eff. Jan. 1, 2009.

REVISION COMMENTS—2008

(a) This Article reproduces the substance of former Civil Code Article 1566 (1870). It is not intended to change the law.

(b) The non-fulfillment of conditions that the donee has the power to perform or prevent does not operate a dissolution of the donation as of right, as is the case in Article 1562 when a suspensive condition can no longer be fulfilled.

(c) The remedy or limitation of the donor under this Article is the same as provided in Article 1562. As in the case of a resolutory condition under Article 1562, this Article authorizes the parties to agree to a dissolution of the donation; otherwise a suit and judicial declaration of dissolution is required.

(d) This Article eliminates use of the term "potestative conditions" contained in the source Article as technically inaccurate under present law, but preserves the underlying theory behind the rule. See Civil Code Article 1770, Comment (e). A "potestative condition" was a condition that depended solely on the will of the obligor.

Art. 1564. Dissolution for non-execution of other condition; prescription

An action to dissolve a donation for failure to fulfill the conditions or perform the charges imposed on the donee prescribes in five years, commencing the day the donee fails to perform the charges or fulfill his obligation or ceases to do so.

Acts 2008, No. 204, § 1, eff. Jan. 1, 2009.

REVISION COMMENTS—2008

(a) This Article, based on former Article 1567, clarifies the law by expressly providing that the prescriptive period for bringing suits to revoke donations for nonfulfillment of a condition is five years. The Article removes the uncertainty in the source Article which referred to the "usual prescription" for actions of this kind. While the Civil Code provides a ten year prescription for personal actions, in Succession of Comeaux, 896 So.2d 1223 (La.App. 3 Cir. 2005), the court held that the "usual" prescription of former Article 1567 is the prescription of five years for actions to annul a testament under Civil Code Article 3497. See also DiMattia v. DiMattia, 282 So.2d 554 (La.App. 1 Cir. 1973), holding that plaintiff's suit to revoke a donation for failure to comply with the conditions imposed on the donee was subject to the prescription of five years.

(b) This Article intentionally makes a distinction between the donee's failure to perform charges and the donee's ceasing to perform them, because of the sophisticated distinction between those terms as actions or non-actions. In case of failure to perform, the donee does not begin performance, but in the case of ceasing to perform, the donee starts the performance and then stops performing.

Art. 1565. Dissolution for non-execution of condition

In case of dissolution of a donation of an immovable for the failure of the donee to fulfill conditions or perform charges, the property shall return to the donor free from all alienations, leases, or encumbrances created by the donee or his successors, subject to the law of registry. If the thing cannot be returned free from alienations, leases, or encumbrances, the donor may, nevertheless, accept it subject to the alienation, lease, or encumbrance, but the donee shall be accountable for any diminution in value. Otherwise, the donee shall restore the value of the thing donated, measured as of the time the action to dissolve is filed.

In case of dissolution of a donation of a movable for failure to fulfill conditions or perform charges, an alienation, lease, or encumbrance created by the donee or his successors is effective against the donor only when it is an onerous transaction made in good faith by the transferee, lessee, or creditor.

Acts 2008, No. 204, § 1, eff. Jan. 1, 2009.

REVISION COMMENTS—2008

(a) This Article changes the law in part by providing that, when immovable property is concerned, in cases of revocation for failure to fulfill conditions, the property must be returned to the donor even if the donee has alienated, leased, or encumbered the immovable by onerous title. Under former Article 1568, as amended by Act 527 of 1985, the revoking donor had no right to a return in kind of the property if the immovable has been alienated to a third party by onerous title. This Article removes that distinction and makes all transferees of the donee of a conditional donation subject to the same rights and obligations. Under this Article the principles of recordation apply to a transfer made by the donee or his successors to a third party, whether the transfer is onerous or gratuitous. See Article 3338; R.S. 9:2721, et seq.

(b) The first paragraph of this Article deals with immovable property, and the second paragraph deals with movable property. The second paragraph purposefully does not refer to the "law of registry." There are some times when the law of registry may affect movable property, as for example, a title certificate to an automobile, a registration of a stock certificate or a creditor's rights under Chapter 9 of the Commercial Laws when a security interest is perfected. Even though there is no reference in the second paragraph to the law of registry where movable property is concerned, the matter is covered by special laws.

(c) The second paragraph of this Article is modeled on the provisions of former Article 1562, when the action is revocation for ingratitude. Thus, for movables the same rule and the same remedy that apply to revocation for ingratitude will apply when dissolution of a donation for failure to fulfill a condition or perform a charge is involved. In the case of dissolution, unlike a revocation for ingratitude, the public records doctrine is clearly applicable because the condition or charge must be of public record in order to affect third parties. That would not be true for ingratitude because there is no condition to be recorded; the activity that gives rise to the action to revoke is not something that a third party might necessarily know.

Art. 1566.   Revocation or dissolution, donee's liability for fruits

When a donation is revoked or dissolved, the donee or his successor is bound to restore or to pay the value of the fruits and products of the things given from the date of written demand.

If the donation is dissolved for nonperformance of a condition or a charge that the donee had the power to perform, the court may order the donee or his successor to restore the value of the fruits and products received after his failure to perform if the failure to perform is due to his fault.

Acts 2008, No. 204, § 1, eff. Jan. 1, 2009.

REVISION COMMENTS—2008

(a) This Article reproduces the principle of former Civil Code Article 1569 (1870) by providing that, as a general rule, in cases of revocation, the donee must return the fruits and products only from the day of judicial demand.

(b) Under the second paragraph, however, the court has discretion to order the return of fruits and products from an earlier date if the conditions imposed by the donor were not fulfilled due to the donee's fault.

Art. 1567.   Donee unable to return thing in same condition

When a donee or his successor is obligated to return a thing and he cannot restore it in essentially the same condition as it was at the time of the donation, the donor may elect to receive the thing in its present condition and require its return. In that event, the donee shall be accountable for any diminution in value at the time of the delivery.

Acts 2008, No. 204, § 1, eff. Jan. 1, 2009.

REVISION COMMENT—2008

This Article is intended to make clear that in a situation where the donor is entitled to dissolve a donation for non-execution of the conditions imposed on the donee, but the thing donated has changed condition, the donor is not limited to an "either-or" choice, i.e. either to accept the thing in its changed state or to receive payment for the value it should have had, as provided in Civil Code article 1565. This Article preserves the donor's right to receive the thing back, if he so chooses, which may be important to the donor for many reasons, and if he elects to receive the thing back, he is not required to accept the thing as is and forfeit the right to be paid for the differential in value that the thing should have had, if it had not changed form. Instead, the donor has the option to receive the thing donated in whatever condition it may be, and if there is a diminution in value, recover payment for the differential resulting from the diminution. This Article implements and clarifies that principle.

Arts. 1568 to 1569.1.   [Blank]

CHAPTER 6—DISPOSITIONS MORTIS CAUSA

SECTION 1—TESTAMENTS GENERALLY

Art. 1570.   Testaments; form

A disposition mortis causa may be made only in the form of a testament authorized by law.

Acts 1997, No. 1421, § 1, eff. July 1, 1999.

REVISION COMMENTS—1997

(a) This Article is based on Article 1570 of the Civil Code of 1870. It simplifies, but does not change, the law.

(b) Dispositions mortis causa are defined in Civil Code Article 1469 of the Civil Code of 1870 as acts to take effect upon death by which the individual disposes of all or a part of his property, but which remain revocable during his lifetime. This Article specifies that dispositions mortis causa may not be made other than in one of the forms of testaments authorized by law, i.e., by statute or Civil Code Article. So long as the testament is in an approved form and demonstrates an intent to dispose of property, it is irrelevant that the testator may have intended it to be in a different form. See Article 1590 of the Civil Code of 1870. The language of this Article is broad enough to include the principle of Article 1590 of the Civil Code of 1870.

(c) No major changes are made in this Article from the provisions of prior law. It was thought unnecessary to continue the definition contained in Article 1571 of the Civil Code of 1870, describing a testament as "the act of last will clothed with certain solemnities, by which the testator disposes of his property, either universally or by universal title, or by particular title." Since the Code already contains a definition of donations mortis causa (C.C. Art. 1469 (1870)), and these donations may only be made by testament, there was no need to repeat the definition.

Art. 1571.   Testaments with others or by others prohibited

A testament may not be executed by a mandatary for the testator. Nor may more than one person execute a testament in the same instrument.

Acts 1997, No. 1421, § 1, eff. July 1, 1999.

REVISION COMMENTS—1997

(a) This Article restates the prohibitions contained in Article 1572 and the first sentence of Article 1573 of the Civil Code of 1870. It recognizes that a testament is a personal and individual act in which no other person can join.

(b) The prohibition set forth in this article does not apply to the situation where the testator is unable to sign the testament personally because of a mental or physical infirmity. See Article 1579. In one sense, Article 1579 may be viewed as expressly relaxing the rule of this article, but more properly, in the situation authorized by Article 1579 the testator is technically the person who "makes" the testament and the person who physically signs for him or makes his mark is nothing more than an extension of the hand of the testator.

Art. 1572.   Testamentary dispositions committed to the choice of a third person

Testamentary dispositions committed to the choice of a third person are null, except as expressly provided by law. A testator may delegate to his executor the authority to allocate specific assets to satisfy a legacy expressed in terms of a value or a quantum, including a fractional share.

The testator may expressly delegate to his executor the authority to allocate a legacy to one or more entities or trustees of trusts organized for educational, charitable, religious, or other philanthropic purposes. The entities or trusts may be designated by the testator or, when authorized to do so, by the

360

executor in his discretion. In addition, the testator may expressly delegate to his executor the authority to impose conditions on those legacies.

Acts 1997, No. 1421, § 1, eff. July 1, 1999.

REVISION COMMENTS—1997

(a) The source of this Article is Article 1573 of the Civil Code of 1870, which originally provided that "the custom of willing by testament, by the intervention of a commissary or attorney in fact, is abolished." In 1982 the article was amended to grant a testator limited power to delegate authority to an executor to select assets to distribute in satisfaction of certain legacies. The 1982 amendment to Article 1573 has been preserved and significantly expanded to permit the delegation of authority to an executor to select assets to distribute in all instances where the legacy of the share of the estate is designated by quantum or value. The revision clarifies that "quantum" includes fractional shares, such as one-fourth or one-half of something, and intentionally removes the language in Article 1573 (1870) that limits the ability to delegate such authority to the instances where the designation of the quantum or value is made "either by formula or by a specific sum". This article permits delegation of authority in all instances where the legacy is a quantum or value, whether or not the bequest is by formula or by specific sum.

(b) The first paragraph of the article refers only to the delegation of authority to select assets and does not permit the delegation of authority to select legatees. The second paragraph of the article, however, goes much further in that regard, but applies only to charitable kinds of legacies. It not only permits a testator to leave a bequest to a specified charity and delegate authority to the executor to select assets to go to the charity, but under this paragraph the testator may even delegate authority to the executor to allocate among charities designated by the testator and, indeed, to grant authority to the executor to select the very charities themselves. The last sentence permits the executor to impose conditions on the legacies, as, for example, that funds be used for heart research, scholarships for indigent children, and so forth. Obviously, the ability "to impose conditions" does not authorize the executor to impose conditions that are contrary to law.

(c) Since a trust is not an entity, the article appropriately refers to "entities or trustees of trusts."

Art. 1573. Formalities

The formalities prescribed for the execution of a testament must be observed or the testament is absolutely null.

Acts 1997, No. 1421, § 1, eff. July 1, 1999.

REVISION COMMENTS—1997

This article is based on the provisions of Article 1595 of the Louisiana Civil Code of 1870. It does not change the law.

SECTION 2—FORMS OF TESTAMENTS

Art. 1574. Forms of testaments

There are two forms of testaments: olographic and notarial.

Acts 1997, No. 1421, § 1, eff. July 1, 1999.

REVISION COMMENTS—1997

(a) This Article changes the law by suppressing the "public and private nuncupative" and "mystic" testaments found in the Civil Code of 1870. The so-called statutory testament is revised and retained by this Article, to be called the notarial testament. The olographic testament is retained without substantive change.

(b) There is no reason to retain the nuncupative wills or the mystic will. The notarial testament provided in the revision can be used in every instance in which those wills would be usable, and is much easier and simpler to obtain and execute. One distinction that arguably might justify keeping the private nuncupative testament is that it does not require a notary public. However, it is almost inconceivable that a lay person would know all of the formal requirements of the Louisiana Civil Code for such a will, when needed. Accordingly, this lack of a notary hardly seems a justification for retaining nuncupative wills. The sole justification of the mystic will is the secrecy that it affords the testator, but that secrecy may as easily be obtained by using an olographic testament. If a testator cannot write such a testament, the notarial testament under Article 1577 or Article 1578 should suffice because it is not necessary that the will be read aloud or that the witnesses read it.

(c) The enactment of this Article does not invalidate testaments that were valid when written. See R.S. 9:2445.

(d) Articles 1597 through 1604 of the Civil Code of 1870 have been suppressed in their entirety as obsolete and unnecessary. They provided special rules for time-limited testaments of military personnel and those at sea. The present law is adequate to provide for the needs of such persons, especially in light of the current military practice to provide for such matters as a part of regular induction procedures. A testament written for military personnel is valid in Louisiana if: (a) it is valid under Louisiana law; or (b) it is valid under the law of the state of making at the time of making or (c) it is valid under the law of the state in which the testator was domiciled at the time of making or at the time of death; or (d) with regard to immovables, it is valid under the law that would be applied by the courts of the state in which the immovables are situated. See Civil Code Article 3528. Moreover, an olographic testament valid under Louisiana law may be written anywhere.

(e) By definition, no oral testament could be valid, since it would not be in one of these forms. See also Articles 1575 and 1576 of the Civil Code of 1870.

(f) A notarial testament may be made in one of four ways. The notarial testament described in Article 1577 may be made only by a person who knows how to sign his name and how to read the testament as written, and is physically able to do both. If the testator lacks the physical ability to sign his name, the testament must be made in the manner described in Article 1578. If the testator's sight is impaired to the extent that he cannot read or if he is a person who does not know how to read, the testament must be made in the manner described in Article 1579. If the testator knows how to and is physically able to read braille, the testament may be made in the manner described in Article 1580. It is envisioned that most testators will use the basic notarial testament described in Article 1577.

Art. 1575. Olographic testament

A.   An olographic testament is one entirely written, dated, and signed in the handwriting of the testator. Although the date may appear anywhere in the testament, the testator must sign the testament at the end of the testament. If anything is written by the testator after his signature, the testament shall not be invalid and such writing may be considered by the court, in its discretion, as part of the testament. The olographic testament is subject to no other requirement as to form. The date is sufficiently indicated if the day, month, and year are reasonably ascertainable from information in the testament, as clarified by extrinsic evidence, if necessary.

B.   Additions and deletions on the testament may be given effect only if made by the hand of the testator.

Acts 1997, No. 1421, § 1, eff. July 1, 1999. Amended by Acts 2001, No. 824, § 1.

REVISION COMMENTS—1997

(a) This Article combines the substance of Articles 1588 and 1589 of the Civil Code of 1870. It does not change the law.

(b) There is no intent to change the rationale of Succession of Burke, 365 So.2d 858 (La.App. 4th Cir. 1978), in which the testament was written in the hand of the testator on a form with printed words intended for another form of testament. The court ignored all printed matter and upheld the olographic testament made up solely of the material in the testator's handwriting and in compliance with the predecessor of this Article.

(c) In Succession of King, 595 So.2d 805 (La.App. 2d Cir. 1992), it was held that in an olographic testament the signature should be at the end, and anything written after the signature would not be effective. This article is not intended to change the rule of Succession of King.

REVISION COMMENT—2001

The 2001 amendment is intended to legislatively overrule Succession of King, 595 So.2d 805 (La.App. 2 Cir. 1992), which held that in an olographic testament the signature should be at the end of the testament. Otherwise, the amendment is not intended to change the law in any manner, but only to clarify it.

Art. 1576. Notarial testament

A notarial testament is one that is executed in accordance with the formalities of Articles 1577 through 1580.1.

Acts 1997, No. 1421, § 1, eff. July 1, 1999. Amended by Acts 1999, No. 745, § 1, eff. July 1, 1999.

REVISION COMMENTS—1997

(a) This Article is new. It does not change the law, however.

(b) A notarial testament may be made in one of four ways. The notarial testament described in Article 1577 may be made only by a person who knows how to sign his name and how to read the testament as written, and is physically able to do both. If the testator lacks the physical ability to sign his name, the testament must be made in the manner described in Article 1578. If the testator's sight is impaired to the extent that he cannot read or if he is a person who does not know how to read, the testament must be made in the manner described in Article 1579. If the testator knows how to and is physically able to read braille, the testament may be made in the manner described in Article 1580. It is envisioned that most testators will use the basic notarial testament described in Article 1577.

Art. 1577. Requirements of form

The notarial testament shall be prepared in writing and dated and shall be executed in the following manner. If the testator knows how to sign his name and to read and is physically able to do both, then:

(1) In the presence of a notary and two competent witnesses, the testator shall declare or signify to them that the instrument is his testament and shall sign his name at the end of the testament and on each other separate page.

(2) In the presence of the testator and each other, the notary and the witnesses shall sign the following declaration, or one substantially similar: "In our presence the testator has declared or signified that this instrument is his testament and has signed it at the end and on each other separate page, and in the presence of the testator and each other we have hereunto subscribed our names this _____ day of _____, ___."

Acts 1997, No. 1421, § 1, eff. July 1, 1999. Amended by Acts 2001, No. 824, § 1.

REVISION COMMENTS—1997

(a) This article reproduces the substance of R.S. 9:2442. It does not change the law.

(b) The testator need not sign after both the dispositive or appointive provisions of this testament and the declaration, although the validity of the document is not affected by such a "double" signature. The testator is disposing of property, appointing an executor or making other directions in the body of the testament itself. He need only sign at the end of the dispositive, appointive or directive provisions. The witnesses and the notary are attesting to the observance of the formalities; they need only sign the declaration.

(c) The testator's indication that the instrument contains his last wishes may be given verbally or in any other manner that indicates his assent to its provisions.

(d) The instrument must be in writing. The form of the writing (typewritten, mimeographed or any other form) is immaterial. Moreover, there is no requirement that the testament be written in the English language, or even in Roman characters. So long as it is written in a language that the testator can read and understand, the protections to assure verity of the provisions are satisfied.

(e) The ability of the testator to verify that the contents of the written document express his last wishes for the disposition of his property is the mechanism to assure accuracy. Thus he must have the intellectual ability to read the will in the manner in which it is written, and must have the same ability to show his assent by signing his name.

(f) This Article does not require that the testator actually read the testament at the time of its execution. Clearly, he should not omit the reading if he is not wholly satisfied that the instrument reflects his wishes accurately. Louisiana courts have frequently observed that "... signatures to obligations are not mere ornaments. If a party can read, it behooves him to examine an instrument before signing it; ..." Snell v. Union Sawmill Company, 159 La. 604, 105 So. 728 (1925); Boult v. Sarpy, 30 La.Ann. 494 (1878).

(g) This Article requires that the testament be dated but intentionally does not specify where the date must appear, nor does it require that the dating be executed in the presence of the notary and witnesses or that the dating be made by the testator. It is common practice to have a typewritten testament that is already dated, and to establish a time frame so that, among other things, in the event of a conflict between two presumptively valid testaments, the later one prevails. A subsequent testament that contains a provision that revokes all prior testaments obviously revokes the earlier testament, and one primary function of the date is to establish which of the two testaments is the later one.

Art. 1578. Notarial testament; testator literate and sighted but physically unable to sign

When a testator knows how to sign his name and to read, and is physically able to read but unable to sign his name because of a physical infirmity, the procedure for execution of a notarial testament is as follows:

(1) In the presence of the notary and two competent witnesses, the testator shall declare or signify to them that the instrument is his testament, that he is able to see and read but unable to sign because of a physical infirmity, and shall affix his mark where his signature would otherwise be required; and if he is unable to affix his mark he may direct another person to assist him in affixing a mark, or to sign his name in his place. The other person may be one of the witnesses or the notary.

(2) In the presence of the testator and each other, the notary and the witnesses shall sign the following declaration, or one substantially similar: "In our presence the testator has declared or signified that this is his testament, and that he is able to see and read and knows how to sign his name but is unable to do so because of a physical infirmity; and in our presence he has affixed, or caused to be affixed, his mark or name at the end of the testament and on each other separate page, and in the presence of the testator and each other, we have subscribed our names this _____ day of _____, ___."

Acts 1997, No. 1421, § 1, eff. July 1, 1999.

REVISION COMMENTS—1997

It is intended that the ordinary requirements for a notarial testament apply to the execution of a testament by a person physically unable to sign his name, except insofar as those requirements are modified by this Article. A person physically unable to make a mark could cause his mark to be affixed by directing someone else to assist him so that the testator in fact affixes the mark. This article also authorizes the testator to direct another person to sign his name in his place. It is believed that with the presence of two witnesses and a notary public there is ample protection against abuse and there is no reason not to permit such liberality.

Art. 1579. Notarial testament; testator unable to read

When a testator does not know how to read, or is physically impaired to the extent that he cannot read, whether or not he is able to sign his name, the procedure for execution of a notarial testament is as follows:

(1) The written testament must be read aloud in the presence of the testator, the notary, and two competent witnesses. The witnesses, and the notary if he is not the person who reads the testament aloud, must follow the reading on copies of the testament. After the reading, the testator must declare or signify to them that he heard the reading, and that the instrument is his testament.

If he knows how, and is able to do so, the testator must sign his name at the end of the testament and on each other separate page of the instrument.

(2) In the presence of the testator and each other, the notary and witnesses must sign the following declaration, or one substantially similar: "This testament has been read aloud in our presence and in the presence of the testator, such reading having been followed on copies of the testament by the witnesses [, and the notary if he is not the person who reads it aloud,] and in our presence the testator declared or signified that he heard the reading, and that the instrument is his testament, and that he signed his name at the end of the testament and on each other separate page; and in the presence of the testator and each other, we have subscribed our names this _____ day of _____, ___."

(3) If the testator does not know how to sign his name or is unable to sign because of a physical infirmity, he must so declare or signify and then affix his mark, or cause it to be affixed, where his signature would otherwise be required; and if he is unable to affix his mark he may direct another person to assist him in affixing a mark or to sign his name in his place. The other person may be one of the witnesses or the notary. In this instance, the required declaration must be modified to recite in addition that the testator declared or signified that he did not know how to sign his name or was unable to do so because of a physical infirmity; and that he affixed, or caused to be affixed, his mark or name at the end of the testament and on each other separate page.

(4) A person who may execute a testament authorized by either Article 1577 or 1578 may also execute a testament authorized by this Article.

Acts 1997, No. 1421, § 1, eff. July 1, 1999.

REVISION COMMENTS—1997

(a) For the protection of sight-impaired or illiterate testators, this article requires that the testament be read aloud in the presence of the testator and the witnesses. The article contemplates that the notary public will be the person to read the testament aloud in their presence, just as previous law has contained that requirement. Nevertheless, as indicated in the Comments below, on occasion the notary public may be unable to read it aloud, or if for any reason the notary chooses to have someone else read it aloud, then the article contemplates that the person who reads it aloud must do so not only in the presence of the testator and the witnesses but in the presence of the notary public. The article contains a form of declaration similar to the declaration that has been used previously, but because of the new provisions expressly authorizing someone other than the notary to read the testament aloud, the form of declaration contained in subsection (2) of the article indicates in bracketed language a suggested change to use when it is not the notary but another person who has read the testament aloud. Obviously, when the notary public is the person who reads the testament aloud, then the bracketed language shown in the form is not necessary and should not be used. The use of brackets in the form should not be misinterpreted. Occasionally brackets are used in the texts of articles that were originally written in French and translated to English to indicate when there is a mistranslation of the original French. The use of the brackets in the form here is simply to indicate a choice of language to use when someone other than the notary public reads the testament aloud, and nothing more than that.

In Succession of Harvey, 573 So.2d 1304 (La.App. 2d Cir. 1991), the attestation clause revealed that the notary did not actually read the testament aloud as required by R.S. 9:2443. Instead, the will was read by one of the witnesses while the testator, the notary, and the other two witnesses followed the reading on copies of the instrument. The notary testified that, on the day of execution, an allergy and asthma condition prevented him from reading the testament aloud. The Court held that there had been substantial compliance with the requirements of R.S. 9:2443 and upheld the validity of the will. According to the Court: "In the instant case, the testator did, in the presence of the notary and three witnesses, indicate that he had heard the reading and that the instrument represented his last will. The evidence clearly establishes that the notary accomplished the intended purpose of the reading of the testament, viz., to ensure that the person executing the document knows its contents. Hence, no error occurred." Succession of Harvey, supra, at 1309. This Article codifies the result reached by the Court in Succession of Harvey.

(b) In light of the fact that the person who executes a testament under this Article lacks the ability to verify its provisions for himself, the assurance of accuracy is achieved by the reading of the

365

testament by the notary to the testator and the witnesses, while the latter follow the reading on copies of the testament. In this instance, the attestation by the witnesses is not only that the testator indicated that the instrument was his testament, but also that the witnesses assured themselves through the reading that the document that the testator signed was the same one that was read aloud.

(c) Section 4 permits this form of testament to be used whenever doubt exists whether a testator is unable to read because the disability, if any, is not so definitive as to be certain that he does not know how to read. There may be situations where doubt exists whether the testator is so physically impaired that he is unable to read, or there may be doubt as to the extent of his literacy. There is often no clear dividing line and it may be difficult to determine the testator's physical condition or literacy level with reasonable accuracy, much less with certainty. To avoid any problem whatsoever in that regard, Section 4 permits even a fully competent testator to execute a will under this section. The primary purpose of the kind of notarial testament authorized in this article is to provide safeguards to protect persons who are illiterate or otherwise unable to read, but it is not intended to disqualify competent testators. Since the procedure for execution of a testament under this article is more exacting and subject to greater formality than it is for a notarial testament executed pursuant to Article 1577 or 1578, any competent testator is permitted to execute a will under this article, not merely a person who is intellectually unable to read or who is so physically impaired that he is unable to read.

Art. 1580. Notarial testament in braille form

A testator who knows how to and is physically able to read braille, may execute a notarial testament according to the following procedure:

(1) In the presence of a notary and two competent witnesses, the testator must declare or signify that the testament, written in braille, is his testament, and must sign his name at the end of the testament and on each other separate page of the instrument.

(2) In the presence of the testator and each other, the notary and witnesses must sign the following declaration, or one substantially similar: "In our presence the testator has signed this testament at the end and on each other separate page and has declared or signified that it is his testament; and in the presence of the testator and each other we have hereunto subscribed our names this _____ day of _____, ___."

(3) If the testator is unable to sign his name because of a physical infirmity, he must so declare or signify and then affix, or cause to be affixed, his mark where his signature would otherwise be required; and if he is unable to affix his mark he may direct another person to assist him in affixing a mark, or to sign his name in his place. The other person may be one of the witnesses or the notary. In this instance, the required declaration must be modified to recite in addition that the testator declared or signified that he was unable to sign his name because of a physical infirmity; and that he affixed, or caused to be affixed, his mark or name at the end of the testament and on each other separate page.

(4) The declaration in the notarial testament in braille form must be in writing, not in braille.

Acts 1997, No. 1421, § 1, eff. July 1, 1999.

This Article reproduces the substance of R.S. 9:2444 relative to statutory testaments in braille form. It does not change the law.

Art. 1580.1. Deaf or deaf and blind notarial testament; form; witnesses

A.   A notarial testament may be executed under this Article only by a person who has been legally declared physically deaf or deaf and blind and who is able to read sign language, braille, or visual English.

B.   The notarial testament shall be prepared and shall be dated and executed in the following manner:

(1) In the presence of a notary and two competent witnesses, the testator shall declare or signify to them that the instrument is his testament and shall sign his name at the end of the testament and on each other separate page of the instrument.

(2) In the presence of the testator and each other, the notary and the witnesses shall then sign the following declaration, or one substantially similar: "The testator has signed this testament at the end and on each other separate page, and has declared or signified in our presence that this instrument is his testament, and in the presence of the testator and each other we have hereunto subscribed our names this _____ day of _____, 2___."

C.   If the testator is unable to sign his name because of a physical infirmity, the testament shall be dated and executed in the following manner:

(1) In the presence of a notary and two competent witnesses, the testator shall declare or signify by sign or visual English to them that the instrument is his last testament, that he is unable to sign because of a physical infirmity, and shall then affix his mark at the end of the testament and on each other separate page of the instrument.

(2) In the presence of the testator and each other, the notary and the witnesses shall then sign the following declaration, or one substantially similar: "The testator has declared or signified by sign or visual English that he knows how to sign his name but is unable to sign his name because of a physical infirmity and he has affixed his mark at the end and on each other separate page of this testament, and declared or signified in our presence that this instrument is his testament and in the presence of the testator and each other we have hereunto subscribed our names this _____ day of _____, 2___."

D.   The attestation clause required by Subparagraphs B(2) and C(2) shall be prepared in writing.

E.   (1) A competent witness for the purposes of this Article is a person who meets the qualifications of Articles 1581 and 1582, and who knows how to sign his name and to read the required attestation clause, and is physically able to do both. At least one of the witnesses to the testament shall also meet the qualifications of a certified interpreter for the deaf as provided for in R.S. 46:2361 et seq.

(2) The testator shall be given the choice of accommodation services afforded by the use of large print, braille, or a tactile interpreter.

Added by Acts 1999, No. 745, § 1, eff. July 1, 1999.

SECTION 3—OF THE COMPETENCE OF WITNESSES AND OF CERTAIN DESIGNATIONS IN TESTAMENTS

Art. 1581.   Persons incompetent to be witnesses

A person cannot be a witness to any testament if he is insane, blind, under the age of sixteen, or unable to sign his name. A person who is competent but deaf or unable to read cannot be a witness to a notarial testament under Article 1579.

Acts 1997, No. 1421, § 1, eff. July 1, 1999.

REVISION COMMENTS—1997

(a) This Article combines the requirements for witnesses to the various testaments found in the Civil Code of 1870 and for the statutory (now the notarial) testament. It does not change the law, except as noted in comments (b) and (c) infra, and with the exception that it imposes a general requirement that a witness know how to read and to sign his name.

(b) The former disqualification in Article 1591 of the Civil Code of 1870 of "persons whom the criminal law declare incapable of exercising civil functions" has been suppressed, because it does not appear that there are any such persons under the present law.

(c) The age of competency has been set at sixteen in accordance with former Civil Code Article 1591 (1870). The former exclusion of persons who were mute ("dumb" under Article 1591 of the Civil Code of 1870) has also been suppressed; the fact that a person cannot speak should not in and of itself disqualify him as a witness. That disqualification had in fact been deleted prior to this revision by Acts 1983, No. 198.

(d) The requirements stated in this Article are not in derogation of, but rather are supplementary to, the general competency requirements of R.S. 13:3665, and Article 691 of the Code of Evidence.

(e) A person who is not able to sign his name for any reason, whether due to physical inability or intellectual inability, does not qualify as a competent witness under this article. The article expressly does not make a distinction regarding the reason for inability to sign (as Article 1578 does, for example). For the same reason, a person who is unable to read, whether because of physical inability to read or intellectual inability to read, does not qualify as a competent witness to a notarial testament under Article 1579, and the reason is obvious: The witness is required to follow the reading of the will on a copy as it is being read aloud to the testator.

Art. 1582.   Effect of witness or notary as legatee

The fact that a witness or the notary is a legatee does not invalidate the testament. A legacy to a witness or the notary is invalid, but if the witness would be an heir in intestacy, the witness may receive the lesser of his intestate share or the legacy in the testament.

Acts 1997, No. 1421, § 1, eff. July 1, 1999.

REVISION COMMENTS—1997

(a) This article reproduces the substance of Article 1592 of the Louisiana Civil Code (1870). It does not change the law in upholding the testament, but it does change the law in permitting the witness to keep the legacy when he would have been an heir by intestacy if the decedent had died intestate.

(b) The second sentence of this Article represents a small change in Louisiana law. Historically, legatees were prohibited altogether from being witnesses to testaments, under penalty that the entire testament was invalid. The harshness of that result was mitigated in 1986 when Article 1592 (1870) was revised by Act No. 709 to permit the testament to be upheld and merely deprive the witness of the legacy. Even that solution, however, may be unnecessarily harsh in some instances, as, for example, when the witness is unaware that he is a legatee. Unless the testament is one that must be read aloud to the witnesses under Civil Code Article 1579, a witness may not know that he or she is a legatee. There is no requirement that the other notarial wills actually be read by the testator (who simply must be able to read), or by the witnesses, or by the notary (who may not have prepared the will). Nevertheless, in light of recent developments in the law of capacity and undue influence, it can be anticipated that there may be more will contests involving challenges to testamentary capacity or allegations of undue influence on the testator. As a result, it is as important as before to encourage the use of disinterested witnesses who can testify not only that the formalities for execution of the testament were satisfied, but who may also be able to furnish insights regarding capacity or undue influence issues when they arise. On the other hand, those issues are often more properly addressed to professionals, such as doctors and nurses, and in any event the potential interest of a witness may affect the credibility of the witness' testimony and the weight to be given the testimony. This article changes the law to permit a witness who is related to the testator to inherit at least as much as he or she would have been able to inherit under the laws of intestacy if the decedent had died intestate. The new rule does not protect a legatee/witness who is unrelated to the testator, but it mitigates somewhat the harshness of the existing rule, and it is in accord with the prevailing rule in most of the United States. A practitioner who assists in the execution of a testament for his client should continue to make every effort to use disinterested witnesses who are fully capable in all respects.

The rule is not relaxed as to the notary public, who performs a more solemn function than the witnesses and is a public officer. The notary remains prohibited from taking under the testament.

Art. 1582.1. Persons prohibited from witnessing; effect

A person may not be a witness to a testament if that person is a spouse of a legatee at the time of the execution of the testament. The fact that a witness is the spouse of a legatee does not invalidate the testament; however, a legacy to a witness' spouse is invalid, if the witness is the spouse of the legatee at the time of the execution of the testament. If the legacy is invalid under the provisions of this Article, and if the legatee would be an heir in intestacy, the legatee may receive the lesser of his intestate share or legacy in the testament. Any testamentary terms or restrictions placed on the legacy shall remain in effect.

Added by Acts 2003, No. 707, § 1, eff. Jan. 1, 2004. Amended by Acts 2004, No. 231, § 1.

Art. 1583.   Certain designations not legacies

The designation of a succession representative or a trustee, or an attorney for either of them, is not a legacy.

Acts 1997, No. 1421, § 1, eff. July 1, 1999.

REVISION COMMENTS—1997

This Article does not represent a change in the law, but it does codify what is believed to be the appropriate rule. It has long been recognized that the designation of a representative, whether the representative is an executor, a trustee, the attorney to handle the estate, or a tutor for a child, is not a bequest. See Succession of Jenkins, 481 So.2d 607 (La. 1986), holding that the designation of an attorney in a will is merely precatory and is not binding on the executor. See also Succession of Wallace, 574 So.2d 348 (La. 1991), holding the enactment of La. R.S. 9:2448, which provided that an executor of an estate may discharge the attorney designated in a testator's will "only for just cause" unconstitutional. There is some unfortunate language, however, in one reported case that indicates that the designation of the attorney might be construed to be a bequest. See Roberts v. Christina, 323 So.2d 888 (4th Cir. 1976), writ denied 328 So.2d 109 (La. 1976); see also Succession of Boyenga, 437 So.2d 260, 263 (La. 1983) (Dixon, C.J., dissenting). Codification of the rule that designation of a representative is not a bequest clarifies the issue so there can be no problem in that regard.

SECTION 4—TESTAMENTARY DISPOSITIONS

Art. 1584.   Kinds of testamentary dispositions

Testamentary dispositions are particular, general, or universal.

Acts 1997, No. 1421, § 1, eff. July 1, 1999.

REVISION COMMENTS—1997

The three categories of legacies under prior law were universal legacies, legacies under universal title, and particular legacies. The names and characteristics of universal legacies and particular legacies are retained in this revision, but the name of the "legacy under universal title" has been changed to "general" legacy, and its characteristics are slightly modified in the new definition. See C.C. Art. 1586. The importance of the three classifications is in allocating liability for the payment of estate debts, and in determining accretion rights among successors when a legacy lapses or is renounced. See, C.C. Arts. 1423 and 1424, infra, regarding payment of estate debts, and C.C. Arts. 1591 through 1595, infra, regarding accretion. And, of course, as before, particular legacies receive preference in being discharged before general or universal legacies. See C.C. Arts. 1600 and 1602, infra. This Article establishes kinds of testamentary dispositions that are not dissimilar to the universal legacy, legacy by universal title, and legacy by particular title found in the Civil Code of 1870. But their designations, and to some extent their substance, are altered somewhat in this revision.

Art. 1585.   Universal legacy

A universal legacy is a disposition of all of the estate, or the balance of the estate that remains after particular legacies.

A universal legacy may be made jointly for the benefit of more than one legatee without changing its nature.

Acts 1997, No. 1421, § 1, eff. July 1, 1999.

REVISION COMMENTS—1997

(a) This Article retains the name of the "universal" legacy and codifies the principle that such a legacy need not be of the entire estate, so long as it is a legacy of the residuum of the estate remaining after particular dispositions. See generally 5 Planiol and Ripert, Traite pratique de droit civil français, Nos. 611, 614, at 614, 644–646 (1933); Cross on Successions, Sec. 140, at 204; Projet Quebec Civil Code, Art. 261. It also codifies the prior jurisprudential rule that a legacy of the residuum following a particular legacy is a universal legacy. See Willis v. McKeithen, 184 So.2d 748 (La.App. 2d Cir. 1966).

It must be noted that when the testament contains a general legacy, then by definition under this article there cannot also be a universal legacy. The two legacies are defined in such a way that they cannot exist in the same testament.

(b) The jurisprudence has recognized that leaving the entire estate or the residue of the estate to multiple legatees does not destroy the universality of the legacy, provided that the legatees are conjoint legatees. Thus, a legacy of the entire estate to A, B and C conjointly is a universal legacy, even though its practical effect is to leave one-third of the estate to A, one-third to B and one-third to C. By the nature of the legacy's being conjoint, if A predeceases B and C, A's share of the estate accretes to B and C. The new code article uses the word "joint" in referring to such legatees, which is consistent with prior jurisprudence and with the new terminology by which the former "conjoint" legacy is now called a "joint" legacy. C.C. Art. 1588.

Art. 1586.   General legacy

A general legacy is a disposition by which the testator bequeaths a fraction or a certain proportion of the estate, or a fraction or certain proportion of the balance of the estate that remains after particular legacies. In addition, a disposition of property expressly described by the testator as all, or a fraction or a certain proportion of one of the following categories of property, is also a general legacy: separate or community property, movable or immovable property, or corporeal or incorporeal property. This list of categories is exclusive.

Acts 1997, No. 1421, § 1, eff. July 1, 1999.

REVISION COMMENTS—1997

(a) The name "legacy under universal title" is the traditional name for fractional legacies in the civil law world, but because of the common use of the word "universal" in both the "legacy under universal title" and the "universal legacy," which are different kinds of legacies, the name was the source of some confusion. For that reason, Quebec recently changed the name of this classification to a "legacy under general title." The Louisiana revision follows the Quebec approach in part: it calls the legacy merely a "general" legacy rather than "legacy under general title," as Quebec does. It is hoped that the use of a new name for this category of legacy will call attention to the fact that there is a change in the law, albeit small. This Article reproduces the substance of Article 1612 of the Civil Code of 1870 concerning legacies by universal title. Functionally, a "general" legacy is similar in most respects to the old "legacy under universal title." As a practical matter, the classification may be important with respect to responsibility for payment of debts, since universal legacies and general legacies primarily bear that responsibility. See Article 1423, infra, but see, also, Article 1422, infra. The classification may also be important for purposes of accretion when a legacy lapses or is renounced. See Articles 1592 and 1595, infra. And, of course, it is important in determining priority for discharge of legacies when the estate is insufficient to discharge all legacies. C.C. Articles 1600–1603, inclusive infra. The new rules for the "general" legacy depart slightly from prior law by expressly providing that a legacy made in terms of one of the enumerated property law classifications, such as "all of my community property to A," is a general legacy. Under prior law that kind of legacy should have been classified as a "legacy under universal title," but in the jurisprudence the classification may have been unclear. This revision clarifies that principle, and establishes that it is properly classified as a general legacy.

(b) A legacy of "one-fourth of my property" is a general legacy because it disposes of a fraction of the estate, even though it does not use one of the enumerated categories, as does a legacy of one-fourth of "all my movables" or "all my immovables," or a legacy of "all my community property" or "all my separate property." The bequest of all or a fraction of the movables or all or a fraction of the immovables would be a disposition of a category of property. If the testator made a specific listing of assets and stated that he thought that the list would equal the portion he had in mind for the legatee, that would not be a general legacy as defined in this Article.

(c) A legacy of a usufruct over a specified portion of the testator's property is not a general legacy, either, nor would a bequest of the naked ownership of the same portion be a general legacy, unless it refers to one of the listed categories.

(d) A bequest of the entirety of an estate is a universal legacy even though in one sense it is the disposition of a specified portion of the estate. It is defined as a universal legacy under the preceding article. The practical effects of classification are essentially the same whether a legacy is a general legacy or a universal legacy, at least with reference to payment of debts and administration expenses, and with reference to determination of priority in discharging legacies.

(e) An executor may be given the power to select assets to satisfy a general legacy without changing the nature of the legacy. See Civil Code Articles 1302 and 1725 (1870) and Article 1571 of this revision. The fact that the executor may offer, and the legatee accept, a specific sum of money in lieu of the general legacy does not change the nature of the legacy itself.

(f) In order for a legacy of a category of property to be classified as a "general" legacy, it must be a legacy of only one of the categories of property enumerated in the Code article. The list of categories is exclusive. When the legacy is phrased in terms of overlapping categories of property, instead of only one category, the focus of the legacy is narrowed and by definition it is not a "general" legacy. Thus, a legacy of "all of my movables to X" is a general legacy, but a legacy of "all of my corporeal movables to X" is a particular legacy. It is narrower in scope, and by definition is a particular legacy under Article 1587. The test, of course, is the language or terminology used by the testator. Even though, as a practical matter, a legacy comprises, say, all of the testator's movables, unless the disposition is couched in those specific terms, that is, in that phraseology, it is not a "general" legacy. For example, if the testator leaves "all of my stocks and bonds to A," and he has no movable property other than the stocks and bonds, the legacy is nevertheless a particular legacy, notwithstanding the fact that its practical effect is to be a legacy of "all" of his movable property. Similarly, if the testator leaves "Blackacre to A," and Blackacre is the only immovable property that he owns, then even though the incidental effect of the legacy is to be a legacy of "all of my immovable property," that is not the phraseology of the disposition and the disposition is not a "general" legacy. The terminology used by the testator, not the net effect or practical result of the disposition, determines the classification.

Art. 1587.   Particular legacy

A legacy that is neither general nor universal is a particular legacy.

Acts 1997, No. 1421, § 1, eff. July 1, 1999.

REVISION COMMENTS—1997

(a) This article reproduces the substance of Article 1625 of the Civil Code of 1870 concerning legacies by particular title. In one sense, however it defines the particular legacy in the negative by providing that it is any disposition that is not either of the other two types of legacies.

(b) The disposition of ownership of a specified asset to multiple legatees by fractions ("one-half of the Jones Road farm to A and one half to B") is a particular legacy, because it is a disposition of a certain object. That classification is not altered by the fact that the testator assigns a fractional interest in the thing to each legatee. A disposition of a right or interest in a certain object or a sum of money, such as the bequest of a usufruct of a sum of money or the usufruct of a specified asset, or the bequest of the naked ownership of that same asset, should also be classified as a particular legacy.

(c) A legacy of "all of my corporeal movables" is a particular legacy. See C.C. Art. 1586, Comment (f).

Art. 1588.   Joint or separate legacy

A legacy to more than one person is either joint or separate. It is separate when the testator assigns shares and joint when he does not. Nevertheless, the testator may make a legacy joint or separate by expressly designating it as such.

Acts 1997, No. 1421, § 1, eff. July 1, 1999.

REVISION COMMENTS—1997

(a) This Article adopts a change in terminology from "conjoint" to "joint"; it does not change the law, however. The consequences of lapse of a joint legacy under the revision are intended to be the same as the consequences of lapse of a conjoint legacy under Article 1707 of the Civil Code of 1870, except with regard to certain modifications to prefer descendants of children and siblings of the testator. See Article 1593.

(b) This Article does not in and of itself overrule the opinion in Succession of Lambert, 210 La. 636, 28 So.2d 1 (1946), and the cases following it, holding that conjointness was destroyed if the testator used a phrase such as "share and share alike" or "to be equally divided between them," which did no more than re-state the legal consequences of his disposition. Under this revision, if the testator assigns shares the legacy is presumed to be "separate," as opposed to joint, so that the same result will be reached as under the Lambert decision, but the testator may nonetheless make the bequest joint in nature by using appropriate language to do so, and the mere use of the phrase "share and share alike" should not preclude that result. Some of the harshness of the Lambert rule is eliminated by this provision and by the coordinating provisions of Article 1593.

(c) The term "joint legacy" has been used to replace the term "conjoint legacy" in order to highlight the fact that new rules have been adopted. It was feared that, because of the familiarity of counsel with the term "conjoint," retaining it might lead lawyers or judges into error. The term "joint legacy" has no relationship to the term "joint obligation" used in Civil Code Articles 1786 et seq.

Art. 1589. Lapse of legacies

A legacy lapses when:

(1) The legatee predeceases the testator.

(2) The legatee is incapable of receiving at the death of the testator.

(3) The legacy is subject to a suspensive condition, and the condition can no longer be fulfilled or the legatee dies before fulfillment of the condition.

(4) The legatee is declared unworthy.

(5) The legacy is renounced, but only to the extent of the renunciation.

(6) The legacy is declared invalid.

(7) The legacy is declared null, as for example, for fraud, duress, or undue influence.

Acts 1997, No. 1421, § 1, eff. July 1, 1999.

REVISION COMMENTS—1997

(a) This Article reproduces the substance of Articles 1697 through 1699 and 1703 of the Louisiana Civil Code of 1870. It does not change the law.

(b) This Article announces the principle that legacies are without effect in designated instances. The subsequent disposition of such legacies is governed by the following Articles.

(c) Incapacity of a legatee is governed by the articles on capacity of successors of the Louisiana Civil Code. See Louisiana Civil Code Articles 1470–83 (Rev. 1991).

(d) In general when the validity of a legacy depends upon the fulfillment of a condition or the completion of an uncertain term, the legacy lapses when that term or condition becomes impossible of fulfillment. Thus if the testator says, "I leave $10,000 to X if she has married Y at my death," the legacy lapses if the marriage has not taken place by the time of the testator's death. Properly viewed, the preceding bequest establishes a condition only to determine a status as of the time of the decedent's death, and in that sense it is neither suspensive nor resolutory. At the moment of the testator's death, a factual determination is made, namely whether X has married Y. A true suspensive condition would be better illustrated by the following example, in which the testator says, "I leave $10,000 to Cindy if the war ends within six months after my death." In that event, Cindy's bequest is suspensive, because "the obligation may not be enforced until the uncertain event

372

occurs. . . ." La. Civ. Code Art. 1767 (rev. 1984). If the war does not end within six months after the testator's death, then the condition is not met and Cindy does not take. When the condition is merely one that suspends the execution of a legacy, the legacy is valid. Thus if the testator says, "I leave $10,000 to X, to be paid him upon his 21st birthday," and X dies at age 19, the $10,000 belongs to X's heirs. See Leonora, f.w.c. v. Scott, 10 La.Ann. 651 (1855). Such a legacy is actually subject to a certain term, not a condition.

(e) Subpart (3) of this Article preserves the probable meaning of Article 2030 of the Civil Code of 1870, repealed by Act 331 of 1984, that the successors of a legatee had no right to a conditional legacy if the legatee died before the condition was fulfilled. Thus if a legacy is conditioned with language such as "to X, if my ship arrives in New Orleans within six months of my death," the legacy lapses if X dies before the ship arrives, i.e. before the event occurs. It also lapses if the ship sinks, since the condition can then no longer be fulfilled.

Art. 1590. Testamentary accretion

Testamentary accretion takes place when a legacy lapses.

Accretion takes place according to the testament, or, in the absence of a governing testamentary provision, according to the following Articles.

Acts 1997, No. 1421, § 1, eff. July 1, 1999.

REVISION COMMENTS—1997

2012 Electronic Pocket Part Update

(a) In this Article the term "accretion" has been expanded to include the disposition of all lapsed legacies, not just joint legacies. Succession of Dougart, 30 La.Ann. 268 (1878), is overruled on this point, as are Articles 1706–1708 of the Civil Code of 1870, to the extent that they mandate the Dougart interpretation.

(b) Although this Article refers to "a lapsed legacy", it should be obvious that the provision includes the lapsed share of a legatee under a joint legacy as well as a lapsed legacy where the legatee is the sole recipient of the bequest. Thus, a legacy of Blackacre "to A," when A predeceases the testator, would be a lapsed legacy, and a legacy of Blackacre "to A and B" jointly, where A predeceases the testator, would also be a lapsed legacy insofar as the undivided one-half interest in Blackacre that was left to A is concerned. In one sense it is only the legatee's share that lapses in the latter case, but in either event the predecease of the legatee causes a lapsed legacy. The second paragraph of this Article then refers the matter to the testament itself, because the testator may have covered the possibility of a lapsed legacy. In the event that the testament does not provide for that contingency, however, the provisions of the following articles would become effective.

Art. 1591. Accretion of particular and general legacies

When a particular or a general legacy lapses, accretion takes place in favor of the successor who, under the testament, would have received the thing if the legacy had not been made.

Acts 1997, No. 1421, § 1, eff. July 1, 1999.

REVISION COMMENTS—1997

This Article clarifies the rule of Article 1704 of the Civil Code of 1870. It does not change the law, but it is important to note the special treatment given a general legacy that is phrased as a "residue" or "balance," under C.C. Art. 1595, infra.

Art. 1592. Accretion among joint legatees

When a legacy to a joint legatee lapses, accretion takes place ratably in favor of the other joint legatees, except as provided in the following Article.

Acts 1997, No. 1421, § 1, eff. July 1, 1999.

(a) Upon death of one of the legatees under a joint legacy, the legacy lapses as provided for in Article 1588. This Article states the consequences that follow, but it does not change the law. It merely restates the provision of the first paragraph of Article 1707 of the Civil Code of 1870 without substantive change. Article 1707 does not specifically define the term, but Article 1588 provides such a definition and is in turn applied in this Article and the following Articles.

(b) The definitions of "joint legacy" and "testamentary accretion" are contained, respectively, in Articles 1588 and 1590 of this revision. With the addition of those definitions, and the exception made in the succeeding Article for certain preferred joint legatees, this Article re-states the provisions of Article 1707 of the Civil Code of 1870 without change.

(c) If the testator wishes to do so, he may specifically provide that the rule of testamentary accretion that would otherwise govern his disposition does not apply. For example, if he has given an item to A and B but does not wish A to receive B's part if B predeceases the testator, he may use a vulgar substitution. In this instance, he might provide ". . . to A and B, but if B should predecease me, his part to go to C."

Art. 1593.   Exception to rule of testamentary accretion

If a legatee, joint or otherwise, is a child or sibling of the testator, or a descendant of a child or sibling of the testator, then to the extent that the legatee's interest in the legacy lapses, accretion takes place in favor of his descendants by roots who were in existence at the time of the decedent's death. The provisions of this Article shall not apply to a legacy that is declared invalid or is declared null for fraud, duress, or undue influence.

Acts 1997, No. 1421, § 1, eff. July 1, 1999. Amended by Acts 2001, No. 824, § 1.

(a) This Article changes the law by establishing a preferred group of legatees as to whom the law implies a vulgar substitution in favor of the descendants of such a legatee when his interest in the legacy lapses.

(b) This Article further changes the law by applying to joint (formerly "conjoint") legatees. If one of the joint legatees is within the preferred group of legatees (children or siblings of the testator, or their descendants), and predeceases the testator with descendants, those descendants succeed to the rights of the deceased legatee per stirpes. If, on the other hand, one of the joint legatees is outside the preferred group of legatees and predeceases the testator, the remaining joint legatees succeed to his share under the preceding Article.

(c) If the joint legacy is universal, the rights to which the preferred successors succeed include not only ownership of the share of property which would have belonged to the predeceased legatee, but also his right to take other legacies that have lapsed or are otherwise without effect under Article 1590.

(d) This Article establishes a species of anti-lapse statute for Louisiana, similar but not identical to Section 2–602 of the Uniform Probate Code.

(e) If a joint legatee within the preferred group predeceases the testator and dies without descendants, the general rule of testamentary accretion applies, rather than the exception in this article.

(f) The phrase "declared invalid" refers to the situation where the legacy is substantively invalid, as in the case of a prohibited substitution. The phrase does not refer to the legatee's being judicially divested of his rights, as for example by a declaration of unworthiness.

(g) The lapsed legacy can not accrete to a descendant by roots who is not in existence at the time of the decedent's death, that is, one who is conceived after the date of the decedent's death. For example, if the successor renounces his legacy, which causes it to lapse, and a descendant of the successor is conceived a year later, the after-conceived descendant has no rights under this article. The time as of which the descendants by roots of the successor are to be identified is the moment of death of the decedent involved. This rule is consistent with Civil Code Article 935, under which the date of the decedent's death is the operative date, also.

(h) The exception made in this article for a lapse that occurs by reason of renunciation reconciles the provisions of this article with those of Article 965 and avoids any inconsistency between the two articles. Article 965 applies to renunciation in a testate succession, and contains a broader scope of protection for descendants than Article 1593 contains. Article 965 applies to all legatees, even those who are not related by consanguinity to the testator, whereas Article 1593 only protects descendants of children and siblings of the testator. Clearly, if a lapse occurs by renunciation, and the renouncing legatee is a child or sibling of the testator, and there is no contrary testamentary provision, both articles reach the same result. But if the legatee who renounces is a friend or distant relative such as an aunt, uncle, or cousin, and there is no contrary testamentary provision, then Articles 965 and 1593 might reach different results. Thus, a friend or relative who does not want his legacy to accrete to his children when it otherwise would do so should not renounce, but should accept the legacy.

In any event, a successor who is considering renunciation should carefully analyze the rules of accretion before he renounces. Among other reasons, the testament itself may provide for accretion in the event of renunciation and, if it does so, then, as Article 965 provides, the testamentary provision would govern.

Art. 1594.   [Blank]

Art. 1595.   Accretion to universal legatee

All legacies that lapse, and are not disposed of under the preceding Articles, accrete ratably to the universal legatees.

When a general legacy is phrased as a residue or balance of the estate without specifying that the residue or balance is the remaining fraction or a certain portion of the estate after the other general legacies, even though that is its effect, it shall be treated as a universal legacy for purposes of accretion under this article.

Acts 1997, No. 1421, § 1, eff. July 1, 1999.

REVISION COMMENTS—1997

(a) This Article establishes a broad anti-lapse provision, preferring universal legatees and certain general legatees over devolution by intestacy.

(b) This Article retains the general substance of the former article dealing with universal legacies and codifies the jurisprudential principle recognizing the most important consequence of such a legacy: the right of the legatee to take lapsed legacies and others that are of no effect. See Succession of Burnside, 35 La.Ann. 705 (1883); City of New Orleans v. Hardie, 43 La.Ann. 251, 9 So. 12 (1891); Willis v. McKeithen, 184 So.2d 748 (La.App. 2d Cir. 1966).

(c) The concept of Article 1704 of the Civil Code of 1870 has been clarified in this revision, with express provision for the lapse of a particular legacy being made in Article 1591 of this revision, and in the catch-all provision provided in this Article. In fact, the substance of both of these Articles is a matter of testamentary choice, because the testator himself can provide specifically what will happen in the event of lapse of a legacy. In the absence of such a testamentary provision, these Articles set forth a rational scheme that should be easy to understand.

(d) If a universal legatee who predeceases the testator is not within the preferred group of legatees under the provisions of Article 1593, then his predecease gives to the other universal legatees both the right to his portion of the universal legacy itself and the right to take lapsed legacies, which is inherent in the universal nature of the legacy.

(e) If a legacy lapsed and there were no universal legacy to take, and there were no "vulgar substitution," then in the absence of the second paragraph in this article, even if the testament contained a general legacy of a "residue" or "balance" of the estate, the accretion would not be to the general legatee but to the intestate successors. See C.C. Art. 1591, supra. The purpose of the second paragraph of this article is to modify the application of that rule in those instances where the general legacy is phrased in terms of "rest," "residue," or "remainder," which, it is believed are terms that imply an intention to pick up lapsed legacies in preference to having them devolve by intestacy. By the nature of their definitions a testament cannot contain both a general legacy and a universal legacy. See revision Comment A to C.C. Article 1585. If there is a general legacy of "all of my movables to A," and no vulgar substitution to provide for an alternative legatee if A predeceases the testator, then if A dies before the testator, the legacy of all the movables lapses and will fall by intestacy. The accretion of a lapsed general legacy can not flow to a universal legacy, because there cannot be a universal legacy by virtue of its definition. The application of the second paragraph can be best illustrated in the following examples: Suppose the testament leaves "10% of the estate" to A, and "90% of the estate" to B. The two legacies are both general legacies, and if either legacy lapses, it does not accrete to the other legatee, but passes by intestacy. On the other hand, suppose that the legacies are "10% to A" and "the balance of my estate" to B. In that situation if A predeceases the testator, the lapsed legacy does accrete to B, under the second paragraph of this article. The legacy to B is by definition a general legacy, not a universal legacy, but a policy decision has been made to permit accretion to a general legacy as if the general legacy were a universal legacy when it is couched or phrased in terms of a "residue" or "balance." Several reasons support that policy decision. Essentially, the rule is based on practice and experience, and attempts to effectuate the testator's most likely intent. The Redactors believe that when a testator has taken the time and effort to execute a testament, it is more likely than not that the testator would prefer that his estate devolve according to his testament rather than the rules of intestacy. Also, the view of experienced practitioners is that a testator who uses words such as "residue," "rest," "balance," or similar expressions, generally believes that if anyone else does not take under the testament, the legatee of the "rest," "residue," or "remainder" of the estate should take it. The same implication would not prevail if the testator has more definitively assigned portions, as in saying "I leave 10% of my estate to A, and 90% of my estate to B." The variance from that expression coupled with use of the words "rest," "residue," or "remainder" implies an intent, or indeed an indirect kind of vulgar substitution, by which the legatee of the "residue" should take the share of the legatee whose legacy has lapsed.

Another example of a general legacy that qualifies under the second paragraph of this article is: "I leave all of my community property to Mary. I leave the balance of my estate to Sue." Since the legacy to Mary is a general legacy, the legacy to Sue is technically a general legacy, also, because it is a legacy of a fraction or certain proportion of the estate. The legacy to Sue is tantamount to being a legacy of "all of my separate property," which would also be a general legacy. Under the second paragraph of this article, if Mary predeceases the testator, the legacy to Mary accretes to Sue as if the legacy to Sue were a universal legacy.

The policy decision of the second paragraph as stated above is to favor testacy over intestacy, and to presume that by leaving the "balance" of the estate rather than expressly stating "all of my separate property" or "all of my movables," the testator has indirectly manifested an intent to favor his testamentary selection of a legatee rather than have any of his property pass by intestacy. In other words, it is thought that the testator would more likely than not want any lapsed legacies to go to a designated legatee of the "residue" of his estate rather than to his heirs by intestacy. For that reason, instead of making this a presumption or rule of evidence, the rule is elevated to code status and made a principle of law. As a special rule, it is an exception to the general rules regarding accretion.

Art. 1596.   Accretion to intestate successors

Any portion of the estate not disposed of under the foregoing rules devolves by intestacy.

Acts 1997, No. 1421, § 1, eff. July 1, 1999.

REVISION COMMENTS—1997

This Article reproduces the substance and clarifies the provisions of Article 1709 of the Civil Code of 1870. It does not change the law.

Art. 1597.   Loss, extinction, or destruction of property given

A.   A legacy is extinguished to the extent that property forming all or part of the legacy is lost, extinguished, or destroyed before the death of the testator. However, the legatee is entitled to any part of the property that remains and to any uncollected insurance proceeds attributable to the loss, extinction, or destruction, and to the testator's right of action against any person liable for the loss, extinction, or destruction.

B.   A legacy of a certain object is not extinguished when the object of the legacy has been transformed into a similar object without an act of the testator.

C.   If the object of the legacy has been condemned or expropriated prior to the testator's death, the legatee is entitled to any uncollected award and to succeed to any right of action concerning the condemnation or expropriation.

Acts 1997, No. 1421, § 1, eff. July 1, 1999. Amended by Acts 2001, No. 824, § 1.

REVISION COMMENTS—1997

(a) While most of this Article is new, the new provisions are in keeping with the principles of Civil Code Article 617 relative to usufruct over property that is lost, extinguished or destroyed, but as to which insurance proceeds are due. The first clause of the second sentence of the Article, on partial destruction, reproduces the provision on partial destruction found in Article 1643 of the Civil Code of 1870.

(b) This new Article does not adopt the principle of Civil Code Article 615 relative to usufruct over property that is converted to money or other property (for example, by expropriation or corporate liquidation) without an act of the usufructuary, or that otherwise changes form where the change is not brought about by an act of the usufructuary. Under usufruct law, in such cases the usufruct does not terminate but attaches to the money or other property. Under this Article the effects of changes brought about by changes of form or conversions into money or other property without an act of the testator, or the sale or donation of the property, are governed by the rules on revocation of legacies.

(c) This Article recognizes the two concepts of total destruction and partial destruction, as to which there are close but not identical counterparts in the Louisiana law of lease. It does not treat the area of damage, where there may be an injury to property that is not so severe as to constitute a partial destruction.

(d) Since this Article by its nature applies only to events that occur prior to the date of the testator's death, and not to events occurring thereafter, one should be careful not to confuse the effects of this Article with the results that occur if there is damage, partial destruction, or total destruction after the testator's death. In those instances, entirely different issues arise, which may be governed by other principles of law, such as the duty of a succession representative to preserve and maintain property of the estate, and the duty to insure property pending the administration of the estate.

Art. 1598.   Right of legatees to fruits and products

All legacies, whether particular, general, or universal, include the fruits and products attributable to the object of the legacy from the date of death, but the right of any legatee to distribution under this Article is subject to administration of the succession.

Nevertheless, the legatee of a specified amount of money is entitled to interest on it, at a reasonable rate, beginning one year after the testator's death, but the executor may, by contradictory proceedings with the legatee and upon good cause shown, obtain an extension of time for such interest to begin to accrue and for such other modification with regard to payment of interest as the court deems appropriate. If, however, the legacy is subject to a usufruct for life of a surviving spouse or is held in trust subject to an income interest for life, to or for the benefit of a surviving spouse, the spouse shall be entitled to interest on the money from the date of death at a reasonable rate.

Acts 1997, No. 1421, § 1, eff. July 1, 1999.

REVISION COMMENTS—1997

(a) This Article combines the provisions of a number of articles of the Civil Code of 1870, retaining some principles and revising others.

(b) The concept that a legatee is the owner of his legacy from the moment of death, regardless of the nature of the legacy, and his ultimate right to the fruits of the legacy, have been retained.

(c) Though legatees are entitled to the natural and civil fruits of their legacies, the practicalities of succession administration require some modifications of that right. To the extent that a particular asset given is actually producing revenues and these can be identified and segregated, there is no

377

reason to deny them to the legatee when his legacy is eventually delivered. For legacies of cash, however, there is no requirement that the succession representative undertake an investment program to produce interest, particularly since the cash may not be readily available at death. A one-year period is granted to the succession representative to arrange for payment of the cash legacy, and thereafter interest would be due. Such a waiting period is fairly common in other states. See Section 3–904 of the Uniform Probate Code (one year from appointment of succession representative). The article uses the term "reasonable" to refer to the rate of interest to permit the court to fix the rate realistically and at an amount that may be different from the legal rate of interest.

(d) For general and universal legatees, such fruits as are actually produced and are attributable to the assets encompassed by their legacies are due to them in their respective proportions. In addition, any expenses directly attributable to those assets are their responsibility.

(e) Within the principles of this Article, legatees retain the right under Article 3191 of the Code of Civil Procedure to assert a breach of the fiduciary duty of the succession representative.

(f) This Article provides a rule in the absence of a provision by the testator. A testator may specifically provide that no interest is due on a particular legacy regardless of the elapsed time period since his death, or that interest shall begin to accrue earlier than one year.

(g) If there is an administration, there is no right to distribution prior to the completion of the administration of the succession. Consistent with the principles of Article 3372 of the Code of Civil Procedure, a legatee may proceed contradictorily with the executor to seek possession of all or part of his legacy.

(h) The Civil Code of 1870 had no provision as to the right of a legatee by universal title (now a general legatee) to the fruits of his legacy from the day of death, but the French have apparently accorded him that right. See Planiol, Vol. 3, No. 2775.

(i) The demand for delivery of the legacy with its role in the determination of the beginning point for accounting for the fruits of the legacy has been suppressed as unnecessary in light of modern succession procedure and the change of the substantive rule effected by this Article.

(j) Mineral substances extracted from the ground and the proceeds of mineral rights are not fruits, because their production results in depletion of the property. Revision Comments to Article 551 (Comment (c)). By virtue of other provisions of law, or by virtue of the testamentary provisions, such mineral rights may belong to the usufructuary, but in any event, although they would not be considered as natural or civil fruits, they are "products" within the purview of this Article.

(k) The last sentence of this Article intentionally refers to a legacy of money that is "subject to a usufruct" of a surviving spouse or that is "held in trust and subject to an income interest" for the benefit of the surviving spouse. It would be inappropriate to state merely that the legacy is a usufruct for life. The legacy is both a naked ownership interest of a sum of money and a usufruct for life. Similarly, the legacy in trust is not only of an income interest; it is an amount or sum of cash that is held in trust subject to an income interest for life. The first operative fact of the last sentence is that the legacy is one of cash, whether in trust or subject to a usufruct, so that the usufructuary has received a legacy of a usufruct of cash or the income beneficiary has received a legacy of an income interest in trust of cash. It should be noted, too, that the usufructuary or the income beneficiary must be a surviving spouse to be entitled to interest on the money from the date of death at a reasonable rate. One of the principal reasons for such a provision is to preserve the ability to obtain federal tax treatment of either interest as a possible "qualifying terminable interest," which, under applicable federal tax regulations, requires that the usufructuary receive the income from the date of death of the decedent. See Internal Revenue Code, 26 U.S.C. § 2702, Federal Tax Regulations, C.F.R. 25.2519–1.

Art. 1599.   Payment of legacies, preference of payment

If the testator has not expressly declared a preference in the payment of legacies, the preference shall be governed by the following Articles.

Acts 1997, No. 1421, § 1, eff. July 1, 1999.

REVISION COMMENTS—1997

This article is new. It does not change the law, however. It codifies a principle implicit under prior law.

Art. 1600.   Particular legacies; preference of payment

A particular legacy must be discharged in preference to all others.

Acts 1997, No. 1421, § 1, eff. July 1, 1999.

REVISION COMMENTS—1997

This Article reproduces the substance of Article 1634 of the Louisiana Civil Code (1870).

Art. 1601.   Preference of payment among particular legacies

If the property remaining after payment of the debts and satisfaction of the legitime proves insufficient to discharge all particular legacies, the legacies of specific things must be discharged first and then the legacies of groups and collections of things. Any remaining property must be applied toward the discharge of legacies of money, to be divided among the legatees of money in proportion to the amounts of their legacies. When a legacy of money is expressly declared to be in recompense for services, it shall be paid in preference to all other legacies of money.

Acts 1997, No. 1421, § 1, eff. July 1, 1999.

REVISION COMMENTS—1997

This Article reproduces the substance of Article 1635 of the Louisiana Civil Code of 1870. It does not change the law. The phrase "property remaining after payment of the debts" is used in preference to the term "the effects" used in the predecessor Article in order to make it clear that payment of debts must precede payment of legacies.

The provision of the source Article giving preference to a legacy that is expressly declared to be in recompense for services has been retained, using the identical language. No change in the law is intended.

Art. 1602.   Discharge of an unsatisfied particular legacy

Intestate successors and general and universal legatees are personally bound to discharge an unpaid particular legacy, each in proportion to the part of the estate that he receives.

Acts 1997, No. 1421, § 1, eff. July 1, 1999.

REVISION COMMENTS—1997

(a) This Article reproduces the substance of Article 1633 of the Louisiana Civil Code of 1870. It does not change the law. It reflects changes in terminology with respect to the former categories of "legatees by universal title" and "legatees by particular title."

(b) The second paragraph of the predecessor Article concerning the liability of the heirs "by mortgage for the whole, to the amount of the value of the immovable property of the succession withheld by them" is not retained in this Article because the concept is adequately covered in the separation of patrimony statutes, R.S. 9:5011, et seq.

(c) The word "heirs" in the predecessor Article is replaced in this Article by a reference to those persons whose legacies or inheritance by intestacy have responsibility for the debts of the deceased.

(d) The substance of the revised Article is consistent with the jurisprudential view of the predecessor Article over the years. Jones v. Mason, 124 So.2d 795 (La.App. 2d Cir. 1960) (action for payment of legacy after heirs are sent into possession is against heirs, not discharged administrator); Baron v. Vaum, 44 La.Ann. 295, 10 So. 766 (1892); Succession of Dupuy, 33 La.Ann. 277 (1881); Anderson's Executors v. Anderson's Heirs, 10 La. 29 (1836). See also C.C. Art. 1381 (1870) (reappearance of left-out heir after partition is cause for re-opening and re-distribution).

(e) It should be obvious that this Article applies only where successors have been put in possession, and can apply only to unpaid cash legacies. If the bequest consists of a specific thing (or "certain object" as it is called in existing law), then either the object exists and is owned by the testator at the time of his death or it does not. If he does not own the thing (for example, if he has sold or donated it during his lifetime), then the legacy lapses and there is no need to assign responsibility to any other successors to discharge that legacy. On the other hand, if the property is found in the estate, then it belongs to the particular legatee. See Article 935. If the succession is under administration, the succession representative will be obligated to deliver the thing to the particular legatee. If it has been distributed to someone erroneously, as for example in the situation where A is placed in possession and a subsequent will or codicil is found leaving the property to B, once it is determined that the subsequent codicil is valid and prevails, the particular legatee under it (here, B) will be able to obtain possession from A of the property in accordance with other rules of the general law. There is no need to provide for successors who have been put in possession when a particular legacy other than cash remains undischarged. It should, however, be noted that when no one has been put in possession, there are internal rules that determine which general and universal legatees bear the brunt of discharging particular legacies. By way of example, if the testator leaves 100 shares of General Motors stock to A, which is a particular legacy, and he leaves "all of my movables" to B, and "all of my immovables to C," then obviously it is B whose legacy is diminished or impaired by the bequest of stock to A, since the stock of General Motors is movable property and diminishes what B will receive. It does not affect C and would not have to be discharged by C. Thus, the responsibility of successors among themselves for the discharge of legacies is governed by rules of preference, but those rules are different from the principle enunciated in this Article.

(f) In many parts of the state it is common practice not to have an administration of an estate, especially when the heirs wish to avoid the time and expense of such an administration. They may be sent into possession without an administration, but when they do, they are required to discharge all of the legacies that have priority over their own. This Article emphasizes the importance of the concept of the duty to discharge a preferred legacy. Nonetheless, so long as the legatee who is obligated to discharge another legacy does not take possession of property of the estate, he has no personal liability for failure to do so. See C.C. Art 1604, infra.

Art. 1603.   [Blank]

Art. 1604.   Discharge of legacies, limitation of liability

In all the foregoing instances, a successor who is obligated to discharge a legacy is personally liable for his failure to do so only to the extent of the value of the property of the estate that he receives, valued as of the time of receipt. He is not personally liable to other successors by way of contribution or reimbursement for any greater amount.

Acts 1997, No. 1421, § 1, eff. July 1, 1999.

REVISION COMMENTS—1997

(a) This revision continues the historic civil law approach to the duty of successors to "discharge" legacies. When an estate is under administration, the succession representative has possession of the property of the estate and is obviously the person obligated to see that all debts are paid and all legacies discharged. See Art. 3211 of the Code of Civil Procedure. But not all estates are administered, and even in an estate that has been administered, there may be no compelling reason to withhold placing a general legatee or a universal legatee in possession of his legacy. When a general legatee or a universal legatee takes possession of property of the estate, his obligation to "discharge" the particular legacies becomes more significant. Although the obligation is a personal obligation in the sense that it is imposed on the legatee himself, in a practical sense it is primarily an obligation imposed upon the property of the estate, and no one should be confused by the in rem nature of the obligation. If a general legatee or a universal legatee never takes possession of any property of the estate, he incurs no personal liability and therefore has essentially no "duty" to see that the particular legacy is discharged. Thus, it is in actuality the property of the estate that is used, so to speak, to discharge the particular legacy. In the scheme of the Code, particular legacies have preference over general and universal legacies. C.C. Art. 1600. This Article, and the Articles that precede it as well as those that follow it, help implement that scheme. See Comments to C. C. Art. 1602, supra.

(b) Article 3031 of the Code of Civil Procedure is being amended as part of this revision to permit general and universal legatees to be sent into possession of their legacies without requiring that particular legatees join in the petition for possession. The general and universal legatees who utilize this change in the procedural law and receive property of the estate are personally obligated to discharge those legacies, and if they fail to do so, they are exposed to personal liability. Consistent with the rules adopted elsewhere in this revision that limit the liability of successors to creditors of the estate, this article provides for a ceiling on the extent of that liability, which is fixed at the value of the property received by the legatees, valued at the time of receipt.

(c) This Article logically follows the provisions of the immediately preceding Articles, and the comments to C.C. Art. 1602 apply with equal force here. This Article, however, also enunciates the limitation on personal liability that is incurred by a general or universal legatee who takes possession of property and then fails to discharge the legacies that he is obligated to discharge. Since there may be more than one general or universal legatee, it is possible that a particular legacy may be discharged by only one of those legatees, but since those legatees are obligated to discharge it on a pro rata basis, the legatee who discharges the particular legacy may be entitled to contribution or in certain instances reimbursement from the other legatees. For example, a general legatee who satisfies a particular legacy may be entitled to reimbursement from the intestate successor or other general legatee who should have satisfied it in its entirety. Whether the claim is for contribution or reimbursement, under any circumstances the legatee who owes the contribution or reimbursement cannot be personally liable for an amount greater than the value of the property that he has received from the estate.

(d) This Article is consistent with the principle expressed in Article 1425 as a corollary of Article 1416 concerning limitation of the liability of successors for estate debts. According to the principle of Article 1425, a successor cannot be held liable for contribution or reimbursement for an amount greater than the value of the property received by him.

SECTION 5—PROBATE OF TESTAMENTS

Art. 1605. Probate of testament

A testament has no effect unless it is probated in accordance with the procedures and requisites of the Code of Civil Procedure.

Acts 1997, No. 1421, § 1, eff. July 1, 1999.

REVISION COMMENTS—1997

(a) Articles 1644 through 1647 of the Civil Code of 1870 concern the procedure for probate of testaments following adequate proof of death. To the extent that their substance is already contained in Articles 2851 et seq. of the Code of Civil Procedure, they do not need to be revised or reenacted. There is, moreover, ample substantive law adopted in the revision in the area of "opening of succession" with appropriate comments. See Chapter 5, First Part, "Commencement of Succession," supra.

(b) When a valid testament is probated, it is effective as of the date of the testator's death. See Article 935.

(c) The relevant prescriptive period for probating a testament is 5 years from the date of judicial opening of the succession of the decedent. See R.S. 9:5643.

(d) Articles 1645–1647 of the Civil Code of 1870 have been suppressed as unnecessary in light of the detailed regulation of this area provided in the Code of Civil Procedure.

SECTION 6—REVOCATION OF TESTAMENTS AND LEGACIES

Art. 1606. Testator's right of revocation

A testator may revoke his testament at any time. The right of revocation may not be renounced.

Acts 1997, No. 1421, § 1, eff. July 1, 1999.

This Article reproduces the substance of Article 1690 of the Civil Code of 1870. It does not change the law.

Art. 1607.　Revocation of entire testament by testator

Revocation of an entire testament occurs when the testator does any of the following:

(1) Physically destroys the testament, or has it destroyed at his direction.

(2) So declares in one of the forms prescribed for testaments or in an authentic act.

(3) Identifies and clearly revokes the testament by a writing that is entirely written and signed by the testator in his own handwriting.

Acts 1997, No. 1421, § 1, eff. July 1, 1999.

This Article supplements the provisions of its predecessor articles by adding new methods of revoking a testament, but otherwise it restates the provisions without substantive change, except for the deletion of the unnecessary division into "express" and "tacit" revocations. Paragraph (1) continues the supposition that physical destruction of the entire instrument indicates that a revocation was intended. Paragraph (2) provides for revocation by subsequent will, but it expands the ability to revoke by adding the use of an authentic act to do so. The more significant new specific ground for revocation of an entire testament is in paragraph (3) which authorizes revocation by a signed writing that identifies and clearly revokes the testament. This new ground is added to permit a finding of revocation when the testator's intent has been made clear in a writing that he has written by hand and signed but which may not be dated. By definition such a signed but undated writing is not in the form of a testament. Nevertheless, such a clear intent to revoke should be honored. As a matter of policy, the formality required to dispose of property is greater than the formality needed to revoke a prior disposition. For example, if there were a contest between two undated testaments, it would be impossible to determine which of them prevailed. But when revocation is involved, the undated writing must of necessity be subsequent to the testament it seeks to revoke, and dating is therefore less significant than a clear identification of the testament to be revoked and a clear manifestation of the intention to revoke. See Comments to Article 1610, infra. To the extent that the rationale of Succession of Melancon, 330 So.2d 679 (La.App. 3rd Cir. 1976), would deny that a revocation would occur by a signed and handwritten notation to that effect that did not have a date, that decision is overruled.

Art. 1608.　Revocation of a legacy or other testamentary provision

Revocation of a legacy or other testamentary provision occurs when the testator:

(1) So declares in one of the forms prescribed for testaments.

(2) Makes a subsequent incompatible testamentary disposition or provision.

(3) Makes a subsequent inter vivos disposition of the thing that is the object of the legacy and does not reacquire it.

(4) Clearly revokes the provision or legacy by a signed writing on the testament itself.

(5) Is divorced from the legatee after the testament is executed and at the time of his death, unless the testator provides to the contrary. Testamentary designations or appointments of a spouse are revoked under the same circumstances.

Acts 1997, No. 1421, § 1, eff. July 1, 1999.

(a) This Article combines and restates the provisions of the predecessor Articles of the Civil Code of 1870 with some substantive change, including the deletion of the unnecessary division into "express" and "tacit" revocations.

(b) The statement in Article 1691 of the Civil Code of 1870 that a revocation results from "some act which supposes a change of will" has not been retained as written, because it was too vague and general and its acceptance by the judiciary was inconsistent. In Succession of Muh, 35 La.Ann. 394 (1883), the court used the phrase to find revocation of an entire testament by the obliteration of the testator's signature on the document. But in Succession of Melancon, 330 So.2d 679 (La.App. 3d Cir. 1976), the lining out of certain legacies accompanied by the notation in the hand of the testator that the legacy was revoked, and his signature beneath that, was held insufficient to constitute a tacit revocation. It was "some act which supposes a change of will," but the court held that since it was not dated, it was not in one of the forms prescribed for testaments. The text of this Article, like Article 1607, is intended to overrule Melancon and to specify the grounds upon which revocation may be found.

(c) The former ground of revocation that applied when an inconsistent disposition of the thing was made by sale or donation, even if null, has not been continued. If the sale, donation or other disposition is valid, the transferee rather than the testator is the owner of the property, and the legacy cannot be given effect. As a technical matter, the disposition is null, and revocation is not the correct approach nor an appropriate legal issue.

(d) The provisions of this and the preceding Article make it unnecessary to continue the provisions of the Civil Code of 1870 relative to general and particular revocations.

(e) This Article is broader than the predecessor Articles because it includes revocation of "other testamentary provisions." A testament customarily includes many important provisions in addition to legacies, such as those designating representatives like executors, tutors, and trustees. Furthermore, the will may provide for short-term survivorship, which is a "testamentary provision" but not a legacy. A codicil may revoke the designation of an executor but not necessarily dispose of property. The new language addresses revocations of such provisions and thus modernizes the traditional rule.

(f) An important new provision in item (5) of this Article covers the situation of divorce that is not otherwise covered by the testament itself. The new rule recognizes that when a testator becomes divorced from a spouse, more often than not, he does not want bequests to that spouse to be maintained, and would very likely not want that spouse to serve as the executor or trustee. The new rule is consistent with Louisiana domestic relations law by providing that the divorce must have occurred after the testament was executed, and that there must have been no reconciliation. Furthermore, the testator may provide to the contrary, so that even though the parties may be divorced, the testator may make a bequest to the spouse, or if he wants that spouse to serve in a representative capacity he may so provide. Most states have adopted similar provisions, and this provision fills a gap in the prior law.

(g) As provided in Article 1609, in order to produce effects under this article, the revocations involved in Sections 1–4 must be effective at the time of the testator's death.

Art. 1609. Revocation of juridical act prior to testator's death

The revocation of a testament, legacy, or other testamentary provision that is made in any manner other than physical destruction of the testament, subsequent inter vivos disposition or divorce is not effective if the revocation itself is revoked prior to the testator's death.

Acts 1997, No. 1421, § 1, eff. July 1, 1999.

REVISION COMMENTS—1997

This Article recognizes the fundamental rule that all testaments are ambulatory, and even a revocation may be revoked. A testament that is revoked by a subsequent testament may be revived by the revocation of the second testament. This article also assures that the rule that testaments are ambulatory will apply to undated but signed writings, since the new law permits an undated but signed writing to revoke a testament or legacy or other testamentary provision. See Arts. 1607 and 1608.

Art. 1610. Other modifications

Any other modification of a testament must be in one of the forms prescribed for testaments.

Acts 1997, No. 1421, § 1, eff. July 1, 1999.

REVISION COMMENTS—1997

Although this Article is new, it must be read in conjunction with Article 1608. A distinction must be made between the revocation of a legacy or a testamentary provision, and the implementation of a new legacy or a new testamentary provision. The rules are relaxed to permit the revocation of a legacy or a testamentary provision by a signed writing that is not dated but which clearly revokes the will, the provision, or the legacy. Where a replacement provision is called for, whether it is a new legacy or a new designation, the formalities should be more stringent. For that reason, this Article continues in place the rule that any modification or amendment other than revocation of a testamentary provision must be in one of the forms prescribed for testaments. For example, if a document containing such a modification were written and signed by the testator it would also have to be dated in order to be in the form prescribed for an olographic testament. The difference between these rules can be shown by the following illustration: suppose that a testator executes a will naming A as the executor. Subsequently, he writes on the testament: "I hereby revoke the designation of A as executor, and I name and appoint B as the executor of my estate." The writing is not dated although it is written by the hand of the testator and is signed by him. Under Article 1608(4), the revocation will be effective and A will not be permitted to serve as executor under the testament. The appointment of B, however, will not be effective, because the "signed writing on the testament" is not in proper form for a testament, which requires that it not only be in writing and signed by the testator, but also that it be dated.

Art. 1610.1. Grounds for revocation of testamentary dispositions

The same causes that authorize an action for the revocation of a donation inter vivos are sufficient to authorize an action for revocation of testamentary dispositions.

Added by Acts 2001, No. 824, § 1.

SECTION 7—RULES FOR THE INTERPRETATION OF LEGACIES

Art. 1611.   Intent of the testator controls

A.   The intent of the testator controls the interpretation of his testament. If the language of the testament is clear, its letter is not to be disregarded under the pretext of pursuing its spirit. The following rules for interpretation apply only when the testator's intent cannot be ascertained from the language of the testament. In applying these rules, the court may be aided by any competent evidence.

B.   When a testament uses a term the legal effect of which has been changed after the date of execution of the testament, the court may consider the law in effect at the time the testament was executed to ascertain the testator's intent in the interpretation of a legacy or other testamentary provision.

Acts 1997, No. 1421, § 1, eff. July 1, 1999. Amended by Acts 2001, No. 560, § 1, eff. June 22, 2001.

REVISION COMMENTS—1997

(a) This Article reproduces the substance Articles 1712 and 1715 of the Louisiana Civil Code (1870). It does not change the law. It emphasizes the strong rule, long recognized in the jurisprudence, that the intent of the testator is the single most important guideline in the interpretation of a testament. It clarifies the role of the other Articles of this section as supplementary in instances of ambiguity or vagueness.

(b) Although the intent of the testator controls the effects of his dispositions, it obviously can do so only to the extent that the dispositions are permissible under Louisiana law. The testator's intent to write a prohibited disposition cannot override substantive law that prevents it.

(c) When the identity of a legatee is ambiguous, the court should give effect to the testator's probable intent by awarding the legacy to the person who had the closer friendship with the deceased. Any competent evidence that could resolve the uncertainty, however, should of course be considered.

See Succession of Baskin, 349 So.2d 931 (La.App. 1st Cir. 1977), cert. den. 350 So.2d 1211 (La. 1977) (reference to legatee who had pre-deceased the testatrix shown not to be reference to adopted son of same name); Succession of Rome, 169 So.2d 665 (La.App. 1st Cir. 1964), cert. den. 171 So.2d 478 (La. 1965) (reference to "Helen" shown to be reference to claimant by testimony of friends of testatrix, and by fact that no other relative or friend bore that name); Succession of Tilton, 133 La. 435, 63 So. 99 (1913) (legacy to "home for insane" shown by extrinsic evidence to be specific state hospital in which testatrix had particular interest and which she believed to be only such hospital in state).

Art. 1612. Preference for interpretation that gives effect

A disposition should be interpreted in a sense in which it can have effect, rather than in one in which it can have none.

Acts 1997, No. 1421, § 1, eff. July 1, 1999.

REVISION COMMENTS—1997

This Article reproduces the substance Article 1713 of the Louisiana Civil Code (1870). It does not change the law. The Article is consistent with the customary position taken elsewhere in the Civil Code. See C.C. Art. 2049 (rev. 1984) (agreement to be interpreted with a meaning that renders it effective and not with one that renders it ineffective). This Article also comports with the general jurisprudential rule for interpretation of statutes. Conley v. City of Shreveport, 216 La. 78, 43 So.2d 223 (1950); Macon v. Costa, 420 So.2d 480 (La.App. 4th Cir. 1982).

Art. 1613. Mistake in identification of object bequeathed

If the identification of an object given is unclear or erroneous, the disposition is nonetheless effective if it can be ascertained what object the testator intended to give. If it cannot be ascertained whether a greater or lesser quantity was intended, it must be decided for the lesser.

Acts 1997, No. 1421, § 1, eff. July 1, 1999.

REVISION COMMENTS—1997

(a) This Article combines and restates the provisions of Civil Code Articles 1716 and 1717 (1870). It does not change the law.

(b) That the testator may have erroneously named the object given and thus himself created the ambiguity is of no moment, so long as the evidence establishes what the object must have been.

(c) If the ambiguity is over the precise amount of the legacy, this article expresses the rule in obscuris, quod minimum est sequimur often followed in the decisions. See Robouam's Heirs v. Robouam's Executor, 12 La. 73 (1838) (two testaments: first with legacy of $500 to each of two brothers, with statement that in event of predecease of either, his $500 should go to the other; second with same legacies but no statement about predecease; only $500 legacies upheld, not $1,000 cumulated from two testaments); Succession of Bobb, 41 La.Ann. 247, 5 So. 757 (1889) (disposition might have made legatees beneficiaries of residuum of entire estate, or only of fund derived from sale of specific asset; latter interpretation preferred).

Art. 1614. Interpretation as to after-acquired property

Absent a clear expression of a contrary intention, testamentary dispositions shall be interpreted to refer to the property that the testator owns at his death.

Acts 1997, No. 1421, § 1, eff. July 1, 1999.

REVISION COMMENTS—1997

This Article combines and restates the provisions of Articles 1720, 1721, and 1722 of the Civil Code of 1870, and it significantly changes their substance. The former rule provided that a disposition that is silent as to time, or one that is written in the present or past tense, applies only to property owned at the time of execution of the testament. The new Article takes the opposite approach and provides that a disposition includes all the property of which the testator dies possessed unless the contrary clearly appears from the instrument, which is believed to be more realistic and more likely to reflect the testator's true intent. It is also more expressive of the rule actually followed by the Louisiana courts, which have generally ignored the provisions of Articles 1720, 1721, and 1722 of the Civil Code of 1870. See, e.g., Succession of Burnside, 35 La.Ann. 708 (1833), and authorities therein cited. But see Succession of Van Baast, 140 So.2d 506 (La.App. 1st Cir. 1962). In Succession of Quintero, 209 La. 279, 24 So.2d 589 (La. 1946) the testament disposed of 20 shares of a corporation (by specific number) which the testatrix owned at the time of execution of the testament, but the court also included in the disposition an additional 20 shares resulting from a 100% stock dividend that accrued between the time of execution of the testament and the time of the testatrix's death.

Art. 1615.   Contradictory provisions

When a testament contains contradictory provisions, the one written last prevails. Nonetheless, when the testament contains a legacy of a collection or a group of objects and also a legacy of some or all of the same objects, the legacy of some or all of the objects prevails.

Acts 1997, No. 1421, § 1, eff. July 1, 1999.

REVISION COMMENTS—1997

(a) This Article reproduces and combines the provisions of Civil Code Articles 1719 and 1723. It does not change the law.

(b) The second sentence of this Article clarifies that there is no contradiction between particular legacies and a general legacy of the same kind. The article follows the rule of choosing the specific over the general. Thus, if the testator leaves "all the books in my collection" to A, but he leaves "the Iliad and the Odyssey" to B, the particular legacy to B prevails and he is entitled to the latter two works.

Art. 1616.   Legacy to creditor

A legacy to a creditor is not applied toward satisfaction of the debt unless the testator clearly so indicates.

Acts 1997, No. 1421, § 1, eff. July 1, 1999.

REVISION COMMENTS—1997

This Article reproduces the substance of Article 1641 of the Louisiana Civil Code (1870). It does not change the law. Obviously the testator may overcome the presumption, by "clearly so indicating," which is illustrated in cases such as Succession of Jackson, 47 La.Ann. 1089, 17 So. 598 (1895). There is no need to retain the second part of Article 1641 (1870) regarding wages to a servant, which is an archaic provision in today's society. See also, Article 956, supra.

SECTION 8—DISINHERISON

Art. 1617.   Disinherison of forced heirs

A forced heir shall be deprived of his legitime if he is disinherited by the testator, for just cause, in the manner prescribed in the following Articles.

Added by Acts 2001, No. 573, § 1, eff. June 22, 2001.

REVISION COMMENT—2001

This Article reproduces the substance of Article 1617 of the Louisiana Civil Code of 1870.

Art. 1618.   Formalities for disinherison

A disinherison must be made in one of the forms prescribed for testaments.

Added by Acts 2001, No. 573, § 1, eff. June 22, 2001.

REVISION COMMENT—2001

This Article reproduces the substance of Article 1618 of the Louisiana Civil Code of 1870.

Art. 1619.   Disinherison, express and for just cause

The disinherison must be made expressly and for a just cause; otherwise, it is null. The person who is disinherited must be either identified by name or otherwise identifiable from the instrument that disinherits him.

Added by Acts 2001, No. 573, § 1, eff. June 22, 2001.

REVISION COMMENTS—2001

(a) This Article reproduces the substance of Article 1619 of the Louisiana Civil Code of 1870. It may change the law in part by providing that the person disinherited must be either identified by name or otherwise identifiable from the instrument of disinherison. Thus, express mention of the name of the person disinherited is no longer required.

(b) The second sentence of this Article is a revised version of language added by the legislature in H.B. 932 (1999). It is intended to improve language that might be interpreted to require that the person be "objectively" ascertainable "solely" from "standards" stated in the instrument that disinherits him, which could give rise to unintended problems.

Art. 1620.   Limitation of causes for disinherison

There are no just causes for disinherison except those expressly recognized in the following Articles.

Added by Acts 2001, No. 573, § 1, eff. June 22, 2001.

REVISION COMMENT—2001

This Article reproduces the substance of Article 1620 of the Louisiana Civil Code of 1870. It does not change the law.

Art. 1621.   Children; causes for disinherison by parents

A.   A parent has just cause to disinherit a child if:

(1) The child has raised his hand to strike a parent, or has actually struck a parent; but a mere threat is not sufficient.

(2) The child has been guilty, towards a parent, of cruel treatment, crime, or grievous injury.

(3) The child has attempted to take the life of a parent.

(4) The child, without any reasonable basis, has accused a parent of committing a crime for which the law provides that the punishment could be life imprisonment or death.

(5) The child has used any act of violence or coercion to hinder a parent from making a testament.

(6) The child, being a minor, has married without the consent of the parent.

(7) The child has been convicted of a crime for which the law provides that the punishment could be life imprisonment or death.

(8) The child, after attaining the age of majority and knowing how to contact the parent, has failed to communicate with the parent without just cause for a period of two years, unless the child was on active duty in any of the military forces of the United States at the time.

B.   For a disinherison to be valid, the cause must have occurred prior to the execution of the instrument that disinherits the heir.

Added by Acts 2001, No. 573, § 1, eff. June 22, 2001.

REVISION COMMENT—2001

This Article reduces the number of causes for which a testator may disinherit a forced heir from twelve to eight.

Art. 1622.   Grandparents; causes for disinherison of grandchildren

A grandparent may disinherit his grandchild for any of the causes, other than the sixth, expressed in the preceding Article, whenever the offending act has been committed against a parent or a grandparent. He may also disinherit the grandchild for the seventh cause expressed in the preceding Article.

Added by Acts 2001, No. 573, § 1, eff. June 22, 2001.

REVISION COMMENT—2001

This Article reproduces the substance of Article 1622 of the Louisiana Civil Code of 1870. It does not change the law.

Art. 1623.   Timing of action; no defense

A person may be disinherited even though he was not a presumptive forced heir at the time of the occurrence of the act or the facts or circumstances alleged to constitute just cause for his disinherison.

Added by Acts 2001, No. 573, § 1, eff. June 22, 2001.

REVISION COMMENTS—2001

(a) This Article was drafted in response to revisions of Article 1623 made in House Bill 932 (1999). It is intended to be shorter, simpler, and technically more accurate. The language of H.B. 932 stated that the person "was not a forced heir at the time of the commission of an offense". A person could not be a forced heir because no one is a forced heir at that time of a living person.

(b) Under this Article a "presumptive forced heir" is a person who would have been a forced heir if the person from whom he would inherit as such had died at that time. Thus, a fifteen-year-old child of a person is a presumptive forced heir, but a twenty-five-year-old child of a person is not a presumptive forced heir.

Art. 1624.   Mention of cause for disinherison; burden of proof; reconciliation

The testator shall express in the instrument the reason, facts, or circumstances that constitute the cause for the disinherison; otherwise, the disinherison is null. The reason, facts, or circumstances expressed in the instrument shall be presumed to be true. The presumption may be rebutted by a preponderance of the evidence, but the unsupported testimony of the disinherited heir shall not be sufficient to overcome the presumption.

Added by Acts 2001, No. 573, § 1, eff. June 22, 2001.

REVISION COMMENT—2001

This Article broadens the ability to express or identify the just cause for which a person is disinherited. The testator does not have to follow the literal language of the grounds set forth in Article 1621. A mere statement of the facts or circumstances will suffice. The Article retains the presumption that has been in the law as it existed before July 1, 1999.

Art. 1625.   Reconciliation

A.   A person who is disinherited may overcome the disinherison by proving reconciliation with the testator after the occurrence of the reason, facts, or circumstances expressed in the instrument, provided he does so by clear and convincing evidence.

B.   A writing signed by the testator that clearly and unequivocally demonstrates reconciliation shall constitute clear and convincing evidence.

Added by Acts 2001, No. 573, § 1, eff. June 22, 2001.

REVISION COMMENTS—2001

(a) Under prior law, proof of reconciliation "must be clear and unequivocal, evidenced in writing, and signed by the testator." Under this Article, proof of reconciliation needs to be by clear and convincing evidence, but there is no longer a requirement of written proof, or that there be some sort of instrument "signed by the testator."

(b) The second paragraph of this Article is intended to be supplementary. It is not intended that a writing be the exclusive way of proving reconciliation.

Art. 1626. Defenses to disinherison

A disinherison shall not be effective if the person who is disinherited shows that because of his age or mental capacity he was not capable of understanding the impropriety of his behavior or if he shows that the behavior was unintentional or justified under the circumstances. Proof of this defense must be by a preponderance of the evidence, but the unsupported testimony of the disinherited heir shall not be sufficient to establish this defense.

Added by Acts 2001, No. 573, § 1, eff. June 22, 2001.

Arts. 1627 to 1723. [Blank]

CHAPTER 7—OF PARTITIONS MADE BY PARENTS AND OTHER ASCENDANTS AMONG THEIR DESCENDANTS

Art. 1724. Right of parents and ascendants to partition property among descendants

Fathers and mothers and other ascendants may make a distribution and partition of their property among their children and descendants, either by designating the quantum of the parts and partitions [portions] which they assign to each of them, or in designating the property that shall compose their respective lots.

Amended by Acts 2004, No. 26, § 1.

Art. 1725. Method of making partition

These partitions may be made by act inter vivos or by testament. If a testator has designated the quantum or value of his estate which he bequeaths to a legatee either by formula or by specific sum, he may expressly delegate to his executor the authority to select assets to satisfy the quantum or value.

Amended by Acts 1982, No. 448, § 1, eff. July 21, 1982.

Art. 1726. Partition by act inter vivos, formalities

Those made by an act inter vivos can have only present property for their object, and are subject to all the formalities and conditions of donations inter vivos.

Art. 1727. Testamentary partitions, formalities

Those made by testament must be made in the forms prescribed for acts of that kind, and are subject to the same rules.

Art. 1728. Property not included in partition

If the partition, whether inter vivos or by testament, has not comprised all the property that the ascendant leaves on the day of his decease, the property not comprised in the partition is divided according to law.

Art. 1729. Necessity for partition to include all descendants

If the partition, whether inter vivos or by testament, be not made amongst all the children living at the time of the decease and the descendants of those predeceased, the partition shall be null and void for the whole; the child or descendant who had no part in it, may require a new partition in legal form.

Amended by Acts 1871, No. 87.

Art. 1730.   Limitation in relation to disposable portion

Partitions, made by ascendants, may be avoided, when the advantage secured to one of the coheirs exceeds the disposable portion.

Art. 1731.   Action to rescind partition, payment of costs

The child who objects to the partition made by the ascendant, must advance the expenses of having the property estimated, and must ultimately support them and the costs of suit, if his claim be not founded.

Art. 1732.   Tender by defendant in action of rescission

The defendant in the action of rescission may arrest it by offering to the plaintiff the supplement of the portion to which he has a right.

Art. 1733.   Donation of extra portion not affected by rescission

The rescission of the partition does not carry with it the nullity of a donation made as an advantage.

CHAPTER 8—OF DONATIONS INTER VIVOS MADE IN CONTEMPLATION OF MARRIAGE BY THIRD PERSONS

SECTION 1—IN GENERAL

Art. 1734.   Donations in contemplation of marriage by third persons; in general

Any third person may make a donation inter vivos in contemplation of a prospective marriage in accordance with the provisions of this Chapter. Such a donation shall be governed by the rules applicable to donations inter vivos in general, including the rules pertaining to the reduction of donations that exceed the disposable portion, but only insofar as those general rules are not modified by the following Articles.

A donation inter vivos by a third person in contemplation of a prospective marriage that is not made in accordance with the provisions of this Chapter shall be governed solely by the rules applicable to donations inter vivos in general.

Acts 2004, No. 619, § 1, eff. Sept. 1, 2005.

Art. 1735.   Form

The donation shall be made by a single instrument in authentic form. The instrument, which shall expressly state that the donor makes the donation in contemplation of the marriage of the prospective spouses, shall be signed at the same time and at the same place by the donor and by both of the prospective spouses.

The donation need not be accepted in express terms.

Acts 2004, No. 619, § 1, eff. Sept. 1, 2005.

Art. 1736.   Condition

The donation shall be made subject to the suspensive condition that the prospective marriage shall take place.

Acts 2004, No. 619, § 1, eff. Sept. 1, 2005.

SECTION 2—DONATIONS OF PRESENT PROPERTY

Art. 1737. Beneficiaries

The donor may donate any of his present property to both or one of the prospective spouses. The donation may not, however, be made to their common descendants, whether already born or to be born.

Acts 2004, No. 619, § 1, eff. Sept. 1, 2005.

SECTION 3—DONATIONS OF PROPERTY
TO BE LEFT AT DEATH

Art. 1738. Beneficiaries

The donor may donate all or any of the property that he will leave at his death (1) to both or one of the prospective spouses or (2) to both or one of them and, in the event that they or he predecease the donor or, once the donor's succession is opened, they or he either renounce the donation or are declared unworthy to receive it, to their common descendants, whether already born or to be born.

The donation is presumed to be made in favor of the common descendants of the spouses, even if, in the act of donation, the donor does not mention them.

Acts 2004, No. 619, § 1, eff. Sept. 1, 2005.

Art. 1739. Limited irrevocability

A donation of property that the donor will leave at his death is irrevocable only in the sense that the donor may no longer dispose of the property by gratuitous title, save for dispositions of modest value. Nevertheless, the donor remains the owner of the property and, as such, retains the full liberty of disposing of it by onerous title, in the absence of an express stipulation to the contrary.

Acts 2004, No. 619, § 1, eff. Sept. 1, 2005.

Art. 1740. Division following substitution of common descendants

If the common descendants of the spouses find themselves substituted to both or one of the spouses, the property to which the common descendants are entitled shall be divided among them in accordance with the provisions of Chapter 2 of Title I of Book III1.

Acts 2004, No. 619, § 1, eff. Sept. 1, 2005.

Art. 1741. Caducity; causes and effects

If every one of the donees, including the substitutes, predeceases the donor or, once the donor's succession is opened, renounces the donation or is declared unworthy to receive it, the donation becomes of no effect at all. The object of the donation falls to the donor's heirs or legatees, as the case may be.

If the donation has been made to both spouses and to their common descendants, and if one of the spouses predeceases the donor or, once the donor's succession is opened, renounces the donation or is declared unworthy to receive it, the donation becomes of no effect only with respect to that spouse. To that extent, accretion takes place in favor of the surviving spouse, if the donation has been made to the spouses jointly, or substitution takes place in favor of their common descendants, if the donation has been made to the spouses separately.

If the donation has been made to both spouses, but not to their common descendants, and if one of the spouses predeceases the donor or, once the donor's succession is opened, renounces the donation or is declared unworthy to receive it, the donation becomes of no effect only with respect to that spouse. To that extent, the object of the donation accretes to the surviving spouse, if the donation has been made to the spouses jointly, or falls to the donor's heirs or legatees, as the case may be, if the donation has been made to the spouses separately.

If the donation has been made to one spouse only and to the spouses' common descendants, and if the donee spouse predeceases the donor or, once the donor's succession is opened, renounces the donation or is declared unworthy to receive it, the donation becomes of no effect with respect to the donee spouse. Substitution takes place in favor of the spouses' common descendants.

Acts 2004, No. 619, § 1, eff. Sept. 1, 2005.

Art. 1742. Acceptance or renunciation of succession

The donee of a donation of property that the donor will leave at his death has the right to accept or renounce the succession of the donor in accordance with the provisions of Chapter 6 of Title I of Book III1.

Acts 2004, No. 619, § 1, eff. Sept. 1, 2005.

Art. 1743. Universal succession; liability for estate debts

The donee of a universal or general donation of property that the donor will leave at his death, as a universal successor of the donor, is answerable for the debts of the estate of the donor in accordance with the provisions of Chapter 13 of Title I of Book III1.

Acts 2004, No. 619, § 1, eff. Sept. 1, 2005.

CHAPTER 9—OF INTERSPOUSAL
DONATIONS INTER VIVOS

Art. 1744. Donations between future or present spouses; in general

A person may make a donation inter vivos to his future or present spouse in contemplation of or in consideration of their marriage in accordance with the provisions of this Chapter. Such a donation shall be governed by the rules applicable to donations inter vivos in general, including the rules that pertain to the reduction of donations that exceed the disposable portion, but only insofar as those general rules are not modified by the following Articles.

A donation inter vivos by a person to his future or present spouse in contemplation of or in consideration of their marriage that is not made in accordance with the provisions of this Chapter shall be governed solely by the rules applicable to donations inter vivos in general.

Acts 2004, No. 619, § 1, eff. Sept. 1, 2005.

Art. 1745. Applicability of rules on donations in contemplation of marriage by third person

The provisions of Chapter 8 of this Title shall apply mutatis mutandis to such donations, with the following modifications.

Acts 2004, No. 619, § 1, eff. Sept. 1, 2005.

Art. 1746. Objects and beneficiaries

The donation, which may consist of any of the donor's present property or all or any of the property that the donor will leave at his death, may be made to the donor's future or present spouse. The donation may not, however, be made to their common descendants, whether already born or to be born.

Acts 2004, No. 619, § 1, eff. Sept. 1, 2005.

Art. 1747.   Form

The donation shall be made by a single instrument in authentic form. The instrument, which shall expressly state that the donor makes the donation in contemplation of his prospective marriage or in consideration of his present marriage, as the case may be, shall be signed at the same time and at the same place by the donor and by the donee.

The donation need not be accepted in express terms.

Acts 2004, No. 619, § 1, eff. Sept. 1, 2005.

Art. 1748.   Right of return not presumed

If the donation consists of present property, it is presumed not to have been made subject to the resolutory condition that the donor survive the donee or survive the donee and his descendants.

Acts 2004, No. 619, § 1, eff. Sept. 1, 2005.

Art. 1749.   Donation of property to be left at death; caducity

When the donation consists of property that the donor will leave at his death, it becomes of no effect and the object thereof thereupon falls to the heirs or legatees of the donor spouse, as the case may be, if the donee predeceases the donor or, once the donor's succession is opened, renounces the donation or is declared unworthy to receive it.

Acts 2004, No. 619, § 1, eff. Sept. 1, 2005.

Art. 1750.   Donations of property to be left at death made during marriage; revocability

A donation made during marriage of property that the donor will leave at his death is freely revocable, notwithstanding any stipulation to the contrary.

Acts 2004, No. 619, § 1, eff. Sept. 1, 2005.

Art. 1751.   Disguised donations and donations to persons interposed

A donation of property that the donor will leave at his death is absolutely null if it is disguised or made to a person interposed to his spouse.

The following are reputed to be such person interposed:

(1) a child of the donee spouse who is not among the spouses' common children; or

(2) a person to whom the donee spouse is a presumptive successor at the time when the donation is made, even if the donee spouse does not thereafter survive that person.

Acts 2004, No. 619, § 1, eff. Sept. 1, 2005.

Arts. 1752 to 1755.   [Blank]

TITLE III—OBLIGATIONS IN GENERAL

CHAPTER 1—GENERAL PRINCIPLES

Art. 1756. Obligations; definition

An obligation is a legal relationship whereby a person, called the obligor, is bound to render a performance in favor of another, called the obligee. Performance may consist of giving, doing, or not doing something.

Acts 1984, No. 331, § 1, eff. Jan. 1, 1985.

REVISION COMMENTS—1984

(a) This definition is based on C.C. Arts. 1756, 1761, and 2132 (1870). It does not change the law.

(b) This Article makes it clear that an obligation is a legal relationship rather than a mere duty to perform. In the Louisiana Civil Code of 1870, "obligation," in general, is made synonymous with "duty," while a "civil" obligation is defined as a "legal tie." C.C. Arts. 1756 and 1757(3) (1870). This dual approach has been eliminated in this revision in order to confine the code definition to obligations that, whether civil or natural, are recognized at law.

(c) This Article follows the modern approach which views obligations as credit-rights. See 1 Litvinoff, Obligations 24–25 (1969). The terms "obligor", synonymous with debtor, and "obligee", synonymous with creditor, have accordingly been preserved. In the case of reciprocal obligations, such as those arising from a bilateral contract, the parties are reciprocally obligors and obligees.

Art. 1757. Sources of obligations

Obligations arise from contracts and other declarations of will. They also arise directly from the law, regardless of a declaration of will, in instances such as wrongful acts, the management of the affairs of another, unjust enrichment and other acts or facts.

Acts 1984, No. 331, § 1, eff. Jan. 1, 1985.

REVISION COMMENT—1984

This Article does not change the law. It reflects ideas previously contained in C.C. Arts. 1760, 2292, and 2300 (1870).

Art. 1758. General effects

A. An obligation may give the obligee the right to:

(1) Enforce the performance that the obligor is bound to render;

(2) Enforce performance by causing it to be rendered by another at the obligor's expense;

(3) Recover damages for the obligor's failure to perform, or his defective or delayed performance.

B. An obligation may give the obligor the right to:

(1) Obtain the proper discharge when he has performed in full;

(2) Contest the obligee's actions when the obligation has been extinguished or modified by a legal cause.

Acts 1984, No. 331, § 1, eff. Jan. 1, 1985.

REVISION COMMENTS—1984

(a) Although new, this Article does not change the law; it articulates ideas expressed in some Articles of the Louisiana Civil Code of 1870 and implied in others.

(b) The Article illustrates the basic rights that the creditor derives from an obligation. See C.C. Arts. 1926, 1927, 1928, and 1930 (1870). For a detailed discussion of the creditor's rights, see 2 Carbonnier, Droit Civil 503–509 (1957); 6 Demogue, Traité des obligations en général 6–59 (1931); 7 Planiol et Ripert, Traité pratique de droit civil français 79–80 (2nd ed. Esmein 1954).

(c) The Article also lists the basic rights of the debtor. These rights are certainly not novel; C.C. Art. 1934(4) (1870) places the creditor under a duty of good faith obviously correlative to the debtor's right, and the debtor's right to perform is implicit in C.C. Art. 2167 (1870).

Art. 1759. Good faith

Good faith shall govern the conduct of the obligor and the obligee in whatever pertains to the obligation.

Acts 1984, No. 331, § 1, eff. Jan. 1, 1985.

REVISION COMMENT—1984

This Article extends to obligations in general the principle of C.C. Art. 1901 (1870), which states that contracts must be performed in good faith.

CHAPTER 2—NATURAL OBLIGATIONS

Art. 1760. Moral duties that may give rise to a natural obligation

A natural obligation arises from circumstances in which the law implies a particular moral duty to render a performance.

Acts 1984, No. 331, § 1, eff. Jan. 1, 1985.

REVISION COMMENTS—1984

(a) Although this Article does not reproduce the substance of C.C. Art. 1757(1870), it does not change the law.

(b) In this revision the word "obligation", without more, is always synonymous with "civil obligation," that is, an obligation which is enforceable by legal action. The scope of the general term has been so much reduced in this revision that it is no longer necessary to insist that it always be preceded by the appropriate modifier.

(c) The reference to the enforceability of civil obligations found in C.C. Art. 1757(3) (1870) has been eliminated. That principle is stated in Chapter 1 of this Title.

(d) The category of "imperfect" obligations listed in C.C. Art. 1757(1) (1870) has been eliminated. If imperfect obligations have no legal effect there is no need for the Civil Code to grant them recognition. See, also, revised C.C. Art. 1756 (Rev.1984), supra, and the discussion of this subject in the Exposé des Motifs.

(e) The expression "binding . . . (in) conscience and according to natural justice," has been eliminated because of its strong philosophical overtones and replaced by the concept of legally recognized moral duty, which reflects the same idea in a more technical and practical way, and which is in keeping with modern doctrine. See Planiol, "Assimilation progressive de l'obligation naturelle et du devoir morale," 42 Revue critique de jurisprudence 157 (1913); Ripert, La règle morale dans les obligations civiles 186–395 (4th ed. 1949); 1 Litvinoff, Obligations 564–568 (1969).

Art. 1761. Effects of a natural obligation

A natural obligation is not enforceable by judicial action. Nevertheless, whatever has been freely performed in compliance with a natural obligation may not be reclaimed.

A contract made for the performance of a natural obligation is onerous.

Acts 1984, No. 331, § 1, eff. Jan. 1, 1985.

REVISION COMMENTS—1984

(a) This Article reproduces the substance of C.C. Art. 1759 (1870). It does not change the law.

(b) The word "freely" in the second sentence of this Article means that the performing party must have acted without outside compulsion by fraud or violence. It does not mean that his performance cannot have been induced by error; as under C.C. Art. 2303 (1870).

(c) This Article changes the language of C.C. Art. 1759(2) (1870), eliminating the word "consideration" in order to achieve a more consistent terminology. This formulation states the first effect of natural obligations in a manner that is more accurate in the light of the civilian tradition.

(d) This Article also states the second effect of natural obligations in a more accurate manner. A natural obligation renders onerous the cause of a promise to fulfill it, thus giving rise to an onerous contract and not to a donation. See Capitant, De la cause des obligations 6 (1923); Smith, "A Refresher Course in Cause", 12 La.L.Rev. 2, 4–9 (1951); 1 Litvinoff, Obligations 550–552 (1969).

Art. 1762. Examples of circumstances giving rise to a natural obligation

Examples of circumstances giving rise to a natural obligation are:

(1) When a civil obligation has been extinguished by prescription or discharged in bankruptcy.

(2) When an obligation has been incurred by a person who, although endowed with discernment, lacks legal capacity.

(3) When the universal successors are not bound by a civil obligation to execute the donations and other dispositions made by a deceased person that are null for want of form.

Acts 1984, No. 331, § 1, eff. Jan. 1, 1985.

REVISION COMMENTS—1984

(a) This Article reproduces the substance of C.C. Art. 1758 (1870). It does, however, change the law in part.

(b) The first sentence of this Article purports to solve a controversy well known in continental doctrine and Louisiana jurisprudence, that is, whether the list contained in C.C. Art. 1758 (1870) was intended to be exclusive or merely illustrative. See 7 Planiol et Ripert, Traité pratique de droit civil français, Part II, at 318 (2d ed. Esmein 1954); 1 Litvinoff, Obligations 610–618 (1969); Succession of Miller v. Manhattan Life Ins. Co., 110 La. 652, 34 So. 723 (1903); Atkins v. Commissioner of Internal Revenue, 30 F.2d 761 (5th Cir.1929). The flexible language used here indicates the illustrative character of the list. This is in accord with progressive continental doctrine, and also with later Louisiana jurisprudence. See Planiol et Ripert, supra, at 316–318; Ripert, La règle morale dans les obligations civiles 186–395 (4th ed. 1949); Succession of Scott, 231 La. 381, 91 So.2d 574 (1956); Succession of Gumbel, 220 La. 266, 56 So.2d 418 (1951); Irwin v. Hunnewell, 207 La. 422, 21 So.2d 485 (1945); White v. White, 7 So.2d 255 (La.App. 2nd Cir.1942). This formulation is intended to enhance the usefulness of the concept of natural obligation in distinguishing between mere generosity, which constitutes a gratuitous cause, and obedience to a moral duty, which may determine the cause as onerous. See Caron, Rapport général, 7 Travaux de l'association Henri Capitant 888–889 (1956); 1 Litvinoff, Obligations 564–568 and 615–618 (1969).

(c) Under the second paragraph of this Article, a performance of an obligation incurred by an incapable which is rendered after his incapacity has ended may not be reclaimed, and a contract reaffirming such an obligation which is made after the incapacity has ended is onerous. The legal representative of an incapable may not fulfill the natural obligation of the latter, however. In the absence of a natural obligation, when a party has rendered voluntary performance under a relatively null obligation, a determination must be made whether that performance constituted a tacit confirmation under revised C.C. Art. 1842 (Rev.1984), infra, which requires an intent to confirm.

(d) The references in the source Article to "reasons of general policy" and "obligations . . . which are not in themselves immoral or unjust" have been eliminated. They were derived from the natural law distinction between malum per se and malum prohibitum, which is not practical enough to be reflected in the positive law. See Perrillat v. Puech, 2 La. 428 (1831). Moreover, certain obligations that the law renders invalid for reasons of general policy, such as gambling debts and loans bearing usurious interest, should not be recognized as producing the two effects of validity of spontaneous performance and enforceability of a new promise. If a new promise were enforceable in such a situation, the general policy that lies at the foundation of the prohibition would be defeated. For this reason, a new promise is not enforceable under such circumstances. See Rosenda v. Zabriskie, 4 Rob. 493 (1843); Bagneris v. Smoot, 159 La. 1049, 106 So. 561 (1925); Whitesides v. McGrath, 15 La.Ann. 401 (1860). As to the validity of spontaneous performance under these circumstances, the centuries-old principle that no one may avail himself of his own wrongdoing, nemo propriam turpitudinem allegare potest; (clean hands rule), furnishes a more solid foundation, than the doctrine of natural obligations. See 1 Litvinoff, Obligations 573–574 (1969). See revised C.C. Art. 2033 (Rev.1984), infra.

CHAPTER 3—KINDS OF OBLIGATIONS

SECTION 1—REAL OBLIGATIONS

Art. 1763. Definition

A real obligation is a duty correlative and incidental to a real right.

Acts 1984, No. 331, § 1, eff. Jan. 1, 1985.

REVISION COMMENTS—1984

(a) This Article is new. It clarifies the law according to contemporary civilian doctrine.

(b) The classification of obligations as strictly personal, heritable, or real confuses the traditional notion of an obligation, which is a vinculum juris between two persons, with a real right, which is a right in a thing that can be held against the world. See 1 Yiannopoulos, Property 380 (2nd ed. 1980). Neither the French Civil Code nor any other modern Civil Code has established this classification. In this respect, the Louisiana Civil Code is entirely isolated in the civilian world. For historical reasons, the concept of real obligation has been preserved to avoid giving the impression that an important change in the law is intended. In a case decided in 1979, Hawthorne Oil and Gas Corporation v. Continental Oil Company, 368 So.2d 726 (La.App. 3rd Cir.1979), the court used the expression "real obligation" as referring to those obligations incurred as a result of ownership or possession of a thing burdened by a real right, which is precisely the manner in which a real obligation is defined in this Article.

Art. 1764. Effects of real obligation

A real obligation is transferred to the universal or particular successor who acquires the movable or immovable thing to which the obligation is attached, without a special provision to that effect.

But a particular successor is not personally bound, unless he assumes the personal obligations of his transferor with respect to the thing, and he may liberate himself of the real obligation by abandoning the thing.

Acts 1984, No. 331, § 1, eff. Jan. 1, 1985.

REVISION COMMENTS—1984

(a) This Article is new. It clarifies the law in the light of contemporary civilian doctrine and repeals C.C. Art. 2011 (1870).

(b) A real obligation attaches to a thing. Because a real obligation is a duty incidental and correlative to a real right, and because such a right may apply to both movables and immovables, a real obligation may attach either to a movable or an immovable. For example, when a movable is subject to a usufruct, the real obligation attaches to the movable; when an immovable is burdened with a predial servitude, the real obligation attaches to the immovable.

(c) A real obligation passes to a subsequent acquirer of the thing to which it is attached without need of a stipulation to that effect. Thus, when an estate burdened with a servitude is transferred, the real obligation that is correlative of the right of servitude is also transferred. See C.C. Art. 650(2) (Rev.1977). It is otherwise with respect to personal obligations.

(d) A particular successor, that is, one who acquires a thing by particular title, is not bound by the personal obligations of his author with respect to the thing, unless he has assumed these obligations by delegation. Conversely, a particular successor does not acquire, without stipulation to that effect, any personal rights that his author has with respect to the thing. For example, if the owner of an immovable who has made a contract for its repair sells the immovable, the purchaser is not bound to perform the obligation of the owner under the repair contract unless he assumes that obligation. Conversely, the purchaser does not acquire any right under the repair contract unless such a right is assigned to him. Civil Code Article 2011 (1870) has been suppressed because its provisions are conceptually inconsistent with other provisions of Louisiana law.

(e) Since a particular successor is bound by real obligations only, he may free himself by abandoning the thing. For example, the title establishing a predial servitude may provide that the owner of the servient estate is bound to construct at his expense works necessary for the exercise of the servitude. C.C. Art. 746 (Rev.1977). Although this duty to render a performance resembles a personal obligation, it does not generate personal responsibility. The obligor is not bound to the extent of his entire patrimony. He is merely bound as owner of a particular immovable, and he may avoid the obligation by abandoning or alienating that immovable. The debt owed to the mortgagee by one acquiring, by particular title, an immovable subject to a mortgage is also a real obligation for the acquirer. The acquirer of the immovable is not personally responsible for the debt, but if it is not paid he must suffer the consequences of a forced sale. His responsibility is limited to the immovable. See C.C. Art. 3405 (1870).

(f) Louisiana courts have held that the indemnity due to the owner of an immovable for the expropriation of a part of that immovable, and damages due to the owner of a thing for its partial destruction or for an interference with the owner's rights, belong to the person who was owner at the time of the expropriation, destruction, or interference. These are personal rights that are not transferred to a successor by particular title without a stipulation to that effect. Rogers v. Louisiana Power and Light Co., 391 So.2d 30 (La.App. 3rd Cir.1980); Yiannopoulos, Predial Servitudes § 147 (1983).

When the owner of the servient estate interferes with the servitude, he violates a real obligation, and may cause damage to the owner of the dominant estate. If the owner of the dominant estate sells it, the claim for damages still belongs to him. It is a personal right that does not pass with the immovable unless assigned. Conversely, when the owner of the dominant estate abuses the servient estate and causes damage, an indemnity may be due to the owner of the servient estate. If the servient estate is sold, the indemnity belongs to the vendor. It is a personal right that does not pass with the immovable unless assigned. See Dunlap v. Red River Waterway Commission, 405 So.2d 655 (La.App. 3rd Cir.1981); Dickson v. Arkansas Louisiana Gas Co., 193 So. 246 (La.App. 2nd Cir.1939); Yiannopoulos, Predial Servitudes § 157 (1983). In contrast, the obligation to demolish works and to restore the premises to their previous condition is a real obligation, following the immovable into the hands of any acquirer. Id.; 3 Planiol et Ripert, Traité pratique de droit civil français 966 (2d ed. Picard 1952).

(g) Civil Code Articles 2011–2014 and 2016–2019 (1870) have not been reproduced because they are unnecessary in light of other provisions of the Civil Code. Civil Code Article 2015 (1870) has also been eliminated without intending any change in the law. That no one may transfer a greater right than he has is a conclusion that results from general principles. And C.C. Art. 2733 (1870) suffices to explain that a lease of immovable property also binds a subsequent acquirer of the property if the lease is recorded.

SECTION 2—STRICTLY PERSONAL AND HERITABLE OBLIGATIONS

Art. 1765. Heritable obligation

An obligation is heritable when its performance may be enforced by a successor of the obligee or against a successor of the obligor.

Every obligation is deemed heritable as to all parties, except when the contrary results from the terms or from the nature of the contract.

A heritable obligation is also transferable between living persons.

Acts 1984, No. 331, § 1, eff. Jan. 1, 1985.

REVISION COMMENTS—1984

(a) This Article reproduces the substance of C.C. Arts. 1997, 1999, and 2009 (1870). It does not change the law.

(b) Under this Article, an obligation is heritable when it is transferable mortis causa. "Transferable" is a better word than "heritable" for the purposes of this Article. See 1 Yiannopoulos, Property, 370 (2nd ed. 1980). The word "heritable," however, has been preserved because of its well-established position in the Louisiana legal system. The word "transferable" is used, nevertheless, in the context of the assignment of a right arising from a particular obligation.

Art. 1766. Strictly personal obligation

An obligation is strictly personal when its performance can be enforced only by the obligee, or only against the obligor.

When the performance requires the special skill or qualification of the obligor, the obligation is presumed to be strictly personal on the part of the obligor. All obligations to perform personal services are presumed to be strictly personal on the part of the obligor.

When the performance is intended for the benefit of the obligee exclusively, the obligation is strictly personal on the part of that obligee.

Acts 1984, No. 331, § 1, eff. Jan. 1, 1985.

REVISION COMMENTS—1984

(a) This Article reproduces the substance of C.C. Arts. 1997, 2000, and 2001 (1870). It does not change the law.

(b) A particular skill is not the only feature of an obligor that may make his obligation strictly personal. A certain social status or professional standing may also be such a feature. The expression "a special qualification of the obligor" is used in this Article to convey this idea.

(c) In Louisiana jurisprudence, the obligation to fulfill a marriage engagement is personal, and the obligation to respond in damages for nonperformance is incidental thereto; if the obligor dies before fulfilling his engagement, the right of action perishes with him. Johnson v. Levy, 118 La. 447, 43 So. 46 (1907). The obligation of a musician under a contract to record music is personal to him. Fletcher v. Rachou, 323 So.2d 163 (La.App. 3rd Cir.1975). A contract for dancing lessons gives rise to an obligation that is personal to the intended recipient of the lessons. Acosta v. Cole, 178 So.2d 456 (La.App. 1st Cir.1965), writ refused 248 La. 432, 433, 179 So.2d 273, 274 (1965); but see Richardson v. Cole, 173 So.2d 336 (La.App. 2nd Cir.1965), where it was asserted that obligations arising from such a contract are personal as to both the obligor and the obligee.

(d) Civil Code Articles 2002 and 2003 (1870) have been eliminated, but without changing the law. The theory of cause and some of its more important consequences, such as the recoverability of a payment of a thing not due and the availability of compensation for unjust enrichment, are more than sufficient to arrive at the solutions contemplated in those Articles.

(e) Civil Code Article 2007 (1870) has been eliminated, first, because the rule it contained is now incorporated into the second paragraph of this Article (see Succession of Zatarain, 138 So.2d 163 (La.App. 1st Cir.1962)) and second, because the 1982 amendment to C.C. Art. 2826 rendered the reference to partnership in C.C. Art. 2007 (1870) inaccurate.

(f) Civil Code Articles 2008 and 2009 (1870) have been eliminated as unnecessary. The conclusions that they contain can be reached on the basis of general principles.

(g) Civil Code Articles 2004, 2005, and 2006 (1870) have been transferred and redesignated as R.S. 9:2785, 2786, and 2787. See Section 4 of this Act.

400

SECTION 3—CONDITIONAL OBLIGATIONS

Art. 1767. Suspensive and resolutory condition

A conditional obligation is one dependent on an uncertain event.

If the obligation may not be enforced until the uncertain event occurs, the condition is suspensive.

If the obligation may be immediately enforced but will come to an end when the uncertain event occurs, the condition is resolutory.

Acts 1984, No. 331, § 1, eff. Jan. 1, 1985.

REVISION COMMENTS—1984

(a) This Article reproduces the substance of C.C. Arts. 2020, 2021, 2043, and 2045 (1870). It does not change the law.

(b) Civil Code Article 2028 (1870), was taken from Toullier. See 3 Toullier, Le droit civil français 503 (1833). It has been eliminated because it is too obvious. Civil Code Article 2029 (1870) has been eliminated for the same reason.

(c) Civil Code Article 2030 (1870) has also been eliminated. That Article is at once obvious and obscure. It is obscure because the English version expresses exactly the opposite of the original French text. See 3 Louisiana Legal Archives Part II, at 1118 (1942). See also 3 Toullier, Le droit civil français 504 (1833), from which this provision was taken literally. The French text provided that the right acquired by a legatee under a conditional bequest does not pass to the heirs of the legatee upon his death if the condition is then unfulfilled and is an act personal to the legatee, which is consistent with general principles. A contrario then, the right does pass to the heirs of the legatee when the condition is an act which is not personal to the legatee. This is consistent with C.C. Arts. 1698 and 1699 (1870). Since both these rules can easily be derived from more general ones, C.C. Art. 2030 (1870) is obvious.

(d) Under this Article, as under the source articles, a "conditional obligation" may be any kind of obligation, and not only one created by contract. Very modern codes such as the Italian and the Ethiopian have confined conditions to contract. Even C.C. Arts. 2028, 2038, and 2039 (1870) contemplate conditions from a contractual perspective. Indeed, it cannot be denied that in the vast majority of instances a condition results from a contractual stipulation. In view of Louisiana legal experience, however, this Article views conditions as affecting obligations in general. In Hebert v. Claude Y. Woolfolk Corp., 176 So.2d 814 (La.App. 3rd Cir.1965), the court made its judgment conditional on the prevailing party's compliance with an order of the court, demonstrating that the operative sphere of conditions exceeds that of contract. Furthermore, civil codes of the German family deal with conditions in that part reserved for the treatment of juridical acts in general. See Litvinoff & Tête, Louisiana Legal Transactions: The Civil Law of Juridical Acts 156–159 (1969).

(e) Under this Article, a condition need not be a future event. Though a condition has universally been defined as a future and uncertain event on which the origination or extinction of an obligation depends (and C.C. Art. 2043 (1870) defines a suspensive condition in those terms),

C.C. Art. 2021 (1870), describes a conditional obligation as one which depends merely on an uncertain event. Moreover, C.C. Art. 2043 (1870), following Article 1181 of the Code Napoleon, alludes to uncertainty as to an event that has already occurred. That approach has been criticized by an important portion of French doctrine. See 7 Planiol et Ripert, Traité pratique de droit civil français 370–371 (2nd ed. Esmein 1954). In more recent civilian doctrine, however, the principle of C.C. Art. 2043 (1870) has been recognized as useful, though with the qualification that in such a case the true "event" upon which the condition depends is the advent of some proof that a past event has actually occurred. See 1 De Gasperi & Morello, Derecho civil 290–291 (1964); see also 5 Merlin, Répertoire universel et raisonné de jurisprudence, Conditions 373 (5th ed. 1825).

(f) This Article does not provide a definition of "condition," but instead defines "conditional obligation." The expression "uncertain event" is flexible enough to encompass an act of a party, especially an act that is enforceable under the contract. This approach has been taken because, in spite of its technical and practical importance, the word "condition" is used differently in different

401

contexts. According to Corbin, "The word 'condition' is used in the law of property as well as in the law of contract and it is used with some variation in meaning. In the law of contract, it is sometimes used in a very loose sense as synonymous with 'term,' 'provision,' or 'clause.' In such sense it performs no useful service; instead, it affords one more opportunity for slovenly thinking. In its proper sense the word 'condition' means some operative fact subsequent to acceptance and prior to discharge, a fact upon which the rights and duties of the parties depend. Such a fact may be an act of one of the two contracting parties, an act of a third party, or any other fact of our physical world. It may be a performance that has been promised or a fact as to which there is no promise." Corbin, "Conditions in the Law of Contract," in Selected Readings on the Law of Contracts 871, 875 (1931). See also, Ashley "Conditions in Contract," Id. at 866 (1931).

It is also quite common to refer to a legal requirement as a "condition". This is the "legal condition" or conditio legis, which, in the mind of Planiol, is a misuse of the word. See 7 Planiol et Ripert, Traité pratique de droit civil français 370–371 (2nd ed. Esmein 1954); see also Litvinoff & Tête, Louisiana Legal Transactions: The Civil Law of Juridical Acts 156–159 (1969). The use of "condition" to signify a performance by one of the parties is also misleading, especially when that performance is enforceable under the agreement. That is the fallacy of the common law expression "conditional sales." See 2 Litvinoff, Obligations 91–96 and 104–110 (1975). The same fallacy taints the "implied resolutory condition" in Civil Code Article 2046 (1870).

Contemporary civilian doctrine, returning to ideas originally expressed by Savigny and further expounded by Winscheid, views a "condition" not as an outside event but as a psychological process whereby the parties impose upon themselves a certain limitation of their will. See 1 De Gasperi & Morello, Derecho civil 284–285 (1964).

Art. 1768.   Expressed and implied conditions

Conditions may be either expressed in a stipulation or implied by the law, the nature of the contract, or the intent of the parties.

Acts 1984, No. 331, § 1, eff. Jan. 1, 1985.

This Article reproduces the substance of C.C. Art. 2026 (1870). It does not change the law. Civil Code Article 2026 (1870) has no equivalent in the Code Napoleon. Its text was taken from Toullier. See 3 Toullier, Le droit civil français 511 (1833). It is an interesting and practical article that may be regarded as one of the fine peculiarities of the Louisiana Civil Code of 1870. Many present articles, including C.C. Arts. 2450, 2460 and 2461 (1870), contain examples of implied conditions. It thus seemed worthwhile to preserve the principle. It is noteworthy that implied conditions have given rise to an important contractual doctrine at common law. See Sturge, "The Doctrine of Implied Condition," Selected Readings on the Law of Contracts 896 (1931).

Art. 1769.   Unlawful or impossible condition

A suspensive condition that is unlawful or impossible makes the obligation null.

Acts 1984, No. 331, § 1, eff. Jan. 1, 1985.

(a) This Article reproduces the substance of C.C. Art. 2031 (1870). It does not change the law. The last words of C.C. Art. 2031 (1870) clearly indicate that only unlawful or impossible conditions that are suspensive make an obligation null. If such a condition is resolutory, the policy reasons calling for nullity are absent. In such a case, the general principles of the law of obligations apply, and if the obligation to which the condition is attached is otherwise valid, the condition is regarded as not written. See Italian Civil Code Article 1354.

(b) This Article formulates a rule that governs obligations in general. The general rule yields to exceptions expressly provided by the law, as in the case of an unlawful or impossible condition attached to a donation inter vivos or mortis causa. C.C. Art. 1519 (1870). See also French Civil Code Article 900; and 7 Planiol et Ripert, Traité pratique de droit civil français 375 (2nd ed. Esmein 1954).

(c) Civil Code Article 2032 (1870) has been eliminated as too obvious to need stating.

(d) Civil Code Article 2033 (1870) has been eliminated because it reflects a wrong approach; that is, it regards a condition as a performance that can be enforced. See Comment (f) to revised C.C. Art. 1767 (Rev.1984), supra.

Art. 1770. Condition that depends on the whim or the will of the obligor

A suspensive condition that depends solely on the whim of the obligor makes the obligation null.

A resolutory condition that depends solely on the will of the obligor must be fulfilled in good faith.

Acts 1984, No. 331, § 1, eff. Jan. 1, 1985.

REVISION COMMENTS—1984

(a) This Article reproduces the substance of C.C. Arts. 2024, 2034, and 2035 (1870). It does not change the law.

(b) Under this Article, a condition that depends upon an event that is left to the obligor's whim makes an obligation null only when that condition is suspensive. The obligation is not null if the condition is resolutory.

(c) A condition involving an event left to the obligee's whim does not make the obligation null. See C.C. Arts. 2034 and 2036 (1870); see also S. Gumbel Realty and Securities Co., Inc. v. Levy, 156 So. 70 (La.App.Orl.1934).

(d) An event which is left to the obligor's whim is one whose occurrence depends entirely on his will, such as his wishing or not wishing something. See 1 Pothier, A Treatise on the Law of Obligations or Contracts 114–115 (Evans translation 1806). An event is not left to an obligor's whim when it is one that he may or may not bring about after a considered weighing of interests, such as his entering a contract with a third party. See C.C. Art. 2035 (1870); Long v. Foster & Associates, Inc., 242 La. 295, 136 So.2d 48 (1961); Humble Oil & Refining Co. v. Guillory et al., 212 La. 646, 33 So.2d 182 (1946).

(e) This Article eliminates the expression "potestative condition" because the Louisiana jurisprudence has been plagued by misinterpretations of it. This Article recasts the concepts expressed in Articles 2024, 2034, and 2035 of the Louisiana Civil Code of 1870 in terms of an implicit dichotomy between the obligor's "whim," that is, his exercise of mere unbridled discretion or arbitrariness (see Administrative Procedure Act, 5 U.S.C. § 706, and Article 903 of the German Buürgerliches Gesetzbuch) and his "judgment" or exercise of a considered and reasonable discretion. Thus, in the traditional example, an obligation to buy a house if the obligor moves to Paris is valid rather than null because it is assumed that moving to Paris or not will be decided according to serious reasons such as obtaining a position there or securing admission to a school in that city. It is assumed, in other words, that the obligor will not decide not to move to Paris for the sole purpose of deceiving the other party. See 3 Toullier, Le droit civil français 508–509 (1833); see also 7 Planiol et Ripert, Traité pratique de droit civil français 376–377 (2nd ed. Esmein 1954).

(f) Under the second paragraph of this Article, a resolutory condition that depends solely on the obligor's will must be fulfilled in good faith, but does not make the obligation null. Thus, a "termination at will" clause is not necessarily null if the right to terminate is exercised in good faith. Nevertheless, doing some violence to the language of the Louisiana Civil Code of 1870, Louisiana courts have sometimes characterized such clauses as "potestative conditions" of the kind that make the obligation null. Thus, on rehearing in Caddo Oil & Mining Co. v. Producers' Oil Co., 134 La. 701, 64 So. 684, 687 (1914), the court dealt with the following clause: "It is expressly understood that the second party (lessee) reserves the right to abandon said premises . . . whenever it desires to cease operations, and to remove all property placed thereon (by it), at its discretion." The court concluded, "(T)he condition . . . is clearly potestative; that is to say, it made the execution of the contract depend upon the will of the (lessee), thereby destroying the obligation (imposed upon him), which was the 'legal tie' that gave . . . (the lessor) the right to enforce the contract, . . . (from which) it follows that, there being no obligation resting upon the lessee, and hence no consideration moving to the lessor, there was no contract." Id. at 688. That conclusion was reached in spite of the fact that the defendant-lessee had drilled wells, paid royalties promptly, and expended large sums in exploring the field. See also Murray v. Barnhart, 117 La. 1023, 42 So. 489 (1906), where the payment of $2 for the right to cancel was not regarded as a "serious" consideration, applying C.C. Art. 2464 (1870) by analogy. In another line of cases, however, the courts have refused to characterize a clause whereby the lease would terminate upon the lessee's failure to pay taxes as a potestative condition that makes the obligation null. See McCain v. Continental Can Company, 299 So.2d 454 (La.App. 2nd Cir.1974); Rome v. New River Lodge No. 402, F. & A.M., 197 So. 174 (La.App. 1st Cir.1940). See also Moses, "Potestative Conditions in Louisiana Oil, Gas and Mineral Leases," 16 Tul.L.Rev. 80 (1941). In still another line of cases, Louisiana courts, for unfathomable reasons, have confused agreements not to compete with "termination at will" clauses and declared such agreements invalid on grounds of "potestativeness." See Blanchard v. Haber, 163 La. 627, 112 So. 509 (1927); Shreveport Laundries, Inc. v. Teagle, 139 So. 563 (La.App. 2nd Cir. 1932).

In modern law, the enforceability of termination clauses often depends upon whether a party attempts to avail itself of the clause before or after performance has started. In the latter situation, the clause is recognized as valid and is enforced; in the former there is a violation of the overriding obligation of good faith and, therefore, a breach of contract. That approach has been explored in depth in Sylvan Crest Sand & Gravel v. United States, 150 F.2d 642 (2nd Cir. 1945). In a Roman law perspective, it can be said that what that approach truly means is that a resolutory condition should not be misused by a party as a suspensive condition.

Practical reasons prevent the conclusion that a resolutory condition that depends on the will of the obligor should always make the obligation null. Thus, in a simple sale where the vendee reserves the choice of paying the price or returning the thing, it is clear that there is a resolutory condition that depends on the will of the vendee, who is obligor of the obligation to pay the price. Neither the contract nor the vendee's obligation is null in such a case, however. Cf. C.C. Art. 2567 (1870). On the other hand, a "termination at will" clause in a contract of long duration may be a fair clause properly bargained for or a trap set by the party with the greater bargaining power. The requirement of good faith stated in the second paragraph of this Article affords the protection needed by the victimized party in the latter kind of situation, and gives the courts necessary discretion to decide when to invoke it. For particular problems, such as dealerships and franchises, 15 U.S.C.A. § 1222 provides particular solutions, though along the same line.

In the second paragraph of this Article, the word "will" is used rather than "whim", the term used in the first paragraph. Once performance of an obligation starts, it does not seem realistic to say that termination is dependent on the "whim" of a party. No doubt some practical considerations are bound to inform his "will", especially if the obligation arises from a bilateral contract.

In order to comply with the requirement of good faith, a party exercising his right to terminate a contract at will should consider not only his own advantage, but also the hardship to which the other party will be subjected because of the termination. Thus, a party to a requirements contract that chooses to terminate it because he has an opportunity to sell the same things elsewhere at a higher profit could violate the good faith requirement if the other party cannot find an alternative source of supply. Likewise, termination because of purely personal rather than business reasons could constitute bad faith. Cf. Corenswet v. Amana Refrigeration, Inc., 594 F.2d 129 (5th Cir.1979), cert. denied, 444 U.S. 938 (1979); Lee Lumber Company, L.T.D. v. International Paper Company, 321 So.2d 42 (La.App.3d Cir.1975); Long v. Foster & Associates, Inc., 242 La. 295, 136 So.2d 48 (La.1961). See also the useful discussion concerning franchise agreements in Sanders, "'At Will' Franchise Terminations and the Abuse of Rights Doctrine: The Maturation of Louisiana Law," 42 La.L.Rev. 210 (1981). If termination is improper under this article, the court may order either continuation of performance for the reasonable time necessary for the other party to overcome the hardship, or may grant damages to the party harmed by the termination. Damages should be assessed on the basis of an estimation of the reasonable duration of the contract had it not been terminated in bad faith.

For employment contracts, see Comment (c) to C.C. Art. 2024 (Rev.1984), infra.

Art. 1771. Obligee's right pending condition

The obligee of a conditional obligation, pending fulfillment of the condition, may take all lawful measures to preserve his right.

Acts 1984, No. 331, § 1, eff. Jan. 1, 1985.

REVISION COMMENT—1984

This Article reproduces the substance of C.C. Art. 2042 (1870). It does not change the law.

Art. 1772. Fault of a party

A condition is regarded as fulfilled when it is not fulfilled because of the fault of a party with an interest contrary to the fulfillment.

Acts 1984, No. 331, § 1, eff. Jan. 1, 1985.

REVISION COMMENTS—1984

(a) This Article reproduces the substance of C.C. Art. 2040 (1870). It changes the law only insofar as it expands the principle of the source Article in order to make it encompass the fault of either party rather than the fault of the obligor alone.

(b) A condition is regarded as fulfilled, and the obligation which is dependent upon it becomes pure and simple, if the operative event specified in the condition is prevented from happening through some fault of the obligor. In the common situation of an agreement to purchase subject to the prospective vendee's securing financing, the vendee might "prevent" the happening of the condition by not applying for credit. But if his failure to do so were caused by illness or some other fortuitous event, the condition would not be regarded as fulfilled.

(c) When a suspensive condition is regarded as fulfilled, the conditional obligation becomes enforceable. Nevertheless, the party not at fault may have to content himself with damages rather than specific performance if the latter has become impossible because of the nonfulfillment of the condition.

(d) Civil Code Article 2037 (1870) has been eliminated. The statement it contained is a clear consequence of the overriding duty of good faith that parties owe each other.

Art. 1773. Time for fulfillment of condition that an event shall occur

If the condition is that an event shall occur within a fixed time and that time elapses without the occurrence of the event, the condition is considered to have failed.

If no time has been fixed for the occurrence of the event, the condition may be fulfilled within a reasonable time.

Whether or not a time has been fixed, the condition is considered to have failed once it is certain that the event will not occur.

Acts 1984, No. 331, § 1, eff. Jan. 1, 1985.

REVISION COMMENTS—1984

(a) This Article reproduces the substance of C.C. Art. 2038 (1870). It changes the law insofar as it provides that, if no time has been fixed for the event to occur, it must occur within a reasonable time.

(b) This Article preserves the basic principle of the source Article. The only change is the limitation of the time allowed for fulfillment of a condition when no time has been fixed. Following the classical approach, C.C. Art. 2038 (1870) provides that in such a case "the condition may always be performed." This suggests that parties could be bound under condition for life, or even for generations on end, which is not practical. Strikingly enough, most French writers, including Planiol, have entirely ignored this matter. Pothier, however, faced it, though very briefly, arriving at the conclusion that when the condition is simply potestative on the part of the obligor, the obligee has the power to address the court and request that a time be fixed. 1 Pothier, A Treatise on the Law of Obligations or Contracts 120 (Evans trans. 1806). In modern times, Baudry-Lacantinerie has reached the same conclusion. 13 Baudry-Lacantinerie et Barde, Traité theorique et pratique de droit civil 29–32 (3rd ed. 1907). That conclusion is reasonable and has therefore been adopted.

Art. 1774. Time for fulfillment of condition that an event shall not occur

If the condition is that an event shall not occur within a fixed time, it is considered as fulfilled once that time has elapsed without the event having occurred.

The condition is regarded as fulfilled whenever it is certain that the event will not occur, whether or not a time has been fixed.

Acts 1984, No. 331, § 1, eff. Jan. 1, 1985.

REVISION COMMENT—1984

This Article reproduces the substance of C.C. Art. 2039 (1870). It does not change the law.

Art. 1775. Effects retroactive

Fulfillment of a condition has effects that are retroactive to the inception of the obligation. Nevertheless, that fulfillment does not impair the validity of acts of administration duly performed by a party, nor affect the ownership of fruits produced while the condition was pending. Likewise, fulfillment of the condition does not impair the right acquired by third persons while the condition was pending.

Acts 1984, No. 331, § 1, eff. Jan. 1, 1985.

REVISION COMMENTS—1984

(a) This Article reproduces the substance of C.C. Art. 2041 (1870). It expresses certain limitations on that principle that have been generally recognized. It does not change the law. See 7 Planiol et Ripert, Traité pratique de droit civil français 395–398 (2nd ed. Esmein 1954); Wampler v. Wampler, 239 La. 315, 118 So.2d 423 (1960); Ober v. Williams, 213 La. 568, 35 So.2d 219 (1948).

(b) The last sentence of this Article is only a consequence of general principle. In expressly protecting the rights of third persons against retroactive effects of the fulfillment of a condition, this Article is consistent with revised C.C. Arts. 1844, 2021, 2028, and 2035 (Rev.1984), infra. Where immovable property is concerned, any conflict must be resolved in light of the public records doctrine.

Art. 1776. Contract for continuous or periodic performance

In a contract for continuous or periodic performance, fulfillment of a resolutory condition does not affect the validity of acts of performance rendered before fulfillment of the condition.

Acts 1984, No. 331, § 1, eff. Jan. 1, 1985.

REVISION COMMENT—1984

This Article is new, but it does not change the law. It expresses an idea implied in C.C. Article 1899 (1870), and states another natural limitation to the principle of retroactivity of the effects of the fulfillment of a condition.

SECTION 4—OBLIGATIONS WITH A TERM

Art. 1777. Express or implied term

A term for the performance of an obligation may be express or it may be implied by the nature of the contract.

Performance of an obligation not subject to a term is due immediately.

Acts 1984, No. 331, § 1, eff. Jan. 1, 1985.

REVISION COMMENTS—1984

(a) This Article reproduces the substance of C.C. Arts. 2048, 2049, and 2050 (1870). It does not change the law.

(b) The word "term" does not actually convey the intended meaning: a period allowed for the performance of an obligation. The French "terme" suffers from the same ambiguity. French doctrine has slowly evolved in favor of the word "délai". Yet, "délai", like its English equivalent delay, suggests unwarranted procrastination. In spite of the word's shortcomings, this Article uses "term" because in traditional doctrine "term" and "condition" are the two modalities of obligation. The last clause of C.C.

406

Art. 2049 (1870) has been suppressed because it adds nothing to the definition of an obligation subject to a term. It merely endeavors to make a comparison with conditional obligations.

(c) Under this Article, performance of an obligation not subject to a term is due immediately. Nevertheless, the obligee must allow the obligor a period of time to complete the performance that is commensurate with its nature, for instance, the time necessary to wrap or crate a thing bought for on-the-spot delivery. The need for a putting in default in that kind of situation is governed by revised C.C. Art. 1990 (Rev.1984), infra, dealing with Putting in Default.

(d) The "term" defined in this Article is the "suspensive term." See 7 Planiol et Ripert, Traité pratique de droit civil français 336 (2nd ed. Esmein 1954); Jean-Louis Baudouin, Traité élémentaire de droit civil-Les obligations 317 (1970). The "resolutory" term, or time of duration of an obligation, is actually one of the means by which obligations are extinguished. The expression: "The time . . . limited for . . ." performance which is used in C.C. Art. 2048 (1870) describes the resolutory term.

Art. 1778. Term for performance

A term for the performance of an obligation is a period of time either certain or uncertain. It is certain when it is fixed. It is uncertain when it is not fixed but is determinable either by the intent of the parties or by the occurrence of a future and certain event. It is also uncertain when it is not determinable, in which case the obligation must be performed within a reasonable time.

Acts 1984, No. 331, § 1, eff. Jan. 1, 1985.

REVISION COMMENTS—1984

(a) This Article reproduces part of the substance of C.C. Art. 2050 (1870). It does not change the law. The Louisiana jurisprudence has repeatedly asserted that where no time is fixed, an obligation must be performed within a reasonable time. See Conques v. Andrus, 162 La. 73, 110 So. 93 (1926); Perrin v. Hellback, 296 So.2d 342 (La.App. 4th Cir.1974), writ denied 300 So.2d 184 (La.1974); Richard v. Food & Services, Inc., 162 So.2d 213 (La.App. 1st Cir.1964), writ denied, 246 La. 347, 164 So.2d 351 (La.1964).

(b) Under this Article, a term may be fixed not only by a period of time allowed for the performance of an obligation but also by an event which is certain, such as a person's death. See C.C. Art. 2049 (1870).

(c) Situations where no date for performance has been fixed are common not only when a term is implied but also when a term is express. Lacking clear guidance from the 1870 Code, the Louisiana courts have developed the "reasonable time" rule presented in this Article. Rabin v. Whitney, 347 So.2d 1253 (La.App. 1st Cir.1977); Luna v. Atchafalaya Realty, 325 So.2d 835 (La.App. 1st Cir.1976); Bagby v. Clark, 327 So.2d 633 (La.App. 4th Cir.1976); Everhardt v. Sighinolfi, 232 La. 996, 95 So.2d 632 (1957). This jurisprudential rule has been applied to the term of duration, or extinctive term, as well as to the suspensive term. See Caston v. Woman's Hospital Foundation, Inc., 262 So.2d 62 (La.App. 1st Cir.1972), writ denied 262 La. 1087, 266 So.2d 220 (La.1972). The Italian Civil Code permits either party to have the court fix a specific deadline for performance in such cases. Though this Article does not expressly authorize such requests, it could be interpreted as permitting them when warranted.

(d) Under this Article, a time for performance is implied when, though not fixed, it is clearly indicated by the circumstances. Thus, if a wedding dress is ordered and the obligor is advised of the date of the wedding, performance is due no later than that date even though the latter has not been fixed as the time for performance.

(e) Under this Article, performance is due within a reasonable time when it is neither expected immediately by the obligee nor due at a certain time. Thus, an obligation to deliver a crop which was promised while still growing is due a reasonable time after the crop has been harvested.

Art. 1779. Term presumed to benefit the obligor

A term is presumed to benefit the obligor unless the agreement or the circumstances show that it was intended to benefit the obligee or both parties.

Acts 1984, No. 331, § 1, eff. Jan. 1, 1985.

REVISION COMMENTS—1984

(a) This Article reproduces the substance of C.C. Art. 2053 (1870). It does not change the law.

(b) A term may benefit the obligee as well as the obligor. See Eugster v. West, 35 La.Ann. 119 (1883).

Art. 1780. Renunciation of a term

The party for whose exclusive benefit a term has been established may renounce it.

Acts 1984, No. 331, § 1, eff. Jan. 1, 1985.

REVISION COMMENTS—1984

(a) This Article is new. It does not change the law, however. It expresses a principle implied in C.C. Arts. 11 and 1901 (1870).

(b) This Article asserts a principle that seems unquestionable. It also reflects the very common contemporary practice of including pre-payment clauses in loan agreements. In Louisiana jurisprudence a term or condition can be waived by a party for whose benefit it has been established. See Morrison v. Mioton, 163 La. 1065, 113 So. 456 (1927); Bach v. Slidell, 1 La.Ann. 375 (1846).

Art. 1781. Performance before end of term

Although performance cannot be demanded before the term ends, an obligor who has performed voluntarily before the term ends may not recover the performance.

Acts 1984, No. 331, § 1, eff. Jan. 1, 1985.

REVISION COMMENTS—1984

(a) This Article reproduces the substance of C.C. Art. 2052 (1870). It does not change the law.

(b) Under this Article, a performance rendered before the expiration of the term governing it must be rendered voluntarily, that is, out of free will not vitiated by duress, error, or fraud, or it is recoverable. Since payment is a juridical act, its validity depends on the existence of a valid consent, that is, consent free from vice. That is what the word "voluntarily" is intended to convey in this Article, in contrast to the meaning of the word "freely" as used in revised C.C. Art. 1761 (Rev. 1984), supra.

(c) The Louisiana jurisprudence does not offer any decision contrary to the rule of this Article.

Art. 1782. If the obligor is insolvent

When the obligation is such that its performance requires the solvency of the obligor, the term is regarded as nonexistent if the obligor is found to be insolvent.

Acts 1984, No. 331, § 1, eff. Jan. 1, 1985.

REVISION COMMENTS—1984

(a) This Article reproduces the substance of C.C. Art. 2054 (1870). It does not change the law.

(b) Under this Article, if an obligor must be solvent in order to perform, as is the case if the obligation is to pay a sum of money or to transfer property which forms a part of the obligor's assets, the term is regarded as nonexistent if the obligor's liabilities exceed his assets. The term may not be so regarded when the contemplated performance does not require solvency, as in the case of an obligation to render services.

(c) Bankruptcy of the obligor is governed by federal law. See Title 11 of the United States Code.

(d) An obligor's insolvency must be judicially declared for this Article to take effect. Insolvency in fact, i.e., a momentary or short-term imbalance of accounts, would not mature a debt subject to a term. See Kleinwort v. Klingender, 14 La.Ann. 96 (1859); Atwill v. Belden and Co., 1 La. 500 (1830); Succ. of Gravolet, 195 La. 832, 197 So. 572 (1940).

Art. 1783.   Impairment or failure of security

When the obligation is subject to a term and the obligor fails to furnish the promised security, or the security furnished becomes insufficient, the obligee may require that the obligor, at his option, either perform the obligation immediately or furnish sufficient security. The obligee may take all lawful measures to preserve his right.

Acts 1984, No. 331, § 1, eff. Jan. 1, 1985.

REVISION COMMENTS—1984

(a) This Article is based on C.C. Arts. 2055 and 2488 (1870). It changes the law in part, giving to the obligor the choice that the source article seemed to give the obligee.

(b) Under this Article, if security given by an obligor has failed or has become insufficient, as when pledged shares of stock have significantly decreased in value, the obligee may give the obligor the choice of either improving the security or performing the obligation at once.

(c) Under this Article, an obligee may stop goods in transit as a means of preserving his right. See C.C. Art. 2488 (1870). See also Blum & Co. v. Marks, 21 La.Ann. 268 (1869); Alice v. Taca International Airlines, 134 So.2d 922 (La.App. 4th Cir.1961). He may also enjoin the obligor from doing an act that would impair his right. See Code of Civil Procedure Articles 3601–3606.

(d) The obligation may remain subject to the term if the obligor cures the impairment of the security to the obligee's satisfaction.

(e) This Article should be particularly useful in commercial transactions. A healthy commercial life demands a continuing sense of reliance and security that promised performances will be forthcoming when due. If either the willingness or ability of a party to perform declines materially between the time of contracting and the time for performance, the other party is threatened with loss of a substantial part of his bargain. This Article provides a hedge against such eventualities. See U.C.C. § 2–609, notes 1–3. See also 4 Carbonnier, Droit Civil § 61, at 212 (9th ed. 1976).

Art. 1784.   Term for performance not fixed

When the term for performance of an obligation is not marked by a specific date but is rather a period of time, the term begins to run on the day after the contract is made, or on the day after the occurrence of the event that marks the beginning of the term, and it includes the last day of the period.

Acts 1984, No. 331, § 1, eff. Jan. 1, 1985.

REVISION COMMENTS—1984

(a) This Article reproduces the substance of C.C. Art. 2058 (1870). It changes the law only in that it eliminates sunset of the last day as the limitation of the useful time to perform. In the atomic age, the reference to "sunset" seems as anachronistic as the equally romantic common law reference to "midnight" of the last day for the same purpose. See Richardson v. American Nat. Ins. Co., 137 So. 370 (1931).

(b) Under this Article, the obligor may perform until that moment of the last day which, according to usage and the next Article, is useful for business.

Art. 1785.   Performance on term

Performance on term must be in accordance with the intent of the parties, or with established usage when the intent cannot be ascertained.

Acts 1984, No. 331, § 1, eff. Jan. 1, 1985.

REVISION COMMENTS—1984

(a) This Article is new. It does not change the law, however, but expresses an idea implicit in C.C. Arts. 21, 1966, 2057, 2058, 2060, and 2061 (1870).

(b) Civil Code Articles 2057, 2058, 2059, 2060, and 2061 (1870) have no equivalent in the Code Napoleon. They were introduced in the revision of 1825. See 3 Louisiana Legal Archives, Part II, at 1132–1133 (1942).

(c) This Article enhances the importance of the parties' intent in a manner consistent with the general principle that a condition must be fulfilled as the parties intended. The last moment at which performance is still timely is a matter to be governed by usage. That is also true of the manner of counting periods of time in some situations. See C.C. Art. 2687 (1870). Following the approach of modern codes, this revised Article avoids narrow rules on these matters.

(d) The intent of the parties, when ascertained, prevails over established usage.

SECTION 5—OBLIGATIONS WITH MULTIPLE PERSONS

Art. 1786.   Several, joint, and solidary obligations

When an obligation binds more than one obligor to one obligee, or binds one obligor to more than one obligee, or binds more than one obligor to more than one obligee, the obligation may be several, joint, or solidary.

Acts 1984, No. 331, § 1, eff. Jan. 1, 1985.

REVISION COMMENTS—1984

(a) This Article restates the rule of C.C. Art. 2077 (1870). It does not change the law.

(b) This and the succeeding Articles of this section reproduce the familiar tripartite classification of obligations involving multiple persons provided by C.C. Arts. 2077–2116 (1870). Only a few changes have been made, notably in the provisions governing joint obligations that are also indivisible. See revised C.C. Arts. 1789, 1797, 1799, 1800, 1802, and 1803 (Rev.1984), infra. This approach has been taken despite the fact that the scheme provided by the source articles is an uneasy amalgam of French and common law concepts and terminology. The alternative, to adopt the original French or common law scheme is inherently confusing. Nevertheless, members of the legal profession, especially those trained in other states, should be aware that there is potential for confusion in the Louisiana scheme itself, if its terminological similarities to the common law scheme are taken literally.

(c) Several, joint, and solidary obligations may be created by contract, by testament, or by law.

Art. 1787.   Several obligations; effects

When each of different obligors owes a separate performance to one obligee, the obligation is several for the obligors.

When one obligor owes a separate performance to each of different obligees, the obligation is several for the obligees.

A several obligation produces the same effects as a separate obligation owed to each obligee by an obligor or by each obligor to an obligee.

Acts 1984, No. 331, § 1, eff. Jan. 1, 1985.

REVISION COMMENTS—1984

(a) This Article reproduces the substance of C.C. Arts. 2078, 2079, and 2084 (1870). It does not change the law.

(b) Under this Article, if the performance owed by each obligor has a different object, the obligation is several, as when one obligor owes delivery of a thing and another owes payment of a sum of money.

(c) This Article does not assume that the only mode of creating several obligations is by the obligors' declarations of will. Several executors, for example, may be bound to deliver separate legacies to the same legatee. Or several executors and a trustee may have various duties to the same legatee. In these hypothetical cases, the obligations are several as a result of the testator's, and not the obligors', declaration of will. The phrase "in the same contract" has been suppressed because it unduly restricts the scope of the classification of several obligations.

(d) The common law category of "several obligations" never was a part of the Louisiana law. The Article uses the word "separate" rather than "distinct" because the French originals of the relevant Articles of the Civil Code of 1825 utilized the word "séparées". See 3 Louisiana Legal Archives, Part II, at 1140–42 (1942).

(e) A several obligation produces the same effects as would separate obligations; thus, inter alia, prescription runs independently on each separate obligation.

Art. 1788. Joint obligations for obligors or obligees

When different obligors owe together just one performance to one obligee, but neither is bound for the whole, the obligation is joint for the obligors.

When one obligor owes just one performance intended for the common benefit of different obligees, neither of whom is entitled to the whole performance, the obligation is joint for the obligees.

Acts 1984, No. 331, § 1, eff. Jan. 1, 1985.

REVISION COMMENTS—1984

(a) This Article does not change the law. It restates the rule of C.C. Arts. 2080 and 2081 (1870).

(b) The term "contract" employed in C.C. Art. 2080 (1870) has been suppressed because it unduly narrows the modes by which joint obligations can arise. See, for example, C.C. Art. 2600 (1870).

(c) The criterion of "common benefit" has been retained because the jurisprudence indicates that it has been found a useful one. Nabors v. Producers' Oil Co., 140 La. 985, 74 So. 527 (1917); A. Veeder Co. v. Pan American Production Co., 205 La. 599, 17 So.2d 891 (1944); Shell Petroleum Corporation v. Calcasieu Real Estate & Oil Co., 185 La. 751, 170 So. 785 (1936).

(d) Whether an obligation is several or joint depends upon the parties' intentions and understanding. A considerable number of decisions construing the source articles have involved oil and gas leases. The leading case of Nabors et al. v. Producers' Oil Co., supra, is instructive. In that case, five parties had granted an oil and gas lease on certain property, requiring the defendant to drill within a certain time to keep the lease alive. He drilled on property belonging to two of the lessors but not on that of the others. The plaintiffs, the remaining lessors, contended that the lease had been several and that the drilling of the well on the property of two of them would not keep the lease in force. In concluding that the obligation was joint for all the lessors, the court observed:

"Whether a contract is severable or joint depends upon the intention of the contracting parties as revealed by the language of their contract and the subject-matter to which it refers. With regard to the subject-matter, the authorities agree that the contract is entire and not severable, although it embodies a conveyance or delivery of several things, if the consideration is paid in a gross sum and it is impossible to affirm that the party making the payment would have done so unless the rights he acquired should apply to all the things mentioned . . . That test is particularly applicable to a mineral lease or option, where the lessee or grantee has paid a gross sum of money for the privilege he acquired on all of the lands described in the contract and it is impossible to affirm that he would have paid a proportionate consideration for the lease or option on only a portion of the land. . . . The contract did not state the amount paid to each of the grantors, nor state the area of land owned by each of them. They joined in one contract to do the same thing, in consideration for advantages to be derived for the common benefit of them all. The language of the instrument leaves no doubt that their contract was joint and not severable." 74 So. 527, 532 (1917).

This emphasis upon intent was of common law origin. It has not always provided a satisfactory means of identifying joint obligations. The parties' intent is often very difficult to determine. The distinction between divisible and indivisible joint obligations presented in the following Articles, however, furnishes a practical means of solving most of the problems such situations might engender.

Art. 1789. Divisible and indivisible joint obligation

When a joint obligation is divisible, each joint obligor is bound to perform, and each joint obligee is entitled to receive, only his portion.

When a joint obligation is indivisible, joint obligors or obligees are subject to the rules governing solidary obligors or solidary obligees.

Acts 1984, No. 331, § 1, eff. Jan. 1, 1985.

REVISION COMMENTS—1984

(a) This Article is new. It reproduces the substance of C.C. Arts. 2085, 2086, 2087, and 2113 (1870), but it changes the law in part, confining the rule of the second clause of C.C. Art. 2085 (1870) to "divisible" obligations. An indivisible joint obligation is given the same effects as if it were solidary.

(b) Under this Article, joint lessors are in the same position as solidary obligees. The rule of A. Veeder Co. v. Pan American Production Co., 205 La. 599, 17 So.2d 891 (1944), and Nabors et al. v. Producers' Oil Co., 140 La. 985, 74 So. 527 (1917), is thus maintained but on different grounds.

(c) All joint obligees or joint obligors are necessary parties to an action to enforce a joint obligation, in the manner provided in Code of Civil Procedure Article 643. The procedural language of C.C. Arts. 2085, 2086, and 2087 (1870) has been eliminated, not in order to change the law, but rather to confine procedural rules to the Code of Civil Procedure.

(d) Under this Article, although no presumption of solidarity is created, the applicability of solidarity principles is enhanced, and this is done in a way which also makes the categories of divisible and indivisible obligations meaningful and functional. See revised C.C. Arts. 1815–1820 (Rev.1984), infra. The solution adopted in this Article lies between the drastic presumption of solidarity that prevails in modern law and the approach of the Louisiana Civil Code of 1870.

Art. 1790. Solidary obligations for obligees

An obligation is solidary for the obligees when it gives each obligee the right to demand the whole performance from the common obligor.

Acts 1984, No. 331, § 1, eff. Jan. 1, 1985.

REVISION COMMENTS—1984

(a) This Article restates the rule of C.C. Art. 2088 (1870).

(b) This Article intentionally uses the word "solidary" rather than the expression "in solido," in order to avoid any pretense of incorporating into the revised Articles on obligations the now meaningless and potentially confusing distinction between obligations in solido and in solidum. The provisions of the Civil Code of 1870 which defines solidary obligations refer only to liability in solido. However, C.C. Art. 254, repealed by Acts 1960, No. 30, stated that, as natural tutrix of her children, a mother who remarried without the consent of a family meeting was liable in solidum with her husband for "all the consequences of the maladministration of the tutorship unduly kept by her." The Civil Code retains a reference to in solidum liability in C.C. Art. 437 (1870), which contemplates that officers of a corporation may expressly agree on such liability. Nevertheless, that and any other such vestigial references to in solidum, as opposed to in solido, liability have been superseded by this revision.

Art. 1791. Extinction of obligation by performance

Before a solidary obligee brings action for performance, the obligor may extinguish the obligation by rendering performance to any of the solidary obligees.

Acts 1984, No. 331, § 1, eff. Jan. 1, 1985.

REVISION COMMENT—1984

This Article restates the rule contained in the first paragraph of C.C. Art. 2089 (1870). The two paragraphs of that Article contemplate situations different enough to warrant its separation into two Articles.

Art. 1792. Remission by one obligee

Remission of debt by one solidary obligee releases the obligor but only for the portion of that obligee.

Acts 1984, No. 331, § 1, eff. Jan. 1, 1985.

REVISION COMMENTS—1984

(a) This Article restates the rule contained in the second paragraph of C.C. Art. 2089 (1870). One solidary obligee cannot dispose, by way of remission, of any part of the obligor's performance that would not have come to that obligee.

(b) The portion of each obligee is determined in the manner described in revised C.C. Art. 1803 (Rev.1984), infra.

Art. 1793. Interruption of prescription

Any act that interrupts prescription for one of the solidary obligees benefits all the others.

Acts 1984, No. 331, § 1, eff. Jan. 1, 1985.

REVISION COMMENT—1984

This Article restates the rule of C.C. Art. 2090 (1870).

Art. 1794. Solidary obligation for obligors

An obligation is solidary for the obligors when each obligor is liable for the whole performance. A performance rendered by one of the solidary obligors relieves the others of liability toward the obligee.

Acts 1984, No. 331, § 1, eff. Jan. 1, 1985.

REVISION COMMENT—1984

This Article restates the principle contained in C.C. Art. 2091 (1870). It does not change the law.

Art. 1795. Solidary obligor may not request division; action against one obligor after action against another

An obligee, at his choice, may demand the whole performance from any of his solidary obligors. A solidary obligor may not request division of the debt.

Unless the obligation is extinguished, an obligee may institute action against any of his solidary obligors even after institution of action against another solidary obligor.

Acts 1984, No. 331, § 1, eff. Jan. 1, 1985.

REVISION COMMENTS—1984

(a) This Article restates the rules of C.C. Arts. 2094 and 2095 (1870). It does not change the law.

(b) Under this Article, a solidary obligor who has been called upon to perform cannot request that the obligee divide the debt among the obligors. See Central Bank v. Winn Farmers Co-op., 299 So.2d 442 (La.App. 2nd Cir.1974), writ denied 302 So.2d 310 (La.1974).

Art. 1796. Solidarity not presumed

Solidarity of obligation shall not be presumed. A solidary obligation arises from a clear expression of the parties' intent or from the law.

Acts 1984, No. 331, § 1, eff. Jan. 1, 1985.

REVISION COMMENTS—1984

(a) This Article restates the basic principles contained in C.C. Arts. 2093 and 2107 (1870). It does not change the law.

(b) A solidary obligation may arise even though the parties have not used the words "solidarity" or "in solido," provided that their intent has been clearly expressed. See Dodd v. Lakeview Motors, 149 So. 278 (La.App. 2nd Cir.1933); George Moroy Cigar and Tobacco Co. v. Henriques, 184 So. 403 (La.App.Orl.1938).

(c) Solidarity may also arise by operation of law with or without the consent of the parties. See C.C. Art. 2324, as amended by Acts 1979, No. 431.

Art. 1797. Solidary obligation arising from different sources

An obligation may be solidary though it derives from a different source for each obligor.

Acts 1984, No. 331, § 1, eff. Jan. 1, 1985.

REVISION COMMENTS—1984

(a) This Article is new. It restates a principle developed by the Louisiana jurisprudence.

(b) Under this Article, a vendor and the manufacturer of a defective product may be solidarily liable to a vendee whom the product injures, even though the liability of each derives from different acts and sources. See Media Production Consultants, Inc. v. Mercedes-Benz of North America, Inc., 262 La. 80, 262 So.2d 377 (1972); Breaux v. Winnebago Industries, Inc., 282 So.2d 763 (La.App. 1st Cir.1973). See also C.C. Art. 2503 (1870). An employer and employee may be solidarily liable to the victim of a quasi-delict committed by the employee, though the obligation of the latter derives from quasi-delict and that of the former is imposed by law. See C.C. Arts. 2315, 2317, and 2320 (1870); Foster v. Hampton, 381 So.2d 789 (La.1980).

Art. 1798. Obligation subject to condition or term

An obligation may be solidary though for one of the obligors it is subject to a condition or term.

Acts 1984, No. 331, § 1, eff. Jan. 1, 1985.

REVISION COMMENTS—1984

(a) This Article restates the principle of C.C. Art. 2092 (1870). It does not change the law.

(b) Under this Article, an obligor may be absolutely bound while his co-obligor is obligated under condition or only during a certain period. The latter is as fully responsible for the whole performance during the term of his obligation as is the former.

Art. 1799. Interruption of prescription

The interruption of prescription against one solidary obligor is effective against all solidary obligors and their heirs.

Acts 1984, No. 331, § 1, eff. Jan. 1, 1985.

REVISION COMMENT—1984

This Article expands the principle of C.C. Art. 2097 (1870) in order to give interruptive effects to acts other than the filing of suit.

Art. 1800. Solidary liability for damages

A failure to perform a solidary obligation through the fault of one obligor renders all the obligors solidarily liable for the resulting damages. In that case, the obligors not at fault have their remedy against the obligor at fault.

Acts 1984, No. 331, § 1, eff. Jan. 1, 1985.

REVISION COMMENTS—1984

(a) This Article is new. It changes the law insofar as it does not limit the damages for nonperformance for which solidary obligors are liable.

(b) Obligors of a solidary obligation represent each other with regard to the obligee. What is done by one of them is considered to have been done by the others. Civil Code Article 2096 (1870) limits this rule of mutual representation in cases where the object of an obligation has been lost or has perished; while all the obligors are responsible for the obligation itself, only the obligor who has caused the loss is liable for damages. This Article eliminates that exception.

(c) An obligor not at fault who pays damages arising from the fault of another solidary obligor may bring an action to compel the latter to reimburse him.

Art. 1801. Defenses that solidary obligor may raise

A solidary obligor may raise against the obligee defenses that arise from the nature of the obligation, or that are personal to him, or that are common to all the solidary obligors. He may not raise a defense that is personal to another solidary obligor.

Acts 1984, No. 331, § 1, eff. Jan. 1, 1985.

REVISION COMMENTS—1984

(a) This Article does not change the law. It restates the rule of the source article and the jurisprudence. E.g., Nations v. Morris, 331 F.Supp. 771 (E.D.La.1971), aff'd 483 F.2d 577 (5th Cir.1973), cert. denied 414 U.S. 1073, 94 S.Ct. 584, 38 L.Ed.2d 477 (1973).

(b) This Article is consistent with the more specific rules governing the same subject which are found in other parts of the Civil Code. E.g., C.C. Arts. 3060 and 3036 (1870) (concerning suretyship); C.C. Art. 3076 (1870) (on transaction and compromise). Even though some modern codes have used other, more succinct language (E.g., Quebec Draft Civil Code (1977) Article 164), it was deemed advisable to retain the expression "nature of the obligation" from the source article in order to avoid any implication that relevant jurisprudence was disturbed. See, for example, Nations v. Morris, supra, in which a Washington federal court, construing Louisiana law, concluded that a defendant co-worker was immune under the federal Longshoremen's and Harbor Workers' Compensation Act (33 U.S.C. § 901 et seq.) from a common-law suit filed by a fellow employee, as the immunity was a substantive nonpersonal defense arising from the nature of the obligations associated with the worker's status.

Art. 1802. Renunciation of solidarity

Renunciation of solidarity by the obligee in favor of one or more of his obligors must be express. An obligee who receives a partial performance from an obligor separately preserves the solidary obligation against all his obligors after deduction of that partial performance.

Acts 1984, No. 331, § 1, eff. Jan. 1, 1985.

REVISION COMMENTS—1984

(a) This Article is new. It changes the law insofar as it eliminates the presumption of renunciation or waiver of solidarity in the absence of a reservation by the obligee and, as a consequence, the requirement of a receipt extended in a particular manner. The rule in this Article is consistent with the principle that a party should not be presumed to have given up a right.

(b) A renunciation or waiver by the obligee, though express, need not be made in a solemn manner. Any clear indication of the obligee's intent to waive solidarity in favor of one or more of his obligors suffices.

(c) An obligor who has paid his share is permitted to rebut the presumption in favor of the subsistence of solidarity.

(d) Under this Article, solidarity is preserved when an obligee accepts a partial performance from one obligor, and the obligee retains his right of action against all the solidary obligors for the balance, regardless of whether the amount he received from the first obligor equaled the latter's portion, or was less or more than that portion.

Art. 1803. Remission of debt to or transaction or compromise with one obligor

Remission of debt by the obligee in favor of one obligor, or a transaction or compromise between the obligee and one obligor, benefits the other solidary obligors in the amount of the portion of that obligor.

Surrender to one solidary obligor of the instrument evidencing the obligation gives rise to a presumption that the remission of debt was intended for the benefit of all the solidary obligors.

Acts 1984, No. 331, § 1, eff. Jan. 1, 1985.

REVISION COMMENTS—1984

(a) This Article is new. It changes the law insofar as it establishes that remission of debt in favor of one obligor does not extinguish the solidary obligation, but only reduces it for the other obligors in the amount of the remitted share. The same effect is given to a transaction or compromise between the obligee and one of the solidary obligors. This Article addresses both remission and transaction because the two terms properly have different meanings: remission, though it may be onerous, is usually understood as an act gratuitous in nature, while transaction or compromise is onerous. See 1 Litvinoff, Obligations 626–628, 636–640 (1969).

(b) In case of transaction, compromise, or settlement between the obligee and one of the solidary obligors, the liability of the other solidary obligors is reduced in the amount of the portion of that obligor, as in the case of settlement between the victim of a tort and one joint tort-feasor. See Wall v. American Employers Insurance Company, 386 So.2d 79 (La.1980); Canter v. Koehring Company, 283 So.2d 716 (La.1973); Cunningham v. Hardware Mutual Casualty Company, 228 So.2d 700 (La.App. 1st Cir.1969); Harvey v. The Travelers Insurance Company, 163 So.2d 915 (La.App. 3rd Cir.1964).

(c) The special presumption created by a "tacit remission," that is, by a surrender of the instrument evidencing the obligation, may be rebutted by any means showing that it was not the obligee's intent to release all the obligors.

(d) In case of insolvency of a solidary obligor after the obligee has remitted the debt in favor of another, the loss must be borne by the obligee. See 13 Baudry-Lacantinerie et Barde, Traité théorique et pratique de droit civil 112 (2nd ed. 1905).

(e) The rule of C.C. Art. 2203 (1870), according to which an obligee who remits a debt in favor of one solidary obligor without expressly reserving his right against the others is deemed to have forfeited the entire obligation reproduces the one contained in Article 1285 of the Code Napoléon. French doctrine has unanimously criticized that Article. See 13 Baudry-Lacantinerie et Barde, Traité théorique et pratique de droit civil—Des obligations 110–111 (2nd ed. 1905); 5 Colmet de Santerre, Manuel élémentaire de droit civil, No. 144 bis-I (4th ed. 1901); 26 Demolombe, Cours de code Napoléon, No. 396 (1877); 17 Laurent, Principes de droit civil français, No. 340 (1876); 8 Huc, Commentaire théorique et pratique du code civil, No. 138 (1894). All of these commentators have said that the French Article is wrong, and have found inexplicable its departure from Pothier, who had made the result in such a case depend upon the obligee's intent. See 2 Œuvres de Pothier, No. 275 (Bugnet ed. 1861).

No doubt responding to those comments, Article 1184 of the Code civil du Quebec provided:

> "An express release granted in favor of one of joint and several debtors does not discharge the others; but the creditor must deduct from the debt the share of him whom he has released." Articles 341 and 342 of the Quebec Draft Civil Code (1977) have preserved this rule. Contemporary common law propounds the same solution. See Restatement, Second, Contracts § 294 (1981).

The change effected by this Article avoids the misunderstanding reflected in Fridge v. Caruthers, 156 La. 746, 101 So. 128 (1924).

(f) It would seem clear that an obligee who surrenders a co-signed promissory note to one of the obligors intends to release all the solidary debtors or to remit the debt in favor of all of them. Eminent French doctrine supports that solution. See 13 Baudry-Lacantinerie et Barde, Traité théorique et pratique de droit civil 120–121 (2nd ed. 1905). See also Article 1183 of the Code civil du Quebec, and Articles 341 and 342 of the Quebec Draft Civil Code (1977).

Art. 1804.   Liability of solidary obligors between themselves

Among solidary obligors, each is liable for his virile portion. If the obligation arises from a contract or quasi-contract, virile portions are equal in the absence of agreement or judgment to the contrary. If the obligation arises from an offense or quasi-offense, a virile portion is proportionate to the fault of each obligor.

A solidary obligor who has rendered the whole performance, though subrogated to the right of the obligee, may claim from the other obligors no more than the virile portion of each.

If the circumstances giving rise to the solidary obligation concern only one of the obligors, that obligor is liable for the whole to the other obligors who are then considered only as his sureties.

Acts 1984, No. 331, § 1, eff. Jan. 1, 1985.

REVISION COMMENTS—1984

(a) This Article synthesizes the rules contained in C.C. Arts. 2104 and 2106 (1870) and the final paragraph of C.C. Art. 2103 (1870). It does not change the law.

(b) Under this Article, the amount of each obligor's virile portion is made to depend on the source of the obligation. The obligors' portions of a contractual or quasi-contractual obligation are presumed to be equal in the absence of an obligor's agreement or, in the case of quasi-contract, any express judicial declaration, to the contrary. That is what is meant by the expression "virile portion" in traditional doctrine. See 13 Baudry-Lacantinerie et Barde, Traité théorique et pratique de droit civil—Des obligations 367 (3rd ed. 1907); 7 Planiol et Ripert, Traité pratique de droit civil français 466 (2nd ed. Esmein 1954). If the obligation originates in an offense or quasi-offense, however, each obligor's virile portion is proportional to his fault, which is consistent with the idea of comparative negligence adopted in C.C. Arts. 2323 and 2324, as amended by Acts 1979, No. 431.

Art. 1805.   Enforcement of contribution

A party sued on an obligation that would be solidary if it exists may seek to enforce contribution against any solidary co-obligor by making him a third party defendant according to the rules of procedure, whether or not that third party has been initially sued, and whether the party seeking to enforce contribution admits or denies liability on the obligation alleged by plaintiff.

Acts 1984, No. 331, § 1, eff. Jan. 1, 1985.

REVISION COMMENTS—1984

(a) This Article reproduces the substance of the second paragraph of C.C. Art. 2103 (1870). It does not change the law.

(b) A defendant seeking to make his co-obligor a third-party defendant must so do according to Articles 1111–1116 of the Code of Civil Procedure.

(c) An obligor who has been released by his obligee is no longer an obligor and therefore cannot be made a third party.

Art. 1806.   Insolvency of a solidary obligor

A loss arising from the insolvency of a solidary obligor must be borne by the other solidary obligors in proportion to their portion.

Any obligor in whose favor solidarity has been renounced must nevertheless contribute to make up for the loss.

Acts 1984, No. 331, § 1, eff. Jan. 1, 1985.

(a) This Article reproduces the substance of C.C. Arts. 2104 and 2105 (1870). It does not change the law.

(b) There is virtually no Louisiana jurisprudence on the issue of the effect of the insolvency of one solidary obligor. Nevertheless, it is important to specify who should bear the loss in such a case, especially when the obligor who becomes insolvent is one upon whose solvency an obligee has relied in releasing a co-obligor. Without the protection afforded by this Article, obligees might be unwilling to discharge any obligor until fully satisfied by all, even in cases in which the obligee is otherwise willing to accept piecemeal payment. Article 176 of the Quebec Draft Civil Code (1977) follows the same approach, reversing the rule of present Article 1119 of the Quebec Code.

(c) This Article merges C.C. Art. 2105 (1870) with the second paragraph of C.C. Art. 2104 (1870) in order to combine all of the provisions regarding the insolvency of a solidary obligor in one article. No change to C.C. Art. 2324, as amended by Acts 1979, No. 431, is intended.

SECTION 6—CONJUNCTIVE AND ALTERNATIVE OBLIGATIONS

Art. 1807. Conjunctive obligation

An obligation is conjunctive when it binds the obligor to multiple items of performance that may be separately rendered or enforced. In that case, each item is regarded as the object of a separate obligation.

The parties may provide that the failure of the obligor to perform one or more items shall allow the obligee to demand the immediate performance of all the remaining items.

Acts 1984, No. 331, § 1, eff. Jan. 1, 1985.

(a) This Article reproduces the substance of C.C. Arts. 2063 and 2065 (1870). It does not change the law.

(b) Under this Article, when a sum is owed in installments or rent is paid periodically, the running of prescription starts separately for each installment or rental payment in the absence of an acceleration clause. See Gardiner v. Montegut, 175 So. 120 (La.App.Orl.1937).

(c) This Article combines the concepts expressed in C.C. Arts. 2063 and 2065 (1870), incorporating examples of conjunctive obligations taken from the Louisiana jurisprudence. See Nesom v. D'Armond, 13 La.Ann. 294 (1858); Kearney v. Fenerty, 185 La. 862, 171 So. 57 (1936); Brandagee v. Chamberlin, 2 Rob. 207 (1842).

(d) The Articles on conjunctive and alternative obligations in the Code of 1870 have been severely criticized. Saunders described them as "the desert of the Civil Code." Saunders, Lectures on the Civil Code 434 (1925). Planiol, discussing corresponding articles of the French Civil Code (which refer only to the alternative obligation), has written that they are "without practical importance and could be suppressed without inconvenience." 2 Planiol, Traité élémentaire de droit civil § 710 (Louisiana State Law Institute trans. 1959).

(e) The conjunctive obligation is rare in modern civil codes, which usually treat only the alternative obligation. See, e.g., Ethiopian Civil Code Articles 1880–1882. Nevertheless, both serve useful purposes. For example, the conjunctive category clarifies the nature of the debtor's obligation in an installment contract and the lessee's obligation to pay rent. Accordingly, both categories have been retained, but the number of articles dealing with them has been reduced. Because some of the source articles were inartfully drafted, an effort has been made to reword them to achieve clarity.

(f) A distinctive characteristic of the conjunctive obligation is the possibility of piecemeal discharge. No magic words are required in order to establish this piecemeal quality.

(g) Civil Code Article 2063 (1870) uses the terms "obligation" and "contract" loosely, and perhaps interchangeably. It is advisable to use the word "obligation" consistently for the sake of clarity. The word "contract" is avoided in the revised article for this reason. The term "object" has also been avoided. As used in the source article, it suggests that the scope of conjunctive obligations is restricted to physical objects. The fulfillment of an obligation may indeed involve an object, as in the case of a sale, but this is not always the case. An obligation may require a purely intangible performance such as forbearance, that is, not doing a certain act. The expression "item of performance" is used in this Section in order to embrace this kind of performance.

(h) Regarding each item of performance as the object of a separate obligation is a useful fiction that allows certain results, such as independent running of prescription as to each, to follow logically. For many other purposes, it is necessary to be aware that a conjunctive obligation is a single entity. This Article uses the expression "each item is regarded as the object of a separate obligation" in order to draw attention to the fiction.

Art. 1808. Alternative obligation

An obligation is alternative when an obligor is bound to render only one of two or more items of performance.

Acts 1984, No. 331, § 1, eff. Jan. 1, 1985.

REVISION COMMENTS—1984

(a) This Article reproduces the substance of C.C. Arts. 2066 and 2074 (1870). It does not change the law.

(b) Civil Code Article 2066 (1870) uses the term "things" to refer to the objects of alternative obligations. A "thing", however, is technically the object of a performance; it is "performance" that is the object of an obligation. One obligation admits of only one performance, but that performance may consist of a number of different "items of performance." In the case of an alternative obligation, the items of performance are specified in the alternative. This Article envisions the possibility of any number of acts as the object of an alternative obligation.

(c) The source Article's reference to separation of the objects of performance by a disjunctive has been suppressed as unnecessary and potentially confusing. Other obligations, such as those created by a penal clause, can be stated in an either/or form.

(d) The distinction between an alternative obligation and a penal clause is that the former is a primary obligation which may be satisfied in one of several ways while the latter is a secondary obligation which can be enforced only if there is also a valid primary obligation which the obligor fails to perform without lawful excuse. In the penal clause, the obligor has no real "choice" as such; he cannot simply elect to pay the penalty rather than perform the primary obligation. If he does, the creditor may still sue for specific performance of the primary obligation. Moreover, in cases which stipulate a penalty merely for delay, both the principal performance and the penalty may be recovered. See revised C.C. Arts. 2005 through 2012 (Rev.1984), infra.

Art. 1809. Choice belongs to the obligor

When an obligation is alternative, the choice of the item of performance belongs to the obligor unless it has been expressly or impliedly granted to the obligee.

Acts 1984, No. 331, § 1, eff. Jan. 1, 1985.

REVISION COMMENT—1984

This Article reproduces the substance of C.C. Art. 2068 (1870). It changes the law in only one respect, permitting the choice between items of performance to be impliedly, as well as expressly, granted to the obligee. This solution is not without support in prior jurisprudence. See Galloway v. Legan, 4 Mart. (N.S.) 167 (1826); Kay & Kay v. Fountain, 28 So.2d 759 (La.App. 1st Cir.1947).

Art. 1810. Delay in exercising choice

When the party who has the choice does not exercise it after a demand to do so, the other party may choose the item of performance.

Acts 1984, No. 331, § 1, eff. Jan. 1, 1985.

REVISION COMMENTS—1984

(a) This Article is new. It does not change the law however. It expresses a consequence of a principle implied in several Articles of the Louisiana Civil Code of 1870, such as C.C. Arts. 2556 and 2694 (1870). See 2 Litvinoff, Obligations 470 (1975). It follows the trend among modern codes.

(b) If the right to make the choice has been granted to the obligee and he fails to exercise it after due demand, the choice reverts to the obligor so that he may release himself from the obligation through performance. By the same token, if the obligor has the choice but will not exercise it after due demand, then the obligee may demand the item of performance of his choice.

(c) The demand upon the party who has the choice must, of course, be seasonably made, that is, neither before any condition prior to performance has been met, nor before arrival of a term if any. According to circumstances, the obligor may be allowed a reasonable delay to make his choice after notice has been given.

Art. 1811. Obligor may not choose part of one item

An obligor may not perform an alternative obligation by rendering as performance a part of one item and a part of another.

Acts 1984, No. 331, § 1, eff. Jan. 1, 1985.

REVISION COMMENT—1984

This Article reproduces the substance of C.C. Art. 2069 (1870). It does not change the law.

Art. 1812. Impossibility or unlawfulness of one item of performance

When the choice belongs to the obligor and one of the items of performance contemplated in the alternative obligation becomes impossible or unlawful, regardless of the fault of the obligor, he must render one of those that remain.

When the choice belongs to the obligee and one of the items of performance becomes impossible or unlawful without the fault of the obligor, the obligee must choose one of the items that remain. If the impossibility or unlawfulness is due to the fault of the obligor, the obligee may choose either one of those that remain, or damages for the item of performance that became impossible or unlawful.

Acts 1984, No. 331, § 1, eff. Jan. 1, 1985.

REVISION COMMENTS—1984

(a) This Article reproduces the substance of C.C. Arts. 2071 and 2072 (1870). It changes the law in part, in that it allows an obligee to whom the choice among items of performance has been given to recover damages, rather than merely the price of a thing which was to be delivered, if one of the items of performance becomes impossible through the obligor's fault. That solution is consistent with the theory of damages reflected in C.C. Art. 1934 (1870) and revised C.C. Arts. 1994 through 2004 (Rev.1984), infra.

(b) When the obligor has the choice, he cannot be made liable even for intentionally destroying one of the items of performance, precisely because the choice is his.

(c) When the choice belongs to the obligee and one of the items of performance becomes impossible without the obligor's fault, the obligee must content himself with the remaining item. That solution is consistent with the theory of impossibility of performance reflected in C.C. Art. 1933(2) (1870) and revised C.C. Art. 1873 (Rev.1984), infra.

Art. 1813. Impossibility or unlawfulness of all items of performance

If all of the items of performance contemplated in the alternative obligation become impossible or unlawful without the obligor's fault, the obligation is extinguished.

Acts 1984, No. 331, § 1, eff. Jan. 1, 1985.

REVISION COMMENTS—1984

(a) This Article reproduces the substance of C.C. Art. 2073 (1870). It does not change the law.

(b) Under this Article, if all of the items of performance become unlawful or impossible without the obligor's fault, he is liberated regardless of which party had the choice.

(c) If all of the items of performance become impossible after the obligor is in default, the obligation is not extinguished. This Article makes no express reference to that situation because the solution clearly follows from revised C.C. Art. 1873 (Rev.1984), infra.

Art. 1814.   Obligor's liability for damages

When the choice belongs to the obligor, if all the items of performance contemplated in the alternative obligation have become impossible and the impossibility of one or more is due to the fault of the obligor, he is liable for the damages resulting from his failure to render the last item that became impossible.

If the impossibility of one or more items is due to the fault of the obligee, the obligor is not bound to deliver any of the items that remain.

Acts 1984, No. 331, § 1, eff. Jan. 1, 1985.

REVISION COMMENTS—1984

(a) This Article reproduces the substance of C.C. Art. 2071 (1870). It changes the law only in part, allowing the obligee to recover damages rather than merely the price of a thing which was to be delivered, when all the items of performance have become impossible and the impossibility of one or more is due to the obligor's fault.

(b) Civil Code Article 2071 (1870) contemplates situations involving only two alternative items of performance. Of course, the same conclusions follow when there are more than two alternatives. This Article makes that clear. Continental doctrine devotes very little discussion to the situation contemplated in C.C. Art. 2071 (1870). In fact, it generally overlooks it. The essence of the rule, however, is that the obligor, as long as he has the choice, is responsible for the last item of performance that cannot be rendered because of his fault. For a cursory discussion of Article 1193 of the Code Napoleon, equivalent to C.C. Art. 2071 (1870), see 7 Planiol et Ripert, Traité pratique de droit civil français 406 (2nd ed. Esmein 1954).

(c) If the impossibility of one or more of the items of performance is caused by the fault of the obligee, the obligor is not bound to deliver any of the remaining items, since his privilege of choosing has been destroyed by the obligee. The obligor may then either exercise his choice among the remaining items, if he so wishes, or demand the return of whatever he may already have given to the obligee. This conclusion is a direct result of the overriding obligation of good faith.

Art. 1815.   Divisible and indivisible obligation

An obligation is divisible when the object of the performance is susceptible of division.

An obligation is indivisible when the object of the performance, because of its nature or because of the intent of the parties, is not susceptible of division.

Acts 1984, No. 331, § 1, eff. Jan. 1, 1985.

REVISION COMMENTS—1984

(a) This Article reproduces the substance of C.C. Arts. 2108 and 2109 (1870). It changes the law in part, eliminating the notion of "intellectual" divisibility of an object.

(b) The notion of "intellectual" divisibility is based on confusion between divisibility of the object of the performance and divisibility of the obligee's right. The latter, since it is an abstraction, is always susceptible of division into shares or aliquot parts. Thus, if a corporeal thing is owed by a seller to three buyers, that obligation is indivisible because it may not be performed in parts without destroying the thing. Nevertheless, the credit-right of the buyers—or obligees—is susceptible of division. Thus, if the thing were delivered, and ownership thereof transferred, to one of the buyers or obligees, he would be bound to recognize the co-ownership of the other two. See 2 Llambras, Tratado de derecho civil—Obligaciones 400 (1967); see also 7 Planiol et Ripert, Traité pratique de droit civil français 473 (2nd ed. Esmein 1954). The right of usufruct is divisible in the same way. See C.C. Arts. 541 and 542 (as amended by Acts 1976, No. 103, § 1). On the other hand, the law considers certain rights to be indivisible. For instance, the right of a mortgagee under a mortgage is indivisible. See C.C. Art. 3282 (1870); Groves v. Sentell, 153 U.S. 465, 14 S.Ct. 898, 38 L.Ed. 785 (1894). Similarly, the obligation of an obligee of warranty is deemed indivisible. Each co-seller is bound to warrant the ownership of the thing sold, and consequently each is obligated to pay the full amount of damages that result if its buyer is evicted. See Soule v. West, 185 La. 655, 170 So. 26 (1936); Collins v. Slocum, 317 So.2d 672 (La.App. 3rd Cir.1975), writ denied, 321 So.2d 362 (La.1975).

(c) Louisiana courts have occasionally confused divisible with conjunctive obligation. See Gaiennie Co. v. Bouchereau, 9 Orl.App. 81 (1911), in which it was said that a contract which sets forth distinct "considerations" for different objects is legally divisible and gives rise to as many different obligations as there are objects. At other times, Louisiana courts have confused civil law "divisible or indivisible obligations" with common law "entire or severable contracts." See Audubon Bldg. Co. v. F.M. Andrews & Co., 187 F. 254, 111 C.C.A. 92 (1911). The Articles of this Section attempt to clarify the provisions of the source Articles in order to avoid that kind of confusion.

Art. 1816.   Effect of divisible obligation between single obligor and obligee

When there is only one obligor and only one obligee, a divisible obligation must be performed as if it were indivisible.

Acts 1984, No. 331, § 1, eff. Jan. 1, 1985.

REVISION COMMENT—1984

This Article reproduces the substance of the first sentence of C.C. Art. 2111 (1870). It does not change the law.

Art. 1817.   Effects of divisible obligation among successors

A divisible obligation must be divided among successors of the obligor or of the obligee.

Each successor of the obligor is liable only for his share of a divisible obligation.

Each successor of the obligee is entitled only to his share of a divisible obligation.

Acts 1984, No. 331, § 1, eff. Jan. 1, 1985.

REVISION COMMENTS—1984

(a) This Article reproduces the substance of the second sentence of C.C. Art. 2111 (1870). It does not change the law.

(b) In this Article, the meaning of the term "successor" is that given it in C.C. Art. 876 (Rev.1981).

Art. 1818.   Effects of indivisible obligations between more than one obligor or obligee

An indivisible obligation with more than one obligor or obligee is subject to the rules governing solidary obligations.

Acts 1984, No. 331, § 1, eff. Jan. 1, 1985.

REVISION COMMENTS—1984

(a) This Article reproduces the substance of C.C. Art. 2113 (1870). It does not change the law.

(b) When distinct obligors owe the same indivisible performance to one obligee, they are solidarily bound to that obligee, regardless of their intentions.

(c) When one obligor owes an indivisible performance to distinct obligees, they are solidary obligees in regard to that obligor, regardless of intention. See Nabors et al. v. Producers' Oil Co., 140 La. 985, 74 So. 527 (1917).

(d) Article 2113 of the Civil Code of 1870 states only that each of the obligors of an indivisible obligation is bound for the whole. This Article makes the other consequences of solidarity equally applicable in such a case. For instance, an interruption of the running of prescription against one obligor benefits all the others, and the putting of one in default affects all the others. This application of principles of solidarity to indivisible obligations is the trend followed by modern codes such as the Italian, Ethiopian, Greek, Japanese, and the Quebec Draft Civil Code (1977). See also Collins v. Slocum, 317 So.2d 672 (La.App. 3rd Cir.1975), writ refused, 321 So.2d 362 (La.1975).

Art. 1819.   Effect of indivisible obligation among successors

An indivisible obligation may not be divided among the successors of the obligor or of the obligee, who are thus subject to the rules governing solidary obligors or solidary obligees.

Acts 1984, No. 331, § 1, eff. Jan. 1, 1985.

REVISION COMMENTS—1984

(a) This Article reproduces the substance of C.C. Arts. 2112–2116 (1870). It does not change the law.

(b) In this Article, the meaning of the term "successor" is that given it in C.C. Art. 876 (Rev.1981).

(c) A divisible obligation secured by a mortgage or pledge is regarded as indivisible for the benefit of the obligee. See C.C. Arts. 1611, 1614, 3171, and 3282, second paragraph (1870).

(d) A successor who is in possession of succession property which is the security for an obligation may be sued for the whole debt, but he has recourse against his co-successor. See C.C. Arts. 1611 and 1614 (1870).

(e) Since an obligation to give a specific thing is indivisible, the divisibility of the obligation cannot be claimed by an heir who is in possession of such a thing.

(f) Civil Code Article 2112 (1870) has been eliminated because it contemplates situations accounted for in other Articles of the Civil Code.

Art. 1820.   Solidarity is not indivisibility

A stipulation of solidarity does not make an obligation indivisible.

Acts 1984, No. 331, § 1, eff. Jan. 1, 1985.

REVISION COMMENTS—1984

(a) This Article reproduces the substance of C.C. Art. 2110 (1870). It does not change the law.

(b) Under this and the preceding Article, a divisible, solidary obligation may be divided among the heirs of an obligor or obligee. This is true even if the obligation arises from a source other than contract.

CHAPTER 4—TRANSFER OF OBLIGATIONS

SECTION 1—ASSUMPTION OF OBLIGATIONS

Art. 1821.   Assumption by agreement between obligor and third person

An obligor and a third person may agree to an assumption by the latter of an obligation of the former. To be enforceable by the obligee against the third person, the agreement must be made in writing.

The obligee's consent to the agreement does not effect a release of the obligor.

The unreleased obligor remains solidarily bound with the third person.

Acts 1984, No. 331, § 1, eff. Jan. 1, 1985.

(a) This Article is new. It changes the law in part. Under this article, the original obligor and the third person who assumes the obligation are solidarily bound rather than bound in imperfect solidarity. See Gay v. Blanchard, 32 La.Ann. 497 (1880).

(b) This Article is the counterpart of revised C.C. Art. 1978 (Rev.1984), infra, dealing with third party beneficiaries. It focuses on the relationship between stipulator and promisor when the beneficiary is a creditor of the former. It does not repeat the general rules on stipulation pour autrui, where the beneficiary need not be a creditor. The Louisiana jurisprudence has long recognized assumption of obligation as a particular transaction. Because of the absence of provisions governing it in the Civil Code of 1870, however, the courts have placed assumption within the general framework of third party beneficiary provisions. Thus, in Latiolais v. The Citizens' Bank of Louisiana, 33 La.Ann. 1444 (1881), the court held that a mortgage creditor could treat as his debtor a vendee of the mortgaged property who had assumed payment of the debt, without thereby creating a novation and discharging the original debtor. A discharge could not be presumed, but must be established by clear and positive proof of such an intention on the part of the creditor. In default of sufficient evidence to the contrary, the court held, it would be presumed that the creditor had retained the old debtor at the same time that he had accepted the new one. See also Moriarty v. Weiss, 196 La. 34, 198 So. 643 (1940); Campti Motor Co. v. Jolley, 120 So. 684 (La.App. 2nd Cir.1929). This and the three following articles provide special regulations for assumptions of obligations.

(c) Under this Article, the original debtor and the "assuming" debtor are solidarily liable for the assumed debt. Thus, inter alia, if prescription is interrupted with regard to the assuming debtor it is interrupted also with regard to the original debtor and, if interrupted with regard to the latter, it is interrupted also with regard to the former. See revised C.C. Art. 1799 (Rev.1984), supra. Contribution between original and assuming obligors depends on the terms of their agreement or the circumstances surrounding their situation. Thus, if the assuming obligor is also a debtor of the original obligor, he has no right to contribution, after performing the obligation, by analogical application of the principle of revised C.C. Art. 1804 (Rev.1984), supra.

(d) Under this Article, an assumption of obligation does not effect a novation by substitution of a new obligor because the original obligation is not extinguished by the assumption. See Latiolais v. The Citizens' Bank of Louisiana, 33 La.Ann. 1444 (1881).

(e) Under this Article, an assumption must be made in writing to be enforceable by the obligee against a third person. The similarity of the assumption to a promise to pay the debt of a third party justifies the requirement. See revised C.C. Art. 1847 (Rev.1984), infra. As between the obligee and a third person, the requirement of a writing is also consistent with views expressed by the Louisiana jurisprudence concerning the very similar stipulation pour autrui. See Fontenot v. Marquette Cas. Co., 258 La. 671, 247 So.2d 572 (1971).

(f) Under this Article, solidarity between the unreleased obligor and the third person is perfect since the difference between perfect and imperfect solidarity has been abandoned by the Louisiana jurisprudence. See Foster v. Hampton, 381 So.2d 789 (La.1980); Sampay v. Morton Salt, 395 So.2d 326 (La.1981).

Art. 1822. Third person bound for amount assumed

A person who, by agreement with the obligor, assumes the obligation of the latter is bound only to the extent of his assumption.

The assuming obligor may raise any defense based on the contract by which the assumption was made.

Acts 1984, No. 331, § 1, eff. Jan. 1, 1985.

(a) This Article is new. It does not change the law, however, but gives general formulation to a rule asserted by the Louisiana jurisprudence. See Moriarty v. Weiss, 196 La. 34, 198 So. 643 (1940); Tiernan v. Martin, 2 Rob. 523 (1842); Union Bank of Louisiana v. Bowman, 9 La.Ann. 195 (1854). See also Litvinoff, The Law of Obligations in the Louisiana Jurisprudence 330 (1979).

(b) Under this Article, if the third person is a debtor of the obligor and the amount of his debt is less than the amount owed by the obligor to the obligee, the third person is bound to the obligee only up to the amount of his original debt to the obligor, in the absence of express agreement to the contrary.

(c) The assuming obligor may avail himself of defenses resulting from his solidary bond with the original obligor. He may also avail himself of any right of action which the principal obligor may have against the original obligee that is obtainable by subrogation, as when the assuming obligor is a subvendee of the original obligor who is the obligee's vendee. See C.C. Art. 2503, as amended by Acts 1924, No. 116. He may not, however, invoke against the original obligee any defenses that are purely personal to the original obligor. See revised C.C. Art. 1801 (Rev.1984), supra; C.C. Art. 3060 (1870). See also Simmons v. Clark, 64 So.2d 520 (La.App. 1st Cir.1953).

(d) Under this Article, an assuming obligor who, because of a breach of contract between the original obligor and obligee, does not have to perform the obligation he has assumed, may not derive an unfair advantage therefrom. If he has received anything from the original obligor for the assumption, he must return it or make compensation to the original obligor. See also revised C.C. Art. 1824 (Rev.1984), infra.

Art. 1823. Assumption by agreement between obligee and third person

An obligee and a third person may agree on an assumption by the latter of an obligation owed by another to the former. That agreement must be made in writing. That agreement does not effect a release of the original obligor.

Acts 1984, No. 331, § 1, eff. Jan. 1, 1985.

REVISION COMMENTS—1984

(a) This Article is new. It does not change the law, however. C.C. Art. 2278(3) (1870) contemplates promises to pay the debt of another. See W.H. Ward Lumber Co. v. International City Bank & Trust Co., 347 So.2d 322 (La.App. 4th Cir.1977), where the defendant bank had undertaken to assure the plaintiff that materials delivered by the latter to another party would be paid for. The bank's promise, which the court did not enforce only because it had not been made in writing, clearly constituted an assumption of an obligation by an agreement between the obligee and an assuming obligor.

(b) The requirement of a writing is consistent with revised C.C. Art. 1847 (Rev.1984) infra, which prohibits using parol evidence to prove a promise to pay the debt of a third person. See C.C. Art. 2278(3) (1870); England v. Neal, 28 La.Ann. 551 (1876); Hogan v. Mississippi Val. Bank, 28 La.Ann. 550 (1876). Through a different line of decisions, however, it has been asserted that the rule of C.C. Art. 2278(3) (1870) is inapplicable when the promisor has a material interest in making the promise and receives consideration for it. See Coreil v. Vidrine, 188 La. 343, 177 So. 233 (1937); Fabacher v. Crampes, 166 La. 397, 117 So. 439 (1928); see also Paul M. Davison Petroleum Products v. L.T. Brown Contractor, Inc., 356 So.2d 572 (La.App. 2nd Cir.1978), reversed on other grounds 364 So.2d 583 (La.1978). This Article does not intend to change that approach.

(c) Although under this Article both the original obligor and the third person are bound to render the same performance, they are not solidary obligors. In the situation contemplated by this Article, the agreement is made by the obligee and the assuming obligor, and the assumption may take place even without the knowledge of the original obligor. Under such conditions, solidarity between the obligors could have unfair effects with regard to the original obligor; for instance, if an interruption of prescription with regard to the assuming obligor were considered as also effective against the original obligor.

(d) Assumption of obligation differs from suretyship in that the assuming obligor may not claim discussion of the property of the original obligor, and his promise is not conditional on the original obligor's failing to perform. See C.C. Art. 3045 (1870). For that reason, this Article does not effect any change in the law of suretyship. See C.C. Arts. 3038 and 3039 (1870).

Art. 1824. Defenses

A person who, by agreement with the obligee, has assumed another's obligation may not raise against the obligee any defense based on the relationship between the assuming obligor and the original obligor.

The assuming obligor may raise any defense based on the relationship between the original obligor and obligee. He may not invoke compensation based on an obligation owed by the obligee to the original obligor.

Acts 1984, No. 331, § 1, eff. Jan. 1, 1985.

REVISION COMMENTS—1984

(a) This Article is new, but it does not change the law. It is consistent with C.C. Art. 3060 (1870). It does not contradict C.C. Art. 2211 (1870) because assumption of obligation is not the same as suretyship. See Schmidt v. City of New Orleans, 33 La.Ann. 17 (1881). See also American Creosote Works v. Aetna Casualty & Surety Co., 167 La. 601, 120 So. 21 (1929), where the court held that the Civil Code Articles relating to the discharge of a surety, if in conflict with Act 224 of 1918, (R.S. 38:2241–38:2247) relating to claims of materialmen and laborers on public works, must yield to the statutory provisions.

(b) Under this Article, the assuming obligor may not raise defenses that are purely personal to the original obligor. See C.C. Art. 3060 (1870) and revised C.C. Art. 1801 (Rev.1984), supra. See also Simmons v. Clark, 64 So.2d 520 (La.App. 1st Cir.1953).

SECTION 2—SUBROGATION

Art. 1825. Definition

Subrogation is the substitution of one person to the rights of another. It may be conventional or legal.

Acts 1984, No. 331, § 1, eff. Jan. 1, 1985.

REVISION COMMENT—1984

This Article is new. It does not change the law, however. It gives express formulation to a definition of subrogation which is traditional in civil law doctrine. See 2 Planiol et Ripert, Traité élémentaire de droit civil § 473, at 178 (11 ed., 1939); 4 Aubry et Rau, Cours de droit civil français § 321, at 277 (5th ed., 1902).

Art. 1826. Effects

A.   When subrogation results from a person's performance of the obligation of another, that obligation subsists in favor of the person who performed it who may avail himself of the action and security of the original obligee against the obligor, but is extinguished for the original obligee.

B.   An original obligee who has been paid only in part may exercise his right for the balance of the debt in preference to the new obligee. This right shall not be waived or altered if the original obligation arose from injuries sustained or loss occasioned by the original obligee as a result of the negligence or intentional conduct of the original obligor.

Acts 1984, No. 331, § 1, eff. Jan. 1, 1985. Amended by Acts 2001, No. 305, § 1.

REVISION COMMENTS—1984

(a) This Article is new. It does not change the law, however. It gives express formulation to the theory underlying C.C. Arts. 2159–2162 (1870). According to traditional doctrine, "The subrogation is a legal fiction admitted or established by the law (in cases exclusively determined) by virtue of which an obligation, extinguished with regard to the original creditor by payment which he has received from a third person (personally foreign to the debt) or from the debtor himself but with funds that a third person has furnished to that effect, is regarded as subsisting in favor of this third person who is entitled to assert . . . the rights and actions of the ancient creditor." 4 Aubry et Rau, Droit civil français—Obligations 187–188 (Louisiana State Law Institute trans. 1965).

(b) Subrogation differs from novation. In the latter, the obligation is extinguished and therefore all securities cease; in the former, through a legal fiction, the obligation and its accessories subsist for the benefit of the subrogee.

(c) As defined in the preceding Article, that is, as the substitution of a person to the rights of another, subrogation may result from an act of payment, but it may also result from a sale. See C.C. Art. 2503 (1870).

(d) Under this Article, "security" may be a personal security such as suretyship, a real security such as mortgage or pledge, or a privilege.

(e) If the subrogee pays only a part of the obligor's debt, the original obligee retains the right to be paid the balance by the obligor. This right takes precedence over that of the subrogee to collect the portion that he paid. These effects would not occur, of course, in a situation where partial performance is not possible, as in the case of an indivisible obligation or a cause of action that may not be split. See Code of Civil Procedure Article 425; Richard v. Travelers Insurance Company, 323 So.2d 176 (La.App. 3rd Cir.1975), affirmed 326 So.2d 370 (La.1976); McConnell v. Travelers Indemnity Company, 222 F.Supp. 979 (E.D.La.1963), affirmed 346 F.2d 219 (C.A.5th Cir.1965).

Art. 1827. Conventional subrogation by the obligee

An obligee who receives performance from a third person may subrogate that person to the rights of the obligee, even without the obligor's consent. That subrogation is subject to the rules governing the assignment of rights.

Acts 1984, No. 331, § 1, eff. Jan. 1, 1985.

REVISION COMMENTS—1984

(a) This Article is new. It is based on C.C. Art. 2160(1) (1870), but changes the law insofar as it eliminates the distinction between conventional subrogation by the obligee and assignment of rights.

(b) Under this Article, conventional subrogation by the obligee carries with it an implied warranty as to the existence of the debt. See C.C. Art. 2646 (1870).

(c) Under this Article, conventional subrogation by the obligee is valid as between the parties without more, but it requires notice to the obligor or his acceptance in an authentic act to be valid against third persons. See C.C. Art. 2643 (1870).

(d) Under this Article, the conventional subrogee is substituted to all of the rights of the original obligee. He is entitled to recover the full amount of the debt from the obligor, regardless of the amount actually paid by the subrogee to the original obligee. Prior decisions that, in cases of conventional subrogation, have limited the subrogee's recovery to the amount he actually paid the obligee are expressly overruled. See, e.g., Roman v. Forstall, 11 La.Ann. 717 (1856); H.B. "Buster" Hughes, Inc., v. Bernard, 306 So.2d 785 (La.App. 4th Cir.1975).

(e) Under this and the preceding Article, a subrogee who has made only partial payment to the obligee yields in ranking to the latter when the obligor's assets are insufficient to afford them both a full recovery. Prior decisions so holding under C.C. Art. 2162 (1870) are preserved. See Hutchinson v. Rice, 105 La. 474, 29 So. 898 (1901); Legendre v. Rodrigue, 358 So.2d 665 (La.App. 1st Cir.1978), writ denied 359 So.2d 1293 (La.1978).

(f) Under this Article, the agreement for subrogation may be made at any time and need not be in writing. Prior decisions holding that conventional subrogation by the obligee must be made in writing and before the time of payment are overruled. See Succession of Virgin, 18 La.Ann. 42 (1866); Bank of Bienville v. Fidelity & Deposit Co. of Maryland, 172 La. 687, 135 So. 26 (1931); Cooper v. Jennings Refining Co., 118 La. 181, 42 So. 766 (1907); Cox v. W.H. Heroman & Co., Inc., 298 So.2d 848 (La.1974).

(g) Under this Article, a transferee of rights cannot claim any advantage based on the allegation that his right was acquired by subrogation rather than by assignment.

Art. 1828.   Conventional subrogation by the obligor

An obligor who pays a debt with money or other fungible things borrowed for that purpose may subrogate the lender to the rights of the obligee, even without the obligee's consent.

The agreement for subrogation must be made in writing expressing that the purpose of the loan is to pay the debt.

Acts 1984, No. 331, § 1, eff. Jan. 1, 1985.

REVISION COMMENTS—1984

(a) This Article reproduces the substance of C.C. Art. 2160(2) (1870). It changes the law in part, abandoning the source article's requirement that the subrogation be effected by authentic act. Requiring only that the agreement be made in writing is more consistent with contemporary business practices.

(b) This Article recognizes that fungible things other than money may be borrowed for the purpose of paying a debt. That approach was taken in the Italian and Ethiopian Codes. In modern business practice such loans, for instance a loan of goods between merchants in the same trade for the purpose of replenishing inventory, are not unusual.

Art. 1829.   Subrogation by operation of law

Subrogation takes place by operation of law:

(1) In favor of an obligee who pays another obligee whose right is preferred to his because of a privilege, pledge, mortgage, or security interest;

(2) In favor of a purchaser of movable or immovable property who uses the purchase money to pay creditors holding any privilege, pledge, mortgage, or security interest on the property;

(3) In favor of an obligor who pays a debt he owes with others or for others and who has recourse against those others as a result of the payment;

(4) In favor of a successor who pays estate debts with his own funds; and

(5) In the other cases provided by law.

Acts 1984, No. 331, § 1, eff. Jan. 1, 1985. Amended by Acts 1989, No. 137, § 16, eff. Sept. 1, 1989; Acts 2001, No. 572, § 1.

REVISION COMMENTS—1984

(a) This Article reproduces the substance of C.C. Art. 2161 (1870). It changes the law in part.

(b) Under this Article, subrogation benefits the purchaser of movable, as well as immovable, property who uses the purchase money to pay a creditor who holds a real right of security on the thing. Since the enactment of Act No. 65 of 1912 (R.S. 9:5351), there is no longer a reason to distinguish between movables and immovables under this Article. See White System of Alexandria v. Fitzhugh, 5 So.2d 555 (La.App. 2nd Cir.1942).

(c) Under this Article, an obligor who pays a debt he owes with others or for others is legally subrogated to the rights of the obligee only if he brings an action against the others as a result of that payment. An obligor is bound "with" another under this Article regardless of whether his obligation arises from the same act as the obligation of the other or from a different act. See Gay & Co. v. Blanchard, 32 La.Ann. 497 (1880).

(d) Under this Article, a creditor who pays another creditor is not legally subrogated to the rights of the latter if the former was the principal obligor of the debt. See Pringle-Associated Mortgage Corporation v. Eanes, 254 La. 705, 226 So.2d 502 (1969).

(e) Besides the situations provided for in this Article, legal subrogation takes place in other instances, such as subrogation of a state supported charity hospital to the rights of a patient (R.S. 46:8, as amended by Acts 1978, No. 786, § 6); subrogation of an employer or insurer who pays an employee workmen's compensation to the rights of that employee against a third person under the

Workmen's Compensation Act (R.S. 23:1101, as amended by Acts 1976, No. 147, § 2); and subrogation of a taxpayer to the right of the collecting authorities under R.S. 47:2105.

Art. 1830. Effects of legal subrogation

When subrogation takes place by operation of law, the new obligee may recover from the obligor only to the extent of the performance rendered to the original obligee. The new obligee may not recover more by invoking conventional subrogation.

Acts 1984, No. 331, § 1, eff. Jan. 1, 1985.

REVISION COMMENTS—1984

(a) This Article is new. It changes the law insofar as it limits the recovery of a person substituting himself to the rights of another to the amount actually paid only when subrogation takes place by operation of law.

(b) The Louisiana jurisprudence has asserted that a person who pays the debt of another and subrogates himself to the rights of the obligee may recover from the obligor only as much as that person paid the obligee. See Roman v. Forstall, 11 La.Ann. 717 (1856); see also H.B. "Buster" Hughes, Inc., v. Bernard, 306 So.2d 785 (La.App. 4th Cir.1975). Under this Article, recovery is so limited in all cases of subrogation by operation of law because that is the fairest solution. When the subrogation is conventional rather than legal, under revised C.C. Art. 1827 (Rev.1984), supra, its effects are the same as those of an assignment; so the subrogee may recover the full amount of the credit regardless of the amount he has paid to the obligee.

(c) Under this Article, a legal subrogee may not claim a greater advantage by availing himself of conventional subrogation. Otherwise, the limitation of recovery in the case of legal subrogation, which is a principle of fairness, could easily be circumvented.

CHAPTER 5—PROOF OF OBLIGATIONS

Art. 1831. Party must prove obligation

A party who demands performance of an obligation must prove the existence of the obligation.

A party who asserts that an obligation is null, or that it has been modified or extinguished, must prove the facts or acts giving rise to the nullity, modification, or extinction.

Acts 1984, No. 331, § 1, eff. Jan. 1, 1985.

REVISION COMMENTS—1984

(a) This Article reproduces the substance and expands the language of C.C. Art. 2232 (1870). It does not change the law.

(b) The Louisiana jurisprudence has established that the party demanding performance bears the burden of proving the obligation by a preponderance of the evidence. E.g., Bordlee v. Pat's Construction Company, Inc., 316 So.2d 16 (La.App. 4th Cir.1975).

Art. 1832. Written form required by law

When the law requires a contract to be in written form, the contract may not be proved by testimony or by presumption, unless the written instrument has been destroyed, lost, or stolen.

Acts 1984, No. 331, § 1, eff. Jan. 1, 1985.

REVISION COMMENTS—1984

(a) This Article is new. It does not change the law, however. It formulates a principle implicit in C.C. Arts. 2275 and 2278(4) (1870), and it reproduces the substance of C.C. Arts. 2279 and 2280 (1870).

(b) The dominant principle in the matter of documentary proof is that where a writing is required for the validity of an act, that act may not be proved by any other means. See Triangle

Farms v. Harvey, 178 La. 559, 152 So. 124 (1934); 7 Planiol et Ripert, Traité pratique de droit civil français 974–975 (2nd ed. Esmein 1954).

Art. 1833. Authentic act

A.   An authentic act is a writing executed before a notary public or other officer authorized to perform that function, in the presence of two witnesses, and signed by each party who executed it, by each witness, and by each notary public before whom it was executed. The typed or hand-printed name of each person shall be placed in a legible form immediately beneath the signature of each person signing the act.

B.   To be an authentic act, the writing need not be executed at one time or place, or before the same notary public or in the presence of the same witnesses, provided that each party who executes it does so before a notary public or other officer authorized to perform that function, and in the presence of two witnesses and each party, each witness, and each notary public signs it. The failure to include the typed or hand-printed name of each person signing the act shall not affect the validity or authenticity of the act.

C.   If a party is unable or does not know how to sign his name, the notary public must cause him to affix his mark to the writing.

Acts 1984, No. 331, § 1, eff. Jan. 1, 1985. Amended by Acts 2003, No. 965, § 1, eff. Jan. 1, 2005.

REVISION COMMENTS—1984

(a) This Article reproduces the substance of C.C. Art. 2234 (1870). It does not change the law.

(b) Under this Article, all persons contemplated in R.S. 35:2, 35:7–9, 35:15–16, and 35:513 are officers authorized to perform notarial functions.

(c) Under this Article, an adjudication made by the sheriff in a judicial sale of succession property has the same effect as an authentic act for the purpose of transferring title. See C.C. Art. 2623 (1870).

Art. 1834. Act that fails to be authentic

An act that fails to be authentic because of the lack of competence or capacity of the notary public, or because of a defect of form, may still be valid as an act under private signature.

Acts 1984, No. 331, § 1, eff. Jan. 1, 1985.

REVISION COMMENT—1984

This Article restates the rule of C.C. Art. 2235 (1870). It does not change the law.

Art. 1835. Authentic act constitutes full proof between parties and heirs

An authentic act constitutes full proof of the agreement it contains, as against the parties, their heirs, and successors by universal or particular title.

Acts 1984, No. 331, § 1, eff. Jan. 1, 1985.

REVISION COMMENTS—1984

(a) This Article reproduces the substance of C.C. Art. 2236 (1870). It does not change the law.

(b) This Article eliminates the reference to forged acts found in C.C. Art. 2236 (1870). A forged act is of course not authentic and can have no evidentiary effect. An act made through a vice of consent is in the same position. See comments under revised C.C. Art. 1948 (Rev.1984), infra.

Art. 1836. Act under private signature duly acknowledged

An act under private signature is regarded prima facie as the true and genuine act of a party executing it when his signature has been acknowledged, and the act shall be admitted in evidence without further proof.

An act under private signature may be acknowledged by a party to that act by recognizing the signature as his own before a court, or before a notary public, or other officer authorized to perform that function, in the presence of two witnesses. An act under private signature may be acknowledged also in any other manner authorized by law.

Nevertheless, an act under private signature, though acknowledged, cannot substitute for an authentic act when the law prescribes such an act.

Acts 1984, No. 331, § 1, eff. Jan. 1, 1985.

REVISION COMMENTS—1984

(a) This Article reproduces the substance of C.C. Arts. 2240 and 2242 (1870). It changes the law in part, making an acknowledged act under private signature not equivalent to an authentic act, but merely admissible in evidence as prima facie genuine. See R.S. 13:3720.

(b) Under this Article, an act under private signature may be acknowledged not only by the party who executed it, but also by a witness in whose presence it was executed. See R.S. 13:3720, R.S. 32:707, R.S. 35:511, and R.S. 35:513.

Art. 1837.   Act under private signature

An act under private signature need not be written by the parties, but must be signed by them.

Acts 1984, No. 331, § 1, eff. Jan. 1, 1985.

REVISION COMMENTS—1984

(a) This Article reproduces the substance of C.C. Art. 2241 (1870). It does not change the law.

(b) This Article is not intended to change the jurisprudential rule that an act under private signature is valid even though signed by one party alone, when the party who signed it asserts the validity of a commutative contract contained in the writing against a party who did not sign it but whose conduct reveals that he has availed himself of the contract. Thus, in Succession of Jenkins v. Dykes, 91 So.2d 416 (La.App. 2nd Cir.1956), a transfer of immovable property in return for the transferee's assumption of a mortgage was held enforceable against a transferee who had not signed the act of transfer, but who had later granted a mineral lease on that property. And in Saunders v. Bolden, 155 La. 136, 98 So. 867 (1923), the court said: "It is well settled in the jurisprudence of this state that written acceptance of a contract or an act of sale is not necessary, but may be established by acts clearly indicating acceptance. In Balch v. Young, 23 La.Ann. 272, it was said that the law does not require that the acceptance of a contract must be expressed on its face, nor is it essential that the act be signed by the party in whose favor it is made. The acceptance may result from his acts in availing himself of its stipulations, or in doing some act which indicates his acceptance." 98 So. at 869. The same criterion prevails in the case of contracts that do not import a transfer. In Atlantic Banana Co. v. Standard Fruit and Steamship Co., 493 F.2d 555 (5th Cir.1974), where the parties had agreed orally on highly specific terms governing various aspects of a complicated joint import business and had both fully performed for a substantial period of time, the court held a written draft of the agreement enforceable although it had been signed by one party alone and never executed by the other. See also Alley v. New Homes Promotion, 247 So.2d 218 (La.App. 4th Cir.1971), writ denied 258 La. 972, 248 So.2d 832 (1971). Thus, a mineral lease may be enforced against a lessee who did not sign it if he has made payments under it or otherwise asserted his right to the lease. See Pennington v. Colonial Pipeline Co., 260 F.Supp. 643 (E.D.La.1966). This exception is based on the same rationale as the French doctrine of commencement de preuve par écrit (commencement of proof in writing). Under that doctrine, a party who does not sign a writing under private signature is nevertheless held to its terms if he has in any manner "intellectually appropriated" those terms. See 7 Planiol et Ripert, Traité pratique de droit civil français 993 (2nd ed. Esmein 1954).

(c) Under this Article, a mark made by a person who cannot write is a sufficient signature. See Zacharie v. Franklin, 37 U.S. 151, 12 Pet. 151, 9 L.Ed. 1035 (1838).

Art. 1838.   Party must acknowledge or deny signature

A party against whom an act under private signature is asserted must acknowledge his signature or deny that it is his.

In case of denial, any means of proof may be used to establish that the signature belongs to that party.

Acts 1984, No. 331, § 1, eff. Jan. 1, 1985.

REVISION COMMENT—1984

This Article reproduces the substance of C.C. Arts. 2244 and 2245 (1870). It does not change the law.

Art. 1839. Transfer of immovable property

A transfer of immovable property must be made by authentic act or by act under private signature. Nevertheless, an oral transfer is valid between the parties when the property has been actually delivered and the transferor recognizes the transfer when interrogated on oath.

An instrument involving immovable property shall have effect against third persons only from the time it is filed for registry in the parish where the property is located.

Acts 1984, No. 331, § 1, eff. Jan. 1, 1985.

REVISION COMMENTS—1984

(a) This Article restates the basic principles of C.C. Arts. 2275, 2264, 2265, and 2266 (1870). It does not change the law. See Lemoine v. Lacour, 213 La. 109, 34 So.2d 392 (1948); Larido v. Perkins, 132 La. 660, 61 So. 728 (1913).

(b) This Article does not change the scheme contained in the statutes governing recordation, or the jurisprudence thereunder. See R.S. 9:2721–2724. See also C.C. Art. 3342 (1870).

Art. 1840. Copy of authentic act

When certified by the notary public or other officer before whom the act was passed, a copy of an authentic act constitutes proof of the contents of the original, unless the copy is proved to be incorrect.

Acts 1984, No. 331, § 1, eff. Jan. 1, 1985.

REVISION COMMENT—1984

This Article reproduces the substance of C.C. Art. 2268 (1870). It does not change the law.

Art. 1841. Copy of recorded writing

When an authentic act or an acknowledged act under private signature has been filed for registry with a public officer, a copy of the act thus filed, when certified by that officer, constitutes proof of the contents of the original.

Acts 1984, No. 331, § 1, eff. Jan. 1, 1985.

REVISION COMMENTS—1984

(a) This Article is new. It changes the law in part. Under it, the evidentiary value of a certified copy no longer depends upon the original's having been lost (See Sampson & Keene v. Noble, 14 La.Ann. 347 (1859); White v. White, 156 La. 324, 100 So. 442 (1924)); and evidentiary value is extended to certified copies of acknowledged acts under private signature.

(b) Under this Article, a certified copy of a recorded act of sale of immovable property under private signature would not be sufficient to establish title to the property unless the private writing had been duly acknowledged. See Tesson v. Gusman, 26 La.Ann. 248 (1874).

(c) Civil Code Article 2253 (1870) has been eliminated because the contrary view prevails in the Louisiana jurisprudence. See Hunt v. Bowie, 358 So.2d 969 (La.App. 1st Cir.1978); Rawls v. Thomas, 3 La.App. 484 (La.App. 2nd Cir.1926); and Stallcup v. Pyron, 33 La.Ann. 1249 (1881).

(d) Civil Code Article 2270 (1870), equivalent to Article 1336 of the Code Napoleon, was enacted in 1808. Civil Code Article 2253 (1870) was introduced in 1825. Civil Code Article 2257 (1870) was introduced in 1870. See 3 Louisiana Legal Archives, Part II, at 1232–1240 (1942). This Article

432

attempts to bring C.C. Art. 2270 (1870) up to date, accounting for the important modifications ensuing the adoption of public records.

Art. 1842. Confirmation

Confirmation is a declaration whereby a person cures the relative nullity of an obligation.

An express act of confirmation must contain or identify the substance of the obligation and evidence the intention to cure its relative nullity.

Tacit confirmation may result from voluntary performance of the obligation.

Acts 1984, No. 331, § 1, eff. Jan. 1, 1985.

REVISION COMMENTS—1984

(a) This Article reproduces the substance of C.C. Art. 2272 (1870). It does not change the law.

(b) The stated requirements must be met for an act, especially a written act, to be accepted as proof of a confirmation, but this does not mean that a confirmation cannot be otherwise proved. Commenting on Article 1338 of the Code Napoleon, which C.C. Art. 2272 (1870) reproduced verbatim, a distinguished French writer has said: "The scope of the article must not be misunderstood. The article deals only with the proof of an act of confirmation. If a writing fails to meet the requirements of the article it will not be accepted as proof, but the confirmation itself is still effective if the party invoking it can prove it by any other means such as witnesses, when allowed, confession and oath. An irregular act of confirmation may even operate as a commencement of proof in writing for the purpose of making parol evidence admissible without limitation of amount of the disputed interest." Weill et Terré, Droit civil—Les obligations 354 (3rd ed. 1980).

(c) This Article is consistent with the interpretation given by Louisiana courts to C.C. Art. 2272 (1870). See, e.g., Carmena v. Blaney, 16 La.Ann. 245 (1861).

(d) Civil Code Article 2271 (1870) had been suppressed as unnecessary. See Exposé des Motifs.

Art. 1843. Ratification

Ratification is a declaration whereby a person gives his consent to an obligation incurred on his behalf by another without authority.

An express act of ratification must evidence the intention to be bound by the ratified obligation.

Tacit ratification results when a person, with knowledge of an obligation incurred on his behalf by another, accepts the benefit of that obligation.

Acts 1984, No. 331, § 1, eff. Jan. 1, 1985.

REVISION COMMENTS—1984

(a) This Article is new, but it does not change the law. It clarifies the concept of ratification contained in C.C. Art. 2272 (1870).

(b) Where ratification proper is concerned, Louisiana courts have been in accord with the views expressed by Toullier which are reproduced in The Exposé des Motifs. Older decisions asserted that: "(T)he acquiescence or long silence of the principal touching an unauthorized or illegal act of his agent (is) a ratification of the act or contract of the agent." Lafitte, Dufilho & Co. v. Godchaux, 35 La.Ann. 1161, 1163 (1883). See also Howland v. Fosdick, 4 La.Ann. 556 (1849). More recently, the jurisprudential rule has been that stated in this Article: "Ratification will occur when the principal, knowing of the contract, does not repudiate it but accepts its benefits." Bamber Contractors, Inc. v. Morrison Engineering and Contracting Co., Inc., 385 So.2d 327, 331 (La.App. 1st Cir.1980).

Art. 1844. Effects of confirmation and ratification

The effects of confirmation and ratification are retroactive to the date of the confirmed or ratified obligation. Neither confirmation nor ratification may impair the rights of third persons.

Acts 1984, No. 331, § 1, eff. Jan. 1, 1985.

REVISION COMMENT—1984

This Article is new. It does not change the law, however. It formulates ideas that were in part express and in part implicit in C.C. Art. 2272 (1870).

Art. 1845. Confirmation of donation

A donation inter vivos that is null for lack of proper form may be confirmed by the donor but the confirmation must be made in the form required for a donation.

The universal successor of the donor may, after his death, expressly or tacitly confirm such a donation.

Acts 1984, No. 331, § 1, eff. Jan. 1, 1985.

REVISION COMMENTS—1984

(a) This Article is new. It changes the law in part, permitting a donor to confirm a donation which is null for lack of proper form, provided that the confirmation is made in the form required for a donation, that is, an authentic act. See C.C. Art. 1536 (1870).

(b) A valid confirmation under this Article has effects retroactive to the date of the original invalid donation.

(c) This Article's recognition of a universal successor's power to confirm invalid donations of his ancestor is consistent with the doctrine of natural obligations as reflected in revised C.C. Art. 1762 (Rev.1984), supra.

Art. 1846. Contract not in excess of five hundred dollars

When a writing is not required by law, a contract not reduced to writing, for a price or, in the absence of a price, for a value not in excess of five hundred dollars may be proved by competent evidence.

If the price or value is in excess of five hundred dollars, the contract must be proved by at least one witness and other corroborating circumstances.

Acts 1984, No. 331, § 1, eff. Jan. 1, 1985.

REVISION COMMENT—1984

This Article reproduces the substance of C.C. Art. 2277 (1870). It does not change the law.

Art. 1847. Debt of a third person and debt extinguished by prescription

Parol evidence is inadmissible to establish either a promise to pay the debt of a third person or a promise to pay a debt extinguished by prescription.

Acts 1984, No. 331, § 1, eff. Jan. 1, 1985.

REVISION COMMENTS—1984

(a) This Article reproduces the substance of C.C. Art. 2278 (1870). It does not change the law.

(b) Under this Article, testimonial evidence may not be admitted to prove a promise to pay a debt extinguished by prescription even if the debt arose from a judgment.

(c) Under this Article, testimonial evidence may not be admitted to prove a promise to pay a debt extinguished by prescription even when the promisor is alive.

(d) According to the Louisiana jurisprudence, a writing is not required to prove a promise to pay the debt of a third person when the promisor had a material interest in making the promise and has received something in return therefor. See Coreil v. Vidrine, 188 La. 343, 177 So. 233 (1937); Fabacher v. Crampes, 166 La. 397, 117 So. 439 (1928). This Article does not intend to change that jurisprudential conclusion that constitutes an exception to the general rule expressed in C.C. Art. 2278(3) (1870) which this Article reproduces.

(e) Civil Code Article 2278 (1870) has no equivalent in the Code Napoleon. It was introduced in the revision of 1870, following the language of Acts 1858, No. 208. See 3 Louisiana Legal Archives,

Part II, at 1246 (1942). Its text, no doubt, reflected the influence of the common law Statute of Frauds. See 12 Ch. 2 (1676).

(f) Since this revision, like the Louisiana Civil Code of 1870, contains no Article comparable to Article 1341 of the French Civil Code, which requires a writing for any contract for a value in excess of a certain sum, the rule here introduced is necessary in order to prevent unfairness in areas where reliance on the fragile memory of witnesses is particularly dangerous. The nature of that danger was clearly discussed by a Louisiana court in the case of Morris v. Abney, 135 La. 302, 65 So. 315 (1914).

(g) See revised C.C. Arts. 1821 through 1830 (Rev.1984), supra.

(h) This Article does not intend any change in the law of suretyship. See C.C. Arts. 3038 and 3039 (1870).

Art. 1848.   Testimonial or other evidence not admitted to disprove a writing

Testimonial or other evidence may not be admitted to negate or vary the contents of an authentic act or an act under private signature. Nevertheless, in the interest of justice, that evidence may be admitted to prove such circumstances as a vice of consent or to prove that the written act was modified by a subsequent and valid oral agreement.

Acts 1984, No. 331, § 1, eff. Jan. 1, 1985. Amended by Acts 2012, No. 277, § 1.

REVISION COMMENTS—1984

(a) This Article is new. It does not change the law, however. It reproduces the substance of C.C. Art. 2276 (1870) and incorporates exceptions recognized by the Louisiana jurisprudence.

(b) Testimonial proof may be used against a writing to show error, fraud, or duress. See Harnischfeger Sale Corporation v. Sternberg Co., 179 La. 317, 154 So. 10 (1934); Broussard v. Sudrique, 4 La. 347 (1832). It may also be admitted to show that a written contract was modified by a subsequent and valid verbal agreement (Succession of Burns, 199 La. 1081, 7 So.2d 359 (1942); Commandeur v. Russell, 5 Mart. (N.S.) 456 (1827)); or that a contract had an unlawful cause (Succession of Fletcher v. Découdreau, 11 La.Ann. 59 (1856)).

(c) Under this Article, testimonial or other evidence is admissible to prove an absolute or relative simulation. See revised C.C. Arts. 2025–2028 (Rev.1984), infra; Smith v. Southern Kraft Corporation, 202 La. 1019, 13 So.2d 335 (1943); Cleveland v. Westmoreland, 191 La. 863, 186 So. 593 (1939). Nevertheless, the nature of the simulation may determine whether only third persons, or the parties to the simulated act themselves, may avail themselves of such evidence. See revised C.C. Arts. 2025–2028 (Rev.1984), infra; C.C. Art. 2239 (1870). In any case, proof of simulation cannot affect the rights of third persons who have relied on the public records. See Chachere v. Superior Oil Co., 192 La. 193, 187 So. 321 (1939); McDuffie v. Walker, 125 La. 152, 51 So. 100 (1909).

Art. 1849.   Proof of simulation

In all cases, testimonial or other evidence may be admitted to prove the existence or a presumption of a simulation or to rebut such a presumption. Nevertheless, between the parties, a counterletter is required to prove that an act purporting to transfer immovable property is an absolute simulation, except when a simulation is presumed or as necessary to protect the rights of forced heirs.

Added by Acts 2012, No. 277, § 1.

REVISION COMMENTS—2012

(a) This Article is new. It reproduces the substance of C.C. Art. 1848 (Rev.1984) and clarifies when a counterletter is necessary to prove a simulation. In light of this Article, comment (c) to Article 1848 should no longer be considered in the context of proving the existence of simulations.

(b) For an example of a presumption of simulation, see C.C. Art. 2480 (Rev.1993).

(c) Under this Article, a relative simulation may be proved by testimonial or other evidence. Saul Litvinoff, Louisiana Law of Obligations, § 12.97 (5 La. Civ. L. Treatise 2009) ("When the act contained in a written instrument is a relative simulation, that is, when the parties intend that their act shall produce between them effects different from those recited in the instrument, testimonial proof is admissible to prove their true intent.") The jurisprudence admits testimonial evidence to prove a relative simulation. See, e.g., Love v. Dedon, 118 So.2d 122 (La. 1960); McWilliams v. McWilliams, 39 La.Ann. 924 (La. 1887); Bennett v. Porter, 58 So.3d 663 (La.App. 3d Cir. 2011); LeBlanc v. Romero, 783 So.2d 419, 421 (La.App. 3d Cir. 2001); Mathews v. Mathews, 1 So. 3d 738 (La.App. 2d Cir. 2008). Other articles in the Civil Code recognize that the true cause of an obligation can be proved without special formalities. See, e.g., C.C. Arts. 1970 (Rev. 1984) and 2464 (Rev. 1993).

(d) Under this Article, even an absolute simulation may generally be proved by testimonial or other evidence, unless the simulation purports to transfer immovable property. Saul Litvinoff, Louisiana Law of Obligations, § 12.97 (5 La. Civ. L. Treatise 2009) ("If the simulation is absolute . . . testimonial proof that the written act is actually a simulation may not be admitted when the apparent or simulated act contained in a writing purports to effect a transfer of immovable property.") See also Ridgedell v. Kuyrkendall, 740 So.2d 173 (La.App. 1st Cir. 1999); Scoggins v. Frederick, 744 So.2d 676 (La.App. 1st Cir. 1999); Kinney v. Bourgeois, 2007 WL 2686113 (La.App. 1st Cir. 2007).

(e) The limitation on the use of testimonial evidence to prove a simulation applies only to parties to the transaction. The privilege of attacking a simulation with parol evidence "has from the very earliest time been available to creditors." Thomas B. Lemann, Some Aspects of Simulation in France and Louisiana, 29 Tul.L. Rev. 22, 43 (1954); Commercial Germania Trust & Sav. Bank v. White, 81 So. 753 (La. 1919) (stating that the rule against parol evidence "is applied only in suits between the parties to the instrument").

(f) Under this Article, forced heirs may protect their legitimes from sham transactions by their parents and may use parol or other evidence to prove an absolute simulation, even if the absolute simulation concerns a transfer of immovable property. This right has existed in the jurisprudence at least since the early nineteenth century. See, e.g., Terrel's Heirs v. Cropper, 9 Mart. (o.s.) 350 (La.1821).

Arts. 1850 to 1852. [Blank]

Art. 1853.   Judicial confession

A judicial confession is a declaration made by a party in a judicial proceeding. That confession constitutes full proof against the party who made it.

A judicial confession is indivisible and it may be revoked only on the ground of error of fact.

Acts 1984, No. 331, § 1, eff. Jan. 1, 1985.

REVISION COMMENTS—1984

(a) This Article reproduces the substance of C.C. Art. 2291 (1870). It does not change the law.

(b) Under this Article, a declaration made by a party's attorney or mandatary has the same effect as one made by the party himself. See C.C. Art. 3021 (1870).

(c) Under this Article, testimony given on the witness stand by a party, without intention of waiving evidence as to the subject matter of that testimony, or factual allegations made in other proceedings, do not constitute judicial confession. See Jackson v. Gulf Ins. Co., 250 La. 819, 199 So.2d 886 (1967).

(d) A judicial confession under this Article is not a bar to a curative amendment under C.C.P. Article 934. See Guidry v. Barras, 368 So.2d 1129 (La.App. 3rd Cir.1979).

(e) Civil Code Article 2290 (1870) has been eliminated since the rule it contained lost its weight owing to jurisprudential developments. See Jackson v. Gulf Ins. Co., 250 La. 819, 199 So.2d 886 (1967); Telford v. New York Life Ins. Co., 227 La. 855, 80 So.2d 711 (1955); Lutrell v. Beard, 273 So.2d 312 (La.App. 4th Cir.1973).

CHAPTER 6—EXTINCTION OF OBLIGATIONS

SECTION 1—PERFORMANCE

Art. 1854. Extinction by performance

Performance by the obligor extinguishes the obligation.

Acts 1984, No. 331, § 1, eff. Jan. 1, 1985.

REVISION COMMENTS—1984

(a) This Article is new. It does not change the law, however. It restates a principle contained in C.C. Art. 2130 (1870).

(b) As used in this Article, "performance" means the performance called for by the obligation. See C.C. Art. 2131 (1870).

Art. 1855. Performance by a third person

Performance may be rendered by a third person, even against the will of the obligee, unless the obligor or the obligee has an interest in performance only by the obligor.

Performance rendered by a third person effects subrogation only when so provided by law or by agreement.

Acts 1984, No. 331, § 1, eff. Jan. 1, 1985.

REVISION COMMENTS—1984

(a) This Article reproduces the substance of C.C. Arts. 2134, 2136, and 2137 (1870). It does not change the law.

(b) Under this Article, performance may be rendered by a third person, even against the obligee's will, provided that the obligation is not of such a nature that the obligee has an interest in receiving performance only from the obligor, and also provided that the third person does not purport to subrogate himself to the right of the obligee.

(c) Under this Article, an obligee may not accept performance from a third person if the obligor has an interest in rendering performance himself.

Art. 1856. Valid transfer of object of performance

An obligation that may be extinguished by the transfer of a thing is not extinguished unless the thing has been validly transferred to the obligee of performance.

Acts 1984, No. 331, § 1, eff. Jan. 1, 1985.

REVISION COMMENTS—1984

(a) This Article is new. It changes C.C. Art. 2138 (1870) to make it compatible with C.C. Arts. 521 and 522, as revised by Acts 1979, No. 180.

(b) Under this Article and C.C. Art. 521, as revised by Acts 1979, No. 180, if an obligor uses a lost or stolen thing belonging to another to perform his obligation, the obligee does not acquire ownership; so the obligation is not extinguished. Nevertheless, if the obligor, for the same purpose, uses a thing whose title he has obtained from the owner by fraudulent means, the thing is not stolen; so the obligee to whom it is transferred acquires a valid title, and the obligation is thus extinguished. See C.C. Art. 521, as amended by Acts 1979, No. 180, and Comment (c), infra.

(c) Under this Article and C.C. Art. 522, as revised by Acts 1979, No. 180, if an obligor who has acquired a corporeal movable as a result of error, fraud, or duress uses that movable to perform an obligation, the obligee who receives that performance in good faith acquires ownership of the movable, and the obligation is therefore extinguished.

Art. 1857.   Performance rendered to the obligee

Performance must be rendered to the obligee or to a person authorized by him.

However, a performance rendered to an unauthorized person is valid if the obligee ratifies it.

In the absence of ratification, a performance rendered to an unauthorized person is valid if the obligee has derived a benefit from it, but only for the amount of the benefit.

Acts 1984, No. 331, § 1, eff. Jan. 1, 1985.

REVISION COMMENTS—1984

(a) This Article reproduces the substance of C.C. Arts. 2140, 2141, 2142, 2143, 2144, and 2146 (1870). It does not change the law.

(b) Civil Code Articles 2141, 2142, 2143, 2144, and 2146 (1870) state obvious principles of mandate which do not belong in the section on performance. This Article returns to the concise formulation of the basic rule contained in Article 1239 of the Code Napoleon and Article 139 of the Digest of 1808. See 3 Louisiana Legal Archives, Part II, at 1172 (1942). In French doctrine, a payment made to an unauthorized person, like a payment made to a person incapable of receiving it, is valid only dans la mesure, that is, to the extent or for the amount of the benefit derived by the obligee. See 7 Planiol et Ripert, Traité pratique de droit civil français 555 (2nd ed. Esmein 1954).

Art. 1858.   Lack of capacity of obligee

Performance rendered to an obligee without capacity to receive it is valid to the extent of the benefit he derived from it.

Acts 1984, No. 331, § 1, eff. Jan. 1, 1985.

REVISION COMMENTS—1984

(a) This Article reproduces the substance of C.C. Art. 2147 (1870). It does not change the law.

(b) Under this Article, the obligor must prove that the obligee has derived a benefit.

(c) An obligee without capacity to receive a payment is deemed to have derived a benefit from it when he has employed it for a useful purpose, such as paying a debt of his own or building improvements on his land. See 7 Planiol et Ripert, Traité pratique de droit civil français 555 (2nd ed. Esmein 1954).

Art. 1859.   Performance in violation of seizure

A performance rendered to an obligee in violation of a seizure is not valid against the seizing creditor who, according to his right, may force the obligor to perform again.

In that case, the obligor may recover the first performance from the obligee.

Acts 1984, No. 331, § 1, eff. Jan. 1, 1985.

REVISION COMMENT—1984

This Article reproduces the substance of C.C. Art. 2149 (1870). It does not change the law.

Art. 1860.   Quality of thing to be given

When the performance consists of giving a thing that is determined as to its kind only, the obligor need not give one of the best quality but he may not tender one of the worst.

Acts 1984, No. 331, § 1, eff. Jan. 1, 1985.

REVISION COMMENTS—1984

(a) This Article reproduces the substance of C.C. Art. 2156 (1870). It does not change the law.

(b) Under this Article, an obligor is deemed to have performed his obligation if he has delivered a thing of marketable quality.

Art. 1861.   Partial performance

An obligee may refuse to accept a partial performance.

Nevertheless, if the amount of an obligation to pay money is disputed in part and the obligor is willing to pay the undisputed part, the obligee may not refuse to accept that part. If the obligee is willing to accept the undisputed part, the obligor must pay it. In either case, the obligee preserves his right to claim the disputed part.

Acts 1984, No. 331, § 1, eff. Jan. 1, 1985.

REVISION COMMENTS—1984

(a) This Article is new. It reproduces the substance of C.C. Art. 2153 (1870), but changes the law in part.

(b) This Article is not intended to apply where there is an "accord and satisfaction." When a creditor asserts that the debtor owes a certain amount, but the debtor only admits owing a certain lesser amount, the latter amount becomes what is known as the "lesser undisputed amount." See 1 C.J.S. 555; Nassoiy v. Tomlinson, 148 N.Y. 326, 42 N.E. 715 (C.A.1896). If the debtor tenders the lesser amount under the express condition that it be accepted in full payment, and the creditor takes the money or cashes the check, the result is accord and satisfaction which extinguishes the debt. But see R.S. 10:1–207. See Meyers v. Acme Homestead Assn., 138 So. 443 (La.App.Orl.1931); see also Berger v. Quintero, 170 La. 37, 127 So. 356 (1930). Louisiana courts have accepted this solution in spite of doubts about its consistency with the Louisiana Civil Code of 1870 and misgivings concerning the "consideration" that validates such an "accord." See 1 Litvinoff, Obligations 657–662 (1969); Litvinoff, "The Work of the Louisiana Appellate Courts for the 1974–1975 Term—Accord and Satisfaction," 36 La.L.Rev. 426–434 (1976); Charles X. Miller, Inc. v. Oak Builders, Inc., 306 So.2d 449 (La.App. 4th Cir.1975).

(c) Under this Article, a debtor may not refuse to pay the undisputed amount when the creditor is willing to accept that amount as partial payment, even if the creditor is unwilling to accept that amount as full payment of the obligation.

Art. 1862.   Place of performance

Performance shall be rendered in the place either stipulated in the agreement or intended by the parties according to usage, the nature of the performance, or other circumstances.

In the absence of agreement or other indication of the parties' intent, performance of an obligation to give an individually determined thing shall be rendered at the place the thing was when the obligation arose. If the obligation is of any other kind, the performance shall be rendered at the domicile of the obligor.

Acts 1984, No. 331, § 1, eff. Jan. 1, 1985.

REVISION COMMENT—1984

This Article reproduces the substance of C.C. Art. 2157 (1870). It does not change the law. See Edwards v. Standard Oil Co. of Louisiana, 175 La. 720, 144 So. 430 (1932); Belvin v. Sikes, 2 So.2d 65 (La.App. 2nd Cir.1941).

Art. 1863.   Expenses

Expenses that may be required to render performance shall be borne by the obligor.

Acts 1984, No. 331, § 1, eff. Jan. 1, 1985.

REVISION COMMENT—1984

This Article reproduces the substance of C.C. Art. 2158 (1870). It does not change the law.

SUBSECTION A—IMPUTATION OF PAYMENT

Art. 1864.   Imputation by obligor

An obligor who owes several debts to an obligee has the right to impute payment to the debt he intends to pay.

The obligor's intent to pay a certain debt may be expressed at the time of payment or may be inferred from circumstances known to the obligee.

Acts 1984, No. 331, § 1, eff. Jan. 1, 1985.

REVISION COMMENTS—1984

(a) This Article is new, but it does not change the law. It reproduces the substance of C.C. Art. 2163 (1870).

(b) This Article applies to debts of sums of money and also to obligations to give fungible things. If the object of the performance is not fungible, as in the case of an obligation to give a unique thing, rules governing imputation are unnecessary. For that reason, this Article, like the others in this Section, preserves the expression "imputation of payment" rather than utilizing "imputation of performance." "Payment" is thus confined to mean the performance of an obligation to pay money or to give fungible things.

Art. 1865.   Imputation to debt not yet due

An obligor may not, without the obligee's consent, impute payment to a debt not yet due.

Acts 1984, No. 331, § 1, eff. Jan. 1, 1985.

REVISION COMMENTS—1984

(a) This Article is new. It does not change the law, however. It expresses a principle implied in C.C. Arts. 2053, 2150, and 2154 (1870).

(b) Under this Article, an obligor may not, by exercising his right to make imputation, impair the obligee's right. It has been established that, when fixed for an interest-bearing debt, a term is for the benefit of the obligee. See In re Liquidation of Hibernia Bank & Trust Co., 189 La. 813, 180 So. 646 (1938). This is a special exception to the general rule that a term is presumed to be for the benefit of the obligor which is stated in revised C.C. Art. 1779 (Rev.1984), supra.

Art. 1866.   Payment imputed to interest

An obligor of a debt that bears interest may not, without the obligee's consent, impute a payment to principal when interest is due.

A payment made on principal and interest must be imputed first to interest.

Acts 1984, No. 331, § 1, eff. Jan. 1, 1985.

REVISION COMMENTS—1984

(a) This Article reproduces the substance of C.C. Art. 2164 (1870). It does not change the law.

(b) This Article is applicable, by analogy, to a situation where the debt produces civil fruits other than interest, as in the case of rents and annuities. See C.C. Arts. 2793–2800 (1870).

Art. 1867.   Imputation by obligee

An obligor who has accepted a receipt that imputes payment to one of his debts may no longer demand imputation to another debt, unless the obligee has acted in bad faith.

Acts 1984, No. 331, § 1, eff. Jan. 1, 1985.

REVISION COMMENTS—1984

(a) This Article reproduces the substance of C.C. Art. 2165 (1870). It does not change the law.

(b) An obligee acts in bad faith under this Article when he imputes payment to one debt although the circumstances clearly indicate the obligor's intent to pay a different debt. See Madison Lumber Co. v. Globe Indemnity Co., 161 So. 775 (La.App.Orl.1935); Grand Lodge B.K. of America v. Murphy Const. Co., 152 La. 123, 92 So. 757 (1922).

Art. 1868.   Imputation not made by the parties

When the parties have made no imputation, payment must be imputed to the debt that is already due.

If several debts are due, payment must be imputed to the debt that bears interest.

If all, or none, of the debts that are due bear interest, payment must be imputed to the debt that is secured.

If several unsecured debts bear interest, payment must be imputed to the debt that, because of the rate of interest, is most burdensome to the obligor.

If several secured debts bear no interest, payment must be imputed to the debt that, because of the nature of the security, is most burdensome to the obligor.

If the obligor had the same interest in paying all debts, payment must be imputed to the debt that became due first.

If all debts are of the same nature and became due at the same time, payment must be proportionally imputed to all.

Acts 1984, No. 331, § 1, eff. Jan. 1, 1985.

REVISION COMMENTS—1984

(a) This Article reproduces the substance of C.C. Art. 2166 (1870). It does not change the law.

(b) Under this Article, payment is imputed as follows: first, on the basis of whether a particular debt is due; second, according to whether it bears interest; third, according to whether it is secured; and fourth, according to the date on which it became due. If all of these factors are equal, then the payment must be imputed to all of the debts proportionally.

(c) Under the sixth paragraph of this Article, payment may be imputed to a debt other than the one that fell due first when the obligor does not have the same interest in paying all his debts, such as when nonpayment of the last that fell due may expose him to contempt of court. See Leach v. Leach, 238 So.2d 26 (La.App. 1st Cir.1970).

(d) Neither C.C. Art. 2166 (1870) nor its French ancestor is sufficiently clear. The criterion "the debt, which the debtor had at the time most interest in discharging" cannot be used with confidence to resolve conflicts between interest-bearing debts and secured ones. There is abundant Louisiana jurisprudence to the effect that payment must be imputed to a secured debt over an unsecured one, and also to the effect that an interest-bearing debt must take precedence over a noninterest-bearing one. See Calatex Oil & Gas Co. v. Smith, 175 La. 678, 144 So. 243 (1932); Everett v. Graye, 3 La.App. 136 (1925); Johnson v. Succession of Robbins, 20 La.Ann. 569 (1868). But no decision has clarified whether a secured debt takes precedence over an interest-bearing one or vice-versa. In French doctrine, payment in such a case should be imputed to the interest-bearing debt. See 7 Planiol et Ripert, Traité pratique de droit civil français 611 (2nd ed. Esmein 1954). The Cour de cassation, however, asserts that the court has the sovereign prerogative of determining which debt the obligor has a greater interest in paying. See Req. July 23, 1884, D. 84.1.459, S. 85.1.365. This Article establishes priorities in a clear manner.

SUBSECTION B—TENDER AND DEPOSIT

Art. 1869.   Offer to perform and deposit by obligor

When the object of the performance is the delivery of a thing or a sum of money and the obligee, without justification, fails to accept the performance tendered by the obligor, the tender, followed by deposit to the order of the court, produces all the effects of a performance from the time the tender was made if declared valid by the court.

A valid tender is an offer to perform according to the nature of the obligation.

Acts 1984, No. 331, § 1, eff. Jan. 1, 1985.

REVISION COMMENTS—1984

(a) This Article is new. It does not change the law, however. It reproduces the substance of C.C. Arts. 2167 and 2168 (1870).

(b) Under this Article, extinguishment of an obligation through tender and deposit is limited to obligations the performance of which consists of delivering a thing or a sum of money. The language of the source Articles is broad enough to include obligations whose performance consists of acts of the obligor other than delivering a thing, such as contracts for services. However, services, although they can be tendered, cannot be deposited. In fact, the effects of the common law tender of services are accomplished under Louisiana law by putting in default. See Jones v. Smalley, 5 La. 28 (1832) (common law approach); revised C.C. Arts. 1989–1993 (Rev.1984), infra; C.C. Arts. 1913 and 1914 (1870). In French doctrine, the mechanism of tender and deposit for extinguishing obligations was meant to be confined to obligations to give. See French Civil Code Articles 1257 and 1258; 7 Planiol et Ripert, Traité pratique de droit civil français 618 (2nd ed. Esmein 1954); 4 Aubry et Rau, Cours de droit civil français—Obligations 210–219 (Louisiana State Law Institute trans. 1965).

(c) A tender is valid only if the requirements for a valid performance, such as capacity, amount, and kind of performance, are fulfilled. See Collins v. Employers' Liability Assur. Corp., 116 So.2d 851 (La.App. 1st Cir. 1959).

(d) Under this Article, if the obligee accepts the deposit or if the court declares the performance valid, the liberative effects of performance take place from that time the tender was made: Inter alia, from that time interest ceases to accrue (see Frey v. Fitzpatrick-Cromwell Co., 108 La. 125, 32 So. 437 (1902)), and the obligee bears the risk of loss of the tendered item. (Breen v. Schmidt, 6 La.Ann. 13 (1851); Smith v. Richardson, 11 Rob. 516 (1845)).

(e) Under this Article and revised C.C. Art. 1871 (Rev.1984), infra, if the deposit is accepted, the obligee is liable for the expenses of safekeeping the thing and other damages the obligor might have sustained because of the obligee's default.

(f) The word "consignment" used in C.C. Art. 2167 (1870) was a literal translation of the French "consignation," which simply means to deposit with a court. In Domingue v. Huval, 261 So.2d 88, 90 (La.App. 3rd Cir.1972), the court said: "A consignment, as that term is used in this Article, generally entails the deposit of funds tendered in the registry of the court in an appropriate proceeding, or otherwise making the funds available to the adverse party."

(g) Civil Code Article 2167 (1870) speaks of "real tender," which means "offres réelles," as in the French original, that is, more than a mere verbal offer to pay. In Sewell v. Willcox, 5 Rob. 83, 89–90 (1843), the court said: "In the French jurisprudence, from which we suppose this doctrine is copied, offers are either labiales or réelles. The latter corresponds to our tender, which, when followed by a consignment, amounts to payment." That notion is clearly expressed in English by the word "tender" without resort to the adjective "real."

(h) This Article, like C.C. Art. 2167 (1870), is based on the idea that an obligor's right to perform is correlative of his duty to do so. See 2 Litvinoff, Obligations 9–11 (1975).

Art. 1870.   Notice as tender

If the obligor knows or has reason to know that the obligee will refuse the performance, or when the object of the performance is the delivery of a thing or a sum of money at a place other than the obligee's domicile, a notice given to the obligee that the obligor is ready to perform has the same effect as a tender.

Acts 1984, No. 331, § 1, eff. Jan. 1, 1985.

REVISION COMMENTS—1984

(a) This Article is new. Though it changes the law insofar as it makes a notice as effective as a tender, that change is consistent with C.C. Art. 2168 (1870), which implies that a tender must be actual only when the obligee can be readily found for that purpose.

(b) Under this Article, if the performance is to be rendered at the obligor's domicile, as when goods are to be delivered at a seller's plant, notice to the obligee substitutes for tender.

(c) Under this Article, if performance is to be rendered at a place which is neither the domicile of the obligee nor that of the obligor, notice to the obligee substitutes for tender.

(d) This Article contemplates situations where the obligor knows or has reason to know that the obligee will not take the performance or where the object of the performance is to be rendered at another place, while the preceding article applies where the obligee has actually refused a tendered performance. In both kinds of situations, to produce the effect of liberating the obligor, a tender must be followed by deposit to the order of the court.

(e) Under this Article, if, before any tender is made, the obligee advises the obligor expressly that that performance will not be accepted, the obligor need not give further notice and may proceed to deposit the thing with the court.

Art. 1871.   Deposit of things by obligor

After the tender has been refused, the obligor may deposit the thing or the sum of money to the order of the court in a place designated by the court for that purpose, and may demand judgment declaring the performance valid.

If the deposit is accepted by the obligee, or if the court declares the performance valid, all expenses of the deposit must be borne by the obligee.

Acts 1984, No. 331, § 1, eff. Jan. 1, 1985.

REVISION COMMENTS—1984

(a) This Article is new. It does not change the law, however. It expresses an idea implied in C.C. Art. 2167 (1870).

(b) Under this Article, a tender must be followed by deposit in order to produce liberative effects. See Domingue v. Huval, 261 So.2d 88 (La.App. 3rd Cir.1972); Pichauffe v. Naquin, 241 So. 574 (La.App. 1st Cir.1970).

(c) Since the object of the performance may be something other than a sum of money, this Article allocates the costs that may be incurred in storing it, say in a warehouse, or of arranging for a custodian or guardian to care for it, as provided in C.C. Arts. 2979–2981 (1870). Code of Civil Procedure Article 4658 provides for the deposit of money in the registry of the court.

(d) Although the express provisions of Articles 404–418 of the Code of Practice of 1870, concerning real tender and deposit, have long been repealed, an obligor's action to protect his right to perform falls within the broad scope of Code of Civil Procedure Article 421. See also C.C.P. Art. 854, Comment (a).

Art. 1872.   Sale of a thing and deposit of proceeds

If performance consists of the delivery of a perishable thing, or of a thing whose deposit and custody are excessively costly in proportion to its value, the court may order the sale of the thing under the conditions that it may direct, and the deposit of the proceeds.

Acts 1984, No. 331, § 1, eff. Jan. 1, 1985.

REVISION COMMENTS—1984

(a) This Article is new. It does not change the law, however, but provides a solution consistent with C.C. Art. 2167 (1870).

(b) Under this Article, an obligor who proceeds to sell things after tender or notice must fulfill the obligation of good faith concerning the circumstances of the sale such as price and opportunity. See revised C.C. Art. 1759 (Rev.1984), supra.

(c) Under this Article, the court may elect to proceed in the manner directed in Code of Civil Procedure Article 3264.

SECTION 2—IMPOSSIBILITY OF PERFORMANCE

Art. 1873.   Obligor not liable when failure caused by fortuitous event

An obligor is not liable for his failure to perform when it is caused by a fortuitous event that makes performance impossible.

An obligor is, however, liable for his failure to perform when he has assumed the risk of such a fortuitous event.

An obligor is liable also when the fortuitous event occurred after he has been put in default.

An obligor is likewise liable when the fortuitous event that caused his failure to perform has been preceded by his fault, without which the failure would not have occurred.

Acts 1984, No. 331, § 1, eff. Jan. 1, 1985.

REVISION COMMENTS—1984

(a) This Article is new. It does not change the law, however. It reproduces the substance of C.C. Arts. 1910, 1912, 1933(2), and 1933(3) (1870).

(b) An obligor's assumption of risk may be expressed or implied. See Eugster & Co. v. Joseph West & Co., 35 La.Ann. 119 (1883).

(c) This Article introduces the defense of impossibility of performance. As a matter of legal semantics, "impossibility of performance" is the English equivalent of the French "cas fortuit ou force majeure." See Corbin, "Frustration of Contract in the United States of America," 29 Journal of Comparative Legislation and International Law 1, 3, 5 (1947); Patterson, "Constructive Conditions in Contracts," 42 Columbia Law Review 903 (1942).

In spite of strenuous doctrinal efforts to distinguish between cas fortuit (fortuitous event) and force majeure (irresistible force), the jurisprudence, in France, Louisiana, and even at common law, uses the two expressions interchangeably. See 7 Planiol et Ripert, Traité pratique de droit civil français 171–172 (2nd ed. Esmein 1954); 3 Bonnecase, Supplement to Traité théorique et pratique de droit civil by Baudry-Lacantinerie 474–506 (1926); El-Gammal, L'adaptation du contrat aux circonstances économiques 142–147 (1967); Bénabent, La chance et le droit 29–38 (1973). See generally Honorat, L'idée d'acceptation des risques dans la responsabilité civile (1969).

Modern codes have eliminated one or the other of the two expressions. The Quebec Draft preserved "fortuitous event" and dropped "irresistible force." The Ethiopian Civil Code preserved "irresistible force" and dropped "fortuitous event." The Italian Civil Code adopted the notion of a "cause not imputable to the debtor." The expression "fortuitous event" has been chosen for this revision because it implicitly encompasses the companion concept, especially when the event must be such as to make performance impossible, as this Article provides.

(d) To relieve an obligor of liability the cas fortuit must make the performance truly impossible. See 7 Planiol et Ripert, Traité pratique de droit civil français 168–172 (2nd ed. Esmein 1954). The Louisiana jurisprudence had so held. See, e.g., Eugster & Co. v. Joseph West & Co., supra. Article 1792 of the Ethiopian Civil Code makes this principle quite clear:

"An irresistible force is an event that could not have been normally foreseen by the obligor and that prevents him from performing his obligation in an absolute manner."

Art. 1874. Fortuitous event that would have destroyed object in hands of obligee

An obligor who had been put in default when a fortuitous event made his performance impossible is not liable for his failure to perform if the fortuitous event would have likewise destroyed the object of the performance in the hands of the obligee had performance been timely rendered.

That obligor is, however, liable for the damage caused by his delay.

Acts 1984, No. 331, § 1, eff. Jan. 1, 1985.

REVISION COMMENT—1984

This Article reproduces the substance of C.C. Art. 1933(4) (1870). It does not change the law.

Art. 1875. Fortuitous event

A fortuitous event is one that, at the time the contract was made, could not have been reasonably foreseen.

Acts 1984, No. 331, § 1, eff. Jan. 1, 1985.

REVISION COMMENTS—1984

(a) This Article is new. It does not change the law, however. It reproduces the substance of C.C. Art. 3556(14) and (15) (1870) in more functional language.

(b) Louisiana courts have shown more concern for the reasonableness of the parties' foresight in a given situation than for the objective foreseeability of a particular event. Thus, in Farnsworth v. Sewerage & Water Board of N.O., 173 La. 1105, 139 So. 638 (1932), the court concluded that, although the parties could have assumed that heavy rains might occur, there was no reason for them to have assumed that such rains would cause a flood. Thus, under this Article, the fact that an event is foreseeable does not preclude a conclusion that the parties could not have reasonably foreseen it, since they may not have thought it sufficiently important a risk to have made it the subject of a clause in the contract.

Art. 1876. Contract dissolved when performance becomes impossible

When the entire performance owed by one party has become impossible because of a fortuitous event, the contract is dissolved.

The other party may then recover any performance he has already rendered.

Acts 1984, No. 331, § 1, eff. Jan. 1, 1985.

REVISION COMMENTS—1984

(a) This Article is new. It does not change the law, however. It states a specific rule which is a direct consequence of the general principle contained in C.C. Art. 2046 (1870), and it generalizes the rule contained in C.C. Art. 2219 (1870).

(b) The rule stated in this Article, although now unarticulated in most of the civil codes, is universally accepted. It allows a very fair solution without having to draw too much from principles excessively general, such as cause, implied resolutory condition, and payment of a thing not due.

Art. 1877. Fortuitous event that has made performance impossible in part

When a fortuitous event has made a party's performance impossible in part, the court may reduce the other party's counterperformance proportionally, or, according to the circumstances, may declare the contract dissolved.

Acts 1984, No. 331, § 1, eff. Jan. 1, 1985.

REVISION COMMENTS—1984

(a) This Article is new. It changes the law to the extent that it allows the court to uphold a contract while reducing the amount for which the parties are bound.

(b) Under this Article, the court may uphold the contract if the partial performance by one party will still be of value to the other after a proportional reduction of the latter's counterperformance. The court may declare the contract dissolved if partial performance by one party would be of no value to the other.

(c) This Article deals with a situation not contemplated in the Civil Code of 1870. It might be said that, upon such facts, the basic rule of dissolution should prevail and the contract should be dissolved, but this solution would allow the obligee to take unfair advantage when a partial performance would still be to his benefit but he prefers dissolution for other reasons. Conversely, if the contract were always allowed to stand to the extent that it was not impaired by the fortuitous event, injustice would result when the partial performance was of no value to the other party. The second alternative has been chosen by the Italian Civil Code. This Article gives the court the option of choosing either according to the circumstances of the individual case.

Art. 1878.   Fortuitous event after obligor performed in part

If a contract is dissolved because of a fortuitous event that occurred after an obligor has performed in part, the obligee is bound but only to the extent that he was enriched by the obligor's partial performance.

Acts 1984, No. 331, § 1, eff. Jan. 1, 1985.

REVISION COMMENTS—1984

(a) This Article is new. It does not change the law, however. The rule stated is consistent with C.C. Arts. 21 and 1965 (1870). It is a generalization of the special rule stated in C.C. Art. 2767 (1870).

(b) This Article addresses a situation not expressly contemplated in the Louisiana Revised Civil Code of 1870. Though the solution which it provides is also provided in C.C. Arts. 2766 and 2767 (1870) for cases of lease of labor by the job or plot, it might be argued that in other cases the basic rule of dissolution should apply, and the obligee should return whatever part performance he has received. Such a solution is not satisfactory. This Article eliminates the danger of controversy on that matter.

SECTION 3—NOVATION

Art. 1879.   Extinguishment of existing obligation

Novation is the extinguishment of an existing obligation by the substitution of a new one.

Acts 1984, No. 331, § 1, eff. Jan. 1, 1985.

REVISION COMMENTS—1984

(a) This Article is based on C.C. Art. 2185 (1870). It changes the law only insofar as it does not define novation as a contract. Indeed, novation is not in itself a transaction but the legal effect of certain acts. Novation may even result by operation of law. Nevertheless, the Articles in this Section contemplate a novation effected by agreement, as is the case in the vast majority of instances.

(b) Civil Code Article 2188 (1870) has been eliminated because it is unnecessary. It is also misleading. If "legal" means "civil" in that Article, it expresses an incorrect conclusion, since natural obligations may be novated. See 1 Litvinoff, Obligations 572–573 (1969). In the original French text of 1825, the Article contained no word equivalent to "legal." See 3 Louisiana Legal Archives, Part II, at 1197 (1942).

Art. 1880.   Novation not presumed

The intention to extinguish the original obligation must be clear and unequivocal. Novation may not be presumed.

Acts 1984, No. 331, § 1, eff. Jan. 1, 1985.

REVISION COMMENTS—1984

(a) This Article reproduces the substance of C.C. Art. 2190 (1870). It does not change the law.

(b) Under this Article, the declaration of will that gives rise to a novation must be made by a person with legal capacity, like any other juridical act. The same rule applies when novation results from a showing of facts unequivocally indicating that a party has intended it.

Art. 1881. Objective novation

Novation takes place when, by agreement of the parties, a new performance is substituted for that previously owed, or a new cause is substituted for that of the original obligation. If any substantial part of the original performance is still owed, there is no novation.

Novation takes place also when the parties expressly declare their intention to novate an obligation.

Mere modification of an obligation, made without intention to extinguish it, does not effect a novation. The execution of a new writing, the issuance or renewal of a negotiable instrument, or the giving of new securities for the performance of an existing obligation are examples of such a modification.

Acts 1984, No. 331, § 1, eff. Jan. 1, 1985.

REVISION COMMENTS—1984

(a) This Article is based on C.C. Arts. 2189(1) and 2187 (1870). It does not change the law, but restates it in a manner that is intended to discourage the finding of novation in the absence of clear indication that a new obligation has been contracted and the original extinguished. See Weaks Supply Co. v. Werdin, 147 So. 838 (La.App. 2nd Cir.1933).

(b) Following the example of the Italian Civil Code, this Section distinguishes between objective and subjective novation. This Article deals with objective novation, and the next with subjective novation.

(c) Novation takes place when a new obligation is substituted for an old one, which is thus extinguished. Such a substitution occurs whenever at least one of the basic elements of the original obligation is changed. The basic elements of an obligation are the parties to it, its object, and its cause. See 7 Planiol et Ripert, Traité pratique de droit civil français 664–669 (2nd ed. Esmein 1954); Weill, Droit civil—Les obligations 951 (1970); 1 Litvinoff, Obligations 35–43 (1969). Following well-established tradition, C.C. Art. 2189 (1870), like Article 1271 of the Code Napoleon, expressly contemplates novation by a change of parties; that is, by the substitution of a new obligor or obligee for the old. It also contemplates novation by the obligor's contracting a "new debt," which is a new obligation having a different cause or whose performance has a different object. The first Paragraph of this Article addresses these last two types of novation. Under it novation takes place when the parties agree that a different performance will be rendered, for instance, that a debtor will give a thing in lieu of money; or that a performance, although the same, will be owed for a different reason, as when a lessor extends credit to a lessee, who will thereafter owe the sum lent not as rent but as repayment of the loan. See 7 Planiol et Ripert, Traité pratique de droit civil français 667–669 (2nd ed. Esmein 1954). See also Colbert v. District Grand Lodge No. 21, Grand United Order of Odd Fellows, 176 So. 633 (La.App. 1st Cir.1937), (novation found where holder of certificate of indebtedness had agreed to receive part payment of the amount represented by the certificate and leave the balance as a loan to the issuer).

(d) Under the second Paragraph of this Article, even if a new performance or a new cause is not substituted, a novation takes place if there is an express declaration of the parties to that effect.

(e) Adding a suspensive condition alters the nature of an obligation in a manner sufficient to effect a novation under this Article. See 7 Planiol et Ripert, Traité pratique de droit civil français 669 (2nd ed. Esmein 1954). Novation does not occur, however, when the parties agree that the original obligation shall be extinguished upon the performance of a new one. In such a case, there is no novation because the first obligation is not completely extinguished by the new. See Hyde & Gleises v. Booraem & Co., 41 U.S. 169, 16 Pet. 169, 10 L.Ed. 925 (1842).

447

(f) Civil Code Article 2187 (1870) had no equivalent in the Code Napoleon or in the Louisiana Digest of 1808. It was first introduced in the Civil Code of 1825. See 3 Louisiana Legal Archives, Part II, at 1197 (1942). The redactors of the 1825 Code no doubt thought that it clarified the distinction between a change that amounts to a novation and one that does not, but only modifies the original obligation without extinguishing it. That distinction, though not stated in the Code Napoleon, had been well understood in earlier French law. See 1 Pothier, A Treatise on the Law of Obligations or Contracts 384–387 (Evans trans. 1806); 3 Toullier, Le droit civil français 120–121 (1833). Nevertheless, the Article introduced in 1825 was misleading. It provided that if any stipulation of the original obligation remained there was no novation. That provision reflects neither the reality of business transactions nor the usual intention of contracting parties. Furthermore, it contradicts C.C. Art. 2189 (1870), which provides that novation takes place by the substitution of a new debt, regardless, apparently, of whether any stipulation regarding the original debt is suffered to remain. Fortunately, Louisiana courts have experienced no difficulty in recognizing a novation despite C.C. Art. 2187 (1870). See, e.g., Sheeks v. McCain-Richards, Inc., 226 La. 578, 76 So.2d 892 (1954); Colbert v. District Grand Lodge No. 21, Grand United Order of Odd Fellows, 176 So. 633 (La.App. 1st Cir.1937), reinstated 178 So. 694 (La.App. 1st Cir.1938). In both those decisions, novations were found to have occurred although the parties had preserved some of the "stipulations" of the original obligations.

Under this Article, modification of an obligation without an intent to extinguish it does not give rise to a novation, but if the parties intend to extinguish it and substitute another in its place there is a novation, even if some stipulations of the original obligation are "suffered to remain," or are carried over to the new obligation.

(g) Under this Article, the execution of a new writing does not give rise to a novation if the parties do not intend thereby to extinguish the original obligation. See Louisiana Store and Market Equipment Co. v. Moore, 167 So. 477 (La.App. 2nd Cir.1936). Thus, the execution of a new note in renewal of an old one does not effect a novation or impair the security for the original note. See Farmers' Nat. Bank of Lebanon, Ky. v. Belle Alliance Co., 142 La. 538, 77 So. 144 (1917); Interstate Trust & Banking Co. v. Sabatier, 189 La. 199, 179 So. 80 (1937); Palfrey v. His Creditors, 8 La. 176 (1835); Consolidated Cos. v. Dowiatt, 187 So. 301 (La.App. 1st Cir.1939). Similarly, the giving of a new security does not per se effect a novation. See Saul v. Nicolet's Executors, 15 La. 246 (1840).

Nevertheless, the giving of a new note or a new security may give rise to a novation if the circumstances or the character of the transaction show that the parties intended to extinguish the existing debt and substitute a new one for it. For instance, in White Co. v. Hammond Stage Lines, 180 La. 962, 158 So. 353 (1934), several secured debts arising from the defendant's prior purchases of a number of vehicles had been consolidated into a new debt secured by a new chattel mortgage on all of the vehicles. The court found that this transaction had been a novation and held that as a result the intervening security interest of a third party, a lessor's privilege, had advanced in rank over the chattel mortgage. Apparently, the court viewed the new "sale" resorted to by the parties to effect the consolidation as having amounted to a change in the cause of the original obligation. That approach was correct and the decision fair. An opposite conclusion would have allowed the mortgagee to increase his security at the expense of another secured obligee. White was distinguished in Union Bldg. Corp. v. Burmeister, 186 La. 1027, 173 So. 752 (1937), where the old notes had not been surrendered to the obligor nor the original chattel mortgage cancelled.

A tacit reconduction of a lease from month to month is not a novation, but a mere extension of the contractual term, according to C.C. Arts. 2684 through 2689 (1870). Therefore, the lessor preserves his privilege on things introduced by the lessee into the leased premises, and intervening chattel mortgages do not advance in rank. See Comegys v. Shreveport Kandy Kitchen, 162 La. 103, 110 So. 104 (1926). In such a situation, the rights of a surety are protected by the special rules of C.C. Arts. 2690 and 3063 (1870).

(h) Under this Article, an agreement to change the amount or quantity of the object of performance of an obligation is not a novation if any substantial part of the original performance is still owed under the new agreement. Thus, a reduction of rent does not constitute a novation. The contrary rule asserted in cases such as Weaks Supply Co. v. Werdin, 147 So. 838 (La.App. 2nd Cir.1933) is thus overruled. See United Credit Co. v. Croswell Co., 219 La. 993, 54 So.2d 425 (1951), where it was held that an agreement to reduce an employee's salary was not a novation.

(i) Under this Article, the granting of an extension of time for the obligor to perform does not effect a novation. See Lee Tire & Rubber Co. of New York v. Frederick-Planche Motor Co., 180 So. 143 (La.App. District Cir.1938); Farmers' Nat. Bank of Lebanon, Ky. v. Belle Alliance Co., 142 La. 538, 77 So. 144 (1917). Nevertheless, the granting of such an extension without the consent of a surety discharges the surety. See C.C. Art. 3063 (1870).

Art. 1882. Subjective novation

Novation takes place when a new obligor is substituted for a prior obligor who is discharged by the obligee. In that case, the novation is accomplished even without the consent of the prior obligor, unless he had an interest in performing the obligation himself.

Acts 1984, No. 331, § 1, eff. Jan. 1, 1985.

REVISION COMMENTS—1984

(a) This Article is based on C.C. Arts. 2189(2) and 2191 (1870). It does not change the law.

(b) Novation takes place under this Article only when the obligation of the original obligor is extinguished and replaced by the obligation of the new obligor. This novation is called "subjective" because it concerns the parties, or "subjects," of the obligation.

(c) Novation by substitution of a new obligor differs from a stipulation pour autrui. In the former, the obligee consents to the extinction of the obligation of the original obligor. In the latter, since the obligee is a third party with regard to the agreement between the original and the new obligor, the original obligor is not released. See revised C.C. Arts. 1978–1982 (Rev.1984), infra.

(d) Subjective novation by substitution of a new obligee is not provided for because the effects of such a novation are readily achieved through an assignment of credit. In modern law, the general acceptance of the notion of transmissibility of obligations has made novation by substitution of an obligee obsolete. See 7 Planiol et Ripert, Traité pratique de droit civil français 664 (2nd ed. Esmein 1954).

Art. 1883. No effect when obligation is invalid

Novation has no effect when the obligation it purports to extinguish does not exist or is absolutely null.

If the obligation is only relatively null, the novation is valid, provided the obligor of the new one knew of the defect of the extinguished obligation.

Acts 1984, No. 331, § 1, eff. Jan. 1, 1985.

REVISION COMMENTS—1984

(a) This Article reproduces the substance of C.C. Art. 2186 (1870) and states a consequence implicit in C.C. Arts. 2188 and 1881 (1870). It does not change the law.

(b) Under this Article, a novation is ineffective if the obligation it purports to extinguish is absolutely null or simply does not exist.

(c) Under this Article, a novation of an obligation that is only relatively null is valid. The intention to effect such a novation must be as unequivocally indicated, however, as in any other situation contemplated in revised C.C. Art. 1880 (Rev.1984), supra.

(d) The novation of a relatively null obligation differs from the confirmation or ratification of a relatively null or unauthorized act under revised C.C. Arts. 1842–1845 (Rev.1984), supra. (See also C.C. Art. 2272 (1870)). Confirmation or ratification is a unilateral act. Novation is not. In the case of confirmation, the obligation is reputed in existence since its inception. In the case of novation, the new obligation arises when it is contracted. See Weill, Droit Civil—Les obligations 326–329 (1970).

Art. 1884. Security for extinguished obligation

Security given for the performance of the extinguished obligation may not be transferred to the new obligation without agreement of the parties who gave the security.

Acts 1984, No. 331, § 1, eff. Jan. 1, 1985.

REVISION COMMENTS—1984

(a) This Article reproduces the substance of C.C. Arts. 2195 and 2196 (1870). It does not change the law.

(b) Civil Code Article 2195 (1870) deals with transfer of security in the case of novation by substitution of a new obligation, and C.C. Art. 2196 (1870) deals with transfer of security in the case of novation by substitution of a new obligor. This Article is drafted in terms general enough to cover both situations.

(c) The references to privileges in the source Articles have been eliminated because privileges cannot be created or freely transferred by the parties. See C.C. Arts. 3185 and 3186 (1870); Capillon v. Chambliss, 211 La. 1, 29 So.2d 171 (1946).

(d) Under this Article, when an obligor has given security, and novation takes place by substitution of a new obligation between the same parties, the security may not be transferred to the new obligation without the obligor's consent.

Art. 1885. Novation of solidary obligation

A novation made by the obligee and one of the obligors of a solidary obligation releases the other solidary obligors.

In that case, the security given for the performance of the extinguished obligation may be retained by the obligee only on property of that obligor with whom the novation has been made.

If the obligee requires that the other co-obligors remain solidarily bound, there is no novation unless the co-obligors consent to the new obligation.

Acts 1984, No. 331, § 1, eff. Jan. 1, 1985.

REVISION COMMENTS—1984

(a) This Article is new. It does not change the law, however. It restates the principles contained in C.C. Arts. 2197 and 2198 (1870).

(b) This Article makes no reference to the effect upon sureties of a novation made by agreement between the obligee and the principal debtor. That case is specially provided for in C.C. Art. 3061 (1870).

(c) This Article contemplates a novation of the entire debt.

Art. 1886. Delegation of performance

A delegation of performance by an obligor to a third person is effective when that person binds himself to perform.

A delegation effects a novation only when the obligee expressly discharges the original obligor.

Acts 1984, No. 331, § 1, eff. Jan. 1, 1985.

REVISION COMMENTS—1984

(a) This Article reproduces the substance of C.C. Art. 2192 (1870). It does not change the law.

(b) Despite this Article, a delegation of performance without the obligee's consent will not be effective if that performance is of a kind that must be rendered personally by the obligor under revised C.C. Art. 1855 (Rev.1984), supra.

(c) Civil Code Article 2193 (1870) has been eliminated as unnecessary. General principles, such as error or failure of cause, suffice to cover the situation where the delegated person is insolvent at the time the delegation is made.

(d) Civil Code Article 2194 (1870) has also been eliminated. If a delegation of performance does not effect a novation, then clearly an obligor's "mere indication . . . of a person who is to pay in his place" does not do so.

(e) This Article complements the rules governing assumption of obligations. It is included among the Articles on Novation in order to clarify the distinction between perfect delegation, which effects a novation, and imperfect delegation, whereby the original obligor is not liberated.

Art. 1887. Discharge of any prior obligor does not affect security

If the new obligor has assumed the obligation and acquired the thing given as security, the discharge of any prior obligor by the obligee does not affect the security or its rank.

Acts 1984, No. 331, § 1, eff. Jan. 1, 1985.

REVISION COMMENTS—1984

(a) This Article is new. It clarifies the law.

(b) Under this Article, the obligee of a secured obligation preserves his security against the new obligor when the latter has acquired the thing given as security and the original obligor is discharged. This result is accomplished even without an express reservation of right on the part of the obligee, thereby protecting him from impairing his right because of a technicality.

This Article applies whether the novation is effected through an assumption of debt or a delegation of performance.

(c) Civil Code Article 2195 (1870) seems to provide that, in the case of the assumption of a debt secured by a mortgage, the obligee who wants to preserve the security against the new obligor must expressly reserve it. Commenting on Article 1278 of the Code Napoleon, equivalent to C.C. Art. 2195 (1870), one authority has said: "Although the novation entails, by its nature, extinction of the privileges and mortgages of the old obligation, the creditor may by means of an express reservation transfer these securities to the new credit . . ."; 4 Aubry et Rau, Droit civil français—Obligations 239–240 (Louisiana State Law Institute trans. 1965); see also 7 Planiol et Ripert, Traité pratique de droit civil français 673–676 (2nd ed. Esmein, 1954). Nevertheless, in Louisiana practice, a discharge of the original obligor by the obligee, after an assumption by a new obligor, has always been given in the belief that the security is preserved against the new obligor even without reservation.

(d) In France, Public Act No. 71–579 of July 16, 1971 amended Article 1279 of the Code Napoleon, equivalent to C.C. Art. 2196 (1870), introducing the following language: "The original priorities and mortgages of a debt may be preserved, with the consent of the owners of the encumbered property, as guaranty for execution of the engagement by the new debtor." That amendment was a step toward the clarification accomplished by this Article.

SECTION 4—REMISSION OF DEBT

Art. 1888. Express or tacit remission

A remission of debt by an obligee extinguishes the obligation. That remission may be express or tacit.

Acts 1984, No. 331, § 1, eff. Jan. 1, 1985.

REVISION COMMENTS—1984

(a) This Article reproduces the substance of C.C. Art. 2199 (1870). It does not change the law.

(b) Although remission is an act gratuitous in principle, it is considered a sort of indirect liberality not subject to the requirements of form prescribed for donations. See 4 Aubry et Rau, Cours de droit civil français—Obligations 223 (Louisiana State Law Institute trans. 1965); 2 Colin et Capitant, Cours élémentaire de droit civil français 403 (10th ed. 1953); 7 Planiol et Ripert, Traité pratique de droit civil français 716 (2nd ed. Esmein 1954); 1 Litvinoff, Obligations 627–628 (1969). See also Hicks v. Hicks, 145 La. 465, 82 So. 415 (1919); Reinecke v. Pelham, 199 So. 521 (La.App.Orl.1941).

(c) This Article modifies only the language of C.C. Art. 2199 (1870). Since Mouton v. Noble, 1 La.Ann. 192 (1846), Louisiana courts have had no difficulty in understanding and applying the civilian notion of remission of debt.

(d) The expression "remission of debt" has been preserved after carefully weighing the advisability of adopting the term "release," which perhaps better conveys the intended meaning. As used at traditional common law, however, a "release" requires consideration. Although the development has been to the contrary since Minnesota's Justice Stone wrote the majority opinion in the seminal case of Rye v. Phillips, 203 Minn. 567, 282 N.W. 459 (1938), it is preferable to avoid even the slightest possibility of confusion due to terminology.

Art. 1889. Presumption of remission

An obligee's voluntary surrender to the obligor of the instrument evidencing the obligation gives rise to a presumption that the obligee intended to remit the debt.

Acts 1984, No. 331, § 1, eff. Jan. 1, 1985.

REVISION COMMENTS—1984

(a) This Article reproduces the substance of the second part of C.C. Art. 2199 (1870). It changes the law insofar as it provides that the surrender of the instrument by the obligee gives rise merely to a rebuttable presumption of remission, rather than a tacit remission. That change is consistent with the principle expressed in C.C. Art. 2200 (1870). It is also consistent with doctrine and the approach taken in modern codes. See 7 Planiol et Ripert, Traité pratique de droit civil français 717 (2nd ed. Esmein 1954); 1 Litvinoff, Obligations 628 (1969); Quebec Draft Civil Code (1977) Article 340.

(b) The distinction between tacit remission and the presumption of remission established by this Article is significant. If the obligee gives the obligor a receipt for payment in full even though he has received no payment, or if he destroys the instrument intentionally, there is occasion to speak of a tacit remission. But if he surrenders the instrument without expressing an intention to remit, that act should not necessarily amount to a remission because it may be prompted by a different intent. It should give rise to no more than a presumption of remission which the obligee may rebut. Article 1282 of the Code Napoleon has always been interpreted in this sense.

Art. 1890. Remission effective when communication is received by the obligor

A remission of debt is effective when the obligor receives the communication from the obligee. Acceptance of a remission is always presumed unless the obligor rejects the remission within a reasonable time.

Acts 1984, No. 331, § 1, eff. Jan. 1, 1985.

REVISION COMMENTS—1984

(a) This Article reproduces the substance of C.C. Art. 2201 (1870). It does not change the law.

(b) This Article modifies the language of the source Article so that it no longer says more than is actually intended. Thus, the phrase "it can not be revoked by the creditor" has been suppressed. That phrase only means that, since the obligor's acceptance of a remission is presumed, the obligee may not revoke the remission once it has been communicated to the obligor. On the other hand, if the remission is gratuitous, it is subject to the rules governing donations (other than the requirement of form). It may therefore be revoked for ingratitude or nonperformance of a condition or charge, according to C.C. Arts. 1559 and 1560 (1870). See 1 Litvinoff, Obligations 632–634 (1969).

Art. 1891. Release of real security

Release of a real security given for performance of the obligation does not give rise to a presumption of remission of debt.

Acts 1984, No. 331, § 1, eff. Jan. 1, 1985.

REVISION COMMENTS—1984

(a) This Article reproduces the substance of C.C. Art. 2204 (1870). It does not change the law.

(b) Under this Article, release of a pledge or mortgage given as security for the performance of an obligation does not give rise to a presumption of remission of that obligation.

(c) This Article enlarges the scope of C.C. Art. 2204 (1870) in order to encompass other real securities besides pledge, such as mortgage. The principle remains unchanged.

Art. 1892. Remission granted to sureties

Remission of debt granted to the principal obligor releases the sureties.

Remission of debt granted to the sureties does not release the principal obligor.

Remission of debt granted to one surety releases the other sureties only to the extent of the contribution the other sureties might have recovered from the surety to whom the remission was granted.

If the obligee grants a remission of debt to a surety in return for an advantage, that advantage will be imputed to the debt, unless the surety and the obligee agree otherwise.

Acts 1984, No. 331, § 1, eff. Jan. 1, 1985.

REVISION COMMENTS—1984

(a) This Article reproduces the substance of C.C. Arts. 2205 and 2206 (1870). It changes the law in part.

(b) Under the third paragraph of this Article, if remission is granted to a surety who would have been bound to make contribution to other sureties if they had paid the debt, the other sureties are released, but only to the extent of that contribution. See C.C. Art. 3058 (1870). Thus, if two or more sureties are several obligors inter se, a remission granted to one does not affect the obligations of the others to any extent. If they are solidary sureties or solidary co-obligors of the principal obligor, on the other hand, then there is a right to contribution, and for the amount of that contribution the other sureties should be released if one obtains a remission. The importance of this distinction was explored in a different context in Teutonia Nat. Bank v. Wagner, 33 La.Ann. 732 (1881).

(c) Under the fourth paragraph of this Article, any payment received by the obligee in return for a remission granted to a surety is imputed to the principal obligation. Nevertheless, obligee and surety may agree to the contrary, that is, that the payment is made only to release the surety of his contingent obligation without reducing the amount of the principal obligation.

SECTION 5—COMPENSATION

Art. 1893. Compensation extinguishes obligations

Compensation takes place by operation of law when two persons owe to each other sums of money or quantities of fungible things identical in kind, and these sums or quantities are liquidated and presently due.

In such a case, compensation extinguishes both obligations to the extent of the lesser amount.

Delays of grace do not prevent compensation.

Acts 1984, No. 331, § 1, eff. Jan. 1, 1985.

REVISION COMMENTS—1984

(a) This Article reproduces the substance of C.C. Arts. 2207, 2208, and 2209 (1870). It does not change the law.

(b) Under this Article, delays of grace do not prevent compensation, whether those delays are judicially or conventionally granted.

Art. 1894. Obligation not subject to compensation

Compensation takes place regardless of the sources of the obligations.

Compensation does not take place, however, if one of the obligations is to return a thing of which the owner has been unjustly dispossessed, or is to return a thing given in deposit or loan for use, or if the object of one of the obligations is exempt from seizure.

Acts 1984, No. 331, § 1, eff. Jan. 1, 1985.

REVISION COMMENTS—1984

(a) This Article reproduces the substance of C.C. Art. 2210 (1870). It does not change the law.

(b) Under this Article, wrongdoers or parties who have acted in bad faith are not allowed to set up the plea of compensation. See Rhodes v. Hooper, 6 La.Ann. 355 (1851); Succession of Cox, 32 La.Ann. 984 (1880); Hitt v. Herndon, 166 La. 497, 117 So. 568 (1928).

(c) Under this Article, a bank may not apply funds on deposit to payment of the depositor's debt to the bank. Gordon & Gomila v. Muchler, 34 La.Ann. 604 (1882); D.T. & A.T. Lee v. First National Bank of Minden, 18 La.App. 586, 139 So. 63 (La.App. 2nd Cir.1932). It may do so, however, pursuant to a special agreement with the depositor to that effect. Succession of Gragard, 106 La. 298, 30 So. 885 (1901); Fory v. American National Bank, 136 La. 298, 67 So. 10 (1914); Watkins v. Bank of Morgan City & Trust Co., 162 So. 262 (La.App. 1st Cir.1935).

(d) In general terms, Louisiana courts have encountered no difficulty in applying C.C. Art. 2210 (1870). Special exceptions to the general rule have sometimes been recognized when insolvency or bankruptcy of a bank was involved. Thus, in Watkins v. Bank of Morgan City & Trust Co., 162 So. 262 (La.App. 1st Cir.1935), the court held that a depositor could not demand application of his deposit to payment of his note to the bank after the latter had become insolvent. That solution is readily explained in light of special provisions governing insolvency and bankruptcy; there is no need to provide for it in this Article.

Art. 1895. Obligations not to be performed at the same place

Compensation takes place even though the obligations are not to be performed at the same place, but allowance must be made in that case for the expenses of remittance.

Acts 1984, No. 331, § 1, eff. Jan. 1, 1985.

REVISION COMMENTS—1984

(a) This Article reproduces the substance of C.C. Art. 2213 (1870). It does not change the law.

(b) No Louisiana decision applying C.C. Art. 2213 (1870) has been found, and French doctrine has devoted little attention to its French counterpart, Article 1296 of the Code Napoleon, probably in the belief that the rule stated is too simple and evident to need discussion. Even though in business practice there may be few opportunities to resort to that rule, the result it propounds is unquestionably fair. Thus, if A and B, both from New Orleans, are reciprocally indebted so that A owes B a certain number of dollars payable in New Orleans and B owes A a certain number of dollars payable in London, compensation takes place, but A must be credited for the cost of remitting dollars to, or situating them in London, if he finds it necessary to do so. Otherwise, A would not receive the full amount of what is actually owed him. The same approach prevails concerning the difference in the price of goods that must be delivered at different places. See 13 Baudry-Lacantinerie et Barde, Traité théorique et pratique de droit civil—Des obligations, Part I, at 176–177 (2nd ed. 1905).

Art. 1896. Rules of imputation of payment

If an obligor owes more than one obligation subject to compensation, the rules of imputation of payment must be applied.

Acts 1984, No. 331, § 1, eff. Jan. 1, 1985.

REVISION COMMENT—1984

This Article reproduces the substance of C.C. Art. 2214 (1870). It does not change the law.

Art. 1897. Compensation extinguishes obligation of surety

Compensation between obligee and principal obligor extinguishes the obligation of a surety.

Compensation between obligee and surety does not extinguish the obligation of the principal obligor.

Acts 1984, No. 331, § 1, eff. Jan. 1, 1985.

This Article reproduces the substance of C.C. Art. 2211 (1870). It does not change the law. Compensation in the context of solidary obligations is dealt with in the next Article.

Art. 1898. Compensation between obligee and solidary obligor

Compensation between the obligee and one solidary obligor extinguishes the obligation of the other solidary obligors only for the portion of that obligor.

Compensation between one solidary obligee and the obligor extinguishes the obligation only for the portion of that obligee.

The compensation provided in this Article does not operate in favor of a liability insurer.

Acts 1984, No. 331, § 1, eff. Jan. 1, 1985.

REVISION COMMENTS—1984

(a) This Article reproduces the substance of C.C. Art. 2211 (1870), third Paragraph. It expands the provisions of that Article in order to cover compensation between obligor and one solidary obligee, but it does not change the law.

(b) The principles of compensation operate also in situations where there is comparative negligence. See generally Chamallas, "Comparative Fault and Multiple Party Litigation in Louisiana: A Sampling of the Problems," 40 La.L.Rev. 373, 396–401 (1980).

(c) Under this Article, when one solidary obligor is a liability insurer, compensation between the obligee and a third person does not operate in the insurer's favor. This exception does not apply to a conventional surety or an indemnitor. See Bronaugh v. Neal, 1 Rob. 23 (1841); Hubert, "The Nature and Essentials of Conventional Suretyship," 13 Tul.L.Rev. 519, 520 (1939); Slovenko, "Suretyship," 39 Tul.L.Rev. 427, 474 (1965).

Art. 1899. Rights acquired by third parties

Compensation can neither take place nor may it be renounced to the prejudice of rights previously acquired by third parties.

Acts 1984, No. 331, § 1, eff. Jan. 1, 1985.

REVISION COMMENTS—1984

(a) This Article reproduces the substance of C.C. Art. 2215 (1870) and gives express formulation to the principle underlying C.C. Art. 2216 (1870). It does not change the law.

(b) Under this Article, if a creditor of the obligee seizes the obligation while the object of performance is still in the hands of the obligor, the latter may not claim compensation if he subsequently becomes a creditor of his obligee. See C.C. Art. 2215 (1870).

(c) Under this Article, an obligor who renounces compensation and pays the debt may no longer avail himself, to the prejudice of third persons, of any securities given for the obligation owed to him by the obligee to whom he paid the debt. See C.C. Art. 2216 (1870).

(d) Assignment of credit and bankruptcy are other examples of situations where compensation cannot take place because it would injure the interest of third persons. See 7 Planiol et Ripert, Traité pratique de droit civil français 693 (2nd ed. Esmein 1954).

(e) The last clause of C.C. Art. 2216 (1870) merely contains an instance of an error that could be grounds for annulment. It falls thus within general principles and does not require a special reference; so it has been eliminated.

Art. 1900. Assignment by obligee

An obligor who has consented to an assignment of the credit by the obligee to a third party may not claim against the latter any compensation that otherwise he could have claimed against the former.

An obligor who has been given notice of an assignment to which he did not consent may not claim compensation against the assignee for an obligation of the assignor arising after that notice.

Acts 1984, No. 331, § 1, eff. Jan. 1, 1985.

REVISION COMMENTS—1984

(a) This Article reproduces the substance of the first paragraph of C.C. Art. 2212 (1870). It does not change the law.

(b) Under this Article, an obligor who, before a compensation takes place by operation of law, consents to an assignment of the obligee's right, may not subsequently claim that compensation against the new obligee. The reason for this rule is that, as between the obligor and the original obligee, the former's obligation to the latter is extinguished when it is assigned with the obligor's consent.

(c) Under this Article, notice given to an obligor of an assignment to which he does not consent does not prevent compensation from taking place between debts that the obligee and obligor owed each other reciprocally before that notice was given. This is so because compensation takes place by operation of law. After notice has been given, the obligor knows that his debt is actually owed to the assignee and, therefore, compensation cannot take place between that debt and any which the original obligee might thereafter come to owe the obligor. See Zibilich v. Rouseo, 157 La. 936, 103 So. 269 (1925).

Art. 1901. Compensation by agreement

Compensation of obligations may take place also by agreement of the parties even though the requirements for compensation by operation of law are not met.

Acts 1984, No. 331, § 1, eff. Jan. 1, 1985.

REVISION COMMENTS—1984

(a) Under this Article, when there is an obstacle that prevents compensation by operation of law, such as when one of the debts is not liquidated or is subject to a term, and the parties consent to remove the obstacle, compensation takes place by their agreement. Such compensation is sometimes called "facultative compensation". See Brock v. Pan American Petroleum Corporation, 186 La. 607, 173 So. 121 (1937); In re Interstate Trust & Banking Co., 194 So. 35 (La.App.Orl.1940).

(b) It is clear in French doctrine that compensation is of three kinds: legal, conventional, and judicial. The Code Napoleon only contemplates the first kind, although without barring the others, and so does the Louisiana Civil Code of 1870. See 7 Planiol, Traité pratique de droit civil français 705–709 (2nd ed. Esmein 1954); 13 Baudry-Lacantinerie et Barde, Traité théorique et pratique de droit civil—Des obligations 215–222 (2nd ed. 1905). In light of the frequent recognition of "facultative compensation" by the Louisiana jurisprudence—see especially In re Canal Bank & Trust Co., 178 La. 961, 152 So. 578 (1934)—it seems appropriate, from a systematic viewpoint, to provide for it in the Civil Code. The Italian and the Ethiopian Civil Codes have followed that approach. Compensation by declaration of the court is dealt with in the next Article.

Art. 1902. Compensation by judicial declaration

Although the obligation claimed in compensation is unliquidated, the court can declare compensation as to that part of the obligation that is susceptible of prompt and easy liquidation.

Acts 1984, No. 331, § 1, eff. Jan. 1, 1985.

REVISION COMMENTS—1984

(a) This Article is new. It does not change the law, but merely generalizes a principle underlying C.C. Art. 1880 (1870) and C.C. Art. 2531 (as amended by Acts 1974, No. 673). It seems practical to allow the operation of that principle even when the amount of one of the obligations, although unliquidated, is susceptible of prompt and easy liquidation. Cf. Italian Civil Code Article 1243 (1942).

(b) This Article recognizes that compensation may not only be legal or conventional, but also judicial, that is, effected by declaration of the court. French doctrine recognizes this form of compensation. See 7 Planiol, Traité pratique de droit civil français 705–709 (2nd ed. Esmein 1954); 13 Baudry-Lacantinerie et Barde, Traité théorique et pratique de droit civil—Des obligations 215–222 (2nd ed. 1905).

SECTION 6—CONFUSION

Art. 1903. Union of qualities of obligee and obligor

When the qualities of obligee and obligor are united in the same person, the obligation is extinguished by confusion.

Acts 1984, No. 331, § 1, eff. Jan. 1, 1985.

REVISION COMMENTS—1984

(a) This Article reproduces the substance of C.C. Art. 2217 (1870). It does not change the law.

(b) Louisiana courts have had no difficulty in understanding and applying the concept of confusion. See Succession of Norton, 18 La.Ann. 36 (1866); Haas v. O'Pry, 10 La.App. 593, 121 So. 631 (La.App. 1st Cir.1929).

Art. 1904. Obligation of the surety

Confusion of the qualities of obligee and obligor in the person of the principal obligor extinguishes the obligation of the surety.

Confusion of the qualities of obligee and obligor in the person of the surety does not extinguish the obligation of the principal obligor.

Acts 1984, No. 331, § 1, eff. Jan. 1, 1985.

REVISION COMMENTS—1984

(a) This Article reproduces the substance of C.C. Art. 2218 (as amended by Acts 1871, No. 87). It does not change the law.

(b) Under this Article, when the same person becomes obligee and surety the principal obligation is not extinguished by confusion. Nor is the principal obligation thus extinguished when the same person becomes surety and principal obligor.

Art. 1905. Solidary obligations

If a solidary obligor becomes an obligee, confusion extinguishes the obligation only for the portion of that obligor.

If a solidary obligee becomes an obligor, confusion extinguishes the obligation only for the portion of that obligee.

Acts 1984, No. 331, § 1, eff. Jan. 1, 1985.

REVISION COMMENT—1984

This Article reproduces the substance of C.C. Art. 2218 as amended by Acts 1871, No. 87. It does not change the law, but only expands the principle of the source article to cover solidary obligees.

TITLE IV—CONVENTIONAL OBLIGATIONS OR CONTRACTS

CHAPTER 1—GENERAL PRINCIPLES

Art. 1906. Definition of contract

A contract is an agreement by two or more parties whereby obligations are created, modified, or extinguished.

Acts 1984, No. 331, § 1, eff. Jan. 1, 1985.

REVISION COMMENTS—1984

(a) This Article reproduces the substance of C.C. Art. 1761 (1870). It does not change the law.

(b) According to this Article, a contract may be entered into not only to create, but also to modify or to extinguish, an obligation. This is consistent with the idea of dissolution of contracts by agreement contained in C.C. Art. 1901 (1870) and with the concept of novation contained in revised C.C. Arts. 1879–1887 (Rev.1984), supra. See 1 Litvinoff, Obligations 140–142 (1969); 6 Planiol & Ripert, Traité pratique de droit civil français—Obligations, Part I, at 17 (2nd ed. Esmein 1952); Planiol, Classification synthétique des contrats, Revue critique 485 (1904).

(c) This Article does not change the concept of the source article. A contract is still defined as an agreement. The reference to things to be given, done, or not done contained in the source article, has been eliminated, however, in order to avoid repeating the idea expressed in revised C.C. Art. 1756 (Rev.1984), supra. The definition presented here emphasizes that a contract is a source of obligations. Thus, the definition of contracts complements the definition of obligations. The wording of C.C. Art. 1761 (1870) has fostered the usage "contract to give," or "contract to do," which is reflected in C.C. Arts. 1905, 1906, and 1907 (1870). That usage is not correct; it is not the contract but the obligation that may be one to give, or to do, or not to do.

Art. 1907. Unilateral contracts

A contract is unilateral when the party who accepts the obligation of the other does not assume a reciprocal obligation.

Acts 1984, No. 331, § 1, eff. Jan. 1, 1985.

REVISION COMMENT—1984

This Article reproduces in part the substance of C.C. Art. 1765 (1870). It does not change the law.

Art. 1908. Bilateral or synallagmatic contracts

A contract is bilateral, or synallagmatic, when the parties obligate themselves reciprocally, so that the obligation of each party is correlative to the obligation of the other.

Acts 1984, No. 331, § 1, eff. Jan. 1, 1985.

REVISION COMMENTS—1984

(a) This Article reproduces in part the substance of C.C. Art. 1765 (1870). It does not change the law. It emphasizes, however, the consequence of the parties having bound themselves reciprocally, which is consistent with the rules of C.C. Arts. 1913 and 2487 (1870).

(b) The doctrine of cause makes the obligations arising out of a bilateral contract correlative. In such a contract, indeed, the obligation of each party is the cause of the other. See Capitant, De la cause des obligations 6 (1923); 1 Litvinoff, Obligations 396–400 (1969).

Art. 1909. Onerous contracts

A contract is onerous when each of the parties obtains an advantage in exchange for his obligation.

Acts 1984, No. 331, § 1, eff. Jan. 1, 1985.

REVISION COMMENTS—1984

(a) This Article reproduces the substance of C.C. Art. 1774 (1870). It does not change the law.

(b) This Article does not alter the definition contained in C.C. Art. 1774 (1870). The language has been changed to make it more concise. The concept of "advantage" clearly includes the "service, interest or condition" mentioned in C.C. Art. 1774 (1870).

(c) This Article introduces the term "exchange," which is the very essence of an onerous contract. See 1 Litvinoff, Obligations 167–168 (1969); 6 Planiol & Ripert, Traité pratique de droit civil français—Obligations, Part I, at 39 (2nd ed. Esmein 1952). The idea of exchange was also incorporated into the definition of onerous contracts in Article 7 of the Franco-Italian Projet of 1927.

Art. 1910. Gratuitous contracts

A contract is gratuitous when one party obligates himself towards another for the benefit of the latter, without obtaining any advantage in return.

Acts 1984, No. 331, § 1, eff. Jan. 1, 1985.

REVISION COMMENTS—1984

(a) This Article reproduces the substance of C.C. Art. 1773 (1870). It does not change the law.

(b) This Article eliminates the second sentence of the source article in order to eliminate a contradiction with C.C. Arts. 1524, 1525, and 1526 (1870). See Smith, "A Refresher Course in Cause," 12 La.L.Rev. 2, 16–17 (1951). See also 1 Litvinoff, Obligations 173, 183 (1969).

(c) Under this Article, a contract is gratuitous only when one party consents to obligate himself without receiving any advantage in return and he does so for the benefit of the other party. The redundancy of expression is intended to avoid any possibility of confusion between a gratuitous contract, which is enforceable, and an onerous contract that is unenforceable on grounds of failure of cause, or an onerous contract which, through the miscalculation of one of the parties, proves advantageous to the other party alone.

Art. 1911. Commutative contracts

A contract is commutative when the performance of the obligation of each party is correlative to the performance of the other.

Acts 1984, No. 331, § 1, eff. Jan. 1, 1985.

REVISION COMMENTS—1984

(a) This Article reproduces the substance of C.C. Art. 1768 (1870). It does not change the law.

(b) According to this Article, correlative performances are the essential feature of commutative contracts. A distinction is thus made between correlative obligations, which make a contract bilateral according to revised C.C. Art. 1908 (Rev.1984), supra, and correlative performances, which make the contract not only bilateral but also commutative. In the absence of correlative obligations, a bilateral contract is null, as when the obligation of one of the parties is subject to a condition that depends solely upon his will. (See revised C.C. Art. 1770 (Rev.1984), supra; Titus v. Jackson, 7 La.App. 37 (1927)); while in default of performance of his correlative obligation by one of the parties, the commutative contract is not null, but is enforceable by the other party.

(c) The reference to correlative performances contained in this Article sets forth the ground for the traditional defense of nonperformance (exceptio non adimpleti contractus) that operates in the sphere of commutative contracts alone. See 1 Litvinoff, Obligations 150 (1969); Pillebout, Recherches sur l'exception d'inéxecution 1–9 (1971). This is consistent with the rule of Civil Code Article 2487

(1870), for matters of sale, and with the rule of revised C.C. Art. 1993 (Rev.1984), infra, which reflects the same principle, although from a different angle, in the context of putting in default.

Art. 1912. Aleatory contracts

A contract is aleatory when, because of its nature or according to the parties' intent, the performance of either party's obligation, or the extent of the performance, depends on an uncertain event.

Acts 1984, No. 331, § 1, eff. Jan. 1, 1985.

REVISION COMMENTS—1984

(a) This Article combines concepts contained in C.C. Arts. 1776 and 2982 (1870). It does not change the law.

(b) This Article permits the elimination of C.C. Art. 2982 (1870), as there is no reason for two different definitions of aleatory contracts. This unnecessary duplication was inherited from Articles 1104 and 1964 of the Code Napoleon.

(c) This Article preserves the concept of C.C. Art. 1776 (1870), that is, that one party must always perform.

(d) This Article alters, although only slightly, the concept of C.C. Art. 2982 (1870). A careful reading of C.C. Art. 2982 (1870) leads to the conclusion that a contract may be aleatory for one of the parties alone, which is not correct. An aleatory contract contemplates reciprocal obligations; thus, what is gain for one of the parties is a loss for the other—a unilateral chance is difficult to conceive. See the criticism to Article 1964 of the Code Napoleon in Kahn, La notion de l'aléa dans les contrats (thesis, 1925); Weill, Droit Civil—Les obligations 42–43 (1970). See also 1 Litvinoff, Obligations 191–193 (1969).

(e) According to this Article, a contract may be aleatory not only because of its nature, but also because of the intention of the parties. Thus, an insurance contract is unquestionably aleatory as the risk involved is inherent in the nature of the contract. It is the same in the case of a wager. In the sale of a thing not yet in existence, however, the parties' intent, and not the nature of the contract, must be scrutinized in order to determine whether the contract is the sale of a future thing (C.C. Art. 2450 (1870)), or the sale of a mere hope (C.C. Art. 2451 (1870)). See Losecco v. Gregory, 108 La. 648, 32 So. 985 (1901). In contemporary continental law, it has been made clear that contracts may be aleatory by the intention of the parties. See Article 1469 of the Italian Civil Code of 1942.

(f) According to this text, the chance that an aleatory contract contemplates may result in one party not having to perform at all, as in the case of an insurance contract when the risk does not occur, or may result in a more or less extensive performance by one of the parties, as in the case of an obligation of support which is assumed in return for a transfer of property. See Thielman v. Gahlman, 119 La. 350, 44 So. 123 (1907). Modern continental doctrine has made it clear that the element of chance may rest in the extent (étendue), and not in the existence, of the obligation. See Article 8 of the Franco-Italian Prôjet of 1927.

(g) It is clear that, through the parties' intent, a contract may not be purely aleatory, but a combination of commutative and aleatory elements, as in the case of a sale where the price is partly a fixed amount and partly an annuity for life. It is for the courts to determine whether a particular clause in a contract makes it aleatory for the whole, or should be given only a limited scope. See 6 Planiol & Ripert, Traité pratique de droit civil français—Obligations, Part I, at 43 (2nd ed. Esmein, 1952). See also Req. July 10, 1899, D.1. 592.

Art. 1913. Principal and accessory contracts

A contract is accessory when it is made to provide security for the performance of an obligation. Suretyship, mortgage, pledge, and other types of security agreements are examples of such a contract.

When the secured obligation arises from a contract, either between the same or other parties, that contract is the principal contract.

Acts 1984, No. 331, § 1, eff. Jan. 1, 1985. Amended by Acts 1989, No. 137, § 16, eff. Sept. 1, 1989.

(a) This Article reproduces the substance of C.C. Art. 1771 (1870). It does not change the law.

(b) Under this Article, a contract may be accessory to an obligation which is not of contractual origin. Examples include the security to be furnished by executors and administrators under Code of Civil Procedure Articles 3151–3153, and the security to be furnished by pawnbrokers under R.S. 37:1754.

Art. 1914.   Nominate and innominate contracts

Nominate contracts are those given a special designation such as sale, lease, loan, or insurance.

Innominate contracts are those with no special designation.

Acts 1984, No. 331, § 1, eff. Jan. 1, 1985.

REVISION COMMENTS—1984

(a) This Article is new. It does not change the law, however. It articulates concepts contained in C.C. Arts. 1777 and 1778 (1870).

(b) All of the contracts that are given special names and special treatment in Book III, Titles VI–XX of the Civil Code are nominate contracts. That category corresponds to the "contrats spéciaux" of French doctrine. See Overstake, Essai de classification des contrats spéciaux I–IV and 9–10 (1969).

(c) All contracts that are neither given a special designation nor subjected to special regulation but which nevertheless result from the exercise of the parties' contractual freedom are innominate contracts. The existence of this category of contracts is recognized by doctrine and jurisprudence. See 2 Demogue, Traité des obligations en général 908 (1923); 6 Planiol & Ripert, Traité pratique de droit civil français—Obligations, Part I, at 44–45 (2nd ed. Esmein, 1952); 1 Litvinoff, Obligations 197–198 (1969); Kirk v. Kansas City, S. & G. Ry. Co., 51 La.Ann. 667, 25 So. 457 (1899); Thielman v. Gahlman, 119 La. 350, 44 So. 123 (1907). See also Nelson v. Texas & P. Ry. Co., 152 La. 117, 92 So. 754 (1922); Blouin v. Hebert, 134 La. 423, 64 So. 230 (1914).

Art. 1915.   Rules applicable to all contracts

All contracts, nominate and innominate, are subject to the rules of this title.

Acts 1984, No. 331, § 1, eff. Jan. 1, 1985.

REVISION COMMENT—1984

This Article reproduces the substance of C.C. Art. 1777 (1870). It does not change the law.

Art. 1916.   Rules applicable to nominate contracts

Nominate contracts are subject to the special rules of the respective titles when those rules modify, complement, or depart from the rules of this title.

Acts 1984, No. 331, § 1, eff. Jan. 1, 1985.

REVISION COMMENT—1984

This Article reproduces the substance of C.C. Art. 1778 (1870). It does not change the law.

Art. 1917.   Rules applicable to all kinds of obligations

The rules of this title are applicable also to obligations that arise from sources other than contract to the extent that those rules are compatible with the nature of those obligations.

Acts 1984, No. 331, § 1, eff. Jan. 1, 1985.

REVISION COMMENTS—1984

(a) This Article is new. It does not change the law, however. It articulates a basic systematic idea underlying the Civil Code. It is clearly understood in French doctrine that the general principles of the theory of obligations that the French redactors incorporated into the French Civil Code are intended to govern obligations in general, regardless of their source. See 6 Planiol & Ripert, Traité pratique de droit civil français—Obligations, Part I, at 18 (2nd ed. Esmein 1952); Weill, Droit Civil—Les obligations 20 (1970).

(b) Under this Article, the general rules of contracts are applicable to declarations of will contained in unilateral acts, an idea which is clearly expressed in C.C. Art. 1788 (10) and (11) (1870). See Carbonnier, Théorie des obligations 69–71 (1963); 6 Planiol & Ripert, Traité pratique de droit civil français—Obligations, Part I, at 18 (2nd ed. Esmein 1952); see also Article 1324 of the Italian Civil Code of 1942.

CHAPTER 2—CONTRACTUAL CAPACITY AND EXCEPTIONS

Art. 1918. General statement of capacity

All persons have capacity to contract, except unemancipated minors, interdicts, and persons deprived of reason at the time of contracting.

Acts 1984, No. 331, § 1, eff. Jan. 1, 1985.

REVISION COMMENTS—1984

(a) This Article does not change the law. It formulates the general principle that capacity is the rule and the lack of it the exception. See C.C. Arts. 25 and 2445 (1870); Litvinoff & Tête, Louisiana Legal Transactions: The Civil Law of Juridical Acts 56 (1969).

(b) The expression "persons deprived of reason" is designed to include all of the varieties of derangement that have been acknowledged by the Louisiana jurisprudence. See, e.g., Interdiction of Scurto, 188 La. 459, 177 So. 573 (1937); Succession of Schmidt, 219 La. 675, 53 So.2d 834 (1951) (dealing with maladies affecting intelligence); Interdiction of Gasquet, 136 La. 957, 68 So. 89 (1915) (habitual drunkenness); Emerson v. Shirley, 188 La. 196, 175 So. 909 (1937) (drunkenness causing loss of reason); Brumfield v. Paul, 145 So.2d 46 (La.App. 4th Cir.1962) (drug sedation); Smith v. Blum, 143 So.2d 419 (La.App. 4th Cir.1962) (senility).

Art. 1919. Right to plead rescission

A contract made by a person without legal capacity is relatively null and may be rescinded only at the request of that person or his legal representative.

Acts 1984, No. 331, § 1, eff. Jan. 1, 1985.

REVISION COMMENTS—1984

(a) This Article is new. It does not change the law, however. It reproduces the substance of C.C. Art. 1791 (1870) and states a principle reflected in C.C. Arts. 1875 and 2221 (1870).

(b) Under this Article, only the incapable person or his legal representative is allowed to raise the former's lack of capacity as a basis for rescinding a contract. See Litvinoff & Tête, Louisiana Legal Transactions: The Civil Law of Juridical Acts 102–103 (1969). In the case of an interdict, the action to rescind the contract is available only to the interdict or his curator. The action to rescind a contract executed by an interdict is susceptible of prescription, the period of which commences to run from the day that the interdiction is removed. See C.C. Art. 2221 (1870), third paragraph.

(c) This Article eliminates the previous uncertainty as to the absolute or relative nature of the nullity caused by lack of legal capacity. For that reason, C.C. Art. 1875 (1870) has been suppressed as unnecessary. See Whitney National Bank of New Orleans v. Schwob, 203 La. 175, 13 So.2d 782 (1943); Chesneau's Heirs v. Sadler, 10 Mart. (O.S.) 726 (1822).

(d) Under this Article, a contract made by an interdict after the date of successful application for interdiction is relatively null. As stated in this Article and in revised C.C. Art. 2031 (Rev.1984), infra, lack of capacity engenders a relative nullity. This is so because the justification of the nullity is the protection of the contracting party unable to understand the nature of his actions. See Litvinoff & Tête, Louisiana Legal Transactions: The Civil Law of Juridical Acts 166–67 (1969).

Art. 1920. Right to require confirmation or rescission of the contract

Immediately after discovering the incapacity, a party, who at the time of contracting was ignorant of the incapacity of the other party, may require from that party, if the incapacity has ceased, or from the legal representative if it has not, that the contract be confirmed or rescinded.

Acts 1984, No. 331, § 1, eff. Jan. 1, 1985.

REVISION COMMENTS—1984

(a) This Article formulates the principle contained in C.C. Art. 1794 (1870). It does not change the law.

(b) Under this Article, a capable party who finds that the other party was incapable at the time of contracting does not have to wait until the incapable or his legal representative chooses to confirm or attack the validity of the contract in order to discover whether or not it is valid.

Art. 1921. Rescission of contract for incapacity

Upon rescission of a contract on the ground of incapacity, each party or his legal representative shall restore to the other what he has received thereunder. When restoration is impossible or impracticable, the court may award compensation to the party to whom restoration cannot be made.

Acts 1984, No. 331, § 1, eff. Jan. 1, 1985.

REVISION COMMENT—1984

This Article changes the law in part. Under C.C. Art. 1793 (1870), the "consideration" must be restored if it has been used for the benefit of the incapable person. As determination of what is beneficial depends so much upon specific facts, whenever restoration in kind is impossible or impracticable it is preferable to allow the court to grant the other party compensation commensurate with the benefit the incapable party has derived from the other's performance. That solution is fair and in keeping with the approach taken by modern codes. See Israeli Contracts Law Article 9(a) (1970).

Art. 1922. Fully emancipated minor

A fully emancipated minor has full contractual capacity.

Acts 1984, No. 331, § 1, eff. Jan. 1, 1985.

REVISION COMMENTS—1984

(a) This Article does not change the law. It consolidates and restates principles derived both from the Louisiana Civil Code of 1870 and the relevant jurisprudence.

(b) According to the Articles in this Chapter, a minor may either be fully emancipated or not emancipated at all. The intermediate category, emancipation conferring the power of administration, is not recognized because its status is uncertain. In 1972 the legislature repealed C.C. Art. 367 (1870) which had authorized this kind of emancipation by judicial declaration for minors over eighteen. Apparently, when the age of majority was lowered to eighteen, the legislature decided that the article was unnecessary. That repeal left only two methods for acquiring this type of emancipation: notarial act and marriage. It also made C.C. Art. 368 (1870) and part of C.C. Art. 378 (1870) vestigial, as they had provided the applicable standards for emancipation under the repealed article. The legal effect of emancipation conferring the power of administration is to invest the minor with capacity to perform acts of administration, such as granting predial leases. He may not perform acts of disposition, such as alienating or mortgaging immovables. These acts require court approval and the tutor's recommendation. The distinction between acts of administration and acts of disposition is imprecise. See 3 Yiannopoulos, Louisiana Civil Law Treatise § 37, 146–47 (1968); Symposium, "Contractual Incapacity in the Louisiana Civil Code," 47 Tul.L.Rev. 1085, 1093, 1098 (1973).

Art. 1923. Incapacity of unemancipated minor; exceptions

A contract by an unemancipated minor may be rescinded on grounds of incapacity except when made for the purpose of providing the minor with something necessary for his support or education, or for a purpose related to his business.

Acts 1984, No. 331, § 1, eff. Jan. 1, 1985.

REVISION COMMENTS—1984

(a) This Article does not change the law. It reformulates it insofar as the capacity of unemancipated minors is concerned.

(b) This Article is consistent with C.C. Art. 3001 (1870), under which an emancipated minor may be appointed as a mandatary. The corresponding language in C.C. Art. 1785 (1870) has been eliminated from this Article in order to avoid repetition, and because C.C. Art. 3001 (1870) contains a special rule whose natural place is among the articles on mandate. In an "undisclosed principal" situation, the prevailing solutions apply. See Doiron v. Lundin, 385 So.2d 450 (La.App. 1st Cir.1980); Chartres Corporation v. Twilbeck, 305 So.2d 730 (La.App. 4th Cir. 1974). See also Bedford, Breedlove & Robeson v. Jacobs, 4 Mart. (N.S.) 528 (1826). Nevertheless, a minor would be relieved from personal liability unless the other party reasonably relied on his representation of capacity. See revised C.C. Art. 1924 (Rev.1984), infra; C.C. Arts. 3012 and 3013 (1870).

Art. 1924. Mere representation of majority; reliance

The mere representation of majority by an unemancipated minor does not preclude an action for rescission of the contract. When the other party reasonably relies on the minor's representation of majority, the contract may not be rescinded.

Acts 1984, No. 331, § 1, eff. Jan. 1, 1985.

REVISION COMMENTS—1984

(a) The first sentence of this Article does not change the law. It states a principle which is also declared in C.C. Art. 2224 (1870), and which is the underlying principle of the source articles.

(b) The second sentence of this Article is new. It changes the law by eliminating the rule of C.C. Art. 1872 (1870). Under this Article, a contract made with a minor who represents himself as of age is valid for the benefit of the contracting party who relied in good faith upon that representation. This solution prevails in modern civil codes. See, e.g., Article 315 of the Civil Code of Ethiopia. It is also consistent with an important strain of Louisiana jurisprudence. See, e.g., Smith v. Hempen, 8 La.App. 120 (La.App. 2nd Cir.1928). Moreover, today the attitude of the law towards minors, who spend millions of dollars every year for necessities and luxuries, is no longer as protective as it once was, although some decisions continue to exhibit an over-protective attitude. Compare Farrar v. Swedish Health Spa, 337 So.2d 911 (La.App. 3rd Cir.1976), with Bunkie Bank and Trust Co. v. Johnston, 385 So.2d 1264 (La.App. 3rd Cir.1980).

Art. 1925. Noninterdicted person deprived of reason; protection of innocent contracting party by onerous title

A noninterdicted person, who was deprived of reason at the time of contracting, may obtain rescission of an onerous contract upon the ground of incapacity only upon showing that the other party knew or should have known that person's incapacity.

Acts 1984, No. 331, § 1, eff. Jan. 1, 1985.

REVISION COMMENTS—1984

(a) This Article is new. It does not change the law, however, but merely restates the distinction between "notorious" and nonevident deprivation of reason found in C.C. Arts. 402, 1788(3), and 1789 (1870).

(b) Under this Article, rescission of an onerous contract entered into by a person deprived of reason who was not interdicted at the time of contracting can only be obtained upon a showing that the capable person knew or reasonably should have known that he was dealing with a person deprived of reason. Proof that the alleged incapable was "notoriously insane" at the time of contracting raises a rebuttable presumption that the other party knew that he was contracting with a person deprived of reason.

(c) Even though the nullity of a contract made by a person deprived of reason is for the benefit of the incapable, security of transactions requires that innocent parties not be deprived of their expectations when they have contracted with a noninterdicted person who appeared sane at the time of contracting. This Article establishes a distinction between insanity that is evident, or, if not evident, susceptible of being known by those who bargain with the incapable, and insanity that can be concealed to the point of deceiving the untrained. In the latter situation, the innocent party deserves the protection of the law against what can be termed a "misrepresentation of sanity." See Litvinoff & Tête, Louisiana Legal Transactions: The Civil Law of Juridical Acts 91 (1969).

Civil Code Article 1789 (1870) has been interpreted in pari materia with C.C. Art. 1788(3) (1870) to allow a noninterdicted person asserting insanity to prove either his co-contractant's personal knowledge of the incapacity or its general notoriety. See Vance v. Ellerbe, 150 La. 388, 90 So. 735 (1922); Note, 24 La.L.Rev. 132, 135–136 (1963); Twomey v. Papalia, 142 La. 621, 77 So. 479 (1918). If the lack of reason was generally known to persons who saw and conversed with the alleged incapable at the time he entered into the contract, there is a presumption that it could not have been unknown to the other party. This presumption does not preclude the other party's proving that the incapable's lack of reason was concealed at the time of contracting.

(d) This Article addresses only capacity to contract. Civil Code Article 402 (1870), which, because of its use of the term "notoriously," may be interpreted as expressing a less strict rule, is not repealed for juridical acts other than contracts.

(e) A person may rescind a gratuitous contract on the basis of his incapacity without showing that the other party knew or should have known of that incapacity.

Art. 1926.   Attack on noninterdicted decedent's contracts

A contract made by a noninterdicted person deprived of reason at the time of contracting may be attacked after his death, on the ground of incapacity, only when the contract is gratuitous, or it evidences lack of understanding, or was made within thirty days of his death, or when application for interdiction was filed before his death.

Acts 1984, No. 331, § 1, eff. Jan. 1, 1985.

REVISION COMMENT—1984

This Article does not change the law. It consolidates the provisions of C.C. Art. 1788(5)–(11) (1870) in a manner consistent with C.C. Art. 403 (1870). Though this Article makes no reference to testaments, no change in the law is intended since the matter covered in C.C. Art. 1788(11) (1870) is now governed by C.C. Art. 1475 (1870), which does not make the time at which a testament was made a criterion for determining whether or not it can be attacked.

CHAPTER 3—CONSENT

Art. 1927.   Consent

A contract is formed by the consent of the parties established through offer and acceptance.

Unless the law prescribes a certain formality for the intended contract, offer and acceptance may be made orally, in writing, or by action or inaction that under the circumstances is clearly indicative of consent.

Unless otherwise specified in the offer, there need not be conformity between the manner in which the offer is made and the manner in which the acceptance is made.

Acts 1984, No. 331, § 1, eff. Jan. 1, 1985.

(a) This Article reproduces the substance of C.C. Arts. 1798, 1812, 1816, and 1817 (1870). It does not change the law.

(b) This Article reflects the view of the Louisiana jurisprudence that when special formalities are prescribed for a contract the same formalities are required for an offer or acceptance intended to form that contract. See Barchus v. Johnson, 151 La. 985, 92 So. 566 (1922); Charbonnet v. Ochsner, 258 La. 507, 246 So.2d 844 (1971).

Art. 1928.   Irrevocable offer

An offer that specifies a period of time for acceptance is irrevocable during that time.

When the offeror manifests an intent to give the offeree a delay within which to accept, without specifying a time, the offer is irrevocable for a reasonable time.

Acts 1984, No. 331, § 1, eff. Jan. 1, 1985.

REVISION COMMENTS—1984

(a) This Article does not change the law. It articulates ideas clearly contained in C.C. Arts. 1802 and 1809 (1870). See 3 Toullier, Le droit civil français 325–326 (1833); Box v. Karam, 252 So.2d 176 (La.App. 3rd Cir.1971); see also 1 Litvinoff, Obligations 237, 249 (1969).

(b) Under this Article, an offeror who specifies a time for acceptance which is too long under the circumstances is not bound beyond a reasonable time. Cf. Union Sawmill Co. v. Mitchell, 122 La. 900, 48 So. 317 (1909).

Art. 1929.   Expiration of irrevocable offer for lack of acceptance

An irrevocable offer expires if not accepted within the time prescribed in the preceding Article.

Acts 1984, No. 331, § 1, eff. Jan. 1, 1985.

REVISION COMMENT—1984

This Article is new. It does not change the law, however. It articulates ideas expressed in C.C. Arts. 1801 and 1802 (1870). See 1 Litvinoff, Obligations 247 (1969).

Art. 1930.   Revocable offer

An offer not irrevocable under Civil Code Article 1928 may be revoked before it is accepted.

Acts 1984, No. 331, § 1, eff. Jan. 1, 1985.

REVISION COMMENTS—1984

(a) This Article is new. It changes the law as reflected in C.C. Arts. 1802, 1809, and 1819 (1870).

(b) This Article and revised C.C. Art. 1928 (Rev.1984), supra, incorporate the interpretation given by the jurisprudence to C.C. Art. 1809 (1870) in the sense that a strong fact situation is necessary in order to imply that an offer is irrevocable for any substantial length of time. See Wagenvoord Broadcasting Co. v. Canal Automatic Transmission Service, Inc., 176 So.2d 188 (La.App. 4th Cir.1965).

Art. 1931.   Expiration of revocable offer

A revocable offer expires if not accepted within a reasonable time.

Acts 1984, No. 331, § 1, eff. Jan. 1, 1985.

REVISION COMMENT—1984

This Article is new. It does not change the law, however. It reflects ideas expressed in C.C. Arts. 1801 and 1802 (1870). See 1 Litvinoff, Obligations 247 (1969).

Art. 1932.   Expiration of offer by death or incapacity of either party

An offer expires by the death or incapacity of the offeror or the offeree before it has been accepted.

Acts 1984, No. 331, § 1, eff. Jan. 1, 1985.

REVISION COMMENT—1984

This Article restates the rule contained in C.C. Art. 1810 (1870). It does not change the law.

Art. 1933.   Option contracts

An option is a contract whereby the parties agree that the offeror is bound by his offer for a specified period of time and that the offeree may accept within that time.

Acts 1984, No. 331, § 1, eff. Jan. 1, 1985.

REVISION COMMENTS—1984

(a) This Article is new. It generalizes the specific rule applicable to sales contained in C.C. Art. 2462 (1870).

(b) An option under this Article is distinguishable from an irrevocable offer, provided for in revised C.C. Art. 1928 (Rev.1984), supra. An option is a veritable contract that may be assigned and that gives rise to rights and obligations that devolve upon the parties' heirs when not personal to the parties. An irrevocable offer is not assignable, and under revised C.C. Art. 1932 (Rev.1984), supra, it expires at the death of either the offeror or the offeree.

(c) The offer contained in an option contract expires upon the death or incapacity of the grantor if the circumstances show that that offer, if accepted, would have given rise to an obligation personal to the grantor; it expires upon the death or incapacity of the grantee if the obligation arising from the proposed contract would have been personal to the grantee. It expires upon the death or incapacity of either if the circumstances show that the proposed obligation would have been personal to both.

Art. 1934.   Time when acceptance of an irrevocable offer is effective

An acceptance of an irrevocable offer is effective when received by the offeror.

Acts 1984, No. 331, § 1, eff. Jan. 1, 1985.

REVISION COMMENTS—1984

(a) This Article does not change the law. It reflects ideas articulated in C.C. Arts. 1809 and 1819 (1870).

(b) Under this Article, an acceptance of an irrevocable offer is effective when received by the offeror within the time named in the offer, or within a reasonable time under revised C.C. Art. 1928 (Rev.1984), supra. See 6 Planiol et Ripert, Traité pratique de droit civil français 155–156 (2nd ed. Esmein, 1952); see also 1 Litvinoff, Obligations 310–313 (1969).

Art. 1935.   Time when acceptance of a revocable offer is effective

Unless otherwise specified by the offer or the law, an acceptance of a revocable offer, made in a manner and by a medium suggested by the offer or in a reasonable manner and by a reasonable medium, is effective when transmitted by the offeree.

Acts 1984, No. 331, § 1, eff. Jan. 1, 1985.

REVISION COMMENTS—1984

(a) This Article is new. It changes the law in part, providing that the acceptance of a revocable offer is effective upon transmission by the offeree rather than upon receipt by the offeror.

(b) When an offer is revocable under revised C.C. Art. 1930 (Rev.1984), supra, the offeree's position is fragile because the offer may be effectively revoked any time before he has accepted it. The famous "mailbox rule" or rule of acceptance upon dispatch, as formulated in Adams v. Lindsell, In re King's Bench, 1 Barn. & Ald. 681 (1818), affords protection to an offeree in such a position by allowing him to rely upon a contract being formed when he transmits his acceptance. The risk of transmission is placed on the offeror. Comparative research in this area shows that in the various systems of law the revocability of offers and the time of formation of contracts are governed by reciprocally complementary rules. Thus, where an ordinary offer is irrevocable for some period of time, as is generally the case in continental systems, acceptance is only effective upon receipt by the offeror; but where an offer is revocable, as is generally the case at the common law, the acceptance is effective upon transmission. See Nussbaum, "Comparative Aspects of the Anglo-American Offer-and-Acceptance Doctrine," 36 Columbia L.R. 920 (1936). See also 1 Litvinoff, Obligations 308–327 (1969).

(c) What constitutes an effective transmission under this Article is to be determined by the courts according to business practices. However, the act of entrusting a communication of acceptance to an employee of the offeree would not constitute transmission until the communication is actually posted.

(d) The burden of stating a particular method of communication is upon the offeror. This approach, which prevails in Anglo-American law, finds strong support in much of French doctrine and jurisprudence. See Aubert, Notions et rôles de l'offre et de l'acceptation dans la formation du contrat 353–354 (1970); 2 Colin et Capitant, Cours élémentaire de droit civil français 38 (10th ed. Julliot de la Morandière 1953); Loches, June 25, 1945, D. 1947, 113.

Art. 1936.   Reasonableness of manner and medium of acceptance

A medium or a manner of acceptance is reasonable if it is the one used in making the offer or one customary in similar transactions at the time and place the offer is received, unless circumstances known to the offeree indicate otherwise.

Acts 1984, No. 331, § 1, eff. Jan. 1, 1985.

REVISION COMMENT—1984

This Article is new. It does not change the law, however. The rule stated is unquestionably implicit in the principle that informs C.C. Arts. 1802, 1804, and 1809 (1870). See 1 Litvinoff, Obligations 292 (1969).

Art. 1937.   Time when revocation is effective

A revocation of a revocable offer is effective when received by the offeree prior to acceptance.

Acts 1984, No. 331, § 1, eff. Jan. 1, 1985.

REVISION COMMENT—1984

This Article is new. It does not change the law, however. It states a rule implicit in C.C. Art. 1797 (1870), and strongly supported in French doctrine. See Aubert, Notions et rôles de l'offre et de l'acceptation dans la formation du contrat 204–205 (1970); 6 Planiol et Ripert, Traité pratique de droit civil français 159 (2nd ed. Esmein 1952). The same rule has prevailed at common law since Byrne v. Van Tienhoven, 5 C.P.D. 344 (1880). See Restatement, Second, Contracts § 42 (1981). See also 1 Litvinoff, Obligations 245 (1969).

Art. 1938.   Reception of revocation, rejection, or acceptance

A written revocation, rejection, or acceptance is received when it comes into the possession of the addressee or of a person authorized by him to receive it, or when it is deposited in a place the addressee has indicated as the place for this or similar communications to be deposited for him.

Acts 1984, No. 331, § 1, eff. Jan. 1, 1985.

REVISION COMMENTS—1984

(a) This Article is new. It does not change the law, however. It reflects an idea that seems implicit in C.C. Art. 1809 (1870).

(b) Under this Article, the "reception theory" of contract formation is adopted rather than the "knowledge theory." See 1 Litvinoff, Obligations 310 (1969); 6 Planiol et Ripert, Traité pratique de droit civil français 192 (2nd ed. Esmein 1952).

Art. 1939.   Acceptance by performance

When an offeror invites an offeree to accept by performance and, according to usage or the nature or the terms of the contract, it is contemplated that the performance will be completed if commenced, a contract is formed when the offeree begins the requested performance.

Acts 1984, No. 331, § 1, eff. Jan. 1, 1985.

REVISION COMMENT—1984

This Article is new. It does not change the law, however. It articulates ideas developed by the jurisprudence, and implicit in C.C. Art. 1816 (1870). See Johnson v. Capital City Ford Company, Inc., 85 So.2d 75 (La.App. 1st Cir.1955); Ever-Tite Roofing Corporation v. Green, 83 So.2d 449 (La.App. 2d Cir.1955).

Art. 1940.   Acceptance only by completed performance

When, according to usage or the nature of the contract, or its own terms, an offer made to a particular offeree can be accepted only by rendering a completed performance, the offeror cannot revoke the offer, once the offeree has begun to perform, for the reasonable time necessary to complete the performance. The offeree, however, is not bound to complete the performance he has begun.

The offeror's duty of performance is conditional on completion or tender of the requested performance.

Acts 1984, No. 331, § 1, eff. Jan. 1, 1985.

REVISION COMMENT—1984

See comment to preceding Article.

Art. 1941.   Notice of commencement of performance

When commencement of the performance either constitutes acceptance or makes the offer irrevocable, the offeree must give prompt notice of that commencement unless the offeror knows or should know that the offeree has begun to perform. An offeree who fails to give the notice is liable for damages.

Acts 1984, No. 331, § 1, eff. Jan. 1, 1985.

REVISION COMMENT—1984

See comment to preceding Articles.

Art. 1942.   Acceptance by silence

When, because of special circumstances, the offeree's silence leads the offeror reasonably to believe that a contract has been formed, the offer is deemed accepted.

Acts 1984, No. 331, § 1, eff. Jan. 1, 1985.

REVISION COMMENT—1984

The Article reproduces the substance of C.C. Art. 1817 (1870). It does not change the law.

Art. 1943.   Acceptance not in accordance with offer

An acceptance not in accordance with the terms of the offer is deemed to be a counteroffer.

Acts 1984, No. 331, § 1, eff. Jan. 1, 1985.

REVISION COMMENT—1984

This Article reproduces the substance of C.C. Arts. 1805, 1806, and 1808 (1870). The law is changed in part, however, by virtue of the elimination of the rule of C.C. Art. 1807 (1870) under which a contract may be established by "crossing" offers and counteroffers.

Art. 1944.   Offer of reward made to the public

An offer of a reward made to the public is binding upon the offeror even if the one who performs the requested act does not know of the offer.

Acts 1984, No. 331, § 1, eff. Jan. 1, 1985.

REVISION COMMENTS—1984

(a) This Article is new. It changes the law in part. It subjects the offeror of a reward to an obligation which is legal rather than contractual. See 1 Litvinoff, Obligations 288 (1969); cf. Taylor v. American Bank and Trust Co., 135 So. 47 (La.App.Orl.1931).

(b) An important segment of modern French doctrine supports the view that the offer of a reward made to the public is binding even when the party who performs the act does not know of the offer. This result is predicated on the binding effect of a unilateral declaration of will. See 6 Planiol et Ripert, Traité pratique de droit civil français 164 (2nd ed. Esmein 1952); 2 Demogue, Traité des obligations en général 204, 264, 267 (1923). See also 1 Litvinoff, Obligations 278–279 (1969).

Art. 1945.   Revocation of an offer of reward made to the public

An offer of reward made to the public may be revoked before completion of the requested act, provided the revocation is made by the same or an equally effective means as the offer.

Acts 1984, No. 331, § 1, eff. Jan. 1, 1985.

REVISION COMMENTS—1984

(a) This Article is new. It does not change the law, however. It articulates an idea developed by the Louisiana jurisprudence. See Youngblood v. Daily and Weekly Signal Tribune, 131 So. 604 (La.App. 2nd Cir.1930); cf. Murphy v. New Orleans, 11 La.Ann. 323 (1856).

(b) If the offeror of a reward dies before it is claimed, under this Article his heirs may revoke the offer by simply publishing a notice of his death. They are bound by the offer, however, to those who performed the requested act without knowing of the offeror's death. They are also bound, up to the amount of the reward, for the expenses incurred before they learned of the death by those who started to perform in good faith before that time. See 1 Litvinoff, Obligations 278 (1969).

(c) If the offer is revoked, under this Article, the offeree may have a remedy under revised C.C. Art. 1967 (Rev.1984), infra.

Art. 1946.   Performance by several persons

Unless otherwise stipulated in the offer made to the public, or otherwise implied from the nature of the act, when several persons have performed the requested act, the reward belongs to the first one giving notice of his completion of performance to the offeror.

Acts 1984, No. 331, § 1, eff. Jan. 1, 1985.

REVISION COMMENT—1984

This Article is new. In the absence of an express provision in the Louisiana Civil Code of 1870, it provides a rule consistent with general principles.

Art. 1947.   Form contemplated by parties

When, in the absence of a legal requirement, the parties have contemplated a certain form, it is presumed that they do not intend to be bound until the contract is executed in that form.

Acts 1984, No. 331, § 1, eff. Jan. 1, 1985.

REVISION COMMENT—1984

This Article is new. It does not change the law, however. The rule stated has been consistently followed by the Louisiana jurisprudence. See, e.g., Laroussini v. Werlein, 52 La.Ann. 424, 27 So. 89

471

(1899); see also Breaux Brothers Const. Co. v. Associated Contractors, Inc., 226 La. 720, 77 So.2d 17 (1954); Waldhauser v. Adams Hats, 207 La. 56, 20 So.2d 423 (1944).

CHAPTER 4—VICES OF CONSENT

SECTION 1—ERROR

Art. 1948.   Vitiated consent

Consent may be vitiated by error, fraud, or duress.

Acts 1984, No. 331, § 1, eff. Jan. 1, 1985.

REVISION COMMENT—1984

This Article restates C.C. Art. 1819 (1870). It does not change the law.

Art. 1949.   Error vitiates consent

Error vitiates consent only when it concerns a cause without which the obligation would not have been incurred and that cause was known or should have been known to the other party.

Acts 1984, No. 331, § 1, eff. Jan. 1, 1985.

REVISION COMMENTS—1984

(a) This Article is new. It does not change the law, however. It articulates ideas contained in C.C. Arts. 1823, 1825, and 1826 (1870).

(b) Under this Article, relief for error may be granted only when the error affects the cause of the obligation, that is, when a party's consent has been determined by it. This is consistent with the principle expressed in C.C. Art. 1823 (1870). See Marty et Raynaud, Droit civil—Les obligations, Part I, at 111–112 (1962).

(c) Under this Article, relief for error may be granted to a party only when the other party knew or should have known that the matter affected by the error was the cause of the obligation for the party in error, that is, that it was the reason he consented to bind himself. This is consistent with the definition of cause contained in revised C.C. Art. 1967 (Rev. 1984), infra, the principle stated in C.C. Art. 1824 (1870); and the jurisprudential interpretation given to C.C. Art. 1826 (1870).

(d) The granting of relief for error presents no problem when both parties are in error, that is, when the error is bilateral. When that is the case the contract may be rescinded, as when the parties misunderstood each other at the time of contracting (Lyons Milling Co. v. Cusimano, 161 La. 198, 108 So. 414 (1926)); or when they were misinformed because of the error of a third party (Calhoun v. Teal, 106 La. 47, 30 So. 288 (1901)). As an alternative, the instrument that contains the contract may be reformed in order to reflect the true intent of the parties. See Wilson v. Levy, 234 La. 719, 101 So.2d 214 (1958); Kolmaister v. Connecticut General Life Insurance Company, 370 So.2d 630 (La.App. 4th Cir.1979).

When only one party is in error, that is, when the error is unilateral, there is theoretically no meeting of the minds, but granting relief to the party in error will unjustly injure the interest of the other party if he is innocent of the error. Louisiana courts have often refused relief for unilateral error for this reason. See Hello World Broadcasting Corp. v. International Broadcasting Corp., 186 La. 589, 173 So. 115 (1937); Kirkland v. Edenborn, 140 La. 669, 73 So. 719 (1916); Scoggin v. Bagley, 368 So.2d 763 (La.App. 2nd Cir.1979). Yet, expanding the rule stated in C.C. Art. 1826 (1870), they have granted relief for unilateral error in cases where the other party knew or should have known that the matter affected by the error was the reason or principal cause why the party in error made the contract. See Marcello v. Bussiere, 284 So.2d 892 (La.1973); Jefferson Truck Equipment Co. v. Guarisco Motor Co., 250 So.2d 211 (La.App. 1st Cir.1971). As expressed in Nugent v. Stanley, 336 So.2d 1058, 1063 (La.App. 3rd Cir.1976): "The jurisprudence . . . establishes that a contract may be invalidated for unilateral error as to a fact which was a principal cause for making the contract, where the other party knew or should have known it was the principal cause." French courts have taken a very similar approach. See 6 Planiol et Ripert, Traité pratique de droit civil français 209–211 (2nd ed. Esmein 1952); Ghestin, La notion d'erreur dans le droit positif actuel 104–131 (1963); Malinvaud, "De l'erreur sur la substance," Recueil Dalloz Sirey, Chronique XXXI (1972); Litvinoff, " 'Error' in the Civil Law," Essays on the Civil Law of Obligations 222, 242–247 (Dainow ed. 1969). At common law, on the other hand, unilateral error does not invalidate consent unless the error was known to the other party. As stated in C.J. 373: "A mistake of one of the parties only in the expression of his agreement or as to the subject matter, not known to the other, does not affect its binding force, and is no ground for its rescission even in equity." At civil law, a party's knowledge of the other's error at the time of making the contract constitutes fraud (dol) see revised C.C. Art. 1953 (Rev.1984), infra; C.C. Arts. 1832 and 1846(6) (1870). Under this revised Article, it is not necessary that the other party have known of the mistake; it suffices that he knew or should have known that the matter affected by the error was the reason that prompted the party in error to enter the contract.

(e) Civil Code Article 1825 (1870) provides that the "principal cause" must be affected by error in order to invalidate the contract. That Article goes on to explain that the "principal cause," when there are several causes, is called the "motive." That, however, is a mistranslation. The original French text of C.C. Art. 1825 (1870) reads: "Pour que l'erreur sur la cause empêche le contrat d'être valide, il faut que cette cause soit la principale, lorsqu'il y en a plusieurs. Cette principale cause est celle sans laquelle le contrat n'aurait pas été fait." 3 Louisiana Legal Archives, Part II, at 1009 (1942). According to the French text, the "principal cause", rather than the "motive," is that cause without which the contract would not have been made. This is sufficiently expressed by "cause" without resorting to "principal cause," which is redundant. Even when an obligation has multiple causes, error that bears on any one of them is sufficient to make the obligation invalid. See Capitant, De la cause des obligations 44 (1923).

Art. 1950. Error that concerns cause

Error may concern a cause when it bears on the nature of the contract, or the thing that is the contractual object or a substantial quality of that thing, or the person or the qualities of the other party, or the law, or any other circumstance that the parties regarded, or should in good faith have regarded, as a cause of the obligation.

Acts 1984, No. 331, § 1, eff. Jan. 1, 1985.

REVISION COMMENTS—1984

(a) This Article is new. It restates principles found in C.C. Arts. 1824–1846 (1870). It does not change the law since it only reflects the repeal of C.C. Art. 1846(3), repealed by Acts 1982, No. 187.

(b) Under this Article, relief may be obtained when a party has consented to a contract different from the one he intended to make, as when, intending to conclude a sale, he has given his consent to a contract of lease.

(c) Under this Article, relief may be obtained when either the thing for which a party has contracted or a substantial quality of that thing is different from what he understood it to be at the time of contracting, as when, intending to buy bars of silver, he has unknowingly bought bars of another metal, or when, intending to buy a gold vase, he has unknowingly bought a gold-plated one. See Deutschmann v. Standard Fur Company, 331 So.2d 219 (La.App. 4th Cir.1976).

(d) Under this Article, relief may be obtained when, intending to contract with a certain person or a person of a certain quality or character, a party has given his consent to a contract with a different person, or with a person who lacks the intended quality or character. If the contract is gratuitous, the presumption obtains that the person of the intended obligee was the reason why the obligor bound himself.

(e) Under this Article, relief may be obtained when a party has drawn erroneous conclusions of law and entered into a contract on the basis of them. Error of law is to be distinguished from ignorance of the law. The former may be excusable, the latter is not. See C.C. Art. 7 (1870).

(f) Under this Article, an error in a party's motive, that is, an error confined within the bounds of a party's subjectivity, does not invalidate consent. As expressed in Capitant, De la cause des obligations at 209–210 (1923): "Error makes the contract annullable when it concerns the act of will through which the party bound himself. Otherwise, that act of will being complete and nonvitiated

473

preserves its obligatory effect. As a consequence, an error which does not affect the manifestation of will remains inoperative. That is the reason why an error in the motive does not annul the contract even though it exerts a decisive influence on the obligation. A party who buys a horse because he erroneously believes that his own has perished, or a donor whose will is determined by an erroneous motive, would not have contracted had he been correctly informed; nevertheless the sale or the donation are nonetheless valid. Although the motives rest in the subjective sphere of the individual, they no doubt prompt him to engage himself, but they nevertheless, remain beyond the contractual field, they are anterior to the act of will by which the party obligates himself; they are not a constitutive element of the act of will." Capitant, supra, at 209–210 (1923). See also 6 Planiol et Ripert, Traité pratique de droit civil français 222–224 (2d ed. Esmein 1952); 1 Litvinoff, Obligations 394–396 (1969). That conclusion is consistent with the approach taken by the Louisiana jurisprudence. In Tri-Parish Bank & Trust Company v. Richard, 280 So.2d 850 (La.App. 3rd Cir.1973), writ denied 283 So.2d 499 (La.1973), where a payee did not know, and could not be presumed to have known, that the maker's motive for signing a promissory note had been to protect a corporation in which the maker owned an interest, the court concluded that even if such was the maker's principal motive, error as to that motive could not invalidate the note.

(g) Relief for error under this Article may be granted only when that error also meets the requirements of revised C.C. Art. 1949 (Rev.1984), supra.

(h) The granting of relief for error of law is subject to the exceptions elsewhere provided in this Code. For example, a transaction or compromise may not be rescinded for error of law. See C.C. Art. 3078 (1870). Nor may a payment made because of an error as to the existence of a civil obligation be recovered, if the party was in fact bound by a natural obligation. See revised C.C. Art. 1761 (Rev.1984), supra; C.C. Art. 2303 (1870).

Art. 1951.   Other party willing to perform

A party may not avail himself of his error if the other party is willing to perform the contract as intended by the party in error.

Acts 1984, No. 331, § 1, eff. Jan. 1, 1985.

REVISION COMMENT—1984

This Article is new. It does not change the law, however. In the context of the theory of mistake, it articulates an idea implied in C.C. Arts. 1901 and 1903 (1870). It is consistent with modern developments in the civilian tradition, as reflected, for instance, in Article 25 of the Swiss Code of Obligations and Article 1702 of the Ethiopian Civil Code.

Art. 1952.   Rescission; liability for damages

A party who obtains rescission on grounds of his own error is liable for the loss thereby sustained by the other party unless the latter knew or should have known of the error.

The court may refuse rescission when the effective protection of the other party's interest requires that the contract be upheld. In that case, a reasonable compensation for the loss he has sustained may be granted to the party to whom rescission is refused.

Acts 1984, No. 331, § 1, eff. Jan. 1, 1985.

REVISION COMMENTS—1984

(a) This Article is new. It generalizes the rules provided in C.C. Arts. 1837 and 1839 (1870). It changes the law insofar as it asserts that the interest of the party not in error and in good faith may be protected by an allowance of damages, and not solely by confirmation of the contract in spite of the error.

(b) Under this Article, a party in error who obtains rescission is liable to the other party for the injury to the latter's interest that the rescission may cause. Previously, when error has been invoked, Louisiana courts have regarded the problem solely as one of rescission vel non. Thus, in Schorr v. Nosacka, 132 So. 524, 525 (La.App.Orl.1931), the court said: "If (the defendant) made a mistake in his bid, it was the result of carelessness from the effect of which we can discover no legal relief." In Cox-Hardie Co. v. Rabalais, 162 So.2d 713, 715 (La.App. 4th Cir.1964), the court asserted: "Defendant cannot be relieved of his carelessness. Where one of two innocent parties must suffer the one who caused the error must suffer the consequences." In First National Mortgage Corporation v. The Manhattan Life Insurance Company, 360 So.2d 264, 267 (La.App. 4th Cir.1978), the court stated the usual jurisprudential rule: "If the contract is null and void, the remedy is to rescind and to put the parties in the position in which they were prior to the attempted agreement. Thus, a request for damages based on this concept states no cause of action." Those assertions contradict the principle underlying C.C. Art. 1837 (1870) and also run counter to the clear rule of C.C. Art. 2452 (1870). The right to recover liquidated damages where performance of a contract to sell was impossible because of an error was asserted in Nelson v. Holden, 219 La. 37, 52 So.2d 240 (1951). This Article allows a more flexible approach to situations of that kind, in keeping with the principles underlying the source Articles. See Palmer, "Contractual Negligence in the Civil Law—The Evolution of a Defense to Actions For Error," 50 Tul.L.Rev. 1, 11–14 (1975).

(c) Under this Article, the award of damages to the party not in error is intended to protect his reliance interest. It is limited to the loss that he actually sustained. See Fuller & Perdue, "The Reliance Interest in Contract Damages: 2," 46 Yale L.J. 373 (1937). Except in exceptional circumstances, full protection of the interest of the party not in error may be better achieved by upholding the contract, as contemplated in the second Paragraph of this Article, rather than by awarding damages.

(d) In determining whether to grant rescission or, when rescission is granted, whether to allow any recovery to the party not in error, the court may consider whether the error was excusable or inexcusable, a distinction received by modern civilian doctrine. See 6 Planiol et Ripert, Traité pratique de droit civil français 227–229 (2nd ed. Esmein 1952); Litvinoff, " 'Error' in the Civil Law," in Essays on the Civil Law of Obligations 222, 226–269 (Dainow ed. 1969); Ghestin, La notion d'erreur dans le droit positif actuel 146–165 (1963). Louisiana courts have granted relief when error has been found excusable (see Boehmer Sales Agency v. Russo, 99 So.2d 475 (La.App.Orl. Cir.1958)) and refused it when error has been found inexcusable (see Watson v. The Planters' Bank of Tennessee, 22 La.Ann. 14 (1870)). The court may also consider whether the other party has changed his position and the importance of such a change. In this context, Louisiana courts have said that in case of doubt as to error in the motive of one of the parties courts will lean heavily in favor of one seeking to avoid loss and against one seeking to obtain a gain. See Dorvin-Huddleston Developments, Inc. v. Connolly, 285 So.2d 359 (La.App. 4th Cir.1973), reversed on other grounds 298 So.2d 734 (La.1974), on remand 320 So.2d 253 (La.App. 4th Cir.1975).

(e) Under this Article, when the interest of the party not in error can be protected only by upholding the contract, a reasonable compensation may be granted to the party in error if the upholding results in unfair detriment to the latter. Thus, if through error a party conveyed to another a piece of property different from the one he intended to sell, and the transferee then built valuable improvements upon the property, it would seem that the transferee could be protected only by upholding the contract. If the property actually conveyed was considerably more valuable than the one intended, however, the transferee would obtain a great advantage if this were done. In such a case, an award of reasonable compensation to the transferor would insure a fair solution. This approach is consistent with the definition of equity contained in C.C. Art. 1965 (1870). Cf. Lawrence v. Mount Zion Baptist Church, 1 La.App. 404 (1925).

SECTION 2—FRAUD

Art. 1953. Fraud may result from misrepresentation or from silence

Fraud is a misrepresentation or a suppression of the truth made with the intention either to obtain an unjust advantage for one party or to cause a loss or inconvenience to the other. Fraud may also result from silence or inaction.

Acts 1984, No. 331, § 1, eff. Jan. 1, 1985.

REVISION COMMENTS—1984

(a) This Article is new. It does not change the law, however. It restates the definition found in C.C. Art. 1847(6) (1870).

(b) Under this Article, fraud may result not only from an act, such as a false assertion or suppression of the truth, but also from a failure to act, such as silence, that is calculated to produce a misleading effect.

(c) Fraud, like its French equivalent "dol," need not be a criminal act. Intentional fault of a quasi-delictual nature suffices to constitute the kind of fraud that vitiates a party's consent. See 6 Planiol et Ripert, Traité pratique de droit civil français 240–243 (2d ed. Esmein 1952); 2 Litvinoff, Obligations 346–347 (1975).

Art. 1954. Confidence between the parties

Fraud does not vitiate consent when the party against whom the fraud was directed could have ascertained the truth without difficulty, inconvenience, or special skill.

This exception does not apply when a relation of confidence has reasonably induced a party to rely on the other's assertions or representations.

Acts 1984, No. 331, § 1, eff. Jan. 1, 1985.

REVISION COMMENTS—1984

(a) This Article is new. It changes the law in part. It generalizes the defense provided in C.C. Art. 1847(4) (1870) for cases involving false assertions of value, cost, or quality. This is consistent with views expressed by the Louisiana jurisprudence. In Rocchi v. Schwabacher & Hirsch, 33 La.Ann. 1364, 1368 (1881), the court asserted: "Where the means of knowledge are at hand, and equally available to both parties, and the subject of purchase is alike open to their inspection, if the purchaser does not avail himself of these means and opportunities, he will not be heard to say, . . . that he was deceived by the vendor's misrepresentations." In Forsman v. Mace, 111 La. 28, 35 So. 372 (1903), the court said: "After reading and carefully weighing the evidence pro and con the other grounds of nullity, we are not satisfied that the fraud complained of has been made out. Two of the plaintiffs were experienced timbermen. They were taken to the logging camp, and afforded the fullest kind of opportunity to examine and be informed as to the condition of the oxen, and as to the location and quantity of the timber. By so simple a thing as looking at the map of the parish they could have known of the distance. They went over the land to look at the timber, and if they did not go over all of it they have but themselves to blame." 35 So. at 374.

(b) Under the exception provided in the second paragraph of this Article, there is fraud even when a party could have readily ascertained the truth without difficulty, inconvenience, or special skill, when a relation of confidence has induced the party to rely on the other's assertions or representations.

(c) This Article does not change special rules under which a false assertion of quality may constitute fraud even in the absence of a relation of confidence or trust, such as C.C. Art. 2547 (1870).

Art. 1955. Error induced by fraud

Error induced by fraud need not concern the cause of the obligation to vitiate consent, but it must concern a circumstance that has substantially influenced that consent.

Acts 1984, No. 331, § 1, eff. Jan. 1, 1985.

REVISION COMMENTS—1984

(a) This Article is new. It does not change the law, however. It restates ideas expressed in C.C. Art. 1847 (1870).

(b) Under this Article, relief may be obtained on grounds of fraud even when the error thus induced did not concern the cause of the obligation or the reason why the party bound himself, provided that it concerned a circumstance that substantially influenced him to do so. Error induced by fraud differs from simple error in this respect. See Strauss v. Insurance Co. of North America, 157 La. 661, 102 So. 861 (1925); Lacoste v. Handy, 1 Man.Unrep.Cas.348 (La.1880).

476

Art. 1956.   Fraud committed by a third person

Fraud committed by a third person vitiates the consent of a contracting party if the other party knew or should have known of the fraud.

Acts 1984, No. 331, § 1, eff. Jan. 1, 1985.

REVISION COMMENTS—1984

(a) This Article is new. It does not change the law, however. It clarifies an idea expressed in C.C. Art. 1847(9) (1870).

(b) Under this Article, when fraud has been committed by a third person without the knowledge of the party who benefited from it, the other party is still bound.

(c) In the situation contemplated in comment (b), relief may nevertheless be obtained on grounds of error if the requirements of revised C.C. Arts. 1949 through 1952 (Rev.1984), supra, are met; and, in a proper case, the party injured in his interest may recover damages from the third person who committed the fraud. C.C. Art. 2315 (1870). See also C.C. Art. 1847(9) (1870).

(d) Under this Article, the victim of fraud committed by a third party is not bound if the other party, though ignorant of the fraud, should have known of it. For instance, in George A. Broas Co., Inc. v. Hibernia Homestead and Savings Ass'n., 134 So.2d 356 (La.App. 4th Cir.1961), the plaintiff corporation sought damages for breach of a contract to provide financing. The court found the contract null because a signature on an important document had been forged at the defendant's offices through the agency of the plaintiff's president's wife, who was also vice president of the defendant corporation. The court clearly surmised that the plaintiff's president could not have ignored, or should have known, the part his wife played in the forgery.

Art. 1957.   Proof

Fraud need only be proved by a preponderance of the evidence and may be established by circumstantial evidence.

Acts 1984, No. 331, § 1, eff. Jan. 1, 1985.

REVISION COMMENTS—1984

(a) This Article is new. It does not change the law, however. It restates a principle expressed in C.C. Art. 1848 (1870).

(b) In some instances, Louisiana courts have recognized the full import of C.C. Art. 1848 (1870). Thus, in Griffing v. Atkins, 1 So.2d 445, 450 (La.App. 1st Cir.1941), the court said: "Whilst it is true that in Article 1848 of the Civil Code it is provided that fraud, like every other allegation, must be proved by him who alleges it, however, that same article further provides that 'it may be proved by simple presumptions, or by legal presumptions as well as by other evidence. The maxim that fraud is not to be presumed, means no more than that it is not to be imputed without legal evidence.' Courts have always acknowledged how difficult it is for one to prove fraud by positive and direct testimony, realizing full well that those who indulge in it generally prepare themselves in such a manner as to cover up and leave no traces of their practice behind them." 1 So.2d 445, at 450.

In an earlier case, H. T. Simon-Gregory Dry-Goods Co. v. Newman, 50 La.Ann. 338, 23 So. 329, 331 (1898), the court said: "While fraud is never to be presumed, courts of justice recognize the cunning concealment in which it shrouds its devious practices and the difficulty of tracing it by direct proof,. . . ." In Vanguard Finance, Inc. v. Smith, 256 So.2d 662, 664 (La.App. 4th Cir.1972), it was asserted that: "(F)raud must be proved by one who alleges fraud, but because of the nature of fraud it sometimes must be inferred from the existence of highly suspicious conditions or events." In Liberty Loan Corporation of Berwick v. Kornbacker, 247 So.2d 404, 405 (La.App. 1st Cir.1971), it was said that: "Fraud must be proven, . . . , by a preponderance of the evidence." Other cases, however, such as Pierce v. Kyle, 241 So.2d 604, 605 (La.App. 2nd Cir.1970), have followed the rule that, "(T)o establish fraud the proof must be exceptionally strong and clear." There is no room for such an interpretation under this Article.

Art. 1958.   Damages

The party against whom rescission is granted because of fraud is liable for damages and attorney fees.

Acts 1984, No. 331, § 1, eff. Jan. 1, 1985.

REVISION COMMENTS—1984

(a) This Article is new. It expresses an idea which is implied in C.C. Art. 1847(9) (1870) and is exemplified in C.C. Art. 2547, as amended by Acts 1968, No. 84. It changes the law in part, authorizing the award of attorney's fees consistently with the amendment to C.C. Arts. 2545 and 2547 by Acts 1968, No. 84.

(b) French doctrine distinguishes between fraud committed to entice a party into a contract (dol) and fraud in performing a contract (fraude). The latter is the kind of fraud contemplated in C.C. Art. 1934 (1870). Where dol is concerned, rescission or nullity is oftentimes a sufficient remedy. Where there are residual damages, however, they may be recovered. See 1 Demogue, Traité des obligations en général 582 (1923); 6 Planiol et Ripert, Traité pratique de droit civil français 250 (2nd ed. Esmein 1952); Weill, Droit civil—Les obligations 200 (1970). See also Smith v. Everett, 291 So.2d 835 (La.App. 4th Cir.1974). This Article incorporates that solution without limiting the recovery to the loss actually sustained. Recovery under this Article is governed by the general provisions on damages.

(c) If the fraud was committed by a third person, that person also is liable for damages. C.C. Art. 2315 (1870). See also C.C. Art. 1847(9) (1870).

SECTION 3—DURESS

Art. 1959.   Nature

Consent is vitiated when it has been obtained by duress of such a nature as to cause a reasonable fear of unjust and considerable injury to a party's person, property, or reputation.

Age, health, disposition, and other personal circumstances of a party must be taken into account in determining reasonableness of the fear.

Acts 1984, No. 331, § 1, eff. Jan. 1, 1985.

REVISION COMMENTS—1984

(a) This Article is new. It does not change the law, however. It restates principles expressed in C.C. Arts. 1850 and 1851 (1870).

(b) This Article substitutes the term "duress" for "violence or threats," the expression used in the source Articles. According to Black's Law Dictionary (Rev. 4th ed. 1968), duress means: "Unlawful constraint exercised upon a man whereby he is forced to do some act that he otherwise would not have done. It may be either 'duress of imprisonment,' where the person is deprived of his liberty in order to force him to compliance, or by violence, beating, or other actual injury, or duress per minas, consisting in threats of imprisonment or great physical injury or death. Duress may also include the same injuries, threats, or restraint exercised upon the man's wife, child, or parent." For the drafters of the Restatement of the Law, Second, Contracts, duress takes two forms. In one, a person physically compels conduct that appears to be a manifestation of assent by a party who has no intention of engaging in that conduct. The result of this type of duress is that the conduct is not effective to create a contract. In the other, a person makes an improper threat that induces a party who has no reasonable alternative to manifest his assent. The result of this type of duress is that the contract that is created is voidable by the victim. This latter type of duress is in practice the more common and more important. Restatement, Second, Contracts, §§ 174 and 175 (1981). In sum, "duress" is a word of art or technical word in the English language which expresses exactly what is meant by "violence or threats" in C.C. Arts. 1850–1852 (1870). Its adoption in this revision is not intended to incorporate notions incompatible with that meaning.

478

Art. 1960.   Duress directed against third persons

Duress vitiates consent also when the threatened injury is directed against the spouse, an ascendant, or descendant of the contracting party.

If the threatened injury is directed against other persons, the granting of relief is left to the discretion of the court.

Acts 1984, No. 331, § 1, eff. Jan. 1, 1985.

REVISION COMMENTS—1984

(a) This Article is new. It does not change the law, however. It restates the substance of C.C. Art. 1853 (1870).

(b) Under this Article, rescission may be obtained when the threats of injury to the spouse, ascendant, or descendant have been communicated either to the contracting party or to the threatened person. See Giroux v. Vinet, 24 Cour Supérieure 1 (Quebec, 1903) (father consented to buy property in response to threats of imprisonment made to his daughter). The vitiating factor is fear, which is equally well provoked regardless of the identity of the addressee of the threats.

(c) The second paragraph of this Article merely expands C.C. Art. 1853 (1870) to cover situations where the fear that is instilled is found upon close friendship or another relationship either based on or productive of strong affection.

Art. 1961.   Duress by third person

Consent is vitiated even when duress has been exerted by a third person.

Acts 1984, No. 331, § 1, eff. Jan. 1, 1985.

REVISION COMMENT—1984

This Article is new. It does not change the law, however, but merely restates the content of C.C. Art. 1852 (1870).

Art. 1962.   Threat of exercising a right

A threat of doing a lawful act or a threat of exercising a right does not constitute duress.

A threat of doing an act that is lawful in appearance only may constitute duress.

Acts 1984, No. 331, § 1, eff. Jan. 1, 1985.

REVISION COMMENT—1984

This Article is new. It does not change the law, however. It restates the substance of C.C. Arts. 1856 and 1857 (1870).

Art. 1963.   Contract with party in good faith

A contract made with a third person to secure the means of preventing threatened injury may not be rescinded for duress if that person is in good faith and not in collusion with the party exerting duress.

Acts 1984, No. 331, § 1, eff. Jan. 1, 1985.

REVISION COMMENTS—1984

(a) This Article reproduces the substance of C.C. Art. 1858 (1870). It does not change the law.

(b) Under this Article, a contract of loan made for the purpose of paying ransom cannot be rescinded for duress if the lender is in good faith.

Art. 1964.   Damages

When rescission is granted because of duress exerted or known by a party to the contract, the other party may recover damages and attorney fees.

When rescission is granted because of duress exerted by a third person, the parties to the contract who are innocent of the duress may recover damages and attorney fees from the third person.

Acts 1984, No. 331, § 1, eff. Jan. 1, 1985.

REVISION COMMENTS—1984

(a) This Article is new. It does not change the law, however. Through reasoning a fortiori it expands a principle contained in C.C. Art. 1847(9) (1870).

(b) Under this Article, when rescission is granted on grounds of duress, the innocent party or parties may recover not only damages but also attorney's fees. That solution is consistent with the policy underlying the amendment to C.C. Arts. 2545 and 2547 by Acts 1968, No. 84.

(c) The rule contained in this Article is strongly recommended by French doctrine. See 6 Planiol et Ripert, Traité pratique de droit civil français 240 (2nd ed. Esmein 1952). It is based on a principle that can be traced to the Seventh Partida, L. 3, Tit. 16 and Rule 18, Tit. 34, and also to the Digest, L. 17, Tit. 3, Book 4. Swiss Civil Code Article 31 and Greek Civil Code Articles 152 and 153 contain similar provisions.

SECTION 4—LESION

Art. 1965.   Lesion

A contract may be annulled on grounds of lesion only in those cases provided by law.

Acts 1984, No. 331, § 1, eff. Jan. 1, 1985.

REVISION COMMENTS—1984

(a) This Article summarizes the content of C.C. Arts. 1860, 1861, and 1863 (1870). It does not change the law. It eliminates the duplication of treatment of lesion in C.C. Arts. 1860–1880 and 2589–2600 (1870).

(b) Under this Article, a contract may be invalidated on grounds of lesion only in the cases provided by law and according to the proportions that in such cases the law specifies for the values of the parties' performances. Thus, lesion may be invoked in sale, exchange, and partition. See C.C. Arts. 2589–2600, 2664–2666, and 1398 (1870).

(c) Civil Code Article 1870 (1870) has been eliminated because it contains a formula which is no longer practical. Civil Code Articles 1864–1868 (1870) have been eliminated because they are unnecessary, as indicated in C.C. Art. 1866 (1870). See also revised C.C. Art. 1922 (Rev.1984), supra, and accompanying comments. Civil Code Article 1867 (1870) has been eliminated because it reflects a policy that is no longer valid. Civil Code Articles 1872–1875 (1870) have been eliminated because they are unnecessary.

CHAPTER 5—CAUSE

Art. 1966.   No obligation without cause

An obligation cannot exist without a lawful cause.

Acts 1984, No. 331, § 1, eff. Jan. 1, 1985.

REVISION COMMENTS—1984

(a) This Article restates the basic principle of C.C. Art. 1893 (1870). It does not change the law.

(b) This Article eliminates the reference to a "false" cause found in C.C. Art. 1893 (1870) in order to avoid conceptual conflict with C.C. Art. 1900 (1870), which has been preserved as revised C.C. Art. 1970 (Rev.1984), infra.

Art. 1967. Cause defined; detrimental reliance

Cause is the reason why a party obligates himself.

A party may be obligated by a promise when he knew or should have known that the promise would induce the other party to rely on it to his detriment and the other party was reasonable in so relying. Recovery may be limited to the expenses incurred or the damages suffered as a result of the promisee's reliance on the promise. Reliance on a gratuitous promise made without required formalities is not reasonable.

Acts 1984, No. 331, § 1, eff. Jan. 1, 1985.

REVISION COMMENTS—1984

(a) This Article is new. It changes the law in two ways: First, it defines cause in terms of "reason," rather than "motive," for the purpose of enhancing the importance of judicial discretion in characterizing an obligation as enforceable. See 1 Litvinoff, Obligations 381–382, 390–396 (1969). Second, it incorporates detrimental reliance as an additional ground for enforceability.

(b) This Article's use of the term "reason," rather than "motive," which is used in the source Articles, is consistent with the source of C.C. Art. 1896 (1870). That source was Toullier's treatise, Le droit civil français. See 3 Toullier, Le droit civil français 378 (1833). Though Toullier spoke of motif, he did so in the sense of pourquoi (why an obligation is assumed). In that context, "motive" and "reason" are practically interchangeable. Furthermore, "reason" is closer than "motive" to the approach taken by modern and contemporary French doctrine, which speaks of "cause" in terms of but (end or goal). See Capitant, De la cause des obligations 5 (1923); 1 Litvinoff, Obligations 388–396 (1969).

(c) Under this Article, "cause" is not "consideration." The reason why a party binds himself need not be to obtain something in return or to secure an advantage for himself. An obligor may bind himself by a gratuitous contract, that is, he may obligate himself for the benefit of the other party without obtaining any advantage in return. See revised C.C. Art. 1910 (Rev.1984), supra. See also Matthews v. Williams, 25 La.Ann. 585 (1873). Cf. Restatement, Second, Contracts § 71 (1981).

(d) Under this Article, a promise becomes an enforceable obligation when it is made in a manner that induces the other party to rely on it to his detriment. That conclusion is consistent with the basic principles of C.C. Art. 1791 (1870) and C.C. Art. 2315 (1870). The case of Ducote v. Oden, 221 La. 228, 59 So.2d 130 (1952) (holding that promissory estoppel is not recognized in Louisiana) is thus overruled.

(e) Under this Article, the court may grant damages, rather than specific performance, to the disappointed promisee, and may even limit damages thus granted to the expenses actually incurred. The court, in other words, need not necessarily grant the promisee both of the elements of damages specified in revised C.C. Art. 1995 (Rev.1984), infra. See 2 Litvinoff, Obligations 338–339 (1975); Fuller and Perdue, "The Reliance Interest in Contract Damages: 1," 46 Yale L.J. 52 (1936).

(f) Under the last sentence of this Article, reliance on a "gratuitous promise" cannot be deemed reasonable if the promise was made without required formalities. In other words, a party should place no reliance on his belief that he has entered a gratuitous contract when some formality prescribed for the validity of such a contract has been omitted. Thus, reliance on a gratuitous donation not made in authentic form is not reasonable. See C.C. Arts. 1523 and 1536 (1870). This provision is not intended to overrule the Louisiana jurisprudence holding that a promise to make a disposition mortis causa is enforceable against the promisor's estate when the formal disposition is not made. See Succession of Joublanc, 199 La. 250, 5 So.2d 762 (1941); Succession of McNamara, 48 La.Ann. 45, 18 So. 908 (1896); Succession of Palmer, 137 La. 190, 68 So. 405 (1915); Succession of Oliver, 184 La. 26, 165 So. 318 (1936); Succession of Gesselly, 216 La. 731, 44 So.2d 838 (1950). See also Succession of Napoli, 286 So.2d 392 (La.App. 4th Cir.1973); R.S. 13:3721; Comment, "Personal Services About the Home," 23 La.L.Rev. 416 (1963). Close analysis reveals that in each of the cases cited the promise was made in return for a counterperformance requested by the promisor.

Art. 1968.   Unlawful cause

The cause of an obligation is unlawful when the enforcement of the obligation would produce a result prohibited by law or against public policy.

Acts 1984, No. 331, § 1, eff. Jan. 1, 1985.

REVISION COMMENT—1984

This Article restates the basic principle contained in C.C. Art. 1895 (1870). It does not change the law.

Art. 1969.   Cause not expressed

An obligation may be valid even though its cause is not expressed.

Acts 1984, No. 331, § 1, eff. Jan. 1, 1985.

REVISION COMMENT—1984

This Article restates the principle contained in C.C. Art. 1894 (1870). It does not change the law.

Art. 1970.   Untrue expression of cause

When the expression of a cause in a contractual obligation is untrue, the obligation is still effective if a valid cause can be shown.

Acts 1984, No. 331, § 1, eff. Jan. 1, 1985.

REVISION COMMENTS—1984

(a) This Article restates the basic principle contained in C.C. Art. 1900 (1870).

(b) Under this Article, a sale that is invalid for the lack of a price may be regarded as a valid donation if the donative intent of the alleged vendor can be shown and the formal requirement for a valid donation has been met. See McWilliams v. McWilliams, 39 La.Ann. 924, 3 So. 62 (1887); Nofsigner v. Hinchee, 199 So. 597 (La.App. 1st Cir.1941).

(c) This Article corrects the mistranslation contained in the English version of C.C. Art. 1900 (1870), where the word contrat (contract) is incorrectly rendered as "consideration." See 3 Louisiana Legal Archives, Part II, at 1048 (1942).

CHAPTER 6—OBJECT AND MATTER OF CONTRACTS

Art. 1971.   Freedom of parties

Parties are free to contract for any object that is lawful, possible, and determined or determinable.

Acts 1984, No. 331, § 1, eff. Jan. 1, 1985.

REVISION COMMENT—1984

This Article reproduces the substance of C.C. Arts. 1884, 1885, 1886, and 1891 (1870). It does not change the law.

Art. 1972.   Possible or impossible object

A contractual object is possible or impossible according to its own nature and not according to the parties' ability to perform.

Acts 1984, No. 331, § 1, eff. Jan. 1, 1985.

REVISION COMMENT—1984

This Article reproduces the substance of C.C. Art. 1891 (1870). It does not change the law.

Art. 1973.   Object determined as to kind

The object of a contract must be determined at least as to its kind.

The quantity of a contractual object may be undetermined, provided it is determinable.

Acts 1984, No. 331, § 1, eff. Jan. 1, 1985.

REVISION COMMENT—1984

This Article reproduces the substance of C.C. Art. 1886 (1870). It does not change the law.

Art. 1974.   Determination by third person

If the determination of the quantity of the object has been left to the discretion of a third person, the quantity of an object is determinable.

If the parties fail to name a person, or if the person named is unable or unwilling to make the determination, the quantity may be determined by the court.

Acts 1984, No. 331, § 1, eff. Jan. 1, 1985.

REVISION COMMENTS—1984

(a) This Article is new. It changes the law in two respects. First, it generalizes the principle underlying C.C. Art. 2465 (1870) so as to make it applicable not only to sales but also to contracts of other kinds. Second, it modifies that principle by providing that, if the parties have failed to name the third person, or if the named person has failed to make the determination, then the determination may be made by the court.

(b) Under this Article, if a party who has agreed to do so refuses to name a third person, then the determination may be made by the court. Cf. Louis Werner Sawmill Co. v. O'Shee, 111 La. 817, 35 So. 919 (1904). For this purpose, the court may resort to the aid of experts. See Code of Civil Procedure Article 192.

(c) Under this Article, if the third person or persons named by the parties are unable to make the determination, as when the parties have appointed more than one person who have failed to agree, or when the person or persons appointed are unwilling to accept the commission, then the determination may be made by the court in the same manner as under the preceding comment.

(d) Under this Article, if at the time of contracting the parties intend the determination to be made only by a certain person or persons, and not by the court, they must make that an express condition, unless the circumstances are such as to make it implied. See C.C. Art. 2026 (1870).

(e) Under this Article, the parties' specification of a class or category of persons from which the third person is to be selected does not amount to the naming of such a person. See Lake v. LeJeune, 226 La. 48, 74 So.2d 899 (1954). Therefore, in such a case the determination of quantity may be made by the court. Cf. Shell Oil Co. v. Texas Gas Transmission Corp., 210 So.2d 554 (La.App. 4th Cir.1968).

Art. 1975.   Output or requirements

The quantity of a contractual object may be determined by the output of one party or the requirements of the other.

In such a case, output or requirements must be measured in good faith.

Acts 1984, No. 331, § 1, eff. Jan. 1, 1985.

REVISION COMMENTS—1984

(a) This Article is new. It does not change the law, however. Louisiana courts have asserted that in a requirements contract, one party may not exact from the other a performance far in excess of a reasonably foreseen amount. See C.A. Andrews Coal Co. v. Board of Directors of Public Schools, 151 La. 695, 92 So. 303 (1922).

(b) Under this Article, a demand or tender of a quantity unreasonably disproportionate to any estimate or prior normal output or requirement constitutes a breach of the obligation of good faith. See United Carbon Co. v. Interstate National Gas Co., 176 La. 929, 147 So. 37 (1933).

Art. 1976. Future things

Future things may be the object of a contract.

The succession of a living person may not be the object of a contract other than an antenuptial agreement. Such a succession may not be renounced.

Acts 1984, No. 331, § 1, eff. Jan. 1, 1985.

REVISION COMMENTS—1984

(a) This Article reproduces the substance of C.C. Art. 1887 (1870) and C.C. Art. 1888, as amended by Acts 1979, No. 711. It does not change the law.

(b) Under this Article, a contract for the succession of a living person is null even if made with that person's consent. Antenuptial agreements constitute an exception in accordance with C.C. Art. 1888, as amended by Acts 1979, No. 711.

Art. 1977. Obligation or performance by a third person

The object of a contract may be that a third person will incur an obligation or render a performance.

The party who promised that obligation or performance is liable for damages if the third person does not bind himself or does not perform.

Acts 1984, No. 331, § 1, eff. Jan. 1, 1985.

REVISION COMMENTS—1984

(a) This Article reproduces the substance of C.C. Art. 1889 (1870). It does not change the law.

(b) This Article contemplates the transaction called promesse de porte-fort: a contract the object of which is an act to be done by another party. A promesse de porte-fort is a security device that resembles suretyship in that the promisor, or porte-fort, is bound only if the third person does not satisfy the obligee, but differs from suretyship in that the promisor never becomes an accessory obligor. For as long as the third person does not bind himself, the promisor remains the sole obligor, and as soon as the third person binds himself the promisor is released. Fabacher v. Crampes, 166 La. 397, 117 So. 439 (1928) and Cambais v. Douglas, 167 La. 791, 120 So. 369 (1929), involved situations similar to the promesse de porte-fort. See also First National Bank of Jefferson Parish v. Louisiana Purchase Corporation, 346 So.2d 345 (La.App. 4th Cir.1977).

(c) The promesse de porte-fort must be distinguished from the stipulation pour autrui. In the latter, a third person derives a benefit from a contract made by others. In the former, a third person, by expressing his consent, initially substitutes himself for an intended party to a contract and therefore binds himself. For a general discussion, see 6 Planiol et Ripert, Traité pratique de droit civil français 52–60 (2nd ed. Esmein 1952).

CHAPTER 7—THIRD PARTY BENEFICIARY

Art. 1978. Stipulation for a third party

A contracting party may stipulate a benefit for a third person called a third party beneficiary.

Once the third party has manifested his intention to avail himself of the benefit, the parties may not dissolve the contract by mutual consent without the beneficiary's agreement.

Acts 1984, No. 331, § 1, eff. Jan. 1, 1985.

REVISION COMMENTS—1984

(a) This Article reproduces the substance of C.C. Arts. 1890 and 1902 (1870). It does not change the law.

(b) Under this Article, the beneficiary's intention to accept the benefit may be made known in any manner, even implied. The filing of suit is a sufficient expression of such an intention. See Vinet v. Bres, 48 La.Ann. 1254, 20 So. 693 (1895).

Art. 1979. Revocation

The stipulation may be revoked only by the stipulator and only before the third party has manifested his intention of availing himself of the benefit.

If the promisor has an interest in performing, however, the stipulation may not be revoked without his consent.

Acts 1984, No. 331, § 1, eff. Jan. 1, 1985.

REVISION COMMENTS—1984

(a) This Article is new. It does not change the law, however. It expresses a principle implied in C.C. Arts. 1890 and 1902 (1870).

(b) Under revised C.C. Art. 1978 (Rev.1984), supra, the parties may not dissolve the contract after the third party has made known his intention to avail himself of the stipulation in his favor which it contains. Under this Article, that stipulation itself also may not be revoked once the beneficiary has manifested his intention to avail himself of it, even if the contract could survive without it.

(c) Under this Article, the provisions of R.S. 22:1521 remain intact. Thus, the validity of a change of beneficiary of life insurance depends on the terms of the policy. See Standard Life Insurance Co. of the South v. Franks, 278 So.2d 112 (La.1973); Morein v. North American Company for Life and Health Insurance, 271 So.2d 308 (La.App. 3rd Cir.1972), writ denied 273 So.2d 845 (La.1973); Sizeler v. Sizeler, 170 La. 128, 127 So. 388 (1930).

Art. 1980. Revocation or refusal

In case of revocation or refusal of the stipulation, the promisor shall render performance to the stipulator.

Acts 1984, No. 331, § 1, eff. Jan. 1, 1985.

REVISION COMMENTS—1984

(a) This Article is new. It does not change the law, however. It makes explicit an idea implied in C.C. Art. 1890 (1870).

(b) Under this Article, when the stipulator lawfully revokes the stipulation, or it lapses for any reason, or the third party refuses the benefit, the promisor must render the performance to the stipulator.

Art. 1981. Rights of beneficiary and stipulator

The stipulation gives the third party beneficiary the right to demand performance from the promisor.

Also the stipulator, for the benefit of the third party, may demand performance from the promisor.

Acts 1984, No. 331, § 1, eff. Jan. 1, 1985.

REVISION COMMENT—1984

This Article is new. It does not change the law, however. It expresses an idea that is implied in C.C. Arts. 1892 and 1902 (1870). The direct right of the beneficiary to demand performance has been consistently recognized by the Louisiana courts since Mayor v. Bailey, 5 Mart. (O.S.) 321 (1818). The right of the stipulator to do so is a natural consequence of this basic principle.

Art. 1982. Defenses of the promisor

The promisor may raise against the beneficiary such defenses based on the contract as he may have raised against the stipulator.

Acts 1984, No. 331, § 1, eff. Jan. 1, 1985.

This Article is new. It does not change the law, however. It expresses a conclusion reached by the Louisiana jurisprudence. See Union Bank of Louisiana v. Bowman, 9 La.Ann. 195 (1854); Tiernan v. Martin, 2 Rob. 523 (1842).

CHAPTER 8—EFFECTS OF CONVENTIONAL OBLIGATIONS

SECTION 1—GENERAL EFFECTS OF CONTRACTS

Art. 1983.   Law for the parties; performance in good faith

Contracts have the effect of law for the parties and may be dissolved only through the consent of the parties or on grounds provided by law. Contracts must be performed in good faith.

Acts 1984, No. 331, § 1, eff. Jan. 1, 1985.

This Article reproduces the substance of C.C. Art. 1901 (1870). It does not change the law.

Art. 1984.   Rights and obligations will pass to successors

Rights and obligations arising from a contract are heritable and assignable unless the law, the terms of the contract or its nature preclude such effects.

Acts 1984, No. 331, § 1, eff. Jan. 1, 1985.

(a) This Article reproduces the substance of C.C. Art. 1763 (1870). It does not change the law.

(b) The classes of successors who are bound by contracts of their ancestor under this Article are universal heirs, universal legatees, and legatees by universal title. See C.C. Arts. 884, 1465, 1606, and 1612 (1870). A legatee by a particular title is not so bound. See C.C. Art. 1626 (1870). See also 1 Planiol, Civil Law Treatise, Part I, at 206–208 (Louisiana State Law Institute trans. 1959).

(c) Rights of action and obligations passing to successors under this Article are transmitted in the manner provided in C.C.P. Arts. 426 and 427.

Art. 1985.   Effects for third parties

Contracts may produce effects for third parties only when provided by law.

Acts 1984, No. 331, § 1, eff. Jan. 1, 1985.

(a) This Article states the principle of relativity of contracts which underlies C.C. Arts. 1763 and 1902 (1870). It does not change the law.

(b) Because of the ever-increasing importance of third party-beneficiary contracts, this Article provides that contracts bind only the parties unless they have lawfully stipulated otherwise. This Article goes back to Article 65 of the Digest of 1808, equivalent to Article 1165 of the Code Napoleon.

SECTION 2—SPECIFIC PERFORMANCE

Art. 1986. Right of the obligee

Upon an obligor's failure to perform an obligation to deliver a thing, or not to do an act, or to execute an instrument, the court shall grant specific performance plus damages for delay if the obligee so demands. If specific performance is impracticable, the court may allow damages to the obligee.

Upon a failure to perform an obligation that has another object, such as an obligation to do, the granting of specific performance is at the discretion of the court.

Acts 1984, No. 331, § 1, eff. Jan. 1, 1985.

REVISION COMMENTS—1984

(a) This Article is new, but it does not change the law. It restates a principle contained in C.C. Arts. 1909, 1926, and 1927 (1870). The Louisiana Supreme Court has clearly established that an obligee has a right to specific performance, rather than a mere right to appeal to the discretion of the court for this remedy. See Girault v. Feucht, 117 La. 276, 41 So. 572 (1906). See also 2 Litvinoff, Obligations 298–324 (1975). Nevertheless, in the Louisiana Civil Code of 1870 the right to obtain specific performance of an obligation to give, though unquestionable, is not clearly and systematically asserted. A clear treatment of specific performance in a remedial context is necessary in order to clarify uncertainties that started with the Code Napoleon. See Dawson, "Specific Performance in France and Germany," 57 Mich.L.Rev. 495 (1959).

(b) Under this Article, if an obligor fails to perform an obligation to deliver a thing, the court shall grant specific performance to the obligee. See Mente & Co., Inc. v. Roane Sugars, Inc., 199 La. 686, 6 So.2d 731 (1942); Oliver v. Home Service Ice Co., Inc., 161 So. 766 (La.App. 2nd Cir.1935). The same rule applies if the obligor fails to perform an obligation not to do an act (McDonogh v. Calloway, 7 Rob. 442 (1844); Levine v. Michel, 35 La.Ann. 1121 (1883); Belvin v. Sikes, 2 So.2d 65 (La.App. 2nd Cir.1941); Salerno v. De Lucca, 211 La. 659, 30 So.2d 678 (1947); Fulton v. Oertling, 131 La. 768, 60 So. 238 (1912); and State v. King, 46 La.Ann. 78, 14 So. 423 (1894)), or to execute an instrument (Peraino v. Plauche, Peltier's Orl.App. No. 8098 (La.App.Orl.1921). See also 2 Litvinoff, Obligations 301–302 (1975)). Nevertheless, the court may allow damages to the obligee instead of specific performance if the latter is impracticable, as when the obligation is to deliver a thing and the obligor has sold the thing to another person protected by the laws of registry, or when he has destroyed the thing. See C.C. Art. 2489 (1870). Specific performance is also impracticable when it requires the continuous supervision of the court. See Branch v. Acme Homestead Ass'n., 169 So. 129 (La.App.Orl.1936); Caddo Oil & Mining Co., v. Producers' Oil Co., 134 La. 701, 64 So. 684 (1914).

(c) If the obligation which the obligee has failed to perform is an obligation to do, the granting of specific performance lies with the discretion of the court, to be exercised in a manner consistent with the principle that the obligor's personal freedom ordinarily may not be encroached upon. See 7 Planiol et Ripert, Traité pratique de droit civil français 95–96 (2d ed. Esmein, 1954). See also 2 Litvinoff, Obligations 312–313 (1975).

(d) Under this Article, the court may permit the obligee himself to perform the obligation, or to have it performed by a third person, at the obligor's expense. See Code of Civil Procedure Article 2504.

Art. 1987. Right to restrain obligor

The obligor may be restrained from doing anything in violation of an obligation not to do.

Acts 1984, No. 331, § 1, eff. Jan. 1, 1985.

REVISION COMMENTS—1984

(a) This Article restates principles contained in C.C. Arts. 1928 and 1929 (1870).

(b) Under this Article, an obligee may be allowed to undo, at the obligor's expense, anything done in violation of the obligation. See Code of Civil Procedure Article 2504.

(c) An obligee need not prove irreparable injury in order to obtain an injunction under this Article. Reilley v. Kroll, 197 La. 790, 2 So.2d 214 (1941); New Orleans Cigarette Service Corp. v. Sicarelli, 73 So.2d 339 (La.App.Orl.1954).

Art. 1988.   Judgment may stand for act

A failure to perform an obligation to execute an instrument gives the obligee the right to a judgment that shall stand for the act.

Acts 1984, No. 331, § 1, eff. Jan. 1, 1985.

REVISION COMMENT—1984

This Article is new. It does not change the law, however. An obligation to execute an instrument is recognized as an obligation to do that can be specifically enforced under C.C. Art. 1927 (1870). See Peraino v. Plauche, Peltier's Orl.App. No. 8098 (La.App.Orl.1921); 2 Litvinoff, Obligations 310–312 (1975). Nevertheless, the importance of the matter warrants express treatment. The Article is conceived in broad terms because it is meant to apply not only to the sale of immovable property but to any juridical act that creates an obligation to execute an instrument.

SECTION 3—PUTTING IN DEFAULT

Art. 1989.   Damages for delay

Damages for delay in the performance of an obligation are owed from the time the obligor is put in default.

Other damages are owed from the time the obligor has failed to perform.

Acts 1984, No. 331, § 1, eff. Jan. 1, 1985.

REVISION COMMENTS—1984

(a) This Article reproduces the substance of the first paragraph of C.C. Art. 1933 (1870). It changes the law in part, by requiring an obligee to put his obligor in default only when the obligee seeks damages for delay, or moratory damages. See Jennings-Heywood Oil Syndicate v. Houssiere-Latreille Oil Co., 119 La. 793, 44 So. 481 (1907). The provisions of C.C. Art. 1912 (1870) have been eliminated.

(b) Moratory damages presuppose a performance actually rendered, although delayed. In such a case, the object of the obligee's recovery is compensation for the injury his interest has sustained because of the obligor's untimeliness in performing. Compensatory damages presuppose, instead, total or partial nonperformance, or defective performance by the obligor. See 2 Litvinoff, Obligations 387 (1975).

Nevertheless, some damages which an obligee may sustain as a result of the untimely satisfaction of his expectations, though grounded on the passage of time, are compensatory rather than moratory. Thus, if an obligor abandons the construction of a building and the obligee must secure completion by another, it is clear that the obligee, besides other items of recovery, is entitled to recover damages sustained by reason of any delay thus caused, such as rent paid for another building. In that case, the damages for the delay should be regarded as compensatory rather than moratory. The same solution is obtained even if the obligor's breach is anticipatory.

(c) Recovery of damages for delay does not preclude recovery of other damages such as damages for defective performance. For the latter, a putting of the obligor in default is not necessary.

(d) Putting the obligor in default is not a prerequisite to filing suit. It is not necessary prior to filing suit for specific performance because in such a case the judicial demand itself amounts to a putting in default. "All the purposes of a nonjudicial act of the obligee, for stronger reasons, are accomplished by the filing a judicial demand, as defendant may meet the demand with an offer to perform and, under certain circumstances, may even be granted additional time to render performance. . . ." 2 Litvinoff, Obligations 517 (1975). Nor is it necessary prior to filing a suit for compensatory damages, as the judicial demand, in such a case, implies a demand for dissolution. 2 Litvinoff, supra. See also Smith, "The Cloudy Concept of Default" 12 Inst.Min.L. 3, 9 (1965). Putting in default is not even a prerequisite to filing suit for delay damages. An obligee who has not put his obligor in default before filing suit is deemed to do so at the moment of filing. See revised C.C. Art. 1991 (Rev.1984), infra. In such a case, moratory damages are calculated against the debtor from the moment of filing.

(e) This Article does not repeal R.S. 31:135–31:139 (of the Louisiana Mineral Code) which provide special legislative exceptions to the general rule that a putting in default is not a prerequisite to filing suit.

(f) The distinction between active and passive breach has been abandoned. In the Louisiana Civil Code of 1870, the question whether a putting in default is necessary is governed by that distinction. See C.C. Arts. 1931–1933 (1870). Though there are reasons to believe that the redactors intended that the distinction be between absolute failure to perform, or total inexecution, and relative failure to perform, or partial inexecution, it is not always easy to ascertain whether a breach is passive or active and, consequently, whether or not a putting in default is necessary under the source articles. See Melancon v. Texas Co., 230 La. 593, 89 So.2d 135 (1956); Lawton v. Louisiana Pacific Corporation, 344 So.2d 1129 (La.App. 3rd Cir.1977). Identifying a breach as active or passive requires a painstaking process of elimination, see 2 Litvinoff, Obligations 401–402 (1975). There is no need for that distinction in this revision, where the usefulness of putting in default is confined to marking a starting point for delay damages.

Art. 1990.   Obligor put in default by arrival of term

When a term for the performance of an obligation is either fixed, or is clearly determinable by the circumstances, the obligor is put in default by the mere arrival of that term. In other cases, the obligor must be put in default by the obligee, but not before performance is due.

Acts 1984, No. 331, § 1, eff. Jan. 1, 1985.

REVISION COMMENTS—1984

(a) This Article is new. It changes the law, adopting the Roman principle dies interpellat pro homine. See 2 Litvinoff, Obligations 371 (1975). The Code Napoleon, and, following it the Louisiana Civil Code of 1870, departed from the Roman principle that no demand for performance is necessary when the obligation requires the obligor to perform within a given time. Whatever the reasons, the French redactors might have had for this omission, modern business practices evidence a marked appreciation for the value of timeliness in the performance of obligations. Louisiana courts have thus often struggled to find implied "time is of the essence" stipulations in contracts. See Chattanooga Car & Foundry Co. v. Lefebvre, 113 La. 487, 37 So. 38 (1904); Ponceti v. Rothschild, 26 So.2d 235 (La.App.Orl.1946); see also 2 Litvinoff, Obligations 462–474 (1975).

(b) Under this Article, an obligee need not put the obligor in default when the contract stipulates a term for performance. See Kinsell & Locke, Inc. v. Kohlman, 12 La.App. 575, 126 So. 257 (La.App.Orl.1930). The same rule applies when a term for the performance of the obligation, though not express, is clearly indicated by the circumstances. Thus, if a wedding dress is ordered from a merchant who is advised of the date of the wedding, he is automatically put in default upon the arrival of that date, even if no date for delivery was expressly stipulated.

(c) When the performance of an obligation is due within a reasonable time, the obligee must allow that time to pass before putting the obligor in default. Even if the performance is due immediately, a reasonable time must be allowed by the obligee, though that time may be very short. See revised C.C. Art. 1778 (Rev.1984), supra.

Art. 1991.   Manners of putting in default

An obligee may put the obligor in default by a written request of performance, or by an oral request of performance made before two witnesses, or by filing suit for performance, or by a specific provision of the contract.

Acts 1984, No. 331, § 1, eff. Jan. 1, 1985.

REVISION COMMENTS—1984

(a) This Article is new. It does not change the law, however. It reproduces the substance of C.C. Art. 1911(2) (1870).

(b) This Article does not include a protest by a notary as one of the means of putting in default. That method has been used fairly often in practice, but it has played a part in only one case; in Laville v. Rightor, 17 La. 303 (1841). At any rate, such a protest would qualify as a written request of performance under this Article.

(c) Since putting in default is no longer necessary for the recovery either of compensatory or moratory damages when there is a term for performance the provision for putting in default by operation of law in C.C. Art. 1911(3) (1870) has been eliminated as unnecessary.

(d) Under this Article, a putting in default is effective only if notified to the obligor. See 2 Litvinoff, Obligations 414–418 (1975).

(e) Under this Article, an obligor may waive the requirement of a putting in default by agreeing in advance that he shall be deemed automatically in default upon his failure to perform.

(f) This Article is not applicable to contract-dissolution which is now governed by revised C.C. Arts. 2013–2024 (Rev.1984), infra, on Dissolution.

Art. 1992.   Risk devolves upon the obligor

If an obligee bears the risk of the thing that is the object of the performance, the risk devolves upon the obligor who has been put in default for failure to deliver that thing.

Acts 1984, No. 331, § 1, eff. Jan. 1, 1985.

REVISION COMMENTS—1984

(a) This Article is new, but it does not change the law. It restates the principle contained in C.C. Art. 1910 (1870).

(b) If the obligee has assumed the risk of the thing from the time the contract is made, he is relieved of that risk from the time the obligor is put in default for not having delivered the thing.

Art. 1993.   Reciprocal obligations

In case of reciprocal obligations, the obligor of one may not be put in default unless the obligor of the other has performed or is ready to perform his own obligation.

Acts 1984, No. 331, § 1, eff. Jan. 1, 1985.

REVISION COMMENTS—1984

(a) This Article is new. It does not change the law, however. It reproduces the substance of C.C. Arts. 1913 and 1914 (1870).

(b) Reciprocal obligations are those that arise from bilateral or synallagmatic contracts. See revised C.C. Art. 1908 (Rev.1984), supra.

(c) Civil Code Article 1914 (1870) has been eliminated. That Article, which was based on an example that can be found in 3 Toullier, Le droit civil français 415 (1833), is superfluous. See 2 Litvinoff, Obligations 428–432 (1975). Furthermore, it incorporates the common law distinction between dependent and independent covenants reflected in C.C. Art. 1767 (1870), which has also been eliminated. That an obligee who intends to put the obligor in default must be ready to accept the performance he requests is a clear consequence of the overriding principle of good faith.

SECTION 4—DAMAGES

Art. 1994.   Obligor liable for failure to perform

An obligor is liable for the damages caused by his failure to perform a conventional obligation.

A failure to perform results from nonperformance, defective performance, or delay in performance.

Acts 1984, No. 331, § 1, eff. Jan. 1, 1985.

REVISION COMMENTS—1984

(a) This Article is new. It does not change the law, however. It reproduces the substance of C.C. Arts. 1930 and 1931 (1870).

(b) This Article states the basic principle of liability for damages and lists the three kinds of noncompliance with a conventional obligation. It attempts to eliminate the obscurities which French doctrine has generated in attempting to distinguish "inexécution" from "demeure." The word "breach" has been replaced by "failure to perform," which has no common law overtones. For a full discussion, see 2 Litvinoff, Obligations 378–387 (1975). The Articles in this Section are primarily intended to govern contractual liability.

Art. 1995.   Measure of damages

Damages are measured by the loss sustained by the obligee and the profit of which he has been deprived.

Acts 1984, No. 331, § 1, eff. Jan. 1, 1985.

REVISION COMMENT—1984

This Article reproduces the substance of the first paragraph of C.C. Art. 1934 (1870). It does not change the law.

Art. 1996.   Obligor in good faith

An obligor in good faith is liable only for the damages that were foreseeable at the time the contract was made.

Acts 1984, No. 331, § 1, eff. Jan. 1, 1985.

REVISION COMMENTS—1984

(a) This Article is new, but it does not change the law. It reproduces the substance of C.C. Art. 1934(1) (1870).

(b) Foreseeable damages are such damages as may fall within the foresight of a reasonable man. In distinguishing foreseeable from unforeseeable damages, the court should consider the nature of the contract, the nature of the parties' business, their prior dealings, and all other circumstances related to the contract and known to the obligor. Any special circumstances made known to the obligor by the obligee should also be taken into account.

Art. 1997.   Obligor in bad faith

An obligor in bad faith is liable for all the damages, foreseeable or not, that are a direct consequence of his failure to perform.

Acts 1984, No. 331, § 1, eff. Jan. 1, 1985.

REVISION COMMENTS—1984

(a) This Article is new. It does not change the law, however. It reproduces the substance of C.C. Art. 1934(2) (1870).

(b) An obligor is in bad faith if he intentionally and maliciously fails to perform his obligation.

(c) This Article uses the term "bad faith" rather than "fraud," the term used in C.C. Art. 1934 (1870). The French version of that Article used dol, which is not exactly fraud. Moreover, the same term of art should not be used to designate two different things. In the context of vices of consent, "fraud" means a stratagem or machination to take unfair advantage of another party. "Bad faith" better conveys the intended meaning here, that is, an intentional and malicious failure to perform. This includes most of the meaning of the French dol. A truly fraudulent failure to perform of course, would constitute bad faith under this Article.

491

Art. 1998. Damages for nonpecuniary loss

Damages for nonpecuniary loss may be recovered when the contract, because of its nature, is intended to gratify a nonpecuniary interest and, because of the circumstances surrounding the formation or the nonperformance of the contract, the obligor knew, or should have known, that his failure to perform would cause that kind of loss.

Regardless of the nature of the contract, these damages may be recovered also when the obligor intended, through his failure, to aggrieve the feelings of the obligee.

Acts 1984, No. 331, § 1, eff. Jan. 1, 1985.

REVISION COMMENTS—1984

(a) This Article is new. It changes the law in part. As interpreted in Meador v. Toyota of Jefferson, Inc., 332 So.2d 433 (La.1976), C.C. Art. 1934(3) (1870) allows recovery of damages for nonpecuniary losses only for breach of a contract which has "intellectual enjoyment" as its principal or exclusive purpose. Under this Article, such damages are recoverable when a contract has been made for the gratification of a nonpecuniary interest and, because of circumstances surrounding its formation or breach, the obligor knew or should have known that his failure to perform would cause nonpecuniary loss. Such damages are also recoverable when regardless of the nature of the contract or the purpose for which it has been made, the obligor, through his breach, intends to aggrieve or hurt the feelings of the obligee.

(b) "Nonpecuniary loss" means that which is known in continental doctrine as "dommage moral," that is, damage of a moral nature which does not affect a "material" or tangible part of a person's patrimony. See Litvinoff, "Moral Damages," 38 La.L.Rev. 1 (1977).

(c) A contract made for the gratification of a nonpecuniary interest means one intended to satisfy an interest of a spiritual order, such as a contract to create a work of art, or a contract to conduct scientific research, or a contract involving matters of sentimental value. In such a case, upon the obligor's failure to perform, the obligee may recover the damages he has sustained of a nonpecuniary—or "moral"—nature. See Litvinoff, supra. Thus, if a horse is bought for the purpose of showing it at an exhibition, the purchaser is entitled to recover for his disappointment and inconvenience if the contract is rescinded because of a redhibitory vice. See Smith v. Andrepont, 378 So.2d 479 (La.App. 1st Cir.1979); see also Lewis v. Holmes, 109 La. 1030, 34 So. 66 (1903). The expression "intellectual enjoyment" used in C.C. Art. 1934(3) (1870) has been suppressed. A mistranslation of the sentence in which that expression is used in that Article has created confusion as to the true meaning of the rule. See Litvinoff, supra; Marks, "Nonpecuniary Damages in Breach of Contract: Louisiana Civil Code Article 1934," 37 La.L.Rev. 625 (1977); Meador v. Toyota of Jefferson, Inc., 332 So.2d 433 (La.1976).

(d) Under this Article, an obligee may recover damages for the nonpecuniary loss he sustains when the obligor fails to perform in circumstances that give rise to the presumption that the obligee's embarrassment or humiliation was intended by the obligor. See Daquano v. Brady, 242 So.2d 302 (La.App. 1st Cir.1970); Vogel v. Saenger Theatres, Inc., 207 La. 835, 22 So.2d 189 (1945).

(e) The jurisprudence has held that mere worry or vexation is not a compensable nonpecuniary loss. See Elston v. Valley Electric Membership Corporation, 381 So.2d 554 (La.App. 2nd Cir.1980).

Art. 1999. Assessment of damages left to the court

When damages are insusceptible of precise measurement, much discretion shall be left to the court for the reasonable assessment of these damages.

Acts 1984, No. 331, § 1, eff. Jan. 1, 1985.

REVISION COMMENTS—1984

(a) This Article is new. It does not change the law, however. The rule that it states is based on a principle contained in C.C. Art. 1934(3) (1870).

(b) Under this Article, the court, in its discretion, may assess damages in more than a mere nominal amount. See Huck v. Louisville & Nashville Railroad Co., 13 Orl.App. 353 (1916); Green v. Farmers' Consolidated Dairy Co., 113 La. 869, 37 So. 858 (1905).

Art. 2000. Damages for delay measured by interest; no need of proof; attorney fees

When the object of the performance is a sum of money, damages for delay in performance are measured by the interest on that sum from the time it is due, at the rate agreed by the parties or, in the absence of agreement, at the rate of legal interest as fixed by R.S. 9:3500. The obligee may recover these damages without having to prove any loss, and whatever loss he may have suffered he can recover no more. If the parties, by written contract, have expressly agreed that the obligor shall also be liable for the obligee's attorney fees in a fixed or determinable amount, the obligee is entitled to that amount as well.

Acts 1984, No. 331, § 1, eff. Jan. 1, 1985. Amended by Acts 1985, No. 137, § 1, eff. July 3, 1985; Acts 1987, No. 883, § 1.

REVISION COMMENTS—1984

(a) This Article is new. It changes the law insofar as it establishes that, when a rate of interest has not been agreed upon, the measure of damages for delay in performing an obligation to pay a sum of money shall be the legal rate of interest in force at the time the sum of money is due. Otherwise, this Article reproduces the substance of C.C. Arts. 1935, 1937, and 1940 (1870).

(b) Civil Code Article 1936 (1870) has been eliminated as unnecessary. Civil Code Article 1938 (1870) has been eliminated for the same reason. Civil Code Article 2924 (1870), in the title on Loan, states the legal rate of interest. Unnecessary duplication or repetition should be avoided. In any case, the legal rate is so often amended that it ideally should be placed in the Revised Statutes, not the Civil Code. See R.S. 9:3503, 3504, 3505, 3516 and 3519, and R.S. 12:703.

(c) The reference to the legal interest rate in effect at the time of contracting in C.C. Art. 1940 (1870) has been eliminated as unnecessary. See C.C. Art. 8 (1870).

(d) Civil Code Article 1942 (1870) has been eliminated. It does not belong in the Civil Code. Civil Code Article 1943 (1870) has also been eliminated. It duplicates the rule of C.C. Art. 1934(2) (1870). Civil Code Article 1944 (1870) has been eliminated as unnecessary; an obligor is put in default by the arrival of the term.

Art. 2001. Interest on interest

Interest on accrued interest may be recovered as damages only when it is added to the principal by a new agreement of the parties made after the interest has accrued.

Acts 1984, No. 331, § 1, eff. Jan. 1, 1985.

REVISION COMMENTS—1984

(a) This Article does not change the law. It reproduces the substance of C.C. Art. 1939 (1870).

(b) Under this Article, an obligor and a surety who has paid the principal and interest of a loan on the former's behalf may agree that the interest shall be added to the principal; and the surety may recover from the obligor the total amount paid, plus interest from the time of payment. Civil Code Article 1941 (1870) is for that reason eliminated.

(c) This Article applies to interest which is the equivalent of moratory damages. It does not apply to interest which is paid for the use of money, as when the parties agree that the interest on a loan shall be compounded, nor does it apply to discounted notes. See Civil Code Article 2924 (1870); Unity Plan Finance Co. v. Green, 179 La. 1070, 155 So. 900 (1934).

(d) This Article does not apply to situations contemplated by the Louisiana Consumer Credit Law. As special legislation, that statute governs all cases within its scope.

Art. 2002. Reasonable efforts to mitigate damages

An obligee must make reasonable efforts to mitigate the damage caused by the obligor's failure to perform. When an obligee fails to make these efforts, the obligor may demand that the damages be accordingly reduced.

Acts 1984, No. 331, § 1, eff. Jan. 1, 1985.

REVISION COMMENTS—1984

(a) This Article is new. It does not change the law, however. It expresses a natural consequence of the principle stated in C.C. Art. 1903 (1870).

(b) Under this Article, if an obligee neglects to mitigate his damages his recovery must be reduced according to the extent both of his negligence and of its consequences.

(c) Under this Article, "reasonable efforts" are such efforts as do not place an excessive burden on the obligee. See Unverzagt v. Young Builders, Inc., 252 La. 1091, 215 So.2d 823 (1968).

Art. 2003. Obligee in bad faith

An obligee may not recover damages when his own bad faith has caused the obligor's failure to perform or when, at the time of the contract, he has concealed from the obligor facts that he knew or should have known would cause a failure.

If the obligee's negligence contributes to the obligor's failure to perform, the damages are reduced in proportion to that negligence.

Acts 1984, No. 331, § 1, eff. Jan. 1, 1985.

REVISION COMMENTS—1984

(a) This Article does not change the law. It reproduces in part the substance of C.C. Art. 1934(4) (1870).

(b) Under this Article, if the obligor's failure to perform is caused by the obligee's bad faith, the obligee may not recover damages for that failure. See Board of Levee Com'rs of Orleans Levee Dist. v. Hulse, 167 La. 896, 120 So. 589 (1929); Atchley v. Horne, 13 So.2d 75 (La.App. 2nd Cir.1943). If negligence on the part of the obligee has played a part in causing the obligor's failure to perform, without constituting its sole cause, the obligee's recovery may be reduced accordingly. Compare C.C. Art. 2323, as amended by Acts 1979, No. 431.

Art. 2004. Clause that excludes or limits liability

Any clause is null that, in advance, excludes or limits the liability of one party for intentional or gross fault that causes damage to the other party.

Any clause is null that, in advance, excludes or limits the liability of one party for causing physical injury to the other party.

Acts 1984, No. 331, § 1, eff. Jan. 1, 1985.

REVISION COMMENTS—1984

(a) This Article is new. It does not change the law, however. It expresses a consequence of the principle of contractual freedom stated in C.C. Art. 1901 (1870). In Freeman v. Department of Highways, 253 La. 105, 217 So.2d 166 (1968), the Supreme Court held that, as a matter of principle, clauses excluding or limiting liability for intentional fault (fraud or dol) are invalid because a party would be free to perform or not to perform at will. Hence, his obligation would be subject to a purely potestative condition that would make it null. That reasoning aside, such clauses are against public policy because the overriding principle of good faith would be destroyed if it were possible to contract away liability for fraud. Foreign civil codes contain abundant indication of the universality of this conclusion. See also Hayes v. Hayes, 8 La.Ann. 468 (1852).

(b) This Article does not apply where federal legislation prevails. See 46 U.S.C. § 1304(5) and 49 U.S.C. §§ 20(11), 319, 1013; Comment, "Limitations of Liability: Passenger Injuries and Baggage Losses on Land, Sea, and Air," 34 Tul.L.Rev. 354 (1960).

(c) Under this Article, a clause relieving a party from liability for damage caused by delay is valid. See Freeman v. Department of Highways, 253 La. 105, 217 So.2d 166 (1968).

(d) Under this Article, a clause relieving a party from liability for damage to property caused through slight fault is valid, unless prohibited by special statutes. See R.S. 10:7–309. See also Litvinoff, "Stipulations as to Liability and as to Damages," 52 Tul.L.Rev. 258 (1978).

(e) This Article does not govern "indemnity" clauses, "hold harmless" agreements, or other agreements where parties allocate between themselves, the risk of potential liability towards third persons. See Polozola v. Garlock, Inc., 343 So.2d 1000 (La.1977); Green v. Taca International Airlines, 304 So.2d 357 (La.1974); Reeves v. Louisiana and Arkansas Railway Company, 282 So.2d 503 (La.1973).

(f) This Article does not supersede R.S. 9:3221. See Terrenova v. Feldner, 28 So.2d 287 (La.App.Orl.Cir.1946); Tassin v. Slidell Mini-Storage, Inc., 396 So.2d 1261 (La.1981).

SECTION 5—STIPULATED DAMAGES

Art. 2005. Secondary obligation

Parties may stipulate the damages to be recovered in case of nonperformance, defective performance, or delay in performance of an obligation.

That stipulation gives rise to a secondary obligation for the purpose of enforcing the principal one.

Acts 1984, No. 331, § 1, eff. Jan. 1, 1985.

REVISION COMMENTS—1984

(a) This Article reproduces the substance of C.C. Art. 2117 (1870). It does not change the law.

(b) This Section effects a change in terminology in an attempt to make a fresh start in this area. The expression "penal clause" used in the source Article is deficient for two reasons. First, it is semantically awkward. Second, it resounds with overtones of "penalty," thus introducing doubt as to whether such a thing exists in the Louisiana system. The expression "stipulated damages" is more neutral, and it is not unknown to the Louisiana jurisprudence. See White v. Rimmer & Garrett, Inc., 328 So.2d 686 (La.App.3rd Cir.1976.) Although it is similar to the common law "liquidated damages," it is not of such common usage in either the civil or the common law tradition as to impart any definite doctrinal meaning of its own. Its meaning in this revision is governed by this and the following Articles.

(c) The Articles of this Section follow in general the civilian doctrine of clause penalé. See 4 Aubry et Rau, Droit Civil—Obligations 91–92 and 120–122 (Louisiana State Law Institute trans. 1965). A stipulated damages clause is given effect if the court deems it to be a true approximation of actual damages.

(d) Civil Code Articles 2118 and 2119 (1870) have been eliminated because of their exclusively doctrinal nature.

Art. 2006. Nullity of the principal obligation

Nullity of the principal obligation renders the stipulated damages clause null.

Nullity of the stipulated damages clause does not render the principal obligation null.

Acts 1984, No. 331, § 1, eff. Jan. 1, 1985.

REVISION COMMENTS—1984

This Article reproduces the substance of C.C. Art. 2123 (1870). It does not change the law. See Lake Forest, Inc. v. Bon Marche Homes, Inc., 356 So.2d 1133 (La.App.4th Cir.1978); Richmond v.

Krushevski, 243 La. 777, 147 So.2d 212 (1962); 4 Aubry et Rau, Droit Civil—Obligations 92, 121 (Louisiana State Law Institute trans. 1965).

Art. 2007.　Stipulated damages or performance

An obligee may demand either the stipulated damages or performance of the principal obligation, but he may not demand both unless the damages have been stipulated for mere delay.

Acts 1984, No. 331, § 1, eff. Jan. 1, 1985.

REVISION COMMENTS—1984

(a) This Article reproduces the substance of C.C. Arts. 2124 and 2125 (1870). It does not change the law.

(b) The conceptual proximity of C.C. Arts. 2124 and 2125(1870) was deemed sufficient to warrant the merger of the two Articles into one. Civil Code Article 2124 (1870) has provoked little jurisprudential controversy, during its lifetime, probably because of its clear wording. It was cited in 1975 in Burris v. Gay, 324 So.2d 11 (La.App.2d Cir.1975), writ denied 326 So.2d 377 (La.1976). The principle of C.C. Art. 2125 (1870) is deeply rooted in the civilian tradition. See 4 Aubry et Rau, Droit Civil—Obligations 121 (Louisiana State Law Institute trans. 1965); Southern Construction Co. v. Housing Authority of the City of Opelousas, 250 La. 569, 197 So.2d 628 (1967); Pennington v. Drews, 218 La. 258, 49 So.2d 5 (1949).

Art. 2008.　Failure to perform justified

An obligor whose failure to perform the principal obligation is justified by a valid excuse is also relieved of liability for stipulated damages.

Acts 1984, No. 331, § 1, eff. Jan. 1, 1985.

REVISION COMMENTS—1984

(a) This Article reproduces the substance of C.C. Art. 2120 (1870). It does not change the law.

(b) Under the Article, impossibility of performance is a valid "excuse" that may relieve an obligor from liability for his nonperformance, and hence also from liability for stipulated damages.

(c) Louisiana courts have encountered no difficulty in applying C.C. Art. 2120 (1870). See Hughes v. Breazeale, 240 La. 126, 121 So.2d 510 (1960); Pennington v. Drews, 218 La. 258, 49 So.2d 5 (1949); Burris v. Gay, 324 So.2d 11 (La.App.2d Cir.1975).

(d) Civil Code Articles 2121 and 2122 (1870) have been eliminated. Those Articles have no counterpart in the French Civil Code. They were no doubt taken from Toullier. See 3 Toullier, Le droit civil français 618 (1833). They deal, respectively, with an outright penal bond and a sort of insurance contract. These revised Articles attempt to depart from the notion of penal bonds. A provision dealing with contracts of insurance, moreover, has no place among the Articles on stipulated damages.

Art. 2009.　Obligee not bound to prove damage

An obligee who avails himself of a stipulated damages clause need not prove the actual damage caused by the obligor's nonperformance, defective performance, or delay in performance.

Acts 1984, No. 331, § 1, eff. Jan. 1, 1985.

REVISION COMMENTS—1984

(a) This Article is new. It does not change the law, however. It states a principle recognized by the Louisiana jurisprudence. See Southern Construction Co. v. Housing Authority of the City of Opelousas, 250 La. 569, 197 So.2d 628 (1967); Stewart-McGhee Construction Co. v. Caddo Parish School Bd., 165 La. 200, 115 So. 458 (1927).

(b) The rule of this Article is implicit in C.C. Arts. 2117, 2118, 2119, 2124, 2125, and 2126 (1870) and has been recognized by traditional doctrine. See 4 Aubry et Rau, Droit Civil—Obligations 122 (Louisiana State Law Institute trans. 1965). It can also be found in Scottish law. See 1 Walker,

Principles of Scottish Private Law 615 (2nd ed. 1975); Craig v. McBeath (1863) 1 M.1020. Modern civil codes such as the Italian, Ethiopian, and Quebec Draft Civil Code (1977) have formulated it clearly.

(c) It might be said that this Article goes back to the notion of the stipulated damages clause as a penalty. To that objection, the answer is that an obligee must be given the advantage of not having to prove damages or the whole idea of stipulated damages must be abandoned as impractical. Any fear of injustice that the rule this Article may provoke should be overcome by revised C.C. Art. 2012 (Rev.1984), infra, which grants the court the power to modify the stipulated damages whenever they are so manifestly unreasonable as to be contrary to public policy.

(d) This Article does not prevent a defendant from proving that a plaintiff who seeks to avail himself of a stipulated damages provision actually has sustained no loss. It merely shifts the burden of proof on the issue of damages from the plaintiff to the defendant.

Art. 2010. Obligor put in default

An obligee may not avail himself of a clause stipulating damages for delay unless the obligor has been put in default.

Acts 1984, No. 331, § 1, eff. Jan. 1, 1985.

REVISION COMMENTS—1984

(a) This Article reproduces in part the substance of C.C. Art. 2126 (1870). Insofar as it makes a putting in default a necessary prerequisite to the recovery of stipulated damages it does not change the law. See Llorente v. Gaitrie, 6 Mart.(N.S.) 623 (1828); Allen v. Wills, 4 La.Ann. 97 (1849); Danziger v. Tessitore, 13 La.App. 450, 126 So. 700 (La.App.Orl.1930); Wendel v. Dixon Real Estate, 232 So.2d 791 (La.App. 4th Cir.1970), writ denied 256 La. 249, 236 So.2d 29 (La.1970). It does, however limit the scope of the traditional rule, requiring a prior putting in default only when stipulated delay damages are sought. This limitation is consistent with revised C.C. Art. 1989 (Rev.1984), supra, which makes putting in default a prerequisite to the recovery of actual damages only when they are moratory in nature.

(b) An obligor may be put in default in any of ways provided in revised C.C. Art. 1991 (Rev.1984), supra, including by expiration of the term stipulated for performance.

Art. 2011. Benefit from partial performance

Stipulated damages for nonperformance may be reduced in proportion to the benefit derived by the obligee from any partial performance rendered by the obligor.

Acts 1984, No. 331, § 1, eff. Jan. 1, 1985.

REVISION COMMENT—1984

This Article reproduces the substance of C.C. Art. 2127 (1870). It does not change the law.

Art. 2012. Stipulated damages may not be modified

Stipulated damages may not be modified by the court unless they are so manifestly unreasonable as to be contrary to public policy.

Acts 1984, No. 331, § 1, eff. Jan. 1, 1985.

REVISION COMMENT—1984

This Article is new, but it does not change the law. It states a principle recognized by the Louisiana jurisprudence. E.g., Pennington v. Drews, 218 La. 258, 49 So.2d 5 (1949).

CHAPTER 9—DISSOLUTION

Art. 2013. Obligee's right to dissolution

When the obligor fails to perform, the obligee has a right to the judicial dissolution of the contract or, according to the circumstances, to regard the contract as dissolved. In either case, the obligee may recover damages.

In an action involving judicial dissolution, the obligor who failed to perform may be granted, according to the circumstances, an additional time to perform.

Acts 1984, No. 331, § 1, eff. Jan. 1, 1985.

REVISION COMMENTS—1984

(a) This Article is new. It does not change the law, however. It reproduces the substance of C.C. Arts. 2046 and 2047 (1870) and also provides that, according to the circumstances, the obligee has a right to regard the contract as dissolved, a right recognized by the Louisiana jurisprudence in numerous decisions. See, e.g., Texala Oil & Gas Co. v. Caddo Mineral Lands Co., 152 La. 549, 93 So. 788 (1922); Hay v. Bush, 110 La. 575, 34 So. 692 (1903).

(b) Under this Article, either party to a contract may seek dissolution upon the other's failure to perform. In C.C. Art. 2046 (1870), this remedy is predicated upon a resolutory condition implied in every commutative contract. This Article abandons both that rationale and that limitation, in accordance with modern doctrine. See Capitant, De la cause des obligations 326 (1923); 2 Litvinoff, Obligations 497–499 (1975); Weill, Droit civil—Les obligations 498 (1970). See also 6 Planiol et Ripert, Traité pratique de droit civil français 572 (2nd ed. Esmein 1952); Starck, Droit civil— Obligations 641–642 (1972). See generally 2 Litvinoff, Obligations 505–506 (1975). Nevertheless, under this Article a party's right to dissolution because of the other party's failure to perform arises from the contract itself, and to that extent it can be said to be implied in it, although not in the form of a resolutory condition.

(c) Under this Article, dissolution takes place upon judicial declaration. Nevertheless, the obligee of an unperformed obligation may, according to the circumstances, regard the contract as dissolved before such a declaration. Thus, when one party has performed but the other has not, and the first party wants to dissolve the contract and recover his performance, the proper course of action for him to follow is to bring suit for judicial dissolution. Under different circumstances, however, such as when neither has performed and it is clear that one will not, the other may declare the contract dissolved in accordance with revised C.C. Art. 2016 (Rev.1984), infra.

(d) This Article preserves the avenue of judicial dissolution because it is useful in a wide variety of situations. See Waseco Chemical and Supply Co. v. Bayou State Oil Corporation, 371 So.2d 305 (La.App.2d Cir.1979); Sliman v. McBee, 311 So.2d 248 (La.1975); Reed v. Classified Parking System, 324 So.2d 484 (La.App.2d Cir.1975); Watson v. Feibel, 139 La. 375, 71 So. 585 (1916).

(e) In any action involving judicial dissolution, whether brought by an obligee or by an obligor who complains that the obligee has wrongly declared the contract dissolved, the obligor who has failed to perform may be granted additional time to do so. Whether to grant such additional time is a matter for the court to determine in light of the circumstances of the individual case, including the good faith vel non of the obligor, and whether he has a valid excuse for his failure.

Art. 2014. Importance of failure to perform

A contract may not be dissolved when the obligor has rendered a substantial part of the performance and the part not rendered does not substantially impair the interest of the obligee.

Acts 1984, No. 331, § 1, eff. Jan. 1, 1985.

REVISION COMMENTS—1984

(a) This Article is new. It does not change the law, however. It is consistent with the overriding principles stated in C.C. Arts. 1901 and 1903 (1870), and with the accepted jurisprudential rule that a building contract may not be dissolved after substantial performance has been rendered. See Airco Refrigeration Service, Inc. v. Fink, 242 La. 73, 134 So.2d 880 (1961); Neel v. O'Quinn, 313 So.2d 286

CONVENTIONAL OBLIGATIONS OR CONTRACTS

(La.App.3d Cir.1975); Lawson v. Donahue, 313 So.2d 263 (La.App.4th Cir.1975); Florida Ice Machine Corp. v. Brandon Insulation Inc., 290 So.2d 415 (La.App.4th Cir.1974).

(b) Although this Article prevents a party from receding from a contract on a mere excuse, it does not prevent the recovery of damages by a party who has not received a full or perfect performance.

(c) For a court to refuse dissolution under this Article, the obligor must have rendered a substantial part of the performance and the unperformed part of the obligation must not impair the interest of the obligee. This double test protects the interests of both parties.

Art. 2015.   Dissolution after notice to perform

Upon a party's failure to perform, the other may serve him a notice to perform within a certain time, with a warning that, unless performance is rendered within that time, the contract shall be deemed dissolved. The time allowed for that purpose must be reasonable according to the circumstances.

The notice to perform is subject to the requirements governing a putting of the obligor in default and, for the recovery of damages for delay, shall have the same effect as a putting of the obligor in default.

Acts 1984, No. 331, § 1, eff. Jan. 1, 1985.

REVISION COMMENTS—1984

(a) This Article is new. It does not change the law, however. Under C.C. Arts. 1912 and 1932 (1870), judicial dissolution is not required in cases of active breach. See 2 Litvinoff, Obligations 537–540 (1975). In numerous decisions, Louisiana courts have recognized that, under certain circumstances, a party has the right to regard a contract as dissolved on his own initiative. See, e.g., Texala Oil & Gas Co. v. Caddo Mineral Lands Co., 152 La. 549, 93 So. 788 (1922); Hay v. Bush, 110 La. 575, 34 So. 692 (1903).

(b) This Article complements the basic mechanism of judicial dissolution. As an alternative to the latter, a party may take steps under this Article to declare the contract dissolved on his own initiative.

(c) Under this Article, an obligee who, upon the obligor's failure to perform, chooses to regard the contract as dissolved under revised C.C. Art. 2013 (Rev.1984), supra, must give the obligor a notice to perform. This requirement is consistent with the overriding obligation of good faith in those situations where, under the revised articles on putting in default, the obligor falls automatically in default without any act of the obligee. See revised C.C. Art. 1990 (Rev.1984), supra. The notice to perform must be given in the manner described in revised C.C. Art. 1991 (Rev.1984), supra, for a valid putting in default.

(d) The giving of a notice to perform under this Article has the same effect as a putting of the obligor in default for the purpose of calculating delay damages. After such notice is given, the obligor will be liable for any delay damages that accrue. If the obligor is already in default at the time the notice to perform is given, of course, the delay damages accrue from the time he fell in default and not from the time of the notice to perform. Under revised C.C. Art. 1990 (Rev.1984), supra, the obligor is put in default by the mere passage of the time for performance, and damages for delay start running then. In such a case, the notice to perform need be given only because it is a prerequisite to the obligee's exercising his right to regard the contract as dissolved. If time is of the essence, no such notice is needed according to the following Article.

Art. 2016.   Dissolution without notice to perform

When a delayed performance would no longer be of value to the obligee or when it is evident that the obligor will not perform, the obligee may regard the contract as dissolved without any notice to the obligor.

Acts 1984, No. 331, § 1, eff. Jan. 1, 1985.

REVISION COMMENT—1984

This Article is new. It does not change the law, however. Louisiana courts have established that a putting in default is not necessary when the obligor has communicated an intention not to perform, or in a situation where time is of the essence. See Allen v. Steers, 39 La.Ann. 586, 2 So. 199 (1887);

Abels v. Glover, 15 La.Ann. 247 (1860); Kinsell & Locke, Inc. v. Kohlman, 12 La.App. 575, 126 So. 257 (La.App.Orl.1930). Since under C.C. Art. 1912 (1870) putting in default is also a prerequisite to dissolution of a contract, the cited decisions amount to judicial recognition that dissolution may be had without a prior putting in default in the contemplated situations.

Art. 2017.   Express dissolution clause

The parties may expressly agree that the contract shall be dissolved for the failure to perform a particular obligation. In that case, the contract is deemed dissolved at the time it provides for or, in the absence of such a provision, at the time the obligee gives notice to the obligor that he avails himself of the dissolution clause.

Acts 1984, No. 331, § 1, eff. Jan. 1, 1985.

REVISION COMMENTS—1984

(a) This Article is new. It changes the law in part, generalizing the rule provided in C.C. Art. 2563 (1870) for contracts of sale, although without that Article's requirement of a judicial demand.

(b) Under this Article, if a contract which contains an express dissolution clause also provides a term for the rendering of performance, then the contract is deemed dissolved if at the expiration of that term the obligor has failed to perform, without the necessity of any prior putting in default or notice to the obligor. If the contract does not provide such a term, it is dissolved at the time the obligee notifies the obligor that he avails himself of the dissolution clause.

Art. 2018.   Effects of dissolution

Upon dissolution of a contract, the parties shall be restored to the situation that existed before the contract was made. If restoration in kind is impossible or impracticable, the court may award damages.

If partial performance has been rendered and that performance is of value to the party seeking to dissolve the contract, the dissolution does not preclude recovery for that performance, whether in contract or quasi-contract.

Acts 1984, No. 331, § 1, eff. Jan. 1, 1985.

REVISION COMMENTS—1984

(a) This Article is new. It does not change the law, however. It expresses a principle that is implied in C.C. Arts. 1901, 1903, 2045, and 2046 (1870).

(b) Under this Article, the buyer of a quantity of things of which only part has been delivered may keep that part, paying for it, and seek dissolution plus damages for the unperformed portion of the contract. See H. T. Cottam & Co. v. Moises, 149 La. 305, 88 So. 916 (1921). Cf. Etie v. Sparks, 4 La. 463 (1832).

(c) Under this Article, if an obligor can no longer perform after rendering a substantial part of the performance, he is entitled to recover for that performance according to the terms of the contract, and the other party is entitled to damages for the unperformed part. See Airco Refrigeration Service, Inc. v. Fink, 242 La. 73, 134 So.2d 880 (1961); Neel v. O'Quinn, 313 So.2d 286 (La.App.3rd Cir.1975); Lawson v. Donahue, 313 So.2d 263 (La.App.4th Cir.1975); Florida Ice Machine Corp. v. Brandon Insulation Inc., 290 So.2d 415 (La.App.4th Cir.1974).

(d) Under this Article, if dissolution takes place after less than a substantial part of the performance has been rendered, the obligor, if that performance is of value to the obligee, is entitled to recover the equivalent of the obligee's enrichment. See Stephenson v. Smith, 337 So.2d 570 (La.App.2nd Cir.1976); Henson v. Gonzalez, 326 So.2d 396 (La.App.1st Cir.1976); Neel v. O'Quinn, 313 So.2d 286 (La.App.3rd Cir.1975).

(e) Under this Article, if dissolution takes place after the obligor has rendered a part of the performance which is of no value to the obligee, the obligor is entitled to no recovery. See Home Services v. Martin, 37 So.2d 413 (La.App.Orl.1948); Toepfer v. Thionville, 299 So.2d 415 (La.App.4th Cir.1974).

(f) This Article contemplates a situation often faced by Louisiana courts—the partial dissolution of a contract. See 2 Litvinoff, Obligations 512–513 (1975). In most such cases, the solution found by the courts has been the right one, as in the cases cited in comment (b), supra. In others, however, courts have inadequately applied the general principle of indivisibility of obligations and reached questionable results, as in Barrow & LeBlanc v. Penick & Ford, 110 La. 572, 34 So. 691 (1903). This Article is intended to provide guidance, so that the wrong approach may be avoided.

Art. 2019. Contracts for continuous or periodic performance

In contracts providing for continuous or periodic performance, the effect of the dissolution shall not be extended to any performance already rendered.

Acts 1984, No. 331, § 1, eff. Jan. 1, 1985.

REVISION COMMENTS—1984

(a) This Article is new. It does not change the law, however. It states a principle that is contained in C.C. Arts. 1899 and 2686 (1870).

(b) A contract that can be performed only through an uninterrupted series of acts of performance, such as a lease, is a "contract providing for continuous performance" under this Article. A contract that is performed through acts that take place at stated intervals, or otherwise intermittently, such as a requirement or output contract, is a contract for periodic performance.

(c) French doctrine has recognized that dissolution cannot always have a retroactive effect. Such is the case of a lease, either of things or of services, or of a contract of insurance. To refer to the dissolution ex tunc—productive of a prospective effect only—that is necessary in such a case, French writers use the word "resiliation," as opposed to "resolution". See Weill, Droit civil—Les obligations 511–512 (1970). This Article preserves the notion of resiliation without utilizing that term.

Art. 2020. Contracts made by more than two parties

When a contract has been made by more than two parties, one party's failure to perform may not cause dissolution of the contract for the other parties, unless the performance that failed was essential to the contract.

Acts 1984, No. 331, § 1, eff. Jan. 1, 1985.

REVISION COMMENTS—1984

(a) This Article is new. It does not change the law, however. It expresses a conclusion that can be derived from principles contained in C.C. Arts. 21, 1901, and 1903 (1870).

(b) Under this Article, when the performance promised by one party to a multilateral contract is essential to its purpose that contract may be dissolved if that performance fails. Thus, a contract for the promotion and exploitation of public appearances by a particular entertainer may be dissolved for all the parties to it if the entertainer cannot or will not perform. On the other hand, failure of a performance which is not essential to achieve the purpose of a multilateral contract need not cause dissolution of that contract. Thus, in the above example the failure of a party who had promised to do the advertising for the entertainer's appearances would not cause the total dissolution of the contract. See C.C. Arts. 2818–2822 (as revised by Acts 1980, No. 150).

Art. 2021. Rights of third party in good faith

Dissolution of a contract does not impair the rights acquired through an onerous contract by a third party in good faith.

If the contract involves immovable property, the principles of recordation apply to a third person acquiring an interest in the property whether by onerous or gratuitous title.

Acts 1984, No. 331, § 1, eff. Jan. 1, 1985. Amended by Acts 2005, No. 169, § 2, eff. July 1, 2006.

This Article is new. It does not change the law, however. It expresses a principle implied in C.C. Arts. 3229 and 2266 (1870).

Art. 2022.   Refusal to perform

Either party to a commutative contract may refuse to perform his obligation if the other has failed to perform or does not offer to perform his own at the same time, if the performances are due simultaneously.

Acts 1984, No. 331, § 1, eff. Jan. 1, 1985.

(a) This Article is new. It does not change the law, however. It reformulates a principle contained in C.C. Arts. 2487, 1913, and 1914 (1870).

(b) This Article gives general formulation to the exceptio non adimpleti contractus (defense of nonperformance). See 2 Litvinoff, Obligations 426–434, 501–506 (1975).

(c) This Article applies only where the performances of the parties are to be rendered simultaneously, either because the contract so provides, or because the contract by its nature demands simultaneous performances. It does not apply where the performances are not to be rendered simultaneously as in the case of a lease.

Art. 2023.   Security for performance

If the situation of a party, financial or otherwise, has become such as to clearly endanger his ability to perform an obligation, the other party may demand in writing that adequate security be given and, upon failure to give that security, that party may withhold or discontinue his own performance.

Acts 1984, No. 331, § 1, eff. Jan. 1, 1985.

(a) This Article is new. It clarifies the law and makes generally applicable the principle contained in C.C. Art. 2488 (1870).

(b) Under this Article, either party may withhold performance of his obligation when there is danger that the other may not be able to perform, regardless of the kind, nature, or object of the contract.

(c) A party's ability to perform an obligation may be "endangered" by a change in his financial situation, as in the case of a buyer whose resources have so diminished as to clearly indicate that he will not be able to pay the price; or by a change in his personal situation, as in the case of an obligor of a personal obligation whose physical or psychological condition has so deteriorated as to indicate that he will not be able to render the promised performance at the agreed time.

(d) As used in this Article, "security" may include not only real or personal security, but also an assurance that the obligor has secured, or will secure, the means of performance. Thus, when raw materials needed to make a thing that the obligor has obligated himself to fabricate become scarce, and it is clear that the obligor has not taken steps to secure such materials, the obligee may request in writing an assurance that the obligor has or will have those materials available in time to perform.

(e) The fairness of C.C. Art. 2488 (1870) is so evident as to warrant applying it to obligations generally. This approach is taken in modern Civil Codes such as the Italian.

Art. 2024.   Contract terminated by a party's initiative

A contract of unspecified duration may be terminated at the will of either party by giving notice, reasonable in time and form, to the other party.

Acts 1984, No. 331, § 1, eff. Jan. 1, 1985.

(a) This Article is new. It does not change the law, however. It makes generally applicable the principle contained in C.C. Art. 2686 (1870).

(b) This Article neither repeals nor supplants the similar rules governing particular kinds of contracts, such as C.C. Art. 2686 (1870), governing lease of things, and C.C. Art. 2747 (1870), governing lease of labor.

(c) Under this Article, a contract of employment for an indefinite duration may be terminated at the will of either party. See Jackson et al. v. The East Baton Rouge Parish Indigent Defender's Board et al., 353 So.2d 344 (La.App.1st Cir.1977), writ denied 354 So.2d 1385 (La.1978).

(d) Under this Article, either party to a requirements or output contract of indefinite duration may terminate it at will by giving reasonable notice of termination to the other party.

(e) In proceeding under this Article, the parties must comply with the overriding duty of good faith. Reasonable advance notice will usually be required to avoid unwarranted injury to the interest of the other party. See U.C.C. § 2–309(3). See also R.S. 32:1256.1 (dealing with automobile franchises).

(f) This Article eliminates from the law of Louisiana the need for any "consideration" for the privilege of terminating contracts of the type stated. See 1 Litvinoff, Obligations 535–539 (1969).

CHAPTER 10—SIMULATION

Art. 2025. Definition; simulation and counterletter

A contract is a simulation when, by mutual agreement, it does not express the true intent of the parties.

If the true intent of the parties is expressed in a separate writing, that writing is a counterletter.

Acts 1984, No. 331, § 1, eff. Jan. 1, 1985.

(a) This Article is new. It does not change the law, however, as the definitions provided are implicit in C.C. Arts. 2464 and 2239 (1870).

(b) This Article defines the traditional institutions of simulation and counterletter. Both institutions are important to the civil law of Louisiana. Though they have long been common in practice, they are not systematically defined in the Louisiana Civil Code of 1870.

(c) Under this Article, a unilateral act addressed to a specified person is a simulation when, by agreement between its author and the person to whom it is addressed, the act is not meant to produce effects. See Italian Civil Code Article 1414.

Art. 2026. Absolute simulation

A simulation is absolute when the parties intend that their contract shall produce no effects between them. That simulation, therefore, can have no effects between the parties.

Acts 1984, No. 331, § 1, eff. Jan. 1, 1985.

(a) This Article is new. It does not change the law, however. It expresses a principle which is implicit in C.C. Art. 2239 (1870). An example of absolute simulation is an act whereby the parties make an apparent sale when they actually intend that the vendor will remain owner. The Louisiana jurisprudence has consistently distinguished such "sham transactions," that is, acts intended by the parties to have no effect at all (See Bourgeois v. Bourgeois, 202 La. 578, 12 So.2d 278 (1943); Smelley v. Ricks, 174 La. 734, 141 So. 445 (1932)), from "disguised donations," that is, conveyances intended by the parties to be valid but in which they have misrepresented the character of their transaction (See Richard v. Richard, 129 La. 967, 57 So. 286 (1912); Byrd v. Pierce, 124 La. 429, 50 So. 452 (1909)). That distinction is in keeping with contemporary doctrine. See 6 Planiol et Ripert, Traité pratique de droit civil français 428–430 (2nd ed. Esmein 1952); 1 Litvinoff, Obligations 225–230 (1969).

(b) Under this Article, the parties' true intent is given effect. It applies, inter alia, to the situation in which an apparent transferee confirms by counterletter that the subject property still belongs to the transferor. The rule that counterletters are effective between the parties given in C.C. Art. 2239 (1870), has been recognized and enforced by the Louisiana jurisprudence. See, e.g., Duncan v. Duncan, 26 La.Ann. 532 (1874). Because of basic principles of written and testimonial proof, however, the apparent transferor may not succeed in attacking an absolute simulation in the absence of a counterletter. See Lemann, "Some Aspects of Simulation in France and Louisiana," 29 Tul.L.Rev. 22 (1954): "(T)here have been a number of attempts by a supposed transferor to prove a non-transfer simulation by other than written evidence. Invariably such attempts have been unsuccessful, for at least three reasons. One is the implication of the Code articles that if written evidence of the secret act is effective between the parties, any other evidence is not. A second reason is the social attitude already mentioned, viz., the distrust of secret acts. A third reason is the codal provisions excluding parol evidence against or beyond written acts of sale. (Citing C.C. Art. 2276 (1870); see revised C.C. Art. 1848 (Rev.1984)). It can be said quite unequivocally today that a supposed transferor cannot establish a simulation unless he produces a written counter letter." 29 Tul.L.Rev. 22, 30–31 (1954).

(c) Under this Article an absolute simulation is without effect only between the parties. Its lack of effect may not be asserted against third persons, such as creditors and bona fide purchasers. See also Litvinoff & Tête, Louisiana Legal Transactions: The Civil Law of Juridical Acts 116–120 (1969). Third persons may, however, attack an absolute simulation made in fraud of their interest. See Heirs of Wood v. Nicholls, 33 La.Ann. 744 (1881). See also Litvinoff, "The Action in Declaration of Simulation in Louisiana Law," Essays on the Civil Law of Obligations 139 (Dainow ed. 1969).

Art. 2027. Relative simulation

A simulation is relative when the parties intend that their contract shall produce effects between them though different from those recited in their contract. A relative simulation produces between the parties the effects they intended if all requirements for those effects have been met.

Acts 1984, No. 331, § 1, eff. Jan. 1, 1985.

REVISION COMMENTS—1984

(a) This Article is new. It does not change the law, however. It expresses a principle contained in C.C. Art. 2464 and 1900 (1870). A relative simulation takes place when the parties make an apparent sale while actually intending a donation.

(b) Under this Article, a simulated sale may be a valid donation if the requirements of form have been met. See C.C. Art. 1536 (1870); McWilliams v. McWilliams, 39 La.Ann. 924, 3 So. 62 (1887).

(c) Under this Article, a simulated sale with right of redemption may be a valid security contract. See Collins v. Pellerin, 5 La.Ann. 99 (1850); Marbury v. Colbert, 105 La. 467, 29 So. 871 (1901); Delcambre v. Dubois, 263 So.2d 96 (La.App.3rd Cir.1972).

(d) Under this Article, the validity of the act actually intended depends on whether it complies with the pertinent formal, as well as substantive, requirements. See Loranger v. The Citizens National Bank of Hammond, 162 La. 1054, 111 So. 418 (1927); Succession of Daste, 254 La. 403, 223 So.2d 848 (1969). See also Lemann, "Some Aspects of Simulation in France and Louisiana," 29 Tul.L.Rev. 22 (1954).

Art. 2028. Effects as to third persons

Any simulation, either absolute or relative, may have effects as to third persons.

Counterletters can have no effects against third persons in good faith. Nevertheless, if the counterletter involves immovable property, the principles of recordation apply with respect to third persons.

Acts 1984, No. 331, § 1, eff. Jan. 1, 1985. Amended by Acts 2012, No. 277, § 1.

REVISION COMMENTS—1984

(a) This Article is new. It reproduces the substance of C.C. Art. 2239 (1870).

(b) Under this Article, creditors and bona fide purchasers are among the third persons who may avail themselves of a simulation, but other third persons are not excluded provided they are in good faith.

(c) Under this Article, an act may not be attacked as a simulation against the interest of a third person who has relied on the public records. See Chachere v. Superior Oil Co., 192 La. 193, 187 So. 321 (1939).

(d) A third person in good faith against whom a counterletter can have no effect under this Article is one who does not know of the existence of the counterletter. Nevertheless, if the counterletter is not recorded, a third person's actual knowledge of it may not deprive him of protection under the principles of the Louisiana public records doctrine. See Redmann, "The Louisiana Law of Recordation: Some Principles and Some Problems," 39 Tul.L.Rev. 491 (1965). See also McDuffie v. Walker, 125 La. 152, 51 So. 100 (1909).

(e) This Article eliminates the reference to the rights of forced heirs which was introduced into C.C. Art. 2239 (1870) by Acts 1884, No. 5. The reasons for that amendment are unclear. It was once suggested that the amendment was prompted by the earlier case of Kerwin v. Hibernia Ins. Co., 35 La.Ann. 33 (1883), and was aimed at situations where recitals in deeds are attacked as false in connection with the question whether certain property is separate or community. Whatever its purpose, the amendment has had almost no impact on the jurisprudence since it was enacted.

REVISION COMMENTS—2012

(a) This Article clarifies the law. It reproduces the substance of C.C. Art. 2028 (Rev. 1984).

(b) Under this Article, simulations may have effects not only between the parties, but also with respect to third persons. For definition of a third person, see C.C. Art. 3343 (Rev. 2005).

(c) Although the predecessor Article stated that counterletters could have no effect against third persons in good faith, C.C. Art. 2028 (Rev. 1984), the predecessor Article was only partially correct. This Article clarifies the general rule that counterletters can "have no effect against third parties in good faith." See Peterson v. Skains, 509 So.2d 197 (La.App. 1st Cir. 1987). When a counterletter affects immovable property, however, a counterletter can have effect with respect to a third person, provided the counterletter is recorded. See, e.g., State v. Recorder of Mortgages, 143 So. 15 (La. 1932) ("Counterletters duly recorded affect all persons even creditors from the time of the recording.") If a counterletter affecting immovable property is unrecorded it can have no effect as to third persons, irrespective of their knowledge or good faith. See, e.g., McDuffie v. Walker, 51 So.100 (La. 1909); Chachere v. Superior Oil Co., 187 So. 321 (La. 1939) ("It is the well settled jurisprudence of this state that third persons dealing with immovable property have a right to depend upon the faith of the recorded title thereof and are not bound by any secret equities that may exist between their own vendor and prior owners of the land."); Musso v. Aiavolasiti, 439 So.2d 1184 (La.App. 4th Cir. 1983) ("An unrecorded document affecting immovable property is not binding upon third parties . . . Whether [the defendant] knew of the document is irrelevant. . . ."); Tate v. Tate, 42 So. 3d 439 (La.App. 1st Cir. 2010) ("Even a third party with actual knowledge of a counterletter is not deprived of the protections of the public records doctrine when the counterletter is unrecorded.") See also William V. Redmann, The Louisiana Law of Recordation: Some Principles and Some Problems, 39 TUL. L. REV. 496–97 (1964); C.C. Art. 2028 Comment (d) (Rev. 1984) ("Nevertheless, if the counterletter is not recorded, a third person's actual knowledge of it may not deprive him of protection under the principles of the Louisiana public records doctrine.")

CHAPTER 11—NULLITY

Art. 2029. Nullity of contracts

A contract is null when the requirements for its formation have not been met.

Acts 1984, No. 331, § 1, eff. Jan. 1, 1985.

REVISION COMMENTS—1984

(a) This Article is new, but it does not change the principles articulated in the source Articles and jurisprudence. It states a conclusion well known in Louisiana law. For systematic reasons, it is convenient to state that conclusion here as a prelude to the difficult subject of nullity. This Article can apply to informal transactions for which the code prescribes no particular form. It can also apply to solemn acts which are incurably null if they are not done in a prescribed form. Among such acts, the most familiar ones are donations null in form. See C.C. Art. 1536 (1870).

(b) The general requirements for the formation of a valid contract are those stated in revised C.C. Arts. 1918, 1927, 1966, and 1971 (Rev.1984), supra.

Art. 2030. Absolute nullity of contracts

A contract is absolutely null when it violates a rule of public order, as when the object of a contract is illicit or immoral. A contract that is absolutely null may not be confirmed.

Absolute nullity may be invoked by any person or may be declared by the court on its own initiative.

Acts 1984, No. 331, § 1, eff. Jan. 1, 1985.

REVISION COMMENTS—1984

This Article is new, but it does not change the law. It codifies the jurisprudential rule that a contract which contravenes the public order is absolutely null. See, e.g., Coco v. Oden, 143 La. 718, 79 So. 287 (1918); Burney's Heirs v. Ludeling, 47 La.Ann. 73, 16 So. 507 (1894); Williams v. Fredericks, 187 La. 987, 175 So. 642 (1937); Ozanne v. Haber, 30 La.Ann. 1384 (1878); Gil v. Williams & Davis, 12 La.Ann. 219 (1857); Gravier's Curator v. Carraby's Executor, 17 La. 118 (1841).

Art. 2031. Relative nullity of contracts

A contract is relatively null when it violates a rule intended for the protection of private parties, as when a party lacked capacity or did not give free consent at the time the contract was made. A contract that is only relatively null may be confirmed.

Relative nullity may be invoked only by those persons for whose interest the ground for nullity was established, and may not be declared by the court on its own initiative.

Acts 1984, No. 331, § 1, eff. Jan. 1, 1985.

REVISION COMMENT—1984

This Article is new, but it does not change the law. It restates the rules of C.C. Arts. 11, 1791, 1795, and 1881 (1870).

Art. 2032. Prescription of action

Action for annulment of an absolutely null contract does not prescribe.

Action of annulment of a relatively null contract must be brought within five years from the time the ground for nullity either ceased, as in the case of incapacity or duress, or was discovered, as in the case of error or fraud.

Nullity may be raised at any time as a defense against an action on the contract, even after the action for annulment has prescribed.

Acts 1984, No. 331, § 1, eff. Jan. 1, 1985.

REVISION COMMENTS—1984

(a) This Article changes the law insofar as it shortens to five years the prescriptive period for actions to declare a relative nullity contained in C.C. Art. 2221, as amended by Acts 1980, No. 308.

(b) The phrase "was discovered," taken from C.C. Art. 2221, as amended by Acts 1980, No. 308, is intended to provide for situations in which a party has been deceived and does not discover the deception until long after the original contract was made, as is often the case where fraud has occurred. An error is also often "discovered" in this way.

Art. 2033. Effects

An absolutely null contract, or a relatively null contract that has been declared null by the court, is deemed never to have existed. The parties must be restored to the situation that existed before the contract was made. If it is impossible or impracticable to make restoration in kind, it may be made through an award of damages.

Nevertheless, a performance rendered under a contract that is absolutely null because its object or its cause is illicit or immoral may not be recovered by a party who knew or should have known of the defect that makes the contract null. The performance may be recovered, however, when that party invokes the nullity to withdraw from the contract before its purpose is achieved and also in exceptional situations when, in the discretion of the court, that recovery would further the interest of justice.

Absolute nullity may be raised as a defense even by a party who, at the time the contract was made, knew or should have known of the defect that makes the contract null.

Acts 1984, No. 331, § 1, eff. Jan. 1, 1985.

REVISION COMMENTS—1984

(a) This Article is new. It does not change the law, however. The rules stated are derived in part from the Louisiana jurisprudence, and in part from principles underlying the source articles. See C.C. Art. 1791 (1870); Gravier's Curator v. Carraby's Executor, 17 La. 118 (1841).

(b) The restoration of the parties to the situation that existed before the contract that is called for by this Article includes restoration of fruits and revenues, as any unjust enrichment of the parties must be prevented. See C.C. Art. 2506 (1870).

(c) Under this Article, a party who knew or should have known at the time of contracting of a defect that made the contract absolutely null may not avail himself of the nullity when the purpose of the illegal contract has been accomplished. See Boatner v. Yarborough, 12 La.Ann. 249 (1857); Gravier's Curator v. Carraby's Executor, 17 La. 118 (1841); Mulhollan v. Voorhies, 3 Mart. (N.S.) 46 (1824). This conclusion flows naturally from the principle expressed in the traditional Roman maxim, nemo propriam turpitudinem allegare potest (no one may invoke his own turpitude), sometimes called the "clean hands" doctrine. If a performance has been rendered under such a contract by a party with knowledge of the cause of nullity, the other party may keep that performance, in accordance with the complementary Roman maxim, In pari causa turpitudinem potior est conditio possidentis (in case of equal wrongdoing the one in possession is in a better position). See 2 Litvinoff, Obligations 163–169 (1975). The philosophy underlying those principles is not to reward the recipient of the performance, who by hypothesis is as guilty as the renderer, but to protect the court from mediating disputes between dealers in iniquity. See Gravier's Curator v. Carraby's Executor, 17 La. 118 (1841). See also Tzarano, Étude sur la règle: "Nemo auditur propriam turpitudinem allegans" 103–115 (1926); Le Tourneau, La règle: "Nemo auditur . . ." 178–179 (1970).

(d) Under this Article, a party who has performed in ignorance of the fact or facts giving rise to an absolute nullity may invoke it to recover either his performance or the equivalent of his performance. See Greffin's Executor v. Lopez, 5 Mart.(O.S.) 145 (1817). See also 1 Domat, The Civil Law in its Natural Order (Strahan trans. 1850): "If the covenant is unlawful only on the part of him who receives, and not of him who gives, as if a depositary demands money for restoring the thing deposited with him, or a thief for giving back what he has stolen, he who has given money on such an account may demand it back, although the receiver have (sic) performed his agreement. But if the covenant be unlawful both on the part of the giver and receiver, as if one who has a lawsuit pending gives money to the judge to engage him to give judgment in his favor; or if one person gives money to another to engage him to do an evil action; he who has given the money is justly stripped of what he has laid out on such an account, and he cannot recover it. And he who received the money cannot reap the profit of the price of his crime; but both the one and the other will be chastised by making restitution, and undergoing the punishments which they shall have deserved." Id. at 514. See also 1 Pothier, A Treatise on the Law of Obligations or Contracts 25–26 (Evans trans. 1806).

(e) Under this Article, a party who has entered into or performed a contract with knowledge of the cause of its nullity may recover his performance if he withdraws from the contract before its purpose is accomplished. Thus, a party who has knowingly lent money to another for the purpose of gambling may recover the amount lent before the intended wager takes place.

(f) Under this Article, absolute nullity of a contract may be raised as a defense even by a party who entered into the contract with knowledge of the cause of its nullity: "The defendants can even be heard to plead, as they have done, that a contract into which they have voluntarily entered is contra bonos mores; for the authorities make this an exception to the general rule nemo allegans suam turpitudinem est audiendus, an exception founded upon the necessity of the case, and the paramount interest of the public." Gil v. Williams and Davis, 12 La.Ann. 219, 221 (1857).

(g) Under this Article, a party who has entered into or performed an absolutely null contract with knowledge of the defect that made it null may recover his performance if denial of recovery would leave the object of that performance in the hands of one whose control of it would be contrary to the public interest, or would render the legal situation of that object so uncertain as to seriously hinder its alienation. Thus, a party who made a wagering agreement under which he deposited property with another who, as stakeholder, promised to give all the stakes to the winner, could recover his property from the stakeholder if he notified him of his claim before the property was delivered to the winner.

Art. 2034. Nullity of a provision

Nullity of a provision does not render the whole contract null unless, from the nature of the provision or the intention of the parties, it can be presumed that the contract would not have been made without the null provision.

Acts 1984, No. 331, § 1, eff. Jan. 1, 1985.

REVISION COMMENT—1984

This Article is new, but it is logically consistent with traditional concepts of motive or cause. It directs the court to consider the totality of the parties' intentions before annulling the agreement when only a portion of it is null. The principle embodied in this Article has been approved in several contract decisions of the United States Supreme Court. See, e.g., Gelpcke v. Dubuque, 68 U.S. 221, 1 Wall. 221, 17 L.Ed. 519 (1863); Daniels v. Tearney, 102 U.S. 415, 12 Otto 415, 26 L.Ed. 187 (1880); Chicago, St. L. & N.O.R. Co. v. Pullman Southern Car Co., 139 U.S. 79, 11 S.Ct. 490, 35 L.Ed. 97 (1891); McCullough v. Virginia, 172 U.S. 102, 19 S.Ct. 134, 43 L.Ed. 382 (1898). See also the dissenting opinion in Davis-Delcambre Motors Inc. v. Simon, 154 So.2d 775 (La.App.3rd Cir.1963); Pennington v. Drews, 218 La. 258, 49 So.2d 5 (1949); C.C. Art. 2123 (1870).

Art. 2035. Rights of third party in good faith

Nullity of a contract does not impair the rights acquired through an onerous contract by a third party in good faith.

If the contract involves immovable property, the principles of recordation apply to a third person acquiring an interest in the property whether by onerous or gratuitous title.

Acts 1984, No. 331, § 1, eff. Jan. 1, 1985. Amended by Acts 2005, No. 169, § 2, eff. July 1, 2006.

REVISION COMMENTS—1984

(a) This Article is new, but it does not change the law. It merely articulates the doctrines of bona fide purchase and the sanctity of the public records. These ideas dominate the jurisprudence and statutory law. See, e.g., R.S. 9:2721–2722; McDuffie v. Walker, 125 La. 152, 51 So. 100 (1909); Owen v. Owen, 336 So.2d 782 (La.1976).

(b) This Article reflects the public policy in favor of security of transactions by protecting the person who acquires rights through a valid onerous contract from the effects of the nullity of any related contract between different persons. However, the parties to either contract may still adjust their rights by means of damages.

CHAPTER 12—REVOCATORY ACTION AND OBLIQUE ACTION

SECTION 1—REVOCATORY ACTION

Art. 2036.   Act of the obligor that causes or increases his insolvency

An obligee has a right to annul an act of the obligor, or the result of a failure to act of the obligor, made or effected after the right of the obligee arose, that causes or increases the obligor's insolvency.

Acts 1984, No. 331, § 1, eff. Jan. 1, 1985. Amended by Acts 2003, No. 552, § 1; Acts 2004, No. 447, § 1.

REVISION COMMENTS—1984

(a) This Article is new. It changes the law insofar as it abandons the notion of fraud contained in the source articles. Otherwise, it reproduces the substance of C.C. Arts. 1969, 1970, 1971, 1972, 1975, 1977, 1985, 1986, 1988, and 1994 (1870).

(b) This Article substitutes an act of the obligor that causes or increases his insolvency for the notion of an act in fraud of creditors contained in the source articles. As used in those articles, the word "fraud" has a meaning which is difficult to determine but which appears different from its meaning in other contexts. In this revision, the criterion for the revocatory action is an objective one. It may be satisfied by an act done negligently as well as intentionally.

(c) The revocatory or Paulian action, an institution derived from Roman law, is the civil law analogue to the common law suit to set aside a fraudulent conveyance.

(d) The term "act" in this Article encompasses contracts, acts of payment, and any "contrivance" employed by an obligor to defeat his obligee's rightful claim. See Newman v. Baer, 50 La.Ann. 323, 23 So. 279 (1897). According to the jurisprudence, any arrangement, whether made through judicial machinery or otherwise, whereby an obligor tries to give an obligee an advantage over others may be attacked by the injured obligees. See, e.g., Muse v. Yarborough, 11 La. 521 (1838), (obligor confessed judgment to one obligee in prejudice of the rights of others); Bank of Patterson v. Urban Co., 114 La. 788, 38 So. 561 (1905), (obligor filed answer and consented to quick trial of suit).

(e) The expression, ". . . the result of a failure to act of the obligor" contemplates situations in which an obligor becomes insolvent, or his insolvency increases, because of his failure to act, as when the obligor fails to defend himself in a law suit, and the resulting judgment creates or increases his insolvency.

(f) Under this Article, anteriority of the debt and insolvency of the debtor are prerequisites to the revocatory action, in accordance with traditional doctrine received by the Louisiana jurisprudence. See Tate, "The Revocatory Action in Louisiana Law," Essays on the Civil Law of Obligations 133 (Dainow ed. 1969); Landry, "The Revocatory Action in the Quebec Civil Code: General Principles," Id. at 115. An obligee's claim does not have to be liquidated to judgment to be considered an anterior debt. Holland v. Gross, 195 So. 828 (La.App.2nd Cir.1940); Ventrilla v. Tortorice, 160 La. 516, 107 So. 390 (1926).

(g) The articles in this section do not address situations in which an already insolvent obligor gives an unfair advantage to one of his creditors. Situations of that kind are regulated by federal bankruptcy law. See 11 U.S.C. § 547.

(h) An obligor's payment of a just and due debt may not be annulled under this Article. Although it reduces his assets, it also reduces his liabilities by the same amount. If the obligor gives a thing in payment of such a debt, C.C. Art. 2658 (1870) controls. See Morgan v. Gates, 396 So.2d 1386 (La.App.2nd Cir.1981).

Art. 2037.   Insolvency

An obligor is insolvent when the total of his liabilities exceeds the total of his fairly appraised assets.

Acts 1984, No. 331, § 1, eff. Jan. 1, 1985. Amended by Acts 2003, No. 552, § 1; Acts 2004, No. 447, § 1.

Art. 2038. Onerous contract made by the obligor

An obligee may annul an onerous contract made by the obligor with a person who knew or should have known that the contract would cause or increase the obligor's insolvency. In that case, the person is entitled to recover what he gave in return only to the extent that it has inured to the benefit of the obligor's creditors.

An obligee may annul an onerous contract made by the obligor with a person who did not know that the contract would cause or increase the obligor's insolvency, but in that case that person is entitled to recover as much as he gave to the obligor. That lack of knowledge is presumed when that person has given at least four-fifths of the value of the thing obtained in return from the obligor.

Acts 1984, No. 331, § 1, eff. Jan. 1, 1985.

Art. 2039. Gratuitous contract made by the obligor

An obligee may attack a gratuitous contract made by the obligor whether or not the other party knew that the contract would cause or increase the obligor's insolvency.

Acts 1984, No. 331, § 1, eff. Jan. 1, 1985.

Art. 2040. Contract made in course of business

An obligee may not annul a contract made by the obligor in the regular course of his business.

Acts 1984, No. 331, § 1, eff. Jan. 1, 1985.

CONVENTIONAL OBLIGATIONS OR CONTRACTS

Art. 2041. Action must be brought within one year

The action of the obligee must be brought within one year from the time he learned or should have learned of the act, or the result of the failure to act, of the obligor that the obligee seeks to annul, but never after three years from the date of that act or result.

The three year period provided in this Article shall not apply in cases of fraud.

Acts 1984, No. 331, § 1, eff. Jan. 1, 1985. Amended by Acts 2013, No. 88, § 1.

REVISION COMMENTS—1984

(a) This Article is new. As "insolvency" is substituted for "fraud" as the criterion for availability of the revocatory action, the prescriptive period should be one year from the day the obligee learned of the harm. Otherwise, a devious obligor could prejudice his obligee's claim and conceal his actions for a year, thereby escaping liability altogether. This approach to prescription conforms with that adopted by Louisiana courts in the field of delicts and quasi-delicts. Nevertheless, to protect the security of transactions, the revocatory action may not be brought after three years from the date of the act or the result of the failure to act of the obligor.

(b) The prescriptive period of C.C. Art. 1994 (1870) runs from date of judgment. Since the revised articles on revocatory action have been drafted to cover unliquidated claims, the "date of judgment" is not a relevant starting point for determining when prescription has run.

(c) If the obligees are represented by a trustee in bankruptcy, then the two-year prescriptive period of 11 U.S.C. § 108 prevails.

Art. 2042. Obligee must join obligor and third persons

In an action to annul either his obligor's act, or the result of his obligor's failure to act, the obligee must join the obligor and the third persons involved in that act or failure to act.

A third person joined in the action may plead discussion of the obligor's assets.

Acts 1984, No. 331, § 1, eff. Jan. 1, 1985.

REVISION COMMENT—1984

This Article is new. It changes the law only insofar as it provides that the obligee must join the obligor and the third persons who concurred with him in the making of the attacked act. Prior jurisprudence merely permitted such joinder. E.J. Hart & Co. v. Mrs. M.J. Bowie et al., 34 La.Ann. 323 (1882); Ventrilla v. Tortorice, 160 La. 516, 107 So. 390 (1926); and Gast v. Gast, 206 La. 285, 19 So.2d 138 (1944).

Art. 2043. Assets transferred must be returned

If an obligee establishes his right to annul his obligor's act, or the result of his obligor's failure to act, that act or result shall be annulled only to the extent that it affects the obligee's right.

Acts 1984, No. 331, § 1, eff. Jan. 1, 1985.

REVISION COMMENTS—1984

(a) This Article reproduces the substance of C.C. Arts. 1977 and 1988 (1870). It does not change the law.

(b) Under this Article, the effect of the revocatory action is that the attacked transaction is annulled only insofar as annulment will benefit the complaining creditor, and the returned property is applied to the payment of that creditor. See Martin Lebreton Ins. Agency v. Phillips, 364 So.2d 1032 (La.1978).

(c) The effect of the revocatory action inures in the first place to the benefit of the creditor who succeeds in that action, even against a creditor of superior rank who did not bring such an action. See Stubbs v. Lee, 105 La. 642, 30 So. 169 (1901).

(d) Under this Article, when attacking creditors bring revocatory actions at about the same time, the effect of the action brought by one of them inures to the benefit of all such creditors. See Walton & Son v. Bemiss, 16 La. 140 (1840).

SECTION 2—OBLIQUE ACTION

Art. 2044.   Insolvency by failure to exercise right

If an obligor causes or increases his insolvency by failing to exercise a right, the obligee may exercise it himself, unless the right is strictly personal to the obligor.

For that purpose, the obligee must join in the suit his obligor and the third person against whom that right is asserted.

Acts 1984, No. 331, § 1, eff. Jan. 1, 1985.

REVISION COMMENTS—1984

(a) This Article is new. It does not change the law, however. It gives express formulation to a principle that the redactors of 1825 regarded as too obvious to need stating.

(b) Identification of those actions which are "strictly personal" is left to the discretion of the courts, guided by the provisions of the relevant articles of this revision. See revised C.C. Arts. 1765 and 1766 (Rev.1984), supra; Succession of Henican, 248 So.2d 385 (La.App.4th Cir.1971).

(c) The creditor's right in the oblique action is similar to the right of a third party beneficiary or the innocent victim of an accident to enforce an insurance contract to which he is not a party. The creditor in an oblique action, like the third party beneficiary or the accident victim, exercises a right which the law gives him to benefit from an obligation to which he is not a party. The debtor in the oblique action should thus not be allowed to claim that he did not intend the creditor's advantage, as such a defense would not be permitted in the case of the third party beneficiary or the accident victim. See, e.g., Andrepont v. Acadia Drilling Co., 255 La. 347, 231 So.2d 347 (1969).

CHAPTER 13—INTERPRETATION OF CONTRACTS

Art. 2045.   Determination of the intent of the parties

Interpretation of a contract is the determination of the common intent of the parties.

Acts 1984, No. 331, § 1, eff. Jan. 1, 1985.

REVISION COMMENTS—1984

(a) This Article is new. It does not change the law, however. It states a principle which underlies C.C. Arts. 1945, 1949, 1950, and 1956 (1870).

(b) Under this Article, the parties' common intent is deemed objective in nature, which means that in some cases it may consist of a reconstruction of what the parties must have intended, given the manner in which they expressed themselves in their contract. In this manner a party's declaration of will becomes an integral part of his will. See Litvinoff and Tête, Louisiana Legal Transactions: The Civil Law of Juridical Acts 105–132 (1969).

Nevertheless, when there is a manifest difference between a party's intent and the pertinent declaration of that intent, the rules governing error may apply. See revised C.C. Arts. 1948–1952 (Rev.1984), supra.

(c) According to C.C. Art. 1950 (1870), when something is doubtful in an agreement "we must endeavor to ascertain what was the common intention of the parties. . . ." This language, though clear in general terms, might, if taken on its face, lead to the conclusion that the intent of the parties is of no moment when nothing is doubtful in their agreement. That conclusion would deny the validity of the principles of autonomy of the will and freedom of contract that permeate the French and Louisiana Civil Codes. If that conclusion is wrong, as no doubt it is, then the intent of the parties governs a contract regardless of whether the terms of that contract are clear or doubtful. Assuming that the parties have used words to express their intent, however, the process of understanding those words, however manifest their meaning, is one of interpretation. Hence, interpretation of a contract is the determination of the parties' intent.

(d) This Article provides a definition of interpretation that may serve as a starting point from which the basic rules of interpretation may be derived as natural consequences. See Geny, Method of Interpretation and Sources of Private Positive Law 399–404 (Louisiana State Law Institute trans. 1963) for a discussion of autonomy of the will in the context of interpretation.

Art. 2046.   No further interpretation when intent is clear

When the words of a contract are clear and explicit and lead to no absurd consequences, no further interpretation may be made in search of the parties' intent.

Acts 1984, No. 331, § 1, eff. Jan. 1, 1985.

REVISION COMMENTS—1984

(a) This Article is new. It does not change the law, however. It makes applicable to contracts the principle contained in C.C. Art. 13 (1870) for interpretation of laws. It also reproduces the substance of C.C. Art. 1945(3) (1870).

(b) Under this Article, when a clause in a contract is clear and unambiguous, the letter of that clause should not be disregarded under pretext of pursuing its spirit. See Maloney v. Oak Builders, Inc., 256 La. 85, 235 So.2d 386 (1970).

(c) This Article effects a synthesis of C.C. Arts. 1945(3) and 13 (1870). If a contract is the private law of the parties, there is no reason not to apply to it the rule of interpretation that C.C. Art. 13 (1870) provides for the interpretation of laws.

Art. 2047.   Meaning of words

The words of a contract must be given their generally prevailing meaning.

Words of art and technical terms must be given their technical meaning when the contract involves a technical matter.

Acts 1984, No. 331, § 1, eff. Jan. 1, 1985.

REVISION COMMENTS—1984

(a) This Article reproduces the substance of C.C. Arts. 1946 and 1947 (1870). It does not change the law.

(b) The rules of error must apply whenever it is evident that one party understood a particular technical word or term as having a meaning different from that given it by the other party, and that misunderstanding can be deemed excusable. See C.C. Art. 1812 (1870).

(c) Civil Code Articles 1946 and 1947 (1870) were introduced in the Civil Code of 1825. They have no equivalents in the Code Napoleon. They were no doubt of common law origin, as is suggested by § 202 of the Restatement of the Law, Second, Contracts (1981). The principles contained in those articles are preserved because Louisiana courts have applied them quite frequently.

Art. 2048.   Words susceptible of different meanings

Words susceptible of different meanings must be interpreted as having the meaning that best conforms to the object of the contract.

Acts 1984, No. 331, § 1, eff. Jan. 1, 1985.

REVISION COMMENTS—1984

(a) This Article reproduces the substance of C.C. Art. 1952 (1870). It does not change the law.

(b) The English text of the source article is a poor translation of the French original. See 3 Louisiana Legal Archives, Part II, at 1081 (1942). This Article merely restates the rule in more idiomatic terms. The Louisiana jurisprudence has had no difficulty in discerning the true intent of the rule. See St. Landry State Bank v. Meyers, 52 La.Ann. 1769, 28 So. 136 (1898); Massy v. Gordy, 1 Man.Unrep.Cas. 313 (La.1880).

Art. 2049.   Provision susceptible of different meanings

A provision susceptible of different meanings must be interpreted with a meaning that renders it effective and not with one that renders it ineffective.

Acts 1984, No. 331, § 1, eff. Jan. 1, 1985.

REVISION COMMENT—1984

This Article restates the rule of C.C. Art. 1951 (1870). It does not change the law.

Art. 2050.   Provisions interpreted in light of each other

Each provision in a contract must be interpreted in light of the other provisions so that each is given the meaning suggested by the contract as a whole.

Acts 1984, No. 331, § 1, eff. Jan. 1, 1985.

REVISION COMMENT—1984

This Article reproduces the substance of C.C. Art. 1955 (1870). It does not change the law.

Art. 2051.   Contract worded in general terms

Although a contract is worded in general terms, it must be interpreted to cover only those things it appears the parties intended to include.

Acts 1984, No. 331, § 1, eff. Jan. 1, 1985.

REVISION COMMENT—1984

This Article restates the rule of C.C. Art. 1959 (1870). It does not change the law.

Art. 2052.   Situation to which the contract applies

When the parties intend a contract of general scope but, to eliminate doubt, include a provision that describes a specific situation, interpretation must not restrict the scope of the contract to that situation alone.

Acts 1984, No. 331, § 1, eff. Jan. 1, 1985.

REVISION COMMENTS—1984

(a) This Article reproduces the substance of C.C. Art. 1962 (1870). It does not change the law.

(b) The rule stated in this Article is a traditional and useful one, which, regrettably, has often been misstated. Its original formulation was Cum species ex abundanti per imperitiam enumerantur, generali legato non derogatur. See 1 Pothier, A Treatise on the Law of Obligations or Contracts 62 (Evans trans. 1806).

(c) Article 64, at page 270, of the Louisiana Digest of 1808, borrowing from the Code Napoleon, provided:

"When in a contract, a case has been expressed for the explanation of the obligation, it is not understood that by that the parties intended to restrict the extent which the engagement receives of right, to the cases not expressed."

That Article was suppressed on recommendation of the redactors of the Civil Code of 1825 and replaced by the text which subsequently became Article 1962 of the Civil Code of 1870. See 3 Louisiana Legal Archives, Part II, at 1085 (1942). The new text improved on the old, but not very significantly. This Article attempts to restate the traditional concept in terms as plain as possible.

In the traditional example, of the application of this rule, if a person makes a legacy of all of his movables, and then, for purpose of clarification, enumerates some of them, such as his furniture, silver, and library, that enumeration does not restrict the legacy to the enumerated items only. See 3 Toullier, Le droit civil français 450 (1833).

(d) Louisiana courts have made fruitful use of C.C. Art. 1962 (1870) in interpreting remedies provisions in contracts. They have held that, when a contract provides certain remedies for its breach, other remedies are not thereby excluded. E.g., Queensborough Land Co. v. Cazeaux, 136 La. 724, 67 So. 641 (1915). Similarly, in Craten v. Aetna Life Ins. Co. of Hartford, Conn., 186 La. 757, 173 So. 306 (1937), the Court cited C.C. Art. 1962 (1870) in holding that when an insurance policy stipulates that an entire and irrevocable loss of use of both hands or both feet or of one hand and one foot shall be deemed to be total and permanent disability, it does not preclude the idea that entire and irrevocable loss of use of only one hand or one foot might mean total and permanent disability to an uneducated and unskilled laborer.

Art. 2053. Nature of contract, equity, usages, conduct of the parties, and other contracts between same parties

A doubtful provision must be interpreted in light of the nature of the contract, equity, usages, the conduct of the parties before and after the formation of the contract, and of other contracts of a like nature between the same parties.

Acts 1984, No. 331, § 1, eff. Jan. 1, 1985.

REVISION COMMENTS—1984

(a) This Article is new. It reproduces the substance of and enlarges upon the provisions of C.C. Arts. 1903, 1953, and 1965 (1870). It clarifies the law by providing that courts may resort to equity for guidance only when the meaning of a provision is in doubt. They may not do so in order to enlarge or restrict the scope of a contract or provision whose meaning is apparent. See 6 Planiol et Ripert, Traité pratique de droit civil français 485 (2d ed. Esmein 1952).

(b) Under this Article, a usage, to be applied in interpreting a contract, must be consistent with the nature of that contract. See New Roads Oilmill & Mfg. Co. v. Kline, Wilson & Co., 154 F. 296, 83 C.C.A. 1 (1907).

(c) Under this Article, stipulations commonly used in contracts of the same kind as the one in question may be regarded as implied in it if not expressed by the parties. Civil Code Article 1954 (1870) has been suppressed as unnecessary.

(d) Louisiana courts have often made use of C.C. Art. 1953 (1870). Thus, in Southern Bitulithic Co. v. Algiers Ry. & Lighting Co., 130 La. 830, 58 So. 588 (1912), it was said that usage enters into every contract and may be shown for the purpose not only of elucidating it, but also of completing it. In Fontenot's Rice Drier, Inc. v. Farmers Rice Milling Co., 329 So.2d 494 (La.App.3rd Cir.1976), writ denied 333 So.2d 239 (La.1976), the court concluded that "custom" may be employed not only to modify or restrict a contract but also to enlarge it. In light of this trend, it seemed advisable to introduce a reference to the nature of a contract as a logical complement to the reference to usages.

(e) In this Article, the meaning of "conduct of the parties before and after the formation of the contract" is similar to that of "course of dealing" as used in Section 1–205 of the Uniform Commercial Code (R.S. 10:1–205). The third paragraph of that section reads: "A course of dealing between parties and any usage of trade in the vocation or trade in which they are engaged or of which they are or should be aware give particular meaning to and supplement or qualify terms of an agreement." Similar ideas are reflected in C.C. Art. 1953 and 1956 (1870), but the idea of considering the conduct of the parties prior to the formation of the contract goes beyond what is contemplated in those Articles.

Art. 2054. No provision of the parties for a particular situation

When the parties made no provision for a particular situation, it must be assumed that they intended to bind themselves not only to the express provisions of the contract, but also to whatever the law, equity, or usage regards as implied in a contract of that kind or necessary for the contract to achieve its purpose.

Acts 1984, No. 331, § 1, eff. Jan. 1, 1985.

REVISION COMMENTS—1984

(a) This Article is new. It changes the law, making the rule of C.C. Art. 1903 (1870) a rule of interpretation rather than one of substantive law.

(b) This Article provides for the instance where the contract is not ambiguous or doubtful, but simply fails to address a particular question.

(c) This Article enhances the rule stated in the second sentence of C.C. Art. 1965 (1870), which has been accorded insufficient recognition because of its location.

(d) Planiol comments on Article 1135 of the French Civil Code, equivalent to C.C. Art. 1903 (1870), as if it were C.C. Art. 21 (1870), which provides, in effect, that the court must act as law-maker when the statutory law is silent. Under this Article, the court is given the same discretion in the context of contractual interpretation, since no situation may be regarded as unregulated by the legal order. See 6 Planiol et Ripert, Traité pratique de droit civil français 485 (2nd ed. Esmein 1952).

Art. 2055. Equity and usage

Equity, as intended in the preceding articles, is based on the principles that no one is allowed to take unfair advantage of another and that no one is allowed to enrich himself unjustly at the expense of another.

Usage, as intended in the preceding articles, is a practice regularly observed in affairs of a nature identical or similar to the object of a contract subject to interpretation.

Acts 1984, No. 331, § 1, eff. Jan. 1, 1985.

This Article reproduces the substance of C.C. Arts. 1964, 1965, and 1966 (1870). It does not change the law.

Art. 2056. Standard-form contracts

In case of doubt that cannot be otherwise resolved, a provision in a contract must be interpreted against the party who furnished its text.

A contract executed in a standard form of one party must be interpreted, in case of doubt, in favor of the other party.

Acts 1984, No. 331, § 1, eff. Jan. 1, 1985.

(a) This Article is new. It does not change the law, however. The rules stated follow from the principle stated in C.C. Art. 1958 (1870). The Louisiana jurisprudence has held that the terms of a printed contract must be interpreted against the party who provided it. Centanni v. A.K. Roy, Inc., 258 So.2d 219 (La.App.4th Cir.1972).

(b) Louisiana courts have long been used to saying that any doubt or ambiguity as to the meaning of a contract must be eliminated by interpreting the contract against the party who prepared it. See, e.g., Ouachita Nat. Bank in Monroe v. Williamson, 338 So.2d 172 (La.App.2nd Cir.1976); Sabine Const. Co., Inc. v. Cameron Sewerage Dist. No. 1, 298 So.2d 319 (La.App.3rd Cir.1974); Crum v. Crum, 330 So.2d 925 (La.App.1st Cir.1976). In many such decisions, the courts have invoked C.C. Art. 1957 (1870), which provides that a doubtful contract is to be interpreted against the obligor, because in those cases the defendant drafted the contract that the plaintiff was trying to enforce. Yet, neither C.C. Art. 1957 (1870) nor C.C. Art. 1958 (1870) squarely supports the traditional jurisprudential rule. Both state broader principles applicable both to written and oral contracts. This Article presents the traditional jurisprudential rule in unequivocal terms.

(c) Under the Article, a contract of adhesion must be interpreted against the party who prepared it. In Golz v. Children's Bureau of New Orleans, Inc., 326 So.2d 865 (La.1976), Louisiana Supreme Court defined this type of contract as follows:

"Broadly defined, a contract of adhesion is a standard contract, usually in printed form, prepared by a party of superior bargaining power for adherence or rejection of the weaker party. Often in small print, these contracts sometimes raise a question as to whether or not the weaker party actually consented to the terms." 326 So.2d 865, 869 (La.1976).

Art. 2057. Contract interpreted in favor of obligor

In case of doubt that cannot be otherwise resolved, a contract must be interpreted against the obligee and in favor of the obligor of a particular obligation.

Yet, if the doubt arises from lack of a necessary explanation that one party should have given, or from negligence or fault of one party, the contract must be interpreted in a manner favorable to the other party whether obligee or obligor.

Acts 1984, No. 331, § 1, eff. Jan. 1, 1985.

REVISION COMMENT—1984

The second paragraph of this Article reproduces the substance of C.C. Art. 1958 (1870). The first paragraph changes the law. It reinstates the rule which was provided by the original text of Article 1952 of the Louisiana Civil Code of 1825, and by Article 1957 of the Civil Code of 1870 before its amendment by Acts 1871, No. 87.

Arts. 2058 to 2291. [Blank]

TITLE V—OBLIGATIONS ARISING WITHOUT AGREEMENT

CHAPTER 1—MANAGEMENT OF AFFAIRS (NEGOTIORUM GESTIO)

Art. 2292. Management of affairs; definition

There is a management of affairs when a person, the manager, acts without authority to protect the interests of another, the owner, in the reasonable belief that the owner would approve of the action if made aware of the circumstances.

Acts 1995, No. 1041, § 1, eff. Jan. 1, 1996.

REVISION COMMENTS—1995

(a) The institution of "management of affairs" (negotiorum gestio) is a typically civilian institution that derives from the Romanist tradition and is found in all civil codes. There is no counterpart in common-law jurisdictions. This Article adopts traditional civilian terminology. The Roman institution of negotiorum gestio has been called "management of affairs" in the Louisiana Civil Codes of 1808, 1825, and 1870 and in other civil codes following the model of the French Civil Code. In the German Civil Code, the expression "management of affairs without mandate" has been used to differentiate negotiorum gestio from mandate.

(b) This Article accords with Article 2295 of the Louisiana Civil Code of 1870. The affair managed may be a material act, such as the protection of property from fire or flood, or the execution of a juridical act, such as the sale of perishable things.

(c) According to French doctrine and jurisprudence that is pertinent for Louisiana, the Civil Code provisions governing the management of affairs apply when there is a necessity or when the owner derives some benefit from the acts of the manager. See 7 Ripert et Planiol, Traité pratique de droit civil français 8 (2d ed. Esmein 1954). In Kirkpatrick v. Young, 456 So.2d 622 (La.1984), the Louisiana Supreme Court declared that a person does not qualify as negotiorum gestor unless he undertakes the management with the "benefit" of the owner in mind.

(d) This Article does not apply when the person who undertakes management acts in his own interest or contrary to the actual or presumed intention of the owner. In such a case, there is a usurpation, and the person who manages an affair under these circumstances may incur liability under the law of delictual obligations.

(e) Dicta in certain Louisiana decisions have confused the institution of negotiorum gestio with that of enrichment without cause. See, e.g., Hobbs v. Central Equip. Rental Inc., 382 So.2d 238 (La.App. 3d Cir.1980); Smith v. Hudson, 519 So.2d 783 (La.App. 1st Cir.1987). The two institutions, however, are distinct. A negotiorum gestor may be entitled to reimbursement of expenses even if the owner has not been enriched at his expense.

Art. 2293. Application of rules governing mandate

A management of affairs is subject to the rules of mandate to the extent those rules are compatible with management of affairs.

Acts 1995, No. 1041, § 1, eff. Jan. 1, 1996.

REVISION COMMENT—1995

This provision is new. It is based on Article 2295(2) of the Louisiana Civil Code of 1870. Corresponding provisions exist in other civil codes.

Art. 2294.   Duties of the manager; notice to the owner

The manager is bound, when the circumstances so warrant, to give notice to the owner that he has undertaken the management and to wait for the directions of the owner, unless there is immediate danger.

Acts 1995, No. 1041, § 1, eff. Jan. 1, 1996.

REVISION COMMENT—1995

This provision is new. It is based on Article 733 of the Greek Civil Code and Section 681 of the German Civil Code.

Art. 2295.   Duties of the manager; liability for loss

The manager must exercise the care of a prudent administrator and is answerable for any loss that results from his failure to do so. The court, considering the circumstances, may reduce the amount due the owner on account of the manager's failure to act as a prudent administrator.

Acts 1995, No. 1041, § 1, eff. Jan. 1, 1996.

REVISION COMMENTS—1995

(a) This provision is new. It is based upon Articles 2298 and 3003 of the Louisiana Civil Code of 1870. There are corresponding provisions in other civil codes.

(b) Under the Louisiana Civil Code of 1870, the responsibility of a mandatary with respect to fault is "enforced less rigorously" when the mandate is gratuitous. Since the management of affairs is gratuitous, the same principle applies in favor of a manager of affairs. See C.C. Art. 3003 (1870).

(c) The manager may also be liable under the law governing delictual obligations for his fraud, fault, or neglect, but not for slight fault. See C.C. Arts. 2315 and 3506(13).

Art. 2296.   Capacity

An incompetent person or a person of limited legal capacity may be the owner of an affair, but he may not be a manager. When such a person manages the affairs of another, the rights and duties of the parties are governed by the law of enrichment without cause or the law of delictual obligations.

Acts 1995, No. 1041, § 1, eff. Jan. 1, 1996.

REVISION COMMENTS—1995

(a) This provision is new. It accords with Article 2300 of the Louisiana Civil Code of 1870 and does not change the law.

(b) Article 2300 of the Louisiana Civil Code of 1870 does not expressly provide that an incompetent or a person of limited capacity may not be a manager of the affair of another person. However, this article, drawn from the common reservoir of the French civilian tradition, implies that there is no management of affairs when the person undertaking the management lacks juridical capacity. See 7 Planiol et Ripert, Traité pratique de droit civil français 12 (2d Ed. Esmein 1954). It is otherwise under the systems of the German Civil Code and the Greek Civil Code.

(c) When an incompetent or a person of limited juridical capacity undertakes the management of the affair of another person, Articles 2292 through 2297 do not apply. The rights and obligations of the parties are governed by laws on enrichment without cause or laws on delictual obligations.

Art. 2297.   Obligations of the owner

The owner whose affair has been managed is bound to fulfill the obligations that the manager has undertaken as a prudent administrator and to reimburse the manager for all necessary and useful expenses.

Acts 1995, No. 1041, § 1, eff. Jan. 1, 1996.

REVISION COMMENTS—1995

(a) This Article is new and is based on Article 2299 of the Louisiana Civil Code of 1870.

(b) This Article following the French legal tradition, imposes liability on the owner, for juridical acts performed by the manager, as if the manager had authority under an express mandate. Obviously, management of affairs and mandate overlap under this approach. It is different under the systems of the German Civil Code and the Greek Civil Code. Under these codes, management of affairs and mandate are clearly distinguishable institutions and the manager of affairs has no authority to enter into juridical acts in the name of the owner. As a result, the owner is never bound by the juridical acts that the manager executes in his name.

(c) When the manager acts as a prudent administrator, whether in his own name or in the name of the owner, the owner is bound to fulfill the obligations undertaken by the manager.

CHAPTER 2—ENRICHMENT WITHOUT CAUSE

SECTION 1—GENERAL PRINCIPLES

Art. 2298. Enrichment without cause; compensation

A person who has been enriched without cause at the expense of another person is bound to compensate that person. The term "without cause" is used in this context to exclude cases in which the enrichment results from a valid juridical act or the law. The remedy declared here is subsidiary and shall not be available if the law provides another remedy for the impoverishment or declares a contrary rule.

The amount of compensation due is measured by the extent to which one has been enriched or the other has been impoverished, whichever is less.

The extent of the enrichment or impoverishment is measured as of the time the suit is brought or, according to the circumstances, as of the time the judgment is rendered.

Acts 1995, No. 1041, § 1, eff. Jan. 1, 1996.

REVISION COMMENTS—1995

(a) This provision is new. It expresses the principle of enrichment without cause that was inherent but not fully expressed in the Louisiana Civil Code of 1870. The formulation of the principle accords with civilian doctrine and jurisprudence.

(b) A person is enriched within the meaning of this Article when his patrimonial assets increase or his liabilities diminish. Correspondingly, a person is impoverished when his patrimonial assets diminish or his liabilities increase. There must be a causal connection, whether direct or indirect, between a person's enrichment and another person's impoverishment.

(c) The Louisiana Supreme Court has recognized the principle of enrichment without cause in Minyard v. Curtis Products, Inc., 251 La. 624, 205 So.2d 422 (1967) in the form of the actio de in rem verso as a subsidiary remedy. Under Article 2298, recovery for "enrichment without cause" is still a subsidiary remedy. If there is an enrichment without cause, a claimant may recover "the amount . . . by . . . which one has been enriched or the other has been impoverished, whichever is less".

SECTION 2—PAYMENT OF A THING NOT OWED

Art. 2299. Obligation to restore

A person who has received a payment or a thing not owed to him is bound to restore it to the person from whom he received it.

Acts 1995, No. 1041, § 1, eff. Jan. 1, 1996.

REVISION COMMENTS—1995

(a) This provision is based on Article 2301 of the Louisiana Civil Code of 1870.

(b) Article 2301 of the Louisiana Civil Code of 1870 declares: "He who receives what is not due to him, whether he receives it through error or knowingly, obliges himself to restore it to him from whom he has unduly received it." Louisiana courts interpreting this provision have correctly ordered persons who received things or payments not owed to return them to the persons who made the delivery or the payment. Under Article 2299, as under Article 2301 of the Louisiana Civil Code of 1870, the person who receives a thing or a payment not owed, whether knowingly or through error, must restore it to the person from whom he received it.

(c) The remedy that Article 2299 provides is not subsidiary; this remedy is available even if other remedies are also available but there can be no double recovery. A plaintiff who may avail himself of several theories of recovery, one of which is the delivery or payment of a thing not owed, may choose the theory of recovery that best suits his interests, See Yiannopoulos, Civil Law Property Sections 356–358 (3d ed. 1991). Thus, a plaintiff may choose to bring an action in revendication, an action in tort, an action grounded on enrichment without cause, or an action grounded on Article 2299 for the return of a thing not owed. Ibid.

(d) Article 2302 of the Louisiana Civil Code of 1870 declares: "He who has paid through mistake, believing himself a debtor, may reclaim what he has paid." This provision derives from the 1825 Revision and has no counterpart in the French Civil Code or in the Louisiana Civil Code of 1808. The provision has been suppressed. Under Article 2299, a person who knowingly or through error has paid or delivered a thing not owed may reclaim it from the person who received it.

Art. 2300. Obligation that does not exist

A thing is not owed when it is paid or delivered for the discharge of an obligation that does not exist.

Acts 1995, No. 1041, § 1, eff. Jan. 1, 1996.

REVISION COMMENTS—1995

(a) This provision reproduces the substance of Articles 2304 and 2305 of the Louisiana Civil Code of 1870. It does not change the law.

(b) Articles 2304 and 2305 of the Louisiana Civil Code of 1870 have no counterpart in the French Civil Code or in modern civil codes. These Articles derive from the 1825 revision. The redactors reproduced the text of Pothier, Prêt de Consommation, Part III, Section II, Article I, note 143. According to Pothier, an example of a payment for the discharge of an obligation that does not exist is the case of an heir who pays a legacy without knowing that the will was revoked. An example of a payment by virtue of a title that is null is the payment of the price of a sale by a purchaser who does not know that he has purchased a thing he owns. The sale is null and the price may be reclaimed. Ibid. For Louisiana jurisprudence interpreting Civil Code Article 2304 (1870), see C.H. Fenstermaker & Assoc. v. Regard, 471 So.2d 1137 (La.App. 3rd Cir.1985); International Harvester Credit Corporation v. Seale, 518 So.2d 1039 (La.1988). Civil Code Article 2305 (1870) has not been cited in any Louisiana decision.

Art. 2301. Obligation under suspensive condition

A thing is not owed when it is paid or delivered for discharge of an obligation that is subject to a suspensive condition.

Acts 1995, No. 1041, § 1, eff. Jan. 1, 1996.

REVISION COMMENTS—1995

(a) This provision is new. It is based on Articles 2308 and 2309 of the Louisiana Civil Code of 1870.

(b) Articles 2308 and 2309 of the Louisiana Civil Code of 1870 have no counterpart in the French Civil Code or in modern civil codes. They derive from the 1825 Revision. The redactors reproduced the text of Pothier, Prêt de Consommation, Part III, Section II, Article I, notes 150 and 151. Civil Code Articles 2308 and 2309 (1870) have been cited in a note in Texas General Petroleum Corp. v. Brown, 408 So.2d 288 (La.App. 2d Cir.1981). See also Merrill Lynch Realty, Inc. v. Williams, 526 So.2d 380 (La.App. 4th Cir.1988) (prospective vendors were entitled to recover deposit when the financing method was subject to a suspensive condition that failed).

(c) The solution that this Article furnishes is a natural consequence of an obligation subject to a suspensive condition. Although the obligation exists, performance is suspended during the pendency of the condition. Conditional obligations are dealt with in Civil Code Articles 1767 through 1776 (Rev.1984), and obligations subject to term are dealt with in Civil Code Articles 1777 through 1785 (Rev.1984). A conditional obligation is one dependent on an uncertain event; a suspensive condition is one that prevents enforcement of the obligation until the happening of the uncertain event. C.C. Art. 1767 (Rev.1984).

(d) A thing paid or delivered for the discharge of an obligation that is subject to a term, whether certain or uncertain, is owed and cannot be reclaimed. Civil Code Article 1781 (Rev.1984) declares that: "Although performance cannot be demanded before the term ends, an obligor who has performed voluntarily before the term ends may not recover the performance."

Art. 2302. Payment of the debt of another person

A person who paid the debt of another person in the erroneous belief that he was himself the obligor may reclaim the payment from the obligee. The payment may not be reclaimed to the extent that the obligee, because of the payment, disposed of the instrument or released the securities relating to the claim. In such a case, the person who made the payment has a recourse against the true obligor.

Acts 1995, No. 1041, § 1, eff. Jan. 1, 1996.

REVISION COMMENTS—1995

(a) Article 2302 is new. It is based on Article 2310 of the Louisiana Civil Code of 1870.

(b) Civil Code Article 1855 (Rev.1984) provides that: "Performance may be rendered by a third person, even against the will of the obligee, unless the obligor or the obligee has an interest in performance only by the obligor." When performance has been rendered by a third person, the same article declares that the third person is subrogated to the rights of the obligee "only when so provided by law or by agreement."

(c) A person who paid the debt of another person in the erroneous belief that he was himself the debtor may recover from the obligee "the payment," that is, the thing given. When the payment may not be reclaimed from the obligee, the person who made the payment has "a recourse against the true obligor," that is, he can recover from him whatever he paid to the obligee.

Art. 2303. Liability of the person receiving payment

A person who in bad faith received a payment or a thing not owed to him is bound to restore it with its fruits and products.

Acts 1995, No. 1041, § 1, eff. Jan. 1, 1996.

REVISION COMMENT—1995

This provision is new. It is based on Article 2311 of the Louisiana Civil Code of 1870 and corresponding provisions in other civil codes. For explanations or definitions of the terms "fruits" and "products", see Civil Code Articles 551 and 488 (Rev.1976).

Art. 2304. Restoration of a thing or its value

When the thing not owed is an immovable or a corporeal movable, the person who received it is bound to restore the thing itself, if it exists.

If the thing has been destroyed, damaged, or cannot be returned, a person who received the thing in good faith is bound to restore its value if the loss was caused by his fault. A person who received the thing in bad faith is bound to restore its value even if the loss was not caused by his fault.

Acts 1995, No. 1041, § 1, eff. Jan. 1, 1996.

REVISION COMMENTS—1995

(a) This provision is based on Article 2312 of the Louisiana Civil Code of 1870. It clarifies the law.

(b) For an interpretation of Article 1379 of the French Civil Code, which corresponds to Article 2312 of the Louisiana Civil Code of 1870, see 7 Planiol et Ripert, Traité pratique de droit civil français, Obligations, 33 (2d ed. 1954): "The defendant must make restitution in natura, if the immovable or corporeal movable he received still exists (Art. 1379). If the thing has been destroyed or if it has deteriorated while in his possession, he incurs no responsibility if the destruction or deterioration occurred while, having received the thing in good faith, was still in good faith; in such a case, he must make restitution of whatever remains of the thing, of the actions resulting from the destruction or deterioration of the thing, and of the sums he may have received on account of that occasion. If, having received the thing in good faith, he had ceased to be in good faith, he is responsible when the thing has been destroyed by his fault. Finally, if he received the thing in bad faith, he is answerable for fortuitous events, but without being responsible in situations in which a debtor in default ceases to be answerable for fortuitous events."

(c) Quite apart from this Article, the owner of a thing may reclaim it by a petitory or a revendicatory action. See La.Civil Code Art. 526 (Rev.1979); Yiannopoulos, Civil Law Property § 350 (3d ed. 1991).

(d) A person may be liable for delictual damages when a thing cannot be returned because it was destroyed as a result of that person's intentional fault.

Art. 2305.   Liability when the thing is alienated

A person who in good faith alienated a thing not owed to him is only bound to restore whatever he obtained from the alienation. If he received the thing in bad faith, he owes, in addition, damages to the person to whom restoration is due.

Acts 1995, No. 1041, § 1, eff. Jan. 1, 1996.

REVISION COMMENTS—1995

(a) This provision is based on Article 2313 of the Louisiana Civil Code of 1870. It clarifies the law.

(b) Article 2313 of the Louisiana Civil Code of 1870 speaks of "sale". The rule has been broadened to include any alienation. "Alienation" includes a transfer by gratuitous title, that is, a donation. As under the Louisiana Civil Code of 1870, under Article 2306, a person who donates a thing he received in good faith owes nothing to the person who made the payment.

(c) Quite apart from Article 2306, the owner of an immovable may reclaim it by the petitory action and the owner of a corporeal movable may reclaim it by a revendicatory action. See Louisiana Civil Code Art. 525 (Rev.1979); Yiannopoulos, Civil Law Property Sec. 350 (3d ed. 1991).

(d) For an interpretation of Article 1380 of the French Civil Code, which corresponds to Article 2313 of the Louisiana Civil Code of 1870, see 7 Planiol et Ripert, Traité pratique de droit civil français, Obligations, 33 (2d ed. 1954): "If he sold the thing, being in good faith, he must make restitution of the price of the sale only (Art. 1380). If he was in bad faith, he owes the actual value if the thing, if that value is higher than the price of the sale. If he made a donation, being in good faith, he owes nothing; if he was in bad faith, he owes the value of the thing."

(e) The second paragraph of Article 2313 of the Louisiana Civil Code of 1870 derives from the 1825 revision. There is no corresponding provision in the Louisiana Civil Code of 1808 or in the French Civil Code. The source of this provision appears to be 11 Toullier, Droit civil français, Des Engagements qui se forment sans convention 133 (1842): "If he [the person who received a thing in bad faith] is, by his own doing, unable to restore the thing itself, for example, if he sold it, he is not relieved of the obligation to restore the thing itself by making restitution of its price, as is the case of a person who received a thing in good faith; and, as he cannot restore the thing he has sold, he is bound to pay full damages and interest to him who was entitled to the restitution of the thing itself."

Arts. 2306 to 2314. [Blank]

CHAPTER 3—OF OFFENSES AND QUASI OFFENSES

Art. 2315.   Liability for acts causing damages

A.   Every act whatever of man that causes damage to another obliges him by whose fault it happened to repair it.

B.   Damages may include loss of consortium, service, and society, and shall be recoverable by the same respective categories of persons who would have had a cause of action for wrongful death of an injured person. Damages do not include costs for future medical treatment, services, surveillance, or procedures of any kind unless such treatment, services, surveillance, or procedures are directly related to a manifest physical or mental injury or disease. Damages shall include any sales taxes paid by the owner on the repair or replacement of the property damaged.

Amended by Acts 1884, No. 71; Acts 1908, No. 120, § 1; Acts 1918, No. 159, § 1; Acts 1932, No. 159, § 1; Acts 1948, No. 333, § 1; Acts 1960, No. 30, § 1, eff. Jan. 1, 1961; Acts 1982, No. 202, § 1; Acts 1984, No. 397, § 1; Acts 1986, No. 211, § 1; Acts 1999, No. 989, § 1, eff. July 9, 1999; Acts 2001, No. 478, § 1.

Art. 2315.1.   Survival action

A.   If a person who has been injured by an offense or quasi offense dies, the right to recover all damages for injury to that person, his property or otherwise, caused by the offense or quasi offense, shall survive for a period of one year from the death of the deceased in favor of:

(1) The surviving spouse and child or children of the deceased, or either the spouse or the child or children.

(2) The surviving father and mother of the deceased, or either of them if he left no spouse or child surviving.

(3) The surviving brothers and sisters of the deceased, or any of them, if he left no spouse, child, or parent surviving.

(4) The surviving grandfathers and grandmothers of the deceased, or any of them, if he left no spouse, child, parent, or sibling surviving.

B.   In addition, the right to recover all damages for injury to the deceased, his property or otherwise, caused by the offense or quasi offense, may be urged by the deceased's succession representative in the absence of any class of beneficiary set out in Paragraph A.

C.   The right of action granted under this Article is heritable, but the inheritance of it neither interrupts nor prolongs the prescriptive period defined in this Article.

D.   As used in this Article, the words "child", "brother", "sister", "father", "mother", "grandfather", and "grandmother" include a child, brother, sister, father, mother, grandfather, and grandmother by adoption, respectively.

E.   For purposes of this Article, a father or mother who has abandoned the deceased during his minority is deemed not to have survived him.

Added by Acts 1986, No. 211, § 2. Amended by Acts 1987, No. 675, § 1; Acts 1997, No. 1317, § 1, eff. July 15, 1997.

Art. 2315.2.   Wrongful death action

A.   If a person dies due to the fault of another, suit may be brought by the following persons to recover damages which they sustained as a result of the death:

(1) The surviving spouse and child or children of the deceased, or either the spouse or the child or children.

(2) The surviving father and mother of the deceased, or either of them if he left no spouse or child surviving.

(3) The surviving brothers and sisters of the deceased, or any of them, if he left no spouse, child, or parent surviving.

(4) The surviving grandfathers and grandmothers of the deceased, or any of them, if he left no spouse, child, parent, or sibling surviving.

B.   The right of action granted by this Article prescribes one year from the death of the deceased.

C.   The right of action granted under this Article is heritable, but the inheritance of it neither interrupts nor prolongs the prescriptive period defined in this Article.

D.   As used in this Article, the words "child", "brother", "sister", "father", "mother", "grandfather", and "grandmother" include a child, brother, sister, father, mother, grandfather, and grandmother by adoption, respectively.

E.   For purposes of this Article, a father or mother who has abandoned the deceased during his minority is deemed not to have survived him.

Added by Acts 1986, No. 211, § 2. Amended by Acts 1997, No. 1317, § 1, eff. July 15, 1997.

Art. 2315.3. Additional damages; child pornography

In addition to general and special damages, exemplary damages may be awarded upon proof that the injuries on which the action is based were caused by a wanton and reckless disregard for the rights and safety of the person through an act of pornography involving juveniles, as defined by R.S. 14:81.1, regardless of whether the defendant was prosecuted for his acts.

Added by Acts 2009, No. 382, § 1.

Art. 2315.4. Additional damages; intoxicated defendant

In addition to general and special damages, exemplary damages may be awarded upon proof that the injuries on which the action is based were caused by a wanton or reckless disregard for the rights and safety of others by a defendant whose intoxication while operating a motor vehicle was a cause in fact of the resulting injuries.

Added by Acts 1984; No. 511, § 1.

Art. 2315.5. Wrongful death and survival action; exception

Notwithstanding any other provision of law to the contrary, the surviving spouse, parent, or child of a deceased, who has been convicted of a crime involving the intentional killing or attempted killing of the deceased, or, if not convicted, who has been judicially determined to have participated in the intentional, unjustified killing or attempted killing of the deceased, shall not be entitled to any damages or proceeds in a survival action or an action for wrongful death of the deceased, or to any proceeds distributed in settlement of any such cause of action. In such case, the other child or children of the deceased, or if the deceased left no other child surviving, the other survivors enumerated in the applicable provisions of Articles 2315.1(A) and 2315.2(A), in order of preference stated, may bring a survival action against such surviving spouse, parent, or child, or an action against such surviving spouse, parent, or child for the wrongful death of the deceased.

An executive pardon shall not restore the surviving spouse's, parent's, or child's right to any damages or proceeds in a survival action or an action for wrongful death of the deceased.

Added by Acts 1987, No. 690, § 1. Amended by Acts 1991, No. 180, § 1.

Art. 2315.6. Liability for damages caused by injury to another

A.   The following persons who view an event causing injury to another person, or who come upon the scene of the event soon thereafter, may recover damages for mental anguish or emotional distress that they suffer as a result of the other person's injury:

(1) The spouse, child or children, and grandchild or grandchildren of the injured person, or either the spouse, the child or children, or the grandchild or grandchildren of the injured person.

(2) The father and mother of the injured person, or either of them.

(3) The brothers and sisters of the injured person or any of them.

(4) The grandfather and grandmother of the injured person, or either of them.

B.   To recover for mental anguish or emotional distress under this Article, the injured person must suffer such harm that one can reasonably expect a person in the claimant's position to suffer serious mental anguish or emotional distress from the experience, and the claimant's mental anguish or emotional distress must be severe, debilitating, and foreseeable. Damages suffered as a result of mental anguish or emotional distress for injury to another shall be recovered only in accordance with this Article.

Added by Acts 1991, No. 782, § 1.

Art. 2315.7. Liability for damages caused by criminal sexual activity occurring during childhood

In addition to general and special damages, exemplary damages may be awarded upon proof that the injuries on which the action is based were caused by a wanton and reckless disregard for the rights and safety of the person through criminal sexual activity which occurred when the victim was seventeen years old or younger, regardless of whether the defendant was prosecuted for his or her acts. The provisions of this Article shall be applicable only to the perpetrator of the criminal sexual activity.

Added by Acts 1993, No. 831, § 1, eff. June 22, 1993.

Art. 2315.8. Liability for damages caused by domestic abuse

A.   In addition to general and special damages, exemplary damages may be awarded upon proof that the injuries on which the action is based were caused by a wanton and reckless disregard for the rights and safety of a family or household member, as defined in R.S. 46:2132, through acts of domestic abuse resulting in serious bodily injury or severe emotional and mental distress, regardless of whether the defendant was prosecuted for his or her acts.

B.   Upon motion of the defendant or upon its own motion, if the court determines that any action alleging domestic abuse is frivolous or fraudulent, the court shall award costs of court, reasonable attorney fees, and any other related costs to the defendant and any other sanctions and relief requested pursuant to Code of Civil Procedure Article 863.

Added by Acts 2014, No. 315, § 1.

Art. 2316. Negligence, imprudence or want of skill

Every person is responsible for the damage he occasions not merely by his act, but by his negligence, his imprudence, or his want of skill.

Art. 2317. Acts of others and of things in custody

We are responsible, not only for the damage occasioned by our own act, but for that which is caused by the act of persons for whom we are answerable, or of the things which we have in our custody. This, however, is to be understood with the following modifications.

Art. 2317.1. Damage caused by ruin, vice, or defect in things

The owner or custodian of a thing is answerable for damage occasioned by its ruin, vice, or defect, only upon a showing that he knew or, in the exercise of reasonable care, should have known of the ruin, vice, or defect which caused the damage, that the damage could have been prevented by the exercise of reasonable care, and that he failed to exercise such reasonable care. Nothing in this Article shall preclude the court from the application of the doctrine of res ipsa loquitur in an appropriate case.

Added by Acts 1996, 1st Ex.Sess., No. 1, § 1, eff. April 16, 1996.

Art. 2318. Acts of a minor

The father and the mother are responsible for the damage occasioned by their minor child, who resides with them or who has been placed by them under the care of other persons, reserving to them recourse against those persons. However, the father and mother are not responsible for the damage occasioned by their minor child who has been emancipated by marriage, by judgment of full emancipation, or by judgment of limited emancipation that expressly relieves the parents of liability for damages occasioned by their minor child.

The same responsibility attaches to the tutors of minors.

Amended by Acts 1984, No. 578, § 1; Acts 2008, No. 786, § 1, eff. Jan. 1, 2009.

REVISION COMMENT—2008

The purpose of the 2008 amendment to this Article is to clarify the types of emancipation that will relieve parents from tort liability for their minor children. There is no intent to change the judicial interpretation of Civil Code Article 2318 as expressed in Turner v. Butcher, 308 So.2d 270 (La. 1975). This Article, in connection with the 2008 Revision of the law of Emancipation, does change the law as expressed in the case of Held v. Wilt, 610 So.2d 1103 (La.App. 5 Cir. 1982) which held that a notarial emancipation relieves a parent from tort liability for the acts of his minor children. Compare Keller v. Rednour, 416 So.2d 357 (La.App. 4 Cir. 1982). Under the Revision, an emancipation by authentic act has limited effects and does not affect the liability of a parent under Civil Code Article 2318. See Civil Code Article 368 (Rev. 2008). This Article is not intended to change the law with respect to other types of emancipation. See Speziale v. Kohnke, 194 So.2d 485 (La.App. 4 Cir. 1967) (father not liable for tort committed by judicially emancipated minor) and Stough v. Young, 185 So.2d 476 (La.App. 2 Cir. 1938) (parent not liable for acts of child emancipated by marriage).

Art. 2319. Acts of interdicts

Neither a curator nor an undercurator is personally responsible to a third person for a delictual obligation of the interdict in his charge solely by reason of his office.

Acts 2000, 1st Ex.Sess., No. 25, § 2, eff. July 1, 2001.

REVISION COMMENTS—2000

(a) This Article is new and changes the law. This Article was revised by the legislature in 2000 as part of a comprehensive revision of Louisiana's interdiction laws. Under Article 2319 of the Civil Code of 1870, "(t)he curators of insane persons are answerable for the damage occasioned by those under their care". See Civil Code Article 2319 (1870). As revised, this Article shields curators and undercurators from vicarious liability for the torts of interdicts in their charge.

(b) Although a curator is not personally responsible for an interdict's torts solely by reason of the relationship, the curator may be liable for damages resulting from his own acts or omissions. For example, if a curator negligently supervises an interdict in his charge and, as a result, the interdict causes damages to himself or to a third party, the curator may be personally responsible for the resulting damages.

Art. 2320. Acts of servants, students or apprentices

Masters and employers are answerable for the damage occasioned by their servants and overseers, in the exercise of the functions in which they are employed.

Teachers and artisans are answerable for the damage caused by their scholars or apprentices, while under their superintendence.

In the above cases, responsibility only attaches, when the masters or employers, teachers and artisans, might have prevented the act which caused the damage, and have not done it.

The master is answerable for the offenses and quasi-offenses committed by his servants, according to the rules which are explained under the title: Of quasi-contracts, and of offenses and quasi-offenses.

Art. 2321. Damage caused by animals

The owner of an animal is answerable for the damage caused by the animal. However, he is answerable for the damage only upon a showing that he knew or, in the exercise of reasonable care, should have known that his animal's behavior would cause damage, that the damage could have been prevented by the exercise of reasonable care, and that he failed to exercise such reasonable care. Nonetheless, the owner of a dog is strictly liable for damages for injuries to persons or property caused by the dog and which the owner could have prevented and which did not result from the injured person's provocation of the dog. Nothing in this Article shall preclude the court from the application of the doctrine of res ipsa loquitur in an appropriate case.

Amended by Acts 1996, 1st Ex.Sess., No. 1, § 1, eff. April 16, 1996.

Art. 2322. Damage caused by ruin of building

The owner of a building is answerable for the damage occasioned by its ruin, when this is caused by neglect to repair it, or when it is the result of a vice or defect in its original construction. However, he is answerable for damages only upon a showing that he knew or, in the exercise of reasonable care, should have known of the vice or defect which caused the damage, that the damage could have been prevented by the exercise of reasonable care, and that he failed to exercise such reasonable care. Nothing in this Article shall preclude the court from the application of the doctrine of res ipsa loquitur in an appropriate case.

Amended by Acts 1996, 1st Ex.Sess., No. 1, § 1, eff. April 16, 1996.

Art. 2322.1. Users of blood or tissue; a medical service

A. The screening, procurement, processing, distribution, transfusion, or medical use of human blood and blood components of any kind and the transplantation or medical use of any human organ, human tissue, or approved animal tissue by physicians, dentists, hospitals, hospital blood banks, and nonprofit community blood banks is declared to be, for all purposes whatsoever, the rendition of a medical service by each and every physician, dentist, hospital, hospital blood bank, and nonprofit community blood bank participating therein, and shall not be construed to be and is declared not to be a sale. Strict liability and warranties of any kind without negligence shall not be applicable to the aforementioned who provide these medical services.

B. In any action based in whole or in part on the use of blood or tissue by a healthcare provider, to which the provisions of Paragraph A do not apply, the plaintiff shall have the burden of proving all elements of his claim, including a defect in the thing sold and causation of his injuries by the defect, by a preponderance of the evidence, unaided by any presumption.

C. The provisions of Paragraphs A and B are procedural and shall apply to all alleged causes of action or other act, omission, or neglect without regard to the date when the alleged cause of action or other act, omission, or neglect occurred.

D. As used in this Article:

(1) "Healthcare provider" includes all individuals and entities listed in R.S. 9:2797, this Article, R.S. 40:1299.39 and R.S. 40:1299.41 whether or not enrolled with the Patient's Compensation Fund.

(2) "The use of blood or tissue" means the screening, procurement, processing, distribution, transfusion, or any medical use of human blood, blood products, and blood components of any kind, and the transplantation or medical use of any human organ, human or approved animal tissue, and tissue products or tissue components by any healthcare provider.

Added by Acts 1981, No. 611, § 1. Amended by Acts 1990, No. 1091, § 1; Acts 1999, No. 539, § 2, eff. June 30, 1999.

Art. 2323. Comparative fault

A. In any action for damages where a person suffers injury, death, or loss, the degree or percentage of fault of all persons causing or contributing to the injury, death, or loss shall be determined, regardless of whether the person is a party to the action or a nonparty, and regardless of the person's insolvency, ability to pay, immunity by statute, including but not limited to the provisions of R.S. 23:1032, or that the other person's identity is not known or reasonably ascertainable. If a person suffers injury, death, or loss as the result partly of his own negligence and partly as a result of the fault of another person or persons, the amount of damages recoverable shall be reduced in proportion to the degree or percentage of negligence attributable to the person suffering the injury, death, or loss.

B.   The provisions of Paragraph A shall apply to any claim for recovery of damages for injury, death, or loss asserted under any law or legal doctrine or theory of liability, regardless of the basis of liability.

C.   Notwithstanding the provisions of Paragraphs A and B, if a person suffers injury, death, or loss as a result partly of his own negligence and partly as a result of the fault of an intentional tortfeasor, his claim for recovery of damages shall not be reduced.

Amended by Acts 1979, No. 431, § 1, eff. Aug. 1, 1980; Acts 1996, 1st Ex.Sess., No. 3, § 1, eff. April 16, 1996.

Art. 2324.   Liability as solidary or joint and divisible obligation

A.   He who conspires with another person to commit an intentional or willful act is answerable, in solido, with that person, for the damage caused by such act.

B.   If liability is not solidary pursuant to Paragraph A, then liability for damages caused by two or more persons shall be a joint and divisible obligation. A joint tortfeasor shall not be liable for more than his degree of fault and shall not be solidarily liable with any other person for damages attributable to the fault of such other person, including the person suffering injury, death, or loss, regardless of such other person's insolvency, ability to pay, degree of fault, immunity by statute or otherwise, including but not limited to immunity as provided in R.S. 23:1032, or that the other person's identity is not known or reasonably ascertainable.

C.   Interruption of prescription against one joint tortfeasor is effective against all joint tortfeasors.

Amended by Acts 1979, No. 431, § 1, eff. Aug. 1, 1980; Acts 1987, No. 373, § 1; Acts 1988, No. 430, § 1; Acts 1996, 1st Ex.Sess., No. 3, § 1, eff. April 16, 1996.

Art. 2324.1.   Damages; discretion of judge or jury

In the assessment of damages in cases of offenses, quasi offenses, and quasi contracts, much discretion must be left to the judge or jury.

Added by Acts 1984, No. 331, § 3, eff. Jan. 1, 1985.

Art. 2324.2.   Reduction of recovery

A.   When the recovery of damages by a person suffering injury, death, or loss is reduced in some proportion by application of Article 2323 or 2324 and there is a legal or conventional subrogation, then the subrogee's recovery shall be reduced in the same proportion as the subrogor's recovery.

B.   Nothing herein precludes such persons and legal or conventional subrogees from agreeing to a settlement which would incorporate a different method or proportion of subrogee recovery for amounts paid by the legal or conventional subrogee under the Louisiana Worker's Compensation Act, R.S. 23:1021, et seq.

Added by Acts 1989, No. 771, § 1, eff. July 9, 1989.

TITLE VI—MATRIMONIAL REGIMES

CHAPTER 1—GENERAL PRINCIPLES

Art. 2325. Matrimonial regime

A matrimonial regime is a system of principles and rules governing the ownership and management of the property of married persons as between themselves and toward third persons.

Acts 1979, No. 709, § 1, eff. Jan. 1, 1980.

REVISION COMMENTS—1979

(a) The definition of a matrimonial regime accords with civilian doctrine. See 8 Planiol et Ripert, Traité pratique de droit civil français No. 2 (2d ed. Boulanger 1957); 12 Toullier, Droit civil français 203 (1833); 21 Laurent, Principes de droit civil français No. 3 (1876).

(b) In the Louisiana Civil Code of 1870, the word "property" is at times a translation of the word propriete and at times a translation of biens. See Yiannopoulos, Civil Law Property § 1 (2d ed. 1980). Following the terminology of the 1870 Code, the word "property" in this revision is at times used to mean things (see, e.g., Articles 2338, 2365 infra), and at times to mean patrimony (see e.g., Articles 2325, 2335, 2374–2376, infra).

Art. 2326. Kinds of matrimonial regimes

A matrimonial regime may be legal, contractual, or partly legal and partly contractual.

Acts 1979, No. 709, § 1, eff. Jan. 1, 1980.

REVISION COMMENTS—1979

This provision is new. It introduces the following articles.

Art. 2327. Legal regime

The legal regime is the community of acquets and gains established in Chapter 2 of this Title.

Acts 1979, No. 709, § 1, eff. Jan. 1, 1980.

REVISION COMMENTS—1979

(a) The legal matrimonial regime is the community of acquets and gains established in Title VI, Chapter 2 of the Louisiana Civil Code. Unless excluded by matrimonial agreement, the legal regime governs the ownership and management of the property of married persons as between themselves and third persons. See Art. 2325, supra.

(b) Jurisprudence and doctrine frequently refer to the community of "acquets and gains". The Louisiana Civil Code of 1870 refers to the community of "acquets or gains". See C.C. Arts. 63–85, pp. 336–340 (1808); (communauté d'acquets ou de gains; translated as "community of acquets or gains"); C.C. Arts. 2369–2423 (1825) (same).

In the Louisiana Civil Code of 1870, Book II, Title VI, Chapter 3 is titled "Of the Community or Partnership of Acquets or Gains". Articles 2332 and 2399 refer to "acquets or gains"; Articles 2386, 2403–2406, 2409–2411, 2413, 2418, 2419, 2421, and 2423 simply refer to the "community of gains"; Article 2401 refers to the "community of acquets"; and only Articles 2386 and 2400 refer to the "community of acquets and gains". This last article was first adopted in the 1870 revision. It has no corresponding provision in the French Civil Code or in the Louisiana Civil Codes of 1808 or 1825. In this revision "acquets" is understood to mean acquisitions; and "gains" is understood to mean an increase in the value of property through the common skill or labor of the spouses.

(c) For the nature of a community property regime, see Article 2336, Comment (c), infra. For the nature of a spouse's right to manage, control, and dispose of community property, see Article 2336, Comment (d), infra.

Art. 2328.   Contractual regime; matrimonial agreement

A matrimonial agreement is a contract establishing a regime of separation of property or modifying or terminating the legal regime. Spouses are free to establish by matrimonial agreement a regime of separation of property or modify the legal regime as provided by law. The provisions of the legal regime that have not been excluded or modified by agreement retain their force and effect.

Acts 1979, No. 709, § 1, eff. Jan. 1, 1980.

REVISION COMMENTS—1979

(a) Spouses are free to establish a matrimonial regime of their choice subject to limitations contained in this Title and other laws. Arts. 2329, 2330, and 2337, infra; cf. C.C. Art. 11 (1870). In the absence of a matrimonial agreement excluding the legal regime, the spouses are subject to it.

(b) A matrimonial agreement is governed by the general rules of conventional obligations unless otherwise provided in this Title. The provisions of a matrimonial agreement may not prejudice third persons. See C.C. Arts. 1502 (1870) and 2036 (Rev.1984).

(c) Under the Louisiana Civil Code of 1870, a matrimonial agreement was a part or a species of marriage contract, that is, an antenuptial agreement determining the property relations of the future spouses as between themselves and toward third persons. Cf. C.C. Arts. 1734–1755 and 2325–2437 (1870); 8 Planiol et Ripert, Traité pratique de droit civil français 51 (2d ed. Boulanger 1957).

In this revision, the term "matrimonial agreement" has the same meaning as a "marriage contract". However, in contrast with the existing law, a matrimonial agreement may be executed before marriage or during marriage. Art. 2329, infra.

Nevertheless, Articles 1734 through 1755 of the Louisiana Civil Code of 1870, employing the term "marriage contract" continue to be applicable to antenuptial agreement only.

Art. 2329.   Exclusion or modification of matrimonial regime

Spouses may enter into a matrimonial agreement before or during marriage as to all matters that are not prohibited by public policy.

Spouses may enter into a matrimonial agreement that modifies or terminates a matrimonial regime during marriage only upon joint petition and a finding by the court that this serves their best interests and that they understand the governing principles and rules. They may, however, subject themselves to the legal regime by a matrimonial agreement at any time without court approval.

During the first year after moving into and acquiring a domicile in this state, spouses may enter into a matrimonial agreement without court approval.

Acts 1979, No. 709, § 1, eff. Jan. 1, 1980. Amended by Acts 1980, No. 565, § 1.

REVISION COMMENTS—1979

(a) Spouses are free to contract with each other during marriage as to all matters that are not prohibited by public policy. For example, they may sell or lease property to each other; they may enter into a compromise agreement; they may even employ each other. The incapacities based on marital status, contained in Article 1790 of the 1870 Code, have been removed. See Acts 1979, No. 711, § 1.

(b) Prior to marriage, spouses may enter into a matrimonial agreement subject to the provisions of this Revision, and they may freely modify it. During marriage, spouses may subject themselves to the legal regime by a matrimonial agreement, otherwise, spouses may terminate or modify a matrimonial regime only upon joint petition and a finding by the court that this serves their best interests and that they understand the governing principles and rules.

(c) Articles 1734 through 1755 of the Louisiana Civil Code deal with marriage contracts, that is, matrimonial agreements made in contemplation of the marriage. These provisions continue being applicable.

(d) A matrimonial regime may be partly legal and partly contractual. This is the case when the spouses exclude, modify, or limit provisions of the legal regime of a community of acquets and gains.

The provisions of the legal regime that have not been excluded, limited, or modified by contract retain their force and effect.

(e) A matrimonial agreement in fraud of creditors may be set aside by the revocatory action. A creditor may sue to annul a matrimonial agreement as in fraud of his rights under Articles 2036–2044 of the Civil Code as revised by Acts 1984, No. 331. Cf. C.C. Arts. 11 and 3183 (1870); Art. 2376, infra.

Art. 2330. Limits of contractual freedom

Spouses may not by agreement before or during marriage, renounce or alter the marital portion or the established order of succession. Nor may the spouses limit with respect to third persons the right that one spouse alone has under the legal regime to obligate the community or to alienate, encumber, or lease community property.

Acts 1979, No. 709, § 1, eff. Jan. 1, 1980.

REVISION COMMENTS—1979

(a) Spouses may not by matrimonial agreement renounce or alter the marital portion or the established order of succession prior to the death of a spouse. After the death of a spouse, the survivor may, of course, renounce the marital portion. The rules establishing the marital portion and the order of succession are rules of public order that may not be derogated from by agreement. C.C. Art. 11 (1870).

(b) A matrimonial agreement is a contract. An antenuptial matrimonial agreement may contain testamentary provisions. See C.C. Arts. 1734–1755 (1870) and C.C. art. 1976 (Rev.1984).

(c) Spouses may not limit, with respect to third persons, the right that a spouse has under the law to obligate the community or to dispose of community property. A limitation on this right produces effects as between the spouses only. Thus, third persons may rely on Articles 2345, 2346, 2360, and 2363, infra, under which a spouse may obligate the community or dispose of community property without the concurrence of the other spouse.

(d) Article 2330 excludes contractual freedom as to certain matters in the light of strong public policy. However, this provision does not deprive the spouses of flexibility in determining the ownership and management of their property. For example, the spouses may by matrimonial agreement provide for contribution to the expenses of the marriage, for apportionment of community property according to fixed shares, or for the reservation of fruits as separate property. The spouses may, further, determine that their existing or future property shall be subject to the matrimonial regime. In such a case, a matrimonial agreement may in fact be a donation governed by the rules of substance and form applicable to donations.

Art. 2331. Form of matrimonial agreement

A matrimonial agreement may be executed by the spouses before or during marriage. It shall be made by authentic act or by an act under private signature duly acknowledged by the spouses.

Acts 1979, No. 709, § 1, eff. Jan. 1, 1980.

REVISION COMMENT—1979

For recordation of a matrimonial agreement affecting immovables in Louisiana, see C.C. Arts. 1839, 2021, 2035 (Rev.1984), and R.S. 9:2756. For the definition of "authentic act", see C.C. Art. 1833 (Rev.1984).

Art. 2332. Effect toward third persons

A matrimonial agreement, or a judgment establishing a regime of separation of property is effective toward third persons as to immovable property, when filed for registry in the conveyance records of the parish in which the property is situated and as to movables when filed for registry in the parish or parishes in which the spouses are domiciled.

Acts 1979, No. 709, § 1, eff. Jan. 1, 1980.

REVISION COMMENTS—1979

(a) This provision is based in part on Acts 1978, No. 627, § 2834.

(b) A matrimonial agreement or judgment establishing a regime of separation of property is effective toward third persons as to movable property when filed for registry in the parish in which the spouses are domiciled. When spouses are domiciled in different parishes, registration must be made in both parishes.

(c) With respect to immovable property, registration must be made in the parish in which the property is situated.

Art. 2333. Minors

Unless fully emancipated, a minor may not enter into a matrimonial agreement without the written concurrence of his father and mother, or of the parent having his legal custody, or of the tutor of his person.

Acts 1979, No. 709, § 1, eff. Jan. 1, 1980.

REVISION COMMENTS—1979

(a) A minor is fully emancipated by judicial decree under Article 385 of the Louisiana Civil Code of 1870, as amended by Acts 1976, No. 155, or by marriage under Article 382 of the same Code, as amended by Acts 1978, No. 73.

(b) Under the prior law, an unemancipated minor capable of contracting marriage could enter into a matrimonial agreement with the consent of those persons whose consent was required for his marriage. C.C. Art. 2330 (1870). Article 2333 provides that minors need the written concurrence of specified persons in a definite order or priority to enter into a valid matrimonial agreement.

CHAPTER 2—THE LEGAL REGIME OF COMMUNITY OF ACQUETS AND GAINS

SECTION 1—GENERAL DISPOSITIONS

Art. 2334. Persons; scope of application of the legal regime

The legal regime of community of acquets and gains applies to spouses domiciled in this state, regardless of their domicile at the time of marriage or the place of celebration of the marriage.

Acts 1979, No. 709, § 1, eff. Jan. 1, 1980.

REVISION COMMENTS—1979

(a) Spouses may exclude the legal regime under Article 2329, supra.

(b) Under this provision, spouses not domiciled in Louisiana at the time of their marriage become subject to the provisions of this Title from the moment they become Louisiana domiciliaries. However, they may enter into a matrimonial agreement within one year without court approval. See Art. 2329, supra.

Art. 2335. Classification of property

Property of married persons is either community or separate, except as provided in Article 2341.1.

Acts 1979, No. 709, § 1, eff. Jan. 1, 1980. Amended by Acts 1991, No. 329, § 1.

REVISION COMMENT—1979

None.

Art. 2336. Ownership of community property

Each spouse owns a present undivided one-half interest in the community property. Nevertheless, neither the community nor things of the community may be judicially partitioned prior to the termination of the regime.

During the existence of the community property regime, the spouses may, without court approval, voluntarily partition the community property in whole or in part. In such a case, the things that each spouse acquires are separate property. The partition is effective toward third persons when filed for registry in the manner provided by Article 2332.

Acts 1979, No. 709, § 1, eff. Jan. 1, 1980. Amended by Acts 1981, No. 921, § 1; Acts 1982, No. 282, § 1.

REVISION COMMENTS—1979

(a) The co-ownership of the community is subject to the rules governing termination of the regime rather than the general rules of the Civil Code governing judicial partition. The spouses may, without court approval, amicably partition the community property, in whole or in part. In such a case, the things that each spouse acquires are separate property. But neither the spouses nor their creditors may force a judicial partition as long as the regime continues to exist.

After a voluntary partition, the fruits and revenues of the property attributed to each spouse fall into the community. C.C. Art. 2339. However each spouse may reserve them as his separate property by an appropriate declaration. Ibid.

(b) This provision, being a rule of public order, may not be derogated from by matrimonial agreement. See Art. 2330, supra; cf. C.C. Art. 11 (1870).

(c) The community of acquets and gains is not a legal entity but a patrimonial mass, that is, a universality of assets and liabilities. An undivided one-half of the mass forms a part of the patrimony of each spouse during the existence of a community property regime, but the entirety of the assets of the mass is liable to creditors for the satisfaction of separate as well as community obligations of the spouses. See Arts. 2345 and 2357, infra. When a separate obligation of a spouse is satisfied from community assets the other spouse has a right of reimbursement under Article 2364, infra. During the existence of a community property regime, the separate property of a spouse is not liable to creditors for the satisfaction of a separate or a community obligation incurred by the other spouse. For satisfaction of obligations after termination of a community property regime, see Article 2357, infra.

(d) Although the patrimony of each spouse includes only an undivided one-half of the mass of the community property, each spouse has by provision of law the right to manage and to dispose of the entire mass and the things that compose it, Article 2346, infra, subject to certain exceptions, Articles 2347, 2349, 2350 and 2352, infra. The spouse's right of equal management is neither a tacit mandate granted by the other spouse nor authority deriving from co-ownership. It is an attribute of any regime of community property, established by provisions of law. It may not be curtailed, insofar as third persons are concerned, by a matrimonial agreement. Art. 2330, supra.

Art. 2337. Disposition of undivided interest

A spouse may not alienate, encumber, or lease to a third person his undivided interest in the community or in particular things of the community prior to the termination of the regime.

Acts 1979, No. 709, § 1, eff. Jan. 1, 1980.

REVISION COMMENTS—1979

(a) This provision is new. The co-ownership of the community is a distinct species. A spouse should not have the right to dispose of his undivided interest in the community or in things of the community by inter vivos act in favor of third persons.

(b) This provision applies to the legal regime as well as to conventional regimes. It may not be derogated from by agreement. Art. 2330, supra; cf. C.C. Art. 11 (1870). The disposition by a spouse of his undivided interest in the community or in things of the community by inter vivos act in favor of a third person is an absolute nullity.

(c) This provision does not prevent the alienation, encumbrance or lease to a third person of a portion of the community or things of the community in full ownership. It is aimed simply at preventing a third party from owning an undivided interest in the community or in particular things of the community.

Art. 2338. Community property

The community property comprises: property acquired during the existence of the legal regime through the effort, skill, or industry of either spouse; property acquired with community things or with community and separate things, unless classified as separate property under Article 2341; property donated to the spouses jointly; natural and civil fruits of community property; damages awarded for loss or injury to a thing belonging to the community; and all other property not classified by law as separate property.

Acts 1979, No. 709, § 1, eff. Jan. 1, 1980.

REVISION COMMENTS—1979

(a) When things are acquired with community and separate funds under Article 2338, the spouse whose separate funds were used is entitled to reimbursement upon dissolution of the community. See Art. 2367, infra.

(b) When spouses live in community, property donated to them jointly falls into the community. If they do not live in community, the donor may not create a community regime for the spouses. In such a case, the property given to them is separate property held in indivision.

Art. 2339. Fruits and revenues of separate property

The natural and civil fruits of the separate property of a spouse, minerals produced from or attributable to a separate asset, and bonuses, delay rentals, royalties, and shut-in payments arising from mineral leases are community property. Nevertheless, a spouse may reserve them as his separate property as provided in this Article.

A spouse may reserve them as his separate property by a declaration made in an authentic act or in an act under private signature duly acknowledged. A copy of the declaration shall be provided to the other spouse prior to filing of the declaration.

As to the fruits and revenues of immovables, the declaration is effective when a copy is provided to the other spouse and the declaration is filed for registry in the conveyance records of the parish in which the immovable property is located. As to fruits of movables, the declaration is effective when a copy is provided to the other spouse and the declaration is filed for registry in the conveyance records of the parish in which the declarant is domiciled.

Acts 1979, No. 709, § 1, eff. Jan. 1, 1980. Amended by Acts 1980, No. 565, § 2; Acts 2008, No. 855, § 1.

REVISION COMMENTS—1979

(a) A declaration affecting the fruits of an immovable must be filed in the conveyance records of the parish in which the immovable is located. C.C. arts. 1839, 2021, 2035 (Rev. 1984) and R.S. 9:2756.

(b) For the definition of "authentic act" see C.C. Art. 1833 (Rev. 1984).

(c) According to Article 551 of the Louisiana Civil Code, fruits are things that are produced by or derived from another thing without diminution of its substance. Mineral substances extracted from the ground and the proceeds of mineral rights are not fruits, because their production results in depletion of the property. See Art. 551, Comment (c). Nevertheless, minerals produced from or attributable to a separate asset, and bonuses, delay rentals, royalties, and shut-in payments arising from mineral leases fall into the community property by application of Article 2339. Thus, the holding of Milling v. Collector of Revenue, 220 La. 773, 57 So.2d 679 (1952) continues to control, and bonuses, delay rentals, royalties, and shut-in payments from separate property fall into the community, though they are not classified as fruits under Article 551. In effect, Article 2339 establishes an exception to the rule of Article 488, which provides that "products derived from a thing as a result of diminution of its substance belong to the owner of that thing."

Art. 2340. Presumption of community

Things in the possession of a spouse during the existence of a regime of community of acquets and gains are presumed to be community, but either spouse may prove that they are separate property.

Acts 1979, No. 709, § 1, eff. Jan. 1, 1980.

REVISION COMMENTS—1979

(a) This provision establishes a rebuttable presumption that everything of value in the possession of a spouse during the existence of the regime of community of acquets and gains is community property.

(b) This provision suppresses the requirement of a double declaration established by Louisiana jurisprudence.

(c) The presumption of community under this provision is rebuttable. For example the presumption is rebutted as to property acquired prior to marriage by evidence establishing the date of acquisition and as to property inherited during marriage by the judgment of possession.

Art. 2341. Separate property

The separate property of a spouse is his exclusively. It comprises: property acquired by a spouse prior to the establishment of a community property regime; property acquired by a spouse with separate things or with separate and community things when the value of the community things is inconsequential in comparison with the value of the separate things used; property acquired by a spouse by inheritance or donation to him individually; damages awarded to a spouse in an action for breach of contract against the other spouse or for the loss sustained as a result of fraud or bad faith in the management of community property by the other spouse; damages or other indemnity awarded to a spouse in connection with the management of his separate property; and things acquired by a spouse as a result of a voluntary partition of the community during the existence of a community property regime.

Acts 1979, No. 709, § 1, eff. Jan. 1, 1980. Amended by Acts 1981, No. 921, § 1.

REVISION COMMENTS—1979

(a) When things are acquired with separate and community funds under Article 2341, the other spouse is entitled to reimbursement of one-half of the community funds used upon dissolution of the community. See Art. 2366, infra.

(b) The value of the community things at the time of acquisition should be used for determining whether it is "inconsequential" in comparison with the value of the separate things used.

(c) The principle of real subrogation is applicable to both separate and community property. Thus, when a thing forming a part of the separate property of a spouse is converted into another thing, the mass of the separate property is not diminished. The new thing takes the place of the old: "Subrogatum capit naturam subrogati". Newson v. Adams, 3 La. 231, 233 (1882); Yiannopoulos, Civil Law Property § 79 (1966).

Art. 2341.1. Acquisition of undivided interests; separate and community property

A.   A spouse's undivided interest in property otherwise classified as separate property under Article 2341 remains his separate property regardless of the acquisition of other undivided interests in the property during the existence of the legal regime, the source of improvements thereto, or by whom the property was managed, used, or enjoyed.

B.   In property in which an undivided interest is held as community property and an undivided interest is held as separate property, each spouse owns a present undivided one-half interest in that portion of the undivided interest which is community and a spouse owns a present undivided interest in that portion of the undivided interest which is separate.

Added by Acts 1991, No. 329, § 2.

Art. 2342. Declaration of acquisition of separate property

A.   A declaration in an act of acquisition that things are acquired with separate funds as the separate property of a spouse may be controverted by the other spouse unless he concurred in the act. It may also be controverted by the forced heirs and the creditors of the spouses, despite the concurrence by the other spouse.

B.   Nevertheless, when there has been such a declaration, an alienation, encumbrance, or lease of the thing by onerous title, during the community regime or thereafter, may not be set aside on the ground of the falsity of the declaration.

C.   (1) The provision of this Article that prohibits setting aside an alienation, encumbrance, or lease on the ground of the falsity of the declaration of separate property is hereby made retroactive to any such alienation, encumbrance, or lease prior to July 21, 1982.

(2) A person who has a right to set aside such transactions on the ground of the falsity of the declaration, which right is not prescribed or otherwise extinguished or barred upon July 21, 1982, and who is adversely affected by the provisions of this Article, shall have six months from July 21, 1982 to initiate proceedings to set aside such transactions or otherwise be forever barred from exercising such right or cause of action. Nothing contained in this Article shall be construed to limit or prescribe any action or proceeding which may arise between spouses under the provisions of this Article.

Acts 1979, No. 709, § 1, eff. Jan. 1, 1980. Amended by Acts 1980, No. 565, § 3; Acts 1982, No. 453, § 1, eff. July 21, 1982; Acts 1995, No. 433, § 1.

REVISION COMMENTS—1979

(a) A declaration in an act of acquisition that things are acquired with separate funds as separate property of a spouse may be controverted by the other spouse unless he concurred in the act. Monk v. Monk, 243 La. 429, 144 So.2d 384 (1962). It may also be controverted by the forced heirs and the creditors of the spouses, despite the concurrence of the other spouse. McGee v. Harris, 333 So.2d 440 (La.App.3rd Cir. 1976); Succession of Broussard, 306 So.2d 399 (La.App.3rd Cir. 1975). Thus, a court may determine that the things were actually acquired with community funds and are community property. This determination produces effects between the spouses and toward creditors and forced heirs as long as the thing is owned by the acquiring spouse. But it is without effect as to things that have been transferred by onerous transaction to a third person. That person acquires ownership from the transferor spouse in reliance on the declaration in the act by which the transferor acquired the thing that it is separate property.

(b) The same legal principles apply when a spouse declares in the act of acquisition that the property acquired is community property when in fact it is acquired with separate funds. Third persons may controvert the declaration to establish that the property is separate. In these circumstances, an act in authentic form evidencing donative intent constitutes a donation of one-half of the property to the other spouse. Succession of Daste, 254 La. 403, 223 So.2d 848 (1969); Funderbuck v. Funderbuck, 214 La. 71, 38 So.2d 502 (1949); Succession of Russo, 246 So.2d 26 (La.App. 4th Cir. 1971).

(c) The general laws on concurrence and ratification will be followed in situations appropriate for the application of the article.

REVISION COMMENT—1995

The amendment to Paragraph B is intended to clarify the law. As a result of the amendment the effect of a declaration in an act of acquisition that the property is separate property clearly extends beyond termination of the community regime. When there has been an alienation, encumbrance or lease of the thing by onerous title after the community terminates, the transaction may not be set aside on the basis of falsity of the declaration.

Art. 2343. Donation by spouse of interest in community

The donation by a spouse to the other spouse of his undivided interest in a thing forming part of the community transforms that interest into separate property of the donee. Unless otherwise provided in the act of donation, an equal interest of the donee is also transformed into separate property and the natural and civil fruits of the thing, and minerals produced from or attributed to the property given as well as bonuses, delay rentals, royalties, and shut-in payments arising from mineral leases, form part of the donee's separate property.

Acts 1979, No. 709, § 1, eff. Jan. 1, 1980. Amended by Acts 1981, No. 921, § 1.

REVISION COMMENTS—1979

(a) The donation by a spouse to the other of his undivided interest in community property may be set aside by the creditors of the donor by the revocatory action. C.C. Arts. 2036–2044 (Rev.1984).

(b) This provision derogates from Article 2339, supra.

Art. 2343.1. Transfer of separate property to the community

The transfer by a spouse to the other spouse of a thing forming part of his separate property, with the stipulation that it shall be part of the community, transforms the thing into community property. As to both movables and immovables, a transfer by onerous title must be made in writing and a transfer by gratuitous title must be made by authentic act.

Added by Acts 1981, No. 921, § 2.

REVISION COMMENTS—1981

(a) This provision is new. It clarifies the law.

(b) Under this article, a spouse may convey to the other spouse a thing that forms part of the transferor's separate property, with the stipulation that the thing shall be part of the community. The thing may be a thing that the transferor owns as sole owner or an undivided interest. In effect, the transferor conveys to the other spouse one-half of what he owns and retains the other half as co-owner under the regime of acquets and gains.

Art. 2344. Offenses and quasi-offenses; damages as community or separate property

Damages due to personal injuries sustained during the existence of the community by a spouse are separate property.

Nevertheless, the portion of the damages attributable to expenses incurred by the community as a result of the injury, or in compensation of the loss of community earnings, is community property. If the community regime is terminated otherwise than by the death of the injured spouse, the portion of the damages attributable to the loss of earnings that would have accrued after termination of the community property regime is the separate property of the injured spouse.

Acts 1979, No. 709, § 1, eff. Jan. 1, 1980.

REVISION COMMENTS—1979

(a) The notion of personal injury includes injuries to the personality of a spouse and workman's compensation benefits.

(b) Under this provision, the classification of damages as separate or community property no longer depends on the sex of a spouse. An award of damages may be partly community and partly separate property of the injured spouse. Apportionment of the award between the community and the separate property of the injured spouse is required when the community terminates otherwise than by the death of the injured spouse. The noninjured spouse does not, ordinarily, have an interest in the portion of the award designed to compensate the injured spouse for loss of earnings that would have accrued after the termination of the community property regime. This segment of the award, which would fall into the community during the existence of a community property regime, upon termination of the regime is classified as the separate property of the injured spouse. When the regime terminates by the death of the injured spouse, the portion of the award designed to compensate the injured spouse for loss of earnings continues to be classified as community property in the interest of the surviving spouse.

Art. 2345. Satisfaction of obligation during community

A separate or community obligation may be satisfied during the community property regime from community property and from the separate property of the spouse who incurred the obligation.

Acts 1979, No. 709, § 1, eff. Jan. 1, 1980.

REVISION COMMENTS—1979

(a) The spouses may not derogate from the provisions of Article 3183 of the Louisiana Civil Code of 1870, according to which the property of the debtor is the common pledge of his creditors.

(b) When community property is used for the satisfaction of a separate obligation of a spouse, the other spouse may have a claim for reimbursement under Article 2364, infra. Likewise, when separate property of a spouse is used for the satisfaction of a community debt, the other spouse may have a claim for reimbursement under Article 2365, infra.

(c) For a determination of the question whether an obligation of a spouse is separate or community, see Articles 2360, 2361, 2362, and 2363, infra.

SECTION 2—MANAGEMENT OF COMMUNITY PROPERTY

Art. 2346. Management of community property

Each spouse acting alone may manage, control, or dispose of community property unless otherwise provided by law.

Acts 1979, No. 709, § 1, eff. Jan. 1, 1980.

REVISION COMMENTS—1979

(a) This provision establishes the principle of equal management of community property. Each spouse has the right to manage community property without the consent or concurrence of the other spouse unless otherwise provided by law. For instances in which the concurrence of the other spouse is required, see Articles 2347 and 2349, infra. For instances in which a spouse has exclusive management, control, or power of disposition of community property, see Articles 2348, 2350, 2351, and 2352, infra.

(b) This provision does not make each spouse the mandatary of the other. A spouse who contracts with a third person, when acting alone in the management of community property, does not obligate the separate property of the other spouse. A spouse acting alone may manage, control, and dispose of community property acquired by virtue of a contract made by the other spouse, unless this is property that the acquiring spouse has the exclusive right to manage or property that requires joint management. Nevertheless, he may not affect the legal relations and responsibilities of the spouse who incurred the obligation and the other party or parties to that contract, because, in principle, contracts produce effects as between the parties only. C.C. Art. 1985 (Rev.1984).

(c) As to separate property of the spouses see C.C. Art. 484 (1870).

Art. 2347. Alienation of community property; concurrence of other spouse

A.   The concurrence of both spouses is required for the alienation, encumbrance, or lease of community immovables, standing, cut, or fallen timber, furniture or furnishings while located in the family home, all or substantially all of the assets of a community enterprise, and movables issued or registered as provided by law in the names of the spouses jointly.

B.   The concurrence of both spouses is required to harvest community timber.

Acts 1979, No. 709, § 1, eff. Jan. 1, 1980. Amended by Acts 2001, No. 558, § 1.

REVISION COMMENTS—1979

(a) Encumbrances imposed by law are not subject to the requirement of concurrence by the spouses. Thus, a transaction by one of the spouses acting alone may give rise to a vendor's privilege, or a mechanic's or materialman's lien on community property. Likewise, the recordation of a judgment against a spouse gives rise to a judicial mortgage on community property situated in the parish in which recordation takes place.

(b) This provision applies to a business that is not a legal entity. If the business possesses legal personality, as a corporation or a partnership, its alienation, encumbrance, or lease may be effected by disposition of shares of stock or a partner's interest. See Arts. 2351 and 2352, infra.

(c) The concurrence of a spouse is a juridical act. In order to concur, a spouse must have capacity to dispose of his property. If the spouse is incompetent, he is represented by his tutor or curator.

Art. 2348. Renunciation of right to concur

A spouse may expressly renounce the right to concur in the alienation, encumbrance, or lease of a community immovable or some or all of the community immovables, or community immovables which may be acquired in the future, or all or substantially all of a community enterprise. He also may renounce the right to participate in the management of a community enterprise. The renunciation may be irrevocable for a stated term not to exceed three years. Further, any renunciation of the right to concur in the alienation, encumbrance, or lease of a community immovable, or some or all of the community immovables or community immovables which may be acquired in the future, or all or substantially all of a community enterprise which was proper in form and effective under the law at the time it was made shall continue in effect for the stated term not to exceed three years or if there was no term stated, then until it is revoked.

A spouse may nonetheless reserve the right to concur in the alienation, encumbrance, or lease of specifically described community immovable property.

Acts 1979, No. 709, § 1, eff. Jan. 1, 1980. Amended by Acts 1981, No. 132, § 1; Acts 1984, No. 554, § 1, eff. Jan. 1, 1985; Acts 1984, No. 622, § 1, eff. Jan. 1, 1985.

REVISION COMMENTS—1979

(a) A spouse may ratify the alienation, encumbrance, or lease of a community immovable by the other spouse, when he has not expressly renounced the right to concur. Art. 2347, supra; cf. Art. 2353, infra.

(b) A spouse may expressly renounce the right to concur in the alienation, encumbrance or lease of a particular community immovable or a particular community business or all, or substantially all, of the assets of that business. Such a renunciation may be irrevocable although no consideration is given. It may be for a specified period of time, or until the happening of a certain or uncertain event. The renunciation, unlike the granting of a power of attorney or mandate, does not render the renouncing spouse a party to the transaction. Consequently, a resulting obligation may not be satisfied from the separate property of the spouse who renounces the right to concur. See Art. 2345, supra.

Art. 2349. Donation of community property; concurrence of other spouse

The donation of community property to a third person requires the concurrence of the spouses, but a spouse acting alone may make a usual or customary gift of a value commensurate with the economic position of the spouses at the time of the donation.

Acts 1979, No. 709, § 1, eff. Jan. 1, 1980.

REVISION COMMENT—1979

A donation of community property in violation of this provision is voidable at the instance of the other spouse. Art. 2353, infra. The donee of movables is not protected by Civil Code Articles 517–525, as amended by Acts 1979, No. 180, § 1.

Art. 2350. Alienation of movable assets of business

The spouse who is the sole manager of a community enterprise has the exclusive right to alienate, encumber, or lease its movables unless the movables are issued in the name of the other spouse or the concurrence of the other spouse is required by law.

Acts 1979, No. 709, § 1, eff. Jan. 1, 1980.

REVISION COMMENTS—1979

(a) The concurrence of the spouses is required under Article 2347, supra, as to the alienation, encumbrance or lease of all the assets or substantially all the assets of a community business. The concurrence of the spouses is also required by Article 2347 as to movables registered in the names of the spouses jointly. A spouse has the exclusive right to alienate, encumber, or lease movables issued or registered in his or her name, and to manage or dispose of his interest in a partnership. Arts. 2352 and 2353, infra.

(b) This provision establishes an exception to the principle of equal management in the interest of commerce. A spouse may act alone, that is, to the exclusion of the other spouse, when the other spouse does not participate in the management of a community business. When both spouses participate in the management of a community business, either spouse acting alone may alienate, encumber, or lease the movable assets of the business, subject to the limitations of Article 2347, supra.

(c) This provision is not intended to limit the right of a creditor of a spouse to seize community property that the other spouse has the exclusive right to manage, alienate, encumber, or lease.

Art. 2351.   Alienation of registered movables

A spouse has the exclusive right to manage, alienate, encumber, or lease movables issued or registered in his name as provided by law.

Acts 1979, No. 709, § 1, eff. Jan. 1, 1980.

REVISION COMMENTS—1979

(a) Shares of stock issued in the name of a spouse may only be transferred by that spouse. Banking laws govern access to accounts in the name of one spouse alone or in the name of either spouse in the alternative. Commercial laws govern the negotiation of instruments issued in the name of one spouse alone.

(b) This provision is not intended to limit the right of a creditor of a spouse to seize community property that the other spouse has the exclusive right to manage, alienate, encumber, or lease.

Art. 2352.   Management and disposition of partnership and limited liability company interest

A spouse who is a partner has the exclusive right to manage, alienate, encumber, or lease the partnership interest.

A spouse who is a member has the exclusive right to manage, alienate, encumber, or lease the limited liability company interest.

Acts 1979, No. 709, § 1, eff. Jan. 1, 1980. Amended by Acts 1993, No. 475, § 1, eff. June 9, 1993.

REVISION COMMENT—1979

Under the general law of obligations, the spouse who is not a party to the other spouse's partnership contract may not affect the legal relationship of the partner spouse and the other partners. See C.C. Art. 1985 (Rev. 1984), and Art. 2346, Comment (d) supra. According to this provision, the spouse who is a partner has the sole right to alienate, encumber, or lease the accompanying partnership interest which might otherwise, as a community asset, be subject to the rule of equal management. See Art. 2346, supra.

Art. 2353.   Unauthorized alienation of community property

When the concurrence of the spouses is required by law, the alienation, encumbrance, or lease of community property by a spouse is relatively null unless the other spouse has renounced the right to concur. Also, the alienation, encumbrance, or lease of the assets of a community enterprise by the non-manager spouse is a relative nullity.

Acts 1979, No. 709, § 1, eff. Jan. 1, 1980.

REVISION COMMENTS—1979

(a) Under Article 2353, when the concurrence of the spouse is required by law for the alienation, encumbrance, or lease of community property, a disposition made by a spouse alone is voidable at the instance of the other spouse, unless, of course, that spouse has renounced the right to concur. Art. 2348, supra. An alienation, encumbrance, or lease of immovable property by a spouse who under the law has the right to act alone is not voidable. The spouses may not limit, with respect to third persons, the right that a spouse has under the law to dispose of property without the concurrence of the other spouse. Art. 2330, supra.

(b) An act entered into by a spouse without the concurrence of the other spouse when such concurrence is required by law is a relative nullity.

Art. 2354. Liability for fraud or bad faith

A spouse is liable for any loss or damage caused by fraud or bad faith in the management of the community property.

Acts 1979, No. 709, § 1, eff. Jan. 1, 1980.

REVISION COMMENT—1979

None.

Art. 2355. Judicial authorization to act without the consent of the other spouse

A spouse, in a summary proceeding, may be authorized by the court to act without the concurrence of the other spouse upon showing that such action is in the best interest of the family and that the other spouse arbitrarily refuses to concur or that concurrence may not be obtained due to the physical incapacity, mental incompetence, commitment, imprisonment, temporary absence of the other spouse, or because the other spouse is an absent person.

Acts 1979, No. 709, § 1, eff. Jan. 1, 1980. Amended by Acts 1990, No. 989, § 2, eff. Jan. 1, 1991.

REVISION COMMENT—1979

The word "family" in this provision refers to the limited family concept of Article 3556(12) of the Louisiana Civil Code of 1870 as amended by Acts 1979, No. 711, § 1.

COMMENT—1990

The word "absence" in Article 2355 of the Louisiana Civil Code, as revised in 1979, appears to be ambiguous. It may be taken to mean temporary absence, the status of a spouse who is an absent person, or both. Article 2355 is amended to clarify the law. When a spouse is "temporarily absent" or when he is an "absent person", that is, his whereabouts are unknown and cannot be ascertained by diligent effort, the other spouse may be authorized by the court in a summary proceeding to act alone upon showing that such action is in the best interest of the family.

Art. 2355.1. Judicial authorization to manage the community

When a spouse is an absent person, the other spouse, upon showing that such action is in the best interest of the family, may be authorized by the court in a summary proceeding to manage, alienate, encumber, or lease community property that the absent spouse has the exclusive right to manage, alienate, encumber, or lease.

Added by Acts 1990, No. 989, § 2, eff. Jan. 1, 1991.

COMMENTS—1990

(a) This provision is new. It is based in part on Article 64 of the Louisiana Civil Code of 1870.

(b) When a spouse in community is an absent person and a curator is appointed to manage his property, the curatorship is limited to the absent person's separate property. The present spouse continues to manage the community property alone in accordance with Civil Code Article 2346 (Rev.1979). However, when a spouse who has the exclusive right to manage, alienate, encumber, or lease community property in accordance with Civil Code Articles 2348–2352 (Rev.1979) is an absent person, the present spouse may be authorized by the court in a summary proceeding to manage, alienate, encumber, or lease the community property and thus replace the absent person. Of course, in matters in which the concurrence of a spouse is required for the alienation, encumbrance, or lease of community property, Civil Code Article 2355 (Rev.1979) applies.

(c) A spouse seeking authorization under this Article must prove that the other spouse is an absent person rather than temporarily absent.

(d) When the concurrence of a spouse is required for the alienation, encumbrance, or lease of community property and concurrence may not be obtained because a spouse is temporarily absent or because he is an absent person, the present spouse may be authorized by the court in a summary proceeding to act alone. See Civil Code Art. 2355 (Rev.1979).

SECTION 3—TERMINATION OF THE COMMUNITY

Art. 2356. Causes of termination

The legal regime of community property is terminated by the death or judgment of declaration of death of a spouse, declaration of the nullity of the marriage, judgment of divorce or separation of property, or matrimonial agreement that terminates the community.

Acts 1979, No. 709, § 1, eff. Jan. 1, 1980. Amended by Acts 1990, No. 989, § 2, eff. Jan. 1, 1991.

REVISION COMMENTS—1979

(a) For suits between spouses during marriage, see R.S. 9:291 as amended by Acts 1979, No. 711, § 1.

(b) For contracts between the spouses during marriage, see Article 2329, supra. A contract terminating or modifying a community property regime is a matrimonial agreement. See Articles 2328 and 2331, supra.

(c) According to Articles 155, 159 and 2432 of the Louisiana Civil Code of 1870, a judgment of divorce, separation from bed and board, or separation of property is retroactive to the date of filing suit.

(d) The word "termination" is preferable to "dissolution". Dissolution connotes termination retroactive to the moment of creation of a community property regime. "Termination" connotes an ending to a regime of community property for the future.

Art. 2357. Satisfaction of obligation after termination of regime

An obligation incurred by a spouse before or during the community property regime may be satisfied after termination of the regime from the property of the former community and from the separate property of the spouse who incurred the obligation. The same rule applies to an obligation for attorney's fees and costs in an action for divorce incurred by a spouse between the date the petition for divorce was filed and the date of the judgment of divorce that terminates the community regime.

If a spouse disposes of property of the former community for a purpose other than the satisfaction of community obligations, he is liable for all obligations incurred by the other spouse up to the value of that community property.

A spouse may by written act assume responsibility for one-half of each community obligation incurred by the other spouse. In such case, the assuming spouse may dispose of community property without incurring further responsibility for the obligations incurred by the other spouse.

Acts 1979, No. 709, § 1, eff. Jan. 1, 1980. Amended by Acts 1990, No. 1009, § 3, eff. Jan. 1, 1991.

This Article contemplates satisfaction of both personal and community obligations after termination of a community property regime. Creditors may seize property of the former community in the hands of either spouse. For satisfaction of obligations during the existence of a community property regime, see Article 2345, supra.

COMMENT—1990

This amendment is intended to accomplish the same result as the former language of Civil Code Article 159 to the effect that the retroactive dissolution of a community by divorce was "without prejudice . . . to the liability of the community for the attorney fees and costs incurred by a spouse in the action in which the judgment is rendered. . . ." That language has been repealed by the 1990 revision of Louisiana divorce law. This amendment of Article 2357, however, assures that both past and future creditors of such obligations may continue to satisfy those obligations from former community property and separate property of the debtor spouse. Without the amendment, the only property available would be the debtor spouse's separate property and his one-half interest in former community property. Under the former text of Civil Code Article 159 community property in its entirety was available to satisfy such an obligation.

Art. 2357.1. [Blank]

Art. 2358. Claims for reimbursement between spouses

A spouse may have a claim against the other spouse for reimbursement in accordance with the following Articles.

A claim for reimbursement may be asserted only after termination of the community property regime, unless otherwise provided by law.

Acts 1979, No. 709, § 1, eff. Jan. 1, 1980. Amended by Acts 1990, No. 991, § 1; Acts 2009, No. 204, § 1.

REVISION COMMENT—1979

This provision is new. The articles governing claims for reimbursement are applicable only between the spouses and their universal successors.

COMMENT—1990

The deletion of the phrase "against the other spouse" is a purely stylistic amendment. There is no change in the law.

REVISION COMMENTS—2009

(a) The effect of the 2009 amendment to this Article is to clarify that a spouse may bring a reimbursement claim only after the community of acquets and gains has terminated. Louisiana courts were split as to whether the introductory language of the 1979 Article referred to when a reimbursement claim may be asserted or to the timing of the use of the property on which the reimbursement claim is based. See, e.g., Gill v. Gill, 895 So. 2nd 807 (La.App. 2 Cir. 2005) (granting reimbursement for the use of separate property to reduce indebtedness on the family home after termination of the marriage); Bordelon v. Bordelon, 942 So.2d 708 (La.App. 3 Cir. 2006) ("the reimbursement scheme contemplated [by the Civil Code] pertains solely to debts paid during the marriage, and not those paid after divorce"). The revision makes it clear that this introductory Article speaks only to when a reimbursement claim may be asserted.

(b) If there is community property to be divided between the spouses and they do not execute a voluntary partition agreement, reimbursement claims will typically be heard as a part of the judicial partition proceeding conducted under R.S. 9:2801. Spouses may assert claims for reimbursement in a petition for divorce, as authorized by R.S. 9:2802.

Art. 2358.1. Source of reimbursement

Reimbursement shall be made from the patrimony of the spouse who owes reimbursement.

Added by Acts 1990, No. 991, § 1.

(a) Article 2358.1 has been enacted for the purpose of clarification of the law. Certain Louisiana courts have misinterpreted Article 2358 and Articles 2364 through 2369 dealing with reimbursement and accounting between separated and divorced spouses. Therefore, clarification of the law is advisable. Article 2358.1 makes it clear that reimbursement is made from the patrimony of the spouse who owes reimbursement, unless the liability of a spouse is limited by exceptional provision of law to the value of his share of the community. See C.C. Arts. 2365, 2367. The patrimony of a spouse consists of his share in the community and his separate property. See Yiannopoulos, Civil Law Property § 125 (2d ed. 1980).

(b) Article 2358.1 does not mean that reimbursement shall be made only after the community is partitioned. It means that reimbursement shall not be made from the total net value of the community; it shall be made from the share in the community of the spouse who owes reimbursement or from his separate property. Cf. C.C. Art. 2366.

(c) According to Article 2364, infra, when community property has been used to satisfy a separate obligation of a spouse, the other spouse is entitled upon termination of the community to reimbursement for one-half of the amount or value used from the patrimony of the other spouse. The principle of accounting is simple and clear. One-half of the community property that was used to satisfy the separate obligation of a spouse belonged to that spouse and, therefore, no reimbursement is due to him. The other half of the community property that was used belonged to the other spouse, and therefore, reimbursement is due to him.

According to the correct interpretation of Article 2364, reimbursement has always been due from the patrimony of the other spouse rather than from the net community assets. See Spaht and Hargrave, Matrimonial Regimes 285 (1989); cf. Patin v. Patin, 462 So.2d 1356 (La.App. 3d Cir.1985); Feazel v. Feazel, 471 So.2d 851 (La.App. 2d Cir.1985); Devezac v. Devezac, 483 So.2d 1197 (La.App. 4th Cir.1986). But see Gachez v. Gachez, 451 So.2d 608 (La.App. 5th Cir.1984); Barry v. Barry, 501 So.2d 897 (La.App. 5th Cir.1987); Nash v. Nash, 486 So.2d 1011 (La.App. 2d Cir.1986). This jurisprudence that has misapplied Article 2364 is legislatively overruled.

Art. 2359. Obligations; community or separate

An obligation incurred by a spouse may be either a community obligation or a separate obligation.

Acts 1979, No. 709, § 1, eff. Jan. 1, 1980.

This provision is new. It introduces the following provisions.

Art. 2360. Community obligation

An obligation incurred by a spouse during the existence of a community property regime for the common interest of the spouses or for the interest of the other spouse is a community obligation.

Acts 1979, No. 709, § 1, eff. Jan. 1, 1980.

None.

Art. 2361. Obligations incurred during marriage; presumption

Except as provided in Article 2363, all obligations incurred by a spouse during the existence of a community property regime are presumed to be community obligations.

Acts 1979, No. 709, § 1, eff. Jan. 1, 1980.

None.

Art. 2362.   Alimentary obligation

An alimentary obligation imposed by law on a spouse is deemed to be a community obligation.

Acts 1979, No. 709, § 1, eff. Jan. 1, 1980.

REVISION COMMENT—1979

Legal alimentary obligations are legislatively classified as incurred during the community regime for the common interest of the spouses. See Justice Tate's concurring opinion in Connell v. Connell, 331 So.2d 4 (La.1976).

Art. 2362.1.   Obligation incurred in an action for divorce

A.   An obligation incurred before the date of a judgment of divorce for attorney fees and costs in an action for divorce and in incidental actions is deemed to be a community obligation.

B.   Notwithstanding the provisions of Paragraph A of this Article, the court may assess attorney fees and costs in an action for divorce granted pursuant to Article 103(4) or (5) and in incidental actions thereafter against the perpetrator of abuse, which shall be a separate obligation of the perpetrator.

Added by Acts 1990, No. 1009, § 3, eff. Jan. 1, 1991; Acts 2009, No. 204, § 1; Amended by Acts 2014, No. 221, § 1; Amended by Acts 2015, No. 221, § 1.

COMMENT—1990

See the 1990 comment to Article 2363, infra.

REVISION COMMENTS—2009

(a) This revision is not intended to change the Louisiana jurisprudential view that the costs and expenses of divorce are community obligations. Vincent v. Vincent, 949 So.2d 535, 541 (La.App. 4 Cir. 2007). Rather, the revision is intended to take into account that it is not always a judgment of divorce that terminates the community property regime. Cf. C.C. Art. 2362.1 (1990) (classifying as community an obligation for attorney fees and costs related to a "judgment of divorce that terminates the community property regime"). Spouses meeting the grounds set out in Article 2374(C) may be granted a judgment of separation of property, which has the effect of terminating the community property regime even before the judgment of divorce is rendered.

(b) Actions incidental to divorce are detailed in Article 105. Louisiana courts have long interpreted this Article to cover incidental proceedings, including protective orders, for instance, even though a narrow construction of the phrase "in an action for divorce incurred before the date of the judgment of divorce" under the former Article may not have covered them. See, e.g., Carroll v. Carroll, 753 So.2d 395, 396 (La.App. 1 Cir. 2000).

Art. 2363.   Separate obligation

A separate obligation of a spouse is one incurred by that spouse prior to the establishment of a community property regime, or one incurred during the existence of a community property regime though not for the common interest of the spouses or for the interest of the other spouse.

An obligation resulting from an intentional wrong or an obligation incurred for the separate property of a spouse is likewise a separate obligation to the extent that it does not benefit both spouses, the family, or the other spouse.

Acts 1979, No. 709, § 1, eff. Jan. 1, 1980. Amended by Acts 1990, No. 1009, § 3, eff. Jan. 1, 1991; Acts 2009, No. 204, § 1.

REVISION COMMENTS—1979

(a) An obligation incurred by a spouse prior to the establishment or after termination of a community property regime is a separate obligation. A separate obligation may be satisfied from community property or from the separate property of the spouse who incurred it. Arts. 2345 and 2357, supra. If it is satisfied from community property, the spouse who did not incur the obligation may have a right of reimbursement. Art. 2364, infra.

547

(b) An obligation incurred during the existence of a community property regime, though not for the common interest of the spouses or for the interest of the other spouse is a separate obligation. Cf. Art. 2360, supra.

(c) An obligation incurred by a spouse for his separate property is a separate obligation to the extent that it does not benefit the community, the family, or the other spouse. Thus, an obligation incurred for the separate property of a spouse may be in part a community obligation and in part a separate obligation of the spouse who incurred it.

(d) The word "family" in this provision refers to the limited family concept of Article 3556(12) of the Louisiana Civil Code of 1870.

COMMENT—1990

The effect of the 1990 amendment to this Article and the enactment of Article 2362.1 is to classify the obligation for attorney's fees and costs in an action for divorce as a community obligation even though as such it is an exception to the general proposition that an obligation incurred after termination of the regime is a separate obligation. The effect of the classification of the obligation as a community one is as follows: (1) it is a community obligation for purposes of the second Paragraph of Article 2357, meaning that if a spouse disposes of former community property in satisfaction of the obligation there is no personal liability incurred by the spouse to creditors of the other spouse; (2) it is a community obligation for purposes of the third Paragraph of Article 2357, meaning that if a spouse assumes responsibility for one-half the community obligations of the other spouse it includes attorney's fees and costs incurred by the other spouse in an action for divorce; (3) it is a community obligation for purposes of reimbursement, meaning that if a spouse uses separate funds for satisfaction of the obligation for attorney's fees (such as earnings acquired after termination) the spouse may seek reimbursement of one-half the funds used under Article 2365, if there are community assets from which reimbursement may be made; (4) it is a community obligation for purposes of R.S. 9:2801, and thus may be allocated by the judge during the partition of community property.

REVISION COMMENT—2009

(a) Under this revision, obligations incurred after the termination of the community property regime are no longer classified as "separate obligations." That classification under the former version of this Article was conceptually flawed. Once the community regime has terminated, an obligation incurred by a spouse is neither separate nor community. It has no impact upon the community property regime, so it is not properly classified as either type of obligation. The same cannot be said of obligations incurred prior to the establishment of a community property regime, however. Those obligations have a direct impact on the community regime. See, e.g., C.C. Art. 2345 (antenuptial separate obligation may be satisfied from the entirety of the spouses' community property). These obligations may, therefore, properly be referred to as "separate obligations," even though their existence may predate the establishment of a community property regime between the spouses.

(b) Rather than focusing on a spouse's intent in committing an "intentional wrong," the second paragraph of this Article now focuses on whether the result of that wrong is to provide a benefit to the family.

(c) The word "family" in this provision refers to the limited family concept of C.C. Art. 3506(12).

Art. 2364. Satisfaction of separate obligation with community property or former community property

If community property has been used during the existence of the community property regime or former community property has been used thereafter to satisfy a separate obligation of a spouse, the other spouse is entitled to reimbursement for one-half of the amount or value that the property had at the time it was used.

Acts 1979, No. 709, § 1, eff. Jan. 1, 1980. Amended by Acts 2009, No. 204, § 1.

REVISION COMMENTS—1979

(a) If community funds are used to satisfy a separate obligation of a spouse, the other spouse or his heirs are entitled to reimbursement upon termination of the community property regime for one-half of the amount. If community things other than money are used, the other spouse or his heirs are entitled to reimbursement for one-half of the value that the property had at the time it was used.

(b) The obligation to reimburse is heritable. See C.C. Arts. 1765 and 1984 (Rev.1984).

(c) For the notion of "separate obligation", see Article 2363, supra.

(d) This provision establishes a right to reimbursement when community property has been used to satisfy a separate obligation of one of the spouses. The other spouse is entitled to one-half of the value of the community property so used. Article 2408 of the Louisiana Civil Code of 1870 created a right to reimbursement when separate property increased in value due to community contributions, and the measure of reimbursement was one-half of the enhanced value. Article 2364 instead treats community property used to satisfy a separate obligation as an interest-free loan.

REVISION COMMENTS—2009

(a) Reimbursement is available under this Article whether community property is used to satisfy a separate obligation during the existence of the community property regime or former community property is used for this purpose after the regime has terminated. The 2009 amendment to the Article eliminates language that created uncertainty as to whether reimbursement was available for post-termination use of former community property. A reimbursement claim may not be asserted until after the community property regime has terminated under Article 2358 (except in the petition for divorce, as authorized by R.S. 9:2802), but when it is asserted it may be based either on use of community property during the community property regime or use of former community property after the regime has terminated.

(b) After termination of a community property regime, each spouse has a duty to preserve and prudently manage former community property under his control. C.C. Art. 2369.3. This reimbursement Article has no effect on that duty, and a spouse may be liable for damages for the breach of the duties described in Article 2369.3, even if this Article provides a reimbursement claim.

(c) A reimbursement claim under this Article exists only when community property is used to satisfy an obligation (1) incurred by a spouse before the establishment of a community property regime, (2) incurred during the existence of the regime though not for the common interest of the spouses or for the interest of the other spouse, or (3) resulting from an intentional wrong or incurred for the separate property of a spouse, to the extent the obligation does not benefit the spouses, the family, or the other spouse. C. C. Art. 2363 (rev. 2009). No reimbursement claim exists under this Article for the use of former community property to satisfy an obligation incurred after termination of the community property regime, because such an obligation is not a "separate obligation" under Article 2363 (rev. 2009). After termination of the community property regime, the spouses are treated as co-owners of all former community property. C.C. Art. 2369.1. Therefore, Article 806 governs their rights and duties toward each other with respect to expenses related to their co-owned property.

Art. 2364.1. [Blank]

Art. 2365. Satisfaction of community obligation with separate property

If separate property of a spouse has been used either during the existence of the community property regime or thereafter to satisfy a community obligation, that spouse is entitled to reimbursement for one-half of the amount or value that the property had at the time it was used.

If the community obligation was incurred to acquire ownership or use of a community corporeal movable required by law to be registered, and separate property of a spouse has been used after termination to satisfy that obligation, the reimbursement claim shall be reduced in proportion to the value of the claimant's use after termination of the community property regime. The value of that use and the amount of the claim for reimbursement accrued during the use are presumed to be equal.

The liability of a spouse who owes reimbursement is limited to the value of his share of all community property after deduction of all community obligations. Nevertheless, if the community obligation was incurred for the ordinary and customary expenses of the marriage, or for the support, maintenance, or education of children of either spouse in keeping with the economic condition of the spouses, the spouse is entitled to reimbursement from the other spouse regardless of the value of that spouse's share of all community property.

Acts 1979, No. 709, § 1, eff. Jan. 1, 1980. Amended by Acts 1990, No. 991, § 1; Acts 2009, No. 204, § 1.

REVISION COMMENTS—1979

(a) For the notion of "community obligation," see Articles 2360, 2361 and 2362, supra. Article 2365 establishes a distinction between community obligations according to whether they are incurred for the ordinary and customary expenses of the marriage, for the support, maintenance, and education of children, in keeping with the economic condition of the community, or for other purposes. When the separate property of a spouse is used to satisfy any community obligation, the spouse is entitled upon termination of the community property regime to reimbursement for one-half of the amount or the value that the property had at the time it was used. In principle, reimbursement may be made only if there are sufficient community assets; there is no obligation for reimbursement from the separate property of the other spouse. However, if the community obligation discharged with separate property is one incurred for the ordinary and customary expenses of the marriage, or for the support, maintenance, and education of children, in keeping with the economic condition of the community, there is an obligation for reimbursement even if there are no sufficient community assets. In such a case, reimbursement may be made from the separate property of the other spouse.

(b) The obligation of reimbursement is heritable. See C.C. Arts. 1765 and 1984 (Rev.1984).

(c) Article 2365 recognizes the right of a spouse to reimbursement when separate property has been used to satisfy an obligation incurred for the common interest of the spouses. Article 2408 of the Louisiana Civil Code of 1870 provided for reimbursement when separate property increased in value. Under the jurisprudence, however, reimbursement was also available when the value of community property increased. The measure of reimbursement was one-half the enhanced value.

COMMENT—1990

Article 2365 has been amended solely for the purpose of clarification of the law. It has always been implicit in the first paragraph of this article that the reimbursement was to be made from the other spouse. Reimbursement from the undivided mass of the community property of only one-half of the amount due would lead to absurd results. See Spaht and Hargrave, Matrimonial Regimes 281–325 (1989); Spaht, Developments in the Law 1988–1989, Matrimonial Regimes, 50 La.L.Rev. 293 (1989).

REVISION COMMENTS—2009

(a) The 2009 amendment to this Article clarifies an ambiguity in prior law as to whether the use of separate property to satisfy a community obligation after termination of the community property regime, but before partition, gave rise to a reimbursement claim. Some Louisiana courts read the "upon termination of the community property regime" language of the 1979 Article to restrict a spouse's right to reimbursement to situations in which separate property was used during the existence of the legal regime. See, e.g., Bordelon v. Bordelon, 942 So.2d 708 (La.App. 3 Cir. 2006). Other courts viewed that language merely as a restriction on the time period within which a reimbursement claim could be asserted. See, e.g., Moody v. Moody, 622 So.2d 1381 (La.App. 1 Cir. 1993); Gill v. Gill, 895 So.2d 807 (La.App. 2 Cir. 2005); Davezac v. Davezac, 483 So.2d 1197 (La.App. 4 Cir. 1986); Gachez v. Gachez, 451 So.2d 608 (La.App. 5 Cir. 1984). This amendment clarifies prior law and resolves the circuit split in favor of allowing reimbursement for post-termination, pre-partition uses of separate property.

(b) The second paragraph of this Article is new. It incorporates the substantial volume of Louisiana jurisprudence which has limited a spouse's right to reimbursement for the use of separate funds after termination of the community property regime to satisfy a community note obligation for an automobile of which the claimant spouse has the exclusive use. See, e.g., Mason v. Mason, 927 So.2d 1235 (La.App. 2 Cir. 2006); Sheridon v. Sheridon, 867 So.2d 38 (La.App. 3 Cir. 2004); Davezac v. Davezac, 483 So.2d 1197 (La.App. 4 Cir. 1986); Gachez v. Gachez, 451 So.2d 608 (La.App. 5 Cir. 1984) (all denying reimbursement claim of a spouse with exclusive use of an automobile after termination of the legal regime). But see Williams v. Williams, 509 So.2d 77 (La.App. 1 Cir. 1987) (reimbursement articles apply to movables and immovables alike). In such cases, the depreciating nature of the automobile works an inequity when a spouse is allowed to retain use of the automobile, all the while contributing to its rapid and substantial decrease in value, and yet receive full reimbursement. To lessen the possibility of such inequities, this Article reduces the reimbursement claim of the spouse with enjoyment of certain corporeal movables in the same way that co-owners are

550

limited in receiving reimbursement for expenses incurred in the preservation and management of co-owned property. See C.C. Art. 806. See also Ostarly v. Ostarly, 988 So.2d 276, 278–79 (La.App. 4 Cir. 2008) (upholding trial court's reduction, but not elimination, of reimbursement owed to claimant with exclusive post-termination use of motorcycle). A presumption of equality between the amount of the reimbursement claim and the value of the claimant spouse's enjoyment exists to forestall questions of valuation when possible.

(c) A reduction or elimination of a spouse's reimbursement claim will occur under this Article only if the obligation for which a spouse expends separate property relates to a "community corporeal movable required by law to be registered." Automobiles are covered, as are many watercraft (see R.S. 34:851.19). But the Louisiana jurisprudence has previously, without any authority in the Civil Code, reduced a spouse's right to reimbursement for exclusive use of community automobiles and community telephone equipment. See, e.g., Mason v. Mason, 927 So.2d 1235 (La.App. 2 Cir. 2006) (automobile); Jurgelsky v. Pinac, 614 So.2d 1331 (La.App. 3 Cir. 1993) (telephone equipment). If the community property acquired is "the family residence, a community immovable occupied as a residence, or a community manufactured home as defined in R.S. 9:1149.2 and occupied as a residence, regardless of whether it has been immobilized," R.S. 9:374 applies and may result in a reduction of the reimbursement claim to offset rent owed.

(d) Regardless of whether a spouse's reimbursement claim is reduced for use, the right to reimbursement for use of separate property to satisfy a community obligation is subject to the limitation of liability set out in the third paragraph of Article 2365. Unless the exception in the third paragraph of this Article applies, a spouse's right to receive reimbursement under both the first and second paragraphs of this Article is limited to his net share of the community property.

(e) The exception to the limitation on reimbursement found in the third paragraph of this Article hinges upon the classification of an expenditure as in line with "the economic condition of the spouses." Prior law referred to the "economic condition of the community." The community is not a legal entity, and thus it is misleading to speak of its "economic condition." See 1979 Revision Comment (c) to C.C. Art. 2336; Bridges v. Bridges, 692 So.2d 1186 (La.App. 3 Cir. 1997).

Art. 2366. Use of community property or former community property for the benefit of separate property

If community property has been used during the existence of the community property regime or former community property has been used thereafter for the acquisition, use, improvement, or benefit of the separate property of a spouse, the other spouse is entitled to reimbursement for one-half of the amount or value that the community property had at the time it was used.

Buildings, other constructions permanently attached to the ground, and plantings made on the separate property of a spouse with community property belong to the owner of the ground. The other spouse is entitled to reimbursement for one-half of the amount or value that the community property had at the time it was used.

Acts 1979, No. 709, § 1, eff. Jan. 1, 1980. Amended by Acts 1984, No. 933, § 1; Acts 2009, No. 204, § 1.

REVISION COMMENTS—1979

(a) This provision establishes a different measure of compensation for improvements made to separate property than that provided for under the law of accession. See C.C. Arts. 493–497, as revised by Acts 1979, No. 180.

(b) This article creates a right to reimbursement if community property has been applied to, or appropriated for, the use of separate property. Reimbursement exists for one-half the value of the community property so used. Under prior Article 2408 when separate property increased in value, the other spouse was entitled to reimbursement for one-half the enhanced value. The measure of reimbursement has been changed from one-half the enhanced value to one-half of the community property so used.

(c) When separate property of one spouse has been applied to, or appropriated for, the use of the community, reimbursement is due if there are community assets from which reimbursement can be made. Although prior Article 2408 did not provide for reimbursement when separate property was used to benefit the community, the jurisprudence recognized such a right. See, e.g., Emerson v. Emerson, 322 So.2d 347 (La.App.2d Cir. 1975).

COMMENT TO 1984 AMENDMENT

This amendment adds a new second paragraph to Article 2366 (Rev.1979) in order to clarify that a special rule of accession applies between spouses. See C.C.Art. 2367.1 (1984) and associated comments. Cf. C.C.Art. 493 (Rev.1984).

REVISION COMMENTS—2009

(a) Consistent with the 2009 revision to Article 2364, which governs the use of community property to satisfy a separate obligation, this Article has been modified to provide for reimbursement whether community property is used to benefit a spouse's separate property during the existence of the community property regime or former community property has been used for this purpose after the community of acquets and gains has been terminated. The 2009 amendment eliminates language that created uncertainty as to whether reimbursement was available for post-termination use of former community property. A reimbursement claim may not be asserted until after the community property regime has terminated under Article 2358 (except in the petition for divorce, as authorized by R.S. 9:2802), but when it is asserted it may be based either on use of community property during the community property regime or use of former community property after the regime has terminated.

(b) The second paragraph of this Article regulates reimbursement rights between the parties for the making of buildings, other constructions permanently attached to the ground, and plantings only when those items are made on a spouse's separate property during the existence of the community property regime. The rights of the former spouses in such works made after termination are governed by Article 493.

(c) The replacement of the word "assets" with "property" is purely a matter of consistency with the existing rules in this Title of the Civil Code and is not intended to change the law.

Art. 2367.   Use of separate property for the benefit of community property

If separate property of a spouse has been used during the existence of the community property regime for the acquisition, use, improvement, or benefit of community property, that spouse is entitled to reimbursement for one-half of the amount or value that the property had at the time it was used. The liability of the spouse who owes reimbursement is limited to the value of his share of all community property after deduction of all community obligations.

Buildings, other constructions permanently attached to the ground, and plantings made on community property with separate property of a spouse during the existence of the community property regime are community property. The spouse whose separate property was used is entitled to reimbursement for one-half of the amount or value that the separate property had at the time it was used. The liability of the spouse who owes reimbursement is limited to the value of his share in all community property after deduction of all community obligations.

Acts 1979, No. 709, § 1, eff. Jan. 1, 1980. Amended by Acts 1984, No. 933, § 1; Acts 1990, No. 991, 1; Acts 2009, No. 204, § 1.

REVISION COMMENT—1979

This provision establishes a different measure of compensation than that provided for under the law of accession. See C.C. Arts. 493–497, enacted by Acts 1979, No. 180, § 1.

COMMENT TO 1984 AMENDMENT

This amendment adds a new second paragraph to Article 2367 (Rev.1979) in order to clarify that a special rule of accession applies between spouses. See C.C.Art. 2367.1 (1984) and associated comments. Cf. C.C.Art. 493 (Rev.1984).

COMMENT—1990

Article 2367 has been amended solely for the purpose of clarification of the law. The phrase "The liability of the spouse who owes reimbursement is limited to the value of his share in the community after deduction of all community obligations" has the same meaning as the phrase "if there are community assets from which reimbursement may be made" that was used in the original version of this Article.

REVISION COMMENTS—2009

(a) This Article regulates reimbursement rights between the parties for the use of separate property or the making of buildings, other constructions permanently attached to the ground, and plantings only when the use or making is done during the existence of the legal regime. The rights of the former spouses for expenses and works made after termination of the community of acquets and gains are governed by the rules of co-ownership in Articles 804 and 806.

(b) The replacement of the word "assets" with "property" is purely a matter of consistency with the existing rules in this Title of the Civil Code and is not intended to change the law.

Art. 2367.1. Use of separate property for the benefit of separate property

If separate property of a spouse has been used during the existence of the community property regime for the acquisition, use, improvement, or benefit of the other spouse's separate property, the spouse whose property was used is entitled to reimbursement for the amount or value that the property had at the time it was used.

Buildings, other constructions permanently attached to the ground, and plantings made on the land of a spouse with the separate property of the other spouse belong to the owner of the ground. The spouse whose property was used is entitled to reimbursement for the amount or value that the property had at the time it was used.

Added by Acts 1984, No. 933, § 1. Amended by Acts 1990, No. 991, § 1; Acts 2009, No. 204, § 1.

REVISION COMMENTS—1984

(a) This article is new. It fills a gap in the law.

(b) The first sentence of this article establishes a special rule of property law in derogation of the general rule stated in Civil Code Article 493 (Rev.1984). Presumably, improvements made on the land of a spouse with the separate assets of the other spouse are made with the consent of the owner of the ground. Nevertheless, under this article the improvements belong to the owner of the ground. Application of Article 493 would have resulted in undesirable complications in the field of matrimonial regimes. It is preferable to establish a special rule of accession in the relations between spouses and accord the remedy of reimbursement to the spouse whose separate assets were used for the improvement of the separate property of the other spouse.

(c) The second sentence of this article applies "upon alienation of the land, legal separation, or termination of the marriage." A spouse does not have the right to reimbursement at any other time, unless, of course, he has reserved that right under a contract with the other spouse.

(d) The second sentence of this article reflects the general principle established in Civil Code Articles 2366, 2367, and 2368 (Rev.1979). During marriage, or prior to the alienation of the improved property, the spouse whose assets were used to improve it has the use of that property; therefore, reimbursement is limited to the value that his separate assets had at the time they were used.

(e) Although this article derogates from Article 493 in light of the special relationship between spouses, nothing prevents the spouses from contracting for application of Article 493, or from making other contractual arrangements.

COMMENT—1990

Article 2367.1 has been amended solely for the purpose of clarification of the law. The words "legal separation, or termination of the marriage" have been changed to "or termination of the community" for purposes of consistent legal terminology. For the same purpose, the word "of" has been changed to "for". Obviously, the reimbursement shall be made from the patrimony of the spouse whose separate property was improved.

REVISION COMMENT—2009

(a) The first paragraph of this Article is new. It fills a gap in the Civil Code Articles on reimbursement when one spouse uses separate property to improve, benefit, use, or acquire the other spouse's separate property. In such a case, full reimbursement is owed by the spouse benefitted. For spouses living under separate property regimes, application of general principles of law, including unjust enrichment, may provide the same result. See, e.g., Lee v. Lee, 868 So.2d 316, 318–20 (La.App. 3 Cir. 2004) (applying unjust enrichment principles to award husband living separate in property from wife full reimbursement for use of his funds to satisfy loan indebtedness on wife's home).

(b) The replacement of the word "assets" with "property" is purely a matter of consistency with the existing rules of this Title of the Civil Code and is not intended to change the law.

(c) This Article is not intended to cover gifts between the spouses. No reimbursement is owed in such situations.

(d) This revision changes the law to make reimbursement under this Article consistent with that under the preceding Articles insofar as it precludes a spouse from asserting a reimbursement claim before termination of the community property regime (except in the petition for divorce, as authorized by R.S. 9:2802). Typically, the claim for reimbursement authorized by this Article will be asserted as a part of the judicial partition conducted under R.S. 9:2801.

Art. 2367.2. Component parts of separate property

When a spouse with his own separate property incorporates in or attaches to a separate immovable of the other spouse things that become component parts under Articles 465 and 466, Article 2367.1 applies.

Added by Acts 1984, No. 933, § 1. Amended by Acts 2009, No. 204, § 1.

REVISION COMMENT—1984

This provision is new. It derogates from the rule stated in Civil Code Article 495 (Rev.1979) in light of the special relationship between spouses. Under this and the preceding article, the rights of a spouse who uses his separate funds to benefit the separate property of the other spouse are the same whether those funds are used to construct improvements upon the property in question or to purchase things that become component parts of it.

REVISION COMMENT—2009

The replacement of the word "assets" with "property" is purely a matter of consistency with the existing rules of this Title of the Civil Code and is not intended to change in law.

Art. 2367.3. Satisfaction of separate obligation with separate property

If a spouse uses separate property during the existence of the community property regime to satisfy the separate obligation of the other spouse, the spouse whose property was used is entitled to reimbursement for the amount or value the property had at the time it was used.

Added by Acts 2009, No. 204, § 1.

REVISION COMMENT—2009

This Article is new. It fills a gap in the Civil Code Articles on reimbursement when one spouse uses separate property to satisfy the other spouse's separate obligation. In such a case, full reimbursement is owed by the spouse whose obligation is satisfied. For spouses living under separate property regimes, application of general principles of law, including unjust enrichment, may provide the same result. See, e.g., Lee v. Lee, 868 So.2d 316, 318–20 (La.App. 3 Cir. 2004) (applying unjust enrichment principles to award husband living separate in property from wife full reimbursement for use of his funds to satisfy loan indebtedness on wife's home).

Art. 2368.   Increase of the value of separate property

If the separate property of a spouse has increased in value as a result of the uncompensated common labor or industry of the spouses, the other spouse is entitled to be reimbursed from the spouse whose property has increased in value one-half of the increase attributed to the common labor.

Acts 1979, No. 709, § 1, eff. Jan. 1, 1980.

REVISION COMMENT—1979

Under this provision, when separate property has increased in value due to the uncompensated common labor and industry of either spouse, the other spouse is entitled to one-half of the increase. To the extent that a spouse is compensated for his labor, no reimbursement is due.

Prior Civil Code Article 2408 provided a right of reimbursement when separate property increased in value due to the common labor, interpreted as the labor of either spouse. Reimbursement could not be obtained if the increase was due to the ordinary course of things only. See Beals v. Fontenot, 111 F.2d 956 (5th Cir. 1940); Abraham v. Abraham, 87 So. 735 (La.1956).

Art. 2369.   Accounting between spouses; prescription

A spouse owes an accounting to the other spouse for community property under his control at the termination of the community property regime.

The obligation to account prescribes in three years from the date of termination of the community property regime.

Acts 1979, No. 709, § 1, eff. Jan. 1, 1980.

REVISION COMMENTS—1979

(a) This provision is new.

(b) This provision establishes the obligation of a spouse who has community property under his control at the termination of the community property regime to account to the other spouse for his administration. This is a heritable obligation. Thus, a spouse, or his heirs, may demand an accounting under this provision from the other spouse, or his heirs.

(c) Under the regime of the Louisiana Civil Code of 1870, courts have at times required a husband to account for his administration of community property during the existence of the community property regime. See, e.g., Hodson v. Hodson, 292 So.2d 831 (La.App.2d Cir. 1974); cf. Broyles v. Broyles, 215 So.2d 526 (La.App. 1st Cir. 1968). In this revision, either spouse may be required to account for community property under his control during the existence of the community property regime. Article 2354, supra, declares: "A spouse is liable for any loss or damage caused by fraud or bad faith in the management of the community property." This obligation may be enforced by action during marriage. R.S. 9:291, as amended by Acts 1979, No. 711, § 2. Prescription is not suspended by marriage.

In contrast with Article 2354, the obligation for accounting under Article 2369 is not predicated upon a showing of fraud or bad faith in the administration of the community. A spouse having control of community property at the termination of a community property regime occupies the position of a co-owner under the general law of property. Thus, he ought to be accountable for any loss or deterioration of the things under his control attributed to his fault, and for the fruits produced by the things, since the termination of the community property regime. Article 2369 thus reiterates a rule that governs the relations between co-owners.

(d) When a community property regime terminates by judgment, the judgment is retroactive to the date of the filing of the petition. See Art. 2375, infra. When, exceptionally, a judgment terminating the community is rendered more than three years from the date of the filing of the suit, argument may be made that the three year prescription governing the obligation to account has already accrued. However, according to Article 3528 of the Louisiana Civil Code of 1870, as interpreted by the jurisprudence, the filing of a suit constitutes a continuous interruption of prescription. See R.S. 9:5801. Thus, in effect, prescription commences to run from the date of the judgment that terminates the community.

555

Art. 2369.1. Application of co-ownership provisions

After termination of the community property regime, the provisions governing co-ownership apply to former community property, unless otherwise provided by law or by juridical act.

When the community property regime terminates for a cause other than death or judgment of declaration of death of a spouse, the following Articles also apply to former community property until a partition, or the death or judgment of declaration of death of a spouse.

Added by Acts 1990, No. 991, § 1. Amended by Acts 1995, No. 433, § 1.

COMMENT—1990

Article 2369.1 has been enacted to provide that in the absence of a contrary provision of law or juridical act the provisions governing co-ownership apply after termination of the community property regime. During the existence of the community property regime, the provisions governing matrimonial regimes take precedence over the provisions governing co-ownership. See C.C. Art. 2336, Comment (a); id. Art. 2337, Comment (a). After termination of the community, the interests of the former spouses in anything held in indivision are treated as co-ownership. See Spaht and Hargrave, Matrimonial Regimes 317 (1989); cf. C.C. Art. 2369, Comment (c).

COMMENTS—1995

(a) This Article clarifies the law. The provisions of the Civil Code setting forth the general principles of co-ownership are contained in Civil Code Articles 797–818 (rev. 1990). During the existence of the community property regime, the provisions of the Civil Code governing matrimonial regimes take precedence over those governing simple co-ownership. See C.C. Art. 2336 (rev. 1979), Comment (a); C.C. Art. 2337 (rev. 1979), Comment (a). After termination of the community, ownership of the former spouses in anything held in indivision generally has been treated as simple co-ownership. Thus, for example, there is no equal management of former community property. See C.C. Art. 801 (rev. 1990); C.C. Art. 2369 (rev. 1979), Comment (c); Spaht and Hargrave, Louisiana Civil Law Treatise, vol. 16, Matrimonial Regimes, sec. 7.19, p. 317 (West 1989). Cf. C.C. Art 2346 (rev. 1979). This Article provides that former community property will be governed by the general principles of co-ownership, but only if it is not otherwise provided by law or by juridical act.

(b) The seven articles that follow in this Section of the Civil Code are examples of instances where the law provides otherwise when the community terminates for a cause other than death or judgment of declaration of death. See C.C. Art. 2356 (rev. 1979) (causes of termination). These articles depart from the principles of co-ownership in a number of important respects, such as the nonalienability of each spouse's share in former community property without the other spouse's consent (C.C. Art. 2369.4 (rev. 1995)), and the special rules governing management of former community assets (C.C. Arts. 2369.5, 2369.6 (rev. 1995)). The need for these departures is explained in Spaht, Developments in the Law 1989–1990—Matrimonial Regimes, 51 La.L.Rev. 321 (1990).

When the community regime terminates because of the death or judgment of declaration of death of a spouse, the general rules of co-ownership, under the first paragraph of this Article, apply to former community property.

(c) The phrase "unless otherwise provided by law" refers to other provisions of Section 3 of this Chapter of Title VI of Book III of the Civil Code, such as Article 2357 (rev. 1979). These articles depart from the principles governing ordinary co-owners on the basis that the unique and peculiar species of co-ownership, the community of acquets and gains, has previously existed between the spouses. Thus, Article 2357 provides that obligations incurred by a spouse prior to termination of the community regime may be satisfied from the entirety of former community property.

(d) The term "spouse" is used in this Article and the other articles of this Section of the Civil Code for the sake of simplicity of expression. In fact, co-owners of former community property are sometimes still spouses, for example, when a separation of property is decreed at the request of a spouse under Civil Code Article 2374 (rev. 1979), but are more often former spouses who must hold former community property in co-ownership during the period of months or years that often ensues between the entry of a judgment of divorce and the judicial or extrajudicial partition of that former community property. Whichever is the situation in a given case, these Articles apply to spouse or former spouse co-owners of former community property until that property is partitioned.

Art. 2369.2. Ownership interest

Each spouse owns an undivided one-half interest in former community property and its fruits and products.

Added by Acts 1995, No. 433, § 1.

COMMENTS—1995

(a) This Article restates in part the rules provided in Civil Code Article 797 (rev. 1990) and the first Paragraph of Civil Code Article 798 (rev. 1990) for ordinary co-owners. Since there are only two co-owners of former community property, this Article simply provides that, in the ordinary case, each spouse continues to own an undivided one-half interest in former community property as that spouse did before termination of the community regime. C.C. Art. 2336 (rev. 1979).

(b) If the spouses have adopted a community regime by matrimonial agreement that alters the fractional ownership interests of the spouses in community property, that same interest will be maintained after termination under the authority of Civil Code Articles 797 and 798 (rev. 1990). See C.C. Art. 2330 (rev. 1979), comment (d).

(c) In keeping with Civil Code Articles 2338 (rev. 1979) and 798 (rev. 1990), this Article also provides that a spouse owns an undivided one-half interest in the fruits and products of former community property. For a definition of fruits and products, see Civil Code Articles 551 (rev. 1976), 488 (rev. 1979), and 2339 (rev. 1979).

(d) A spouse's right to recover costs of producing fruits and products is governed by Civil Code Article 798 (rev. 1990) (ordinary co-owners). The claim by the producing spouse is properly assertable in an action of partition under R.S. 9:2801. Under Civil Code Article 798 (rev. 1990), the producing spouse co-owner may not claim reimbursement for the value of his services or labor in producing fruits or products. See C.C. Art. 798 (rev. 1990), comment (c). For a critique, see Symeonides & Martin, The New Law of Co-ownership: A Kommentar, 68 Tul.L.Rev. 701, 729–32 (1993). See also Samuel, Restoration of the Separate Estate from Community Property after the Equal Management Reform: Some Thoughts on Louisiana's Reimbursement Rules, 56 Law and Contemp. Problems 273 (1993).

Art. 2369.3. Duty to preserve; standard of care

A spouse has a duty to preserve and to manage prudently former community property under his control, including a former community enterprise, in a manner consistent with the mode of use of that property immediately prior to termination of the community regime. He is answerable for any damage caused by his fault, default, or neglect.

A community enterprise is a business that is not a legal entity.

Added by Acts 1995, No. 433, § 1.

COMMENTS—1995

(a) This Article changes the law. First, it imposes on a spouse who has control of former community property an affirmative duty "to preserve and to manage" such property. In contrast, Civil Code Article 800 (rev. 1990), applicable to ordinary co-owners, provides for a right but not a duty to act for the preservation of the property. Such a duty arises only if the co-owner undertakes to act as a negotiorum gestor or he is appointed as administrator. See Symeonides & Martin, The New Law of Co-ownership: A Kommentar, 68 Tul.L.Rev. 701, 746 (1993). Similarly, the co-ownership articles of the Civil Code do not impose on one co-owner an affirmative duty to manage the co-owned thing unless that owner assumed the qualities of a gestor or was appointed as an administrator. See C.C. Arts. 801, 803 (rev. 1990); Symeonides & Martin, supra at 738–748. Second, this Article imposes a higher standard of care than that provided by Civil Code Article 799 (rev. 1990) for ordinary co-owners. See comment (g), infra.

This Article also imposes a higher standard of care in managing and maintaining such former community property than the standard imposed during the marriage for managing community property. See C.C. Art. 2354 (rev. 1979). The reason for imposing a higher standard of care in managing former community property is that, after termination of the community property regime,

557

the law no longer assumes that a spouse who has former community property under his control will act in the best interest of both spouses in managing it.

(b) This Article applies to "former community property, including a former community enterprise." "[F]ormer community enterprise" refers to a former community business that is not a legal entity. See C.C. Art. 2347 (rev. 1979), comment (b). Recognition of the business as a collective of things, although it has no juridical personality, continues after termination of the community regime for the purposes of this Section.

(c) The provisions of this Article overlap to some extent those of Civil Code Article 2369 (rev. 1979). Article 2369, however, focuses on a moment in time at which a spouse may have control over community property. That moment is the date of termination of the community. As to former community property over which the spouse had control at that moment, a duty is imposed upon that spouse "to account", i.e., to explain what happened to the property that was then under his control. To invoke that duty a spouse need prove only that the other spouse had control of former community property at the moment of termination of the regime. Then the burden shifts to the other spouse to prove what disposition was made of the property. This obligation is subject to a very short prescriptive period of three years from the date of termination of the community regime. See C.C. Art. 2369 (rev. 1979).

By contrast, the duty to preserve and manage former community property under one spouse's control imposed by this Article arises at the moment of termination of the community regime and continues until a partition of the former community property occurs. A claim for breach of the obligation imposed by this Article is subject to a longer prescriptive period of ten years. C.C. Art. 3499 (rev. 1983). Furthermore, the claim requires a spouse to prove that the other spouse failed to act prudently in a manner consistent with the mode of use of the property immediately prior to termination of the regime, not simply that he had former community property under his control.

(d) The phrase "in a manner consistent with the mode of use of that property immediately prior to termination of the community regime" is intended to particularize the standard against which to judge the acts of a spouse undertaken to preserve and especially to manage the former community property. The language "mode of use" appears in Civil Code article 803 (rev. 1990) (use and management of co-owned thing in absence of agreement) and is intended to have the same meaning as in that article. To preserve and manage former community property in accordance with its mode of use immediately prior to termination of the community regime does not require a spouse with such property under his control to make previously unproductive property productive.

(e) Under this Article a spouse is liable for any damage caused by his "fault, default, or neglect." This language is almost identical to that found in Civil Code Article 576 (rev. 1976) (standard of care), explaining the responsibility of a usufructuary to the naked owner for losses to the property. See Article 576, comments (b) and (c), describing the standard of care of the usufructuary as that of a "prudent administrator." See also Symeonides & Martin, The New Law of Co-ownership: A Kommentar, 68 Tul.L.Rev. 701, 732–743 (1993), comparing the standard applicable to usufructuaries with that applicable to ordinary co-owners as well as co-owners acting as gestors or administrators. The spouse who has control over former community property occupies a position similar to that of the usufructuary and thus should have the same standard of care in managing and preserving former community property. The same types of reasons exist for imposing a high standard of care upon both the usufructuary and a spouse who controls former community property.

(f) A spouse who incurs expenses in compliance with the obligation imposed by this Article is entitled to reimbursement for one-half the costs in accordance with general principles of the law of co-ownership. C.C. Art. 806 (rev. 1990).

(g) The standard of care that a spouse must satisfy in the management and maintenance of former community property not under his control is that of an ordinary co-owner under Civil Code Article 799 (rev. 1990). The spouse is liable for damages occasioned to such former community property due to his fault. See C.C. Art. 799 (rev. 1990) and comments thereto; Symeonides & Martin, The New Law of Co-ownership: A Kommentar, 68 Tul.L.Rev. 701, 732–743 (1993).

Art. 2369.4. Alienation, encumbrance, or lease prohibited

A spouse may not alienate, encumber, or lease former community property or his undivided community interest in that property without the concurrence of the other spouse, except as provided in the following Articles. In the absence of such concurrence, the alienation, encumbrance, or lease is a relative nullity.

Added by Acts 1995, No. 433, § 1.

COMMENTS—1995

(a) The principle expressed in the first Paragraph of this Article differs from the general principle of equal management that prevails during the existence of the community regime, under which either spouse acting alone may validly alienate, encumber, or lease community property. See C.C. Art. 2346 (rev. 1979). Nonetheless, the first Paragraph is consistent with the major exception to that general principle—that concurrence of the spouses is required for the alienation, encumbrance, or lease of certain specified classes of community assets during the existence of the community regime. See C.C. Art. 2347 (rev. 1979). The reason for adopting a much broader requirement of concurrence for alienation, encumbrance, or lease of former community property is that, during the existence of the community regime while it may be assumed that a spouse will exercise his management powers in such a way as to promote the mutual purposes of the community regime, no such assumption exists after termination of the community regime.

On the other hand, vis-a-vis a spouse's undivided interest in former community property, this Article is similar to Civil Code Article 2337 (1979), which provides that during the existence of the community regime a spouse may not unilaterally alienate his undivided interest in community property to a third person. However, the provisions of this Article differ in one important respect from those of Article 2337. Under this Article there is a clear implication that a spouse may concur in an alienation, encumbrance, or lease of the other spouse's undivided interest in former community property, and thereby render it valid. Comment (b) to Article 2337, by contrast, suggests that even if a spouse consents to the alienation of the other spouse's one-half interest in community property during the existence of the community, the transaction is an absolute nullity.

(b) This Article is consistent with the second sentence of Civil Code Article 805 (rev. 1990) which requires "consent of all the co-owners for the lease, alienation or encumbrance of the entire thing held in indivision." However, this Article departs from the part of Article 805 that provides "[a] co-owner may freely lease, alienate, or encumber his share of the thing held in indivision" [emphasis added]. The reason for this departure is the need to prevent a stranger from owning former community property in indivision with a spouse, and to protect the right of the spouses to a partition of former community property under the flexible principles of R.S. 9:2801, rather than the more rigid partition rules governing ordinary co-owners. See C.C. Arts. 810–811 (rev. 1990).

(c) The language "alienation, encumbrance, or lease" in the first Paragraph of this Article corresponds to the use of the same words in Civil Code Article 2347 (rev. 1979) concerning concurrence of both spouses during the existence of the regime. Therefore, concurrence of both spouses is not required to subject former community property in its entirety to the satisfaction of obligations incurred by either spouse prior to termination of the community regime. See C.C. Art. 2357 (rev. 1979); C.C. Art. 2336 (rev. 1979), comment (c); C.C. Art. 2347 (rev. 1979), comment (a).

(d) The general requirement of concurrence stated in this Article is subject to exceptions which are contained in the following three Articles. If a movable is issued or registered in the name of one spouse, that spouse may alienate that movable without concurrence of the other spouse. See C.C. Art. 2369.5 (rev. 1995). If a spouse is the sole manager of a former community enterprise, under Civil Code Article 2369.6 (rev. 1995), that spouse has the exclusive right to alienate, encumber, or lease the movable assets of the enterprise in the regular course of business. The other exception is if a spouse obtains court authorization to act alone under Civil Code Article 2369.7 (rev. 1995).

(e) Under the second Paragraph of this Article an alienation, encumbrance, or lease of former community property or of a spouse's undivided interest in such property by one spouse alone is a relative nullity. The result is the same as for a transaction by one spouse alone of a kind that requires concurrence during the existence of the community regime. See C.C. Art. 2353 (rev. 1979).

Art. 2369.5. Alienation of registered movables

A spouse may alienate, encumber, or lease a movable issued or registered in his name as provided by law.

Added by Acts 1995, No. 433, § 1.

COMMENTS—1995

(a) Under this Article a co-owner spouse in whose name a movable is issued or registered as provided by law may alienate, encumber, or lease by onerous title the movable without concurrence of the other spouse. This exception to the principle enunciated in Civil Code Article 2369.4 (rev. 1995) is for the protection of third parties. The same exception exists during the existence of the community regime. See C.C. Art. 2351 (rev. 1979). Nevertheless, the spouse with authority to alienate, encumber, or lease movables issued in his name that are former community property owes the duty to preserve and manage such property prudently. See C.C. Art. 2369.3.

(b) Issued or registered movables include movables regulated by the Commercial Laws (R.S. 10:8–101 et seq.) and the Vehicle Certificate of Title Law (R.S. 32:701 et seq.) (investment securities). See also, Civil Code Article 2351 (rev. 1979), comment (a), for other examples.

Art. 2369.6. Alienation, encumbrance, or lease of movable assets of former community enterprise

The spouse who is the sole manager of a former community enterprise may alienate, encumber, or lease its movables in the regular course of business.

Added by Acts 1995, No. 433, § 1.

COMMENTS—1995

(a) This Article enunciates the second of three exceptions to the requirement of Civil Code Article 2369.4 (rev. 1995) for concurrence of the spouses for the alienation, encumbrance, or lease of former community property. It establishes a rule of sole and exclusive power in one spouse to alienate, encumber, or lease by onerous title movable assets of a former community enterprise, but only if the transaction is in the regular course of business. It is similar to the exception of sole and exclusive authority of a manager spouse to alienate movable assets of a community enterprise during the existence of the community regime. See C.C. Art. 2350 (rev. 1979). No such exception is present in the law of simple co-ownership.

(b) There is an important limitation in this Article upon actions by a spouse who is sole manager of a former community enterprise with regard to its movable assets. An alienation, encumbrance, or lease of such property by the manager spouse acting alone must be "in the regular course of business." This phrase is borrowed from Civil Code Article 2040 (rev. 1984), governing the revocatory action. Jurisprudence interpreting the phrase in Article 2040 may be relied upon to determine its meaning in this Article. This Article limits the power of a spouse who manages a former community enterprise in an effort to protect the other spouse, yet it permits the enterprise to continue to operate and produce co-owned income.

Art. 2369.7. Court authorization to act alone

A spouse may be authorized by the court in a summary proceeding to act without the concurrence of the other spouse, upon showing all of the following:

(1) The action is necessary.

(2) The action is in the best interest of the petitioning spouse and not detrimental to the interest of the nonconcurring spouse.

(3) The other spouse is an absent person or arbitrarily refuses to concur, or is unable to concur due to physical incapacity, mental incompetence, commitment, imprisonment, or temporary absence.

Added by Acts 1995, No. 433, § 1.

COMMENTS—1995

(a) This Article departs from the law of ordinary co-ownership, which allows court intervention only for matters of "use and management" and only when "partition is not available." C.C. Art. 803 (rev. 1990). See Symeonides & Martin, The New Law of Co-ownership: A Kommentar, 68 Tul.L.Rev. 761–764 (1993). This Article establishes a broader right of judicial recourse when the spouses cannot agree on management or other decisions affecting former community property, but also provides specific criteria for guiding judicial action in such cases.

(b) A spouse may seek judicial authorization to act alone under this Article whenever concurrence is required to alienate, encumber, or lease former community property. However, to obtain judicial authorization under this Article requires more stringent proof than that required for obtaining the same authorization during the existence of the community regime. Under this Article a spouse must additionally prove that the action is "necessary." Compare C.C. Art. 2355 (rev. 1979). Authorization may be sought by summary proceeding.

Art. 2369.8. Right to partition; no exclusion by agreement; judicial partition

A spouse has the right to demand partition of former community property at any time. A contrary agreement is absolutely null.

If the spouses are unable to agree on the partition, either spouse may demand judicial partition which shall be conducted in accordance with R.S. 9:2801.

Added by Acts 1995, No. 433, § 1.

COMMENTS—1995

(a) This Article provides that a spouse may demand partition of former community property at any time, and no agreement of the spouses may provide otherwise. The latter provision is a conscious departure from the corresponding rule applicable to ordinary co-owners. See C.C. Art. 807 (rev. 1990).

(b) The spouses may partition former community property by contract or judicially, just as may ordinary co-owners. However, the judicial partition of community property is to be governed by the special procedures of R.S. 9:2801, not Civil Code Articles 810–813 (rev. 1990).

CHAPTER 3—SEPARATION OF PROPERTY REGIME

Art. 2370. Separation of property regime

A regime of separation of property is established by a matrimonial agreement that excludes the legal regime of community of acquets and gains or by a judgment decreeing separation of property.

Acts 1979, No. 709, § 1, eff. Jan. 1, 1980.

REVISION COMMENTS—1979

(a) A separation of property regime is established by a matrimonial agreement that excludes or terminates the legal regime of community of acquets and gains or by a judgment to that effect. The spouses may, of course, provide in a matrimonial agreement that they opt for the regime of separation of property or that they do not wish to be subject to the legal regime of community of acquets and gains. When the spouses modify by agreement the legal regime of community of acquets and gains, the regime is partly legal and partly contractual. See Arts. 2326 and 2329, supra. In such a case, the provisions of the legal regime that have not been excluded or modified retain their force and effect, and the rights and obligations of the spouses are determined by the rules of the legal regime that have not been excluded or modified, by contractual provisions, or by application of the rules governing separation of property.

(b) When the spouses live under a separation of property regime, they may establish this fact toward third persons by virtue of a recorded matrimonial agreement or judgment, in accordance with C.C. Art. 2332, supra.

Art. 2371. Management of property

Under the regime of separation of property each spouse acting alone uses, enjoys, and disposes of his property without the consent or concurrence of the other spouse.

Acts 1979, No. 709, § 1, eff. Jan. 1, 1980.

REVISION COMMENT—1979

Individuals have the right to freely dispose of the property which belongs to them, under the restrictions established by law. See C.C. Art. 454, as revised in 1978.

Art. 2372. Necessaries

A spouse is solidarily liable with the other spouse who incurs an obligation for necessaries for himself or the family.

Acts 1979, No. 709, § 1, eff. Jan. 1, 1980.

REVISION COMMENTS—1979

(a) This provision is new. It imposes on spouses solidary liability toward creditors for obligations incurred by either spouse for necessaries for himself or the family. As between the spouses, however, the debt is apportioned in accordance with Article 2373, infra.

(b) The word "family" in this provision refers to the limited family concept of Article 3556(12) of the Louisiana Civil Code of 1870.

Art. 2373. Expenses of the marriage

Each spouse contributes to the expenses of the marriage as provided in the matrimonial agreement. In the absence of such a provision, each spouse contributes in proportion to his means.

Acts 1979, No. 709, § 1, eff. Jan. 1, 1980.

REVISION COMMENT—1979

Prior law permitted spouses conventionally separate in property to agree as to the sharing of expenses of the marriage and provided that the wife contribute to the extent of one-half of her income in the absence of agreement. See C.C. Art. 2395 (1870). Article 2373 changes prior law by requiring each spouse, in the absence of agreement, to contribute in proportion to his means.

Art. 2374. Judgment of separation of property

A.   When the interest of a spouse in a community property regime is threatened to be diminished by the fraud, fault, neglect, or incompetence of the other spouse, or by the disorder of the affairs of the other spouse, he may obtain a judgment decreeing separation of property.

B.   When a spouse is an absent person, the other spouse is entitled to a judgment decreeing separation of property.

C.   When a petition for divorce has been filed, upon motion of either spouse, a judgment decreeing separation of property may be obtained upon proof that the spouses have lived separate and apart without reconciliation for at least thirty days from the date of, or prior to, the filing of the petition for divorce.

D.   When the spouses have lived separate and apart continuously for a period of six months, a judgment decreeing separation of property shall be granted on the petition of either spouse.

Acts 1979, No. 709, § 1, eff. Jan. 1, 1980. Amended by Acts 1990, No. 989, § 2, eff. Jan. 1, 1991; Acts 1992, No. 295, § 1; Acts 1993, No. 25, § 1; Acts 1993, No. 627, § 1; Acts 2010, No. 603, § 1, eff. June 25, 2010.

REVISION COMMENT—1979

None.

Art. 2375. Effect of judgment

A. Except as provided in Paragraph C of this Article, a judgment decreeing separation of property terminates the regime of community property retroactively to the day of the filing of the petition or motion therefor, without prejudice to rights validly acquired in the interim between filing of the petition or motion and rendition of judgment.

B. If a judgment has been rendered on the ground that the spouses have lived separate and apart either after the filing of a petition for divorce without having reconciled or for six months, a reconciliation reestablishes the regime of community property between the spouses retroactively to the day of the filing of the motion or petition therefor, unless prior to the reconciliation the spouses execute a matrimonial agreement to the contrary. This agreement need not be approved by the court and is effective toward third persons when filed for registry in the manner provided by Article 2332. The reestablishment of the community is effective toward third persons when a notice thereof is filed for registry in the same manner.

C. If a judgment is rendered on the ground that the spouses were living separate and apart without having reconciled for at least thirty days from the date of, or prior to, the filing of the petition for divorce, the judgment shall be effective retroactively to the date the petition for divorce was filed, without prejudice to rights validly acquired in the interim. All subsequent pleadings or motions involving matters incidental to the divorce shall be filed in the first filed suit.

Acts 1979, No. 709, § 1, eff. Jan. 1, 1980. Amended by Acts 1992, No. 295, § 1; Acts 1993, No. 25, § 1; Acts 1993, No. 627, § 1; Acts 1997, No. 35, § 1; Acts 2010, No. 603, § 1, eff. June 25, 2010.

REVISION COMMENT—1979

When a spouse obtains a judgment substituting the regime of separation of property, the spouses will be regulated by the provisions of the legal regime of separation of property, in such matters as management and disposition of property and contributing to the expenses of the marriage.

Art. 2376. Rights of creditors

The creditors of a spouse, by intervention in the proceeding, may object to the separation of property or modification of their matrimonial regime as being in fraud of their rights. They also may sue to annul a judgment of separation of property within one year from the date of the rendition of the final judgment. After execution of the judgment, they may assert nullity only to the extent that they have been prejudiced.

Acts 1979, No. 709, § 1, eff. Jan. 1, 1980.

REVISION COMMENT—1979

A creditor may sue to annul a contract of separation of property as in fraud of his rights under C.C. Arts. 2036–2044 (Rev. 1984).

Arts. 2377 to 2431. [Blank]

CHAPTER 4—MARITAL PORTION

Art. 2432. Right to marital portion

When a spouse dies rich in comparison with the surviving spouse, the surviving spouse is entitled to claim the marital portion from the succession of the deceased spouse.

Acts 1979, No. 710, § 1, eff. Jan. 1, 1980.

REVISION COMMENTS—1979

(a) This provision reproduces the substance of the first sentence of Article 2382 of the Louisiana Civil Code of 1870, as interpreted by jurisprudence. It does not change the law.

(b) See Yiannopoulos, Personal Servitudes § 114 (2d ed. 1978): According to Article 2382 of the Louisiana Civil Code, "if either the husband or the wife die rich, leaving the survivor in necessitous circumstances, the latter has a right to take out of the succession of the deceased what is called the marital portion". The source of this provision may be found in the Novellae of Justinian and in the Spanish laws prevailing in Louisiana at the time of the purchase. Their object is "to prevent a spouse on the death of the other from being left in abject poverty after having become accustomed to the wealth of the decedent". Malone v. Cannon, 215 La. 939, 959, 41 So.2d 837, 843 (1949). See also Succession of Henry, 287 So.2d 214 (La.App. 3rd Cir. 1973).

(c) According to Article 2382 of the Louisiana Civil Code of 1870, recovery of the marital portion depends on the conditions that the deceased spouse dies "rich" and the survivor is left in "necessitous circumstances." These conditions are relative; their fulfillment depends on a comparison of the patrimonial assets of the deceased with those of the survivor. See Malone v. Cannon, 215 La. 939, 41 So.2d 837 (1949); Smith v. Smith, 43 La.Ann. 1140, 10 So. 248 (1891); Succession of Leppelman, 30 La.Ann. 468 (1878); Harrell v. Harrell, 17 La. 374 (1841); Moore v. Succession of Moore, 7 So.2d 716 (La.App.2d Cir. 1942); Wimprenne v. Jouty, 12 La.App. 326, 125 So. 154 (La.App.Orl. Cir. 1929). See also Smitherman v. Smitherman, 240 So.2d 69 (La.App.2d Cir. 1970): " 'Rich', as heretofore noted, is a relative term. Property which would make a person in one walk of life rich would be inadequate to supply the wants of one in another condition of life"; Succession of Thumfart, 289 So.2d 850 (La.App. 4th Cir. 1974); Succession of Harris, 283 So.2d 325 (La.App. 4th Cir. 1973). For comparison of assets, see Succession of Neal, 242 So.2d 328 (La.App.2d Cir. 1971); Smitherman v. Smitherman, 240 So.2d 6 (La.App.2d Cir. 1970) (claim for marital portion denied; the value of the property left by the deceased spouse was less than twice that owned by the survivor in her own right). While no concrete test has ever been devised by Louisiana courts, the survivor will ordinarily be awarded the marital portion when the comparison of patrimonial assets show a ratio of five to one or more. For illustrations of comparative wealth, see Comment, Codal Exceptions to the Louisiana law of Heirship: The Marital Fourth and the Widow's Homestead, 18 Tul.L.Rev. 290, 302 (1943). Whether the survivor is left in necessitous circumstances or not is determined as of the time of dissolution of marriage by death. See Connor's Widow v. Connor's Admr's & Heirs, 10 La.Ann. 440 (1855). See also Succession of Kunemann, 115 La. 604, 39 So. 702 (1905). For a critical discussion of the controlling time for this determination, see Comment, The Marital Fourth and the Widow's Homestead, 25 La.L.Rev. 259, 272–74 (1964). Future earning capacity of the survivor and support he may expect from grown up children are not patrimonial assets; accordingly, these items are not taken into account in determining the financial situation of the survivor. See Succession of Fortier, 3 La.Ann. 104 (1848). In succession of Thumfart, 289 So.2d 850, 853 (La.App. 4th Cir. 1974), the court declared that "the earnings or earning capacity of a spouse are not a factor in determining whether the marital portion of Civil Code Article 2382 is due from the other spouse's estate."

See also Dupuy v. Dupuy, 52 La.Ann. 869, 27 So. 287 (1899); cf. Yiannopoulos, Civil Law Property Sec. 78 (1966).

Art. 2433.   Incident of marriage; charge on the succession

The marital portion is an incident of any matrimonial regime and a charge on the succession of the deceased spouse. It may be claimed by the surviving spouse, even if separated from the deceased, on proof that the separation occurred without his fault.

Acts 1979, No. 710, § 1, eff. Jan. 1, 1980.

REVISION COMMENTS—1979

(a) This provision is new. It codifies Louisiana jurisprudence interpreting Article 2382 of the Louisiana Civil Code of 1870. See Succession of Lichtentag, 363 So.2d 706 (La.1978).

(b) See Yiannopoulos, Personal Servitudes § 114 (2d ed. 1978): Recovery of the marital portion is predicated on "the existence of a normal marriage—both in law and in fact—in which the spouses discharge the mutual duties specified in Civil Code Articles 119 and 120, particularly those of fidelity, support and assistance". Malone v. Cannon, 215 La. at 959, 41 So.2d at 843. See also Pickens v. Gillam, 43 La.Ann. 350, 8 So. 928 (1891); Armstrong v. Steeber, 3 La.Ann. 713 (1848). The spouses may be putative in good faith. Smith v. Smith, 43 La.Ann. 1140, 10 So. 248 (1891). If there has been separation in fact, the survivor, in order to obtain the marital portion, must prove that the separation occurred without his fault. Malone v. Cannon, 215 La. 939, 41 So.2d 837 (1949). See also Pickens v. Gillam, 43 La.Ann. 350, 8 So. 928 (1891); McMahon, The Original Case of the Misunderstood Wife, 11 Loyola L.J. 109 (1930). See also Succession of Harris, 283 So.2d 325 (La.App.4th Cir. 1973) (judicial separation; recovery). The same rule ought to apply in the case of judicial separation, and the blameless survivor ought to be entitled to obtain the marital portion. Early Louisiana decisions stand for the proposition that, since judicial separation from bed and board does not dissolve the bonds of matrimony, the faithful survivor is entitled to the portion if a divorce has not been obtained prior to the dissolution of the marriage by death. See Gee v. Thompson, 11 La.Ann. 657 (1856). Cf. Succession of Liddell, 22 La.Ann. 9 (1870). See also Succession of Harris, 283 So.2d 325 (La.App. 4th Cir. 1973).

(c) The survivor may claim the marital portion even if the deceased spouse disposed of his property by will in favor of persons other than the surviving spouse. In Malone v. Cannon, 215 La. 939, 41 So.2d 837, 839 (1949), the Louisiana Supreme Court declared that "the marital fourth appears to be a benefit which the law obligates an estate to provide under certain conditions to a surviving spouse, irrespective of the rights of heirs, forced or otherwise, and of legatees. . . . Moreover, by its very terms, Article 2382 shows that the marital fourth is demandable in a testate, as well as in an intestate succession."

(d) Early Louisiana decisions classified the survivor's right as an inheritance right in order to preclude demands by heirs of a survivor who did not himself claim the portion. See Connor's Widow v. Connor's Admr's & Heirs, 10 La.Ann. 440 (1855); affirmed 18 How. 591, 15 Law Ed. 497. Dunbar v. Dunbar's Heirs, 5 La.Ann. 158 (1850); Abercrombie v. Caffray, 3 Mart. (N.S.) 1 (1824). Cf. Siete Partidas, Pt. 6, tit. 13, 1.7. However, Louisiana courts declared later that "it is not an inheritance. . . . It is a gift, a bounty, bestowed, not by the deceased, but by the law". Malone v. Cannon, 215 La. 939, 949, 41 So.2d 837, 840 (1949). See also Succession of Lichtentag, 363 So.2d 706 (La.1978), Succession of Henry, 287 So.2d 214 (La.App.3rd Cir.1973).

(e) When the heirs simply have the succession and make no effort to settle the succession, the courts do not permit the spouse's claim to the marital portion to be defeated. In such cases, the survivor's right follows the property into the hands of the heirs. See Shaw v. Reneau, 10 La.Ann. 190 (La.1844); Wiezler v. Harvey, 9 Orl.App. 190 (1912).

Art. 2434. Quantum

The marital portion is one-fourth of the succession in ownership if the deceased died without children, the same fraction in usufruct for life if he is survived by three or fewer children, and a child's share in such usufruct if he is survived by more than three children. In no event, however, shall the amount of the marital portion exceed one million dollars.

Acts 1979, No. 710, § 1, eff. Jan. 1, 1980. Amended by Acts 1987, No. 289, § 1.

REVISION COMMENTS—1979

(a) This provision reproduces the substance of the pertinent dispositions in Article 2382 of the Louisiana Civil Code of 1870. It does not change the law.

(b) See Yiannopoulos, Personal Servitudes § 114 (2d ed. 1978). If the deceased died without children, the marital portion is one-fourth of the succession in perfect ownership; if there are three or fewer children, the survivor takes the fourth in usufruct; and if there are more than three children, the survivor receives only a child's portion in usufruct. The word "children" in Article 2382 of the Louisiana Civil Code ought to be understood in the light of the definition in Article 3556(8) of the same Code and should include grandchildren and other direct descendants. Further, for the determination of the survivor's marital portion, adopted children and the issue of a previous marriage of the deceased spouse are "children" within the meaning of Article 2382. Taylor v. Taylor, 189 La. 1084, 181 So. 543 (1938); Abercrombie v. Caffray, 3 Mart. (N.S.) 1 (La.1824).

(c) The survivor receiving the marital portion in usufruct incurs, in principle, the rights and duties of usufructuaries under the general law. Taylor v. Taylor, 189 La. 1084, 1093, 181 So. 543, 546 (1938). Cf. Hartford Accident & Indemnity Co. v. Abdalla, 203 La. 999, 14 So.2d 815 (1943). He is exempt, however, from the requirement of posting security. The usufruct attaches to the proceeds of a liquidated succession and is one of money. The principle of "le mort saisit le vif" does not apply to the marital portion. Since Article 2382 makes no provision for termination of the usufruct upon remarriage, this usufruct is for life and terminates in accordance with the general provisions governing usufruct. See C.C. Arts. 607–629, as revised in 1976.

(d) The surviving spouse is entitled to the usufruct of one-fourth or of a lesser fraction of the succession, depending on the number of children. He is not entitled to the value of such a fraction in usufruct or to a usufruct having a value equal to that of such a fraction of the succession. Succession of Henry, 287 So.2d 214 (La.App. 3d Cir. 1973), is overruled to the extent that it is inconsistent with Article 2434.

Art. 2435. Deduction of legacy

A legacy left by the deceased to the surviving spouse and payments due to him as a result of the death are deducted from the marital portion.

Acts 1979, No. 710, § 1, eff. Jan. 1, 1980.

REVISION COMMENTS—1979

(a) This provision reproduces the substance of the first paragraph, last sentence, of Article 2382 of the Louisiana Civil Code of 1870. It changes the law as it requires deduction of payments due to the surviving spouse as a result of the death of the other spouse.

(b) See Yiannopoulos, Personal Servitudes § 114 (2d ed. 1978). Legacies left to the survivor by the deceased must be deducted from the marital portion. See Succession of Lichtentag, 363 So.2d 706 (La.1978) and Succession of Henry, 287 So.2d 214 (La.App. 3d Cir. 1973); Melancon's Widow v. His Executor, 6 La. 105 (1833).

(c) "Payments" includes benefits derived from life insurance, social security and pension plans.

Art. 2436. Nonheritable right; prescription

The right of the surviving spouse to claim the marital portion is personal and nonheritable. This right prescribes three years from the date of death.

Acts 1979, No. 710, § 1, eff. Jan. 1, 1980.

REVISION COMMENTS—1979

(a) This provision is new. The first sentence codifies Louisiana jurisprudence interpreting Article 2382 of the Louisiana Civil Code of 1870. The second sentence establishes a three year prescriptive period in derogation from Article 3544 of the Louisiana Civil Code of 1870.

(b) The survivor's right to claim the portion is personal and nonheritable. Thus, "if the widow or widower does not take advantage of it while in necessitous circumstances, it is forever lost. Such a right if not exercised by the beneficiary, is not inherited by his or her heirs." Succession of Bancker, 154 La. 77, 80, 97 So. 321, 322 (1923). See also Succession of Justus, 44 La.Ann. 721, 11 So. 95 (1892). But if the survivor died after having made a demand, the claim becomes a patrimonial asset and is inherited by his or her heirs, who may thus recover the portion. See Succession of Piffet, 39 La.Ann. 556, 2 So. 210 (1887), distinguished in Succession of Justus, 44 La.Ann. 721, 725, 11 So. 95, 96 (1892). See also Succession of Bancker, 154 La. 77, 97 So. 321 (1923). For a critique, see Comment, The Marital Fourth and the Widow's Homestead, 25 La.L.Rev. 259, 269 (1964).

Art. 2437. Periodic allowance

When, during the administration of the succession, it appears that the surviving spouse will be entitled to the marital portion, he has the right to demand and receive a periodic allowance from the succession representative.

The amount of the allowance is fixed by the court in which the succession proceeding is pending. If the marital portion, as finally fixed, is less than the allowance, the surviving spouse is charged with the deficiency.

Acts 1979, No. 710, § 1, eff. Jan. 1, 1980.

REVISION COMMENT—1979

This Article reproduces the substance of the second paragraph of Article 2382 of the Louisiana Civil Code of 1870. It does not change the law.

TITLE VII—SALE

CHAPTER 1—OF THE NATURE AND FORM
OF THE CONTRACT OF SALE

Art. 2438. Rules of other titles

In all matters for which no special provision is made in this title, the contract of sale is governed by the rules of the titles on Obligations in General and Conventional Obligations or Contracts.

Acts 1993, No. 841, § 1, eff. Jan. 1, 1995.

REVISION COMMENT—1993

This Article reproduces the substance of Article 2438 of the Louisiana Civil Code of 1870. It does not change the law.

Art. 2439. Definition

Sale is a contract whereby a person transfers ownership of a thing to another for a price in money.

The thing, the price, and the consent of the parties are requirements for the perfection of a sale.

Acts 1993, No. 841, § 1, eff. Jan. 1, 1995.

REVISION COMMENT—1993

This Article reproduces the substance of Article 2439 of the Louisiana Civil Code of 1870. It does not change the law.

Art. 2440. Sale of immovable, method of making

A sale or promise of sale of an immovable must be made by authentic act or by act under private signature, except as provided in Article 1839.

Acts 1993, No. 841, § 1, eff. Jan. 1, 1995.

REVISION COMMENTS—1993

(a) This Article reproduces the substance of Article 2440 of the Louisiana Civil Code of 1870. It does not change the law.

(b) Under this Article, a description of immovable property in an act of sale is sufficient if it enables a person to locate and identify the property. See Hargrove v. Hodge, 121 So. 224 (La.App. 2d Cir.1928).

Art. 2441. [Blank]

Art. 2442. Recordation of sale of immovable to affect third parties

The parties to an act of sale or promise of sale of immovable property are bound from the time the act is made, but such an act is not effective against third parties until it is filed for registry according to the laws of registry.

Acts 1993, No. 841, § 1, eff. Jan. 1, 1995. Amended by Acts 2005, No. 169, § 2, eff. July 1, 2006.

REVISION COMMENT—1993

This Article changes the text of the source provision in part by providing that a sale of immovable property is effective against third parties "only from the time it is filed for recordation according to the laws of registry." Under Article 2442 of the Louisiana Civil Code of 1870, a sale made under private signature was effective against third parties "only from the day such sale was registered according to law, and the actual delivery of the thing sold took place." There is no change in the law, however. See R.S. 9:2721; C.C. Art. 1839.

Art. 2443. Purchase of a thing already owned

A person cannot purchase a thing he already owns. Nevertheless, the owner of a thing may purchase the rights of a person who has, or may have, an adverse claim to the thing.

Acts 1993, No. 841, § 1, eff. Jan. 1, 1995.

REVISION COMMENTS—1993

(a) This Article reproduces the substance of Article 2443 of the Louisiana Civil Code of 1870. It does not change the law.

(b) This Article does not reproduce the second sentence of Article 2443 of the Louisiana Civil Code of 1870 because the nullity of a transaction whereby a person purchases a thing he already owns clearly results from the legal impossibility to make such a purchase.

Arts. 2444 to 2446. [Blank]

CHAPTER 2—OF PERSONS CAPABLE OF BUYING AND SELLING

Art. 2447. Sale of litigious rights, prohibitions

Officers of a court, such as judges, attorneys, clerks, and law enforcement agents, cannot purchase litigious rights under contestation in the jurisdiction of that court. The purchase of a litigious right by such an officer is null and makes the purchaser liable for all costs, interest, and damages.

Acts 1993, No. 841, § 1, eff. Jan. 1, 1995.

REVISION COMMENTS—1993

(a) This Article reproduces the substance of Article 2447 of the Louisiana Civil Code of 1870. It does not change the law.

(b) Any act done in contravention of the provisions of this Article is a nullity, but that nullity can be invoked only by the party to the suit against whom the right is to be exercised. Saint v. Martel, 122 La. 93, 47 So. 413 (La.1918).

CHAPTER 3—OF THINGS WHICH MAY BE SOLD

Art. 2448. Things that may be sold

All things corporeal or incorporeal, susceptible of ownership, may be the object of a contract of sale, unless the sale of a particular thing is prohibited by law.

Acts 1993, No. 841, § 1, eff. Jan. 1, 1995.

REVISION COMMENTS—1993

(a) This Article reproduces the substance of Articles 2448 and 2449 of the Louisiana Civil Code of 1870. It does not change the law.

(b) The expression "of commerce" used in Article 2448 of the Civil Code of 1870 has been abandoned in order to avoid any interpretation that would limit applicability of this Article to commercial transactions only. Under traditional civilian notions, things are "in commerce" when traffic thereon is neither illegal nor unlawful. Thus, under Article 1764 of the Louisiana Civil Code of 1870 (repealed by Acts 1984, No. 331), the sale of human body tissue was prohibited unless made as authorized by that Article. In instances where the transaction was made otherwise, the sale of human body tissue was unlawful as being the sale of an article out of commerce. Several sections of the revised statutes prohibit the sale of certain drugs; thus, for example, R.S. 40:961–971.1 make it unlawful to sell any of the substances, mostly narcotic drugs, described therein. In the same vein, R.S. 40:1033 prohibits the sale of drug paraphernalia. See also R.S. 14:81.1 prohibiting the sale of pornography in material involving juveniles, and R.S. 14:229 prohibiting the sale of counterfeit trademarks.

Art. 2449. [Blank]

Art. 2450. Sale of future things

A future thing may be the object of a contract of sale. In such a case the coming into existence of the thing is a condition that suspends the effects of the sale. A party who, through his fault, prevents the coming into existence of the thing is liable for damages.

Acts 1993, No. 841, § 1, eff. Jan. 1, 1995.

REVISION COMMENTS—1993

This Article reproduces the substance of Article 2450 of the Louisiana Civil Code of 1870. It does not change the law.

Art. 2451. Sale of a hope

A hope may be the object of a contract of sale. Thus, a fisherman may sell a haul of his net before he throws it. In that case the buyer is entitled to whatever is caught in the net, according to the parties' expectations, and even if nothing is caught the sale is valid.

Acts 1993, No. 841, § 1, eff. Jan. 1, 1995.

REVISION COMMENTS—1993

(a) This Article reproduces the substance of Article 2451 of the Louisiana Civil Code of 1870. It changes the law insofar as it provides a solution for the case where something other than fish is caught in the net.

(b) Under this Article the sale of a hope is an aleatory contract; see C.C. Art. 1912 (Rev.1984). Louisiana courts have made fruitful use of the idea of the sale of a hope in order to explain the nature of contract in a variety of situations. Thus, in Losecco v. Gregory, 108 La. 648, 32 So. 985 (1901), the court concluded that the sale of future crops where the buyer had assumed all risks was the sale of a hope. In Humble Oil & Ref. Co. v. Guillory, 212 La. 646, 33 So.2d 182 (1946), the nature of a mineral royalty was explained in the same terms; see also Section 82 (La.R.S. 31:82) of the Louisiana Mineral Code. In New Orleans & Carrollton R.R. Co. v. Jourdain's Heirs, 34 La.Ann. 648 (1882), with a reference to Marcad, the court concluded that a sale without warranty where the buyer is aware of the danger of eviction amounts to the sale of a hope.

Art. 2452. Sale of the thing of another

The sale of a thing belonging to another does not convey ownership.

Acts 1993, No. 841, § 1, eff. Jan. 1, 1995.

REVISION COMMENTS—1993

(a) This article is new. In spite of its different language it does not change the law as stated in the source article. It gives formulation to a principle that was implicit in the text of Article 2452 (1870). It recognizes that the sale of a thing belonging to another may have some effects in certain circumstances.

(b) This Article applies to sales of things that are individualized. It does not apply to sales of things indicated by their kind but not yet individualized, as in the case of sales by weight, tale, or measure. When the things that are the contractual object are not yet individualized at the time of the sale, it suffices for the validity of the sale that the seller be owner at the moment of individualization or identification of the things to the contract. See 17 Baudry-Lacantinerie et Saignat, Traité théorique et pratique de droit civil—De la vente et de l'échange 90–91 (1900); Beudant, Cours de droit civil français—La vente et le louage 67 (1908); 10 Planiol et Ripert, Traité pratique de droit civil français—Vente et échange 41 (1932).

(c) Under this Article a seller is still owner when, under the laws of registry, he appears as owner of record even though, because of a prior unrecorded sale, the thing may be regarded as no longer his. See McDuffie v. Walker, 125 La. 152, 51 So. 100 (1909).

(d) Under this Article, a seller who purports to sell a thing he does not own is liable for damages if the buyer did not know that the thing did not belong to the seller. See Nelson v. Holden, 219 La. 37, 52 So.2d 240 (1951).

(e) Under this Article, the sale of a thing belonging to another becomes valid if the seller acquires ownership from the true owner before the buyer brings action for nullity. See St. Landry Oil & Gas Co. v. Neal, 166 La. 799, 118 So. 24 (1928); Bonin v. Eyssaline, 12 Mart. (O.S.) 185, 227 (1822). Once the buyer brings the action, however, the after-acquired title doctrine does not operate, and ownership thereof does not vest automatically in the buyer. See 17 Baudry-Lacantinerie et Saignat, Traité théorique et pratique de droit civil—De la vente et de l'échange 98 (1900); Bonin v. Eyssaline, supra.

Art. 2453. Sale of a thing pending litigation of ownership

When the ownership of a thing is the subject of litigation, the sale of that thing during the pendency of the suit does not affect the claimant's rights. Where the thing is immovable, the rights of third persons are governed by the laws of registry.

Acts 1993, No. 841, § 1, eff. Jan. 1, 1995.

REVISION COMMENT—1993

This Article reproduces the substance of Article 2453 of the Louisiana Civil Code of 1870. It does not change the law.

Arts. 2454 to 2455. [Blank]

CHAPTER 4—HOW THE CONTRACT OF SALE IS TO BE PERFECTED

Art. 2456. Transfer of ownership

Ownership is transferred between the parties as soon as there is agreement on the thing and the price is fixed, even though the thing sold is not yet delivered nor the price paid.

Acts 1993, No. 841, § 1, eff. Jan. 1, 1995.

REVISION COMMENTS—1993

(a) This Article is new. It changes the law insofar as it confines the effects of the parties' consent to the transfer of ownership alone, excluding risk, which is now subject to a different regime (see Article 2471, infra), while the source provision, Article 2456 of the Civil Code of 1870, because of its allusion to the "perfection" of the sale, could be interpreted to govern not only ownership but also risk, which was corroborated by C.C. Art. 2467 (1870). See 2 Litvinoff, Obligations 271–273 (1975).

(b) Under this Article, the transferring effects of the parties' consent is limited to the parties themselves. Vis-à-vis third parties, a transfer is effective only when the requirements of Civil Code Articles 517 and 518 (Rev.1979) are met.

Art. 2457. Transfer of ownership; things not individualized

When the object of a sale is a thing that must be individualized from a mass of things of the same kind, ownership is transferred when the thing is thus individualized according to the intention of the parties.

Acts 1993, No. 841, § 1, eff. Jan. 1, 1995.

(a) This Article is new. It clarifies the law by providing that, in the case of sale of unspecified or nonindividualized things, ownership is not transferred until the things are individualized, thereby eliminating the ambiguity contained in Article 2458 of the Louisiana Civil Code of 1870. See 2 Litvinoff, Obligations 63–66 (1975).

(b) Under this Article, the act of individualization may not effect a valid transfer without the consent of both parties. That is so because that process must be regarded as contradictoire—that is, the agreement of the parties is required. See Baudry-Lacantinerie et Saignat, Traité théorique et pratique de droit civil—De la vente et de l'échange 131 (1900); Planiol et Ripert, Traité pratique de droit civil français 334 (1932). See also Edgwood Co. v. Falkenhagen, 151 La. 1072, 92 So. 703 (1922); George D. Witt Shoe Co. v. J.A. Seegars & Co., 122 La. 145, 47 So. 445 (1908). The buyer's consent to individualization by the seller may be express or implied. See C.C. Art. 1927 (Rev.1984). It is express, for example, when the buyer so declares it in the agreement. It is implied, for example, when the buyer sends a carrier to pick up goods already selected by the seller; see 17 Baudry-Lacantinerie et Saignat, Traité théorique et pratique de droit civil—De la vente et de l'échange 131 (1900); 2 Litvinoff, Obligations 68–70 (1975); 10 Planiol et Ripert, Traité pratique de droit civil français 334 (1932). The buyer's consent may be implied, also, as the result of well-established usages or practices. That consent may be implied, thus, when the buyer, from a distance, places an order for unspecified goods with the seller.

Art. 2458.   Sale by weight, tale or measure; lump sales

When things are sold by weight, tale, or measure, ownership is transferred between the parties when the seller, with the buyer's consent, weighs, counts or measures the things.

When things, such as goods or produce, are sold in a lump, ownership is transferred between the parties upon their consent, even though the things are not yet weighed, counted, or measured.

Acts 1993, No. 841, § 1, eff. Jan. 1, 1995.

(a) This Article reproduces the substance of Articles 2458–2459 of the Louisiana Civil Code of 1870. It does not change the law.

(b) Under this Article there is a lump sale only where there is a lump price. See Peterkin v. Martin, 30 La.Ann. 894 (1878); Goodwyn v. Pritchard, 10 La.Ann. 249 (1855). The Louisiana solution on this matter departs from the French. See 2 Litvinoff, Obligations 62–63 (1975).

(c) Under this Article, when things are sold in a lump, any required weighing, counting, or measuring is conducted only for the purpose of ascertaining whether the seller performed in full. See Mobile Machinery & Supply Co. v. York Oilfield Salvage Co., 171 So. 872 (La.App. 1st Cir.1937).

Art. 2459.   [Blank]

Art. 2460.   Sale on view or trial

When the buyer has reserved the view or trial of the thing, ownership is not transferred from the seller to the buyer until the latter gives his approval of the thing.

Acts 1993, No. 841, § 1, eff. Jan. 1, 1995.

(a) This Article reproduces the substance of Article 2460 of the Louisiana Civil Code of 1870. It does not change the law.

(b) Under this Article, the viewing or trying of the thing by the buyer is subject to the overriding obligation of good faith. See C.C. Art. 1983 (Rev.1984). The buyer may not reject the thing arbitrarily. See Hamilton Co. v. Medical Arts Bldg. Co., Inc., 135 So. 94, 98 (La.App. 2d Cir.1931).

(c) Under this Article, the viewing or trying of the thing by the buyer following a sale "on approval" must be distinguished from the buyer's right to inspect things delivered by the seller in performance of a contract of sale. The former is incidental to a special kind of sale where the transfer of ownership depends on approval by the buyer. The latter is the buyer's right to check whether the seller has complied with the contract. The former may lead to "no sale" as a result in case the buyer does not approve the thing in good faith. The latter may lead to "breach of contract" as a result in case the seller does not deliver the right thing, even after a transfer of ownership has taken place. See Brown-McReynolds Lumber Co. v. Commonwealth Bond and Casualty Co., 11 Orl.App. 49 (1913).

Art. 2461. Inclusion of accessories

The sale of a thing includes all accessories intended for its use in accordance with the law of property.

Acts 1993, No. 841, § 1, eff. Jan. 1, 1995.

REVISION COMMENT—1993

This Article changes the law in part, since according to Articles 2461 and 2490 of the Louisiana Civil Code of 1870 the sale of a thing also includes its accessories, while under property law the solution depends on whether the thing is movable or immovable. See C.C. Arts. 469, 507–508.

Art. 2462. [Blank]

Art. 2463. Expenses

The expenses of the act and other expenses incidental to the sale must be borne by the buyer.

Acts 1993, No. 841, § 1, eff. Jan. 1, 1995.

REVISION COMMENTS—1993

(a) This Article reproduces the substance of Article 2466 of the Louisiana Civil Code of 1870. It does not change the law.

(b) The rule of this Article is of a suppletive nature. The parties may, therefore, depart from it through agreement to the contrary. See C.C. Art. 7 (Rev.1988).

CHAPTER 5—OF THE PRICE OF THE CONTRACT OF SALE

Art. 2464. Price, essential elements

The price must be fixed by the parties in a sum either certain or determinable through a method agreed by them. There is no sale unless the parties intended that a price be paid.

The price must not be out of all proportion with the value of the thing sold. Thus, the sale of a plantation for a dollar is not a sale, though it may be a donation in disguise.

Acts 1993, No. 841, § 1, eff. Jan. 1, 1995.

REVISION COMMENTS—1993

(a) This Article reproduces the substance of Article 2464 of the Louisiana Civil Code of 1870. It does not change the law.

(b) This Article does not restate the second paragraph of Article 2464 of the Louisiana Civil Code of 1870, under which when the price consists of a thing other than money the contract is an exchange rather than a sale. Two reasons have prompted that omission. In the first place, general principle suffices to arrive at the same conclusion. See also C.C. Art. 2660 (1870). In the second, the omission should facilitate the conclusion that a contract is still a sale when, in return for the transfer of a thing, a party gives a sum of money plus another thing, and the former is larger than the value of the latter. See 10 Planiol et Ripert, Traité pratique de droit civil français 29 (1932).

(c) Under this Article, the transfer of a thing in return for services to be rendered, or an obligation of support, is not a sale but an innominate contract. See C.C. Art. 1914 (Rev.1984);

Thielman v. Gahlman, 119 La. 350, 44 So. 123 (1907). See also Hearsey v. Craig, 126 La. 824, 53 So. 17 (1910); 10 Planiol et Ripert, Traité pratique de droit civil français 29 (1932).

(d) Under this Article, when the parties do not intend that a price be paid the alleged sale is a simulation either absolute or relative. See C.C. Arts. 2025–2028 (Rev.1984). An apparent sale that is a relative simulation may be a valid donation if the relevant requirement of form is satisfied. See C.C. Arts. 1536 (1870) and 1970 (Rev.1984); Reinerth v. Rhody, 52 La.Ann. 2029, 28 So. 277 (1900); McWilliams v. McWilliams, 39 La.Ann. 924, 3 So. 62 (1887); Nofsinger v. Hinchee, 199 So. 597 (La.App. 1st Cir.1941).

Art. 2465.   Price left to determination by third person

The price may be left to the determination of a third person. If the parties fail to agree on or to appoint such a person, or if the one appointed is unable or unwilling to make a determination, the price may be determined by the court.

Acts 1993, No. 841, § 1, eff. Jan. 1, 1995.

REVISION COMMENT—1993

This Article is new. It changes the law by providing that, if the parties fail to name the third person, or if the named person fails to make an estimation of the price, then the determination of the price may be made by the court. The change is consistent with the principle contained in Civil Code Article 1974 (Rev. 1984).

Art. 2466.   No price fixed by the parties

When the thing sold is a movable of the kind that the seller habitually sells and the parties said nothing about the price, or left it to be agreed later and they fail to agree, the price is a reasonable price at the time and place of delivery. If there is an exchange or market for such things, the quotations or price lists of the place of delivery or, in their absence, those of the nearest market, are a basis for the determination of a reasonable price.

Nevertheless, if the parties intend not to be bound unless a price be agreed on, there is no contract without such an agreement.

Acts 1993, No. 841, § 1, eff. Jan. 1, 1995.

REVISION COMMENT—1993

This Article is new. Although it changes the text of the law as expressed in Article 2464 of the Louisiana Civil Code of 1870, it gives legislative formulation to a rule established by the Louisiana jurisprudence through an interpretation of that Article in the light of the principles that govern consent in general; see Benglis Sash & Door Co. v. A.P. Leonards, 387 So.2d 1171 (La.1980).

CHAPTER 6—AT WHOSE RISK THE THING IS, AFTER THE SALE IS COMPLETED

Art. 2467.   Transfer of risk

The risk of loss of the thing sold owing to a fortuitous event is transferred from the seller to the buyer at the time of delivery.

That risk is so transferred even when the seller has delivered a nonconforming thing, unless the buyer acts in the manner required to dissolve the contract.

Acts 1993, No. 841, § 1, eff. Jan. 1, 1995.

REVISION COMMENTS—1993

(a) This Article is new. It changes the law insofar as it provides that the risk of loss is transferred to the buyer at the moment of delivery rather than upon consent.

(b) The principle contained in Article 2467 of the Louisiana Civil Code of 1870 under which the buyer was burdened with the risk of loss of the thing sold from the moment of consent and even before delivery was criticized for its disregard of practical business considerations. See 3 Mazeaud et Mazeaud, Leçons de droit civil, Vol. 2, Part 1, 173 (5th ed. 1979). The same principle was criticized at common law where it also prevailed. See White & Summers, Uniform Commercial Code 175–177 (1980). Between the lines of many Louisiana decisions the conclusion can be read that Louisiana courts have deemed that transfer of risk upon delivery rather than consent is a fairer principle, and they have made all reasonable efforts to assert it as a solution whenever the circumstances of a case have so allowed. See C.W. Greeson Company v. Harnischfeger Corp., 231 La. 934, 93 So.2d 221 (1957); California Fruit Exchange v. John Meyer, Inc., 166 La. 9, 116 So. 575 (1928). See also Goodwyn v. Pritchard, 10 La.Ann. 249 (1855).

Arts. 2468 to 2473. [Blank]

CHAPTER 7—OF THE OBLIGATIONS OF THE SELLER

Art. 2474.   Construction of ambiguities respecting obligations of seller

The seller must clearly express the extent of his obligations arising from the contract, and any obscurity or ambiguity in that expression must be interpreted against the seller.

Acts 1993, No. 841, § 1, eff. Jan. 1, 1995.

REVISION COMMENTS—1993

(a) This Article reproduces the substance of Article 2474 of the Louisiana Civil Code. It does not change the law. It merely clarifies it by substituting the word "express" for "explain" in order to adjust the rule to the practice of everyday transactions.

(b) Under this Article, a waiver of warranty by the buyer must be clear and unambiguous. Guidry v. St. John Auto Exchange, 379 So.2d 878 (La.App. 4th Cir.1980); Hendricks v. Horseless Carriage, Inc., 332 So.2d 892 (La.App. 2d Cir.1976); Sanders v. Sanders Tractor Company, Inc., 480 So.2d 913 (La.App. 2d Cir.1985).

Art. 2475.   Seller's obligations of delivery and warranty

The seller is bound to deliver the thing sold and to warrant to the buyer ownership and peaceful possession of, and the absence of hidden defects in, that thing. The seller also warrants that the thing sold is fit for its intended use.

Acts 1993, No. 841, § 1, eff. Jan. 1, 1995.

REVISION COMMENTS—1993

(a) This Article combines the substance of Articles 2475–2476 of the Louisiana Civil Code of 1870. It does not change the law, but simply clarifies it by stating that ownership is comprised in the warranty, as clearly provided in the Articles on eviction. See C.C. Arts. 2500–2517, infra.

(b) Under this Article "intended use" shall be presumed to mean "ordinary use", unless the seller has reason to know the particular use the buyer intends for the thing. See C.C. Art. 2524.

Art. 2476.   [Blank]

Art. 2477.   Methods of making delivery

Delivery of an immovable is deemed to take place upon execution of the writing that transfers its ownership.

Delivery of a movable takes place by handing it over to the buyer. If the parties so intend delivery may take place in another manner, such as by the seller's handing over to the buyer the key to the place where the thing is stored, or by negotiating to him a document of title to the thing, or even by the mere consent of the parties if the thing sold cannot be transported at the time of the sale or if the buyer already has the thing at that time.

Acts 1993, No. 841, § 1, eff. Jan. 1, 1995.

REVISION COMMENTS—1993

(a) This Article combines the substance of Articles 2477–2479 of the Civil Code of 1870. It changes the law insofar as it extends to acts under private signature the presumption that Civil Code Article 2479 (1870) created for authentic acts. This change is consistent with the legislative history of former Civil Code Article 2479 (1870). See La. Legal Archives, Vol. 3, p. 1365.

(b) This Article presupposes that delivery is the transferring of the thing sold into the power and possession of the buyer or the making of the thing available to the buyer by the seller. See C.C. Art. 2477 (1870). It has always been clearly understood, since Roman times, that delivery may be actual or fictitious or symbolic. The text of former Civil Code Article 2477 (1870) is not reproduced simply because it merely contained a definition, but no change in the law is intended.

(c) Under this Article, negotiation of a document of title by the seller to the buyer takes place in accordance with the provisions of Chapters 3 and 7 of Title 10 of the Louisiana Revised Statutes of 1950.

(d) This Article does not apply to assignment of rights. See C.C. Arts. 2642 (1870), et seq.

Arts. 2478 to 2479. [Blank]

Art. 2480. Retention of possession by seller, presumption of simulation

When the thing sold remains in the corporeal possession of the seller the sale is presumed to be a simulation, and, where the interest of heirs and creditors of the seller is concerned, the parties must show that their contract is not a simulation.

Acts 1993, No. 841, § 1, eff. Jan. 1, 1995.

REVISION COMMENTS—1993

(a) This Article reproduces the substance of Article 2480 of the Louisiana Civil Code of 1870. It clarifies the law by changing the reference from "third persons" to "heirs and creditors of the seller", since the interest of other third persons is subject to the rules of recordation.

(b) A simulated sale occurs where the parties have no good faith intent to transfer ownership. Wilson v. Progressive State Bank & Trust Company, 446 So.2d 867 (La.App. 2d Cir.1984).

(c) A simulated sale is a sham, and, as a result, an absolute nullity. Wilson v. Progressive State Bank & Trust Company, 446 So.2d 867 (La.App. 2d Cir.1984).

Art. 2481. Incorporeals, method of making delivery

Delivery of incorporeal movable things incorporated into an instrument, such as stocks and bonds, takes place by negotiating such instrument to the buyer. Delivery of other incorporeal movables, such as credit rights, takes place upon the transfer of those movables.

Acts 1993, No. 841, § 1, eff. Jan. 1, 1995.

REVISION COMMENT—1993

This Article reproduces the substance of Article 2481 of the Louisiana Civil Code of 1870. It does not change the law.

Art. 2482. Things not in possession of seller

When at the time of the sale the seller is not in possession of the thing sold he must obtain possession at his cost and deliver the thing to the buyer.

Acts 1993, No. 841, § 1, eff. Jan. 1, 1995.

575

(a) This Article reproduces the substance of Article 2482 of the Louisiana Civil Code of 1870. It does not change the law.

(b) The seller's failure to put the buyer in possession of the thing sold may entitle the buyer to damages caused by his being deprived of the use of the property from the date of acquisition. See C.C. Arts. 1994–2004 (Rev.1984).

Art. 2483. Costs of delivery and of removal

The cost of making delivery is borne by the seller and that of taking delivery by the buyer, in the absence of agreement to the contrary.

Acts 1993, No. 841, § 1, eff. Jan. 1, 1995.

REVISION COMMENT—1993

This Article reproduces the substance of Article 2483 of the Louisiana Civil Code of 1870. It does not change the law.

Art. 2484. Place of delivery

Delivery must be made at the place agreed upon by the parties or intended by them. In the absence of such agreement or intent, delivery must be made at the place where the thing is located at the time of the sale.

Acts 1993, No. 841, § 1, eff. Jan. 1, 1995.

REVISION COMMENT—1993

This Article reproduces the substance of Article 2484 of the Louisiana Civil Code of 1870. It does not change the law.

Art. 2485. Buyer's rights upon default, damages

When the seller fails to deliver or to make timely delivery of the thing sold, the buyer may demand specific performance of the obligation of the seller to deliver, or may seek dissolution of the sale.

In either case, and also when the seller has made a late delivery, the buyer may seek damages.

Acts 1993, No. 841, § 1, eff. Jan. 1, 1995.

REVISION COMMENTS—1993

(a) This Article combines the substance of Articles 2485 and 2486 of the Louisiana Civil Code of 1870. It clarifies the law concerning the remedies available to the buyer upon the seller's failure to fulfill his obligation to deliver or to timely deliver.

(b) The remedies prescribed by this Article are subject to the general rules of obligations concerning the granting of specific performance, recovery of damages, and contract dissolution. See C.C. Arts. 1986–88, 1994–2012, and 2013–2024 (Rev.1984).

(c) Every contract of sale implies an obligation to deliver within a reasonable time. Lanier Business Products, Inc. v. First National Bank of Rayville, 388 So.2d 442 (La.App. 2d Cir.1980).

Art. 2486. [Blank]

Art. 2487. Delivery excused until payment of price and for insolvency

The seller may refuse to deliver the thing sold until the buyer tenders payment of the price, unless the seller has granted the buyer a term for such payment.

Acts 1993, No. 841, § 1, eff. Jan. 1, 1995.

REVISION COMMENTS—1993

(a) This Article reproduces the substance of Article 2487 of the Louisiana Civil Code of 1870. It does not change the law.

(b) Under this Article, even when the seller has granted the buyer a term for payment he may refuse to deliver the thing sold unless the buyer gives security for the payment of the price, if the buyer has become insolvent, or bankrupt, or has filed for protection under the bankruptcy law, since the time of the sale. See C.C. Arts. 1782, 2023 (Rev.1984). Article 2488 of the Civil Code of 1870 is not reproduced, because the solution propounded in that Article is now expanded and contained in Civil Code Article 2023 (Rev.1984). That right is not available to the seller, however, if the buyer's inability to perform existed at the time of the sale and was known to the seller.

(c) Under this Article, the buyer who fails to pay the price when due must reimburse the seller for expenses incurred in the preservation of the thing in the interim between the time stipulated for delivery and the time the price was paid. See Charles Carter and Company, Inc. v. Cast Crete Corporation of Florida, 369 So.2d 1138 (La.App. 1st Cir.1979).

Art. 2488. [Blank]

Art. 2489. Condition of thing at time of delivery

The seller must deliver the thing sold in the condition that, at the time of the sale, the parties expected, or should have expected, the thing to be in at the time of delivery, according to its nature.

Acts 1993, No. 841, § 1, eff. Jan. 1, 1995.

REVISION COMMENTS—1993

(a) This Article reformulates the principle contained in Article 2489 of the Louisiana Civil Code of 1870 in order to make that principle responsive to the reality of everyday transactions.

(b) Under this Article, the seller must care for and preserve the thing sold as a reasonably prudent administrator, in accordance with the overriding obligation of good faith.

(c) In accordance with the overriding duty of good faith, between sale and delivery the seller must care for and preserve the thing sold as a reasonably prudent administrator. See C.C. Arts. 1759, 1983 (Rev.1984) and 2468 (1870).

(d) When the buyer has not seen the thing, as when goods are purchased at a distance, in the absence of a contrary agreement it is presumed that the thing is of merchantable quality. See C.C. Art. 1860 (Rev.1984).

Art. 2490. [Blank]

Art. 2491. Immovables, extent of delivery

The seller must deliver to the buyer the full extent of the immovable sold. That obligation may be modified in accordance with the provisions of the following Articles.

Acts 1993, No. 841, § 1, eff. Jan. 1, 1995.

REVISION COMMENT—1993

This Article reproduces the substance of Article 2491 of the Louisiana Civil Code of 1870. It does not change the law.

Art. 2492. Sale of immovables at a price per measure

If the sale of an immovable has been made with indication of the extent of the premises at the rate of so much per measure, but the seller is unable to deliver the full extent specified in the contract, the price must be proportionately reduced.

If the extent delivered by the seller is greater than that specified in the contract, the buyer must pay to the seller a proportionate supplement of the price. The buyer may recede from the sale when the actual extent of the immovable sold exceeds by more than one twentieth the extent specified in the contract.

Acts 1993, No. 841, § 1, eff. Jan. 1, 1995.

REVISION COMMENT—1993

This Article reproduces the substance of Article 2492 of the Louisiana Civil Code of 1870. It does not change the law.

Art. 2493.   [Blank]

Art. 2494.   Sale of immovable for lump price

When the sale of an immovable has been made with indication of the extent of the premises, but for a lump price, the expression of the measure does not give the seller the right to a proportionate increase of the price, nor does it give the buyer the right to a proportionate diminution of the price, unless there is a surplus, or a shortage, of more than one twentieth of the extent specified in the act of sale.

When the surplus is such as to give the seller the right to an increase of the price the buyer has the option either to pay that increase or to recede from the contract.

Acts 1993, No. 841, § 1, eff. Jan. 1, 1995.

REVISION COMMENT—1993

This Article reproduces the substance of Article 2494 of the Louisiana Civil Code of 1870. It does not change the law.

Art. 2495.   Sale of a certain and limited body or of a distinct object for a lump price

When an immovable described as a certain and limited body or a distinct object is sold for a lump price, an expression of the extent of the immovable in the act of sale does not give the parties any right to an increase or diminution of the price in case of surplus or shortage in the actual extension of the immovable.

Acts 1993, No. 841, § 1, eff. Jan. 1, 1995.

REVISION COMMENTS—1993

(a) This Article is new. It changes the law in part insofar as it effects a merger of Articles 2494 and 2495 of the Civil Code of 1870 to the effect of making every sale of immovable property described as constituting a certain and limited body a sale per aversionem.

(b) Under this Article, the sale of an immovable with indication of boundaries is a sale of a certain and limited body. See Guerin v. Guerin, 449 So.2d 1053 (La.App. 1st Cir.1984); Standard Oil Company of Louisiana v. Futral, 204 La. 215, 15 So.2d 65 (1943).

(c) Under this Article, the sale of an immovable designated by the adjoining owners is a sale of a certain and limited body.

(d) Under this Article, the sale of immovable property designated by a particular proper name is a sale of a certain and limited body.

Art. 2496.   [Blank]

Art. 2497.   Restitution of price and expenses in case of rescission

When the buyer has the right to recede from the contract the seller must return the price, if he has already received it, and also reimburse the buyer for the expenses of the sale.

Acts 1993, No. 841, § 1, eff. Jan. 1, 1995.

This Article reproduces the substance of Article 2497 of the Louisiana Civil Code of 1870. It does not change the law.

Art. 2498.   Prescription of actions for supplement or diminution of price or for dissolution

The seller's action for an increase of the price and the buyer's actions for diminution of the price or dissolution of the sale for shortage or excessive surplus in the extent of the immovable sold prescribe one year from the day of the sale.

Acts 1993, No. 841, § 1, eff. Jan. 1, 1995.

REVISION COMMENT—1993

This Article reproduces the substance of Article 2498 of the Louisiana Civil Code of 1870. It does not change the law.

Art. 2499.   [Blank]

CHAPTER 8—EVICTION

Art. 2500.   Eviction, definition, scope of warranty

The seller warrants the buyer against eviction, which is the buyer's loss of, or danger of losing, the whole or part of the thing sold because of a third person's right that existed at the time of the sale. The warranty also covers encumbrances on the thing that were not declared at the time of the sale, with the exception of apparent servitudes and natural and legal nonapparent servitudes, which need not be declared.

If the right of the third person is perfected only after the sale through the negligence of the buyer, though it arises from facts that took place before, the buyer has no claim in warranty.

Acts 1993, No. 841, § 1, eff. Jan. 1, 1995.

REVISION COMMENTS—1993

(a) This Article reproduces the substance of Articles 2500, 2501, 2502, and 2515 of the Civil Code of 1870. It changes the law only insofar as it gives legislative recognition to the danger of loss as a circumstance that is as operative as an actual loss. See Bonvillain v. Bodenheimer, 117 La. 793, 42 So. 273 (1906); McDonold & Coon v. Vaughan, 14 La.Ann. 716 (1859); Landry v. Gamet, 1 Rob. 362 (1842).

(b) Under this Article, the buyer need not be actually dispossessed of the thing in order to sustain an eviction loss; eviction may take place while the buyer remains in possession of the property, as when the buyer inherits it, or acquires it by purchase from the true owner. See Landry v. Gamet, 1 Rob. 362 (1842); Thomas v. Clement, 11 Rob. 397 (1845); McDonold & Coon v. Vaughan, 14 La. 716 (1859).

(c) Under this Article, the assignee of an option to buy immovable property cannot sue the assignor for eviction where the property owner-grantor's title is defective, since the seller or transferor of an option to buy immovable property does not warrant title to the immovable. Ratcliff v. McIlhenny, 157 La. 708, 102 So. 878 (1925).

(d) The text of this Article allows the elimination of Article 2515 of the Louisiana Civil Code of 1870 without intending any change in the law. It is clear that an eviction caused by a nonapparent servitude is a partial eviction. See Art. 2511, infra.

(e) Under this Article a pipeline servitude that prohibits the erection of improvements above the line is a nonapparent servitude. See Collins v. Slocum, 317 So.2d 672 (La.App. 3d Cir.1975).

(f) This Article is consistent with the holding in Collins v. Slocum, 317 So.2d 672 (La.App. 3d Cir.1975), to the effect that the buyer of an immovable encumbered by a nonapparent servitude, which was not declared at the time of the contract, is entitled to rescission of the sale plus damages.

Art. 2501.   [Blank]

Art. 2502.   Transfer of rights to a thing

A person may transfer to another whatever rights to a thing he may then have, without warranting the existence of any such rights. In such a case the transferor does not owe restitution of the price to the transferee in case of eviction, nor may that transfer be rescinded for lesion.

Such a transfer does not give rise to a presumption of bad faith on the part of the transferee and is a just title for the purposes of acquisitive prescription.

If the transferor acquires ownership of the thing after having transferred his rights to it, the after-acquired title of the transferor does not inure to the benefit of the transferee.

Acts 1993, No. 841, § 1, eff. Jan. 1, 1995.

REVISION COMMENTS—1993

(a) This Article is new. It does not change the law, however. It gives legislative formulation to conclusions clearly established by the Louisiana jurisprudence. See Waterman et al. v. Tidewater Associated Oil Co. et al., 213 La. 588, 35 So.2d 225 (La.1947); Read v. Hewitt, 120 La. 288, 45 So. 143 (La.1907); Land Development Co. v. Schulz, 169 La. 1, 124 So. 125 (La.1929).

(b) This Article describes the effects of an act of the kind called a quitclaim deed at common law. See Waterman et al. v. Tidewater Associated Oil Co. et al., 213 La. 588, 35 So.2d 225 (La.1947); Read v. Hewitt, 120 La. 288, 45 So. 143 (La.1907); Land Development Co. v. Schulz, 169 La. 1, 124 So. 125 (La.1929).

(c) At common law, the distinguishing factor of a quitclaim deed is that it is an instrument that purports to convey nothing more than the interest or estate of the grantor, if any he has, at the time of the conveyance, rather than the property itself. See 3 A.L.R. 945 (1919); Moelle v. Sherwood, 148 U.S. 21, 13 Sup.Ct. 426, 37 L.Ed. 350 (1893); Van Rensselaer v. Kearney, 11 How. 297, 13 L.Ed. 703 (1850). Conveyance by quitclaim does not include any implication that the vendor has good title to the property, or even that he has any title at all. Thus, the purchaser by quitclaim deed is put on immediate notice that he is not acquiring land but merely the interest of his vendor in the land. See Waterman et al. v. Tidewater Associated Oil Co. et al., 213 La. 588, 35 So.2d 225 (La.1947).

What is called quitclaim at common law is an assignment of rights without warranty in the civil law. See Spanish Civil Code, Article 1529.

(d) While the fact that a sale is by quitclaim deed may be regarded as an indication that the seller lacked faith in his title, it does not necessarily indicate that the purchaser lacked faith in the seller's title to the property. Land Development Co. v. Schulz, 169 La. 1, 124 So. 125 (La.1929); Cherami v. Cantrelle, 174 La. 995, 142 So. 150 (La.1932).

Art. 2503. Modification or exclusion of warranty, seller's liability for personal acts, restitution of price in case of eviction

The warranty against eviction is implied in every sale. Nevertheless, the parties may agree to increase or to limit the warranty. They may also agree to an exclusion of the warranty, but even in that case the seller must return the price to the buyer if eviction occurs, unless it is clear that the buyer was aware of the danger of eviction, or the buyer has declared that he was buying at his peril and risk, or the seller's obligation of returning the price has been expressly excluded.

In all those cases the seller is liable for an eviction that is occasioned by his own act, and any agreement to the contrary is null.

The buyer is subrogated to the rights in warranty of the seller against other persons, even when the warranty is excluded.

Acts 1993, No. 841, § 1, eff. Jan. 1, 1995.

REVISION COMMENTS—1993

(a) This Article reproduces the substance of Articles 2503–2505 of the Louisiana Civil Code of 1870. It does not change the law.

(b) Under this Article, the seller is estopped to deny the sufficiency of his vendee's title. Boyet v. Perryman, 240 La. 339, 123 So.2d 79 (1960); Louisiana Canal Company v. Leger, 237 La. 936, 112 So.2d 667 (1959); Arnett v. Marshall, 210 La. 932, 28 So.2d 665 (1946).

(c) Under this Article, only actual and not merely constructive knowledge of the danger of eviction at the time of the sale will suffice to defeat a warranty action when a sale is made with an exception to the warranty clause. Bielawski v. Landry, 397 So.2d 861 (La.App. 4th Cir.1981); Collins v. Slocum, 317 So.2d 672 (La.App. 3d Cir.1975).

(d) In New Orleans & Carrollton R.R. Co. v. Jourdain's Heirs, 34 La.Ann. 648 (1882), the Louisiana Supreme Court held that, in a sale without warranty, knowledge by the buyer of the danger of eviction amounted to the buyer's purchasing at his peril and risk. According to the Court: "We think . . . that our Article (2505) means the same as if it read:

'Unless the buyer was aware, at the time of the sale, of the danger of eviction, and thus or therefore purchased at his peril and risk.'" 34 La.Ann. 648, at 650.

This Article codifies the result reached in New Orleans & Carrollton R.R. Co. v. Jourdain's Heirs.

(e) Under this Article, the seller's liability for an eviction that is occasioned by his own act is based on contract. Such liability does not exclude quasi-delictual liability of the seller when his acts are of a tortious nature.

(f) The last sentence incorporates a conclusion of Louisiana jurisprudence in Atlas Oil Co. v. Logan, 166 La. 28, 166 So. 582 (1928).

Arts. 2504 to 2505. [Blank]

Art. 2506. Rights of buyer against seller in case of eviction

A buyer who avails himself of the warranty against eviction may recover from the seller the price he paid, the value of any fruits he had to return to the third person who evicted him, and also other damages sustained because of the eviction with the exception of any increase in value of the thing lost.

Acts 1993, No. 841, § 1, eff. Jan. 1, 1995.

REVISION COMMENTS—1993

(a) This Article reproduces the substance of Article 2506 of the Louisiana Civil Code of 1870. It does not change the law.

(b) Under this Article, in the absence of special agreement, attorney's fees is not an item of damages recoverable by the evicted vendee. Guthrie v. Rudy Brown Builders, Inc., 416 So.2d 590 (La.App. 5th Cir.1982); Miller v. Patterson, 240 So.2d 22 (La.App. 2d Cir.1970).

Art. 2507. Restitution of full price despite deterioration, deduction of damage when benefit to buyer

A seller liable for eviction must return the full price to the buyer even if, at the time of the eviction, the value of the thing has been diminished due to any cause including the buyer's neglect.

Nevertheless, if the buyer has benefited from a diminution in value caused by his own act, the amount of his benefit must be deducted from the total owed to him by the seller because of the eviction.

Acts 1993, No. 841, § 1, eff. Jan. 1, 1995.

REVISION COMMENTS—1993

(a) This Article combines the substance of Articles 2507 and 2508 of the Louisiana Civil Code of 1870. It changes the law insofar as it modifies the rule of Article 2508 of the Louisiana Civil Code of 1870 in order to make it compatible with the principle that a mere threat, rather than actual, eviction suffices to allow action by the buyer. See Art. 2500, supra.

(b) Under this Article, when the buyer has benefited from a diminution in value of the thing because of his own act, as when he has sold a component part of the thing, the seller is allowed to withhold the value of that benefit from the price he must return to the buyer, even in the absence of an action brought by the true owner, because the seller is the one primarily exposed to such an action. A buyer who claims that he also is exposed to an action by the true owner may protect himself by bringing an action against the seller and making the true owner a third party in that suit, a procedure advisable to either party whenever a buyer considers himself evicted on the strength of a threat alone. See Bologna Bros. v. Stephens, 206 La. 112, 18 So.2d 914 (1944).

Art. 2508. [Blank]

Art. 2509. Reimbursement to buyer for useful improvements, liability of seller in bad faith

A seller liable for eviction must reimburse the buyer for the cost of useful improvements to the thing made by the buyer. If the seller knew at the time of the sale that the thing belonged to a third person, he must reimburse the buyer for the cost of all improvements.

Acts 1993, No. 841, § 1, eff. Jan. 1, 1995.

REVISION COMMENTS—1993

(a) This Article combines the substance of Articles 2509 and 2510 of the Louisiana Civil Code of 1870; it does not change the law.

(b) Ordinary repairs necessary to the enjoyment of the object sold cannot be classified as improvements. McKenzie v. Bacon, 41 La.Ann. 6, 5 So. 640 (1889).

(c) The term "cost" has been substituted for the word "expenses" used in the source Article, since "cost" has a clearer and more technically precise meaning.

(d) The rules of this Article also prevail when eviction results from an encumbrance, such as a nonapparent servitude. See Collins v. Slocum, 317 So.2d 672 (La.App. 3d Cir.1975).

Art. 2510. [Blank]

Art. 2511. Partial eviction, rights of buyer

When the buyer is evicted from only a part of the thing sold, he may obtain rescission of the sale if he would not have bought the thing without that part. If the sale is not rescinded, the buyer is entitled to a diminution of the price in the proportion that the value of the part lost bears to the value of the whole at the time of the sale.

Acts 1993, No. 841, § 1, eff. Jan. 1, 1995.

REVISION COMMENTS—1993

(a) This Article combines the substance of Articles 2511 and 2514 of the Louisiana Civil Code of 1870. It does not change the law.

(b) This Article contains an example of a situation of failure of cause. See Guglielmi v. Geismer, 47 La.Ann. 147, 16 So. 742 (1895). See also C.C. Art. 1966 (Rev.1984).

(c) The amount of the buyer's recovery in instances where he is evicted from a part of the thing purchased depends on the relative value of the part from which he is evicted. For instance, where for a lump price the buyer has bought immovable property, part of which is valuable road frontage land and part of which is relatively inexpensive swampland, the buyer is entitled to recover the relative value of the particular part from which he was evicted, regardless of the proportion that the evicted area bears to the total area of the immovable.

Art. 2512.   Warranty against eviction from proceeds

The warranty against eviction extends also to those things that proceed from the thing sold.

Acts 1993, No. 841, § 1, eff. Jan. 1, 1995.

REVISION COMMENTS—1993

(a) This Article reproduces the substance of Article 2512 of the Louisiana Civil Code of 1870. It does not change the law.

(b) "Things that proceed from the thing sold" include "fruits" as defined by Civil Code Article 551 (Rev.1976) and "products" as defined by Civil Code Article 488 (Rev.1979).

(c) For the damages recoverable under this Article, the rules contained in the preceding Articles—as explained in the pertinent comments—are applicable.

Art. 2513.   Scope of warranty in sale of succession rights

In a sale of a right of succession, the warranty against eviction extends only to the right to succeed the decedent, which entitles the buyer to those things that are, in fact, a part of the estate, but it does not extend to any particular thing.

Acts 1993, No. 841, § 1, eff. Jan. 1, 1995.

REVISION COMMENT—1993

This Article reproduces the substance of Article 2513 of the Louisiana Civil Code of 1870. It does not change the law.

Arts. 2514 to 2516. [Blank]

Art. 2517.   Call in warranty, failure of buyer to call seller in warranty, suit to quiet possession

A buyer threatened with eviction must give timely notice of the threat to the seller. If a suit for eviction has been brought against the buyer, his calling in the seller to defend that suit amounts to such notice.

A buyer who elects to bring suit against a third person who disturbs his peaceful possession of the thing sold must give timely notice of that suit to the seller.

In either case, a buyer who fails to give such notice, or who fails to give it in time for the seller to defend himself, forfeits the warranty against eviction if the seller can show that, had he been notified in time, he would have been able to prove that the third person who sued the buyer had no right.

Acts 1993, No. 841, § 1, eff. Jan. 1, 1995.

REVISION COMMENTS—1993

(a) This Article combines the substance of Articles 2517–2519 of the Louisiana Civil Code of 1870. It does not change the law.

(b) Under this article, the buyer who fails to notify the seller of the disturbance of his peaceful possession as provided in the article forfeits the warranty against eviction in all cases regardless of whether the buyer has actually been sued by the third person disturbing the buyer's possession.

Arts. 2518 to 2519. [Blank]

CHAPTER 9—REDHIBITION

Art. 2520.　Warranty against redhibitory defects

The seller warrants the buyer against redhibitory defects, or vices, in the thing sold.

A defect is redhibitory when it renders the thing useless, or its use so inconvenient that it must be presumed that a buyer would not have bought the thing had he known of the defect. The existence of such a defect gives a buyer the right to obtain rescission of the sale.

A defect is redhibitory also when, without rendering the thing totally useless, it diminishes its usefulness or its value so that it must be presumed that a buyer would still have bought it but for a lesser price. The existence of such a defect limits the right of a buyer to a reduction of the price.

Acts 1993, No. 841, § 1, eff. Jan. 1, 1995.

REVISION COMMENTS—1993

(a) This Article does not change the law. It adopts a more functional approach than the source provision, Civil Code Article 2520 (1870), in outlining the content of the seller's warranty against hidden defects in the thing sold.

(b) Under this Article, the presence of an express warranty in the sale does not convert the action for redhibition into an action for breach of contract. PPG Industries, Inc. v. Industrial Laminates Corp., 664 F.2d 1332 (U.S.C.A. 5th Cir.1982).

(c) The warranty against redhibitory vices can be avoided only by an express and explicit waiver. Williams v. Ring Around Products, Inc., 344 So.2d 1125 (La.App. 3d Cir.1977); California Chemical Co. v. Lovett, 204 So.2d 633 (La.App. 3d Cir.1967).

(d) This and the other Civil Code Articles on redhibition do not apply to contracts to sell. Stack v. Irwin, 246 La. 777, 167 So.2d 363 (La.1964).

(e) The Articles on redhibition do not apply to hidden defects discovered in a new home governed by the New Home Warranty Act, R.S. 9:3141–3150.

(f) Article 2544 of the Louisiana Civil Code of 1870 has been eliminated as unnecessary. This is so, because, since there is only one cause of action, the governing rules are the same regardless of the remedy granted.

Art. 2521.　Defects that are made known to the buyer or that are apparent

The seller owes no warranty for defects in the thing that were known to the buyer at the time of the sale, or for defects that should have been discovered by a reasonably prudent buyer of such things.

Acts 1993, No. 841, § 1, eff. Jan. 1, 1995.

REVISION COMMENTS—1993

(a) This Article combines the substance of Articles 2521 and 2522 of the Louisiana Civil Code of 1870, to the effect that apparent defects are not redhibitory vices. It does not change the law.

(b) Under this Article, a defect, or vice, is redhibitory when it is hidden, that is, not apparent, nor known to the buyer. Thus, a defect is not hidden, and therefore not redhibitory, when the buyer knows of it either because it was disclosed by the seller or because the buyer discovered it by himself.

(c) Under this Article the standard of diligence that must be exercised by the buyer in determining whether the thing purchased is defective is that of a prudent administrator. See Barker v. Tangi Exterminating Co., 448 So.2d 690 (La.App. 1st Cir.1984).

(d) Under this Article the buyer must make more than a casual observation of the object; he must examine the thing to ascertain its soundness. Matthews v. Calamari, 411 So.2d 620 (La.App. 4th Cir.1982), Guillory v. Sarpy, 177 So.2d 403 (La.App. 4th Cir.1965).

(e) Under this Article, testimonial proof concerning the seller's declaration of defects to the buyer, or of the buyer's knowledge of the defects, may be received.

(f) Under this Article, the seller need not respond for defects in the thing of which the buyer was aware, irrespective of the gravity of the defects.

Art. 2522.   Notice of existence of defect

The buyer must give the seller notice of the existence of a redhibitory defect in the thing sold. That notice must be sufficiently timely as to allow the seller the opportunity to make the required repairs. A buyer who fails to give that notice suffers diminution of the warranty to the extent the seller can show that the defect could have been repaired or that the repairs would have been less burdensome, had he received timely notice.

Such notice is not required when the seller has actual knowledge of the existence of a redhibitory defect in the thing sold.

Acts 1993, No. 841, § 1, eff. Jan. 1, 1995.

REVISION COMMENTS—1993

(a) This Article changes the law by providing that the buyer must give the seller notice of the existence of a redhibitory defect, and that such notice must also be timely. Under prior law, the buyer needed only tender the defective thing to the seller for repairs. See Louisiana Civil Code, Article 2531 (1870); Chalmers v. Stephens Chevrolet, Inc., 461 So.2d 395 (La.App. 4th Cir.1984).

(b) Under this Article, a seller who has actual knowledge of the existence of a defect in the thing sold need not be notified. On the other hand, a seller who is merely presumed to have knowledge of a defect in the thing—as, for instance, a manufacturer—by operation of law is entitled to receive notice.

(c) Under this Article, when the manufacturer sells his products through a dealer the manufacturer is deemed to receive notice when the dealer is properly notified of the existence of a defect in the thing.

Art. 2523.   [Blank]

Art. 2524.   Thing fit for ordinary use

The thing sold must be reasonably fit for its ordinary use.

When the seller has reason to know the particular use the buyer intends for the thing, or the buyer's particular purpose for buying the thing, and that the buyer is relying on the seller's skill or judgment in selecting it, the thing sold must be fit for the buyer's intended use or for his particular purpose.

If the thing is not so fit, the buyer's rights are governed by the general rules of conventional obligations.

Acts 1993, No. 841, § 1, eff. Jan. 1, 1995.

REVISION COMMENTS—1993

(a) This Article is new. It does not change the law, however. It gives express formulation to the seller's obligation of delivering to the buyer a thing that is reasonably fit for its ordinary use. The Louisiana jurisprudence has recognized the existence of that obligation although, in most instances, it has been confused with the warranty against redhibitory vices. See Crawford v. Abbott Automobile Co., Ltd., 157 La. 59, 101 So. 871 (1924); Jackson v. Breard Motor Co., Inc., 167 La. 857, 120 So. 478 (1929); Falk v. Luke Motor Co., Inc., 237 La. 982, 112 So.2d 683 (La.1959); Radalec Incorporated v. Automatic Firing Corporation, 228 La. 116, 81 So.2d 830 (La.1955); Media Production Consultants, Inc. v. Mercedes-Benz of North America, Inc., 262 La. 80, 262 So.2d 377 (La.1972).

(b) Under this Article when the thing sold is not fit for its ordinary use, even though it is free from redhibitory defects, the buyer may seek dissolution of the sale and damages, or just damages, under the general rules of conventional obligations. The buyer's action in such a case is one for breach of contract and not the action arising from the warranty against redhibitory defects.

(c) The seller's obligation under this Article is not the common law warranty of fitness. See Media Production Consultants, Inc. v. Mercedes-Benz of North America, Inc., 262 La. 80, 262 So.2d 377 (La.1972); Hob's Refrigeration and Air Conditioning, Inc. v. Poche, 304 So.2d 326 (La.1974). At common law the remedies arising from the warranty of fitness offer quasi-delictual overtones entirely absent from this Article.

(d) The second Paragraph of this Article contemplates a situation where the seller, without giving the buyer an express warranty, has reason to know that the buyer intends to put the thing sold to a particular use or that he is buying it for a particular purpose and the buyer relies on the seller's skill or judgment for the selection of the thing. The first Paragraph addresses the very frequent situation where, due to the absence of special circumstances, the presumption must prevail that the buyer's intention is to put the thing to its ordinary use.

Arts. 2525 to 2528. [Blank]

Art. 2529. Thing not of the kind specified in the contract

When the thing the seller has delivered, though in itself free from redhibitory defects, is not of the kind or quality specified in the contract or represented by the seller, the rights of the buyer are governed by other rules of sale and conventional obligations.

Acts 1993, No. 841, § 1, eff. Jan. 1, 1995.

REVISION COMMENTS—1993

(a) This Article is new. It does not change the law, however. It has been introduced in order to enhance the distinction between redhibition and breach of contract, and to eliminate the possibility of confusion that arose from the pertinent Articles in the Louisiana Civil Code of 1870. In addition, it gives legislative formulation to a principle implicit in the Articles of the Louisiana Civil Code of 1870 governing redhibition.

(b) The provisions of Article 2529 of the Louisiana Civil Code of 1870, to the effect that a seller's mistaken declaration as to quality gives rise to redhibition when such quality was the buyer's principal motive for entering the sale, have been eliminated. That Article was of uncertain origin. It was introduced into the Civil Code in 1825; the French Civil Code contains no corresponding provision. Revised Article 2529 provides that where a thing of a different kind or quality from that specified in the contract is delivered, but the thing is free of redhibitory defects, the rights of the buyer are governed by other rules of sales and conventional obligation but not by the Articles on redhibition.

(c) Under this Article, decisions such as the one rendered in Rey v. Cuccia, 298 So.2d 840 (La.1974), concluding that redhibition is available even though the thing sold is in itself free of defects, are legislatively overruled. In all such cases the buyer may reject the thing or may sue for damages or dissolution or both.

(d) Under this Article, where a thing is damaged before or during delivery the issue is not one of redhibition, but rather an issue of breach of contract. Walker v. Universal Business Association, 482 So.2d 992 (La.App. 3d Cir.1986).

(e) The seller's failure to complete the renovation of a condominium unit, which adversely impacted upon plaintiff's unit by rendering it virtually uninhabitable for the reason that plaintiff's unit effectively lacked a roof, was not a redhibitory defect. Voitier v. Hagan, 489 So.2d 1280 (La.App. 1st Cir.1986).

(f) When a product is contracted for and a product other than what was agreed upon is supplied, such a situation gives rise to an action for breach of contract. It does not matter that the delivery of the wrong commodity may have been caused by negligence, arguably giving rise to an action in tort. In such cases, a ten-year prescriptive period applies. McDermott, Inc. v. M-Electric & Construction Co., Inc., 496 So.2d 1105 (La.App. 4th Cir.1986).

Art. 2530. Defect must exist before delivery

The warranty against redhibitory defects covers only defects that exist at the time of delivery. The defect shall be presumed to have existed at the time of delivery if it appears within three days from that time.

Acts 1993, No. 841, § 1, eff. Jan. 1, 1995.

REVISION COMMENTS—1993

(a) This Article reproduces the substance of Article 2530 of the Louisiana Civil Code of 1870, but changes the law in part in order to make the Article consistent with the principle that risk passes at the time of delivery. See Revised Article 2467, supra.

(b) Under this Article, to make out a prima facie case of redhibition the buyer need not prove the underlying cause of the redhibitory defect involved, but only that the defect existed. Rey v. Cuccia, 298 So.2d 840 (La.1974); Ezell v. General Motors Corp., 446 So.2d 954 (La.App. 3d Cir.1984); Jordan v. Security Co., 425 So.2d 333 (La.App. 3d Cir.1982); Gamble v. Bill Lowrey Chevrolet, Inc., 410 So.2d 1155 (La.App. 3d Cir.1981).

(c) Under this Article the nature of a defect may allow the court to draw an inference that it existed at the time of delivery even if it appeared after three days from that time. Rey v. Cuccia, 298 So.2d 840 (La.1974); Griffin v. Coleman Oldsmobile, Inc., 424 So.2d 1116 (La.App. 1st Cir.1982).

Art. 2531. Liability of seller who knew not of the defect

A seller who did not know that the thing he sold had a defect is only bound to repair, remedy, or correct the defect. If he is unable or fails so to do, he is then bound to return the price to the buyer with interest from the time it was paid, and to reimburse him for the reasonable expenses occasioned by the sale, as well as those incurred for the preservation of the thing, less the credit to which the seller is entitled if the use made of the thing, or the fruits it has yielded, were of some value to the buyer.

A seller who is held liable for a redhibitory defect has an action against the manufacturer of the defective thing, if the defect existed at the time the thing was delivered by the manufacturer to the seller, for any loss the seller sustained because of the redhibition. Any contractual provision that attempts to limit, diminish or prevent such recovery by a seller against the manufacturer shall have no effect.

Acts 1993, No. 841, § 1, eff. Jan. 1, 1995.

REVISION COMMENTS—1993

(a) This Article reproduces the substance of Article 2531 of the Louisiana Civil Code of 1870. It does not change the law.

(b) Under this Article, the seller is not entitled to indemnification from the manufacturer where the loss is attributable to the seller's fault. Wheeler v. Clearview Dodge Sales, 462 So.2d 1298 (La.App. 5th Cir.1985).

(c) Under this Article, a manufacturer need not be provided an opportunity to repair a defect in the thing sold. Newman v. Dixie Sales Service, 387 So.2d 1333 (La.App. 1st Cir.1980); Benard v. Bradley Automotive, 365 So.2d 1382 (La.App. 2d Cir.1978); Burns v. Lamar-Lane Chevrolet, Inc., 354 So.2d 620 (La.App. 1st Cir.1977).

(d) Under this Article a seller liable for redhibition has an action against his own seller, and other sellers in the chain of title of the thing, even if such sellers are not manufacturers. In such a case the liability of any such seller depends on whether he did or did not know of the existence of the defect at the time of delivery of the thing to his buyer.

Art. 2532. Return of the thing; destruction of the thing

A buyer who obtains rescission because of a redhibitory defect is bound to return the thing to the seller, for which purpose he must take care of the thing as a prudent administrator, but is not bound to deliver it back until all his claims, or judgments, arising from the defect are satisfied.

If the redhibitory defect has caused the destruction of the thing the loss is borne by the seller, and the buyer may bring his action even after the destruction has occurred.

If the thing is destroyed by a fortuitous event before the buyer gives the seller notice of the existence of a redhibitory defect that would have given rise to a rescission of the sale, the loss is borne by the buyer.

After such notice is given, the loss is borne by the seller, except to the extent the buyer has insured that loss. A seller who returns the price, or a part thereof, is subrogated to the buyer's right against third persons who may be liable for the destruction of the thing.

Acts 1993, No. 841, § 1, eff. Jan. 1, 1995.

REVISION COMMENTS—1993

(a) This Article is new. It combines the substance of Articles 2532, 2533, and 2536 of the Louisiana Civil Code of 1870, and eliminates the contradiction between the last two of those Articles. It clarifies the law by making the giving notice of the defect to the seller a prerequisite to the rescission of the sale rather than a requirement for pertinent action. It changes the law in part by shifting the risk of loss of the thing sold from the buyer to the seller upon notice given by the former to the latter rather than upon the filing of suit. It also makes the conclusion express that the buyer may keep the defective thing in his possession until all his claims arising from the defect are satisfied. See also C.C. Art. 1993 (Rev.1984).

(b) Under this Article, a buyer in possession of a defective thing after giving notice to the seller or filing suit for redhibition must take care of the thing as a prudent administrator. See C.C. Arts. 1759, 1983 (Rev.1984).

(c) Under this Article, an action for quanti minoris may be brought even if the buyer no longer owns the thing. Stratton-Baldwin Co., Inc. v. Brown, 343 So.2d 292 (La.App. 1st Cir.1977).

(d) Under this Article once the thing has perished through the badness of its quality, rescission may be granted even if nothing remains of the thing to be returned to the seller. Greenburg v. Fourroux, 300 So.2d 641 (La.App. 3d Cir.1974); Molbert Bros. Poultry & Egg Co. v. Montgomery, 261 So.2d 311 (La.App. 3d Cir.1972).

(e) Under this Article, if the thing is destroyed through the fault of a third person after the buyer gave notice to the seller of the existence of a redhibitory defect, upon returning the price or a part thereof to the buyer, the seller subrogates himself to the right the buyer may have against that third person. See C.C. Arts. 1825, 1829(3) (Rev.1984).

Art. 2533.   [Blank]

Art. 2534.   Prescription

A.   (1) The action for redhibition against a seller who did not know of the existence of a defect in the thing sold prescribes in four years from the day delivery of such thing was made to the buyer or one year from the day the defect was discovered by the buyer, whichever occurs first.

(2) However, when the defect is of residential or commercial immovable property, an action for redhibition against a seller who did not know of the existence of the defect prescribes in one year from the day delivery of the property was made to the buyer.

B.   The action for redhibition against a seller who knew, or is presumed to have known, of the existence of a defect in the thing sold prescribes in one year from the day the defect was discovered by the buyer.

C.   In any case prescription is interrupted when the seller accepts the thing for repairs and commences anew from the day he tenders it back to the buyer or notifies the buyer of his refusal or inability to make the required repairs.

Acts 1993, No. 841, § 1, eff. Jan. 1, 1995. Amended by Acts 1995, No. 172, § 1; Acts 1997, No. 266, § 1.

REVISION COMMENTS—1993

(a) This Article combines the substance of Articles 2534 and 2546 of the Louisiana Civil Code of 1870. It changes the law in part by extending the prescriptive period for actions in redhibition against a seller in good faith from one to four years in order to make this prescriptive period consistent with the one prevailing in other American jurisdictions governed by the U.C.C. The article also eliminates the suspension of prescription provided by former Article 2534 for certain cases where the seller is a nondomiciliary. It changes the law in part by eliminating the suspension of prescription provided by the former Article 2534 for certain cases where the seller is a nondomiciliary and by providing a longer prescriptive period for actions in redhibition.

(b) Under this Article, an action in redhibition prescribes ten years from the time of perfection of the contract regardless of whether the seller was in good or bad faith. See C.C. Art. 3499.

(c) The purpose of a longer prescriptive period is to discourage precipitate action by disappointed buyers, to facilitate the settlement of disputes between buyers and sellers, and to make the prescriptive period consistent with the one prevailing in other jurisdictions.

Arts. 2535 to 2536. [Blank]

Art. 2537. Judicial sales

Judicial sales resulting from a seizure are not subject to the rules on redhibition.

Acts 1993, No. 841, § 1, eff. Jan. 1, 1995.

REVISION COMMENTS—1993

(a) This Article reproduces the substance of Article 2537 of the Louisiana Civil Code of 1870. It does not change the law.

(b) Under this Article, judicial sales of succession property are subject to the action for rescission on account of redhibitory defects. See C.C. Art. 2624 (1870).

Art. 2538. Multiple sellers, multiple buyers, successors

The warranty against redhibitory vices is owed by each of multiple sellers in proportion to his interest.

Multiple buyers must concur in an action for rescission because of a redhibitory defect. An action for reduction of the price may be brought by one of multiple buyers in proportion to his interest.

The same rules apply if a thing with a redhibitory defect is transferred, inter vivos or mortis causa, to multiple successors.

Acts 1993, No. 841, § 1, eff. Jan. 1, 1995.

REVISION COMMENTS—1993

(a) This Article changes the law in part by providing that the warranty obligation of co-sellers is divisible. Under prior law, the warranty obligation of multiple sellers was indivisible. See Schultz v. Ryan, 131 La. 78, 59 So. 21 (1912); Soule v. West, 185 La. 655, 170 So. 26 (1936); Collins v. Slocum, 317 So.2d 672 (La.App. 3d Cir.1975). See also Articles 2538 and 2539 of the Louisiana Civil Code of 1870.

(b) Paragraph three makes clear that the rules set forth in this Article for multiple sellers and purchasers are also applicable where the thing with redhibitory vices is transferred to multiple successors by an act inter vivos or mortis causa.

Art. 2539. [Blank]

Art. 2540. Redhibitory vice of one of several matched things sold together

When more than one thing are sold together as a whole so that the buyer would not have bought one thing without the other or others, a redhibitory defect in one of such things gives rise to redhibition for the whole.

Acts 1993, No. 841, § 1, eff. Jan. 1, 1995.

REVISION COMMENTS—1993

(a) This Article reproduces the substance of Article 2540 of the Louisiana Civil Code of 1870. It does not change the law.

(b) Where the things sold are independent of each other, the rule of this Article does not apply. Huntington v. Lowe, 3 La.Ann. 377 (La.1848).

Art. 2541. Reduction of the price

A buyer may choose to seek only reduction of the price even when the redhibitory defect is such as to give him the right to obtain rescission of the sale.

In an action for rescission because of a redhibitory defect the court may limit the remedy of the buyer to a reduction of the price.

Acts 1993, No. 841, § 1, eff. Jan. 1, 1995.

REVISION COMMENTS—1993

(a) This Article reproduces the substance of Article 2541 of the Louisiana Civil Code of 1870. It does not change the law.

(b) The price reduction that may be demanded under this Article is the difference between the sale price and the price that a reasonable buyer would have paid if he had known of the defects. Capitol City Leasing Corp. v. Hill, 404 So.2d 935 (La.1981).

(c) Under this Article, one of the principal elements in formulating a reduction of the purchase price is the cost of repairs. Griffin v. Coleman Oldsmobile, Inc., 424 So.2d 1116 (La.App. 1st Cir.1982).

(d) Under this Article, in sales of immovable property the amount to be awarded is the amount necessary to convert an unsound structure into a sound one. Lemonier v. Coco, 237 La. 760, 112 So.2d 436 (La.1956).

Arts. 2542 to 2544. [Blank]

Art. 2545. Liability of seller who knows of the defect; presumption of knowledge

A seller who knows that the thing he sells has a defect but omits to declare it, or a seller who declares that the thing has a quality that he knows it does not have, is liable to the buyer for the return of the price with interest from the time it was paid, for the reimbursement of the reasonable expenses occasioned by the sale and those incurred for the preservation of the thing, and also for damages and reasonable attorney fees. If the use made of the thing, or the fruits it might have yielded, were of some value to the buyer, such a seller may be allowed credit for such use or fruits.

A seller is deemed to know that the thing he sells has a redhibitory defect when he is a manufacturer of that thing.

Acts 1993, No. 841, § 1, eff. Jan. 1, 1995.

REVISION COMMENTS—1993

(a) This Article gives formulation to a well-established jurisprudential interpretation of the source provision, Article 2545 of the Louisiana Civil Code of 1870. It changes the law in part by allowing a buyer to bring an action in redhibition also against a seller who, knowingly, made a false declaration regarding a quality of the thing. This provision does not preclude an action for fraud against such a seller whenever the requirements of Article 1953 are met.

(b) Under this Article, a manufacturer is presumed to know of the defects in the things it manufactures. In the words of Pothier, a manufacturer "spondet peritiam artis", that is, by exercising his trade he represents that he has the skill of one learned in his art, and he is for this reason presumed to know of the defects in the things he sells. Pothier, Traité du contrat de vente 126–28 (1806). Louisiana jurisprudence is to the same effect. See Doyle v. Fuerst & Kraemer, 129 La. 838, 56 So. 906 (1911); LaFrance v. Abraham Lincoln Mercury, Inc., 462 So.2d 1291 (La.App. 5th Cir.1985); Cox v. Lanier Business Products, Inc., 423 So.2d 690 (La.App. 1st Cir.1982); Anselmo v. Chrysler Corp., 414 So.2d 872 (La.App. 4th Cir.1982); Associates Financial Services Co., Inc. v. Ryan, 382 So.2d 215 (La.App. 3d Cir.1980); John Deere Indus. Equipment Co. v. Willett Timber Co., Inc., 380 So.2d 182 (La.App. 3d Cir.1980); Harris v. Bardwell, 373 So.2d 777 (La.App. 2d Cir.1979). Thus, regardless of what his actual knowledge may be, a manufacturer is deemed to be in bad faith in selling a defective product. Alexander v. Burroughs Corp., 359 So.2d 607 (La.1978). Thus, under this

590

Article, since a manufacturer is presumed to know of the defects in the things he sells, he can never be in good faith if a defect in fact exists. Associates Financial Services Co., Inc. v. Ryan, 382 So.2d 215 (La.App. 3d Cir.1980).

(c) When the thing sold contains a redhibitory defect, the manufacturer and the seller are solidarily liable to the buyer for a return of the purchase price. Womack and Adcock v. 3M Business Products Sales, Inc., 316 So.2d 795 (La.App. 1st Cir.1975); Media Production Consultants, Inc. v. Mercedes-Benz of North America, Inc., 262 La. 80, 262 So.2d 377 (La.1972).

(d) The buyer may bring action against all sellers in the chain of sales back to the primary manufacturer to rescind a sale for breach of implied warranty. Womack and Adcock v. 3M Business Products Sales, Inc., 316 So.2d 795 (La.App. 1st Cir.1975).

(e) Under this Article, a vendor-builder of a residence is a "manufacturer" who cannot avoid conclusively presumptive knowledge of defects in the things he manufactures. Cox v. Moore, 367 So.2d 424 (La.App. 2d Cir.1979).

(f) Under this Article, a buyer is not required to give a bad faith seller or a manufacturer an opportunity to repair before instituting an action in redhibition. Benard v. Bradley Automotive, 365 So.2d 1382 (La.App. 2d Cir.1978); Riche v. Krestview Mobile Homes, Inc., 375 So.2d 133 (La.App. 3d Cir.1979); Dickerson v. Begnaud Motors, Inc., 446 So.2d 536 (La.App. 3d Cir.1984).

(g) The trial court has discretion to allow the bad faith seller and the manufacturer a credit for the buyer's use of the thing if such a credit is warranted under the facts. John Deere Indus. Equipment Co. v. Willett Timber Co., Inc., 380 So.2d 182 (La.App. 3d Cir.1980); Alexander v. Burroughs Corp., 359 So.2d 607 (La.1978).

(h) The developer of a subdivision is a "manufacturer" of the lots therein, and thus is presumed to know the defects of the thing sold. Hostetler v. W. Gray & Company, 523 So.2d 1359 (La.App. 2d Cir.1988); Amin v. Head, 419 So.2d 529 (La.App. 2d Cir.1982), writ denied, 423 So.2d 1151 (La.1982).

(i) Under this Article, the assembler of things manufactured by another is a seller in bad faith. Spillers v. Montgomery Ward & Co., Inc., 294 So.2d 803 (La.1974); Radalec, Inc. v. Automatic Firing Corp., 228 La. 116, 81 So.2d 830 (1955).

(j) Under this Article, nonpecuniary damages are recoverable, as in other cases of contractual breach, whenever the requirements set forth in Civil Code Article 1998 (Rev.1984) are met. See Lafleur v. John Deere, Inc., 491 So.2d 624 (La.1986); Gagliano v. Namias, 479 So.2d 23 (La.App. 4th Cir.1985); Rasmussen v. Cashio Concrete Corp., 484 So.2d 777 (La.App. 1st Cir.1986).

Arts. 2546 to 2547. [Blank]

Art. 2548. Exclusion or limitation of warranty; subrogation

The parties may agree to an exclusion or limitation of the warranty against redhibitory defects. The terms of the exclusion or limitation must be clear and unambiguous and must be brought to the attention of the buyer.

A buyer is not bound by an otherwise effective exclusion or limitation of the warranty when the seller has declared that the thing has a quality that he knew it did not have.

The buyer is subrogated to the rights in warranty of the seller against other persons, even when the warranty is excluded.

Acts 1993, No. 841, § 1, eff. Jan. 1, 1995.

REVISION COMMENTS—1993

(a) This Article gives legislative formulation to a well-established interpretation of the source provisions by the Louisiana jurisprudence. It does not change the law.

(b) Under this Article, in consumer transactions, in order to be effective, a waiver clause must either be brought to the buyer's attention or explained to him. Sallinger v. Mayer, 304 So.2d 730 (La.App. 4th Cir.1974).

(c) Under this Article, the subvendee is subrogated to the rights of his vendor and his vendor's warranty against redhibitory defects from the vendor who sold the thing to him, and so on in the chain of title. DeSoto v. Ellis, 393 So.2d 847 (La.App. 2d Cir.1981).

(d) Under this Article, the buyer is subrogated to the seller's rights and actions in warranty against the manufacturer. Cotton States Chemical Co., Inc. v. Larrison Enterprises, Inc., 342 So.2d 1212 (La.App. 2d Cir.1977).

CHAPTER 10—OF THE OBLIGATIONS OF THE BUYER

Art. 2549. Obligations of the buyer

The buyer is bound to pay the price and to take delivery of the thing.

Acts 1993, No. 841, § 1, eff. Jan. 1, 1995.

REVISION COMMENTS—1993

(a) This Article changes the law by eliminating the buyer's liability for expenditures made by the seller for the preservation of the thing before delivery. That elimination is consistent with the change effected by this revision in the allocation of risk of loss. While under the Louisiana Civil Code of 1870 risk was transferred on perfection of the contract, under the revision risk is transferred upon delivery. See Louisiana Civil Code Article 2467, supra.

(b) Where, due to the buyer's failure to take delivery, the seller is forced to incur storage expenditures in order to preserve the thing, the buyer is not entitled to delivery until he honors claims for those storage charges. See Charles Carter and Co., Inc. v. Cast Crete Corp. of Florida, 369 So.2d 1138 (La.App. 1st Cir.1979).

(c) Under this Article, where the buyer unreasonably refuses to take delivery of the thing, the seller may resell it in order to mitigate the damages. Adler Export Co. v. Eagle Rice & Feed Mills, 10 La.App. 119, 119 So. 551 (La.App. 1st Cir.1929).

Art. 2550. Time and place of payment of price

Payment of the price is due at the time and place stipulated in the contract, or at the time and place of delivery if the contract contains no such stipulation.

Acts 1993, No. 841, § 1, eff. Jan. 1, 1995.

REVISION COMMENTS—1993

(a) This Article reproduces the substance of Article 2550 of the Louisiana Civil Code of 1870. It does not change the law.

(b) Civil Code Article 2551 (1870) has been eliminated. The problem of forcing payment of the price by tendering delivery is taken care of by the revised Articles on obligations, primarily Civil Code Articles 1993 and 2022 (Rev.1984).

Arts. 2551 to 2552. [Blank]

Art. 2553. Interest on price

The buyer owes interest on the price from the time it is due.

Acts 1993, No. 841, § 1, eff. Jan. 1, 1995.

REVISION COMMENTS—1993

(a) This Article combines the substance of former Civil Code Articles 2553 and 2554 (1870). It changes the law in part, in that interest is due from the time the price is due, regardless of whether the thing produces fruits.

(b) This Article does not purport to change any provisions of the Louisiana Consumer Credit Law and other special laws.

Art. 2554.   [Blank]

Art. 2555.   Liability of the buyer who fails to take delivery

A buyer who fails to take delivery of the thing after a tender of such delivery, or who fails to pay the price, is liable for expenses incurred by the seller in preservation of the thing and for other damages sustained by the seller.

Acts 1993, No. 841, § 1, eff. Jan. 1, 1995.

REVISION COMMENTS—1993

(a) This Article reproduces the substance of Article 2555 of the Louisiana Civil Code of 1870. It does not change the law.

(b) Under this Article, upon the buyer's failure to take delivery, the seller must take reasonable measures to mitigate the damages. See C.C. Art. 2002 (Rev.1984). See also Adler Export Co. v. Eagle Rice & Feed Mills, 10 La.App. 119, 119 So. 551 (La.App. 1st Cir.1929).

(c) The reference to "other damages" in this Article remits to the general rules of damages contained in Civil Code Article 1989 (Rev.1984) et seq.

(d) Article 2565 of the Louisiana Civil Code of 1870 has been eliminated because it stated a matter of general principle. The diminution in value suffered by the thing is just one item of damages to be considered in granting an award of damages. See C.C. Art. 1989 (Rev.1984) et seq.

Art. 2556.   [Blank]

Art. 2557.   Eviction and threat of eviction as grounds for suspension of payment

A buyer who is evicted by the claim of a third person may withhold payment of the price until he is restored to possession, unless the seller gives security for any loss the buyer may sustain as a result of the eviction.

A seller who, in such a case, is unable or unwilling to give security may compel the buyer to deposit the price with the court until the right of the third person is adjudged. Also the buyer may deposit the price with the court, on his own initiative, to prevent the accrual of interest.

A buyer may not withhold payment of the price when the seller is not liable for a return of the price in case of eviction.

Acts 1993, No. 841, § 1, eff. Jan. 1, 1995.

REVISION COMMENTS—1993

(a) This Article reproduces the substance of Articles 2557–2559 of the Louisiana Civil Code of 1870. It does not change the law.

(b) Under this Article, even in case of a threat of eviction, the buyer may not withhold payment of the price when he bought at his peril and risk. See former C.C. Art. 2503 (1870). On the other hand, if he bought without warranty he may withhold the price, since even in such a case the seller is bound to return the price in case of eviction. See Gautreaux v. Boote, 10 La.Ann. 137 (1855).

Arts. 2558 to 2559.   [Blank]

Art. 2560.   Payment of the price before disturbance of possession

A buyer who paid the price before being evicted of the thing may not demand that the seller return the price or give security for it.

Acts 1993, No. 841, § 1, eff. Jan. 1, 1995.

(a) This Article reproduces the substance of Article 2560 of the Louisiana Civil Code of 1870; it does not change the law.

(b) Under this Article, though the buyer may not demand return of the price, or security for its repayment, he still has available the remedies for eviction.

Art. 2561. Dissolution of sale for nonpayment of price

If the buyer fails to pay the price, the seller may sue for dissolution of the sale. If the seller has given credit for the price and transfers that credit to another person, the right of dissolution is transferred together with the credit. In case of multiple credit holders all must join in the suit for dissolution, but if any credit holder refuses to join, the others may subrogate themselves to his right by paying the amount due to him.

If a promissory note or other instrument has been given for the price, the right to dissolution prescribes at the same time and in the same period as the note or other instrument.

Acts 1993, No. 841, § 1, eff. Jan. 1, 1995.

(a) This Article reproduces the substance of Article 2561 of the Louisiana Civil Code of 1870. It changes the law in part by providing that the right to dissolution prescribes with the note or other instrument given for the price. Under prior law, the seller's right to receive payment of the price and the right to dissolution were independent, so that prescription of the former would not extinguish the latter. See Louis Werner Sawmill v. White, 205 La. 242, 17 So.2d 264 (1944); Templeman v. Peques, 24 La.Ann. 537 (1872).

(b) The vendor's right to dissolution for nonpayment of the price, and his privilege under Civil Code Articles 3249 and 3271 (1870), are remedies that are independent of each other. Robertson v. Buoni, 504 So.2d 860 (La.1987).

(c) After perfection of the sale, where the buyer fails to pay the price, the seller may either sue for payment of the price or for dissolution under this Article. Madere v. Cole, 424 So.2d 1125 (La.App. 1st Cir.1982); Toler v. Toler, 337 So.2d 666 (La.App. 3d Cir.1976); Sliman v. McBee, 311 So.2d 248 (La.1975).

(d) Under this Article, the seller's right to dissolution for nonpayment of the price is not contingent on the absence of a third-party purchaser, and may be exercised even after the property has left the hands of the original purchaser. Robertson v. Buoni, 504 So.2d 860 (La.1987).

(e) Upon judicial dissolution, the property is restored to the seller and the buyer is discharged from his obligation to pay the price. If the buyer has paid part of the price, he is entitled to have that part returned to him. Sliman v. McBee, 311 So.2d 248 (La.1975).

(f) The seller's right to sue for dissolution under this Article is not dependent upon the existence of a security device, such as a mortgage or privilege. Robertson v. Buoni, 504 So.2d 860 (La.1987); Hollanger v. Hollanger Rice Farms, Inc., 445 So.2d 117 (La.App. 2d Cir.1984).

(g) Under this Article the public records doctrine prevails when the thing is immovable. Thus, a party who buys immovable property from another who is not an owner of record is exposed to an action for dissolution by the true owner. See Johnson v. Bloodworth, 12 La.Ann. 699 (1857). On the other hand, if according to a recorded act translative of ownership the price has been paid, or the counterperformance rendered, a third party who acquires from the transferee is protected against an action from the transferor who, contrary to the recitals of the act, was in fact not paid. See Schwing Lumber & Shingle Co. v. Arkansas Nat. Gas Co., 166 La. 201, 116 So. 851 (1928).

(h) Under this Article the right to dissolution is effective regardless of recordation in the mortgage records. See Stevenson v. Brown, 32 La.Ann. 461 (1880).

(i) While the thrust of this Article is on judicial dissolution, it does not negate the possibility that dissolution might be effected through some other means provided by law. See C.C. Arts. 2013–2024 (Rev.1984).

Art. 2562. Dissolution of sale of immovables for non-payment of price; extension of time for payment

When an action is brought for the dissolution of the sale of an immovable and there is no danger that the seller may lose the price and the thing, the court, according to the circumstances, may grant the buyer an extension of time, not in excess of sixty days, to make payment, and shall pronounce the sale dissolved if the buyer fails to pay within that time. When there is such a danger, the court may not grant the buyer an extension of time for payment.

Acts 1993, No. 841, § 1, eff. Jan. 1, 1995.

REVISION COMMENTS—1993

(a) This Article changes the law in part by providing that the trial court, in sales of immovables, may grant the buyer an extension to pay the price of no more than sixty days.

(b) Under this Article, the "danger" that the seller may lose the price is a relative term and refers to something more than a mere possibility of losing. Chiantella v. Mississippi Mud, Inc., 157 So.2d 279 (La.App. 4th Cir.1963).

(c) Under this Article, the ability of the buyer to make payment is an element which must be considered in determining whether there is danger for the seller of losing the price. Mid-State Homes, Inc. v. Davis, 250 So.2d 836 (La.App. 4th Cir.1971).

(d) This Article contemplates a completed sale, not a contract to sell; a contract to sell is governed by the general Articles on contract dissolution. Southport Mill v. Ansley, 160 La. 131, 106 So. 720 (1925).

Art. 2563. Payment of price after expiration of term but prior to default

When the contract of sale of an immovable expressly provides for dissolution in case of failure to pay the price, the buyer still has the right to pay, in spite of the express dissolution clause, for as long as the seller has not given the buyer notice that he avails himself of that clause or has not filed suit for dissolution.

Acts 1993, No. 841, § 1, eff. Jan. 1, 1995.

REVISION COMMENTS—1993

(a) This Article changes the law in part by providing that the buyer may avoid an automatic dissolution clause by paying the price before he is put in default by the seller's giving him the specified notice or suing him. Under Article 2563 of the Civil Code of 1870, it was necessary for the seller to file a judicial demand against the buyer in order to preclude the latter from defeating a dissolutory clause.

(b) Under this Article, because of a traditional policy that favors the stability of transactions concerning immovable property, an exception is made to the basic rules that govern the consequences of putting an obligor in default. See C.C. Arts. 1990–1991 (Rev.1984). That is so, because in spite of the stipulation by the parties of an express dissolution clause, under this Article the unpaid seller must still actively put the buyer in default, which leaves no room for the buyer's falling automatically into default by the mere expiration of the specified term for performance. See 2 Litvinoff, Obligations 532–35 (1975).

Art. 2564. Dissolution of sale of movables

If the thing is movable and the seller chooses to seek judicial dissolution of the sale because of the failure of the buyer to perform, the court may not grant to the buyer any extension of time to perform.

Acts 1993, No. 841, § 1, eff. Jan. 1, 1995.

This Article reproduces the substance of Article 2564 of the Louisiana Civil Code of 1870. It does not change the law, in spite of the change made in the terminology in order to achieve consistency with the new Articles on dissolution. See C.C. Arts. 2013–2024 (Rev.1984).

Arts. 2565 to 2566. [Blank]

CHAPTER 11—OF THE SALE WITH A RIGHT OF REDEMPTION

Art. 2567. Right of redemption, definition

The parties to a contract of sale may agree that the seller shall have the right of redemption, which is the right to take back the thing from the buyer.

Acts 1993, No. 841, § 1, eff. Jan. 1, 1995.

(a) This Article reproduces the substance of Article 2567 of the Louisiana Civil Code of 1870. It does not change the law.

(b) A sale with a right of redemption is distinguishable from a sale with option to repurchase. While the intent of the parties controls the classification of the transaction as redemption or option— see Delcambre v. Dubois, 263 So.2d 96 (La.App. 3d Cir.1972)—in the usual sale subject to redemption, the vendor must reserve the right to repurchase. If, on the contrary, the right to repurchase is granted by the vendee, the contract is a sale with option to repurchase and not a sale with a right of redemption. See Culpepper's dissent in Delcambre v. Dubois, (supra), at 107; Glover v. Abney, 160 La. 175, 106 So. 735 (1925). In Pitts v. Lewis, 7 La.Ann. 552 (1852), the Court stated: "It is elementary that there is no vente a remere unless the right to take back the property, on refunding the price, be stipulated in the act of sale, so as to form one of the reservations of it, and that if it is appended by a subsequent act to a sale originally pure and simple, it is either a resale or a promise to sell. 7 La.Ann. 552, at pp. 552–553."

(c) The exercise of redemption does not involve a new sale. When the right to redeem is exercised it effects a dissolution of the sale and of the transfer of the property which was the consequence of it. See 2 Planiol et Ripert, Traité élémentairé de droit civil, § 1582 (1959) (English translation by the Louisiana State Law Institute).

(d) The price of redemption or remere of the property sold may be higher or lower than the purchase price paid by the original vendee. See 2 Planiol et Ripert, Traité élémentairé de droit civil, § 1579 (1959) (English translation by the Louisiana State Law Institute). Thus, in a highly inflationary period contracting for a higher price might be very realistic, since it would tend to protect the buyer's investment against inflation.

Art. 2568. Limitation on duration

The right of redemption may not be reserved for more than ten years when the thing sold is immovable, or more than five years when the thing sold is movable. If a longer time for redemption has been stipulated in the contract that time must be reduced to either ten or five years, depending on the nature of the thing sold.

Acts 1993, No. 841, § 1, eff. Jan. 1, 1995.

(a) This Article changes the law in part by providing that the maximum period for redemption in sales of immovables is ten years, and five years in sales of movables.

(b) Under this Article, if no delay for the exercise of redemption is stipulated, the right is presumed to last the maximum time allowed by law. Delcambre v. Dubois, 263 So.2d 96 (La.App. 3d Cir.1972).

(c) Under this Article, the running of the period allowed for redemption is not subject to suspension or interruption. See C.C. Art. 2571, infra.

Art. 2569. Redemption, presumption of security

A sale with right of redemption is a simulation when the surrounding circumstances show that the true intent of the parties was to make a contract of security. When such is the case, any monies, fruits or other benefit received by the buyer as rent or otherwise may be regarded as interest subject to the usury laws.

Acts 1993, No. 841, § 1, eff. Jan. 1, 1995.

REVISION COMMENT—1993

This Article changes the law in part by establishing that a sale subject to the right of redemption is to be considered a simulation under certain circumstances.

Art. 2570. Effect of failure to exercise right within time stipulated

If the seller does not exercise the right of redemption within the time allowed by law, the buyer becomes unconditional owner of the thing sold.

Acts 1993, No. 841, § 1, eff. Jan. 1, 1995.

REVISION COMMENT—1993

Under this Article, the running of the period allowed for redemption is not subject to suspension or interruption.

Art. 2571. Application of time limit against all persons including minors

The period for redemption is peremptive and runs against all persons including minors. It may not be extended by the court.

Acts 1993, No. 841, § 1, eff. Jan. 1, 1995.

REVISION COMMENT—1993

Under this Article, the running of the period allowed for redemption is not subject to suspension or interruption.

Art. 2572. Redemption against second purchaser

When the thing is immovable, the right of redemption is effective against third persons only from the time the instrument that contains it is filed for registry in the parish where the immovable is located.

When the thing is movable, the right of redemption is effective against third persons who, at the time of purchase, had actual knowledge of the existence of that right.

Acts 1993, No. 841, § 1, eff. Jan. 1, 1995.

REVISION COMMENT—1993

This Article is new. Although it reproduces the substance of Article 2572 of the Louisiana Civil Code of 1870, it clearly subjects the rights of third persons to the public records doctrine when the thing is immovable.

Art. 2573. [Blank]

Art. 2574. Buyer's benefit of discussion against creditors of the seller

A buyer under redemption may avail himself of the right of discussion against creditors of the seller.

Acts 1993, No. 841, § 1, eff. Jan. 1, 1995.

(a) This Article reproduces the substance of Article 2574 of the Louisiana Civil Code of 1870. It does not change the law.

(b) Under this Article, if a creditor of the seller avails himself of the oblique action and exercises the seller's right of redemption, the buyer may prevent redemption by availing himself of the right of discussion. See C.C. Arts. 2042, 2044 (Rev.1984).

Art. 2575. Ownership of fruits and products pending redemption

The fruits and products of a thing sold with right of redemption belong to the buyer.

Acts 1993, No. 841, § 1, eff. Jan. 1, 1995.

(a) This Article is new. It changes the law in part by establishing that the buyer under right of redemption is entitled to the products of the thing as well as the thing itself. Thus, where mineral royalties are concerned, the buyer does not owe an accounting of the products to the seller who exercises the right of redemption. See Fuselier v. Estate of Lionel Peschier, 525 So.2d 577 (La.App.3d Cir.1988).

(b) Article 2573 of the Louisiana Civil Code of 1870 has been eliminated because it is quite obvious that, in a sale with right of redemption, the buyer acquires all the rights of an owner.

(c) Article 2579 of the Louisiana Civil Code of 1870 has been eliminated because the rule it contains belongs to the regulation of judicial sales.

Art. 2576. [Blank]

Art. 2577. Ownership of improvements and augmentations pending redemption

The buyer is entitled to all improvements he made on the thing that can be removed when the seller exercises the right of redemption. If such improvements cannot be removed, the buyer is entitled to the enhancement of the value of the thing resulting from the improvements. The buyer is also entitled to the enhancement of the value of the thing resulting from ungathered fruits and unharvested crops.

If the thing sold under right of redemption is naturally increased by accession, alluvion, or accretion before the redeeming seller exercises the right, the increase belongs to the seller.

Acts 1993, No. 841, § 1, eff. Jan. 1, 1995.

(a) This Article is based on the same principle that underlay Articles 2576 and 2577 of the Louisiana Civil Code of 1870. It does not change the law.

(b) Under this Article the rights of the buyer may be greater than those of a possessor in good faith, since while the evicted good faith possessor is entitled only to reimbursement of expenses, the buyer under this Article is entitled to the increase in value. See C.C. Arts. 486, 526, and 527 (Rev.1979).

Art. 2578. Liability for deterioration at the time of redemption

During the time allowed for redemption, the buyer must administer the thing sold with the degree of care of a prudent administrator. He is liable to the redeeming seller for any deterioration of the thing caused by the lack of such care.

Acts 1993, No. 841, § 1, eff. Jan. 1, 1995.

REVISION COMMENT—1993

This Article reproduces the substance of Article 2578 of the Louisiana Civil Code of 1870. It changes the law in part by allowing the purchaser under the right of redemption in a lower standard of diligence than the one set forth in the source Article.

Arts. 2579 to 2583. [Blank]

Art. 2584. Multiple successors, applicability of rules governing lesion

If more than one seller concurred in the sale with right of redemption of an immovable, or if a seller has died leaving more than one successor, the exercise of the right of redemption is governed by the rules provided for the division of the action for lesion among multiple sellers, or among successors of the seller or of the buyer.

Acts 1993, No. 841, § 1, eff. Jan. 1, 1995.

REVISION COMMENT—1993

This Article reproduces the substance of Article 2600 of the Louisiana Civil Code of 1870. It changes the law in part by providing that the renvoi in cases involving multiple successors is to the Articles on lesion.

Arts. 2585 to 2586. [Blank]

Art. 2587. Reimbursement to buyer on redemption

A seller who exercises the right of redemption must reimburse the buyer for all expenses of the sale and for the cost of repairs necessary for the preservation of the thing.

Acts 1993, No. 841, § 1, eff. Jan. 1, 1995.

REVISION COMMENTS—1993

(a) This Article reproduces the substance of Article 2587 of the Louisiana Civil Code of 1870. It does not change the law.

(b) Under this Article, the items recoverable by the buyer when the seller exercises redemption may be fewer than the items recoverable by an evicted possessor under Civil Code Article 527 (Rev.1979). That is so because a buyer under redemption is an owner for as long as the seller does not exercise his right. Therefore, such a buyer may not recover expenses such as taxes and insurance and other expenses customarily defrayed by owners, provided such expenses do not cover benefits to be received by the seller once he exercises his right. For example, the buyer may not recover the cost of insurance covering the thing for the time he owned it, but may recover the proportional cost of insurance, and a proportion of taxes paid, if such expenses cover a time that will elapse after the redemption.

Art. 2588. Encumbrances created by buyer

The seller who exercises the right of redemption is entitled to recover the thing free of any encumbrances placed upon it by the buyer. Nevertheless, when the thing is an immovable, the interests of third persons are governed by the laws of registry.

Acts 1993, No. 841, § 1, eff. Jan. 1, 1995.

REVISION COMMENTS—1993

(a) This Article reproduces the substance of Article 2588 of the Louisiana Civil Code of 1870. It does not change the law.

(b) The provisions of this Article are subject to the public records doctrine. McDuffie v. Walker, 125 La. 152, 51 So. 100 (1909).

CHAPTER 12—RESCISSION FOR LESION BEYOND MOIETY

Art. 2589. Rescission for lesion beyond moiety

The sale of an immovable may be rescinded for lesion when the price is less than one half of the fair market value of the immovable. Lesion can be claimed only by the seller and only in sales of corporeal immovables. It cannot be alleged in a sale made by order of the court.

The seller may invoke lesion even if he has renounced the right to claim it.

Acts 1993, No. 841, § 1, eff. Jan. 1, 1995.

REVISION COMMENTS—1993

(a) This Article combines the substance of Articles 2589, 2593, and 2594 of the Louisiana Civil Code of 1870. It does not change the law.

(b) Under this Article, the valuation may not be based on conjecture, possibility, or speculation. Armwood v. Kennedy, 231 La. 102, 90 So.2d 793 (1956).

(c) An action in lesion cannot be exercised against a third-party purchaser unless fraud or bad faith is proven. Evergreen Plantation, Inc. v. Zunamon, 319 So.2d 543 (La.App. 2d Cir.1975).

(d) The rule of this Article is not applicable to a simulated sale that is actually a donation in disguise. See McWilliams v. McWilliams, 39 La.Ann. 924, 3 So. 62 (1887).

(e) Under this Article, a renunciation of the right to claim lesion made a reasonable time after the price has been paid must meet the requirements of Civil Code Article 1842, which is applicable by analogy. See 17 Baudry-Lacantinerie et Saignat, Traité théorique et pratique de droit civil—de la vente et de l'échange 604 (1900).

Art. 2590. Time of valuation for determination of lesion

To determine whether there is lesion, the immovable sold must be evaluated according to the state in which it was at the time of the sale. If the sale was preceded by an option contract, or by a contract to sell, the property must be evaluated in the state in which it was at the time of that contract.

Acts 1993, No. 841, § 1, eff. Jan. 1, 1995.

REVISION COMMENTS—1993

(a) This Article reproduces the substance of Article 2590 of the Louisiana Civil Code of 1870. It does not change the law.

(b) Under this Article, if credit is given for payment of the price the length of the term, in its relation to established practices in a certain place, should be taken into account in order to determine whether, at the time of the sale, the price was truly lesionary. See Article 1870 of the Louisiana Civil Code of 1870. See also Guerin v. Guerin, 449 So.2d 1053 (La.App. 1st Cir.1984).

Art. 2591. Option of buyer to supplement price

When a sale is subject to rescission for lesion the buyer may elect either to return the immovable to the seller, or to keep the immovable by giving to the seller a supplement equal to the difference between the price paid by the buyer and the fair market value of the immovable determined according to the preceding Article.

Acts 1993, No. 841, § 1, eff. Jan. 1, 1995.

REVISION COMMENTS—1993

(a) This Article reproduces the substance of Article 2591 of the Louisiana Civil Code of 1870. It does not change the law.

(b) Tender of the price received is not a condition precedent to the bringing and maintenance of an action to rescind a sale for lesion beyond moiety. Ware v. Couvillion, 112 La. 43, 36 So. 220 (La.1904).

Art. 2592.   Lesion, return of fruits by buyer and payment of interest by seller

If the buyer elects to return the immovable he must also return to the seller the fruits of the immovable from the time a demand for rescission was made. In such a case, the seller must return to the buyer the price with interest from the same time.

If the buyer elects to keep the immovable he must also pay to the seller interest on the supplement from the time a demand for rescission was made.

Acts 1993, No. 841, § 1, eff. Jan. 1, 1995.

REVISION COMMENT—1993

This Article reproduces the substance of Article 2592 of the Louisiana Civil Code of 1870. It does not change the law.

Art. 2593.   [Blank]

Art. 2594.   Lesion, action against vendee who has resold the immovable

When the buyer has sold the immovable, the seller may not bring an action for lesion against a third person who bought the immovable from the original buyer.

In such a case the seller may recover from the original buyer whatever profit the latter realized from the sale to the third person. That recovery may not exceed the supplement the seller would have recovered if the original buyer had chosen to keep the immovable.

Acts 1993, No. 841, § 1, eff. Jan. 1, 1995.

REVISION COMMENTS—1993

(a) This Article is new. It does not change the law, however. It gives formulation to a principle established by Louisiana jurisprudence. See Evergreen Plantation, Inc. v. Zunamon, 319 So.2d 543 (La.App.2d Cir.1975); O'Brien v. LeGette, 254 La. 252, 223 So.2d 165 (1969).

(b) The Articles of the Louisiana Civil Code of 1870 do not clearly stipulate the rights of the vendor in a lesionary sale where the vendee has alienated the property to a third party. After the vendee alienates the property, he is no longer capable of exercising the right to return the immovable. In instances where the vendee who has resold the property has acted in good faith, the Louisiana Supreme Court has required him to give to the vendor whatever profits he may have realized in the second sale. See O'Brien v. LeGette, 254 La. 252, 223 So.2d 165 (1969).

Where, on the other hand, the vendee has acted fraudulently or in bad faith the situation is quite different. In such a case the vendee has knowingly deprived the vendor of a valuable right by intentionally inducing the vendor to sell under false pretenses. See C.C. Arts. 1953 (Rev.1984) et seq. In such a situation, as in other instances of fraud, the vendor should be entitled to a damage award, measured, in this instance, by the fair market value of the property at the time of the sale.

Art. 2595.   Peremption of action for lesion

The action for lesion must be brought within a peremptive period of one year from the time of the sale.

Acts 1993, No. 841, § 1, eff. Jan. 1, 1995.

REVISION COMMENT—1993

This Article changes the law by providing a peremptive period of one year in actions for lesion. See C.C. Art. 3458 (Rev.1982). Article 2595 of the Civil Code of 1870 provided a prescriptive period of four years.

Art. 2596. Lesion, action against vendee who has granted a right on the immovable

When the buyer has granted a right on the immovable to a third person, rescission may not impair the interest of that person. The seller who receives back the immovable so encumbered is entitled to recover from the buyer any diminution in value suffered by the immovable because of the right of the third person. That recovery may not exceed the supplement the seller would have recovered if the buyer had not encumbered the immovable and had decided to keep it.

Acts 1993, No. 841, § 1, eff. Jan. 1, 1995.

REVISION COMMENT—1993

This Article is new. It changes the law in providing that if the buyer has encumbered the property and chooses not to keep it, the seller, upon rescission, receives the immovable back subject to the right of the third person under the encumbrance.

Art. 2597. Condition in which property is returned to seller; reimbursement of buyer for improvements

When rescission is granted for lesion the seller must take back the immovable in the state it is at that time. The buyer is not liable to the seller for any deterioration or loss sustained by the immovable before the demand for rescission was made, unless the deterioration or loss was turned into profit for the buyer.

The seller must reimburse the buyer for the expenses of the sale and for those incurred for the improvement of the immovable, even if the improvement was made solely for the convenience of the buyer.

Acts 1993, No. 841, § 1, eff. Jan. 1, 1995.

REVISION COMMENTS—1993

(a) This Article reproduces the substance of Articles 2597 and 2598 of the Louisiana Civil Code of 1870. It does not change the law.

(b) Under this Article, the expenses of the sale which the seller must reimburse to the buyer are those which are caused by the conclusion of the contract, such as title checking, title opinion, and notarial fees. When the buyer has obtained financing to procure the purchase price, "expenses" include credit checking fees charged by a lending institution. See, for the purpose of analogy, Williams v. Toyota of Jefferson, Inc., 655 F.Supp. 1081 (U.S.Dist.Ct., E.D.La.1987); Chance v. Stevens of Leesville Inc., 491 So.2d 116 (La.App. 3d Cir.1986); Lee v. Blanchard, 264 So.2d 364 (La.App. 1st Cir.1972).

Art. 2598. [Blank]

Art. 2599. Buyer's right of retention pending reimbursement

The buyer may retain possession of the immovable until the seller reimburses the buyer the price and the recoverable expenses.

Acts 1993, No. 841, § 1, eff. Jan. 1, 1995.

REVISION COMMENT—1993

This Article reproduces the substance of Article 2599 of the Louisiana Civil Code of 1870. It does not change the law.

Art. 2600. Divisibility of action in lesion among joint sellers and successors, joinder

If more than one seller concurred in the sale of an immovable owned by them in indivision, or if each of them sold separately his share of the immovable, each seller may bring an action for lesion for his share.

Likewise, if a seller died leaving more than one successor, each successor may bring an action for lesion individually for that share of the immovable corresponding to his right.

Acts 1993, No. 841, § 1, eff. Jan. 1, 1995.

REVISION COMMENT—1993

This Article reproduces the substance of Articles 2580–2583 of the Louisiana Civil Code of 1870, but changes the law insofar as it does not prevent an action for lesion from continuing if some of the co-sellers do not join.

CHAPTER 13—SALES OF MOVABLES

Art. 2601. Additional terms in acceptance of offer to sell a movable

An expression of acceptance of an offer to sell a movable thing suffices to form a contract of sale if there is agreement on the thing and the price, even though the acceptance contains terms additional to, or different from, the terms of the offer, unless acceptance is made conditional on the offeror's acceptance of the additional or different terms. Where the acceptance is not so conditioned, the additional or different terms are regarded as proposals for modification and must be accepted by the offeror in order to become a part of the contract.

Between merchants, however, additional terms become part of the contract unless they alter the offer materially, or the offer expressly limits the acceptance to the terms of the offer, or the offeree is notified of the offeror's objection to the additional terms within a reasonable time, in all of which cases the additional terms do not become a part of the contract. Additional terms alter the offer materially when their nature is such that it must be presumed that the offeror would not have contracted on those terms.

Acts 1993, No. 841, § 1, eff. Jan. 1, 1995.

REVISION COMMENTS—1993

(a) This Article is new. It changes the law in that it departs from the general rule of Civil Code Article 1943 (Rev.1984) that requires the acceptance to conform to the terms of the offer. That departure is however limited to the particular case of contracts for the sale of movables.

(b) The rule of this Article is applicable to all kinds of offer and acceptance where the sale of movables is involved and is not limited to communications contained in printed forms like those habitually used by merchants.

(c) Under this Article, when the parties are not merchants, or one of them is not, a contract is formed in the original terms of the offer unless the offeror assents to the additional or different terms contained in the acceptance.

(d) Under this Article, when both parties are merchants, an expression of acceptance containing additional or different terms that materially alter the offer does not prevent the formation of a contract of sale without such terms.

(e) Under this Article, when both parties are merchants and the offer limits the acceptance to the terms of the offer or the offeror timely objects to the additional or different terms, the contract is formed in the original terms of the offer.

(f) Under this Article, a term contained in an expression of acceptance is "additional" when it contemplates a matter not addressed in the offer, as when the acceptance names a date for delivery, but the offer does not. A term in an acceptance is "different" when it varies a term contained in the offer, as when the offer names a date for delivery, but the acceptance names a date that does not coincide with the one in the offer.

(g) Under this Article, a term contained in an acceptance alters the offer materially when it is of such a nature that it gives rise to the presumption that the offeror would not enter a contract with that term. An arbitration clause, or a clause relative to the extent of the parties' liability, are examples of such terms.

(h) Under this Article, a party to a contract of sale is regarded as a merchant when he habitually manufactures, or buys and sells things of the kind involved in the contract. A merchant,

603

however, may be regarded as a consumer when purchasing things of a kind different from those he manufactures, or buys and sells.

(i) The provisions of this article apply to offers to sell as well as to offers to buy.

Art. 2602.   Contract by conduct of the parties

A contract of sale of movables may be established by conduct of both parties that recognizes the existence of that contract even though the communications exchanged by them do not suffice to form a contract. In such a case the contract consists of those terms on which the communications of the parties agree, together with any applicable provisions of the suppletive law.

Acts 1993, No. 841, § 1, eff. Jan. 1, 1995.

REVISION COMMENTS—1993

(a) This Article is new. It changes the law so that a performance rendered after the sending of an acceptance not conforming to the terms of the offer does not imply the formation of a contract in the terms of the counteroffer, but gives rise to a contract consisting of those terms of the offer and the acceptance that agree plus all applicable provisions of the suppletive law.

(b) In this Article, the expression "suppletive law" means the rules contained in the provisions of this Title and the general principles of the law of obligations, namely provisions intended to supply solutions for situations the parties did not expressly provide for. See Garro, "Codification Technique and the Problem of Imperative and Suppletive Laws," 41 La.L.R. 1007 (1981).

Art. 2603.   Obligation to deliver conforming things

The seller must deliver to the buyer things that conform to the contract.

Things do not conform to the contract when they are different from those selected by the buyer or are of a kind, quality, or quantity different from the one agreed.

Acts 1993, No. 841, § 1, eff. Jan. 1, 1995.

REVISION COMMENTS—1993

(a) This Article is new. It does not change the law, however. It gives formulation to a principle that underlay former Civil Code Articles 2439, 2475, and 2477 (1870). See also Mabry v. Midland Valley Lumber Co., 217 La. 877, 47 So.2d 673 (1950), where the Court held that delivery by the seller of green and wet lumber under a contract calling for delivery of dry pine of a certain grade constituted a breach of contract. The same result was reached in Victory Oil Co. v. Perret, 183 So.2d 360 (La.App. 4th Cir.1966), where a different kind of diesel fuel than that contracted for was delivered.

(b) Under this Article, any determination of a certain kind, quality, or quantity as agreed by the parties must be made in light of prevailing usages and prior dealings between the parties. See C.C. Arts. 2053 and 2054 (Rev.1984).

Art. 2604.   Buyer's right of inspection

The buyer has a right to have a reasonable opportunity to inspect the things, even after delivery, for the purpose of ascertaining whether they conform to the contract.

Acts 1993, No. 841, § 1, eff. Jan. 1, 1995.

REVISION COMMENTS—1993

(a) This Article is new. It does not change the law, however, as it formulates a principle that, though not expressly stated in the Louisiana Civil Code of 1870, has been recognized by the Louisiana jurisprudence. See California Fruit Exchange v. John Meyer, Inc., 166 La. 9, 116 So. 575 (1928); Hamilton Co. v. Medical Arts Bldg. Co., 17 La.App. 508, 135 So. 94 (La.App. 2d Cir.1931).

(b) The buyer's right to inspect may be exercised at any reasonable place and in any reasonable manner, and when shipment is involved the inspection may be made after the goods arrive at their destination. See Henson, The Law of Sales 153 (1985).

Art. 2605. Rejection of nonconforming things by the buyer

A buyer may reject nonconforming things within a reasonable time. The buyer must give reasonable notice to the seller to make the rejection effective. A buyer's failure to make an effective rejection within a reasonable time shall be regarded as an acceptance of the things.

Acts 1993, No. 841, § 1, eff. Jan. 1, 1995.

REVISION COMMENTS—1993

(a) This Article clarifies the law by providing that the buyer has a right to reject nonconforming goods. Although no provision of the Louisiana Civil Code of 1870 gave the buyer this right, such a right is implicit in—and is correlative to—the seller's obligation to deliver the thing that is the object of the sale. See C.C. Arts. 2456, 2475, 2549 (1870); C.C. Arts. 1759, 1983 (Rev.1984). There is no change in the law.

(b) Under this Article, an effective rejection cannot be made before the buyer has had an opportunity to inspect the goods in order to determine whether they conform to the specifications of the contract. See C.C. Arts. 1759, 1983 (Rev.1984); Henson, The Law of Sales 158 (1985).

(c) The right of rejection applies only to nonconforming goods. A rejection of conforming goods by the buyer would constitute a breach of the contract of sale. See C.C. Arts. 2549 (1870); C.C. Arts. 1759 and 1983 (Rev.1984). Under this Article a consumer buyer is subject to a lower standard of diligence than a merchant buyer.

Art. 2606. Buyer's acceptance of nonconforming things

A buyer who, with knowledge, accepts nonconforming things may no longer reject those things on grounds of that nonconformity, unless the acceptance was made in the reasonable belief that the nonconformity would be cured.

Acts 1993, No. 841, § 1, eff. Jan. 1, 1995.

REVISION COMMENTS—1993

(a) This Article is new. It does not change the law, however. It formulates a principle that is consistent with the contractual freedom of the parties.

(b) Under this Article, though a buyer who, with knowledge of a particular nonconformity, has accepted non-conforming things may no longer reject them on grounds of that non-conformity, he may still reject them on other grounds, such as unsuitableness of the nonconforming things for their apparent purpose.

Art. 2607. Buyer may accept part of things delivered

Out of a quantity of things delivered by the seller, the buyer may accept those things that conform to the contract and form a commercial unit and may reject those that do not conform. The buyer must pay at the contract rate for any things that are accepted.

Acts 1993, No. 841, § 1, eff. Jan. 1, 1995.

REVISION COMMENTS—1993

(a) This Article is new. It does not change the law, however. It formulates a principle that has long been accepted by Louisiana courts. See Bates v. Lilly Brokerage Co., 159 So. 457 (La.App. 2d Cir.1935); Huntington v. Lowe et al., 3 La.Ann. 377 (1848).

(b) Under this Article, the buyer may accept conforming commercial units and reject defective ones. See Bates v. Lilly Brokerage Co., 159 So. 457 (La.App. 2d Cir.1935).

Art. 2608. Merchant buyer's duty upon rejection of things

When the seller has no agent or business office at the place of delivery, a buyer who is a merchant and has rejected the things must follow any reasonable instructions received from the seller with respect to those things. If the seller gives no such instructions, and the things rejected are perishable or susceptible of rapid decline in value, the merchant buyer must make reasonable efforts to sell those things on the seller's behalf.

In all instances of rejection, a buyer who is a merchant must handle the rejected things as a prudent administrator.

Acts 1993, No. 841, § 1, eff. Jan. 1, 1995.

REVISION COMMENTS—1993

(a) This Article is new. It does not change the law, however. It gives formulation to principles recognized by the Louisiana jurisprudence. See United Suriname Trading Company v. C.B. Fox Company, 242 So.2d 259 (La.App. 4th Cir.1970).

(b) Under this Article, a merchant buyer who proceeds to sell perishable things that he has rejected acts as the seller's negotiorum gestor. See C.C. Arts. 2295–2299 (1870). Cf. H.T. Cottam & Co. v. Moises, 149 La. 305, 88 So. 916 (1921).

(c) If the buyer resells the goods pursuant to the obligations placed upon him by this Article, he neither accepts nor converts them. 3 Hawkland, Uniform Commercial Code Series 29 (1984).

(d) The buyer's failure to follow the guidelines set forth in this Article may result in his being held liable to the seller for damages. 3 Hawkland, Uniform Commercial Code Series 29 (1984).

(e) Under this Article, instructions by a seller are not reasonable if they require the buyer to incur expenses for which the seller does not advance the necessary funds.

(f) The affirmative duties required of a merchant-buyer under this Article seem too burdensome to be applied to a situation involving a consumer who rejects a nonconforming Article. While the merchant-buyer, as a professional seller himself, may be presumed to know the market and the facilities available for the preservation and care of the goods delivered, no such presumption is applicable where the buyer is a consumer. The consumer must, however, act in good faith at all times. See C.C. Arts. 1759, 1983 (Rev.1984).

Art. 2609.   Purchase of substitute things by the buyer

When the seller fails to render the performance required by a contract of sale of movable things, the buyer may purchase substitute things within a reasonable time and in good faith. In such a case the buyer is entitled to recover the difference between the contract price and the price of the substitute things. The buyer may recover other damages also, less the expenses saved as a result of the failure of the seller to perform.

Acts 1993, No. 841, § 1, eff. Jan. 1, 1995.

REVISION COMMENTS—1993

(a) This Article is new. It changes the law in part by providing that, when the seller fails to make delivery as required by the contract, the buyer is entitled to obtain substitute goods in the market and recover from the seller the difference between the contract price and the price paid for replacement goods.

(b) Under this Article, the substitute goods purchased by the buyer must not be of an entirely different kind. See Comment 2 to U.C.C. 2–712, where it is said that the goods must be "commercially usable as reasonable substitutes under the circumstances of the particular case."

(c) Under this Article, a buyer's failure to purchase substitute things does not deprive him of other remedies to which he may be entitled to avail himself according to the circumstances.

Art. 2610.   Cure of nonconformity

Upon rejection of nonconforming things by the buyer, the seller may cure the nonconformity when the time for performance has not yet expired or when the seller had a reasonable belief that the nonconforming things would be acceptable to the buyer. In such a case the seller must give reasonable notice of his intention to cure to the buyer.

Acts 1993, No. 841, § 1, eff. Jan. 1, 1995.

(a) This Article is new. It changes the law in part by providing that delivery of nonconforming things by the seller before expiration of the term for performance is not necessarily an anticipatory breach, as the seller is given the right to cure the nonconforming delivery or tender. The correlative duty of the buyer to give the seller an opportunity to cure is consistent with the overriding obligation of good faith. See C.C. Art. 1983 (Rev.1984).

(b) Under this Article, if the seller has tendered or delivered the goods ahead of the contract deadline and the buyer has rejected them because of nonconformity, the seller may, by giving reasonable notice of his intention to cure, make a conforming tender within the contract period. See Traynor v. Walters, 342 F.Supp. 455, 10 U.C.C.Rep.Serv. 965 (U.S.D.C. M.D.Pa.1972); Carnes Constr. Co. v. Richards & Canover Steel & Supply Co., 10 U.C.C.Rep.Serv. 797 (Okl.Ct.App.1972).

(c) Under this Article, the seller might have "a reasonable belief" that a nonconforming tender or delivery would be acceptable based on a prior course of dealing between the parties or a general usage in the particular area or business. Henson, The Law of Sales 126 (1985).

(d) Under this Article, the seller's right to cure only arises when the buyer rejects the goods. See Bonebrake v. Cox, 499 F.2d 951, 14 U.C.C. 1318 (U.S.C.A. 8th Cir., 1974), asserting that no right to cure exists when the buyer accepts defective goods.

Art. 2611.   Resale by the seller

When the buyer fails to perform a contract of sale of movable things, the seller, within a reasonable time and in good faith, may resell those things that are still in his possession. In such a case the seller is entitled to recover the difference between the contract price and the resale price. The seller may recover also other damages, less the expenses saved as a result of the buyer's failure to perform.

Unless the things are perishable or subject to rapid decline in value, the seller must give the buyer reasonable notice of the public sale at which the things will be resold, or of his intention to resell the things at a private sale.

Acts 1993, No. 841, § 1, eff. Jan. 1, 1995.

(a) This Article is new. It does not change the law, however, as it gives formulation to a principle often recognized by the Louisiana jurisprudence. See H.T. Cottam Co. v. Moises, 149 La. 305, 88 So. 916 (1921); Bartley v. City of New Orleans, 30 La.Ann. 264 (1878); Hoffman v. The Western Marine and Fire Insurance Co., 1 La.Ann. 216 (1846).

(b) Under this Article a seller who elects to resell must act according to the overriding obligation of good faith. See C.C. Arts. 1759, 1983 (Rev.1984). If the seller is a merchant, the terms of the resale must be commercially reasonable.

(c) Under this Article, a purchaser who buys in good faith at a resale takes the things free of any rights of the original buyer. See C.C. Art. 518 (Rev.1979).

(d) The basic assumption of this Article is that the resale price is lower than the contract price. Should the resale price be greater than the contract price the seller would of course not be entitled to recover the difference in price from the original buyer, and would also not be accountable to that buyer for any profit made on the resale. Friedman Iron & Supply Co. v. J.B. Beaird Co., 222 La. 627, 63 So.2d 144 (1953). See also U.C.C. 2–706.

(e) Under this Article the seller is not under a duty to resell. That is why he does not forego other remedies if he chooses not to resell. On the other hand, if the things are perishable or subject to rapid diminution in value, a resale by the seller, if possible, would conform to his duty to minimize damages. See C.C. Art. 2002 (Rev.1984). See also Friedman Iron & Supply Co. v. J.B. Beaird Co., 222 La. 627, 63 So.2d 144 (1953); Leon Godchaux Clothing Co. v. DeBuys, 120 So. 539 (La.App.Orl.Cir.1929). Also Judd Linseed and Sperm Oil Co. v. Kearney, 14 La.Ann. 352 (1859); Benton v. Bidault, 6 La.Ann. 30 (1851).

Art. 2612. Deposit of the things by seller

When the buyer neglects to take delivery of movable things that are the contractual object the seller may request court authority to put the things out of his possession and at the buyer's risk. The seller must give the buyer notice of the time at which the things will leave possession of the seller.

Acts 1993, No. 841, § 1, eff. Jan. 1, 1995.

REVISION COMMENT—1993

This Article reproduces the substance of former Civil Code Article 2556 (1870). It does not change the law.

Art. 2613. Things in transit, ownership

When, according to the terms of the contract, the seller sends the things to the buyer through a common carrier, the form of the bill of lading determines ownership of the things while in transit.

When the bill of lading makes the things deliverable to the buyer, or to his order, ownership of the things is thereby transferred to the buyer.

When the bill of lading makes the things deliverable to the seller, or to his agent, ownership of the things thereby remains with the seller.

When the seller or his agent remains in possession of a bill of lading that makes the things deliverable to the buyer, or to the buyer's order, the seller thereby reserves the right to retain the things against a claim of the buyer who has not performed his obligations.

Acts 1993, No. 841, § 1, eff. Jan. 1, 1995.

REVISION COMMENTS—1993

(a) This Article is new. It does not change the law, however. It reproduces the substance of a rule once contained in R.S. 45:940, although limiting the scope of that rule to ownership of things in transit, without addressing the matter of risk. This Article is designed to fill the gap that resulted from the repeal of R.S. 45:940.

(b) Under this Article, when the seller obtains a bill of lading that makes the things deliverable to himself, or to his order, or to his agent, or to his agent's order, the seller thereby retains ownership of the things. See C.W. Greeson Co. v. Harnischfeger Corp., 231 La. 934, 93 So.2d 221 (1957); State v. Federal Sales Co., 172 La. 921, 136 So. 4 (1931); California Fruit Exchange v. John Meyer, Inc., 166 La. 9, 116 So. 575 (1928).

(c) Under this Article, when the seller obtains a bill of lading that makes the things deliverable to the buyer or to the buyer's order, or to any person designated by the buyer, the seller thereby transfers ownership of the things to the buyer. See cases cited in the preceding comment.

(d) Under this Article, when the seller remains in possession of a bill of lading that makes the things deliverable to the buyer, or to the buyer's order, or to a person designated by the buyer, the seller thereby reserves a right of retention of the things as security for payment, a right consistent with the general principle expressed in Civil Code Article 529 (Rev.1979).

(e) Under this Article, the things which are the object of the contract of sale travel at the buyer's risk regardless of which party owns the things under the bill of lading, as risk is transferred upon delivery to a carrier. See C.C. Art. 2616, infra.

(f) Under this Article ownership is not transferred upon the sole consent of the parties, as under Civil Code Article 2456, supra, but either upon the seller's obtaining a bill of lading that makes the things deliverable to the buyer, or upon the seller's endorsing to the buyer a bill of lading that makes the things deliverable to the seller or his agent. Indeed, delivery to a carrier under a bill of lading that makes the things deliverable to the buyer is a clear act of individualization of the contractual object. It is clear that, for the Louisiana jurisprudence, delivery to a carrier amounts to an appropriation. See Edgwood Co. v. Falkenhagen, 151 La. 1072, 92 So. 703 (1922). On the other hand, delivery to a carrier under a bill of lading that makes the things deliverable to the seller or his agent can be regarded as inconclusive individualization of the thing.

608

Art. 2614.   Stoppage in transit

The seller may stop delivery of the things in the possession of a carrier or other depositary when he learns that the buyer will not perform the obligations arising from the contract of sale or is insolvent.

Acts 1993, No. 841, § 1, eff. Jan. 1, 1995.

REVISION COMMENTS—1993

(a) This Article is new. It does not change the law, however. It formulates a principle that underlay the rule contained in former Civil Code Article 2488 (1870) and that has been recognized by the Louisiana jurisprudence. See I. Blum & Co. v. Marks, 21 La.Ann. 268, 269 (1869); Alice v. Taca International Airlines S.A., 134 So.2d 922, 925 (La.App. 4th Cir.1961), reversed on other grounds, 243 La. 97, 141 So.2d 829 (1962). See also 2 Litvinoff, Obligations 274 and 502 (1975).

(b) Under this Article, the seller must give notice to the carrier or depositary with reasonable diligence in order to prevent delivery of the things.

(c) Under this Article, if a document has been issued that represents ownership of the things the depositary is not bound to obey the order to stop delivery until surrender of that document. See U.C.C. 2–705(2)(c).

(d) Under this Article, a carrier who has issued a non-negotiable bill of lading is not bound to obey an order to stop delivery from a person other than the consignor. See U.C.C. 2–705(3)(d).

(e) Under this Article, where a carrier or other depositary honors the seller's stoppage instructions, the depositary is entitled to be reimbursed by the seller for any resulting loss or expense. See R.S. 10:7–504.

Art. 2615.   Judicial dissolution

In an action for judicial dissolution of a sale of movable things the court must grant dissolution, upon proof of the defendant's failure to perform, without allowing that party any additional time to render performance.

Acts 1993, No. 841, § 1, eff. Jan. 1, 1995.

REVISION COMMENT—1993

This Article reproduces the substance of former Civil Code Article 2564 (1870). It does not change the law. It only confines the scope of the rule to situations where a party seeks judicial dissolution in order to make it compatible with the treatment of contract-dissolution in Civil Code Articles 2013–2018 (Rev.1984).

Art. 2616.   Things in transit, risk of loss

When the contract requires the seller to ship the things through a carrier, but does not require him to deliver the things at any particular destination, the risk of loss is transferred to the buyer upon delivery of the things to the carrier, regardless of the form of the bill of lading.

When the contract of sale requires the seller to deliver the things at a particular destination, the risk of loss is transferred to the buyer when the things, while in possession of the carrier, are duly tendered to the buyer at the place of destination.

When the parties incorporate well established commercial symbols into their contract, the risk of loss is transferred in accordance with the customary understanding of such symbols.

Acts 1993, No. 841, § 1, eff. Jan. 1, 1995.

REVISION COMMENTS—1993

(a) This Article is new. It changes the law in part as it provides that, when the seller is not required to deliver at a particular destination, the things that are the contractual object will travel at the buyer's risk even under a bill of lading that makes the things deliverable to the seller or his agent, thereby departing from conclusions reached by the Louisiana jurisprudence in cases such as

California Fruit Exchange v. John Meyer, Inc., 166 La. 9, 116 So. 575 (1928) and Gerde-Newman & Co. v. Louisiana Stores, 144 So. 756 (La.App. 2d Cir.1932).

(b) The well-established commercial symbols referred to in this Article are those that represent particular kinds of agreements that contemplate the transportation of things, such as F.O.B., C.I.F., F.A.S., and others recognized and frequently used in the practice of commerce. Such symbols allude to the contractual duties of the parties, who in their freedom thus may depart from the basic rules that are provided in this Article for situations where the parties made no express provision. Such symbols are defined in great detail in U.C.C. 2–319 and U.C.C. 2–320; INCOTERMS (International Chamber of Commerce Terms); and R.A.F.T.D. (Revised American Foreign Trade Definitions). Those bodies of rules and definitions are to be regarded as subsidiary to the suppletive nature of this Article, as they reflect the customs and usages of commerce, which, in Civil Code Articles 2053, 2054, and 2055 (Rev.1984), are recognized as sources of guidance to ascertain the intention of the parties.

(c) Under this Article, when the seller has agreed to deliver the things free on board (F.O.B.) the place of shipment, he must ship the things at that place and bear the expense of putting them in the possession of the carrier there, at which moment the risk of loss is passed to the buyer. When the seller has agreed to deliver the things free on board (F.O.B.) the place of destination he must transport the things at his own expense and risk to that place and tender delivery to the buyer there. See U.C.C. 2–319; INCOTERMS F.O.B., R.A.F.T.D. F.O.B.; Commercial Code of Honduras, Article 790.

(d) Under this Article, when the seller has agreed to deliver the things free alongside the vessel at a named port (F.A.S.) he must at his own risk and expense so deliver the things in the manner usual in that port, or on a dock designated by the buyer, and obtain and tender a receipt for the things. See U.C.C. 2–319; INCOTERMS F.A.S.; R.A.F.T.D. F.A.S.

(e) Under this Article, when the parties have agreed on a lump sum that includes the cost of the things plus insurance and freight of the same to the named destination (C.I.F.) the seller must put the things in the possession of a carrier and obtain a bill or bills of lading covering the transportation of the things. He must also obtain a receipt from the carrier showing that the freight has been paid or provided for, and secure a policy of insurance covering the things. All such documents must be forwarded by the seller to the buyer with reasonable promptness.

When the parties have agreed on a sum that includes the cost of the things and freight (C. & F.) the obligations of the seller are the same as above with the exception of that concerning insurance. See U.C.C. 2–320; INCOTERMS C.I.F.; R.A.F.T.D. C.I.F.; Commercial Code of Honduras, Articles 787, 789.

(f) Under this Article, when the seller has agreed to deliver the things free on board a vessel, or railroad car, or other vehicle, the buyer must name the intended vessel or other vehicle. See Hawkland, Sales and Bulk Sales, 21 (1976).

(g) Under this Article the buyer must give the seller any instructions needed for making delivery. See Henson, The Law of Sales 66 (1985).

(h) Under the first Paragraph of this Article ownership and risk pass to the buyer upon the seller's making proper delivery of the things alongside the vessel. See 3 Anderson, Uniform Commercial Code Series 466 (1981).

(i) Under this Article the seller must provide a clean dock or ship's receipt of a kind that the carrier will not hesitate in exchanging for a bill of lading. See Hawkland, Sales and Bulk Sales 121 (1976).

(j) Under this Article, at the buyer's request and expense, the seller must render whatever assistance may be necessary to obtain the documents issued in the country of origin, or of shipment, or of both, which the buyer may require for purposes either of exportation or of importation at destination.

(k) Under the first Paragraph of this Article the buyer must give the seller adequate notice of the name, sailing date, and loading berth of the vessel and also of the delivery time to the same. Henson, The Law of Sales 66 (1985).

(l) Under this Article the C.I.F. contract is not a destination but a shipment contract, that is, delivery to the carrier is delivery to the buyer for purposes of ownership and risk. Thus, the risk of subsequent loss or damage to the things passes to the buyer upon shipment if the seller has properly performed all his obligations. 3 Anderson, Uniform Commercial Code Series 479 (1981).

(m) Under this Article, the insurance comprised in the C.I.F. term is for the buyer's benefit, to protect him against the risk of loss or damage to the things while in transit. If the parties express in such a contract that insurance is for the account of the seller, that expression only means that the seller is supposed to pay for the insurance and not that the insurance is for the seller's benefit. See U.C.C. 2–320, Official Comment 3.

(n) Under this Article the seller must procure insurance for the things in the currency of the contract, covering the entire transportation of the things to the named destination. See Hawkland, Sales and Bulk Sales 123 (1976).

Art. 2617.   Payment against documents

In all cases where the parties have agreed that the seller will obtain a document showing that the things have been delivered to a carrier or a depositary the buyer must make payment against tender of that document and others as required. The seller may not tender, nor may the buyer demand, delivery of the things in lieu of the documents.

Acts 1993, No. 841, § 1, eff. Jan. 1, 1995.

REVISION COMMENTS—1993

(a) This Article is new. It does not change the law, however. It gives formulation to a well-established and recognized business practice.

(b) Under this Article, besides the document showing delivery of the things to a carrier, such as a bill of lading or a receipt, the seller must tender all other documents provided for in the F.O.B., C.I.F., C. & F. or F.A.S. contract, plus any other document the parties might have agreed on. 3 Anderson, Uniform Commercial Code Series 481, 487 (1981).

(c) Under this Article the seller is entitled to receive payment upon tendering the required documents and even before the things have been actually received by the buyer, as the basic assumption, based on business experience, is that the documents will arrive in the hands of the buyer before the things that are the contractual object. Henson, The Law of Sales 67–68 (1985).

(d) Under this Article, a depositary is a person to whom the things are entrusted with instructions for delivery, such as a warehouseman.

Arts. 2618 to 2619.   [Blank]

CHAPTER 14—AGREEMENTS PREPARATORY TO THE SALE

SECTION 1—OPTION

Art. 2620.   Option to buy or sell

An option to buy, or an option to sell, is a contract whereby a party gives to another the right to accept an offer to sell, or to buy, a thing within a stipulated time.

An option must set forth the thing and the price, and meet the formal requirements of the sale it contemplates.

Acts 1993, No. 841, § 1, eff. Jan. 1, 1995.

REVISION COMMENTS—1993

(a) This Article is a particularized application, for the contract of sale, of the definition of option found in Civil Code Art. 1933 (Rev.1984). It changes the law insofar as it eliminates the requirement of a "consideration" contained in Article 2462 of the Louisiana Civil Code of 1870.

(b) An option to buy differs from an irrevocable offer to buy in that, while the latter is a mere pollicitation, the option is a contract. See C.C. Art. 1933 (Rev.1984).

(c) Under this Article, an option for a perpetual or indefinite term is null. See Crawford v. Deshotels et al., 359 So.2d 118 (La.1978); Becker and Assoc., Inc. v. Lou-Ark Equipment Rentals, Inc., 331 So.2d 474 (La.1976); Bristo v. Christine Oil & Gas Co., 139 La. 312, 71 So. 521 (1916).

(d) Under this Article, an extension of the time stipulated in an option to buy immovable property must be in writing. Hoth v. Schmidt et al., 220 La. 249, 56 So.2d 412 (La.1951).

(e) Upon the optionee's exercise of the option, the option is transformed into a contract to sell. McMikle v. O'Neal, 207 So.2d 922 (La.App. 2d Cir.1968).

(f) In this Article, the requirement of a clearly stipulated time within which the option may be exercised helps to distinguish the option from an irrevocable offer, see C.C. Art. 1928 (Rev.1984).

(g) Under this Article, an option must satisfy the requirements for perfection of the contract of sale as set forth in Civil Code Article 2439, supra, as well as the formal requirements as provided in Civil Code Article 1839 (Rev.1984).

(h) Under this Article, the consent of the party to whom the option is given, which is not yet an acceptance of the offer to sell or buy contained in the option, may be signified by his giving something in return for the right of option or by his express or tacit acceptance of such right. The requirement of "consideration" contained in Article 2462 of the Louisiana Civil Code of 1870 is eliminated since it is inconsistent with the Louisiana system. Nevertheless, parties may agree that the grantee of the option will give the grantor, besides his consent, a corporeal or incorporeal thing of the kind that, at common law, would be regarded as a "consideration", but that at civil law, is a counter-performance that makes a contract onerous. See 2 Litvinoff, Obligations 193–198 (1975).

(i) Under this Article, an option is heritable and may be assigned, unless the parties have intended the contrary, or the circumstances clearly show that such was the parties' intent. See C.C. Arts. 1765–66 (Rev.1984).

Art. 2621. Acceptance, when effective; option turns into contract to sell; rejection

The acceptance or rejection of an offer contained in an option is effective when received by the grantor. Upon such an acceptance the parties are bound by a contract to sell.

Rejection of the offer contained in an option terminates the option but a counteroffer does not.

Acts 1993, No. 841, § 1, eff. Jan. 1, 1995.

REVISION COMMENTS—1993

(a) This Article is new. It changes in part the rule set forth in Bankston v. Estate of Bankston, 401 So.2d 436 (La.App. 1st Cir.1981), by providing that the acceptance of the offer contained in an option is effective upon reception of that acceptance by the grantor of the option.

(b) Under this Article, acceptance by the grantee of the offer contained in an option turns the option into a contract to sell, regardless of whether the object of the option involves movables or immovables.

Art. 2622. Warranty of assignor

The assignor of an option to buy a thing warrants the existence of that option, but does not warrant that the person who granted it can be required to make a final sale.

If, upon exercise of the option, the person who granted it fails to make a final sale, the assignee has against the assignor the same rights as a buyer without warranty has against the seller.

Acts 1993, No. 841, § 1, eff. Jan. 1, 1995.

REVISION COMMENTS—1993

(a) This Article is new. It changes the interpretation and application of the law made by the jurisprudence in Ratcliff v. McIlhenny, 157 La. 708, 102 So. 878 (1925), since it provides that, if the grantor of the option cannot make a final sale once the option is exercised, the assignee has against the assignor the same rights as a buyer without warranty has against the seller, that is, he may recover whatever he gave for the assignment although he may not recover other damages from the assignor. See C.C. Art. 2503.

(b) Under this Article, the assignee may recover from the assignor whatever he gave for the option if the grantor cannot be required to make a final sale, which may happen, for example, when the grantor has no title to the thing on which he granted the option, or cannot tender a merchantable title, or can avail himself of an excuse for nonperformance such as impossibility. See C.C. Arts. 1873–1878 (Rev.1984).

SECTION 2—CONTRACT TO SELL

Art. 2623.   Bilateral promise of sale; contract to sell

An agreement whereby one party promises to sell and the other promises to buy a thing at a later time, or upon the happening of a condition, or upon performance of some obligation by either party, is a bilateral promise of sale or contract to sell. Such an agreement gives either party the right to demand specific performance.

A contract to sell must set forth the thing and the price, and meet the formal requirements of the sale it contemplates.

Acts 1993, No. 841, § 1, eff. Jan. 1, 1995.

REVISION COMMENTS—1993

(a) This Article reproduces the substance of paragraph one of Article 2462 of the Louisiana Civil Code of 1870. It does not change the law.

(b) Under this Article, no time limitation need be stipulated to conclude the sale. Miller v. Miller, 335 So.2d 767 (La.App. 3d Cir.1976).

(c) In a contract to sell, ownership and risk remain with the vendor, since a contract to sell does not effect a transfer of ownership.

(d) In Peck v. Bemiss, 10 La.Ann. 160 (1855), addressing the usefulness of the bilateral promise of sale, the court stated:

> "The law would be censurable for a strange violation of the principles of reason and justice, and for a shortsighted view of expediency, if it deprived individuals of the right of making prospective agreements for a sale, or told them that if they make each other a reciprocal promise to buy and sell a thing a year hence, for example, that they should be absolutely considered as having made a present sale, with all the incidents of a shifting of the risk, revenues, accretion, etc., which pertain to a contract of sale. 10 La.Ann. 160, at 163."

Art. 2624.   Deposit, earnest money

A sum given by the buyer to the seller in connection with a contract to sell is regarded to be a deposit on account of the price, unless the parties have expressly provided otherwise.

If the parties stipulate that a sum given by the buyer to the seller is earnest money, either party may recede from the contract, but the buyer who chooses to recede must forfeit the earnest money, and the seller who so chooses must return the earnest money plus an equal amount.

When earnest money has been given and a party fails to perform for reasons other than a fortuitous event, that party will be regarded as receding from the contract.

Acts 1993, No. 841, § 1, eff. Jan. 1, 1995.

REVISION COMMENTS—1993

(a) This Article is new. Though it restates the principle contained in Civil Code Article 2463 (1870), it departs from the former jurisprudential rule according to which a sum of money given in connection with a contract to sell, even when named a "deposit" by the parties, must be regarded as earnest money. See Maloney v. Aschaffenburg, 143 La. 509, 78 So. 761 (1918). See also Breaux v. Burkenstock, 165 La. 266, 115 So. 482 (1928). Under this Article, thus, when the parties' intention is that a sum of money be given as earnest they must clearly express that intention. For greater reason a deposit made at the time of exercising an option is not to be regarded as earnest money. Haeuser v. Schiro, 235 La. 909, 106 So.2d 306 (La.1958), is thus overruled. See Edco Properties v. Landry, 371 So.2d 1367 (La.App.3d Cir.1979).

(b) Under this Article, a party who does not intend to recede but who fails to perform for any reason other than a fortuitous event is regarded as receding from the contract, that is, depending upon whether he was to be a buyer or a seller, he will either forfeit the earnest money or have to return it plus an equal amount, which gives to earnest money a nature similar to that of stipulated damages, a similarity, or identity, that has been asserted by the Louisiana jurisprudence. See Bounds v. Makar, 493 So.2d 268 (La.App. 3d Cir.1986). If the reason that prevents a seller's performance is a fortuitous event, he is then bound simply to return the earnest money. See C.C. Art. 1876 (Rev.1984).

SECTION 3—RIGHT OF FIRST REFUSAL

Art. 2625. Right of first refusal

A party may agree that he will not sell a certain thing without first offering it to a certain person. The right given to the latter in such a case is a right of first refusal that may be enforced by specific performance.

Acts 1993, No. 841, § 1, eff. Jan. 1, 1995.

REVISION COMMENTS—1993

(a) This Article is new. It does not change the law, however. It gives legislative formulation to a kind of agreement long recognized by Louisiana jurisprudence. See Ebrecht v. Pontchatoula Farm Bureau Association, Inc. et al., 498 So.2d 55 (La.App. 1st Cir.1986); Crawford v. Deshotels, et al., 359 So.2d 118 (La.1978); Price v. Town of Ruston, 171 La. 985, 132 So. 653 (1931).

(b) An agreement of first refusal may be attached to another contract, such as a sale or a lease. See C.C. Art. 2627.

(c) The grantor of a right of first refusal is conditionally bound; he need only offer the thing for sale to the promisee if he—the promisor—should decide to make a certain transaction. See 2 Litvinoff, Obligations 188 (1975); Litvinoff, "Consent Revisited", 97 La.L.Rev. 699, at 753–54 (1987).

(d) Under this Article, since an offer to sell made pursuant to a right of first refusal need not be irrevocable, it may be revoked before it is accepted by the holder of the right of first refusal, in which case the grantor of the right remains bound not to sell to another without first making another offer to the promisee. Litvinoff, "Consent Revisited", 47 La.L.Rev. 699, at 754 (1987).

(e) Under this Article, a right of first refusal is heritable and assignable, unless the parties provide otherwise. See C.C. Art. 1765 (Rev.1984).

Art. 2626. Terms of offered sale

The grantor of a right of first refusal may not sell to another person unless he has offered to sell the thing to the holder of the right on the same terms, or on those specified when the right was granted if the parties have so agreed.

Acts 1993, No. 841, § 1, eff. Jan. 1, 1995.

REVISION COMMENTS—1993

(a) This Article is new. It does not change the law, however, since it states a clear consequence of the overriding obligation of good faith. See C.C. Arts. 1759 and 1983 (Rev.1984).

(b) Under this Article, the promisor is under no duty to communicate to the promisee the offer made by the third party if he—the promisor—does not intend to accept it.

(c) Under this Article, if the property subject to the right of first refusal becomes the object of a judicial sale, Articles 2372 and 2376 of the Code of Civil Procedure apply.

SECTION 4—EFFECTS

Art. 2627.   Right of first refusal, time for acceptance

Unless otherwise agreed, an offer to sell the thing to the holder of a right of first refusal must be accepted within ten days from the time it is received if the thing is movable, and within thirty days from that time if the thing is immovable.

Unless the grantor concludes a final sale, or a contract to sell, with a third person within six months, the right of first refusal subsists in the grantee who failed to exercise it when an offer was made to him.

Acts 1993, No. 841, § 1, eff. Jan. 1, 1995.

REVISION COMMENT—1993

This Article is new. It does not change the law, however. It sets a term for acceptance of an offer by the holder of a right of first refusal.

Art. 2628.   Time limitation for option and right of first refusal

An option or a right of first refusal that concerns an immovable thing may not be granted for a term longer than ten years. If a longer time for an option or a right of first refusal has been stipulated in a contract, that time shall be reduced to ten years. Nevertheless, if the option or right of first refusal is granted in connection with a contract that gives rise to obligations of continuous or periodic performance, an option or a right of first refusal may be granted for as long a period as required for the performance of those obligations.

Acts 1993, No. 841, § 1, eff. Jan. 1, 1995. Amended by Acts 2003, No. 1005, § 1, eff. July 2, 2003.

REVISION COMMENTS—1993

(a) This Article changes the law by providing a maximum term for options to buy and rights of first refusal that concern immovable things.

(b) A right of first refusal or an option to buy for a perpetual or indefinite term is null. See Crawford v. Deshotels et al., 359 So.2d 118 (La.1978); Becker and Assoc. Inc. v. Lou-Ark Equipment Rentals, Inc., 331 So.2d 474 (La.1976); Bristor v. Christine Oil & Gas Co., 139 La. 312, 71 So. 521 (1916).

(c) The failure to expressly state a termination date in an option or a right of first refusal made part of a lease having a definite term does not render the option or right of first refusal invalid if the time for its acceptance is necessarily limited by the term of the lease. Becker and Assoc. Inc. v. Lou-Ark Equipment Rentals, Inc., 331 So.2d 474 (La.1976); Smith Enterprises, Inc. v. Borne, 245 So.2d 9 (La.App. 1st Cir.1971); Kinberger v. Drouet, 149 La. 986, 90 So. 367 (1922).

Art. 2629.   Effect against third persons

An option, right of first refusal, or contract to sell that involves immovable property is effective against third persons only from the time the instrument that contains it is filed for registry in the parish where the immovable is located.

An option, right of first refusal, or contract to sell that involves movable property is effective against third persons who, at the time of acquisition of a conflicting right, had actual knowledge of that transaction.

Acts 1993, No. 841, § 1, eff. Jan. 1, 1995.

REVISION COMMENTS—1993

(a) This Article is new. It does not change the law, however. It gives legislative formulation to a principle established by Louisiana jurisprudence. Versai Management, Inc. v. Monticello Forest Products, Corp., 479 So.2d 477 (La.App. 1st Cir.1985).

(b) Louisiana courts have recognized the enforceability of a right of first refusal affecting immovable property contained in a recorded instrument. See Crawford v. Deshotels et al., 359 So.2d 118 (La.1978).

Art. 2630. Indivisibility of right

The right to exercise an option and the right of first refusal are indivisible. When either of such rights belongs to more than one person all of them must exercise the right.

Acts 1993, No. 841, § 1, eff. Jan. 1, 1995.

REVISION COMMENTS—1993

(a) This Article is new. It derives from the basic principles of indivisibility of obligations. See C.C. Arts. 1815–1820 (Rev.1984); C.C. Art. 1815 (Rev.1984), comment (b). It does not change the law.

(b) Under this Article, the indivisibility of the right protects the grantor of the option, as it prevents one grantee from attempting to exercise the option for the part of the thing that may correspond to his share. Among grantees, if one of them refuses to exercise the option, the others may exercise the right to buy the whole thing provided that the refusal is final and clearly evinced.

Arts. 2631 to 2641. [Blank]

CHAPTER 15—ASSIGNMENT OF RIGHTS

Art. 2642. Assignability of rights

All rights may be assigned, with the exception of those pertaining to obligations that are strictly personal. The assignee is subrogated to the rights of the assignor against the debtor.

Acts 1993, No. 841, § 1, eff. Jan. 1, 1995.

REVISION COMMENTS—1993

(a) This Article is new. It does not change the law, however. It simply gives legislative recognition to the fact that incorporeal rights, except for strictly personal obligations, are generally assignable.

(b) Under this Article, an assignment is valid even without the debtor's consent, since, as a general rule, the identity of the creditor should be immaterial to the debtor who owes the performance involved. See IV Messineo, Manuale Di Diritto Civile E Comerciale, vol. 2, part II, Section 136 (8th ed. 1952).

(c) Under this Article, a right cannot be assigned where assignment is prohibited by law. See Article 2447 of the Louisiana Civil Code of 1870.

Art. 2643. Assignment effective from the time of knowledge or notice

The assignment of a right is effective against the debtor and third persons only from the time the debtor has actual knowledge, or has been given notice of the assignment.

If a partial assignment unreasonably increases the burden of the debtor he may recover from either the assignor or the assignee a reasonable amount for the increased burden.

Acts 1993, No. 841, § 1, eff. Jan. 1, 1995.

REVISION COMMENTS—1993

(a) This Article is new. It changes the law insofar as it requires either actual knowledge by the debtor, or that notice be given to him, for the effectiveness even of a partial assignment, thereby restoring the rule that prevailed before the 1985 amendment to Article 2643 of the Louisiana Civil Code of 1870. It also changes the law insofar as it eliminates the requirement of notice where the debtor has actual knowledge of the assignment.

(b) Under this Article, where the debtor has knowledge of the assignment the assignment is effective against him, regardless of whether or not he accepts the transfer in an authentic act.

(c) Under this Article, no particular form of notification is required. Peoples Bank and Trust Company, Natchitoches v. Harper, 370 So.2d 1291 (La.App. 3d Cir., 1979); In Re Pan American Life Insurance Company, 88 So.2d 410 (La.App. 2d Cir., 1956); Rosenblath v. Rice, 73 So.2d 812 (La.App. 2d Cir., 1954); Strudwick Funeral Home v. Liberty Ind. Life Ins. Co., 176 So. 679 (La.App.Orl.1937).

(d) Under this Article, when a contract contemplates that a party may assign his right provided that he gives notice to the other at a certain place, the assignment is effective against that other party if notice is so given even though the party so notified does not learn of the assignment because of his absence from that place or because of other personal circumstances.

Art. 2644. Performance by debtor before knowledge of assignment

When the debtor, without knowledge or notice of the assignment, renders performance to the assignor, such performance extinguishes the obligation of the debtor and is effective against the assignee and third persons.

Acts 1993, No. 841, § 1, eff. Jan. 1995.

REVISION COMMENT—1993

This Article reproduces the substance of Article 2644 of the Louisiana Civil Code of 1870. It changes the law in part by eliminating the requirement of notice where the debtor has knowledge of the assignment.

Art. 2645. Accessories included in assignment of right

The assignment of a right includes its accessories such as security rights.

Acts 1993, No. 841, § 1, eff. Jan. 1, 1995.

REVISION COMMENTS—1993

(a) This Article reproduces the substance of Article 2645 of the Louisiana Civil Code of 1870. It does not change the law.

(b) Under this Article, the transfer of a promissory note also transfers the accessory rights of mortgage and privilege that secure the debt involved. Holliday v. Logan, 134 La. 427, 64 So. 277 (1914).

(c) Under this Article, the transfer of a hand note also transfers the collateral mortgage note pledged to secure it. Mardis v. Hollanger, 426 So.2d 392 (La.App. 2d Cir., 1983); In Re Elliott, 385 F.Supp. 1194 (U.S.D.C.M.D.La.1974); Smith v. Shippers' Oil Co., 120 La. 640, 45 So. 533 (1908); Richey v. Venture Oil & Gas Corp., 346 So.2d 875 (La.App. 4th Cir.1977).

Art. 2646. Warranty of existence of debt, solvency of debtor

The assignor of a right warrants its existence at the time of the assignment.

The assignor does not warrant the solvency of the debtor, however, unless he has agreed to give such a warranty.

Acts 1993, No. 841, § 1, eff. Jan. 1, 1995.

REVISION COMMENTS—1993

(a) This Article combines the substance of Articles 2646 and 2647 of the Louisiana Civil Code of 1870. It does not change the law.

(b) Under this Article, the assignor of a right guarantees not only the existence of the right but also the existence of the accessory securities transferred with it. Templeman v. Hamilton & Co., 37 La.Ann. 754 (1885); Toler v. Swayze, 2 La.Ann. 880 (1847); Corcoran v. Ridell, 7 La.Ann. 268 (1852).

(c) This Article is not intended to affect the provisions of the Louisiana revised statutes on commercial paper, bank deposits and collections, and other commercial matters. (See R.S.10:3–413–10:3–418). The obligation in warranty of one who sells or otherwise assigns negotiable instruments or other commercial paper are governed by R.S. 10:3. See, esp., R.S. 10:3–413–10:3–418.

Art. 2647. [Blank]

Art. 2648. Scope of warranty of debtor's solvency

An assignor who warrants the solvency of the debtor warrants that solvency at the time of the assignment only and, in the absence of agreement to the contrary, does not warrant the future solvency of the debtor.

Acts 1993, No. 841, § 1, eff. Jan. 1, 1995.

REVISION COMMENT—1993

This Article reproduces the substance of Article 2648 of the Louisiana Civil Code of 1870. It does not change the law.

Art. 2649. Assignor's knowledge of the debtor's insolvency; effects

When the assignor of a right did not warrant the solvency of the debtor but knew of his insolvency, the assignee without such knowledge may obtain rescission of the contract.

Acts 1993, No. 841, § 1, eff. Jan. 1, 1995.

REVISION COMMENTS—1993

(a) This Article reproduces the substance of Article 2649 of the Louisiana Civil Code of 1870. It does not change the law.

(b) Under this Article, which contains statements of suppletive and not mandatory law, the assignee may waive his rights to rescind the contract in case of insolvency of the debtor.

Art. 2650. Warranty in assignment of succession rights

A person who assigns his right in the estate of a deceased person, without specifying any assets, warrants only his right of succession as heir or legatee.

Acts 1993, No. 841, § 1, eff. Jan. 1, 1995.

REVISION COMMENTS—1993

(a) This Article reproduces the substance of Article 2650 of the Louisiana Civil Code of 1870. It does not change the law.

(b) Under this Article, if the assignor has no right as heir or legatee, the cause of the assignee's obligation fails, and he is, therefore, entitled to recover whatever he gave for the assignment.

(c) Under this Article, if the assignor specified any assets of the succession as allegedly comprised in his right as successor, he then warrants that the assignee will receive those assets.

(d) Civil Code Article 2651 (1870), according to which the assignor of succession rights who had received fruits from the estate, was bound to give such fruits to the assignee, has been eliminated, thereby changing the law in order to make it consistent with the intent of parties to a contemporary contract of that kind.

Art. 2651.   [Blank]

Art. 2652.   Sale of litigious rights

When a litigious right is assigned, the debtor may extinguish his obligation by paying to the assignee the price the assignee paid for the assignment, with interest from the time of the assignment.

A right is litigious, for that purpose, when it is contested in a suit already filed.

Nevertheless, the debtor may not thus extinguish his obligation when the assignment has been made to a co-owner of the assigned right, or to a possessor of the thing subject to the litigious right.

Acts 1993, No. 841, § 1, eff. Jan. 1, 1995.

REVISION COMMENTS—1993

(a) This Article combines the substance of Articles 2652 through 2654 of the Louisiana Civil Code of 1870. It changes the law in part insofar as it eliminates the exception that Civil Code Article 2654 (1870) recognized for an assignment to a creditor of the assignor.

(b) Under this Article, a party seeking to redeem a litigious right that has been transferred must be prompt in making his intention known. A.M. & J. Solari, Limited v. Fitzgerald, 150 So.2d 896 (La.App. 4th Cir., 1963); Clement v. Sneed Brothers et al., 238 La. 614, 116 So.2d 269 (La.1959); Charrier v. Bell, 380 So.2d 155 (La.App. 1st Cir.1979).

(c) Under this Article, if after learning of a transfer of a litigious right a party continues to contest the suit, he will not be permitted to redeem that right. Clement v. Sneed Brothers et al., 238 La. 614, 116 So.2d 269 (La.1959).

(d) This Article is inapplicable to transactions that do not, in fact, import a sale, such as pignorative contracts. Lerner Shops of Louisiana, Inc. v. Reeves, 73 So.2d 490 (La.App. 1st Cir., 1954).

(e) Under this Article, a right transferred before a suit has been filed is not litigious. United States Fidelity & Guaranty Co. et al. v. Richardson, 486 So.2d 929 (La.App. 1st Cir., 1968); Wood v. Zor, Inc., 154 So.2d 632 (La.App. 4th Cir., 1963).

(f) Under this Article, it is immaterial whether the assignment transfers totally, or only partially, the right involved. Smith v. Cook, 189 La. 632, 180 So. 469 (1938).

(g) Under this Article, a contingency fee agreement between an attorney and his client is not a prohibited sale of a litigious right. See R.S. 37:218.

(h) Under this Article, when a litigious right is assigned to a creditor of the assignor, the obligor of that right may extinguish his obligation by paying to the assignee the amount of the debt discharged by way of the assignment.

Art. 2653.   Assignability prohibited by contract; exceptions

A right cannot be assigned when the contract from which it arises prohibits the assignment of that right. Such a prohibition has no effect against an assignee who has no knowledge of its existence.

Acts 1993, No. 841, § 1, eff. Jan. 1, 1995.

REVISION COMMENTS—1993

(a) This Article is new. It clarifies the law by stating a rule that is consistent with general principles of Louisiana law. See C.C. Arts. 1839, 1983 (Rev.1984).

(b) Under this Article, where the right assigned is an immovable, the requirement of notice is governed by the public records doctrine.

Art. 2654. Documents evidencing the right

The assignor of a right must deliver to the assignee all documents in his possession that evidence the right. Nevertheless, a failure by the assignor to deliver such documents does not affect the validity of the assignment.

When a right is assigned only in part, the assignor may give the assignee an original or a copy of such documents.

Acts 1993, No. 841, § 1, eff. Jan. 1, 1995.

REVISION COMMENT—1993

This Article is new. It changes the law in part in that it provides that a failure by the assignor to deliver documents in his possession that evidence the right assigned does not affect the validity of the assignment. See Marshall v. Parish Morehouse, 14 La.Ann. 689 (1859). Under this Article, an assignment is valid as between assignor and assignee even though the pertinent documents have not been delivered, thereby departing from the rule of Scott v. Corkern, 231 La. 368, 91 So.2d 569 (La.1956).

CHAPTER 16—OF THE GIVING IN PAYMENT

Art. 2655. Giving in payment, definition

Giving in payment is a contract whereby an obligor gives a thing to the obligee, who accepts it in payment of a debt.

Acts 1993, No. 841, § 1, eff. Jan. 1, 1995.

REVISION COMMENTS—1993

(a) This Article reproduces the substance of Article 2655 of the Louisiana Civil Code of 1870. It does not change the law.

(b) Under this Article, the critical consideration in determining whether a transaction is a giving in payment is the intent of the parties, particularly of the creditor, who has the right to demand exactly what was due by virtue of the obligation. Dunaway v. Spain, 493 So.2d 577 (La.1986).

(c) All of the elements necessary to perfect a valid sale—that is, agreement as to the thing and the price—are essential to the perfection of a giving in payment. Slaton v. King, 214 La. 89, 36 So.2d 648 (1948). Article 2656, infra, imposes an additional requirement for a giving in payment that need not be met in the case of a sale.

(d) A valid giving in payment presupposes the existence of a real indebtedness. Krauss Co. v. Godchaux, 13 La.App. 607, 128 So. 673 (La.App.Orl.Cir.1930).

(e) Under this Article, unless the parties intended only a partial extinguishment of the debt, the giving of a thing in payment extinguishes the obligation completely, even when the value of the thing given in payment is less than the debt being discharged. Succession of Burns, 199 La. 1081, 7 So.2d 359 (La.1942).

(f) Under this Article, any debt or obligation, disputed or undisputed, liquidated or unliquidated, may be extinguished by a giving in payment. St. Landry Credit Plan, Inc. v. Darbonne, 221 So.2d 880 (La.App. 1st Cir., 1969); Huval Tractor, Inc. v. Journet, 452 So.2d 373 (La.App. 3d Cir.1984).

(g) A giving in payment transfers ownership and has the same effect as an ordinary sale. Quality Finance Co. of Donaldsonville, Inc. v. Bourque, 315 So.2d 656 (La.1975).

Art. 2656. Delivery essential to giving in payment

Delivery of the thing is essential to the perfection of a giving in payment.

Acts 1993, No. 841, § 1, eff. Jan. 1, 1995.

(a) This Article reproduces the substance of Article 2656 of the Louisiana Civil Code of 1870. It does not change the law.

(b) Under this Article no giving in payment is possible after a sequestration, since the owner of the thing sequestered cannot deliver possession of it to his creditor. LaGardeur Intern., Inc. v. Ascension Const. Corp., 504 So.2d 587 (La.App. 4th Cir.1987).

(c) Under this Article, delivery is of the essence of a giving in payment; ownership is not transferred until the moment of delivery. Durnford v. Syndics of Brooks, 3 Mart. (O.S.) 222 (1814); Wilson v. Smith, 12 La. 375 (1838).

(d) Under this Article, where the thing given in payment is an immovable, delivery is deemed to take place upon execution of the writing transferring ownership of the thing. Miller v. Miller, 234 La. 883, 102 So.2d 52 (1957); Shultz v. Morgan, 27 La.Ann. 616 (1875).

Art. 2657.   Giving in partial payment

An obligor may give a thing to the obligee in partial payment of a debt.

A giving in partial payment extinguishes the debt in the amount intended by the parties. If the parties' intent concerning the amount of the partial extinguishment cannot be ascertained, it is presumed that they intended to extinguish the debt in the amount of the fair market value of the thing given in partial payment.

Acts 1993, No. 841, § 1, eff. Jan. 1, 1995.

(a) This Article is new. It does not change the law, however. It is intended to give legislative recognition to the decision of the Louisiana Supreme Court in Dunaway v. Spain, 493 So.2d 577 (La.1986).

(b) Under this Article the parties may stipulate specifically the part of the debt that is to be discharged by the thing given in partial payment. In the absence of such an agreement, it is presumed that the parties intended for the debt to be discharged in an amount proportional to the fair market value of the thing given in payment. See Dunaway v. Spain, 493 So.2d 577 (La.1986).

(c) Article 2657 of the Civil Code of 1870, according to which the risk of loss of the thing given in payment remained with the debtor until the moment of delivery, has been eliminated because it is now unnecessary. See C.C. Art. 2467, supra.

(d) Article 2658 of the Civil Code of 1870 has been eliminated because of its lack of consistency with the rules that, since 1985, have governed the revocatory action. See C.C. Arts. 2036–2043 (Rev.1984).

Art. 2658.   [Blank]

Art. 2659.   Application of general rules of sale

The giving in payment is governed by the rules of the contract of sale, with the differences provided for in this Chapter.

Acts 1993, No. 841, § 1, eff. Jan. 1, 1995.

(a) This Article reproduces the substance of Article 2659 of the Louisiana Civil Code of 1870. It does not change the law.

(b) Under this Article, a conveyance of land given in payment is subject to rescission on grounds of lesion beyond moiety. Jones v. First National Bank, Ruston, La., 215 La. 862, 41 So.2d 811 (1949); Hullaby v. Mosely, 505 So.2d 874 (La.App. 2d Cir., 1987).

TITLE VIII—EXCHANGE

Art. 2660. Exchange, definition

Exchange is a contract whereby each party transfers to the other the ownership of a thing other than money.

Ownership of the things exchanged is transferred between the parties as soon as there is agreement on the things, even though none of the things has been delivered.

If it is the intent of the parties that the transfer of ownership will not take place until a later time, then the contract is a contract to exchange.

Acts 2010, No. 186, § 1.

REVISION COMMENTS—2010

(a) This Article combines the provisions of Articles 2660–2661 of the Louisiana Civil Code (1870). It does not change the law.

(b) Consent alone is sufficient to effect a transfer of ownership to the things given and received by each of the parties to the exchange. Thus, as under present law, exchange remains a consensual contract.

(c) Under a contract of exchange, each party transfers to each other the ownership of a thing other than money. If the "thing" given by one of the parties is money, then the transaction is a sale rather than an exchange.

(d) The transfer of a thing in return for services to be rendered is not an exchange but an innominate contract. See Louisiana Civil Code Article 1914; Thielman v. Gahlman, 119 La. 350, 44 So. 123 (1907); Hearsey v. Craig, 126 La. 824, 53 So. 17 (1910); 10 Planiol et Ripert, Traité pratique de droit civil français 29 (1932).

Art. 2661. Rights and obligations of the parties

Each of the parties to a contract of exchange has the rights and obligations of a seller with respect to the thing transferred by him and the rights and obligations of a buyer with respect to the thing transferred to him.

Acts 2010, No. 186, § 1.

REVISION COMMENT—2010

This Article is new. It is not intended to change the law, however. It gives formulation to a principle implicit in Articles 2660 and 2667 (1870).

Art. 2662. Rights of party evicted

A person evicted from a thing received in exchange may demand the value of the thing from which he was evicted or the return of the thing he gave, with damages in either case.

Acts 2010, No. 186, § 1.

REVISION COMMENTS—2010

(a) This Article changes the law in part by providing an evicted party to a contract of exchange the election between two remedies, without foreclosing the recoverability of damages, if appropriate.

(b) The election by the evicted party to dissolve the contract and obtain the return of the thing given by him in exchange does not prevent the recoverability of damages, if appropriate. Recoverability of damages is appropriate in accordance with the Civil Code Articles governing damages in eviction cases. See Civil Code Articles 2506–2509.

Art. 2663 EXCHANGE

(c) If the immovable given in exchange by the party evicted has been transferred to a third party, the right of the evicted party to recover the immovable given by him is subject to the public records law. See Louisiana Civil Code Articles 3338–3353. It is the intent of this Article that the rights of the transferee prime the rights of the evicted party to recover the immovable in the same situation as in a sales transaction.

Art. 2663. Rescission for lesion in contracts of exchange

A party giving a corporeal immovable in exchange for property worth less than one half of the fair market value of the immovable given by him may claim rescission on grounds of lesion beyond moiety.

Acts 2010, No. 186, § 1.

(a) This Article changes the law in part by providing a different rule for determining when a party may claim lesion. Under Articles 2664–2666 (1870), rescission for lesion can be obtained in two situations: (1) In case of an exchange of immovable property for movables, the person that gave immovable property can obtain rescission if the movables received are not worth more than one half of the value of the immovables; and (2) When an immovable is exchanged for another immovable with a balance paid in movables. In the second situation, only the person that paid the balance is entitled to demand rescission. The exchanger that received the balance does not have an action for lesion. Saizan v. Century 21 Gold Key Realty, Inc., 447 So.2d 41 (La.App. 1 Cir. 1984).

(b) Under this Article, a party that gives a corporeal immovable in exchange may claim lesion if the things that he receives in return, movable or immovable, are worth less than one half the fair market of the immovable given by him.

(c) It is the intent of this Article that rescission for lesion not be allowed in the contract of exchange except as provided in this Article. The text of Article 2664 (1870), which provided that lesion was not available in exchange transactions except in the cases provided in the Civil Code, has not been reproduced as unnecessary. This omission is not intended to change the law.

Art. 2664. Application of the rules of sale

The contract of exchange is governed by the rules of the contract of sale, with the differences provided in this Title.

Acts 2010, No. 186, § 1.

REVISION COMMENTS—2010

This Article amends the language of present Article 2667 without intending to change the law. The rules of the contract of sale govern exchange transactions with the differences provided in the Articles of Exchange.

Arts. 2665 to 2667. [Blank]

TITLE IX—LEASE

CHAPTER 1—GENERAL PROVISIONS

Art. 2668.   Contract of lease defined

Lease is a synallagmatic contract by which one party, the lessor, binds himself to give to the other party, the lessee, the use and enjoyment of a thing for a term in exchange for a rent that the lessee binds himself to pay.

The consent of the parties as to the thing and the rent is essential but not necessarily sufficient for a contract of lease.

Acts 2004, No. 821, § 1, eff. Jan. 1, 2005.

REVISION COMMENTS—2004

(a) This Article reproduces in condensed form the substance of Articles 2669, 2670, 2674, and 2677 of the Civil Code of 1870. It differs from the source articles in that it excludes the hiring of services from the scope of the term "lease." Under this Revision, the hiring of services is no longer a form of lease, but is instead an innominate contract. This change also makes it possible to replace the term "price" with the more appropriate term "rent" in describing the lessee's performance.

(b) According to this Article, a lease is a synallagmatic, or bilateral, contract . . . that is, "[a] contract . . . [by which] the parties obligate themselves reciprocally, so that the obligation of each party is correlative to the obligation of the other." C.C. Art. 1908 (Rev. 1984). In return for the lessee's obligation to pay the rent, the lessor binds himself to allow the lessee, and to ensure for him, the use and enjoyment of the thing for the agreed or contemplated term. The lessee's right is a personal rather than a real right, see Civil Code Article 476 (Rev. 1978) and comments thereunder, and the lessor's obligation is a personal rather than a real one, see Civil Code Articles 1766 and 1763 (Rev. 1984). Externally, a lease may resemble certain real rights, such as the personal servitudes of usufruct or habitation or the limited personal servitude of rights of use, all of which also confer on a person the right to use a thing belonging to another. However, unlike those servitudes—which are true dismemberments of ownership conferring on the holder of them a direct and immediate authority over the thing that is assertible against future owners of the thing—a lease simply confers on the lessee the right to demand performance from the lessor and his universal successors. Only exceptionally, and where the law so provides, is this right assertible against subsequent acquirers of the thing. See C.C. Arts. 2711 and 2712 (Rev. 2004), (providing that the transfer of a leased movable or an immovable subject to a recorded lease does not terminate the lease).

(c) The second paragraph of this Article is based on Civil Code Article 2670 (1870), but clarifies that: (1) the necessary consent must be consent as to the thing to be leased and the rent to be paid; and (2) such consent, though essential, is not necessarily sufficient for a contract of lease.

(d) Without an agreement as to the thing and the rent, there cannot be a contract of lease. On the other hand, the existence of such an agreement does not necessarily mean that a contract of lease has come into existence if the parties did not so intend. For example, if, despite agreement on the thing and the rent, it is understood that the parties will not be bound until they agree on other terms of the contract, then there is no lease until these terms are agreed upon. Similarly, even if the parties intended to be bound upon their agreement as to the thing and the "rent," the resulting contract may or may not be one of lease, depending again on the intent of the parties. For example, if the right intended to be conveyed has the attributes of a real right such as a personal servitude or a limited personal servitude of use, then the contract is not a lease, even though the parties used terms like "rent" or "lease." Cf. C.C. Art. 730 (Rev. 1977).

(e) If the contract is one of lease, then the rules of this Title become applicable for filling any gaps in the parties' agreement and for determining its overall validity and effectiveness. Agreement as to the rent does not necessarily mean agreement on the exact amount (see Civil Code Article 2676 (Rev. 2004) providing for the fixing of the rent), but does presuppose an understanding that what is to be paid will be "rent" rather than a "price." Likewise, as stated in the first paragraph of this Article, the parties must have agreed that the giving of the "use and enjoyment" of the thing is not a permanent one but is rather "for a term," albeit an indeterminate one. See Civil Code Articles 2678–2680 (Rev. 2004).

Art. 2669. Relation with other titles

In all matters not provided for in this Title, the contract of lease is governed by the rules of the Titles of "Obligations in General" and "Conventional Obligations or Contracts".

Acts 2004, No. 821, § 1, eff. Jan. 1, 2005.

REVISION COMMENTS—2004

(a) This Article reproduces the substance of Article 2668 of the Civil Code of 1870. The slight change in language is not intended to change the law, but rather to parallel the corresponding article of the Title "Sale" (see C.C. Art. 2438 (Rev. 1993)). The cross-reference contained in the source provision has been broadened to take account of the rearrangement of articles effected by the 1984 obligations revision which expanded the content of Title III of Book III of the Civil Code of 1870, "Of Obligations," and has placed in it many of the general articles formerly contained in Title IV, "Of Conventional Obligations."

(b) This Article restates the obvious proposition that, like any other contract, a lease is subject to the general rules provided by the Civil Code for all contracts. Since particular rules prevail over general rules, then, with regard to leases, the rules of the Title on "Lease" should prevail over the general rules on contracts and obligations in general. See C.C. Art. 1916 (Rev. 1984) (providing that "nominate contracts are subject to the special rules of the respective titles when those rules modify, complement, or depart from the [general] rules[.]") By the same token, the rules of this Title, being the general rules for all leases, may be displaced by more specific rules provided in other statutes for certain types of leases, such as the Mineral Code (see C.C. Art. 2672 (Rev. 2004)), the Louisiana Lease of Movables Act (R.S. 9:3301 et seq.), the Louisiana Rental-Purchase Agreement Act (R.S. 9:3351 et seq.), and R.S. 9:3201 et seq.

Art. 2670. Contract to lease

A contract to enter into a lease at a future time is enforceable by either party if there was agreement as to the thing to be leased and the rent, unless the parties understood that the contract would not be binding until reduced to writing or until its other terms were agreed upon.

Acts 2004, No. 821, § 1, eff. Jan. 1, 2005.

REVISION COMMENTS—2004

(a) This Article is new. It is derived from pertinent Louisiana jurisprudence and from the general principle of Civil Code Article 1971 (Rev. 1984), which provides that "[p]arties are free to contract for any object that is lawful, possible, and determined or determinable." Cf. also C.C. Arts. 1976 (Rev. 1984) and 2450 (Rev. 1993). A contract to enter into a lease at a future time is not only lawful and possible, but also meets the requirement of determinability provided by Civil Code Article 1971 (Rev. 1984), if the parties agree as to the thing to be leased and the rent to be paid. Agreement as to the term is not necessary since the term may be supplied by law. See C.C. Art. 2680 (Rev. 2004).

(b) A contract to lease that meets the requirements of this Article generates binding obligations and may be enforced by either party pursuant to the provisions of the Title of "Conventional Obligations or Contracts." See C.C. Arts. 1983 et seq. (Rev. 1984). For cases recognizing this principle, see Coffee v. Smith, 109 La. 440, 33 So. 554 (1903); Gladney v. Steinau, 149 La. 79, 88 So. 694 (1921); Knights of Pythias v. Fishel, 168 La. 1095, 123 So. 724 (1929); Johnson v. Williams, 178 La. 891, 152 So. 556 (1934); City of New Orleans v. Cheramie, 509 So.2d 58 (La.App. 1 Cir. 1987), writ denied 512 So.2d 463 (La. 1987). See also Vernon Palmer, Leases: The Law in Louisiana, § 2–4 (1982).

(c) Enforcement is not available, however, if the parties understood that the contract would not be binding until reduced to writing or until its other terms were agreed upon. In such cases, "the contract is [merely] inchoate, incomplete, and either party, before signing, may . . . recede . . ." Laroussini v. Werlein, 52 La.Ann. 424, 27 So. 89, at p. 90 (1899). See also In re Woodville, 115 La. 810, 40 So. 174 (1905); Waldhauser v. Adams Hats, 207 La. 56, 20 So.2d 423 (1944).

Art. 2671. Types of leases

Depending on the agreed use of the leased thing, a lease is characterized as: residential, when the thing is to be occupied as a dwelling; agricultural, when the thing is a predial estate that is to be used for agricultural purposes; mineral, when the thing is to be used for the production of minerals; commercial, when the thing is to be used for business or commercial purposes; or consumer, when the thing is a movable intended for the lessee's personal or familial use outside his trade or profession. This enumeration is not exclusive.

When the thing is leased for more than one of the above or for other purposes, the dominant or more substantial purpose determines the type of lease for purposes of regulation.

Acts 2004, No. 821, § 1, eff. Jan. 1, 2005.

REVISION COMMENT—2004

This Article is new. It defines the various categories of leases, many of which are used in this Title.

Art. 2672. Mineral lease

A mineral lease is governed by the Mineral Code.

Acts 2004, No. 821, § 1, eff. Jan. 1, 2005.

REVISION COMMENTS—2004

(a) This Article reiterates the obvious by providing that mineral leases are governed by the applicable provisions of the Mineral Code (R.S. 31:114, et seq.). Being more specific with regard to mineral leases, those provisions prevail over the provisions of this Title.

(b) R.S. 31:2, Article 2 of the Mineral Code, provides that "[i]f [the Mineral] Code does not expressly or impliedly provide for a particular situation, the Civil Code . . . [is] applicable." As part of the Civil Code, this Title may apply in a supplementary fashion to mineral lease issues that are not provided for by the Mineral Code. However, before resorting to this Title, as opposed to other titles of the Civil Code, one should bear in mind the fact that a mineral lease is a real right and that it differs in many respects from an ordinary lease.

CHAPTER 2—ESSENTIAL ELEMENTS

SECTION 1—THE THING

Art. 2673. The thing

All things, corporeal or incorporeal, that are susceptible of ownership may be the object of a lease, except those that cannot be used without being destroyed by that very use, or those the lease of which is prohibited by law.

Acts 2004, No. 821, § 1, eff. Jan. 1, 2005.

REVISION COMMENTS—2004

(a) This Article reproduces the substance of Articles 2678 and 2679 of the Civil Code of 1870. It differs from the source articles in three respects, as explained in the next three comments, respectively.

(b) This Article clarifies the law by declaring that things that are insusceptible of ownership are also insusceptible of being leased. Examples of such things, called "common things" by Civil Code Article 449 (Rev. 1978), are "such as the air and the high seas." Id. See also La. Const. Art. 9 § 1. For a parallel provision in the law of sales, see C.C. Art. 2448 (Rev. 1995). On the other hand, things that are susceptible of ownership but not private ownership, i.e. "public things" (see C. C. Art. 450 (Rev. 1978)), may be leased provided that such a lease is permitted by "applicable laws and regulations." C.C. Art. 452 (Rev. 1978).

(c) This Article also differs from the source provisions in that it does not prohibit a priori the lease of a credit, nor does it contain any presumption against the lease of incorporeals. Under this Article, all things, corporeal or incorporeal, movable or immovable, may be the object of lease, "except those that cannot be used without being destroyed by that very use. . . ." This prohibition may encompass certain incorporeals, such as a credit, but can also encompass certain corporeal movables, such as "those that cannot be used without being expended or consumed" (C.C. Art. 536 (Rev. 1976)) by that use. The question of whether the particular use will so consume or destroy the thing is left for judicial determination.

(d) The second prohibition refers to things "the lease of which is prohibited by law." Examples of such prohibitions can be found in the Civil Code, as well as the Revised Statutes. See, e.g., C.C. Art. 637 (Rev. 1976) (prohibiting the lease of the right of habitation); C.C. Art. 650 (Rev. 1977) (which is amended by this Revision to clarify that not only alienation but also the leasing of a predial servitude separately from the dominant estate is prohibited). See Comment (e); C.C. Art. 1766 (Rev. 1984) (defining obligations strictly personal to the obligee); and C.C. Art. 2337 (Rev. 1979) (prohibiting the lease of a spouse's undivided interest in the community).

(e) Article 2680 of the Civil Code of 1870 provides that "[a] right of servitude can not be leased separately from the property to which it is annexed." The substance of that article has been retained and transferred to Civil Code Article 650 (Rev. 1977), where it more properly belongs, which now provides in part that "[t]he right of using the servitude cannot be alienated, leased, or encumbered separately from the dominant estate." The word "leased" has been added to Civil Code Article 650 by this Act.

Art. 2674. Ownership of the thing

A lease of a thing that does not belong to the lessor may nevertheless be binding on the parties.

Acts 2004, No. 821, § 1, eff. Jan. 1, 2005.

REVISION COMMENTS—2004

(a) This Article is derived from Articles 2681 and 2682 of the Louisiana Civil Code of 1870. See also C.C. Arts. 2703 and 2704 (1870). Article 2681 of the Civil Code of 1870 provided that "[h]e who possesses a thing belonging to another, may let it to a third person, but he can not let it for any other use than that to which it is usually applied." The quoted article seems to contemplate subleases by lessees or leases by other precarious possessors. Civil Code Article 2674 (Rev. 2004) is broader in scope and includes even leases by adverse possessors, in good or in bad faith. Consequently, the provision of the source article that prohibited the lease of the thing "for any other use than that to which it is usually applied" is not reproduced in Civil Code Article 2674 (Rev. 2004). For the right of a lessee, vis-à-vis the lessor, to sublease the thing, see Civil Code Article 2713 (Rev. 2004).

(b) Article 2682 of the Louisiana Civil Code of 1870 provided that "[h]e who lets out the property of another, warrants the enjoyment of it against the claim of the owner." This principle is implicit in Civil Code Article 2674 (Rev. 2004), particularly the phrase "binding on the parties." According to Civil Code Article 2700 (Rev. 2004), a binding lease imposes on the lessor the obligation to warrant the lessee's peaceful possession. The combined reading of Civil Code Articles 2700 and 2674 (Rev. 2004) leads inescapably to the conclusion that, even if he does not own the thing, the lessor is bound to warrant the lessee's peaceful possession of the thing against any person with pretensions of ownership or other legal right. See C.C. Arts. 2700–2702 (Rev. 2004). See also Civil Code Article 2711 (Rev. 2004) which provides that the transfer of the leased thing does not terminate the lease, and Comment (b) which reiterates that the lessor remains bound to warrant the lessee's peaceful possession.

(c) By the same token, as long as the lessor is willing and able to protect the lessee's peaceful possession for the remainder of the term, the lessee may not refuse to pay rent or carry out his other obligations under the lease solely because of the lessor's claimed or real lack of ownership. Thus, the gist of Civil Code Article 2674 (Rev. 2004) is that ownership of the thing by the lessor is not an essential element of the contract of lease. In the absence of contrary understanding, the lease is binding even if such ownership is lacking. The use of the word "may" in Civil Code Article 2674 (Rev. 2004) is intended to cover cases in which there is a contrary understanding and generally cases in which ownership of the thing by the lessor was part of the cause of the contract of lease. In such cases, the lessee is entitled to the remedies provided by the Title of "Conventional Obligations or Contracts."

(d) The rule of this Article is subject to exceptions provided by more specific provisions of Louisiana legislation which prohibit the lease of a thing belonging to another. For example, Civil Code Article 2337 (Rev. 1979) provides that "[a] spouse may not ... lease to a third person his undivided interest in the community or in particular things of the community prior to the termination of the regime." Similarly, Civil Code Article 2369.4 (Rev. 1995) provides that "[a] spouse may not ... lease former community property ... without the concurrence of the other spouse[.]" Leases entered into in violation of these articles are null. Comment (b) under Civil Code Article 2337 (Rev. 1979) declares that leases in violation of that article are absolutely null, and Civil Code Article 2369.4 (Rev. 1995) provides that leases in violation of that article are relatively null. A similar conclusion might be reached with regard to Civil Code Article 805 (Rev. 1990), which provides that "[t]he consent of all the co-owners is required for the lease ... of the entire thing held in indivision." However, Civil Code Article 802 (Rev. 1990), which provides that "[a]s against third persons, a co-owner has the right to use and enjoy the thing as if he were the sole owner," may lead to the conclusion that leases in violation of Civil Code Article 805 (Rev. 1990) are binding on the lessor and the lessee, although they are not binding on the non-leasing co-owners.

SECTION 2—THE RENT

Art. 2675.   The rent

The rent may consist of money, commodities, fruits, services, or other performances sufficient to support an onerous contract.

Acts 2004, No. 821, § 1, eff. Jan. 1, 2005.

REVISION COMMENTS—2004

(a) This Article is based in part on Article 2671 of the Louisiana Civil Code of 1870 but adds "services, or other performances" to the list contained in the source provision. This addition is consistent with the jurisprudence, which characterized as illustrative the list contained in that article. See Louisiana Ass'n for Mental Health v. Edwards, 322 So.2d 761 (La. 1975). Cf. C.C. Art. 1756 (Rev. 1984). The term "rent" is substituted for "price" because, unlike the source provision, the scope of Civil Code Article 2675 (Rev. 2004) and of this Title is confined to the lease of things and does not encompass the hiring of services. See C.C. Art. 2668 (Rev. 2004), Comment (a).

(b) Because a lease is an onerous contract (see C.C. Art. 2668 (Rev. 2004)), all the performances contemplated by Civil Code Article 2675 (Rev. 2004) must be "sufficient to support an onerous contract." This is consistent with the jurisprudence, which held that in the absence of rent there is no lease and that the rent "must be serious and not out of proportion to the thing's value." Arnold v. Board of Levee Com'rs of Orleans Levee Dist., 366 So.2d 1321, 1327 (La. 1978). See also Myers v. Burke, 189 So. 482 (La.App. 1 Cir. 1939); Benoit v. Burke, 189 So. 484 (La.App. 1 Cir. 1939); University Pub. Co. v. Piffet, 34 La.Ann. 602 (1882); Fisk v. Moores, 11 Rob. 279 (1845); Paige & Wells v. Scott's Heirs, 12 La. 490 (1838). See also C.C. Art. 2464 (Rev. 1993), which provides that "[t]here is no sale unless the parties intended that a price be paid" and that "[t]he price must not be out of all proportion with the value of the thing sold."

Art. 2676.   Agreement as to the rent

The rent shall be fixed by the parties in a sum either certain or determinable through a method agreed by them. It may also be fixed by a third person designated by them.

If the agreed method proves unworkable or the designated third person is unwilling or unable to fix the rent, then there is no lease.

If the rent has been established and thereafter is subject to redetermination either by a designated third person or through a method agreed to by the parties, but the third person is unwilling or unable to fix the rent or the agreed method proves unworkable, the court may either fix the rent or provide a similar method in accordance with the intent of the parties.

Acts 2004, No. 821, § 1, eff. Jan. 1, 2005.

REVISION COMMENTS—2004

(a) This Article is derived from Articles 2671 and 2672 of the Civil Code of 1870. The first sentence of this Article restates the principle of Article 2671 of the Louisiana Civil Code of 1870 by requiring that the rent be either certain or determinable. If this requirement is not met, there is no lease. For pertinent jurisprudence, see, inter alia, Haughery v. Lee, 17 La.Ann. 22 (1865); Weaks Supply Co. v. Werdin, 147 So. 838 (La.App. 2 Cir. 1933); Faroldi v. Nungesser, 144 So.2d 568 (La.App. 4 Cir. 1962); Southern States Equipment Co., Inc. v. Unique Services, Inc., 525 So.2d 1198 (La.App. 5 Cir. 1988); Paige & Wells v. Scott's Heirs, 12 La. 490 (1838); Fisk v. Moores, 11 Rob. 279 (1845); Groghan v. Billingsley, 313 So.2d 255 (La.App. 4 Cir. 1975), writ denied 318 So.2d 46 (La. 1975). This jurisprudence continues to be relevant.

(b) The first sentence also clarifies the law by providing that the requirement of determinability is satisfied if the parties specified a method for fixing the rent. For example, an agreement for a rental price of one cent per gallon on all gasoline sold during the month was held to be sufficiently certain to support a lease contract. See Lee v. Pearson, 143 So. 516 (La.App. 1 Cir. 1932); Selber Bros. v. Newstadt's Shoe Stores, 203 La. 316, 14 So.2d 10 (1943). This clarification is consistent not only with the jurisprudence but also with the 1993 revision of the law of Sales. See C.C. Art. 2464 (Rev. 1993); Bonfanti v. Davis, 487 So.2d 165 (La.App. 3 Cir. 1986); Mouton v. P.A.B., Inc., 450 So.2d 410 (La.App. 3 Cir. 1984), writ denied 458 So.2d 118 (La. 1984); Arata v. Louisiana Stadium and Exposition Dist., 254 La. 579, 225 So.2d 362 (1969), certiorari denied 90 S.Ct. 569, 396 U.S. 279, 24 L.Ed.2d 467 (1970); Succession of Pietri, Orleans No. 7991 (La.App. Orleans 1921).

(c) The second sentence of this Article reproduces the substance of the first sentence of Article 2672 of the Civil Code of 1870. Although the source provision required that the third person be "named and determined," this sentence requires only that the third person be "designated." Designation may be by name or by title or position. For example, a stipulation in a commercial lease that the rent shall be fixed "by the president of the local chamber of commerce or her designee" is sufficient under this sentence, even if at the time of the stipulation the parties did not know who would be the president or her designee. For related provisions, see C.C. Arts. 1974 (Rev. 1984) and 2465 (Rev. 1993).

(d) The second paragraph of this Article restates in broader terms the principle of the last phrase of the first paragraph of Article 2672 of the Civil Code of 1870 so as to include situations in which the method agreed by the parties proves unworkable.

(e) The third paragraph of this Article changes the law by allowing court intervention in the limited circumstances specified therein. This change is consistent with the 1984 revision of the law of Obligations and the 1993 revision of the law of Sales. See Cf. C.C. Arts. 1974 (Rev. 1984) and 2465 (Rev. 1993). However, unlike these articles, this paragraph authorizes court intervention only for redetermination, as opposed to initial determination, of the rent.

Art. 2677.   Crop rent

When the parties to an agricultural lease agree that the rent will consist of a portion of the crops, that portion is considered at all times the property of the lessor.

Acts 2004, No. 821, § 1, eff. Jan. 1, 2005.

REVISION COMMENT—2004

This Article reproduces the substance of the first sentence of R.S. 9:3204. It does not change the law.

SECTION 3—THE TERM

Art. 2678.   Term

The lease shall be for a term. Its duration may be agreed to by the parties or supplied by law.

630

The term may be fixed or indeterminate. It is fixed when the parties agree that the lease will terminate at a designated date or upon the occurrence of a designated event.

It is indeterminate in all other cases.

Acts 2004, No. 821, § 1, eff. Jan. 1, 2005.

REVISION COMMENTS—2004

(a) The first sentence of this Article reiterates the principle established in the first article of this Title that, in order for a contract to qualify as a lease, the contract must, inter alia, be "for a term," that is, it may not be perpetual. This principle is derived from Article 2674 of the Civil Code of 1870 (for "a certain time") and from Louisiana judicial decisions that have held that a perpetual "lease" is a nudum pactum. Becker & Associates, Inc. v. Lou-Ark Equipment Rentals Co., Inc., 331 So.2d 474 (La. 1976); Bristo v. Christine Oil & Gas Co., 139 La. 312, 71 So. 521 (1916); Calhoun v. Christine Oil & Gas Co., 139 La. 316, 71 So. 522 (1916); Dunham v. McCormick, 139 La. 317, 71 So. 523 (1916); Parrott v. McCormick, 139 La. 318, 71 So. 523 (1916); Nervis v. McCormick 139 La. 318, 71 So. 523 (1916); Leslie v. Blackwell, 370 So.2d 178 (La.App. 3 Cir. 1979).

(b) The second sentence of this Article provides that the duration of the term need not be specified in the contract. If it is not so specified, then the duration is supplied by law (legal term). See C.C. Art. 2680 (Rev. 2004). This principle is derived from Articles 2685 and 2687 of the Civil Code of 1870. In combination with Civil Code Articles 2679 and 2680 (Rev. 2004), this sentence enunciates the distinction between (a) conventional terms, that is, terms the duration of which is validly established by the parties; and (b) legal terms, that is, terms the duration of which is established by operation of law when the parties either did not specified the duration or provided for one not allowed by law, such as one exceeding ninety-nine years or one depending solely on the will of the lessee or the lessor who have not fixed a maximum. See C.C. Arts. 2679 and 2680 (Rev. 2004).

(c) The second and third paragraphs of this Article address the term's duration and enunciate a distinction between fixed terms and indeterminate terms. This distinction is important, inter alia, for purposes of termination of the lease. A lease with a fixed term terminates upon the expiration of the term but is susceptible of being reconducted. See C.C. Arts. 2720–2724 (Rev. 2004). A lease with an indeterminate term continues indefinitely until terminated through notice. See C.C. Arts. 2727–2729 (Rev. 2004).

(d) A term is fixed when, pursuant to the agreement of the parties, its terminal point is marked in advance by a particular date on the calendar or by the occurrence of a future event that is bound to occur, albeit on a date not yet known (e.g., the death of the lessee).

(e) A term is indeterminate if its terminal point is not fixed in advance but depends on the will of the parties subsequently expressed, such as a month-to-month lease or another periodical lease. An indeterminate term may be conventional, as when the parties agreed to a month-to-month lease, or it may be a legal term, as when the parties to a residential lease do not specify a term and thus trigger the application of the suppletive legal rules (see, e.g., C.C. Art. 2680 (Rev. 2004)) which provide that residential leases with an unspecified term are on a month-to-month basis. Although all the legal terms prescribed in Civil Code Article 2680 (Rev. 2004) are indeterminate, the reverse is not true—all indeterminate terms are not legal.

Art. 2679. Limits of contractual freedom in fixing the term

The duration of a term may not exceed ninety-nine years. If the lease provides for a longer term or contains an option to extend the term to more than ninety-nine years, the term shall be reduced to ninety-nine years.

If the term's duration depends solely on the will of the lessor or the lessee and the parties have not agreed on a maximum duration, the duration is determined in accordance with the following Article.

Acts 2004, No. 821, § 1, eff. Jan. 1, 2005.

REVISION COMMENTS—2004

(a) The first sentence of this Article imposes a quantitative limit on the otherwise unrestricted power of the parties to fix in advance the duration of the term of a lease. This limitation is dictated by public policy considerations. A lease for a duration longer than ninety-nine years differs little from a perpetual lease. It binds the parties and their successors for a period much longer than most people are able to envision and thereby imposes on them the risk of changing circumstances that they cannot anticipate. Such a lease also binds the property for too long a period, and thus keeps it out of commerce for most practical purposes. This is why many other civil codes impose similar, and usually shorter, maximum limitations on the duration of leases. See, e.g., Argentine C.C. Art. 1539 (ten years); Greek C.C. Art. 610 (thirty years or for the life of the lessee); Italian C.C. Arts. 1573, 1607, 1629 (30 years or for the life of the lessee, and ninety-nine years for rural lands intended for reforestation); Quebec C.C. Art. 1880 (100 years). The ninety-nine year maximum in this Article is derived from French law (see Decree of 18–29 December 1790) as well as from Louisiana jurisprudence. See State v. Board of Adm'rs of Tulane Education Fund, 125 La. 432, 51 So. 483 (1910) (upholding the validity of a ninety-nine year lease).

(b) The second sentence of this Article prescribes the consequences of a violation of the rule of the first sentence. A lease providing for an initial term that exceeds ninety-nine years is not for that reason invalid. Its term will simply be reduced by operation of law to ninety-nine years. The same is true for a lease that provides for a shorter initial term but allows either party the option of extending the lease's duration. (See C.C. Art. 2725 (Rev. 2004).) If the option is exercised so as to extend the lease to more than ninety-nine years from the beginning of the initial term, the lease will not be invalidated for that reason alone. Its duration will simply be reduced to ninety-nine years from the beginning of the initial term as provided by the second sentence of Civil Code Article 2679 (Rev. 2004).

(c) A lease for an indeterminate term, such as a year-to-year lease, that is allowed by the parties to last longer than ninety-nine years does not violate the rule of the first sentence of this Article. Since a lease for an indeterminate term can be terminated by either party through notice (see C.C. Arts. 2727–2729 (Rev. 2004)), the continuation of such a lease depends on the mutual and constantly-renewed consent of both parties. The fact that the lease is thus allowed to last for longer than ninety-nine years is due not to the parties' initial agreement, but rather to their subsequently expressed volition not to terminate the lease. The same is true of a lease for a fixed term shorter than ninety-nine years that is reconducted by the parties (see C.C. Arts. 2720–2723 (Rev. 2004)) so as to eventually last for a longer period. Here again, the ultimate duration of the lease is due not to the initial agreement of the parties in fixing the initial term, but rather to their subsequently-expressed volition to reconduct the lease. The same should be true for leases at will. See Comment (d).

(d) The second paragraph of this Article addresses situations in which the duration of the term is left entirely to the will of one party and in which the parties have not fixed a maximum term. This paragraph is intended to overrule Louisiana judicial decisions that have invalidated leases whose duration depended entirely on the will of the lessee on the theory that such leases have the potential of becoming perpetual. See Bristo v. Christine Oil & Gas Co., 139 La. 312, 71 So. 521 (1916); Leslie v. Blackwell, 370 So.2d 178 (La.App. 3 Cir. 1979). But see G.I.'s Club of Slidell v. American Legion Post #374, 504 So.2d 967 (La.App. 1 Cir. 1987). In Bristo, the court held that "to recognize that the defendant [lessee] has the right, without any obligation, to hold the plaintiff's land under a perpetual lease or option, would take the property out of commerce, and would be violative of the doctrine of ownership . . ." 71 So. 521, at 522 (1916). The problem of the potential perpetuity of such a lease is also addressed by Civil Code Article 2678 (Rev. 2004), which prohibits perpetual leases, and by the first paragraph of Civil Code Article 2679 (Rev. 2004), which provides that a term agreed, or extended so as, to last longer than ninety-nine years is reduced to ninety-nine years. The rationale for the second paragraph of Civil Code Article 2679 (Rev. 2004) rests on a broader ground (which also explains why this provision has a broader scope than the jurisprudence it overrules) so as to encompass leases whose duration depends solely on the will of the lessor. The rationale is grounded on the inherent similarity of such leases to leases whose term has not been agreed to by the parties. Indeed, it can be said that, when the term's duration depends solely on the will of one party, there is in fact no agreement as to duration. Thus, it is appropriate to treat such a lease in the same fashion as a lease in which the parties were silent as to the duration of the term, and then to relegate it to Civil Code Article 2680 (Rev. 2004) for supplying the applicable term. This is a more equitable solution than that reached by those Louisiana cases (supra) that have treated as invalid agreements in which the terms' duration depended entirely on the will of the lessee. The same is true for leases whose duration depends solely on the will of the lessor. Since all the terms supplied by Civil Code Article 2680 (Rev. 2004) are indeterminate terms, and thus can be terminated by either party, the relegation to Civil Code Article 2680 (Rev. 2004) restores the necessary equilibrium between the parties without completely negating the volition of the party on whose will the duration was to depend.

(e) Leases in which the parties have fixed a maximum term but provided that one or the other party may terminate the lease at an earlier point do not fall within the scope of the second paragraph of Civil Code Article 2679 (Rev. 2004) and thus are not relegated by this provision to Civil Code Article 2680 (Rev. 2004). Such leases are perfectly valid. If the party that has the contractual right to terminate the lease before the end of the maximum term does not exercise this right, then the lease remains one with a fixed term and terminates upon the expiration of that term without the need of notice. See Article 2720 (Rev. 2004). If that party wants to exercise this right before the end of the term, then the lease becomes one with an indeterminate term and that party must give advance notice to the other party. See Article 2727 (Rev. 2004).

Art. 2680. Duration supplied by law; legal term

If the parties have not agreed on the duration of the term, the duration is established in accordance with the following rules:

(1) An agricultural lease shall be from year to year.

(2) Any other lease of an immovable, or a lease of a movable to be used as a residence, shall be from month to month.

(3) A lease of other movables shall be from day to day, unless the rent was fixed by longer or shorter periods, in which case the term shall be one such period, not to exceed one month.

Acts 2004, No. 821, § 1, eff. Jan. 1, 2005.

REVISION COMMENTS—2004

(a) This Article clarifies and supplements the provisions of Articles 2685 and 2687 of the Civil Code of 1870. It changes the law in two respects as explained in Comments (d) and (e).

(b) This Article applies when the parties have not agreed on the duration of the term. An agreement may be express or implied. See, e.g., C.C. Art. 2054 (Rev. 1984) which provides that "[w]hen the parties made no provision for a particular situation, it must be assumed that they intended to bind themselves not only to the express provisions of the contract, but also to whatever the law, equity, or usage regards as implied in a contract of that kind. . . ."

(c) By virtue of the express reference contained in the second paragraph of Civil Code Article 2679 (Rev. 2004), Civil Code Article 2680 (Rev. 2004) also applies to leases in which the parties, without fixing a maximum term, have agreed that the duration of the lease will depend solely on the will of either the lessor or the lessee.

(d) Once this Article becomes applicable, it provides the applicable term in a definite as opposed to a presumptive manner. This represents a change from the letter of Article 2687 of the Civil Code of 1870, which speaks of a presumptive term of one year in the case of an agricultural lease, and may represent a change from Article 2685 of the same code, which uses similar language ("considered") in the case of a residential lease. However, this change is more apparent than real. Civil Code Article 2680 (Rev. 2004) retains much of the flexibility of the source provisions, but this flexibility is available in determining whether the article is applicable, rather than in making it possible to displace it after it is found applicable. Moreover, several Louisiana cases have treated the presumptions of the source provisions as nearly irrebuttable. See, e.g., Jackson & Anderson v. Beling, 22 La.Ann. 377 (1870).

(e) Subparagraph (1) of Civil Code Article 2680 (Rev. 2004) deals with agricultural leases as defined in Civil Code Article 2671 (Rev. 2004) and supplies an indeterminate term from year to year. The one-year term is drawn from Article 2687 of the Civil Code of 1870, which, however, provides for a fixed term of one year rather than an indeterminate term from year to year. It is believed that this change is consistent with agricultural usage.

(f) Subparagraph (2) of Civil Code Article 2680 (Rev. 2004) reproduces the substance of Article 2685 of the Civil Code of 1870. It differs from the source provision in that it is not limited to a "house or other edifice" but encompasses any immovable (other than one that is the object of an agricultural lease). It also encompasses certain movables, such as trailers, that are rented for use as residences.

(g) Subparagraph (3) of Civil Code Article 2680 (Rev. 2004) is new. It fills a gap in the law which currently does not supply a term for leases of movables. The general term supplied by this provision is from day to day. However, if the rent is fixed by the parties by shorter periods, such as by the hour, the term shall be by the hour. Similarly, if the rent is fixed by longer periods not exceeding a month, such as by the week, then the term shall be from week to week.

SECTION 4—FORM

Art. 2681.   Form

A lease may be made orally or in writing. A lease of an immovable is not effective against third persons until filed for recordation in the manner prescribed by legislation.

Acts 2004, No. 821, § 1, eff. Jan. 1, 2005.

REVISION COMMENTS—2004

(a) The first sentence of this Article restates the rule of Article 2683 of the Civil Code of 1870. The second sentence restates the rule currently found in the second paragraph of Civil Code Article 1839 (Rev. 1984) and R.S. 9:2721. Neither sentence changes the law.

(b) The recordation of leases is regulated by R.S. 9:2721, 2721.1, and 2722.

CHAPTER 3—THE OBLIGATIONS OF THE LESSOR AND THE LESSEE

SECTION 1—PRINCIPAL OBLIGATIONS

Art. 2682.   The lessor's principal obligations

The lessor is bound:

(1) To deliver the thing to the lessee;

(2) To maintain the thing in a condition suitable for the purpose of which it was leased; and

(3) To protect the lessee's peaceful possession for the duration of the lease.

Acts 2004, No. 821, § 1, eff. Jan. 1, 2005.

REVISION COMMENTS—2004

(a) This Article restates the substance of Article 2692 of the Civil Code of 1870 with some cosmetic changes in language. These changes are not intended to change the law. The words "without any clause to that effect" contained in the source provision have been omitted as self-evident.

(b) This Article serves to enunciate the three basic obligations of the lessor. These obligations, as well as the consequences of their breach, are defined further hereafter.

Art. 2683.   The lessee's principal obligations

The lessee is bound:

(1) To pay the rent in accordance with the agreed terms;

(2) To use the thing as a prudent administrator and in accordance with the purpose for which it was leased; and

(3) To return the thing at the end of the lease in a condition that is the same as it was when the thing was delivered to him, except for normal wear and tear or as otherwise provided hereafter.

Acts 2004, No. 821, § 1, eff. Jan. 1, 2005.

This Article restates the three principal obligations of the lessee as defined in Article 2710 of the Civil Code of 1870 and pertinent Louisiana jurisprudence. This jurisprudence has long recognized that the obligation to return the thing at the end of the lease as that obligation is defined in Articles 2719 and 2720 of the Civil Code of 1870 is also one of the lessee's principal obligations. These obligations are defined further or modified in the more specific articles of this Title.

SECTION 2—DELIVERY

Art. 2684. Obligations to deliver the thing at the agreed time and in good condition

The lessor is bound to deliver the thing at the agreed time and in good condition suitable for the purpose for which it was leased.

Acts 2004, No. 821, § 1, eff. Jan. 1, 2005.

REVISION COMMENTS—2004

(a) This Article restates the substance of the first sentence of Article 2693 of the Civil Code of 1870. It does not change the law. The jurisprudence interpreting the source provision continues to be relevant.

(b) The lessor's obligation to deliver the thing consists of: delivering the agreed thing; delivering the thing at the agreed time; and delivering the thing in good condition. Although not expressly mentioned in the source provision, delivery "at the agreed time" is a self-evident element of the obligation to deliver. What is "good condition" is determined by reference to the purpose for which the thing was leased as that purpose is defined in, or derived from, the contract.

(c) In keeping with the intent of the source provision as indicated by the phrase "free from any repairs" (C.C. Art. 2693 (1870)), the lessor's obligation to deliver the thing in good condition includes the obligation to make, before delivery, the repairs that are necessary in order for the thing to serve the purpose for which it was leased. This obligation is distinct from the lessor's obligation to make the repairs that become necessary during the lease. The latter obligation is addressed in Civil Code Article 2691 (Rev. 2004).

Art. 2685. Discrepancy between agreed and delivered quantity

If the leased thing is an immovable and its extent differs from that which was agreed upon, the rights of the parties with regard to such discrepancy are governed by the provisions of the Title "Sale".

Acts 2004, No. 821, § 1, eff. Jan. 1, 2005.

REVISION COMMENTS—2004

(a) This Article is derived from Article 2701 of the Civil Code of 1870. However, unlike the source provision which provides only for situations in which the extent of the delivered immovable is smaller than that which was agreed upon by the parties, Civil Code Article 2685 (Rev. 2004) addresses both that situation and the situation in which the extent of the delivered immovable is greater than that which was agreed upon. In both such situations, the rights of the parties will be governed by the provisions of the Title "Sale" (see, e.g., C.C. Arts. 2491–97 (Rev. 1993)).

(b) Like the source provision, this Article does not apply to leases of movables. When the extent or quantity of the delivered movable or movables differs from that which was agreed upon, then, pursuant to Civil Code Article 2669 (Rev. 2004), the rights of the parties with regard to such a discrepancy will be governed by the provisions of the Titles of "Obligations in General" and "Conventional Obligations or Contracts."

SECTION 3—USE OF THE THING BY THE LESSEE

Art. 2686. Misuse of the thing

If the lessee uses the thing for a purpose other than that for which it was leased or in a manner that may cause damage to the thing, the lessor may obtain injunctive relief, dissolution of the lease, and any damages he may have sustained.

Acts 2004, No. 821, § 1, eff. Jan. 1, 2005.

REVISION COMMENTS—2004

(a) This Article is derived in part from Article 2711 of the Civil Code of 1870 properly translated. The French text of the corresponding article of the 1825 Code (C.C. Art. 2681 (1825)) provided that the lessor could obtain dissolution of the lease "[if] the lessee makes another use of the thing than that for which it was intended, *or* a use which may cause damage to [*the lessor*]." The italicized phrase was erroneously translated into English as "and if any loss is thereby sustained by [the lessor]." This error, which unduly narrowed the lessor's right of dissolution, was either not detected or knowingly ignored by Louisiana jurisprudence. To the extent that it restores the original meaning conveyed by the French text, Civil Code Article 2686 (Rev. 2004) suppresses that jurisprudence.

(b) According to this Article, the lessor has in principle the right to obtain relief in two potentially different situations: (1) if the lessee uses the thing for a purpose other than that for which it was leased (and regardless of whether such use causes damage to the thing or the lessor); or (2) if the lessee uses the thing in a manner that may cause damage to the thing. However, the actual granting of relief, as well as the choice of the appropriate relief, is left to the discretion of the court upon proper weighing of all the circumstances of the particular case. Depending on the circumstances, the court may decide to grant none, one, any two, or all three of the remedies described in Civil Code Article 2686 (Rev. 2004).

(c) According to this Article, and in keeping with the principles enunciated in Civil Code Article 1987 (Rev. 1984) and Code of Civil Procedure Article 3601, the lessor need not show irreparable harm in order to obtain an injunction. The jurisprudence has adopted this principle even under the regime of Civil Code Article 2711 (1870), which did not expressly authorize injunctive relief. That jurisprudence continues to be relevant.

Art. 2687. Damage caused by fault

The lessee is liable for damage to the thing caused by his fault or that of a person who, with his consent, is on the premises or uses the thing.

Acts 2004, No. 821, § 1, eff. Jan. 1, 2005.

REVISION COMMENTS—2004

(a) This Article combines the substance of Articles 2721–2723 of the Civil Code of 1870, after omitting unnecessary verbiage. The omission of the word "only" found in Civil Code Article 2721 (1870) has only symbolic significance.

(b) However, this Article differs from the source provisions in that it defines more broadly the persons for whose fault the lessee is responsible for damage to the thing. According to the source provisions, the lessee was responsible for damage caused: by "his own fault" (C.C. Arts. 2721 and 2723 (1870)); by the fault of members of "his family" (C.C. Arts. 2722 and 2723 (1870)) or "household" (French text of C.C. Arts. 2692 and 2693 (1825)); and by the fault of his sublessees (C.C. Art. 2722 (1870)). According to Civil Code Article 2687 (Rev. 2004), the lessee is responsible for the fault of all of the above persons, and in addition for the fault of all other persons "who, with his consent, [are] on the premises or [use] the thing," such as his invitees. The lessee is not responsible for damage caused by persons who use the thing without his consent, such as a passerby or a trespasser.

Art. 2688. Obligation to inform lessor

The lessee is bound to notify the lessor without delay when the thing has been damaged or requires repair, or when his possession has been disturbed by a third person. The lessor is entitled to damages sustained as a result of the lessee's failure to perform this obligation.

Acts 2004, No. 821, § 1, eff. Jan. 1, 2005.

REVISION COMMENTS—2004

(a) This Article is new. It is derived in part from Article 2724 of the Civil Code of 1870, which imposed on agricultural lessees a duty to prevent encroachment upon the leased estate and to notify the lessor of such encroachment. Civil Code Article 2688 (Rev. 2004) reproduces not only the obligation to notify the lessor but extends that obligation to non-agricultural leases and expands its scope so as to encompass a duty to inform the lessor of any damage to, or a need for repair of, the thing.

(b) The imposition of the latter duty is a departure from present Louisiana jurisprudence under which the lessee is required to inform the lessor of damages or disrepairs only when the lessee seeks to repair and deduct the costs from the rent. This change is made in the interest of fairness. The lessee's obligation to inform the lessor is a proper counterweight to the lessor's obligation to keep the thing in proper condition and to make the necessary repairs. See C.C. Art. 2691 (Rev. 2004).

(c) The lessee's failure to give timely notice to the lessor as provided by Civil Code Article 2688 (Rev. 2004) gives rise to a right on the part of the lessor to demand damages. Such a failure does not give rise to a right of dissolution of the lease, nor does it relieve the lessor from the obligation to make repairs, or from any other responsibility the lessor may have under other provisions of law.

Art. 2689. Payment of taxes and other charges

The lessor is bound to pay all taxes, assessments, and other charges that burden the thing, except those that arise from the use of the thing by the lessee.

Acts 2004, No. 821, § 1, eff. Jan. 1, 2005.

REVISION COMMENT—2004

This Article reproduces the substance of Article 2702 of the Civil Code of 1870. The words "unless there be a stipulation to the contrary" in the source provision have not been reproduced as unnecessary. The words "except those that arise from the use of the thing by the lessee" have been added in order to ensure that fees such as sewerage fees or water use fees which depend on the degree of use by the lessee would not be automatically borne by the lessor.

SECTION 4—ALTERATIONS, REPAIRS, AND ADDITIONS

Art. 2690. Alterations by the lessor prohibited

During the lease, the lessor may not make any alterations in the thing.

Acts 2004, No. 821, § 1, eff. Jan. 1, 2005.

REVISION COMMENT—2004

This Article restates the substance of Article 2698 of the Civil Code of 1870. It does not change the law. The jurisprudence interpreting the source provision continues to be relevant. Civil Code Article 2690 (Rev. 2004) may be displaced by a contrary agreement that allows the making of such alterations, or by a statute, such as the Americans with Disabilities Act, that requires the making of such alterations.

Art. 2691.   Lessor's obligation for repairs

During the lease, the lessor is bound to make all repairs that become necessary to maintain the thing in a condition suitable for the purpose for which it was leased, except those for which the lessee is responsible.

Acts 2004, No. 821, § 1, eff. Jan. 1, 2005.

REVISION COMMENTS—2004

(a) This Article reproduces the substance of the second sentence of Article 2693 of the Civil Code of 1870, except for the word "accidentally" which had no counterpart in the French text of the 1825 Code, Civil Code Article 2663 (1825).

(b) This Article is also intended to incorporate the substance of Civil Code Articles 2717 and 2718 (1870) which are not reproduced in this Revision as unnecessary. Since all repairs that are not expressly assigned to the lessee are borne by the lessor, it follows that the repairs mentioned in Civil Code Articles 2717 and 2718 (1870) should be borne by the lessor without any express provision to that effect. Although Civil Code Article 2692 (Rev. 2004) requires the lessee to "repair any deterioration," that article limits that requirement to deterioration caused by the lessee or his invitees and only "to the extent" such a deterioration "exceeds the normal or agreed use of the thing." Thus, Civil Code Articles 2691 and 2692 (Rev. 2004) together maintain the philosophy of the Civil Code of 1870 according to which the lessor, having bound himself to secure the lessee's enjoyment of the thing, must make all the necessary repairs, except those that are attributed to the fault of the lessee or are expressly assigned to the lessee by law or contract.

Art. 2692.   Lessee's obligation to make repairs

The lessee is bound to repair damage to the thing caused by his fault or that of persons who, with his consent, are on the premises or use the thing, and to repair any deterioration resulting from his or their use to the extent it exceeds the normal or agreed use of the thing.

Acts 2004, No. 821, § 1, eff. Jan. 1, 2005.

REVISION COMMENTS—2004

(a) The principle of this Article is derived from Articles 2715–2717 of the Civil Code of 1870. Although it uses different language than the source provisions, Civil Code Article 2692 (Rev. 2004) is nevertheless based on the same philosophy, namely that the lessee should bear responsibility for only that damage to, or repairs of, the thing that are attributable to his own fault or use or that of persons accountable to him. The Civil Code of 1870 assigns to the lessee those "necessary repairs . . . which it is incumbent on lessees to make . . ." Art. 2715 (1870) and then, perhaps in an attempt to provide legal certainty, provides a list of those repairs (C.C. Art. 2716 (1870)). However, because that list was merely illustrative (". . . and everything of that kind, according to the custom of the place." id.), the 1870 Code did not in fact produce the desired certainty. Moreover, even if that list were perfect, the fact that it was confined to leases of buildings would limit its utility in serving as a basis for this Revision which provides equally for all types of leases. This is why, rather than attempting to reproduce the casuistic listing of repairs contained in Civil Code Article 2716 (1870), Civil Code Article 2692 (Rev. 2004) extracts from that list the common denominators of the repairs enumerated in Civil Code Article 2716 (1870) and recasts them in language that is sufficiently general so as to apply all leases, including leases of movables.

(b) According to this Article, the lessee is bound to repair "[any] damage to the thing [that is] caused by his fault or that of persons who, with his consent, are on the premises or use the thing . . ." This obligation is consistent with the lessee's responsibility "for the injuries and losses sustained through his own fault." C.C. Art. 2721 (1870). See also C.C. Art. 2687 (Rev. 2004).

(c) The lessee is also bound to repair "any deterioration" resulting from his use and the use of "persons who, with his consent, are on the premises or use the thing," but only to the extent that such deterioration exceeds the "normal or agreed use of the thing." In other words, as was the case under the Civil Code of 1870 (see C.C. Arts. 2719 and 2720 (1870)), the lessee is not responsible for repairing the deterioration that is caused by normal wear and tear of the thing. See also C.C. Art. 2683 (Rev. 2004). However, in some instances the parties may have agreed, expressly or tacitly, that the lessee

638

may engage in uses that exceed, or differ from, the normal uses of a thing. In those instances, the lessee should not be responsible for deterioration resulting from uses that remain within the limits of the "agreed" use.

(d) Through the use of the phrase "unless the contrary hath been stipulated," Article 2715 of the Civil Code of 1870 allowed the lessor and the lessee to deviate from the division of responsibility for repairs prescribed by that article and its companion articles. The quoted words have not been reproduced in Civil Code Article 2692 (Rev. 2004) as being unnecessary. Since the provisions of Civil Code Article 2692 (Rev. 2004) are not "enacted for the protection of the public interest" (C.C. Art. 7 (Rev. 1987)), the parties retain the same freedom as under the old law to agree to a different division of responsibility for repairs than that provided by Civil Code Articles 2691 and 2692 (Rev. 2004).

Art. 2693. Lessor's right to make repairs

If during the lease the thing requires a repair that cannot be postponed until the end of the lease, the lessor has the right to make that repair even if this causes the lessee to suffer inconvenience or loss of use of the thing.

In such a case, the lessee may obtain a reduction or abatement of the rent, or a dissolution of the lease, depending on all of the circumstances, including each party's fault or responsibility for the repair, the length of the repair period, and the extent of the loss of use.

Acts 2004, No. 821, § 1, eff. Jan. 1, 2005.

REVISION COMMENTS—2004

(a) The first paragraph of this Article reproduces the substance of the first sentence of Article 2700 of the Civil Code of 1870. It does not change the law.

(b) The second paragraph of this Article reproduces the principle contained in the second and third sentences of Article 2700 (1870), but without the confining details found therein. Thus, the reference to "repairs . . . be[ing] of such nature as to oblige the tenant to leave the house or the room and to take another house," has been deliberately avoided because Civil Code Article 2693 (Rev. 2004) is not confined to residential leases. Similarly, the reference to "repairs . . . continu[ing] for a longer time than one month" has also been avoided because Civil Code Article 2693 (Rev. 2004) applies as much to short-term leases as to long-term leases. Rather than reproducing the confining casuistry of the source provision, the second paragraph of Civil Code Article 2693 (Rev. 2004) enunciates a flexible formula which requires the court to consider all the circumstances before deciding which, if any, of the three options provided in that paragraph would be the most appropriate in the particular case.

Art. 2694. Lessee's right to make repairs

If the lessor fails to perform his obligation to make necessary repairs within a reasonable time after demand by the lessee, the lessee may cause them to be made. The lessee may demand immediate reimbursement of the amount expended for the repair or apply that amount to the payment of rent, but only to the extent that the repair was necessary and the expended amount was reasonable.

Acts 2004, No. 821, § 1, eff. Jan. 1, 2005.

REVISION COMMENT—2004

This Article restates the principles of Article 2694 of the Civil Code of 1870 with minor modifications and clarifications, such as the references to "reasonable time," the possibility of "immediate reimbursement," and the substitution of "necessary" for "indispensable" repairs.

Art. 2695. Attachments, additions, or other improvements to leased thing

In the absence of contrary agreement, upon termination of the lease, the rights and obligations of the parties with regard to attachments, additions, or other improvements made to the leased thing by the lessee are as follows:

(1) The lessee may remove all improvements that he made to the leased thing, provided that he restore the thing to its former condition.

(2) If the lessee does not remove the improvements, the lessor may:

(a) Appropriate ownership of the improvements by reimbursing the lessee for their costs or for the enhanced value of the leased thing whichever is less; or

(b) Demand that the lessee remove the improvements within a reasonable time and restore the leased thing to its former condition. If the lessee fails to do so, the lessor may remove the improvements and restore the leased thing to its former condition at the expense of the lessee or appropriate ownership of the improvements without any obligation of reimbursement to the lessee. Appropriation of the improvement by the lessor may only be accomplished by providing additional notice by certified mail to the lessee after expiration of the time given the lessee to remove the improvements.

(c) Until such time as the lessor appropriates the improvement, the improvements shall remain the property of the lessee and the lessee shall be solely responsible for any harm caused by the improvements.

Acts 2004, No. 821, § 1, eff. Jan. 1, 2005.

REVISION COMMENTS—2004

(a) This Article applies to "attachments, additions, or other improvements" made to the leased thing by the lessee during the lease. Attachments and additions are examples of "improvements." "Other improvements" may include items mentioned in Civil Code Articles 463, 465, 466 (Rev. 1978), 491 (Rev. 1979), 493 (Rev. 1984), 495, 496, and 510 (Rev. 1979), such as buildings, other constructions, plantings, or other "works." Consistently with other provisions of the Civil Code as well as prevailing judicial usage, Civil Code Article 2695 (Rev. 2004) uses the term "improvement" in its technical meaning which differs from popular usage to the extent it encompasses items that may not actually "improve" the thing or enhance its value. See C.C. Arts. 2726 (Amended 1984), 493 (Rev. 1984), 495, 497 (Rev. 1979), 558, 601, 602 (Rev. 1976), and 804 (Rev. 1990).

(b) Civil Code Article 2695 (Rev. 2004) provides a suppletive rule of law that applies only in the absence of a contrary agreement regarding the fate of the improvements at the end of the lease. The agreement may be made at any time, such as at the making of the lease contract, or at any time before or after the making of the improvement. The agreement may be express or implied. See, e.g., C.C. Art. 2054 (Rev. 1984) which provides that "[w]hen the parties made no provision for a particular situation, it must be assumed that they intended to bind themselves not only to the express provisions of the contract, but also to whatever the law, equity, or usage regards as implied in a contract of that kind . . ."

(c) Civil Code Article 2695 (Rev. 2004) establishes a self-contained rule that departs from the rule of Article 2726 of the Civil Code of 1870. The latter article regulated this issue through a cross-reference to the Civil Code's provisions on accession to immovables, in particular Articles 493, 493.1, 493.2 (Rev. 1984), and 495 (Rev. 1979). Besides failing to provide for cases in which the leased thing is a movable, this cross-reference imported to the law of leases the numerous deficiencies and inequities of the law of accession. These deficiencies are noted in Symeonides, Developments in the Law, 1982–83: Property, 44 La.L.Rev. 505, 519–27 (1983); See Symeonides, Developments in the Law, 1983–84: Property, 45 La.L.Rev. 541, 541–49 (1984); Symeonides, Developments in the Law, 1985–86: Property, 47 La.L.Rev. 429, 444–52 (1986). Civil Code Article 2695 (Rev. 2004) attempts to cure these deficiencies by providing a special self-contained rule applicable directly to leases of immovables as well as of movables. Civil Code Article 2695 (Rev. 2004) applies only if the relationship between the two parties qualifies as a lease. For other relationships, such as those involving precarious possessors who are not lessees, Civil Code Articles 493 et seq. remain applicable.

(d) The phrasing and arrangement of Civil Code Article 2695 (Rev. 2004) make clear that the first option in determining the fate of the improvements upon termination of the lease belongs to the lessee. In the absence of a contrary agreement: (a) the lessee has the right to remove the improvements, even if he had made them without the lessor's consent; and (b) the lessor may not prevent their removal, even if they were made with his consent. Depending on the circumstances, the making of improvements without the lessor's consent may amount to a breach of the lessee's obligations under Civil Code Articles 2683(2), 2686, or 2687 (Rev. 2004) and if so the lessor has the remedies available through those articles. But at the termination of the lease, restoration of the thing to its former condition is also one of the lessee's obligations under Civil Code Article 2683(3) (Rev.

2004) and removal of the improvements is a means of discharging that obligation. Conversely, in the absence of a contrary agreement, the fact that the lessor consented to the making of the improvements does not deprive the lessee of the right to remove them, or the lessor of the right to force their removal at the end of the lease. See Comment (f).

(e) If the lessee removes the improvements but does not restore the thing to its former condition, the lessee is liable for damages under Civil Code Article 2687 (Rev. 2004).

(f) If the lessee does not exercise his right to remove the improvements, then, again in the absence of contrary agreement, the lessor gets to exercise the two main options provided in subparagraph (2) of Civil Code Article 2695 (Rev. 2004), namely: (a) appropriate ownership of the improvements by reimbursing the lessee for their costs or for the enhanced value of the leased thing, whichever is less; or (b) demand that the lessee remove the improvements within a reasonable time and restore the thing to its former condition. If the lessee fails to do so, the lessor gets two further options: (i) have the improvements removed and the thing restored to its former condition at the expense of the lessee; or (ii) appropriate ownership of the improvements by providing notice to the lessee. In the latter case, the lessor owes no reimbursement to the lessee.

SECTION 5—LESSOR'S WARRANTIES

SUBSECTION 1—WARRANTY AGAINST VICES OR DEFECTS

Art. 2696. Warranty against vices or defects

The lessor warrants the lessee that the thing is suitable for the purpose for which it was leased and that it is free of vices or defects that prevent its use for that purpose.

This warranty also extends to vices or defects that arise after the delivery of the thing and are not attributable to the fault of the lessee.

Acts 2004, No. 821, § 1, eff. Jan. 1, 2005.

REVISION COMMENT—2004

This Article restates in part the principles of Articles 2692 and 2695 of the Civil Code of 1870.

Art. 2697. Warranty for unknown vices or defects

The warranty provided in the preceding Article also encompasses vices or defects that are not known to the lessor.

However, if the lessee knows of such vices or defects and fails to notify the lessor, the lessee's recovery for breach of warranty may be reduced accordingly.

Acts 2004, No. 821, § 1, eff. Jan. 1, 2005.

REVISION COMMENT—2004

The first paragraph of this Article restates in part the principle of Article 2695 of the Civil Code of 1870 with regard to vices or defects that are not known to the lessor. The second paragraph of this Article departs from the source provision by making an exception for vices or defects that were known to the lessee but not to the lessor.

Art. 2698. Persons protected by warranty

In a residential lease, the warranty provided in the preceding Articles applies to all persons who reside in the premises in accordance with the lease.

Acts 2004, No. 821, § 1, eff. Jan. 1, 2005.

REVISION COMMENT—2004

This Article addresses a problem encountered by Louisiana judicial decisions which had difficulty in deciding whether the lessor's warranty extends to members of the lessee's family or household and, if so, on what legal basis. See Vernon Palmer, Leases: The Law in Louisiana, § 3–17 (1982). This Article resolves this problem by expressly extending the warranty to the above persons as well as other persons who reside in the premises in accordance with the lease.

Art. 2699.   Waiver of warranty for vices or defects

The warranty provided in the preceding Articles may be waived, but only by clear and unambiguous language that is brought to the attention of the lessee.

Nevertheless, a waiver of warranty is ineffective:

(1) To the extent it pertains to vices or defects of which the lessee did not know and the lessor knew or should have known;

(2) To the extent it is contrary to the provisions of Article 2004; or

(3) In a residential or consumer lease, to the extent it purports to waive the warranty for vices or defects that seriously affect health or safety.

Acts 2004, No. 821, § 1, eff. Jan. 1, 2005.

REVISION COMMENTS—2004

(a) This Article is new. It is derived from Louisiana jurisprudence, but also departs from it in some respects as explained below. This Article applies to the warranty for vices or defects as defined in Civil Code Articles 2696–2698 (Rev. 2004). It does not apply to the warranty of peaceful possession, which is defined in Civil Code Articles 2700–2702 (Rev. 2004) and which may not be waived.

(b) Civil Code Article 2699 (Rev. 2004) introduces the principle that, as a general proposition, the warranty for vices or defects is waivable. However, to be effective, a waiver: (a) must meet the conditions specified in the first paragraph of the Article; and (b) must not fall within any one of the three exceptions or prohibitions specified in the second paragraph.

(c) The first paragraph of Civil Code Article 2699 (Rev. 2004) provides that, to be effective, a waiver must be written in "clear and unambiguous language" and that language must be "brought to the attention of the lessee." The quoted phrases parallel language found in Civil Code Article 2548 (Rev. 1993) with regard to sales, and codifies pertinent Louisiana jurisprudence in lease cases. In summarizing the jurisprudence, Judge King stated: "It is well established that for the waiver of implied warranty in a contract of sale or lease to be effective that it must be (1) written in clear and unambiguous terms, (2) the waiver must be contained in the written contract, and (3) the waiver either must be brought to the attention of the buyer or lessee or explained to him. Cf. Louisiana National Leasing Corporation v. ADF Service, Inc., et al, supra, (Dissenting Opinion of Chief Justice Dixon); Theriot v. Commercial Union Ins. Co., 478 So.2d 741 (La.App. 3 Cir.1985) and cases cited therein; Thibodeaux v. Meaux's Auto Sales, Inc., 364 So.2d 1370 (La.App. 3 Cir.1978); Hendricks v. Horseless Carriage, Inc., 332 So.2d 892 (La.App. 2 Cir.1976); Prince v. Paretti Pontiac Co., 281 So.2d 112 (La.1973). Louisiana cases are generally in accord and constitute a recognition that where limitations of warranty are not the result of actual bargaining that they should not be given literal effect. Wolfe v. Henderson Ford, Inc., 277 So.2d 215 (La.App. 3 Cir.1973); The Work of the Louisiana Appellate Courts for the 1968–1969 Term-Particular Contracts, 30 La.L.Rev. 171, 214. An exclusion or waiver of warranty by which parties take themselves out of the coverage of specific or general law and make a law unto themselves must be strictly construed and our courts have been reluctant to give effect to stipulated waivers of the warranty implied by law. Wolfe v. Henderson Ford, Inc., supra; Harris v. Automatic Enterprises of Louisiana, Inc., 145 So.2d 335 (La.App. 4 Cir.1962)." J.L. Andrus v. Cajun Insulation Co., Inc., 524 So.2d 1239, at 1245–46 (La.App. 3rd Cir. 1988) (King, J., concurring).

(d) The second paragraph of Civil Code Article 2699 (Rev. 2004) introduces three independent exceptions to the principle of waivability enunciated in the first paragraph of the Article. When applicable, any one of these exceptions renders a waiver ineffective, even a waiver that meets the requirements of the first paragraph of Civil Code Article 2699 (Rev. 2004), namely a waiver written in "clear and unambiguous language that is brought to the attention of the lessee." The first two exceptions (clauses (1) and (2)) apply to all leases, including residential or consumer leases. The third exception (clause (3)) applies to residential leases or consumer leases only. These leases are defined in Civil Code Article 2671 (Rev. 2004).

(e) The first exception (stated in clause (1)) pertains to vices or defects which were not known to the lessee but of which the lessor "knew or should have known." The knowledge standard is subjective with regard to the lessee (actual knowledge) and objective with regard to the lessor ("knew or should have known."). A waiver is ineffective if: (a) the lessee did not know of the vice or defect; and (b) the lessor either knew or should have known of it. Conversely, a waiver is effective: (a) if, regardless of the lessor's knowledge, the lessee knew of the vice or defect; or (b) if, regardless of the lessee's knowledge, the lessor did not know nor should he have known of the vice or defect.

(f) The second exception (stated in clause (2)) applies to cases in which the waiver exceeds the limits of Civil Code Article 2004 (Rev. 1984). Civil Code Article 2004 (Rev. 1984) provides that "[a]ny clause is null that, in advance, excludes or limits the liability of one party for intentional or gross fault that causes damage to the other party . . . [or] excludes or limits the liability of one party for causing physical injury to the other party." A waiver that exceeds the limits of Civil Code Article 2004 (Rev. 1984) is ineffective, even if the waiver is otherwise effective under the other provisions of Civil Code Article 2699 (Rev. 2004).

(g) The third exception (stated in clause (3)) applies to residential or consumer leases only. See Civil Code Article 2671 (Rev. 2004). This exception reflects the philosophy of Louisiana jurisprudence which, "in recognition of the inequality of bargaining power between landlords and tenants," has been "very reluctant to find that the tenant has waived his legal rights," so much so that some authors speak of "[t]he aversion of Louisiana courts to waiver of this warranty." G. Armstrong & J. LaMaster, "The Implied Warranty of Habitability: Louisiana Institution, Common Law Innovation," 46 La.L.Rev. 195, 214, 215 (1985). Modern civil law codifications, as well as the majority of the states of the United States, now directly prohibit waivers of this warranty in residential and consumer leases. See, e.g., Quebec Civ. Code Arts. 1900, 1901, and 1910; N.Y. Real Prop.Law Sec. 235–b; Vt.St. 9:4457; Me.St. 10:9097(7); Wi.St. 101.953(3); Ca.Civ.Code Secs. 1797.4 and 1812.646. Rather than completely prohibiting waivers of this warranty, clause (3) adopts the middle position of limiting the prohibition to situations in which the waiver encompasses vices or defects that seriously affect health or safety. To the extent that a waiver purports to encompass those vices or defect, the waiver is ineffective even if it is otherwise effective under the other provisions of Civil Code Article 2699 (Rev. 2004). Conversely, a waiver that does not fall within the prohibition of clause (3) is nevertheless ineffective if it fails to meet the other requirements for an effective waiver specified in the other provisions of Civil Code Article 2699 (Rev. 2004).

(h) Civil Code Article 2699 (Rev. 2004) deals with the contractual obligations between the parties rather than with the delictual or quasi-delictual obligations that one party may incur vis a vis the other party, or vis a vis third parties. Consequently, Civil Code Article 2699 (Rev. 2004) does not supersede the provisions of R.S. 9:3221 which provides for delictual or quasi-delictual obligations incurred as a result of injury occurring in the leased premises. Section 3 of this Act amends and reenacts R.S. 9:3221 to provide that the amendment and reenactment of Civil Code Article 2699 does not change the law of R.S. 9:3221. Similarly, but also for additional reasons, Civil Code Article 2699 (Rev. 2004) does not supersede the provisions of R.S. 9:2795, which limits the delictual liability of the owner of property used for recreational purposes.

SUBSECTION 2—WARRANTY OF PEACEFUL POSSESSION

Art. 2700. Warranty of peaceful possession

The lessor warrants the lessee's peaceful possession of the leased thing against any disturbance caused by a person who asserts ownership, or right to possession of, or any other right in the thing.

In a residential lease, this warranty encompasses a disturbance caused by a person who, with the lessor's consent, has access to the thing or occupies adjacent property belonging to the lessor.

Acts 2004, No. 821, § 1, eff. Jan. 1, 2005.

REVISION COMMENTS—2004

(a) The first paragraph of this Article restates the principles found in Articles 2692, 2696, and 2704 of the Civil Code of 1870. It reiterates one of the lessor's principal obligations (see C.C. Art. 2682 (Rev. 2004)) to ensure and protect the lessee's peaceful possession for the duration of the lease. The lessor is bound to not only refrain from interfering with the lessee's peaceful possession but also to defend and protect that possession against disturbances caused by third persons who claim a right in the leased thing.

(b) When the lessor interferes with the lessee's peaceful possession through the lessor's own acts or those of persons acting on the lessor's behalf, the lessor is in direct breach of this warranty obligation. The consequences of this breach are determined under the provisions of the Titles of "Obligations in General" and "Conventional Obligations or Contracts" which are made applicable by Civil Code Articles 2669 and 2719 (Rev. 2004). Depending on the circumstances, the lessee's remedies may consist of damages, injunctive relief, or dissolution of the lease. See Lacour v. Myer, 98 So.2d 308 (La.App. 1st Cir. 1957); Butler v. Jones, 21 So.2d 181 (La.App. Orl. 1945); Eddy v. Monaghan, 60 So.2d 717 (La.App. Orl. 1952); Fontenot v. Benoit, 128 So.2d 815 (La.App. 3 Cir. 1961); Lansalot v. Mihaljevich, 125 So. 183 (La.App. Orl. 1929).

(c) The lessor's warranty obligation extends to disturbances caused by third persons who do not act on the lessor's behalf but who assert ownership, or right to possession of, or any other right in, the leased thing. In such a case, the lessor is "bound to take all steps necessary to protect the lessee's possession" (C.C. Art. 2701 (Rev. 2004)). If the lessor fails to do so, the lessor breaches this warranty obligation and is answerable to the lessee accordingly. See Comment (c) under C.C. Art. 2701 (Rev. 2004).

(d) When the person who disturbs the lessee's possession does not claim a right in the thing, as in the case of a passerby, a trespasser, or a squatter, the lessor is not bound to protect the lessee's possession. See C.C. Art. 2702 (Rev. 2004). The second paragraph of Civil Code Article 2700 (Rev. 2004) introduces an exception to this principle in the case of a residential lease. The sentence provides that if the person who causes the disturbance had access to the leased thing with the lessor's consent or if that person, again with the lessor's consent, occupies adjacent property belonging to the lessor, then the lessor is bound to protect the lessee's possession even if the disturber does not claim a right in the thing. This exception is derived from Louisiana jurisprudence which has held the lessor responsible for disturbances committed by persons over whom the lessor had control, such as occupants of adjacent apartments owned by the lessor. See, e.g., Keenan v. Flanigan, 157 La. 749, 103 So. 30 (1925); Gayle v. Auto-Lec Stores, 174 La. 1044, 142 So. 258 (1932). The second paragraph of Civil Code Article 2700 (Rev. 2004) speaks only of residential leases. It is not intended to authorize an a contrario argument with regard to other leases in appropriate cases.

(e) As used in Civil Code Articles 2700, 2701, and 2702 (Rev. 2004), the term "disturbance" of possession is intended to have the same meaning as in Article 3659 of the Code of Civil Procedure, even though the latter article is applicable to immovables only. Code of Civil Procedure Article 3659 distinguishes between a "disturbance in fact" and a "disturbance in law." A "disturbance in fact" maybe an "eviction" or any other physical act which, though falling short of eviction, "prevents the possessor . . . from enjoying his possession quietly, or which throws any obstacle in the way of that enjoyment." Id. A "disturbance in law" is "the execution, recordation, registry, or continuing existence of record of any instrument which asserts or implies a right of ownership or to the possession of . . . property or of a real right therein, or any claim or pretension of ownership or right to the possession thereof . . ." Id. Both of these types of disturbances fall within the scope of the lessor's warranty of peaceful possession under Civil Code Article 2700 (Rev. 2004).

Art. 2701.   Call in warranty

The lessor is bound to take all steps necessary to protect the lessee's possession against any disturbance covered by the preceding Article, as soon as the lessor is informed of such a disturbance. If the lessor fails to do so, the lessee may, without prejudice to his rights against the lessor, file any appropriate action against the person who caused the disturbance.

If a third party brings against the lessee an action asserting a right in the thing or contesting the lessee's right to possess it, the lessee may join the lessor as a party to the action and shall be dismissed from the action, if the lessee so demands.

Acts 2004, No. 821, § 1, eff. Jan. 1, 2005.

(a) This Article is derived from Articles 2692, 2696, and 2704 of the Civil Code of 1870. The scope of this Article is co-extensive with the scope of the lessor's warranty obligation as defined in Civil Code Article 2700 (Rev. 2004). Thus, both paragraphs of Civil Code Article 2701 (Rev. 2004) apply only when the disturbance or action in question is one of those that fall within the lessor's warranty.

(b) The lessee is "bound to notify the lessor without delay ... when his possession has been disturbed by a third person," C.C. Art. 2688 (Rev. 2004) and the lessor is bound to take prompt and effective steps to defend and protect the lessee's possession. If the lessor fails to do so, the lessee may file against the person who caused the disturbance any appropriate action, including a possessory action or an action for injunction. See Civil Code Article 3440 (Rev. 1982) which provides that "the possessory action is available to a precarious possessor, such as a lessee ..., against anyone except the person for whom he possesses." For the rationale and import of the latter article, see comments under Civil Code Article 3440 (Rev. 1982).

(c) The filing of such an action by the lessee is "without prejudice to his rights against the lessor." A lessor who fails to take prompt and effective steps to protect the lessee's possession is in breach of his warranty obligation and thus is answerable to the lessee accordingly. Article 2696 of the Civil Code of 1870 provided that "[i]f the lessee be evicted, the lessor is answerable for the damage and loss which he sustained by the interruption of the lease." Although this provision has not been reproduced in this Revision, the same result obtains under the provisions of the Titles of "Obligations in General" and "Conventional Obligations or Contracts" which are made applicable by Civil Code Article 2669 (Rev. 2004). Under these provisions, the lessee may be entitled to a remedy even if the disturbance in question fell short of eviction. For the difference between a disturbance that amounts to eviction and a disturbance that falls short of eviction, see C.C.P. Art. 3659. Additionally, under Civil Code Article 2719 (Rev. 2004), the lessee "may obtain dissolution of the lease pursuant to the provisions of the Title of 'Conventional Obligations or Contracts.'"

(d) The second paragraph of Civil Code Article 2701 (Rev. 2004) reproduces in part Article 2704 of the Civil Code of 1870, which provided that "if the lessee is cited to appear before a court of justice to answer to the complaint of the person thus claiming the whole or a part of the thing leased, or claiming some servitude on the same, he shall call the lessor in warranty, and shall be dismissed from the suit if he wishes it, by naming the person under whose rights he possesses."

Art. 2702. Disturbance by third persons without claim of right

Except as otherwise provided in Article 2700, the lessor is not bound to protect the lessee's possession against a disturbance caused by a person who does not claim a right in the leased thing. In such a case, the lessee may file any appropriate action against that person.

Acts 2004, No. 821, § 1, eff. Jan. 1, 2005.

(a) The first sentence of this Article restates the principle of Article 2703 of the Civil Code of 1870. The lessor is not bound to protect the lessee's possession against a disturbance caused by a person such as a bystander, a squatter, or a trespasser who does not claim a right in the leased thing. With regard to residential leases, however, this principle, is subject to the exception provided in the second paragraph of Civil Code Article 2700 (Rev. 2004).

(b) The second sentence of this Article recasts in broader and more accurate terms the principle enunciated in the last phrase of Article 2703 of the Civil Code of 1870. The English version of that sentence in the Civil Code of 1870 left the impression that the lessee's remedy was confined to an action for damages ("the lessee has a right of action for damages sustained against the person occasioning such disturbance"). However, the French version of the corresponding article of the 1808 and 1825 codes made it clear that an action for damages was only one of the lessee's remedies ("sauf au preneur a les poursuivre en son nom, et a demander, s'il y echet, des dommages—interets de ces voies de fait.") Consistently with this principle, Louisiana courts have not hesitated to grant injunctive relief to a lessee, even though at that time lessees and other precarious possessors were not allowed to bring a possessory action in their own name. See Indian Bayou Hunting Club, Inc. v. Taylor, 261 So.2d 669 (La.App. 3 Cir. 1972) (relying on C.C.P. Art. 3663(2)); Caney Hunting Club, Inc.

v. Tolbert, 294 So.2d 894 (La.App. 2 Cir. 1974) (relying on C.C.P. Art. 3601). With the enactment of Civil Code Article 3440 (Rev. 1982), which allows a precarious possessor to file in his own name a possessory action "against anyone except the person for whom he possesses," there should be no doubt that the lessee may file in his own name any appropriate action against the disturber. The second sentence of Civil Code Article 2702 (Rev. 2004) reaffirms this principle.

SECTION 6—PAYMENT OF RENT

Art. 2703.   When and where rent is due

In the absence of a contrary agreement, usage, or custom:

(1) The rent is due at the beginning of the term. If the rent is payable by intervals shorter than the term, the rent is due at the beginning of each interval.

(2) The rent is payable at the address provided by the lessor and in the absence thereof at the address of the lessee.

Acts 2004, No. 821, § 1, eff. Jan. 1, 2005.

REVISION COMMENT—2004

This Article is derived in part from Louisiana jurisprudence and in part from foreign civil codes. It is believed that this Article conforms with current usage in Louisiana.

Art. 2704.   Nonpayment of rent

If the lessee fails to pay the rent when due, the lessor may, in accordance with the provisions of the Title "Conventional Obligations or Contracts", dissolve the lease and may regain possession in the manner provided by law.

Acts 2004, No. 821, § 1, eff. Jan. 1, 2005.

REVISION COMMENT—2004

This Article is based on Paragraph A of Article 2712 of the Louisiana Civil Code of 1870. (Paragraph B of that article will be transferred to the Revised Statutes; See R.S. 9:3259.2 as enacted by this Act). This Article provides that the lessee's failure to pay the rent when due entitles the lessor to cause a dissolution of the lease as provided in the Title on "Conventional Obligations or Contracts" (see, e.g., C.C. Arts. 2013–2024 (Rev. 1984)) and to regain possession of the thing in the manner provided by law (see, e.g., C.C.P. Arts. 4701–4705 and 4731–4735).

Art. 2705.   Abatement of rent for unforeseen loss of crops

In the absence of a contrary agreement, the agricultural lessee may not claim an abatement of the rent for the loss of his unharvested crops unless the loss was due to an unforeseeable and extraordinary event that destroyed at least one-half of the value of the crops. Any compensation that the lessee has received or may receive in connection with the loss, such as insurance proceeds or government subsidies, shall be taken into account in determining the amount of abatement.

Acts 2004, No. 821, § 1, eff. Jan. 1, 2005.

REVISION COMMENT—2004

The first sentence of this Article reproduces the substance of Articles 2743 and 2744 of the Louisiana Civil Code of 1870. The second sentence is new. As was the case under the source provisions, the lessee's right to claim abatement of the rent for accidental loss of his crop is an extremely limited right which exists only with regard to unharvested, not harvested, crops.

Art. 2706.   Loss of crop rent

When the rent consists of a portion of the crops, then any loss of the crops that is not caused by the fault of the lessor or the lessee shall be borne by both parties in accordance with their respective shares.

Acts 2004, No. 821, § 1, eff. Jan. 1, 2005.

REVISION COMMENT—2004

This Article is drawn from the general principles of co-ownership and from R.S. 9:3204 (replaced by Civil Code Article 2677 (Rev. 2004)), which provides that "[i]n a lease of land for part of the crop, that part which the lessor is to receive is considered at all times the property of the lessor." Since in leases of the type contemplated by Civil Code Article 2706 (Rev. 2004), the parties co-own the crop, they should bear proportionally the risk of accidental loss of the co-owned, unharvested or harvested, crop.

SECTION 7—LESSOR'S SECURITY RIGHTS

Art. 2707. Lessor's privilege

To secure the payment of rent and other obligations arising from the lease of an immovable, the lessor has a privilege on the lessee's movables that are found in or upon the leased property.

In an agricultural lease, the lessor's privilege also encompasses the fruits produced by the land.

Acts 2004, No. 821, § 1, eff. Jan. 1, 2005.

REVISION COMMENTS—2004

(a) This Article continues the privilege granted by Civil Code Article 2705 (1870), but slightly modifies its expression and consequences. Former Civil Code Article 2705 (1870) granted to the lessor a "right of pledge" over the movables of the lessee that were found on the property leased. This impliedly gave the lessor the privilege of a pledgee (C.C. Art. 3157). Civil Code Article 3218 (1870) then declared that the lessor's right, was of a "higher nature than a mere privilege" because the lessor could "take the effects themselves and retain them until he is paid." The Code thus rather clearly stated that the lessor not only enjoyed a privilege over the lessee's property, but that he had the same right as a pledgee who, if the debtor defaults, may simply continue to hold the pledged property until he is paid and is not required to execute upon it. Notwithstanding that the rather clear provisions of the Code equating the lessor's rights to a form of pledge, it was also obvious that his "possession" which is the essence of pledge existed only in principle and fictitiously, if at all.

(b) Attempts by a lessor to enforce his "pledge" extra-judicially by taking actual possession of the lessee's movables, were almost universally rejected by the courts as being an unlawful interference with or implied termination of the lease. They thus held that the lessor had no right of self-help and could not obtain actual possession of the lessee's property by "padlocking" the premises and excluding the lessee from them or by physically removing the lessee's effects from the premises, except under the very narrow circumstances where the lessee had clearly abandoned the premises without removing his property. See: Bunel of New Orleans, Inc. v. Cigali, 348 So.2d 993 (La.App. 4 Cir. 1977); Lucas v. Ludwig, 313 So.2d 12 (La.App. 4 Cir. 1975), Reh. Den. (1975), Writ Ref. (1975); Mena v. Barnard, 113 So.2d 332 (La.App. 2 Cir. 1959), Reh. Den. (1959); Reed v. Walthers, 193 So. 253 (La.App. Orl.1940); Lansalot v. Mihaljevich, 125 So. 183 (La.App. Orl. 1929); Pelletier v. Sutter et al., 121 So. 364 (La.App. Orl. 1929); and Wolf v. Cuccia, 144 La. 336, 80 So. 581 (1919).

(c) Civil Code Articles 2705 and 3218 (1870) were thus construed as ordinarily requiring the lessor to proceed judicially, originally by a writ of provisional seizure, or after the latter was abolished, by way of sequestration and as an incident to a suit for the rent, unless the lessee voluntarily surrendered his property to the lessor in satisfaction of the debt or recognition of the privilege. (See C.C.P. Art. 3572). This pragmatically placed the so-called pledge of the lessor in about the same category as any that of any other non-possessory privilege.

(d) Under Civil Code Article 2707 (Rev. 2004), the lessor rights are defined simply as a privilege on the lessee's movables that are found in or upon the leased property. Civil Code Article 3218 (1870) is repealed and Civil Code Article 3219 (1870) is amended to provide that the manner in which the privilege is enforced is regulated by the Title of Lease. Consequently, absent a contemporaneous agreement or voluntary surrender of the property by the debtor, enforcement of the privilege requires, like all other non-possessory privileges, a judicial seizure and sale of property as an incident to the enforcement of the secured obligation itself. The change in the Article does not affect either the

647

nature or priority of the privilege vis a vis other creditors of the lessee, nor the existence of a privilege in favor of the lessor, which is continued unabated by Civil Code Article 2707 (Rev. 2004).

(e) The second and third paragraphs of former Civil Code Article 2705 (1870) also are omitted from Civil Code Article 2707 (Rev. 2004). The second paragraph of the Civil Code Article 2705 (1870) contained a list of movable property subject to the privilege. With the exception of a reference to growing crops, explained below, Civil Code Article 2707 (Rev. 2004) simply subjects to the privilege "the lessee's movables that are found in or upon the leased property."

(f) The third paragraph of former Civil Code Article 2705 (1870) contained a list of property of the lessee that was exempt from seizure. R.S. 13:3881 describes property that is exempt from seizure "under any writ, mandate, or process whatsoever" and largely duplicates the third paragraph of former Civil Code Article 2705 (1870). Although Civil Code Article 2707 (Rev. 2004) provides that the privilege encompasses all of the lessee's movables that are found in or upon the leased property, it also assumes that absent a particular waiver, R.S. 13:3881 is applicable to the property it lists when the lessor attempts to execute his privilege by writ of sequestration or fieri facias and thus provides the lessee substantially the same protection as did Civil Code Article 2705 (1870). It should be noted, perhaps, that R.S. 13:3881(B)(2) which makes the exemption inapplicable to "property on which the debtor has voluntarily granted a lien" is not intended to apply to the lessor's privilege. The paragraph is based on an implied waiver of the exemption, since granting a "lien" implicitly is a consent to the sale of the property over which the "lien" is granted. However, the action of the lessee in merely agreeing to lease property, can hardly be construed as being expressive of a present intention to waive the exemption from seizure given him by law of all of the future property he may bring onto the premises of whatever nature it may be or value it may have. Nor is it reasonable to assume that merely placing such property on the premises represents a present expression of an intention by a debtor to waive a beneficial right given to him by law in favor of a creditor who has already extended the credit.

(g) Although Civil Code Article 2707 (Rev. 2004) grants a privilege over all of the movables of the lessee that or found in or upon the leased property, the second paragraph of Civil Code Article 2707 (Rev. 2004) also specifically extends the privilege, in the case of an agricultural lease, to the fruits produced by the land. This was done to set at rest any lingering doubts as to the nature of the fruits produced by an agricultural lessee before they are gathered and recognize the applicability of Civil Code Article 474 (Rev. 1978) which rather clearly characterizes growing crops as being "movables by anticipation" when grown by a lessee.

(h) Neither does Civil Code Article 2707 (Rev. 2004) modify the rule of Civil Code Article 2710 (Rev. 2004), which extinguishes the privilege as to movables that are removed from the leased property for more than fifteen days, or that cannot be identified, or that no longer belong to the lessee.

Art. 2708. Lessor's privilege over sublessee's movables

The lessor's privilege extends to the movables of the sublessee but only to the extent that the sublessee is indebted to his sublessor at the time the lessor exercises his right.

Acts 2004, No. 821, § 1, eff. Jan. 1, 2005.

REVISION COMMENTS—2004

(a) This Article maintains the rule of former Civil Code Article 2706 (1870) that the lessor's privilege extends to the property of a sub-lessee of the premises, but only to the extent that the sublessee is indebted to the sublessor when the lessor exercises his right. The provision of Civil Code Article 2706 (1870) that the sublessee could not claim the benefit, in such a case, of payments made to the sublessor in anticipation of the time they were due under the contract of sublease has been omitted. Since the contract of lease need not be in writing, it is difficult to see how, in the first instance, that a payment of a future installment of rent made by the sublessee and accepted by the sublessor, is not an implied amendment of the terms of the lease as to the time and method of payment of the installment, which was not prohibited by Civil Code Article 2706 (1870).

(b) The underlying premise of Civil Code Article 2708 (Rev. 2004) is that the lessor is in fact doing little more than indirectly exercising the privilege enjoyed by the sublessor (who as a lessor of the sublessee is entitled to a privilege over the sublessee's property). A lessor seldom executes the lease in reliance upon the financial worth of a sublessee and in the rare case in which he might do so, other means of security are available if he wishes to use the sublessee's rent as security and protect against a waiver or payment by anticipation in advance of a default by the lessee.

(c) Civil Code Article 2708 (Rev. 2004) by its terms grants a privilege over the sublessee's property, directly to the lessor in his own right independently of the rights of the sublessor to the extent of the rent due by the sublessee. The sublessee may, of course raise any defense to the claim of the lessor that he could raise against the sublessor, since his property is liable to no greater extent that his obligation. Furthermore, since the privilege created by Civil Code Article 2708 (Rev. 2004) is security for the rental obligation of the lessee, there is no implication that there is a subrogation of the lessor to any other the rights of the sublessor or an imposition of personal liability by the sublessee to the lessor.

Art. 2709. Lessor's right to seize movables of third persons

The lessor may lawfully seize a movable that belongs to a third person if it is located in or upon the leased property, unless the lessor knows that the movable is not the property of the lessee.

The third person may recover the movable by establishing his ownership prior to the judicial sale in the manner provided by Article 1092 of the Code of Civil Procedure. If he fails to do so, the movable may be sold as though it belonged to the lessee.

Acts 2004, No. 821, § 1, eff. Jan. 1, 2005.

REVISION COMMENTS—2004

(a) The provisions of former Civil Code Articles 2707 and 2708 (1870) that subjected movables of third persons to the privilege if the movables were in a house, store, or shop unless they were there only transiently or accidentally have been suppressed. Civil Code Article 2709 (Rev. 2004) omits reference to the existence of the privilege over the property of a third person.

(b) Civil Code Article 2709 (Rev. 2004) extends its provisions not only to property that is located in a house, store, or shop as did former Civil Code Article 2707 (1870), but to any movables in or upon the leased property.

(c) Civil Code Article 2709 (Rev. 2004) provides that the lessor "may lawfully" seize a third person's property if the lessor does not know that the property is not that of the lessee. It further provides that if a third person's property is in fact seized, it may be sold "as though it belonged to the lessee", unless the third person intervenes pursuant to the provisions of C.C.P. Art. 1092 and proves his ownership before the judicial sale occurs. Civil Code Article 2709 (Rev. 2004) relieves the lessor who in good faith causes a third person's property to be seized and sold from any liability for damages for wrongful seizure.

Art. 2710. Enforcement of the lessor's privilege

The lessor may seize the movables on which he has a privilege while they are in or upon the leased property, and for fifteen days after they have been removed if they remain the property of the lessee and can be identified.

The lessor may enforce his privilege against movables that have been seized by the sheriff or other officer of the court, without the necessity of a further seizure thereof, as long as the movables or the proceeds therefrom remain in the custody of the officer.

Acts 2004, No. 821, § 1, eff. Jan. 1, 2005.

REVISION COMMENTS—2004

(a) The provisions of this Article continue and restate the provisions of paragraphs A and B of the former Civil Code Article 2709 (1870) continuing the privilege over the lessee's property for fifteen days after it is removed from the leased property as long as it can be identified and remains the lessee's property. Civil Code Article 2710 (Rev. 2004) modifies former Civil Code Article 2709 (1870) to the extent that Civil Code Article 2709 (1870) extinguished the privilege when the property was taken from the leased premises with the consent of the lessor. This condition is omitted from Civil Code Article 2710 (Rev. 2004) so that the privilege continues even if the removal from the premises is done with the consent of the lessor. Part of the difficulty with Civil Code Article 2709 (1870) was that an action for eviction (which is not in itself an action for the rent) is a demand by the lessor that the lessee quit the premises and remove his property from it. It was not deemed reasonable that by demanding a defaulting lessee vacate the premises, or failing that by recovering possession of his premises by the expeditious remedy of eviction, the lessor has waived his rights of security because he has "consented to the removal" of the property from the premises.

(b) The second paragraph of Civil Code Article 2710 (Rev. 2004) continues the provisions of former Civil Code Article 2709 (1870) that if movables subject to the privilege are seized by another creditor of the lessee and as long as the property remains in custodia legis, the lessor may intervene in the proceedings and assert his privilege, without the necessity of himself provoking a seizure.

SECTION 8—TRANSFER OF INTEREST BY THE LESSOR OR THE LESSEE

Art. 2711.   Transfer of thing does not terminate lease

The transfer of the leased thing does not terminate the lease, unless the contrary had been agreed between the lessor and the lessee.

Acts 2004, No. 821, § 1, eff. Jan. 1, 2005.

REVISION COMMENTS—2004

(a) This Article is based on Article 2733 of the Louisiana Civil Code of 1870, which provided that "[i]f the lessor sells the thing leased, the purchaser can not turn out the tenant before his lease has expired, unless the contrary has been stipulated in the contract." The history of the source provision suggests that it was intended as an exception to the requirement of recordation, that is, it was intended to make an unrecorded lease of an immovable assertible against the transferee. See Stadnik, The Doctrinal Origins of the Juridical Nature of Lease in the Civil Law, 54 Tul.L.Rev. 1094, 1135 (1980). However, both the jurisprudence and the legislature have taken a contrary position which is now codified in R.S. 9:2721 et seq., the public records statute. This statute provides that "[n]o . . . lease . . . affecting immovable property shall be binding on or affect third persons . . . unless and until filed for registry in the office of the parish recorder of the parish where the land or immovable is situated." This principle is reiterated in Civil Code Article 2712 (Rev. 2004), which applies to immovables only and to that extent functions as an exception from the rule of Civil Code Article 2711 (Rev. 2004) by providing that an unrecorded lease is not assertible against the transferee.

(b) If the leased thing is a movable or an immovable subject to a recorded lease, then Civil Code Article 2712 (Rev. 2004) is inapplicable, and, in the absence of a contrary agreement between the lessor and the lessee, the lease continues in effect between the original parties despite the transfer of the thing by the lessor. This is consistent with the principle that "a lease of a thing that does not belong to the lessor may nevertheless be binding on the parties," Civil Code Article 2674 (Rev. 2004), and that "ownership of the thing by the lessor is not an essential element of the contract of lease." Comment (c) under Civil Code Article 2674 (Rev. 2004). For example, the lessor remains bound to warrant the lessee's peaceful possession. This principle was expressly stated in Article 2682 of the Civil Code of 1870 which provided that "[h]e who lets out the property of another, warrants the enjoyment of it against the claim of the owner." Although Civil Code Article 2682 (1870) is not reproduced in this Revision, the underlying principle is implicit in both Civil Code Article 2674 (Rev. 2004) and Civil Code Article 2711 (Rev. 2004). Similarly, the lessor is entitled to collect rent, and the lessee may not refuse to pay rent or perform his other obligations because of the lessor's lack of ownership. Comment (c), C.C. Art. 2674 (Rev. 2004).

(c) Conversely, the transferee of a movable or an immovable subject to a recorded lease may not evict the lessee "because [his] right to use [the leased thing] has been alienated prior to his acquisition." Port Arthur Towing Co. v. Owens-Illinois, Inc., 352 F.Supp. 392 at 398 (W.D. La. 1972), affirmed 492 F.2d 688 (5 Cir. 1974). See also R.S. 9:2721(C) (providing that the acquirer of immovable property "subject to a recorded lease agreement that is not divested by the acquisition, shall take the property subject to all of the provisions of the lease,") Carmouche v. Jung, 157 La. 441, 102 So. 518 (1924); Clague v. Townsend, 1 Mart. (N.S.) 264 (1823); Walker v. Van Winkle, 8 Mart. (N.S.) 560 (1830). See also Hardy v. Lemons, 36 La.Ann. 146 (1884) (a lessee of a horse or other movable property cannot be divested of possession thereof, by the lessor's sale of it to a third party). The transferee does not, by virtue of the transfer alone, become the lessor and does not assume the lessor's obligations (see C.C. Arts. 1821 et seq. (Rev. 1984)). Nor is the transferee subrogated to the lessor's rights (see C.C. Arts. 1821 et seq. (Rev. 1984)), except the right to protect the thing from abuse or waste by the lessee. See C.C. Arts. 2686 and 2687 (Rev. 2004).

Art. 2712. Transfer of immovable subject to unrecorded lease

A third person who acquires an immovable that is subject to an unrecorded lease is not bound by the lease.

In the absence of a contrary provision in the lease contract, the lessee has an action against the lessor for any loss the lessee sustained as a result of the transfer.

Acts 2004, No. 821, § 1, eff. Jan. 1, 2005.

REVISION COMMENTS—2004

(a) Civil Code Article 2681 (Rev. 2004) provides that "[a] lease of an immovable is not effective against third persons until filed for recordation in the manner prescribed by legislation." The public records statutes, R.S. 9:2721 et seq., also provide to the same effect, define the pertinent terms such as "third person," and prescribe in detail the specific requirements and standards. The first paragraph of Civil Code Article 2712 (Rev. 2004) reiterates the principles of the public records statutes and should be interpreted accordingly in pari materia with those statutes.

(b) Civil Code Article 2711 (Rev. 2004) deals with the relationship between the lessor and the lessee and provides that, in the absence of a contrary agreement between them, the transfer of the leased thing does not terminate the lease. In contrast, the first paragraph of Civil Code Article 2712 (Rev. 2004) deals with the relationship between the lessee and a "third person" who—usually through a transfer from the lessor—acquires an immovable that is subject to an unrecorded lease. This paragraph provides that the third person is not—by virtue of this acquisition alone—bound by the lease.

(c) The second paragraph of Civil Code Article 2712 (Rev. 2004) returns to the relationship between the lessor and the lessee and defines the lessee's rights vis a vis the lessor for any loss the lessee may have sustained as a result of the transfer. For example, if the third person transferee exercises his right to evict the lessee before the end of the term, then the lessor—who has put the transferee in that position—is in breach of his obligation of warranty of peaceful possession. See C.C. Art. 2700 (Rev. 2004). Because of the seriousness of this breach, Civil Code Article 2712 (Rev. 2004) gives the lessee an express cause of action to recover any loss the lessee sustained. This remedy is in keeping with the general law of obligations, as well as Articles 2735 et seq. of the Civil Code of 1870. (These articles required the lessor to indemnify the lessee even in cases in which the lease granted to the lessor the right to terminate the lease by transferring the thing, as long as the lease was silent on the issue of indemnification.) Like all other obligations under the lease, the lessor's obligation to warrant the lessee's peaceful possession is binding between the lessor and the lessee even if the lease is not recorded or is not in writing. (See C.C. Art. 2681 (Rev. 2004) which provides that even an oral lease is binding between the parties, although with regard to third parties a lease is ineffective unless recorded.) The lessee's failure to record the lease explains why the lessee will not be protected vis-a-vis the third person transferee who relied on the public records. Such failure, however, may not be invoked by the lessor as an excuse for breaching his obligations with impunity.

(d) The lessee's rights described in comment (c) may be negated or modified by "a contrary provision in the lease contract," such as a provision that reserves to the lessor the right to transfer the immovable before the end of the term. If, in exercising this right, the lessor remains within the confines of that provision and complies with the notice requirements of Civil Code Article 2718 (Rev. 2004), the lessor should ordinarily be able to defeat an action by the lessee. Article 2734 of the Civil Code of 1870 provided a similar solution for cases in which the lessor "ha[d] reserved to himself in the agreement, the right of taking possession of the thing leased whenever he should think proper." In such cases, the Article provided, the lessor who had complied with the notice requirements was "not bound to make any indemnification to the lessee, unless it be specified by the contract." A somewhat different solution was provided by the Civil Code of 1870 for cases in which the lease allowed the lessor to transfer the thing and the transferee to take immediate possession of it. In such cases, the

Code provided in Civil Code Article 2735 (1870) that "if no indemnification has been stipulated, the lessor shall be bound to indemnify the lessee in the . . . manner [provided in Civil Code Articles 2736–2741 (1870)]." The second paragraph of Civil Code Article 2712 (Rev. 2004) is similar to Civil Code Article 2735 (1870) in that both provisions give primacy to an agreement of the parties on the issue of indemnification. However, unlike Civil Code Article 2735 (1870), the above paragraph contains no presumption in favor of indemnification in those cases in which the lease allowed the lessor to transfer the thing and the transferee to take immediate possession of it.

Art. 2713.   Lessee's right to sublease, assign, or encumber

The lessee has the right to sublease the leased thing or to assign or encumber his rights in the lease, unless expressly prohibited by the contract of lease. A provision that prohibits one of these rights is deemed to prohibit the others, unless a contrary intent is expressed. In all other respects, a provision that prohibits subleasing, assigning, or encumbering is to be strictly construed against the lessor.

Acts 2004, No. 821, § 1, eff. Jan. 1, 2005.

REVISION COMMENT—2004

The first sentence of this Article restates the principle of Article 2725 of the Civil Code of 1870. The second sentence is new. The third sentence restates the principle of the second paragraph of Civil Code Article 2725 (1870) properly understood. That paragraph provided that "[t]he interdiction [of the right to sublease] . . . is always construed strictly." In derogation of general principles of interpretation, some cases have erroneously construed such interdiction against the lessee. The third sentence of Civil Code Article 2713 (Rev. 2004) corrects this error.

CHAPTER 4—TERMINATION AND DISSOLUTION

SECTION 1—RULES APPLICABLE TO ALL LEASES

Art. 2714.   Expropriation; loss or destruction

If the leased thing is lost or totally destroyed, without the fault of either party, or if it is expropriated, the lease terminates and neither party owes damages to the other.

Acts 2004, No. 821, § 1, eff. Jan. 1, 2005.

REVISION COMMENTS—2004

(a) This Article is derived from Civil Code Article 2728 (1870) and from the first sentence of Civil Code Article 2697 (1870). The former article provided that the lease terminates by "the loss of the thing leased," apparently contemplating a total loss of the thing. The latter article provided that the lease also terminates if the thing is "totally destroyed by an unforseen event" or is "taken for a purpose of public utility." The scope of Civil Code Article 2714 (Rev. 2004) is coextensive with that of the source provisions in that it contemplates total loss or total destruction of the thing, or expropriation of the whole thing. (If the loss or destruction is only partial, or only part of the thing is expropriated, the applicable article is Civil Code Article 2715 (Rev. 2004).)

(b) If the loss or destruction is total, or if the whole thing is expropriated, then under Civil Code Article 2714 (Rev. 2004), the lease terminates, regardless of whether the events that brought about the loss or destruction are attributable to the fault of either party. Although this Article contains the phrase "without the fault of either party," that phrase addresses the parties' right to claim damages. That is, if the loss or destruction was not attributable to the fault of either party, then "neither party owes damages to the other." Conversely, if the loss or destruction was attributable to the fault of one party then, of course, that party would owe damages to the other, but the lease would also terminate for the simple reason that the destruction of the whole object of the contract renders performance impossible. Cf. C.C. Art. 1876 (Rev. 1984). This is consistent with Civil Code Article 2728 (1870), which provided that the loss of the thing terminated the lease, without making any reference to the parties' fault. See also C.C. Art. 751 (Rev. 1977) (providing that a predial servitude is extinguished by "the total destruction of the dominant estate or the part of the servient estate burdened with the servitude," again without any reference to the parties' fault); Austrian Civil Code Article 1112 (providing that the lease terminates if the thing is destroyed and that "[i]f this happens through the fault of one party, the other is entitled to indemnification; if it happens by accident, neither of the parties is liable to the other therefor.") While it is true that Civil Code Article 2697 (1870) spoke of destruction caused "by an unforeseen event," thus contemplating something beyond the control of the parties, that reference was tied to the last sentence of the article which releases the lessor from the obligation to pay damages. The same is true under Civil Code Article 2714 (Rev. 2004), in the sense that if the loss or destruction is "without the fault of either party," then "neither party owes damages to the other."

(c) Expropriation of the whole thing also results in the total loss of use of the thing and thus terminates the lease. (For partial expropriation, see Civil Code Article 2715 (Rev. 2004)). The jurisprudence has held that the fact that the lease terminates does not deprive the lessee of the right to demand compensation from the expropriating authority if such compensation is otherwise due. See Holland v. State, Dept. of Transp., 554 So.2d 727 (La.App. 2 Cir. 1989), writ denied 559 So.2d 125 (La. 1990); State, Through Dept. of Highways v. Champagne, 371 So.2d 626 (La.App. 1 Cir. 1979), reversed in part on other grounds 379 So.2d 1069 (La. 1980), on remand, 391 So.2d 1234 (La.App. 1 Cir. 1980). This jurisprudence continues to be relevant.

(d) When the requirements of Civil Code Article 2714 (Rev. 2004) are met, the lease terminates "of right" or "by operation of law," that is, without the need for judicial intervention. The quoted words are translations of the French terms de plein droit, which were contained in the French text of the predecessor of Civil Code Articles 2697 and 2728 (1870) in the 1825 Code, but were not reproduced in the English translation of that Code. They are also not reproduced in Civil Code Article 2714 (Rev. 2004), because they are self-evident. Cf. C.C. Arts. 613 (Rev. 1976) and 751 (Rev. 1977).

(e) The fact that the lease terminates by operation of law does not mean that such termination is inescapable. The jurisprudence has held that the parties may prevent such termination by inserting appropriate clauses in the lease contract. See Cerniglia v. Napoli, 517 So.2d 1209 (La.App. 4 Cir. 1987); S. Gumbel Realty & Securities Co. v. Levy, 156 So. 70 (La.App. Orleans 1934). This jurisprudence continues to be relevant.

Art. 2715. Partial destruction, loss, expropriation, or other substantial impairment of use

If, without the fault of the lessee, the thing is partially destroyed, lost, or expropriated, or its use is otherwise substantially impaired, the lessee may, according to the circumstances of both parties, obtain a diminution of the rent or dissolution of the lease, whichever is more appropriate under the circumstances. If the lessor was at fault, the lessee may also demand damages.

If the impairment of the use of the leased thing was caused by circumstances external to the leased thing, the lessee is entitled to a dissolution of the lease, but is not entitled to diminution of the rent.

Acts 2004, No. 821, § 1, eff. Jan. 1, 2005.

REVISION COMMENTS—2004

(a) This Article is derived in part from two separate provisions of the Civil Code of 1870: (a) the second sentence of Civil Code Article 2697 (1870), which dealt with cases of partial destruction of the leased thing; and (b) Civil Code Article 2699 (1870), which dealt with cases in which the leased thing "cease[s] to be fit for the purpose for which it was leased, or . . . [its] use [is] much impeded . . ." Both provisions contemplated situations in which neither the lessor nor the lessee were at fault. However, while the former provision allowed for either diminution of the rent or dissolution of the lease, the second provision allowed only for dissolution of the lease. Reasoning that dissolution is a more drastic remedy than diminution of the rent, the jurisprudence concluded that the permission of the major also includes the minor and thus has granted the remedy of diminution in cases covered by Civil Code Article 2699 (1870). See, e.g., Hinricks v. City of New Orleans, 50 La.Ann. 1214, 24 So. 224 (1898); Foucher v. Choppin, 17 La.Ann. 321 (1865). Civil Code Article 2715 (Rev. 2004) grants both remedies, but only with regard to cases falling within the scope of the first paragraph of the Article.

(b) Civil Code Article 2715 (Rev. 2004) applies to cases of partial destruction, loss, or expropriation of the leased thing. For cases of total destruction, loss, or expropriation, see Civil Code Article 2714 (Rev. 2004). Civil Code Article 2715 (Rev. 2004) also applies to other cases in which the

653

use of the thing is "otherwise substantially impaired." The quoted phrase is intended to have the same meaning as the phrase "much impeded" in the source provision. The first paragraph of Civil Code Article 2715 (Rev. 2004) provides that if these events were not attributable to the fault of the lessee, then the lessee is entitled to either diminution of the rent or dissolution of the lease, "whichever is more appropriate under the circumstances." If these events were attributable to the fault of the lessor, then the lessee may also demand damages, in addition to diminution of the rent or dissolution of the lease.

(c) The second paragraph of Civil Code Article 2715 (Rev. 2004) introduces an exception from the rule of the first paragraph to the extent it allows only for dissolution of the lease but not for diminution of the rent. The exception applies only to cases in which the use of the leased thing is "otherwise substantially impaired" (that is, in cases other the partial destruction, loss, or expropriation of the thing) and in which the impairment of use is caused by "circumstances external to the leased thing." One example of such a circumstance is the one provided by Article 2699 of the Civil Code of 1870 (a neighbor who, "by raising his walls . . . intercept[s] the light of a house leased . . ."). Another is a zoning or other governmental regulation that results in or imposes substantial restrictions on the use of the leased thing. As these examples indicate, the circumstances contemplated by this paragraph must not be attributable to the fault of the lessor. If such fault is shown, however, then the lessee's remedies are not confined to dissolution of the lease.

Art. 2716. Termination of lease granted by a usufructuary

A lease granted by a usufructuary terminates upon the termination of the usufruct.

The lessor is liable to the lessee for any loss caused by such termination, if the lessor failed to disclose his status as a usufructuary.

Acts 2004, No. 821, § 1, eff. Jan. 1, 2005.

REVISION COMMENTS—2004

(a) The first paragraph of this Article restates the rule found in the first sentence of Civil Code Article 2730 (1870) and in the second sentence of Civil Code Article 567 (Rev. 1976).

(b) The second paragraph of Civil Code Article 2716 (Rev. 2004) recasts in affirmative terms the language of the second paragraph of Civil Code Article 2730 (1870), and resolves an ambiguity inherent in the source provision. Under the new paragraph, the lessor is liable for the termination of the lease not only when he affirmatively represented himself as the owner of the thing, but also when he failed to disclose the fact that he was merely a usufructuary.

(c) The source provision also refers to the "heirs of the lessor" as being responsible for indemnification, thus giving the impression that the article contemplated only situations in which the usufruct had terminated by the death of the usufructuary. Although justifiable from a literal perspective, that impression was not accurate. Indeed, both the language of the first paragraph of Civil Code Article 2730 (1870) and the source from which it was derived suggest that the article was not confined to cases in which the usufruct terminates by death, but was instead intended to encompass terminations from any other cause. The same is true of Civil Code Article 2716 (Rev. 2004). Consequently, the words "heirs of the lessor" have been replaced by the word "lessor." If the lessor dies, his heirs will, of course, be responsible, since this obligation is heritable.

Art. 2717. Death of lessor or lessee

A lease does not terminate by the death of the lessor or the lessee or by the cessation of existence of a juridical person that is party to the lease.

Acts 2004, No. 821, § 1, eff. Jan. 1, 2005.

REVISION COMMENTS—2004

(a) This Article reproduces the principle of Article 2731 of the Civil Code of 1870 and codifies the jurisprudence that extended that principle to juridical persons. As provided in the source provision, the death of either the lessor or the lessee does not dissolve or terminate the lease. The obligations created by the lease contract are not "strictly personal" as this term is defined by Civil Code Article 1766 (Rev. 1984). Rather they are heritable obligations (see Civil Code Article 1765 (Rev. 1984)) and hence they may be enforced by or against the heirs of the lessor or the lessee. See Cheney v. Haley, 142 So. 312 (La.App. 2 Cir. 1932); Dyer v. Wilson, 190 So. 851 (La.App. 2 Cir. 1939).

(b) The same principle applies when a party to the lease is a juridical person, such as a partnership or corporation or any other "entity to which the law attributes personality." C.C. Art. 24 (Rev. 1987). When, for whatever reason, that personality ceases to exist, the lease does not necessarily terminate. Since the obligations created by the lease are "heritable," they may be enforced by or against that person's successors.

(c) Article 2732 of the Louisiana Civil Code of 1870 provided that "[t]he lessor can not dissolve the lease for the purpose of occupying himself the premises, unless that right has been reserved to him by the contract." That Article is not reproduced in this Revision because it is self-evident.

Art. 2718.   Leases with reservation of right to terminate

A lease in which one or both parties have reserved the right to terminate the lease before the end of the term may be so terminated by giving the notice specified in the lease contract or the notice provided in Articles 2727 through 2729, whichever period is longer. The right to receive this notice may not be renounced in advance.

Acts 2004, No. 821, § 1, eff. Jan. 1, 2005.

REVISION COMMENTS—2004

(a) This Article deals with leases in which the parties have agreed on a maximum term, but have also agreed that the lessor, the lessee, or both, will have the right to terminate the lease at an earlier time for reasons other than a breach by the other party. If the party entitled to this right does not exercise it, then the lease is treated as one with a fixed term, which terminates upon the expiration of the term as provided in Civil Code Article 2720 (Rev. 2004) without the need to give notice. Civil Code Article 2718 (Rev. 2004) becomes operative when the party that has the contractual right to terminate the lease before the end of the term wants to exercise this right. Civil Code Article 2718 (Rev. 2004) provides that this party must give to the other party the notice specified in the lease contract, if any is specified, or the notice prescribed in Civil Code Articles 2727–2729 (Rev. 2004), whichever provides for a longer notice period. Civil Code Article 2718 (Rev. 2004) also provides that this right to be given notice may not be renounced in advance.

(b) Article 2732 of the Civil Code of 1870 provided indirectly that the lessor could "dissolve the lease for the purpose of occupying himself the premises," if that right has been "reserved to him by the contract." Civil Code Article 2718 (Rev. 2004) preserves this right, subject to the notice requirements provided in the Article. Article 2735 of the Civil Code of 1870 provided—in effect and indirectly—that the lessor could reserve in the contract of lease the right to terminate the lease by transferring the thing. Civil Code Article 2718 (Rev. 2004) preserves this right, subject to the notice requirements provided in the Article. However, Civil Code Article 2718 (Rev. 2004) is broader than either of the source provisions in that it also encompasses cases in which the lessor has reserved the right to terminate the lease for other reasons. In addition, Civil Code Article 2718 (Rev. 2004) encompasses cases in which the same right to terminate has been reserved to the lessee.

(c) Civil Code Article 2718 (Rev. 2004) does not address questions of any indemnification that may be owed by the party who exercises the right to terminate the lease before the end of the term. Whether such indemnification is owed will depend on a proper interpretation of the lease contract, including consideration of applicable customs and usages. Articles 2734–2740 of the Civil Code of 1870, which provided for such indemnification for certain cases, are not reproduced in this Revision. The starting premise of Civil Code Article 2718 (Rev. 2004) is that, subject to the overriding obligation of good faith enunciated in Civil Code Article 1770 (Rev. 1984), the mere exercise of the right granted by the contract to either the lessor or the lessee to terminate the contract as provided in Civil Code Article 2718 (Rev. 2004) does not, in and of itself, give rise to a duty to indemnify the other party.

Art. 2719. Dissolution for other causes

When a party to the lease fails to perform his obligations under the lease or under this Title, the other party may obtain dissolution of the lease pursuant to the provisions of the Title of "Conventional Obligations or Contracts".

Acts 2004, No. 821, § 1, eff. Jan. 1, 2005.

REVISION COMMENTS—2004

(a) This Article reproduces the substance of Article 2729 of the Civil Code of 1870. It may be changing the law as explained in Comment (b).

(b) Article 2729 of the Civil Code of 1870 provided for the dissolution of leases "in the manner expressed concerning contracts in general." At the time this cross-reference was made, the pertinent articles of the Civil Code of 1870 (e.g., C.C. Arts. 2046 and 2047) provided only for a judicial dissolution of contracts but did not authorize extra-judicial dissolution on the initiative of one party only. Although it has been argued that cases interpreting Article 2046 of the Civil Code of 1870 allowed such extra-judicial dissolution in cases of "active breach" (see Comment (a) under C.C. Arts. 2013 and 2015 (Rev. 1984) and cases cited therein), none of these cases involved a contract of lease. The jurisprudence on leases has steadfastly adhered to the principle that judicial intervention is necessary. See Vernon Palmer, Leases: The Law in Louisiana, § 5–18 (1982). The first express legislative authorization for extra-judicial dissolution of contracts in general was made by the 1984 revision of the Civil Code's Obligations provisions in the circumstances described in C.C. Arts. 2013 and 2015–2017 (Rev. 1984). Whether the above-quoted cross-reference in Article 2729 of the Civil Code of 1870 should somehow be "updated" so as to encompass these new articles on extra-judicial dissolution, or whether the cross-reference should instead be read in light of the pre-1984 obligations articles of the 1870 code which did not authorize extra-judicial dissolution, is a question that has not been answered by the jurisprudence on leases. Civil Code Article 2719 (Rev. 2004) resolves this question by authorizing the application of all the pertinent articles of the Title of "Conventional Obligations or Contracts" dealing with dissolution (see, e.g., C.C. Arts. 2013–2024 (Rev. 1984)), including those that authorize extra-judicial dissolution on the initiative of one party and at his or her own risk.

(c) Civil Code Article 2719 (Rev. 2004) applies when a party "fails to perform" his obligations under the lease or under this Title. Failure to perform is defined by Civil Code Article 1994 (Rev. 1984) as "nonperformance, defective performance, or delay in performance." However, under Civil Code Article 2014 (Rev. 1984), "[a] contract may not be dissolved when the obligor has rendered a substantial part of the performance and the part not rendered does not substantially impair the interest of the obligee." This is consistent with the position of the jurisprudence that has refused to dissolve leases for minor violations, a position that is often synopsized in the phrase "abrogation of leases is not favored by law." Tullier v. Tanson Enterprises, Inc., 359 So.2d 654 (La.App. 1 Cir. 1978) reversed on other grounds 367 So.2d 773 (La. 1979); Arbo v. Jankowski, 39 So.2d 458 (La.App. Orl. 1949); Lillard v. Hulbert, 9 So.2d 852 (La.App. 1 Cir. 1942); Kling v. Maloney, 7 La.App. 751 (La.App. Orleans 1927); United Shoe Stores v. Burt, 142 So. 370 (La.App. 2 Cir. 1932); Vernon Palmer, Leases, § 5–19 (1982). This jurisprudence continues to be relevant in granting judicial dissolution under Civil Code Article 2719 (Rev. 2004). A fortiori, this jurisprudence is relevant in judging the propriety of extra-judicial dissolution.

(d) Because a lease is a contract "providing for continuous or periodic performance," (Civil Code Article 2019 (Rev. 1984)), the effect of its dissolution "shall not be extended to any performance already rendered." Id. See also Comment (b) under Civil Code Article 2019 (Rev. 1984). In other words, dissolution is ex tunc only or what is called in French legal literature resiliation. See Comment (c) under C.C. Art. 2019 (Rev. 1984). This is consistent with the jurisprudence on leases. See Palmer, supra, at § 5–18.

656

SECTION 2—LEASES WITH A FIXED TERM

Art. 2720.   Termination of lease with a fixed term

A lease with a fixed term terminates upon the expiration of that term, without need of notice, unless the lease is reconducted or extended as provided in the following Articles.

Acts 2004, No. 821, § 1, eff. Jan. 1, 2005.

(a) This Article, as well as this Section, applies only to leases "with a fixed term" as defined by Civil Code Article 2678 (Rev. 2004) as opposed to leases with an indeterminate term. The latter are governed by Civil Code Articles 2727–2729 (Rev. 2004).

(b) The term of a lease is fixed when the parties agreed that the lease would "terminate at a designated date or upon the occurrence of a designated event." Civil Code Article 2678 (Rev. 2004). Basic principles of contract law dictate that when the specified date arrives, or the specified event occurs, the lease should terminate without the need of notice and without the need of any judicial action or declaration. This is what Civil Code Article 2720 (Rev. 2004) provides and in so doing reproduces the substance of the first sentence of Civil Code Article 2686 (1870) ("[t]he parties must abide by the agreement as fixed at the time of the lease") and by Civil Code Article 2727 (1870) which provided that "[t]he lease ceases *of course*, at the expiration of the time agreed on." The italicized words are a translation of the French words de plein droit, which could be more accurately translated as "by operation of law." These words have not been reproduced in Civil Code Article 2720 (Rev. 2004) as unnecessary.

(c) The last clause of Civil Code Article 2720 (Rev. 2004) provides that the lease does not terminate if it has been reconducted or extended as provided in Civil Code Articles 2721 and 2725 (Rev. 2004). The principle of the continuity of a reconducted lease is reiterated in Civil Code Article 2724 (Rev. 2004).

Art. 2721.   Reconduction

A lease with a fixed term is reconducted if, after the expiration of the term, and without notice to vacate or terminate or other opposition by the lessor or the lessee, the lessee remains in possession:

(1) For thirty days in the case of an agricultural lease;

(2) For one week in the case of other leases with a fixed term that is longer than a week; or

(3) For one day in the case of a lease with a fixed term that is equal to or shorter than a week.

Acts 2004, No. 821, § 1, eff. Jan. 1, 2005.

REVISION COMMENTS—2004

(a) This Article is derived from Articles 2688, 2689, and 2691 of the Civil Code of 1870 and pertinent Louisiana jurisprudence. It clarifies and changes the law, as explained below.

(b) This Article applies only to leases the term of which: (a) is "fixed" as defined by Civil Code Article 2678 (Rev. 2004), (as opposed to leases whose term is "indeterminate"); and (b) has expired.

(c) In contrast to Articles 2688 and 2689 of the Civil Code of 1870 which were confined to a "lease of a predial estate" and a lease of "a house or of a room," respectively, this Article applies to leases of all immovables and, for that matter, all movables. To this extent, this Article changes the law and overrules the jurisprudential thesis that there could be no reconduction of a lease of movables. See National Automatic Fire Alarm Co. v. New Orleans & N.E.R.R. Co., 2 Orleans App. 421 (La.App. Orleans 1905).

(d) Article 2691 of the Civil Code of 1870 provided that "[w]hen notice has been given, the tenant . . . can not pretend that there has been a tacit renewal of the lease." Articles 2689 and 2688 of the Civil Code of 1870 provided respectively that reconduction occurs only if the lessee's continued possession after the expiration of the term was "without any opposition being made thereto by the lessor" or "without any step having been taken . . . by the lessor . . . to cause [the lessee] to deliver up the possession . . ." From these articles flows the principle that reconduction does not occur if *the lessor* has given notice of termination or has in other ways expressed his opposition to the lessee's continuous possession. This principle is now contained in Civil Code Article 2721 (Rev. 2004) in the phrase "without notice of termination or other opposition by the lessor *or the lessee*." The italicized words indicate a change from the language of the source provisions all of which contemplated notice or opposition by the lessor only. However, the change is more apparent than real. Since reconduction owes its source to a presumed tacit agreement of the parties, it should follow that either party, through a clear manifestation of a contrary intent, should be able to prevent such an agreement from being formed. Louisiana jurisprudence has long recognized this principle and has held that the Civil Code articles providing for reconduction have "no application whatever when either party has clearly announced his intention not to renew the lease on same terms . . . [since] the purpose of law is not to force a contract upon parties unwilling to contract, but merely to establish a rule of evidence, or presumption, as to their intention . . ." Ashton Realty Co. v. Prowell, 165 La. 328, 115 So. 579, at p. 581 (1928) (emphasis added). See also Prisock v. Boyd, 199 So.2d 373 (La.App. 2 Cir. 1967); Waller Oil Co., Inc. v. Brown, 528 So.2d 584 (La.App. 2 Cir. 1988). While it is true that the lessee's continued possession after the expiration of the term normally justifies the inference that he intends to continue the lease, such inference is negated by an express contrary statement. For example if, in a residential lease with a fixed term of one year, the lessee requests the lessor's permission to occupy the premises for ten days after the end of the year "so as to have enough time to move out his furniture," and the lessor does not object or does not respond, the lessee's remaining in possession for these ten days should not lead to reconduction in light of his intent, expressed in his request and communicated to the lessor, not to continue the lease.

(e) In order for reconduction to occur, the lessee must have remained in unopposed possession for a certain period of time after the expiration of the term of the lease. Under the Civil Code of 1870, this period was "one month" for agricultural leases and "a week" for leases "of a house or of a room." C.C. Arts. 2688 and 2689 (1870). Under Civil Code Article 2721 (Rev. 2004), the length of this period depends on the type of lease or the length of the expired term. Thus, for agricultural leases, this period is thirty days, regardless of the length of the expired term. For other leases that have a fixed term that is longer than a week, such as a residential lease for a year, a semester, or a month, this period is one week. Finally, for leases with a fixed term of one week or shorter, such as a lease of a movable for a weekend, this period is one day.

Art. 2722.   Term of reconducted agricultural lease

The term of a reconducted agricultural lease is from year to year, unless the parties intended a different term which, according to local custom or usage, is observed in leases of the same type.

Acts 2004, No. 821, § 1, eff. Jan. 1, 2005.

REVISION COMMENTS—2004

(a) This Article is derived from Article 2688 of the Louisiana Civil Code of 1870 and pertinent Louisiana jurisprudence. It clarifies and changes the law, as explained below.

(b) Civil Code Article 2722 (Rev. 2004) defines the term of an agricultural lease that has been reconducted pursuant to Civil Code Article 2721 (Rev. 2004). Article 2688 of the Civil Code of 1870 provided that a reconducted agricultural lease "shall continue only for the year next following the expiration of the lease." The word "only" has been construed away by Louisiana courts. In Dyer v. Wilson, 190 So. 851 (La.App. 2 Cir. 1939), the court rejected an argument to the contrary and held that the quoted language means that "reconduction . . . is . . . only for one year at a time. It does not, however, fix any maximum number of yearly periods." Dyer, supra, at p. 853. Civil Code Article 2722 (Rev. 2004) adopts the position that there should be no maximum yearly periods by using the words "from year to year." The quoted phrase also signifies that the reconducted lease is one for an indeterminate rather than a fixed term and thus answers a question that was not answered by the text of Civil Code Article 2688 (1870).

(c) However, in contrast to the source provision, Civil Code Article 2722 (Rev. 2004) also allows for the possibility that the term of the reconducted lease may be something other than from year to year, if it is shown that "the parties intended a different term which, according to local custom or usage, is observed in leases of the same type." This provision may prove useful when the initial term was shorter than a year, such as "one farming season," but also when it was longer than a year.

658

(d) Because a reconducted lease is a lease for an indeterminate term, the reconducted lease continues indefinitely until terminated by notice as directed in Civil Code Articles 2727–2729 (Rev. 2004).

Art. 2723. Term of reconducted nonagricultural lease

The term of a reconducted nonagricultural lease is:

(1) From month to month in the case of a lease whose term is a month or longer;

(2) From day to day in the case of a lease whose term is at least a day but shorter than a month; and

(3) For periods equal to the expired term in the case of a lease whose term is less than a day.

Acts 2004, No. 821, § 1, eff. Jan. 1, 2005.

REVISION COMMENTS—2004

(a) This Article is derived from Article 2689 of the Louisiana Civil Code of 1870 and pertinent Louisiana jurisprudence. However, in contrast to the source provision which was confined to the lease of "a house or room," Civil Code Article 2723 (Rev. 2004) applies to all non-agricultural leases of immovables as well as movables.

(b) This Article defines the term of a lease that has been reconducted pursuant to Civil Code Article 2721 (Rev. 2004). Under Civil Code Article 2723 (Rev. 2004), the term of a reconducted lease is always an indeterminate term of the periodical type, that is, it is measured in periods such as from month-to-month. The length of these periods depends on the length of the original term, as explained below.

(c) Article 2689 of the Civil Code of 1870 did not define the term of a reconducted lease of "a house or of a room" but simply provided that the lease "shall be presumed to have been continued." The jurisprudence has treated such leases as leases for an indeterminate term and then applied to them the month-to-month period provided by Civil Code Article 2685 (1870) for leases of an unspecified duration. See Bowles v. Lyon, 6 Rob. 262 (1843); Garner v. Perrin, 403 So.2d 814 (La.App. 2 Cir. 1981); Weaks Supply Co. v. Werdin, 147 So. 838 (La.App. 2 Cir. 1933); Standard Oil Co. of N.J. v. Edwards, 32 So.2d 102 (La.App. 1 Cir. 1947). Clause (1) of Civil Code Article 2723 (Rev. 2004) is consistent with this jurisprudence for those leases falling within the scope of this clause.

(d) Clause (2) of Civil Code Article 2723 (Rev. 2004) applies to leases whose expired term was shorter than a month but equal to or longer than a day. In such cases, the reconducted lease shall be from day to day. Clause (3) of Civil Code Article 2723 (Rev. 2004) applies to all leases whose term was shorter than a day and provides that the reconducted lease shall be for periods equal to the expiring term. Thus, a lease of a movable for one hour becomes a lease by the hour if reconducted pursuant to the preceding article.

(e) Because a reconducted lease is a lease for an indeterminate term, the reconducted lease continues indefinitely until terminated by notice as directed in Civil Code Articles 2727–2729 (Rev. 2004). This is consistent with Civil Code Article 2689 (1870) and Louisiana jurisprudence.

Art. 2724. Continuity of the reconducted lease

When reconduction occurs, all provisions of the lease continue for the term provided in Article 2722 or 2723.

A reconducted lease is terminated by giving the notice directed in Articles 2727 through 2729.

Acts 2004, No. 821, § 1, eff. Jan. 1, 2005.

REVISION COMMENT—2004

This Article is new. It codifies the position taken by Louisiana jurisprudence to the effect that a reconducted lease is not a new lease but rather a continuation of the old lease under the same terms and conditions, except for duration. See Comegys v. Shreveport Kandy Kitchen, 162 La. 103, 110 So. 104 (1926); Weaks Supply Co. v. Werdin, 147 So. 838 (La.App. 2 Cir. 1933). This principle has important ramifications, not only as between the parties who can insist on compliance with the terms of the original lease, but also with regard to third parties. Thus, a lessor's privilege created during the original lease continues in existence after reconduction. See Comegys, supra; Acadiana Bank v. Foreman, 352 So.2d 674 (La. 1977).

Art. 2725.　Extension

If the lease contract contains an option to extend the term and the option is exercised, the lease continues for the term and under the other provisions stipulated in the option.

Acts 2004, No. 821, § 1, eff. Jan. 1, 2005.

REVISION COMMENTS—2004

(a) This Article is new. It is derived from principles inherent in the Civil Code and elaborated upon by Louisiana courts under the doctrine of renewal. See Blanchard v. Shrimp Boats of La., 305 So.2d 748 (La.App. 4 Cir. 1974); Vernon Palmer, Leases, § 2–15 (1982). This Article avoids use of the word "renewal" precisely in order to avoid the connotation that the extended lease is a "new" lease rather than a continuation of the old lease.

(b) This Article applies only when the lease contract contains an option to extend the term of the lease, popularly known as "option to renew." If the option is validly exercised before the expiration of the term, the lease continues and is considered the same lease, not only as between the parties, but also vis-a-vis third parties. However, with regard to leases of immovables, the continuity of the old lease vis-à-vis third parties will depend, at a minimum, on whether or not the option to renew (and the lease that contained it) was recorded. If it was not recorded, then under Civil Code Articles 2681 and 2712 (Rev. 2004) and basic principles of the law of registry, the option would not be assertible against third parties. If the option was recorded, the next question is whether the exercise of the option must also be recorded in order to be assertible against third parties. One Louisiana court gave an affirmative answer (Julius Gindi & Sons v. E.J.W. Enterprises, 438 So.2d 594 (La.App. 4 Cir. 1983)), while another gave a negative answer to this question (Thomas v. Lewis, 475 So.2d 52 (La.App. 2 Cir. 1985)). The latter court reasoned that the fact that the original option was recorded was sufficient to put third parties on notice of potential claims against the property and that it was not necessary to also record the exercise of the option to renew.

Art. 2726.　Amendment

An amendment to a provision of the lease contract that is made without an intent to effect a novation does not create a new lease.

Acts 2004, No. 821, § 1, eff. Jan. 1, 2005.

REVISION COMMENT—2004

This Article is new but does not change the law. It recasts in more specific language the general principles of the law of novation, and particularly those found in Civil Code Articles 1880 and 1881 (Rev. 1984). The latter articles have already overruled cases such as Weaks Supply Co. v. Verdin, 147 So. 838 (La.App. 2 Cir. 1933) which had held that an agreement to alter the stipulated rent is a novation of the lease. See Comment (a) under C.C. Art. 1881 (Rev. 1984). However, because Civil Code Article 1881 (1870) is often overlooked by some courts (see, e.g., Misse v. Dronet, 493 So.2d 271 (La.App. 3 Cir. 1986) which adheres to the overruled jurisprudence), it is thought necessary to expressly incorporate the principles of that article in an article applicable specifically to lease contracts. This is the purpose of Civil Code Article 2726 (Rev. 2004). For an excellent discussion of the difference between an amendment or "modification" and a novation of leases, see George Armstrong, Louisiana Landlord and Tenant Law, § 2.4 (1987).

SECTION 3—LEASES WITH INDETERMINATE TERM

Art. 2727.　Termination of lease with an indeterminate term

A lease with an indeterminate term, including a reconducted lease or a lease whose term has been established through Article 2680, terminates by notice to that effect given to the other party by the party desiring to terminate the lease, as provided in the following Articles.

Acts 2004, No. 821, § 1, eff. Jan. 1, 2005.

REVISION COMMENT—2004

This Article is based on Civil Code Articles 2686 (as amended 1924) and 2024 (Rev. 1984). It applies to all leases that have an indeterminate term. This encompasses leases whose term has been established through Civil Code Article 2680 (Rev. 2004) and leases that are reconducted as provided in Civil Code Articles 2721–2724 (Rev. 2004).

Art. 2728.   Notice of termination; timing

The notice of termination required by the preceding Article shall be given at or before the time specified below:

(1) In a lease whose term is measured by a period longer than a month, thirty calendar days before the end of that period;

(2) In a month-to-month lease, ten calendar days before the end of that month;

(3) In a lease whose term is measured by a period equal to or longer than a week but shorter than a month, five calendar days before the end of that period; and

(4) In a lease whose term is measured by a period shorter than a week, at any time prior to the expiration of that period.

A notice given according to the preceding Paragraph terminates the lease at the end of the period specified in the notice, and, if none is specified, at the end of the first period for which the notice is timely.

Acts 2004, No. 821, § 1, eff. Jan. 1, 2005.

REVISION COMMENTS—2004

(a) This Article is new. It changes the law as explained below. It is derived from the general principle of Civil Code Article 2024 (Rev. 1984) which provides that "[a] contract of unspecified duration may be terminated at the will of either party by giving notice, reasonable in time . . ." In the interest of legal certainty, Civil Code Article 2728 (Rev. 2004) determines and defines this reasonableness rather than leaving that determination to be made by the courts on a case by case basis.

(b) Civil Code Article 2686 (as amended 1924) provided that the notice must be given "at least ten days before the expiration of the month, which has begun to run." This enigmatic provision is also problematic in that, inter alia, it would not work in leases whose term is measured by periods shorter than ten days, such as a lease by the week or by the day. Civil Code Article 2728 (Rev. 2004) replaces this provision with a set of rules that define the time at which notice must be given in a way that correlates with the length of the term of the lease that is to be terminated. Thus, in a year-to-year lease, the notice must be given at least thirty days before the end of the year (clause (1)); in a month-to-month lease, ten days before the end of that month (clause (2)); in a week-to-week or bi-weekly lease, five days before the end of the week or bi-weekly period (clause (3)); and in a lease by the day or by the hour, at any time before the end of the day or the hour (clause (4)).

(c) A notice given at the time specified in the first paragraph of Civil Code Article 2728 (Rev. 2004) causes the termination of the lease at the time specified in the second paragraph. The second paragraph provides that termination occurs "at the end of the period specified in the notice, and, if none is specified, at the end of the first period for which the notice is timely." For example, on September 15, 2005, a lessee gives notice of termination of a month-to-month lease that began on January 1, 2005. This notice is timely for terminating the lease on September 30, 2005 and will so terminate it if no other period is specified in the notice. However, if the notice provides that the lease is to be terminated on October 31 rather than September 30, then the lease will terminate on October 31. If the lessor does not want the lease to last until October 31, he can give his own notice of termination before September 20 and thus cause termination on September 30.

Art. 2729.   Notice of termination; form

If the leased thing is an immovable or is a movable used as residence, the notice of termination shall be in writing. It may be oral in all other cases.

In all cases, surrender of possession to the lessor at the time at which notice of termination shall be given under Article 2728 shall constitute notice of termination by the lessee.

Acts 2004, No. 821, § 1, eff. Jan. 1, 2005.

REVISION COMMENTS—2004

(a) This Article is new. It departs from the requirement of written notice prescribed by Civil Code Article 2686 (as amended 1924) in that it sanctions other forms of notice: (1) in leases of movables other than those used as residences; and (2) in the cases provided in the second paragraph.

(b) The second paragraph provides that "[i]n all cases," that is, even in leases of immovables or movables used as residence, surrender of possession to the lessor shall be deemed a sufficient notice of termination by the lessee, provided it is timely under Civil Code Article 2728 (Rev. 2004). This rule is consistent with Louisiana jurisprudence. See e.g., Lafayette Realty Co. v. Travia, 11 Orleans App. 275 (La.App. Orleans 1914).

Arts. 2730 to 2744. [Blank]

CHAPTER 5—OF THE LETTING OUT OF LABOR OR INDUSTRY

Art. 2745. Kinds of lease of services or labor

Labor may be let out in three ways:

1.   Laborers may hire their services to another person.

2.   Carriers and watermen hire out their services for the conveyance either of persons or of goods and merchandise.

3.   Workmen hire out their labor or industry to make buildings or other works.

SECTION 1—OF THE HIRING OF SERVANTS AND LABORERS

Art. 2746. Limited duration of contract

A man can only hire out his services for a certain limited time, or for the performance of a certain enterprise.

Art. 2747. Contract of servant terminable at will of parties

A man is at liberty to dismiss a hired servant attached to his person or family, without assigning any reason for so doing. The servant is also free to depart without assigning any cause.

Art. 2748. Contract of farm or factory laborer, restrictions on termination

Laborers, who hire themselves out to serve on plantations or to work in manufactures, have not the right of leaving the person who has hired them, nor can they be sent away by the proprietor, until the time has expired during which they had agreed to serve, unless good and just causes can be assigned.

Art. 2749. Liability for dismissal of laborer without cause

If, without any serious ground of complaint, a man should send away a laborer whose services he has hired for a certain time, before that time has expired, he shall be bound to pay to such laborer the whole of the salaries which he would have been entitled to receive, had the full term of his services arrived.

Art. 2750. Liability of laborer leaving employment without cause

But if, on the other hand, a laborer, after having hired out his services, should leave his employer before the time of his engagement has expired, without having any just cause of complaint against his employer, the laborer shall then forfeit all the wages that may be due to him, and shall moreover be compelled to repay all the money he has received, either as due for his wages, or in advance thereof on the running year or on the time of his engagement.

SECTION 2—OF CARRIERS AND WATERMEN

Art. 2751.   Obligations of carriers and watermen

Carriers and watermen are subject, with respect to the safe keeping and preservation of the things intrusted to them, to the same obligations and duties which are imposed on tavern keepers in the title: Of Deposit and Sequestration.

Art. 2752.   Liability for things delivered for shipment

They are answerable, not only for what they have actually received in their vessel or vehicle, but also for what has been delivered to them at the port or place of deposit, to be placed in the vessel or carriage.

Art. 2753.   Birth of child during sea voyage

The price of a passage agreed to be paid by a women [woman], for going by sea from one country to another, shall not be increased in case the woman has a child during the voyage, whether her pregnancy was known or not by the master of the ship.

Art. 2754.   Liability for loss or damage

Carriers and waterman [watermen] are liable for the loss or damage of the things intrusted to their care, unless they can prove that such loss or damage has been occasioned by accidental and uncontrollable events.

Art. 2755.   Master's and crew's privilege on vessel for payment of wages

The masters of ships and other vessels, and their crews, have a privilege on the ship, for the wages due to them on the last voyage.

SECTION 3—OF CONSTRUCTING BUILDINGS ACCORDING TO PLOTS, AND OTHER WORKS BY THE JOB, AND OF FURNISHING MATERIALS

Art. 2756.   Building by plot and work by job, definitions

To build by a plot, or to work by the job, is to undertake a building or a work for a certain stipulated price.

Art. 2757.   Agreement to furnish work or materials or both

A person, who undertakes to make a work, may agree, either to furnish his work and industry alone, or to furnish also the materials necessary for such a work.

Art. 2758.   Destruction of work before delivery, liability of contractor furnishing materials

When the undertaker furnishes the materials for the work, if the work be destroyed, in whatever manner it may happen, previous to its being delivered to the owner, the loss shall be sustained by the undertaker, unless the proprietor be in default for not receiving it, though duly notified to do so.

Art. 2759. Destruction of work before delivery, liability of contractor furnishing work only

When the undertaker only furnishes his work and industry, should the thing be destroyed, the undertaker is only liable in case the loss has been occasioned by his fault.

Art. 2760. Destruction of work before delivery, contractor's right to payment of salary

In the case mentioned in the preceding article, if the thing be destroyed by accident, and not owing to any fault of the undertaker, before the same be delivered, and without the owner be [being] in default for not receiving it, the undertaker shall not be entitled to his salaries, unless the destruction be owing to the badness of the materials used in the building.

Art. 2761. Delivery of work in separate parts

If the work be composed of detached pieces, or made at the rate of so much a measure, the parts may be delivered separately; and that delivery shall be presumed to have taken place, if the proprietor has paid to the undertaker the price due for the parts of the work which have already been completed.

Art. 2762. Liability of contractor for damages due to badness of workmanship

If a building, which an architect or other workman has undertaken to make by the job, should fall to ruin either in whole or in part, on account of the badness of the workmanship, the architect or undertaker shall bear the loss if the building falls to ruin in the course of ten years, if it be a stone or brick building, and of five years if it be built in wood or with frames filled with bricks.

Art. 2763. Changes or extensions of original plans, effect

When an architect or other workman has undertaken the building of a house by the job, according to a plot agreed on between him and the owner of the ground, he can not claim an increase of the price agreed on, on the plea of the original plot having been changed and extended, unless he can prove that such changes have been made in compliance with the wishes of the owner.

Art. 2764. Substantial and necessary alterations

An exception is made to the above provision, in a case where the alteration or increase is so great, that it can not be supposed to have been made without the knowledge of the owner, and also where the alteration or increase was necessary and has not been foreseen.

Art. 2765. Cancellation of contract by owner

The proprietor has a right to cancel at pleasure the bargain he has made, even in case the work has already been commenced, by paying the undertaker for the expense and labor already incurred, and such damages as the nature of the case may require.

Art. 2766. Termination of contract by death of workman

Contracts for hiring out work are canceled by the death of the workman, architect or undertaker, unless the proprietor should consent that the work should be continued by the heir or heirs of the architect, or by workmen employed for that purpose by the heirs.

Art. 2767. Payment to heirs of contractor for work or materials completed

The proprietor is only bound, in the former case, to pay to the heirs of the undertaker the value of the work that has already been done and that of the materials already prepared, proportionably to the price agreed on, in case such work and materials may be useful to him.

Art. 2768.   Contractor's liability for acts of employees

The undertaker is responsible for the acts of the persons employed by him.

Art. 2769.   Contractor's liability for non-compliance with contract

If an undertaker fails to do the work he has contracted to do, or if he does not execute it in the manner and at the time he has agreed to do it, he shall be liable in damages for the losses that may ensue from his non-compliance with his contract.

Art. 2770.   Workmen employed by contractor, rights against owner

Masons, carpenters and other workmen, who have been employed in the construction of a building or other works, undertaken by the job, have their action against the proprietor of the house on which they have worked, only for the sum which may be due by him to the undertaker at the time their action is commenced.

Art. 2771.   Masons, carpenters and other artificers as contractors

Masons, carpenters, blacksmiths and all other artificers, who undertake work by the job, are bound by the provisions contained in the present section, for they may be considered as undertakers each in his particular line of business.

Art. 2772.   Privilege of contractors, laborers and materialmen; settlement of accounts

The undertaker has a privilege, for the payment of his labor, on the building or other work, which he may have constructed.

Workmen employed immediately by the owner, in the construction or repair of any building, have the same privilege.

Every mechanic, workman or other person doing or performing any work towards the erection, construction or finishing of any building erected under a contract between the owner and builder or other person, (whether such work shall be performed as journeyman, laborer, cartman, subcontractor or otherwise,) whose demand for work and labor done and performed towards the erection of such building has not been paid and satisfied, may deliver to the owner of such building an attested account of the amount and value of the work and labor thus performed and remaining unpaid; and thereupon, such owner shall retain out of his subsequent payments to the contractor the amount of such work and labor, for the benefit of the person so performing the same.

Whenever any account of labor performed on a building erected under a contract as aforesaid, shall be placed in the hands of the owner or his authorized agent, it shall be his duty to furnish his contractor with a copy of such papers, in order that if there be any disagreement between such contractor and his creditor, they may, by amicable adjustment between themselves or by arbitration, ascertain the true sum due; and if the contractor shall not, within ten days after the receipt of such papers, give the owner written notice that he intends to dispute the claim, or if, in ten days after giving such notice, he shall refuse or neglect to have the matter adjusted as aforesaid, he shall be considered as assenting to the demand, and the owner shall pay the same when it becomes due.

If any such contractor shall dispute the claim of his journeyman or other person for work or labor performed as aforesaid, and if the matter can not be adjusted amicably between themselves, it shall be submitted, on the agreement of both parties, to the arbitrament of three disinterested persons, one to be chosen by each of the parties, and one by the two thus chosen; the decision, in writing, of such three persons, or any two of them, shall be final and conclusive in the case submitted.

Whenever the amount due shall be adjusted and ascertained as above provided, if the contractor shall not, within ten days after it is so adjusted and ascertained, pay the sum due to his creditor with the costs incurred, the owner shall pay the same out of the funds as provided; and the amount due may be recovered from the owner by the creditor of the contractor, and the creditor shall be entitled to the same

665

privileges as the contractor, to whose rights the creditor shall have been subrogated, to the extent in value of any balance due by the owner to his contractor under the contract with him, at the time of the notice first given as aforesaid, or subsequently accruing to such contractor under the same, if such amount shall be less than the sum due from the contractor to his creditor.

All the foregoing provisions shall apply to the person furnishing materials of any kind to be used in the performance of any work or construction of any building, as well as the work done and performed towards such building, by any mechanic or workman; and the proceedings shall be had on the account, duly attested, of such person furnishing materials, and the same liabilities incurred by, and enforced against the contractor or owner of such building, or other person, as those provided for work or labor performed.

If, by collusion or otherwise, the owner of any building erected by contract as aforesaid, shall pay to his contractor any money in advance of the sum due on the contract, and if the amount still due the contractor after such payment has been made, shall be insufficient to satisfy the demand made for work and labor done and performed, or materials furnished, the owner shall be liable to the amount that would have been due at the time of his receiving the account of such work, in the same manner as if no payment had been made.

Art. 2773. Rights of workmen and materialmen against contractor and owner

Workmen and persons furnishing materials, who have contracted with the undertaker, have no action against the owner who has paid him. If the undertaker be not paid, they may cause the moneys due him to be seized, and they are of right subrogated to his privilege.

Art. 2774. Anticipated payments by owner to contractor, effect on rights of laborers and materialmen

The payments, which the proprietor may have made in anticipation to the undertaker, are considered, with regard to workmen and to those who furnish materials, as not having been made, and do not prevent them from exercising the right granted them by the preceding article.

Art. 2775. Contract exceeding $500, recordation essential for privilege

No agreement or undertaking for work exceeding five hundred dollars, which has not been reduced to writing, and registered with the recorder of mortgages, shall enjoy the privilege above granted.

Art. 2776. Contract under $500, recordation of statement essential for privilege

When the agreement does not exceed five hundred dollars, it is not required to be reduced to writing, but the statement of the claim must be recorded, in the manner required by law, to preserve the privilege.

Art. 2777. Privilege of workmen on ships and boats

Workmen employed in the construction or repair of ships and boats, enjoy the privilege established above, without being bound to reduce their contracts to writing, whatever may be their amount, provided the statement of the claim is recorded in the manner required by law; but this privilege ceases, if they have allowed the ship or boat to depart, without exercising their right.

TITLE X—ANNUITIES

CHAPTER 1—ANNUITY CONTRACT

Art. 2778. Annuity contract; definition

An annuity contract is an agreement by which a party delivers a thing to another who binds himself to make periodic payments to a designated recipient. The recipient's right to these payments is called an annuity.

A contract transferring ownership of a thing other than money for a certain or determinable price payable over a term is not an annuity contract.

Acts 2012, No. 258, § 1, eff. Jan. 1, 2013.

REVISION COMMENTS—2012

(a) This Article is new. Under this Article, an annuity contract for an uncertain period of time may be established by delivering to the obligee all kinds of things, corporeals and incorporeals, consumables and nonconsumables, movables and immovables. Modern civil codes, including the Quebec Civil Code, the Dutch Civil Code, the German Civil Code, and the Italian Civil Code are in accord.

(b) Under the principle of contractual freedom that prevails in Louisiana, parties are free to enter into contract whereby a person binds himself to make periodic payments to a designated recipient for a certain or determinable price payable over a term. Such contracts are not annuity contracts under this Article. They may be credit sales, or they may be innominate contracts governed by contractual provisions and general principles of law and conventional obligations.

(c) Article 2793 of the Louisiana Civil Code of 1870 defines the nominate annuity contract. In Louisiana practice, however, the word annuity is at times used to denote an annuity contract and at other times the same word is used to denote the right to the payments that derive from an annuity contract or other provision of contract or law. See C.C. Art. 3494(2) (Rev. 1983). See also C.C. Art. 593 (Rev. 1976) that refers to "the legacy of an annuity," namely, a testamentary provision intended to provide successive payments to a legatee.

(d) Article 2793 of the Louisiana Civil Code of 1870 contemplates two parties to the annuity contract: the first party delivers a sum of money to the second party who binds himself to make successive payments to the first party. In contrast, under C.C. Art. 2778 (Rev. 2012), the recipient of the payments may be a third person. In that respect, the annuity contract may be a stipulation pour autrui, a third-party beneficiary contract.

(e) C.C. Art. 593 (Rev. 1976) refers to "the legacy of an annuity," namely, a testamentary provision for successive payments to a designated legatee. In the absence of other provision, payments under such legacy to a natural person terminate upon his death and payments to a juridical person terminate upon the dissolution of that person. See Yiannopoulos, Personal Servitudes, § 1:7, § 4:34, § 6:4 (5th ed. 2011). However, a legacy of an annuity for a determined period of time may exceed the lifetime of the legatee and may be heritable.

(f) The contract of annuity in this Article is distinguishable from a legacy of revenues under C.C. Art. 609 (Rev. 1976). A legacy of revenues may be a charge on the succession of a deceased or a charge on specified property of the deceased. A legacy of revenues burdening specified property of the deceased is a real right and a kind of usufruct. See Yiannopoulos, 3 Personal Servitudes, § 6:4 (5th ed. 2011).

(g) The right to the stream of income from an annuity contract is an incorporeal. C.C. Art. 473 (Rev. 1978). Moreover, the annuity contract is itself an incorporeal. An action for an arrearage of an annuity payment is subject to a liberative prescription of three years. C.C. Art. 3494(2) (Rev. 1983).

667

Art. 2779. Applicability of the rules governing obligations

In all matters for which no special provision is made in this Title, an onerous annuity contract is governed by the Titles of Obligations in General and Conventional Obligations or Contracts, and when the contract provides for delivery of a thing other than money, it is governed by the Title of Sales. A gratuitous annuity contract is governed by the Title of Donations.

Acts 2012, No. 258, § 1, eff. Jan. 1, 2013.

REVISION COMMENTS—2012

(a) This Article is new. It restates a principle of existing law governing special contracts. Cf. C.C. Arts. 2892 (Rev. 2004) and 2927 (Rev. 2003).

(b) The definition of the annuity contract in C.C. Art. 2778 (Rev. 2012) indicates that such a contract is always at least partly onerous. In accord with that Article, this Article declares that a gratuitous annuity contract is governed by the Title of Donations. For application to an onerous donation of the rules peculiar to donations inter vivos, see C.C. Art. 1526 (Rev. 2008).

(c) An onerous contract transferring ownership of a thing other than money for a certain or determinable price payable over a term is not an annuity contract. C.C. Art. 2778 (Rev. 2012).

(d) According to this Article, in the absence of a special provision in this Title, an onerous annuity contract providing for delivery of a thing other than money is governed by the Title of Sales. An annuity contract providing for the transfer of a corporeal immovable may be rescinded for lesion beyond moiety. See C.C. Arts. 1965, 2589 et seq., and 2663.

Art. 2780. Recipient of payments

The recipient of payments under an annuity contract may be a natural person or a juridical person.

Acts 2012, No. 258, § 1, eff. Jan. 1, 2013.

REVISION COMMENT—2012

This Article is new. It is based upon C.C. Arts. 24, 26, 29 (Rev. 1987), and 549 (Rev. 1976; amended 2010) and restates a principle of existing law.

Art. 2781. Annuity for life or time period

The payments under an annuity contract may be for the lifetime of a designated natural person, or, alternatively, for a period of time.

Acts 2012, No. 258, § 1, eff. Jan. 1, 2013.

REVISION COMMENTS—2012

(a) This Article is new. In accord with Article 2794 of the Louisiana Civil Code of 1870, which declares that "[the] annuity may be either perpetual or for life" the payments under an annuity contract may be for the life of a designated recipient or for a period of time, certain or indefinite.

(b) The right to periodic payments under an annuity contract is heritable and assignable in the absence of contrary provision of law or juridical act. See C.C. Art. 2783 (Rev. 2012).

(c) An annuity contract is assignable and heritable. C.C. Art. 2783 (Rev. 2012). However, an annuity charge cannot burden an immovable beyond the limitations of time provided in C.C. Art. 2790 (Rev. 2012).

Art. 2782. Termination of annuity; absence of a designated term

In the absence of a designated term, an annuity established in favor of a natural person terminates upon the death of that person, but one in favor of a juridical person is without effect.

Acts 2012, No. 258, § 1, eff. Jan. 1, 2013.

668

This Article is new. According to C.C. Art. 2781 (Rev. 2012), an annuity established in favor of a juridical person may be "for a period of time." However, such an annuity cannot be for an indefinite period. In the absence of a designated term, an annuity established in favor of a juridical person is without effect because a substantive legal requirement for the formation of the contract has not been met.

Art. 2783. Assignable and heritable rights and obligations

In the absence of a contrary provision of law or juridical act, the rights and obligations of the parties under an annuity contract are assignable and heritable.

Acts 2012, No. 258, § 1, eff. Jan. 1, 2013.

REVISION COMMENTS—2012

(a) The obligations of the parties to an annuity contract are heritable and assignable. Accordingly, the obligations of the party bound to make payments do not necessarily end with his death. In the absence of other provision of law or juridical act, the obligation to make payments passes to his successors in the same manner as other debts. Correspondingly, in the absence of other provision of law or juridical act, the right of a designated recipient of payments for a term of years does not terminate on his death. On his death, that right passes to his successors.

(b) These provisions are suppletive. The parties to an annuity contract may freely provide that rights and obligations shall terminate upon the death of either party. Thus, they may provide that the obligation to make successive payments is extinguished upon the obligor's death or that the recipient's right to receive payments is likewise extinguished upon his death.

Art. 2784. Annuity in favor of successive recipients

An annuity may be established in favor of successive recipients.

Acts 2012, No. 258, § 1, eff. Jan. 1, 2013.

REVISION COMMENT—2012

This Article is new. It restates a principle of existing law. Cf. C.C. Art. 546 (Rev. 1976).

Art. 2785. Annuity contract in favor of several recipients of payments

An annuity contract may be established in favor of several natural persons, whether in divided shares or in indivision. When an annuity contract is established for the lifetimes of several recipients of payments in indivision, the termination of the interest of a recipient inures to the benefit of those remaining unless the annuity contract expressly provides otherwise.

Acts 2012, No. 258, § 1, eff. Jan. 1, 2013.

REVISION COMMENTS—2012

(a) This Article is new. It is analogous to the law governing the rights of several usufructuaries in indivision. Cf. C.C. Art. 547 (Rev. 1976). When an annuity contract is established for the lives of several recipients of payments in indivision, the termination of the interest of a recipient inures upon his death to the benefit of those remaining unless the annuity contract expressly provides otherwise.

(b) This Article contemplates the constitution of a single annuity contract for the lives of several natural persons in indivision. Accordingly, this Article does not apply when an annuity is established in favor of several recipients for a designated period, whether in divided shares or in indivision, or when an annuity is established in divided shares for the lives of several recipients. Furthermore, this Article does not apply when an annuity is established in favor of several juridical persons.

Art. 2786. Existence of recipient

When an annuity is established in favor of a natural person, that person must exist or be in utero at the time of the formation of the annuity contract.

When an annuity is established in favor of a juridical person, that person must likewise exist at the time of the formation of the annuity contract.

Acts 2012, No. 258, § 1, eff. Jan. 1, 2013.

REVISION COMMENT—2012

This Article is new. It restates principles of existing law. Cf. C.C. Art. 548 (Rev. 1976).

CHAPTER 2—ANNUITY CHARGE

Art. 2787. Annuity charge

An annuity contract transferring an immovable may provide for the establishment of a charge on the immovable for the periodic payments due under the contract. In such a case, the recipient in whose favor the annuity was established acquires a real right for periodic payments. The establishment of the annuity charge must be express and in writing.

Acts 2012, No. 258, § 1, eff. Jan. 1, 2013.

REVISION COMMENTS—2012

(a) This Article is new. It is intended to provide for Louisiana owners a modern, effective, and efficient tool for acquisition of financial resources as an alternative to the so-called reverse mortgage. The annuity charge is similar in nature to a legacy of revenues under C.C. Art. 609 (Rev. 1976).

(b) An owner may transfer immovable property to another person who undertakes a personal obligation to make periodic payments to the transferor or to another recipient. The parties may agree that the obligation will be a charge on the immovable that has been transferred. In such a case, the transferor acquires a real right for periodic payments over the transferred immovable property. The annuity charge is an incorporeal immovable subject to the laws governing immovable property and a real obligation under C.C. Arts. 1763 and 1764 (Rev. 1984). Accordingly, in order to be effective toward third persons, the annuity charge must be recorded in the appropriate public records as provided by law. See C.C. Art. 2788 (Rev. 2012), infra.

(c) In principle, the holder of the real right providing for periodic payments has an assignable right that he may dispose of as he pleases. If the immovable property is transferred to another person, the annuity charge continues to burden that property, and if the owner of the immovable fails to make payments, the annuity recipient has recourse against the obligor and the immovable burdened by the annuity charge.

(d) For security and certainty of transaction and acquisition, certain juridical acts, including the establishment of an annuity charge, must be express and in writing. Cf. C.C. Arts. 771, 963, 1839, 3038, and 3450.

Art. 2788. Annuity charge; recordation

An annuity charge on an immovable is without effect as to third persons unless the annuity contract establishing it is recorded in the conveyance records of the parish in which the immovable is located.

Acts 2012, No. 258, § 1, eff. Jan. 1, 2013.

REVISION COMMENTS—2012

(a) This Article is new. It accords with the principles established in C.C.Art. 3346(A) (Rev. 2005).

(b) In order to be effective against third persons, the contract establishing the annuity charge must be recorded in the conveyance records of the parish in which the immovable is located. This accords with the principles established in C.C. Art. 3346(A) (Rev. 2005). The annuity charge is not merely security like a mortgage or privilege; therefore, recordation of the annuity contract in the conveyance records is appropriate and required by law.

(c) Recordation of the contract establishing the annuity charge in the mortgage records is not required. Accordingly, an annuity charge recorded in the conveyance records is effective against third persons without recordation in the mortgage records.

Art. 2789.   Applicable law

In all matters for which no special provision is made in this Chapter, the annuity charge is governed by the provisions of Chapter 1 of this Title.

REVISION COMMENT—2012

This Article corresponds with C.C. Art. 2779 (Rev. 2012).

Art. 2790.   Annuity charge for life or time period

The annuity charge may not exceed thirty years, except that it may continue for the lifetime of a recipient who is a natural person.

Acts 2012, No. 258, § 1, eff. Jan. 1, 2013.

REVISION COMMENTS—2012

(a) This Article is new. The payments under an annuity contract may be for the life of a designated recipient or for a period of time. See C.C. Art. 2781 (Rev. 2012). In contrast, under C.C. Art. 2790 (Rev. 2012), the annuity charge may not exceed thirty years, except that it may continue for the life of a recipient who is a natural person.

(b) The right to periodic payments under an annuity contract is heritable and assignable in the absence of a contrary provision of law or juridical act. See C.C. Art. 2783 (Rev. 2012). However, an annuity charge cannot burden an immovable beyond the time limitations provided in this Article.

(c) The termination of the annuity charge does not affect the annuity contract for periodic payments. Accordingly, the personal obligation for periodic payments continues to exist until the termination of the annuity contract. See C.C. Arts. 2781 and 2782 (Rev. 2012).

Art. 2791.   Enforcement of the annuity charge

Upon failure of payment of amounts due under a contract establishing an annuity charge, the recipient may obtain judgment for the amounts due and may enforce the judgment by execution upon the immovable subject to the annuity charge in accordance with law.

The adjudication extinguishes the annuity charge for all amounts for which judgment was rendered as well as all charges and encumbrances on the immovable inferior to the annuity charge but does not extinguish the annuity charge for amounts thereafter becoming due under the contract.

Acts 2012, No. 258, § 1, eff. Jan. 1, 2013.

REVISION COMMENTS—2012

(a) This Article is new. It creates a legal framework for the enforcement of the annuity charge by judicial process when the obligor fails to render payments due. Execution will be governed by the applicable provisions of the Louisiana Code of Civil Procedure.

(b) The adjudication extinguishes the annuity charge as to all amounts for which judgment was rendered as well as all charges and encumbrances on the immovable inferior to the annuity charge. However, the adjudication does not extinguish the annuity charge for amounts thereafter becoming due under the contract. The annuity charge on the immovable property continues to exist for payments due under the annuity contract.

(c) If the qualities of obligee and obligor are united in the same person, the principles of confusion are applicable. See C.C. Art. 1903 (Rev.1984). Cf. C.C. Arts. 622, 765, and 3319(2).

Arts. 2792 to 2800.   [Blank]

TITLE XI—PARTNERSHIP

CHAPTER 1—GENERAL PRINCIPLES

Art. 2801. Partnership; definition

A partnership is a juridical person, distinct from its partners, created by a contract between two or more persons to combine their efforts or resources in determined proportions and to collaborate at mutual risk for their common profit or commercial benefit.

Trustees and succession representatives, in their capacities as such, and unincorporated associations may be partners.

Acts 1980, No. 150, § 1, eff. Jan. 1, 1981.

REVISION COMMENTS—1980

(a) This article presents the concept that a partnership is created by a contract of partnership, a nominate contract. In some instances the contract must meet formal requirements in order to produce the effects intended. For example, the contract of partnership must be in writing for the partnership to acquire immovable property, and it must be filed for registry for a partner to acquire an in commendam status regarding third persons. See Articles 2806 and 2841, infra and R.S. 9:3401, et seq. (Acts 1980, No. 151, § 1). The consensual element underlying the creation of a partnership distinguishes it from the fortuitous creation of a community of interest. Cf. C.C. Art. 2806 (1870). The contract of partnership is based upon a community of interest and gives rise to a juridical person distinct from its partners.

(b) Under this article any juridical person, such as a corporation, a partnership, or a natural person may become a party to a contract of partnership if not otherwise disqualified by law. Trustees and succession representatives, in their capacities as such, and unincorporated associations may be partners. See R.S. 9:2123. The exclusion of curators and tutors in the text of this article does not necessarily mean that they may not be partners.

(c) This article requires that each member of the partnership make a contribution. This is a traditional requirement. See C.C. Arts. 2801 and 2809 (1870) B.G.B. § 706; French Civil Code Art. 1833; Quebec Civil Code Art. 1830; Q.R.P. Art. 1. "Efforts or resources" as used in Article 2801 means contributions that have value in an economic sense and that may aid in the achievement of partnership goals; hence, a sham or meaningless contribution would not qualify under this article.

(d) The partnership is an entrepreneurial association and, as such, all partners have, in addition to organizational and managerial responsibilities, the responsibility to share the risk among themselves. The phrase "at mutual risk" reflects this concept.

Although certain other contracts, such as leases and employment contracts, resemble the contract of partnership, the risk element of the partnership contract is one factor that distinguishes it from those other types.

The notion of mutual risk does not preclude the possibility of one or more partners agreeing to protect other partners against losses that the partnership may incur, although a stipulation of that kind would not affect third persons. See Art. 2815, infra.

(e) This article codifies a well-established rule of Louisiana jurisprudence. As a juridical person, a partnership is a legal entity distinct from the partners who compose it. Smith v. McMicken, 3 La.Ann. 319, 321–322 (1848); Trappey v. Lumber, 229 La. 632, 86 So.2d 515, 517 (1956). Among other things, a partnership has its own domicile, its own patrimony, the right to sue and be sued in its own behalf, and the capacity to make donations and to receive legacies and donations. See C.C.P. Arts. 78, 79, 83, 688, 692, 737, and 740.

Art. 2802. Applicability of rules of conventional obligations

The contract of partnership is governed by the provisions in the Title: Of Conventional Obligations, in all matters that are not otherwise provided for by this Title.

Acts 1980, No. 150, § 1, eff. Jan. 1, 1981.

REVISION COMMENTS—1980

(a) This article reproduces the substance of Article 2803 of the Louisiana Civil Code of 1870 and is consistent with the concept that a partnership is created by a contract. The contract must conform with the provisions of Title IV: Of Conventional Obligations to the extent that those provisions are consistent with the rules of this Title.

(b) The provisions of Chapters 1, 2, 4, 5, 6 are generally suppletive, that is, in accordance with the principle of Article 11 of the Louisiana Civil Code of 1870, parties may depart from the provisions of these Chapters that do not concern matters of public policy. Nevertheless, provisions such as contained in Article 2813, infra, deal with matters involving the public order and should therefore be construed as mandatory rather than suppletive. In some instances provisions may not be departed from not because they are "mandatory" but because they are "essential" as the proper legal frame for a particular situation. Article 1764 of the Louisiana Civil Code of 1870 contemplates such "essential" stipulations or provisions. Except for the provisions of R.S. 31:215 as provided for by section 2 of Acts 1980, No. 150, Article 2801, supra, is an example of a provision of which no departure is possible because it is essential. The suppletive nature of a provision is at times indicated by the expression "unless otherwise agreed" or other words to the same effect, but the absence of such wording does not necessarily indicate that the provision in question is mandatory or is not suppletive. Courts ultimately determine which matters involve public policy. It is clear that provisions concerning ownership of immovable property and protection of the interests of third parties are matters of public policy. See for example Arts. 2806, 2833 and the provisions of Chapters 3 and 7.

Art. 2803. Participation of partners

Each partner participates equally in profits, commercial benefits, and losses of the partnership, unless the partners have agreed otherwise. The same rule applies to the distribution of assets, but in the absence of contrary agreement, contributions to capital are restored to each partner according to the contribution made.

Acts 1980, No. 150, § 1, eff. Jan. 1, 1981.

REVISION COMMENTS—1980

(a) The partners have complete freedom to contract regarding the manner and extent to which they are to participate in the profits, benefits, assets, and losses of the partnership. If the parties agree, the participation may be unequal, and it may differ among the four categories, namely, profits, benefits, assets, and losses. It is only when the parties have not agreed on fixed percentages that the parties are presumed to have intended equal participation.

(b) Contributions to capital are specially treated under this article in that unless otherwise agreed partners are entitled to the restoration of their contributions to capital even when the restoration might result in an unequal distribution or be disproportionate to the sharing of profits.

Art. 2804. Participation in one category only

If a partnership agreement establishes the extent of participation by partners in only one category of either profits, commercial benefits, losses, or the distribution of assets other than capital contributions, partners participate to that extent in each category unless the agreement itself or the nature of the participation indicates the partners intended otherwise.

Acts 1980, No. 150, § 1, eff. Jan. 1, 1981.

REVISION COMMENTS—1980

(a) If the partnership agreement sets the participation for only one category and is silent as to the others, the same participation applies to all categories unless the contrary is clearly implied.

Thus, if the agreement sets a partner's participation in profits at twenty-five percent, but does not refer to losses, nor to any other category, it is presumed that as between partners, his participation in losses, as well as in each other category, is twenty-five percent.

(b) The parties are free to determine who are to participate and to what extent and in which categories they are to participate; thus, the allocations and percentages may vary among the four categories of profits, losses, benefits, and assets. This article merely creates a presumption that applies in the absence of a pertinent stipulation.

(c) An exception is made in this article regarding the distribution of capital contributions. If the participation of a partner has been set for only one category, e.g., for profits, the presumption that the partner is to participate to that extent in other categories does not cover necessarily his participation in capital contributions. Unless the parties indicate otherwise, capital contributions are restored to partners proportionally, i.e., based on the percentage that the capital contribution of each partner bears to the total amount of capital contributions. See Art. 2803, supra.

Art. 2805. Name of the partnership

A partnership may adopt a name with or without the inclusion of the names of any of the partners. If no name is adopted, the business must be conducted in the name of all the partners.

Acts 1980, No. 150, § 1, eff. Jan. 1, 1981.

REVISION COMMENTS—1980

(a) If the partnership adopts a name, it is not necessary that the adopted name include the name of any partner or the names of one or more partners. If a trade name is adopted, however, the trade name statute should be complied with in all respects because this article does not supersede that statute. See R.S. 9:3406 prior to repeal and reenactment by Acts 1980, No. 151, § 1 and R.S. 51:281 and 283. This article is intended to remove any uncertainty that may have existed previously regarding any requirement that the names of partners be included in the firm or trade name.

(b) If no partnership name is adopted, the business must be conducted in the name of all of the partners. See C.C. Art. 2837 (1870).

Art. 2806. Ownership of immovable property; retroactivity of partnership's existence; acquisition of immovable property prior to partnership's existence

A.   An immovable acquired in the name of a partnership is owned by the partnership if, at the time of acquisition, the contract of partnership was in writing. If the contract of partnership was not in writing at the time of acquisition, the immovable is owned by the partners.

B.   As to third parties, the individual partners shall be deemed to own immovable property acquired in the name of the partnership until the contract of partnership is filed for registry with the secretary of state as provided by law.

C.   Whenever any immovable property is acquired by one or more persons acting in any capacity for and in the name of any partnership which has not been created by contract as required by law, and the partnership is subsequently created by contract in accordance with Title XI of Book III of the Civil Code, the partnership's existence shall be retroactive to the date of acquisition of an interest in such immovable property, but such retroactive effect shall be without prejudice to rights validly acquired by third persons in the interim between the date of acquisition and the date that the partnership was created by contract.

Acts 1980, No. 150, § 1, eff. Jan. 1, 1981. Amended by Acts 2005, No. 136, § 1, eff. June 22, 2005.

REVISION COMMENTS—1980

(a) According to Louisiana jurisprudence, the ownership of immovable property acquired in the name of a partnership, when there is no written contract of partnership, is vested in the individual partners. Madison Lumber Co. v. Pincheloup, 125 So. 175, 12 La.App. 196 (La.App.Orl.1929).

(b) Under prior law a commercial partnership could not own immovable property, whereas an ordinary partnership could own immovable property provided it had a recorded contract of partnership. Because the revision no longer recognizes the distinction between commercial and other kinds of partnership, any partnership may own immovable property if the contract of partnership is in writing at the time of acquisition. If the contract of partnership is written but has not been filed with the secretary of state, the contract of partnership is effective between the parties, but it is not effective toward third persons so as to enable the partnership to own immovable property with respect to those third persons.

(c) If a partnership attempts to acquire immovable property at a time when the contract of partnership is not in writing, the mere subsequent execution of a written contract of partnership would not transfer ownership of the immovable to the partnership. Instead, the partners would have to transfer the asset to the partnership by a separate act.

(d) As to third persons, if immovable property is acquired by a partnership that has a written, but unfiled, contract of partnership, the subsequent filing and registration of the contract of partnership with the secretary of state automatically vests the ownership of the immovable in the partnership; thus, the partners would not have to transfer the asset to the partnership by a separate act as would be the case if there were no written contract of partnership at the time of the attempted acquisition by the partnership.

Art. 2807.   Decisions affecting the partnership

Unless otherwise agreed, unanimity is required to amend the partnership agreement, to admit new partners, to terminate the partnership, or to permit a partner to withdraw without just cause if the partnership has been constituted for a term.

Decisions affecting the management or operation of a partnership must be made by a majority of the partners, but the parties may stipulate otherwise.

Acts 1980, No. 150, § 1, eff. Jan. 1, 1981.

REVISION COMMENTS—1980

(a) This article is new. Its rules are applicable only in the absence of contrary agreement. Decisions affecting the management or operation of a partnership are to be made by majority vote, each partner having a single vote, but the parties may provide for a different arrangement or for greater or lesser percentages. For example, the parties may give one partner complete managerial authority; likewise, they may stipulate that voting is to be by percentage interests instead of by heads, and they may require a two-thirds vote instead of a majority.

(b) This article requires unanimity on four types of major decisions. Decisions to amend the partnership agreement or to terminate the partnership are obviously of sufficient importance to require the unanimous agreement of partners. The same is true of a decision to admit a new partner. Article 2821, infra, permits a partner to withdraw from a partnership constituted for a term provided the partner has just cause for withdrawal or the other partners consent to the withdrawal. The consent required under Article 2821 is a unanimous consent, unless there exists a contrary agreement. Art. 2807, supra. If a partnership does not have a term, a partner need not have the consent of his partners to withdraw. Art. 2822, infra.

(c) This article does not require that a general meeting be held to vote on the decisions described in this article.

CHAPTER 2—OBLIGATIONS AND RIGHTS OF PARTNERS TOWARD EACH OTHER AND TOWARD THE PARTNERSHIP

Art. 2808.   Obligation of a partner to contribute

Each partner owes the partnership all that he has agreed to contribute to it.

Acts 1980, No. 150, § 1, eff. Jan. 1, 1981.

(a) This article is based on the first paragraph of Article 2856 of the Louisiana Civil Code of 1870. Articles 2856 through 2861 of the Louisiana Civil Code of 1870 deal with certain obligations of partners, such as those involving warranty, the payment of interest on money that the partner has agreed to contribute to the partnership, and the accountability of a partner for profits resulting from the exercise of his skill, industry, or credit when the skill, industry, or credit is owed to the partnership. The instances enumerated in those articles have not been retained because it was thought that to do so might unduly restrict the instances in which it is found that a partner owes an obligation to the partnership. Another reason for not retaining the enumerated instances is that the associated remedies are too restrictive. By eliminating the enumerated instances and remedies, more leeway is created so that appropriate remedies can be granted in situations that arise.

(b) The partnership agreement may stipulate penalties, and the partnership, as a legal entity, may sue a partner for breach of contract.

Art. 2809. Fiduciary duty; activities prejudicial to the partnership

A partner owes a fiduciary duty to the partnership and to his partners. He may not conduct any activity, for himself or on behalf of a third person, that is contrary to his fiduciary duty and is prejudicial to the partnership. If he does so, he must account to the partnership and to his partners for the resulting profits.

Acts 1980, No. 150, § 1, eff. Jan. 1, 1981.

(a) This article is new but is based upon Article 1901 of the Louisiana Civil Code of 1870 and upon Article 2862 of the Louisiana Civil Code of 1870. Article 1901 of the Louisiana Civil Code of 1870 requires good faith performance by parties to a contract. A contract of partnership is an agreement by which parties agree to join efforts in an attempt to produce profits or commercial benefits for the partnership, and the parties must perform their obligations in this regard in good faith. Article 2862 of the Louisiana Civil Code of 1870 makes a partner answerable to the partnership for damages suffered by it due to the fault of the partner, and this rule has been carried over in Article 2809 and Article 2810, infra.

(b) This article prohibits activities that are prejudicial to the partnership. The relationship of the partners is fiduciary and imposes upon them the obligation of good faith and fairness in their dealings with one another with respect to the affairs of the partnership. This fiduciary duty continues until the partnership is finally liquidated. This places the partner in a similar relationship to the partnership that a director holds to a corporation and its shareholders.

Consent by the partners or the partnership to permit activities that otherwise would be contrary to a partner's fiduciary duty should be given effect to avoid the consequences of this article only when the consent is given after there has been a full disclosure of all relevant information.

(c) If a partner engages in an activity in breach of his fiduciary duty, and profits result therefrom, for the partnership to recover the profits for which the partner is accountable, either the partner must be allowed to recoup his original investment in the activity or the partnership must contribute its share of the investment.

(d) This article does not exclude the remedy provided in Articles 2046 and 2047 of the Louisiana Civil Code of 1870 concerning implied resolutory conditions, whenever the necessary requirements are met.

(e) This article also does not exclude the possibility of injunctive relief in appropriate cases. See C.C.P. Art. 3601, et seq. See also Art. 2810, infra.

Art. 2810. Other rights not prejudiced

The provisions of Articles 2808 and 2809 do not prejudice other rights granted by law to recover damages or to obtain injunctive relief in appropriate cases.

Acts 1980, No. 150, § 1, eff. Jan. 1, 1981.

This article insures that the rights of the partnership against a partner are not limited to the recovery of profits resulting from a partner's breach of his fiduciary duty. The partnership may recover damages from the partner for the harm it has suffered.

Art. 2811. Partner as creditor of the partnership

A partner who acts in good faith for the partnership may be a creditor of the partnership for sums he disburses, obligations he incurs, and losses he sustains thereby.

Acts 1980, No. 150, § 1, eff. Jan. 1, 1981.

This article reproduces the substance of Article 2864 of the Louisiana Civil Code of 1870. A partner has the right to be reimbursed for expenses and losses incurred in good faith for the partnership. There is no right of reimbursement for services rendered by a partner, unless the partnership agreement so provides.

Art. 2812. The sharing of a partner's interest with a third person

A partner may share his interest in the partnership with a third person without the consent of his partners, but he cannot make him a member of the partnership. He is responsible for damage to the partnership caused by the third person as though he caused it himself.

Acts 1980, No. 150, § 1, eff. Jan. 1, 1981.

This article reproduces the substance of Article 2871 of the Louisiana Civil Code of 1870. In the absence of an express prohibition in the partnership agreement, a partner may associate a third person in his interest in the partnership, but the association would not make the third person a partner. This approach follows French Civil Code Article 1861; Quebec Civil Code Article 1853; Q.R.P. Article 18; and U.P.A. § 18(g).

Art. 2813. The right of a partner to obtain information

A partner may inform himself of the business activities of the partnership and may consult its books and records, even if he has been excluded from management. A contrary agreement is null.

He may not exercise his right in a manner that unduly interferes with the operations of the partnership or prevents other partners from exercising their rights in this regard.

Acts 1980, No. 150, § 1, eff. Jan. 1, 1981.

This article is new. Although it does not require the keeping of books and records by the partnership, it does set forth a rule of public policy that a partner has the right to inform himself of the conduct and the course of the business of the partnership. The partner may not abuse this right by causing undue interference with the operations of the partnership, nor may he prevent other partners from exercising the rights given to them by Article 2813.

CHAPTER 3—RELATIONS OF THE PARTNERSHIP AND THE PARTNERS WITH THIRD PERSONS

Art. 2814. Partner as mandatary of the partnership

A partner is a mandatary of the partnership for all matters in the ordinary course of its business other than the alienation, lease, or encumbrance of its immovables. A provision that a partner is not a mandatary does not affect third persons who in good faith transact business with the partner. Except as provided in the articles of partnership, any person authorized to execute a mortgage or security agreement on behalf of a partnership shall, for purposes of executory process, have authority to execute a confession of judgment in the act of mortgage or security agreement without execution of the articles of partnership by authentic act.

Acts 1980, No. 150, § 1, eff. Jan. 1, 1981. Amended by Acts 1981, No. 888, § 1; Acts 1989, No. 137, § 16, eff. Sept. 1, 1989.

REVISION COMMENTS—1980

(a) This Article establishes a relationship of mandate between the partnership and its partners. The scope of authority of the mandate created by this Article is limited to acts within the ordinary course of the business of the partnership. This Article abolishes the distinctions made in the Louisiana Civil Code of 1870 and in the jurisprudence between the commercial partnership, whose partners had the implied power to bind the partnership for acts within the ordinary course of its business, and the ordinary partnership, whose partners did not have that implied power. A partner who has no authority to act for the partnership due to a stipulation in the partnership agreement can bind the partnership if the third person with whom he deals neither knows nor has reason to know of the partner's lack of authority to bind the partnership.

(b) If the alienation, lease or encumbrance of immovables of the partnership is involved, the third person must inquire into and establish the authority of the partner who attempts to act as mandatory of the partnership. The article, however, does not apply to acquisitions that are all cash transactions.

(c) Although a stipulation to the effect that a partner is not a mandatary of the partnership does not affect third persons, the stipulation is nevertheless

Art. 2815. Effect of loss stipulation on third persons

A provision that a partner shall not participate in losses does not affect third persons.

Acts 1980, No. 150, § 1, eff. Jan. 1, 1981.

REVISION COMMENT—1980

This article renders the provision ineffective only with regard to third persons. As between the partners, the provision would be effective; hence, an agreement by which a partner agrees to protect another partner against losses for which the latter is liable by virtue of his membership in the partnership is enforceable between the partners. This changes the law. Under prior law, the stipulation would have been ineffective not only with regard to third persons, but also as between the partners themselves. See C.C. Art. 2814(1870). Allowing the stipulation to be effective between the partners is not inconsistent with defining "partnership" in a manner that requires the partners to collaborate at mutual risk because there is always a risk of liability toward third persons; a partner is liable toward third persons for his virile share of the debts of the partnership. Art. 2817, infra.

Art. 2816. Contract by partner in his own name; effect on the partnership

An obligation contracted for the partnership by a partner in his own name binds the partnership if the partnership benefits by the transaction or the transaction involves matters in the ordinary course of its business. If the partnership is so bound, it can enforce the contract in its own name.

Acts 1980, No. 150, § 1, eff. Jan. 1, 1981.

REVISION COMMENT—1980

This article reproduces the substance of Article 2874 of the Louisiana Civil Code of 1870. It imposes liability on the partnership for obligations contracted by a partner if the partnership benefits by the transaction or the transaction involves matters in the ordinary course of its business. If in those circumstances the partnership is bound to perform under the contract entered into by the partner in his own name, it follows that it also should have the right to enforce the contract in its own name.

Art. 2817. Partnership debts; liability

A partnership as principal obligor is primarily liable for its debts. A partner is bound for his virile share of the debts of the partnership but may plead discussion of the assets of the partnership.

Acts 1980, No. 150, § 1, eff. Jan. 1, 1981.

REVISION COMMENTS—1980

(a) This article sets forth the rule that creditors must look to the partnership first for the debts of the partnership. The partners are only secondarily liable. This continues the present jurisprudence, but the article adds a new provision to the effect that if a partner is sued on a partnership debt, the partner may plead discussion of the partnership's assets. A third person may sue the partnership and the partners at the same time, as provided in Article 737 of the Louisiana Code of Civil Procedure, but can recover against a partner who has properly pleaded discussion only if the partnership's assets have been exhausted or the partnership has been dissolved. By requiring the partner to plead discussion in order to get the benefit of having the assets of the partnership exhausted before there can be recovery against him, the article, in fairness to creditors, places the burden of pointing out partnership property on the partner.

(b) This article does not affect the principle in Article 737 of the Louisiana Code of Civil Procedure to the effect that a partner cannot be sued unless the partnership is joined in the suit.

(c) This article provides that each partner is bound for his virile share of the debts of the partnership. Prior law distinguished the liability of a member of an ordinary partnership from the liability of a member of a commercial partnership. A partner of an ordinary partnership had virile share liability, whereas a partner of a commercial partnership had solidary liability. Under the new law, there is no distinction between commercial and ordinary partnerships, and solidary liability has been suppressed, so that for all partnerships, each partner is liable only for his virile share. Except where solidary liability may arise in other contexts, such as in delictual matters in which solidary liability is imposed by operation of law, if a creditor of the partnership wants solidary liability, he is now required to obtain express agreement from the partners to the effect that they are solidarily liable for the debt.

(d) A partner's right of discussion is governed by Civil Code Articles 3045, 3046, 3047, 3048, and 3051, and Code of Civil Procedure Articles 3743, 5151, 5152, 5153, 5154, 5155, and 5156.

CHAPTER 4—CESSATION OF MEMBERSHIP

SECTION 1—CAUSES OF CESSATION

Art. 2818. Causes of cessation of membership

A. A partner ceases to be a member of a partnership upon: his death or interdiction; his being granted an order for relief under Chapter 7 or confirmation of a plan of liquidation or the appointment of a trustee of his estate under Chapter 11 of the Bankruptcy Code; his interest in the partnership being seized and not released as provided in Article 2819; his expulsion from the partnership; or his withdrawal from the partnership.

B. A partner also ceases to be a member of a partnership in accordance with the provisions of the contract of partnership.

Acts 1980, No. 150, § 1, eff. Jan. 1, 1981. Amended by Acts 2004, No. 827, § 1.

REVISION COMMENTS—1980

(a) This article substantially changes the law. Under prior law the occurrence of one of the enumerated events of itself may have terminated the partnership. Under the new law, the partnership itself does not terminate upon occurrence of the event unless there results one of the causes for terminating a partnership set forth in Article 2826, infra, such as the reduction of membership to one party. The effect of the occurrence of any of the enumerated events under the new law is to terminate the membership of the partner, not the partnership itself.

(b) The only voluntary cause of cessation of membership is withdrawal. There are two kinds of withdrawal, one with the consent of other partners and the other without their consent. The partner's right of withdrawal and the circumstances under which the right can be exercised, including the circumstances in which the consent of other partners is required, are given in Articles 2821 and 2822, infra.

(c) Causes other than withdrawal are involuntary. The death of a partner obviously terminates membership. In the absence of contrary agreement, the heirs of the deceased partner do not become partners but only inherit the interest of the deceased partner, which entitles them to be paid as provided in Articles 2823, et seq., infra. A partner may be expelled as provided in Article 2820, infra.

(d) The contract of partnership may provide for the termination of membership. For example, the partnership agreement may provide for mandatory retirement at a certain age, with resulting loss of membership, or it may contain a noncompetition clause to the effect that if a partner engages in business in competition with the partnership, he ceases to be a partner.

Art. 2819.   Seizure of the interest of a partner

A partner ceases to be a member of a partnership if his interest in the partnership is seized under a writ of execution and is not released within thirty days. The cessation is retroactive to the date of seizure.

Acts 1980, No. 150, § 1, eff. Jan. 1, 1981.

REVISION COMMENTS—1980

(a) This article is new. Under prior law, a seizure of a partner's interest effectuated a dissolution of the partnership. C.C. Art. 2823 (1870). Under the new law, the seizure does not operate to dissolve the partnership but only terminates the partner's membership if the seized interest is not released within thirty days. The seizing creditor is entitled to be paid as provided in Article 2823, infra.

(b) The seizure of a partner's interest ends his status as a partner only if the seized interest is not released within thirty days. This gives the partner time to negotiate a release of his interest and affords him some protection against losing his status as a partner due to a bad faith seizure.

(c) This article applies only to a seizure made under a writ of execution and does not apply to a seizure made under some other writ, such as a writ of attachment.

Art. 2820.   Expulsion of a partner for just cause

A partnership may expel a partner for just cause. Unless otherwise provided in the partnership agreement, a majority of the partners must agree on the expulsion.

Acts 1980, No. 150, § 1, eff. Jan. 1, 1981.

REVISION COMMENTS—1980

(a) This article grants the remedy of expulsion to the partnership when the conduct of a partner is detrimental to the interests of the partners or the partnership. Examples of conduct of a partner that would constitute "just cause" for expulsion would be failure to perform obligations, engaging in activities that prejudice the business of the partnership, or the willful or repeated breach of the partnership agreement. Unless stipulated otherwise, a majority of the partners must agree on the expulsion, and the partner against whom the expulsion attempt is made is to have a vote on the matter; thus, a sufficient number of votes must be cast in favor of the expulsion to amount to a majority vote of all partners.

(b) If a partner engages in conduct that constitutes just cause for expulsion, and damages result therefrom, the partner may be liable for the damages under Articles 2808, 2809, and 2810, supra.

(c) An expelled partner is entitled to an amount equal to the value of his share as provided in Articles 2823, 2824, and 2825, infra, even though he has been expelled for just cause. The value of his share is to be fixed as provided in those articles.

(d) The meaning of the term "just cause" used in this article differs from the "just cause" of Article 2821, infra, in that the just cause for expulsion under this article is not as restrictive as the just cause for withdrawal under Article 2821.

Art. 2821. Partnership constituted for term; withdrawal

If a partnership has been constituted for a term, a partner may withdraw without the consent of his partners prior to the expiration of the term provided he has just cause arising out of the failure of another partner to perform an obligation.

Acts 1980, No. 150, § 1, eff. Jan. 1, 1981.

REVISION COMMENTS—1980

(a) The requirement that a partner have just cause to withdraw from a partnership that has been constituted for a term is necessary because in those cases there is a greater likelihood that withdrawal prior to the expiration of the term would damage the partnership and prejudice the interests of the remaining partners. Just cause, however, is limited to causes that arise out of the failure of a partner to perform an obligation and does not cover the broader range of causes such as the hardship of a partner, the nonprofitability of the partnership, or the failure of the partnership to realize its objectives.

(b) A partner who attempts to withdraw without just cause remains liable as a partner and may be liable for resulting damages pursuant to Articles 2809 and 2810, supra.

Art. 2822. Partnership without term; withdrawal

If a partnership has been constituted without a term, a partner may withdraw from the partnership without the consent of his partners at any time, provided he gives reasonable notice in good faith at a time that is not unfavorable to the partnership.

Acts 1980, No. 150, § 1, eff. Jan. 1, 1981.

REVISION COMMENTS—1980

(a) If the partnership has not been subjected to a term, a partner can withdraw at any time that is not unfavorable, provided he gives reasonable notice in good faith. The failure to give reasonable notice in good faith at a favorable time would amount to a breach of the partner's fiduciary duty. Whether the notice is reasonable depends upon the circumstances. In some instances a few days or weeks notice may suffice; in other instances, several months may be required.

(b) If a partner attempts to withdraw under this article and does not give reasonable notice in good faith or at a favorable time, he remains a partner and therefore his liability as a partner continues. He may be liable for resulting damages pursuant to Articles 2809 and 2810, supra.

SECTION 2—EFFECTS OF CESSATION OF MEMBERSHIP AND RIGHTS OF THE FORMER PARTNER

Art. 2823. Rights of a partner after withdrawal

The former partner, his successors, or the seizing creditor is entitled to an amount equal to the value that the share of the former partner had at the time membership ceased.

Acts 1980, No. 150, § 1, eff. Jan. 1, 1981.

REVISION COMMENTS—1980

(a) In all cases of cessation of membership, whether voluntary or involuntary, the former partner or other interested person is entitled to be paid an amount equal to the value of the former partner's interest as of the time of cessation. The former partner is not entitled to an interest in the assets of the partnership but is only entitled to be paid an amount equal to the value of his interest as of the time his membership ceased. The value of the interest may be set by the partnership agreement or by separate agreement, or it may be judicially determined pursuant to the provisions of Article 2825, infra.

(b) The term "successors", as used in this article, includes heirs, assigns, or anyone standing in the shoes of the former partner.

Art. 2824.   Payment of interest of partner

If a partnership continues to exist after the membership of a partner ceases, unless otherwise agreed, the partnership must pay in money the amount referred to in Article 2823 as soon as that amount is determined together with interest at the legal rate from the time membership ceases.

Acts 1980, No. 150, § 1, eff. Jan. 1, 1981.

REVISION COMMENTS—1980

(a) The partnership is required to pay the former partner in money as soon as the amount can be determined. The rule that the partnership need only make a payment in money protects the partnership in that it does not have to partition its assets in order to make a payment in kind. The imposition of a requirement that the partnership make an in kind payment might seriously impair the viability of the partnership and might unduly prejudice the rights of creditors and the interests of remaining partners. This article does not prevent the partnership and the withdrawing partner from agreeing to an in kind distribution because the parties retain their freedom to contract in that regard.

(b) The amount bears interest from the time the party ceases to be a partner. The rate of interest shall be the legal rate of interest unless otherwise agreed. Although the amount may not be determined at the time of cessation, the partner's rights vest at that time; thus, this article provides that interest is to be computed from the time of cessation.

(c) This article is applicable only if the partnership continues to exist for purposes other than liquidation; thus, if the cessation of membership of a partner coincides with a cause of termination, or itself constitutes a cause of termination, this article is inapplicable even though the partnership continues to exist for purposes of liquidation as provided in Article 2834, infra.

Art. 2825.   Judicial determination of amount

If there is no agreement on the amount to be paid under Articles 2823 and 2824, any interested party may seek a judicial determination of the amount and a judgment ordering its payment.

Acts 1980, No. 150, § 1, eff. Jan. 1, 1981.

REVISION COMMENT—1980

This article permits the partners to agree on the value of the partnership interest, and the agreement may be made in advance either in the partnership agreement or by a separate agreement, or it may be made when the membership of the partner ceases. Subject to the provisions of Article 2802, infra, the agreement would be binding not only on the partners, but also on all interested persons. If there is no agreement, this article is broad enough to protect the interests of a creditor of the partner by permitting the creditor to have the value of the former partner's share judicially determined and to obtain a judgment ordering its payment.

CHAPTER 5—TERMINATION OF A PARTNERSHIP

SECTION 1—CAUSES OF TERMINATION

Art. 2826.   Termination of a partnership; causes

Unless continued as provided by law, a partnership is terminated by: the unanimous consent of its partners; a judgment of termination; the granting of an order for relief to the partnership under Chapter 7 of the Bankruptcy Code; the reduction of its membership to one person; the expiration of its term; or the attainment of, or the impossibility of attainment of the object of the partnership.

A partnership also terminates in accordance with provisions of the contract of partnership.

A partnership in commendam, however, terminates by the retirement from the partnership, or the death, interdiction, or dissolution, of the sole or any general partner unless the partnership is continued with the consent of the remaining general partners under a right to do so stated in the contract of partnership or if, within ninety days after such event, all the remaining partners agree in writing to continue the partnership and to the appointment of one or more general partners if necessary or desired.

Acts 1980, No. 150, § 1, eff. Jan. 1, 1981. Amended by Acts 1981, No. 797, § 1; Acts 1982, No. 273, § 1.

REVISION COMMENTS—1980

(a) A partnership terminates for the reasons listed in this article unless it is continued as provided in Articles 2827 and 2828, infra.

(b) A partnership is created by agreement and may be terminated by agreement. A partnership does not terminate when there is less than unanimous consent to that effect unless the partnership agreement so provides.

(c) Termination due to the bankruptcy of a partnership occurs when there has been an order of relief granted under Chapter 7 of the Bankruptcy Code. The mere seizure of the assets of a partnership does not effectuate its termination.

(d) If membership is reduced to one person, the entity no longer meets the definition of "partnership", which requires that there be two or more persons, but the business may be continued as a sole proprietorship as provided in Article 2828, infra.

Art. 2827. Continuation of a partnership

A partnership may be expressly or tacitly continued when its term expires or its object is attained, or when a resolutory condition of the contract of partnership is fulfilled. If the object becomes impossible, the partnership may be continued for a different object.

Unless otherwise agreed, a partnership that is expressly or tacitly continued has no term.

Acts 1980, No. 150, § 1, eff. Jan. 1, 1981.

REVISION COMMENTS—1980

(a) The intent to continue a partnership may be manifested by a declaration to that effect or it may be inferred from circumstances such as the continuation of the business of the partnership. If prior objectives have been attained or have become impossible, the adoption or pursuit of other objectives would evidence an intent to continue the partnership; thus, if the partners use the entity to pursue other objectives, a tacit continuation results.

(b) A partnership continued under this article is the same partnership created by the prior partnership agreement and is governed by that agreement. Creditors of the partnership are not to be prejudiced by the continuation of the partnership.

(c) The withdrawal of partners from a partnership after it has been continued is governed by Articles 2821 and 2822, supra. If, when the partnership is continued, it is also constituted for a term, and withdrawal of partners would be governed by Article 2821, supra. On the other hand, if it is not constituted for a term when it is continued, Article 2822, supra, would govern the withdrawal of partners.

(d) Article 2826, supra, provides that a partnership terminates in accordance with the provisions of the contract of partnership. It is impossible to list all the conditions that partners may choose to effectuate the termination of the partnership. This article applies to resolutory conditions in general, and once a resolutory condition of the contract of partnership is fulfilled, the parties may continue the partnership under this article, or they may waive the condition with the result that the partnership continues.

Art. 2828. Continuation for liquidation; sole proprietorship

When a partnership terminates, the business of the partnership ends except for purposes of liquidation.

If a partnership terminates because its membership is reduced to one person, that person is not bound to liquidate the partnership and may continue the business as a sole proprietor. If the person elects to continue the business, his former partners are entitled to amounts equal to the value of their shares as of time the partnership terminated, and they have the right to demand security for the payment of partnership debts.

Acts 1980, No. 150, § 1, eff. Jan. 1, 1981.

REVISION COMMENTS—1980

(a) This article provides that when one of the causes of termination occurs, the business of the partnership continues, but only for purposes of liquidation.

(b) The article further provides that when there is only one remaining person, the person may elect to continue the business.

In case the business is continued, former partners may demand security for the payment of the debts of the partnership. Since the withdrawing partners have virile share liability for debts incurred prior to withdrawal, they are accordingly given rights to demand security for the payment of those debts.

(c) If membership is reduced to one person, the former partners cannot compel liquidation if the sole ground for doing so is that the partnership has terminated because of the reduction; however, if there is some other ground for liquidation, such as the inability of the remaining person to furnish the required security, the remaining person can be forced to liquidate the business.

Art. 2829.   Change in number or identity of partners

A change in the number or identity of partners does not terminate a partnership unless the number is reduced to one.

Acts 1980, No. 150, § 1, eff. Jan. 1, 1981.

REVISION COMMENT—1980

This article presents a new concept. A change in the number or identity of the partners should not terminate a partnership unless the partners have so agreed. This rule is consistent with the concept that a partnership is an entity distinct from its partners. It prevents unfortunate results from occurring if partners and third persons continue to deal with the partnership after there has been a change in the identity or number of its partners.

SECTION 2—EFFECTS OF TERMINATION OF PARTNERSHIP AND RIGHTS OF FORMER PARTNERS

Art. 2830.   Effects of termination; authority of partners

When a partnership terminates, the authority of the partners to act for it ceases, except with regard to acts necessary to liquidate its affairs.

Anything done in what would have been the usual course of business of the partnership by a partner acting in good faith, who is unaware that the partnership has terminated, binds the partnership as if it still existed.

Acts 1980, No. 150, § 1, eff. Jan. 1, 1981.

REVISION COMMENTS—1980

(a) Once the partnership terminates, the partners who have knowledge of the termination no longer have authority to bind the partnership, except for purposes of liquidating it and completing the transactions initiated prior to the termination. Partners who have no knowledge of the termination can still bind the partnership for acts within what would have been its normal course of business. A partner who continues the business despite having knowledge of the termination cannot bind the partnership unless Article 2831, infra, is applicable. In any event, the partner who transacts business with knowledge of the termination is the principal obligor of any resulting obligation.

(b) The activities of liquidation include the concluding of business transactions, the realization of assets, the paying of creditors, and the division of net assets among the partners.

(c) A partner who transacts business with knowledge of the termination of the partnership may be liable for resulting damages pursuant to Articles 2809 and 2810, supra.

Art. 2831. Termination of the partnership; rights of third parties

The termination of a partnership, for any reason, does not affect the rights of a third person in good faith who transacts business with a partner or a mandatary acting on behalf of the former partnership.

Acts 1980, No. 150, § 1, eff. Jan. 1, 1981.

REVISION COMMENTS—1980

(a) This article is designed to protect the rights of a third person in good faith who transacts business with a partner or a mandatary acting on behalf of a partnership that has been terminated. If the third person was in good faith, he will have a right of action against the partnership and the person with whom he made the transaction. See Arts. 2814, 2815, 2817, and 2830, supra.

(b) The third person must comply with the other provisions of this Title. See Art. 2814, supra. The third persons' actual knowledge of the termination of the former partnership will be evidence of whether he was in good faith.

CHAPTER 6—DISSOLUTION, LIQUIDATION, AND DIVISION OF ASSETS

Art. 2832. Creditors of the partnership; preference

The creditors of the partnership must be paid in preference to the creditors of the partners.

Acts 1980, No. 150, § 1, eff. Jan. 1, 1981.

REVISION COMMENTS—1980

(a) Although this article basically reproduces the substance of Article 2823 of the Louisiana Civil Code of 1870, there is a subtle difference in its applicability because the seizure of the interest of a partner no longer terminates the partnership, but only the partner's membership if the seizure is not released within thirty days. Art. 2819, supra. The creditors of an individual partner do not, as such, have any claim to the assets of the partnership, but they do have a claim to the partner's interest in the partnership; consequently, judgment creditors may seize that interest.

(b) The creditors of the partnership can hold the individual partners liable for their virile shares under Article 2817, supra, but are on equal footing with other unsecured creditors of the partners.

Art. 2833. Division of the partnership assets

The creditors of a partnership shall be paid in the following order of priority: secured creditors in accordance with their security rights; unsecured creditors who are not partners; unsecured creditors who are partners.

If any assets remain after the payment of all secured and unsecured creditors, the capital contributions shall be restored to the partners. Finally, any surplus shall be divided among the partners proportionally based on their respective interests in the partnership.

Acts 1980, No. 150, § 1, eff. Jan. 1, 1981.

REVISION COMMENT—1980

This article makes the principles set forth in Articles 2803, 2804, and 2832, supra, applicable to the dissolution process. The order of priority for payment of partnership debts cannot be varied by agreement of the partners. The article sets forth as a matter of public policy the rule that unsecured creditors who are not partners are to be paid in preference to unsecured creditors who are partners. The rights granted to secure creditors under this article are consistent with the rights conferred upon them by other provisions of law.

Art. 2834.   Liquidation of the partnership

In the absence of contrary agreement, a partnership is liquidated in the same manner and according to the same rules that govern the liquidation of corporations.

A partnership retains its juridical personality for the purpose of liquidation.

Acts 1980, No. 150, § 1, eff. Jan. 1, 1981.

REVISION COMMENTS—1980

(a) Retaining the juridical personality of the partnership facilitates the process of liquidation and insures that the fiduciary relationship between the partners and the partnership continues until final liquidation. Retaining juridical personality also allows the liquidator to act on behalf of the partnership to recover assets and permits the creditors to institute proceedings against the partnership itself.

(b) The contract of partnership may provide for the appointment of liquidators and may set the manner and method of liquidation. For example, the partners may appoint one or more partners, one or more third persons, or a combination of partners and third persons, to serve as liquidators. This article applies only in the absence of a pertinent stipulation.

(c) Once a cause of termination occurs, the partnership is required to liquidate, unless it is continued as provided in Articles 2827 and 2828, supra. If the partnership does not liquidate after a cause of termination has occurred, any interested party may seek a court order directing liquidation and a judicial appointment of a liquidator. An "interested party" includes a partner, a third party creditor, an heir or assign of a partner, or any one who has a legitimate interest in the liquidation of the partnership. If the interested party has good reason for demanding liquidation, he may force liquidation even in case the partnership or the business has been continued as provided in Articles 2827 and 2828, supra.

Art. 2835.   Final liquidation

The liquidation of a partnership is not final until all its assets have been collected and applied to its obligations and its remaining assets, if any, have been appropriately distributed to the partners.

Acts 1980, No. 150, § 1, eff. Jan. 1, 1981.

REVISION COMMENTS—1980

(a) This article insures that the relationship of partners to the partnership, including their fiduciary relationship, does not end fully until final liquidation has occurred. A partner's obligation to the partnership continues with regard to those matters to be carried out in the liquidation process. This is consistent with the rule that the juridical personality of the partnership continues until final liquidation; consequently there is an attendant fiduciary duty of partners not to interfere with the orderly liquidation of the partnership.

(b) This article confers power and authority on the liquidator to handle the liquidation process until the assets of the partnership have been collected, the obligations of the partnership have been satisfied, and the remaining assets, if any, have been distributed.

CHAPTER 7—PARTNERSHIP IN COMMENDAM

Art. 2836.   Provisions applicable to partnerships in commendam

The provisions of the other chapters of this Title apply to partnerships in commendam to the extent they are consistent with the provisions of this Chapter.

Acts 1980, No. 150, § 1, eff. Jan. 1, 1981.

(a) This article states the principle that the general provisions set forth in Chapters 1–6 of this Title are applicable to partnerships in commendam to the extent they are consistent with the provisions of this Chapter.

(b) Because of the nature of the partnership in commendam and the manner in which it affects the interests of third parties, the provisions in this Chapter should be construed as mandatory. See Comment (b) of Art. 2802, supra.

Art. 2837. Partnership in commendam; definition

A partnership in commendam consists of one or more general partners who have the powers, rights, and obligations of partners, and one or more partners in commendam, or limited partners, whose powers, rights, and obligations are defined in this Chapter.

Acts 1980, No. 150, § 1, eff. Jan. 1, 1981.

REVISION COMMENT—1980

A partnership in commendam is a partnership that has one or more partners in commendam. The rules of this Chapter permit an existing partnership to receive one or more partners in commendam, and it also permits one or more parties to acquire the in commendam status at the inception of the partnership by being parties to the original contract of partnership, but at least one other party would have to acquire the status of a general partner by the original contract of partnership because the definition of partnership in commendam requires that there be at least one general partner.

Art. 2838. Name; designation as partnership in commendam

For the liability of a partner in commendam to be limited as to third parties, the partnership must have a name that appears in the contract of partnership; the name must include language that clearly identifies it as a partnership in commendam, such as language consisting of the words "limited partnership" or "partnership in commendam"; and the name must not imply that the partner in commendam is a general partner.

Acts 1980, No. 150, § 1, eff. Jan. 1, 1981.

REVISION COMMENTS—1980

(a) This article is new. It enables third parties, when inspecting the records of partnership, to be apprised of the fact that the partnership has partners in commendam in addition to general partners.

(b) The partnership in commendam may adopt any style or trade name, but must include the required identification language. Art. 2838. See Art. 2805, supra. If the name suggests that one or more partners in commendam are general partners, those partners are liable to third persons as general partners.

Art. 2839. Name of partner in commendam; use

A.   A partner in commendam becomes liable as a general partner if he permits his name to be used in business dealings of the partnership in a manner that implies he is a general partner.

B.   If the name of a partner in commendam is used without his consent, he is liable as a general partner only if he knew or should have known of its use and did not take reasonable steps to prevent the use.

C.   If the name of the partner in commendam is the same as that of a general partner or if it had been included in the name of a predecessor business entity or in the name of the partnership prior to the admission of the partner in commendam, its use does not imply that he is a general partner.

Acts 1980, No. 150, § 1, eff. Jan. 1, 1981. Amended by Acts 1984, No. 429, § 1.

REVISION COMMENTS—1980

(a) This article covers the use of the name of a partner in commendam in business dealings. A partner in commendam becomes liable as a general partner if he permits his name to be used in a manner that implies he is a general partner. The article is broad enough to cover cases in which the use of the partner's name involves its inclusion as part of the name of the partnership and also cases in which the use does not involve the inclusion of his name as part of the partnership's name. For example, in a particular business activity it may be asserted that the in commendam partner is a general partner, yet the name of the partnership may be correctly used when reference is made to the partnership itself. If in that case the remaining requirements of this article are satisfied, the partner in commendam would become liable as a general partner, not only with respect to the third persons involved, but also with respect to third persons in general. In other words, the partner incurs the same liability as a general partner, i.e., liability in general toward third persons. Of course, if the partner had not consented to this use of his name, he would not be liable as a general partner unless he knew or should have known of the use and did not take reasonable steps to prevent it.

(b) Article 2838, supra, governs the case in which the name of the partner in commendam is used in the name of the partnership that appears in the contract of partnership.

Art. 2840.   Partner in commendam; liability; agreed contribution

A partner in commendam must agree to make a contribution to the partnership. The contribution may consist of money, things, or the performance of nonmanagerial services. The partnership agreement must describe the contribution and state either its agreed value or a method of determining it. The contract should also state the time or circumstances upon which the money or other things are to be delivered, or the services are to be performed, and if it fails to do so, payment is due on demand.

A partner in commendam is liable for the obligations of the partnership only to the extent of the agreed contribution. If he does not make the contribution, or contributes only part of it, he is obligated to contribute money, or other things equal to the portion of the stated value that he has failed to satisfy. The court may award specific performance if appropriate.

Acts 1980, No. 150, § 1, eff. Jan. 1, 1981.

REVISION COMMENTS—1980

(a) This article continues the present status enjoyed by partners in commendam, namely, the privilege of limited liability to the extent of the agreed contribution with respect to third persons, the partners, and the partnership itself. A partner in commendam who has made the required contribution need not contribute more; thus, if that contribution is lost during the course of the activities of the partnership, the partner in commendam cannot be forced to make an additional contribution. Of course, if the partner in commendam has provided only a portion of the agreed contribution, he is liable for the balance. Darden v. Cox, 240 La. 310, 123 So.2d 68 (1960); Marshall v. Lambeth, 7 Rob. 471 (La.1844).

(b) This article continues and expands the rules governing the agreed contribution of a partner in commendam. The article clarifies existing law and recognizes the ability of a partner in commendam to perform nonmanagerial services as his contribution. The article also permits a method of evaluation to be given in lieu of a stated value so that the exact value need not be determined at the inception of the partnership or at the time the partner in commendam is admitted.

(c) The requirement that a contribution be made is a mandatory rule of public policy. If the agreement fails either to require a contribution or to describe it, yet otherwise meets the requirements of this Chapter, the partner is liable in the same manner as a general partner.

Art. 2841.   Contract form; registry

A contract of partnership in commendam must be in writing and filed for registry with the secretary of state as provided by law. Until the contract is filed for registry, partners in commendam are liable to third parties in the same manner as general partners.

Acts 1980, No. 150, § 1, eff. Jan. 1, 1981.

REVISION COMMENTS—1980

(a) This article continues the requirement of written articles and recordation, although recordation is no longer required in the principal place of business of the partnership. Shalett v. Brownell-Kidd Co., 153 So.2d 425 (La.App. 1st Cir. 1963), writ refused 244 La. 1004, 156 So.2d 57 (1963); Ray's Appliance and Air Conditioning Service, Inc. v. K & D Enterprises, Inc., 350 So.2d 228 (La.App. 3d Cir. 1977). Under the new law recordation is made in the office of the secretary of state. See R.S. 9:3401–3408 on Registry for Contracts of Partnership, as enacted by Acts 1980, No. 151, § 1. Notice to third persons is the principal object of the registry. Thus, if a contract creating a partnership in commendam is unregistered, the partner in commendam is liable as a general partner. Lachomette v. Thomas, 5 Rob. 172 (La.1843).

(b) The time requirement of Article 2847 of the Louisiana Civil Code of 1870 has been eliminated.

Art. 2842.   Restrictions on the right of a partner in commendam to receive contributions

A partner in commendam may not receive, directly or indirectly, any part of the capital or undistributed profits of the partnership if to do so would render the partnership insolvent. If he does so, he must restore the amount received together with interest at the legal rate.

If the partnership or the partners do not force the partner in commendam to restore the amount received, the creditors may proceed directly against the partner in commendam to compel the restoration.

Acts 1980, No. 150, § 1, eff. Jan. 1, 1981.

REVISION COMMENTS—1980

(a) Prior law restricted only the withdrawal of the contribution of a partner in commendam when the partnership was in failing circumstances, but the new law broadens that restriction to include not only the agreed contribution of the partner in commendam but also any part of the capital or undistributed profits of the partnership. To allow the partner in commendam to withdraw funds in circumstances in which the withdrawal would cause the insolvency of the partnership would be prejudicial to third party creditors and would be in derogation of the principle that the patrimony of the debtor, which in this case is that partner's interest in the partnership, is the common pledge of the creditors.

(b) Except as provided in this article, a partner in commendam cannot be forced to restore distributions he has received. For example, if a distribution were made at a time when the partnership was solvent, and the distribution did not result in insolvency, the creditors would not be able to compel restoration under this article.

Art. 2843.   Restrictions on the partner in commendam with regard to management or administration of the partnership

A partner in commendam does not have the authority of a general partner to bind the partnership, to participate in the management or administration of the partnership, or to conduct any business with third parties on behalf of the partnership.

Acts 1980, No. 150, § 1, eff. Jan. 1, 1981.

REVISION COMMENT—1980

This article continues the basic principle that a partner in commendam may not exercise the same rights and privileges available to a general partner. His role is that of a passive contributor whose powers are generally restricted to the protection of his interest. See Arts. 2844–2848, infra.

Art. 2844.   Liability of the partner in commendam to third parties

A.   A partner in commendam is not liable for the obligations of the partnership unless such partner is also a general partner or, in addition to the exercise of such partner's rights and powers as a partner, such partner participates in the control of the business. However, if the partner in commendam participates in the control of the business, such partner is liable only to persons who transact business with the partnership reasonably believing, based upon the partner in commendam's conduct, that the partner in commendam is a general partner.

B.   A partner in commendam does not participate in the control of the business within the meaning of Paragraph A of this Article solely by doing one or more of the following:

(1) Being a contractor for or an agent or employee of the partnership or of a general partner.

(2) Being an employee, officer, director, or shareholder of a general partner that is a corporation or a member or manager of a general partner that is a limited liability company.

(3) Consulting with and advising a general partner with respect to the business of the partnership.

(4) Acting as surety for the partnership or guaranteeing or assuming one or more specific obligations of the partnership.

(5) Taking any action required or permitted by law to bring or pursue a derivative action in the right of the partnership.

(6) Requesting or attending a meeting of partners.

(7) Proposing, approving, or disapproving, by voting or otherwise, one or more of the following matters:

(a) The continuation, dissolution, termination, or liquidation of the partnership.

(b) The alienation, exchange, lease, mortgage, pledge, or other transfer of all or substantially all of the assets of the partnership.

(c) The incurrence of indebtedness by the partnership other than in the ordinary course of its business.

(d) A change in the nature of the business.

(e) The admission, expulsion, or withdrawal of a general partner.

(f) The admission, expulsion, or withdrawal of a partner in commendam.

(g) A transaction involving an actual or potential conflict of interest between a general partner and the partnership or the partners in commendam.

(h) An amendment to the contract of partnership.

(i) Matters related to the business of the partnership not otherwise enumerated in this Paragraph, which the contract of partnership states in writing may be subject to the approval or disapproval of partners.

(8) Liquidating the partnership.

(9) Exercising any right or power permitted to partners in commendam under this Chapter and not specifically enumerated in this Paragraph.

C.   The enumeration in Paragraph B does not mean that the possession or exercise of any other powers by a limited partner constitutes participation by such partner in the business of the partnership.

Acts 1980, No. 150, § 1, eff. Jan. 1, 1981. Amended by Acts 1995, No. 847, § 1, eff. June 27, 1995.

REVISION COMMENT—1980

This article continues the consequence of loss of limited liability for violating the basic restrictions on activities of the partner in commendam, prohibiting him from managing or administering the affairs of the partnership. The article, however, does not prohibit a partner in commendam from advising and consulting with his partners, or from examining the progress of the partnership. See also Art. 2845, et seq., infra.

Arts. 2845 to 2890. [Blank]

TITLE XII—LOAN

CHAPTER 1—LOAN FOR USE (COMMODATUM)

Art. 2891.   Loan for use; definition

The loan for use is a gratuitous contract by which a person, the lender, delivers a nonconsumable thing to another, the borrower, for him to use and return.

Acts 2004, No. 743, § 1, eff. Jan. 1, 2005.

REVISION COMMENTS—2004

(a) This Article is new. It combines ideas expressed in Articles 2893, 2894, and 2895 of the Louisiana Civil Code of 1870. For the definition of nonconsumables, see C.C. Art. 537 (Rev. 1976); Yiannopoulos, Civil Law Property § 28 (4th ed. 2001).

(b) This Chapter governs "the loan for use" as distinguished from a "contract to lend." Ordinarily, the contract of loan for use is preceded by a promise or contract to lend. See 11 Planiol, Traite Pratique de Droit Civil Francais 445 (2d ed. Rouast, Savatier, Lepargneur and Besson 1954). Parties enjoy contractual freedom to enter into a contract to lend. Id. Parties may also derogate from the rules governing loan for use. The contract of loan for use may be for the benefit of either party or for the benefit of both parties.

(c) This Article does not state to whom the thing is returned because that matter is determined either by the contract or under the general law of obligations.

Art. 2892.   Applicability of the rules governing obligations

In all matters for which no special provision is made in this Title, the contract of loan for use is governed by the Titles of "Obligations in General" and "Conventional Obligations or Contracts".

Acts 2004, No. 743, § 1, eff. Jan. 1, 2005.

REVISION COMMENTS—2004

(a) This Article is new. It is based on Civil Code Articles 2438 (Rev. 1993) and 2990 (Rev. 1997).

(b) Article 2897 of the Louisiana Civil Code of 1870 has not been reproduced because the heritability of obligations is governed by Civil Code Article 1765 (Rev. 1984). Further, Article 2903 of the Louisiana Civil Code of 1870 has not been reproduced because compensation is governed by Civil Code Article 1894 (Rev. 1984).

Art. 2893.   Things that may be lent

Any nonconsumable thing that is susceptible of ownership may be the object of a loan for use.

Acts 2004, No. 743, § 1, eff. Jan. 1, 2005.

REVISION COMMENT—2004

This Article reproduces the substance of Article 2896 of the Louisiana Civil Code of 1870. It accords with C.C. Art. 2448 (Rev. 1993) governing sales. For things susceptible of ownership, See Yiannopoulos, Civil Law Property § 19–24 (4th ed. 2001).

Art. 2894.   Preservation and limited use

The borrower is bound to keep, preserve, and use the thing lent as a prudent administrator. He may use it only according to its nature or as provided in the contract.

Acts 2004, No. 743, § 1, eff. Jan. 1, 2005.

REVISION COMMENTS—2004

(a) This Article reproduces the substance of Article 2898 of the Louisiana Civil Code of 1870.

(b) There was an error in the English translation of the French text of Article 2898 of the 1870 Code. The words "in the best possible order" should be "as a prudent administrator." The error has been corrected in the revised text.

Art. 2895. Ordinary wear and tear; damage caused by the failure to keep, preserve, or use as a prudent administrator

The borrower is not liable for ordinary wear and tear of the thing lent. He is liable for damage to the thing lent caused by his failure to keep, preserve, or use it as a prudent administrator.

Acts 2004, No. 743, § 1, eff. Jan. 1, 2005.

REVISION COMMENT—2004

This Article reproduces the substance of Article 2902 of the Louisiana Civil Code of 1870.

Art. 2896. Use for longer time or in other manner

When the borrower uses the thing for a longer time or in a manner other than agreed upon, he is liable for any damage to the thing, even if it is caused by a fortuitous event.

Acts 2004, No. 743, § 1, eff. Jan. 1, 2005.

REVISION COMMENT—2004

According to the civilian tradition embodied in the Louisiana Civil Code of 1870 and in modern civil codes, the borrower is not liable for deterioration or even destruction of the thing lent as a result of ordinary wear and tear; he is liable, however, for loss attributed to his fault. Exceptionally, the borrower is also liable for loss resulting from fortuitous events when the borrower uses the thing for longer time or in a manner other than agreed upon. See La. C.C. Art. 2899 (1870); French C.C. Art.1881; Italian C.C. Art. 1805; Quebec C.C. Art. 2322; cf. German C.C. § 603; cf. Greek C.C. Art. 813. The policy underlying these Articles is that when the borrower violates his obligations and the thing is lost or damaged, the loss should be sustained by the borrower rather than the lender. In such a case, under continental civil codes the borrower is in default and there is a shift of the risk of loss. This accords with the general principles of the Louisiana law of conventional obligations. See La. C.C. Arts. 1873, 1874, 1990, and 1992 (Rev. 1984). See also Quebec C.C. Art. 2322.

Art. 2897. Loss caused by fortuitous event

When the thing lent is damaged by a fortuitous event from which the borrower could have protected the thing lent by using a thing of his own or, when being unable to preserve both things, the borrower chose to preserve a thing of his own, he is liable for the damage to the thing lent.

Acts 2004, No. 743, § 1, eff. Jan. 1, 2005.

REVISION COMMENT—2004

This Article reproduces the substance of Article 2900 of the Louisiana Civil Code of 1870.

Art. 2898. Valuation of the thing

When the contract of loan for use states a value for the thing lent, the borrower bears the risk of loss of the thing, including loss by fortuitous event.

Acts 2004, No. 743, § 1, eff. Jan. 1, 2005.

REVISION COMMENTS—2004

(a) This Article reproduces the substance of Article 2901 of the Louisiana Civil Code of 1870.

(b) It is implicit in this provision that when the parties appraise the thing lent, they intend to shift to the borrower the risk of loss of the thing lent, even loss by fortuitous event. There is no doubt, however, that parties enjoy contractual freedom to provide for the risk of loss of the thing lent as they see fit. Accordingly, the "unless" clause in the source Article is unnecessary and it has not been reproduced.

Art. 2899. Reimbursement for expenses

The borrower may not claim reimbursement from the lender for expenses incurred in the use of the thing.

The borrower may claim reimbursement for expenses incurred for the preservation of the thing lent, if the expenses were necessary and urgent.

Acts 2004, No. 743, § 1, eff. Jan. 1, 2005.

REVISION COMMENTS—2004

(a) This Article reproduces the substance of Articles 2904 and 2908 of the Louisiana Civil Code of 1870.

(b) The basic ideas expressed in Articles 2904 and 2908 of the Louisiana Civil Code of 1870 and in corresponding provisions of other civil codes are these:

(1) The borrower must bear the expenses that are incidental to the use of the thing. For example, the borrower must pay expenses for the transportation of the thing lent or for its storage and safekeeping. He may not claim reimbursement from the lender for such expenses. La. C.C. Art. 2904; French C.C. Art. 1886; Quebec C.C. Art. 2320(2); Italian C.C. Art. 1808(1).

(2) The borrower may under certain circumstances claim from the lender reimbursement for expenses incurred for the preservation of the thing lent. According to Article 2908 of the Louisiana Civil Code of 1870, the borrower may claim from the lender reimbursement for "extraordinary" expenses needed for the "preservation" of the thing lent that were "necessary" and so "urgent" that he could not give notice to the lender before incurring the expenses.

It follows that the borrower may "not" claim reimbursement: for ordinary expenses, even if needed for the preservation of the thing lent; or for extraordinary expenses needed for the preservation of the thing lent, unless they were necessary and so urgent that there was not time to communicate with the lender.

(c) The words "necessary expenses" are found in several articles of the Civil Code. See, e.g., La. C.C. Arts. 527 (Rev. 1979), 806 (Rev. 1990), 1257, 1259, 3217, and 3262 (1870). These Articles make it clear that necessary expenses are those incurred for the preservation of property.

Art. 2900. Liability of joint borrowers

When several persons jointly borrow the same thing, they are solidarily liable toward the lender.

Acts 2004, No. 743, § 1, eff. Jan. 1, 2005.

REVISION COMMENT—2004

This Article reproduces the substance of Article 2905 of the Louisiana Civil Code of 1870.

Art. 2901. Retaking before or after conclusion of use or expiration of time

The lender may demand the return of the thing lent after expiration of the term and, in the absence of a term, after conclusion of the use for which the thing was lent. In case of urgent and unforeseen need, the lender may demand the return of the thing at any time.

Acts 2004, No. 743, § 1, eff. Jan. 1, 2005.

REVISION COMMENTS—2004

(a) This Article reproduces the substance of Articles 2906 and 2907 of the Louisiana Civil Code of 1870.

(b) For other Civil Codes, see French C.C. Arts. 1888 and 1889; Italian C.C. Arts. 1809, 1810; Greek C.C. Arts. 816, 817; German C.C. §§ 604, 605; Quebec C.C. Art. 2319.

Art. 2902.   Lender's liability for damage caused by defects in the thing

The lender is liable to the borrower when defects in the thing lent cause damage or loss sustained by the borrower, if the lender knew or should have known of the defects and failed to inform the borrower.

Acts 2004, No. 743, § 1, eff. Jan. 1, 2005.

REVISION COMMENT—2004

This Article is new. It is based in part on Article 2909 of the Louisiana Civil Code of 1870.

Art. 2903.   Liberative prescription

An action of the lender for damages because of alteration or deterioration of the thing lent and an action of the borrower for reimbursement of expenses are subject to a liberative prescription of one year. These prescriptions commence to run from the day of the return of the thing.

Acts 2004, No. 743, § 1, eff. Jan. 1, 2005.

REVISION COMMENTS—2004

(a) This Article is new. It reflects articles in contemporary civil codes, including the German Civil Code and the Greek Civil Code. In the absence of the shorter prescription established in this Article, actions of the lender for damages on account of alteration or deterioration of the thing lent and the claim of the borrower for reimbursement of expenses would be subject to the ten-year liberative prescription under Civil Code Article 3499 (Rev. 1983).

(b) The short prescriptions of Civil Code Article 2903 (Rev. 2004) apply to actions of the lender for alteration or deterioration of the thing lent and of the borrower for expenses that he may have a right to claim under Civil Code Article 2899 (Rev. 2004). All other personal actions of the lender against the borrower and of the borrower against the lender are subject to other prescriptive periods provided in legislation. For example, delictual actions for the destruction of property are subject to the prescriptive periods provided for in Civil Code Articles 3492, 3493 (Rev. 1983), and 3493.10 (1999). Actions for the annulment of a contract, including the contract of loan for use, are subject to the five-year prescriptive period of Civil Code Article 2032 (Rev. 1984). Actions for violation of conventional obligations, including those arising under the contract of loan for use, are generally subject to the ten-year prescriptive period of Civil Code Article 3499 (Rev. 1983), unless otherwise provided by legislation.

(c) An action of the lender for the return of the thing grounded on the "contract of loan for use" is a "personal action" subject to the ten-year liberative prescription of Civil Code Article 3499 (Rev. 1983). Thus, when the borrower fails to return the thing to the lender at the termination of the contract of loan for use, the lender has ten years from that date to institute a personal action for the recovery of the thing. The lender, however, has also an imprescriptible real action, the "revendicatory action," for the recovery of his property. According to Civil Code Article 526 (Rev. 1979): "The owner of a thing is entitled to recover it from anyone who possesses or detains it without right and to obtain judgment recognizing his ownership and ordering delivery of the thing to him." This action, grounded on "ownership" rather than the personal obligation of the lender to return the thing lent to the borrower, is imprescriptible. See Songbyrd v. Bearsville Records, Inc., 104 F.3d 773 (5th Cir. 1997); Yiannopoulos, Civil Law Property § 358 (4th ed. 2001).

CHAPTER 2—LOAN FOR CONSUMPTION (MUTUUM)

Art. 2904.   Loan for consumption; definition

The loan for consumption is a contract by which a person, the lender, delivers consumable things to another, the borrower, who binds himself to return to the lender an equal amount of things of the same kind and quality.

Acts 2004, No. 743, § 1, eff. Jan. 1, 2005.

REVISION COMMENTS—2004

(a) This Article reproduces the substance of Article 2910 of the Louisiana Civil Code of 1870.

(b) For the definition of consumables, see C.C. Art. 536 (Rev. 1976); Yiannopoulos, Civil Law Property § 28 (4th ed. 2001). Parties enjoy contractual freedom to treat nonconsumables as consumables. Id.

(c) The loan for consumption is not necessarily gratuitous. Cf. Quebec C.C. Art. 2315.

Art. 2905. Ownership and risk of loss of the thing lent

The borrower in a loan for consumption becomes owner of the thing lent and bears the risk of loss of the thing.

Acts 2004, No. 743, § 1, eff. Jan. 1, 2005.

REVISION COMMENTS—2004

(a) This Article reproduces the substance of Article 2911 of the Louisiana Civil Code of 1870.

(b) For the transfer of ownership, see C.C. Art. 518 (Rev. 1979); cf. id. C.C. Arts. 2456 and 2457 (Rev. 1993). For the transfer of the risk of loss when a thing is sold, see C.C. Art. 2467 (Rev. 1993).

(c) This Article does not involve delictual liability. The "risk of loss of the thing" may be total or partial and refers to the obligation of the borrower to return to the lender an equal amount of things of the same kind and quality as those borrowed. See Civil Code Article 2904 (Rev. 2004).

Art. 2906. Loan of nonfungible things

A loan of a nonfungible thing, in the absence of contrary agreement, is not a loan for consumption, but is a loan for use.

Acts 2004, No. 743, § 1, eff. Jan. 1, 2005.

REVISION COMMENTS—2004

(a) This Article is new.

(b) Fungibles are things which according to law or the intention of the parties are interchangeable. Nonfungibles are things that are not interchangeable. See Yiannopoulos, Civil Law Property § 29 (4th ed. 2001). Ordinarily, fungibles are handled in trade by number, weight, or measure. See 3 Planiol et Ripert, Traite pratique de droit civil francais 63 (2d ed. Picard 1952).

(c) The words "fungibles" and "consumables" are not synonymous. A fungible thing may be consumable or nonconsumable and a consumable thing may be fungible or nonfungible. See Yiannopoulos, Civil Law Property § 29 (4th ed. 2001). Parties enjoy contractual freedom to treat consumables as nonconsumables and fungibles as nonfungibles. Parties may also treat nonconsumables as consumables and nonfungibles as fungibles. Id.

(d) Nonfungible things are ordinarily lent for use. Accordingly, in the absence of contrary agreement, a loan of a nonfungible thing is a loan for use. However, parties may agree otherwise, that a loan of nonfungibles will be a loan for consumption. In that case, nonfungible things are treated as fungibles and consumables.

Art. 2907. Loan of money or commodities

When the loan is of money, the borrower is bound to repay the same numerical amount in legal tender of the country whose money was lent regardless of fluctuation in the value of the currency.

When commodities are lent, the borrower is bound to return the same quantity and quality regardless of any increase or diminution of value.

Acts 2004, No. 743, § 1, eff. Jan. 1, 2005.

REVISION COMMENT—2004

This Article reproduces the substance of Articles 2913, 2914, and 2915 of the Louisiana Civil Code of 1870.

Art. 2908.   Lender's liability for damage caused by defects in the thing

The lender is liable to the borrower when defects in the thing lent for consumption cause damage or loss sustained by the borrower, if the lender knew or should have known of the defects and failed to inform the borrower.

Acts 2004, No. 743, § 1, eff. Jan. 1, 2005.

REVISION COMMENTS—2004

(a) This Article reproduces the substance of Article 2916 of the Louisiana Civil Code of 1870. Rather than making a cross-reference to Civil Code Article 2902 (Rev. 2004), Civil Code Article 2908 (Rev. 2004) repeats the language of Civil Code Article 2902 (Rev. 2004).

(b) Civil Code Article 2902 (Rev. 2004) governs the liability of the lender in the framework of the "loan for use." Civil Code Article 2908 (Rev. 2004) governs the liability of the lender in the framework of the "loan for consumption."

Art. 2909.   Inability to demand performance until expiration of term

The lender may not demand from the borrower the performance of his obligation to return an equal amount of things of the same kind and quality before expiration of the term. In the absence of a certain term or of an agreement that performance will be exigible at will, a reasonable term is implied.

Acts 2004, No. 743, § 1, eff. Jan. 1, 2005.

REVISION COMMENTS—2004

(a) This Article is new. It is based in part on Articles 2917 and 2918 of the Louisiana Civil Code of 1870.

(b) This Article accords with Article 1777 of the Louisiana Civil Code (Rev. 1984). Under that Article, a term may be express or implied. Performance of an obligation not subject to a term is due immediately.

Art. 2910.   Substance and place of performance

The borrower is bound to render performance at the place agreed upon. When the place for performance is not fixed in the contract, performance shall be rendered at the place where the loan is contracted.

Acts 2004, No. 743, § 1, eff. Jan. 1, 2005.

REVISION COMMENTS—2004

(a) This Article reproduces the substance of Article 2920 of the Louisiana Civil Code of 1870.

(b) The second paragraph of the source Article has no equivalent in other Civil Codes. It derives from the Louisiana Civil Code of 1808. Its source is the Projet du Gouvernement (1800), Book III, Title XV, Art. 28.

Art. 2911.   Payment of value when restitution is impossible

When it is impossible for the borrower to return to the lender things of the same quantity and quality as those lent, the borrower is bound to pay the value of the things lent, taking into account the time and place they should have been returned according to the contract.

When the time and place are not fixed in the contract, the borrower owes the value of the things at the time the demand for performance is made and at the place where the loan is contracted.

Acts 2004, No. 743, § 1, eff. Jan. 1, 2005.

REVISION COMMENT—2004

This Article reproduces the substance of Article 2921 of the Louisiana Civil Code of 1870.

Art. 2912.   Payment of interest in case of default

When the borrower does not return the things lent or their value at the time when due, he is bound to pay legal interest from the date of written demand.

Acts 2004, No. 743, § 1, eff. Jan. 1, 2005.

REVISION COMMENT—2004

This Article reproduces the substance of Article 2922 of the Louisiana Civil Code of 1870.

CHAPTER 3—LOAN ON INTEREST

Art. 2913.   Payment of interest presumed in release of principal

When the principal of the loan is released without reservation as to interest, it is presumed that the interest is also released.

Acts 2004, No. 743, § 1, eff. Jan. 1, 2005.

REVISION COMMENT—2004

This Article reproduces the substance of Article 2925 of the Louisiana Civil Code of 1870.

Arts. 2914 to 2925. [Blank]

TITLE XIII—DEPOSIT AND SEQUESTRATION

CHAPTER 1—DEPOSIT

Art. 2926. Deposit; definition

A deposit is a contract by which a person, the depositor, delivers a movable thing to another person, the depositary, for safekeeping under the obligation of returning it to the depositor upon demand.

Acts 2003, No. 491, § 1, eff. Jan. 1, 2004.

REVISION COMMENTS—2003

(a) This provision reproduces the substance of Articles 2926 and 2928 of the Louisiana Civil Code of 1870. It accords with corresponding provisions in modern Civil Codes. See Greek C.C. Art. 822; Quebec C.C. Art. 2280 (1). These provisions are, in the absence of contrary indication, suppletive. Accordingly, contracting parties enjoy a wide measure of contractual freedom and can derogate from these provisions.

(b) According to the Louisiana Civil Code and firmly established civilian tradition, the contract of deposit applies to corporeal movables only. See C.C. Art. 2928 (1870). There can be no deposit of incorporeals or of immovable property. However, incorporeals that are evidenced by, or incorporated in, a document, a token, or other item that is susceptible of delivery to another person may become objects of a contract of deposit. In such cases, the thing deposited is a corporeal movable that evidences, represents, or even embodies a right or obligation. Accordingly, things such as stock certificates, investment certificates, and even certificate s of deposit, may be deposited.

(c) According to the Louisiana Civil Code, a "person" may be a human being or a juridical person, that is, an entity possessing juridical personality, such as a corporation or a partnership. See C.C. Art. 24 (Rev. 1987). Accordingly, depositors and depositaries may be natural persons or juridical persons.

(d) The word "delivers" in Civil Code Article 2926 (Rev. 2003), signifies the transfer by the depositor to the depositary of the physical control of a corporeal movable. The depositary thus becomes a precarious possessor. He exercises possession on behalf of the depositor. See C.C. Arts. 3437–3440 (Rev. 1982).

(e) The provisions of the Louisiana Civil Code governing the contract of deposit apply to what may be described as "civil law" deposit. The word "deposit" is also used in a variety of commercial relations and transactions that are subject to special legislation rather than the provisions of the Civil Code. For example, warehouse deposits, deposits of goods carried under bills of lading, and deposits of securities at savings and investment institutions are governed by commercial laws and regulations.

Art. 2927. Applicability of the rules governing obligations

In matters for which no special provision is made in this Title, the contract of deposit is governed by the Titles of "Obligations in General" and "Conventional Obligations or Contracts".

Acts 2003, No. 491, § 1, eff. Jan. 1, 2004.

Art. 2928. Nature of the contract

The contract of deposit may be either onerous or gratuitous. It is gratuitous in the absence of contrary agreement, custom, or usage.

Acts 2003, No. 491, § 1, eff. Jan. 1, 2004.

REVISION COMMENTS—2003

(a) This provision is new. Under the Louisiana Civil Code of 1870, the deposit is always gratuitous. Under that Code, a "deposit for remuneration" is a contract for services other than deposit. See C. C. Art. 2929 (1870). Civil Code Article 2928 (Rev. 2003) changes the law in accordance with contemporary needs and the provisions of modern civil codes. See, e.g., Greek C.C. Art. 822; Quebec C.C. Art. 2280 (2).

(b) Quite frequently, things are delivered by one person to another in the framework of a contract for services or repairs. For example, a car is delivered to a parking attendant for parking or a television set is delivered to a repairman for repairs. In these circumstances, certain Louisiana courts have at times applied, without good reason, the provisions of the Louisiana Civil Code governing deposit. In reality, such contracts for services or repairs are quite different from contracts of deposit and should be governed by the agreement of the parties, the provisions governing particular nominate contracts (other than deposit), and the general law of obligations.

(c) "Usage" is defined in C.C. Art. 2055 (Rev. 1984).

Art. 2929.   Formation of the contract; delivery

The formation of a contract of deposit requires, besides an agreement, the delivery of the thing to the depositary.

Acts 2003, No. 491, § 1, eff. Jan. 1, 2004.

REVISION COMMENTS—2003

(a) This provision reproduces the substance of Article 2930 of the Louisiana Civil Code of 1870. Changes in terminology are not intended to change the law.

(b) According to firmly established civilian doctrine, the contract of deposit is a "real" contract, that is, a contract perfected by the delivery of the thing to the depositary. Prior to delivery, there is no contract of deposit, but there may be a variety of legal relations between the parties. For example, the parties may have exchanged offers to enter into a contract of deposit, they may have concluded a contract to deposit, or they may have exchanged unilateral promises to deliver or to accept a thing in deposit. In this respect, the law of sales offers useful analogies.

(c) The word "delivery" in Article 2929 signifies the transfer by the depositor to the depositary of the physical control of a corporeal movable. The depositary thus becomes a precarious possessor. He exercises possession on behalf of the depositor. See C.C. Arts. 3437–3440 (Rev. 1982). As under the 1870 Code, the delivery may be actual or fictitious. It is actual, when the depositor transfers the possession of the thing to the depositary. It is fictitious, when the thing is already in the possession of the depositary at the time the contract of deposit is made.

Art. 2930.   Diligence and prudence required

When the deposit is onerous, the depositary is bound to fulfill his obligations with diligence and prudence.

When the deposit is gratuitous, the depositary is bound to fulfill his obligations with the same diligence and prudence in caring for the thing deposited that he uses for his own property.

Whether the deposit is gratuitous or onerous, the depositary is liable for the loss that the depositor sustains as a result of the depositary's failure to perform such obligations.

Acts 2003, No. 491, § 1, eff. Jan. 1, 2004.

REVISION COMMENTS—2003

(a) This provision is new. The first paragraph establishes the principle that a compensated depositary is bound to fulfill his obligations under the contract of deposit with diligence and care. Accordingly, the depositor is liable to the depositary for the loss that the depositor sustains as a result of the depositary's failure to fulfill his obligations. However, the second paragraph, following Article 2937 of the Louisiana Civil Code of 1870 and modern civil codes, relieves a gratuitous depositary from liability for the loss that the depositor sustains, if the depositary exercises the same diligence and care for the thing deposited that he exercises for his own property. Analogous solutions have been adopted with respect to onerous and gratuitous mandataries. See C.C. Arts. 3001 and 3002 (Rev. 1997).

(b) According to well-established civilian tradition and Article 2937 of the Louisiana Civil Code of 1870, a gratuitous depositary is held to a lighter standard of care than a compensated depositary. A gratuitous depositary is held to the standard of diligentia quam in suis (the same care that he exercises for his own property). This means that if he is neglectful in his own affairs, he is not expected to be more careful in caring for the property of the depositor. A compensated depositary, however, is held to a higher standard of care, that of diligent and prudent depositary. Such a depositary is liable for any failure to perform and he is not excused if he is neglectful in the care of his own property.

(c) Neither the gratuitous nor the onerous depositary is liable for loss or deterioration of the thing deposited that has resulted from an "irresistible force," that is, force majeure, in the absence of a special undertaking. This is a general principle of the law of obligations that need not be restated. Cf. C.C. Arts. 1873–1878 (Rev. 1984).

(d) This provision determines the liability of the depositary under the contract of deposit. This liability is contractual and is not exclusive of other forms of liability. Obviously, in addition to contractual liability, a depositary may incur liability under other provisions of law, including delictual liability for negligence or intentional misconduct.

Art. 2931. Use of the thing deposited

The depositary may not use the thing deposited without the express or implied permission of the depositor.

Acts 2003, No. 491, § 1, eff. Jan. 1, 2004.

REVISION COMMENT—2003

This provision reproduces the substance of Article 2940 of the Louisiana Civil Code of 1870. It does not change the law.

Art. 2932. Use of consumable

When the thing deposited is a consumable and the depositary has permission to consume or dispose of it, the contract is a loan for consumption rather than deposit and is governed by the laws applicable to that contract.

Acts 2003, No. 491, § 1, eff. Jan. 1, 2004.

REVISION COMMENTS—2003

(a) This provision reproduces the substance of Article 2941 of the Louisiana Civil Code of 1870.

(b) For definitions of consumables and nonconsumables, see C.C. Arts. 536 and 537 (Rev. 1976); Yiannopoulos, Civil Law Property § 28 (4th ed. 2001).

(c) Ordinarily, parties enjoy contractual freedom to treat in their transactions consumable things as nonconsumables, and vice versa. For example, shares of stock are nonconsumables; however, the depositor may endorse a stock certificate and authorize the depositary to dispose of the shares subject to the obligation to return shares of the same kind upon demand.

Art. 2933. Return of the thing deposited

The depositary is bound to return the precise thing that he received in deposit.

Acts 2003, No. 491, § 1, eff. Jan. 1, 2004.

REVISION COMMENT—2003

This provision reproduces the substance of the first paragraph of Article 2944 of the Louisiana Civil Code of 1870. The second paragraph of that Article is merely didactic and has not been reproduced. There should be no doubt that when coins are deposited, and the depositary has not been given permission to use the coins, the depositary is bound to return the identical coins. When the depositary is given permission to use the coins, he must return coins of the same kind, whether they sustained "an increase or diminution in value."

Art. 2934.   Delivery of value received

When the thing deposited is lost or deteriorated without any fault of the depositary, the depositary is nevertheless bound to deliver to the depositor whatever value the depositary received as a result of that loss, including the proceeds of any insurance.

Acts 2003, No. 491, § 1, eff. Jan. 1, 2004.

REVISION COMMENTS—2003

(a) This provision is new. It is based on Article 2946 of the Louisiana Civil Code of 1870 and reflects solutions under the law of obligations in general. See C.C. Arts. 1973 through 1978 (Rev. 1984). Further, this provision is an application of the principle of real subrogation. Cf. C.C. Arts. 614 through 617 (Rev. 1976); Quebec C.C. Art. 2286(2).

(b) The depositary is bound to return to the depositor the precise thing that he received in deposit if that thing still exists, Civil Code Article 2933 (Rev. 2003). In addition, under Civil Code Article 2934 (Rev. 2003), the depositary is bound to deliver to the depositor the proceeds of casualty insurance that he received as compensation for the loss or deterioration of the thing that was deposited.

Art. 2935.   Delivery of civil and natural fruits

The depositary is bound to deliver to the depositor the civil and natural fruits that he received from the thing deposited.

Acts 2003, No. 491, § 1, eff. Jan. 1, 2004.

REVISION COMMENTS—2003

(a) This provision reproduces the substance of the first sentence of Article 2948 of the Louisiana Civil Code of 1870. It accords with Article 2287(2) of the Quebec Civil Code. There is no change in the law. For the definition of fruits, see C.C. Art. 551 (Rev. 1977); Yiannopoulos, Personal Servitudes § 50 (4th ed. 2000).

(b) The depositary is also bound to deliver to the depositor products derived from the thing deposited as a result of diminution of its substance. These belong to the owner of the thing by right of accession. See C.C. Art. 488 (Rev. 1979).

(c) Money is corporeal and consumable. See C.C. Arts. 461 (Rev. 1978) and 536 (Rev. 1976). According to Civil Code Article 2932 (Rev. 2003), when money is deposited and the depositary has permission to consume or dispose of it, "the contract is a loan for consumption rather than deposit and is governed by the laws applicable to that contract." In such a case, the "depositary" is actually a borrower under a gratuitous loan for consumption and owes no obligation to deliver any interest he received or should have received from the money in deposit. However, the depositary of money owes interest from the date he defaulted in his obligation to deliver the money to the depositor.

(d) Nothing prevents the parties from entering into an actual contract of deposit, whether gratuitous or onerous, for the safekeeping of money. This happens, for example, when coins or bank notes are given in deposit and the depositary has no permission to consume or dispose of the money. Further, this may also happen when the parties agree that the depositary will have permission to consume or dispose of the money but he shall be bound to pay interest or deliver any civil fruits of the money that he received or should have received. Cf. Greek C.C. Art. 830.

Art. 2936.   Proof of ownership of the thing deposited not required; a stolen thing

The depositary may not require the depositor to prove that he is the owner of the thing deposited. If the depositary discovers that the thing deposited was stolen, the depositary may refuse to return the thing to the depositor and is exonerated from liability if he delivers the thing to its owner.

Acts 2003, No. 491, § 1, eff. Jan. 1, 2004.

REVISION COMMENTS—2003

(a) This provision is based on the first sentence of Article 2950 of the Louisiana Civil Code of 1870. It has no equivalent in the German Civil Code or in the Greek Civil Code. However, Article 2284 of the Quebec Civil Code provides: "The depositary may not require the depositor to prove that he is the owner of the property deposited, or require such proof of the person to whom the property is to be restored."

(b) The second and the third sentences of Article 2950 of the Louisiana Civil Code of 1870 declare: "Yet if he discovers that the thing was stolen and who the owner of it is, he must give him notice of the deposit, requiring him to claim within due time. If the owner, having received due notice, neglects to claim the deposit, the depositary is fully exonerated on returning it to the person from whom he received it." The matter is now governed by provisions of criminal law. See R.S. 14: 69(A) and (C).

(c) This provision applies when the thing given in deposit is a stolen thing. In such a case, the depositary may refuse to return the thing to the depositor, and he is exonerated from liability toward the depositor if he delivers the thing to its owner. This provision does not determine the question of the liability of the depositary toward the owner of the stolen thing, if the depositary returns the thing to the depositor rather than its owner.

(d) For the notion of "stolen" thing, see Louisiana Civil Code Art. 521 (Rev. 1979), Revision Comment (b). See also, Yiannopoulos, Civil Law Property § 352 (4th ed. 2001).

Art. 2937. Place and expense of return

When the contract of deposit specifies the place of return, the thing deposited is to be returned there and the depositor bears the expense of transportation. If the contract of deposit does not specify the place of return, the thing deposited is to be returned at the place where the deposit was made.

Acts 2003, No. 491, § 1, eff. Jan. 1, 2004.

REVISION COMMENT—2003

This provision reproduces the substance of Articles 2953 and 2954 of the Louisiana Civil Code of 1870. It does not change the law.

Art. 2938. Time of return

The depositary is bound to return the thing deposited upon demand, even if the agreed term of the deposit has not expired, unless expressly provided otherwise in the contract of deposit.

A depositary may not return the thing deposited before the lapse of the agreed term unless unforeseen circumstances make it impossible for him to keep the thing safely and without prejudice to himself.

When no term is fixed, the depositary may return the thing deposited at any time.

Acts 2003, No. 491, § 1, eff. Jan. 1, 2004.

REVISION COMMENTS—2003

(a) This provision is based on Article 2955 of the Louisiana Civil Code of 1870. The "unless" clause of that Article has not been reproduced as self-evident.

(b) According to the civilian tradition, a clause relieving the depositary of the obligation to deliver the thing deposited upon demand is not valid. See C.C. Art. 2955 (1870); Quebec C.C. Art. 2285; Greek C.C. Art. 827. However, the legislature has determined that parties should enjoy contractual freedom to enter into a contract of deposit for a fixed term, thus excluding the depositor's right to demand return of the thing deposited before the expiration of the term.

Art. 2939.   Retention of the deposit

The depositary may retain the thing deposited until his claims arising from the contract of deposit are paid. He may not retain the thing until payment of a claim unrelated to the contract of deposit or by way of setoff.

Acts 2003, No. 491, § 1, eff. Jan. 1, 2004.

REVISION COMMENT—2003

This provision reproduces the substance of Article 2956 of the Louisiana Civil Code of 1870. It has no equivalents in modern civil codes.

Art. 2940.   Reimbursement of the depositary

The depositor is bound to reimburse the depositary for the reasonable expenses he has incurred for the safekeeping of the thing deposited, to indemnify him for the losses the thing may have caused him, and to pay him the agreed remuneration.

Acts 2003, No. 491, § 1, eff. Jan. 1, 2004.

REVISION COMMENTS—2003

(a) This provision is based on Article 2960 of the Louisiana Civil Code of 1870. It accords with Articles 2293(1) of the Quebec Civil Code and Article 826 of the Greek Civil Code.

(b) The obligation of the depositor to reimburse the depositary the expenses that the depositary has incurred for the preservation of the thing deposited arises when the contract is gratuitous. When the contract is for remuneration, the compensation of the depositary includes the costs for the preservation of the thing deposited.

CHAPTER 2—DEPOSIT WITH INNKEEPERS

Art. 2941.   Obligation of innkeeper to accept the deposit

An innkeeper is bound to accept for deposit the personal belongings of guests unless he is unable to provide such a service because of the excessive value, size, weight, or nature of the things sought to be deposited. He may examine the things handed over for deposit and require that they be placed in a closed or sealed receptacle.

Acts 2003, No. 491, § 1, eff. Jan. 1, 2004.

REVISION COMMENTS—2003

(a) This provision is new. It is based in part on Article 2968 of the Louisiana Civil Code of 1870 and on Articles 2298 and 2299 of the Quebec Civil Code.

(b) An innkeeper is bound to accept for deposit documents, money, jewelry, and other valuables. However, he may refuse to accept the deposit of things that he cannot accommodate on account of their excessive size, weight, or particular nature. For example, an innkeeper may refuse to accept the deposit of excessively heavy or bulky materials, and of perishable, dangerous, or illegal things.

(c) Under this provision, an innkeeper may refuse to accept a thing for deposit when it is imprudent to do so because of the value of the thing.

(d) For the definition of innkeepers, see C.C. Art. 3232 (1870).

Art. 2942.   Innkeeper as compensated depositary

An innkeeper is a compensated depositary as to things that guests deliver to him for safekeeping.

Acts 2003, No. 491, § 1, eff. Jan. 1, 2004.

(a) This provision is new. It is based in part on Article 2965 of the Louisiana Civil Code of 1870 and on Article 2298 of the Quebec Civil Code.

(b) An innkeeper is bound as a compensated depositary whether the things are delivered to him personally or to his servants. See C.C. Arts. 2317 and 2320 (1870). The provision of Article 2966 of the Louisiana Civil Code of 1870 has not been reproduced as self-evident.

(c) For the right of an innkeeper to dispose of left and unclaimed things, see C.C. Art. 3236 (1974).

Art. 2943.   Availability of a safe

An innkeeper who places a safe at the disposal of a guest in the guest's room is not a depositary of the things that the guest places in the safe.

Acts 2003, No. 491, § 1, eff. Jan. 1, 2004.

REVISION COMMENT—2003

This provision is new. It is based on Article 2300 of the Quebec Civil Code. An innkeeper who provides a safe to guests for the safekeeping of their valuables is not a depositary. He provides a service that is accessorial to the contract of lodging.

Art. 2944.   Damaged or stolen things

An innkeeper is not responsible for things of a guest that are stolen or damaged, unless the loss is attributed to the innkeeper's fault.

Acts 2003, No. 491, § 1, eff. Jan. 1, 2004.

REVISION COMMENT—2003

This Article is based upon Articles 2967 and 2969 of the Louisiana Civil Code of 1870. According to these provisions and applicable jurisprudence, an innkeeper is strictly liable, that is, without regard to fault, for stolen or damaged things brought into the premises by guests. However, an innkeeper who provides safes for the safekeeping of valuables and posts the requisite notices is liable only if the loss or damage to the goods is attributed to his fault. By way of an exception to the exception, an innkeeper is liable for stolen or damaged personal belongings, including pocket money, watches, jewelry, and apparel, that the guests wear and do not deposit them with the innkeeper for safekeeping.

Art. 2945.   Limitation of innkeeper's liability

The innkeeper's liability to guests, whether contractual or delictual, for stolen or damaged personal belongings that were not delivered to the innkeeper, is limited to five hundred dollars if he provides a safe deposit facility for such belongings and if he posts notice of the availability of a safe, unless the innkeeper has assumed greater liability by a separate written contract.

Acts 2003, No. 491, § 1, eff. Jan. 1, 2004.

REVISION COMMENTS—2003

(a) This provision is based on Article 2971 of the Louisiana Civil Code as amended by Acts 1982, No. 382. It is not intended to change the law.

(b) The depositary is liable for fault only, that is, he is not liable without fault.

(c) This provision applies regardless of the kind of safe that the innkeeper has provided. That safe may be the innkeeper's primary safe, a safe in a guest's room, or a safe located elsewhere on the premises.

CHAPTER 3—CONVENTIONAL SEQUESTRATION

Art. 2946. Conventional sequestration; definition

Conventional sequestration takes place when two or more persons by agreement deliver to a depositary a thing, movable or immovable, the rights to which are disputed or uncertain. In that case, the depositary is bound to deliver the thing according to their agreement or according to a court order.

Acts 2003, No. 491, § 1, eff. Jan. 1, 2004.

REVISION COMMENT—2003

This provision is based on Articles 2972 and 2973 of the Louisiana Civil Code of 1870. It accords with Article 831 of the Greek Civil Code.

Art. 2947. Applicable law

Conventional sequestration is governed by the rules applicable to deposit, to the extent that their application is compatible with the nature of conventional sequestration.

Acts 2003, No. 491, § 1, eff. Jan. 1, 2004.

REVISION COMMENTS—2003

(a) This provision is new. It is based on Article 832 of the Greek Civil Code.

(b) The provisions governing conventional sequestration are suppletive. Accordingly, parties may, by agreement, deviate from these provisions as they see fit.

Art. 2948. Termination of conventional sequestration by the depositary

The depositary may terminate the conventional sequestration unilaterally only if he is unable to perform his obligations. He is bound to deliver the thing to the successor depositary agreed upon by the parties and, when the parties cannot agree, he must apply to the court for the appointment of another depositary.

Acts 2003, No. 491, § 1, eff. Jan. 1, 2004.

REVISION COMMENTS—2003

(a) This provision reproduces the substance of Article 2978 of the Louisiana Civil Code of 1870. It has no equivalents in modern civil codes.

(b) This provision applies even if the conventional sequestration is subject to a term.

CHAPTER 4—JUDICIAL SEQUESTRATION

Art. 2949. Judicial sequestration

A judicial sequestration takes place according to a court order as provided in the Code of Civil Procedure.

Acts 2003, No. 491, § 1, eff. Jan. 1, 2004.

REVISION COMMENTS—2003

(a) This provision reproduces the substance of Article 2979 of the Louisiana Civil Code of 1870. It is not intended to change the law.

(b) Civil Code Articles 2949 through 2951 (Rev. 2003) are intended to apply when a writ of sequestration is issued in accordance with Articles 3571 through 3576 of the Louisiana Code of Civil Procedure. In contrast, Civil Code Articles 2946 through 2948 (Rev. 2003) apply to conventional sequestration, that is, when two or more persons agree to deliver to a depositary a thing, the rights to which are disputed or uncertain. Nevertheless, the judicial sequestration is governed by the rules applicable to deposit and conventional sequestration to the extent that their application is compatible with the nature of judicial sequestration, Civil Code Article 2950 (Rev. 2003).

Art. 2950. Applicable law

Judicial sequestration is governed by the rules applicable to deposit and conventional sequestration to the extent that their application is compatible with the nature of judicial sequestration.

Acts 2003, No. 491, § 1, eff. Jan. 1, 2004.

REVISION COMMENT—2003

This provision is new. It is not intended to change the law. Cf. C.C. Art. 2947 (Rev. 2003).

Art. 2951. Judicial depositary

The judicial depositary is the public official charged with the duty to execute the orders of the court. He is subject to the obligations of a conventional depositary. He is bound to deliver the thing to the person designated by the court. He is entitled to a fee to be paid by the person ordered to pay that fee by the court.

Acts 2003, No. 491, § 1, eff. Jan. 1, 2004.

REVISION COMMENTS—2003

(a) This provision reproduces the substance of Article 2981 of the Louisiana Civil Code of 1870. It is not intended to change the law.

(b) This provision is based in part on the substance of Civil Code Article 2980 (1979).

(c) The judicial sequestration is an onerous deposit and the judicial depositary incurs the obligations of a compensated depositary.

Arts. 2952 to 2981. [Blank]

TITLE XIV—OF ALEATORY CONTRACTS

Art. 2982.   Aleatory contract, definition

The aleatory contract is a mutual agreement, of which the effects, with respect both to the advantages and losses, whether to all the parties or to one or more of them, depend on an uncertain event.

Art. 2983.   Actions for payment of gaming debts and bets

The law grants no action for the payment of what has been won at gaming or by a bet, except for games tending to promote skill in the use of arms, such as the exercise of the gun and foot, horse and chariot racing.

And as to such games, the judge may reject the demand, when the sum appears to him excessive.

Art. 2984.   Actions for recovery of payments made on gaming debts and bets

In all cases in which the law refuses an action to the winner, it also refuses to suffer the loser to reclaim what he has voluntarily paid, unless there has been, on the part of the winner, fraud, deceit, or swindling.

TITLE XV—REPRESENTATION AND MANDATE

CHAPTER 1—REPRESENTATION

Art. 2985.   Representation

A person may represent another person in legal relations as provided by law or by juridical act. This is called representation.

Acts 1997, No. 261, § 1, eff. Jan. 1, 1998.

REVISION COMMENTS—1997

(a) This provision is new. It states the principle of representation, that is, the authority of a person to represent another person in legal relations. This authority may rest on a provision of law or on a juridical act, such as a contract or a procuration.

(b) In modern civil codes, the word "representation" is used to convey the same meaning as the word "agency" in common-law systems. See e.g. Italian Civil Code Art. 1387; Greek Civil Code Article 211; German Civil Code Section 164. In accord, the word "representation" is used in Civil Code Article 2985 (Rev. 1997) to refer to all situations in which a person may be authorized by law or by juridical act to represent another person in legal relations. This usage is not unknown in Louisiana. For example, parents are authorized by law to represent their children. See Civil Code Article 235 (1870) (Parental protection and representation of children in litigation). See also Civil Code Article 3088 (1870): "Absent creditors . . . are to be represented by an attorney. . . ." In the revision of the law of Obligations, the word representation has also been used in accord with the civilian tradition. See Civil Code Article 1800 (Rev. 1984), Comment (b): "Obligors of a solidary obligation represent each other with regard to the obligee . . . Civil Code Article 2096 (1870) limits this rule of mutual representation in cases where the object of an obligation has been lost or has perished. . . ."

(c) The legal institution of representation under Civil Code Article 2985 (Rev. 1997) has nothing to do with the use of the word "representation" in the law of successions to denote "a fiction of the law, the effect of which is to put the representative in the place, degree, and rights of the person represented," that is the deceased ancestor. See Civil Code Article 881 (Rev. 1981); cf. R.S. 9:1894 (Trust Code). See Civil Code Articles 882 through 888 (Rev. 1981); Civil Code Articles 973, 1028, 1240, and 1241 (1870); Civil Code Article 1238 (as amended in 1995); and Civil Code Article 1493 (Rev. 1996). Likewise, the legal institution of representation has nothing to do with the use of the word representation to denote statements made by one person to another. See, e.g., Civil Code Articles 1924 and 1954 (Rev. 1984); id. Civil Code Article 1923 (Rev. 1984), Comment (b); Civil Code Article 3069 (Rev. 1987), Comment (d).

Art. 2986.   The authority of the representative

The authority of the representative may be conferred by law, by contract, such as mandate or partnership, or by the unilateral juridical act of procuration.

Acts 1997, No. 261, § 1, eff. Jan. 1, 1998.

REVISION COMMENTS—1997

(a) In the Louisiana Civil Code of 1870, the words "power of attorney", "letter of attorney", "mandate", "procuration", and "agency" were used interchangeably. However, each of these words also has a technical meaning that differentiates one from another. Following the legislative technique employed in modern civil codes, in this revision, the word "mandate" applies exclusively to the "contract of mandate" whereby a person, called principal, authorizes another person, called mandatary, to transact an affair on behalf of the principal. The word "agency" has not been used in this revision, in an effort to prevent confusion with the common-law institution of agency. The words "letter of attorney" and "power of attorney" in the Louisiana Civil Code of 1870 are a translation from the French "procuration". These words connote a unilateral juridical act whereby a person, called

713

principal, confers authority on another person to represent him in legal relations. Thus, a person may have authority to represent another person by virtue of a contract of mandate or by virtue of a unilateral juridical act.

(b) The Quebec Civil Code, following the model of the French Civil Code, regulates the contract of mandate only. However, all other modern civil codes, following the model of the German Civil Code, establish principles of representation generally and deal with mandate simply as a special contract. In those civil codes, a person may confer authority on another person to represent him by a mere declaration of will.

Art. 2987. Procuration defined; person to whom addressed

A procuration is a unilateral juridical act by which a person, the principal, confers authority on another person, the representative, to represent the principal in legal relations.

The procuration may be addressed to the representative or to a person with whom the representative is authorized to represent the principal in legal relations.

Acts 1997, No. 261, § 1, eff. Jan. 1, 1997.

REVISION COMMENTS—1997

(a) This provision is new. It is based on Article 2985 of the Louisiana Civil Code of 1870. The civilian term "procuration" has been used instead of the colloquial "power of attorney", which is a common-law term of art. This usage avoids confusion with common-law institutions and the designation of the representative as "attorney".

(b) A procuration is a "unilateral juridical act" that confers on the representative authority to represent the principal in legal relations. It differs from a mandate which is a "contract" that confers on the mandatary authority to transact one or more affairs for the principal. See Civil Code Article 2989 (Rev. 1997), infra.

(c) The procuration is not required to be in a particular form. Nevertheless, when the law prescribes a certain form for the authorized act, a procuration authorizing the act must be in the same form. See Civil Code Article 2993 (Rev. 1997), infra.

(d) The recipient of the procuration does not bind himself to do anything. However, if he accepts the procuration or acts accordingly, a contract may be formed between the principal and the representative. This contract may be a mandate or another nominate contract.

(e) The term "legal relations" includes creating, modifying, or terminating "legal relations."

Art. 2988. Applicability of the rules of mandate

A procuration is subject to the rules governing mandate to the extent that the application of those rules is compatible with the nature of the procuration.

Acts 1997, No. 261, § 1, eff. Jan. 1, 1998.

Revision Comment—1997

This provision is new. Though unilateral juridical acts, procurations are governed by the rules governing the contract of mandate, unless such application is incompatible with the procuration. Thus, the obligations of the principal and the representative toward each other, the rights and obligations of the principal and the representative toward third persons, and the termination of the power of attorney are determined by analogous application of the rules governing mandate.

CHAPTER 2—MANDATE

SECTION 1—GENERAL PRINCIPLES

Art. 2989.   Mandate defined

A mandate is a contract by which a person, the principal, confers authority on another person, the mandatary, to transact one or more affairs for the principal.

Acts 1997, No. 261, § 1, eff. Jan. 1, 1998.

REVISION COMMENTS—1997

(a) This provision is based on Article 2985 of the Louisiana Civil Code of 1870, as interpreted by Louisiana jurisprudence.

(b) Article 2985 of the Louisiana Civil Code of 1870 uses synonymously the terms mandate, procuration, and letter of attorney. This is both inaccurate and confusing. A mandate is a contract; a procuration or a letter of attorney is a unilateral juridical act. In this revision, the word mandate applies to a contract by which the principal confers authority on the mandatary to transact one or more affairs for the principal. The word procuration applies to unilateral juridical acts by which the principal confers authority on an attorney or other person to represent him in legal relations.

(c) Article 2985 of the Louisiana Civil Code of 1870 declares that a mandate is an act by which one person gives power to another to transact for him and in his name one or several affairs. The Louisiana Supreme Court has written out of Civil Code Article 2985 (1870) the words "and in his name", in order to adopt the common-law notion of undisclosed principal. See Sentell v. Richardson, 211 La. 288, 29 So.2d 852 (1947). Civil Code Article 2989 (Rev. 1997), follows Louisiana jurisprudence rather than the text of Article 2985 of the Louisiana Civil Code of 1870. Under Civil Code Article 2989 (Rev. 1997), a principal may confer authority on a mandatary to act either in his own name or in the name of the principal. The principal may, therefore, be either disclosed or undisclosed. For the rights and obligations of a disclosed principal and of an undisclosed principal, see Section 3 of Chapter 2, infra.

(d) Article 2985 of the Louisiana Civil Code of 1870 declares that a mandate is an act by which one person gives power to another to transact for him and in his name one or several affairs. According to traditional civilian notions, an "affair" may be either a juridical act or a material act. Louisiana decisions may be found in which a mandatary was charged with the responsibility for certain material acts. See, e.g., Alaynick v. Jefferson Bank & Trust Co., 451 So.2d 627 (La.App. 5th Cir. 1984) (collection of indebtedness); Craft v. Trahan, 351 So.2d 277 (La.App. 3d Cir. 1977) (making repair estimates); Roth v. B & L Enterprises, Inc., 420 So.2d 1094 (La. 1982) (receiving payment). The word "affairs" has also been used in the revision of the law governing "management of affairs" (negotiorum gestio). See Civil Code Articles 2292 through 2297 (Rev. 1995).

(e) The contract of mandate may involve the performance of material acts as well as the making of juridical acts. Limiting the contract of mandate to juridical acts would be an unnecessary departure from the civilian tradition. However, one should be aware of the fact that most of the provisions on mandate have been drafted with the making of juridical acts in mind.

(f) For provisional custody by mandate, see R.S. 9:951–954.

Art. 2990.   Applicability of the rules governing obligations

In all matters for which no special provision is made in this Title, the contract of mandate is governed by the Titles of "Obligations in General" and "Conventional Obligations or Contracts."

Acts 1997, No. 261, § 1, eff. Jan. 1, 1998.

REVISION COMMENTS—1997

(a) This provision is new. It is based on Article 2438 of the 1993 revision of the law of Sales.

(b) Articles 2987, 2988, 2989, and 2990 of the Louisiana Civil Code of 1870 have been suppressed because matters pertaining to the contract of mandate, including its object, offer, and acceptance, are governed by the Titles of "Obligations in General" and "Conventional Obligations or Contracts." For example, the obligations of a mandatary who resigns are subject to the provisions of Civil Code Article 2024 (Rev. 1984).

Art. 2991.   Interest served

The contract of mandate may serve the exclusive or the common interest of the principal, the mandatary, or a third person.

Acts 1997, No. 261, § 1, eff. Jan. 1, 1998.

REVISION COMMENTS—1997

(a) This provision reproduces the substance of Civil Code Article 2986 (1871). This provision was first enacted as Article 2955 of the Louisiana Civil Code of 1825. There is no corresponding provision in the French Civil Code or in the Quebec Civil Code.

(b) The mandatary is bound to discharge his obligations in good faith. See Civil Code Article 1759 (Rev. 1984). Questions concerning the conflict of the mandatary's interests with those of the principal must be resolved in accordance with the overriding obligation of good faith.

Art. 2992.   Onerous or gratuitous contract

The contract of mandate may be either onerous or gratuitous. It is gratuitous in the absence of contrary agreement.

Acts 1997, No. 261, § 1, eff. Jan. 1, 1998.

REVISION COMMENT—1997

This provision reproduces the substance of Civil Code Article 2991 (1870).

Art. 2993.   Form

The contract of mandate is not required to be in any particular form.

Nevertheless, when the law prescribes a certain form for an act, a mandate authorizing the act must be in that form.

Acts 1997, No. 261, § 1, eff. Jan. 1, 1998.

REVISION COMMENTS—1997

(a) This provision reproduces the substance of Article 2992 of the Louisiana Civil Code of 1870.

(b) The form of the contract of mandate is subject to the general law governing proof of obligations. See La. Civil Code Arts. 1832, 1837, and 1846 (Rev. 1984).

(c) The law requires that a donation be made by authentic act. C.C. Art. 1536 (1870). Therefore, under Civil Code Article 2993 (Rev. 1997), a mandate authorizing the mandatary to make a donation must be made by authentic act. Further, the law requires a written act for a compromise. C.C. Art. 3071 (Amended 1981). Therefore, under Civil Code Article 2993 (Rev. 1997), a mandate authorizing the mandatary to enter into a compromise agreement must be in writing.

Art. 2994.   General authority

The principal may confer on the mandatary general authority to do whatever is appropriate under the circumstances.

Acts 1997, No. 261, § 1, eff. Jan. 1, 1998.

Revision Comment—1997

This provision resolves questions concerning the validity of a mandate conferring general authority.

Art. 2995.   Incidental, necessary, or professional acts

The mandatary may perform all acts that are incidental to or necessary for the performance of the mandate.

The authority granted to a mandatary to perform an act that is an ordinary part of his profession or calling, or an act that follows from the nature of his profession or calling, need not be specified.

Acts 1997, No. 261, § 1, eff. Jan. 1, 1998.

REVISION COMMENT—1997

This provision based upon Civil Code Article 3000 of the Louisiana Civil Code of 1870 and Articles 2136 and 2137 of the Quebec Civil Code.

Art. 2996.   Authority to alienate, acquire, encumber, or lease

The authority to alienate, acquire, encumber, or lease a thing must be given expressly. Neither the property nor its location need be specifically described.

Acts 1997, No. 261, § 1, eff. Jan. 1, 1998.

REVISION COMMENTS—1997

(a) This provision reproduces the substance of Civil Code Articles 2996 (1870) and 2997(A)(1) and (B) (as amended in 1981, 1990, and 1992), and Civil Code Article 2135(2) of the Quebec Civil Code.

(b) For the distinction between acts of administration and acts of disposition, see Yiannopoulos, 3 Louisiana Civil Law Treatise, Personal Servitudes § 87 (3d ed. 1989).

(c) Express authority is also required for other specific acts. See Civil Code Article 2997 (Rev. 1997), infra.

Art. 2997.   Express authority required

Authority also must be given expressly to:

(1) Make an inter vivos donation, either outright or to a new or existing trust or other custodial arrangement, and, when also expressly so provided, to impose such conditions on the donation, including, without limitation, the power to revoke, that are not contrary to the other express terms of the mandate.

(2) Accept or renounce a succession.

(3) Contract a loan, acknowledge or make remission of a debt, or become a surety.

(4) Draw or endorse promissory notes and negotiable instruments.

(5) Enter into a compromise or refer a matter to arbitration.

(6) Make health care decisions, such as surgery, medical expenses, nursing home residency, and medication.

Acts 1997, No. 261, § 1, eff. Jan. 1, 1998. Amended by Acts 2001, No. 594, § 1.

REVISION COMMENTS—1997

(a) These provisions are based upon Article 2997 of the Louisiana Civil Code (as amended in 1981, 1990, and 1992). There should be no doubt that under the Louisiana Civil Code of 1870, a principal may expressly authorize the mandatary to make a donation on behalf of the principal. The Internal Revenue Service has been questioning the practice of having gifts made under a power of attorney for tax purposes. This has created problems in estate planning. Civil Code Article 2997(1) (Rev. 1997) makes it clear that, under Louisiana law, a mandatary may be given authority to make gifts by virtue of an express mandate.

(b) The provisions of Article 2997(A)(9) of the Louisiana Civil Code (as amended in 1992) have not been reproduced because they are provided for in R.S. 9:951, et seq.

Art. 2998.   Contracting with one's self

A mandatary who represents the principal as the other contracting party may not contract with himself unless he is authorized by the principal, or, in making such contract, he is merely fulfilling a duty to the principal.

Acts 1997, No. 261, § 1, eff. Jan. 1, 1998.

REVISION COMMENT—1997

This provision is new. It is based on Article 235 of the Greek Civil Code, Article 1395 of the Italian Civil Code, and Section 181 of the German Civil Code.

Art. 2999.   Person of limited capacity

A person of limited capacity may act as a mandatary for matters for which he is capable of contracting. In such a case, the rights of the principal against the mandatary are subject to the rules governing the obligations of persons of limited capacity.

Acts 1997, No. 261, § 1, eff. Jan. 1, 1998.

REVISION COMMENTS—1997

(a) This provision is based on Article 3001 of the Louisiana Civil Code (as amended in 1979). The provision originated in Article 1990 of the French Civil Code. There is no corresponding provision in the Quebec Civil Code.

(b) For capacity to contract, see Civil Code Articles 1918, 1922, 1923, and 1925 (Rev. 1984).

Art. 3000.   Mandatary of both parties

A person may be the mandatary of two or more parties, such as a buyer and a seller, for the purpose of transacting one or more affairs involving all of them. In such a case, the mandatary must disclose to each party that he also represents the other.

Acts 1997, No. 261, § 1, eff. Jan. 1, 1998.

REVISION COMMENTS—1997

(a) This provision is new. It is based on Article 3016 of the Louisiana Civil Code of 1870.

(b) Book III, Title XV, Chapter 3 (Of the Mandatary or Agent of Both Parties) dealing with the institution of brokerage has been suppressed in this revision. Civil Code Article 3000 (Rev. 1997) establishes the principle that a person may be the mandatary of two or more parties. Under this provision, depending on particular arrangements, a broker may be a mandatary of the buyer, of the seller, or of both the buyer and the seller. The rules governing particular types of brokerage contracts are found in special legislation.

SECTION 2—RELATIONS BETWEEN THE PRINCIPAL AND THE MANDATARY

Art. 3001.   Mandatary's duty of performance; standard of care

The mandatary is bound to fulfill with prudence and diligence the mandate he has accepted. He is responsible to the principal for the loss that the principal sustains as a result of the mandatary's failure to perform.

Acts 1997, No. 261, § 1, eff. Jan. 1, 1998.

(a) This provision is based on the first paragraph of Article 3002 of the Louisiana Civil Code of 1870 and Article 2138 of the Quebec Civil Code.

(b) Quite apart from Civil Code Articles 3001 and 3002 (Rev. 1997), the mandatary is bound to discharge his obligations in good faith. See C.C. Art. 1759 (Rev. 1984). Questions concerning the conflict of the mandatary's interests with those of the principal must be resolved in accordance with the overriding obligation of good faith.

Art. 3002. Gratuitous mandate; liability of a mandatary

When the mandate is gratuitous, the court may reduce the amount of loss for which the mandatary is liable.

Acts 1997, No. 261, § 1, eff. Jan. 1, 1998.

REVISION COMMENT—1997

This provision is based on Article 3003 of the Louisiana Civil Code of 1870 and Article 2148 of the Quebec Civil Code.

Art. 3003. Obligation to provide information

At the request of the principal, or when the circumstances so require, the mandatary is bound to provide information and render an account of his performance of the mandate. The mandatary is bound to notify the principal, without delay, of the fulfillment of the mandate.

Acts 1997, No. 261, § 1, eff. Jan. 1, 1998.

REVISION COMMENTS—1997

(a) This provision is new. It is based on Article 2139 of the Quebec Civil Code.

(b) For the obligation to account after the termination of the mandate, see Civil Code Article 3032 (Rev. 1997), infra.

Art. 3004. Obligation to deliver; right of retention

The mandatary is bound to deliver to the principal everything he received by virtue of the mandate, including things he received unduly.

The mandatary may retain in his possession sufficient property of the principal to pay the mandatary's expenses and remuneration.

Acts 1997, No. 261, § 1, eff. Jan. 1, 1998.

REVISION COMMENTS—1997

(a) This provision is based on Articles 3005 and 3023 of the Louisiana Civil Code of 1870.

(b) The mandatary may not retain more property than is needed to pay his expenses and remuneration.

Art. 3005. Interest on money used by mandatary

The mandatary owes interest, from the date used, on sums of money of the principal that the mandatary applies to his own use.

Acts 1997, No. 261, § 1, eff. Jan. 1, 1998.

REVISION COMMENTS—1997

(a) This provision is based on Article 3015 of the Louisiana Civil Code of 1870.

(b) In the absence of contrary agreement, the mandatary is not entitled to apply to his own use the money or other property of the principal. When the mandatary, without right, applies to his own use sums of money that belong to the principal, the mandatary owes interest from the time of such use. In addition to his obligation to pay interest, the mandatary may, of course, be liable to the principal under the Titles governing "Obligations in General" and "Conventional Obligations or Contracts."

(c) In the absence of contrary provision, the interest contemplated in this Article is the applicable rate of legal interest.

Art. 3006. Fulfillment of the mandate by the mandatary

In the absence of contrary agreement, the mandatary is bound to fulfill the mandate himself.

Nevertheless, if the interests of the principal so require, when unforeseen circumstances prevent the mandatary from performing his duties and he is unable to communicate with the principal, the mandatary may appoint a substitute.

Acts 1997, No. 261, § 1, eff. Jan. 1, 1998.

REVISION COMMENT—1997

This Article is new. The first paragraph expresses an idea that is implicit in the Louisiana Civil Code of 1870. The second paragraph is based on Article 2140 of the Quebec Civil Code.

Art. 3007. Mandatary's liability for acts of the substitute

When the mandatary is authorized to appoint a substitute, he is answerable to the principal for the acts of the substitute only if he fails to exercise diligence in selecting the substitute or in giving instructions.

When not authorized to appoint a substitute, the mandatary is answerable to the principal for the acts of the substitute as if the mandatary had performed the mandate himself.

In all cases, the principal has recourse against the substitute.

Acts 1997, No. 261, § 1, eff. Jan. 1, 1998.

REVISION COMMENTS—1997

(a) This provision is new. It is based on Article 2141 of the Quebec Civil Code and, in part, on Articles 3007, 3008, and 3009 of the Louisiana Civil Code of 1870.

(b) The first paragraph of this provision accords with Article 3008 of the Louisiana Civil Code of 1870. Under that Article, the mandatary is answerable to the principal if, authorized to appoint a substitute, he has not exercised diligence in the selection of the substitute. The second paragraph of this provision reflects the idea contained in Article 3007 of the Louisiana Civil Code of 1870. The third paragraph of this provision accords with Article 3009 of the Louisiana Civil Code of 1870.

Art. 3008. Liability for acts beyond authority; ratification

If the mandatary exceeds his authority, he is answerable to the principal for resulting loss that the principal sustains.

The principal is not answerable to the mandatary for loss that the mandatary sustains because of acts that exceed his authority unless the principal ratifies those acts.

Acts 1997, No. 261, § 1, eff. Jan. 1, 1998.

REVISION COMMENT—1997

This provision is based on Article 3010 of the Louisiana Civil Code of 1870. It applies to the relationship between the principal and the mandatary.

Art. 3009. Liability of multiple mandataries

Multiple mandataries are not solidarily liable to their common principal, unless the mandate provides otherwise.

Acts 1997, No. 261, § 1, eff. Jan. 1, 1998.

REVISION COMMENT—1997

This provision is based on Article 3014 of the Louisiana Civil Code of 1870.

Art. 3010. Performance of obligations contracted by the mandatary

The principal is bound to the mandatary to perform the obligations that the mandatary contracted within the limits of his authority. The principal is also bound to the mandatary for obligations contracted by the mandatary after the termination of the mandate if at the time of contracting the mandatary did not know that the mandate had terminated.

The principal is not bound to the mandatary to perform the obligations that the mandatary contracted which exceed the limits of the mandatary's authority unless the principal ratifies those acts.

Acts 1997, No. 261, § 1, eff. Jan. 1, 1998.

REVISION COMMENTS—1997

(a) This provision is new. It is based in part on Article 3021 of the Louisiana Civil Code of 1870 and Article 2152 of the Quebec Civil Code.

(b) The principal is primarily bound to the third person with whom the contract has been made and not to the mandatary.

Art. 3011. Advantageous performance despite divergence from authority

The mandatary acts within the limits of his authority even when he fulfills his duties in a manner more advantageous to the principal than was authorized.

Acts 1997, No. 261, § 1, eff. Jan. 1, 1998.

REVISION COMMENT—1997

This provision is based on Article 3011 of the Louisiana Civil Code of 1870 and Article 2153 of the Quebec Civil Code.

Art. 3012. Reimbursement of expenses and remuneration

The principal is bound to reimburse the mandatary for the expenses and charges he has incurred and to pay him the remuneration to which he is entitled.

The principal is bound to reimburse and pay the mandatary even though without the mandatary's fault the purpose of the mandate was not accomplished.

Acts 1997, No. 261, § 1, eff. Jan. 1, 1998.

REVISION COMMENTS—1997

(a) This provision is based on Article 3022 of the Louisiana Civil Code of 1870 and Articles 2150 and 2154 of the Quebec Civil Code.

(b) The second phrase of the second paragraph of Article 3022 of the Louisiana Civil Code of 1870 has not been reproduced as unnecessary. This is an echo from the days that the contract of mandate was essentially gratuitous. Today, the contract of mandate may be a contract for remuneration. Corresponding Article 2150 of the Quebec Civil Code provides that the principal pays the mandatary "the remuneration to which he is entitled." This is a much more preferable formulation. Indeed, the mandatary may be entitled to remuneration not only under the terms of the mandate, but also in accordance with usages, customary law, or even under the law of enrichment without cause.

Art. 3013. Compensation for loss sustained by the mandatary

The principal is bound to compensate the mandatary for loss the mandatary sustains as a result of the mandate, but not for loss caused by the fault of the mandatary.

Acts 1997, No. 261, § 1, eff. Jan. 1, 1998.

(a) This provision is based on Article 3024 of the Louisiana Civil Code of 1870 and Article 2154 of the Quebec Civil Code.

(b) The fault of the mandatary does not exclude the mandatary's right to claim reimbursement. The notion of comparative fault should apply, and the mandatary should not have the right to claim reimbursement to the extent that his loss is attributed to his own fault. In case of contributing fault, recovery is apportioned according to the degree of the mandatary's fault.

Art. 3014.   Interest on sums expended by the mandatary

The principal owes interest from the date of the expenditure on sums expended by the mandatary in performance of the mandate.

Acts 1997, No. 261, § 1, eff. Jan. 1, 1998.

REVISION COMMENT—1997

This provision is based on Article 3025 of the Louisiana Civil Code of 1870 and Article 2151 of the Quebec Civil Code.

Art. 3015.   Liability of several principals

Multiple principals for an affair common to them are solidarily bound to their mandatary.

Acts 1997, No. 261, § 1, eff. Jan. 1, 1998.

REVISION COMMENT—1997

This provision is based on Article 3026 of the Louisiana Civil Code of 1870 and Article 2156 of the Quebec Civil Code.

SECTION 3—RELATIONS BETWEEN THE PRINCIPAL, THE MANDATARY, AND THIRD PERSONS

SUBSECTION A—RELATIONS BETWEEN THE MANDATARY AND THIRD PERSONS

Art. 3016.   Disclosed mandate and principal

A mandatary who contracts in the name of the principal within the limits of his authority does not bind himself personally for the performance of the contract.

Acts 1997, No. 261, § 1, eff. Jan. 1, 1998.

REVISION COMMENTS—1997

(a) This provision is new. It is based on Article 3012 of the Louisiana Civil Code of 1870 and Article 2157(1) of the Quebec Civil Code.

(b) This provision applies when the mandatary discloses both his status as a mandatary and the identity of the principal. Thus, when a mandatary enters into a contract with a third person in the name of the principal and within the limits of his authority, the contract binds the principal to the third person and the third person to the principal. In effect obligor and obligee are the principal and the third person. The mandatary does not bind himself personally to the third person for the performance of the contract.

(c) A mandatary who enters into a contract with a third person in the name of the principal and expressly promises the performance of the contract binds himself personally for that performance. See C.C. Arts. 1977 and 1983 (Rev. 1984); C.C. Art. 3012 (1870).

Art. 3017.   Undisclosed mandate

A mandatary who contracts in his own name without disclosing his status as a mandatary binds himself personally for the performance of the contract.

Acts 1997, No. 261, § 1, eff. Jan. 1, 1998.

REVISION COMMENT—1997

This provision is new. It is based in part on Article 3013 of the Louisiana Civil Code of 1870 and Article 2157(2) of the Quebec Civil Code.

Art. 3018.   Disclosed mandate; undisclosed principal

A mandatary who enters into a contract and discloses his status as a mandatary, though not his principal, binds himself personally for the performance of the contract. The mandatary ceases to be bound when the principal is disclosed.

Acts 1997, No. 261, § 1, eff. Jan. 1, 1998.

REVISION COMMENT—1997

This provision is new. Under this Article, a mandatary who discloses the mandate but fails to disclose the principal binds himself personally for the performance of the contracts he has made with third persons. However, the mandatary ceases to be so bound when the principal is disclosed. In such a case, the mandatary incurs the same obligations to third persons as a mandatary who acts in the name of and on behalf of the principal. See Civil Code Article 3016 (Rev. 1997), supra.

Art. 3019.   Liability when authority is exceeded

A mandatary who exceeds his authority is personally bound to the third person with whom he contracts, unless that person knew at the time the contract was made that the mandatary had exceeded his authority or unless the principal ratifies the contract.

Acts 1997, No. 261, § 1, eff. Jan. 1, 1998.

REVISION COMMENT—1997

This provision is new; it is based on Article 2158 of the Quebec Civil Code and in part on Article 3013 of the Louisiana Civil Code of 1870.

SUBSECTION B—RELATIONS BETWEEN THE PRINCIPAL AND THIRD PERSONS

Art. 3020.   Obligations of the principal to third persons

The principal is bound to perform the contract that the mandatary, acting within the limits of his authority, makes with a third person.

Acts 1997, No. 261, § 1, eff. Jan. 1, 1998.

REVISION COMMENTS—1997

(a) This provision is new. It is based on Article 2160 of the Quebec Civil Code.

(b) Under this provision a principal, whether disclosed or undisclosed, is bound to perform the contracts that the mandatary, acting within the limits of his authority, made with third persons. A third person who contracts with the mandatary has a cause of action directly against the principal, whether disclosed or undisclosed. Cf. C.C. Art. 3023 (Rev. 1997), infra.

(c) For the liability of a mandatary, who does not disclose his principal or who exceeds his authority, see Civil Code Articles 3018 and 3019 (Rev. 1997), supra. For the liability of a principal who ratifies the acts of the mandatary, see Civil Code Articles 3018 and 3019 (Rev. 1997), supra.

(d) This provision applies to all mandates, regardless of the commercial or non-commercial nature of the mandate or of the contract between the mandatary and the third person.

Art. 3021.   Putative mandatary

One who causes a third person to believe that another person is his mandatary is bound to the third person who in good faith contracts with the putative mandatary.

Acts 1997, No. 261, § 1, eff. Jan. 1, 1998.

REVISION COMMENT—1997

This provision is new. It is based on Article 2163 of the Quebec Civil Code.

Art. 3022.   Disclosed mandate or principal; third person bound

A third person with whom a mandatary contracts in the name of the principal, or in his own name as mandatary, is bound to the principal for the performance of the contract.

Acts 1997, No. 261, § 1, eff. Jan. 1, 1998.

REVISION COMMENT—1997

This provision is new. It is based on Article 2165 of the Quebec Civil Code and Louisiana jurisprudence.

Art. 3023.   Undisclosed mandate or principal; obligations of third person

A third person with whom a mandatary contracts without disclosing his status or the identity of the principal is bound to the principal for the performance of the contract unless the obligation is strictly personal or the right non-assignable. The third person may raise all defenses that may be asserted against the mandatary or the principal.

Acts 1997, No. 261, § 1, eff. Jan. 1, 1998.

REVISION COMMENT—1997

This provision is new. An undisclosed principal may demand performance of the contract from the third party with whom the mandatary contracted unless the obligation is strictly personal or the right non-assignable. See Civil Code Article 1766 (Rev. 1984); id. Civil Code Article 2642 (Rev. 1993). For the obligations of the mandatary to the third person, see Civil Code Articles 3016 through 3019 (Rev. 1997), supra.

SECTION 4—TERMINATION OF THE MANDATE AND THE AUTHORITY OF THE MANDATARY

Art. 3024.   Termination of the mandate and of the mandatary's authority

In addition to causes of termination of contracts under the Titles governing "Obligations in General" and "Conventional Obligations or Contracts," both the mandate and the authority of the mandatary terminate upon the:

(1) Death of the principal or of the mandatary.

(2) Interdiction of the mandatary.

(3) Qualification of the curator after the interdiction of the principal.

Acts 1997, No. 261, § 1, eff. Jan. 1, 1998.

REVISION COMMENTS—1997

(a) This provision is based on Civil Code Article 3027(A) (as amended in 1981).

(b) For possible liability of the mandatary toward the principal when the mandatary "resigns or renounces his authority", see Civil Code Article 3029 (Rev. 1997), infra.

(c) The mandate is a contract governed by the Titles of "Obligations in General" and "Conventional Obligations or Contracts" with respect to all matters for which no special provision is made in this Title. Civil Code Article 2990 (Rev. 1997), supra. Therefore, the contract of mandate and the authority of the mandatary may terminate by application of the Titles governing "Obligations in General" and "Conventional Obligations or Contracts." Civil Code Article 3024 (Rev. 1997) provides additional grounds for termination of the contract of mandate and of the authority of the mandatary.

(d) See also, Civil Code Article 3030 (Rev. 1997), infra.

Art. 3025. Termination by principal

The principal may terminate the mandate and the authority of the mandatary at any time. A mandate in the interest of the principal, and also of the mandatary or of a third party, may be irrevocable, if the parties so agree, for as long as the object of the contract may require.

Acts 1997, No. 261, § 1, eff. Jan. 1, 1998.

REVISION COMMENTS—1997

(a) This provision is new. It is based in part of Article 724 of the Greek Civil Code and Article 1723 of the Italian Civil Code. It accords with Article 2024 (Rev. 1984) of the Louisiana Civil Code.

(b) In principle, the mandate is freely revocable; the principal may terminate the mandate at any time. Exceptionally, however, a mandate may be irrevocable if the parties so agree and the mandate also concerns the interest of the mandatary or of a third party.

Art. 3026. Incapacity of the principal

In the absence of contrary agreement, neither the contract nor the authority of the mandatary is terminated by the principal's incapacity, disability, or other condition that makes an express revocation of the mandate impossible or impractical.

Acts 1997, No. 261, § 1, eff. Jan. 1, 1998.

REVISION COMMENTS—1997

(a) This provision reproduces the substance of the first sentence of Civil Code Article 3027(B) (as amended in 1981).

(b) The authority of the mandatary terminates upon the qualification of the curator after the interdiction of the principal. See Civil Code Article 3024(3) (Rev. 1997), supra.

Art. 3027. Reliance on public records

Until filed for recordation, a revocation or modification of a recorded mandate is ineffective as to the persons entitled to rely upon the public records.

Acts 1997, No. 261, § 1, eff. Jan. 1, 1998.

REVISION COMMENTS—1997

(a) This Article is based upon the substance of the second sentence of Civil Code Article 3027(B) (as amended in 1981).

(b) In Louisiana, the public records doctrine is negative. Parties are entitled to rely on the absence in the public records of documents which according to law must be recorded. The source provision creates the mistaken impression that the public records doctrine has an affirmative function and that a third person may rely on the presence of a recorded mandate. It is implicit in Civil Code Article 3027 (Rev. 1997) that: (a) the reference is to a mandate which according to law must be recorded in order to have effect toward third persons and (b) a notice of termination of such a mandate must be placed in the public records.

Art. 3028.   Rights of third persons without notice of revocation

The principal must notify third persons with whom the mandatary was authorized to contract of the revocation of the mandate or of the mandatary's authority. If the principal fails to do so, he is bound to perform the obligations that the mandatary has undertaken.

Acts 1997, No. 261, § 1, eff. Jan. 1, 1998.

REVISION COMMENTS—1997

(a) This provision is based on Article 3029 of the Louisiana Civil Code of 1870.

(b) A mandatary who purports to represent the principal despite the revocation of the mandate acts without authority. Such a mandatary is personally bound to a third person with whom he contracted. See Civil Code Article 3019 (Rev. 1997), supra. Further, the mandatary is liable to the principal under Civil Code Articles 3001 and 3008 (Rev. 1997), supra.

Art. 3029.   Termination by the mandatary

The mandate and the authority of the mandatary terminate when the mandatary notifies the principal of his resignation or renunciation of his authority. When a mandatary has reasonable grounds to believe that the principal lacks capacity, the termination is effective only when the mandatary notifies another mandatary or a designated successor mandatary. In the absence of another mandatary or a designated successor mandatary, the termination is effective when the mandatary notifies a person with a sufficient interest in the welfare of the principal.

Acts 1997, No. 261, § 1, eff. Jan. 1, 1998. Amended by Acts 2014, No. 356, § 2.

REVISION COMMENTS—1997

(a) This provision is new. It is based in part on Article 3031 of the Louisiana Civil Code of 1870.

(b) The mandatary is bound to give notice of termination in accordance with Civil Code Article 2024 (Rev. 1984). This provision is applicable even if a mandate is given for a specified period of time.

(c) If the termination of a mandate for remuneration causes injury to the principal, the liability of the mandatary is governed by the Titles of "Obligations in General" and "Conventional Obligations or Contracts." In the case of a gratuitous mandate, the court may reduce the amount of loss for which the mandatary is liable. See Civil Code Articles 2990 and 3002 (Rev. 1997), supra.

COMMENTS—2014

The duty of the mandatary to notify someone other than the principal when the mandatary believes the principal lacks capacity does not impose a duty on the person notified to accept any responsibility or to take any action. The mandatary remains responsible for the consequences of his failure to fulfill the mandate until proper notice is given.

Art. 3030.   Acts of the mandatary after principal's death

The mandatary is bound to complete an undertaking he had commenced at the time of the principal's death if delay would cause injury.

Acts 1997, No. 261, § 1, eff. Jan. 1, 1998.

REVISION COMMENT—1997

This provision reproduces the substance of the second paragraph of Article 3002 of the Louisiana Civil Code of 1870.

Art. 3031.   Contracts made after termination of the mandate or the mandatary's authority

If the mandatary does not know that the mandate or his authority has terminated and enters into a contract with a third person who is in good faith, the contract is enforceable.

Acts 1997, No. 261, § 1, eff. Jan. 1, 1998.

REVISION COMMENT—1997

This provision is based upon Articles 3032 and 3033 of the Louisiana Civil Code of 1870.

Art. 3032.   Obligation to account

Upon termination of the mandate, unless this obligation has been expressly dispensed with, the mandatary is bound to account for his performance to the principal.

Acts 1997, No. 261, § 1, eff. Jan. 1, 1998.

REVISION COMMENT—1997

This provision reproduces the substance of Article 3004 of the Louisiana Civil Code of 1870.

Arts. 3033 to 3034.   [Blank]

TITLE XVI—SURETYSHIP

CHAPTER 1—NATURE AND EXTENT OF SURETYSHIP

Art. 3035. Definition of suretyship

Suretyship is an accessory contract by which a person binds himself to a creditor to fulfill the obligation of another upon the failure of the latter to do so.

Acts 1987, No. 409, § 1, eff. Jan. 1, 1988.

REVISION COMMENTS—1987

(a) This Article reproduces the substance of C.C. Art. 3035 (1870). It clarifies the law by deleting from the source Article the words "already bound." See C.C. Art. 3036 (Rev.1987), comment (b).

(b) A contract is accessory when it is made to provide security for the performance of an obligation. See C.C. Art. 1913 (Rev.1984).

Art. 3036. Obligations for which suretyship may be established

Suretyship may be established for any lawful obligation, which, with respect to the suretyship, is the principal obligation.

The principal obligation may be subject to a term or condition, may be presently existing, or may arise in the future.

Acts 1987, No. 409, § 1, eff. Jan. 1, 1988.

REVISION COMMENTS—1987

(a) The first Paragraph of this Article reproduces the substance of the first sentence of C.C. Art. 3036 (1870).

(b) The second Paragraph of this Article is new. It emphasizes the unqualified nature of the principal obligation and sets at rest speculation that has from time to time been raised as to whether suretyship can be given for future obligations although such contracts have been recognized in Louisiana from the earliest times. See Hubert, "Nature and Essentials of Conventional Suretyship," 13 Tul.L.Rev. 519 (1939). A contract guaranteeing an obligation that is to arise in the future is a contract on a suspensive condition, and in this respect it makes no difference whether the creditor to whom it is given is bound to permit its creation or whether his arrangement with his debtor is facultative. The question of the validity of such contracts usually arises in the context of an attempt by the surety to terminate his promise before the obligation is incurred. See Bonura v. Christiana Bros. Poultry Co. of Gretna, Inc., 336 So.2d 881 (La.App. 4th Cir.1976), writ den. 339 So.2d 11. The right of a surety to terminate the contract is now regulated by Article 3061 (Rev.1987).

Art. 3037. Surety ostensibly bound as a principal with another; effect of knowledge of the creditor

One who ostensibly binds himself as a principal obligor to satisfy the present or future obligations of another is nonetheless considered a surety if the principal cause of the contract with the creditor is to guarantee performance of such obligations.

A creditor in whose favor a surety and principal obligor are bound together as principal obligors in solido may presume they are equally concerned in the matter until he clearly knows of their true relationship.

Acts 1987, No. 409, § 1, eff. Jan. 1, 1988.

REVISION COMMENTS—1987

(a) The Exposé des Motifs contains a general discussion of the purposes and functions of this Article. The Article recognizes that contracts of guaranty or suretyship may be confected in an infinite variety of forms, having little or no difference in their intended effect. The surety's obligation may be contained in the basic contract with the principal obligor or in a separate undertaking. Sureties may sign one or several separate agreements. Some may sign separate contracts of guaranty, while others may endorse notes, sign them as co-makers or even sign as a maker, when the principal obligor signs as an endorser. Sureties are frequently asked to sign contracts with the principal obligor that identify them as "guarantors," "sureties in solido," "co-signers," "co-makers" etc. This Article makes it clear that the form in which the surety's undertaking is cast is irrelevant, and that the inherent nature of the undertaking determines whether or not the provisions of this Title regulate its provisions.

(b) The second paragraph of the Article makes it clear that the creditor will be protected if he deals in good faith with parties who are in fact principal and surety, but who contract jointly as principals and fail to disclose their true relationship to him. The effect of this Article may be illustrated as follows:

A and B purchase an automobile from C, agreeing to be solidarily bound for the price. The car is obtained exclusively for A, with B joining in the transaction only to lend his credit to it. C, in ignorance of their relationship accepts half of the price from A and gives him a release. He may still hold B for one-half of the debt. If, however, A initially approaches C to purchase the vehicle and C requires him to obtain B as a "co-maker" because of A's weak credit rating, C is entitled to treat A as a principal and B as a surety, even though A and B sign the contract of sale as "co-purchasers" solidarily bound for the price.

Art. 3038. Formal requirements of suretyship

Suretyship must be express and in writing.

Acts 1987, No. 409, § 1, eff. Jan. 1, 1988.

REVISION COMMENTS—1987

(a) This Article restates the rules contained in C.C. Art. 3039 (1870) and C.C. Art. 1847 (Rev.1984).

(b) It is sometimes doubtful whether an individual has guaranteed payment of another's debt or has merely given an opinion as to the person's ability and willingness to perform. In such cases doubts are resolved against holding the individual as a surety on the theory that suretyship is a burden that one does not lightly undertake. See Ball Marketing Enterprise v. Rainbow Tomato, 340 So.2d 700 (La.App.3rd Cir.1976); Exchange Nat. Bank v. Waldron Lumber Co., 150 So. 3 (La.1933).

(c) Civil Code Article 3041 (1870) has been eliminated because it is unnecessary. Suretyship and mortgage are separate and distinct obligations. Suretyship does not create a mortgage on the property of the surety unless the surety secures his promise by an express contract of mortgage. See Etheridge v. Ariail, 138 So. 517 (La.1931).

(d) The term "writing" as applied to a contract means either an act under private signature or an authentic act. See C.C. Arts. 1837 and 1833 (Rev.1984).

Art. 3039. Suretyship requires no formal acceptance

Suretyship is established upon receipt by the creditor of the writing evidencing the surety's obligation. The creditor's acceptance is presumed and no notice of acceptance is required.

Acts 1987, No. 409, § 1, eff. Jan. 1, 1988.

REVISION COMMENT—1987

This Article is new. The surety who desires an acceptance in a particular form or a notice of acceptance may of course require it as a condition of his promise. This Article implicitly permits the surety to withdraw until the writing evidencing his obligation has been received by the creditor. Upon receipt of the writing by the creditor the suretyship comes into being. Thereafter the right of the surety to terminate the suretyship is regulated by Article 3061 (Rev.1987).

Art. 3040.   Rules may be varied

Suretyship may be qualified, conditioned, or limited in any lawful manner.

Acts 1987, No. 409, § 1, eff. Jan. 1, 1988.

REVISION COMMENT—1987

This Article is new. See C.C. Art. 11 (1870). It recognizes the suppletive nature of the provisions of the Civil Code in contractual matters. However, an agreement that is contrary to the essential accessorial nature of suretyship is not a suretyship but may be some other kind of conventional obligation. The imperative requirements of the Code may not be modified. See, e.g., Articles 3038, 3052, 3065, 3066, 3067 (Rev.1987).

CHAPTER 2—KINDS OF SURETYSHIP

Art. 3041.   Kinds of suretyship

There are three kinds of suretyship: commercial suretyship, legal suretyship, and ordinary suretyship.

Acts 1987, No. 409, § 1, eff. Jan. 1, 1988.

REVISION COMMENT—1987

This Article is new. It lists the three kinds of suretyship which are defined in the following Articles.

Art. 3042.   Commercial suretyship

A commercial suretyship is one in which:

(1) The surety is engaged in a surety business;

(2) The principal obligor or the surety is a business corporation, partnership, or other business entity;

(3) The principal obligation arises out of a commercial transaction of the principal obligor; or

(4) The suretyship arises out of a commercial transaction of the surety.

Acts 1987, No. 409, § 1, eff. Jan. 1, 1988.

REVISION COMMENT—1987

This Article is new. It implicitly recognizes that the rule of strict construction set forth for ordinary suretyship in Article 3044 (Rev.1987) does not apply to commercial transactions. The Louisiana courts have rejected the applicability of such rules in the case of "compensated" sureties, i.e., those who are paid a premium or fee for their services. This Article broadens the concept to encompass transactions that are essentially commercial in nature.

Art. 3043.   Legal suretyship

A legal suretyship is one given pursuant to legislation, administrative act or regulation, or court order.

Acts 1987, No. 409, § 1, eff. Jan. 1, 1988.

REVISION COMMENT—1987

This Article is new. It combines into one classification legal and judicial suretyship, which were formerly separately classified.

Art. 3044.   Ordinary suretyship; interpretation

An ordinary suretyship is one that is neither a commercial suretyship nor a legal suretyship.

An ordinary suretyship must be strictly construed in favor of the surety.

Acts 1987, No. 409, § 1, eff. Jan. 1, 1988.

REVISION COMMENT—1987

This second sentence of this Article is new. It is based on C.C. Art. 3039 (1870). It continues the rule, long in force in Louisiana, that strict construction prevails regarding the contract of the ordinary surety. Basso v. Export Warrant Co., 193 So. 654 (La.1940). It implicitly excludes commercial and legal suretyship from application of the rule. See comment to Article 3042 (Rev.1987).

CHAPTER 3—THE EFFECTS OF SURETYSHIP BETWEEN THE SURETY AND CREDITOR

Art. 3045.   Liability of sureties to creditor; division and discussion abolished

A surety, or each surety when there is more than one, is liable to the creditor in accordance with the provisions of this Chapter, for the full performance of the obligation of the principal obligor, without benefit of division or discussion, even in the absence of an express agreement of solidarity.

Acts 1987, No. 409, § 1, eff. Jan. 1, 1988.

REVISION COMMENTS—1987

(a) This Article restates the principle of the first sentence of C.C. Art. 3049 (1870). It abolishes the pleas of division and discussion formerly recognized in C.C. Arts. 3045–3051 (1870). This is consistent with R.S. 9:4813(A), which abolished the benefits of division and discussion for sureties on private construction bonds.

(b) This Article is an extension of the principle of Art. 3035 (Rev.1987). The nature of the surety's promise is to satisfy the entire obligation if the debtor fails to do so. A surety may, of course, agree to secure only a part of the debt or limit his own liability to a specific sum. See Art. 3040 (Rev.1987).

(c) The creditor may include in the same suit both the principal obligor and the surety or he may sue the surety without joinder of the principal obligor. Continental Supply Co. v. Fisher Oil Co., 91 So. 287 (La.1922); State v. McDonnell, 12 La.Ann. 741 (1857); C.C. Art. 3051 (1870).

Art. 3046.   Defenses available to surety

The surety may assert against the creditor any defense to the principal obligation that the principal obligor could assert except lack of capacity or discharge in bankruptcy of the principal obligor.

Acts 1987, No. 409, § 1, eff. Jan. 1, 1988.

REVISION COMMENTS—1987

(a) This Article reproduces the substance of C.C. Art. 3060 (1870) and the second sentence to C.C. Art. 3036 (1870).

(b) This Article lists the defenses to the principal obligation that may not be asserted by the surety. See Federal Schools v. Kuntz, 134 So. 118 (La.1931) (surety could not raise as a defense the fact that the principal obligor was a minor); Devoe & Reynolds Co. v. Loup, 129 So. 450 (La.1930) (surety could not raise as a defense the fact that the principal obligor had no legal existence); Watkins v. Brumfield, 86 So.2d 263 (La.App. 1st Cir.1956); Serra E Hijo v. Hoffman & Co., 30 La.Ann. 67 (1878); Ludeling v. Felton, 29 La.Ann. 719 (1877) (discharge in bankruptcy of principal obligor cannot be raised as a defense by the surety). See also 11 U.S.C.A. § 524(e). A discharge in bankruptcy does not operate as or have the effect of a payment. Bankruptcy does not extinguish the debt but is simply a bar to the enforcement of it. It is this very contingency, the insolvency of the debtor, that necessitates suretyship.

(c) The "lack of capacity" exception includes contracts made by a principal obligor who is an unemancipated minor, an interdict, or a person deprived of reason at the time of contracting. See C.C. Art. 1918 et seq.

CHAPTER 4—THE EFFECTS OF SURETYSHIP BETWEEN THE SURETY AND PRINCIPAL OBLIGOR

Art. 3047. Rights of the surety

A surety has the right of subrogation, the right of reimbursement, and the right to require security from the principal obligor.

Acts 1987, No. 409, § 1, eff. Jan. 1, 1988.

REVISION COMMENT—1987

This Article is new. It is didactic in that it classifies for analytical purposes the rights of the surety against the principal obligor that are particularly set forth in C.C. Arts. 3048–3053 (Rev.1987) and that were recognized in former Civil Code Articles 3052–3053 and 3057 (1870).

Art. 3048. Surety's right of subrogation

The surety who pays the principal obligation is subrogated by operation of law to the rights of the creditor.

Acts 1987, No. 409, § 1, eff. Jan. 1, 1988.

REVISION COMMENT—1987

This Article reproduces the substance of C.C. Art. 1829(3) (Rev.1984) and Art. 3053 (1870). See Curtis v. Kitchen, 8 Mart. (O.S.) 706 (La.1820).

Art. 3049. Surety's right of reimbursement for payment of obligation

A surety who pays the creditor is entitled to reimbursement from the principal obligor. He may not recover reimbursement until the principal obligation is due and exigible.

A surety for multiple solidary obligors may recover from any of them reimbursement of the whole amount he has paid the creditor.

Acts 1987, No. 409, § 1, eff. Jan. 1, 1988.

REVISION COMMENTS—1987

(a) The first sentence of this Article reproduces the substance of C.C. Art. 3052 (1870).

(b) The second sentence of this Article reproduces the substance of C.C. Art. 3054 (1870). See Representatives of Dickey v. Rogers, 7 Mart. (N.S.) 588 (La.1829).

(c) Under this Article a surety has a right to reimbursement whether the suretyship was given with or without the knowledge of the principal obligor. This was expressly stated in former Art. 3052 (1870) and implied in Art. 3038 (1870). The unqualified expression of this Article is adequate to convey the same meaning. See C.C. Arts. 2295 (1870) et seq.

Art. 3050. Surety's right of reimbursement for payment of obligation not owed

A surety who in good faith pays the creditor when the principal obligation is extinguished, or when the principal obligor had the means of defeating it, is nevertheless entitled to reimbursement from the principal obligor if the surety made a reasonable effort to notify the principal obligor that the creditor was insisting on payment or if the principal obligor was apprised that the creditor was insisting on payment.

The surety's rights against the creditor are not thereby excluded.

Acts 1987, No. 409, § 1, eff. Jan. 1, 1988.

REVISION COMMENT—1987

This Article clarifies and broadens former C.C. Art. 3056 (1870). It permits the surety to recover by way of reimbursement what he has paid the creditor in cases not covered by the preceding article—if the debt has been extinguished or there was a defense to its enforcement—provided the surety is in good faith, i.e., honestly believes the debt is due and either makes an effort to notify the obligor or the obligor in fact knows the creditor is pursuing the surety. If the debtor advises the surety he is not liable, then the payment by the surety is not in "good faith" as required by the Article and he pays at his own risk.

Art. 3051. Payment by debtor without notice of payment by surety

A surety may not recover from the principal obligor, by way of subrogation or reimbursement, the amount paid the creditor if the principal obligor also pays the creditor for want of being warned by the surety of the previous payment.

In these circumstances, the surety may recover from the creditor.

Acts 1987, No. 409, § 1, eff. Jan. 1, 1988.

REVISION COMMENT—1987

This Article restates the rule of C.C. Art. 3055 (1870).

Art. 3052. Limitation on right of surety to recover what he paid creditor

A surety may not recover from the principal obligor more than he paid to secure a discharge, but he may recover by subrogation such attorney's fees and interest as are owed with respect to the principal obligation.

Acts 1987, No. 409, § 1, eff. Jan. 1, 1988.

REVISION COMMENTS—1987

(a) This Article is new. It states a rule that has been consistently followed by the Louisiana jurisprudence. See, e.g., Nolte v. Their Creditors, 7 Mart. N.S. 9 (La.1828); Picket v. Bates, 3 La.Ann. 627 (1848); Long v. Templeman, 24 La.Ann. 564 (1872); Succession of Dingrave, 31 La.Ann. 703 (1879). It is consistent with C.C. Art. 1830 (Rev.1984).

(b) Under this Article a surety may not claim a greater advantage by availing himself of conventional subrogation. See comment (c) to C.C. Art. 1830 (Rev.1984).

(c) The exception clause of this Article is new but is consistent with the principle upon which the jurisprudence was based—that a surety should not profit by his contract at the expense of the debtor. Interest owed on monies paid by the surety and attorney's fees incurred from the failure of the debtor to reimburse the surety are not excluded by the principle referred to. The courts have also recognized a distinction between the surety's right to recover by way of subrogation and reimbursement. See Harrell, "Developments in the Law, 1982–1983," 44 La.L.Rev. 535 (1983). The action for reimbursement, being an independent personal action, is subject to the usual rule that attorney's fees are not recoverable in the absence of a contract. The surety who proceeds against the principal obligor by way of subrogation is entitled to the same rights the creditor could exercise, including the creditor's right to collect attorney's fee and interest.

Art. 3053. Surety's right to require security

A surety, before making payment, may demand security from the principal obligor to guarantee his reimbursement when:

(1) The surety is sued by the creditor;

(2) The principal obligor is insolvent, unless the principal obligation is such that its performance does not require his solvency;

(3) The principal obligor fails to perform an act promised in return for the suretyship; or

(4) The principal obligation is due or would be due but for an extension of its term not consented to by the surety.

The principal obligor may refuse to give security if the principal obligation is extinguished or if he has a defense against it.

Acts 1987, No. 409, § 1, eff. Jan. 1, 1988.

REVISION COMMENTS—1987

(a) This Article is intended to clarify Louisiana law. It is based on Civil Code Article 3057 (1870) and traditional Civil Law principles. See Jones, "Roman Law Bases of Suretyship in Some Modern Civil Codes," 52 Tul.L.Rev. 129, 142 (1977); Buckland, "A Text-Book of Roman Law from Augustus to Justinian" 449 (1950); French Civil Code Art. 2032; Quebec Draft Proposed Civil Code Art. 858; Italian Civil Code Art. 1953.

(b) This Article makes one change in terminology. Art. 3057 (1870) used the word "indemnification" in the combined sense of reimbursement and security before payment. This Article uses the word "security" as a more accurate description of the surety's right.

(c) The conditions enumerated in this Article are exclusive. The surety must establish the occurrence of at least one of them to maintain an action for security. See Taylor v. Drane, 13 La. 62 (1839); Edwards v. Prather, 22 La.Ann. 334 (1915).

(d) Paragraphs (1) and (3) restate Civil Code Article 3057(1) and (2) (1870). See Thompson v. Wilson's Executor, 13 La. 138 (1839). Cf. Bannon v. Barnett, 7 La.Ann. 648 (1852). See Mudd v. Rogers, 10 La.Ann. 648 (1855).

(e) Paragraph A(3) extends the principle of C.C. Art. 3057(3) (1870). A surety who has entered into a suretyship with the creditor in reliance on a contract with the principal obligor, has a cause of action if the obligor breaches his obligations under the contract, by failing to pay the surety his fee, or by failing to secure the discharge of the surety at an expressed time, etc. Since he may not have suffered damages before payment, the surety would have no effective remedy for the breach and should be permitted to demand security from the obligor.

(f) Paragraph (4) recodifies Art. 3057(4) (1870). See Mudd v. Rogers, 10 La.Ann. 648 (1855). Louisiana courts have relied on the surety's right to security before payment as a basis for holding that a delay or a mere forbearance to sue by the creditor is not a "prolongation of the terms" under Art. 3063 (1870) that will discharge the surety even if some privilege or security is lost. Cooly v. Lawrence, 4 Mart. O.S. 639 (1817). See also Gillet v. Rachal, 9 Rob. 276 (1844). Since this right is available it should make no difference whether the extension is "binding" upon the creditor or not. The surety is free to seek protection. Consequently, Article 3063 (1870) (discharging the surety if an extension of time is granted) is repealed.

(g) This Article does not contain a provision similar to C.C. Art. 3057(5) (1870). There apparently have been no cases decided under that provision. The provision is unnecessary.

Art. 3054. Failure to provide security

If, within ten days after the delivery of a written demand for the security, the principal obligor fails to provide the required security or fails to secure the discharge of the surety, the surety has an action to require the principal obligor to deposit into the registry of the court funds sufficient to satisfy the surety's obligation to the creditor as a pledge for the principal obligor's duty to reimburse the surety.

Acts 1987, No. 409, § 1, eff. Jan. 1, 1988.

REVISION COMMENT—1987

This Article is new. It clarifies the law by establishing the procedure by which the surety may enforce his right to security granted by the preceding Article, a matter not made clear by the former Code. See Art. 3057 (1870).

CHAPTER 5—THE EFFECTS OF SURETYSHIP AMONG SEVERAL SURETIES

Art. 3055.   Liability among co-sureties

Co-sureties are those who are sureties for the same obligation of the same obligor. They are presumed to share the burden of the principal obligation in proportion to their number unless the parties agreed otherwise or contemplated that he who bound himself first would bear the entire burden of the obligation regardless of others who thereafter bind themselves independently of and in reliance upon the obligation of the former.

Acts 1987, No. 409, § 1, eff. Jan. 1, 1988.

REVISION COMMENTS—1987

(a) This Article is new. It presumes that a person who becomes surety for an obligation already secured by a suretyship previously given is relying upon the security for the debt as well as the credit of the debtor. The same result can be obtained under present law if the surety becomes a sub-surety for the previous surety rather than for the principal obligor. It is in accord with the rules presently prevailing for negotiable instruments. See R.S. 10:3–414.

(b) The presumption provided in this Article is rebuttable. Parol evidence is admissible to overcome the presumption and to show that the sureties agreed among themselves that liability would be proportionately shared or that certain sureties were induced to make their contract with the understanding that others would entirely bear the burden. See the official comments to U.C.C. 3–414 (1978 version) and Aiavolasiti v. Versailles Gardens Land Dev. Co., 371 So.2d 755 (La.1979).

(c) The exception clause in the second sentence of the Article is applicable only if the later surety can prove he had knowledge of and relied on the existence of the earlier surety. If the later surety is ignorant of the earlier suretyship or if they all contract in contemplation of each other's agreements, then the presumption of an equality in sharing the burden among the several sureties should apply. The order of liability should be what the parties contemplate, and the extent to which a surety has relied upon the presence of other sureties who are to bear all (or a part) of the burden of the debt.

Art. 3056.   Right of contribution among co-sureties

A surety who pays the creditor may proceed directly or by way of subrogation to recover from his co-sureties the share of the principal obligation each is to bear. If a co-surety becomes insolvent, his share is to be borne by those who would have borne it in his absence.

Acts 1987, No. 409, § 1, eff. Jan. 1, 1988.

REVISION COMMENTS—1987

(a) This Article reproduces the rule stated in C.C. Art. 3058 (1870). Implicit in this Article is the requirement that the co-sureties are bound for the same debt and the same principal obligor. See Art. 3056 (Rev.1986); Stockmeyer v. Oertling, 35 La.Ann. 467 (1883). It is immaterial whether the sureties bind themselves at different times or by different contracts except insofar as such matters may regulate the order and extent of their liability among themselves.

(b) This Article removes the requirement of C.C. Art. 3058 (1870) that before a surety may seek contribution from his co-sureties, he must have paid in consequence of a lawsuit.

Art. 3057.   Limitation upon right of contribution

A surety who pays the creditor more than his share may recover the excess from his co-sureties in proportion to the amount of the obligation each is to bear as to him. If a surety obtains the conventional discharge of other co-sureties by paying the creditor, any reduction in the amount owed by those released benefits them proportionately.

Acts 1987, No. 409, § 1, eff. Jan. 1, 1988.

REVISION COMMENT—1987

Ordinarily payments by a surety are first imputed to his part of the debt vis a vis his co-surety. Thus if one of two sureties (who are to share the debt equally) pays one half of the obligation and secures a release from the creditor it neither affects the obligation of the other (who remains liable for his half) nor gives rise to a right to reimbursement in favor of the one who pays. If however, by paying one half of the debt, the surety is able to secure a release both for himself and his co-surety, the latter benefiting equally from the discount, should reimburse the other one half of what he has paid.

CHAPTER 6—TERMINATION OR EXTINCTION OF SURETYSHIP

Art. 3058. Extinction of the suretyship

The obligations of a surety are extinguished by the different manners in which conventional obligations are extinguished, subject to the following modifications.

Acts 1987, No. 409, § 1, eff. Jan. 1, 1988.

REVISION COMMENT—1987

This Article reproduces the substance of C.C. Art. 3059 (1870). It suppresses, as being redundant, the second clause of that Article relative to confusion between the surety and principal obligor.

Art. 3059. Extinction of principal obligation

The extinction of the principal obligation extinguishes the suretyship.

Acts 1987, No. 409, § 1, eff. Jan. 1, 1988.

REVISION COMMENTS—1987

(a) This Article is new. It is implicit from the accessorial nature of suretyship. Under the Revised Civil Code of 1870 the discharge of the surety because of the extinction of the principal obligation was left to implication but recognized in terms of defenses available to the surety. See former C.C. Art. 3060 (1870).

(b) Payment of the principal obligation by a surety does not affect the rights of the sureties among themselves.

Art. 3060. Prescription of the surety's obligation, right of reimbursement, and contribution

Prescription of the principal obligation extinguishes the obligation of the surety. A surety's action for contribution from his co-sureties and his action for reimbursement from the principal obligor prescribe in ten years.

The interruption of prescription against a surety is effective against the principal obligor and other sureties only when such parties have mutually agreed to be bound together with the surety against whom prescription was interrupted.

Acts 1987, No. 409, § 1, eff. Jan. 1, 1988.

REVISION COMMENTS—1987

(a) This Article is new. Because the surety's obligation is accessory to the principal obligation, the surety's obligation prescribes with the principal obligation. See Gilbert v. Meriam, 2 La.Ann. 160 (1847); J.R. Watkins Co. v. Lewis, 16 So.2d 495 (La.App.2d Cir.1944).

(b) The surety's claims for reimbursement and contribution, being personal actions, prescribe in ten years. See C.C. Art. 3499 (Rev.1983); Cleveland v. Comstock, 22 La.Ann. 597 (1870); Allen v. McDonald, 89 So. 799 (La.1921).

(c) The last paragraph recognizes the principle inherent in the concept of "perfect" solidarity, that when parties contract together, whether as principals or as principal and surety, payment or acknowledgment by one should be sufficient to interrupt prescription against the other. Its practical effect is limited to cases where the surety who has contracted jointly with the principal is sued, makes a payment, or otherwise acknowledges the debt. This will have the effect of interrupting prescription upon the principal obligation.

Art. 3061. Termination of suretyship

A surety may terminate the suretyship by notice to the creditor. The termination does not affect the surety's liability for obligations incurred by the principal obligor, or obligations the creditor is bound to permit the principal obligor to incur at the time the notice is received, nor may it prejudice the creditor or principal obligor who has changed his position in reliance on the suretyship.

Knowledge of the death of a surety has the same effect on a creditor as would a notice of termination received from the surety. A termination resulting from notice of the surety's death does not affect a universal successor of the surety who thereafter unequivocally confirms his willingness to continue to be bound thereby. The confirmation need not be in writing to be enforceable.

Acts 1987, No. 409, § 1, eff. Jan. 1, 1988.

REVISION COMMENTS—1987

(a) This Article is new. It codifies and clarifies the implicit understanding that a suretyship is revocable by the surety until the creditor or debtor has acted upon it. See comments to Article 3039 (Rev.1987) and Exposé des Motifs, infra.

(b) The second paragraph of this Article codifies a principle recognized by the jurisprudence. See Interstate Electric Co. v. Tucker, 2 So.2d 56 (La.1941); Buckeye Cotton Oil Co. v. Amrheim, 121 So. 602 (La.1929); Menard v. Scudder, 7 La.Ann. 385 (1852). Whether a universal successor of a surety unequivocally confirms his willingness to continue to be bound on the suretyship is factual.

Art. 3062. Effect of modifications of principal obligation

The modification or amendment of the principal obligation, or the impairment of real security held for it, by the creditor, in any material manner and without the consent of the surety, has the following effects.

An ordinary suretyship is extinguished.

A commercial suretyship is extinguished to the extent the surety is prejudiced by the action of the creditor, unless the principal obligation is one other than for the payment of money, and the surety should have contemplated that the creditor might take such action in the ordinary course of performance of the obligation. The creditor has the burden of proving that the surety has not been prejudiced or that the extent of the prejudice is less than the full amount of the surety's obligation.

Acts 1987, No. 409, § 1, eff. Jan. 1, 1988.

REVISION COMMENTS—1987

(a) This Article is based upon C.C. Art. 3061 (1870).

(b) Louisiana jurisprudence has created a special rule, applicable to compensated sureties who guarantee construction or other contracts, that changes or alterations that do not materially affect the surety's liability and that bear a reasonable relationship to the extent of the original project will not release the surety. See State v. Preferred Acc. Ins. Co. of N.Y., 149 So.2d 632 (La.App. 1st Cir.1963). This jurisprudential rule was made statutory in R.S. 9:4812(E)(2). This Article extends that rule to commercial suretyships generally and amplifies its provisions.

CHAPTER 7—LEGAL SURETYSHIP

Art. 3063.   Commercial suretyship rules apply to legal suretyship

The provisions governing commercial suretyship contained in this Title apply to legal suretyship except as otherwise provided in this Chapter.

Acts 1987, No. 409, § 1, eff. Jan. 1, 1988.

REVISION COMMENT—1987

This Article is new. It complements the following Article. The two Articles establish that legal suretyship is essentially regulated by the Articles pertaining to commercial suretyship, unless the particular provisions of the Chapter on legal suretyship provide otherwise, or unless such Articles are in conflict with the particular statute or regulation establishing the legal suretyship.

Art. 3064.   Supplementary nature of this Chapter

The provisions of this Chapter apply to the extent they are not contrary to special laws governing particular kinds of legal suretyship.

Acts 1987, No. 409, § 1, eff. Jan. 1, 1988.

REVISION COMMENT—1987

This Article expands and articulates the general principle implicit in C.C. Arts. 3066 and 3068 (1870), that the laws establishing or regulating particular kinds of legal and judicial suretyships prevail over the general provisions of this chapter to the extent they are incompatible.

Art. 3065.   Qualifications of legal surety; evidenced by affidavit; lack thereof not a defense

Legal suretyship may be given only by a person authorized to conduct a surety business in Louisiana or by a natural person domiciled in this state who owns property in this state that is subject to seizure and is of sufficient value to satisfy the obligation of the surety.

The qualification of a natural person to act as legal surety must be evidenced by his affidavit and the affidavit of the principal obligor.

A legal surety may not raise his lack of qualification as a defense to an action on his contract.

Acts 1987, No. 409, § 1, eff. Jan. 1, 1988.

REVISION COMMENTS—1987

(a) This Article reproduces the substance of C.C. Art. 3042 (1870). It changes the law insofar as Article 3042 (1870) required that the surety be domiciled in the parish where security was to be given.

(b) The second Paragraph is new. It extends to legal sureties generally the procedure applicable to sureties on bonds in judicial proceedings. The qualifications of a corporate surety (who must be licensed to conduct a surety business in this state) need not be proven by affidavit, since the fact of their qualifications may be easily verified. See C.C.P. Art. 5122.

(c) The third Paragraph is new. It does not change the law. See Madison Parish School Directors v. Brown, 33 La.Ann. 383 (1881). It makes clear that while a suretyship may not comply with the law requiring it the surety can not escape liability from his contract by pleading his lack of qualification.

Art. 3066.   Legal suretyship to conform to law

A legal suretyship is deemed to conform to the requirements of the law or order pursuant to which it is given, except as provided by Article 3067.

Acts 1987, No. 409, § 1, eff. Jan. 1, 1988.

REVISION COMMENTS—1987

(a) This Article is new. It follows the provisions adopted in R.S. 9:4812(D). See Miller v. Bonner, 111 So. 776 (La.1927). Davis v. West Louisiana Bank, 99 So. 207 (La.1924).

(b) An error, inaccuracy, or omission in naming the obligee on the bond is not a defense to an action thereon. The proper obligee may be inserted by the court. See C.C.P. Art. 5121; Scooler v. Alstrom, 38 La.Ann. 907 (1886).

Art. 3067.   Permissible variations

A surety is not liable for a sum in excess of that expressly stated in his contract. A legal suretyship may contain terms more favorable to the creditor than those required by the law or order pursuant to which it is given, but it may not provide for a time longer than is provided by law for bringing an action against the surety.

Acts 1987, No. 409, § 1, eff. Jan. 1, 1988.

REVISION COMMENT—1987

This Article is new. The first sentence of this Article provides that the surety may not be bound for a sum in excess of the total amount stated in his contract even if the statute under which he gave the bond required more. U.S. v. National Surety Co. of N.Y., 187 So.2d 9 (La.1939); Dougherty v. Peters, 2 Rob. 537 (1842); Conn v. U.S. Fidelity & Guaranty Co., 13 Orl.App. 99 (1916). See also R.S. 9:4812(D). If the bond is insufficient, the remedy is to get a new bond. When the amount of the bond is left blank, however, the law will supply the amount in accordance with the statute requiring the bond. Ricks v. Gantt, 35 La.Ann. 920 (1883).

Art. 3068.   Pledge of funds in lieu of suretyship

Legal suretyship may be given whenever the law requires or permits a person to give security for an obligation. The principal obligor may in lieu of legal suretyship deposit a sum equal to the amount for which he is to furnish security to be held in pledge as security for his obligation.

Acts 1987, No. 409, § 1, eff. Jan. 1, 1988.

REVISION COMMENT—1987

This Article reproduces the substance of C.C. Art. 3065 (1870).

Art. 3069.   Necessity for judgment against legal surety

No judgment shall be rendered against a legal surety unless the creditor obtains judgment against the principal obligor fixing the amount of the latter's liability to the creditor or unless the amount of that liability has otherwise been fixed. The creditor may join the surety and principal obligor in the same action.

Acts 1987, No. 409, § 1, eff. Jan. 1, 1988.

REVISION COMMENTS—1987

(a) The first sentence of this Article restates the rule of C.C. Art. 3066 (1870) and requires the creditor to obtain a judgment against the principal obligor fixing the amount of the latter's liability to the creditor before a judgment may be rendered against the surety. Posey v. Hamner, 27 So.2d 158 (La.1946). See C.C.P. Art. 2592(4). It establishes an exception where the amount of the creditor's "liability has otherwise been fixed" in some manner other than by judgment, as for example, when a suretyship is given in response to an order of an administrative agency, and the liability of the creditor is fixed by an order of the agency that is not appealed.

(b) C.C. Art. 3066 (1870), as interpreted by the courts, required, in addition to a judgment against the principal debtor, issuance of a writ of execution and its return nulla bona. American Indemnity Co. v. Robertson, 309 So.2d 737 (4th Cir.1975); Nicholson v. Ogden, 6 La.Ann. 486 (1851); Gaillard v. Bordelon, 35 La.Ann. 390 (1883). The requirement of a nulla bona return of the writ of execution was limited to actions on those bonds listed in Art. 3066 (1870). Macready v. Schenck, 41 La.Ann. 456 (1889); Ocean Coffee Co. v. Employers Liability Assur. Corp., 171 So. 144 (La.App. 2nd

Cir.1936). However, in some circumstances the judgment alone was sufficient, for example when the debtor's estate was obviously insolvent. Alley v. Hawthorne, 1 La.Ann. 122 (1846); Trimble v. Brichta, 11 La.Ann. 271; Murison v. Butler, 20 La.Ann. 512; Lepretre v. Barthet, 25 La.Ann. 124 (1873). Under this Article the creditor is not required to issue a writ of execution and have it returned nulla bona.

(c) The first sentence of this Article would not be applicable in those situations authorized by specific legislation where the creditor is allowed to sue the surety directly without the necessity of first obtaining a judgment against or joinder of the principal debtor. See La Rose v. Alliance Casualty Co., 150 So. 455 (Orl.App.1933); State v. McDonnell, 12 La.Ann. 741 (1857). Ocean Coffee Co. v. Employers Liability Assur. Corp., 171 So. 144 (La.App. 2nd Cir.1936).

(d) The second sentence of this Article allows joinder of the principal debtor with the surety in the same suit. This rule is grounded upon modern procedural notions of judicial efficiency. See Succession of Moody, 158 So.2d 601 (La.1963). However, it is not proper, unless authorized by special legislation, to sue the surety alone without joinder of the principal debtor. Such an action is premature, under the first sentence of this Article, until a judgment is obtained against the principal debtor. Posey v. Hamner, 27 So.2d 158 (La.1946). This rule differs from the rule for conventional sureties which allows the surety to be sued before there is judgment against the principal obligor. See comment (d) to Art. 3045 (Rev.1987). There is good reason, however, for preserving the distinction. The overwhelming number of legal suretyships are given for obligations that are neither contractual nor liquidated. To permit the surety to be sued alone would in such cases force the surety, in effect, to defend the principal debtor and would thus convert the contract of suretyship into one of insurance. Furthermore, the debtor could thereafter deny his liability and force the surety to again litigate the merits of the claim. These events are much less likely to occur under conventional suretyships, which are ordinarily given to secure moneyed obligations where the amount of the liability is seldom in dispute, and where the obligation itself is frequently incurred as a result of representations of the surety that the debtor is responsible.

(e) The last sentence of Art. 3066 (1870), dealing with sureties on official bonds, is not expressly reproduced here. There is no intent to affect R.S. 42:196, which gives sureties on official bonds the right to discussion. See Art. 3064 (Rev.1987).

Art. 3070. Right to demand new security

If a legal surety ceases to possess required qualifications or becomes insolvent or bankrupt, any interested person may demand that the principal obligor furnish additional security in the same amount and upon the same terms as those given by the existing surety for the performance of the obligation.

Acts 1987, No. 409, § 1, eff. Jan. 1, 1988.

REVISION COMMENTS—1987

(a) This Article reproduces and expands the rule stated in C.C. Art. 3043 (1870) but limits its application to legal suretyship.

(b) The procedure for testing the sufficiency of bonds in judicial proceedings is contained in C.C.P. Arts. 5123–5126.

TITLE XVII—COMPROMISE

Art. 3071. Compromise; definition

A compromise is a contract whereby the parties, through concessions made by one or more of them, settle a dispute or an uncertainty concerning an obligation or other legal relationship.

Acts 2007, No. 138, § 1.

REVISION COMMENTS—2007

(a) This Article is new. It is not intended to change the law. It is based on contemporary notions regarding the elements of the contract of compromise expressed in modern Civil Codes. See, for example, Article 1809 of the Spanish Civil Code and Article 3307 of the Ethiopian Civil Code.

(b) This Article does not retain the traditional Louisiana approach of referring to this contract as "transaction or compromise." Since either term would be sufficient in and of itself, this Revision refers to this contract as "compromise," since the term "transaction" is superfluous and could lead to confusion.

(c) A valid and enforceable settlement may also be a compromise if it is reduced to writing. Louisiana courts have held that "settlement" must be equated with compromise in connection with the rules governing compromise. See Townsend v. Square, 643 So.2d 787 (La.App. 4 1994).

Art. 3072. Formal requirements; effects

A compromise shall be made in writing or recited in open court, in which case the recitation shall be susceptible of being transcribed from the record of the proceedings.

Acts 2007, No. 138, § 1.

REVISION COMMENTS—2007

(a) This Article preserves the requirement of Article 3071 of the Louisiana Civil Code of 1870 that a compromise must be reduced to writing. It is not intended to change the law.

(b) When the parties reach a valid oral settlement in court they may mutually compel each other to reduce the agreement to writing. Abadie v. Metropolitan Life Insurance Company, 712 So.2d 932 (La.App. 5 Cir. 1998).

(c) A compromise, as any other contract, may be contained in two instruments rather than one. A consent judgment may also have the nature of a compromise. DeSoto v. DeSoto, 694 So.2d 1043 (La.App. 5 Cir. 1997).

(d) The requirement of a writing for a valid compromise may be satisfied by complying with the provisions of R.S. 9:2601–2620 which regulate electronic contracts.

Art. 3073. Capacity and form

When a compromise effects a transfer or renunciation of rights, the parties shall have the capacity, and the contract shall meet the requirement of form, prescribed for the transfer or renunciation.

Acts 2007, No. 138, § 1.

REVISION COMMENTS—2007

(a) This Article is new. It reflects in part the principle contained in Article 3072 of the Louisiana Civil Code of 1870.

(b) The tutor of a minor and the curator of an absentee must obtain court approval, as required by law, to enter into a compromise.

(c) A corporation must comply with any formal or other requirements necessary for the alienation of its assets.

Art. 3074.   Lawful object

The civil consequences of an unlawful act giving rise to a criminal action may be the object of a compromise, but the criminal action itself shall not be extinguished by the compromise.

A compromise may relate to the patrimonial effects of a person's civil status, but that civil status cannot be changed by the compromise.

Acts 2007, No. 138, § 1.

REVISION COMMENTS—2007

(a) This Article is new. It is not intended to change the law. It is based on well-established principles of Louisiana law recognized by Louisiana courts. See Civil Code Article 7. See also Ackel v. Ackel, 696 So.2d 140 (La.App. 5 Cir. 1997).

(b) A compromise will not be invalidated in the absence of a clear showing that it violates public policy. State through the Department of Social Services on Behalf of Harden v. Southern Baptist Hospital, 663 So.2d 443 (La.App. 4 Cir. 1995).

(c) The validity of a compromise concerning future alimony or child support is governed by the provisions of this Code and the Revised Statutes on family law.

Art. 3075.   Relative effect

A compromise entered into by one of multiple persons with an interest in the same matter does not bind the others, nor can it be raised by them as a defense, unless the matter compromised is a solidary obligation.

REVISION COMMENT—2007

This Article reproduces the substance of Article 3077 of the Civil Code of 1870. It is not intended to change the law.

Art. 3076.   Scope of the act

A compromise settles only those differences that the parties clearly intended to settle, including the necessary consequences of what they express.

Acts 2007, No. 138, § 1.

REVISION COMMENTS—2007

(a) This Article reproduces the substance of Article 3073 of the Louisiana Civil Code of 1870. It is not intended to change the law.

(b) Under this Article, a compromise must clearly express the rights that the parties intended to settle.

Art. 3077.   [Blank]

Art. 3078.   After-acquired rights

A compromise does not affect rights subsequently acquired by a party, unless those rights are expressly included in the agreement.

Acts 2007, No. 138, § 1.

REVISION COMMENTS—2007

(a) This Article reproduces the substance of Article 3074 of the Louisiana Civil Code of 1870. It is not intended to change the law.

(b) The provisions of this Article do not dispense with the requirement that a party act in good faith as required by law. See Civil Code Articles 1759 and 1983.

Art. 3079.   Tender and acceptance of less than the amount of the claim

A compromise is also made when the claimant of a disputed or unliquidated claim, regardless of the extent of his claim, accepts a payment that the other party tenders with the clearly expressed written condition that acceptance of the payment will extinguish the obligation.

Acts 2007, No. 138, § 1.

REVISION COMMENTS—2007

(a) This Article is new. It is not intended to change the law. It gives recognition to the validation by the Louisiana jurisprudence of the dispute-settling mechanism known at common law as accord and satisfaction. See Burger v Quintero, 170 La. 37, 127 So. 356 (1930); McLelland v. Security Industrial Insurance Company, 426 So.2d 665 (La.App. 1 Cir. 1982); Brown v. Drillers, Inc., 630 So.2d 741 (La. 1994).

(b) An act that fails to meet the requirements for accord and satisfaction may be a valid compromise if it meets the general requirements for the validity of a compromise.

(c) It is essential to a valid accord and satisfaction that the creditor understands that the payment is tendered in full settlement of the dispute. See, for example, McLelland v. Security Industrial Insurance Company, 426 So.2d 665 (La.App. 1 Cir. 1982); Adams v. Sconza, 380 So.2d 679 (La.App. 4 Cir. 1980); Louisiana National Bank of Baton Rouge v. Heindel, 365 So.2d 37 (La.App. 4 Cir. 1978).

(d) The recipient of payment makes his informed consent manifest when he accepts the payment intended to be made in full, that is, to put an end to a difference between the parties. Walters v. Greer, 726 So.2d 1094 (La.App. 2 Cir. 1999).

Art. 3080.   Preclusive effect of compromise

A compromise precludes the parties from bringing a subsequent action based upon the matter that was compromised.

Acts 2007, No. 138, § 1.

REVISION COMMENTS—2007

(a) This Article precludes subsequent actions on the subject matter that was the object of the compromise, in accordance with the intent of the parties. This preclusive effect of a compromise can be raised in a peremptory exception, under Code of Civil Procedure Article 927.

(b) The preclusive effect of this Article is tantamount to that of former Article 3078 of the Louisiana Civil Code of 1870, prior to the revision of the law of res judicata in 1990. See R.S. 13:4231.

(c) The fact that a compromise has been reached does not preclude correction of an error in calculation in appropriate cases.

Art. 3081.   Effect on novation

A compromise does not effect a novation of the antecedent obligation. When a party fails to perform a compromise, the other party may act either to enforce the compromise or to dissolve it and enforce his original claim.

Acts 2007, No. 138, § 1.

REVISION COMMENTS—2007

(a) This Article clarifies the law by expressly providing that a compromise does not novate the antecedent obligation. Thus under this Article when a party breaches the compromise, the other party is not limited to an action to enforce the compromise. Enforcing the compromise may prove the more attractive alternative, since a party seeking to enforce the compromise would not need to prove the elements of the original cause of action settled by the compromise involved.

(b) In order to regard the contract as dissolved the party electing that remedy shall give the notice prescribed in Civil Code Article 2015.

(c) The parties may expressly agree that the compromise is to effect a novation. In such a case, the only remedy available for nonperformance is an action to enforce the compromise.

(d) Under this Article, the rights and duties of sureties, mortgagees or holders of other security rights, are governed by Civil Code Articles 3059, 3062, and other provisions of law.

Art. 3082. Rescission

A compromise may be rescinded for error, fraud, and other grounds for the annulment of contracts. Nevertheless, a compromise cannot be rescinded on grounds of error of law or lesion.

Acts 2007, No. 138, § 1.

REVISION COMMENTS—2007

(a) Under this Article, rescission of a compromise is based on general grounds for the annulment of contracts. See Civil Code Articles 1948–1958. The prescriptive period to bring an action to rescind or annul a contract is five years as provided in Civil Code Article 2032.

(b) As under current law, this Article provides that a compromise cannot be rescinded for error of law or lesion.

(c) A compromise against public policy can be set aside on those grounds. Kozina v. Zeagler, 646 So.2d 1217, 1220 (La.App. 5 Cir. 1994).

(d) Under this Article, the discovery of new titles or documents is not grounds for annulment or rescission of a compromise in the absence of bad faith. See Mexican Civil Code Article 2957.

Art. 3083. Compromise suspends prescription

A compromise entered into prior to filing suit suspends the running of prescription of the claims settled in the compromise. If the compromise is rescinded or dissolved, prescription on the settled claims begins to run again from the time of rescission or dissolution.

Acts 2007, No. 138, § 1.

REVISION COMMENTS—2007

(a) This Article is new. It is not intended to change the law. It is based on fundamental notions of fairness and good faith. See Civil Code Articles 1759 and 1983.

(b) Under this Article, the running of prescription is suspended, not interrupted. Accordingly, the running of prescription resumes on the claims settled by the dissolved or rescinded compromise.

TITLE XVIII—OF RESPITE
[REPEALED]

Arts. 3084 to 3098. [Blank]

TITLE XIX—OF ARBITRATION

Art. 3099.   Submission to arbitrate

A *submission* is a covenant by which persons who have a lawsuit or difference with one another, name arbitrators to decide the matter and bind themselves reciprocally to perform what shall be arbitrated.

Art. 3100.   Writing necessary

A submission must be reduced to writing.

Art. 3101.   Capacity of parties; authority of mandataries, tutors and curators

They who cannot bind themselves cannot make a submission.

An attorney in fact cannot make a submission without a special power.

The tutors of minors and the curators of persons interdicted or absent, cannot do it without being authorized by the judge.

Amended by Acts 1979, No. 711, § 1, eff. Jan. 1, 1980.

Art. 3102.   Scope of submission

Parties may submit either all their differences, or only some of them in particular; and likewise they may submit to arbitration a lawsuit already instituted or only in contemplation, and generally every thing which they are concerned in, or which they may dispose of.

Art. 3103.   Arbitration of damages incurred by public offense

One may submit to arbitration the damages incurred for a public offense; but it is without any prejudice to the prosecution of it in behalf of the State.

Art. 3104.   Power of arbitrators

The power of arbitrators is limited to what is explained in the submission.

Art. 3105.   Duration of power of arbitrators; prescription

A.   If the submission does not limit any time, the power of the arbitrators may continue in force during three months from the date of the submission, unless the parties agree to revoke it.

B.   Prescription is interrupted as to any matter submitted to arbitration from the date of the submission and shall continue until the submission and power given to the arbitrators are put at an end by one of the causes in Article 3132, unless suit has been filed, in which case the provisions of Articles 3462 and 3463 shall apply.

Amended by Acts 1984, No. 782, § 1.

Art. 3106.   Penal clauses in submission

It is usual to undergo a penalty of a certain sum of money in the submission, which the person who shall contravene the award, or bring appeal therefrom, shall be bound to pay to the other who is willing to abide by it; but this covenant is not essential, and the submission may subsist without the penalty.

Art. 3107.   Capacity of arbitrators

A.   All persons may be arbitrators, except such as are under some incapacity or infirmity, which renders them unfit for that function.

B.   Therefore, minors under the age of eighteen years, persons interdicted, those who are deaf and unable to speak, can not be arbitrators.

Amended by Acts 2014, No. 811, § 30, eff. June 23, 2014.

Art. 3108.   [Blank]

Art. 3109.   Arbitrators and amicable compounders

There are two sorts of arbitrators:

The arbitrators properly so called;

And the amicable compounders.

Art. 3110.   Powers of arbitrators and amicable compounders

The arbitrators ought to determine as judges, agreeably to the strictness of the law.

Amicable compounders are authorized to abate something of the strictness of the law in favor of natural equity.

Amicable compounders are, in other respects, subject to the same rules which are provided for the arbitrators by the present title.

Art. 3111.   Oath of arbitrators

Before examining the difference to them submitted, the arbitrators ought to take an oath before a judge or justice of the peace, to render their award with integrity and impartiality in the cause which is laid before them.

Art. 3112.   Presentation and proof of claims by parties

The parties, who have submitted their differences to arbitrators, must make known their claims, and prove them, in the same manner as in a court of justice, by producing written or verbal evidence in the order agreed on between them or fixed by the arbitrators.

Art. 3113.   Time, place and notice of hearing

The arbitrators shall appoint a time and place for examining the matter to them submitted, and give notice thereof to the parties or to their attorneys.

Art. 3114.   Attendance of parties and witnesses

The parties must attend the arbitrators either in person, or by their attorney, with their witnesses and documents. If one or both of them should not appear, the arbitrators may proceed and inquire into the affair in their absence.

Art. 3115.   Attendance and swearing in of witnesses

Arbitrators have no authority to compel witnesses to appear before them or to administer an oath; but, at the request of arbitrators, it will be the duty of justices of the peace to compel witnesses to appear and to administer the oath to them.

Art. 3116.   Disagreement among arbitrators; umpire

If the arbitrators disagree another shall decide, and that other is called an umpire.

Art. 3117. Nomination of umpire

The nomination of the umpire is either made by the parties themselves at the time of the submission, or left to the discretion of the arbitrators.

Art. 3118. Appointment of umpire

Whenever the umpire has not been appointed by the submission, the arbitrators have the power to appoint him, though such power is not mentioned in the submission. But if the arbitrators can not agree on this election, the umpire shall be appointed *ex officio* by the judge.

Art. 3119. Oath of umpire

The umpire shall take an oath similar to that taken by the arbitrators, before examining the matter or the point submitted to him.

Art. 3120. Time for decision of arbitrators

The arbitrators who have consented to act as such, ought to determine the suit or the difference which is submitted to them, as soon as possible and within the time fixed by the submission.

Art. 3121. Arbitrators acting in excess of power, effect

Arbitrators can not exceed the power which is given to them; and if they exceed it, their award is null for so much.

Art. 3122. Scope of arbitrators' authority

The authority of arbitrators extend [extends] only to the things contained in the submission, unless it has been stated that they shall have power to decide all disputes which may arise between the parties in the course of the arbitration.

Art. 3123. Award null after time limit

The arbitrators ought to give their award within the time limited by the submission, and it would be null if it were given after the time is expired.

Art. 3124. Extension of time for making award

Nevertheless the parties may give power to the arbitrators to prolong the time, and in this case their power lasts during the time of the prorogation.

Art. 3125. Award made prior to time specified for examination

If the submission specifies a certain time for the examination of the cause which the arbitrators are to decide, they can not give their award till that time is expired.

Amended by Acts 1871, No. 87.

Art. 3126. Participation in proceedings; signature of award

If there are several arbitrators named by the submission, they can not give their award, unless they all see the proceedings and try the cause together; but it is not necessary that the award be signed by them all.

Art. 3127. Amount of award

The arbitrators shall fix by their award the amount of the sum which they sentence one or several of the parties to pay to the other or others, though the omission of this does not annul the award.

Art. 3128.   Interest and costs

The arbitrators may likewise pronounce by their award on the interest and costs; but their silence on that subject is not a cause of nullity. If legal interest would have been payable by law from date of judicial demand, such legal interest awarded by the arbitrators shall attach from the date the matter was submitted to arbitration.

Amended by Acts 1985, No. 571, § 1.

Art. 3129.   Approval of award by judge

The award in order to be put in execution, ought to be approved by the judge; but this formality is only intended to invest the award with a sufficient authority to ensure its execution and not to submit to the judge the examination of its merits, except in case an appeal is brought before him.

Art. 3130.   Appeal from award; prepayment and repayment of penalty

He who is not satisfied with the award, may appeal from it, though the parties had renounced such appeal by the submission; but the appellant before being heard on his appeal, ought to pay the penalty stipulated in the submission, if any has been stipulated; and this penalty shall ever be due, though the appellant afterwards renounces his appeal; but if he succeeds to have the award reversed, either in whole or in part, the court who shall pronounce on the appeal, shall order the re-payment of the penalty; but if the award is confirmed, the penalty which has been paid, shall operate no diminution on the amount of the award.

Art. 3131.   Retraction or change of award prohibited

The arbitrators having once given their award, can not retract it nor change any thing in it.

Art. 3132.   Termination of arbitration

The submission and power given to the arbitrators are put at an end by one of the following causes:

1.   By the expiration of the time limited, either by the submission or by law, though the award should not be yet rendered.

2.   By the death of one of the parties or arbitrators.

3.   By the final award rendered by the arbitrators.

4.   When the parties happen to compromise touching the thing in dispute, or when this thing ceases to exist.

TITLE XX—SECURITY

Art. 3133. Liability of an obligor for his obligations

Whoever is personally bound for an obligation is obligated to fulfill it out of all of his property, movable and immovable, present and future.

Acts 2014, No. 281, § 1, eff. Jan. 1, 2015.

REVISION COMMENT—2014

This Article, which restates the substance of Article 3182 of the Louisiana Civil Code of 1870, provides the general principle that an obligor is bound to fulfill his obligations out of all of his property. This general principle is subject to exceptions established by law for certain kinds of property that are exempt from seizure for the satisfaction of creditors' claims. See, e.g., La. Const. Art. 12, Section 9 (1974); R.S. 9:2004–2006; R.S. 13:3881; R.S. 20:1; R.S. 20:33. La. Const. Art. 12, Section 10(C) (1974) exempts all public property from seizure, and that provision as well as R.S. 13:5109(B)(2) limits the enforcement of a judgment against the state, a state agency, or a political subdivision of the state to funds appropriated for that purpose by the legislature or political subdivision. See Newman Marchive Partnership, Inc. v. City of Shreveport, 979 So.2d 1262 (La. 2008).

Art. 3134. Ratable treatment of creditors

In the absence of a preference authorized or established by legislation, an obligor's property is available to all his creditors for the satisfaction of his obligations, and the proceeds of its sale are distributed ratably among them.

Acts 2014, No. 281, § 1, eff. Jan. 1, 2015.

REVISION COMMENTS—2014

(a) This Article, derived from Article 3183 of the Louisiana Civil Code of 1870, carries forward the familiar principle that the property of the debtor is the "common pledge of his creditors." The reference in the source Article to the concept of "pledge" has been deleted, because the term was used in that Article in a non-technical sense that was different from the security device known as pledge. See Slovenko, Of Pledge, 33 Tul. L. Rev. 59, 62–63 (1958).

(b) This Article does not imply that all of an obligor's creditors will have an immediate right to share in the proceeds of each sale of the obligor's property. In the case of a voluntary sale of property, the obligor retains whatever portion of the price remains after satisfying those creditors having secured rights in the thing sold, and both the price that he retains, and anything he may later acquire with it, form part of his patrimony that remains available to his creditors for satisfaction of the obligations owed to them. Even in the case of the enforcement of a mortgage or other security in a thing, the proceeds from the sale that remain after payment of the claims of the seizing creditor and those holding inferior security rights in the thing are delivered to the obligor, rather than to his other creditors. See C.C.P. Art. 2373.

Art. 3135. Limitations upon recourse

A written contract may provide that the obligee's recourse against the obligor is limited to particular property or to a specified class or kind of property.

Acts 2014, No. 281, § 1, eff. Jan. 1, 2015.

REVISION COMMENTS—2014

(a) This Article is new. It expands a concept that was introduced by the 1991 revision of the Articles on mortgage. A similar provision is found in Article 2645 of the Québec Civil Code.

(b) When a contract limits an obligee's recourse to certain property, the limitation serves as an exception to the provisions of Article 3134 (Rev. 2014), and the obligee has no right to have the obligation owed to him satisfied from the obligee's other property.

(c) An obligee's right of recourse may be limited to the security given for the performance of the obligation owed to the obligee. Under this Article, however, an obligee's right of recourse could be limited to specified property of the obligor even if the obligee holds no security at all.

(d) The limitation contemplated by this Article may be made either by identifying the property against which the obligee will have recourse or, inversely, by identifying property against which the obligee will have no recourse. The property may be identified with specificity or by employing general classifications of property, such as those found in Articles 448 (Rev. 1978) and 2335 (Rev. 1979).

Art. 3136. Security defined

Security is an accessory right established by legislation or contract over property, or an obligation undertaken by a person other than the principal obligor, to secure performance of an obligation. It is accessory to the obligation it secures and is transferred with the obligation without a special provision to that effect.

Acts 2014, No. 281, § 1, eff. Jan. 1, 2015.

REVISION COMMENTS—2014

(a) This Article is new, but it furthers the concepts stated in Article 1913 (Rev. 1984), which identifies certain types of security agreements as examples of accessory contracts. This Article is broader in its scope, however, because it is not limited to rights established by contract. For instance, privileges, which are established only by law and never by contract, are a form of security.

(b) The concept of security arises in numerous other Articles found throughout the Civil Code. See, e.g., C.C. Arts. 474 (Rev. 1978); 571 (Rev. 1976; Amended 2004); 573 and 624 (Rev. 1976; Amended 2010); 1499 (Rev. 1996; Amended 2003); 1514 (Rev. 1996; Amended 2003); 1783, 1884, 1887, 1891, 1913, and 2023 (Rev. 1984); 2557 and 2569 (Rev. 1993); 3047, 3053, 3054, 3062, 3068, and 3070 (Rev. 1987).

(c) When security consists of rights over property, it is a preference authorized or established by legislation and thus constitutes an exception to the ratable treatment principle of Article 3134 (Rev. 2014).

Art. 3137. Personal or real security

Security is personal or real.

It is personal when it consists of an obligation undertaken to secure performance of the obligation of another.

It is real when it consists of a right of preference established over property of the obligor or of a third person to secure performance of an obligation.

Acts 2014, No. 281, § 1, eff. Jan. 1, 2015.

REVISION COMMENTS—2014

(a) This Article is new, but it is not intended to change the law. On the distinction between real and personal security, see Slovenko, Of Pledge, 33 Tul. L. Rev. 59, 60 (1958).

(b) Suretyship is personal security. Security consisting of a right over property, such as mortgage, pledge, security interest, or privilege, is real security.

(c) Forms of real security are not necessarily real rights. Many privileges do not constitute real rights, even though they are a form of real security. See Liquid Carbonic Corporation v. Leger, 169 So. 170 (La.App. 1st Cir. 1936). See also Planiol et Ripert, Traité élémentaire de droit Civil, Volume 2, Part 2, No. 2548, 2618 (1939)(English translation by the Louisiana State Law Institute, 1959); Yiannopoulos, Real Rights in Louisiana and Comparative Law: Part 1, 23 La. Law Rev. 161, 223 (1963).

Art. 3138.   Kinds of security

Kinds of security include suretyship, privilege, mortgage, and pledge. A security interest established to secure performance of an obligation is also a kind of security.

Acts 2014, No. 281, § 1, eff. Jan. 1, 2015.

REVISION COMMENTS—2014

(a) This Article is new, but it is not intended to change the law.

(b) Article 3184 of the Louisiana Civil Code of 1870 defined lawful causes of preferences to include only privilege and mortgage. Those lawful causes of preference are forms of security that are mentioned in this Article along with privileges and security interests, as well as the contract of suretyship, which is a form of personal security.

(c) The list contained in this Article is merely illustrative. Other forms of security exist, such as a pignorative contract in the form of a sale with a right of redemption in favor of a seller who remains in possession. See C.C. Art. 2569 (Rev. 1993); Latiolais v. Breaux, 154 La. 1006, 98 So. 620 (La. 1924); Jackson v. Golson, 91 So.2d 394 (La.App. 2d Cir. 1956).

(d) This Article gives express recognition to the concept of security interest, which has been the exclusive means of creating security by contract in most kinds of movable property since Louisiana's adoption of Chapter 9 of the Uniform Commercial Code effective January 1, 1990. See Acts 1988, No. 528 and Acts 1989, No. 135, enacting Chapter 9 of Title 10 of the Louisiana Revised Statutes of 1950. The definition of "security interest" in the Uniform Commercial Code, however, is broader than interests in movable property intended as security; it also includes outright sales of certain kinds of property, such as accounts receivable. See R.S. 10:1–201(35). Only those security interests established for the purpose of securing an obligation qualify as "security" under this Title.

Art. 3139.   Law governing security interest

Security interest is defined by the Uniform Commercial Code, which specifies the kinds of property susceptible of encumbrance by a security interest and governs the manner of creation of security interests and the rights of the holders of security interests against obligors and third persons.

Acts 2014, No. 281, § 1, eff. Jan. 1, 2015.

REVISION COMMENTS—2014

(a) This Article is new. It signals that security interests, though obviously a form of security when granted for the purpose of securing an obligation, are governed by special legislation.

(b) Security interest, as defined in the Uniform Commercial Code, also includes certain transactions that do not secure the performance of an obligation. See R.S. 10:1–201(35). This Title is not intended to limit the definition of the term "security interest" found in the Uniform Commercial Code or the application of the Uniform Commercial Code to those transactions.

Art. 3140.   Nullity of agreement of forfeiture

Unless expressly permitted by law, a clause in a contract providing in advance that ownership of a thing given as security will transfer upon default in performance of the secured obligation is absolutely null.

A clause in a contract obligating the owner of a thing to give it to an obligee in payment of a debt upon a future default in performance of an obligation is absolutely null.

Acts 2014, No. 281, § 1, eff. Jan. 1, 2015.

REVISION COMMENTS—2014

(a) The first paragraph of this Article furthers a longstanding civilian concept that an agreement of forfeiture of a thing given as security, known in Roman law as the lex commissoria, is null. An express prohibition of agreements of that nature in contracts of pledge was contained in Article 3132 of the Louisiana Civil Code of 1825 and also in the second paragraph of Article 3165 of

755

the Louisiana Civil Code of 1870, until the repeal of that paragraph by Acts 1872, No. 9. Despite the repeal, agreements of forfeiture have continued to be viewed as unenforceable in Louisiana. See Alcolea v. Smith, 150 La. 482, 90 So. 769 (La. 1922), holding that agreements of forfeiture have been prohibited by the civil law "since the edict of Constantine" and that "it would require something more than a doubtful implication (i.e., the 1872 amendment of Article 3165) to justify any court in any civilized country in now reading it into a statute."

(b) The prohibition of this Article is not limited to contracts of pledge but rather applies to all forms of security. Thus, a mortgage may not provide that ownership of the mortgaged property will transfer to the mortgagee upon default.

(c) Many civil law jurisdictions continue to prohibit the lex commissoria. See, e.g., Québec Civil Code Art. 1801; Luxembourg Civil Code Art. 2078; Argentine Civil Code Art. 3222; B.G.B. § 1229; Spanish Civil Code Art. 1859. In France, the agreement of forfeiture, known as the pacte commissoire, is now sometimes permitted. See French Civil Code Arts. 2348, 2459, and 2460 (Rev. 2006).

(d) The second paragraph of the Article addresses a related concept: the inability of a debtor to promise before default to make a giving in payment. This paragraph follows, and makes more general, the holding of Guste v. Hibernia National Bank in New Orleans, 655 So.2d 724 (La.App. 4th Cir. 1995), writ denied 660 So.2d 852 (La. 1995), which found to be absolutely null a dation en paiement executed at the time of an act of credit sale and held in escrow under an agreement providing for its release upon a future default. The reasoning of the court was that the law provides for the exclusive means of foreclosure of a mortgage and any attempt to "completely bypass and waive the laws concerning foreclosure" violates public policy. This Article does not by its terms prohibit an obligor from promising after default to make a future giving in payment in favor of the obligee, but other public policy considerations may nonetheless make such a promise unenforceable according to the circumstances. On the invalidity of a promise to make a giving in payment, see Slovenko, Of Pledge, 33 Tul. L. Rev. 59, 116 (1958).

(e) Chapter 9 of the Uniform Commercial Code permits a creditor, after default, to propose a "strict foreclosure" whereby he will acquire the collateral in full or partial satisfaction of the secured obligation without the necessity of a judicial sale or other disposition. See R.S. 10:9–620 through 9–622. This Article does not limit the availability of strict foreclosure under the Uniform Commercial Code.

TITLE XX–A—PLEDGE

CHAPTER 1—GENERAL PROVISIONS

Art. 3141. Pledge defined

Pledge is a real right established by contract over property of the kind described in Article 3142 to secure performance of an obligation.

Acts 2014, No. 281, § 1, eff. Jan. 1, 2015.

REVISION COMMENTS—2014

(a) This Article is new. Article 3133 of the Louisiana Civil Code of 1870 defined pledge as a contract by which a debtor gives something to his creditor as security for his debt. Though that Article defined the term as a type of contract, ensuing Articles referred to "the obligation of pledge", and certain Articles referred to "the pledge" as the thing pledged. See, e.g., C.C. Art. 3175 (1870). This Article defines pledge as the real right that arises from a contract of pledge, rather than the contract itself.

(b) Pledge is defined by the domain of things that are susceptible of pledge, as specified in Article 3142 (Rev. 2014). A pledge under this Title cannot exist over other kinds of property.

(c) Since Louisiana's adoption of Chapter 9 of the Uniform Commercial Code effective January 1, 1990, the Articles on pledge contained in the Louisiana Civil Code of 1870 have been greatly reduced in their operation and to a large extent supplanted by the Uniform Commercial Code. The revision of this Title harmonizes the law of pledge with the Uniform Commercial Code by eliminating any overlap between the two wholly different regimes. Because of the very broad scope of Chapter 9 of the Louisiana Uniform Commercial Code, this Title has quite limited applicability to movables. It nonetheless fills a gap in the law that would otherwise exist with respect to encumbrance of movable property that is presently, or in the future becomes, excluded from coverage under the Uniform Commercial Code. See generally R.S. 10:9–109.

(d) Under the Louisiana Civil Code of 1870, two kinds of pledge existed: the pledge of a movable, known as the pawn, and the pledge of an immovable, known as the antichresis. See C.C. Arts. 3134 and 3135 (1870). With an antichresis, the creditor was given possession of an immovable for the purpose of reaping its fruits and other revenues and undertook the correlative obligations of paying taxes and providing for the upkeep and repair of the immovable. See C.C. Arts. 3176–3181 (1870). Because of the obligations imposed on the creditor, antichresis fell into disuse. See Slovenko, Of Pledge, 33 Tul. L. Rev. 59, 130 (1958). Over a century ago, the Louisiana Supreme Court termed it "an antiquated contract." See Harang v. Ragan, 134 La. 201, 63 So. 875, 877 (La. 1913). Antichresis is suppressed in this revision and is no longer a form of pledge. Despite the suppression of the nominate contract of antichresis, parties might nonetheless, through the exercise of the freedom of contract recognized by Article 1971 (Rev. 1984), enter into an innominate contract providing for an arrangement similar to what was previously known as an antichresis, but the contract would create neither a pledge under this Title nor a real right in the immovable enforceable against third persons who acquire rights in it. See Comment (d) to C.C. Art. 476 (Rev. 1978).

(e) In modern times, the antichresis has given way to other forms of security that allow the creditor to be secured by the revenues of an immovable without the disadvantages of an antichresis. For instance, in France, antichresis was effectively replaced by the cession of anticipated rent. Planiol et Ripert, Traité élémentaire de droit civil, Volume 2, Part 2, No. 2507–07 (1939)(English translation by the Louisiana State Law Institute, 1959). A similar evolution has taken place in Louisiana; the assignment of leases and rents, which has become almost universal in commercial real estate financings and which requires no dispossession of the debtor, has supplanted antichresis. Since 1980, the assignment of leases and rents has been governed by former R.S. 9:4401. This Title gives express recognition and treatment within the Civil Code to this modern form of pledge.

Art. 3142. Property susceptible of pledge

The only things that may be pledged are the following:

(1) A movable that is not susceptible of encumbrance by security interest.

(2) The lessor's rights in the lease of an immovable and its rents.

(3) Things made susceptible of pledge by law.

Acts 2014, No. 281, § 1, eff. Jan. 1, 2015.

REVISION COMMENTS—2014

(a) This Article is new. It contains an exhaustive list of things susceptible of pledge.

(b) Civil law jurisdictions typically permit all movable property, corporeal or incorporeal, to be encumbered by pledge. See, e.g., French Civil Code Arts. 2333 and 2355 and B.G.B. § 1204. Similarly, Articles 3154 and 3155 of the Louisiana Civil Code of 1870 provided that every corporeal or incorporeal movable could be pawned. With the adoption of Chapter 9 of the Uniform Commercial Code in Louisiana effective January 1, 1990, however, security interest became the exclusive means of encumbrance of most kinds of movable property, thereby greatly narrowing the kinds of movable property that can be pledged under the Civil Code. Nonetheless, the exclusions that do remain, or that might exist in the future, require the continued existence of the legal framework under which property outside the scope of Chapter 9 of the Uniform Commercial Code can be encumbered. This Article makes the set of things susceptible of pledge and the set of things susceptible of encumbrance by a security interest mutually exclusive.

(c) There are presently few, if any, corporeal movables that are excluded from coverage under Chapter 9 of the Uniform Commercial Code. The few incorporeal movables that are excluded include rights under policies of insurance other than life insurance. Even then, Chapter 9 still has limited applicability to the extent that amounts payable under an insurance policy constitute proceeds of other collateral. See R.S. 10:9–109(d)(8).

(d) Under this Article, the lessor's rights in the lease of an immovable and its rents are also susceptible of pledge. Chapter 2 of this Title contains rules that are specifically applicable to a pledge of that nature. Under prior law, the lessor's rights in the leases and rents of an immovable could be encumbered by an assignment or pledge effected under former R.S. 9:4401, a statute whose provisions suggested heavy influence from both the common law and the Uniform Commercial Code. This revision places the encumbrance of the lessor's rights in the lease of an immovable and its rents within the civil law framework of pledge and gives nearly complete treatment to pledges of that nature within the Civil Code itself.

Art. 3143. Pledge of property susceptible of encumbrance by security interest

A contract by which a person purports to pledge a thing that is susceptible of encumbrance by security interest does not create a pledge under this Title but may be effective to create a security interest in the thing.

Acts 2014, No. 281, § 1, eff. Jan. 1, 2015.

REVISION COMMENT—2014

This Article is new. In the case of property susceptible of encumbrance by a security interest, the Uniform Commercial Code contains the exclusive regime under which it can be encumbered as security, and parties are not permitted to negate the applicability of the Uniform Commercial Code by styling their contract as one of pledge. Nevertheless, it remains a common practice for property to be "pledged" under a contract styled as a "pledge," even though the property in question is susceptible of encumbrance under the Uniform Commercial Code and the security right created by the contract is actually a security interest. An example of this is the "pledge" of a collateral mortgage note. This Article provides that a contract purporting to pledge property that is susceptible of encumbrance under the Uniform Commercial Code does not create a pledge under this Title. Whether the contract is sufficient to create a security interest is a matter governed exclusively by the Uniform Commercial Code.

Art. 3144.   Accessory nature of pledge

Pledge is accessory to the obligation that it secures and may be enforced by the pledgee only to the extent that he may enforce the secured obligation.

Acts 2014, No. 281, § 1, eff. Jan. 1, 2015.

REVISION COMMENT—2014

This Article is new. As a form of security, pledge is always accessory to the obligation that it secures. Consequently, a pledge may be enforced only to the extent of the obligation that it secures. Another consequence of the accessory nature of pledge is that it is transferred with the obligation that it secures without a special provision to that effect. See C.C. Art. 3136 (Rev. 2014).

Art. 3145.   Preference afforded by pledge

Pledge gives the pledgee the right to be satisfied from the thing pledged and its fruits in preference to unsecured creditors of the pledgor and to other persons whose rights become effective against the pledgee after the pledge has become effective as to them.

Acts 2014, No. 281, § 1, eff. Jan. 1, 2015.

REVISION COMMENTS—2014

(a) This provision, which is based on Article 3157 of the Louisiana Civil Code of 1870, adds a ranking rule similar to that applicable to mortgages in Article 3307(3)(Rev. 1992).

(b) Because the kinds of property subject to security interest and pledge are mutually exclusive, there is no need for a rule ranking security interests against pledges except perhaps in the special case of insurance proceeds payable with respect to collateral that is subject to a security interest under the Uniform Commercial Code. Under R.S. 10:9–315, a security interest continues in the insurance proceeds, even though claims under insurance policies, other than life insurance, are otherwise outside the scope of Chapter 9 of the Uniform Commercial Code. See R.S. 10:9–109(d)(8). If, however, the owner of the collateral desires to encumber a claim to insurance proceeds in favor of another creditor, he must do so by granting a pledge under this Title. In that limited instance, there is the possibility of a ranking dispute between the secured party claiming rights to the insurance as proceeds of his collateral and the pledgee of the claim under the insurance policy. This Article supplies the ranking rule: if the security interest was perfected under the Uniform Commercial Code before the pledge was made effective against third persons, the security interest primes the pledge of rights under the insurance policy.

Art. 3146.   Obligations for which pledge may be given

A pledge may be given to secure the performance of any lawful obligation, including obligations that arise in the future. As to all obligations, present and future, secured by the pledge, notwithstanding the nature of the obligations or the date they arise, the pledge has effect between the parties from the time that the requirements for formation of the contract of pledge are satisfied and has effect as to third persons from the time that the applicable requirements of Articles 3153 through 3155 are satisfied.

Acts 2014, No. 281, § 1, eff. Jan. 1, 2015.

REVISION COMMENTS—2014

(a) This Article restates the substance of Article 3136 of the Louisiana Civil Code of 1870 and expressly permits a pledge to secure future obligations, an arrangement that was also permitted under the complicated provisions of Article 3158 of the 1870 Code, as amended.

(b) Article 3158 of the Louisiana Civil Code of 1870 required, as a condition for effectiveness against third persons, that a pledge state the amount of the debt that it secured or a limit on the amount of the secured obligations. In contrast, Chapter 9 of the Uniform Commercial Code does not require that a security agreement state the amount or limit of secured obligations. This Article follows the approach of the Uniform Commercial Code by omitting any requirement for a statement of the amount of the secured obligation. Chapter 2 of this Title requires, however, that a contract pledging the lessor's interest in the leases and rents of an immovable state the amount of the secured obligation or the maximum amount of secured obligations that may be outstanding from time to time. See C.C. Art. 3168 (Rev. 2014).

(c) In the case of a pledge securing future obligations, the rights created by the pledge as security for the future obligations relate back to the time the pledge became effective between the parties or, insofar as third persons are concerned, from the time the pledge was made effective against third persons. On that issue, this Article follows the pattern of Article 3298(B) (Rev. 1991; As Amended), which provides a similar rule for mortgages.

(d) Article 3140 of the Louisiana Civil Code of 1870 permitted a pledge to be given not only for an obligation consisting of money but also for one having another object. By permitting a pledge to secure any lawful obligation, this Article also allows a pledge to secure an obligation that is not for the payment of money. Article 3147 (Rev. 2014) specifies the effect of such a pledge.

Art. 3147. Pledge securing obligation that is not for the payment of money

A pledge that secures an obligation other than one for the payment of money, such as an obligation for the performance of an act, secures the claim of the pledgee for the damages he may suffer from the breach of the obligation.

Acts 2014, No. 281, § 1, eff. Jan. 1, 2015.

REVISION COMMENT—2014

This Article is new. Although it has no counterpart in the Civil Code of 1870, it is patterned after Article 3294 (Rev. 1991), which provides a similar rule for contracts of mortgage.

Art. 3148. Pledge securing an obligation of another person

A person may pledge his property to secure an obligation of another person. In such a case, the pledgor may assert against the pledgee any defense that the obligor could assert except lack of capacity or discharge in bankruptcy of the obligor. The pledgor may also assert any other defenses available to a surety.

Acts 2014, No. 281, § 1, eff. Jan. 1, 2015.

REVISION COMMENTS—2014

(a) The first sentence of this Article is derived from Article 3141 of the Louisiana Civil Code of 1870. The second sentence expresses the same principle found in Article 3295 (Rev. 1991), which applies when a person mortgages his property as security for another person's obligation.

(b) When a person encumbers his property as security for the obligation of another, his status is similar to that of a surety against whom recourse has been limited by contract to the thing given as security. French commentators refer to a third person who has mortgaged an immovable as security for the debt of another without obligating himself personally as a caution réelle, or real surety. Planiol, Traité élémentaire de droit civil, Vol. 2, Part 2, No. 2368 (English translation by the Louisiana State Law Institute, 1959); Baudry-Lacantinerie, Traité de droit civil français § 1292 (3d ed. 1906); T. 2. 18 Laurent, Principes de droit civil français § 126 at 160 (3d ed. 1878). See also Boyter v. Shreveport Bank & Trust, 65 B.R. 944 (W.D. La.1986). Because the status of a person who has pledged his property as security for the debt of another is akin to that of a surety, this Article grants to him the same defenses that are available to a surety under Article 3046 (Rev. 1987). In the event of a modification of the principal obligation without his consent, the pledgor is also entitled to assert the defenses available to a surety under Article 3062 (Rev. 1987).

Art. 3149. Formal requirements of contract of pledge

The pledge of a corporeal movable is effective between the parties only if the thing pledged has been delivered to the pledgee or a third person who has agreed to hold the thing for the benefit of the pledgee.

The pledge of other things is effective between the parties only if established by written contract, but delivery is not required.

Acts 2014, No. 281, § 1, eff. Jan. 1, 2015.

REVISION COMMENTS—2014

(a) This Article greatly simplifies the complicated rules that were provided in Article 3158 and other Articles of the Louisiana Civil Code of 1870 governing the formal requirements of the contract of pledge, at the same time adopting a number of concepts from Chapter 9 of the Uniform Commercial Code. Between the parties, this Article retains the requirement that a pledged corporeal movable must be placed into the pledgee's possession; indeed, that remains the essence of a pledge, as it is in many civil law systems. See, e.g., Argentine Civil Code Art. 3212; B.G.B. § 1205; Luxembourg Civil Code Art. 2076; Spanish Civil Code Art. 1863. In the case of the pledge of an incorporeal, however, delivery is unnecessary, and the requirement of a written pledge agreement is substituted as the essential element that must exist for the pledge to have effect between the parties.

(b) Under Article 3152 of the Louisiana Civil Code of 1870, delivery of the thing pledged was essential to the very existence of the contract of pledge, even between the parties. This provision was tempered, however, by Article 3153 (1870), which provided that delivery was necessary only with respect to corporeal things and that, in the case of incorporeal rights, delivery was merely fictitious and symbolical. Nevertheless, if the incorporeal right was evidenced by a writing, Articles 3156 and 3162 (1870) required delivery to the pledgee of the note or other instrument evidencing the right. This Article continues the requirement of delivery of a pledged corporeal movable but removes that requirement entirely in the case of the pledge of an incorporeal. In modern practice, contracts are often executed in multiple originals, and parties frequently treat mere scanned facsimiles exchanged by electronic means as the equivalent of signed original documents. Thus, a requirement of delivery of a contract or other instrument to the pledgee would further no purpose, except perhaps in the case of special types of writings such as promissory notes and certificates evidencing securities. The rights evidenced by those writings, however, are susceptible of encumbrance under the Uniform Commercial Code and therefore cannot be encumbered under this Title in any event. See C.C. Art. 3142 (Rev. 2014).

(c) Though this Article requires delivery in the case of the pledge of a corporeal movable, there may actually be no corporeal movables to which that rule would presently apply, for Chapter 9 of the Uniform Commercial Code may cover all corporeal movables without exception. The first sentence of this Article is intended to apply only if, under present law or under some future change in the law, a particular corporeal movable is insusceptible of encumbrance under the Uniform Commercial Code and therefore is properly susceptible of encumbrance by pledge. See Article 3142 (Rev. 2014). The first sentence of this Article is not intended to apply to a corporeal movable that is susceptible of encumbrance by a security interest under the Uniform Commercial Code. In that case, Chapter 9 of the Uniform Commercial Code applies exclusively.

(d) Article 3162 of the Civil Code of 1870 allowed the thing pledged to be placed into the possession of "a third person agreed on by the parties." Though not expressly required by the text of the Article, the jurisprudence held that the third person must have knowledge of the arrangement and accept delivery with the obligation to hold the property in trust for the pledgee. See Wells v. Dean, 211 La. 132, 29 So.2d 590 (La. 1947). This rule did not, however, necessarily require a written acknowledgment, and one case even presumed, in the absence of any other explanation why the pledgor of a life insurance policy had come into possession of the original policy before his death, that the pledgor's possession was as an agent pro hac vice for the pledgee. See Scott v. Corkern, 231 La. 368, 91 So.2d 569 (La. 1956). By comparison, when a third party's possession is used as the means of perfection of a security interest, the Uniform Commercial Code requires that the third party authenticate a record acknowledging that he holds possession of the collateral for the secured party's benefit. See R.S. 10:9–313(c)(1). This Article requires that the third person agree to hold the thing for the benefit of the pledgee but does not require that agreement to be in writing.

(e) As a condition to the effectiveness of a pledge between the parties, this Article requires a written contract of pledge except in one instance: when the thing pledged is a corporeal movable that has been placed into the possession of the pledgee or a third person who has agreed to hold the thing for the benefit of the pledgee. In all other cases, a pledge cannot exist, even between the parties, unless it is established by a written contract. The Louisiana Civil Code of 1870 generally did not require a writing for a pledge to exist between the parties; delivery of possession sufficed to evidence the pledge.

(f) Rules concerning the effectiveness of a pledge against third persons are contained in Articles 3153 through 3155 (Rev. 2014).

Art. 3150.   Acceptance

A written contract of pledge need not be signed by the pledgee, whose consent is presumed and whose acceptance may be tacit.

Acts 2014, No. 281, § 1, eff. Jan. 1, 2015.

REVISION COMMENTS—2014

This Article is new. Although it has no counterpart in the Civil Code of 1870, it is patterned after Article 3289 (Rev. 1991), which provides a similar rule for contracts of mortgage.

Art. 3151.   Power to pledge

A contract of pledge may be established only by a person having the power to alienate the thing pledged.

Acts 2014, No. 281, § 1, eff. Jan. 1, 2015.

REVISION COMMENTS—2014

This Article is new, although the Louisiana Civil Code of 1870 contained a number of Articles addressing a person's power to pledge the property of another. See C.C. Arts. 3148–3150 (1870). This Article follows the simpler approach of Article 3290 (Rev. 1992), which provides the identical rule for contracts of mortgage. Similar provisions limiting the power to encumber a thing to those persons having the power to alienate it exist in the civil codes of other jurisdictions. See, e.g., Argentine Civil Code Art. 3213; Québec Civil Code Art. 2681; Zakona o Založnom Pravu na Pokretnim Stvarima Upisanim u Registar (The Law on Pledge of Movable Assets in the Pledge Registry) art. 17 (Serbia); Spanish Civil Code Art. 1857.

Art. 3152.   Pledge of a thing not owned

A pledge given over a thing that the pledgor does not own is established when the thing is acquired by the pledgor and the other requirements for the establishment of the pledge have been satisfied.

Acts 2014, No. 281, § 1, eff. Jan. 1, 2015.

REVISION COMMENTS—2014

This Article is derived from Article 3144 of the Louisiana Civil Code of 1870.

Art. 3153.   General requirements for effectiveness of pledge against third persons

A pledge is without effect as to third persons unless it has become effective between the parties and is established by written contract.

Acts 2014, No. 281, § 1, eff. Jan. 1, 2015.

REVISION COMMENTS—2014

(a) This Article is derived from Paragraph A of Article 3158 of the Louisiana Civil Code of 1870, which stated the general rule that a pledge could have effect against third persons only if evidenced by a writing. Paragraph B of the same Article contained a number of exceptions to the writing requirement, in the case of promissory notes, bills of exchange, bills of lading, stocks, bonds, or other "written obligations of any kind." Other than the catch-all category of "written obligations of any kind," those kinds of collateral are all now encumbered under the Uniform Commercial Code, and an exception to the writing requirement for them in this Title is unnecessary. Thus, this Article follows the simpler approach of Paragraph A of Article 3158 of the 1870 Code, requiring in all cases a written contract for a pledge to be effective against third persons. In the case of the pledge of an incorporeal, a written pledge is required under Article 3153 even for the pledge to be effective between the parties. In that case, therefore, this Article adds no additional requirement in order for the pledge to have effect against third persons.

(b) This Article sets forth only the general requirements imposed upon all pledges in order for them to have effect against third persons. Additional requirements must be satisfied in the case of the pledge of the lessor's rights in the lease of an immovable and its rents and in the case of the pledge of other third-party obligations. See C.C. Arts. 3154 and 3155 (Rev. 2014).

Art. 3154. Effectiveness against third persons of the pledge of the lease of an immovable

The pledge of the lessor's rights in the lease of an immovable and its rents has effect against third persons in accordance with the provisions of Chapter 2 of this Title.

Acts 2014, No. 281, § 1, eff. Jan. 1, 2015.

REVISION COMMENTS—2014

This Article is new. Chapter 2 of this Title specifies the requirements that must be satisfied for a pledge of the lessor's rights in the lease of an immovable and its rents to have effect against third persons. See C.C. Art. 3169 (Rev. 2014).

Art. 3155. Effectiveness against third persons of the pledge of other obligations

If the thing pledged is another person's obligation not arising under the lease of an immovable, the pledge is effective against third persons only from the time that the obligor has actual knowledge of the pledge or has been given notice of it.

Acts 2014, No. 281, § 1, eff. Jan. 1, 2015.

REVISION COMMENTS—2014

(a) This Article is new. The Louisiana Civil Code of 1870 did not require notification to the person obligated on a pledged obligation in order for the pledge to have effect against third persons. In contrast, Article 2643 (Rev. 1993) requires notice to or knowledge by the person obligated on an assigned right in order for an assignment of that right to be effective against him or other third persons. This Article applies the same rule to pledges, other than a pledge of the lessor's rights in the lease of an immovable and its rents. See C.C. Art. 3169 (Rev. 2014).

(b) This Article does not require the obligor's consent to the pledge, nor an acknowledgment by the obligor that notice has been given.

(c) This Article does not address the issue of when the obligor is obligated to render performance to the pledgee. That issue is governed by Article 3161 (Rev. 2014), which requires not only the obligor's knowledge of the existence of the pledge but also a written direction to the obligor to render performance to the pledgee.

(d) In the case of a mortgage that includes a pledge of the mortgagor's rights under policies of insurance covering the mortgaged immovable, R.S. 9:5386 provides an exception to the notice requirement of this Article: the pledge has effect as to third persons when the act of mortgage is recorded, without the necessity of notice to the insurer.

Art. 3156. Pledgee's right of retention

If the thing pledged has been delivered to the pledgee or a third person for the benefit of the pledgee, the pledgee is not obligated to return it until all secured obligations have been extinguished.

Acts 2014, No. 281, § 1, eff. Jan. 1, 2015.

REVISION COMMENTS—2014

(a) This Article restates the principle of Civil Code Article 3164 (1870) without intending to change the law. The pledgee's right of retention is commonly recognized under the law of pledge in civilian jurisdictions. See, e.g., French Civil Code Art. 2339; Argentine Civil Code Art. 3229; Luxembourg Civil Code Art. 2083; Spanish Civil Code Art. 1866;

(b) This Article does not alter the longstanding rule that a pledgee may not resist seizure under judicial process, even if instituted by a creditor holding an inferior security right. See Pickens v. Webster, 31 La.Ann. 870 (1879) and Case v. Kloppenburg, 27 La.Ann. 482 (1875).

Art. 3157.   Indivisibility of pledge

The contract of pledge is indivisible, notwithstanding the divisibility of the secured obligations, and the pledgor may not demand return of all or part of the thing pledged until all secured obligations have been extinguished.

Acts 2014, No. 281, § 1, eff. Jan. 1, 2015.

REVISION COMMENTS—2014

This Article restates the principle of indivisibility found in Civil Code Article 3163 (1870), without intending to change the law. This principle is a common feature of the law of pledge in civilian jurisdictions. See, e.g., French Civil Code Art. 2349; Argentine Civil Code Art. 3233; Luxembourg Civil Code Art. 2083; Spanish Civil Code Art. 1860.

Art. 3158.   Enforcement of pledge of a movable

If agreed in a written contract of pledge of a movable, the pledgee may, upon failure of performance of the secured obligation, dispose of the thing pledged at public auction or by private sale, but he shall act reasonably in disposing of the thing and shall account to the pledgor for any proceeds of the disposition in excess of the amount needed to satisfy the secured obligation. Otherwise, the pledgee may cause the sale of the thing pledged only by having it seized and sold under judicial process.

Acts 2014, No. 281, § 1, eff. Jan. 1, 2015.

REVISION COMMENTS—2014

This Article is derived from Articles 3165 and 3172 of the Louisiana Civil Code of 1870. The requirement to act reasonably in the disposition of the thing pledged is similar to the requirement of the Uniform Commercial Code that every aspect of a secured party's actions in disposing of collateral after default must be "commercially reasonable." See R.S. 10:9–610.

Art. 3159.   Fruits of things pledged

The pledgee is entitled to receive the fruits of the thing pledged and to retain them as security. He may also apply them to the secured obligation, even if not yet due.

Acts 2014, No. 281, § 1, eff. Jan. 1, 2015.

REVISION COMMENTS—2014

This Article is a restatement and simplification of Article 3168 of the Louisiana Civil Code of 1870. The entitlement of a pledgee to fruits of the thing pledged is a common feature of the law of pledge in civilian jurisdictions. See, e.g., French Civil Code Art. 2345 (2006); Argentine Civil Code Art. 3231; Zakona o Zalošznom Pravu na Pokretnim Stvarima Upisanim u Registar (The Law on Pledge of Movable Assets in the Pledge Registry) art. 21 (Serbia).

Art. 3160.   Pledge of obligation of a third person

If the thing pledged is an obligation of a third person, the pledgee is entitled to enforce performance of the third person's obligation when it becomes due and to retain as security any payment or other thing received from the third person. The pledgee may apply any money collected to the secured obligation, even if not yet due. He must account to the pledgor for any payment or other thing remaining after the secured obligation has been satisfied.

Acts 2014, No. 281, § 1, eff. Jan. 1, 2015.

REVISION COMMENTS—2014

(a) This Article is derived from Articles 3168 through 3170 of the Louisiana Civil Code of 1870. It clarifies that the pledgee may apply collections from the third person's obligation to the secured obligation, even if the secured obligation has not yet matured.

(b) Article 3169 of the Louisiana Civil Code of 1870 provided that interest accruing on a pledged credit was imputed to the interest owing on the obligation secured by the pledge and to principal if the latter obligation did not bear interest. That Article, which obviously did not cover all possible circumstances, has been omitted, because the second paragraph of Article 1866 (Rev. 1985) supplies the operative imputation rule: The payment received from the third-party obligor is imputed first to interest and then to principal of the secured obligation.

Art. 3161. Performance by obligor of a pledged obligation

A third person obligated on a pledged obligation is bound to render performance to the pledgee only from the time that the pledgor or pledgee notifies him of the pledge and directs him in writing to render performance to the pledgee. Performance that the third person renders to the pledgor before that time extinguishes the pledged obligation and is effective against the pledgee.

Acts 2014, No. 281, § 1, eff. Jan. 1, 2015.

REVISION COMMENTS—2014

(a) This Article expands the principle expressed in Article 3170 of the Louisiana Civil Code of 1870 that the pledgee was "justified in receiving" the amount due from the obligor of a pledged obligation. That Article did not, however, directly address the duty of the obligor to render performance of the pledged obligation to the pledgee. This Article and Article 3162 (Rev. 2014) supply the operative rules, borrowing heavily from the Articles on assignment of rights. See C.C. Arts. 2642–2654 (Rev. 1993).

(b) Under Article 2643 (Rev. 1993), an assignment of a right is effective against the debtor only from the time the debtor has actual knowledge or has been given notice of the assignment. Article 2644 (Rev. 1993) provides that if the debtor renders performance to the assignor without knowledge or notice of the assignment, the performance extinguishes the obligation of the debtor and is effective against the assignee. Thus, notice of an assignment automatically obligates the third person to render performance to the assignee. In contrast, in order to bind an account debtor to pay the assignee following an assignment of the account debtor's obligation under the Uniform Commercial Code, the account debtor must not only receive a notification of the assignment but also a direction that payment is to be made to the assignee. See R.S. 10:9–406(a). The reason for this added requirement is obvious: in the case of a mere secured transaction, rather than an outright assignment of ownership, the parties may very well intend that the assignor retain the right to collect payments on the pledged obligation until some later event, such as the occurrence of a default by the assignor. This Article adopts the same concept: the obligor is not obligated to render performance to the pledgee until he has been notified of the pledge and directed in writing to render performance to the pledgee. Since mere notification to the third-party obligor of the existence of a pledge is not sufficient to require him to render performance to the pledgee, a fortiori the third party's actual knowledge of the pledge would not so obligate him in the absence of an express, written direction to render performance to the pledgee.

(c) In addition to the pledge of other kinds of obligations, this Article applies to the pledge of the lessor's interest in the lease of an immovable and its rents. It replaces former R.S. 9:4401(G), which provided that a lessee was not discharged from his debt if he paid anyone other than an assignee after receiving written notice that the assignment had become "absolute."

Art. 3162.   Defenses available to obligor of a pledged obligation

Unless the obligor of a pledged obligation makes a contrary agreement with the pledgor or pledgee, he may assert against the pledgee any defense arising out of the transaction that gave rise to the pledged obligation. He may also assert against the pledgee any other defense that arises against the pledgor before the obligor has been given written notice of the pledge.

Acts 2014, No. 281, § 1, eff. Jan. 1, 2015.

REVISION COMMENTS—2014

(a) This Article is new. It combines concepts found in the Uniform Commercial Code and elsewhere in the Civil Code.

(b) Article 1900 (Rev. 1984) provides that an obligor who has been given notice of an assignment to which he did not consent may not claim compensation against the assignee for an obligation of the assignor arising after that notice. The Civil Code does not expressly address the circumstances under which other defenses might be asserted by the obligor against the assignee. By contrast, the Uniform Commercial Code provides that an account debtor, in the absence of an agreement to the contrary, retains the right to assert against a secured party any defense or claim arising from the transaction that gave rise to the account debtor's obligation irrespective of when the claim or defense arises. He may also assert against the secured party any other defense or claim he has against the assignor, even if not related to the contract in question, to the extent that the defense or claim accrues before he receives a notification of the assignment. See R.S. 10:9–404(a). This Article largely adopts the approach of the Uniform Commercial Code.

Art. 3163.   Clause prohibiting pledge

A clause in a contract restricting the pledge of the rights of a party to payments that are or will become due under the contract, making the pledge or its enforcement a default under the contract, or providing that the other party is excused from performance or may terminate the contract on account of the pledge, is without effect.

Acts 2014, No. 281, § 1, eff. Jan. 1, 2015.

REVISION COMMENTS—2014

(a) This Article is new. It adopts concepts expressed in Chapter 9 of the Uniform Commercial Code and in former R.S. 9:4401. Under certain circumstances, it may effect a change in the law.

(b) Under Article 2653 (Rev. 1993), a right cannot be assigned when the contract from which it arises prohibits the assignment of that right. Interpreting that Article, the Supreme Court has held that there is no public policy precluding a clause prohibiting assignment of rights under an insurance contract. See In Re Katrina Canal Breaches Litigation, 63 So.3d 955 (La. 2011). By its terms, however, Article 2653 (Rev. 1993) applies to sales and does not necessarily apply to a mere pledge or the granting of a security interest. Chapter 9 of the Uniform Commercial Code generally voids anti-assignment clauses that prohibit a security interest and specifically provides this rule prevails over Article 2653 (Rev. 1993). See R.S.10:9–406. Similarly, former R.S. 9:4401(G)(4) provided that any term in a lease was ineffective if it prohibited assignment of rent, prohibited creation of a security right in rent or required the lessee's consent to the assignment or security right.

(c) This Article applies to all pledges of an obligation of a third person to make payment, including both pledges of movables that are outside the scope of Chapter 9 of the Uniform Commercial Code and pledges of the lessor's interest in the lease of an immovable and its rents. The effect of this Article is, however, limited to the pledge of payments that are or will become due under a contract. This Article does not apply to the encumbrance of other rights that the pledgor may have under the contract.

(d) This Article does not invalidate the arrangement commonly known as a "negative pledge" by which an obligor agrees with one of his creditors that he will not encumber one or more of his assets in favor of another creditor. Thus, a lessor may validly agree with one of his creditors that he will not pledge to another creditor his rights to rents arising under a lease of an immovable. The reason that this Article does not apply to such an agreement is that the contract restricting the pledge is not the contract under which the pledged payments will become due. In the example given, the payments arise under the lease between the lessor and lessee, while the prohibition against pledging those payments arises under the contract between the lessor and his creditor. On the other hand, this Article invalidates a stipulation in a lease whereby the lessor agrees with the lessee that the rents under the lease may not be pledged to the lessor's creditors. Such a stipulation, if it were permitted under this Article, would in effect make the rents under the lease insusceptible of pledge. There is no similar consequence with a negative pledge, which is a mere contractual covenant that does not have the effect of nullifying a pledge made in violation of its terms.

Art. 3164. Modification of contract from which a pledged obligation arises

The parties to a contract from which a pledged obligation arises may agree to modify or terminate the contract or to substitute a new contract. If made in good faith, the agreement is effective against the pledgee without his consent. Nevertheless, after written notice of the pledge is given to the obligor of a pledged obligation that has been fully earned by the pledgor's performance, an agreement modifying or extinguishing the pledged obligation is without effect against the pledgee unless made with his consent.

Acts 2014, No. 281, § 1, eff. Jan. 1, 2015.

REVISION COMMENTS—2014

(a) This Article is new. It addresses an issue for which no treatment was given in the Louisiana Civil Code of 1870: the circumstances under which the contract from which a pledged obligation arises can be modified or terminated by the parties to that contract without the consent of the pledgee.

(b) For contracts that are susceptible of encumbrance by a security interest, Chapter 9 of the Uniform Commercial Code states the general rule that a modification of or substitution for an assigned contract is effective against the assignee (i.e., the secured party) if made in good faith. R.S. 10:9–405(a). R.S. 10:9–405(b) hinges the applicability of this rule, however, on two factors: whether the right to payment has been fully earned by performance and whether the account debtor has received notification of the assignment. Only where the right to payment has been fully earned by performance and the account debtor has been notified of the assignment is the general rule of R.S. 10:9–405(a) inapplicable. In other words, only in that event is the consent of the assignee necessary for a modification made in good faith. Of course, under any circumstances in which a modification is made by the parties in bad faith, the modification is, by inference from R.S. 10:9–405(a), unenforceable against the assignee.

(c) This Article restates the substance of R.S. 10:9–405. An agreement made in good faith by the parties to a contract from which a pledged obligation arises is generally effective against the pledgee without the necessity of his consent. An exception arises after written notice of a pledge has been given to the obligor of a pledged obligation that has been fully earned by performance. In that specific case, an agreement for the modification of that obligation is without effect as to the pledgee unless made with his consent.

(d) The rules expressed in this Article apply to all pledges of a third person's obligation, including the obligations of a lessee under a lease that is the subject of a pledge made under Chapter 2 of this Title. In the case of an assignment of leases and rents, former R.S. 9:4401(G) addressed the topic using terminology and concepts similar to those found in R.S. 10:9–405 but with somewhat different results.

Art. 3165. Attachment of pledge to obligations arising under modified or substituted contract

Upon the modification of a contract from which a pledged obligation arises, or the substitution of a new contract, the pledge encumbers the corresponding rights of the pledgor under the modified or substituted contract.

Acts 2014, No. 281, § 1, eff. Jan. 1, 2015.

REVISION COMMENTS—2014

This Article is new. It makes more general a principle that applied to assignments of leases and rents under former R.S. 9:4401(G)(3). Chapter 9 of the Uniform Commercial Code contains a similar principle. See R.S. 10:9–405.

Art. 3166. Modification as default by pledgor

The pledgor and pledgee may agree that a modification or termination of the contract from which a pledged obligation of a third person arises, or the substitution of a new contract, is a default by the pledgor.

Acts 2014, No. 281, § 1, eff. Jan. 1, 2015.

REVISION COMMENTS—2014

(a) This Article is new. It makes more general a principle that applied to assignments of leases and rents under former R.S. 9:4401(G)(3). Chapter 9 of the Uniform Commercial Code contains a similar principle. See R.S. 10:9–405.

(b) Under Article 3164 (Rev. 2014), a modification or termination of a contract from which a pledged obligation arises is generally effective against the pledgee without his consent if it is made in good faith. Nevertheless, a pledge may provide that a modification or termination of the contract, or the substitution of a new contract, is a default by the pledgor.

Art. 3167. Pledgee not bound for pledgor's obligations

In the absence of an assumption by the pledgee, the existence of a pledge does not impose upon the pledgee liability for the pledgor's acts or omissions, nor does it bind the pledgee to perform the pledgor's obligations.

Acts 2014, No. 281, § 1, eff. Jan. 1, 2015.

REVISION COMMENTS—2014

This Article is new. It expands to all pledges a principle that applied to assignments of leases and rents under former R.S. 9:4401(G)(5). Chapter 9 of the Uniform Commercial Code contains a similar principle. See R.S. 10:9–402.

CHAPTER 2—THE PLEDGE OF THE LESSOR'S RIGHTS IN THE LEASE OF AN IMMOVABLE AND ITS RENTS

Art. 3168. Requirements of contract

A contract establishing a pledge of the lessor's rights in the lease of an immovable and its rents must state precisely the nature and situation of the immovable and must state the amount of the secured obligation or the maximum amount of secured obligations that may be outstanding from time to time.

Acts 2014, No. 281, § 1, eff. Jan. 1, 2015.

REVISION COMMENTS—2014

(a) This Chapter, which supplements the general provisions of Chapter 1, contains provisions that are specifically applicable to the pledge of the lessor's rights in the lease of an immovable and its rents.

(b) There is no requirement that a pledge encumber both leases and rents, for the parties may choose to encumber in a pledge only leases or only rents. There is also no requirement that all leases or all rents of an immovable be pledged; the parties may choose to encumber only one or more specific leases or the rents from those specific leases. See C.C. Art. 3170 (Rev. 2014). The scope of what is pledged is a matter of contract between the parties.

(c) This Article restates a number of formal requirements contained in former R.S. 9:4401(A) but in a manner that more closely follows the formal requirements applicable to a contract of mortgage.

Cf. C.C. Art. 3288 (Rev. 1991). The degree of specificity required in the description of the immovable subject to the pledge and the requirements for description of the secured obligation are identical to the corresponding requirements that apply to a contract of mortgage. See Comments (b) and (c) to C.C. Art. 3288 (Rev. 1991).

(d) A pledge under this Chapter may be created by a sublessor. In that event, the pledge encumbers his rights under the sublease, but not his rights under the underlying lease of the property from his own lessor. The rights of a lessee under a lease, as well as the rights of a sublessee under a sublease, are not susceptible of pledge under this Chapter but instead are encumbered by mortgage. See C.C. Art. 3286 (Rev. 1991; Amended 1993); R.S. 9:4401 (Rev. 2014).

Art. 3169. Effectiveness against third persons

The pledge of the lessor's rights in the lease of an immovable and its rents is without effect as to third persons unless the contract establishing the pledge is recorded in the manner prescribed by law.

Nevertheless, the pledge is effective as to the lessee from the time that he is given written notice of the pledge, regardless of whether the contract establishing the pledge has been recorded.

Acts 2014, No. 281, § 1, eff. Jan. 1, 2015.

REVISION COMMENTS—2014

(a) This Article is new. Recordation of a contract establishing a pledge of the lessor's rights in the lease of an immovable and its rents is required for the pledge to have effect against third persons other than the lessee. To that extent, the Article restates a requirement that was contained in former R.S. 9:4401. Unlike that statute, however, this Article does not specify the place where recordation must occur. The place of recordation is specified in Article 3346 (Rev. 2014), which changes the law by requiring recordation in the mortgage records, rather than in the conveyance records, as former R.S. 9:4401 previously provided.

(b) This Article does not address the issue of when the lessee is obligated to render performance to the pledgee. That issue is governed by Article 3161 (Rev. 2014). Article 3164 (Rev. 2014) prescribes the circumstances under which an agreement by the lessor and lessee to modify a lease has effect against a pledgee.

Art. 3170. Pledge contained in act of mortgage

A pledge of the lessor's rights in the lease of an immovable and its rents may be established in an act of mortgage of the immovable. In that event, the pledge is given the effect of recordation for so long as the mortgage is given that effect and is extinguished when the mortgage is extinguished.

Acts 2014, No. 281, § 1, eff. Jan. 1, 2015.

REVISION COMMENTS—2014

This Article is new. It recognizes the longstanding practice of the inclusion within a contract of mortgage of the pledge of the mortgagor's rights in the leases and rents of the mortgaged immovable. Similar recognition was contained in former R.S. 9:4401(A). This Article omits, however, the provision of former R.S. 9:4401(A) to the effect that recordation of the contract of mortgage in the mortgage records obviated the need for separate recordation in the conveyance records in order for the pledge to have effect against third persons. Under this revision, all pledges of the lessor's interest in the lease of an immovable and its rents must be recorded in the mortgage records, rather than the conveyance records, in order to have effect against third persons, regardless of whether the pledge is contained in a contract of mortgage or in a separate contract of pledge. See C.C. Art. 3346 (Rev. 2014).

Art. 3171. Pledge of all or part of the leases of an immovable

A pledge may be established over all or part of the leases of an immovable, including those not yet in existence, without the necessity of specific description of the leases in the contract establishing the pledge. If the pledge is established over leases not yet in existence, the pledge encumbers future leases as they come into existence. The pledge has effect as to third persons, even with respect to leases not in existence at the time of formation of the contract establishing the pledge, from the time that the contract establishing the pledge is recorded in the manner prescribed by law.

Acts 2014, No. 281, § 1, eff. Jan. 1, 2015.

REVISION COMMENTS—2014

This Article is new. It restates the provisions of former R.S. 9:4401(A)(2), without any intent to change the law.

Art. 3172.   Pledge of mineral payments by owner of land or holder of mineral servitude

By express provision in a contract establishing a pledge, the owner of land or holder of a mineral servitude may pledge bonuses, delay rentals, royalties, and shut-in payments arising from mineral leases, as well as other payments that are classified as rent under the Mineral Code. Other kinds of payments owing under a contract relating to minerals are not susceptible of pledge under this Title.

Acts 2014, No. 281, § 1, eff. Jan. 1, 2015.

REVISION COMMENTS—2014

(a) This Article, which is derived from former R.S. 9:4401(D), clarifies the law.

(b) Like the source provision, this Article permits a landowner or holder of a mineral servitude to pledge mineral payments. This Article makes clear, however, that a contract of pledge encumbers mineral payments only if the contract includes an express statement to that effect. A mere statement that all leases and rents of the immovable are pledged will not suffice for the pledge to encumber mineral payments.

(c) "Accounts" as defined in Chapter 9 of the Uniform Commercial Code and the kinds of mineral payments susceptible of encumbrance by pledge under this Chapter are mutually exclusive. See R.S. 10:9–102(a)(2) (Rev. 2014).

(d) This Article clarifies an issue that was uncertain under former R.S. 9:4401: whether mineral lease bonus payable to a landowner or holder of a mineral servitude is susceptible of encumbrance by a pledge, rather than by a security interest under Chapter 9 of the Uniform Commercial Code. Under prior law, mineral payments that were classified as rent under the Mineral Code were susceptible of encumbrance under former R.S. 9:4401 and were excluded from the definition of "account" in Section 9–102 of the Uniform Commercial Code. Both that definition and the provisions of former R.S. 9:4401 were written, however, in a manner that seemed to presuppose that mineral lease bonus payable to a landowner or holder of a mineral servitude was not rent and would therefore be an "account" susceptible of encumbrance only by a security interest under Chapter 9 of the Uniform Commercial Code. Nevertheless, after the adoption of those statutes, the Supreme Court held, in a case involving claims of collation among heirs, that mineral lease bonus is a form of rent. Succession of Doll v. Doll, 593 So.2d 1239 (La. 1992).

(e) This Article provides that mineral lease bonus payable to a landowner or holder of a mineral servitude is encumbered by a pledge under this Chapter, rather than by a security interest under Chapter 9 of the Uniform Commercial Code, without regard to whether the bonus is classified as rent under the Mineral Code. Similarly, delay rentals, royalties, and shut-in payments arising from mineral leases are encumbered by a pledge under this Chapter, as is any other payment that is owed to a landowner or holder of a mineral servitude and that is classified as rent under the Mineral Code. This treatment is in accord with cases holding a mineral lease bonus to be a civil fruit (See, e.g., Milling v. Collector of Revenue, 220 La. 773, 57 So.2d 679 (La. 1952)), as well as the law of community property, which classifies as community property bonuses, delay rentals, royalties, and shut-in payments arising from mineral leases covering separate property. See C.C. Art. 2339 (Rev. 1979; Amended 2008).

(f) Mineral payments owing to a person other than a landowner or holder of a mineral servitude are not susceptible of pledge under this Title.

Art. 3173.   Accounting to other pledgees for rent collected

Except as provided in this Article, a pledgee is not bound to account to another pledgee for rent collected.

A pledgee shall account to the holder of a superior pledge for rent the pledgee collects more than one month before it is due and for rent he collects with actual knowledge that the payment of rent to him violated written directions given to the lessee to pay rent to the holder of the superior pledge.

After all secured obligations owed to a pledgee have been extinguished, he shall deliver any remaining rent collected to another pledgee who has made written demand upon him for the rent before he delivers it to the pledgor.

Acts 2014, No. 281, § 1, eff. Jan. 1, 2015.

REVISION COMMENTS—2014

(a) This Article is new. It changes the law by generally permitting an inferior pledgee to collect rent from the lessee without a duty to account to a superior pledgee for the rent collected. Nevertheless, the inferior pledgee must account to the superior pledgee for any rent he collects more than one month before it is due. The inferior pledgee must also account for any rent he collects with actual knowledge that payment of the rent to him violated written instructions to the lessee to pay rent to the superior pledgee.

(b) Former R.S. 9:4401(G)(2) provided that, if a pledgee had not notified the lessee to make direct payment to him, the lessee was exonerated of liability for rent paid to the lessor or a subsequent assignee; however, the person to whom payment was remitted was nevertheless liable to the pledgee for the sums received. Thus, an inferior pledgee who collected rent was exposed to liability to a superior pledgee for any rent he might collect. This Article now permits the inferior pledgee to retain rent he collects as it falls due, unless a superior pledgee has notified the lessee to make payment to him and the inferior pledgee has knowledge of these instructions. At any time, of course, the superior pledgee can give a direct payment notification to the lessee, in which event the lessee will no longer be able safely to pay the inferior pledgee. See C.C. Art. 3161 (Rev. 2014). The inferior pledgee would still be able to retain any payments that the lessee might make to him in violation of these instructions if the inferior pledgee were unaware of those instructions.

(c) The principles expressed in this Article are analogous to rules under Chapter 9 of the Uniform Commercial Code, which generally permit an inferior secured party to collect proceeds of collateral without liability to a superior secured party, provided that the inferior secured party does not know that his receipt of the proceeds violates the rights of the superior secured party. See Uniform Commercial Code Official Comment 5 to R.S. 10:9–331; Uniform Commercial Code Official Comment 7 to R.S. 10:9–330 and Uniform Commercial Code Official Comment 5 to R.S. 10:9–607.

(d) This Article does not grant inferior pledgees the right to collect rent more than one month in advance of the date due. Without a rule limiting the ability of an inferior pledgee to collect future rents, a superior pledgee might have discovered that all future rents for the balance of the term of the lease had been paid in advance to an inferior pledgee.

(e) Under Article 3160 (Rev. 2014), after the secured obligation has been satisfied, a pledgee must account to the pledgor for any excess payment received on a pledged obligation of a third person. This obligation applies to any excess proceeds of rent collected from a lessee. Under this Article, if before delivering the excess proceeds to the pledgor the pledgee receives a demand for them from another pledgee, the pledgee who collected the rent is bound to turn the excess proceeds over to the other pledgee, rather than delivering them to the lessor. Chapter 9 of the Uniform Commercial Code contains a similar rule. See R.S. 10:9–608.

(f) R.S. 9:4402 (Rev. 2014) addresses the rights of competing pledgees to rental collections that have been deposited into a deposit account maintained with a financial institution.

(g) The provisions of this Article may be altered by agreement between pledgees.

Art. 3174.   Judicial sale prohibited

A pledge of the lessor's rights in the lease of an immovable and its rents does not entitle the pledgee to cause the rights of the lessor to be sold by judicial process. Any clause to the contrary is absolutely null.

Acts 2014, No. 281, § 1, eff. Jan. 1, 2015.

REVISION COMMENTS—2014

(a) This Article, which is new and has no counterpart in either the Louisiana Civil Code of 1870 or former R.S. 9:4401, highlights a fundamental distinction between the enforcement of the pledge of a movable and the enforcement of the pledge of the lessor's rights under the lease of an immovable. In the case of the pledge of a movable, Article 3158 (Rev. 2014) permits an extra-judicial disposition by the pledgee, if authorized in the contract of pledge, as well as seizure and sale by judicial process of the thing pledged. This Article precludes the pledgee of the lessor's rights in the lease of an immovable and its rents from proceeding with either kind of disposition. Allowing the pledgee to sell the lessor's rights under the lease, whether by private or judicial sale, would, in a sense, effect an undesirable dismemberment of ownership of the immovable.

(b) The pledge of lessor's rights in the lease of an immovable and its rents is enforced only by collection of rents and enforcement of other obligations of the lessee under the lease. The pledgee is given the right to collect rents by Article 3160 (Rev. 2014) and, to effectuate this right, is permitted by Article 3161 (Rev. 2014) to direct the lessee to pay rent to him. If necessary, the pledgee may enforce his rights by bringing suit directly against the lessee. He may also employ remedies available under the Code of Civil Procedure to seize the rents in the hands of the lessee, but he cannot cause the lessor's rights under the lease to be sold by judicial process. See C.C.P. Arts. 2411 and 3503.

Art. 3175.   Applicability of general rules of pledge

In all matters for which no special provision is made in this Chapter, the pledge of the lessor's rights in the lease of an immovable and its rents is governed by the provisions of Chapter 1 of this Title.

Acts 2014, No. 281, § 1, eff. Jan. 1, 2015.

REVISION COMMENTS—2014

This Article is new. It states explicitly that the entirety of Chapter 1 of this Title applies fully to the pledge of the lessor's rights in the lease of an immovable and its rents except to the extent inconsistent with the provisions of this Chapter.

Arts. 3176 to 3181. [Blank]

TITLE XXI—OF PRIVILEGES

CHAPTER 1—GENERAL PROVISIONS

Arts. 3182 to 3184. [Blank]

Art. 3185. Privileges established only by law, stricti juris

Privilege can be claimed only for those debts to which it is expressly granted in this Code.

CHAPTER 2—OF THE SEVERAL KINDS OF PRIVILEGES

Art. 3186. Privilege, definition

Privilege is a right, which the nature of a debt gives to a creditor, and which entitles him to be preferred before other creditors, even those who have mortgages.

Art. 3187. Basis of preferences among privileges

Among creditors who are privileged, the preference is settled by the different nature of their privileges.

Art. 3188. Concurrent privileges

The creditors who are in the same rank of privileges, are paid in concurrence, that is on an equal footing.

Art. 3189. Property affected by privileges

Privileges may exist, either on movables or immovables, or on both at once.

CHAPTER 3—OF PRIVILEGES ON MOVABLES

Art. 3190. General or special privileges on movables

Privileges are either general, or special on certain movables.

SECTION 1—OF GENERAL PRIVILEGES ON MOVABLES

Art. 3191. General privileges on all movables, enumeration and ranking

The debts which are privileged on all the movables in general, are those hereafter enumerated, and are paid in the following order:

1. Funeral charges.

2. Law charges.

3. Charges, of whatever nature, occasioned by the last sickness, concurrently among those to whom they are due.

4. The wages of servants for the year past, and so much as is due for the current year.

5. Supplies of provisions made to the debtor or his family, during the last six months, by retail dealers, such as bakers, butchers, grocers; and, during the last year, by keepers of boarding houses and taverns.

6.   The salaries of clerks, secretaries, and other persons of that kind.

Amended by Acts 1979, No. 711, § 1, eff. Jan. 1, 1980.

§ 1. Of Funeral Charges

Art. 3192.   Funeral charges, definition

Funeral charges are those which are incurred for the interment of a person deceased.

Art. 3193.   Reduction of funeral charges of insolvent decedent

If the property of the deceased is so incumbered as not to suffice for the payment of his creditors, the funeral charges may, upon the request of any of them, be reduced by the judge to a reasonable rate, regard being had to the station in life which the deceased held and which his family holds.

Art. 3194.   Limitation in event of reduction

But, in case of the reduction, the judge can never allow, at the expense of the estate, on any account whatever, more than Five Hundred Dollars for all the expenses occasioned by the interment of the deceased.

Amended by Acts 1954, No. 114, § 1.

§ 2. Of Law Charges

Art. 3195.   Law charges, definition

Law charges are such as are occasioned by the prosecution of a suit before the courts. But this name applies more particularly to the costs, which the party cast has to pay to the party gaining the cause. It is in favor of these only that the laws [law] grants the privilege.

Art. 3196.   Costs which enjoy privilege

The creditor enjoys this privilege, not with regard to all the expenses which he is obliged to incur in obtaining judgment against his debtor, but with regard only to such as are taxed according to law, and such as arise from the execution of the judgment.

Art. 3197.   Costs for the general benefit of creditors

The cost of affixing seals and making inventories for the better preservation of the debtor's property, those which occur in cases of failure or cession of property, for the general benefit of creditors, such as fees to lawyers appointed by the court to represent absent creditors, commissions to syndics; and finally, costs incurred for the administration of estates which are either vacant or belonging to absent heirs, enjoy the privileges established in favor of law charges.

Art. 3198.   Costs not taxed in suit

Not only has the creditor no privilege for the costs which are not taxed, or which are not included among those mentioned above, but he has no right to demand them even from the debtor.

§ 3. Of Expenses During the Last Sickness

Art. 3199.   Last sickness, definition

The last sickness is considered to be that of which the debtor died; the expenses of this sickness enjoy the privilege.

Art. 3200.   Chronic sickness

But if the sickness with which the deceased was attacked and of which he died, was a chronic disease, the progress of which was slow and which only occasioned death after a long while, then the privilege shall only commence from the time when the malady became so serious as to prevent the deceased from attending to his business and confined him to his bed or chamber.

Art. 3201.   Maximum period of privileged expenses

However long the sickness may have lasted after arriving at the point which prevented him from attending to his affairs, the privilege granted for the expense it has occasioned, can only extend to one year before the decease.

Art. 3202.   List of expenses privileged

The expenses of the last sickness comprehend the fees of physicians and surgeons, the wages of nurses, and the price due to the apothecary for medicines supplied by him to the deceased for his personal use during his last illness.

Art. 3203.   Amount due for expenses, fixed by contract or by judge

The accounts relating to these expenses must be fixed by the judge, in case of dispute, after hearing testimony as to the value of the services rendered or care afforded, or as to the true value of the medicines supplied, unless there has been a contract between the parties, in which case it must be observed.

Art. 3204.   Last sickness of debtor's children

This privilege subsists, not only for the expenses of the last sickness of the debtor, it subsists also for those of the last sickness of children, under his authority, but it is exercised subject to the rules laid down above.

§ 4. Of the Wages of Servants

Art. 3205.   Servants, definition

Servants or domestics are those who receive wages, and stay in the house of the person paying and employing them for his service or that of his family; such are valets, footmen, cooks, butlers, and others who reside in the house.

Art. 3206.   Prescription of action; extent of privilege

Domestics or servants must make a demand of their wages within a year from the time when they left service, but their privilege is only for the year past, and so much as is due for the present year.

Art. 3207.   Wages recoverable but not privileged

As to the wages of preceding years which may be due, the wages may be recovered, if there is any balanced account, note or obligation of the debtor, but they enjoy no privilege. They form an ordinary debt, for which domestics or servants come in by contribution with other ordinary creditors.

§ 5. Of Supplies of Provisions

Art. 3208.   Supplies furnished by retail dealers

Such supplies of provisions as confer a privilege, are those which are made by retail dealers; that is, persons keeping an open shop, and selling, by small portions, provisions and liquors.

Art. 3209.   Prescription of action; extent of privilege

Retail dealers who have furnished such supplies, ought to demand their money within a year from the time of the first supply; but they have a privilege only for the last six months, and for the rest they are placed on the footing of ordinary creditors.

Art. 3210.   Wholesale dealers

Dealers by wholesale in provisions and liquors do not enjoy any privilege on the property of their debtor, further than what they have acquired by mortgage, or by a judgment duly recorded.

Art. 3211.   Innkeepers and masters of boarding houses

It is not keepers of taverns and hotels alone, who are comprehended in the term *masters of boarding houses*, and who enjoy a privilege for their supplies, but all persons who make a business of receiving persons at board for a fixed price.

Art. 3212.   Teachers and preceptors

Teachers and preceptors, who receive into their houses young persons to be brought up, fed and instructed, enjoy the same privilege which is given to keepers of boarding houses.

Art. 3213.   Extent of privilege for supplies

The privilege of keepers of boarding houses, taverns, and other persons comprised in this class, extends to the last year due, and so much as has expired of the current year.

§ 6. Of the Privilege of Clerks

Art. 3214.   Clerks and secretaries, extent and rank of privilege for salaries

Although clerks, secretaries and other agents of that sort can not be included under the denomination of servants, yet a privilege is granted them for their salaries for the last year elapsed, and so much as has elapsed of the current year. This privilege, however, can not be enforced until after that of the furnishers of provisions.

Art. 3215.   [Blank]

SECTION 2—OF THE PRIVILEGE ON
PARTICULAR MOVABLES

Art. 3216.   Special privileges on movables

The privileges enumerated in the preceding section, extend to all the movables of the debtor, without distinction.

There are some which act only on particular movables and no other; and it is of these last that we shall treat in this and the following sections.

Art. 3217.   List of special privileges on particular movables

The debts which are privileged on certain movables, are the following:

1.   The appointments or salaries of the overseer for the current year, on the crops of the year and the proceeds thereof; debts due for necessary supplies furnished to any farm or plantation, and debts due for money actually advanced and used for the purchase of necessary supplies and the payment of necessary expenses for any farm or plantation, on the crops of the year and the proceeds thereof.

2.   The debt of a workman or artisan for the price of his labor, on the movable which he has repaired or made, if the thing continues still in his possession.

3.   The rents of immovables and the wages of laborers employed in working the same, on the crops of the year, and on the furniture, which is found in the house let, or on the farm, and on every thing which serves to the working of the farm.

4.   The debt, on the pledge which is in the creditor's possession.

5.   That of a depositor, on the price of the sale of the thing by him deposited.

6.   The debt due for money laid out in preserving the thing.

7.   The price due on movable effects, if they are yet in the possession of the purchaser.

8.   The things which have been furnished by an innkeeper, on the property of the traveler which has been carried to his inn.

9.   The carrier's charges and the accessory expenses, on the thing carried, including necessary charges and expenses paid by carriers; such as taxes, storage and privileged claims required to be paid before moving the thing; and in case the thing carried be lost or destroyed without the fault of the carrier, this privilege for money paid by the carrier shall attach to insurance effected on the thing for the benefit of the owner, provided written notice of the amount so paid by the carrier and for whose account, with a description of the property lost or destroyed, be given to the insurer or his agent within thirty days after the loss, or if it be impracticable to give the notice in that time, it shall be sufficient to give the notice at any time before the money is paid over.

The privilege hereinbefore granted to the overseer, the laborers, the furnishers of supplies and the party advancing money necessary to carry on any farm or plantation, shall be concurrent and shall not be divested by any prior mortgage, whether conventional, legal or judicial, or by any seizure and sale of the land while the crop is on it.

The privileges granted by this article, on the growing crop, in favor of the classes of persons mentioned shall be concurrent, except the privilege in favor of the laborer, which shall be ranked as the first privilege on the crop.

§ 1. Of the Privilege of the Lessor

Art. 3218.   [Blank]

Art. 3219.   Method of enforcement of lessor's privilege

The privilege of the lessor and the manner in which it is enforced against the property subject to it are described in the Title "Lease".

Acts 2004, No. 821, § 2, eff. Jan. 1, 2005.

§ 2. Of the Privilege of the Creditor on the Thing Pledged

Art. 3220.   Privilege of pledgee

The creditor acquires the right of possessing and retaining the movable which he has received in pledge, as a security for his debt, and may cause it to be sold for the payment of the same.

Hence proceeds the privilege which he enjoys on the thing.

Art. 3221.   Enforcement of pledge

For the exercise of this privilege it is necessary that all the requisites stated in the title: *Of Pledge,* should be fulfilled.

§ 3. Of the Privilege of a Depositor

Art. 3222.   Privilege of depositor on thing deposited

He who deposits a thing in the hands of another still remains the owner of it.

Consequently his claim to it is preferred to that of the other creditors of the depositary, and he may demand the restitution of it, if he can prove the deposit, in the same manner as is required in agreements for sums of money, and if the thing reclaimed be identically the same which he deposited.

Art. 3223.   Depositor's privilege on price in case of sale

If the depositary abuses his trust, by alienating the thing confided to his care, or if his heirs sell it, not knowing that it had been given in deposit, the depositor retains his privilege on the price which shall be due.

§ 4. Of Expenses Incurred for the Preservation of a Thing

Art. 3224.   Preservation of property of another

He who, having in his possession the property of another, whether in deposit or on loan or otherwise, has been obliged to incur any expense for its preservation, acquires on this property two species of rights.

Art. 3225.   Rights of pledge and retention against owner

Against the owner of the thing, his right is in the nature of that of pledge, by virtue of which he may retain the thing until the expenses, which he has incurred, are repaid.

He possesses this qualified right of pledge, even against the creditors of the owner, if they seek to have the thing sold. He may refuse to restore it, unless they either refund his advance, or give him security that the thing shall fetch a sufficient price for that purpose.

Art. 3226.   Right of preference against creditors

Finally, he who has incurred these expenses has a privilege against these same creditors, by virtue of which he has preference over them out of the price of the thing sold, for the amount of such necessary charges as he shall have incurred for its preservation. This is the privilege in question in the present paragraph.

§ 5. Of the Privilege of the Vendor of Movable Effects

Art. 3227.   Vendor's privilege on movables; agricultural products of the United States

He who has sold to another any movable property, which is not paid for, has a preference on the price of his property, over the other creditors of the purchaser, whether the sale was made on a credit or without, if the property still remains in the possession of the purchaser.

So that although the vendor may have taken a note, bond or other acknowledgment from the buyer, he still enjoys the privilege.

Any person who may sell the agricultural products of the United States in the city of New Orlenas [Orleans], shall be entitled to a special lien and privilege thereon to secure the payment of the purchase money, for and during the space of five days only, after the day of delivery; within which time the vendor shall be entitled to seize the same in whatsoever hands or place they may be found, and his claim for the purchase money shall have preference over all others. If the vendor gives a written order for the delivery of any such products and shall say therein that they are to be delivered without vendor's privilege, then no lien shall attach thereto.

Art. 3228. Loss of privilege by sale with other property of purchaser

But if he allows the things to be sold, confusedly with a mass of other things belonging to the purchaser, without making his claim, he shall lose the privilege, because it will not be possible in such a case to ascertain what price they brought.

Art. 3229. Vendor's claim for restitution

If the sale was not made on credit, the seller may even claim back the things in kind, which were thus sold, as long as they are in possession of the purchaser, and prevent the resale of them; provided the claim for restitution be made within eight days of the delivery at farthest, and that the identity of the objects be established.

Art. 3230. Restitution dependent on identification

When the things reclaimed consist in merchandise, which is sold in bales, packages or cases, the claim shall not be admitted if they have been untied, unpacked or taken out of the cases and mixed with other things of the same nature belonging to the purchaser, so that their identity can no longer be established.

Art. 3231. Restitution of things easily recognized

But if the things sold are of such a nature as to be easily recognized, as household furniture, even although the papers or cloths, which covered them at the time of delivery, be removed, the claim for restitution shall be allowed.

§ 6. Of the Privilege of the Innkeeper on the Effects of the Traveler

Art. 3232. Innkeepers, definition

Those are called innkeepers, who keep a tavern or hotel, and make a business of lodging travelers.

Art. 3233. Innkeepers' rights on property of guests

Innkeepers and all others who let lodgings or receive or take boarders have a privilege, or more properly, a right of pledge on the property of all persons who take their board or lodging with them, by virtue of which they may retain property, and have it sold, to obtain payment of what such persons may owe them on either accounts above mentioned and this privilege shall extend to extras not to exceed Ten ($10) Dollars supplied by the proprietors of hotels, inns and boarding house keepers.

Amended by Acts 1896, No. 29; Acts 1898, No. 110.

Art. 3234. Property covered by innkeepers' privilege

Innkeepers', hotel, boarding house and lodging house keepers enjoy this privilege on all the property which the sojourner has brought to their place, whether it belongs to him or not, because the property so brought into their place has become pledged to them by the mere fact of its introduction into their place.

Amended by Acts 1896, No. 35.

Art. 3235. Travelers, definition

The term *travelers* applies to strangers and such as being transiently in a place where they have no domicile, take their board and lodging at an inn.

Art. 3236.　Sale or donation of unclaimed and unredeemed property, procedure

Whenever any trunk, carpetbag, valise, box, bundle or other baggage which shall hereafter come into the possession of the keeper of any hotel, motel, inn, boarding or lodging house, as such, and shall remain unclaimed or unredeemed for the period of six months, such keeper may proceed to sell the same at public auction, and without judicial proceedings, and out of the proceeds of such sale may retain the amount due him for board, lodging and extras, and the charges for storage, if any, and the expense of advertising and sale thereof, but no such sale shall be made until the expiration of four weeks from the publication of notice of such sale in a newspaper published in or nearest the city, town, village or place in which said hotel, motel, inn, boarding or lodging house is situated. Said notice shall be published once, in some newspaper, daily or weekly, of general circulation, and shall contain a description of each trunk, carpetbag, valise, box, bundle or other baggage as near as may be; the name of the owner, if known; the name of the keeper, and the time and place of sale. The expense incurred for advertising shall be a lien upon such trunk, carpetbag, valise, box, bundle or other baggage in a ratable proportion according to the value of such property, or thing or article sold. In case any balance arising upon such sale shall not be claimed by the rightful owner within one week from the day of said sale the same shall be paid to any authorized charity or state institution.

Alternatively, the hotel, motel, inn, boarding house, or lodging house at its discretion may store the unclaimed or unredeemed possessions for six months and at the expiration of this period donate, give or turn them over to an authorized charity, or state institution.

Amended by Acts 1896, No. 28; Acts 1974, No. 713, § 1.

SECTION 3—OF THE PRIVILEGE ON SHIPS AND MERCHANDISE

Art. 3237.　Privileges on ships and vessels, enumeration and ranking; prescription

The following debts are privileged on the price of ships and other vessels, in the order in which they are placed:

　1.　Legal and other charges incurred to obtain the sale of a ship or other vessel, and the distribution of the price.

　2.　Debts for pilotage, towage, wharfage and anchorage.

　3.　The expenses of keeping the vessel from the time of her entrance into port until sale, including the wages of persons employed to watch her.

　4.　The rent of stores, in which the rigging and apparel are deposited.

　5.　The maintenance of the ship and her tackle and apparatus, since her return into port from her last voyage.

　6.　The wages of the captain and crew employed on the last voyage.

　7.　Sums lent to the captain for the necessities of the ship during the last voyage, and reimbursement of the price of merchandise sold by him for the same purpose.

　8.　Sums due to sellers, to those who have furnished materials and to workmen employed in the construction, if the vessel has never made a voyage; and those due to creditors for supplies, labor, repairing, victuals, armament and equipment, previous to the departure of the ship, if she has already made a voyage.

　9.　Money lent on bottomry for refitting, victualing, arming and equipping the vessel before her departure.

10.   The premiums due for insurance made on the vessel, tackle and apparel, and on the armament and equipment of the ship.

11.   The amount of damage due to freighters for the failure in delivering goods which they have shipped, or for the reimbursement of damage sustained by the goods through the fault of the captain or crew.

12.   Where any loss or damage has been caused to the person or property of any individual by any carelessness, neglect or want of skill in the direction or management of any steamboat, barge, flatboat, water craft or raft, the party injured shall have a privilege to rank after the privileges above specified.

The term of prescription of privileges against ships, steamboats and other vessels shall be six months.

Art. 3238.   Proportionate payment to creditors of same rank

The creditors, named in each number of the preceding article, except number twelve, come in together, and must all suffer a ratable diminution, if the fund be insufficient.

Art. 3239.   Right of pursuit after sale of ship

Creditors having privileges on ships or other vessels, may pursue the vessel in the possession of any person who has obtained it by virtue of a sale; in this case, however, a distinction must be made between a forced and a voluntary sale.

Art. 3240.   Privilege on price of adjudication in case of forced sale

When the sale was a forced one, the right of the purchaser to the property becomes irrevocable; he owes only the price of adjudication, and over it the creditors exercise their privilege, in the order above prescribed.

Art. 3241.   Voluntary sale, distinction between sale in port or on voyage

When the sale is voluntary on the part of the owner, a distinction is to be made, whether the vessel was in port or on a voyage.

Art. 3242.   Voluntary sale of ship in port, rights of privileged creditors

When a sale has been made, the vessel being in port, the creditors of the vendor, who enjoy the privilege for some cause anterior to the act of sale, may demand payment and enforce their rights over the ship, until a voyage has been made in the name and at the risk of the purchaser, without any claim interposed by them.

Art. 3243.   Loss of privilege after voyage in name of purchaser

But when the ship has made a voyage in the name and at the risk of the purchaser, without any claim on the part of the privileged creditors of the vendor, these privileges are lost and extinct against the ship, if she was in port at the time of sale.

Art. 3244.   Voluntary sale of ship while on voyage, rights of privileged creditors

On the other hand, if the ship was on a voyage at the time of sale, the privilege of the creditor against the purchaser shall only become extinct after the ship shall have returned to the port of departure, and the creditors of the vendor shall have allowed her to depart on another voyage for the account and risk of the purchaser, and shall have made no claim.

Art. 3245.   Voyage, definition

A ship is considered to have made a voyage, when her departure from one port and arrival at another shall have taken place, or when, without having arrived at another, more than sixty days have elapsed between the departure and return to the same port; or when the ship, having departed on a long voyage, has been out more than sixty days, without any claim on the part of persons pretending a privilege.

Art. 3246.   Captain's privilege on cargo for freight charges

The captain has a privilege for the freight during fifteen days after the delivery of the merchandise, if they have not passed into third hands. He may even keep the goods, unless the shipper or consignee shall give him security for the payment of the freight.

Art. 3247.   Privilege of consignee or agent on merchandise consigned

Every consignee or commission agent who has made advances on goods consigned to him, or placed in his hands to be sold for account of the consignor, has a privilege for the amount of these advances, with interest and charges on the value of the goods, if they are at his disposal in his stores, or in a public warehouse, or if, before their arrival, he can show, by a bill of lading or letter of advice, that they have been dispatched to him.

This privilege extends to the unpaid price of the goods which the consignee or agent shall have thus received and sold.

Every consignee, commission agent or factor shall have a privilege, preferred to any attaching creditor, on the goods consigned to him for any balance due him, whether specially advanced on such goods or not; provided they have been received by him, or an invoice or bill of lading has been received by him previous to the attachment; provided, that the privilege established by this article shall not have a preference over a privilege pre-existing on the goods aforesaid in behalf of a resident creditor of this State.

Art. 3248.   Rights of consignor on insolvency of consignee or agent

In the event of the failure of the consignee or commission agent, the consignor has not only a right to reclaim the goods sent by him, and which remain unsold in the hands of the consignee or agent, if he can prove their identity, but he has also a privilege on the price of such as have been sold, if the price has not been paid by the purchaser, or passed into account current between him and the bankrupt.

CHAPTER 4—OF PRIVILEGES ON IMMOVABLES

Art. 3249.   Special privileges on immovables

Creditors who have a privilege on immovables, are:

1.   The vendor on the estate by him sold, for the payment of the price or so much of it as is unpaid, whether it was sold on or without a credit.

2.   Architects, undertakers, bricklayers, painters, master builders, contractors, subcontractors, journeymen, laborers, cartmen and other workmen employed in constructing, rebuilding or repairing houses, buildings, or making other works.

3.   Those who have supplied the owner or other person employed by the owner, his agent or subcontractor, with materials of any kind for the construction or repair of an edifice or other work, when such materials have been used in the erection or repair of such houses or other works.

The above named parties shall have a lien and privilege upon the building, improvement or other work erected, and upon the lot of ground not exceeding one acre, upon which the building, improvement or other work shall be erected; provided, that such lot of ground belongs to the person having such building, improvement or other work erected; and if such building, improvement or other work is caused to be erected by a lessee of the lot of ground, in that case the privilege shall exist only against the lease and shall not affect the owner.

4.   Those who have worked by the job in the manner directed by the law, or by the regulations of the police, in making or repairing the levees, bridges, ditches and roads of a proprietor, on the land over which levees, bridges and roads have been made or repaired.

Art. 3250. Extent of vendor's privilege

The privilege granted to the vendor on the immovable sold by him, extends to the beasts and agricultural implements attached to the estate, and which made part of the sale.

Art. 3251. Successive sales, preference among vendors

If there are several successive sales, on which the price is due wholly or in part, the first vendor is preferred to the second, the second to the third, and so throughout and as provided by Article 3186, and assuming timely recordation as provided in Article 3274, each such vendor is preferred to the previously recorded mortgages of his vendees and their successors.

Amended by Acts 1989, No. 538, § 1.

CHAPTER 5—OF PRIVILEGES WHICH EMBRACE BOTH MOVABLES AND IMMOVABLES

Art. 3252. General privileges on both movables and immovables

The privileges which extend alike to movables and immovables are the following:

1.   Funeral charges.
2.   Judicial charges.
3.   Expenses of last illness.
4.   The wages of servants.
5.   The salaries of secretaries, clerks and other agents of that kind.

Whenever a surviving spouse or minor children of a deceased person shall be left in necessitous circumstances, and not possess in their own rights property to the amount of one thousand dollars, the surviving spouse or the legal representatives of the children, shall be entitled to demand and receive from the succession of the deceased spouse or parent, a sum which added to the amount of property owned by them, or either of them, in their own right, will make up the sum of one thousand dollars, and which amount shall be paid in preference to all other debts, except those secured by the vendor's privilege on both movables and immovables, conventional mortgages, and expenses incurred in selling the property. The surviving spouse shall have and enjoy the usufruct of the amount so received from the deceased spouse's succession, until remarriage, which amount shall afterwards vest in and belong to the children or other descendants of the deceased spouse.

Amended by Acts 1917, Ex.Sess., No. 17; Acts 1918, No. 242; Acts 1979, No. 711, § 1, eff. Jan. 1, 1980.

Art. 3253. Order of payment of privileges; debtor's movables taken before immovables

When, for want of movables, the creditors, who have a privilege according to the preceding article, demand to be paid out of the proceeds of the immovables of the debtor, the payment must be made in the order laid down in the following chapter.

CHAPTER 6—OF THE ORDER IN WHICH PRIVILEGED CREDITORS ARE TO BE PAID

Art. 3254. Special privileges prime general privileges on movables; ranking among general privileges when movables sufficient

If the movable property, not subject to any special privilege, is sufficient to pay the debts which have a general privilege on the movables, those debts are paid in the following order:

Funeral charges are the first paid.

Law charges, the second.

Expenses of the last illness, the third.

The wages of servants, the fourth.

Supplies of provisions, the fifth.

The salaries of clerks, secretaries, and others of that nature, the sixth.

The thousand dollars secured by law to the surviving spouse or minor children, as set forth in Article 3252, shall be paid in preference to all other debts, except those for the vendor's privileges and expenses incurred in selling the property.

Amended by Acts 1979, No. 711, § 1, eff. Jan. 1, 1980.

Art. 3255. Order of payment when available movables insufficient

But when part of the movables are subject to special privileges, and the remainder of the movables are not sufficient to discharge the debts having a privilege on the whole mass of movables, or if there be equality between the special privileges, the following rules shall direct the determination.

Art. 3256. Lessor's privilege primed by costs of sale

Whatever may be the privilege of the lessor, charges for selling the movables subjected to it are paid before that which is due for the rent, because it is these charges which procure the payment of the rent.

Art. 3257. Lessor's privilege primed by funeral charges

The case is the same with respect to the funeral expenses of the debtor and his family; when there is no other source from which they can be paid, they have a preference over the debt for rent or hire, on the price of the movables contained in the house or on the farm.

Art. 3258. Lessor's privilege primes other general privileges

But the lessor has a preference on the price of these movables, over all the other privileged debts of the deceased, such as expenses of the last illness, and others which have a general privilege on the movables.

Art. 3259. Lessor's privilege on crops primed by supplies and labor

With regard to the crops which are subject to the lessor's privilege, the expenses for seed and labor, the wages of overseers and managers are to be paid out of the product of the year, in preference to the lessor's debt.

So, also, he who supplied the farming utensils, and who has not been paid, is paid in preference to the lessor out of the price of their sale.

Art. 3260. Ranking between privileges of lessor and depositor

If, among the movables with which the house or farm, or any other thing subject to the lessor's privilege, is provided, there should be some which were deposited by a third person in the hands of the lessor or farmer, the lessor shall have a preference over the depositary on the things deposited for the payment of his rent, if there are no other movables subject to his privilege, or if they are not sufficient; unless it be proved that the lessor knew that the things deposited did not belong to his tenant or farmer.

Amended by Acts 1871, No. 87.

Art. 3261. Depositor's privilege and other privileges

With the exception stated in the foregoing article, the privilege of the depositor on the thing deposited is not preceded by any other privileged debt, even funeral expenses, unless it be that the depositor must contribute to the expense of sealing and making inventory, because this expense is necessary to the preservation of the deposit.

Art. 3262. Privilege for expenses of preservation and other privileges

The privilege of him who has taken care of the property of another, has a preference over that property, for the necessary expenses which he incurred, above all the other claims for expenses, even funeral charges; his privilege yields only to that for the charges on the sale of the thing preserved.

Art. 3263. Vendor's privilege and other privileges

The privilege of the vendor on movables sold by him, which are still in the possession of the vendee, yields to that of the owner of the house or farm which they serve to furnish or supply, for his rents. It yields also to the charges for affixing seals and making inventories, but not to the funeral or other expenses of the debtor.

Art. 3264. Privilege of innkeepers

The privilege of innkeepers on the effects of travelers deceased in their house, is postponed to funeral and law charges, but is preferred to all the other privileged debts of the deceased.

Art. 3265. Privilege of carriers

The privilege of carriers, for the cost of transportation and incidental expenses, yields only to the charges which would arise on the sale of the goods.

The case is the same respecting the freight of goods carried on board a ship or other vessels [vessel].

Art. 3266. Immovables liable when movables insufficient

If the movables of the debtor, by reason of the special privileges affecting them or for any other cause, are not sufficient to discharge the debts having a privilege on the whole movable property, the balance must be raised on the immovables of the debtor, as hereafter provided.

Art. 3267. Special privileges on immovables and other privileges

If the movables of the debtor are subject to the vendor's privilege, or if there be a house or other work subjected to the privilege of the workmen who have constructed or repaired it, or of the individuals who furnished the materials, the vendor, workmen and furnishers of materials, shall be paid from the price of the object affected in their favor, in preference to other privileged debts of the debtor, even funeral charges, except the charges for affixing seals, making inventories, and others which may have been necessary to procure the sale of the thing.

Art. 3268.   Vendor's privilege on land and workmen's privilege on buildings

When the vendor of lands finds himself opposed by workmen seeking payment for a house or other work erected on the land, a separate appraisement is made of the ground and of the house, the vendor is paid to the amount of the appraisement on the land, and the other to the amount of the appraisement of the building.

Art. 3269.   Order of payment out of immovables; distribution of loss among mortgage creditors

With the exception of special privileges, which exist on immovables in favor of the vendor, of workmen and furnishers of materials, as declared above, the debts privileged on the movables and immovables generally, ought to be paid, if the movables are insufficient, out of the product of the immovables belonging to the debtor, in preference to all other privileged and mortgage creditors.

The loss which may then result from their payment must be borne by the creditor whose mortgage is the least ancient, and so in succession, ascending according to the order of the mortgages, or by *pro rata* contributions where two or more mortgages have the same date.

Art. 3270.   Effect of priorities among privileges

When the debts privileged on the movables and immovables can not be paid entirely, either because the movable effects are of small value, or subject to special privileges which claim a preference, or because the movables and immovables together do not suffice, the deficiency must not be borne proportionally among the debtors, but the debts must be paid according to the order established above, and the loss must fall on those which are of inferior dignity.

CHAPTER 7—HOW PRIVILEGES ARE PRESERVED AND RECORDED

Art. 3271.   Vendor's privilege on immovables, recordation

The vendor of an immovable only preserves his privilege on the object, when he has caused to be duly recorded at the office for recording mortgages, his act of sale, in the manner directed hereafter, whatever may be the amount due to him on the sale.

Art. 3272.   Privileges of contractors, mechanics and materialmen; recordation and ranking

Architects, undertakers, bricklayers, painters, master builders, contractors, subcontractors, journeymen, laborers, cartmen, masons and other workmen employed in constructing, rebuilding and repairing houses, buildings, or making other works; those who have supplied the owner or other person employed by the owner or his agent or subcontractor with materials of any kind for the construction or repair of his buildings or other works; those who have contracted, in the manner provided by the police regulations, to make or put in repair the levees, bridges, canals and roads of a proprietor, preserve their privileges, only in so far as they have recorded, with the recorder of mortgages in the parish where the property is situated, the act containing the bargains they have made, or a detailed statement of the amount due, attested under the oath of the party doing or having the work done, or acknowledgment of what is due to them by the debtor.

The privileges mentioned in this article are concurrent.

Art. 3273.   Recordation, effect against third persons

Privileges are valid against third persons, from the date of the recording of the act or evidence of indebtedness as provided by law.

Art. 3274. Time and place of recordation; effectiveness

No privilege shall have effect against third persons, unless recorded in the manner required by law in the parish where the property to be affected is situated. It shall confer no preference on the creditor who holds it, over creditors who have acquired a mortgage, unless the act or other evidence of the debt is recorded within seven days from the date of the act or obligation of indebtedness when the registry is required to be made in the parish where the act was passed or the indebtedness originated and within fifteen days, if the registry is required to be made in any other parish of this State. It shall, however, have effect against all parties from date of registry.

Amended by Acts 1877, No. 45.

Art. 3275. Inclusion of date of birth of parties

In addition to any other requirement that may be provided by general or special law, every act or other document evidencing a privilege that is filed for recordation in accordance with this Chapter shall contain the date of birth of all parties named in the act or document. The failure to include the date of birth of all parties shall not affect the validity of the act or instrument. No clerk of court or recorder of mortgages shall refuse to accept for recordation any act or instrument which does not contain the date of birth of all parties.

Added by Acts 1995, No. 1295, § 2.

Art. 3276. Priority of claims against succession arising after death

The charges against a succession, such as funeral charges, law charges, lawyer fees for settling the succession, the thousand dollars secured in certain cases to the surviving spouse or minor heirs of the deceased, and all claims against the succession originating after the death of the person whose succession is under administration, are to be paid before the debts contracted by the deceased person, except as otherwise provided for herein, and they are not required to be recorded.

Amended by Acts 1979, No. 711, § 1, eff. Jan. 1, 1980.

CHAPTER 8—OF THE MANNER IN WHICH PRIVILEGES ARE EXTINGUISHED

Art. 3277. Methods of extinction

Privileges become extinct:

1. By the extinction of the thing subject to the privilege.
2. By the creditor acquiring the thing subject to it.
3. By the extinction of debt which gave birth to it.
4. By prescription.

TITLE XXII—MORTGAGES

CHAPTER 1—GENERAL PROVISIONS

Art. 3278. Mortgage defined

Mortgage is a nonpossessory right created over property to secure the performance of an obligation.

Acts 1991, No. 652, § 1, eff. Jan. 1, 1992.

REVISION COMMENTS—1991

(a) This Article substantially reproduces the provisions of former Civil Code Articles 3278 and 3284 (1870). The phrase "property of the debtor" appearing in the source Article has been deleted because a mortgage may be given over the property of someone other than the principal debtor. See C.C. Arts. 3295 and 3297, infra.

(b) The statement that a mortgage is a "nonpossessory right created over property" emphasizes the traditional distinction between mortgage and pledge, formerly expressed in Civil Code Article 3281 (1870). Former Civil Code Articles 3279–3281 (1870) have been omitted because they essentially added nothing to the definition and served only a didactic purpose. Moore v. Boagni, 111 La. 490, 35 So. 716 (1903); Webre v. Beltran, 47 La.Ann. 195, 16 So. 860 (La.1894). A mortgage neither gives "title" nor possession to the mortgagee, whose rights are defined in the succeeding articles. See Howe v. Austin, 40 La.Ann. 323, 4 So. 315 (La.1888); Miller v. Shotwell, 38 La.Ann. 890 (1886); Duclaud v. Rousseau, 2 La.Ann. 168 (1847); Conrad v. Prieur, 5 Rob. 49 (La.1843).

Art. 3279. Rights created by mortgage

Mortgage gives the mortgagee, upon failure of the obligor to perform the obligation that the mortgage secures, the right to cause the property to be seized and sold in the manner provided by law and to have the proceeds applied toward the satisfaction of the obligation in preference to claims of others.

Acts 1991, No. 652, § 1, eff. Jan. 1, 1992.

REVISION COMMENTS—1991

(a) The Article defines the substantive nature of mortgage. The term "mortgagee" as used in this Article and others in this Title means the creditor or creditors to whom obligations are owed that from time to time are secured by the mortgage. The mortgage, being an accessory to such creditors' rights, is inseparable from them. C.C. Art. 3282, infra. The transfer in whole or in part of the obligation that the mortgage secures includes an implicit transfer of the mortgagee's rights under the mortgage to the extent that it secures the transferred obligation. The obligee therefore always is the mortgagee. The effects of a mortgage are also defined by Article 3307. The two Articles complement each other.

(b) This Article reproduces the substance of Civil Code Article 3278 (1870). The preceding article defines the nature of mortgage. This Article defines the substance and content of the right of mortgage, which essentially gives the creditor two rights: First, he may have the mortgaged property seized and sold. Second, he will enjoy a preference to the proceeds ahead of the claims of others. The requirement that the seizure and sale must be "in the manner provided by law" emphasizes the long tradition in Louisiana of requiring recourse to judicial procedures and generally rejecting private sale or self-help as a method of execution.

Art. 3280. Mortgage is an indivisible real right

Mortgage is an indivisible real right that burdens the entirety of the mortgaged property and that follows the property into whatever hands the property may pass.

Acts 1991, No. 652, § 1, eff. Jan. 1, 1992.

REVISION COMMENTS—1991

(a) This Article reproduces the substance of former Civil Code Article 3282 (1870). For a discussion of real rights in Louisiana, see Yiannopoulos, Real Rights in Louisiana and Comparative Law, 23 La.L.Rev. 161 (1963). See also Comment (b) to Civil Code Article 535 (rev. 1976). The concept of indivisibility is central to the understanding of mortgage. In essence "indivisibility" expresses the notion that each portion of the mortgaged property secures every part of the mortgaged debt. "It is well settled ... that a mortgage is in its nature indivisible and prevails over all the immovables subjected to it, and over each and every portion." Lawton v. Smith, 146 So. 361, 363 (La.App. 2nd Cir.1933). Correlatively, each part of the obligation is secured by all of the mortgage over all of the property. "Each and every portion of the property mortgaged, is liable for each and every portion of the debt." Bagley v. Tate, 10 Rob. 45 (La.1845). The concept of indivisibility does not prevent the parties from agreeing to the partial release or division of the right to enforce the mortgage, or otherwise modifying its effect within the limits permitted by law, and subject to the rights of third possessors under the laws of registry.

(b) The mortgage creditor may not be compelled to execute on only a part of the seized property, nor can the debtor obtain a reduction of the property on the grounds that it is an excessive seizure. See C.C.P. Articles 2295 and 2296. The mortgagee may direct that the property be sold either separately or in globo. Bank of New Orleans & Trust Co. v. Lambert, 409 So.2d 294 (La.App. 1st Cir.1981).

(c) The mortgage creditor may execute on only a part of the mortgaged property at his option. "The creditor with a special mortgage has the right to foreclose it on a part only of the property mortgaged, and is not compelled to make the whole of said property contribute to the payment of his debt." Federal Land Bank v. Rester, 164 La. 926, 114 So. 839, 840 (La.1927). See also Burgess v. Gordy, 32 La.Ann. 1296 (1880). The holder of any part of the debt may execute on the mortgaged property, but it will be sold subject to the mortgage as to the remaining part of the debt. See C.C.P. Art. 2341.

(d) It is only the mortgage that is indivisible and not the personal obligation that the mortgage secures. "While a mortgage is indivisible, the debt which it secures may be divisible. So that, two or more persons may secure their personal obligations, solidary or joint, by a mortgage on property owned by them in its entirety ... And, certainly, separate pieces of property belonging to two or more persons may be embraced within the same mortgage given to secure the individual debt of one of such persons." Nelson v. Stewart, 173 La. 203, 136 So. 565, 567 (La.1931). "An indivisible mortgage frequently secures a divisible debt." Randolph v. Starke, 51 La.Ann. 1121, 26 So. 59, 62 (La.1899).

Art. 3281.   Mortgage established only in authorized cases

Mortgage may be established only as authorized by legislation.

Acts 1991, No. 652, § 1, eff. Jan. 1, 1992.

REVISION COMMENT—1991

This Article reproduces the substance of former Civil Code Article 3283 (1870) and continues the well-established principle that security may only exist in those cases where it has been expressly authorized by law. See C.C. Arts. 3183–3185 (1870). "Our lawgivers have thought it wise to restrain the power of hypothecating property, which is one of the rights of dominion, by the following general and sweeping rule ... (article quoted). The mortgage right then is to be measured, in every case, by the express grant of power in our Codes and other statute books." Voorhies v. De Blanc, 12 La.Ann. 864, 865 (1857).

Art. 3282.   Accessory nature

Mortgage is accessory to the obligation that it secures. Consequently, except as provided by law, the mortgagee may enforce the mortgage only to the extent that he may enforce any obligation it secures.

Acts 1991, No. 652, § 1, eff. Jan. 1, 1992.

REVISION COMMENTS—1991

(a) This Article reproduces the substance of former Civil Code Articles 3284 and 3285 (1870). It completes the definitional Articles by emphasizing the accessory character of mortgage. Like all accessory contracts, a mortgage may only be enforced to satisfy another, principal obligation. Although the rights of the mortgagee may not be enforced until the principal obligation is due and unperformed, the rights of mortgage may exist before the obligation is incurred or before there has been a default upon it. See C.C. Art. 3298, infra. An agreement that enforcement of the obligation will be restricted to proceeds realized from execution upon the mortgaged property is not contrary to the accessory nature of the security. See C.C. Art. 3297, infra.

(b) The reference to exceptions provided by law in the second sentence recognizes the provisions of Civil Code Article 3295, infra, making a mortgage given to secure the debt of another enforceable even though the principal obligor lacks capacity to contract or has been discharged in bankruptcy.

Art. 3283. Kinds of mortgages

Mortgage is conventional, legal, or judicial, and with respect to the manner in which it burdens property, it is general or special.

Acts 1991, No. 652, § 1, eff. Jan. 1, 1992.

REVISION COMMENT—1991

This Article maintains the traditional categories of mortgage established by the former code.

Art. 3284. Conventional, legal, and judicial mortgages

A conventional mortgage is established by contract.

A legal mortgage is established by operation of law.

A judicial mortgage is established by law to secure a judgment.

Acts 1991, No. 652, § 1, eff. Jan. 1, 1992.

REVISION COMMENT—1991

This Article defines the kinds of mortgages established by the preceding Article. It reproduces the substance of former Article 3287 (1870).

Art. 3285. General and special mortgages distinguished

A general mortgage burdens all present and future property of the mortgagor.

A special mortgage burdens only certain specified property of the mortgagor.

Acts 1991, No. 652, § 1, eff. Jan. 1, 1992.

REVISION COMMENTS—1991

(a) This Article continues the distinction long recognized in Louisiana law between general mortgages that burden both the present and indefinite future property of the debtor and special mortgages that affect only certain specified property. The essential difference lies in the necessity for particularly identifying the property subject to a special mortgage. A general mortgage attaches to all of the existing and future property of the mortgagor susceptible of mortgage, or certain categories of such property, without particular identification or designation. In essence, proof that the mortgagor owned the property during the time a general mortgage is effective suffices to prove its validity, subject of course to the principles of recordation. A special mortgage must describe the property it affects (C.C. Art. 3288, infra), although it is not necessary that the property then be owned by the mortgagee. C.C. Art. 3292, infra.

(b) In the absence of particular legislation conventional mortgages are limited to special ones, and judicial and legal mortgages are general. Special laws presently permit certain general, conventional mortgages. See, for example, R.S. 12:702 (mortgages executed by public utility corporations), and R.S. 9:5103 (newspaper may give mortgage of plant, equipment, name and good will). That the specific property over which a mortgage may be given is not then owned by the mortgagor does not prevent the parties from contracting for it, nor make the mortgage a general mortgage. See C.C. Art. 3292, infra.

Art. 3286. Property susceptible of mortgage

The only things susceptible of mortgage are:

(1) A corporeal immovable with its component parts.

(2) A usufruct of a corporeal immovable.

(3) A servitude of right of use with the rights that the holder of the servitude may have in the buildings and other constructions on the land.

(4) The lessee's rights in a lease of an immovable with his rights in the buildings and other constructions on the immovable.

(5) Property made susceptible of conventional mortgage by special law.

Acts 1991, No. 652, § 1, eff. Jan. 1, 1992. Amended by Acts 1992, No. 649, § 1, eff. July 1, 1993; Acts 1993, No. 948, § 6, eff. June 25, 1993.

REVISION COMMENTS—1991

(a) This Article defines the property that is susceptible of mortgage. It restates somewhat the provisions of former Civil Code Article 3289 (1870) and brings into the Code the provisions of former R.S. 9:5102 permitting the mortgaging of predial leases. For the most part the restatements adopt the terminology and categories of things used in the revision of Book II of the Civil Code dealing with "Things And The Different Modifications Of Ownership" and work little substantive change in the law.

(b) Paragraph (1) provides that corporeal immovables and their component parts may be mortgaged. This essentially comprehends land and its component parts (C.C. Art. 462); buildings and their component parts when on the land of another (C.C. Art. 464); and standing timber when it belongs to someone other than the owner of the land. C.C. Art. 464. Things that become component parts of land or a building are covered by a mortgage on the land or building simply because they are components of the mortgaged thing itself. Consequently, former Civil Code Article 3310 (1870) providing that a conventional mortgage "includes all the improvements which [the mortgaged immovable] may afterwards receive" has been omitted as being unnecessary and incomplete, since the effect is not limited to conventional mortgages, but arises from the nature of the classifications of the property itself.

(c) Paragraph (2) continues the authority to mortgage the usufruct of a corporeal immovable. It is the usufruct itself which is the subject of the mortgage under this Paragraph. Consequently, the mortgage covers things which become a component part of such an immovable to the extent that the usufructuaries' rights extend over them.

(d) A servitude of right of use may be mortgaged "with the rights that the holder of the servitude may have in the buildings and other constructions on the land." The classification of things established by Civil Code Articles 462–475 (rev. 1978), makes a building constructed on the land subject to a servitude of right of use is a distinct immovable. C.C. Art.464 (rev. 1978). Other constructions are movables, and thus neither a part of the servitude nor of the land. See discussion in Part II of the Expose des Motifs. Paragraph (3) is intended to make it clear that a mortgage of such a servitude covers the mortgagor's rights in such things, and in essence, treats them as though they were an integral part of the servitude for the purposes of the mortgage. It does not change their classification for other purposes.

(e) A predial servitude is not classified as a component part of the dominant estate. However, Civil Code Article 650 (Rev. 1977) notes that such a servitude is "inseparable from the dominant estate and passes with it" and that it "cannot be ... encumbered separately from the dominant estate." A mortgage of the dominant estate implicitly covers all predial servitudes belonging to it. Neither can such a servitude be mortgaged separately. See the comments to C.C. Art. 650 (Rev. 1977).

(f) The provisions of former R.S. 9:5102 permitting the mortgaging of predial leases has been incorporated into the body of the Code in Paragraph (4). The reference to the lessee's rights in the buildings and other constructions on the immovable has been included for the same reasons as are discussed in comment (d), above, relative to the personal servitude of right of use. The term "lessee" as used in this Article includes a sublessee or assignee of the lease.

(g) Paragraph (5) recognizes that the legislature has from time to time extended the rights of mortgage to other kinds of property by special laws. Despite the reference to "conventional mortgage", the nature, extent, and substance of such mortgages are regulated by the laws creating them. See, for example, R.S. 31:203 (mineral rights susceptible of mortgage to the same extent as corporeal immovables). The Paragraph does serve the purpose of indicating that such mortgages will be regulated in accordance with the general provisions established by the Code, in the absence of contrary provisions in the laws authorizing them.

CHAPTER 2—CONVENTIONAL MORTGAGES

Art. 3287.   Conventional mortgage

A conventional mortgage may be established only by written contract. No special words are necessary to establish a conventional mortgage.

Acts 1991, No. 652, § 1 eff. Jan. 1, 1992.

REVISION COMMENTS—1991

(a) This Article substantially restates the definition of a conventional mortgage given in former Civil Code Article 3290 (1870). It recognizes a conventional mortgage is both created and established by the contract of the parties. Neither delivery nor any other formality beyond the contract is required. The phrase "but without divesting himself of the possession" has been deleted as being redundant, since mortgage is by its nature non-possessory. See C.C. Art. 3278, supra.

(b) The requirement that the mortgage be in writing is based on former Civil Code Article 3305 (1870). The writing may be either an authentic act or an act under private signature. No witnesses are necessary. It is customary in Louisiana for mortgages to be in authentic form for purposes of executory process. Article 3321 now dispenses with the necessity for authentication as a prerequisite to recordation. The statement in former Civil Code Article 3305 (1870) that no proof can be admitted of a verbal mortgage has been omitted as unnecessary in light of Civil Code Article 1832 (rev. 1984).

(c) The second sentence of this Article is new, but codifies the well-established rule of Louisiana law that contracts are to be classified according to their substantive nature, rather than by the names or labels the parties choose to place upon them. As to the applicability of this rule to mortgages, see Succession of Benjamin, 39 La.Ann. 612, 2 So. 187 (La.1887).

Art. 3288.   Requirements of contract of mortgage

A contract of mortgage must state precisely the nature and situation of each of the immovables or other property over which it is granted; state the amount of the obligation, or the maximum amount of the obligations that may be outstanding at any time and from time to time that the mortgage secures; and be signed by the mortgagor.

Acts 1991, No. 652, § 1, eff. Jan. 1, 1992.

REVISION COMMENTS—1991

(a) The formal requirements for a conventional mortgage previously found in several articles have been combined into this Article and the preceding one. The contract must be in writing and must be signed by the mortgagor. See C.C. Arts. 1833, 1837 (Rev. 1984). It must describe or otherwise identify the thing mortgaged. It must declare the maximum amount for which the property stands mortgaged.

(b) The requirement that the mortgage describe the property it affects is taken verbatim from former Civil Code Article 3306 (1870). The language of the Article, taken alone, is perhaps somewhat misleading. There is a considerable body of jurisprudence interpreting the language and the continuation of the exact wording of the former Article is intended to insure that this jurisprudence will continue to be authoritative in determining what kinds of descriptions are sufficient, both between the parties and as to third persons, to validly mortgage property.

(c) The requirement of former Civil Code Article 3309 (1870) that the mortgage must declare "the exact sum for which it is given" has been modified to make it clear that the mortgage need only state a maximum amount secured by the mortgage of the debtor's obligations that are outstanding at any time or from time to time. Thus a mortgage may secure what is sometimes called a "revolving" line of credit, or other running balance of the debtor's obligations outstanding from time to time that it secures. This is contrary to dicta that has been occasionally expressed that a mortgage securing future obligations may secure only a definite, limited amount of the debtor's obligations. The purpose of the clause is to define the limit to which the debtor has encumbered his property. It is not necessary to identify the particular obligations that the mortgage secures, and indeed, the extent and nature of the precise obligations which are secured at any given time has never been determined from either the mortgage or the public records. The provision is consistent with what is permitted under current practices by utilization of the collateral mortgage, in which the amount of the mortgage note fixes the maximum amount of the obligations that the mortgage secures, but permits the pledge of the note to secure fluctuating and indefinite obligations of the debtor. This is not to say, however, that the mortgagee must not prove that any particular debt he is owed is one that is intended to be secured by the mortgage.

Art. 3289.   Acceptance

A contract of mortgage need not be signed by the mortgagee, whose consent is presumed and whose acceptance may be tacit.

Acts 1991, No. 652, § 1, eff. Jan. 1, 1992.

REVISION COMMENT—1991

A conventional mortgage is established by contract which, as with all other conventional obligations, requires the consent of both parties. This Article codifies two well-established jurisprudential rules pertaining to that consent. First, the acceptance of the mortgagee is presumed. This is an evidentiary presumption and simply means that the mortgagee presenting a mortgage for enforcement, or claiming rights through it, need not allege or prove that he has accepted it. The presumption does not dispense with the necessity for acceptance nor preclude the mortgagor or a third person from demonstrating that the contract was rejected, or the offer lapsed or was revoked before acceptance or even that it occurred at a particular time. The second rule codifies the well-established principle that, except for donations, unilateral contracts may be tacitly or verbally accepted, even though the law may require the contract to be in writing. See generally Comment (b) to C.C. Art. 1837 (Rev. 1984) and the cases cited therein.

Art. 3290.   Power to mortgage

A conventional mortgage may be established only by a person having the power to alienate the property mortgaged.

Acts 1991, No. 652, § 1, eff. Jan. 1, 1992.

REVISION COMMENT—1991

This Article substantially restates former Civil Code Article 3300 (1870) and is an expression of the basic principle that the establishment of a mortgage is an alienation or transfer of real rights over the property. Former Civil Code Articles 3301–3303 (1870) have been omitted as being unnecessary. The capacity, power, and authority of persons acting in their own right or in a representative capacity to mortgage or otherwise encumber property is established by the laws regulating their capacity or relationship to the persons for whom they act. Thus, Civil Code Article 1918 (Rev. 1984) states the rule of contractual capacity. Code of Civil Procedure Article 4267 requires court authorization for a tutor to mortgage the property of a minor. Code of Civil Procedure Article 4554 makes that rule applicable to a curator of an interdict.

Art. 3291. Presumption that things are subject to conventional mortgage

A conventional mortgage of a corporeal immovable, servitude of right of use, or lease, as the case may be, includes the things made susceptible of mortgage with them by Article 3286, unless the parties expressly agree to the contrary.

Acts 1991, No. 652, § 1, eff. Jan. 1, 1992.

REVISION COMMENT—1991

This Article is new. It is intended to eliminate any confusion as to the proper interpretation of Civil Code Article 3286, supra. Some of the things listed in that Article as being "susceptible of mortgage" with a servitude of right of use or a lease technically may be classified as movables or distinct immovables. For purposes of mortgage, however, functionally they are considered as components of the servitude or lease they serve and implicitly are covered by its mortgage in the absence of a contrary stipulation.

Art. 3292. Mortgage of future property permitted in certain cases

A special mortgage given over property the mortgagor does not own is established when the property is acquired by the mortgagor. A general conventional mortgage is permitted only when expressly provided by law.

Acts 1991, No. 652, § 1, eff. Jan. 1, 1992.

REVISION COMMENT—1991

This Article combines and clarifies the provisions of former Civil Code Articles 3308 (prohibiting the mortgage of "future property") and 3304 (1870) (validating a mortgage of property of which the mortgagor is not then the owner if the property is subsequently acquired). Former Civil Code Article 3308 (1870) was construed as prohibiting a general mortgage of indefinite future property. It did not prohibit a special mortgage of particular property later acquired by the mortgagor. The present Article clarifies the distinction. A special mortgage of property the debtor does not own is authorized, and such a mortgage becomes established if and when the property is acquired by the mortgagor. Being a special, conventional mortgage, it is subject to all of the requirements of this Section for such mortgages. Accordingly, it is necessary to describe the property as required by Article 3288.

Art. 3293. Obligations for which mortgage may be established

A conventional mortgage may be established to secure performance of any lawful obligation, even one for the performance of an act. The obligation may have a term and be subject to a condition.

Acts 1991, No. 652, § 1, eff. Jan. 1, 1992.

REVISION COMMENT—1991

Former Civil Code Article 3291 (1870) declared that a mortgage could be given to secure fulfillment of any obligation, even one for the performance of an act. Although the concept is consistent with the nature of security generally, it was deemed desirable to expressly continue its expression. This Article must be read in conjunction with Civil Code Article 3294, infra, regulating the consequences of a mortgage given to secure such an obligation.

Art. 3294. Mortgage securing obligation that is not for the payment of money

A mortgage that secures an obligation other than one for the payment of money secures the claim of the mortgagee for the damages he may suffer from a breach of the obligation, up to the amount stated in the mortgage.

Acts 1991, No. 652, § 1, eff. Jan. 1, 1992.

REVISION COMMENT—1991

This Article is new. It clarifies the effect of a mortgage given to secure an obligation other than one for the payment of money. Since the right of the mortgagee is limited to the seizure and sale of the mortgaged property, it follows that his recourse must be measured by some amount of money. If the obligation which the mortgage secures is one for the performance of an act, the mortgagee obviously will have to convert his claim into one for damages. The Article also makes it clear that the contract of mortgage must state a specific sum for which the property is to be held. It inferentially negates the idea that the amount stated in the mortgage is to be taken as equivalent to liquidated damages or a penalty. The amount stated is merely the maximum amount which the mortgagee may claim under the mortgage from the property for the satisfaction of the damages he has suffered. (Cf. C.C. Art. 3288)

Art. 3295.   Mortgage securing another's obligation

A person may establish a mortgage over his property to secure the obligations of another. In such a case, the mortgagor may assert against the mortgagee any defense to the obligation which the mortgage secures that the obligor could assert except lack of capacity or discharge in bankruptcy of the obligor.

Acts 1991, No. 652, § 1, eff. Jan. 1, 1992.

REVISION COMMENTS—1991

(a) This Article combines and restates the substance of former Civil Code Articles 3295 and 3299 (1870). The provisions of former Civil Code Articles 3296–3298 (1870) relative to the distinction between giving a mortgage and personally guaranteeing the obligation of a third person have been suppressed as being didactic. The right of mortgage does not give rise to personal liability in any case. See the Comments to Art. 3297, infra. If the mortgagor also guarantees the debts of another that guarantee will constitute a suretyship and be so regulated. A question may be present in such a case as to whether the mortgage secures the promise of the surety or that of the principal obligor, but that is a matter of contract to be determined by the intention of the parties as expressed in their agreements.

(b) The second sentence of this Article provides two exceptions to the rule that the mortgage is not enforceable unless the principal obligation is enforceable. The exceptions, lack of capacity and discharge in bankruptcy, are the same as is provided for by Civil Code Article 3046 (rev. 1987).

Art. 3296.   Right of mortgagor to raise defenses

Neither the mortgagor nor a third person may claim that the mortgage is extinguished or is unenforceable because the obligation the mortgage secures is extinguished or is unenforceable unless the obligor may assert against the mortgagee the extinction or unenforceability of the obligation that the mortgage secures.

Acts 1991, No. 652, § 1, eff. Jan. 1, 1992.

REVISION COMMENTS—1991

(a) This Article is new. It clarifies the law. Ordinarily, the extinction of the principal obligation extinguishes the mortgage. See former C.C. Art. 3285 (1870). The mortgage is a contract separate from the principal obligation it secures. The mortgage is not negotiable. Frequently, the obligation it secures is negotiable. Although the matter has never been expressly decided, there is dicta in a few cases indicating that under the prior law the mortgagor or a third person, such as a second mortgage holder, could raise as a defense to the enforcement of the mortgage, the claim that it had been extinguished by extinction of the principal obligation, under circumstances where the obligor of that obligation was precluded from pleading the defense against the mortgagee, either because the latter was a holder in due course of the instrument the mortgage secured, or for other reasons. This Article legislatively overrules that dicta.

(b) If the obligation that the mortgage secures is enforceable against the obligor, so that the mortgagee may obtain a judgment against him on it, neither a third person who has mortgaged his property nor one who has acquired an interest in the mortgaged property should be able to defeat the mortgage on the grounds that the debt it secures has been extinguished. This, of course does not preclude such persons from raising as a defense to the enforcement of the mortgage, some vice or defect in the mortgage itself.

Art. 3297. Restrictions upon recourse of mortgagee

The mortgagee's recourse for the satisfaction of an obligation secured by a mortgage may be limited in whole or in part to the property over which the mortgage is established.

Acts 1991, No. 652, § 1, eff. Jan. 1, 1992.

REVISION COMMENTS—1991

(a) This Article is new. It reproduces, in a more positive manner, the substance of the second sentence of former Civil Code Article 3291 added by Act 238 of 1980, which declared that a mortgage could be given on the stipulation that the mortgagor would not be personally bound, and that stipulations limiting the rights of recourse of the mortgagee against the mortgagor or precluding or limiting personal liability of a mortgagor would not affect the validity of the mortgage.

(b) As is discussed more fully in the Expose des Motifs, a mortgage does not create personal liability on the part of the mortgagee for the principal obligation (whether or not it is his or that of a third person). As is defined in Articles 3278 and 3279, supra, a mortgage is a right to have property seized and sold in satisfaction of a principal obligation, which may be that of the mortgagor or of another. Contracts or agreements limiting the right of recourse of the creditor to the mortgaged property (or any other property) for satisfaction of the principal obligation pertain to the obligation, not the accessory right securing it. Of course, a mortgagor may undertake personal obligations (such as those pertaining to insuring or preserving the property, etc.) in the contract of mortgage. These also are distinct from the principal obligation and from the mortgage itself. These relationships are best seen in the case of a mortgage by one person to secure the obligations of another. The mortgagor is not liable for the obligations of the debtor that the mortgage secures nor is the debtor liable for the obligation of the mortgagor undertaken in the act of mortgage, unless, of course, he should personally undertake them by making himself a party to the contract of mortgage.

Art. 3298. Mortgage may secure future obligations

A.   A mortgage may secure obligations that may arise in the future.

B.   As to all obligations, present and future, secured by the mortgage, notwithstanding the nature of such obligations or the date they arise, the mortgage has effect between the parties from the time the mortgage is established and as to third persons from the time the contract of mortgage is filed for registry.

C.   A promissory note or other evidence of indebtedness secured by a mortgage need not be paraphed for identification with the mortgage and need not recite that it is secured by the mortgage.

D.   The mortgage may be terminated by the mortgagor or his successor upon reasonable notice to the mortgagee when an obligation does not exist and neither the mortgagor nor the mortgagee is bound to the other or to a third person to permit an obligation secured by the mortgage to be incurred. Parties may contract with reference to what constitutes reasonable notice.

E.   The mortgage continues until it is terminated by the mortgagor or his successor in the manner provided in Paragraph D of this Article, or until the mortgage is extinguished in some other lawful manner. The effect of recordation of the mortgage ceases in accordance with the provisions of Articles 3357 and 3358.

Acts 1991, No. 652, § 1, eff. Jan. 1, 1992. Amended by Acts 1992, No. 779, § 1; Acts 1995, No. 1087, § 1; Acts 2010, No. 385, § 1.

REVISION COMMENTS—1991

(a) As the Expose des Motifs more fully explains, this Article, and certain supplemental legislation adopted with it (R.S. 9:5555–5557), is intended to provide a direct and convenient substitute for the so-called collateral mortgage, which in recent years has become widely used, and to permit a person to mortgage his property to secure a line of credit, or even to secure obligations that may not then be contemplated by him except in the broadest sense of an expectation that he may some day incur an obligation to the mortgagee. The supplemental legislation also facilitates the granting of mortgages to secure obligations that are not evidenced by a note paraphed for identification with it. See R.S. 9:5555–5557 (1991).

(b) The expression in Paragraph A that "a mortgage may secure" is intended to emphasize that a mortgage securing future obligations is not a distinct or different form of mortgage. A mortgage may secure existing obligations; obligations contemporaneously incurred with the execution of the mortgage or specific identifiable or particular and limited future obligations; or general and indefinite future obligations; or any combination of them. The matter is one of contract, not law, and the provisions of this Title regulating mortgages are equally applicable in each case.

(c) Paragraph B declares that a mortgage securing future obligations has the same effect and priority it would have if the obligations were in existence when the contract of mortgage was entered into. Thus, it is effective between the parties from the date it is created by the contract of the parties (Art. 3287), and is established over future property when the property is acquired. (Art. 3292).

(d) The effect and rank of a mortgage securing future obligations thus essentially corresponds to the effect and rank which it would have if it secured a collateral note that was pledged to secure the future obligations, with the exception that the Article does not require that there initially be a debt or commitment in order to give vitality to the mortgage. Of course, the contract of mortgage must be in existence and, to affect third persons acquiring rights in and to the thing mortgaged, it must be recorded. Once recorded, however, it serves notice to the world that, until released or cancelled, it encumbers the property it describes to secure the obligations it contemplates.

(e) Paragraph D concerns the termination of the mortgage. The contract of mortgage securing obligations which neither the mortgagor nor mortgagee are bound to permit to be incurred is treated as being terminable by the mortgagor unless and until such obligations are in fact incurred. If no such obligations exist, or if neither the debtor nor creditor is obligated to permit the other to incur them, then the mortgagor or his successor may demand a conventional release from the mortgagee, who is bound to give it to him. The term "successor" is broad enough to include one who has acquired the property from the mortgagor or a right in it (the obligation of mortgage is a real right, and correlatively the obligation is a real one) owed by the owner of the land, although personal obligations undertaken by the mortgagor continue after disposition of the land. See C.C. Arts. 1763 and 1764 (Rev. 1984). The provision impliedly recognizes that a mortgage contract securing future, indefinite obligations is similar to one of continuous or periodic performance as described in Civil Code Article 1776 (Rev. 1984), and is terminable at the will of either party upon reasonable notice, as contemplated by Civil Code Article 2024 (Rev. 1984). It also recognizes that the mortgage is indivisible and that the mortgagor may not demand a release unless no debt it secures is in existence and neither party is bound to the other to permit a debt to be incurred. R.S. 9:5557 supplements this provision by establishing a procedure by which the mortgagor or his successor may demand such a release.

(f) Paragraph E reinforces the principle implicit in Paragraphs B and C of this Article as discussed in the preceding comment, and more fully explained in the Expose des Motifs, that the mortgage is fully in existence, though its enforcement may be conditional, and even though no obligations are then secured, the Paragraph provides that the mortgage continues until all of the obligations present and future for which it is established are incurred and have been extinguished. Resort must be had to the contract of mortgage to determine what obligations it may secure. If it is given for specific, identifiable existing or future obligations, or those of an aggregate fixed amount, then when those obligations have been incurred and are extinguished, the mortgage is extinguished. If on the other hand, the mortgage secures future, indefinite obligations with a maximum limit on their aggregate balance from time to time, then in essence, the mortgage continues indefinitely until it is terminated by notice of the mortgagor or the consent of the parties, or in some other manner recognized by law. See the comments to Art. 3411, infra.

CHAPTER 3—JUDICIAL AND LEGAL MORTGAGES

Art. 3299.   Judicial and legal mortgages

A judicial mortgage secures a judgment for the payment of money. A legal mortgage secures an obligation specified by the law that provides for the mortgage.

Acts 1992, No. 1132, § 2, eff. Jan. 1, 1993.

REVISION COMMENTS—1992

(a) A judicial mortgage is defined by Civil Code Article 3284 (rev. 1991). The qualification that the judgment be for the payment of money codifies a long-established interpretation of prior law. See Lirette v. Carrane, 27 La.Ann. 298 (1875); Jartroux v. Dupeire, 2 La.Ann. 608 (1847).

(b) R.S. 9:321 et seq. provide that an alimony judgment does not give rise to a judicial mortgage until a further judgment condemning the defendant to pay a fixed amount is recorded. The present Article does not repeal or modify those special provisions.

(c) Special statutes allow for the creation of a mortgage by virtue of recordation of something other than a judgment. See, for example, R.S. 47:1577 and 1581, which provide that the recordation of a tax assessment has the same effect as the recordation of a judgment. Flowers, Inc. v. Rausch, 364 So.2d 928 (La.1978). See also R.S. 35:73 which provides that a notarial bond operates as a mortgage when suit is filed and notice of lis pendens is recorded.

(d) A legal mortgage is defined by Civil Code Article 3284 (Rev. 1991). It functionally operates in the same manner as a judicial mortgage.

Art. 3300. Creation of judicial mortgage

A judicial mortgage is created by filing a judgment with the recorder of mortgages.

Acts 1992, No. 1132, § 2, eff. Jan. 1, 1993.

REVISION COMMENT—1992

This Article substantially restates prior law. C.C. Art. 3322 (1870). By declaring that a judicial mortgage is created by the filing of the judgment emphasizes that, unlike a conventional mortgage, which is created by contract, a judicial mortgage does not exist merely by virtue of the judgment. Consequently, none of the effects of mortgage can be said to flow from the judgment itself. Recordation creates the mortgage as a right in favor of the creditor and establishes it over the property then owned by the debtor. If the debtor does not then own property, the mortgage exists as a right in favor of the creditor to a mortgage over the future property of his debtor, and is then imposed (established) over particular property when the debtor acquires it. Consequently, although such mortgages take their effect as to third persons from the time of recordation, they do not constitute a charge upon any particular property until it is acquired by the debtor. The mortgage, being effective as to the judgment debtor and being recorded will rank ahead of any other charges imposed by the debtor over the property after the judgment is recorded, even as to future property.

Art. 3301. Creation of legal mortgage

A legal mortgage is created by complying with the law providing for it.

Acts 1992, No. 1132, § 2, eff. Jan. 1, 1993.

REVISION COMMENT—1992

This Article recognizes that a legal mortgage is a product of special legislation and is primarily regulated by the law providing for it.

Art. 3302. Property burdened by judicial and legal mortgages

Judicial and legal mortgages burden all the property of the obligor that is made susceptible of mortgage by Paragraphs 1 through 4 of Article 3286 or that is expressly made subject to judicial or legal mortgage by other law.

Acts 1992, No. 1132, § 2, eff. Jan. 1, 1993.

REVISION COMMENTS—1992

(a) Former Civil Code Article 3328 (1870) declared that a judicial mortgage affected all "the immovables" of the debtor. This was construed to include only that property that the Code declared to be susceptible of mortgage. It is more accurate to expressly refer to the provisions of Civil Code Article 3286 (rev. 1991), in describing the property that is burdened by a judicial or legal mortgage.

(b) This Article and Article 3286 change the law by extending the effect of judicial and legal mortgages to predial leases. Before the 1991 revision, the lessee's interest in a lease could only be mortgaged conventionally under R.S. 9:5102. Article 3286 makes the lease and the lessee's interest in any building or other construction on the leased premise generally susceptible to mortgage.

(c) Mineral rights, although not expressly made susceptible of mortgage by Article 3286, are made mortgageable "to the same extent . . . as is prescribed by law for mortgages of immovables under Article 3286" by R.S. 31:203 (Rev. 1991). This is intended to make such mineral rights subject to judicial and legal mortgages.

Art. 3303.　Nature of judicial and legal mortgages

Judicial and legal mortgages are general mortgages. They are established over property that the obligor owns when the mortgage is created and over future property of the obligor when he acquires it.

Acts 1992, No. 1132, § 2, eff. Jan. 1, 1993.

REVISION COMMENTS—1992

(a) This Article substantially restates the provisions of former Articles 3320 and 3328.

(b) Former Article 3328 (1870) provided that a judicial mortgage affected the property "actually" owned by the judgment debtor. This was a mistranslation of the French word "actuel," used in the Code Napoleon meaning "current" or "present". See Comment, 34 Tul.L.Rev. 768 (1960), and cases cited therein. Based upon this the courts rejected the argument that the requirement that the debtor "actually" own the property made the judicial mortgage ineffective as to property owned of record by the debtor if that ownership could be disproven by an unrecorded counterletter or other instrument. See State ex rel. Hebert v. Recorder of Mortgages, 175 La. 94, 143 So. 15 (1932); Martin v. Fuller, 214 La. 404, 37 So.2d 851 (1948). This Article does not change that rule, but simply states that the mortgage encumbers all of the property owned by the debtor. Whether an unrecorded document that affects the judgment debtor's ownership can be asserted against the mortgagee is dependent upon whether or not he is a third person, under the ordinary rules pertaining to the effect of registry.

Art. 3304.　Judgment; suspensive appeal

A judicial mortgage is not affected or suspended by a suspensive appeal or stay of execution of the judgment.

Acts 1992, No. 1132, § 2, eff. Jan. 1, 1993.

REVISION COMMENTS—1992

(a) The effect of a suspensive appeal upon the judicial mortgage created by recordation of the judgment creating it formerly was controlled by Goldking Properties v. Primeaux, 477 So.2d 76 (La.1985). That case held that a party who perfected a suspensive appeal had a right to have a judicial mortgage securing the trial judgment cancelled on the grounds that it was an effect of the judgment that was suspended according to the provisions of C.C.P.Art. 2123. This Article overrules the Goldking case. A devolutive appeal, of course, had no effect upon the mortgage.

(b) This Article must be read in conjunction with R.S. 13:4434–4435 which permit the judgment debtor who has taken a suspensive appeal and filed a proper appeal bond to obtain an order terminating the mortgage and erasing the judgment from the records. This, in effect, accomplishes the same result as the Goldking case, but protects the judgment creditor by affording him an opportunity to test the validity and sufficiency of the appeal bond before the debtor's property is freed from the mortgage. The mortgage remains effective notwithstanding the suspensive appeal if the debtor takes no steps to secure its termination.

Art. 3305.　Judgments of other jurisdictions

The filing of an authenticated copy of a judgment of a court of a jurisdiction foreign to this state, such as the United States, another state, or another country, creates a judicial mortgage only when so provided by special legislation, or when accompanied by a certified copy of a judgment or order of a Louisiana court recognizing it and ordering it executed according to law.

In all other cases the judgment of a court of a jurisdiction foreign to this state creates a judicial mortgage only when a Louisiana court has rendered a judgment making the foreign judgment the judgment of the Louisiana court, and the Louisiana judgment has been filed in the same manner as other judgments.

Acts 1992, No. 1132, § 2, eff. Jan. 1, 1993.

REVISION COMMENTS—1992

(a) This Article restates the substance of former Article 3326 (1870). Whether filing a foreign judgment creates a judicial mortgage, or whether the creditor is required to obtain and file a judgment of a Louisiana court recognizing or adopting it, is determined by special laws.

(b) R.S. 13:4204 permits a judgment rendered by a United States court of original jurisdiction in Louisiana to be filed and have the same effect as a judgment of a Louisiana court.

(c) R.S. 13:4241 et seq. provide that a Louisiana court may enter an order recognizing a foreign judgment and ordering it executed. In such a case the recordation of the foreign judgment together with the Louisiana order recognizing it is the operative act that creates the mortgage. Code of Civil Procedure Article 2541 provides an alternative procedure in that the judgment creditor may file an ordinary action against the debtor based upon the foreign judgment. By this procedure a Louisiana judgment is obtained. The filing of that judgment creates the mortgage in the same manner as the filing of any other Louisiana judgment. See Kenzie v. Havard, 12 Mart. (O.S.) 101 (1822); Bonnafe v. Lane, 5 La.Ann. 225 (1850); Succession of Macheca, 84 So. 574 (La.1920); State v. Dunn, 87 So. 236 (La.1921).

Art. 3306. Judgment against person deceased

A judicial mortgage burdens the property of the judgment debtor only and does not burden other property of his heirs or legatees who have accepted his succession.

Acts 1992, No. 1132, § 2, eff. Jan. 1, 1993.

REVISION COMMENT—1992

This Article continues and more clearly states the provisions of former Article 3327 (1870). A universal successor succeeds to all of the assets and becomes liable for all of the obligations of the person to whom he is a successor. A judgment rendered against a person who dies is the obligation of his heirs or legatees who accept his succession unconditionally or with benefit of inventory, although in the latter case their liability may be limited in amount. This Article accommodates that rule with the public records doctrine and limits the mortgage enjoyed by the judgment creditor to the property of the decedent that is transmitted to his successors. Such a judgment does not affect the other assets of the heir or legatee.

CHAPTER 4—THE EFFECT AND RANK OF MORTGAGES

Art. 3307. The effect and rank of mortgages

A mortgage has the following effects:

(1) Upon failure of the obligor to perform the obligation secured by the mortgage, the mortgagee may cause the mortgaged property to be seized and sold in the manner provided by law and have the proceeds applied toward the satisfaction of the obligation.

(2) The mortgaged property may not be transferred or encumbered to the prejudice of the mortgage.

(3) The mortgagee is preferred to the unsecured creditors of the mortgagor and to others whose rights become effective after the mortgage becomes effective as to them.

Acts 1992, No. 1132, § 2, eff. Jan. 1, 1993.

REVISION COMMENT—1992

This Article is based on former Article 3397 (1870). It also restates the substance of Article 3279 (rev. 1991). In addition to summarizing the basic rights given by a mortgage, it lays the foundation for the ranking of mortgages, which is amplified in the Articles that follow.

Arts. 3308 to 3310. [Blank]

Art. 3311. Mortgage securing several obligations

In the absence of contrary agreement, the proceeds realized from enforcement of the mortgage shall be apportioned among several obligations secured by the mortgage in proportion to the amount owed on each at the time of enforcement.

Acts 1992, No. 1132, § 2, eff. Jan. 1, 1993.

REVISION COMMENTS—1992

(a) This Article is new. It changes the law. There has never been any question that a mortgage can secure several obligations. The Civil Code did not expressly regulate the rights of the mortgagee in cases where such obligations initially were incurred in favor of several persons or later were transferred to several persons. The jurisprudence generally held that in the absence of contrary agreement, all obligations were secured equally and in the proportion to their original principal amounts, although any excess left after satisfaction of one would be applied to the others until all were paid. See Leonard v. Brooks, 105 So. 54 (La.1925) and cases cited therein; Jacobs v. Calderwood, 4 La.Ann. 509 (La.1849); "The Problem Of A Series Of Mortgage Notes" 3 La.L.Rev. 464 (1940).

(b) The present Article changes the law. Under it the proceeds realized upon enforcement of the mortgage are allocated among the obligations according to the relative amounts owed on each at that time. The Article is relevant only if the property is sold in execution of all of the obligations that the mortgage secures (see comment (c), infra), and if the proceeds of the sale are insufficient to satisfy all of those obligations.

(c) A mortgage is indivisible. That is, each part of the mortgaged property indivisibly secures every part of the secured obligation. A contract of mortgage that secures separate and distinct obligations gives rise to a conjunctive obligation. "An obligation is conjunctive if it binds the obligor to multiple items of performance that may be separately rendered or enforced." C.C. Art. 1807. This principle has been construed to give each obligee of separate obligations secured by a mortgage, a distinct right to execute on the mortgage to satisfy what he is owed, the property being sold "subject to" the remaining obligations. This Article does not change those rules. See Utz v. Utz, 34 Ann. 752 (1882); Smith v. Sanders-Lenahan Lmbr. Co., 72 So. 445 (La.1918); City Savings Bank & Trust Co. v. Wilkinson 115 So. 629 (La.1928). Where multiple obligations secured by a single mortgage are held by one person, some of which are not due, "he may demand that the property be sold for the entire debt, on the same terms for the payment of the unmatured installments as provided in the original contract." C.C.P.Art. 2341.

Art. 3312. Transfer of the secured obligation

A transfer of an obligation secured by a mortgage includes the transfer of the mortgage. In such a case, the transferor warrants the existence, validity and enforceability of the mortgage only to the extent that he warrants the existence, validity, or enforceability of the obligation.

Acts 1992, No. 1132, § 2, eff. Jan. 1, 1993.

REVISION COMMENTS—1992

(a) The first sentence of this Article essentially reiterates the provisions of Article 2645: "The sale or transfer of a credit includes every thing which is an accessory to the same; as suretyship, privileges and mortgages." See also Nolen v. Davidson's Succession, 190 So. 826 (La.App.2d Cir.1939) ("When the notes, or the principal obligations, were transferred by delivery, the securities, which were accessories thereto, followed them."); Gardner v. Maxwell, 27 La.Ann. 561 (1875); Auguste v. Renard, 3 Rob. 389 (La.1843); Succession of Forstall, 3 So. 277 (La.1887); Perkins v. Gumbel, 21 So. 743 (La.1897); Perot v. Levasseur, 21 La.Ann. 529 (1869). Succession of Forstall, supra; Scott v.

Turner, 15 La.Ann. 346 (1860). See also LNB v. Heroman, 280 So.2d 362 (App. 1st Cir.1973). An express assignment of the mortgage therefore is unnecessary although if the mortgage secures obligations not evidenced by instruments paraphed for identification with the mortgage, a separate assignment of the mortgage is desirable. See R.S. 9:5555.

(b) The second sentence of this Article clarifies, and perhaps changes, the law. Some courts have viewed the transfer of the security contemplated by Article 2645 as an implied one and have imposed upon the transferor the warranties and obligations of an ordinary assignor. Thus a transfer "without recourse" of a negotiable note ostensibly secured by a mortgage imposed liability under the Civil Code on the transferor to return the purchase price if he knew that the mortgage securing the note had no legal validity. Citizens Bank v. Cook, 121 So. 306 (La.App.2d Cir.1928). Templeman v. Hamilton Co., 37 La. 754 (1885). This article makes it clear that in the absence of a contrary agreement the warranties expressly or impliedly made in connection with the transfer of the principal obligation are the warranties the parties intend to apply to the transfer of the mortgage.

Art. 3313.   Transfer does not imply subordination

A transferor of part of an obligation secured by a mortgage does not subordinate his rights to those of the transferee with respect to the portion of the mortgaged obligation he retains.

Acts 1992, No. 1132, § 2, eff. Jan. 1, 1993.

REVISION COMMENT—1992

This provision changes the law. Under the former law the transferor of part of the obligations secured by a mortgage impliedly subordinated the remaining obligations held by him to those transferred and he therefore could not compete with the transferee in the distribution of the mortgaged proceeds if they were insufficient to satisfy all of the obligations. Salzman v. His Creditors, 2 Rob. 241 (La.1842); Barkdull v. Herwig, 30 La.Ann. 618 (1878); Leonard v. Brooks, 105 So. 54 (La.1925). This, however, was held to be a personal obligation of the transferor to the transferee. A later transferee of one of the remaining obligations was not bound by the subordination. Begnaud v. Roy, 21 La.Ann. 624 (1864) ("transferees of portions of a mortgage debt are entitled to be paid, pro rata, out of the proceeds of the property mortgaged without regard to the time when they were transferred"); Adams v. Lear, 3 La.Ann. 144 (1848); Pepper v. Dunlap, 16 La. 163 (1840). This Article overrules the cases holding that there is an implied subordination agreement. In the absence of a contrary agreement, the transferor and transferee will share in the proceeds in the same manner as if they had received their obligations directly from the mortgagor. See C.C. Art. 3311.

Art. 3314.   [Blank]

CHAPTER 5—THIRD POSSESSORS

Art. 3315.   Third possessor defined

A third possessor is one who acquires mortgaged property and who is not personally bound for the obligation the mortgage secures.

Acts 1992, No. 1132, § 2, eff. Jan. 1, 1993.

REVISION COMMENT—1992

This Article is new. The definition of third possessor is derived from the jurisprudence. One who acquires the mortgaged property without knowing of the mortgage, or who expressly takes it "subject to" the mortgage, but without assuming the principal obligation secured by the mortgage, is a third possessor. See Duncan v. Elam, 1 Rob. 135 (La.1841); Twichel v. Andry, 6 Rob. 407 (La.1844); Boissac v. Downs, 16 La.Ann. 187 (1861); Thompson v. Levy, 23 So. 913 (La.1898); Federal Land Bank v. Cook, 155 So. 249 (La.1934). One who mortgages his property for the debt of another is not a third possessor even though he is not personally liable for the principal obligation because he has not acquired the mortgaged property subject to the mortgage, and more importantly, has expressly consented that his property be sold to satisfy the debt it secures.

Art. 3316.   Liability of third possessor

The deteriorations, which proceed from the deed or neglect of the third possessor to the prejudice of the creditors who have a privilege or a mortgage, give rise against the former to an action of indemnification.

Acts 1992, No. 1132, § 2, eff. Jan. 1, 1993.

REVISION COMMENTS—1992

(a) This Article continues the provisions of former Article 3407 making the third possessor liable for damages that he causes to the mortgaged property by his "deed or neglect."

(b) The mortgagee may obtain an injunction to prevent the mortgagor or his grantee from damaging the property. Fulton v. Oertling, 60 So. 238 (La.1912). The mortgagee may also have the property seized under a writ of sequestration if it is within the power of the defendant to waste the property during the pendency of an action. C.C.P.Art. 3571.

(c) The mortgage creditor has no right to the fruits of the property until it is seized. Ittman v. Kracke & Flanders Co., 127 So. 106 (Orl.App.1930). Code of Civil Procedure Article 327 expressly provides that the seizure of the property by the sheriff effects the seizure of the fruits it produces. Former Civil Code Article 3408 (1870), providing that the fruits of the property mortgaged are due by a third possessor from the time he is notified of the seizure of the property, have been suppressed as being in conflict with C.C.P. Article 327.

Art. 3317.   Rights of third possessor

A third possessor who performs the obligation secured by the mortgage is subrogated to the rights of the obligee. In such a case, the mortgage is not extinguished by confusion as to other mortgages, privileges, or charges burdening the mortgaged property when the third possessor acquired the mortgaged property and for which he is not personally bound.

Acts 1992, No. 1132, § 2, eff. Jan. 1, 1993.

REVISION COMMENTS—1992

(a) This Article is new. It clarifies the law.

(b) A third possessor is one who acquires mortgaged property without becoming personally bound for the obligation that the mortgage secures. Art. 3315, supra. Compare C.C.P.Art. 2702 with C.C.P.Art. 2703. Since the third possessor who pays the debt secured by the mortgage on his property is not an obligor of that debt, the qualities of obligor and obligee of the debt are not united by virtue of the payment and confusion therefore does not occur with respect to the debt. The third possessor is also technically subrogated to the mortgage by virtue of his payment. However, in the absence of the second sentence of this Article, the mortgage would be extinguished by confusion, since an owner of land ordinarily cannot hold a mortgage over his own property. See Art. 3319(2), infra. This would then elevate to a first position other inferior mortgages or privileges against the property as to which the payor was also a third possessor. This article prevents that result and recognizes the general principle that confusion does not extinguish a right as to intervening claimants. See Pugh v. Sample, 49 So. 626 (1909).

(c) The third possessor who has either discharged the mortgage debt or suffered the mortgaged property to be sold under execution may have an action in warranty against the principal debtor. See C.C. Art. 2501 (1870); Long v. Grisham, 123 So. 492 (La.App.2d Cir.1929); former C.C. Art. 3410 (1870).

Art. 3318.   Right of third possessor for costs of improvements

A third possessor may recover the cost of any improvements he has made to the property to the extent the improvements have enhanced the value of the property, out of the proceeds realized from enforcement of the mortgage, after the mortgagee has received the unenhanced value of the property.

Acts 1992, No. 1132, § 2, eff. Jan. 1, 1993.

804

REVISION COMMENT—1992

Former Article 3407 permitted the third possessor who has improved the mortgaged property to recover the costs of such improvements out of the proceeds received from enforcing the mortgage, to the extent the improvements have enhanced its value. This article continues the rule but expresses it to conform to the procedures for determining the amount of reimbursement prescribed by the Louisiana Supreme Court in Glass v. Ives, 126 So. 69 (La.1929). When a third possessor claims such a reimbursement, the property is to be appraised at its value exclusive of the improvements. The mortgagee or mortgagees as to which the owner is a third possessor is entitled to receive that amount from the proceeds of the sale. The third possessor is then to receive the excess until he has recovered the costs he incurred in making the improvements. Any excess then is to be used to satisfy the balance of the mortgages. This article is not intended to change the rule recognizing that if there is an inferior mortgagee as to whom the owner is not a third possessor (as where he himself has mortgaged the property) that mortgagee is entitled to the proceeds that would otherwise be distributable to the third possessor under the principles enunciated in the preceding paragraph, to the extent they are required to satisfy the obligation his mortgage secures.

CHAPTER 6—EXTINCTION OF MORTGAGES

Art. 3319. Methods of extinction

A mortgage is extinguished:

(1) By the extinction or destruction of the thing mortgaged.

(2) By confusion as a result of the obligee's acquiring ownership of the thing mortgaged.

(3) By prescription of all the obligations that the mortgage secures.

(4) By discharge through execution or other judicial proceeding in accordance with the law.

(5) By consent of the mortgagee.

(6) By termination of the mortgage in the manner provided by Paragraph D of Article 3298.

(7) When all the obligations, present and future, for which the mortgage is established have been incurred and extinguished.

Acts 1992, No.1132, § 2, eff. Jan. 1, 1993. Amended by Acts 1995, No. 1087, § 1.

REVISION COMMENTS—1992

(a) This Article largely reproduces the substance of former Article 3411 (1870). Paragraph (6) has been added to conform to the provisions of Article 3296, and to clarify the fact that a mortgage may be in existence and have juridical effect although some or all of the obligations for which it is given have not yet been incurred. If the mortgage secures a "revolving line" of future indefinite obligations, such a mortgage ordinarily will remain effective until it is released by consent of the mortgagee (Para. 5); is terminated by the mortgagor (Para. 6) or, the property is sold to satisfy all of the obligations that the mortgage then secures or to satisfy a mortgage or privilege of superior rank (Para. 4).

(b) Paragraph (4) is new but reflects existing law. See Quality Finance Corp. of Donaldsonville v. Bourque, 315 So.2d 656 (La.1975).

CHAPTER 7—INSCRIPTION OF MORTGAGES
AND PRIVILEGES

Art. 3320. Recordation; limits of effectiveness

A.   Repealed by Acts 2005, No. 169, § 8, eff. July 1, 2006.

B.   Repealed by Acts 2005, No. 169, § 8, eff. July 1, 2006.

C.   Recordation has only the effect given it by legislation. It is not evidence of the validity of the obligation that the encumbrance secures. It does not give the creditor greater rights against third persons than he has against the person whose property is encumbered.

Acts 1992, No. 1132, § 2, eff. Jan. 1, 1993.

REVISION COMMENTS—1992

(a) This Article combines in one provision several basic principles establishing the fundamental effects of recordation, all of which were formerly stated in the source articles and well-established by the jurisprudence. See former C.C. Arts. 3346–3348 (1870).

(b) Article 3308 declares that mortgages have no effect against third persons until they are registered as provided by law. C.C. Arts. 3308, 3309, supra. This Article fixes the particular time when registry occurs as being when the act evidencing the mortgage or other encumbrance is filed. This is consistent with existing law. See R.S. 9:2721.

(c) Paragraph B of this Article continues the rule that the effect of recordation is limited to property located in the parish where the recordation occurs. See former C.C. Art. 3347 (1870).

(d) Paragraph C of this Article restates three well-established principles. The first is that recordation is only given such effect as the law provides. Louisiana's registry system is not based upon knowledge, actual or implied. A document recorded in the mortgage records has effect as to third persons not because they have or are deemed to have notice of it, but merely because the law provides it has such effect. Conversely, an unrecorded instrument that is required to be recorded has no effect as to third persons, whether or not they are aware of its existence. See Art. 3308. Under that system, to be effective, an instrument also must be filed in the place prescribed by law. Thus, a mortgage recorded in the conveyance records, or a sale recorded in the mortgage records, is without effect as to third persons. The second and third sentences of Paragraph C of this Article restate principles previously articulated by Civil Code Article 3357 (1870). They do not represent any change in those principles.

Arts. 3321 to 3324. [Blank]

Art. 3325. Paraph of notes or written obligations secured by a mortgage, privilege, or other encumbrance

A.   Except as provided in Paragraph B of this Article, a note or other written obligation which is secured by an act of mortgage, or an act evidencing a privilege or other encumbrance, need not be paraphed for identification with such mortgage, privilege, or other encumbrance, and need not recite that it is secured by such mortgage, privilege, or other encumbrance.

B.   A notary before whom is passed an act of mortgage, or an act evidencing a privilege or other encumbrance that secures a note or other written obligation, shall paraph the obligation for identification with his act if the obligation is presented to him for that purpose. The paraph shall state the date of the act and shall be signed by the notary. The notary shall also mention in his act that he has paraphed the obligation. Failure to do so shall render the paraph ineffective. The paraph is prima facie evidence that the paraphed obligation is the one described in the act.

Acts 1992, No. 1132, § 2, eff. Jan. 1, 1993. Amended by Acts 1995, No. 1087, § 1.

REVISION COMMENTS—1992

(a) This Article restates the former provisions of law relative to the notary's paraph and also makes a change in the law. It does not prescribe a particular form for the paraph, which through long practice in the state is an inscription beginning "Ne Varietur." Any reference on the instrument, signed by the notary, and evidencing that it is to be identified with a particular act of a certain date of the notary will suffice.

(b) R.S. 9:5555 and 9:5556 provide for proof in executory proceedings of obligations not paraphed for identification with the mortgage, and for the manner of dealing with the mortgagee of record in such cases. A mortgage may secure obligations that are not in writing. It may secure future obligations of indefinite terms. It need not describe the terms of the obligations, nor must it be in

806

authentic form. In all of these cases it would be impractical, if not impossible to require the paraph of a notary. This Article permits the paraph in those cases where the parties desire to continue prior practice—which is unaffected by this revision. Persons who take notes or other written obligations secured by a mortgage, but who prefer to be regulated by R.S. 9:5555 and 5556, may do so simply by directing the notary not to paraph the instrument. The failure of the notary to mention the paraph in his instrument renders the paraph ineffective and therefore makes those Sections applicable even if the note or instrument itself erroneously is paraphed.

Art. 3326.   Effect of mortgage filed after death of mortgagor

A judgment or a conventional mortgage filed for recordation more than twenty days after the mortgagor dies gives no preference to the mortgagee over the other creditors of the estate of the deceased if the estate is insufficient to satisfy all the creditors.

Acts 1992, No. 1132, § 2, eff. Jan. 1, 1993.

REVISION COMMENT—1992

Former Article 3363 (1870) declared that the recordation of a mortgage after the mortgagor's death was ineffective as to other creditors when a "succession . . . administered by a curator or beneficiary heir, is not sufficient to satisfy the creditors. . . ." The principle has been retained but the Article has been somewhat expanded to cover insolvent successions, however administered, and has been amended to give the holder of a conventional mortgage twenty days after the death of the mortgagor in which to record the mortgage. It will, however, still take its rank from the date of filing.

Arts. 3327 to 3336.   [Blank]

Art. 3337.   Cancellation of mortgages and privileges from the records

The recorder shall cancel a mortgage or privilege from his records in the manner prescribed by law.

Acts 1992, No. 1132, § 2, eff. Jan. 1, 1993. Amended by Acts 2005, No. 169, § 2, eff. July 1, 2006.

REVISION COMMENTS—1992

(a) This Article summarizes the various methods by which a document may be erased from the records by the recorder. As the Article indicates each method must be accomplished "in the manner prescribed by legislation" and thus requires reference to other provisions of law for its implementation.

(b) The judgment referred to in Paragraph (4) contemplates a case where the court itself orders the inscription erased. It does not refer to the mandamus action, which results in a judgment directing the clerk to erase the mortgage when he has a ministerial duty to do so, that is, when he has been furnished evidence which under the rules regulating Paragraphs (1) through (3) require him to cancel the mortgage. Where the mortgagor or other interested party seeks erasure of the mortgage or privilege when proper evidence of its extinction is not available, or the mortgagee refuses to provide a proper release, the suit should be directed against the mortgagee, not the recorder. Compare C.C.P.Art. 3863, ("A writ of mandamus may be directed to a public officer to compel the performance of a ministerial duty required by law") with R.S. 9:5557, (a mortgagee may be required by summary process to deliver an act directing a recorder to erase a mortgage from his records, when the mortgage or privilege does not secure an instrument paraphed for identification with it); and 9:5385, (holder of a mortgage note who fails to produce note when it is satisfied liable for damages resulting therefrom).

CHAPTER XXII–A—OF REGISTRY

CHAPTER 1—GENERAL PROVISIONS

Art. 3338. Instruments creating real rights in immovables; recordation required to affect third persons

The rights and obligations established or created by the following written instruments are without effect as to a third person unless the instrument is registered by recording it in the appropriate mortgage or conveyance records pursuant to the provisions of this Title:

(1) An instrument that transfers an immovable or establishes a real right in or over an immovable.

(2) The lease of an immovable.

(3) An option or right of first refusal, or a contract to buy, sell, or lease an immovable or to establish a real right in or over an immovable.

(4) An instrument that modifies, terminates, or transfers the rights created or evidenced by the instruments described in Subparagraphs (1) through (3) of this Article.

Acts 2005, No. 169, § 1, eff. July 1, 2006.

Art. 3339. Matters not of record

A matter of capacity or authority, the occurrence of a suspensive or a resolutory condition, the exercise of an option or right of first refusal, a tacit acceptance, a termination of rights that depends upon the occurrence of a condition, and a similar matter pertaining to rights and obligations evidenced by a recorded instrument are effective as to a third person although not evidenced of record.

Acts 2005, No. 169, § 1, eff. July 1, 2006.

Art. 3340. Effect of recording other documents

If the law or a recorded instrument expressly makes the recordation of an act or instrument a condition to the creation, extinction, or modification of rights or obligations, such act or instrument is not effective as to a third person until it is recorded.

The recordation of a document, other than an instrument described in Article 3338, that is required by law to be registered, filed, or otherwise recorded with the clerk of court or recorder of conveyances or of mortgages or in the conveyance or mortgage records shall have only the effect provided for by such law.

Acts 2005, No. 169, § 1, eff. July 1, 2006.

Art. 3341. Limits on the effect of recordation

The recordation of an instrument:

(1) Does not create a presumption that the instrument is valid or genuine.

(2) Does not create a presumption as to the capacity or status of the parties.

(3) Has no effect unless the law expressly provides for its recordation.

(4) Is effective only with respect to immovables located in the parish where the instrument is recorded.

Acts 2005, No. 169, § 1, eff. July 1, 2006.

Art. 3342. Parties to an instrument are precluded from raising certain matters

A party to a recorded instrument may not contradict the terms of the instrument or statements of fact it contains to the prejudice of a third person who after its recordation acquires an interest in or over the immovable to which the instrument relates.

Acts 2005, No. 169, § 1, eff. July 1, 2006.

Art. 3343. Third person defined

A third person is a person who is not a party to or personally bound by an instrument.

A witness to an act is a third person with respect to it.

A person who by contract assumes an obligation or is bound by contract to recognize a right is not a third person with respect to the obligation or right or to the instrument creating or establishing it.

Acts 2005, No. 169, § 1, eff. July 1, 2006.

Art. 3344. Refusal for failure of original signature or proper certification; effect of recordation; necessity of proof of signature recordation of a duplicate

A. The recorder shall refuse to record:

(1) An instrument that does not bear the original signature of a party.

(2) A judgment, administrative decree, or other act of a governmental agency that is not properly certified in a manner provided by law.

B. Recordation does not dispense with the necessity of proving that the signatures are genuine unless they are authenticated in the manner provided by law.

Acts 2005, No. 169, § 1, eff. July 1, 2006.

Art. 3345. Recordation of a duplicate

The recordation of a duplicate of an instrument, as defined in Code of Evidence Article 1001(5), that does not bear the original signature of a party, shall nonetheless have the same effect as recordation of the original instrument. Recordation does not dispense with proving that the recorded instrument is a duplicate.

Acts 2005, No. 169, § 1, eff. July 1, 2006.

Art. 3346. Place of recordation; duty of the recorder

A. An instrument creating, establishing, or relating to a mortgage or privilege over an immovable, or the pledge of the lessor's rights in the lease of an immovable and its rents, is recorded in the mortgage records of the parish in which the immovable is located. All other instruments are recorded in the conveyance records of that parish.

B. The recorder shall maintain in the manner prescribed by law all instruments that are recorded with him.

Acts 2005, No. 169, § 1, eff. July 1, 2006. Amended by Acts 2014, No. 281, § 1, eff. Jan. 1, 2015.

REVISION COMMENTS—2014

Effective as of January 1, 2015, this Article provides that a pledge of the lessor's rights in the lease of an immovable and its rents is recorded in the mortgage records of the parish in which the immovable is located. This represents a change in the law, which formerly required recordation in the conveyance records. For transitional rules applicable to the continued effectiveness of assignments of leases and rents filed in the conveyance records in accordance with former R.S. 9:4401 prior to

January 1, 2015, as well as rules that apply to the reinscription, release, transfer, amendment, or other modification of those assignments, see R.S. 9:4403. After January 1, 2015, despite the filing of the original assignment of leases and rents in the conveyance records, an instrument effecting the reinscription, release, transfer, amendment, or other modification of the assignment must be filed in the mortgage records, and a filing in the conveyance records is neither necessary nor effective to cause the instrument to have effect against third persons.

Art. 3347.   Effect of recordation arises upon filing

The effect of recordation arises when an instrument is filed with the recorder and is unaffected by subsequent errors or omissions of the recorder. An instrument is filed with a recorder when he accepts it for recordation in his office.

Acts 2005, No. 169, § 1, eff. July 1, 2006.

Art. 3348.   Time of filing; determination

Upon acceptance of an instrument the recorder shall immediately write upon or stamp it with the date and time it is filed and the registry number assigned to it.

Acts 2005, No. 169, § 1, eff. July 1, 2006.

Art. 3349.   Failure to endorse; effect

If the recorder upon acceptance of an instrument fails to endorse an instrument with the date and time of filing or if it bears the same date and time of filing as another instrument, it is presumed that the instrument was filed with respect to other instruments in the order indicated by their registry numbers and that the filing of the instrument occurred immediately before an instrument bearing the next consecutive registry number.

Acts 2005, No. 169, § 1, eff. July 1, 2006.

Art. 3350.   Presumption as to time of filing

When the date and time of filing cannot be determined under Articles 3348 and 3349, it is presumed that the instrument was filed at the first determinable date and time that it appears in the records of the recorder.

Acts 2005, No. 169, § 1, eff. July 1, 2006.

Art. 3351.   Ancient documents; presumptions

An instrument that has been recorded for at least ten years is presumed to have been signed by all persons whose purported signatures are affixed thereto, and, if a judgment, that it was rendered by a court of competent jurisdiction.

Acts 2005, No. 169, § 1, eff. July 1, 2006.

Art. 3352.   Recorded acts; required information

A.   An instrument shall contain the following information when appropriate for its type and nature:

(1) The full name, domicile, and permanent mailing address of the parties.

(2) The marital status of all of the parties who are individuals, including the full name of the present spouse or a declaration that the party is unmarried.

(3) A declaration as to whether there has been a change in the marital status of any party who is a transferor of the immovable or interest or right since he acquired it, and if so, when and in what manner the change occurred.

(4) The municipal number or postal address of the property, if it has one.

(5) The last four digits of the social security number or the taxpayer identification number of the mortgagor, whichever is applicable.

(6) The notary's identification number or the attorney's bar roll number and the typed, printed, or stamped name of the notary and witnesses if the instrument is an authentic act of, or an authenticated act by, a notary.

B.   The recorder shall not refuse to record an instrument because it does not contain the information required by this Article. The omission of that information does not impair the validity of an instrument or the effect given to its recordation.

C.   The recorder shall only display the last four digits of the social security numbers listed on instruments that his office makes available for viewing on the Internet.

Acts 2005, No. 169, § 1, eff. July 1, 2006.

Art. 3353.   Effect of indefinite or incomplete name

A recorded instrument is effective with respect to a third person if the name of a party is not so indefinite, incomplete, or erroneous as to be misleading and the instrument as a whole reasonably alerts a person examining the records that the instrument may be that of the party.

Acts 2005, No. 169, § 1, eff. July 1, 2006.

CHAPTER 2—MORTGAGES RECORDS

SECTION 1—GENERAL PROVISIONS

Art. 3354.   Applicability

The provisions of this Chapter apply only to the mortgages and privileges encumbering immovables and to pledges of the lessor's rights in the lease of an immovable and its rents.

Acts 2005, No. 169, § 1, eff. July 1, 2006. Amended by Acts 2014, No. 281, § 1, eff. Jan. 1, 2015.

REVISION COMMENTS—2014

(a) The primary purpose of the 2014 revision of this Chapter is to include the pledge of the lessor's rights in the lease of an immovable and its rents within its scope. Effective as of January 1, 2015, Article 3346 provides that the pledge of the lessor's rights in the lease of an immovable and its rents is recorded in the mortgage records of the parish in which the immovable is located. This represents a change in the law, which formerly required recordation in the conveyance records. For transitional rules applicable to the continued effectiveness of assignments of leases and rents filed in the conveyance records in accordance with former R.S. 9:4401 prior to January 1, 2015, as well as rules that apply to the reinscription, release, transfer, amendment, or other modification of those assignments, see R.S. 9:4403. After January 1, 2015, despite the filing of the original assignment of leases and rents in the conveyance records, an instrument effecting the reinscription, release, transfer, amendment, or other modification of the assignment must be filed in the mortgage records, and a filing in the conveyance records is neither necessary nor effective to cause the instrument to have effect against third persons.

(b) This Chapter applies only to encumbrances upon immovables. Privileges and pledges that encumber movable property are not subject to the registry or reinscription requirements of this Chapter or other provisions of this Title. See C.C. Arts. 3153 and 3155 (Rev. 2014); Art. XIX, Sec. 19 of the La. Const. of 1921, made statutory by Art. XIV, Sec. 16 of the La. Const. of 1974. References to pledges in later Articles of this Chapter are limited to pledges of the lessor's rights in the lease of an immovable and its rents.

Art. 3355. Mortgage, pledge, or privilege affecting property in several parishes

An act of mortgage, contract of pledge, instrument evidencing a privilege, or other instrument that affects property located in more than one parish may be executed in multiple originals for recordation in each of the several parishes. An original that is filed with a recorder need only describe property that is within the parish in which it is filed.

A certified copy of an instrument that is recorded in the records of a parish need only describe property that is within the parish in which it is filed.

Acts 2005, No. 169, § 1, eff. July 1, 2006. Amended by Acts 2014, No. 281, § 1, eff. Jan. 1, 2015.

REVISION COMMENTS—2014

This provision is consistent with Article 3345 (Rev. 2005) and reflects practices that have long been followed by practitioners. It expressly recognizes that recordation of a multiple original that omits the description of encumbered property located in other parishes does not affect the validity of the recordation.

Art. 3356. Transfers, amendments, and releases

A. A transferee of an obligation secured by a mortgage, pledge, or privilege is not bound by any unrecorded act releasing, amending, or otherwise modifying the mortgage, pledge, or privilege if he is a third person with respect to that unrecorded act.

B. A recorded transfer, modification, amendment, or release of a mortgage, pledge, or privilege made by the obligee of record is effective as to a third person notwithstanding that the obligation secured by the mortgage, pledge, or privilege has been transferred to another.

C. For the purpose of this Chapter, the obligee of record of a mortgage, pledge, or privilege is the person identified by the mortgage records as the obligee of the secured obligation.

Acts 2005, No. 169, § 1, eff. July 1, 2006. Amended by Acts 2014, No. 281, § 1, eff. Jan. 1, 2015.

REVISION COMMENTS—2014

Prior to the revision of the Title on Mortgages effective January 1, 1993, some courts, relying upon the general principle that one cannot transfer a greater right than he has under a contract, held that a transferee of the secured obligation was bound by unrecorded acts between the mortgagor and previous mortgagee. Other courts, seemingly recognizing that a mortgage is a real right and hence subject to the principle that contracts modifying or amending such rights must be recorded to affect third persons, held that a transferee of an obligation secured by a mortgage was not bound by a separate unrecorded contract between the mortgagor and mortgagee modifying, releasing or amending the mortgage. See Harrell, "Developments in the Law, Security Devices," 47 La.L.Rev. 452, 464 (1986). This Article adopts the latter view and requires that any act releasing a mortgage, pledge, or privilege, or amending or otherwise modifying the contract creating or evidencing it, be recorded in order to affect subsequent assignees of the secured obligation.

SECTION 2—METHOD AND DURATION OF RECORDATION

Art. 3357. Duration; general rule

Except as otherwise expressly provided by law, the effect of recordation of an instrument creating a mortgage or pledge or evidencing a privilege ceases ten years after the date of the instrument.

Acts 2005, No. 169, § 1, eff. July 1, 2006. Amended by Acts 2014, No. 281, § 1, eff. Jan. 1, 2015.

REVISION COMMENTS—2014

(a) This and the succeeding four Articles state the rules relative to the lapse of inscriptions of mortgages, pledges, and privileges in the mortgage records.

(b) This Article establishes a general rule that the effect of an inscription ceases ten years after the date of the document evidencing the mortgage, pledge, or privilege. This departs from the rule of Article 3369 of the Louisiana Civil Code of 1870 that the period of inscription was counted from the date of the secured obligation.

Art. 3358. Duration of recordation of certain mortgages, pledges, and privileges

If an instrument creating a mortgage or pledge or evidencing a privilege describes the maturity of any obligation secured by the mortgage, pledge, or privilege and if any part of the described obligation matures nine years or more after the date of the instrument, the effect of recordation ceases six years after the latest maturity date described in the instrument.

Acts 2005, No. 169, § 1, eff. July 1, 2006. Amended by Acts 2014, No. 281, § 1, eff. Jan. 1, 2015.

REVISION COMMENTS—2014

Under this Article, the effect of recording a mortgage, pledge, or privilege that secures an obligation having a stated maturity of nine years or more ceases six years after the maturity of the obligation. This Article recognizes, however, that the particular terms of the secured obligations may or may not be apparent from the recorded instruments creating the mortgage or pledge or evidencing the privilege securing them. Consequently, this Article extends the period of inscription beyond the ten-year limit prescribed by Article 3357 (Rev. 2014) only in those cases in which the recorded instrument describes the maturity of a particular obligation that it secures. If the maturity occurs nine years or more from the date of the instrument, the effect of registry continues for six years from the date of the described maturity.

Art. 3359. Duration of recordation of judicial mortgage

The effect of recordation of a judgment creating a judicial mortgage ceases ten years after the date of the judgment.

Acts 2005, No. 169, § 1, eff. July 1, 2006.

REVISION COMMENTS—2014

(a) This Article expressly declares that the effect of recording a judgment ceases ten years after the date of the judgment. This continues the interpretation of Article 3369 of the Louisiana Civil Code of 1870 and is implicit in present Article 3357 (Rev. 2014).

(b) The failure to reinscribe a judicial mortgage within ten years of its date causes the effect of recordation to cease. As the courts have observed, there is a common misunderstanding as to the relationship between reinscribing a judicial mortgage and obtaining a judgment of revival under C.C.P.Art. 3334. Bank One Louisiana v. Lacobee, 811 So.2d 164 (La.App. 2d Cir. 2002). See also Brunston v. Hoover, 945 So.2d 852 (La.App. 3d Cir. 2006) and Mouton v. Watson, 500 So.2d 792 (La.App. 1st Cir.1986). Under Article 3300 (Rev. 2014), a judicial mortgage is created by the filing of a money judgment in the mortgage records. This Article provides that the effect of recordation of a judgment creating a judicial mortgage ceases ten years after the date of the judgment. A notice of reinscription filed in accordance with Article 3362 (Rev. 2014) continues the effect of recordation of a judicial mortgage, without the necessity of filing a judgment reviving the original judgment. The judgment itself prescribes, however, if a suit to revive it is not filed within ten years of its date and a judgment reviving it obtained in due course. If the judicial mortgage is not reinscribed, the effect of recordation ceases whether or not prescription on the underlying judgment is interrupted by a suit for revival. If the judicial mortgage is reinscribed, it nevertheless becomes unenforceable when the underlying judgment prescribes. Accordingly, Article 3368 (Rev. 2014) permits the recorder to cancel the inscription from his records upon the request of any person if the request is accompanied by a certificate from the clerk of the court rendering the judgment that no suit has been filed for its revival within the time required by Article 3501 (Rev. 1983) or is accompanied by a final and definitive judgment of that court rejecting the demands of the plaintiff in a suit to revive it.

Art. 3360. Duration of recordation of mortgage given by tutor, curator, or succession representative

A.   The effect of recordation of a legal mortgage over the property of a natural tutor, or of a special mortgage given for the faithful performance of his duties by a tutor or a curator of an interdict, ceases four years after the tutorship or curatorship terminates, or, if the tutor or curator resigns or is removed, four years after the judgment that authorizes the resignation or removal.

B.   The effect of recordation of a special mortgage given for the faithful performance of his duties by a curator of an absent person or by a succession representative ceases four years after homologation of his final account, or, if the curator or representative resigns or is removed, four years after the judgment that authorizes that resignation or removal. In any event, the effect of recordation ceases ten years after the date of the act of mortgage.

Acts 2005, No. 169, § 1, eff. July 1, 2006.

Art. 3361. Effect of amendment

If before the effect of recordation ceases an instrument is recorded that amends a recorded mortgage, pledge, or privilege to describe or modify the maturity of a particular obligation that it secures, then the time of cessation of the effect of the recordation is determined by reference to the maturity of the obligation last becoming due described in the mortgage, pledge, or privilege as amended.

Acts 2005, No. 169, § 1, eff. July 1, 2006. Amended by Acts 2014, No. 281, § 1, eff. Jan. 1, 2015.

REVISION COMMENTS—2014

If, before the effect of recordation ceases, an amendment to a mortgage, pledge, or privilege is filed that would bring about a longer period of effectiveness, as in the case of an amendment describing a note with a maturity of nine years or more from the date of the original instrument, then the period of inscription is calculated with reference to the maturity of the obligations described by the instrument as amended.

Art. 3362. Method of reinscription

A person may reinscribe a recorded instrument creating a mortgage or pledge or evidencing a privilege by recording a signed written notice of reinscription. The notice shall state the name of the mortgagor or pledgor, or the name of the obligor of the debt secured by the privilege, as it appears in the recorded instrument, as well as the registry number or other appropriate recordation information of the instrument or of a prior notice of reinscription, and shall declare that the instrument is reinscribed.

Acts 2005, No. 169, § 1, eff. July 1, 2006. Amended by Acts 2014, No. 281, § 1, eff. Jan. 1, 2015.

REVISION COMMENTS—2014

The method of reinscription provided for in this Article, which has been the exclusive means of reinscription since January 1, 1993, is much simpler than the method that was previously required. Formerly, one had to file a copy of the original mortgage with the recorder accompanied by a request for reinscription. Reinscription occurred when the recorder again copied the reinscribed act into his records. No useful purpose was served by refiling an instrument that was already filed, or by copying an existing document into the records again. This Article instead simply requires the person desiring to reinscribe an instrument to do so by expressing that intent in a signed document that identifies the instrument and the records where its inscription is found.

Art. 3363. Method of reinscription exclusive

The method of reinscription provided in this Chapter is exclusive. Neither an amendment of an instrument creating a mortgage or pledge, or evidencing a privilege, nor an acknowledgment of the existence of a mortgage, pledge, or privilege by the mortgagor, pledgor, or obligor, constitutes a reinscription of the instrument.

Acts 2005, No. 169, § 1, eff. July 1, 2006. Amended by Acts 2014, No. 281, § 1, eff. Jan. 1, 2015.

REVISION COMMENTS—2014

(a) This Article makes clear that the filing of a signed, written notice of reinscription is the exclusive means of reinscription. The Article rejects jurisprudence under former Civil Code Article 3369 (1870) to the effect that any document filed by the mortgagor which recognized an existing mortgage effected a reinscription of that mortgage. One case even appears to hold that a reinscription could occur if the acknowledgement was in an act filed in the conveyance records. Exxon Process & Mechanical v. Moncrieffe, 498 So.2d 158 (La.App. 1 Cir.1986).

(b) Under Article 3367 (Rev. 2014), the recorder is required upon simple request to cancel from his records any mortgage, pledge, or privilege that has not been reinscribed within the required period. The rule under the 1870 Code placed a considerable burden upon both the recorder and the persons examining the records. Nor was the rule necessarily advantageous to the obligee. The present rule, which has been in effect since January 1, 1993, requires that there be an express notice that reinscription is sought, which is then accomplished when that notice is filed.

Art. 3364.   Effect of timely recordation of notice of reinscription

A notice of reinscription that is recorded before the effect of recordation ceases continues that effect for ten years from the date the notice is recorded.

Acts 2005, No. 169, § 1, eff. July 1, 2006.

REVISION COMMENTS—2014

Under this Article, reinscription is effective when a notice of reinscription is filed. The effect of the original recordation is extended for ten years from that time.

Art. 3365.   Effect of notice recorded after cessation of effect of recordation

A notice of reinscription that is recorded after the effect of recordation of the instrument sought to be reinscribed has ceased, again produces the effects of recordation, but only from the time that the notice of reinscription is recorded. The effect of recordation pursuant to this Article shall continue for ten years from the date on which the notice of reinscription is recorded, and the instrument may be reinscribed thereafter from time to time as provided by Article 3362.

Reinscription pursuant to this Article does not require that the mortgage or pledge or evidence of privilege be again recorded, even if the original recordation has been cancelled.

Acts 2005, No. 169, § 1, eff. July 1, 2006. Amended by Acts 2014, No. 281, § 1, eff. Jan. 1, 2015.

REVISION COMMENTS—2014

This Article restates a rule that the courts held was implied by provisions of the Louisiana Civil Code of 1870. If the notice of reinscription is timely recorded, it extends the period of inscription for ten years from its date of recordation in all cases. If it is recorded after the effect of recordation ceases, the reinscription gives the mortgage, pledge, or privilege the effect it would have if that were the first time the instrument was recorded.

SECTION 3—CANCELLATION

Art. 3366.   Cancellation upon written request; form and content

A.   The recorder of mortgages shall cancel, in whole or in part and in the manner prescribed by law, the recordation of a mortgage, pledge, or privilege upon receipt of a written request for cancellation in a form prescribed by law and that:

(1) Identifies the mortgage, pledge, or privilege by reference to the place in the records where it is recorded; and

(2) Is signed by the person requesting the cancellation.

B.   The effect of recordation of the instrument ceases upon cancellation by the recorder pursuant to the provisions of this Article.

Acts 2005, No. 169, § 1, eff. July 1, 2006. Amended by Acts 2014, No. 281, § 1, eff. Jan. 1, 2015.

Art. 3367.   Cancellation of recordation after effect of recordation has ceased

If the effect of recordation of a mortgage, pledge, or privilege has ceased for lack of reinscription, the recorder upon receipt of a written signed application shall cancel its recordation.

Acts 2005, No. 169, § 1, eff. July 1, 2006. Amended by Acts 2014, No. 281, § 1, eff. Jan. 1, 2015.

Art. 3368.   Cancellation of judicial mortgage arising from judgment that has prescribed

Notwithstanding the reinscription of a judicial mortgage created by the filing of a judgment of a court of this state, the recorder shall cancel the judicial mortgage from his records upon any person's written request to which is attached a certificate from the clerk of the court rendering the judgment that no suit or motion was filed for its revival within the time required by Article 3501 or of a certified copy of a final and definitive judgment of the court rejecting the demands of the plaintiff in a suit or motion to revive the judgment.

Acts 2005, No. 169, § 1, eff. July 1, 2006. Amended by Acts 2014, No. 281, § 1, eff. Jan. 1, 2015.

REVISION COMMENTS—2014

As Comment (b) to Article 3359 (Rev. 2014) explains, reinscription of a judicial mortgage and revival of the underlying judgment are entirely different concepts. Both timely reinscription and a timely suit for revival are necessary for a judicial mortgage to continue to have effect. Under this Article, even if a judicial mortgage is reinscribed, the recorder must cancel the inscription of the judicial mortgage from his records upon any person's request accompanied by a certificate from the clerk of the court rendering the underlying judgment that no suit was filed for its revival within the time required by Article 3501 (Rev. 1983) or by a final and definitive judgment of that court rejecting the demands of the plaintiff in a suit to revive it.

Arts. 3369 to 3411. [Blank]

TITLE XXIII—OCCUPANCY AND POSSESSION

CHAPTER 1—OCCUPANCY

Art. 3412. Occupancy

Occupancy is the taking of possession of a corporeal movable that does not belong to anyone. The occupant acquires ownership the moment he takes possession.

Acts 1982, No. 187, § 1, eff. Jan. 1, 1983.

REVISION COMMENTS—1982

(a) This provision reproduces the substance of Articles 3412, 3413, and 3414 of the Louisiana Civil Code of 1870. It does not change the law.

(b) Occupancy is a mode of acquiring ownership by taking possession of a corporeal movable that does not belong to anyone. According to Article 3421, infra, possession is defined as the exercise of physical acts of use, detention, or enjoyment of a corporeal thing with the intent to own it; thus, the language "with the intention of acquiring a right of ownership over it", found in Article 3412 of the 1870 Code, is redundant and has not been reproduced.

(c) Occupancy is a mode of acquiring ownership by talking possession of a corporeal thing. See 3 Planiol et Ripert, Traité pratique de droit civil français, 603 (2d ed. Picard 1952). The language "and when it is of a nature which admits of its being taken possession of", figuring in Article 3413 of the 1870 Code, is redundant and has not been reproduced.

(d) According to traditional civilian conceptions, occupancy applies to res nullius, that is, things that are not owned by anyone, such as wild animals and abandoned things. In Louisiana, however, certain species of wild animals are declared to be owned by the state in its capacity as a public person. See Civil Code Article 450, Comment (g), as amended by Acts 1978, No. 728, § 1. Nevertheless, the law of occupancy applies to wild animals provided they are captured in accordance with applicable laws and regulations. See Article 3414, infra. Thus, occupancy applies to corporeal movables that do not belong to anyone as well as to wild animals that either are not owned by anyone or are owned by the state in its capacity as a public person.

(e) The word "wildlife" is used in Louisiana statutes in preference to "wild animals" to include reference to creatures of the earth, sea, or air that are not commonly thought of as being animals, such as shellfish. See La. R.S. 56:102, 312, 421, and 492 as amended [subsequently repealed; see, now, R.S. 41.14, 56:3, and 56:56].

(f) Article 3414 of the Louisiana Civil Code of 1870 furnished examples of acquisition of ownership by occupancy. This provision is unnecessary and has not been reproduced. Hunting, fishing, and finding an abandoned thing or a treasure are dealt with in Articles 3413, 3418, and 3420, infra. Capture from the enemy is a matter of prize governed by federal law.

(g) According to the Mineral Code, fugacious minerals are not owned by anyone. See Mineral Code Article 6 [R.S. 31:6]. However, "the landowner has the exclusive right to explore and develop his property for the production of such minerals and to reduce them to possession and ownership". Ibid. Thus, as to fugacious minerals, occupancy applies only to the landowner and to those to whom he assigns or transfers his mineral rights.

Art. 3413. Wild animals, birds, fish, and shellfish

Wild animals, birds, fish, and shellfish in a state of natural liberty either belong to the state in its capacity as a public person or are things without an owner. The taking of possession of such things is governed by particular laws and regulations.

The owner of a tract of land may forbid entry to anyone for purposes of hunting or fishing, and the like. Nevertheless, despite a prohibition of entry, captured wildlife belongs to the captor.

Acts 1982, No. 187, § 1, eff. Jan. 1, 1983.

REVISION COMMENTS—1982

(a) This provision reproduces the substance of Article 3415 of the Louisiana Civil Code of 1870. It does not change the law.

(b) Following a general trend in the United States, the Louisiana legislature has asserted state ownership over a variety of living creatures of the land, sea, and air. See Acts 1926, No. 273; 1932, No. 68; 1918, No. 83; 1926, No. 80; 1932, No. 50; 1932, No. 67; and 1918, No. 104. See also La. Revised Statutes of 1950, 56:101 [repealed; see, now, R.S. 56:103] et seq. In a sense, these are now public things rather than res nullius. Ownership of wildlife, however, is a new concept. This form of state ownership, asserted in an effort to conserve natural resources, confers mainly administrative advantages and rests upon the notion that certain assets of society are not subject to private appropriation except when done under regulations that protect the general interest. See Yiannopoulos, Civil Law Property, § 38 (2d ed. 1980). In Hughes v. Oklahoma, 441 U.S. 322 (1979), the United States Supreme Court declared that the "ownership theory" of wildlife "is now generally regarded as but a fiction expressive in legal shorthand of the importance to its people that a State have power to preserve and regulate the exploitation of an important resource."

In accordance with special legislation, jurisprudence, and Civil Code Article 450, as revised by Acts 1978, No. 728, Article 3413 indicates that certain creatures of the earth, sea, or air in a state of natural liberty are public things, that is, things owned by the state in its capacity as a public person. See Civil Code Article 450, as revised by Acts 1978, No. 728; Leger v. Louisiana Department of Wildlife and Fisheries, 306 So.2d 391 (La.App.3rd Cir. 1975); and La. R.S. 56:102, 312, 421, and 492 [repealed; see, now, R.S. 41:14, 56:3, and 56:56]. However, creatures of the earth, sea, or air that are not governed by special legislation continue to be res nullius, that is, things susceptible of ownership but which have no owner.

(c) The owner of a tract of land may post it against entry by unauthorized persons. Nevertheless, despite the prohibition of entry, captured wildlife belongs to the captor. In such a case, the owner of the land may have a delictual action for damages against the violator of the prohibition under Article 2315 of the Louisiana Civil Code of 1870 as well as other remedies, such as injunction or an action for unjust enrichment. See Rosenthal-Brown Fur Co. v. Jones-Frere Fur Co., 162 La. 403, 110 So. 603 (1926); Buras v. Salinovich, 154 La. 495, 97 So. 748 (1923); and Harrison v. Petroleum Surveys, 80 So.2d 153 (La.App. 1st Cir. 1955).

(d) The term "animals" includes alligators and other reptiles and amphibians.

Art. 3414. Loss of ownership of wildlife

If wild animals, birds, fish, or shellfish recover their natural liberty, the captor loses his ownership unless he takes immediate measures for their pursuit and recapture.

Acts 1982, No. 187, § 1, eff. Jan. 1, 1983.

REVISION COMMENTS—1982

(a) This provision is based on Article 3416 of the Louisiana Civil Code of 1870 and on Article 1077 of the Greek Civil Code. It changes the law.

(b) The ownership of the captor is lost when the captured wild animals, birds, fish, or shellfish recover their natural liberty unless he takes immediate measures for their pursuit and recapture. If the captor fails to take such measures, the wild animals cease to be privately owned, and they may be captured by another person who then acquires ownership by occupancy. The language "and they become the property of the first who seizes them", figuring in R.C.C. (1870) Article 3416, is unnecessary and has not been reproduced.

Art. 3415. Wildlife in enclosures

Wild animals or birds within enclosures, and fish or shellfish in an aquarium or other private waters, are privately owned.

Pigeons, bees, fish, and shellfish that migrate into the pigeon house, hive, or pond of another belong to him unless the migration has been caused by inducement or artifice.

Acts 1982, No. 187, § 1, eff. Jan. 1, 1983.

REVISION COMMENTS—1982

This provision is based on Article 519 of the Louisiana Civil Code of 1870 and on Article 1077 of the Greek Civil Code.

Art. 3416. Tamed wild animals

Tamed wild animals and birds are privately owned as long as they have the habit of returning to their owner. They are considered to have lost the habit when they fail to return within a reasonable time. In such a case, they are considered to have recovered their natural liberty unless their owner takes immediate measures for their pursuit and recapture.

Acts 1982, No. 187, § 1, eff. Jan. 1, 1983.

REVISION COMMENTS—1982

(a) This provision is based on Article 3417 of the Louisiana Civil Code of 1870. It changes the law in certain respects.

(b) According to Article 3417 of the Louisiana Civil Code of 1870, "peacocks and pigeons are considered as wild fowls, though after every flight it is their custom to return." Article 3416 suppresses this rule and thereby changes the law. There is no reason why peacocks and pigeons should be considered as wild fowl as long as they have the habit of returning.

(c) Tamed wild animals that have lost the habit of returning are considered to have recovered their natural liberty. Accordingly, they may be captured by anyone unless their owner takes immediate measures for their pursuit and recapture. If he fails to take such measures, a new captor acquires ownership by occupancy. The phrase "but if this habit ceases, they cease to be yours, and will again become the property of them who take them", figuring in Article 3417 of the 1870 Code, is unnecessary and has not been reproduced.

Art. 3417. Domestic animals

Domestic animals that are privately owned are not subject to occupancy.

Acts 1982, No. 187, § 1, eff. Jan. 1, 1983.

REVISION COMMENTS—1982

(a) This provision is based on Article 3419 of the Louisiana Civil Code of 1870. It does not change the law.

(b) Domestic animals, even if lost, are privately owned. Accordingly, the captor of such an animal does not acquire ownership by occupancy. See Peloquin v. Calcasieu Parish Police Jury, 367 So.2d 1246 (La.App. 3rd Cir. 1979).

(c) One who takes possession of the domestic animal of another with the intent to own it commits theft. The last sentence of R.C.C. (1870) Article 3419 is unnecessary and has not been reproduced. The matter is covered by provisions of criminal law.

(d) At common law, animals that have the power of locomotion are divided into two classes: domestic animals and wild animals. Domestic animals include those which are tame by nature, or from time immemorial have been accustomed to the association of man, or by his industry have been subjected to his will, and have no disposition to escape his dominion. The expression "domestic animals" is generic, and its particular application may vary in different parts of the world. Wild animals comprehend those wild by nature, which, because of habit, mode of life, or natural instinct, are incapable of being completely domesticated and which require the exercise of art, force, or skill to keep them in subjection. See 3A C.J.S. Animals, § 3.

However, according to civilian tradition, animals are divided into three classes: wild animals, tamed wild animals, and domestic animals. Article 1077 of the Greek Civil Code deals with wild animals and tamed wild animals. Domestic animals are not dealt with in Article 1077 because they are not subject to the law of occupancy.

Art. 3418. Abandoned things

One who takes possession of an abandoned thing with the intent to own it acquires ownership by occupancy. A thing is abandoned when its owner relinquishes possession with the intent to give up ownership.

Acts 1982, No. 187, § 1, eff. Jan. 1, 1983.

REVISION COMMENTS—1982

(a) This provision is based on Article 3421 of the Louisiana Civil Code of 1870. It does not change the law.

(b) Abandoned things are subject to the law of occupancy. Thus, one who takes possession of an abandoned thing with the intent to own it acquires the ownership of the thing. This rule is set forth in Article 3421 of the 1870 Code and has been retained in this revision.

(c) According to Article 3421 of the 1870 Code, an abandoned thing is one "which its owner has left with the intention not to keep it any longer." A thing is abandoned when its owner relinquishes possession with the intent to give up ownership. The relinquishment of possession is a fact, and the determination of the intent to give up ownership is based upon objective criteria.

(d) According to Article 3424 of the Louisiana Civil Code of 1870, things jettisoned and things lost in a shipwreck are not considered abandoned. This provision is unnecessary and has not been reproduced. Indeed, the owner of things that are jettisoned does not relinquish possession with the intent to give up ownership, and the owner of things lost in a shipwreck or other accident does not give up possession voluntarily.

Art. 3419. Lost things

One who finds a corporeal movable that has been lost is bound to make a diligent effort to locate its owner or possessor and to return the thing to him.

If a diligent effort is made and the owner is not found within three years, the finder acquires ownership.

Acts 1982, No. 187, § 1, eff. Jan. 1, 1983.

REVISION COMMENTS—1982

(a) This provision is based on Article 3422 of the Louisiana Civil Code of 1870. It changes the law in certain respects.

(b) Article 3422 of the 1870 Code, apparently requires the finder to make publication in newspapers and to do "all that is possible to find out the true owner". Under Article 3419, the finder is bound to make a diligent effort to locate the owner or possessor of the thing.

(c) Under Article 3422 of the 1870 Code, the finder seems to acquire ownership of the thing upon finding it, but this ownership terminates when the true owner reclaims the thing. Revocable ownership is not recognized in this revision. The finder is merely a possessor of the lost thing. Since, however, the thing escaped the possession of the owner without his consent, the finder may not transfer it to an acquirer in good faith for fair value. See Civil Code Article 521, as amended by Acts 1979, No. 180: "One who has possession of a lost or stolen thing may not transfer its ownership to another. For purposes of this Chapter, a thing is stolen when one has taken possession of it without the consent of its owner. A thing is not stolen when the owner delivers it or transfers its ownership to another as a result of fraud."

(d) A diligent effort to locate the owner may involve publishing or advertising in newspapers, posting notes, or notifying public authorities.

(e) Things jettisoned and things lost in a shipwreck or other accident may be considered lost in certain circumstances. Article 3424 of the 1870 Code read: "We must not reckon in the number of things abandoned those which one has lost, nor those which are thrown into the sea in peril of shipwreck to save the vessel, nor those which are lost in a shipwreck. For although the owners of such things lose the possession of them, yet they retain the ownership and the right to recover them. Therefore, those who find things of this kind can not make themselves masters of them, but are obliged to restore them to their lawful owners, in the manner provided for by the special laws made on that subject." This article is unnecessary and has not been reproduced.

(f) Civil Code Article 2280, as revised by Acts 1970 and 1979 [subsequently vacated; see, now, R.S. 13:3741], requires advertisement or security, or both, when lost commercial instruments are made the basis of a suit or legal defense.

Art. 3420. Treasure

One who finds a treasure in a thing that belongs to him or to no one acquires ownership of the treasure. If the treasure is found in a thing belonging to another, half of the treasure belongs to the finder and half belongs to the owner of the thing in which it was found.

A treasure is a movable hidden in another thing, movable or immovable, for such a long time that its owner cannot be determined.

Acts 1982, No. 187, § 1, eff. Jan. 1, 1983.

REVISION COMMENTS—1982

(a) This provision is based on Article 3423 of the Louisiana Civil Code of 1870 and on Article 1093 of the Greek Civil Code. It changes the law in certain respects.

(b) According to Article 3423 of the Louisiana Civil Code of 1870, a treasure is a thing hidden or buried in the earth. According to modern civil law, however, a treasure may be hidden in a movable or in an immovable. See, e.g., Greek Civil Code Article 1093. Article 3420 deviates from the text of Article 3423 of the 1870 Code and follows the modern approach.

(c) A treasure is not a lost thing, an abandoned thing, or a thing that has no owner. It is a thing hidden in another thing by someone who cannot prove his ownership. See R.C.C. (1870) Article 3423.

CHAPTER 2—POSSESSION

SECTION 1—NOTION AND KINDS OF POSSESSION

Art. 3421. Possession

Possession is the detention or enjoyment of a corporeal thing, movable or immovable, that one holds or exercises by himself or by another who keeps or exercises it in his name.

The exercise of a real right, such as a servitude, with the intent to have it as one's own is quasi-possession. The rules governing possession apply by analogy to the quasi-possession of incorporeals.

Acts 1982, No. 187, § 1, eff. Jan. 1, 1983.

REVISION COMMENTS—1982

(a) This provision is based on Articles 3432, 3426, 3430, and 3436 of the Louisiana Civil Code of 1870. It does not change the law.

(b) This definition of possession accords with the civilian tradition and with definitions in contemporary civil codes. But cf. 3 Planiol et Ripert, Traité pratique de droit civil français, 158 (2d ed. Picard 1952): "Possession is a state of fact which consists in the detention of a thing in an exclusive manner and in the performance on this thing of the material acts of use and enjoyment as if the possessor were owner."

(c) Strictly speaking, one may not possess a real right because one cannot exercise physical acts over an incorporeal. However, one may hold a real right with the intent to have it as his own. Such a holding of a real right corresponds to the possession of a corporeal thing and is referred to as quasi-possession. According to Louisiana jurisprudence, the rules governing possession apply by analogy to the quasi-possession of incorporeals. See, e.g., Louisiana Irrigation and Mill Co. v. Pousson, 262 La. 973, 265 So.2d 756 (1972); Yiannopoulos, Civil Law Property, § 211 (2d ed. 1980).

Art. 3422. Nature of possession; right to possess

Possession is a matter of fact; nevertheless, one who has possessed a thing for over a year acquires the right to possess it.

Acts 1982, No. 187, § 1, eff. Jan. 1, 1983.

REVISION COMMENTS—1982

(a) This provision is new. It is based in part on Article 3434(2) of the Louisiana Civil Code of 1870. It does not change the law.

(b) Louisiana legislation and well-settled jurisprudence distinguish between possession, which is the exercise of factual authority over a thing, and the right to possess, which one may acquire by exercising such authority for over a year. See, e.g., R.C.C. (1870) Articles 3454(2) and 3455. See also Liner v. Louisiana Land and Exploration Co., 319 So.2d 766 (La. 1975):

"For example, the word possession in Civil Code Articles 3426–3431, 3436–3438, means physical control over a thing that one has acquired with the intent to own it. (Possession as physical control leads, of course, to acquisitive prescription if it has the attributes required by Article 3487 of the Louisiana Civil Code of 1870.) This physical control alone, however, does not give rise to possessory protection or to acquisitive prescription. Possessory protection is predicated on acquisition of the right to possess. This right to possess is acquired by one who has been for a year in peaceable and uninterrupted possession of an estate. Civil Code Articles 3454(2), 3456; cf. id. Art. 3449(2)."

Article 3434 of the 1870 Code confused possession with the right to possess. Article 3422 distinguishes clearly between the two.

(c) Article 481 of the Louisiana Civil Code, as revised in 1979, declares: "The ownership and the possession of a thing are distinct". Therefore, Articles 3434(1) and 3435 of the 1870 Code are unnecessary and have not been reproduced.

Art. 3423. Rights of possessors

A possessor is considered provisionally as owner of the thing he possesses until the right of the true owner is established.

Acts 1982, No. 187, § 1, eff. Jan. 1, 1983.

REVISION COMMENTS—1982

(a) This provision reproduces the substance of Article 3454(1) of the Louisiana Civil Code of 1870. It does not change the law.

(b) The provisions of Article 3454(2), (3), and (4), being merely didactic, have not been reproduced. Indeed, a possessor may acquire the right to possess and thus be entitled to seek protection by the possessory action; a possessor may acquire the ownership of the thing he possesses by acquisitive prescription; and a possessor is entitled to be reimbursed for certain expenses and to retain the thing until he is reimbursed. Civil Code Articles 486, 488, 527, 528, and 529, supra, as amended by Acts 1979, No. 180.

(c) This provision applies to both movables and immovables. Thus, the possessor of a stray cat may sue for damages on account of the destruction of the cat by a third person. See Peloquin v. Calcasieu Parish Police Jury, 367 So.2d 1246 (La.App. 3rd Cir. 1979).

SECTION 2—ACQUISITION, EXERCISE, RETENTION, AND LOSS OF POSSESSION

Art. 3424.   Acquisition of possession

To acquire possession, one must intend to possess as owner and must take corporeal possession of the thing.

Acts 1982, No. 187, § 1, eff. Jan. 1, 1983.

REVISION COMMENTS—1982

(a) This provision reproduces the substance of Article 3436 of the Louisiana Civil Code of 1870. It does not change the law.

(b) According to well-settled civilian doctrine, one who takes corporeal possession of a thing is presumed to have the intent to own it. See R.C.C.(1870) Art. 3488; 3 Planiol et Ripert, Traité pratique de droit civil français, 163 (2d ed. Picard 1952). The presumption is rebuttable.

(c) One may acquire possession without taking corporeal possession of the thing by means of a transfer from one who has satisfied the requirements of this article. In such a case, the transferor's corporeal possession is tacked to the transferee's intent to own the thing. See Ellis v. Prevost, 19 La. 251 (1841); Articles 3441 through 3443, infra.

Art. 3425.   Corporeal possession

Corporeal possession is the exercise of physical acts of use, detention, or enjoyment over a thing.

Acts 1982, No. 187, § 1, eff. Jan. 1, 1983.

REVISION COMMENTS—1982

(a) This provision reproduces the substance of Article 3428 of the Louisiana Civil Code of 1870. It does not change the law.

(b) Corporeal possession is that by which one possesses a thing corporeally, for example, by residing in a house, cultivating land, or using a movable. Cf. R.C.C. (1870) Art. 3428.

(c) Article 3430 of the 1870 Code defined corporeal possession as "the corporeal detention of a thing which we possess as belonging to us, without any title to that possession, or with a title which is void." This definition of corporeal possession is useless and has not been reproduced. Its purpose in the 1870 Code was to draw a distinction between corporeal possession, as defined in R.C.C. (1870) Article 3430, and civil possession, as defined in R.C.C. (1870) Article 3431. Article 3431 defined "civil possession" as "the detention of a thing by virtue of a just title, and under the conviction of possessing as owner." This definition was in conflict with the definition set forth in R.C.C. (1870) Article 3429 and for good reason was written out of the Civil Code by the Louisiana Supreme Court in Ellis v. Prevost, 19 La. 251 (1841).

(d) The expression "natural possession", occurring in Article 3428 of the Louisiana Civil Code of 1870 has the same meaning as "corporeal possession." The former expression is not used in this revision.

Art. 3426.   Constructive possession

One who possesses a part of an immovable by virtue of a title is deemed to have constructive possession within the limits of his title. In the absence of title, one has possession only of the area he actually possesses.

Acts 1982, No. 187, § 1, eff. Jan. 1, 1983.

REVISION COMMENTS—1982

(a) The first sentence of this provision reproduces the substance of Article 3437 of the Louisiana Civil Code of 1870. It does not change the law. The second sentence of this provision codifies Louisiana jurisprudence. Likewise, it does not change the law.

(b) The notion of constructive possession is well settled in Louisiana jurisprudence. One who possesses by virtue of a title, that is, an act sufficient to transfer ownership, possesses within the limits of his title. See, e.g., Board of Commissioners v. S. D. Hunter Foundation, 354 So.2d 156 (La. 1978); Bolding v. Eason Oil Co., 248 La. 269, 178 So.2d 246 (1965); Jackson v. Bouanchaud, 178 La. 26, 150 So. 567 (1933); Ryan v. Pekinto, 387 So.2d 1325 (La.App. 1st Cir. 1980); and Winjum v. J. G. Duplantis, 393 So.2d 405 (La.App. 1st. Cir. 1980). One may have constructive corporeal or constructive civil possession. Moreover, one may have constructive possession by virtue of a defective title. Marks v. Collier, 216 La. 1, 43 So.2d 16 (1949). Finally, one may have constructive possession regardless of good or bad faith.

(c) The notion of constructive possession is pertinent for both the ten and thirty years' acquisitive prescription. Thus, one who possesses an immovable by virtue of a title in bad faith may prescribe in thirty years on proof that he had possession of a part, and therefore constructive possession of the whole within the limits of his title.

(d) In the absence of title, there is no constructive possession: one has possession only of the area he actually possesses. Actual possession must be either inch by inch possession (pedis possessio) or possession within enclosures. According to well-settled Louisiana jurisprudence, an enclosure is any natural or artificial boundary. See Yiannopoulos, Civil Law Property, §§ 212–214 (2d ed. 1980).

Art. 3427. Presumption of intent to own the thing

One is presumed to intend to possess as owner unless he began to possess in the name of and for another.

Acts 1982, No. 187, § 1, eff. Jan. 1, 1983.

REVISION COMMENTS—1982

(a) This provision reproduces the substance of Article 3488 of the Louisiana Civil Code of 1870. It does not change the law.

(b) C.C. (1870) Article 3488 is located in the part of the Civil Code that deals with ten years' acquisitive prescription of immovable property. However, it is also applicable to the thirty year's prescription of immovables by virtue of C.C. (1870) Article 3505. The rule of C.C. (1870) Article 3488 should apply equally to movables and immovables in all matters of possession. Accordingly, it has been placed in the Chapter of the Civil Code that deals with possession in general.

(c) Article 3488 of the Louisiana Civil Code of 1870 corresponds to Article 2230 of the French Civil Code. The provision derives from the 1808 Digest. Its source is Projet du Gouvernement, Book III, Title Xara. 12.

(d) When it is shown that the possession was begun for another, the presumption set forth in this article does not arise. In cases in which the presumption does arise, it is rebuttable.

Art. 3428. Acquisition of possession through another

One may acquire possession of a thing through another who takes it for him and in his name. The person taking possession must intend to do so for another.

Acts 1982, No. 187, § 1, eff. Jan. 1, 1983.

REVISION COMMENTS—1982

(a) This provision reproduces the substance of Articles 3438 and 3445 of the Louisiana Civil Code of 1870. It does not change the law.

(b) When one acquires possession for another and in the name of another, his possession is precarious. See Article 3437, infra. For example, one who has taken possession of a servitude has quasi-possession of the servitude for himself and the possession of the land for the owner. As to the landowner, therefore, the holder of the servitude is a precarious possessor. See 3 Planiol et Ripert, Traité pratique de droit civil français, 177 (2d ed. Picard 1952); and Board of Commissioners v. S. D. Hunter Foundation, 354 So.2d 156 (La. 1978).

Art. 3429. Exercise of possession by another

Possession may be exercised by the possessor or by another who holds the thing for him and in his name. Thus, a lessor possesses through his lessee.

Acts 1982, No. 187, § 1, eff. Jan. 1, 1983.

REVISION COMMENTS—1982

(a) This provision reproduces the substance of Article 3433 of the Louisiana Civil Code of 1870. It does not change the law.

(b) Possession may be exercised by the possessor himself or by another who detains the thing in his name. Thus, the lessor possesses through his lessee. One who exercises possession for another is a precarious possessor. See Article 3437, infra.

Art. 3430. Juridical persons

A juridical person acquires possession through its representatives.

Acts 1982, No. 187, § 1, eff. Jan. 1, 1983.

REVISION COMMENT—1982

This provision reproduces the substance of Article 3440 of the Louisiana Civil Code of 1870. It does not change the law.

Art. 3431. Retention of possession; civil possession

Once acquired, possession is retained by the intent to possess as owner even if the possessor ceases to possess corporeally. This is civil possession.

Acts 1982, No. 187, § 1, eff. Jan. 1, 1983.

REVISION COMMENTS—1982

(a) This provision reproduces the substance of Articles 3429 and 3442 of the Louisiana Civil Code of 1870. It does not change the law.

(b) Two things are necessary to acquire possession: corporeal possession and the intent to own the thing. Article 3424, supra. However, to retain an acquired possession, the intent to own suffices. Thus, even if the possessor no longer exercises physical acts over the thing, he nevertheless may be considered to be in possession.

(c) Civil possession is the retention of the possession of a thing merely by virtue of the intent to own it, as when a person, without intending to abandon possession, ceases to reside in a house or on the land which he previously occupied or when a person ceases to exercise physical control over a movable without intending to abandon possession. Cf. R.C.C. (1870) Art. 3429. A second definition of civil possession, contained in Article 3431 of the Louisiana Civil Code of 1870, has long been written out by the Louisiana Supreme Court. See Ellis v. Prevost, 19 La. 251 (1841).

(d) Acts of civil possession include acts such as the payment of taxes on an immovable or the execution of a juridical act affecting the thing, such as a lease. Cf. R.C.C. (1870) Art. 3501. Moreover, vestiges of works, such as the ruins of a house, may signify civil possession. Cf. R.C.C. (1870) Art. 3502.

Art. 3432. Presumption of retention of possession

The intent to retain possession is presumed unless there is clear proof of a contrary intention.

Acts 1982, No. 187, § 1, eff. Jan. 1, 1983.

REVISION COMMENTS—1982

(a) This provision reproduces the substance of Article 3443 of the Louisiana Civil Code of 1870. It does not change the law.

(b) The intent to retain possession is presumed. Thus, one who ceases to cultivate a tract of land nevertheless is presumed to have the intention to retain possession and retains it in fact. The presumption is rebuttable. The second sentence of R.C.C. (1870) Article 3443 contains an unnecessary illustration and has not been reproduced.

(c) According to the text of Article 3444 of the Louisiana Civil Code of 1870, the presumption of intent to retain possession ceases when the possessor "has failed to exercise an actual possession for ten years." In other words, without acts of possession, the presumption exists for a maximum period of ten years. This part of Article 3444 was not included in the projet of the Louisiana Civil Code of 1825. Obviously it was added by the legislature. In the past, Louisiana courts found this portion of Article 3444 to be inapplicable when one possessed under title. See Manson Realty Co. v. Plaisance, 196 So.2d 555 (La.App. 4th Cir. 1967). Thus, the rule was applicable only when the possessor possessed without title. Louisiana courts frequently managed to avoid application of this portion of C.C. (1870) Article 3444 by finding that the possessor exercised corporeal possession within the appropriate ten year period. See, e.g., Womack v. Walsh, 255 La. 217, 230 So.2d 83 (1969). Under this revision the presumption that one intends to retain possession continues as long as possession has not been lost to another.

Art. 3433.   Loss of possession

Possession is lost when the possessor manifests his intention to abandon it or when he is evicted by another by force or usurpation.

Acts 1982, No. 187, § 1, eff. Jan. 1, 1983.

REVISION COMMENTS—1982

(a) This provision is based on Articles 3447, 3448, and 3449 of the Louisiana Civil Code of 1870. It does not change the law.

(b) Possession continues as long as it is not abandoned and as long as the possessor is not evicted by an adverse possessor. According to Article 3448(1) of the Louisiana Civil Code of 1870, possession also is lost when the possessor "transfers this possession to another with the intention to divest himself of it." This provision has not been reproduced under the heading of loss of possession because a transfer of possession is not a loss of possession. It is true that the possessor ceases to possess, but his possession is continued by the transferee who benefits by tacking. See Article 3442, infra. Thus, the two modes of loss of possession are abandonment and eviction by another who commences to possess for himself.

(c) What constitutes abandonment is a question to be determined in the light of all the circumstances. Abandonment is predicated on a manifestation of intent to abandon, which may be established in the light of objective criteria.

(d) What constitutes eviction is a question of fact to be determined by the trier of facts. Ordinarily, the erection of a fence or other enclosure constitutes an eviction. See Hongo v. Carlton, 241 So.2d 34 (La.App. 3rd Cir. 1970); Kilchrist v. Conrad, 191 So.2d 705 (La.App. 3rd Cir. 1966). Likewise, the use of property by an adverse possessor according to its nature ordinarily constitutes an eviction. Certain acts, however, such as the mowing of grass at the boundary between two tracts of land may or may not constitute an eviction. See Richard v. Comeaux, 260 So.2d 350 (La.App. 1st Cir. 1972); and Yiannopoulos, Civil Law Property, § 216 (2d ed. 1980).

Art. 3434.   Loss of the right to possess

The right to possess is lost upon abandonment of possession. In case of eviction, the right to possess is lost if the possessor does not recover possession within a year of the eviction.

When the right to possess is lost, possession is interrupted.

Acts 1982, No. 187, § 1, eff. Jan. 1, 1983.

REVISION COMMENTS—1982

(a) This provision is based on Articles 3449(2) and 3517 of the Louisiana Civil Code of 1870. It does not change the law.

(b) According to Louisiana jurisprudence, Article 3449 of the Louisiana Civil Code of 1870 contemplates two distinct situations: loss of possession by eviction and loss of the right to possess. See Liner v. Louisiana Land and Exploration Co., 319 So.2d 766 (La.1975). Articles 3433 and 3434 of this revision deal respectively with the loss of possession and the loss of the right to possess.

SECTION 3—VICES OF POSSESSION

Art. 3435.   Vices of possession

Possession that is violent, clandestine, discontinuous, or equivocal has no legal effect.

Acts 1982, No. 187, § 1, eff. Jan. 1, 1983.

REVISION COMMENTS—1982

(a) This provision is new. It is based on Articles 3487, 3491, and 3500 of the Louisiana Civil Code of 1870. It does not change the law.

(b) As explained in 2 Planiol, Traité élémentaire de droit civil, 346–351 (An English translation by the Louisiana State Law Institute 1959), Article 3487 of the Louisiana Civil Code of 1870, corresponding to Article 2229 of the French Civil Code, takes a backward approach to the problem of classifying the vices of possession. Article 3435, in contrast, specifies what are the vices of possession and indicates that a vicious possession fails to produce legal effects.

Art. 3436.   Violent, clandestine, discontinuous, and equivocal possession

Possession is violent when it is acquired or maintained by violent acts. When the violence ceases, the possession ceases to be violent.

Possession is clandestine when it is not open or public, discontinuous when it is not exercised at regular intervals, and equivocal when there is ambiguity as to the intent of the possessor to own the thing.

Acts 1982, No. 187, § 1, eff. Jan. 1, 1983.

REVISION COMMENT—1982

This provision is new. It is based on Articles 3487, 3491, and 3500 of the Louisiana Civil Code of 1870. It does not change the law.

SECTION 4—PRECARIOUS POSSESSION

Art. 3437.   Precarious possession

The exercise of possession over a thing with the permission of or on behalf of the owner or possessor is precarious possession.

Acts 1982, No. 187, § 1, eff. Jan. 1, 1983.

REVISION COMMENTS—1982

(a) This provision is new. The idea that detention is the exercise of factual authority over a thing without the intent to own it is implicit in the Louisiana Civil Code of 1870. Article 3437 does not change the law.

(b) According to civilian tradition and modern civil codes, there is a clear distinction between possession and detention. Possession is the exercise of physical acts of use, enjoyment, or detention over a thing with the intent to own it; detention or precarious possession is the exercise of factual authority over a thing with the permission of or on behalf of the owner or possessor. The precarious possessor (called in France possesseur precaire or detenteur) does not intend to own the thing he detains. See 3 Planiol et Ripert, Traité pratique de droit civil français, 175 (2d ed. Picard 1952).

Art. 3438.   Presumption of precariousness

A precarious possessor, such as a lessee or a depositary, is presumed to possess for another although he may intend to possess for himself.

Acts 1982, No. 187, § 1, eff. Jan. 1, 1983.

REVISION COMMENTS—1982

(a) This provision is based on Articles 3446 and 3489 of the Louisiana Civil Code of 1870. It does not change the law.

(b) A precarious possessor is presumed to possess on behalf of another even if he changes his mind and intends to possess for himself. The presumption is rebuttable. Cf. Article 2287 of the Civil Code of 1870.

Art. 3439.   Termination of precarious possession

A co-owner, or his universal successor, commences to possess for himself when he demonstrates this intent by overt and unambiguous acts sufficient to give notice to his co-owner.

Any other precarious possessor, or his universal successor, commences to possess for himself when he gives actual notice of this intent to the person on whose behalf he is possessing.

Acts 1982, No. 187, § 1, eff. Jan. 1, 1983.

REVISION COMMENTS—1982

(a) This provision is new. The rule it establishes is inherent in the Louisiana Civil Code of 1870. It does not change the law.

(b) According to well-settled Louisiana jurisprudence, a precarious possessor commences to possess for himself when he gives notice and manifests his intention to possess as owner by overt and unambiguous acts. In such a case, there is a usurpation of possession. See, e.g., Thayer v. Waples, 26 La.Ann. 502 (1874); Succession of Seals, 243 La. 1056, 150 So.2d 13 (1963); and Dupuis v. Broadhurst, 213 So.2d 528 (La.App. 3rd Cir. 1968).

(c) According to Articles 3441 and 3490 of the Louisiana Civil Code of 1870, a precarious possessor cannot acquire "the legal possession" of the thing he detains. He does not have the rights of a possessor. Thus, a precarious possessor cannot prescribe (R.C.C. (1870) Article 3490), has no claims to the fruits of the property as a possessor in good faith (Civil Code Article 486, as revised by Acts 1979, No. 180), and is not entitled to reimbursement for expenses or improvements as a good or bad faith possessor (Civil Code Articles 486, 488, 527, 528, and 529, as revised by Acts 1979, No. 180). In this article, there is no reference to "legal possession". It is clear, however, that a precarious possessor, having merely the detention of the thing, does not enjoy the rights of a possessor.

Art. 3440.   Protection of precarious possession

Where there is a disturbance of possession, the possessory action is available to a precarious possessor, such as a lessee or a depositary, against anyone except the person for whom he possesses.

Acts 1982, No. 187, § 1, eff. Jan. 1, 1983.

REVISION COMMENTS—1982

(a) This provision is new. It accords possessory protection to a mere precarious possessor against anyone other than the person for whom he possesses. It changes the law.

(b) According to the Louisiana Civil Code of 1870, a precarious possessor, such as a lessee or a depositary, does not have "legal" possession. See R.C.C. (1870) Article 3441. Accordingly, the possessory action is not available to such a person. See C.C.P. Article 3656. However, according to certain Louisiana decisions, a precarious possessor may obtain injunctive relief against trespassers or other persons who disturb his possession by application of Article 3663(2) of the Louisiana Code of Civil Procedure. See, e.g., Indian Bayou Hunting Club, Inc. v. Taylor, 261 So.2d 669 (La.App. 3rd Cir.

1972); but see Caney Hunting Club, Inc. v. Tolbert, 294 So.2d 894 (La.App. 2nd Cir. 1974) (relief only under Article 3601 of the Code of Civil Procedure).

(c) In most modern civil law countries, including France, the possessory action is available to a precarious possessor for the protection of his detention vis-a-vis third persons. In France, the legislature added two articles to the Code Civil in 1975 (Articles 2282 and 2283). See Yiannopoulos, Civil Law Property, §§ 203–206 (2d ed. 1980).

(d) According to Article 3440 a precarious possessor may bring a possessory action against anyone other than the person for whom he possesses. Thus, a lessee may bring a possessory action against a trespasser or an adverse possessor, but he cannot bring a possessory action against his lessor. The judgment in a possessory action brought by a precarious possessor is not res judicata vis-a-vis the person for whom he possesses, unless the latter has been made a party to the proceedings. See R.C.C. (1870) Article 2286.

(e) Article 3440 does not modify in any way R.C.C. (1870) Article 2704. When the possession of the lessee is disturbed by a third person claiming a right to the thing leased, the lessee is bound to call the lessor in warranty. See R.C.C. (1870) Article 2704.

SECTION 5—TRANSFER, TACKING, AND PROOF OF POSSESSION

Art. 3441.   Transfer of possession

Possession is transferable by universal title or by particular title.

Acts 1982, No. 187, § 1, eff. Jan. 1, 1983.

REVISION COMMENTS—1982

(a) This provision is new. It is based on Articles 3493, 3494(2), and 3496 of the Louisiana Civil Code of 1870, which indicate that possession is transferable. It does not change the law.

(b) Possession is not interrupted by the death of the possessor. The possession of the deceased is continued by his universal successor, such as an heir, universal legatee, or legatee under universal title. A particular legatee is placed in possession by the universal successor of the deceased. The possession of the deceased is tacked to the possession of the universal successor, and the possession of the latter to that of the particular legatee. Thus, there is no interruption of possession when a possessor dies.

(c) For the distinction between succession by universal title and succession by particular title, see R.C.C. (1870) Article 3556(28).

Art. 3442.   Tacking of possession

The possession of the transferor is tacked to that of the transferee if there has been no interruption of possession.

Acts 1982, No. 187, § 1, eff. Jan. 1, 1983.

REVISION COMMENTS—1982

(a) This provision is new. It is based on Articles 3493, 3494, and 3495 of the Louisiana Civil Code of 1870. It does not change the law.

(b) In case of universal succession, the possession of the successor is tacked to the possession of the deceased; in case of succession by particular title, the succession of the buyer or donee is tacked to that of the seller or donor.

(c) Possession is interrupted when the possessor loses the right to possess. See Article 3434, supra.

(d) Tacking of possession presupposes a juridical link. This link may arise through universal succession or particular succession. For the definition of universal succession and of particular succession, see R.C.C. (1870) Article 3556(28). Despite the nonexistence of a juridical link, tacking is permitted in boundary actions within the limits of Article 794 of the Civil Code, as amended by Acts 1977, No. 169.

(e) An author is a person from whom the possessor has derived his right. Thus, the word "author" has the same meaning as ancestor in title. The possessor may have acquired his right from the author by universal or by particular title, onerous or gratuitous. The possession of the heir may be tacked to that of the deceased, and the possession of the buyer to that of the seller.

Art. 3443.   Presumption of continuity of possession

One who proves that he had possession at different times is presumed to have possessed during the intermediate period.

Acts 1982, No. 187, § 1, eff. Jan. 1, 1983.

REVISION COMMENTS—1982

(a) This provision reproduces the substance of Article 3492 of the Louisiana Civil Code of 1870. It does not change the law.

(b) Article 3492 of the Louisiana Civil Code of 1870 corresponds to Article 2234 of the French Civil Code.

(c) The presumption of ownership is established in favor of the possessor of a corporeal movable by Civil Code Article 530, as revised by Acts 1979, No. 180.

Art. 3444.   Possessory action

Possession of immovables is protected by the possessory action, as provided in Articles 3655 through 3671 of the Code of Civil Procedure.

Possession of movables is protected by the rules of the Code of Civil Procedure that govern civil actions.

Acts 1982, No. 187, § 1, eff. Jan. 1, 1983.

REVISION COMMENTS—1982

(a) This provision is new. It clarifies the law.

(b) The possessory action under Articles 3655 through 3671 of the Louisiana Code of Civil Procedure is applicable exclusively to immovable property. There is no nominate action for the protection of the possession of movables; however a possessor of movables who has been disturbed in his possession may bring a civil action to recover possession. See Navratil v. Smart, 373 So.2d 544 (La. 1979); cf. Peloquin v. Calcasieu Parish Police Jury, 367 So.2d 1246 (La.App. 3rd Cir. 1979); Yiannopoulos, Civil Law Property, § 233 (2d ed. 1980).

TITLE XXIV—PRESCRIPTION

CHAPTER 1—GENERAL PROVISIONS

SECTION 1—PRESCRIPTION

Art. 3445. Kinds of prescription

There are three kinds of prescription: acquisitive prescription, liberative prescription, and prescription of nonuse.

Acts 1982, No. 187, § 1, eff. Jan. 1, 1983.

REVISION COMMENTS—1982

(a) This provision is new. It is based in part on Articles 3457 and 3546 of the Louisiana Civil Code of 1870. It does not change the law.

(b) Article 3457 of the Louisiana Civil Code of 1870 indicates that there are two kinds of prescription: acquisitive prescription and liberative prescription. Article 3546 of the Louisiana Civil Code of 1870 indicates that the prescription of nonuse is a species of liberative prescription. However, liberative prescription, being a bar to an action, is clearly distinguishable from prescription of nonuse, which is a mode of extinction of real rights other than ownership. For this reason, in accordance with modern conceptual technique, Article 3445 declares that there are three kinds of prescription: acquisitive prescription, liberative prescription, and prescription of nonuse. The slight change in conceptual technique does not involve a change in the law.

(c) Prescription, whether acquisitive, liberative, or of nonuse, forms the basis of a peremptory exception. See Montgomery v. Breaux, 297 So.2d 185 (La.1974).

Art. 3446. Acquisitive prescription

Acquisitive prescription is a mode of acquiring ownership or other real rights by possession for a period of time.

Acts 1982, No. 187, § 1, eff. Jan. 1, 1983.

REVISION COMMENTS—1982

(a) This provision is new. It is based in part on C.C. (1977) Article 742 on R.C.C. (1870) Article 3458. It does not change the law.

(b) Article 3458 of the Louisiana Civil Code of 1870 declares that acquisitive prescription "is a right by which a mere possessor acquires the ownership of a thing which he possesses by the continuance of his possession during the time fixed by law." This language has not been reproduced in this draft because it is too narrow and also because it is unnecessary. Acquisitive prescription applies to both ownership and other real rights, such as usufruct and apparent servitudes. C.C. (1976) Article 544, Comment (c); id. C.C. (1977) Article 742. The incidents of acquisitive prescription are dealt with in Chapter 3 and hence are not summarized in Article 3446.

(c) For a discussion of the distinction between acquisitive prescription and liberative prescription, see Baudry-Lacantinerie et Tissier, Prescription, 14–30 (an English translation by the Louisiana State Law Institute 1972).

Art. 3447. Liberative prescription

Liberative prescription is a mode of barring of actions as a result of inaction for a period of time.

Acts 1982, No. 187, § 1, eff. Jan. 1, 1983.

(a) This provision is new. It is based in part on Articles 3457 and 3459 of the Louisiana Civil Code of 1870. It does not change the law.

(b) According to Article 3457 of the Louisiana Civil Code of 1870, liberative prescription is a manner of "discharging debts", and according to Article 3459 of the same Code, liberative prescription is "a peremptory and perpetual bar to every species of action, real or personal, when the creditor has been silent for a certain time without urging his claim." This language is not accurate and has not been reproduced in this revision.

In the first place, liberative prescription is not merely a mode of discharging debts; it is a mode of extinguishing claims. After the accrual of prescription, a natural obligation remains. R.C.C. (1870) Article 1758(3).

Second, any kind of prescription may form the basis of a peremptory exception. Thus, not only liberative prescription, but also acquisitive prescription and the prescription of nonuse may establish a peremptory exception.

Third, liberative prescription is not a bar to "every species of action, real or personal". Certain real actions, such as the petitory action and the action of boundary are imprescriptible; other real actions, such as the possessory action and the action for the recognition of a servitude, are barred by the prescription of nonuse rather than by liberative prescription.

Fourth, the language "when the creditor has been silent for a certain time without urging his claim" peculiarly is applicable to liberative prescription rather than to the prescription of nonuse. Moreover, the same words represent elements of liberative prescription and need not be mentioned in Article 3447.

(c) According to the Code of Civil Procedure, an action is "a demand for enforcement of a legal right". C.C.P. Article 421. It is the equivalent of the Roman actio expressed in terms of substantive law. See Yiannopoulos, Civil Law Property, § 182 (2d ed. 1980).

Art. 3448. Prescription of nonuse

Prescription of nonuse is a mode of extinction of a real right other than ownership as a result of failure to exercise the right for a period of time.

Acts 1982, No. 187, § 1, eff. Jan. 1, 1983.

(a) This provision is new. It is based in part on Article 3546 of the Louisiana Civil Code of 1870. It does not change the law.

(b) Article 3546 of the Louisiana Civil Code of 1870 declares that "the rights of usufruct, use, and habitation and servitudes are lost by nonuse for ten years." This language is too narrow. In reality, all real rights other than ownership may be lost by nonuse. Special provisions in the Mineral Code govern the prescription of nonuse as it applies to mineral rights.

(c) Liberative prescription bars actions. See Article 3447, supra. However, the prescription of nonuse extinguishes the right itself. Thus, after the accrual of prescription of nonuse, no natural obligation remains. See Dainow, The Work of the Louisiana Supreme Court for the 1952–1953 Term, 14 La.L.Rev. 129–132 (1953).

(d) Ownership cannot be extinguished by nonuse. See Civil Code Article 481, as revised by Acts 1979, No. 180.

Art. 3449. Renunciation of prescription

Prescription may be renounced only after it has accrued.

Acts 1982, No. 187, § 1, eff. Jan. 1, 1983.

(a) This provision is based on Article 3460 of the Louisiana Civil Code of 1870. It does not change the law.

(b) According to well-settled Louisiana Jurisprudence interpreting Article 3460 of the 1870 Code, one may not renounce prescription prior to its accrual. However, one is free to renounce prescription after it has accrued. R.C.C. (1870) Article 3460 expresses the same idea.

(c) Renunciation of prescription is a technical term designating the abandonment of rights derived from an accrual of prescription. It is to be distinguished from an acknowledgment of a right or obligation, which is made prior to the accrual of prescription and which wipes out the time that has run prior to the acknowledgment.

(d) According to the civilian tradition, the renunciation of prescription is not an act translative of ownership. It is a unilateral act that does not require acceptance by the other party; moreover, it does not require any formality. See 3 Planiol et Ripert, Traité pratique de droit civil français, 748 (2d ed. Picard 1952):

"Renunciation is a unilateral act that does not require acceptance by the other party. . . .

"The possessor who renounces prescription when it has run in his favor, seems to divest himself of his right and to agree to an act translative of ownership in favor of somebody else. But this is so merely in appearance. As has already been seen (no. 2709) prescription does not take place by operation of law. It must be set up by the party. The Court cannot do so of its own motion. Consequently, if it be a means of acquiring, it is still necessary that use be made of it. When he, in whose favor prescription has run, renounces it, he refrains from making use of a means that the law offers him to become owner. It may accordingly be said that he threw away an opportunity to acquire, that he refused to have a piece of property become part of his patrimony. It would, however be a mistake to say that he had alienated it, that he had transmitted the ownership to another. Article 2221 speaks of the renunciation of prescription as 'the abandonment of an acquired right.' But this term 'acquired' connotes merely the right to set up the plea of prescription. It is of the right, and not of the ownership which is not as yet acquired, that the possessor despoils himself by his renunciation.

"Even though the renunciation of an acquired prescription is not the juridical equivalent of an alienation, it nevertheless has the same practical effect. It deprives the person who makes it of the ownership of a piece of property which he could have definitively retained. Renunciation is therefore essentially dangerous. And thus does the law prohibit it to 'him who cannot alienate' (Art. 2222)."

Art. 3450. Express or tacit renunciation

Renunciation may be express or tacit. Tacit renunciation results from circumstances that give rise to a presumption that the advantages of prescription have been abandoned.

Nevertheless, with respect to immovables, renunciation of acquisitive prescription must be express and in writing.

Acts 1982, No. 187, § 1, eff. Jan. 1, 1983.

This provision is based in part on Article 3461 of the Louisiana Civil Code of 1870. The first paragraph does not change the law. The second paragraph changes the law in the interest of security of titles.

Art. 3451. Capacity to renounce

To renounce prescription, one must have capacity to alienate.

Acts 1982, No. 187, § 1, eff. Jan. 1, 1983.

(a) This provision is based on Article 3462 of the Louisiana Civil Code of 1870. It does not change the law.

(b) The renunciation of prescription has the same effect as an act of alienation. Accordingly, to renounce prescription, one must have the capacity to alienate. Interdicts and certain minors lack the capacity to renounce prescription. See Planiol, Treatise on the Civil Law; Vol. 1, No. 2715; Vol. 2, No. 702.

Art. 3452. Necessity for pleading prescription

Prescription must be pleaded. Courts may not supply a plea of prescription.

Acts 1982, No. 187, § 1, eff. Jan. 1, 1983.

REVISION COMMENT—1982

This provision reproduces the substance of Article 3463 of the Louisiana Civil Code of 1870. It does not change the law.

Art. 3453. Rights of creditors and other interested parties

Creditors and other persons having an interest in the acquisition of a thing or in the extinction of a claim or of a real right by prescription may plead prescription, even if the person in whose favor prescription has accrued renounces or fails to plead prescription.

Acts 1982, No. 187, § 1, eff. Jan. 1, 1983.

REVISION COMMENTS—1982

(a) This provision reproduces the substance of Article 3466 of the Louisiana Civil Code of 1870. It does not change the law.

(b) See also R.C.C. (1870) Article 1990.

Art. 3454. Computation of time

In computing a prescriptive period, the day that marks the commencement of prescription is not counted. Prescription accrues upon the expiration of the last day of the prescriptive period, and if that day is a legal holiday, prescription accrues upon the expiration of the next day that is not a legal holiday.

Acts 1982, No. 187, § 1, eff. Jan. 1, 1983.

REVISION COMMENTS—1982

(a) This provision is new. It is based in part on Article 3467 of the Louisiana Civil Code of 1870, Article 5059 of the Louisiana Code of Civil Procedure, and Articles 241 and 242 of the Greek Civil Code. It is not intended to change the law.

(b) The day which marks the commencement of prescription is not counted. The Louisiana Code of Civil Procedure has adopted this rule for periods of time "allowed or prescribed by law or by order of the court." C.C.P.Art. 5059. Cf. 1(2) Planiol, Traité élémentaire de droit civil, 574 (an English translation by the Louisiana State Law Institute 1959).

(c) Prescription accrues upon lapse of the last day of the prescriptive period. However, according to Article 5059 of the Louisiana Code of Civil Procedure and Article 242 of the Greek Civil Code, if the last day of the prescriptive period is a legal holiday, prescription accrues upon the lapse of the next working day. But see 1(2) Planiol, Traité élémentaire de droit civil, 577 (an English translation by the Louisiana State Law Institute 1959): "Prescription is completed on the fixed day, even if it be a holiday."

Art. 3455. Computation of time by months

If the prescriptive period consists of one or more months, prescription accrues upon the expiration of the day of the last month of the period that corresponds with the date of the commencement of prescription, and if there is no corresponding day, prescription accrues upon the expiration of the last day of the period.

Acts 1982, No. 187, § 1, eff. Jan. 1, 1983.

(a) This provision is new. It is based in part on Article 3468 of the Louisiana Civil Code of 1870 and on Article 243 of the Greek Civil Code. It does not change the law.

(b) Article 3468 of the Louisiana Civil Code of 1870 speaks of the day "when the possession commenced." However, there should be no doubt that the article was intended to apply to both acquisitive and liberative prescription. Article 3455, conceived in broader terms, clearly is applicable to any kind of prescription.

Art. 3456. Computation of time by years

If a prescriptive period consists of one or more years, prescription accrues upon the expiration of the day of the last year that corresponds with the date of the commencement of prescription.

Acts 1982, No. 187, § 1, eff. Jan. 1, 1983.

(a) This provision is new. It is based in part on Article 3469 of the Louisiana Civil Code of 1870 and on Article 243 of the Greek Civil Code. It does not change the law.

(b) Article 3469 of the Louisiana Civil Code of 1870 speaks of "the time of possession required by law." It is apparent that the provision was meant to apply to both liberative and acquisitive prescription. Accordingly, Article 3456 is conceived in broader terms and applies to any kind of prescription.

(c) When there is no date that corresponds to the commencement of prescription, the preceding article applies by analogy. For example, a five-year prescription that commenced to run on February 29, 1980, will accrue upon the lapse of the last day of February in 1985. See Mangin v. Auter, 360 So.2d 577 (La.App. 4th Cir. 1978).

Art. 3457. Prescription established by legislation only

There is no prescription other than that established by legislation.

Acts 1982, No. 187, § 1, eff. Jan. 1, 1983.

(a) This provision reproduces the substance of Article 3470 of the Louisiana Civil Code of 1870. It does not change the law.

(b) Under the Louisiana legal system, there is no room for the common law doctrine of laches. See System Federation No. 59 of Railway Employees' Department of American Federation of Labor v. Louisiana & A. Ry. Co., 57 F.Supp. 151 (W.D.C.La.1944) and Landry v. Mutual Life Ins. Co. of New York, 54 F.Supp. 356 (W.D.C.La.1944).

SECTION 2—PEREMPTION

Art. 3458. Peremption; effect

Peremption is a period of time fixed by law for the existence of a right. Unless timely exercised, the right is extinguished upon the expiration of the peremptive period.

Acts 1982, No. 187, § 1, eff. Jan. 1, 1983.

(a) This provision is new. It is based on Louisiana jurisprudence. It does not change the law.

(b) Peremption is a period of time, fixed by law, within which a right must be exercised or be forever lost. Guillory v. Avoyelles Ry. Co., 104 La. 11, 28 So. 899 (1900). Liberative prescription merely prevents the enforcement of a right by action; in contrast, peremption destroys the right itself. See Pounds v. Schori, 377 So.2d 1195 (La.1979); Flowers Inc. v. Rausch, 364 So.2d 928 (La.1978). The prescription of nonuse applicable to mineral rights and other real rights is to be distinguished from peremption.

(c) It is not always easy to determine whether a period of time fixed by law is peremptive or prescriptive. The determination must be made in each case in the light of the purpose of the rule in question and in light of whether the intent behind the rule is to bar action or to limit the duration of a right. For a discussion of this subject, see Comment, Legal Rights and the Passage of Time, 41 La.L.Rev. 220, 252 (1980).

(d) For a discussion of pertinent French doctrine and jurisprudence, see Baudry-Lacantinerie et Tissier, Prescription, 38–39 (An English Translation by the Louisiana State Law Institute (1972)).

Art. 3459. Application of rules of prescription

The provisions on prescription governing computation of time apply to peremption.

Acts 1982, No. 187, § 1, eff. Jan. 1, 1983.

REVISION COMMENTS—1982

(a) This provision is new. It is based in part on Article 279 of the Greek Civil Code. It does not change the law.

(b) The provisions on prescription governing computation of time apply to peremption as well. See Articles 3454–3456, supra.

Art. 3460. Peremption need not be pleaded

Peremption may be pleaded or it may be supplied by a court on its own motion at any time prior to final judgment.

Acts 1982, No. 187, § 1, eff. Jan. 1, 1983.

REVISION COMMENTS—1982

(a) This provision is new. It is based on Article 280 of the Greek Civil Code. It clarifies the law.

(b) In contrast with prescription which must be pleaded, peremption may be recognized by the court on its own motion. See Comment, Legal Rights and the Passage of Time, 41 La.L.Rev. 220, 238 (1980).

Art. 3461. Renunciation, interruption, or suspension ineffective

Peremption may not be renounced, interrupted, or suspended.

Acts 1982, No. 187, § 1, eff. Jan. 1, 1983.

REVISION COMMENTS—1982

(a) This provision is new. It is based on Louisiana jurisprudence and Article 280 of the Greek Civil Code. It does not change the law.

(b) For purposes of comparison, see Greek Civil Code Article 280:

"A peremptive period established by law is taken into account by the court on its own motion, and renunciation is null."

(c) In contrast with prescription, peremption may be neither interrupted nor suspended. See Pounds v. Schori, 377 So.2d 1195 (La.1979); Flowers Inc. v. Rausch, 364 So.2d 928 (La.1978). Comment, Legal Rights and the Passage of Time, 41 La.L.Rev. 220, 239 (1980).

Nevertheless, when an action asserting a right subject to peremption has been commenced or served as provided in Article 3462, the right has been exercised and so long as the action is pending the lapse of the period of peremption does not extinguish the right.

CHAPTER 2—INTERRUPTION AND SUSPENSION OF PRESCRIPTION

SECTION 1—INTERRUPTION OF PRESCRIPTION

Art. 3462.   Interruption by filing of suit or by service of process

Prescription is interrupted when the owner commences action against the possessor, or when the obligee commences action against the obligor, in a court of competent jurisdiction and venue. If action is commenced in an incompetent court, or in an improper venue, prescription is interrupted only as to a defendant served by process within the prescriptive period.

Acts 1982, No. 187, § 1, eff. Jan. 1, 1983.

REVISION COMMENTS—1982

(a) This provision is new. It is based on Article 3518 of the Louisiana Civil Code of 1870 and on R.S. 9:5801. It does not change the law. Accordingly, Louisiana decisions interpreting the source provisions continue to be relevant, and R.S. 9:5801 is repealed.

(b) The filing of suit in a court of competent jurisdiction and venue interrupts any kind of prescription as to the causes of action therein sued upon, provided the plaintiff is a proper party plaintiff and the defendant is a proper party defendant. Moreover, all kinds of prescription are interrupted by the service of process, as to the defendant served, even if the action is commenced in an incompetent court or in an improper venue. See Kupperman, Interruption of Prescription by Judicial Action in Louisiana, 14 Tul.L.Rev. 601 (1940).

(c) For solidary debtors, see R.C.C. (1870) Article 2097 [see, now, C.C. Art. 1799].

(d) Interruption of prescription by the service of process is discussed in Conner v. Continental Southern Lines, Inc., 294 So.2d 485 (La.1974). In that case the court stated:

"Service of process interrupts the running of prescription even though the process is defective and subject to exception, if it is sufficient to inform the person served of the legal demands made upon him from the described occurrence. See, Vernon v. Illinois Central Railroad Co., supra; Anding v. Texas and Pacific Railway Co., supra; Babin v. Lyons Lumber Co., 132 La. 873, 61 So. 855 (1913). Cf. Lunkin v. Triangle Farms, Inc., 208 La. 538, 23 So.2d 209 (1945); Jackson v. American Employers' Insurance Co., 202 La. 23, 11 So.2d 225 (1942). However, the proper person, as designated by law, must be served before service of process will interrupt the running of prescription."

Art. 3463.   Duration of interruption; abandonment or discontinuance of suit

An interruption of prescription resulting from the filing of a suit in a competent court and in the proper venue or from service of process within the prescriptive period continues as long as the suit is pending. Interruption is considered never to have occurred if the plaintiff abandons, voluntarily dismisses the action at any time either before the defendant has made any appearance of record or thereafter, or fails to prosecute the suit at the trial.

Acts 1982, No. 187, § 1, eff. Jan. 1, 1983. Amended by Acts 1999, No. 1263, § 2, eff. Jan. 1, 2000.

REVISION COMMENTS—1982

(a) The first paragraph of this provision is new. It is based on Louisiana jurisprudence. It does not change the law. The second paragraph is based on Article 3519 of the Louisiana Civil Code of 1870. It does not change the law.

(b) According to Louisiana decisions, after being interrupted by the filing of suit in a competent court, prescription is suspended while the suit is pending. See Marshall v. Southern Farm Bureau Casualty Company, 204 So.2d 665 (La.App. 3rd Cir. 1967); Hebert v. Cournoyer Oldsmobile-Cadillac-G.M.C., Inc., 405 So.2d 359 (La.App. 4th Cir. 1981). However, it is preferable to speak of a continuous interruption rather than a suspension. See Dainow, The Work of the Louisiana Appellate Courts for the 1967–1968 Term, 29 La.L.Rev. 230 (1969). In such a case, if the suit is dismissed with prejudice, the interruption of prescription is immaterial because of res judicata. If the action is successful, the interruption of prescription has produced its effect: the plaintiff's right is recognized by the judgment in his favor. However, if an interruption results and the action is dismissed without prejudice, the period during which the action was pending does not count toward the accrual of prescription. The plaintiff then has the full prescriptive period within which to bring a new action. See Hebert v. Cournoyer Oldsmobile-Cadillac-G.M.C., Inc., 405 So.2d 359 (La.App. 4th Cir. 1981).

(c) An interruption of prescription resulting from the service of process in an action filed in an incompetent court or in an improper venue continues as long as the suit is pending. But if the action is brought before an incompetent court and process is served after the accrual of the prescription, prescription is neither interrupted nor suspended. Hazel v. Allstate Insurance Company, 240 So.2d 431 (La.App. 3rd Cir. 1970).

(d) For the definition of "abandonment of suit," see C.C.P. Article 561.

(e) For the definition of "failure to prosecute", as distinguished from "abandonment", see McCallon v. Travelers Ins. Co., 302 So.2d 676 (La.App. 3rd Cir. 1974).

(f) Issues of interruption of prescription are determined as of the time of filing of the suit sought to be dismissed, not as of the time of filing the exception based upon prescription. Article 3519 of the Louisiana Civil Code of 1870 has been held to apply prospectively to suits filed after a plaintiff abandons, voluntarily dismisses, or fails to prosecute his demand. Levy v. Stelly, 277 So.2d 194 (La.App. 4th Cir. 1973).

Art. 3464. Interruption by acknowledgment

Prescription is interrupted when one acknowledges the right of the person against whom he had commenced to prescribe.

Acts 1982, No. 187, § 1, eff. Jan. 1, 1983.

REVISION COMMENTS—1982

(a) This provision reproduces the substance of Article 3520 of the Louisiana Civil Code of 1870. It does not change the law.

(b) Acquisitive prescription is interrupted when the possessor acknowledges the right of the owner; liberative prescription is interrupted when the debtor acknowledges the right of the creditor; and prescription of nonuse is interrupted when the owner of an estate burdened with a servitude or other real right acknowledges the servitude or other real right.

(c) According to civilian tradition, an acknowledgement may be formal or informal, express or tacit. See 3 Planiol et Ripert, Traité pratique de droit civil français 732 (2d ed. Picard 1952). However, as in the case of a renunciation of prescription, an acknowledgement may be made only by a person who has capacity to alienate. Ibid. See also Blum, Interruption of Prescription by Acknowledgment in Louisiana, 14 Tul.L.Rev. 430 (1940).

(d) Article 54 of the Mineral Code declares that an acknowledgment "must be in writing, and, to affect third parties, must be filed for registry." Moreover, Article 55 of the same Code declares that "an acknowledgment must express the intent of the landowner to interrupt prescription and clearly identify the party making it and the mineral servitude or servitudes acknowledged." These provisions are applicable specifically to the interruption of the prescription of nonuse running against mineral servitudes and other mineral rights.

(e) Louisiana jurisprudence is settled that an acknowledgment interrupting liberative prescription may be oral or written, formal or informal, and express or tacit. See Lake Providence Equipment Co. v. Tallulah Production Credit Ass'n, 257 La. 104, 241 So.2d 506 (1970). For an excellent doctrinal discussion of this subject, see Flowers v. United States Fidelity and Guaranty Company, 381 So.2d 378 (La. 1980). Likewise, an acknowledgment interrupting acquisitive prescription may be oral or written, formal or informal, and express or tacit. See W.J. Gayle & Sons v. Deperrodil, 300 So.2d 599 (La.App. 3rd Cir. 1974) and cases cited; Harris v. Mount Zion Baptist Church, 198 So. 780 (La.App. Orl. Cir. 1940). Louisiana courts at one time were in accord that an acknowledgment that interrupts the prescription of nonuse could be express or tacit, written or oral, and formal or informal. See Gillis & Co. v. Nelson and Donalson, 16 La.Ann. 27 (1861); Baker v. Pena,

20 La.Ann. 52 (1868). However, in Goldsmith v. McCoy, 190 La. 320, 182 So. 519 (1938), a case involving an interruption of a mineral servitude, the court declared that only the prescription of nonuse running against continuous and apparent servitudes could be interrupted by tacit or informal acknowledgment. The acknowledgment for the interruption of discontinuous servitudes or continuous nonapparent servitudes must be written and, in order to affect third persons, it must be filed for registry. Insofar as predial servitudes are concerned, these declarations are dicta that have been overruled legislatively by Article 3464. This insures a return to traditional concepts and accords with the spirit of the new legislation governing predial servitudes.

(f) When interrupted by an acknowledgment, prescription commences to run anew. Depending on the type of acknowledgment, the new prescriptive period may be the same as or longer than before. See Blum, Interruption of Prescription by Acknowledgment in Louisiana, 14 Tul.L.Rev. 430 (1940).

(g) R.S. 9:5807 covers the interruption of prescription on pledged obligations and is not affected by this revision.

Art. 3465. Interruption of acquisitive prescription

Acquisitive prescription is interrupted when possession is lost.

The interruption is considered never to have occurred if the possessor recovers possession within one year or if he recovers possession later by virtue of an action brought within the year.

Acts 1982, No. 187, § 1, eff. Jan. 1, 1983.

REVISION COMMENTS—1982

(a) This provision is new. It is based in part on Article 3517 of the Louisiana Civil Code of 1870 and on Articles 3433 and 3434 of this revision. It does not change the law.

(b) Article 3517 of the Louisiana Civil Code of 1870 contemplates deprivation of possession, that is, eviction by the owner or by a third person. However, there should be no doubt that acquisitive prescription is also interrupted when the possessor abandons his possession. Accordingly, Article 3465 is conceived in broader terms and utilizes the concept of the loss of the right to possess, which is established in the part of the revision that deals with possession.

(c) When a possessor abandons possession or is evicted by another before he has acquired the right to possess, acquisitive prescription is interrupted upon the loss of possession.

(d) The prescription of nonuse of real rights is interrupted by the exercise of the right according to its nature.

Art. 3466. Effect of interruption

If prescription is interrupted, the time that has run is not counted. Prescription commences to run anew from the last day of interruption.

Acts 1982, No. 187, § 1, eff. Jan. 1, 1983.

REVISION COMMENTS—1982

(a) This provision is new. It is based on Article 270 of the Greek Civil Code. It does not change the law.

(b) According to well settled Louisiana jurisprudence, when prescription is interrupted, the time that has run is wiped out, and prescription commences to run anew from the date of interruption. See Blum, Interruption of Prescription by Acknowledgment in Louisiana, 14 Tul.L.Rev. 430 (1940).

(c) Article 270 of the Greek Civil Code declares: "When prescription is interrupted, the time that has run is not counted, and, from the end of the interruption, a new prescription commences to run."

PRESCRIPTION

SECTION 2—SUSPENSION OF PRESCRIPTION

Art. 3467. Persons against whom prescription runs

Prescription runs against all persons unless exception is established by legislation.
Acts 1982, No. 187, § 1, eff. Jan. 1, 1983.

REVISION COMMENTS—1982

(a) This provision reproduces the substance of Article 3521 of the Louisiana Civil Code of 1870. It does not change the law.

(b) Pertinent legislative exceptions may be found in R.S. 9:5802, 9:5803, 9:5804, and 9:5685. These provisions are not affected by this revision. See La. Const. Art. 12, § 13 (1974) and La. Const. Art. 9, § 4(b) for applicable constitutional provisions.

(c) Provisions relating to the suspension of prescription on account of an obstacle may be found in Civil Code Articles 755 and 756, as revised by Acts 1977, No. 514, and in Article 59 of the Mineral Code.

(d) Despite the clear language of Article 3521 of the Louisiana Civil Code of 1870, courts have, in exceptional circumstances, resorted to the maxim contra non valentem non currit praescriptio. See Corsey v. State Dept. of Corrections, 375 So.2d 1319 (La. 1979). This jurisprudence continues to be relevant.

Art. 3468. Incompetents

Prescription runs against absent persons and incompetents, including minors and interdicts, unless exception is established by legislation.

Acts 1982, No. 187, § 1, eff. Jan. 1, 1983. Amended by Acts 1983, No. 173, § 3, eff. Jan. 1, 1984; Acts 1991, No. 107, § 1.

COMMENTS—1983 AMENDMENT

(a) This Article is new. It establishes the principle that prescription runs against absentees and incompetents, including minors and interdicts, unless exception is established by legislation.

(b) Article 3468 of the Louisiana Civil Code, as revised in 1982, followed prior law in declaring that prescription was suspended in favor of minors and interdicts, unless exception was established by legislation. In reality, exceptions had swallowed that rule. According to former Civil Code Article 3541 (1870), the liberative prescriptions of one, three, five, and thirty years ran against minors and interdicts. Aside from the liberative prescriptions of five years provided by C.C. Art. 3542 (1870) (Art. 3497 in this revision), which were specially suspended in favor of minors alone, only the liberative prescription of ten years was actually suspended in favor of minors and interdicts.

Similarly, special legislation provided that the prescription of nonuse of predial servitudes (C.C. Art. 763 (rev.1977)), and of mineral servitudes, (Mineral Code Article 58, R.S. 9:5805), ran against minors and interdicts, so that only the prescription of nonuse of personal servitudes was actually suspended in favor of minors and interdicts.

Likewise, the acquisitive prescriptions of immovables, ten and thirty years, ran against absentees, minors, and interdicts, (C.C. Arts. 3474 (rev. 1982) and 3541 (1870)) so that only the acquisitive prescription of movables, three and ten years, were actually suspended in favor of minors and interdicts.

(c) As a result of this revision, the following prescriptions which did not previously do so now run against minors and interdicts: (1) the ten year liberative prescription; (2) the prescription of nonuse of personal servitudes; and (3) the acquisitive prescriptions of movables, three and ten years. All other prescriptions, also run against minors, interdicts, and absentees unless an exception is established by legislation.

REVISION COMMENTS—1982

(a) This provision reproduces the substance of Article 3522 of the Louisiana Civil Code of 1870. It does not change the law. Thus, as a general rule, prescription does not run against minors and interdicts unless exception is established by legislation.

(b) In quite a few instances prescription runs against minors and interdicts. The liberative prescription of five years runs against minors and interdicts. R.C.C. (1870) Article 3540. The one and three years liberative prescriptions run against minors and interdicts. R.C.C. (1870) Articles 3534–3539. The thirty years liberative or acquisitive prescription runs against minors and interdicts. R.C.C. (1870) Article 3541. The prescription of nonuse of predial servitudes runs against minors and interdicts. C.C. (1977) Finally, the prescription of nonuse of mineral servitudes runs against minors and interdicts. Mineral Code Article 58; R.S. 9:5805. The ten year acquisitive prescription established in Article 3475, this revision, runs against minors and interdicts.

It seems that the only remaining general prescription that is suspended on account of minority or interdiction is the liberative prescription of ten years established in Article 3544 of the Civil Code of 1870. There are, however, additional provisions in the Civil Code and in the Revised Statutes that may be interpreted to suspend prescription as to minors and interdicts by application of Article 3468 of this revision.

Art. 3469. Suspension of prescription

Prescription is suspended as between: the spouses during marriage, parents and children during minority, tutors and minors during tutorship, and curators and interdicts during interdiction, and caretakers and minors during minority.

A "caretaker" means a person legally obligated to provide or secure adequate care for a child, including a tutor, guardian, or legal custodian.

Acts 1982, No. 187, § 1, eff. Jan. 1, 1983. Amended by Acts 1988, No. 676, § 1.

REVISION COMMENTS—1982

(a) This provision is new. It is based in part on Article 3523 of the Louisiana Civil Code of 1870 and on Article 256 of the Greek Civil Code. It clarifies the law as it suspends prescription between parents and children during minority, between tutors and minors during tutorship, and between curators and interdicts during interdiction.

(b) Insofar as minors and interdicts are concerned, Article 3469 establishes a specific application of the principal adopted in Article 3468.

(c) The suspension of prescription is effective only as between spouses, parents and children, tutors and minors, and curators and interdicts. There is no suspension of prescription vis-a-vis third persons. Thus liberative prescription, acquisitive prescription, and prescription of nonuse may accrue in favor of a third person to the prejudice of a spouse, a minor, or an interdict.

Art. 3470. Prescription during delays for inventory; vacant succession

Prescription runs during the delay the law grants to a successor for making an inventory and for deliberating. Nevertheless, it does not run against a beneficiary successor with respect to his rights against the succession.

Prescription runs against a vacant succession even if an administrator has not been appointed.

Acts 1982, No. 187, § 1, eff. Jan. 1, 1983.

REVISION COMMENTS—1982

(a) This provision reproduces the substance of Articles 3526 and 3527 of the Louisiana Civil Code of 1870. It does not change the law.

(b) Prescription does not run against a beneficiary successor. However, prescription runs against all other successors, even during the period that the law grants for making an inventory and for deciding whether to accept or to renounce the succession.

(c) Article 3526 of the Louisiana Civil Code of 1870 speaks of the "debt" due to the beneficiary heir by the succession. This provision obviously was meant to apply to all prescriptions. Accordingly, the language has been broadened to include rights and actions rather than "debts" alone.

(d) The definition of "beneficiary successor", is provided in Civil Code Article 879, as revised in 1981.

(e) The definition of "vacant succession", is provided in R.C.C. (1870) Article 1095.

Art. 3471.   Limits of contractual freedom

A juridical act purporting to exclude prescription, to specify a longer period than that established by law, or to make the requirements of prescription more onerous, is null.

Acts 1982, No. 187, § 1, eff. Jan. 1, 1983.

REVISION COMMENTS—1982

(a) This provision is new. It is based on Article 275 of the Greek Civil Code and does not change the law.

(b) According to French doctrine and jurisprudence, parties enjoy contractual freedom to shorten, and, under certain circumstances, to extend, a prescriptive period. See Baudry-Lacantinerie et Tissier, Prescription, 56–66 (an English translation by the Louisiana State Law Institute 1972). In Louisiana, the jurisprudence is well-settled that parties may not extend a period of prescription that is established by law. See E.L. Burns Co. v. Anthony Cashio, 302 So.2d 297 (La.1974); and Nabors Oil & Gas Co. v. Louisiana Oil Refining Co., 151 La.361, 91 So. 765 (1922). For a discussion of the validity of agreements intended to shorten prescriptive periods, see Note, 16 Tul.L.Rev. 625 (1942).

(c) A juridical act is a lawful volitional act intended to have legal consequences. It may be a unilateral act, such as an affidavit, or a bilateral act, such as a contract. It may be onerous or gratuitous. See Yiannopoulos, Civil Law System—Part I, § 77 (Claitor 1977).

(d) For purposes of comparison, Article 275 of the Greek Civil Code may be considered. It reads as follows:

"A juridical act purporting to exclude prescription, or fixing a shorter or longer period than that provided by law, or making the conditions or prescription more or less onerous, is null."

Art. 3472.   Effect of suspension

The period of suspension is not counted toward accrual of prescription. Prescription commences to run again upon the termination of the period of suspension.

Acts 1982, No. 187, § 1, eff. Jan. 1, 1983.

REVISION COMMENTS—1982

(a) This provision is new. It is based on civilian tradition and on principles inherent in the Louisiana Civil Code. It does not change the law.

(b) For purposes of comparison, Article 257 of the Greek Civil Code may be considered. It reads:

"The period of suspension is not counted as a part of the period of prescription. After the end of suspension, prescription continues to run but does not accrue in less than six months."

CHAPTER 3—ACQUISITIVE PRESCRIPTION

SECTION 1—IMMOVABLES: PRESCRIPTION OF TEN YEARS IN GOOD FAITH AND UNDER JUST TITLE

Art. 3473.   Prescription of ten years

Ownership and other real rights in immovables may be acquired by the prescription of ten years.

844

Acts 1982, No. 187, § 1, eff. Jan. 1, 1983.

REVISION COMMENTS—1982

(a) This provision reproduces the substance of Articles 3474 and 3478, first sentence, of the Louisiana Civil Code of 1870. It does not change the law.

(b) Articles 3472 and 3473 of the Louisiana Civil Code of 1870 are essentially didactic. For this reason, they have not been reproduced. The provisions of R.C.C. (1870) Articles 3475 and 3476 are dealt with, respectively, under the headings: "Immovables; Prescription of Twenty Years" and "Movables; Prescription of Three Years and Ten Years", infra.

Art. 3474. Incompetents

This prescription runs against absent persons and incompetents, including minors and interdicts.

Acts 1982, No. 187, § 1, eff. Jan. 1, 1983. Amended by Acts 1991, No. 107, § 1.

REVISION COMMENTS—1982

(a) This provision is based on the second sentence of Article 3478 of the Louisiana Civil Code of 1870. It changes the law.

(b) Under Article 3478 of the Louisiana Civil Code of 1870, the acquisitive prescription of ten years ran against all incompetents. However, as to certain minors, this prescription accrued one year from the date of majority. In effect, there was an extension of the period of prescription in favor of certain minors in cases in which the adverse possessor began to possess the property during the owner's minority. This exception did not apply if the adverse possessor began to possess against a person from whom the minor inherited the property.

Article 3474 suppresses this exception. Minors should occupy the same position as other incompetents. Accordingly, prescription runs against all incompetents, and the prescriptive period is not extended in favor of any minors.

Art. 3475. Requisites

The requisites for the acquisitive prescription of ten years are: possession of ten years, good faith, just title, and a thing susceptible of acquisition by prescription.

Acts 1982, No. 187, § 1, eff. Jan. 1, 1983.

REVISION COMMENT—1982

This provision reproduces the substance of Article 3479 of the Louisiana Civil Code of 1870. It does not change the law.

Art. 3476. Attributes of possession

The possessor must have corporeal possession, or civil possession preceded by corporeal possession, to acquire a thing by prescription.

The possession must be continuous, uninterrupted, peaceable, public, and unequivocal.

Acts 1982, No. 187, § 1, eff. Jan. 1, 1983.

REVISION COMMENTS—1982

(a) This provision is new. It is based on Article 3487 of the Louisiana Civil Code of 1870. It does not change the law.

(b) "Corporeal possession" is defined in Article 3425, supra. "Civil possession" is defined in Article 3431, supra.

(c) A possession that is discontinuous, interrupted, violent, clandestine, or equivocal is vicious, and has no legal effect. See Articles 3435 and 3436, supra. The requirements that the possession be continuous, uninterrupted, peaceable, public, and unequivocal, restate the rule that, for purposes of acquisitive prescription, the possession must be free of vice.

(d) A possessor is presumed to possess as owner. See Article 3427, supra. For this reason, the provisions of Article 3481 of the Louisiana Civil Code of 1870 have not been reproduced in Article 3476 of this revision.

(e) A possessor is one who possesses for himself. The exercise of possession over a thing with the permission of or on behalf of the owner or possessor is precarious possession. See Article 3437, supra. Articles 3477–3479, infra, cover prescription as it relates to precarious possession.

(f) Articles 3441 and 3442, supra cover the tacking of possession. Article 3426, supra, covers constructive possession.

(g) One who possesses under a just title is not a clandestine possessor because his title gives notice to the world of his intention to possess as owner. The language of Article 3487 of the Louisiana Civil Code of 1870 that states "he who possesses by virtue of a title cannot be considered as a clandestine possessor, for his title leads to the supposition that the possession commenced in good faith, and that is sufficient to enable him to plead prescription" has not been reproduced. This language confuses the requirements of good faith and just title and is not needed.

(h) Article 3491 of the Louisiana Civil Code of 1870 has been suppressed. The matter is covered by Articles 3435 and 3436, supra. Article 3492 of the Louisiana Civil Code of 1870 has been suppressed. The matter is covered by Article 3443, supra. C.C. (1870) Articles 3493 through 3496 have been suppressed. The matter is covered by Articles 3441 and 3442, supra. C.C. (1870) Article 3498 has been suppressed. The matter is covered by Article 3426, supra.

Art. 3477. Precarious possessor; inability to prescribe

Acquisitive prescription does not run in favor of a precarious possessor or his universal successor.

Acts 1982, No. 187, § 1, eff. Jan. 1, 1983.

REVISION COMMENTS—1982

(a) This provision reproduces the substance of Article 3510 of the Louisiana Civil Code of 1870. It does not change the law.

(b) Acquisitive prescription does not run in favor of a precarious possessor. A precarious possessor is one who exercises "possession over a thing with the permission or on behalf of the owner or possessor." Article 3437, supra. A precarious possessor, such as a lessee or a depositary, "is presumed to possess for another although he may intend to possess for himself." Article 3438, supra.

(c) A lessee possesses for the lessor, and a depositary possesses for the depositor. A usufructuary possesses the usufruct for himself and the thing for the naked owner; however, and a person having a predial servitude possesses the servitude for himself and the land for the owner. See C.C.P.Art. 3656; Board of Commissioners v. S. D. Hunter Foundation, 354 So.2d 156 (La.1978). A co-owner possesses his undivided share for himself and the immovable both for himself and for his co-owners.

(d) Acquisitive prescription does not run in favor of the universal successor of a precarious possessor. The universal successor of a precarious possessor occupies the same position as his ancestor.

(e) R.C.C. (1870) Article 3556(28) [see, now, C.C. Art. 3506] defines "universal successor".

Art. 3478. Termination of precarious possession; commencement of prescription

A co-owner, or his universal successor, may commence to prescribe when he demonstrates by overt and unambiguous acts sufficient to give notice to his co-owner that he intends to possess the property for himself. The acquisition and recordation of a title from a person other than a co-owner thus may mark the commencement of prescription.

Any other precarious possessor, or his universal successor, may commence to prescribe when he gives actual notice to the person on whose behalf he is possessing that he intends to possess for himself.

Acts 1982, No. 187, § 1, eff. Jan. 1, 1983.

REVISION COMMENTS—1982

(a) This provision is new. It is based in part on Article 3512 of the Louisiana Civil Code of 1870. It does not change the law.

(b) Article 3512 of the Louisiana Civil Code of 1870 indicates that a precarious possessor, or his universal successor, may commence to prescribe when the "cause of their possession is changed by the act of a third person". The example given in the article refers to "a farmer who acquires from another the estate which he rented." Louisiana courts have interpreted this provision expansively and have held that a precarious possessor may change the nature of his possession by his own overt and unambiguous acts that are sufficient to give notice to the owner. See, e.g., Thayer v. Waples, 26 La.Ann. 502 (1874); Succession of Seals, 243 La. 1056, 150 So.2d 13 (1963); Dupuis v. Broadhurst, 213 So.2d 528 (La.App. 3rd Cir. 1968). Article 3478 accords with the jurisprudence.

(c) Article 3515(3) of the Louisiana Civil Code of 1870 declares that an owner in indivision may acquire the entire property by prescription. This can happen when the owner in indivision acquires from a nonowner title to the part of the property that belongs to his co-owners or when he possesses adversely to his co-owners, without title, for thirty years. In either case, courts require overt and unambiguous acts, sufficient to give notice to co-owners. See Dunham v. Nixon, 371 So.2d 1288 (La.App. 3rd Cir. 1979); Hill v. Dees, 188 La. 708, 178 So. 250 (1937); Southern Natural Gas Co. v. Naquin, 167 So.2d 434 (La.App. 1st Cir. 1964). The registration of an adverse title has been held to be sufficient notice to co-owners. Detraz v. Pere, 183 So.2d 401 (La.App. 3rd Cir. 1966); but see John T. Moore P. Co. v. Morgan's Louisiana & T.R. & S.S. Co., 126 La. 840, 53 So. 22 (1910).

Art. 3479. Particular successor of precarious possessor

A particular successor of a precarious possessor who takes possession under an act translative of ownership possesses for himself, and prescription runs in his favor from the commencement of his possession.

Acts 1982, No. 187, § 1, eff. Jan. 1, 1983.

REVISION COMMENTS—1982

(a) This provision is new. It is based on Article 3513 of the Louisiana Civil Code of 1870. It does not change the law.

(b) When a usufructuary, a lessee, or other precarious possessor conveys the thing he possesses to another person, the transferee is not a precarious possessor. He is a person who possesses for himself. Indicatively, in Jordan v. Richards, 114 La.329, 38 So. 206, 208 (1905), one Mrs. Bealle, a usufructuary and owner in indivision of an immovable, had conveyed the whole property to another person. The court declared: "from that moment he and the vendees succeeding him acquired, so far as prescription was concerned, a right of their own, separate and distinct from any which Mrs. Bealle may have had on that subject in respect to the property." See also Allen v. Paggi Bros. Oil Co., 244 So.2d 116 (La.App. 3rd Cir. 1971).

(c) A particular successor of a precarious possessor may not satisfy the requirement of possession for a period of time by tacking the possession of his ancestor to his own. Liles v. Pitts, 145 La. 650, 82 So. 735 (1919). In such a case, the possession of the particular successor is considered to be precarious.

(d) A particular successor under this provision is a person such as "a buyer, donee or legatee", see R.C.C. (1870) Article 3556(28), to whom the precarious possessor conveys the property, rather than his interest, by an act translative of ownership.

Art. 3480. Good faith

For purposes of acquisitive prescription, a possessor is in good faith when he reasonably believes, in light of objective considerations, that he is owner of the thing he possesses.

Acts 1982, No. 187, § 1, eff. Jan. 1, 1983.

REVISION COMMENTS—1982

(a) This provision is based on Article 3451 of the Louisiana Civil Code of 1870. It changes the law.

(b) This definition of good faith is limited to matters of prescription. There is a different definition for matters of accession. See Civil Code Article 487, as revised in 1979. The reasons why two definitions are needed are explained in the comments under Article 487. In short, for purposes of prescription, good faith and just title are separate ideas, whereas for purposes of accession, the two ideas are blended.

(c) Article 3451 of the Louisiana Civil Code of 1870 leaves room for ambiguity as to the nature of good faith. According to certain decisions interpreting this article, good faith is a subjective belief of the possessor that he owns the thing he possesses. However, according to prevailing jurisprudence, good faith is determined in the light of objective considerations. See Comment, The Ten Year Acquisitive Prescription of Immovables; 36 La. L. Rev. 1000 (1976). Article 3480 codifies this jurisprudence. It declares that a possessor is in good faith when he reasonably believes that he is owner of the thing he possesses. The trier of facts thus must ascertain in the light of objective considerations whether a reasonable person in the position of the possessor could believe himself to be the owner.

(d) This provision does not affect the public records doctrine. According to Louisiana jurisprudence, an acquirer of immovable property is not charged with constructive knowledge of the public records, nor is he bound to search the public records in order to ascertain ownership. According to certain decisions, however, an acquirer of immovable property who knows facts sufficient to excite inquiry is bound exceptionally to search the public records and is charged with the knowledge that a reasonable person would acquire from the records. See Comment, Good Faith for Purposes of Acquisitive Prescription in Louisiana and France, 28 La. L. Rev. 662–674 (1968). The crucial consideration is whether the presumption of good faith has been rebutted; thus the matter should be decided under Article 3481, infra.

Art. 3481. Presumption of good faith

Good faith is presumed. Neither error of fact nor error of law defeats this presumption. This presumption is rebutted on proof that the possessor knows, or should know, that he is not owner of the thing he possesses.

Acts 1982, No. 187, § 1, eff. Jan. 1, 1983.

REVISION COMMENTS—1982

(a) The first sentence of this provision reproduces the substance of Article 3481 of the Louisiana Civil Code of 1870. It does not change the law. The second sentence abrogates Article 1846(3) of the Louisiana Civil Code of 1870 and changes the law. The third sentence is based on Article 3452 of the Louisiana Civil Code of 1870 and on pertinent jurisprudence. It does not change the law.

(b) Good faith is presumed. Thus, one who alleges that the possessor is not in good faith has the burden of proving his allegation.

(c) Neither error of fact nor error of law defeats the presumption of good faith. It has long been settled in Louisiana that an error of fact does not defeat good faith. However, according to Louisiana jurisprudence interpreting Article 1846(3) of the Louisiana Civil Code of 1870, an error of law defeats good faith. In such a case, the acquirer of the immovable is said to be in legal bad faith. See Martin v. Schwing Lumber and Shingle Co., 228 La. 175, 81 So.2d 852 (1955). Article 3481 abrogates Article 1846(3) and overrules legislatively the doctrine of legal bad faith.

(d) The presumption of good faith is rebutted on proof that the possessor knows, or should know, that he is not owner of the thing he possesses. According to Article 3480, supra, good faith is determined in the light of objective considerations. Correspondingly, bad faith is determined in the light of similar considerations. Thus, the presumption of good faith is rebutted on proof that a reasonable person in the position of the possessor should know that he is not owner of the property.

(e) According to Louisiana jurisprudence, an acquirer of immovable property is not bound to search the public records unless he knows facts sufficient to excite inquiry. See Attaway v. Culpepper,

386 So.2d 674 (La.App. 3rd Cir. 1980). In such a case, the acquirer is charged with the knowledge that a reasonable person would acquire from the public records, and the presumption of good faith may be rebutted. The same is true when an acquirer voluntarily undertakes to search the public records: he also is charged with the knowledge that a reasonable person would acquire from the public records, and the presumption of good faith may be rebutted. See Comment, Good Faith for Purposes of Acquisitive Prescription in Louisiana and France, 28 La. L. Rev. 662–674 (1968).

Art. 3482. Good faith at commencement of prescription

It is sufficient that possession has commenced in good faith; subsequent bad faith does not prevent the accrual of prescription of ten years.

Acts 1982, No. 187, § 1, eff. Jan. 1, 1983.

REVISION COMMENTS—1982

(a) This provision reproduces the substance of Article 3482 of the Louisiana Civil Code of 1870. It does not change the law.

(b) In civil law systems mala fides superveniens non nocet. Good faith is material at the time possession commences. If the possessor subsequently learns that he is not owner of the thing he possesses, his bad faith does not prevent accrual of the prescription of ten years.

Art. 3483. Just title

A just title is a juridical act, such as a sale, exchange, or donation, sufficient to transfer ownership or another real right. The act must be written, valid in form, and filed for registry in the conveyance records of the parish in which the immovable is situated.

Acts 1982, No. 187, § 1, eff. Jan. 1, 1983.

REVISION COMMENTS—1982

(a) This provision is new. It is based on Articles 3483, 3484, 3485, and 3486 of the Louisiana Civil Code of 1870. It changes the law as it requires that the title be written and recorded.

(b) A just title is a juridical act, that is, a licit act intended to have legal consequences. Moreover, it is an act translative of ownership or of another real right, such as a sale, donation, or exchange. A just title need not be derived from the true owner because if that were the case, prescription would have no place. The law merely requires an act which, if it had been executed by the true owner, would have conveyed ownership or established another real right. Neither a lease nor a loan constitutes a just title: these juridical acts do not transfer the ownership of a thing. Likewise, neither an act of partition nor a judgment constitutes a just title. These acts are declarative rather than translative of rights.

A universal successor has no title of his own. He continues the possession of the deceased who transmitted to him the title that the deceased had. A universal successor thus possesses as a purchaser or donee, depending on the nature of the title by which the deceased had acquired the property. See 1(2) Planiol, Traité élémentaire de droit civil, 578–580 (An English translation by the Louisiana State Law Institute 1959).

(c) The act must be written. Under the Louisiana Civil Code of 1870, immovable property may be conveyed by oral agreement, and it would seem that such an agreement could be a just title. However, Article 3483 changes the law in this respect. For purposes of acquisition of immovable property by the prescription of ten years, the title must be written.

Further, the act must be valid in form. This requirement applies only in situations in which the law requires the observance of certain formalities. For example, one who possesses an immovable under a purported donation, made by an act under private signature, does not have a just title for purposes of acquiring the immovable by the acquisitive prescription of ten years.

According to French doctrine and jurisprudence, an absolutely null juridical act does not constitute a just title. See 1(2) Planiol, Traité élémentaire de droit civil, 578–580 (An English translation by the Louisiana State Law Institute 1959). This view has been followed by Louisiana courts. See, e.g., Lloyd v. Register, 184 So.2d 279 (La.App. 1st Cir. 1966); Wilkie v. Cox, 222 So.2d 85

(La.App. 3rd Cir. 1969). Thus, only a juridical act that is relatively null may be a just title. In this respect, it should be noted that Article 2452 of the Louisiana Civil Code of 1870 establishes a relative nullity rather than an absolute nullity.

(d) The act must be filed for registry in the conveyance records of the parish in which the immovable is situated. There is no requirement of registration under the Louisiana Civil Code of 1870. Article 3483 changes the law in the interest of certainty of ownership. Prescription commences to run from the date of filing for registry rather than from the date of entry into possession.

(e) The act must be certain and proved. These are obvious requirements. For this reason, the provisions of Article 3486(2) and (3) of the Louisiana Civil Code of 1870 have not been reproduced. A putative title, that is, one which is believed to exist but which in reality does not exist, is not a just title.

(f) One who possesses under a just title, whether as a universal or particular successor of another, may add his author's possession to that of his own. Articles 3441 and 3442, supra, cover the tacking of possession. Tacking of possession presupposes a juridical link. This link may be established by universal succession or by particular succession. For the definitions of universal succession and particular succession, see R.C.C. (1870) Article 3556(28). Despite the nonexistence of a juridical link, tacking is permitted within the limits of Civil Code Article 794, as revised in 1977.

An "author" is the person from whom the possessor has derived his right. This word has the same meaning as "ancestor in title." The possessor may have acquired the right from the author by universal or by particular title, onerous or gratuitous. The possession of the heir may be tacked to that of the deceased, and the possession of the buyer to that of the seller.

(g) When a person has a just title and his possession conforms to it, he is presumed to possess according to the title and to the full extent of its limits. See Article 3426, supra. Constructive possession applies to both the ten and the thirty years prescription. Thus, one who possesses by virtue of a just title but in bad faith possesses within the limits of his title. In contrast, one who possesses without title must prove possession within enclosures or inch by inch possession.

Art. 3484.   Transfer of undivided part of an immovable

A just title to an undivided interest in an immovable is such only as to the interest transferred.

Acts 1982, No. 187, § 1, eff. Jan. 1, 1983.

REVISION COMMENTS—1982

(a) This provision is new. It clarifies the law.

(b) When a co-owner of an immovable transfers the ownership of the entire immovable to a third person, the transferee acquires the undivided interest of the transferor, and in addition, he acquires a just title to the remaining parts. Thus, the transferee acquires the ownership of the entire immovable in ten years if he is in good faith and if his possession is sufficiently adverse to the interests of the remaining co-owners. See Succession of Seals, 243 La. 1056, 150 So.2d 13 (1963); Tremont Lumber Co. v. Powers & Critchett Lumber Co., 173 La. 937, 139 So. 12 (1931); Dupuis v. Broadhurst, 213 So.2d 528 (La.App. 3rd Cir. 1968). If the transferee is in bad faith, he cannot acquire the ownership of the entire immovable in ten years. See Martin v. Schwing Lumber and Shingle Co., 228 La. 175, 81 So.2d 852 (1955).

(c) When a co-owner of an immovable transfers only his undivided part to a third person, the transferee acquires only the part of transferor. In such a case, the transferee does not have a just title to the entire immovable. Thus, even if he possesses the entire immovable adversely to the remaining co-owners, he cannot acquire the ownership of the entire immovable by the prescription of ten years.

(d) When a nonowner transfers to another person an undivided part of an immovable, the transferee acquires a just title to the part transferred. Article 3484 declares that a juridical act transferring an undivided part of an immovable is a just title only as to the part transferred. It should be clear that the transferee does not have just title to the entire immovable and that he cannot acquire the ownership of the entire immovable by the prescription of ten years regardless of the adversity of his possession or of his good faith, or both.

However, the transferee of an undivided part may acquire that part by the prescription of ten years if he is in good faith and if he has exercised possession either by himself or by virtue of the possession of his co-owners. Of course, such a possession must be sufficiently adverse to the interests of the owner of the share. In Bel v. Manuel, 234 La. 135, 99 So.2d 58 (1958), nonowners transferred an undivided part to another person who took possession of the entire immovable. The court held that the transferee could acquire nothing by the prescription of ten years on the ground that he was in legal bad faith. Language in the decision indicates that the transferee of an undivided interest is in legal bad faith as to the interest transferred and as to the interest not transferred. The decision is overruled legislatively by Article 3484.

(e) Successive transfers of undivided parts may constitute a just title as to the whole of an immovable. Cf. Land Development Company v. Schulz, 169 La. 1, 124 So. 125 (1929).

Art. 3485.   Things susceptible of prescription

All private things are susceptible of prescription unless prescription is excluded by legislation.

Acts 1982, No. 187, § 1, eff. Jan. 1, 1983.

REVISION COMMENTS—1982

(a) This provision is based on Article 3497 of the Louisiana Civil Code of 1870. It does not change the law.

(b) Common things and public things are insusceptible of acquisitive prescription. See Civil Code Articles 449 and 450, as revised by Acts 1978, No. 728.

(c) All private things are susceptible of prescription unless the prescription is excluded by provision of law. See e.g., La. Const.Art. 9, § 4; id. Art. 12, § 13 (1974); R.S. 9:5804.

SECTION 2—IMMOVABLES: PRESCRIPTION
OF THIRTY YEARS

Art. 3486.   Immovables; prescription of thirty years

Ownership and other real rights in immovables may be acquired by the prescription of thirty years without the need of just title or possession in good faith.

Acts 1982, No. 187, § 1, eff. Jan. 1, 1983.

REVISION COMMENTS—1982

(a) This provision reproduces the substance of Article 3499 of the Louisiana Civil Code of 1870. It does not change the law.

(b) The provisions of Articles 3500, 3501, and 3502 have not been reproduced. The attributes of possession for the prescription of thirty years are the same as those set forth in Article 3476, supra.

Art. 3487.   Restriction as to extent of possession

For purposes of acquisitive prescription without title, possession extends only to that which has been actually possessed.

Acts 1982, No. 187, § 1, eff. Jan. 1, 1983.

REVISION COMMENTS—1982

(a) This provision reproduces the substance of Article 3503 of the Louisiana Civil Code of 1870. It does not change the law.

(b) The notion of constructive possession is inapplicable in the absence of title. See Article 3426, supra.

(c) Actual possession is determined according to the nature of the property. See Yiannopoulos, Civil Law Property, § 212 (2d ed. 1980); Chamberlain v. Abadie, 48 La.Ann. 587, 19 So. 574 (1896); Tremont Lumber Co. v. Powers & Critchett Lumber Co., 173 La. 937, 139 So. 12 (1931).

Art. 3488. Applicability of rules governing prescription of ten years

The rules governing acquisitive prescription of ten years apply to the prescription of thirty years to the extent that their application is compatible with the prescription of thirty years.

Acts 1982, No. 187, § 1, eff. Jan. 1, 1983.

REVISION COMMENTS—1982

(a) This provision is based on Article 3505 of the Louisiana Civil Code of 1870. It does not change the law.

(b) The notion of constructive possession applies to the acquisitive prescription of thirty years. See Article 3426, supra.

SECTION 3—MOVABLES: ACQUISITIVE PRESCRIPTION OF THREE YEARS OR TEN YEARS

Art. 3489. Movables; acquisitive prescription

Ownership and other real rights in movables may be acquired either by the prescription of three years or by the prescription of ten years.

Acts 1982, No. 187, § 1, eff. Jan. 1, 1983.

REVISION COMMENT—1982

This provision is new. It is based on Articles 3476, 3505, and 3509 of the Louisiana Civil Code of 1870. It does not change the law.

Art. 3490. Prescription of three years

One who has possessed a movable as owner, in good faith, under an act sufficient to transfer ownership, and without interruption for three years, acquires ownership by prescription.

Acts 1982, No. 187, § 1, eff. Jan. 1, 1983.

REVISION COMMENTS—1982

(a) This provision reproduces the substance of Article 3506 of the Louisiana Civil Code of 1870. It changes the law.

(b) As to movables, the requirement of a just title is easily satisfied. There is no requirement that the title be written or recorded.

Art. 3491. Prescription of ten years

One who has possessed a movable as owner for ten years acquires ownership by prescription. Neither title nor good faith is required for this prescription.

Acts 1982, No. 187, § 1, eff. Jan. 1, 1983.

REVISION COMMENT—1982

This provision reproduces the substance of Article 3509 of the Louisiana Civil Code of 1870. It does not change the law.

CHAPTER 4—LIBERATIVE PRESCRIPTION

SECTION 1—ONE YEAR PRESCRIPTION

Art. 3492. Delictual actions

Delictual actions are subject to a liberative prescription of one year. This prescription commences to run from the day injury or damage is sustained. It does not run against minors or interdicts in actions involving permanent disability and brought pursuant to the Louisiana Products Liability Act or state law governing product liability actions in effect at the time of the injury or damage.

Acts 1983, No. 173, § 1, eff. Jan. 1, 1984. Amended by Acts 1992, No. 621, § 1.

REVISION COMMENTS—1983

(a) The first sentence of this Article reproduces the substance of Article 3536(1), and the second sentence that of Article 3537(2), of the Louisiana Civil Code of 1870. This Article does not change the law. Louisiana jurisprudence interpreting the source provisions continues to be relevant.

(b) The one year prescription applies to all delictual actions. Article 3536(1) of the Louisiana Civil Code of 1870 speaks of liability caused by libellous statements, animals, and offenses and quasi-offenses. These are merely examples of delictual actions. This Article expresses the principle embodied in Article 3536(1) of the 1870 Code. The notion of delictual liability includes: intentional misconduct, negligence, abuse of right, and liability without negligence. See F. Stone, Louisiana Tort Doctrine, § 229 (1977); Langlois v. Allied Chemical Corp., 258 La. 1067, 249 So.2d 133 (1971); Hero Lands Co. v. Texaco, Inc., 310 So.2d 93 (La.1975).

(c) The second paragraph of Article 3536 of the Louisiana Civil Code of 1870 has not been reproduced in this revision. The matter is covered by Article 3658 of the Louisiana Code of Civil Procedure.

(d) This Article is sufficiently broad to cover delictual actions arising from nondelivery, misdelivery, or short delivery of merchandise shipped under a contract of carriage. Accordingly, the third and fourth paragraphs of Article 3536 of the Louisiana Civil Code of 1870 have not been reproduced in this revision.

Art. 3493. Damage to immovable property; commencement and accrual of prescription

When damage is caused to immovable property, the one year prescription commences to run from the day the owner of the immovable acquired, or should have acquired, knowledge of the damage.

Acts 1983, No. 173, § 1, eff. Jan. 1, 1984.

REVISION COMMENTS—1983

(a) This Article is based on Article 3537(3) of the Louisiana Civil Code of 1870. It does not change the law.

(b) When damage is caused to immovable property, the one year prescription that is applicable to a delictual action commences to run from the day the owner of the immovable acquired, or should have acquired, knowledge of the damage. Dean v. Hercules, Inc., 328 So.2d 69 (La.1976).

(c) Louisiana decisions draw a distinction between damages caused by continuous, and those caused by discontinuous, operating causes. When the operating cause of the injury is continuous, giving rise to successive damages, prescription begins to run from the day the damage was completed and the owner acquired, or should have acquired, knowledge of the damage. See South Central Bell Telephone Co. v. Texaco, 418 So.2d 531 (La.1982), and cases cited therein. When the operating cause of the injury is discontinuous, there is a multiplicity of causes of action and of corresponding prescriptive periods. Prescription is completed as to each injury, and the corresponding action is barred, upon the passage of one year from the day the owner acquired, or should have acquired, knowledge of the damage. See A.N. Yiannopoulos, Predial Servitudes, § 63 (1982).

(d) The second paragraph of Article 3537 of the Louisiana Civil Code of 1870 has not been reproduced in this revision. There is no reason to provide a special rule for merchandise shipped under a contract of carriage. The matter is covered by the second sentence of revised Art. 3492 (1983), supra.

Art. 3493.1. [Blank]

SECTION 1–A—TWO YEAR PRESCRIPTION

Art. 3493.10.   Delictual actions; two-year prescription; criminal act

Delictual actions which arise due to damages sustained as a result of an act defined as a crime of violence under Chapter 1 of Title 14 of the Louisiana Revised Statutes of 1950 are subject to a liberative prescription of two years. This prescription commences to run from the day injury or damage is sustained.

Added by Acts 1999, No. 832, § 1.

SECTION 2—THREE YEAR PRESCRIPTION

Art. 3494.   Actions subject to a three-year prescription

The following actions are subject to a liberative prescription of three years:

(1) An action for the recovery of compensation for services rendered, including payment of salaries, wages, commissions, tuition fees, professional fees, fees and emoluments of public officials, freight, passage, money, lodging, and board;

(2) An action for arrearages of rent and annuities;

(3) An action on money lent;

(4) An action on an open account; and

(5) An action to recover underpayments or overpayments of royalties from the production of minerals, provided that nothing herein applies to any payments, rent, or royalties derived from state-owned properties.

Acts 1983, No. 173, § 1, eff. Jan. 1, 1984. Amended by Acts 1984, No. 147, § 1, eff. June 25, 1984; Acts 1986, No. 1031, § 1.

REVISION COMMENTS—1983

(a) This Article is based on Articles 3534 and 3538 of the Louisiana Civil Code of 1870. In lieu of liberative prescriptions of one and three years, this article establishes a single prescription of three years. This accords with modern practices.

(b) For actions by or against common carriers, see R.S. 45:1099. That provision is not affected by this revision of Article 3494 of the Civil Code.

Art. 3495.   Commencement and accrual of prescription

This prescription commences to run from the day payment is exigible. It accrues as to past due payments even if there is a continuation of labor, supplies, or other services.

Acts 1983, No. 173, § 1, eff. Jan. 1, 1984.

REVISION COMMENTS—1983

(a) This Article is based on Article 3535 of the Louisiana Civil Code of 1870. It does not change the law.

(b) On principle, liberative prescription commences to run from the day a cause of action arises and its judicial enforcement is possible. See 2 M. Planiol, Traité élémentaire de droit civil 3 Pt. 2, at 358 (Louisiana State Law Institute trans. 1959):

Liberative prescription begins to run as soon as the action accrues, or, as Pothier said "the day on which the creditor could institute his demand." It cannot commence sooner, because the time given for prescription should be a time during which the action can be exercised, and one cannot reproach the creditor for not having acted at a time when he did not have the right to do so. Otherwise, it could happen that the right would be lost before it could be exercised, which would be as unjust as absurd (Cass.Civ., 11 Dec. 1918, D. 1923.1.96, P. and S. 1921.1.161).

Art. 3496.   Action against attorney for return of papers

An action by a client against an attorney for the return of papers delivered to him for purposes of a law suit is subject to a liberative prescription of three years. This prescription commences to run from the rendition of a final judgment in the law suit or the termination of the attorney-client relationship.

Acts 1983, No. 173, § 1, eff. Jan. 1, 1984.

REVISION COMMENT—1983

This Article reproduces the substance of Article 3539 of the Louisiana Civil Code of 1870. It does not change the law.

Art. 3496.1.   Action against a person for abuse of a minor

An action against a person for abuse of a minor is subject to a liberative prescriptive period of three years. This prescription commences to run from the day the minor attains majority, and this prescription, for all purposes, shall be suspended until the minor reaches the age of majority. This prescriptive period shall be subject to any exception of peremption provided by law.

Added by Acts 1988, No. 676, § 1. Amended by Acts 1992, No. 322, § 1.

SECTION 3—FIVE YEAR PRESCRIPTION

Art. 3497.   Actions subject to a five year prescription

The following actions are subject to a liberative prescription of five years:

An action for annulment of a testament;

An action for the reduction of an excessive donation;

An action for the rescission of a partition and warranty of portions; and

An action for damages for the harvesting of timber without the consent of the owner.

This prescription is suspended in favor of minors, during minority.

Acts 1983, No. 173, § 1, eff. Jan. 1, 1984. Amended by Acts 2009, No. 107, § 1.

REVISION COMMENT—1983

This Article reproduces the substance of Article 3542 of the Louisiana Civil Code of 1870. It does not change the law.

Art. 3497.1.   Actions for arrearages of spousal support or of installment payments for contributions made to a spouse's education or training

An action to make executory arrearages of spousal support or installment payments awarded for contributions made by one spouse to the education or training of the other spouse is subject to a liberative prescription of five years.

Added by Acts 1984, No. 147, § 1, eff. June 25, 1984. Amended by Acts 1990, No. 1008, § 3, eff. Jan. 1, 1991; Acts 1997, No. 605, § 1, eff. July 3, 1997.

REVISION COMMENT—1990

This amendment merely adds an additional class of arrearages to those covered by this Article. It is not intended to change the law otherwise.

Art. 3498. Actions on negotiable and nonnegotiable instruments

Actions on instruments, whether negotiable or not, and on promissory notes, whether negotiable or not, are subject to a liberative prescription of five years. This prescription commences to run from the day payment is exigible.

Acts 1983, No. 173, § 1, eff. Jan. 1, 1984. Amended by Acts 1992, No. 1133, § 1, eff. July 1, 1993; Acts 1993, No. 901, § 1, eff. July 1, 1993; Acts 1993, No. 948, § 6, eff. June 25, 1993.

REVISION COMMENT—1983

This Article reproduces the substance of Article 3540 of the Louisiana Civil Code of 1870. It does not change the law.

Art. 3498.1. [Blank]

SECTION 4—TEN YEAR PRESCRIPTION

Art. 3499. Personal action

Unless otherwise provided by legislation, a personal action is subject to a liberative prescription of ten years.

Acts 1983, No. 173, § 1, eff. Jan. 1, 1984.

REVISION COMMENTS—1983

(a) This Article reproduces the substance of Article 3544 of the Louisiana Civil Code of 1870. It does not change the law.

(b) A personal action is subject to a liberative prescription of ten years in the absence of a legislative provision that either establishes a shorter or longer period or declares the action to be imprescriptible. Shorter prescriptive periods are established in revised C.C. Arts. 3492 through 3498 (1983), supra. Longer prescriptive periods are established, for example, in Articles 78 [subsequently repealed], 1030, 1305, 1306, and 2271 of the Louisiana Civil Code of 1870. For an example of an imprescriptible action, see C.C. Art. 1304 (1870) [subsequently repealed].

(c) For a discussion of the distinction between personal actions and real actions, see A.N. Yiannopoulos, Civil Law Property, §§ 171–175 (2d ed. 1980).

Art. 3500. Action against contractors and architects

An action against a contractor or an architect on account of defects of construction, renovation, or repair of buildings and other works is subject to a liberative prescription of ten years.

Acts 1983, No. 173, § 1, eff. Jan. 1, 1984.

REVISION COMMENTS—1983

(a) This Article is based on Article 3545 of the Louisiana Civil Code of 1870. It broadens the scope of the source article by adding the phrases "renovation, or repair" and "other works" and by suppressing the phrase "of brick or stone". It does not change the law because an action against a contractor or an architect on account of defects of construction, renovation, or repair of buildings or other works is a personal action subject to a liberative prescription of ten years.

(b) For rules concerning the commencement of the prescriptive period, see R.S. 9:2772 and 9:4808. Those statutes are not affected by this revision of Article 3500 of the Civil Code.

Art. 3501. Prescription and revival of money judgments

A money judgment rendered by a trial court of this state is prescribed by the lapse of ten years from its signing if no appeal has been taken, or, if an appeal has been taken, it is prescribed by the lapse of ten years from the time the judgment becomes final.

An action to enforce a money judgment rendered by a court of another state or a possession of the United States, or of a foreign country, is barred by the lapse of ten years from its rendition; but such a judgment is not enforceable in this state if it is prescribed, barred by the statute of limitations, or is otherwise unenforceable under the laws of the jurisdiction in which it was rendered.

Any party having an interest in a money judgment may have it revived before it prescribes, as provided in Article 2031 of the Code of Civil Procedure. A judgment so revived is subject to the prescription provided by the first paragraph of this Article. An interested party may have a money judgment rendered by a court of this state revived as often as he may desire.

Acts 1983, No. 173, § 1, eff. Jan. 1, 1984.

REVISION COMMENT—1983

This Article is based on Article 3547 of the Louisiana Civil Code of 1870. It clarifies the law as to the time from which prescription begins to run.

Art. 3501.1. Actions for arrearages of child support

An action to make executory arrearages of child support is subject to a liberative prescription of ten years.

Added by Acts 1997, No. 605, § 1, eff. July 3, 1997.

SECTION 5—THIRTY YEAR PRESCRIPTION

Art. 3502. Action for the recognition of a right of inheritance

An action for the recognition of a right of inheritance and recovery of the whole or a part of a succession is subject to a liberative prescription of thirty years. This prescription commences to run from the day of the opening of the succession.

Acts 1983, No. 173, § 1, eff. Jan. 1, 1984.

REVISION COMMENTS—1983

(a) This Article is based on Article 3548 of the Louisiana Civil Code of 1870. It does not change the law.

(b) The thirty year prescription barring an action for the recognition of a right of inheritance and recovery of the whole or a part of a succession commences to run from the day of the opening of the succession, simultaneously with the prescription provided by C.C. Art. 1030 (1870). When an heir is barred from accepting a succession, he is also barred from bringing an action for the recognition of his right of inheritance and for the recovery of the whole or a part of that succession.

(c) According to well-settled Louisiana legislation, jurisprudence, and doctrine, a petitory action for the recovery of immovable property is imprescriptible. See C.C. Art. 481 (rev. 1979); A.N. Yiannopoulos, Civil Law Property, § 201 (2d ed. 1980).

(d) For the method of determining the day of "opening of the succession", see C.C. Art. 934 (1870).

SECTION 6—INTERRUPTION AND SUSPENSION OF LIBERATIVE PRESCRIPTION

Art. 3503. Solidary obligors

When prescription is interrupted against a solidary obligor, the interruption is effective against all solidary obligors and their successors.

When prescription is interrupted against a successor of a solidary obligor, the interruption is effective against other successors if the obligation is indivisible. If the obligation is divisible, the interruption is effective against other successors only for the portions for which they are bound.

Acts 1983, No. 173, § 1, eff. Jan. 1, 1984.

REVISION COMMENTS—1983

(a) This Article reproduces the substance of Article 3552 of the Louisiana Civil Code of 1870. It accords with Article 2097 of the same Code and does not change the law.

(b) Prescription is interrupted by the filing of suit or service of process in accordance with C.C. Art. 3462 (rev. 1982); or by acknowledgment in accordance with C.C. Art. 3464 (rev. 1982).

(c) For the rule concerning interruption of prescription in favor of solidary obligees see C.C. Art. 2090 (1870).

Art. 3504. Surety

When prescription is interrupted against the principal debtor, the interruption is effective against his surety.

Acts 1983, No. 173, § 1, eff. Jan. 1, 1984.

REVISION COMMENT—1983

This Article reproduces the substance of Article 3553 of the Louisiana Civil Code of 1870. It does not change the law.

SECTION 7—EXTENSION OF LIBERATIVE PRESCRIPTION

Art. 3505. Acts extending liberative prescription

After liberative prescription has commenced to run but before it accrues, an obligor may by juridical act extend the prescriptive period. An obligor may grant successive extensions. The duration of each extension may not exceed one year.

Added by Acts 2013, No. 88, § 1.

REVISION COMMENTS—2013

(a) Under this Article, an obligor may extend the liberative prescriptive period only after a cause of action exists and prescription has begun to run. This approach is consistent with those of a variety of other civil law jurisdictions and international conventions. See, e.g., Cour de Cassation (Comm.), No. 03–21156 (30 Mars 2005); Sophie Stijns et Ilse Samoy, La Prescription Extinctive: Le Rôle de la Volonté; et du Comportement des Parties 355, in Patrice Jourdain et Patrick Wéry, La Prescription Extinctive: Études de Droit Comparé; (2010); Convention on the Limitations Period in the International Sale of Goods Art. 22 (2). Prescription may not be extended before it has begun to run, see C.C. Art. 3471, or after it has accrued. Nonetheless, after prescription has accrued, an obligor may renounce prescription. See, e.g., C.C. Art. 3449.

(b) An extension of prescription may be granted by the obligor only in a juridical act that complies with the form requirements of C.C. Art. 3505.1. See, e.g., Convention on the Limitations Period in the International Sale of Goods Art. 22(2) (allowing modification of the limitations period by means of a "declaration"). For the definition of a juridical act, see C.C. Art. 3471, Comment (c) (Rev. 1982).

(c) An obligor may grant multiple extensions of prescription, each for no more than one year. Although this Article gives priority to individual freedom, that freedom is not absolute. Limitations on the ability to extend prescription are common. See, e.g., Convention on the Limitations Period in the International Sale of Goods Art. 22(2); Civil Code (Fr.)Art. 2254; BGB § 202; Principles of European Contract Law Art. 14:601; Unidroit Principles Art. 10.3. The one-year limitation on each extension is designed to allow parties sufficient time to negotiate and settle a dispute rather than having to file suit to interrupt prescription. At the same time, however, the one-year limitation prevents an obligor from rashly granting an excessively long or indefinite period of extension. A renewable one-year limitation provides an appropriate balance. For commencement of the duration of each extension, see C.C. Art. 3505.2 (Rev. 2013).

(d) As an extension of prescription is explicitly recognized by this Article, it thus not violative of the prohibition in Article 3457, which is designed to prohibit the recognition of the common law doctrine of laches. See C.C. Art. 3457 (Rev. 1982), Comment (b).

Art. 3505.1. Formal requirements

An extension of liberative prescription must be express and in writing.

Added by Acts 2013, No. 88, § 1.

REVISION COMMENTS—2013

(a) The policy behind this Article is not one of public interest but one of evidence. Oral or implied extensions would allow evidentiary debates and unnecessary doubts as to the existence of an agreement. The requirement that an extension be express and in writing exists for proof purposes and is common throughout the Louisiana Civil Code. See, e.g., C.C. Arts. 963 (renunciation of succession rights); 3038 (creation of suretyship); 3450 (renunciation of acquisitive prescription with respect to immovables).

(b) The phrase "in writing" requires the existence of either an authentic act or an act under private signature. See C.C. Arts. 1833 and 1837. Under certain circumstances, an electronic transmission may satisfy the requirement of a writing. See, e.g., R.S. 9:2601 et seq.

Art. 3505.2. Commencement of period of extension

The period of extension commences to run on the date of the juridical act granting it.

Added by Acts 2013, No. 88, § 1.

REVISION COMMENT—2013

This Article specifies the time at which the period of extension commences to run. Successive extensions each restart the period of extension but only from the date of the act granting it.

Art. 3505.3. Effect of extension on other obligors and obligees

An extension of liberative prescription is effective against only the obligor granting it but benefits all joint obligees of an indivisible obligation and all solidary obligees.

An extension of liberative prescription by a principal obligor is effective against his surety. An extension of liberative prescription by a surety is effective only if the principal obligor has also granted it.

Added by Acts 2013, No. 88, § 1.

REVISION COMMENTS—2013

(a) This Article provides that an extension granted by an obligor does not grant an obligee an extension against other solidary or joint obligors. The same is true with respect to joint tortfeasors. Thus, an obligee who obtains an extension from one solidary obligor may, after the original prescriptive period has run, pursue a claim against only the obligor granting the extension. To that extent, the effects of an extension are not analogous to an interruption. Cf. C.C. Arts. 1799, 2324(C), and 3503. Similarly, an obligor who renders performance outside the original prescriptive period but during a period of extension he granted may not recover from his co-obligors who did not concur in the extension, as subrogation will be inoperative. See generally Perkins v. Scaffolding Rental and Erection Service, Inc., 568 So.2d 549 (La. 1990); Cf. C.C. Art. 1804.

(b) Unlike co-obligors, joint obligees of an indivisible obligation and solidary obligees all benefit from an extension granted by an obligor. To that extent, the effect of an extension of liberative prescription is similar to an interruption. See, e.g., C.C. Art. 1793.

(c) The second paragraph of this Article makes an exception to the general rule that extensions of liberative prescription will be effective only against the obligor granting the extension. Because of the nature of the surety arrangement, a special rule is necessary. A principal obligor's extension of prescription is effective against his surety because of the accessory nature of the contract. See, e.g., C.C. Arts. 3035 and 3504. This Article does not, however, preclude the application of Article 3062, which must be read in pari materia with this and other Articles that may serve to modify a principal obligation. This Article also makes clear that for an extension of prescription granted by a surety to be effective, the principal obligor must also grant the extension. Because suretyship is an accessorial obligation, a prescriptive period cannot effectively be extended, even as to the surety who granted the extension, without a similar grant by the principal obligor.

Art. 3505.4. Interruption or suspension during a period of extension

Prescription may be interrupted or suspended during the period of extension.

Added by Acts 2013, No. 88, § 1.

REVISION COMMENTS—2013

(a) Because an extension of prescription is an extension of the original prescriptive period, an interruption may occur or a suspension may exist during a contractually granted extension. See, e.g., Taranto v. Louisiana Citizens Prop. Ins. Corp., 62 So. 3d 721 (La. 2011) (holding that a contractually shortened prescriptive period is a liberative rather than contractual period and thus may be suspended under C.C.P.Art. 596). But see id. at 737 (Victory, J., dissenting); Dixey v. Allstate Ins. Co., 681 F. Supp.2d 740 (E.D. La. 2010).

(b) If an interruption occurs during a period of extension, after the last day of the interruption, only the original prescriptive period commences to run anew, not the extension. If prescription is suspended during a period of extension, after the termination of the period of suspension, the remainder of the period of extension runs again. See, e.g., C.C. Art. 3472.

(c) For the effect of an interruption of prescription, see C.C. Art. 3466. For the effect of a suspension of prescription, see C.C. Art. 3472.

TITLE XXV—OF THE SIGNIFICATION OF SUNDRY TERMS OF LAW EMPLOYED IN THIS CODE

Art. 3506. General definitions of terms

Whenever the terms of law, employed in this Code, have not been particularly defined therein, they shall be understood as follows:

1.   The masculine gender comprehends the two sexes, whenever the provision is not one, which is evidently made for one of them only:

Thus, the word man or men includes women; the word son or sons includes daughters; the words he, his and such like, are applicable to both males and females.

2.   The singular is often employed to designate several persons or things: the heir, for example, means the heirs, where there are more than one.

3.   Abandoned.—In the context of a father or mother abandoning his child, abandonment is presumed when the father or mother has left his child for a period of at least twelve months and the father or mother has failed to provide for the child's care and support, without just cause, thus demonstrating an intention to permanently avoid parental responsibility.

4.   Repealed by Acts 1999, No. 503, § 1.

5.   Assigns.—Assigns means those to whom rights have been transmitted by particular title; such as sale, donation, legacy, transfer or cession.

6, 7. Repealed by Acts 1999, No. 503, § 1.

8.   Children. Under this name are included those persons born of the marriage, those adopted, and those whose filiation to the parent has been established in the manner provided by law, as well as descendants of them in the direct line.

A child born of marriage is a child conceived or born during the marriage of his parents or adopted by them.

A child born outside of marriage is a child conceived and born outside of the marriage of his parents.

9 to 11.   Repealed by Acts 1999, No. 503, § 1.

12.   Family.—Family in a limited sense, signifies father, mother, and children. In a more extensive sense, it comprehends all the individuals who live under the authority of another, and includes the servants of the family.

It is also employed to signify all the relations who descend from a common root.

13 to 22.   Repealed by Acts 1999, No. 503, § 1.

23.   Repealed by Acts 1987, No. 125, § 2, eff. Jan. 1, 1988.

24 to 27.   Repealed by Acts 1999, No. 503, § 1.

28.   Successor.—Successor is, generally speaking, the person who takes the place of another.

There are in law two sorts of successors: the universal successor, such as the heir, the universal legatee, and the general legatee; and the successor by particular title, such as the buyer, donee or legatee of particular things, the transferee.

The universal successor represents the person of the deceased, and succeeds to all his rights and charges.

The particular successor succeeds only to the rights appertaining to the thing which is sold, ceded or bequeathed to him.

29 to 31. Repealed by Acts 1999, No. 503, § 1.

32. Third Persons.—With respect to a contract or judgment, third persons are all who are not parties to it. In case of failure, third persons are, particularly, those creditors of the debtor who contracted with him without knowledge of the rights which he had transferred to another.

Amended by Acts 1979, No. 607, § 1; Acts 1979, No. 711, § 1, eff. Jan. 1, 1980; Acts 1981, No. 919, § 2, eff. Jan. 1, 1982; Acts 1997, No. 1317, § 1, eff. July 15, 1997; Acts 1997, No. 1421, § 2, eff. July 1, 1999; Acts 2004, No. 26, § 1.

COMMENT—1981 AMENDMENT

This provision changes the definition of children which appeared in Article 3556(8) of the Civil Code of 1870. Acts 1979, No. 607 had changed the definition to exclude illegitimate children. This definition includes them, so long as their filiation to the alleged parent is established.

Arts. 3507 to 3514. [Blank]

BOOK IV—CONFLICT OF LAWS

TITLE I—GENERAL PROVISIONS

Art. 3515.   Determination of the applicable law; general and residual rule

Except as otherwise provided in this Book, an issue in a case having contacts with other states is governed by the law of the state whose policies would be most seriously impaired if its law were not applied to that issue.

That state is determined by evaluating the strength and pertinence of the relevant policies of all involved states in the light of: (1) the relationship of each state to the parties and the dispute; and (2) the policies and needs of the interstate and international systems, including the policies of upholding the justified expectations of parties and of minimizing the adverse consequences that might follow from subjecting a party to the law of more than one state.

Acts 1991, No. 923, § 1, eff. Jan. 1, 1992.

REVISION COMMENTS—1991

(a) The residual and general nature of this Article. This Article applies only to cases that fall within the scope of this Book and that are not "otherwise provided [for] in this Book". Thus, this is the residual article. If any other article in this Book is found to be applicable to a particular case or issue, that article prevails. However, Article 3515 also serves as the general article, in the sense that it contains the general principles from which the other articles of this Book have been derived and in light of which they should be applied.

(b) The objective. The first paragraph of this Article enunciates the objective of the choice-of-law process. The objective is to identify "the state whose policies would be most seriously impaired if its law were not applied to that [particular] issue", that is, the state which, in light of its relationship to the parties and the dispute and its policies rendered pertinent by that relationship, would bear the most serious legal, social, economic, and other consequences if its law were not applied to that issue.

The negative phrasing of this objective is deliberate and is intended to disassociate the approach of this Article and of this Book from the so-called "governmental interest analysis" and other modern American approaches that seem to perceive the choice-of-law problem as a problem of interstate competition rather than as a problem of interstate cooperation in conflict avoidance. Because of this negative formulation, the approach of this Book bears some resemblance to the "comparative impairment" approach originally advanced by Professor William F. Baxter and since followed by the courts of California. However, to the extent it is anything more than acoustic, this resemblance is confined to the most basic premise, namely, that the choice-of-law process should strive for ways to minimize impairment of the interests of all involved states, rather than to maximize the interests of one state at the expense of the interests of the other states. See Symeonides, "Problems and Dilemmas in Codifying Choice of Law for Torts: The Louisiana Experience in Comparative Perspective", 38 Am.J.Comp.L. 431, 436–41 (1990).

(c) The process. The second paragraph of this Article prescribes the process or method for achieving the objective enunciated in the first paragraph. The process will begin by identifying, through the resources of statutory interpretation, the various state policies that might be implicated in the conflict. This should include not only the policies embodied in the particular rules of law claimed to be applicable, but also the more general policies, domestic as well as multistate, of each involved state that might be pertinent to the particular issue. The "involved states" include ex hypothesi the forum state, as well as any other state having pertinent contacts with the parties or the dispute.

The next step of the process is to evaluate the "strength and pertinence" of these policies in light of "the relationship of each state to the parties and the dispute", and in light of "the policies and needs of the interstate and international systems". What is to be evaluated is not the wisdom or goodness of a state policy, either in the abstract or vis-a-vis the policy of another state, but rather the "strength and pertinence" of this policy in space. A legislative policy that is strongly espoused by the enacting state for intra-state cases may in fact be attenuated in a particular multistate case that has only minimal contacts with that state. Similarly, the same policy may prove to be far less pertinent if the case has sufficient contacts with that state, but not contacts of the type that would actually implicate that policy.

The evaluation of state policies is to be conducted in light of "the relationship of each state to the parties and the dispute". The relationship with the parties may consist of anything from the formal bond of citizenship or domicile, past or present, to habitual or mere residence. The relationship to the dispute may consist of any factual or legal connection to the events or the transaction giving rise to the dispute or to its subject matter.

Finally, the evaluation of state policies is also to be conducted "in the light of . . . the . . . needs of the interstate and international systems". Obviously, this admonition goes beyond the self-evident requirement of complying with the limits prescribed by the federal Constitution for state choice-of-law decisions. See, e.g., Allstate Insurance Co. v. Hague, 449 U.S. 302 (1981). What might be constitutionally permissible may not necessarily be appropriate from the perspective of choice of law. The court should strive for decisions that not only stay within the limits prescribed by the federal Constitution but also are deferential and sensitive to the needs and policies of the interstate and international systems. Some of these policies, like the policy of discouraging forum shopping or favoring interstate uniformity of result, are so universally acknowledged that they need not be mentioned expressly. Other policies, however, are more susceptible to being overlooked if they are not brought to the attention of the decision-maker. This is why this Article expressly mentions "the policies of upholding the justified expectations of the parties and of minimizing the adverse consequences that might follow from subjecting a party to the law of more than one state."

"[U]pholding the justified expectations of parties" is a self-explanatory policy that is imbedded in the internal law of all states, but it is also an important multistate policy. It is in this latter sense that it is invoked here. All other factors being equal, the parties should not be subjected to the law of a state that they had no reason to anticipate would be applied to their case. In some instances, however, the parties may have had, or should have had, reason to anticipate the application of the law of a certain state, but they may have had no way of complying with that law. For example, a corporation may have reason to anticipate that the laws of states in which it does business may be applicable to some aspects of its internal organization, but that corporation might have no way of complying with the law of all of those states, short of reincorporating in each such state. See Order of Commercial Travelers v. Wolfe, 331 U.S. 586 (1947). Similarly, the parties to an ordinary juridical act intended to be performed in more than one state may find it difficult to comply with the requirements of each state. Even complying with the most stringent of these laws may sometimes be problematic if what is required by that law is outlawed by the law of another state. In these and similar instances, the court should try to "minimiz[e] the adverse consequences that might follow from subjecting a party to the law of more than one state." Sometimes it will not be possible to minimize, much less eliminate, these consequences. But striving to do so should be one of the goals of the choice-of-law process, especially when all of the other factors are equal.

(d) Issue-by-issue analysis and dépeçage. The use of the term "issue" in the first paragraph of this Article is intended to focus the choice-of-law-process on the particular issue as to which there exists an actual conflict of laws. When a conflict exists with regard to only one issue, the court should focus on the factual contacts and policies that are pertinent to that issue. When a conflict exists with regard to more than one issue, each issue should be analyzed separately, since each may implicate different states, or may bring into play different policies of these states. Seen from another angle, each state having factual contacts with a given multi-state case may not have an equally strong interest in regulating all issues in the case, but only those issues that actually implicate its policies in a significant way.

This so-called issue-by-issue analysis is an integral feature of all modern American choice-of-law methodologies and facilitates a more nuanced and individualized resolution of conflicts problems. One result of this analysis might be that the laws of different states may be applied to different issues in the same dispute. This phenomenon is known in conflicts literature by its French name of dépeçage. Although infrequently referred to by this name, this phenomenon is now a common occurrence in the United States and has received official recognition in Europe. This Article does not prohibit dépeçage.

However, dépeçage should not be pursued for its own sake. The unnecessary splitting of the case should be avoided, especially when it results in distorting the policies of the involved states.

Art. 3516. Meaning of "State"

As used in this Book, the word "state" denotes, as may be appropriate: the United States or any state, territory, or possession thereof; the District of Columbia; the Commonwealth of Puerto Rico; and any foreign country or territorial subdivision thereof that has its own system of law.

Acts 1991, No. 923, § 1, eff. Jan. 1, 1992.

REVISION COMMENTS—1991

This Article defines the term "state" for the purposes of this Book by using language similar to that employed by most uniform statutes in the United States. By way of illustration, a Canadian province or an Australian state is a "territorial subdivision" of a foreign country which, with regard to most private law matters, has "its own system of law." If the conflict at issue involves one of those matters, then the particular province is to be treated as a "state" for the purposes of this Book.

With regard to matters governed by federal law, the United States may also be considered a "state" for the purposes of this Book. The question as to which matters are governed by federal law is determined by federal rather than state law. Since this "vertical" delineation between these two sets of laws is beyond the scope of state conflicts law, it is also beyond the scope of this Book. However, American federal law may well conflict with the law of a foreign country, as in the area of maritime or bankruptcy law. In these cases, the United States may be considered a "state" for the purposes of this Book.

Art. 3517. Renvoi

Except as otherwise indicated, when the law of another state is applicable under this Book, that law shall not include the law of conflict of laws of that state.

Nevertheless, in determining the state whose law is applicable to an issue under Articles 3515, 3519, 3537, and 3542, the law of conflict of laws of the involved foreign states may be taken into consideration.

Acts 1991, No. 923, § 1, eff. Jan. 1, 1992.

REVISION COMMENTS—1991

(a) Renvoi. This Article addresses the question of renvoi. Translated as "remission" or "transmission", this French word has become an internationally accepted term of art in conflicts literature. This term is generally used as short-hand for the question of whether the forum state should follow the conflicts law of another state. The answers given to this question by the various national conflicts systems range from a complete disapproval of renvoi to its enthusiastic endorsement. This Article is based on the following two premises: (1) when the choice-of-law decision is made expressly by the legislature of this state, renvoi should be excluded unless the legislature indicates otherwise; and (2) when the choice-of-law decision is left to the discretion of the court, renvoi should not be excluded.

(b) Premise 1: renvoi excluded. The first premise is implemented by the first paragraph of this Article, which articulates the basic rule. When the legislature of this state expressly designates that the law of another state is applicable to an issue, as in Articles 3523, 3528–3532, 3536, 3538, 3539, 3543, 3544, and 3546, that designation prevails over any contrary wishes of the courts or legislature of that other state. To that end, the application of the foreign law is confined to the internal or substantive law of the foreign state and does not include its law of conflict of laws, "except as otherwise indicated".

(c) The exception: renvoi authorized. The phrase last quoted articulates the exception to the rule of excluding renvoi. According to this exception, renvoi is authorized when the articles of this Book so indicate. These articles do so by authorizing the application of "the law that would be applied by the courts" of the foreign state (see, e.g. Art. 3528, subpar. (4); Art. 3534, first par.; Art. 3535, second par.) or by referring to a particular result that may be obtainable "in" the foreign state (see, e.g., Art. 3520 and Art. 3549, second par., subpars. (1) and (2)). Since in both instances the courts of that foreign state would operate in accordance with the conflicts rules of that state, the courts of the forum should do likewise.

(d) Premise 2: renvoi considered. When this Book does not expressly designate the applicable law but, as in Articles 3515, 3519, 3537, and 3542, simply lists the factors to be used by the court for determining that law, there is no compelling reason to prohibit renvoi. Since the objective of the choice-of-law process prescribed by these Articles is to identify "the state whose policies would be most seriously impaired if its law were not applied", and since the conflicts rules of each state reflect that state's own delineation of the territorial scope of its policies, those rules can be a very helpful factor in "evaluating the strength and pertinence of . . . [these] policies". This is why the second paragraph of this Article provides that in these cases "the law of conflict of laws of the involved foreign states may be taken into consideration." The flexible phrasing of this directive is intended to indicate that the court is not bound to follow the conflicts rules of the foreign state.

Art. 3518.　Domicile

For the purposes of this Book, the domicile of a person is determined in accordance with the law of this state. A juridical person may be treated as a domiciliary of either the state of its formation or the state of its principal place of business, whichever is most pertinent to the particular issue.

Acts 1991, No. 923, § 1, eff. Jan. 1, 1992.

REVISION COMMENTS—1991

(a) Purpose of this Article. This Article designates the law under which domicile is to be determined and establishes a special rule for determining the domicile of juridical persons. As indicated by the introductory phrase, the scope of this Article is co-extensive with the scope of this Book. Thus, for instance, this Article does not apply for determining domicile for purposes of jurisdiction in this or another state.

(b) Domicile determined according to the law of the forum. This Article provides that the place where a person, natural or juridical, is domiciled is to be determined according to Louisiana law (see, e.g., La.Civ.Code Arts. 38–46 (1870)), even in cases where that person is ultimately found to be domiciled in another state. This provision is consistent with present jurisprudence as well as with the principle that characterization is normally conducted in accordance with the law of the forum. See, e.g., Restatement Second, Conflict of Laws, § 13.

(c) Domicile of juridical persons. This Book employs domicile as a connecting factor both for natural and for juridical persons. Because the concept of domicile of a juridical person is not defined by Louisiana statutory law, this Article defines this concept for the purposes of this Book. Article 3548, infra, contains an additional definition for the purposes of the Title on the law applicable to delictual obligations.

Although it is often said that a juridical person has its domicile in the state of its incorporation, closer examination reveals that such an assertion is usually confined to matters pertaining to the internal affairs of corporations. Even in this context, the assertion is subject to exceptions. When the issue pertains to the external relations of a corporation with third parties, the place of incorporation is usually less important than the principal place of business. Rather than choose a priori between the places of incorporation and principal place of business, this Article leaves the choice to the court. The choice will be guided by the principles of Article 3515 and will depend on the issue involved and the circumstances of the particular case.

For the definition of a juridical person, see La.Civ.Code Art. 24 (Rev.1987). Because this term encompasses corporations, partnerships, and other associations that possess a personality distinct from that of their members, this Article uses the term "formation" rather than the more narrow term "incorporation".

TITLE II—STATUS

Art. 3519. Status of natural persons; general principle

The status of a natural person and the incidents and effects of that status are governed by the law of the state whose policies would be most seriously impaired if its law were not applied to the particular issue.

That state is determined by evaluating the strength and pertinence of the relevant policies of the involved states in the light of: (1) the relationship of each state, at any pertinent time, to the dispute, the parties, and the person whose status is at issue; (2) the policies referred to in Article 3515; and (3) the policies of sustaining the validity of obligations voluntarily undertaken, of protecting children, minors, and others in need of protection, and of preserving family values and stability.

Acts 1991, No. 923, § 1, eff. Jan. 1, 1992.

REVISION COMMENTS—1991

(a) Scope of this Article. The scope of this Article encompasses the "status of a natural person and the incidents and effects of that status". The meaning of the term "status" is defined by doctrine and jurisprudence. Planiol defines status as "those attributes of a person which the law takes into consideration in order to attach juridical effects to them. Thus the attributes of Frenchman, major, husband, legitimate son are juridical statuses." M. Planiol, Traite elementaire de droit civil v. 1 § 419 (English translation by the Louisiana State Law Institute 1959). Traditionally, at least the following sub-topics are subsumed under the rubric of status: "personality" or "capacity to have rights and duties" (see La.Civ.Code.Arts. 25, 27 (Rev.1987)); capacity to enter into juridical acts (La.Civ.Code Art. 28 (Rev.1987)); citizenship; the name of a person; marriage (including its formation, validity, incidents, and termination); legitimacy, filiation, and adoption; and generally the relationship between parents and children, including parental authority, custody, and support. As stated in Civil Code Article 3514 (Rev.1991), supra, this and the following Articles of this Title apply to those of the above sub-topics for which the law of this state does not provide otherwise.

By way of illustration, this Article does not apply to citizenship, which is regulated by federal law, or child custody and child support, which are covered by more specific Louisiana statutes. See, e.g., R.S. 13:1700 et seq.; 28 U.S.C. 1738A; and R.S. 13:1641 et seq. Similarly, this Article does not apply to the issue of capacity to make a testament, to inherit or to receive as legatee under a testament, or to enter into a contract or another juridical act, because all of these issues are covered by other articles. See respectively Arts. 3529, 3530, 3539, and 3541, infra. However, this Article does apply to other aspects of capacity or personality, such as the existence, beginning and termination of personality, the capacity to own property in general and the capacity to sue or to be sued.

Similarly, and again by way of illustration only, this Article applies to: the validity of marriages that do not fall under Article 3520 (see comments under Article 3520, infra); the effects and incidents of all marriages, "unless otherwise provided by the law of this state" (see the cross reference in Article 3522, infra); the effects and incidents of divorce, except as otherwise provided by law (see id.); the establishment, existence, proof, and contestation of a parent-child relationship, whether such relationship is legitimate or illegitimate, or has been created by adoption; and, except as otherwise provided by law, the effects and incidents of the parent-child relationship.

Finally, this Article, as well as the other articles of this Title, is applicable not only in proceedings seeking a direct determination of status, such as a filiation or disavowal action or an action to annul a marriage, but also in proceedings where the issue of status is merely incidental to the resolution of another issue. The most typical example of this is a wrongful death or similar action in which the plaintiff's status as the surviving spouse or a child of the deceased is subject to dispute. Such dispute is to be resolved according to the law selected under this Article.

(b) Relation to Article 3515. The first paragraph of this Article prescribes the objective of the choice-of-law process for issues of status in language that is purposefully identical to the language used in Article 3515 for the objective of the choice-of-law process in general. For the meaning of this language, see comment (b) under Article 3515, supra. Similarly, the second paragraph of this Article prescribes the method or process for attaining this objective in language that is slightly more specific than that of the second paragraph of Article 3515. For a step-by-step description of this method, see comments (c) and (d) under Article 3515.

This Article adds specificity to this description in two respects. First, this Article adds to the list of "policies referred to in Article 3515" an illustrative list of some general policies that are likely to be implicated in many status conflicts even when such policies are not evidenced by any particular language in the specific laws competing for application in the particular case. It is in order to ensure that they will not be overlooked by the court that these policies are mentioned expressly in this Article.

Second, this Article describes in more specific terms the relationship in light of which to evaluate the strength and pertinence of the implicated state policies. Thus, the language "the parties, and the person whose status is at issue" serves as a reminder that the two may or may not coincide. For example, in a suit to declare the nullity of a marriage brought by one spouse against the other, the parties and the person[s] whose status is at issue would coincide. This would also be true, for instance, in a filiation action, a disavowal action, or an emancipation action. However, in many other instances, the outcome of the dispute between the plaintiff and the defendant depends on the status of a third person. For example, the plaintiff's right of inheritance through representation may depend on the status of the plaintiff's father as a child of the de cujus. Similarly, the right of a person to an action for the wrongful death of his brother might depend on the validity of that brother's marriage or divorce, the validity of that brother's adoption by another person, or the validity of the adoption of a child by that brother. In these cases, the outcome of the dispute between the parties will depend on the status of another person. Similarly, the phrase "at any pertinent time" ensures that the court's examination of the parties' relationship to the forum and to other involved states should not be confined to the time of litigation but should extend to any other pertinent time, such as the time of the events from which the dispute originated. For example, in a filiation action or in any other action in which the paternity of a child is at stake, the court should consider not only the present domicile of the child and the parents but also their respective domiciles at the time of the child's conception. Similarly, in a dispute about the validity of marriage, the court should consider the spouses' domicile not only at the time of the trial but also at the time of the marriage.

Art. 3520. Marriage

A.   A marriage that is valid in the state where contracted, or in the state where the parties were first domiciled as husband and wife, shall be treated as a valid marriage unless to do so would violate a strong public policy of the state whose law is applicable to the particular issue under Article 3519.

B.   A purported marriage between persons of the same sex violates a strong public policy of the state of Louisiana and such a marriage contracted in another state shall not be recognized in this state for any purpose, including the assertion of any right or claim as a result of the purported marriage.

Acts 1991, No. 923, § 1, eff. Jan. 1, 1992. Amended by Acts 1999, No. 890, § 1.

REVISION COMMENTS—1991

(a) Scope. This Title draws a distinction between the validity of marriage and the "effects and incidents" of marriage. This Article applies only to the validity of the marriage. Article 3522, infra, applies to the incidents and effects of marriage. The reasons for this distinction are explained in the comments under Article 3522.

This Article is confined to marriages that are "valid in the state where contracted, or in the state where the spouses were first domiciled as husband and wife" and purposefully does not encompass marriages that would not be valid in either one of these states. The validity or invalidity of these marriages will therefore be determined under the law designated by Article 3519, which is the residual article for all matters of status that are not otherwise provided for in this Title or elsewhere by Louisiana legislation. Although these marriages will not benefit from an a priori presumption of validity, their eventual validation need not be precluded in advance.

(b) Favor matrimonii. Based on the universally espoused policy of favoring the validity of marriages if there is any reasonable basis for doing so (favor matrimonii), this Article authorizes the validation of marriages that are valid either in the state where contracted or in the state where the spouses were first domiciled as husband and wife. The word "contracted" as opposed to the word "celebrated" is used so as not to exclude common-law marriage from the scope of this Article. Similarly, the use of the words "in the state" rather than "under the law of the state" is intended to include consideration of the conflicts law of that state (i.e., renvoi, see Art. 3517, supra). This ancient policy of favor matrimonii and favor validatis is well entrenched in the substantive law of every state of the United States. This policy is equally important at the multistate level, where it is reenforced by the policy of avoiding "limping marriages". This Article enunciates this policy of validation and defines its limits. These limits are co-extensive with the "strong public policy of the state whose law is applicable to the particular issue under Article 3519." In order to rebut the presumptive rule of validation established by Article 3520, the party who asserts the invalidity of the marriage must prove that: (1) under Article 3519, the law of a state other than the one where the marriage was contracted or where the parties were first domiciled as husband and wife would be applicable to the particular issue; and (2) that law would invalidate the marriage for reasons of "a strong public policy".

Art. 3521.   Divorce or separation

A court of this state may grant a divorce or separation only for grounds provided by the law of this state.

Acts 1991, No. 923, § 1, eff. Jan. 1, 1992.

REVISION COMMENTS—1991

(a) Scope. This Article is confined to the narrow question of the right to obtain a divorce or separation and the grounds on which they may be obtained. This Article does not extend to other claims or remedies that might arise in an action for divorce or separation, such as the claim for alimony, child support, or property settlement. To the extent they are incidents of marriage or divorce, these other remedies are covered by Article 3522. This Article also does not apply to an action to declare the nullity of a marriage. Since nullity is simply the other side of validity, nullity actions are governed by the same law that governs the validity of marriage, namely the law designated by Articles 3520 and 3519, supra. Act 1009 of 1990, effective January 1, 1991, repealed Civil Code Article 138 which provided for separation from bed and board. Since such separation is no longer available under the law of this state, then, under Article 3521, a Louisiana court may not grant a separation under the law of another state.

(b) Operation. This Article may be read in both a positive and a negative way. The positive reading is that, as long as it has jurisdiction, "[a] court of this state may grant a divorce . . . for grounds provided by the law of this state", even if another state or states involved would not allow divorce on the same grounds. The negative reading is that "[a] court of this state may [not] grant a divorce . . . for grounds provided by the law of . . . [another] state", unless of course those grounds are also recognized by the law of this state. Both readings are permissible and both are interrelated with the existence of jurisdiction. Under present Louisiana law, a Louisiana court has jurisdiction to grant a divorce "if, at the time of filing, one or both of the spouses are domiciled in this state." La.Code Civ.Proc.Art. 10(7) (Rev.1990).

Art. 3522.   Effects and incidents of marriage and of divorce

Unless otherwise provided by the law of this state, the effects and incidents of marriage and of divorce with regard to an issue are governed by the law applicable to that issue under Article 3519.

Acts 1991, No. 923, § 1, eff. Jan. 1, 1992.

REVISION COMMENTS—1991

(a) Scope. This Article applies to the "effects and incidents of marriage" as distinguished from the validity of marriage, which is governed by Articles 3520 and 3519, supra. This Article also applies to the "effects and incidents" of divorce as distinguished from the right to obtain a divorce, which is governed by Article 3521.

(b) Incidents of marriage. The definition of the term "effects and incidents of marriage" is left to judicial interpretation. In a broad sense, this term may include any legal consequence of marriage, whether pertaining to the status and rights of children, the reciprocal rights and duties of spouses during marriage, or their respective rights following dissolution of the marriage by divorce or death. Act 886 of 1987, which revised the pertinent provisions of the Louisiana Civil Code, subsumes under the heading "Incidents and Effects of Marriage" the reciprocal duties of "fidelity, support, and assistance" (C.C. Art. 98 (Rev.1987)), the rights and obligations stemming from parental authority (C.C. Art. 99 (Rev.1987)) and the effect of marriage on a spouse's name (C.C. Art. 100 (Rev.1987)). See also C.C. Art. 97 (Rev.1987) which uses the roughly synonymous term "civil effects" of marriage.

(c) The reason for differentiating between validity and incidents of marriage. The distinction between validity and incidents of marriage can be justified by the fact that these two categories of issues often implicate different policies and needs. For instance, with regard to validity, there seems to be a universal consensus in favor of upholding the validity of marriage whenever reasonably possible. On the other hand, it is almost meaningless to speak of a policy of "favor matrimonii" with regard to the effects or incidents of a—valid or invalid—marriage. One need only be reminded of the concept of putative spouses to realize that the effects and incidents that a state chooses to attribute to a particular marriage need not depend on the validity of that marriage. States may agree on the validity of a particular marriage but may disagree on its incidents, and vice versa. The policy of "favor matrimonii" has little to contribute to a rational resolution of such conflicts. To resolve these conflicts, it is necessary to consider values beyond validation and factual contacts other than, or in addition to, the place of the marriage or the place of the first matrimonial domicile, such as policies that are pertinent and the contacts that are present at the time of the events from which the particular incident flows and at the time the particular incident is asserted. See comment (b) under Article 3519, supra. By differentiating between validity and incidents of marriage and relegating the latter to Article 3519, Article 3522 facilitates a separate consideration of these policies and factual contacts.

(d) Right to divorce and its incidents. Similar reasons may be advanced for differentiating between the right to obtain a divorce and the effects and incidents of divorce. The former is an issue on which the laws of the various states, at least in this country, are uniform, except perhaps in matters of detail. Thus, to equate jurisdiction with choice of law with regard to that issue, as is done in Article 3521, seems to be not only acceptable but also efficient. On the other hand, the effects and incidents of divorce are matters on which the various states continue to differ, not only in details but also in basic policy. Because of these differences and the multitude of law-fact patterns that might come before Louisiana courts, it would have been unwise to assign a priori all of these incidents to the law of the forum, or, for that matter, to any single law. By referring these issues to the flexible approach of Article 3519, Article 3522 seeks to ensure that each such issue will receive the flexible, individualized treatment prescribed by that article.

(e) Residual nature of this Article. As indicated by its introductory phrase, this Article becomes operable only when the law of Louisiana, including applicable federal law, does not provide otherwise. Among the instances in which Louisiana law does provide otherwise are: Civil Code Article 2334 (Rev.1979) with regard to the matrimonial regime; the Title in this Book on marital property (infra); the Uniform Reciprocal Enforcement of Support Act (URESA) enacted in Louisiana as La.R.S. 13:1641 et seq.; and the Uniform Child Custody Jurisdiction Act (La.R.S. 13:1700 et seq.).

TITLE III—MARITAL PROPERTY

Art. 3523. Movables

Except as otherwise provided in this Title, the rights and obligations of spouses with regard to movables, wherever situated, acquired by either spouse during marriage are governed by the law of the domicile of the acquiring spouse at the time of acquisition.

Acts 1991, No. 923, § 1, eff. Jan. 1, 1992.

REVISION COMMENTS—1991

(a) Relationship with Civil Code Articles 2334 and 2329. The articles of this Title presuppose and complement Articles 2334 and 2329 of the Civil Code (Rev.1979), which are not affected by this revision, as well as Article 3522, supra, which designates the law applicable to the incidents of marriage and divorce. Article 2334 provides that "[t]he legal regime of community of acquets and gains applies to spouses domiciled in this state, regardless of their domicile at the time of marriage or the place of celebration of the marriage." Thus, this article codifies the principle of the mutability of the matrimonial regime, that is, the notion that the matrimonial regime changes when the matrimonial domicile is moved from one state to another. This principle has been part of Louisiana and American conflicts law since Saul v. His Creditors, 5 Mart. (n.s.) 569 (La.1827), which, however, confined the application of the new regime to "future acquisitions," namely assets acquired after the change of domicile. See Symeonides, "Louisiana's Draft on Successions and Marital Property", 35 Am.J.Comp.L. 259, 270–72 (1987). Article 3523 is consistent with Saul and the principle of partial or prospective mutability. However, this principle is subject to exceptions provided in the following articles of this Title. One of these exceptions is the one established by subparagraph (1) of Article 3526, infra, which essentially authorizes a total or retrospective mutability for the cases falling within the scope of that subparagraph. Another exception to the principle of partial mutability is established by Article 2329 of the Civil Code (Rev.1979), which recognizes the freedom of spouses to "enter into a matrimonial agreement . . . as to all matters that are not prohibited by public policy" and allows spouses who move to Louisiana "[d]uring the first year after moving into and acquiring a domicile in this state . . . [to] enter into a matrimonial agreement without court approval." As long as they remain within the limits of public policy, these spouses may agree to preserve their previous matrimonial regime in whole or in part, or may replace it in whole or in part, prospectively or retrospectively.

(b) Comparison with previous law. Articles 2334 and 2329 of the Civil Code (Rev.1979) were complemented by paragraph 4 of Civil Code Article 15 (Redesignated 1987), which addressed the rights and obligations of spouses with regard to particular property. The Articles of this Title replace that paragraph. The first sentence of that paragraph provided for immovables situated in Louisiana. That sentence is replaced by Articles 3524 and 3526–3527, infra. In addition, Article 3525, infra, provides for one category of immovables situated outside Louisiana that were not heretofore provided for by that paragraph.

With regard to movables, the second sentence of paragraph 4 of Civil Code Article 15 (Redesignated 1987) provided that "[m]ovables, wherever situated, are subject to the law of the domicile of the acquiring spouse." That provision is replaced by Articles 3523 and 3526 of this Title. Article 3523 restates that provision and adds the necessary clarification that, "[e]xcept as otherwise provided in this Title," the pertinent domicile of the acquiring spouse is the domicile at the time of acquisition and not later. This Title "provides otherwise", inter alia, in Articles 3524 and 3526, infra, which authorize the application of Louisiana law as the law of the situs of an immovable, rather than that of the domicile, in classifying funds (i.e. movables) used for the acquisition of a Louisiana immovable, and in Article 3526, infra, which authorizes the application of Louisiana law as the law of the domicile at the time of the termination of the marriage. Thus, Article 3523 is the general and residual rule of this Title.

(c) Application. Unlike Articles 3525, 3526, and 3527, infra, but like Article 3524, infra, this Article designates the law applicable not only upon the termination of, but also during the marriage. This Article is primarily a rule of classification and functions as a rule of distribution only when it is not displaced by Article 3526, infra. For example, if the acquiring spouse was domiciled in this state at the time he acquired the movable, then regardless of its location, this movable will be classified as community or separate property according to the law of this state. If the spouses retain their Louisiana domicile until their marriage terminates by divorce or death, Louisiana law will continue to be applicable through this Article, which will then function as a rule of distribution. If the spouses move their domicile to another state where their marriage terminates, this Article will not, of course, be binding on the courts of that state, but will remain as a statement of the policy of this state for foreign courts that care to inquire. On the other hand, if the acquiring spouse was domiciled in another state at the time he acquired the movable, then the respective rights of the spouses to that movable during marriage are to be determined under the law of that state. However, if at the time the marriage terminates one or both spouses are domiciled in Louisiana, Article 3526, infra, becomes applicable as a rule of distribution that displaces this Article. If Article 3526 is inapplicable for whatever reason, this Article continues to be applicable. For a general discussion of the provisions of this Title, see Symeonides, "Louisiana's Draft on Successions and Marital Property", 35 Am.J.Comp.L. 259, 266–85 (1987); Symeonides, "In Search of New Choice-of-Law Solutions to Some Marital Property Problems of Migrant Spouses: A Response to the Critics", 13(3) Comm.Prop.J. 11 (1986).

Art. 3524.   Immovables situated in this state

Except as otherwise provided in this Title, the rights and obligations of spouses with regard to immovables situated in this state are governed by the law of this state. Whether such immovables are community or separate property is determined in accordance with the law of this state, regardless of the domicile of the acquiring spouse at the time of acquisition.

Acts 1991, No. 923, § 1, eff. Jan. 1, 1992.

REVISION COMMENTS—1991

(a) Comparison with present law. According to paragraph 4 of Civil Code Article 15 (Redesignated 1987), which was added to the article during the 1979 revision of the law of matrimonial regimes, "[i]mmovables situated in this state . . . , acquired by a married person, are subject to the legal regime of acquets and gains regardless of his domicile." However, the comments to the 1979 revision provide that "this provision does not require that immovable property acquired in the name of a married nonresident be classified as community property in all instances. When a nonresident purchases an immovable situated in Louisiana with separate funds, the immovable is his separate property." Thus, besides correcting what was obviously an overstatement in the text of paragraph 4, the 1979 comments authorized the courts to follow the principle known as the "source doctrine" and to classify the property as community or separate depending on the source of the funds used for its acquisition. However, neither these comments nor the text of paragraph 4 of Civil Code Article 15 (Redesignated 1987) answered the most critical question, namely which state's law, Louisiana's or that of the domicile of the nonresident spouse, should be employed to classify the funds as community or separate? The second sentence of this Article answers this question in favor of the "law of this state," that is, Louisiana's substantive law of matrimonial regimes (see, e.g., La.Civ.Code Arts. 2334–2345 (Rev.1979)).

(b) Rationale. Since the funds used for the acquisition of an immovable are themselves movables, they should perhaps be classified according to the law governing movables, that is, the law of the domicile of the acquiring spouse (see Article 3523, supra). However, at least when the acquiring spouse was domiciled in a separate-property state at the time of acquiring the funds, this solution would make little sense since, under the law of that state, all funds are separate funds. Moreover, despite the acoustic similarity, the concept of separate property in a common-law system is not identical to the concept of separate property under Louisiana law. Under Louisiana law the separate property of a spouse is free of any claims in favor of the other spouse, whereas in a common-law state the separate property of a spouse is subject to liens or inchoate rights in favor of the other spouse which ripen into a statutory share or dower in death cases, and into similar rights, through the doctrine of equitable distribution, in divorce cases. Symeonides, "In Search of New Choice-of-Law Solutions to Some Marital Property Problems of Migrant Spouses: A Response to the Critics", 13(3) Comm.Prop.J. 11, 12–14, 24–25 (1986). Thus, if the funds, and therefore, under the "source doctrine", the Louisiana immovable, are to be classified according to the law of the foreign domicile of the acquiring spouse, the immovable should also be subject to the same equitable claims that are granted to the other spouse by the law of that state over the funds used for its acquisition. However, the practical problems that would be created by this otherwise logically consistent solution are quite formidable, and are complicated by the fact that Louisiana does not recognize the concept of equitable title. In order to avoid these problems and to preserve certainty of title, this Article opts for the much simpler rule under which the funds are classified under the internal law of this state, regardless of the domicile of the acquiring spouse. This Article should withstand constitutional challenges by the acquiring spouse since it does not affect that spouse's rights to the funds at the moment they are brought into the state (see Article 3523, supra), but only if and when these funds are used to buy an immovable in this state, and then only in the absence of a valid matrimonial agreement providing otherwise.

(c) This Article applies to Louisiana immovables only. Immovables situated in another state are provided for in Article 3525, infra, which, however, applies only when the acquiring spouse was domiciled in Louisiana at the time of acquisition.

Like Article 3523, supra, and unlike Arts. 3525, 3526, and 3527, infra, this Article designates the law that determines the spouses' rights to the immovable during the marriage. Thus, if the immovable is classified as community property, the provisions of the Louisiana Civil Code (see La.Civ.Code Arts. 2346–2355 (Rev.1979)) pertaining to the management of community property become applicable. This Article may also be applicable upon termination of the marriage, but only in the cases that are not covered by Articles 3526 or 3527, infra, which prevail over this Article because they are more specific.

Art. 3525. Termination of community; immovables in another state acquired by a spouse while domiciled in this state

Upon the termination of the community between spouses, either of whom is domiciled in this state, their rights and obligations with regard to immovables situated in another state acquired during marriage by either spouse while domiciled in this state, which would be community property if situated in this state, shall be determined in accordance with the law of this state. This provision may be enforced by a judgment recognizing the spouse's right to a portion of the immovable or its value.

Acts 1991, No. 923, § 1, eff. Jan. 1, 1992.

REVISION COMMENTS—1991

(a) Scope. This Article applies to immovables which: (1) are situated outside Louisiana; (2) would be classified as community property under Louisiana law (e.g., were acquired with funds classified as community funds under Louisiana law); and (3) were acquired by a spouse (a) who, at the time of the acquisition, was domiciled in Louisiana and (b) who, at the time of the termination of the community, was domiciled in Louisiana or was subject to the jurisdiction of its courts. If any one of the above conditions is missing, this Article does not apply and, depending on the circumstances, another article in this Title might be applicable. If no other article is directly applicable, the case may fall under Article 3523, supra, as the residual article of this Title, and, if that Article is not applicable, the court should resort to Article 3515, supra, the residual Article of this Book.

(b) Application. This Article designates the law applicable only upon termination of the community and not before. The status of the immovable during the community will depend on the law of the situs state and particularly on whether or how that state applies the source doctrine. If that state is a community-property state, the immovable will likely be classified as community property. If that state is a common-law state, the classification of the immovable will depend on whether that state applies the source doctrine. Most common-law states consider the acquiring spouse to be the legal owner of the immovable, subject to an equitable interest of one half for the benefit of the other spouse. See Depas v. Mayo, 11 Mo. 314, 49 Am.Dec. 88 (1848); Uniform Disposition of Community Property Rights at Death Act §§ 1(2), 3, 6, and 7. The acquiring spouse may, however, encumber or convey the immovable to innocent third parties, who acquire it free of any claims of the other spouse. The latter spouse has the same rights to the proceeds of the sale as that spouse had to the funds used for the acquisition of the immovable. Cf. Jackson v. Jackson, 425 So.2d 379 (La.App. 3rd Cir.1982).

(c) This Article applies only when the termination of the community occurs while at least one of the spouses is domiciled in this state and there exists jurisdiction over the other spouse. When the spouses have moved to another state, the matter will be decided by the courts of that state. This Article, together with Article 3523, serve as statements of the policy of this state for foreign courts that choose to inquire. On the other hand, when the spouses are domiciled in this state at the termination of the community, Louisiana has every legitimate interest, and is constitutionally empowered, to apply its own law of classification and distribution so as to prevent cheating by one Louisiana spouse who uses community funds to buy immovable property in his own name in another state. When only one spouse is domiciled here and there is no jurisdiction over the other, this Article, as well as any article pertaining to property, is inapplicable because a court cannot affect the property rights of the absent spouse in ex parte proceedings.

(d) Potential enforcement problems: (1) Divorce in Louisiana. As long as Louisiana remains the matrimonial domicile, Louisiana has personal jurisdiction over both spouses. This should mitigate, if not eliminate, most problems of enforcing the Louisiana judgment at the foreign situs. Rather than rendering a judgment purporting to directly affect the foreign immovable, the Louisiana court should render a judgment ordering the owning spouse to convey half of the foreign immovable, or an equivalent value, to the other spouse. (See, e.g., California Civil Code § 4800.5; Texas Family Code § 3.63). Such a judgment is enforceable in Louisiana by contempt proceedings and would be enforceable at the foreign situs through recognition proceedings under the full faith and credit clause of the United States Constitution. The same result would follow in any case where, although no longer the matrimonial domicile, Louisiana had personal jurisdiction over both spouses on other grounds. (2) Probate proceedings in Louisiana. Louisiana courts may also be able to implement this Article in all cases in which the court has jurisdiction over the owning spouse or his successors. They may be ordered to convey to the surviving spouse one half of the immovable or equivalent value, and such a judgment would be enforceable as explained above.

(e) The acquiring spouse's own half. By essentially treating the foreign immovable as if it were community property, this Article adequately protects the non-owner spouse. To give that spouse more under the substantive successions law of the foreign situs would be giving that spouse much more than is contemplated by the law of either state. In order to avoid this result, § 3 of the Uniform Disposition of Community Rights at Death Act provides that "the one half of the property which is the property of the decedent is not subject to the surviving spouse's right to elect against the will." On this issue the Act accurately reflects the judicial practice in most sister states. The same result should follow under this Title. Being more specific, Article 3525 should prevail over the general situs rule embodied in Article 3534, infra.

Art. 3526. Termination of community; movables and Louisiana immovables acquired by a spouse while domiciled in another state

Upon termination of the community, or dissolution by death or by divorce of the marriage of spouses either of whom is domiciled in this state, their respective rights and obligations with regard to immovables situated in this state and movables, wherever situated, that were acquired during the marriage by either spouse while domiciled in another state shall be determined as follows:

(1) Property that is classified as community property under the law of this state shall be treated as community property under that law; and

(2) Property that is not classified as community property under the law of this state shall be treated as the separate property of the acquiring spouse. However, the other spouse shall be entitled, in value only, to the same rights with regard to this property as would be granted by the law of the state in which the acquiring spouse was domiciled at the time of acquisition.

Acts 1991, No. 923, § 1, eff. Jan. 1, 1992.

REVISION COMMENTS—1991

(a) Scope and application. This Article applies only to property, movable or immovable, "acquired during the marriage by either spouse while domiciled in another state". If, at the time of acquisition, the acquiring spouse was domiciled in Louisiana, the case will be governed by Article 3523, supra, with regard to movables "wherever situated," by Article 3524, supra, with regard to Louisiana immovables, and by Article 3525, supra, with regard to certain foreign immovables that meet the conditions specified therein.

For movables falling within its scope, this Article does not require a Louisiana situs, either at the time of the acquisition or at the time of the termination of the marriage. When applicable to such movables, this Article derogates from the general principle of Article 3523, supra, and prevails over it, being more specific.

With regard to immovables, this Article applies only to "immovables situated in this state". Immovables situated in another state may be subject to Article 3525, supra, if they meet the conditions specified therein. Otherwise, foreign immovables will be governed by the law selected under Article 3515, which is the residual article. In applying Article 3515, the policies of this Title, particularly those of Article 3526, should be given proper consideration.

The final substantive condition for the application of this Article is that at least one of the spouses be domiciled in Louisiana at the time of the so-called "significant event". The significant event could be the termination of the community (without termination of the marital relationship) or the dissolution of the marriage (whether or not the spouses lived under the community regime) either by death or by divorce. Annulment could also be analogized to divorce for the purposes of this Article.

Obviously, as with any other provision of this Book, in order for this Article to become applicable, Louisiana must possess adjudicatory jurisdiction. Moreover, since the application of this Article inevitably affects the property rights of the parties, Louisiana must have either in rem jurisdiction or in personam jurisdiction over the parties affected. Thus, if the marriage has been terminated by death of either spouse, Louisiana must have probate jurisdiction. See La.Code Civ.Pro. Arts. 2811 and 3401. In cases of divorce or termination of the community, Louisiana must have jurisdiction over both spouses in order to render any judgment affecting their property rights. See La.Code Civ.Pro. Art. 10(A); Estin v. Estin, 334 U.S. 541 (1948); Simons v. Miami Beach First Nat'l Bank, 381 U.S. 81 (1965).

(b) Classification of property. This Article envisions two separate mental steps. The first step is the classification of the property that falls within the scope of the Article as either "community property" or "separate property". This classification is to be conducted "under the law of this state", that is, the substantive rules Louisiana has devised for cases that do not contain any foreign elements. See, e.g., La.Civ.Code Arts. 2325–2437 (Rev.1979). In other words, the classification is to be conducted as if the spouses were domiciled in Louisiana at all critical times. Aside from logistical simplicity, one reason for applying Louisiana law here is to avoid the anomaly of having to apply the law of a another state (e.g., a common-law separate-property state) to matters of classification when that state might not have any comparable scheme for classifying property.

(c) Distribution of property. The second step is the determination of the respective rights of spouses with regard to the property that has been classified in the first step. For brevity's sake this step is called "distribution", although in actuality the property may not always be distributed. Although, as explained above, the classification of the property is governed exclusively by Louisiana law, the distribution of the property may be governed either by Louisiana law or by the law of another state. Subparagraph (1) applies to property that is classified as community property under Louisiana classification law and calls for the application of the same law for distributing that property at Louisiana's 50:50 ratio between the spouses or their successors. Subparagraph (2) applies to property classified as separate property under Louisiana law and calls for the application of the distribution law of the state where the acquiring spouse was domiciled at the time of acquisition. The reason for this difference is explained below.

(d) Subparagraph (1): "Quasi-Community". Subparagraph (1) attempts to secure for the non-acquiring, formerly non-Louisianian, spouse the same protection as is provided by Louisiana substantive law for similarly situated Louisiana spouses. This scheme is similar to what is known in other states as the scheme of "quasi-community". One difference is that this provision is applicable to both divorce and death situations, whereas, with the exception of Idaho and California, other community property states confine their scheme to divorce situations only. See also § 17, 18 of the Uniform Marital Property Act. Another and more important difference stems from the fact that the quasi-community rule of subparagraph (1) is supplemented by the rule of subparagraph (2), which is explained infra.

(e) Subparagraph (2). Subparagraph (2) of this Article applies only to property that is not classified as community property under Louisiana substantive law. As long as the marriage lasts, this property is governed by the law designated by Article 3524 for immovables, and by Article 3523 for movables. Upon dissolution of the marriage, subparagraph (2) of this Article becomes operative and calls for the application of the distribution law of the state in which the acquiring spouse was domiciled at the time of acquisition. For similar results under the jurisprudence, see Schueler v. Schueler, 460 So.2d 1120 (La.App. 2d Cir.1985); Gilbert v. Gilbert, 442 So.2d 1330 (La.App. 3rd Cir.1984). See also Hughes v. Hughes, 91 N.M. 339, 573 P.2d 1194 (1978).

(f) The objective of subparagraph (2) is the same as that of subparagraph (1), namely to afford some protection to the non-acquiring spouse. Subparagraph (1) accomplishes this objective through the application of the community-property law of this state. Subparagraph (2) accomplishes the same objective through the application of the distribution laws of the domicile of the acquiring spouse at the time of acquisition. The co-existence of the two subparagraphs might create an impression of overprotection of the non-acquiring spouse. For a critique on exactly this point, see Reppy, "Louisiana's Proposed 'Hybrid' Quasi-Community Property Statute Could Cause Unfairness", 13(3) Comm.Prop.J. 1 (1986). For a response, see Symeonides, "In Search of New Choice-of-Law Solutions to Some Marital Property Problems of Migrant Spouses: A Response to the Critics", 13(3) Comm.Prop.J. 11 (1986).

(g) Insofar as it encompasses "inheritance" rights of the surviving spouse to Louisiana immovables, subparagraph (2) of this Article derogates from the general situs rule applicable to succession to immovables. See Article 3533, infra. Being more specific, this subparagraph prevails over Article 3533, which, of course, remains applicable to the inheritance rights of persons other than the surviving spouse. Also, insofar as it pertains to the "inheritance" rights of the surviving spouse to movables, this subparagraph derogates from, and should prevail over, the general rule of Article 3532, infra.

(h) The phrase "in value only" in subparagraph (2) is used in order to avoid the problems that may arise when the law of the domicile at the time of acquisition grants to the non-acquiring spouse a property interest (e.g., tenancy by the entirety) that is not recognized by the law of this state.

Art. 3527. Louisiana immovables acquired by a spouse while domiciled in another state; death of the acquiring spouse while domiciled in another state

Upon the death of a spouse domiciled outside this state, that spouse's immovables situated in this state and acquired by that spouse while domiciled outside this state, which are not community property under the law of this state, are subject to the same rights, in value only, in favor of the surviving spouse as provided by the law of the domicile of the deceased at the time of death.

Acts 1991, No. 923, § 1, eff. Jan. 1, 1992.

REVISION COMMENTS—1991

(a) Scope and rationale. While similar in scope and rationale to subparagraph (2) of Article 3526, this Article applies to death situations only and applies only when the acquiring spouse dies while domiciled outside this state. The applicable law is also different. It is the law of the domicile of the deceased at the time of death rather than at the time of acquisition of the property.

(b) This Article applies only when the acquiring spouse was domiciled outside Louisiana, both at the time of the acquisition of the property and at the time of death. If he was domiciled in Louisiana at the time of acquisition and at the time of death, Article 3524, supra, applies, and the other spouse would have no rights to this (separate) property under Louisiana succession law or matrimonial regimes law because he would have rights to the community property. If the acquiring spouse was domiciled outside Louisiana at the time of acquisition, but within Louisiana at the time of death, subparagraph (2) of Article 3526, supra, will apply, and the surviving spouse's rights will be determined according to the law of the domicile at the time of acquisition. Finally, if the acquiring spouse (and in all likelihood, the other spouse as well) was, at the time of acquisition and at the time of death, domiciled in another state, this Article becomes applicable to give the other spouse the protection given by the law of that state. When that other state is a community-property state, this protection may amount to virtually nothing. When the other state is a separate-property state, this protection will likely consist of a statutory share, usually a one-third share.

(c) Exception from the situs rule. Insofar as it calls for the application of a foreign law to Louisiana immovables, this Article derogates from the general situs rule of Article 3533, and, being more specific, it should prevail over that article. However, Article 3527 is entirely consistent with the forced share exception contained in Article 3533 and is inspired by the same philosophy. The phrase "in value only" has the same meaning and purpose as it has in Article 3526, supra. See comment (h) under Article 3526, supra.

TITLE IV—SUCCESSIONS

Art. 3528. Formal validity of testamentary dispositions

A testamentary disposition is valid as to form if it is in writing and is made in conformity with: (1) the law of this state; or (2) the law of the state of making at the time of making; or (3) the law of the state in which the testator was domiciled at the time of making or at the time of death; or (4) with regard to immovables, the law that would be applied by the courts of the state in which the immovables are situated.

Acts 1991, No. 923, § 1, eff. Jan. 1, 1992.

REVISION COMMENTS—1991

(a) Scope. This Article addresses only issues of formal validity, such as the mode of writing, the number of witnesses, the presence of a notary, and, generally, all other formalities and solemnities required by law for the confection of a valid testament. Whether a particular issue is an issue of form is determined according to the law of this state.

(b) Change in the law. Under Civil Code Article 15 (Redesignated 1987), paragraph 1, the formal validity of testaments was governed exclusively by the law of the place of the making, regardless of whether that law would validate the testament. This unduly harsh and narrow rule was liberalized only slightly with the enactment of La.R.S. 9:2401, which allows the upholding of a testament as to form if the testament conforms to either the law of the place of its making or the law of the place where the testator was domiciled at the time of the making. See Symeonides, "Exploring the 'Dismal Swamp': Revising Louisiana's Conflicts Law on Successions", 47 La.L.Rev. 1029, 1044–1047 (1987). This Article liberalizes prior law by adding three more possible states to the list of states whose law may be applied to validate a testament as to form. The additions are: this state; the state where the deceased was domiciled at the time of death; and, with regard to immovables, the situs state. (See comments (d) through (g), infra). Thus, a testament will be considered valid as to form if it conforms to the pertinent requirements prescribed by any one of the states enumerated in this Article.

(c) Rationale. This liberalization is long overdue. It has already taken place in most sister states, as well as in most western legal systems. See Symeonides, "Exploring the 'Dismal Swamp': Revising Louisiana's Conflicts Law on Successions", 47 La.L.Rev. 1029, 1043–1044 (1987). Besides being firmly grounded in comparative experience, this liberalization is amply justified by one of the most basic policies of the substantive law of successions, the policy of favor testamenti. At the domestic level, this policy favors testate over intestate succession whenever there are reasonable assurances that the testament contains the genuine will of the deceased. At the multistate level, this policy translates into a so-called "rule of validation", that is, a rule that upholds the testament as to form if it conforms to the pertinent requirements of any state that is sufficiently related with the deceased and his testament. This rule also finds support in the assumption that nowadays the laws of the various states on questions of testamentary formalities usually differ only on matters of detail rather than fundamental policy. If this assumption is true, then failure to comply with the technical requirements of one state should not be fatal to the formal validity of a testament as long as it conforms with the law of another state also related to the testator.

(d) Under this Article, a testament is formally valid if it satisfies the form requirements prescribed by "the law of this state". Pursuant to the general command of Article 3517, supra, this must be understood as a reference to the "internal law" of this state exclusive of its conflicts law. Theoretically, the application of the internal law of this state may validate even a testament that has no connection with this state, such as a testament made outside this state by a testator domiciled at all times outside this state and not disposing of any property within this state. However, since the law of this state can be applied only when a Louisiana court has jurisdiction, one or more of the above Louisiana contacts are likely to be present.

(e) Insofar as it authorizes the application of the law of the place of the making of the testament, this Article restates the rule contained in the first paragraph of Civil Code Article 15 (Redesignated 1987) and La.R.S. 9:2401. This Article also clarifies a question implicit in the source provisions, namely that the pertinent law of the place of making is the law in force at the time of making and not later. Thus, a testament that was valid under that law will not be affected by a subsequent change in that law that would make such a testament invalid. By the same token, if the testament was invalid under the law at the time of its making (and was also invalid under all other laws enumerated in this Article), the testament will not be validated by a subsequent change in that law, unless of course the new law is clearly intended to validate invalid testaments previously made.

(f) To the extent it refers to the law of the domicile of the testator at the time of making the testament, this Article restates the supplementary rule of former R.S. 9:2401. However, this Article changes the law by authorizing the application of the law of the domicile at the time of death in order to validate the testament. This change brings Louisiana into line with all other sister states and is justified by the policy of favor testamenti. See comments (b) and (c), supra. Moreover, unlike former La.R.S. 9:2401, which was confined by its terms to "will[s] made outside this state", this Article is applicable to testaments made within or without Louisiana.

(g) This Article also changes the law by authorizing the application of the law of the situs of an immovable to the extent that law would uphold a testament disposing of that immovable. This change brings Louisiana into line with all other states of the Union. Obviously, the application of the law of the situs may validate the testament only to the extent it disposes of immovables situated therein, but not with regard to immovables situated elsewhere, or movables situated anywhere. The phrase "the law that would be applied by the courts of the state . . ." is meant to refer to the "whole law" of the situs including its conflicts law. Thus, the quoted phrase authorizes a renvoi. See Article 3517, supra. Compare with Restatement Second, Conflict of Laws, §§ 236, 239. When the immovable is situated in this state, the "law that would be applied by the courts of [this] state" is any law designated as applicable by this Article. When the immovable is situated in another state, the "law that would be applied by the courts of [that] state" is any law applicable under the relevant conflicts rule of that state. This renvoi would prove to be particularly useful, and would sustain the disposition, if the foreign situs has a choice-of-law rule that is more liberal than this Article, such as § 2–506 of the Uniform Probate Code, which encompasses the law of the testator's residence or nationality. The formal sufficiency, under the law of the foreign state qua situs, of a disposition of immovables located therein, will not sustain the validity of dispositions of movables, or of immovables located elsewhere, which are not sustainable under the other provisions of this Article.

(h) In order to be validated by any of the laws enumerated in this Article, the testament must meet one minimum requirement, that is, it must be in writing. La.R.S. 9:2401 imposed the additional requirement that the testament be "subscribed by the testator." The Uniform Probate Code has dropped this latter requirement.

(i) The rules established by this Article also govern the formal sufficiency of a subsequent testamentary disposition that purports to revoke the first. However, the effect of the subsequent disposition on a previous disposition, that is, whether the former actually revoked the latter in whole or in part, would be determined by the law designated by other Articles in this Title, such as Articles 3529, 3531, and 3533–3534, infra, as the case may be. Articles 3533–3534 also apply to other forms of revocation, such as revocation by operation of law or by physical act.

Art. 3529.   Capacity and vices of consent

A person is capable of making a testament if, at the time of making the testament, he possessed that capacity under the law of the state in which he was domiciled either at that time or at the time of death.

If the testator was capable of making the testament under the law of both states, his will contained in the testament shall be held free of vices if it would be so held under the law of at least one of those states.

If the testator was capable of making the testament under the law of only one of the states specified in the first paragraph, his will contained in the testament shall be held free of vices only if it would be so held under the law of that state.

Acts 1991, No. 923, § 1, eff. Jan. 1, 1992.

REVISION COMMENTS—1991

(a) Scope. The first paragraph of this Article designates the law under which to determine whether, at the time of making the testament, the testator possessed the juridical capacity to make a testament. The second and third paragraphs designate the law under which to determine whether a testator, who possessed the required capacity under the law applicable to that issue, was also able to express his will freely and without impediments, that is, whether his volition contained in his testament was "free of vices". In this Article and throughout this Book, "[t]he masculine gender comprehends [either of] the two sexes". La.Civ.Code Art. 3556(1) (1870).

(b) Scope: Capacity. The capacity referred to in the first paragraph of this Article is the capacity to make a testament in general, as distinguished from the "capacity" to make a particular type of testament (e.g., an olographic testament), or "capacity" to dispose in favor of particular persons or to dispose of particular assets. The capacity contemplated in this Article can best be described in a negative manner by referring to what the Civil Code calls "absolute incapacities", namely those incapacities which "prevent the giving . . . indefinitely with regard to all persons". (La.Civ.Code Art. 1471 (1870)). Examples of such incapacities are unsound mind (La.Civ.Code Art. 1475 (1870)) and lack of minimum age (La.Civ.Code Art. 1476 (1870)). The article also encompasses similar incapacities recognized by other legal systems. Whether a particular issue is an issue of capacity is determined under the law of this state.

This Article is not intended to apply to questions relating to the type or form of testaments required for persons with particular handicaps such as blindness, deafness, illiteracy, etc. These are questions of form, and as such fall under Article 3528, supra. The testator laboring under such a handicap is in fact capable of making a testament and of disposing of his property, except that he must do so in the proper form prescribed by law for persons with such a handicap. Compare with article 5 of the Hague Convention on the Conflict of Laws Relating to the Form of Testamentary Dispositions.

Similarly, this Article does not encompass what the Civil Code calls "relative incapacities," namely incapacities which "prevent the giving to certain persons" (La.Civ.Code Art. 1471 (1870)), such as tutors (La.Civ.Code Art. 1478–79 (1870)), and doctors and ministers (La.Civ.Code Art. 1489 (1870)). These incapacities are covered by Article 3530, infra.

Finally, this Article does not affect the rules pertaining to the disposable portion (La.Civ.Code Art. 1493 et seq. (1870)), that is, the rules that prescribe how much property an otherwise capable person is permitted to dispose of. These questions are governed by Article 3532, infra, with regard to movables, and Articles 3533 and 3534, infra, with regard to immovables.

(c) Scope: Vices of consent. One of the basic prerequisites for the substantive validity of a testament is that it must reflect the free and unrestrained will of the testator unaffected by vices of consent. See La.Civ.Code Arts. 1948–65, 1917 (Rev.1984) and comments thereunder. However, although duress, fraud, and error are the typical examples of vices of consent in most legal systems, these systems differ on other vices of consent as well as on precise legal meaning and ultimate impact of each vice on the validity of the testament. Thus, in a multistate context, this multiplicity of meanings and consequences may raise, in addition to a factual question, a genuine choice-of-law question: which law should govern the issues of the existence vel non of vices of consent and their impact on the validity of the testament? The second and third paragraphs of this Article address this question.

(d) Comparison with prior law. Civil Code Article 15 (Redesignated 1987) provided that the "form" of a testament is governed by the law of the place of making, while the "effect" of the testament was governed by the law of the place where the testament was "to have effect." Since issues of testamentary capacity and vices of consent do not fit neatly into either the "form" or the "effect" of the testament, one could assume that there was simply no statutory choice-of-law rule for these issues. This appears to have been the assumption of Louisiana jurisprudence, which reached inconsistent decisions on the issue of testamentary capacity and virtually ignored vices of consent as an issue. The majority view for capacity seems to have been to apply the law of the situs with regard to immovables and the law of the testator's domicile with regard to movables. See Symeonides, "Exploring the 'Dismal Swamp': Revising Louisiana's Conflicts Law on Successions", 47 La.L.Rev. 1029, 1055–1056 (1987). Thus, on the issue of testamentary capacity, this Article changes the jurisprudence with regard to immovables and clarifies the jurisprudence with regard to movables. On the issue of vices of consent, this Article fills a gap in the law.

(e) Operation and rationale. The operation of this Article may be illustrated by the following hypothetical: In 1985, Mr. T made a testament while he was domiciled in State X. T died in 1990, after he had already acquired a new domicile in state Y. The first paragraph of this Article provides that, on the issue of capacity, T's testament will be considered valid if, at the time of the making of the testament in 1985, T was considered capable of making a testament under the then-existing law of either state X or state Y. The rationale for this rule of validation is explained in Symeonides, "Exploring the 'Dismal Swamp': Revising Louisiana's Conflicts Law on Successions", 47 La.L.Rev. 1029, 1057–1060 (1987).

If T was considered incapable under the law of both states, the testament will of course be invalid and the issue of vices of consent will never be reached. If T was considered capable under the law of both states X and Y, and there happens to be a question about the authenticity of his consent, the second paragraph of this Article will become applicable. This paragraph provides that T's will contained in his testament shall be held free of vices if it would be so held under the law of either state X or state Y.

If T was considered capable of making a testament under the law of state X but not under the law of state Y, then, under the first paragraph of this Article, his testament will be valid as to capacity. However, according to the third paragraph of this Article, any vices of consent and their impact on the validity of the testament must be judged exclusively under the law of state X, not Y. Thus, if under the law of state X, T's will contained in his testament is considered free of vices, the testament will be considered valid. On the other hand, if under the law of state X, T's will is not free of vices, then the testament will be considered invalid even if on that same issue the testament would be considered valid under the law of state Y. Proponents of the testament should not be allowed to "pick and choose" from the laws of the two states only those provisions that favor validation and thus to salvage a testament that is not valid in either state. In many states, the rules concerning vices of consent are closely interrelated with the rules on incapacities. Applying the one set of rules without the other may disturb the equilibrium accomplished by them and may distort the policies of both states.

Art. 3530.   Capacity of heir or legatee

The capacity or unworthiness of an heir or legatee is determined under the law of the state in which the deceased was domiciled at the time of his death.

Nevertheless, with regard to immovables situated in this state, the legatee must qualify as a person under the law of this state.

Acts 1991, No. 923, § 1, eff. Jan. 1, 1992.

REVISION COMMENTS—1991

(a) Scope. This Article encompasses questions of: (1) capacity to inherit (see, e.g., La.Civ.Code Arts. 950–963 (1870) (existence at the moment the succession is opened)); (2) capacity to receive donations (see, e.g., La.Civ.Code Arts. 1471–1490 (1870)); and (3) unworthiness of heirs (see, e.g., La.Civ.Code Arts. 965–975 (1870)). This Article does not apply to questions such as who should inherit, in which class, or how much, when the testator has left no testament. These questions are governed by Articles 3532–3534, infra.

(b) Rationale. As with Article 3539, supra, the issues that form the scope of this Article pertain more to the personal and family relations of the deceased rather than to his property as such. For instance, the rules imposing an incapacity to receive reflect a reprobation of certain relationships (e.g., concubinage, see former La.Civ.Code art. 1481 (repealed in 1987)), or a determination that certain dispositions are inherently suspect because of the likelihood of undue influence (see, e.g., La.Civ.Code Arts. 1479, 1489 (1870), declaring invalid legacies to certain tutors, doctors, and ministers). Similarly, the rules on unworthiness of heirs are legislatively articulated value judgments about family relationships. In all three instances these legislative determinations have nothing to do with land utilization, and little if anything to do with security of title. Because of this, they should be reserved to the law-making jurisdiction of the state where the deceased was last domiciled rather than the state where his property was located. This is the premise of this Article. For a defense of this premise and of the choice of the law of the domicile of the deceased rather than the domicile of the heir or legatee, see Symeonides, "Exploring the 'Dismal Swamp': Revising Louisiana's Conflicts Law on Successions", 47 La.L.Rev. 1029, 1062–1066 (1987).

(c) The domicile of the heir or legatee. Although not a pertinent factor under this Article, the domicile of the heir or legatee may assume a dominant role in adjudicating questions pertaining to the status of such persons under Article 3519, supra. For instance, if the law of the decedent's domicile were to reserve a certain portion of his estate to legitimate children and another portion to adopted children, then, leaving aside questions of constitutionality, whether a child would qualify as a "legitimate" or "adopted" child would be determined in accordance with the law selected for the particular issue under Article 3519. In that selection, the domicile of the child is likely to be a significant factor. The same is true with regard to juridical persons and unincorporated associations, except that the pertinent article for determining their status would be Article 3515, supra.

(d) The proviso in the second paragraph of this Article is confined to immovables situated in "this state," i.e., Louisiana, and is intended to preserve the public policy of this state in extreme cases, such as when the law of the testator's foreign domicile would permit legacies to animals. The proviso also applies to unincorporated associations that might not be permitted to own property under the law of this state. In this latter case, however, the incapacity may be cured if the foreign association is subsequently incorporated under Louisiana law.

Art. 3531.   Interpretation of testaments

The meaning of words and phrases used in a testament is determined according to the law of the state expressly designated by the testator for that purpose, or clearly contemplated by him at the time of making the testament, and, in the absence of such an express or implied selection, according to the law of the state in which the testator was domiciled at the time of making the testament.

Acts 1991, No. 923, § 1, eff. Jan. 1, 1992.

REVISION COMMENTS—1991

(a) Scope. Like any juridical act, testaments may be ambiguous for a number of reasons, including the incorrect use of legal terms, the use of ambiguous language, or the making of contradictory dispositions. The process of resolving these ambiguities is called "interpretation" by the Civil Code of 1870, which devotes twelve articles to this subject. (See La.Civ.Code Arts. 1712–1723 (1870)). The general literature on the subject distinguishes between "interpretation" and "construction". "Interpretation" is the process of defining the meaning of words and terms contained in a testament. "Construction" is the process of completing or presuming the intent of the testator as to matters on which he could have, but has not, spoken. The introductory phrase of the Article confines its scope to matters of interpretation.

(b) Interpretation distinguished from effect of testament. It must be emphasized that this Article does not apply to the effect of a disposition once its meaning has been established. For instance, through interpretation the court may determine whether a disposition contained in a testament was intended by the testator to be a successive usufruct or some other form of successive disposition. Once this is determined, the substantive validity and the effectiveness of the disposition is judged by the law applicable to the merits under Articles 3532, 3533 and 3534, infra. If, under these Articles, the applicable law is the law of this state and the arrangement is found to be a prohibited substitution, then it will not be given effect.

(c) The intent of the testator. The cardinal principle of interpretation of testaments is to ascertain and honor, to the extent possible, the intent of the testator. Article 1712 of the Louisiana Civil Code of 1870 reflects this principle by providing that "[i]n the interpretation of acts of last will, the intention of the testator must principally be endeavored to be ascertained . . ." Ascertaining the intent of the testator is essentially a factual inquiry. However, because this inquiry is often inconclusive, different legal systems provide sets of suppletive rules to aid the court in "supplying" the missing intent of the testator. In a multistate context, the choice-of-law question is, "which state's suppletive rules should be utilized in interpreting the testament?" To this problem, this Article provides three solutions in the order in which they appear in the text. The first is to allow the testator to expressly designate the law that should be used in interpreting his testament. This solution, which has by now been adopted in most modern codes, is the most direct way of honoring the testator's intent, consistently with La.Civ.Code Art. 1712 (1870). If the testator failed to expressly designate the applicable law, it is equally consistent with the cardinal principle of honoring the intent of the testator to instruct the court to try to ascertain the legal system upon which the testator was relying at the time of making the testament. This is the second solution provided by this Article. The third solution is to apply "the law of the state in which the testator was domiciled at the time of making the testament" as the residual law for those cases in which there was no express or implied selection by the testator.

Art. 3532. Movables

Except as otherwise provided in this Title, testate and intestate succession to movables is governed by the law of the state in which the deceased was domiciled at the time of death.

Acts 1991, No. 923, § 1, eff. Jan. 1, 1992.

REVISION COMMENTS—1991

(a) Scope. This Article establishes both the general and the residual rule for determining the law applicable to testate and intestate succession to movables. The law designated by this Article applies "except as otherwise provided in [the preceding articles of] this Title". Thus, when the particular issue does not qualify as an issue of form, capacity, or interpretation falling within the scope of Articles 3528–3531, supra, the issue will be decided under this Article.

(b) Comparison with prior law: (1) Intestate successions. Civil Code Article 15 (Redesignated 1987) did not deal expressly with intestate succession. However, paragraph 5 of Civil Code Article 15 (Redesignated 1987), together with Civil Code Article 14 (Redesignated 1987), could have been read as establishing a unilateral conflicts rule requiring the application of Louisiana law to Louisiana movables. The jurisprudence, however, ignored both these provisions and applied the law of the last domicile of the deceased. See Symeonides, "Exploring the 'Dismal Swamp': Revising Louisiana's Conflicts Law on Successions", 47 La.L.Rev. 1029, 1085–1086 (1987). (2) Testate successions. With regard to testate successions, Civil Code Article 15 (Redesignated 1987) would, if applied literally, have subjected the foreign movables of a Louisiana testator to the law of the foreign situs (see La.Civ.Code Art. 15 (Redesignated 1987) par. 2), and the Louisiana movables of a foreign testator to the law of the foreign state where the testament was made (see La.Civ.Code Art. 15 (Redesignated 1987) par. 3). For discussion and jurisprudence, see Symeonides, "Exploring the 'Dismal Swamp': Revising Louisiana's Conflicts Law on Successions", 47 La.L.Rev. 1029, 1076–1085 (1987). This Article removes this uncertainty with a single, bilateral choice-of-law rule calling for the application of the law of the decedent's last domicile to both testate and intestate succession to all movables, wherever situated.

(c) Rationale. The domiciliary rule adopted by this Article realigns Louisiana with the rest of the nation and the civilian world and satisfies two important succession-law policies: the ensurement of a uniform treatment of the succession as a single unit in cases involving movables located in more than one state; and the protection of the justified expectations of the testator who, in making or not making a disposition, is more likely to have relied on the law of his domicile than, say, the law of the situs of the movables. More importantly, the domiciliary rule recognizes the obvious, which is that, of all the states potentially involved in a multistate succession, the last domicile of the testator has a more legitimate claim to have its law applied than either the state where the movable property was located at the time of death or, even less, the state where the testament was made. Although to some extent this principle applies to immovables, nonetheless Articles 3533 and 3534, infra, retain the situs rule for them, but allow the exceptions specified therein.

(d) This Article does not affect the application of Louisiana inheritance tax law. According to R.S. 47:2404, Louisiana imposes inheritance tax on "all tangible movable property physically in the State of Louisiana, whether . . . inherited, bequeathed, given or donated under the laws of this state or of any other state or country."

Art. 3533. Immovables situated in this state

Except as otherwise provided in this Title, testate and intestate succession to immovables situated in this state is governed by the law of this state.

The forced heirship law of this state does not apply if the deceased was domiciled outside this state at the time of death and he left no forced heirs domiciled in this state at the time of his death.

Acts 1991, No. 923, § 1, eff. Jan. 1, 1992. Amended by Acts 1997, No. 257, § 1.

(a) Scope. This Article establishes the general and residual rule for the law applicable to testate and intestate succession to immovables situated in this state. This Article applies "except as otherwise provided in this Title," that is, it applies to questions other than form, capacity, consent, and interpretation, which are governed by Articles 3528–3531, supra. Immovables situated in another state are provided for in Article 3534, infra. The terms movable and immovable are used here and throughout this Title in their usual signification under Louisiana law, and include incorporeals. However, whether an interest in land or an attachment thereto actually qualifies as an immovable is determined by the law of the situs of the land.

(b) The situs rule and its exceptions. This Article retains, for the most part, the traditional situs rule followed by this and most other states of the United States. See Symeonides, "Exploring the 'Dismal Swamp': Revising Louisiana's Conflicts Law on Successions", 47 La.L.Rev. 1029, 1090–1092 (1987). During the last three decades the situs rule has been severely criticized by most academic commentators as being too mechanical, arbitrary, and non-responsive to the true policies implicated in most multistate successions disputes. Indeed, while it has a legitimate interest in matters of land utilization (e.g., prohibited substitutions, perpetuities, etc.), the situs state has little interest in deciding matters of testamentary formalities, capacity, or wealth distribution among members of a family not domiciled therein. Also, while the situs has an interest in preserving the integrity of its recording system, that interest is fully satisfied by requiring recordation of the judgment at the situs and does not require application of situs substantive law on the merits. For these reasons, this Title removes the following issues from the scope of the situs rule: issues of testamentary formalities (see Article 3528, supra); capacity, vices of consent, and unworthiness (see Articles 3529–3530, supra); and interpretation (see Article 3531, supra). This Article introduces a further exception pertaining to forced heirship.

(c) The forced heirship exception. According to this Article, the forced heirship law of this state shall not apply to cases which present cumulatively the following three fact-patterns: (1) the testator was domiciled outside this state at the time he acquired the immovable; (2) he was domiciled outside this state at the time of his death; and (3) he left no forced heirs domiciled in this state at the time of his death. In such cases, Louisiana has no true interest in applying its forced heirship law against the will of the foreign testator for the protection of his foreign heirs. The mere fact that the property is situated here is not sufficient to justify the application of Louisiana's forced heirship law, a law that is geared toward people, that is, Louisiana people, rather than property.

The exception is narrowly drawn so as to apply only to cases which, aside from the fact that they involve a Louisiana immovable, are completely alien to Louisiana. For instance, in order for the exception to apply, the testator must have been domiciled outside Louisiana both at the time he acquired the immovable and at the time of death. This is designed to prevent long-time Louisiana domiciliaries from effectively disinheriting their children by establishing a domicile outside Louisiana shortly before their death.

Art. 3534. Immovables situated in another state

Except as otherwise provided in this Title, testate and intestate succession to immovables situated in another state is governed by the law that would be applied by the courts of that state.

If the deceased died domiciled in this state and left at least one forced heir who at the time was domiciled in this state, the value of those immovables shall be included in calculating the disposable portion and in satisfying the legitime.

Acts 1991, No. 923, § 1, eff. Jan. 1, 1992.

(a) Scope and comparison with present law. This Article applies to testate and intestate succession to immovables situated in another state. The first paragraph calls for the application of the law that would be applied by the courts of the situs and thus restates the traditional rule followed in all states of the United States. Except perhaps for the renvoi component, the prior Louisiana rule was the same. See Symeonides, "Exploring the 'Dismal Swamp': Revising Louisiana's Conflicts Law on Successions", 47 La.L.Rev. 1029, 1090–1092 (1987).

(b) Renvoi. By authorizing the application of "the law that would be applied by the courts" of the foreign situs, the first paragraph of this Article authorizes a renvoi, that is, a consideration of the conflicts rules of the foreign state. See Article 3517, supra. More often than not, these rules will point to the internal, substantive successions law of the situs state. If so, the Louisiana court should apply that law. Occasionally, however, the foreign conflicts rules might point to the law of another state on certain issues. If so, the Louisiana court should follow that reference to the law of the third state and stop the reference there. Although renvoi might introduce some complexity into the choice-of-law process, renvoi has the advantage of ensuring a uniform treatment of questions pertaining to land, regardless of the forum in which these questions are litigated. Compare with Restatement Second, Conflict of Laws, §§ 236, 239 (1971).

(c) The forced heirship exception. The second paragraph establishes an exception to the situs rule of the first paragraph in favor of the forced heirship law of this state for cases in which both the deceased and at least one of his forced heirs are domiciled in this state at the time of death. The exception authorizes the inclusion of the value of the foreign immovable into the fictitious mass of the estate of the Louisiana deceased for purposes of calculating his disposable portion and satisfying the legitime of his forced heirs.

(d) Rationale. The rationale for this exception is the same as in Article 3533, supra. The forced heirship law is designed for the protection of the descendants of the testator. When any such descendants are domiciled in Louisiana, this state has a genuine interest in protecting them. When the testator is also domiciled in Louisiana, the interest of this state in protecting his descendants by imposing on his freedom of disposition the limits considered appropriate by the collective will outweighs any interest the foreign situs might have. The fact that the property is not situated in Louisiana does not detract from either the strength or the legitimacy of this interest. Indeed, the only interest the foreign situs might have in such cases is the interest of preserving the integrity of its recordation system. This interest, however, will not be affected by the application of Louisiana law because a Louisiana court may not, under this or any other Article, render a judgment directly affecting foreign immovables, and because any judgment will have to be recorded in the situs state to be effective there.

(e) Once the second paragraph of this Article becomes applicable, the paragraph will benefit even those forced heirs of the deceased who are domiciled in another state. Although these foreign heirs do not clearly come under the protective scope of the Louisiana law of forced heirship, the application of that law for their protection may be justified on grounds of evenhandedness and uniform treatment of the estate, as well as other grounds.

(f) Enforcement. Very often, the rule of the second paragraph of this Article may be implemented without the need of enforcing the Louisiana judgment at the foreign situs, such as when the testator had enough movables or Louisiana immovables to satisfy the legitime. The Louisiana court will then include the value of the foreign immovables in calculating the mass of the estate and the value of the disposable portion, and will satisfy the legitime out of property within its jurisdiction. When the property within its jurisdiction is insufficient to satisfy the legitime, a Louisiana court may still be able to implement this provision with regard to the foreign immovables if the court has in personam jurisdiction over the parties affected, by ordering them to execute the necessary conveyances. If carefully cast in terms not purporting to bind directly the foreign immovable, but only the parties before the court, the judgment would be valid. It would be enforceable in Louisiana by contempt proceedings and in the situs state through recognition proceedings under the full faith and credit clause of the Constitution.

TITLE V—REAL RIGHTS

Art. 3535. Real rights in immovables

Real rights in immovables situated in this state are governed by the law of this state.

Real rights in immovables situated in another state are governed by the law that would be applied by the courts of that state.

Whether a thing is an immovable is determined according to the substantive law of the state in which the thing is situated.

Acts 1991, No. 923, § 1, eff. Jan. 1, 1992.

REVISION COMMENTS—1991

(a) Terminology. This Article applies to real rights as defined by Louisiana substantive law (see, e.g., La.Civ.Code Art. 476 (Rev.1978) and official comments thereunder). Whether a right in a thing qualifies as a real right is determined according to Louisiana law, even if the thing to which the right applies is situated in another state. However, whether a thing qualifies as an immovable is determined according to the substantive law of the state where the thing is situated. For Louisiana immovables, see, e.g., La.Civ.Code Arts. 462–470 (Rev.1978). An immovable may be corporeal or incorporeal, see La.Civ.Code Art. 470 (Rev.1978), and includes its component parts, see, e.g., La.Civ.Code Art. 469 (Rev.1978).

(b) Scope. Under this Article, the law of the situs of the immovable governs the real right itself, that is, its effects, incidents, and extinction. However, except for rights created by operation of law, such as by prescription or accession, the law of the situs does not necessarily govern the juridical act that purports to create the real right. For example, when the juridical act purporting to establish the real right is a contract, its formal and substantive validity and the rights flowing therefrom are determined according to the law designated by Articles 3537–3541, infra. Although these Articles will often point to the law of the situs, they may sometimes authorize the application of another law. Similarly, when the act purporting to establish the real right is a testament, its formal validity and interpretation will be determined according to the law designated respectively by Articles 3528 and 3531, supra, and the testator's capacity according to the law designated by Article 3529, supra. That law will determine, for instance, whether the testament is formally valid, whether the testator was of sound mind, and whether he intended to establish a successive usufruct or some other dismemberment of ownership. Once these facts are established, the law designated by this Article, that is, the law of the situs, will determine whether the dismemberment constitutes a prohibited substitution, or, in the case of a usufruct, what its incidents and the respective rights of the usufructuary are vis-a-vis the naked owner.

This distinction between the real right itself and the juridical act by which the right is established is inherent in the very nature of real rights. The real significance of classifying a right as real appears not in the relationship between the grantor and the grantee of the right, but rather in the relationship between the grantee-holder of the right and third parties. The former relationship is always juridical and is governed by the law applicable to the juridical act. The latter relationship is often not juridical, but rather extrajuridical, and forms the subject matter of this Article.

(c) Application. This Article establishes a bilateral conflicts rule applicable to both Louisiana and foreign immovables. The first paragraph applies to immovables situated in this state and calls for the application of the internal law of this state. The second paragraph applies to immovables situated in another state and calls for the application of the "whole law" of that state, that is, including its conflicts law. See Article 3517, supra. This renvoi is a well-accepted feature of American conflicts law in cases involving immovables.

(d) Rationale. Although severely criticized by most modern commentators, the situs rule restated in this Article remains one of the most well-entrenched rules in Louisiana and American conflicts law. In any event, most of these criticisms are directed against the excessive breadth of the traditional situs rule rather than against its core. These criticisms were taken into account in formulating the specific exceptions to the situs rule that are contained in the Titles on marital property, supra, successions, supra, and conventional obligations, infra. In a mineral-rich state like Louisiana with a substantive law quite different from that of its neighboring states, it would be unwise to go beyond these exceptions and to abandon the situs rule altogether. Within the confines prescribed by these exceptions, the situs rule has a useful role to play in any choice-of-law system, traditional or "modern".

Art. 3536.   Real rights in corporeal movables

Real rights in corporeal movables are governed by the law of the state in which the movable was situated at the time the right was acquired.

Nevertheless, after the removal of a movable to this state, a real right acquired while the movable was situated in another state is subject to the law of this state if: (1) the right is incompatible with the law of this state; or (2) the holder of the right knew or should have known of the removal to this state; or (3) justice and equity so dictate in order to protect third parties who, in good faith, have dealt with the thing after its removal to this state.

Acts 1991, No. 923, § 1, eff. Jan. 1, 1992.

REVISION COMMENTS—1991

(a) Terminology. This Article applies to real rights as defined by Louisiana substantive law (see, e.g., La.Civ.Code Article 476 (Rev.1978) and official comments thereunder). Whether a right in a thing qualifies as a real right is determined according to Louisiana law, even if the thing to which the right applies is situated in another state.

Real rights are subdivided into principal and accessory. The principal real rights pertain to the substance of the thing, which is thereby placed at the service of the holder of the right. They consist of ownership and its permissible dismemberments. The accessory real rights are accessory to the obligation they secure and include pledges, chattel mortgages, special privileges or liens, and other security interests recognized by other legal systems. Although most conflicts cases involve accessory real rights such as chattel mortgages, these rights are subject to special legislation that contains conflicts provisions. As explained in comment (c) below, these special conflicts provisions are not superseded by this Article, which is intended to serve as a residual Article for cases not provided for elsewhere by legislation.

This Article applies to corporeal movables only. Incorporeal movables are intentionally excluded from the scope of this Article. Consequently, the inherently more complex conflicts that involve incorporeals should be resolved under the flexible formula of Article 3515, the residual article. Whether a thing is a corporeal movable is determined according to the law of the state where the thing is situated. For Louisiana movables, see, e.g., La.Civ.Code Arts. 471–475 (Rev.1978).

(b) Scope. This Article applies to real rights in corporeal movables, that is, to the relation between the holder of the right and third parties other than those involved in the juridical act that gave rise to the right. Except for rights created by operation of law, as by prescription or accession, the relationship between the holder and the grantor of the right is not governed by this Article, but by other articles applicable to the relationship. For example, if the relationship was created by contract, its formal and substantive validity and the rights flowing therefrom are determined according to the law designated by the Articles of the Title on conventional obligations, infra. Similarly, when the relationship between the grantor and the grantee of the right is based on a testament, its formal validity and interpretation as well as the testator's capacity are determined according to the law designated respectively by Articles 3528, 3531 and 3529, supra. That law determines, for instance, whether the testament was formally valid, whether the testator was of sound mind, and whether he intended to establish a successive usufruct or rather some other dismemberment of ownership. Once these facts are established, the law designated by this Article will determine whether the dismemberment constitutes a prohibited substitution, or, in the case of a usufruct, what its incidents and the respective rights of the usufructuary are vis-a-vis the naked owner.

(c) Residual character of this Article. This Article is not intended to supersede more specific statutory conflicts rules presently found in Louisiana law, such as in the Vehicle Certificate of Title Law (La.R.S. 32:704 et seq.), the Lease of Movables Act (La.R.S. 9:3301 et seq.), and, more importantly, La.R.S. 10:9–103, which was derived from § 9–103 of the U.C.C. and became effective on January 1, 1990.

(d) Content and structure. The first paragraph of this Article establishes a bilateral choice-of-law rule applicable to movables which, at the time the question arises, may or may not be situated in this state. The second paragraph establishes a unilateral choice-of-law rule applicable to movables which, at the time the question arises, are situated in Louisiana, but which were formerly situated in another state. This Article does not address directly the reverse fact-pattern, that is, cases in which a thing subject to a real right acquired in this state is subsequently moved to another state. Such cases are rarely encountered by Louisiana courts. When they do arise, Louisiana courts may devise appropriate solutions drawn from the principles of Article 3515, supra, as well as from the first and the second paragraphs of this Article.

(e) Rationale of the first paragraph. The first paragraph provides that real rights in a corporeal movable are governed by the law of the situs of the movable at the time that the asserted right was acquired. The situs rule is well-entrenched in Louisiana jurisprudence, and seems to be the focal point of the expectations of parties when dealing with corporeal movables.

(f) Rationale of the second paragraph. Because movables may be moved from one state to another, any choice-of-law rule based on situs as the exclusive connecting factor leads inevitably to many problems known collectively as the "conflit mobile". Rigid adherence to the law of the former situs rule would ignore the legitimate interest of the second situs in protecting its own citizens who have acquired rights in justifiable reliance upon the law of that state. By the same token, rigid adherence to the law of the second situs would mean that rights created while a thing was situated in one state could be extinguished by subsequent transactions in another state after the thing has been removed to that state. The conflict between the two situses must be resolved in a way that takes into account the legitimate interests of each situs. The expectations of the parties provide the key for resolving the conflict. The first state has an interest in protecting the holder of the right validly acquired while the thing was located in that state, while the second state has an interest in protecting innocent third parties who have dealt with the thing after its removal to the second state.

These are the lines along which the second paragraph of this Article attempts to strike a compromise between the interests of the first situs as well as the constitutionally sanctioned principle of continuity of rights on the one hand, and the interests of the second situs on the other. The compromise consists of (a) defining narrowly the circumstances under which the foreign-created right will be subject to the law of the second situs, Louisiana; and (b) applying the law of the former situs to all other situations where the exceptions contained in this paragraph are not applicable. This compromise is consistent with Louisiana jurisprudence.

(g) Application of the second paragraph. When the conditions described in the second paragraph are met, the foreign-created right will be "subject" to Louisiana law. However, subjecting the foreign-created right to Louisiana law does not necessarily entail the extinction or subordination of the foreign-created right, but simply means that the right is subjected to the same requirements, and to the same protection and rank, as provided by Louisiana law for those rights. For instance, if Louisiana law requires recordation to make the right assertible vis-a-vis third parties, recordation must be effected within the time limits specified by Louisiana law. Similarly, if Louisiana law ranks the right lower than other specific rights in the same thing, whether previously or subsequently acquired, such a ranking will have to be recognized by Louisiana courts.

(h) Compatibility with the law of this state. The second paragraph of this Article provides that the continuing vitality in this state of rights acquired in another state after the thing has been removed to this state depends on the extent to which they are compatible with the law of this state. This is so regardless of whether the holder of the right knew or should have known of the thing's removal to this state and regardless of the good or bad faith of third parties who have subsequently dealt with the thing in this state.

A foreign-created right may be totally or partly incompatible with the law of this state. Incompatibility may also encompass only some aspects of the right, such as the means available to the holder of the right for its enforcement. Joint tenancies and, until 1985, lease-purchase agreements may be cited as examples of rights the substance of which is not compatible with Louisiana law. Louisiana should not be forced to recognize rights that do not fit into its own scheme of real rights, especially in light of the numerus clausus of real rights under La.Civ.Code Article 476 (Rev.1978). However, this principle should not prevent Louisiana courts from giving the holder of the right protection that approximates as much as possible the protection accorded by the law of the other state. In the case of joint tenancy, for example, Louisiana would not recognize the survivorship feature of joint tenancy under the common law but might give each joint tenant the Louisiana version of co-ownership. Examples of foreign-created rights which, though themselves recognized by Louisiana law, are nevertheless partly incompatible with the law of this state are foreign security interests that allow the creditor to use self-help in repossessing the thing and to sell it at a private sale without appraisal. In such cases, enforcement of the right must comply with Louisiana law.

(i) Notice to the holder of the right of the removal of the thing to this state. The second paragraph of this Article also provides that if the holder of a real right acquired according to the law of another state where the thing was originally situated knew or should have known of the subsequent removal of the thing to this state, his rights are subject to the law of this state. As said earlier, this rule, which is derived directly from pertinent Louisiana jurisprudence, does not mean that these rights will necessarily be subordinated to rights of third parties subsequently acquired under the law of this state. The rule simply means that the holder of the foreign-created right will have to comply with Louisiana law in order to secure the continuing protection and enjoyment of his rights. For instance, if Louisiana law requires recordation in order to protect him vis-a-vis third parties, he would have to comply with that requirement within the time limits specified by Louisiana law. Similarly, if Louisiana law ranks his right lower than other specific rights in the same thing, whether previously or subsequently acquired, such a ranking will have to be recognized by Louisiana courts. Subjecting the foreign-created right to Louisiana law in such circumstances is not unfair to the holder of the right, in light of his actual or constructive knowledge of the removal of the thing to Louisiana and of the opportunity available to him to take protective measures.

(j) Removal of the thing to this state without notice to the holder of the right; protection of third parties in the interest of justice. On the other hand, when the holder of the foreign-created right did not know and had no reason to know of the removal of the thing to this state, Louisiana courts have taken the position that he ought to be protected even as against innocent third parties, and without any limitation as to time. This position of the Louisiana jurisprudence was contrary to § 9–103 of the Uniform Commercial Code, which protects the holder of a foreign-created security interest for only four months after the removal of the thing to the forum state. Thus, under this jurisprudence, the holder of a foreign-created right was treated more generously than all other sister states would treat the holder of a Louisiana-created right in the reverse situation. This difference has been removed by the enactment in Act 135 of 1989, of R.S. 10:9–103, which is based on U.C.C. § 9–103, and which became effective on January 1, 1990. The second paragraph of this Article addresses this problem with regard to those areas of the law that are not covered by R.S. 10:9–103.

The second paragraph of this Article provides that the foreign-created right will be subject to Louisiana law if "justice and equity so dictate in order to protect third parties who, in good faith, have dealt with the thing after its removal to this state." When these conditions are met, the law of this state applies even if the holder of the foreign-created right had no reason to know of the removal of the thing to this state. Because of this, his right should be subjected to the law of this state only in exceptional cases and only when necessary in order to avoid gross inequity. The reference to the dictates of "justice and equity" is intended to convey this idea, namely that the foreign-created right may be subordinated only if a compelling case can be made in the interest of justice and equity. The reference to third parties indicates that only they are the intended beneficiaries of this provision and not the immediate parties to the transaction that created the right. Moreover, the third parties may invoke the protection of this provision only if they have dealt with the thing in good faith, even if good faith is not required by the substantive law for the acquisition of the right asserted by them. Thus, the reference to good faith is intended to raise the standard for subordinating the foreign-created right to a right created by Louisiana law.

The following example illustrates the intended application of this provision: A stolen movable that is not subject to a registration requirement (see La.Civ.Code Article 525 (Rev.1979)) is sold in Louisiana by "a merchant customarily selling similar things" (see La.Civ.Code Article 524 (Rev.1979)), and bought by a third party in good faith. Civil Code Article 524 (Rev.1979) protects the purchaser by requiring the owner, in order to recover the thing, to reimburse to the purchaser the purchase price. Without the above provision, this protection would probably not be available to the Louisiana purchaser if the owner of the stolen thing had acquired ownership of it in another state and did not know or have any reason to know that, after it was stolen from him, it was brought to Louisiana. The few Louisiana cases in which this problem was addressed have protected the purchaser but did so without any discussion of the conflicts problem. See, e.g., Southeast Equipment Co. Inc. v. Office of State Police, 437 So.2d 1184 (La.App. 4th Cir.1983). This provision sanctions these cases and supplies a rationale for deciding similar cases by providing that the purchaser should be protected if he was in good faith, and justice and equity so dictate. The defendant's good faith in such a case would make the true owner's rights in the thing subject to the law of this state, if justice and equity so dictate. In this case, because of the fact that under La.Civ.Code Article 524 (Rev.1979) the purchaser's good faith is a necessary prerequisite to his having a right to reimbursement, the requirement of good faith imposed by this provision may appear superfluous. However, the need for this requirement appears more clearly in other cases in which good faith is not a condition for the acquisition of a right by a third party.

TITLE VI—CONVENTIONAL OBLIGATIONS

Art. 3537. General rule

Except as otherwise provided in this Title, an issue of conventional obligations is governed by the law of the state whose policies would be most seriously impaired if its law were not applied to that issue.

That state is determined by evaluating the strength and pertinence of the relevant policies of the involved states in the light of: (1) the pertinent contacts of each state to the parties and the transaction, including the place of negotiation, formation, and performance of the contract, the location of the object of the contract, and the place of domicile, habitual residence, or business of the parties; (2) the nature, type, and purpose of the contract; and (3) the policies referred to in Article 3515, as well as the policies of facilitating the orderly planning of transactions, of promoting multistate commercial intercourse, and of protecting one party from undue imposition by the other.

Acts 1991, No. 923, § 1, eff. Jan. 1, 1992.

REVISION COMMENTS—1991

(a) Scope. This Article establishes the general approach for selecting the law applicable to conventional obligations. Being more general, this Article will be superseded by the more specific Articles contained in this Title. Articles 3538 and 3539, infra, are more specific with regard to issues of form and capacity respectively. Both Articles contain language that regulates more specifically their relationship to this Article. (See comment (e) under Article 3538 and comment (b) under Article 3539, infra). The same is true with regard to Article 3540. See comments (d) and (f) under Article 3540, infra. In essence, this Article applies in the absence of an effective choice of law by the parties. The existence, validity, and effectiveness of a choice-of-law agreement is decided according to the law applicable to the particular issue under Articles 3537–3539. See comments (c) and (d) under Article 3540, infra.

According to Article 14, supra, this and any other Article of this Title apply "[u]nless otherwise expressly provided by the law of this state". The following are among the Revised Statutes that "provide otherwise": R.S. 10:1–105 (U.C.C.); R.S. 22:611 et seq. (Insurance Code); R.S. 9:3302 et seq. (Lease of Movables Act); R.S. 9:3511 (consumer credit transactions); R.S. 51:1418 (consumer transactions). When applicable, these statutes will prevail, being more specific, over the provisions of this Section.

(b) Comparison with prior law. Paragraph 2 of Civil Code Article 15 (Redesignated 1987) provided that the "effect" of juridical acts was "regulated by the laws of the country where such acts are to have effect." Without any guidance as to how to identify the place of the "effect" of the contract, Louisiana courts reached conflicting determinations that included the place of performance, the place intended by the parties, the common domicile of the parties, the place where the object of the contract was situated, and sometimes the place that, from the totality of the circumstances, had the strongest connection with the contract and the parties. See Note, "Conflict of Laws—Contracts", 47 La.L.Rev. 1181 (1987); Comment, "Conflict of Laws: Contracts and Other Obligations", 35 La.L.Rev. 112 (1974). In recent years, a significant minority of cases found in Jagers v. Royal Indemnity Co., 276 So.2d 309 (La.1973), which is the leading case that introduced into Louisiana the modern American choice-of-law doctrine in tort conflicts, the needed excuse for ignoring Civil Code Article 15 (Redesignated 1987) and applying instead the so-called "governmental interest analysis", or the approach of the Second Conflicts Restatement, or both. See Note, "Conflict of Laws—Contracts", 47 La.L.Rev. 1181 (1987). In retrospect, the inherent vagueness of Civil Code Article 15 (Redesignated 1987) may well have been a blessing in disguise, since it protected the Louisiana courts from being locked into the wooden lex loci contractus rule that was then being followed in other states. This Article maintains this flexibility but also provides sufficient guidance on how to use it.

(c) Relation to Article 3515. The first paragraph of this Article enunciates the objective of the choice-of-law process for contract conflicts in language that is purposefully identical to that of the first paragraph of Article 3515. These two Articles and the comments accompanying them are intended to

893

be read together. As in Article 3515, supra, the objective is to identify "the state whose policies would be most seriously impaired", that is, the state that, in light of its connection to the parties and the transaction and its interests implicated in the conflict, would bear the most serious legal, social, economic, and other consequences "if its law were not applied" to the issue at hand. As envisioned by this Article, the search for the applicable law should not be a mechanical, quantitative process, but should be based on an objective and impartial evaluation of the consequences of the choice-of-law decision on each of the involved states with a view towards accommodating their respective interests rather than selfishly promoting the interests of one state at the expense of the others.

The second paragraph of this Article prescribes the process or method for attaining the objective enunciated in the first paragraph in language that is parallel to, though more specific than, the language employed in the second paragraph of Article 3515. Article 3537 adds specificity to the description of this process by: providing an illustrative list of the factual contacts that are usually pertinent in contract conflicts; by adding to the list of "policies mentioned in Article 3515" certain sets of policies that are ex hypothesi pertinent in contract conflicts; and by providing that the evaluation of the strength and pertinence of the involved policies is to be made "in the light of . . . the nature, type, and purpose of the contract".

(d) The process. Thus, the first step of the process is to identify "the relevant policies of the involved states". A state is considered "involved" when it has any of the factual contacts expressly listed in the second paragraph of this Article or included by implication in the phrase "pertinent contacts". The "relevant policies" of that state are identified through the resources of the interpretative process by focusing on the specific rules of substantive contract law whose applicability is being urged in the particular case.

The second step of the process is to evaluate "the strength and pertinence of [these] policies . . . in the light of" the three sets of factors listed in the second paragraph, to wit: (i) the factual contacts of each involved state to the parties and the transaction; (ii) the "nature, type and purpose of the contract"; and (iii) the policies listed in clause (3).

(e) Factual contacts. Clause (1) of the second paragraph lists the most important factual contacts or connecting factors in light of which the strength and the spatial pertinence of the policies of the involved states are to be evaluated. This list is neither exhaustive nor hierarchical and is intended to discourage rather than encourage a mechanistic counting of contacts as a means of selecting the applicable law. The fact that one state has more contacts with the dispute than another state does not necessarily mean that the law of the first state should be applied to any or all issues of the dispute, unless the contacts are of the kind that bring into play policies of that state that "would be most seriously impaired if its law were not applied" to the issue at hand. For example, in a contract pertaining to immovables, the fact that the "location of the object of the contract" is in one state may well be more important than all other factual contacts of another state, if the issue in dispute is such as to bring into play a strong policy of the situs state concerning land utilization or security of land titles. Similarly, the place of the performance of a contract would normally be more important than most other factual contacts combined, if the issue in dispute is the availability of specific performance and the contract is considered immoral under the law of the place of performance.

(f) Multistate considerations. Through its cross-reference to Article 3515, clause (3) of the second paragraph of this Article incorporates by reference the list of policies contained therein as well as the analysis prescribed by that Article. See comment (c) under Article 3515, supra. The listing of additional multistate policies is not intended to alter that analysis, but rather to add specificity to it by mentioning expressly policies that are likely to be implicated in most multistate contract conflicts. The listing of these policies is neither exhaustive nor hierarchical. Their relative importance will depend on the particular contacts of the enacting jurisdiction, the nature, type, and purpose of the contract, and the particular issue with regard to which there exists an actual conflict.

(g) The nature, type, and purpose of the contract. Deliberately placed between the lists of factual contacts and multistate considerations, "the nature, type, and purpose of the contract" (clause (2)) should help orient the dialectical process of evaluating the strength and pertinence of state policies. Indeed, the nature, type, or purpose of the particular contract may provide useful pointers for assessing the relative importance of factual contacts and the relative pertinence of multistate considerations. For example, in a contract with family-law aspects (e.g., a child-support agreement), the domicile of the parties would normally be more important than any of the other factual contacts listed in clause (1), and the policy of facilitating and promoting multistate commercial intercourse (clause 3) would be far less relevant than any of the other multistate considerations listed in clause (3). Similarly, in an employment contract, the place where the services were to be rendered would usually be among the more important factual contacts, and the policy of "protecting one party from undue imposition by the other" would acquire particular significance. Finally, the latter policy would usually be more important in small consumer contracts than in commercial contracts between parties with equal bargaining power.

Art. 3538.   Form

A contract is valid as to form if made in conformity with: (1) the law of the state of making; (2) the law of the state of performance to the extent that performance is to be rendered in that state; (3) the law of the state of common domicile or place of business of the parties; or (4) the law governing the substance of the contract under Articles 3537 or 3540.

Nevertheless, when for reasons of public policy the law governing the substance of the contract under Article 3537 requires a certain form, there must be compliance with that form.

Acts 1991, No. 923, § 1, eff. Jan. 1, 1992.

REVISION COMMENTS—1991

(a) Scope. This Article applies only to issues of form of the contract. Whether an issue is one of form is determined by the law of the forum. When the issue is one of form, this Article prevails, as more specific, over Article 3537, supra, except as specified in this Article. See comment (e), infra.

(b) Comparison with prior law. Paragraph 1 of Civil Code Article 15 (Redesignated 1987) provided that "[t]he form . . . of public and private written instruments . . . [is] governed [exclusively] by the laws . . . of the places where they are passed or executed[,]" whether or not those laws would uphold the contract. For jurisprudence see Note, "Conflict of Laws—Contracts", 47 La.L.Rev. 1181, 1208–10 (1987). Under this Article, the law of the place of the making is no longer the exclusive law for determining the formal validity of the contract. Moreover, that law is applied only to validate, not invalidate, the contract. This Article establishes what is known in conflicts literature as a "rule of validation", that is, a rule that favors validation by authorizing the application of whichever of the laws mentioned therein would validate the contract. This rule liberalizes Louisiana law and brings it into line with the judicial practice of most sister states and with the statutory rules of most continental countries.

(c) Rationale. The premise underlying this approach is that, more often than not, the laws of the various states about contractual formalities differ only in detail rather than in fundamental policy. Because of this, failure to meet the technical requirements of one state should not, without more, defeat the intent of the parties to have a binding contract, as long as their contract complies with the form requirements of another state reasonably related to the parties and the transaction. Each of the states enumerated in the first paragraph of this Article would be sufficiently related to the transaction and the parties to warrant application of its law in order to validate the contract. This would be true even if the contract would be formally invalid under the law of all other states mentioned therein. However, validation should not be an end in itself. Sometimes, formal requirements are used as means of ensuring observance of strongly-held substantive policies. Any rule of validation must therefore be subject to appropriate exceptions in order to preserve those policies. This is the purpose of the exception provided in the second paragraph of this Article.

(d) Operation of first paragraph. The first paragraph of this Article refers to "the law governing the substance of the contract under Articles 3537 or 3540." Article 3537, supra, provides the applicable law in the absence of a valid choice by the parties, and defines the limits of their choice when one is made. This law is usually referred to in the literature as the lex causae or the "proper law of the contract". Article 3540, infra, authorizes, under certain conditions specified therein, the application of the law chosen or clearly relied upon by the parties. If the contract satisfies the form requirements of the chosen law, the contract will be considered valid even if it does not satisfy the requirements of any other state enumerated in Article 3538. However, as with any of the other laws enumerated in the first paragraph of this Article, the application of the chosen law is subject to the public policy limitation prescribed in the second paragraph of this Article. For the risks and advantages of this apparent "bootstrapping", see comment (c) under Article 3540, infra.

(e) Operation of second paragraph. The second paragraph of this Article introduces a limited exception to the rule of validation established in the first paragraph. The exception is in favor of the lex causae only, that is, the law that, under the factors enumerated in Article 3537, supra, would be applicable to the particular issue in the absence of an effective choice of law by the parties. The exception comes into operation when the party who challenges the formal validity of a contract that is formally valid under any one of the laws enumerated in the first paragraph of this Article proves that: (1) under the principles of Article 3537, supra, the law of another state would have been applicable to the issue; and (2) that state would invalidate the contract "for reasons of public policy". In the Draft submitted to the Council of the Louisiana State Law Institute, the words "public policy" were preceded by the qualifier "strong". The Council deleted the latter word based on the understanding that, by definition, only strongly held beliefs of a particular state qualify for the characterization of "public policy".

The following two examples illustrate the operation of the second paragraph of this Article. An employment contract that complies with the law of the place of making but not with the law of the state where the services are to be rendered would be formally valid under the first paragraph of this Article. However, if under the principles of Article 3537, the law of the latter state would be the law applicable to the substance of the contract, and if that state would invalidate the contract "for reasons of public policy", such as the policy of protecting the weaker party from fraudulent exploitation, then the contract would have to be declared formally invalid under the second paragraph of this Article. The same result would be reached in a situation in which a contract pertaining to immovables complies with the form requirements of the law of the place of making but not with those of the law of the situs of the immovable. If, under the principles of Article 3537, the law of the situs would be the law applicable to the substance of the contract, and assuming further that the particular rule of the situs that had not been complied with reflected a public policy of the situs state, such as a policy designed to preserve security of titles, then the contract would be declared formally invalid under the second paragraph of this Article. For purposes of comparison, see Article 9, par. 6 of the EEC Convention on Contractual Obligations of 1980.

Art. 3539. Capacity

A person is capable of contracting if he possesses that capacity under the law of either the state in which he is domiciled at the time of making the contract or the state whose law is applicable to the contract under Article 3537.

Acts 1991, No. 923, § 1, eff. Jan. 1, 1992.

REVISION COMMENTS—1991

(a) Scope. This Article applies to issues of contractual capacity and incapacity as defined by Louisiana Civil Code Articles 1918–26 (Rev.1984) (that is, minority, interdiction, and being deprived of reason) as well as to similar incapacities prescribed by other legal systems. Being more specific on the issue of capacity, this Article prevails over Article 3540, infra. Consequently, the capacity of the parties to choose the applicable law is to be determined under this Article. (See comment (d) under Article 3540, infra).

(b) Operation. This Article provides in effect that the search for the law applicable to capacity should begin by looking first to the law of the state that presumptively has the greatest interest in determining the issue, that is, the domicile of each contracting party. If all parties are considered capable of contracting under the laws of their respective domiciles, this will normally put an end to the matter. However, if one party is incapable of contracting under the law of his domicile, then the court should return to Article 3537, supra, with two questions in mind. The first question is whether the law of a state other than that of the domicile of the incapable party would be applicable to this particular issue of capacity under the principles of Article 3537, including especially the individualized issue-by-issue analysis that is built into that Article. If the answer to this question is negative, that is, if the law of the domicile of the incapable party is also the lex causae, then the contract is to be considered invalid. If the answer is affirmative, that is, if the lex causae is the law of a state other than that of the domicile of the incapable party, the court will ask the second question, namely, whether under the lex causae that party would be considered capable of contracting. If the answer to this question is yes, the contract will be considered valid, otherwise invalid.

The same two-step process should be followed if both contracting parties lack contractual capacity under the law of their respective domiciles. It is conceivable, though perhaps not likely, that the law of a third state would be the lex causae with regard to that issue under the principles of Article 3537, supra. If so, and if that law would uphold the contract as to capacity, the contract should be upheld.

(c) Rationale. The objective of this Article is to attain an appropriate equilibrium between two often competing policies. The first is the policy of protecting security of transactions and commercial expectations. This policy would be served by a choice-of-law rule that favors validation. The second is the policy of protecting parties whom the law considers to be in need of protection. This policy would have been served by an unqualified application of the law of the domicile of the incapable party. Because it authorizes the application of whichever of the two laws (the lex domicilii or the lex causae) validates the contract, this Article would seem to favor the former policy too much at the expense of the latter. However, despite a tilt towards validation, this Article neither compels nor guarantees validation a priori but instead makes it dependent on the highly flexible and individualized approach of selecting the applicable law for the particular issue under Article 3537, supra.

The initial resort to the law of the domicile provided for in this Article is consistent with Louisiana jurisprudence and its civilian origin. See Symeonides, "Exploring the 'Dismal Swamp': Revising Louisiana's Conflicts Law on Successions", 47 La.L.Rev. 1029, 1055–56 (1987); Note, "Conflict of Laws—Contracts", 47 La.L.Rev. 1181, 1203–08 (1987). It is also consistent with the teachings of most modern American choice-of-law theories which have come to recognize the important role of domicile, at least as a starting point, in any choice-of-law decision involving capacity. The rules of substantive law on capacity are essentially a priori societal judgments about the maturity, soundness of mind, and need of protection of various classes of persons. They are also conscious legislative determinations that the need of protecting particular classes of persons and their families is strong enough to override the general policy of promoting the security of transactions. In delineating the scope of operation of these rules, the conflicts legislator must begin with the premise that they have been enacted with a view toward protecting people domiciled in the enacting state rather than with the idea of affecting contracts made therein by people domiciled elsewhere. Consequently, that state has an interest in applying these rules in every contract which, whether made within or without its territory, involves one of its domiciliaries whom it considers in need of protection. That interest will not of course always prevail, but it must be the starting point of the search for the applicable law. It goes without saying that the interest of one state in protecting the incapable party may often run contrary to the interest that another—and sometimes of the same—state may have in, for instance, promoting the justified expectations of the other party and the security of transactions in general. By referring to the principles of Article 3537, this Article attempts to provide a flexible formula for resolving such conflicts in favor of the lex causae, that is, in favor of the law of the only other state which has a greater and more legitimate interest in regulating this particular issue than does the state where the incapable party is domiciled.

Art. 3540. Party autonomy

All other issues of conventional obligations are governed by the law expressly chosen or clearly relied upon by the parties, except to the extent that law contravenes the public policy of the state whose law would otherwise be applicable under Article 3537.

Acts 1991, No. 923, § 1, eff. Jan. 1, 1992.

REVISION COMMENTS—1991

(a) Scope. This Article applies to issues other than capacity and form, except as specified in comments (c) and (d), infra. Like any other article in this Book, this Article may be superseded by more specific legislative provisions, such as La.R.S. 10:1–105 (U.C.C.); La.R.S. 22:629 (insurance contracts); La.R.S. 9:3303 (lease of movables); La.R.S. 9:3511 (consumer credit transactions); and La.R.S. 51:1418 (consumer transactions).

(b) Comparison with prior law. This Article restates for multistate contracts the ancient principle of party autonomy that is referred to obliquely in Civil Code Article 7 (Rev. 1987) for domestic contracts. That Article provides that "[p]ersons may not by their juridical acts derogate from laws enacted for the protection of the public interest," and thus affirms the freedom of the parties to derogate from laws not falling within the above characterization. When the contract contains foreign elements, this freedom includes the ability to choose the applicable law. Louisiana courts have recognized this freedom in dozens of cases decided under the similarly phrased Article 11 of the Civil Code of 1870. See Note, "Conflict of Laws—Contracts", 47 La.L.Rev. 1181, 1183–96 (1987). This Article recasts this principle in affirmative terms for conflicts purposes.

(c) Formal validity. The formal validity of a choice-of-law clause in a contract is judged under the law applicable to issues of form under Article 3538, supra. Among the states whose law may be applied to validate the contract as to form under that Article is the state whose "law govern[s] . . . the substance of the contract under Article . . . 3540." This means that if the choice-of-law clause is contained in a contract that is formally valid only under the chosen law, but not under any of the other laws enumerated in Article 3538, the contract and the choice-of-law clause will be considered valid as to form. If this phenomenon is a type of "bootstrapping", it is one that is both innocuous and practically useful. It is innocuous because, under both the exception clause of this Article (see comment (f), infra) and the second paragraph of Article 3538 (see comment (e) under Art. 3538, supra), the chosen law is not allowed to contravene "the public policy of the state whose law would otherwise be applicable under Article 3537." It is practically useful because it allows a contract that is formally valid under the chosen law to be treated as valid unless and until the opposing party demonstrates that the law of another state would have been applicable to the issue under Article 3537 and that the chosen law contravenes the public policy of that state.

(d) Existence and substantive validity. The capacity of the parties to choose the applicable law is governed by the same law that is applicable to contractual capacity in general under Article 3539, supra. Thus the "bootstrapping" phenomenon is avoided with regard to capacity. In order to avoid a similar "bootstrapping" with regard to other "preliminary" issues that pertain to the existence of the choice of law clause, such as consent and vices of consent, these issues should be judged according to the law applicable under Article 3537, supra.

(e) Mode, timing, and scope of the parties' choice. To be recognized under this Article, the contractual choice of law must either be express or implied. It is express when it is literally declared in the contract; it is implied when, on the basis of the surrounding circumstances, especially the provisions of the contract or the conduct of the parties, it is evident that the parties have clearly relied upon the law of a particular state. An implied choice is distinguished from a hypothetical choice. The latter is not recognized by this Article.

The parties may, of course, choose the applicable law after the conclusion of the contract and may modify a choice made earlier. The parties may also choose more than one law to govern their contract. For example, in a contract that is to be performed in more than one state, the parties may provide that details of performance are to be governed by the law of the state in which performance is to take place. Recent continental codifications take the same position on this issue. By the same token, the parties may choose a law to govern only part of their contract. Their choice will be honored if it is otherwise valid under the provisions of this Title. The rest of the contract will be governed by the law applicable to the issue under the other Articles of this Title. Naturally, this partial choice of law, as well as the choice of more than one law, may well result in depecage, namely, the application of different laws to different parts or aspects of the contract. As long as it remains within the limits of party autonomy as defined in this Article, this "private" form of depecage should not be any more objectionable than the depecage brought about by the court. See comment (d), under Article 3515, supra.

As long as they remain within the limits established for party autonomy by the provisions of this Title, the parties are free to include in their choice the conflicts rules of the chosen law. However, unless they expressly provide for that inclusion, it is more logical to assume that they intended to avoid rather than to invite the complexities of renvoi and that, consequently, their choice was intended to be confined to the substantive law of the designated state.

(f) Limits of party autonomy. The parties are in principle free to choose the law of any state, whether or not that state has a particular factual, geographical, or legal relationship with the contract. However, the application of the chosen law is subject to limitations imposed by "the public policy" of the state whose law would "otherwise", that is, in the absence of an effective choice of law by the parties, "be applicable under Article 3537." The parties may not, by simply choosing another law, evade the public policy of the state whose law would have been applicable to the issue "but for" the parties' choice. In the Draft submitted to the Council of the Louisiana State Law Institute, the words "public policy" were preceded by the qualifier "strong". The Council deleted the latter word based on the understanding that, by definition, only strongly held beliefs of a particular state qualify for the characterization of "public policy".

Art. 3541.   Other juridical acts and quasi-contractual obligations

Unless otherwise provided by the law of this state, the law applicable to juridical acts other than contracts and to quasi-contractual obligations is determined in accordance with the principles of this Title.

Acts 1991, No. 923, § 1, eff. Jan. 1, 1992.

REVISION COMMENTS—1991

(a) Scope. This Article applies to juridical acts other than contracts and to quasi-contractual obligations, such as those arising from negotiorum gestio or from the payment of a thing not due. See, e.g., La.Civ.Code Arts. 2293–2313 (1870). This Article applies "[u]nless otherwise provided by the law of this state". For examples of situations in which the law provides otherwise, see the Titles on successions and marital property, supra.

(b) Operation. Obligations falling within the scope of this Article are governed by the law that would be selected on the basis of the principles enunciated in this Title (i.e., Articles 3537–3540, supra) to the extent that those principles are applicable to the particular obligation in question.

(c) Rationale. Other more complete conflicts codifications contain separate special rules for juridical acts other than contracts and for quasi-contractual obligations. In this state, the relative scarcity of conflicts cases involving such issues militates against the drafting of such special rules. Nevertheless, a general "catch-all" article is needed to govern these classes of cases. This Article is intended to meet this need.

TITLE VII—DELICTUAL AND QUASI-DELICTUAL OBLIGATIONS

Art. 3542. General rule

Except as otherwise provided in this Title, an issue of delictual or quasi-delictual obligations is governed by the law of the state whose policies would be most seriously impaired if its law were not applied to that issue.

That state is determined by evaluating the strength and pertinence of the relevant policies of the involved states in the light of: (1) the pertinent contacts of each state to the parties and the events giving rise to the dispute, including the place of conduct and injury, the domicile, habitual residence, or place of business of the parties, and the state in which the relationship, if any, between the parties was centered; and (2) the policies referred to in Article 3515, as well as the policies of deterring wrongful conduct and of repairing the consequences of injurious acts.

Acts 1991, No. 923, § 1, eff. Jan. 1, 1992.

REVISION COMMENTS—1991

(a) The approach of this Article. This Article enunciates the general choice-of-law approach of this Title in the same way Article 3515 enunciates the general approach of this Book. This Article implements for tort conflicts the general approach prescribed by Article 3515 for other conflicts in general. These two Articles and the comments accompanying them are intended to be read together. The first paragraph of this Article enunciates the objective of the choice-of-law process for tort conflicts in language that is purposefully identical to that of the first paragraph of Article 3515. For the meaning of this language, see comment (b) under Article 3515. Similarly, the second paragraph of Article 3542, prescribes the method or process for attaining this objective in language that is only slightly more specific than that of the second paragraph of Article 3515. For a description of this method, see comments (c) and (d) under Article 3515, supra; Symeonides, "Problems and Dilemmas in Codifying Choice of Law for Torts: The Louisiana Experience in Comparative Perspective", 38 Am.J.Comp.L. 431, 436–41 (1990) [hereinafter cited as "Symeonides, Choice of Law for Torts"].

Article 3542 adds specificity to the description of this process in two respects. First, this Article adds to the list of "policies referred to in Article 3515" two sets of policies that are ex hypothesi pertinent in tort conflicts: "the policies of deterring wrongful conduct and of repairing the consequences of injurious acts." Second, this Article provides an illustrative list of the most important factual contacts in light of which to evaluate the strength and pertinence of the above policies. These contacts will serve the dual role of helping, first, to identify the potentially concerned states, and, then, to assess the pertinence and strength of their respective policies and the impact of the decision on such policies. The listing of contacts is neither exhaustive nor hierarchical, and is intended to discourage a mechanistic counting of contacts as a means of selecting the applicable law. The fact that one state has more contacts with the dispute than other states does not necessarily mean that the law of the first state should be applied to any or all issues of the dispute, unless such contacts are of the kind that bring into play policies of that state which "would be most seriously impaired if its law were not applied to the particular issue." In other words, the evaluation of factual contacts should be qualitative rather than quantitative, and should be made in the light of the policies of each contact-state that are pertinent to the particular issue in dispute.

(b) Relation to other articles of this Title. The approach of this Article is further implemented by specific rules contained in Articles 3543–3546, infra, which are a priori legislative determinations of "the state whose policies would be most seriously impaired if its law were not applied". Being more specific, these Articles should, when applicable, prevail over this Article. However, as with any a priori rules, Articles 3543–3546 may in exceptional cases produce a result that is incompatible with the general objective of Article 3542, in pursuance of which they were drafted. In order to avoid such a result, Article 3547 contains an "escape clause" which, when applicable, refers these cases back to Article 3542. Moreover, Articles 3543–3546 do not cover the entire spectrum of cases or issues that might fall under the general headings of these Articles, but only those cases that appeared to be susceptible to a clear and non-controversial choice-of-law rule. The remaining cases or issues are governed by this Article as the residual article. Thus, Article 3542 is intended to perform a general as well as a residual role. In its residual role, this Article applies to all cases and issues that are not included within the scope of Articles 3543–3546. In its general role, this Article will help determine whether issues that do fall within the general scope of Articles 3543–3546 should be decided under the rules contained therein or under the escape clause of Article 3547 which refers them back to Article 3542.

Art. 3543.   Issues of conduct and safety

Issues pertaining to standards of conduct and safety are governed by the law of the state in which the conduct that caused the injury occurred, if the injury occurred in that state or in another state whose law did not provide for a higher standard of conduct.

In all other cases, those issues are governed by the law of the state in which the injury occurred, provided that the person whose conduct caused the injury should have foreseen its occurrence in that state.

The preceding paragraph does not apply to cases in which the conduct that caused the injury occurred in this state and was caused by a person who was domiciled in, or had another significant connection with, this state. These cases are governed by the law of this state.

Acts 1991, No. 923, § 1, eff. Jan. 1, 1992.

REVISION COMMENTS—1991

(a) Scope and terminology. This Article applies to "issues pertaining to standards of conduct and safety" as distinguished from "issues of loss distribution and financial protection" which are governed by Article 3544, infra. This distinction draws from the substantive law of torts and its two fundamental objectives—deterrence and compensation. By way of illustration, so-called "rules of the road" establish or pertain to "standards of conduct and safety", whereas rules that impose a ceiling on the amount of compensatory damages or provide immunity from suit are "rules of loss-distribution and financial protection". From the choice-of-law perspective, the reason for distinguishing between conduct-regulating rules and loss-distribution rules is the fact that their operation in space abides by different principles. Thus, while conduct-regulating rules are territorially oriented, compensation or loss-distribution rules are usually not so oriented. A state's policy of deterrence embodied in its conduct-regulating rules is implicated in all substandard conduct that occurs within its territory, even if the parties involved are not domiciled in that state. Conversely, a state's loss-distribution policy may or may not extend to non-domiciliaries acting within its territory, but does extend to domiciliaries even when they act outside the state. For the origin and rationale of this distinction in American conflicts law, see Symeonides, "Choice of Law for Torts", 441–44.

(b) Relation to Article 3542. Although derived from the general principles of Article 3542, the rules contained in this Article prevail over Article 3542 because they are more specific. However, according to Article 3547, infra, the rules of this Article may, in exceptional cases, be subordinated to the principles of Article 3542. See comment under Article 3547, infra. Moreover, as the residual Article, Article 3542 applies "by default" to cases that involve issues of conduct and safety for which Article 3543 does not provide a rule (see comment (g), infra).

(c) Operation: The applicable law. Based on the premise that conduct-regulating rules are territorially oriented, this Article focuses on the law of the state in which the conduct and/or the injury occurred rather than on the law of the domicile of the involved parties. The law of the domicile is in principle irrelevant to issues of conduct, except when domicile and conduct coincide in the same state. When acting outside the state of their domicile, neither the tortfeasor nor the victim should be allowed to carry with them the conduct-regulating law of that state. Thus, when both the wrongful conduct and the resulting injury occur in the same state, this Article calls for the application of the law of that state. When the conduct occurs in one state and the injury in another, this Article calls for the application of the law of the place of conduct in most cases and for the application of the law of the place of injury in some cases, as explained below.

(d) Conduct and injury in the same state: Application of the law of that state. The first paragraph of this Article provides that when both the tortfeasor's conduct and the victim's injury occur in the same state, the law of that state applies, regardless of the domicile of the parties or any other factors. As long as the issue is one pertaining to regulation of conduct and safety, the state where both the conduct and the injury occur has the best, if not the exclusive, claim for applying its law. This is true regardless of the content of that law, that is, regardless of whether that law provides for a standard of conduct that is lower or higher than, for instance, the law of the state in which either party is domiciled.

(e) *Conduct and injury in different states.* The balance of this Article deals with situations where the tortfeasor's conduct and the victim's injury occur in different states. In these cases the application of the law of one state or the other depends in part on the content of their respective laws, that is, whether they establish a lower or a higher standard of conduct. For example, a "negligence per se" rule establishes a higher standard of conduct than does a rule of ordinary negligence. When the law of the state of conduct is the one prescribing the higher standard, this Article authorizes the application of that law without any qualifications, but subject always to the escape clause of Article 3547. When the law of the state of injury is the one prescribing the higher standard, this Article authorizes the application of that state's law, but only in cases in which: (a) the tortfeasor should have foreseen the occurrence of the injury in that state (see comment (g), infra); and (b) the tortfeasor was not a Louisiana domiciliary or another similarly situated person engaging in conduct within Louisiana (see comment (j), infra).

(f) *Conduct and injury in different states: Application of the law of the state of conduct.* The first paragraph of this Article provides that, if the injurious conduct and the resulting injury occur in different states, the law of the state of conduct applies, if the law of the state of injury "did not provide for a higher standard of conduct" than the state of conduct. Phrased affirmatively, this means that the law of the state of conduct applies if it provides for the same or a higher standard of conduct than does the state of injury. Indeed, when the standards prescribed by the two states are the same, there is no actual conflict and the application of the law of the state of conduct need not be explained or defended. When the law of the state of conduct provides for a higher standard of conduct than does the law of the state of injury, the application of the law of the state of conduct may be justified both in terms of the interest of the two states and from the perspective of the individuals involved. In terms of the interests of the two states, applying the law of the state of conduct when that state imposes the higher standard promotes the policy of that state in policing conduct and preserving safety within its borders, without subordinating whatever policies may be embodied in the law of the state of injury which allows a lower standard of conduct. The effectiveness of the conduct-regulating law of the state of conduct would be seriously impaired if exceptions to it were made for out-of-state injuries. Such exceptions are not warranted by the fact that the state of injury happens to allow a lower standard of conduct, since such a lower standard is designed to protect conduct within, not without, that state. Finally, from the perspective of the individuals involved, there is nothing unfair about subjecting a tortfeasor to the law of the state in which he acted. Having violated the standards of conduct of that state, he should bear the consequences of such violation and should not be allowed to invoke the lower standards of another state. See Symeonides, "Choice of Law for Torts", 445–46 and authorities cited therein.

(g) *Conduct and injury in different states: Application of the law of the state of injury.* The second paragraph of this Article begins with a reference to "all other cases," that is, cases not covered by the first paragraph. These are the cases in which the tortfeasor's conduct and the resulting injury occur in different states, but, unlike the cases covered by the previous paragraph, it is now the state of injury that has the higher standard. From these cases, the third paragraph of this Article exempts cases that involve conduct in Louisiana by a Louisiana tortfeasor (see comment (j), infra). The second paragraph itself confines these "other cases" to those in which the tortfeasor should have foreseen the occurrence of the injury in the state with the higher standard and subjects those cases to the law of that state. This foreseeability requirement makes the application of the law of that state not only constitutional but also appropriate from the choice-of-law perspective. It is a factor of sufficient weight to tip the scales in favor of applying the law of the state that feels the impact of the tortfeasor's conduct and a good enough response to an argument of unfair surprise on his behalf. See Symeonides, "Choice of Law for Torts", 446–47.

As indicated by the use of the verb "should have foreseen", the foreseeability proviso of the second paragraph of this Article contemplates an objective rather than a subjective test. Furthermore, since this is a choice-of-law article, this foreseeability should be understood in a "spatial" sense and should not be confused with the foreseeability of substantive tort law. The pertinent question here is not whether the tortfeasor should have foreseen the occurrence of the injury, but whether he should have foreseen that the injury would have occurred in the particular state in which the injury did occur. If the occurrence of the injury in that state was not reasonably foreseeable, then the law of that state would not apply under this Article. Such a case will then be governed by Article 3542, the residual article, which, depending on the other factors in the case, may or may not produce the same result.

(h) Conduct in more than one state. Cases in which the injurious conduct occurs in more than one state should be approached under the principles of causation of the law of the forum. Ordinarily, these principles will make it possible to determine which particular conduct was, legally speaking, the principal cause of the injury. Following such a determination, the case will be governed by either the law of the state of that conduct or the law of the state of injury, depending on which paragraph of this Article is applicable, and subject always to the "escape clause" of Article 3547, infra. In the latter case, as well as in all cases in which the principles of causation would not yield a clear answer, the applicable law will be determined in accordance with Article 3542. It is also possible that the fact that the injurious conduct was not localized in any single state could, in appropriate circumstances, evoke the escape clause of Article 3547, even without resorting to the principles of causation.

(i) Injury sustained in more than one state. Cases involving multiple victims who sustained their respective injuries in different states should be handled independently for each victim. Cases where the same victim sustained injury in more than one state should be resolved by a factual determination of where the injury was primarily suffered. Following such a determination, the case will be governed by either the law of the state of injury or the law of the state of conduct, depending on which paragraph of this Article is applicable, and subject always to the escape clause of Article 3547.

(j) The third paragraph: Conduct in Louisiana. The third paragraph of this Article is intended to ensure that conduct in Louisiana by persons domiciled in, or having another similarly significant relationship with, this state will not be subjected to higher standards of another state where the injury might occur. For a critique of this provision, see Weintraub, "The Contributions of Symeonides and Kozyris to Making Choice of Law Predictable and Just: An Appreciation and Critique", 38 Am.J.Comp.L. 511, 515–16 (1990). For a response, see Symeonides, "Choice of Law for Torts", 447–48.

Art. 3544.   Issues of loss distribution and financial protection

Issues pertaining to loss distribution and financial protection are governed, as between a person injured by an offense or quasi-offense and the person who caused the injury, by the law designated in the following order:

(1) If, at the time of the injury, the injured person and the person who caused the injury were domiciled in the same state, by the law of that state. Persons domiciled in states whose law on the particular issue is substantially identical shall be treated as if domiciled in the same state.

(2) If, at the time of the injury, the injured person and the person who caused the injury were domiciled in different states: (a) when both the injury and the conduct that caused it occurred in one of those states, by the law of that state; and (b) when the injury and the conduct that caused it occurred in different states, by the law of the state in which the injury occurred, provided that (i) the injured person was domiciled in that state, (ii) the person who caused the injury should have foreseen its occurrence in that state, and (iii) the law of that state provided for a higher standard of financial protection for the injured person than did the law of the state in which the injurious conduct occurred.

Acts 1991, No. 923, § 1, eff. Jan. 1, 1992.

REVISION COMMENTS—1991

(a) Scope: issues. This Article applies to issues of "loss distribution and financial protection" arising out of offenses and quasi-offenses. These issues are distinguished from "issues pertaining to standards of conduct and safety" which are governed by Article 3543. For the meaning and rationale of this distinction, see comment (a) under Article 3543. For its application in American conflicts law, see Symeonides, "Choice of Law for Torts", 441–44; Kozyris & Symeonides, "Choice of Law in the American Courts in 1989: An Overview", 38 Am.J.Comp.L. 601, 616–17 (1990).

(b) Scope: persons. This Article applies to issues of loss-distribution "as between a person injured by an offense or quasi-offense and the person who caused the injury". Thus, the scope of this Article is confined to obligations between the tortfeasor and the victim and their respective universal or particular successors. Obligations arising between joint tortfeasors, or between a tortfeasor and a person vicariously liable for his acts (e.g., employer or parent), are not covered by this Article but by Article 3542, the residual Article. However, in applying Article 3542, the court may be guided by the rules of this Article.

When one tortfeasor causes injury to more than one person, the applicable law should be determined separately with regard to each victim. When one person is injured by more than one tortfeasor, the latter's obligations vis-a-vis the victim and the law governing these obligations should be determined separately with regard to each tortfeasor.

For the purposes of this Article, the "injured person" in a survival action (see La.Civ.Code Art. 2315.1 (Rev.1986)) is the deceased victim. However, in a wrongful death action (see La.Civ.Code Art. 2315.2 (Rev.1986)) or in an action for loss of consortium (see La.Civ.Code Art. 2315 (1870)), the "injured persons" are the persons who qualify as plaintiffs under these Articles.

(c) Relation to Article 3542. Like Article 3543, this Article is derived from the general principles of Article 3542. When applicable, this Article, being more specific, prevails over Article 3542. However, according to Article 3547, infra, the rules provided in this Article may, in exceptional cases, be subordinated to the principles of Article 3542. See comment under Article 3547, infra. Moreover, this Article does not cover the entire spectrum of cases involving issues of loss distribution. As with Article 3543, the objective of this Article is to lighten the court's choice-of-law burden by attempting to identify those cases for which a safe choice-of-law rule could be established in advance based on accumulated experience. Because this experience does not yield safe choice-of-law rules for all cases, this Article is purposefully left open-ended. For instance, this Article does not cover situations in which the wrongful conduct, the resulting injury, and the domicile of each party are each located in different states. Such cases are, therefore, governed by Article 3542, the residual Article.

(d) Domicile. Based on the premise that laws of loss distribution are usually not territorially oriented, this Article pays less attention to territorial factors and focuses instead on the domicile of the parties. Domicile is defined in Civil Code Articles 38–46 (1870). For the domicile of juridical persons, see Article 3518, supra, and Article 3548, infra. For the purposes of this Article, the pertinent domicile is the domicile at the time of the injury. This is stated expressly in the Article or implied by the use of the past tense. However, a post-injury change of domicile may well be pertinent for the purposes of Article 3542. See Allstate Insurance v. Hague, 449 U.S. 302 (1981).

Domicile has been chosen as the primary connecting factor for the purposes of this Article because domicile connotes a permanent, factual, consensual, and formal bond between a person and a given society. Because of this bond, the person participates, however indirectly, in the shaping of that society's values and may reasonably expect the protection of its laws. Correspondingly, that society has both a right and a duty to be concerned about that person's welfare. When the domiciliary bond is attenuated for whatever reason, both the person's expectations and the society's concerns may also be diminished accordingly. Thus, when a person is only nominally domiciled in one state, but habitually resides in another or has another substantial factual connection with another state that is pertinent to the particular issue, the interest of the latter state in protecting him may be stronger than that of the former state. Depending on the other factors in the case, such a case may be a good candidate for invoking the "escape clause" of Article 3547, infra.

(e) Common domicile. The first sentence of subparagraph (1) of this Article deals with situations in which, at the time of the injury, both the tortfeasor and the victim were domiciled in the same state. This provision calls for the application of the law of the common domicile regardless of whether that law provides for a higher or a lower standard of financial protection for the victim than does the law of the state where the conduct and/or the injury occurred. In cases where the law of the state of the common domicile provides for a higher standard of financial protection than does the state of conduct and/or the injury, the application of the law of the common domicile has become routine in all states that have abandoned the traditional lex loci delicti rule. Symeonides, "Choice of Law for Torts", 448–50; Kozyris & Symeonides, "Choice of Law in the American Courts in 1989: An Overview", 38 Am.J.Comp.L. 601, 604–05 (1990); Symeonides, "Choice of Law in the American Courts in 1988", 37 Am.J.Comp.L. 457, 460–63 (1989). Jagers v. Royal Indemnity Ins. Co., 276 So.2d 309 (La.1973), the leading Louisiana case, involved this law-fact pattern and was decided the same way. Cases in which the law of the common domicile provides for a lower standard of financial protection than does the law of the state of conduct and/or injury are more controversial. See Symeonides, "Choice of Law for Torts", 452. This Article adopts the view that, as a general rule, these cases should also be resolved under the law of the common domicile, unless the special circumstances of the case warrant resort to the escape clause of Article 3547, infra.

(f) Parties domiciled in states with identical law. The second sentence of subparagraph (1) provides that persons domiciled in states whose law on the particular issue of loss distribution is substantially identical should be treated as if domiciled in the same state. This legal fiction is justified by both policy and practical considerations. From a policy viewpoint, this rule is supported by the same factors as the common-domicile rule. See comment (e), supra. From a practical viewpoint, this rule will alleviate the court's choice-of-law burden by properly identifying and resolving as "false conflicts" all cases in which the victim and the tortfeasor were domiciled in states whose law on the issue of financial protection was substantially identical. This rule will also prove useful in cases involving multiple victims or multiple tortfeasors because it will enable the court to treat as domiciliaries of the same state those victims or tortfeasors who are domiciled in states with substantially identical law.

(g) Domicile of either party. Subparagraph (2) deals with cases in which, at the time of the injury, the tortfeasor and the victim were not domiciled in the same state. Clause (a) of that subparagraph provides that when both the injurious conduct and the resulting injury occurred in a state where either the tortfeasor or the victim was domiciled, the law of that state shall apply, regardless of whether it provides for a higher or a lower standard of financial protection than the law of the domicile of the other party. For rationale and supporting authority, see Symeonides, "Choice of Law for Torts", 453–56. When a person is injured in his home state by conduct in that state, his rights should be determined by the law of that state, even if the person who caused the injury happened to be from another state. The law of the latter state should not be interjected to the victim's detriment or benefit. By the same token, when a person acting within his home state causes injury in that state, he should be held accountable according to the law of that state, even if the injured person happened to be from another state. The law of the latter state should not be interjected to the tortfeasor's detriment or benefit. See D. Cavers, The Choice of Law Process (1965).

(h) Domicile of the injured person. Of the numerous cases that fall outside the scope of subparagraph (1) and clause (a) of subparagraph (2), clause (b) of the latter subparagraph addresses only the relatively few cases that meet the three requirements prescribed by that clause. The remaining cases are left to Article 3542, the residual Article. Clause (b) addresses only the cases in which the injury occurred in the state of the victim's domicile and authorizes the application of that state's law if both conditions specified in parts (ii) and (iii) of that clause are satisfied.

The first condition is that the tortfeasor should have foreseen the occurrence of the injury in the state of the victim's domicile. This condition is necessary in order to protect the tortfeasor from unfair surprise, see Allstate Ins. Co. v. Hague, 449 U.S. 302 (1981), and is intended to have the same meaning as the similar condition in Article 3543 (see comment (g) under Article 3543, supra). If this condition is not met, clause (b) will be inapplicable and the case will fall under Article 3542, the residual Article. The second condition for applying the law of the victim's domicile under clause (b) is a showing that that law provided for a higher standard of financial protection for the victim than the law of the state where the tortfeasor's conduct occurred. If this condition is not met, clause (b) will be inapplicable and the case will be decided under Article 3542, the residual Article.

It should be noted that requiring that the victim's domicile provide for a higher standard before its law is applied under clause (b) does not preclude the application of that state's law in cases in which it provides for a lower standard. It simply means that, rather than being subjected to a black-letter rule, these cases will be referred to the more flexible approach of Article 3542. In applying Article 3542, the court will have the opportunity to look at the totality of the circumstances of the particular case and to evaluate them in the light of the policies enumerated in that Article. Following such an evaluation, the court may well conclude that applying the law of the victim's domicile is the best solution under the circumstances.

Art. 3545. Products liability

Delictual and quasi-delictual liability for injury caused by a product, as well as damages, whether compensatory, special, or punitive, are governed by the law of this state: (1) when the injury was sustained in this state by a person domiciled or residing in this state; or (2) when the product was manufactured, produced, or acquired in this state and caused the injury either in this state or in another state to a person domiciled in this state.

The preceding paragraph does not apply if neither the product that caused the injury nor any of the defendant's products of the same type were made available in this state through ordinary commercial channels.

All cases not disposed of by the preceding paragraphs are governed by the other Articles of this Title.

Acts 1991, No. 923, § 1, eff. Jan. 1, 1992.

REVISION COMMENTS—1991

(a) Scope and terminology. This Article applies to delictual and quasi-delictual as distinguished from contractual liability that may arise from an injury caused by a product. Contractual liability is governed by the Title on Conventional Obligations, supra. For cases falling within its scope, this Article applies to issues of conduct and safety, to issues of loss distribution, e.g., compensatory damages, as well as to issues of exemplary, punitive, or special damages. Thus when applicable, this Article prevails over Articles 3543 and 3544, supra, and Article 3546, infra.

For the purposes of this Article, the word "product" is not confined to industrial products but includes natural substances, whether raw, processed, or otherwise altered by the industry of man. A product may be movable or immovable, a single or a composite thing, and includes its component parts. The product need not be "defective". It suffices that the product has caused the injury, as for instance when the injury results from a mis-description. This Article applies to any injury caused by a product, rather than to the product itself. The latter type of damage is likely to be characterized as contractual in nature and thus would be governed by the Title on conventional obligations, supra. This Article applies to any injury directly sustained by a person or his property, whether or not that person is the owner of the product, and whether or not he was using the product at the time of the injury. This Article covers the liability of any person who can be made a defendant in a products liability action under Louisiana law. It is understood that this coverage may include not only the producer or manufacturer of the product and its component parts, but also retailers, wholesale distributors, and other persons in the commercial chain of preparation and distribution of the product.

(b) Operation and relation to other articles. This Article delineates the scope of Louisiana's products liability law by using four factual contacts: place of injury; victim's domicile or residence; acquisition of the product; and production or manufacturing of the product. With only one exception (cases in which Louisiana has no contacts other than the manufacturing and acquisition of the product), the first paragraph of this Article authorizes the application of Louisiana law to all cases in which any two or more of these contacts are situated in this state. (See comments (d)-(g), infra). The second paragraph provides a "foreseeability" exception from all of these cases. (See comment (h), infra). Finally, the third paragraph relegates to the other articles of this Title all cases not disposed of by the first two paragraphs of this Article. These are the cases in which Louisiana has fewer contacts than the ones required by the first paragraph or cases that are subject to the foreseeability defense of the second paragraph. Obviously, this relegation does not preclude the application of Louisiana law to some of these cases. Hence, Article 3545 should be understood as defining the minimum, not the maximum, reach of Louisiana substantive law. On the other hand, the fact that this Article is also subject to the "escape clause" of Article 3547, infra, means that some cases or issues that are subjected to Louisiana law by Article 3545 might actually be decided under a foreign law if the court chooses to utilize Article 3547. See comments under Article 3547, infra. For a critique of this Article, see Kozyris, "Values and Methods in Choice of Law for Products Liability: A Comparative Comment on Statutory Solutions", 38 Am.J.Comp.L. 475 (1990). For a response, see Symeonides, "Choice of Law for Torts", 464–69.

(c) Injury in Louisiana. The occurrence of a product-induced injury in Louisiana will usually implicate the pertinent policies of this state in regulating the consequences of the injury and minimizing similar injuries in the future. Whether or not the policies of this state should prevail over the countervailing policies of another state will depend on what other connections the two states have with the particular case. Clauses (1) and (2) of the first paragraph of this Article identify those cases in which it is believed that the policies of this state would be most seriously impaired if its law were not applied. These are the cases in which, in addition to being the place of injury, Louisiana is also either: (a) the domicile or residence of the victim; or (b) the place of manufacturing of the product; or (c) the place of acquisition of the product. In these cases, Louisiana law should apply regardless of the factual contacts of the other state or states. The application of Louisiana law in such cases has been sanctioned by the United States Supreme Court in Watson v. Employers Liab. Assur. Corp., 348 U.S. 66 (1954).

Cases in which Louisiana's only connection consists of being the place of the product-induced injury present a more difficult problem. Although from a constitutional view-point, Watson contains language that seems to permit the application of Louisiana law to these cases, it is nevertheless believed that, from a choice-of-law perspective, these cases should not be subjected a priori to Louisiana law without considering the contacts and policies of the other state or states. That is why these cases are not covered by this Article but are referred to "the other Articles of this Title", that is, Articles 3542–3544 and 3546–3548. Those Articles provide for a more flexible approach based on an evaluation of all pertinent factors and combinations thereof. Depending on these combinations, those articles may lead to the application of Louisiana law or to the application of the law of another state.

(d) Injury and victim's domicile or residence in Louisiana. When, in addition to the injury, the victim's domicile or residence is in Louisiana, then the application of Louisiana law not only passes the constitutional test of Watson, but is also amply justified, from the choice-of-law perspective, by Louisiana's legitimate interest in protecting consumers living and injured within its borders. This need exists whether or not the product was manufactured or acquired in this state. Any potential argument of unfair surprise that might be made by the defendant is adequately taken care of by the defense provided in the second paragraph. Besides, the application of Louisiana law may well benefit the defendant if it turns out to be less protective of the plaintiff than, for instance, the law of the place of manufacture or acquisition of the product.

(e) Injury and manufacture in Louisiana. Here, the application of Louisiana law is justified by the need to ensure that products that are manufactured in this state and which actually cause injury here conform to the standards prescribed by the law of this state. This need exists whether or not the injured person is a Louisiana domiciliary or a domiciliary of another state whose law would provide him with more or less protection.

(f) Injury and acquisition in Louisiana. Here, the application of Louisiana law is justified by the need to ensure that products that are marketed in this state and which actually cause injury here conform to the standards prescribed by the law of this state. This need exists whether or not the injured person is a Louisiana domiciliary or a domiciliary of another state. Again, any potential argument of unfair surprise by the defendant is adequately taken care of by the defense provided in the second paragraph.

(g) Victim's domicile and manufacture or acquisition in Louisiana. Clause (2) of the first paragraph of this Article also authorizes the application of Louisiana law to cases in which the victim was domiciled in this state and the product was either manufactured or acquired in this state. Here the application of Louisiana law is justified by the need to ensure that products which are manufactured or marketed in this state and which cause injury to a Louisiana domiciliary conform to the standards prescribed by the law of this state. This need exists even if the injury actually occurred outside this state.

(h) Foreseeability defense. In the interest of fairness, the second paragraph of this Article enables a defendant to avoid the application of Louisiana law under this Article if he meets the conditions specified in that paragraph. For similar defenses in other systems, see Symeonides, "Choice of Law for Torts", 467–69. Obviously, the burden of proof would rest with the defendant, but nothing would preclude the plaintiff from voluntarily assuming that burden if this would be to his advantage. When this burden is discharged, "the preceding paragraph does not apply" and the particular case must be handled as a non-products case under the other articles of this Title.

Art. 3546.   Punitive damages

Punitive damages may not be awarded by a court of this state unless authorized:

(1) By the law of the state where the injurious conduct occurred and by either the law of the state where the resulting injury occurred or the law of the place where the person whose conduct caused the injury was domiciled; or

(2) By the law of the state in which the injury occurred and by the law of the state where the person whose conduct caused the injury was domiciled.

Acts 1991, No. 923, § 1, eff. Jan. 1, 1992.

REVISION COMMENTS—1991

(a) Scope. This Article applies to claims for punitive or exemplary damages arising out of offenses and quasi-offenses in all cases except those product liability cases that are governed by Louisiana law under Article 3545, supra. Article 3546 does not apply to claims for punitive damages arising from other sources, such as contracts or quasi-contracts. This Article is not intended to prevent either "a court of this state" or, a fortiori, a federal court, from awarding punitive damages in cases where such damages are authorized by applicable federal substantive law.

(b) Rationale. Although there is a wide divergence of opinion as to the fairness or effectiveness of punitive damages, there also seems to be a consensus that their objective is deterrence or punishment rather than compensation. Punitive damages are not intended for the protection of the individual victim who, ex hypothesi, has been compensated for his loss through ordinary damages. Instead, punitive damages are for the most part designed to "punish" the individual tortfeasor, to deter him and other potential tortfeasors in the future. Punitive damages protect victims only indirectly. This is why the domicile of the victim is not a pertinent factor under this Article. See Symeonides, "Choice of Law for Torts", 460–61.

Since punitive damages have more to do with the tortfeasor than with the victim, this Article focuses on the three potentially different places that bear relation to the tortfeasor: the place of his domicile, the place of his conduct, and the place of the injury resulting from that conduct. The state of the tortfeasor's domicile must have a say in whether the tortfeasor is to be "punished" (or not punished/protected) and if so, to what degree, or in whether similarly situated potential tortfeasors should be deterred. The state where the injury-causing conduct occurred has the equally obvious right and interest in regulating conduct within its borders. Finally, being the state that bears many of the consequences of such conduct, the state where the injury occurs has a legitimate claim to determine the legal consequences of tortious conduct.

This Article authorizes the award of punitive damages when such damages are imposed by the laws of all three or of any two of these states. When all three of the above states impose punitive damages on particular conduct, the award of such damages need not be defended. When only two of these states provide for punitive damages, the award may be defended both in terms of the interests of those states and in terms of the expectations of the tortfeasor. See comments (c)–(e), infra.

When only one of these three states provides for punitive damages, the awarding of such damages might seem more controversial but is by no means uncommon either in this or, especially, in other states. See, e.g., Cooper v. American Express, 593 F.2d 612 (5th Cir.1979) (imposing punitive damages under the law of Alabama, the place of injury, although such damages were not available under the law of Louisiana where the defendant acted and was domiciled); Ashland Oil, Inc. v. Miller Oil Purchasing Co., 678 F.2d 1293 (5th Cir.1982) (same result with regard to one defendant); Bryant v. Silverman, 146 Ariz. 41, 703 P.2d 1190 (1985) (awarding punitive damages under the law of defendant's domicile although such damages were not available under the law of the place of injury, which, according to defendant's contentions, was also the place of conduct). Nevertheless, because of the prevailing hostility towards punitive damages in Louisiana (see Symeonides, "Choice of Law for Torts", 459) this Article prohibits, as a general matter, the awarding of punitive damages in these cases in the absence of exceptional circumstances that may render applicable the escape clause of Article 3547 (see comment (g), infra).

(c) Places of conduct and injury. Subparagraph (1) authorizes the awarding of punitive damages if such damages are imposed by the law of the place of the conduct that caused the injury and by the

909

law of the place where the resulting injury occurred. For rationale and supporting authority, see Symeonides, "Choice of Law for Torts", 463; Kozyris & Symeonides, "Choice of Law in the American Courts in 1989: An Overview", 38 Am.J.Comp.L. 601, 615 (1990). It is not necessary that the conduct and injury have occurred in the same state. However, when the conduct and injury have occurred in different states, then both of those states must provide for punitive damages in order for that case to fall under this subparagraph. For cases in which either the conduct or the injury, or both, occurred in more than one state, see comments (e) and (h) under Article 3543, supra.

(d) Places of conduct and domicile of the tortfeasor. Subparagraph (1) also authorizes the awarding of punitive damages if such damages are imposed by the law of the place where the conduct that caused the injury occurred and by the law of the state where the person who caused that injury was domiciled. For rationale and supporting authority, see Ardoyno v. Kyzar, 426 F.Supp. 78 (E.D.La.1976); Symeonides, "Choice of Law for Torts", 463–64; Kozyris & Symeonides, supra at 615. Again, it is not necessary that conduct and domicile of the tortfeasor coincide in the same state, but, when they do not, both states must provide for punitive damages in order for that case to fall under this subparagraph. For cases in which the conduct occurs in more than one state, see comment (h) under Article 3543, supra. For the domicile of juridical persons, see Article 3518, supra, and Article 3548, infra.

(e) Places of injury and domicile of the tortfeasor. Subparagraph (2) authorizes the awarding of punitive damages if such damages are imposed by the law of the place where the injury occurred and by the law of the state where the person who caused that injury was domiciled. Again, it is not necessary that both of these factors coincide in the same state, but, when they do not, both states must provide for punitive damages in order for that case to fall under this subparagraph. For cases in which the injury occurred in more than one state, see comment (i) under Article 3543, supra. For the domicile of juridical persons, see Article 3518, supra, and Article 3548, infra.

(f) Measure of punitive damages. This Article allows, but does not compel, the awarding of punitive damages in the cases which fall within its scope. The Article also does not establish the measure for punitive damages nor does it designate the state whose substantive law is to provide such measure. The former is a factual question whose resolution does not belong in a conflicts article. The latter is a choice-of-law question only in the relatively rare cases in which, by legislation or precedent, the states enumerated in the article fix in advance, and do so differently, the recoverable measure of punitive damages. In such cases, the choice from among the differing standards of punitive damages is left to the court and should be guided by the principles of Article 3542.

(g) Exceptional cases. This Article is subject to the "escape clause" of Article 3547, infra. That clause "cuts both ways" and thus may lead not only to a contraction, but also to an expansion of the scope of this Article. Thus, in a case where the award of punitive damages is authorized by the laws of two or more of the classes of states enumerated by this Article, the court may determine that, under the principles of Article 3542 and the special circumstances of the particular case, the policies of these states in imposing punitive damages would be less seriously impaired by an adverse decision than would the policies of another state that does not impose punitive damages. In such an exceptional case, punitive damages may be denied.

What might be less obvious is that the escape clause may also lead to the awarding of punitive damages in cases other than the ones enumerated in this Article. Indeed, despite its prohibitory language, the first sentence of this Article is not immune from the escape clause of Article 3547. This means that under appropriate circumstances the court may determine that, although punitive damages may not be recoverable under this Article, the denial of punitive damages would so impair the policies of another state favoring such damages as to defeat the principles of Article 3542. In such an exceptional case, punitive damages may be awarded under the law of the latter state.

Art. 3547.   Exceptional cases

The law applicable under Articles 3543–3546 shall not apply if, from the totality of the circumstances of an exceptional case, it is clearly evident under the principles of Article 3542, that the policies of another state would be more seriously impaired if its law were not applied to the particular issue. In such event, the law of the other state shall apply.

Acts 1991, No. 923, § 1, eff. Jan. 1, 1992.

Function and rationale of this Article. As stated earlier, the choice-of-law rules contained in Articles 3543–3546 were drawn from the general principles enunciated in Article 3542. By designating in advance the applicable law, these rules will enable the courts to avoid the laborious analysis required by Article 3542, and thus will alleviate their choice-of-law burden while providing the desired measure of predictability. However, as with any a priori choice-of-law rules, the rules contained in Articles 3543–3546 may, in exceptional cases, produce a result that is incompatible with the principles of Article 3542 from which these rules have been derived. In order to avoid such a result, this Article provides an "escape mechanism". The court will avail itself of this mechanism if it is convinced from the totality of the circumstances of the particular case that the policies of a state other than the one whose law is designated as applicable by Articles 3543–3546 would be significantly more impaired if its law were not applied. In such a case, Articles 3543–3546 must yield to Article 3542 and the law of the former state must be applied. This mechanism should be reserved for the truly exceptional cases, and the burden of persuasion for its utilization should be placed on the party who invokes it. For a critique of this provision, see Weintraub, "The Contributions of Symeonides and Kozyris to Making Choice of Law Predictable and Just: An Appreciation and Critique", 38 Am.J.Comp.L. 511, 517–18 (1990).

Art. 3548.   Domicile of juridical persons

For the purposes of this Title, and provided it is appropriate under the principles of Article 3542, a juridical person that is domiciled outside this state, but which transacts business in this state and incurs a delictual or quasi-delictual obligation arising from activity within this state, shall be treated as a domiciliary of this state.

Acts 1991, No. 923, § 1, eff. Jan. 1, 1992.

(a) Scope. This Article applies to juridical persons that: are domiciled outside Louisiana; transact business in Louisiana; and incur a delictual or quasi-delictual obligation arising from their activity in Louisiana. For the definition of the domicile of a juridical person, see Article 3518, supra. For the meaning of "transact[ing] business in this state", see, e.g., La.R.S. 12:301–302 and pertinent Louisiana jurisprudence. This Article requires the court to treat such foreign juridical persons as Louisiana domiciliaries for the purposes of this Title, if the court determines that, under the principles of Article 3542, such treatment is appropriate in the particular case.

(b) Operation. One of the effects of this Article is to facilitate the task of the court by enabling it to resolve cases involving issues of loss distribution or financial protection for which Article 3544, supra, does not provide a rule. For example, Article 3544 does not provide a rule for cases in which the injurious conduct as well as the resulting injury occurred in Louisiana but in which neither the victim nor the tortfeasor was domiciled in this state. In such a case, if the tortfeasor were a juridical person that met the qualifications prescribed by this Article, the court could decide to treat that person as a Louisiana domiciliary for the purposes of the particular case. This would mean that the cases would then fall under Article 3544(2), and would be governed by Louisiana law, whether that law favored the plaintiff or the defendant.

Similarly, Article 3544 does not designate the applicable law for cases in which Louisiana's only contact with the case consists of being the domicile of the victim. Again, if the tortfeasor in such a case were a juridical person that met the qualifications prescribed in Article 3548, the court could decide to treat that person as a Louisiana domiciliary for the purposes of the particular case. This would mean that the case would then fall under the common-domicile rule of Article 3544(1) and would be governed by Louisiana law, whether that law favored the plaintiff or the defendant.

On the other hand, Article 3548 may result in taking some cases out of the scope of the common-domicile rule of Article 3544(1). For example, under Article 3544(1), loss distribution issues between a Texas tortfeasor and a Texas victim injured in Louisiana by the tortfeasor's Louisiana conduct would be governed by Texas law. But, if the tortfeasor were a juridical person that met the qualifications prescribed in Article 3548, the court could decide to treat that person as a Louisiana domiciliary for the purposes of the particular case. This would render inoperative the common domicile rule of Article 3544(1) and would render applicable clause (a) of subparagraph (2) of the same Article. This would mean that the case would be governed by Louisiana law, irrespective of whether that law favored the plaintiff or the defendant, because both the conduct and the resulting injury would have occurred in the state of "domicile" of one of the two parties.

TITLE VIII—LIBERATIVE PRESCRIPTION

Art. 3549. Law governing liberative prescription

A. When the substantive law of this state would be applicable to the merits of an action brought in this state, the prescription and peremption law of this state applies.

B. When the substantive law of another state would be applicable to the merits of an action brought in this state, the prescription and peremption law of this state applies, except as specified below:

(1) If the action is barred under the law of this state, the action shall be dismissed unless it would not be barred in the state whose law would be applicable to the merits and maintenance of the action in this state is warranted by compelling considerations of remedial justice.

(2) If the action is not barred under the law of this state, the action shall be maintained unless it would be barred in the state whose law is applicable to the merits and maintenance of the action in this state is not warranted by the policies of this state and its relationship to the parties or the dispute nor by any compelling considerations of remedial justice.

C. Notwithstanding the foregoing provisions, if the substantive law of another state would be applicable to the merits of an action brought in this state and the action is brought by or on behalf of any person who, at the time the cause of action arose, neither resided in nor was domiciled in this state, the action shall be barred if it is barred by a statute of limitation or repose or by a law of prescription or peremption of the other state, and that statute or law is, under the laws of the other state, deemed to be substantive, rather than procedural, or deemed to bar or extinguish the right that is sought to be enforced in the action and not merely the remedy.

Acts 1991, No. 923, § 1, eff. Jan. 1, 1992. Amended by Acts 2005, No. 213, § 1.

REVISION COMMENTS—1991

(a) Scope. This Article applies to issues of liberative prescription, including all questions of commencement, suspension, interruption, and accrual of prescription. Cf. La.Civ.Code Arts. 3447, 3449–72 (Rev.1982). For the purposes of this Article, peremption (see La.Civ.Code Arts. 3458–61 (Rev.1982)) is treated as a species of liberative prescription.

This Article does not apply to acquisitive prescription or prescription of non-use. See La.Civ.Code Arts. 3446, 3448 (Rev.1982). According to Articles 3535–3536, supra, these questions are governed by the law of the situs of the thing.

This Article also does not apply to prescription of judgments. Civil Code Article 3501 (Rev.1983), which establishes the time periods for the enforcement, revival, and prescription of Louisiana as well as foreign judgments, is not affected by this Article.

(b) The two poles of this Article: Lex fori and lex causae. This Article is built around two poles: the lex fori and the lex causae. The lex fori is the law of the state where litigation takes place, including the choice-of-law rules of that state. The lex causae is the substantive law which, through the choice-of-law rules of the forum, is found applicable to the merits of a particular action that contains foreign elements. The law thus chosen may be the law of the forum or the law of another state. In Louisiana, the lex causae will be chosen through the choice-of-law rules contained in the preceding Articles of this Book or in other Louisiana statutes.

In the United States, issues of liberative prescription have been traditionally assigned to the lex fori with occasional exceptions in favor of the lex causae. Paragraphs 6 and 7 of Civil Code Article 15 (Redesignated 1987) were fairly representative of the traditional common-law approach. In civil-law systems, on the other hand, issues of liberative prescription are usually assigned to the lex causae with occasional exceptions in favor of the lex fori. Recently, this latter approach has also been adopted by the (American) Uniform Conflict of Laws Limitations Act of 1982. Finally, a fresh, more nuanced approach has been taken by the 1987 and 1988 revisions of § 142 of the Restatement, Second, of

Conflict of Laws. For a comparison of these approaches, see Symeonides, "Revising Puerto Rico's Conflicts Law: A Preview", 28 Colum.J.Transn'l L. 413, 433–37 (1990). This Article draws from all three approaches.

(c) When the lex causae is the lex fori. The first paragraph of this Article states the obvious, namely that, when Louisiana substantive law would be applicable to the merits of an action brought in this state, that is, when the lex causae coincides with the lex fori, then the forum's law of prescription and peremption applies, without any further inquiry and regardless of whether it bars the action.

(d) When the lex causae is a law other than the lex fori. The second paragraph of this Article deals with actions the merits of which would be governed by the law of another state. Here again the lex fori remains the basic rule, subject, however, to exceptions in favor of the lex causae which are defined in subparagraphs (1) and (2). Subparagraph (1) deals with the situation in which the action is barred under Louisiana prescription law but not under the prescription law of the state of the lex causae, while subparagraph (2) deals with the converse situation. The two exceptions are deliberately phrased differently so that the burden of displacing Louisiana law will be heavier in cases where Louisiana law provides for a longer prescriptive period (see subparagraph 2) than in cases in which it provides for a shorter prescriptive period (see subparagraph 1) than the foreign lex causae.

(e) Actions barred under Louisiana law: The rule and its exception. Subparagraph (1) of the second paragraph of this Article begins by reaffirming the lex-fori rule by providing for the dismissal of actions brought after the accrual of the relevant prescriptive or peremptive period of Louisiana law. The rationale for the rule in these cases is that the application of the shorter prescriptive period of the forum promotes the forum's interest in judicial economy and protects the integrity of its judicial system.

Subparagraph (1) also introduces a new exception to the lex-fori rule, an exception that departs from prior Louisiana conflicts law, which did not allow the displacement of Louisiana prescription law in cases where Louisiana law provided for a shorter prescription than the lex causae. That limitation was apparently motivated by a desire to protect the judicial system of this state from the burden of, and the dangers inherent in, adjudicating claims which were deemed too old under Louisiana's principles of liberative prescription. However, in some cases this otherwise legitimate desire should yield to an equally important need to provide a forum. By authorizing a new exception to the lex-fori rule, subparagraph (1) recognizes this need. The exception is based on two grounds which both must be shown to exist before it may be utilized.

(f) The two grounds for the subparagraph (1) exception. The first necessary prerequisite to the application of the exception is that the action "would not be barred in the state whose law would be applicable to the merits [of the action]." It is immaterial why the action would be maintained in that other state, that is, whether it is because that state's statute of limitations actually provides for a longer time limit, or because under that state's rules pertaining to interruption or suspension, including its tolling statutes, the action would be maintained in the courts of that state.

The second necessary prerequisite to the application of the exception is that "maintenance of the action in this state is warranted by compelling considerations of remedial justice." This language is borrowed from the 1987 Revision of § 142 of the Restatement, Second, of Conflict of Laws. The examples given by the Restatement are pertinent to the application of this provision and illustrate its exceptional character. These examples refer to cases where "through no fault of the plaintiff an alternative forum is not available as, for example, where jurisdiction could not be obtained over the defendant in any state other than the forum or where for some reason a judgment obtained in the other state having jurisdiction would be unenforceable in other states . . . also situations where suit in the alternative forum, although not impossible would be extremely inconvenient for the parties." Restatement (Second) of Conflict of Laws, 1986 Revisions, § 142 comment f (Supp. March 31, 1987). As might be surmised from the initial phrase of the quotation, none of these examples should be seen as requiring the forum to entertain an action solely because it is time-barred in all or most other states. The disapproving reference to Keeton v. Hustler, 465 U.S. 770 (1984), as an "egregious example of forum shopping" in the comments to this section of the Restatement leaves little doubt that the plaintiff's own procrastination is not likely to ever make his case compelling enough to reach the threshold of this exception.

(g) Actions not barred under Louisiana law: The rule and its exception. The opening sentence of subparagraph (2) of the second paragraph of this Article reaffirms the basic rule of the lex fori for actions that have been filed timely under Louisiana prescription or peremption law. Here the rationale for following that rule is that entertaining such actions promotes whatever substantive policies this state has in not providing for a shorter prescriptive period and preserves to the plaintiff the opportunity to fully pursue his judicial remedies as long as he does so within the time specified by the law of this state. These substantive and procedural policies underlying Louisiana prescription law are entitled to preference in a Louisiana court, unless it is amply demonstrated that neither set of policies is actually implicated in the particular case and that the opposing substantive policies of another state, that of the lex causae, are implicated more intimately. Only then may Louisiana law be displaced.

These are essentially the three grounds for the exception to the rule of the lex fori which is enunciated in the balance of subparagraph (2). Again, all three grounds must be satisfied before this exception is utilized. Before dismissing an action that has been timely filed under Louisiana law, the court must be satisfied that the action has prescribed in the state of the lex causae, and that neither the substantive nor the procedural or remedial policies of the forum state would be served by maintaining the action. Only then would the policy of providing a forum be outweighed by the policy of discouraging forum shopping. The very fact that all three hurdles must be overcome before this exception is utilized indicates that this exception is not expected to be applied often.

(h) Action barred in the state of lex causae. The first necessary prerequisite to application of the exception is that the action would be barred by the statute of limitations or some other time-bar recognized "in the state whose law is applicable to the merits [of the action]." Again, it is immaterial why the action would be barred in that other state, that is, whether it is because that state's domestic law provides for a shorter prescriptive period, or because, under its own borrowing statute, that state would borrow the shorter prescriptive period of another state.

(i) Maintenance of action "not warranted by the policies of this state". The second prerequisite to displacing Louisiana's prescription law in cases where it provides for a prescriptive period that is longer than that of the foreign lex causae is a showing that "maintenance of the action in this state is not warranted by the policies of this state and its relationship to the parties or the dispute". This test can be viewed either from a negative or from a positive angle. The court must be satisfied that the policies of this state in providing a longer prescriptive period for actions of the type before the court would not be adversely affected by dismissing the particular action, or that these policies would be served by entertaining the action. Either way, this evaluation will be based on an examination of the relationship, if any, that this state has with the parties or their dispute. The pertinent question will be whether that relationship is of the kind that would implicate in a significant way the policies of this state in providing a longer prescriptive period.

By way of illustration, it would seem that if none of the parties are domiciled in this state and neither they nor their dispute are related to this state in any other significant way, the policies of this state would not be served by imposing on its overburdened courts the adjudication of a dispute which, but for the existence of jurisdiction, is essentially a foreign dispute. Dismissing the action in such a case—which on its face appears to be a case of forum shopping—would not seriously affect whatever interest this state has in providing a longer prescriptive period, especially since, ex hypothesi, this state is not the state of the lex causae.

On the other hand, if the plaintiff is a Louisiana domiciliary, then dismissing his action would deprive him of the opportunity to litigate in the most convenient forum, and would close to him the doors of the judicial system which he helps sustain through his taxes. Depending on the other circumstances of the particular case, dismissal here might not be warranted in light of the policies of this state derived from its relationship to the plaintiff. Similarly, if the defendant is a Louisiana domiciliary, there would seem to be less of a concern about forum shopping by the plaintiff and less of an argument of unfair surprise by the defendant. These two factors would suggest that allowing the action would be warranted by the policies of this state, but whether or not this would actually be so should be determined by the court by examining all the circumstances surrounding the particular case.

(j) Maintenance of action not warranted by "compelling considerations of remedial justice." Finally, the third prerequisite that must be satisfied in order to displace Louisiana prescription law in cases where it provides for a prescriptive period that is longer than that of the foreign lex causae is a showing that maintenance of the action in this state is not warranted by "compelling considerations of remedial justice." This phrase is intended to have the same meaning as in subparagraph (1). See comment (f), supra. Again, under no circumstances should this phrase be seen as a command or even as a license for entertaining a particular action simply because it is barred in all or most other states. Such egregious examples of forum shopping as Keeton v. Hustler, 465 U.S. 770 (1984), are neither encouraged nor condoned by this Article.

(k) Multiple leges causae. Article 421 of the Louisiana Code of Civil Procedure defines a civil action as "a demand for the enforcement of a legal right." Obviously more than one such "legal right," claim, or cause of action may be cumulated in one and the same proceeding, such as when the plaintiff asserts one claim based on tort and another on contract. Each of these causes of action would not only be subject to a different prescriptive period, but might also be governed by a different substantive law on the merits. If so, each such cause of action should be handled separately under this Article.

This phenomenon of multiple leges causae might be encountered even within the confines of a single cause of action, since, under the issue-by-issue approach adopted throughout this Book, it is possible that a cause of action may be governed in part by the law of one state and in part by the law of another state. For example, the Title on delictual obligations provides different choice-of-law rules for issues of conduct than for issues of loss distribution, and these rules may on occasion lead to the application of the substantive law of a different state to each category of issues. In such cases, the decision of which of these states will be treated as the state(s) of the lex causae for the purposes of this Article is left to the discretion of the court.

(l) Necessity of pleading prescription. It is a well-established principle of Louisiana law that "[p]rescription must be pleaded. Courts may not supply a plea of prescription." La.Civ.Code Art. 3452 (Rev.1982). This principle applies to Louisiana prescription and, perhaps a fortiori, to foreign prescriptions. Nothing contained in this Article is intended to derogate from the above principle. Thus, when it refers to an action as being "barred . . . under the law of this state," this Article contemplates situations in which the obligor has properly and timely invoked a valid defense of prescription under the law of this state. Similarly, when it refers to the action as being "barred in the state whose law is applicable to the merits of the action", this Article contemplates situations in which the party who relies on the foreign law has not only proven that that law would be applicable to the merits, but also has properly and timely invoked the applicable statute of limitations of that state.

On the other hand, in Louisiana, peremption "may be supplied by a court on its own motion". La.Civ.Code Art. 3460 (Rev.1982). This Article should certainly apply with regard to Louisiana peremptions. However, it is a different question whether a Louisiana court should apply on its own motion a limitation period provided by the foreign lex causae and treated by that law as applicable ex officio. Theoretically, a Louisiana court may do so with regard to sister-state, as opposed to foreign-country, "peremptions". Article 202 of the Louisiana Code of Evidence provides that the court "shall take judicial notice" of sister-state law, including presumably the preemptive period provided in that law. As a practical matter, however, Louisiana courts have all but ignored the above provision which compels judicial notice of sister-state law and have relied on the litigants to timely invoke and prove the content of that law.

Arts. 3550 to 3556. [Blank]